New Venture Creation

Entrepreneurship for the 21st Century

FOURTH EDITION

Jeffry A. Timmons, A.B., M.B.A., D.B.A.
Professor of Entrepreneurial Studies
Director, The Price-Babson Fellows Program
Babson College
Babson Park, Massachusetts

and

Class of 1954 Professor of New Ventures
Harvard University Graduate School
of Business Administration
Boston, Massachusetts

IRWIN

Chicago • Bogotá • Boston • Buenos Aires • Caracas
London • Madrid • Mexico City • Sydney • Toronto

IRWIN
Concerned About Our Environment

In recognition of the fact that our company is a large end-user of fragile yet replenishable resources, we at IRWIN can assure you that every effort is made to meet or exceed Environmental Protection Agency (EPA) recommendations and requirements for a "greener" workplace.

To preserve these natural assets, a number of environmental policies, both companywide and department-specific, have been implemented. From the use of 50% recycled paper in our textbooks to the printing of promotional materials with recycled stock and soy inks to our office paper recycling program, we are committed to reducing waste and replacing environmentally unsafe products with safer alternatives.

Senior sponsoring editor:	Kurt L. Strand
Editorial assistant:	Michele Dooley
Marketing manager:	Kurt Messersmith
Project editor:	Mary Conzachi
Production manager:	Jon Christopher
Designer:	Larry J. Cope
Cover designer:	Jamie O'Neal
Art coordinator:	Heather Burbridge
Art studio:	Benoit and Associates
Compositor:	Graphic World, Inc.
Typeface:	11/13 Times Roman
Printer:	Wm. C. Brown Communications, Inc.

Library of Congress Cataloging-in-Publication Data

Timmons, Jeffry A.
New venture creation : entrepreneurship for the 21st century / Jeffry A. Timmons. – 4th ed.
p. cm.
Includes index.
ISBN 0-256-11548-6 ISBN 0-256-19348-7 (Revised 4th ed.)
1. New business enterprises–Handbooks, manuals, etc. 2. Entrepreneurship–Handbooks, manuals, etc. I. Title.
HD62.5.T55 1994
658.1'1–dc20 93-39387

Printed in the United States of America
2 3 4 5 6 7 8 9 0 WCB 1 0 9 8 7 6 5

DEDICATION

To the MBA Class of 1954, Harvard University Graduate School of Business Administration. Your generous and unyielding support of the Entrepreneurial Management mission at Harvard created the MBA Class of 1954 Professorship in New Ventures, which has made possible the revision of this edition and numerous other projects. You have set a standard for future classes to emulate. Congratulations!

Preface

A BOOK FOR THE 'NOT-SO-SILENT REVOLUTION'

In the 1990 edition I began the preface with "a book for the silent revolution." During the two decades that had passed since work began on the first edition of the book, I noted that an explosion had occurred in entrepreneurship in America, and around the world the *extraordinary power of the entrepreneurial process* had been seen. We were in the midst of an unusual revolution of the human spirit: a discovery of the *extraordinary power of the entrepreneurial mind*. I called this the silent revolution. By creating and seizing opportunities, by providing imagination, tenacity, and leadership, and by insisting on the higher ground of ethics and square dealing, successful entrepreneurs play for the long haul. In this complicated process they create and allocate value and benefits for individuals, groups, organizations, and society.

Writing in early 1989, I could not imagine just how prophetic these words would be. The toppling of the Berlin Wall in November 1989, symbolizing the subsequent disintegration of totalitarian, centralized governments and economies in the Soviet Union and Eastern Europe, was breathtaking. By 1993 entrepreneurship had exploded throughout these formerly communist nations. Hundreds, perhaps thousands, of US academics, entrepreneurs, and consultants had crafted programs to transfer the American models of business and entrepreneurship to these nations.

Numbers of their counterparts traveled to the United States to participate in programs to accelerate the silent revolution. Babson College was the first to launch a program for entrepreneurship educators, entrepreneurs, and policy makers in Poland, Slovenia, and Croatia. A joint effort by Harvard, MIT, Wharton, and Stanford subsequently created a program for educators from the Eastern bloc nations.

In Europe the European Foundation for Entrepreneurship Research (EFER) led a pioneering effort with uncanny foresight by announcing—*before the Berlin Wall fell*—the very first conference on entrepreneurship in the Eastern bloc and the former USSR to be held in East Berlin in December 1990. Reports and data now emerging from these nations clearly indicate that individual entrepreneurship, especially the formation of new enterprises, is the driving force behind the transformation to private, market-based economies. Privatization and conversion of large, existing state-owned enterprises are occurring at a painfully slow pace, in comparison.

The domain of entrepreneurship is not just limited to new and small firms. It can also happen in old and large companies (though we see it far less frequently); in slower growing and even troubled companies; in profit-seeking and nonprofit organizations; and in the Eastern, Western, and developing economies. Most significantly, however, it also can *FAIL TO OCCUR* in each of these.

THE ENTREPRENEURIAL WAVE ROLLS ON

As the 1990s exposed the excesses of the 1980s, critics, skeptics, and the ever predictable cynics began to ask their even more predictable question, Is entrepreneurship a fad? The evidence and the trends speak for themselves. Among the adult working population in the United States about one in eight is self-employed, and it can be said that a cultural imperative exists in the minds of millions of other Americans: the entrepreneurial dream of working for oneself, of "growing up big." And it is no wonder, once you discover how the self-employed feel about themselves, their work lives, and the economic rewards. Uniformly, self-employed persons report the highest levels of personal satisfaction, challenge, pride, and remuneration. As a lot they love their work because it is invigorating, energizing, and meaningful. Compared to managers and those working for others, as many as three times more plan never to retire. They seem to love the "entrepreneurial game" for the game's sake. The vast majority of the nearly two million "millionaires" in the United States in 1993 have accumulated their wealth through entrepreneurial acts of self-employment.

What may be more surprising is that even graduates of the Harvard Business School (HBS)—long thought of as the "West Point for the Fortune 500"—thrive on this entrepreneurial dream. About one-third end up working for themselves, and the vast majority of all graduates 10 years out of HBS work for smaller companies employing fewer than 1,000 persons. At the author's 25th MBA reunion in 1992, a staggering 59 percent said they were self-employed. Further evidence of just how wide and deep is the quest for entrepreneurship is reflected by the readership of the *Harvard Business Review*: about 70 percent are owners, executives, or managers of firms with fewer than 1,000 employees. And among the students at HBS over 90 percent say they have the entrepreneurial dream of self-employment. A recent survey of Fortune 500 CEOs showed two dominant activities they considered the most prestigious: first, owning or investing in a small company, and second, international travel. One has to ask: what is going on here?

The rebirth of the "entrepreneurial wave" in America in the past two decades has brought unprecedented benefits not just to individuals but to society as a whole. Entrepreneurs, it turns out, are the fuel, engine, and throttle for the economic backbone of the country. Consider the following:

- About 1.2 million new enterprises from one-person operations and up will be launched in the United States in 1994.
- Virtually all of the net new jobs created in this country come from these new and expanding firms—not from the large, established companies. One recent study reported that just 7 percent of these new and expanding ventures accounted for a remarkable 118 percent of all the net new jobs in the early 1980s. In 1987 employment in 7 million small firms grew three times faster than employment in the 500 largest companies in the nation, according to American Express.
- In 1989 the 5 million women-owned businesses generated $89 billion in revenue. By 1992 women-owned firms created more jobs than did the Fortune 500, and employed 12 million people, also more than the Fortune 500.

- Since World War II, 95 percent of all radical innovations and half of all innovations have come from new and smaller firms. Innumerable innovations and industries began this way: heart pacemakers, microcomputers, overnight express delivery, the quick-oil-change, fast-food, the oral contraceptive, the x-ray machine, and hundreds of others.
- The 50 individuals who have been inducted into the Babson College Academy of Distinguished Entrepreneurs from 1977 to 1993 have created and/or built companies—many from nothing—to combined sales that would place their 37 companies as the *20th largest country GNP* in the world. Their names are entrepreneurial legends: Royal Little, An Wang, Frank Perdue, Ken Olsen, Sochio Honda, Ewing Kauffman, Ray Kroc, Fred Smith, Nolan Bushnell, Trammel Crow, Willard Marriott, Ed Lowe, Wally Amos, H. R. Block, Don Burr, John Cullinane, Rupert Murdoch, Peter Sprague, John Templeton, Anita Roddick, Robert Swanson, and others with equal deeds but lesser familiarity.
- The entrepreneurial fever has also spread to colleges and high schools in the 1990s, and now shows promise of gaining the attention of administrators and teachers in elementary schools. A Wichita State University survey indicated that as many as 800 to 1,000 two- and four-year colleges and/or universities now offer courses in new ventures and entrepreneurship, compared to as few as 50 in 1975.
- Five states have passed, or have pending, legislation that mandates entrepreneurship education for K through 12, a truly historic precedent.
- The Ewing Marion Kauffman Foundation of Kansas City became a true pioneer as the first among America's dozen largest foundations to commit its resources to the support of entrepreneurship. Its comprehensive strategy will launch initiatives in K–12, colleges, and universities, seed money and classic venture capital, and will fund education and applied research to benefit practitioners. Through its Center for Entrepreneurial Leadership it is creating strategic alliances to help implement its strategy, such as the Babson-Kauffman Foundation Entrepreneurship Conference, beginning in 1994.
- Since its inception 10 years ago, the Price-Babson College Fellows Program has had matched pairs of faculty and highly successful entrepreneurs (with an itch to teach) attend a week-long Symposium for Entrepreneurship Educators (SEE) at Babson College. By SEE-10 in 1994, over 300 faculty and fellows from over 140 universities from over 30 nations have attended the program and have experienced a unique "intellectual and practical collision between academia and the real world" and are now helping to spread the not-so-silent revolution worldwide.
- Between $50 billion and $60 billion of informal risk capital exists in our economy, coming almost entirely from self-made entrepreneurs we call angels.
- Another $35 billion of venture capital funds are available from professional sources seeking to back small-company entrepreneurs with big ambitions—Apple Computer, Federal Express, Lotus 1-2-3, DEC, Data General, and the like, started with just such sources. These funds are now a worldwide phenomenon, including the United Kingdom, Scandinavia, Western Europe, Spain, Kenya, Brazil, Australia, Philippines, Japan, Korea, and others.
- For the first time ever, in June and July of 1987, 46 senior policy makers, researchers, entrepreneurs, and executives from 26 countries met at the Salzburg Seminar in Austria for an eight-day session entitled Entrepreneurship, led by Howard H. Stevenson of Harvard. Only three Americans attended. The rest looked like a United Nations contingent: China, Russia, Romania, Turkey, Norway, West Germany, Poland, Scotland, Ireland, England, Egypt, Greece, Yugoslavia, Spain, Portugal, Sweden, Netherlands, Belgium, Austria, Malaysia, Singapore, and others.
- These roots and backbones of economic progress are now being discovered worldwide and show unprecedented promise of a sustained, global entrepreneurial wave, including

China and other nations. Lighting the flame of the entrepreneurial spirit empowers nations and peoples with "the knowledge and ability to fish, rather than just giving them a fish."

A BOOK ABOUT THE ENTREPRENEURIAL PROCESS: ITS OPPORTUNITIES, RISKS, REWARDS, AND REALITIES

New Venture Creation is a book about the actual process of getting a new venture started, growing the venture, successfully harvesting it, and starting again.

There is a substantial body of knowledge, concepts, and tools that entrepreneurs need to know, prior to and while taking the start-up plunge and after, if they are to get the odds in their favor. Accompanying the explosion in entrepreneurship has been a significant increase in research and knowledge about the entrepreneurship process. Much of what was known previously has been reinforced and refined, some has been challenged, and numerous new insights have emerged.

New Venture Creation has been the product of experience and considerable research in this field, rooted in real-world application, nearly two decades of research, and refinement in the classroom. The fourth edition updates and refines the best of the first three editions and includes new insights that have emerged.

As before, the design and flow of the book are aimed at creating knowledge, skills, awareness, and involvement in the process, and the critical aspects of creating a new venture and then making it grow. In a pragmatic way—through text, case studies, and hands-on exercises—the book guides students in discovering the concepts of entrepreneurship and the competencies, skills, know-how and experience, attitudes, resources, and networks that are sufficient to pursue different entrepreneurial opportunities. No doubt about it: There is no substitute for the real thing—actually starting a company. But short of that, it is possible to expose students to many of the vital issues and immerse them in key learning experiences, such as the development of a business plan.

The book is divided into six parts. The first three parts detail the driving forces of entrepreneurship—the opportunity recognition, the team, and resource requirements. Part I addresses the process by which *real* opportunities—not just ideas—can be discovered and selected. This section concerns opportunities around which higher potential ventures can be built, where the risks and trade-offs are acceptable, and where entrepreneurs will be able to exit their businesses profitably and when they want to, rather than when they have to or, worse, not at all.

Part II concerns the team and what makes entrepreneurs tick—how they think and act—and what they do to get the odds of success in their favor.

Part III is about resources and developing a business plan.

The next two parts concern some details. Part IV concerns entrepreneurial finance and the process of financing new ventures. Part V talks about start-up, strategies for success and managing rapid growth, and harvest issues.

Part VI helps in crafting a personal entrepreneurial strategy. Once an entrepreneur knows how winning entrepreneurs think, act, and perform, then he or she can establish goals to practice emulating those actions, attitudes, habits, and strategies. This section asks entrepreneurs to think of the process of becoming an entrepreneur, much as a coach of an athlete would in preparing for a winning season, and also to consider the following: What are my real talents, strengths, and weaknesses and how can my talents and strengths be exploited (and my weaknesses minimized)? What are the opportunities to use my strengths and to capitalize on the competition's weaknesses?

New Venture Creation seeks to enable entrepreneurs to immerse themselves in the dynamics of launching and growing a company and to address the following practical issues:

- What does an entrepreneurial career take?
- What is the difference between a good opportunity and just another idea?
- Is the opportunity I am considering the right opportunity for me, now?
- Why do some firms grow quickly to several million dollars in sales but then stumble, never growing beyond a single-product firm?
- What are the critical tasks and hurdles in seizing an opportunity and building the business?
- How much money do I need and when, where, and how can I get it – on acceptable terms?
- What financing sources, strategies, and mechanisms can I use from prestart, through the early growth stage, to the harvest of my venture?
- What are the minimum resources I need to gain control over the opportunity, and how can I do this?
- Is a business plan needed? If so, what kind is needed and how and when should I develop one?
- Who are the constituents for whom I must create or add value to achieve a positive cash flow and to develop harvest options?
- What is my venture worth and how do I negotiate what to give up?
- What are the critical transitions in entrepreneurial management as a firm grows from $1 million to $5 million to $25 million in sales?
- What are some of the pitfalls, minefields, and hazards I need to anticipate, prepare for, and respond to?
- What are the contacts and networks I need to access and to develop?
- Do I know what I do and do not know, and do I know what to do about it?
- How can I develop a personal "entrepreneurial game plan" to acquire the experience I need to succeed?
- How critical and sensitive is the timing in each of these areas?
- Why do entrepreneurs who succeed in the long term seek to maintain reputations for integrity and ethical business practices?
- Why do entrepreneurship and entrepreneurial management seem surrounded by paradoxes, well-known to entrepreneurs, such as:
  - Ambiguity and uncertainty versus planning and rigor?
  - Creativity versus disciplined analysis?
  - Patience and perseverance versus urgency?
  - Organization and management versus flexibility?
  - Innovation and responsiveness versus systemization?
  - Risk avoidance versus risk management?
  - Current profits versus long-term equity?

This edition is a major overhaul and enhancement with several new 1990s cases and updates on earlier cases and textual material to capture the new financial and technological context and global competitive environment of the 1990s. A special effort was made to include cases that capture the dynamic ups and downs new firms experience over an extended period of time. By grappling with decisions faced in new companies over both the first year or two and the next 5 to 20 years, you begin to develop a much broader and richer perspective on the often turbulent and unpredictable nature of the entrepreneurial process. These include the following:

- **FAX International** examines how a recent MBA (1990) and his wife are attempting to launch an innovative telecommunications service between Japan and the United States and raise over $5 million from private investors, none from venture capitalists. It explores identifying an opportunity, finding sources of private capital, valuing a start-up company, and early out-of-cash crises.

- **PC-Build** is a business plan by two graduating MBAs (1992) who just won a business plan competition. They are contemplating starting the business using a bootstrap-financing strategy to create a build-it-yourself kit for PC users. The case examines the start-up decision, valuing the business, and raising capital from friends and associates.
- **EASEL Corporation** series examines the anatomy of a fast-growing young software company, built by Kevin Mooney (familiar to 2nd and 3rd edition users), now contemplating its first public stock offering in 1990. It traces the issues and realities in the IPO process, including selecting an underwriter and managing and orchestrating the offering. It also enables you to follow the entrepreneurial career of Kevin Mooney from his first small company after his MBA, at age 25, to his early 40s, a unique and revealing journey from the late 1970s into the 1990s, with valuable lessons on how young, aspiring entrepreneurs acquire relevant experience and know-how.
- The **Fenchell Lampshades** case examines how an Afro-American couple, after graduation, turn down lucrative big-time consulting firm offers and pursue the purchase of a small company. It examines the issues in finding, evaluating, negotiating, and financing a small million-dollar business in Chicago.
- **Morris Alper, Inc.,** is an extraordinary case series that traces the career of an ambitious man who joins a third-generation family firm with 40 people and builds it to a national leader, with 350 employees by 1994. It examines the very difficult and complicated issues of succession planning in a family firm, the passing of the baton to the first nonfamily president, and the challenges and paradoxes the prior president faces in letting go to become chairman.
- **Jiffy Lube International** is a series of follow-on cases examining the incredible saga of this company from its inception in the late 1970s to the early 1990s. This is one of the most sobering and valuable case series on the risks and rewards of a rapid-growth strategy and a highly leveraged financial strategy.

The textual material is also substantially updated to capture the realities and opportunities of the 1990s. Major revisions and enhancement are included in several areas:

- *Opportunity recognition*. The criteria and benchmarks for distinguishing between an idea and an opportunity.
- *Assessing and obtaining outside resources*. Especially new material on bootstrapping strategies and techniques used by entrepreneurs who have limited resources over which they can gain control, or do not want to give up equity.
- *Entrepreneurial finance*. Extensive revision and new material on financing sources and strategies, valuation methods, debt financing, negotiating and structuring deals, going public, how investors look at deals, and the like.
- *Ethics*. Some of the newest material and insights available in this new field.

AN APPROACH WITH REAL-WORLD RESULTS

New Venture Creation is about the dignity of practical knowledge and the utility of the question: *Is entrepreneurship for me, and, if so, how do I get the odds in my favor?*

The domain is you and the whole is integrated, or woven together, like the threads of a fabric. The interrelationships among the functional parts of a business are studied with an eye for achieving a winning balance.

New Venture Creation will help you achieve this winning balance by assisting you in addressing these central, yet very practical, questions about new ventures and entrepreneurship. One result will be a *compression and acceleration of learning* that would be far more costly and time consuming than is either necessary or desirable if left to the school of hard knocks alone.

The approaches taught here have been used by successful entrepreneurs, investors, and students who have gone forth to start their own businesses. The content and material have won accolades from experienced graduate students, college seniors, and hundreds of founders and owners of new and emerging companies pursuing their entrepreneurial dreams. Earlier editions of *New Venture Creation* (1977 and 1985) became leading books for courses on entrepreneurship and starting new ventures courses worldwide. According to *The Wall Street Journal*, October 1987, *New Venture Creation* is a "textbook classic." The consensus of real-world entrepreneurs and students about the material in the book is: It works!

HISTORY OF *NEW VENTURE CREATION*

New Venture Creation has two principal roots going back over 25 years. This is reflected best in a feature article in the Babson College alumni bulletin: "This Professor Practices What He Teaches". Since 1971, and earlier during doctoral research at the Harvard Business School, I have been immersed in the world of entrepreneurs and the start-up, development, and financing of new and growing (and sometimes shrinking) companies—as a student, researcher, teacher and scholar, and as an investor, advisor, director, and founding shareholder. The cases and material in this edition are the cumulative result of my "post-doc degree" working directly with entrepreneurs, entrepreneurial firms, and venture capital providers.

Over the past 25 years my clientele has included presidents and partners of venture capital firms and emerging companies in the United States, United Kingdom, and Sweden, including Investkontakt & Svetab, Zero Stage Capital, Venture Economics (publisher of *Venture Capital Journal*), Vlasic Foods (part of Campbell Soup) and the Sunmark Companies, a $160 million private firm in St. Louis which was acquired by Nestle. In 1984, as the first outside member of the partnership committee of Cellular One in Boston, I became actively involved in starting and building the first independent car phone company in New England. In 1987, I became a founding shareholder and director of Boston Communications Group (BCG), which owned and operated cellular phone systems in southern Maine and New Hampshire, until their sales in 1989, and which managed Cellular One in Boston for Southwestern Bell. BCG now owns a rural cellular phone company in Massachusetts, a cellular installation and service center, and Roamer-Plus, an innovative service firm. Since 1985, I have assisted Ernst & Young's national entrepreneurial services group to develop and implement professional development programs for partners in this leading Big Six accounting firm, including entrepreneurial concepts, entrepreneurial opportunities, and financing alternatives. This effort has now expanded to E&Y International in a similar effort for the United Kingdom. In 1988 I joined the advisory board of BCI Advisors, Inc., a $285 million fund in Teaneck, New Jersey, which specializes in providing growth capital for emerging companies with sales in the $5 million to $100 million range.

In 1991 I became involved as an advisor to the Ewing Marion Kauffman Foundation and have subsequently worked with the founder and board to develop and implement a mission and strategy to foster entrepreneurship in America. It is a great honor to serve on the board of its Center for Entrepreneurial Leadership and on the national advisory board and to be a part of this ground-breaking effort.

In 1971, I became a founding shareholder of a Boston venture capital firm with subsidiaries in the United Kingdom and Belgium, and worked from 1971 to 1982 in developing ways to identify, evaluate, and finance seed-stage and start-up ventures. This was an important testing ground for applying and refining my approaches to launching and growing higher potential ventures. Of particular note is that these investing activities have spanned a range of high-, low-, and no-technology businesses, and product and service businesses in the United States, Canada, United Kingdom, and Europe. In 1981–82 I accepted a full-time assignment in Stockholm with one of the first venture capital firms there.

Since 1989, I have held the first joint appointment at Babson College and Harvard Business School. At Babson College I was the first to hold the Paul T. Babson Professorship for two years, then became the first holder of the Frederic C. Hamilton Professorship, and then first holder of the MBA Class of 1954 Professorship in New Ventures at Harvard, where I continue my love for and study of entrepreneurship. I continue to serve as director of the Price-Babson College Fellows Program, which I founded in 1984. Earlier I served as director of the Center for Entrepreneurial Studies at Babson, and as cochairman of the Babson Entrepreneurship Research Conference, now the Babson-Kauffman Foundation Entrepreneurship Conference, and am coeditor of a new book series which will feature leading contributions from the conference. I have developed and teach courses on starting new ventures, entrepreneurship, financing entrepreneurial ventures, and entrepreneurial finance, and have taught entrepreneurial finance (a second-year MBA elective at HBS) the last five years. In addition, I have worked with founders and presidents in Harvard's President's Seminar, and I founded and have taught in Babson's Entrepreneurial Management Program.

In addition to this practical experience, I have conducted research in entrepreneurship on new and emerging firms and venture financing which has resulted in nearly 100 publications in such periodicals as the *Harvard Business Review* and the *Journal of Business Venturing*, and in the proceedings of national and international conferences, including *Frontiers of Entrepreneurship Research* (1981–87). Quotations from my work have appeared in publications such as *The Wall Street Journal, INC., Venture, Business Week, Entrepreneur, In Business, New York Times, Boston Globe, Los Angeles Times, Success*, and elsewhere. I have authored and coauthored several books, including *Venture Capital at the Crossroads*, *New Venture Creation*, *The Encyclopedia of Small Business Resources*, *The Insider's Guide to Small Business Resources, A Region's Struggling Savior*, and I have coedited three yearly editions in the Babson College series *Frontiers of Entrepreneurship Research* (1983, 1984, and 1985). I have also written chapters in several books, including *The Portable MBA-Finance* and *The Portable MBA-Entrepreneurship*. My speaking and consulting assignments have included travels throughout the United States, Austria, Australia, Canada, the former East Germany, Malaysia, Philippines, Thailand, the United Kingdom, Scandinavia, Singapore, Spain, and elsewhere.

As a product of these experiences, *New Venture Creation* is rooted in both real-world application and over two and one-half decades of refinement in the classroom and in the field. The content and material have won accolades from experienced MBAs, college seniors, and hundreds of founders and owners of new and emerging companies pursuing their entrepreneurial dreams. Much of what is here has been tempered and enhanced by my "post-graduate degree" working directly with entrepreneurs and entrepreneurial firms, usually while risking both my reputation and my wallet.

I graduated from Colgate University, where I have served as a trustee since 1991, and received my MBA and doctorate from Harvard Business School.

In the Spirit of Crazy Horse
Jeffry A. Timmons
Harvard, Massachusetts
August 1993

Acknowledgments

The fourth edition of this book is an accumulation of over 25 years of intellectual capital acquired through research, teaching, and practice—the latter while risking both my reputation and my wallet in a wide range of ventures. It reflects the support, encouragement, thinking, and achievement of many people: colleagues, associates, entrepreneurs, former students, and friends. But first and foremost, a very special thank you goes to Christine C. Remey, my former research associate and now an analyst with Norwest Venture Capital in Boston. She set an entirely new standard in helping to pull this new edition together on time (in half the time of the prior edition) and with a new quality standard. With unparalleled self-discipline and organization, she did a spectacular job, while always being a tremendously human, energetic, and fun colleague to work with. Christy is one of a kind: thank you for two great years! Also deserving a special thanks is the Harvard Business School MBA Class of 1954, to whom I have dedicated this fourth edition. This class has a long, rich, and very deep tradition of entrepreneurship among its members. Their class gifts funded the first endowed professorship in New Ventures at Harvard, the MBA Class of 1954 Professorship, which I have held since 1989. Without their on-going generous support, projects such as this one could not be completed. Their support has been tremendous and is greatly appreciated by me and my colleagues at HBS.

The original book (1977) stemmed from research and concepts developed in my doctoral dissertation at Harvard Business School, and later with work with the coauthors of the earlier editions. My course development work and research in new ventures at Northeastern University in the 1970s, and in new ventures and financing entrepreneurial ventures at Babson College in the 1980s contributed heavily to the evolution of the book. Since 1989, my research in venture capital and my course development work in the entrepreneurial finance MBA elective at Harvard have enabled me to make major additions and improvements in this edition, especially in the venture-financing chapters.

I have drawn intellectual capital from many roots and contributors, and I have received support and encouragement, as well as inspiration. To list them all might well take a chapter by itself. I wish to express special thanks to those who have been so helpful in recent years, especially my colleagues and all of my MBAs at Harvard Business School who have been a constant source of encouragement, great inspiration, and friendship. I would also like to thank Dean John H. McArthur, Associate Dean Thomas R. Piper, and Warren F. Mcfarlan, my research dean. Thanks to all my colleagues in entrepreneurial management, but especially William Sahlman for his superb work in entrepreneurial finance, much of which is evident in this edition, and Howard Stevenson for his tremendous support and encouragement. At Babson College, numerous colleagues have been supportive of my work: Bill Bygrave, Alan Cohen, Jeff Ellis, Bill Glavin, Alan Grant, Mike Gordon, Wendy Handler, J. B. Kassarjian, Ed Marram, Dean Tom Moore, Dan Muzyka, Bonnie Pandya, Steve Spinelli, Jennifer Starr, Natalie Taylor, and Barbara Ward, as well as all of our Price-Babson College Fellows, especially Les Charm for his generous giving of time, entrepreneurial energy, and resources to Babson.

Outside Harvard and Babson, several key people have given more to this effort than they shall ever know. Paul J. Tobin, president of Cellular One, Boston, and the Boston Communications Group, has been a model entrepreneur and entrepreneurial manager in pioneering the car phone industry in America, along with the superb team at Cell-One. I learn new lessons on entrepreneurial creativity each time I work with PJ and see him in action. Also, Harold Price, Gloria Appel, and the late Edwin Appel of the Price Institute have been staunch and unwavering champions of entrepreneurship at Babson College and across America. Their generous, pioneering support of the Price-Babson Fellows Program has made a major contribution toward creating entrepreneurial minds—in both faculty and students—at colleges and universities worldwide. By the 10th anniversary of the program in 1994, over 300 faculty and the entrepreneur fellows from over 140 universities in over 30 nations had attended this pioneering symposium.

My colleagues and fellow board members at BCI Advisors, Inc., have provided a window on emerging companies beyond the start-up stage: Don Remey, Hoyt Goodrich, Bart Goodwin, Ted Horton, Steve Ely, Bill Foxley, Bill Johnson, and Craig Foley.

Since 1991 I have had the privilege of working closely with Ewing M. Kauffman and his extraordinary team at the Ewing Marion Kauffman Foundation (EMKF) in Kansas City: Michael Herman, Marilyn Kourilsky, James McGraw, Steve Roling, Bob Rogers, Michie Slaughter, Raymond Smilor. Thanks also go to those who serve with me on the board of the Center for Entrepreneurial Leadership (CEL) at the Foundation: Bert Berkley, Wilie Davis, and Paul Henson. Having built from scratch Marion Labs, Inc., into one of the largest US pharmaceutical firms, "Mr. K" and his top-management team have created one of the largest foundations in America and have committed half of its resources to the support of entrepreneurship. This unprecedented initiative sets EMKF apart as a pioneer and the leader among all major US foundations in this mission. I have said many times since 1991 that the world of entrepreneurship education, practice, and research will never be the same. This is already proving to be an understatement.

Hal Seigle, retired chairman of the Sunmark Companies, St. Louis, and now a professional director and adviser to growing companies, has taught me a great deal about the difference between working hard and working smart. Watching him do both, always with a lot of class and integrity, has been a post-graduate course by itself. The inspiring example of Jake and Diana Bishop which continually reminds me of the wisdom of Casey Stengel's advice: They say it can't be done; but that don't always work!

My colleagues at Ernst & Young's national US and UK offices in the Entrepreneurial Services Group have opened my eyes to a whole new perspective on how it is possible for a Big Six firm to be very entrepreneurial: Ed Beanland, Herb Braun, Bill Casey, Henry Clark, Richard Combes, Gary Dando, Dan Garner, Ron Deigleman, Peter Gillette, Jan Gregory, Chris Harrison, Horace Johnson, Jock Lennox, Karl Mayhall, Dick Nigon, Bob Phillips, Alice Downes-Rice, Ralph Sabin, and Hy Schweil have all helped me to understand the entrepreneurial process.

A debt of appreciation is due to all of my former students from whom I learn with each encounter and marvel both at their accomplishments, and how little damage I imparted! Without them this work would be meaningless.

The work of over 50 researchers who have contributed to the Babson Entrepreneurship Research Conferences, begun in 1981 by Karl Vesper while he was Paul T. Babson Professor, and reported in *Frontiers of Entrepreneurship Research*, 1981 through 1993 (Babson College), has added to my thinking. A driving force behind entrepreneurship research, these conferences were sponsored by Babson College beginning in 1981 and later were cosponsored by Georgia Tech's School of Management (1984), the Wharton Center for Entrepreneurship (1985), Pepperdine University (1987), University of Calgary (1988), St. Louis University (1989), St. Louis University (1990), University of Pittsburg (1991), INSEAD France (1992), and University of Houston (1993). In 1994, the conference will become The Babson-Kauffman Foundation Entrepreneurship Conference as a new strategic alliance begins for both institutions. While the names of the researchers are too numerous to note, I am especially mindful of the work of Professors Birley, Block, Boyd, Brockhaus, Brown, Bruno, Bygrave, Churchill, Cooper, Dunkleberg, Feigen, Gasse, Hornaday, Hoy, Krasner, MacMillan, Miner, Mitton, Muzyka, Peterson, Roberts, Sahlman, Sexton, Shapero, Smith, H. Stevenson, Tarpley, Tyebjee, Vesper, and Wetzel.

Research studies reported elsewhere, such as the Baylor Conference (1980) and the 75th Anniversary Entrepreneurship Symposium held at Harvard Business School in 1983, have also been invaluable.

Practical knowledge and earlier research of the venture capital industry have been enhanced by the publications and work of my friends and colleagues Stanley E. Pratt and Norman D. Fast, founders of Venture Economics and publishers of *Venture Capital Journal.* The founding management teams of Investkontakt AB and Svetab in Sweden made innumerable innovations in applying my earlier concepts and approaches to their venture capital and business development activities. These include Hakan Raihle, Morgan Olsson, Ingvar Svenson, Gunnar Olofgors, Lars Bostrom, Per Wahlstrom, and their staffs. Further fine-tuning of earlier concepts and approaches occurred in practice in the United Kingdom. Contributing to this effort were the late Brian Haslett, Jack Peterson, Jack Hayes, and Paul Croke of Ventures Founders Corporation, and Joseph Frye of VF Limited in the United Kingdom. Professor Chris Harling of Cranfield Business School was an extraordinary co-worker in these efforts.

Entrepreneurs and others whose experience and insight have touched me over the years are many. I am most appreciative of them all. I especially want to thank Doug Kahn, Brian Dwyer, Michael Harde, John Bray, J. C. Egnew, John Moore, Art Beisang, Ken DaFoe, Fred Alper, Karl Baumgartner, Don Spigarelli, Bill Egan, Harry Healer, Kevin Rhone, Jan Pirrong, Dan Gregory, Arthur Little, Jim Morgan, Bill Congleton, Earl Linehan, Jim Hindman and Ed Kelley, Allan Harle, Colin Chapman, Ken Fisher, Bill Poduska, Bill Foster, Richard Testa, Burt McMurtry, Brent Rider, Howard Head, Paul Kelley, and Gordon Baty.

My work with my good friend and colleague David Gumpert of the *Harvard Business Review* on two other books and articles helped to make easier the writing of this manuscript. I am grateful to Wendy C. Handler, assistant professor, Babson College, who wrote the material for Chapter 8, "The Family Venture."

I am also most appreciative of Richard J. Testa, of Testa, Hurwitz & Thibeault, Boston, for contributing his excellent article "The Legal Process of Venture Capital Investment," reproduced as Appendix III, from *Pratt's Guide to Venture Capital Sources,* 8th edition. I am grateful also to Kenneth Goodpaster, professor, Harvard Business School, for permission to use his material on ethics in Chapter 9. I also wish to acknowledge the earlier contributions to Chapter 9 of Grace M. Dingee, Nancy Tieken, and David Boyd, professor and dean of the College of Business, Northeastern University, Boston. I am thankful also to Robert Morris Associates of Philadelphia for permission to use information about their statement studies

(Appendix I). I would also like to thank Douglas Ranalli, founder of Fax International, and Frederic M. Alper and Victor R. Del Regno of Morris Alper, Inc.

Without the attentive and highly professional support of Lisa Lamoureaux Garrahan, Donna MacLearn, and Stephanie Bomhoff at my HBS office Christy Remey and I would not have been able to get the project done on time. You are in a class by yourselves. Thanks!

J.A.T.

Contents

PART I THE OPPORTUNITY 1

1 **The Entrepreneurial Process 3**
The Silent Revolution 3
What Is Entrepreneurship? 7
The Problem of Survival 9
Exceptions to the Failure Rule 11
An Analytical Framework 15
Myths and Realities 22
The Entrepreneurial Mind 24
Case—Outdoor Scene, Inc. 26
Exercise—A Visit with an Entrepreneur 34

2 **New Venture Ideas 39**
The Role of Ideas 39
Pattern Recognition 42
Finding Ideas 45
Case—PC-Build, Inc. 49
Exercise—Creative Squares 79
Exercise—Idea Generation Guide 81

3 **Opportunity Recognition 87**
Recognizing Opportunities 87
Screening Opportunities 94
Gathering Information 105
Case—Fibercom Applications, Inc. 109

4 **Screening Venture Opportunities 139**
Screening Venture Opportunities 139
Exercise—Venture Opportunity Screening Guide 140

PART II THE FOUNDERS 183

5 **The Entrepreneurial Mind in Thought and Action 185**
The Search for Understanding 185
Converging on the Entrepreneurial Mind 190
The Concept of Apprenticeship 199
Entrepreneur's Creed 202
Case—Kevin Mooney 203

6 **The Entrepreneurial Manager 207**
The Entrepreneurial Domain 207
Stages of Growth 210
Management Competencies 217
Case—PMI, Inc. 222
Exercise—Managerial Skills and Know-How Assessment 228

7 **The New Venture Team 253**
The Importance of the Team 253
Forming/Building Teams 254
Rewards and Incentives 262
Case—Setting the Stage 265
Exercise—Rewards 275

8 **The Family Venture 283**
Popular and Numerous 283
The Impact of Goals 284
The Family Venture Team 288
Strategies for Success 291
Case—Passing the Baton 293

9 Personal Ethics and the Entrepreneur 305
Exercise—Ethics **305**
Overview of Ethics **313**
Ethical Stereotypes **314**
Should Ethics Be Taught? **316**
Thorny Issues for Entrepreneurs **319**
Ethics Exercise Revisited **322**
Case—When the Party's Over **322**

PART III RESOURCE REQUIREMENTS 329

10 Resource Requirements 331
The Entrepreneurial Approach to Resources **331**
Outside People Resources **334**
Financial Resources **345**
General Sources of Information **351**
Case—Fenchel Lampshade Company **351**
Exercise—Financial Statements **370**
Exercise—How Entrepreneurs Turn Less Into More **374**

11 The What, Whether, and Why of the Business Plan 375
Planning and the Business Plan **375**
Pitfalls of Effective Planning **379**
A Closer Look at the What **382**
Case—FAX International, Inc. **386**
Preparing a Business Plan **418**
Exercise—The Business Plan Guide **419**

PART IV FINANCING ENTREPRENEURIAL VENTURES 441

12 Entrepreneurial Finance 443
Venture Financing: The Entrepreneur's Achilles' Heel **443**
Determining Capital Requirements **450**
Crafting Financial and Fund-Raising Strategies **453**
Case—Douglas J. Ranalli **456**

13 Obtaining Risk Capital 479
Cover Your Equity **479**
Angels and Informal Investors **481**
Venture Capital: Gold Mines and Tar Pits **483**
Other Equity Sources **492**
Case—Hindman & Company **498**

14 The Deal: Valuation, Structure, and Negotiation 509
The Art and Craft of Valuation **509**
Structuring the Deal **517**
Negotiations **521**
Sandtraps **523**
Case—Bridge Capital Investors, Inc. **528**

15 Obtaining Debt Capital 543
The 1990s: The New Credit Environment **543**
Sources of Debt Capital **544**
Managing and Orchestrating the Banking Relationship **553**
Tar Pits: Entrepreneurs Beware **561**
Case—Michigan Lighting, Inc. **562**

PART V START-UP AND AFTER 573

16 Managing Rapid Growth 575
Growing Up Big **575**
The Importance of Culture and Organizational Climate **580**
Entrepreneurial Management for the 21st Century: Three Breakthroughs **583**
Case—Jiffy Lube International, Inc. **587**

17 The Entrepreneur and the Troubled Company 597
When the Bloom Is Off the Rose **597**
The Gestation Period of Crisis **600**
Predicting Trouble **601**
The Threat of Bankruptcy **603**
Intervention **604**
Case—EASEL Corporation **610**

18 The Harvest and Beyond 653
A Journey, Not a Destination **653**
First Build a Great Company **654**
Harvest Options **658**
Beyond the Harvest **662**
Seven Secrets of Success **662**
Case—R. Douglas Kahn **663**

PART VI CRAFTING A PERSONAL ENTREPRENEURIAL STRATEGY 681

19 Crafting a Personal Entrepreneurial Strategy 683

Planning Revisited **683**
Crafting an Entrepreneurial Strategy **685**
Exercise—Personal Entrepreneurial Strategy **688**
Case—When the Circus Comes to Town **735**

APPENDIXES 739

I **Information about RMA "Projection of Financial Statements" and RMA Statement Studies 741**
II **Information about *Industry Norms and Key Business Ratios*, Published by Dun & Bradstreet 753**
III **"The Legal Process of Venture Capital Investment," by Richard J. Testa 755**
IV **Sample Terms Sheet 771**
V **Outline of an Investment Agreement 774**
VI **Sample Vesting and Stock Restriction Agreement 777**
VII **Sample Loan Agreement 781**
VIII **Vases and Faces Exercise, by Betty Edwards 785**

INDEX 789

THE OPPORTUNITY

PART I

One often hears, especially from younger, newer entrepreneurs, the exhortation: "Go for it! You have nothing to lose now. So what if it doesn't work out. You can do it again. Why wait?" While the spirit reflected in these comments is commendable and while there can be no substitute for doing, such itchiness can be a real mistake unless it is focused on a solid opportunity.

Most entrepreneurs who start businesses, particularly if they are their first, run out of cash at a faster rate than they bring in customers and profitable sales. While there are many reasons for this, the first is that they have not focused on the right opportunities. Unsuccessful entrepreneurs usually equate an idea with an opportunity; successful entrepreneurs know the difference.

While there are boundless opportunities for those with the entrepreneurial zest, the fact of the matter is that a single entrepreneur will be able to launch and build only a few good businesses—probably no more than three or four—during his or her energetic and productive years. (Fortunately, all you need to do is grow and harvest one quite profitable venture whose sales have exceeded several million dollars. The result will be a most satisfying professional life, as well as a quite financially rewarding one.)

How important is it, then, that you screen and choose an opportunity with great care? Very important. It is no accident that venture capital investors have consistently invested in just 1 percent to 3 percent of all the ventures they review.

As important as it is to find a good opportunity, each good opportunity has its risk and problems as well. The perfect deal has yet to be seen. Identifying risks and problems before you start so steps can be taken, early on, to eliminate them or reduce any negative effects is another dimension of opportunity screening.

The Entrepreneurial Process 1

Anyone [can be an entrepreneur] who wants to experience the deep, dark canyons of uncertainty and ambiguity; and who wants to walk the breathtaking highlands of success. But I caution, do not plan to walk the latter, until you have experienced the former.

An Entrepreneur

RESULTS EXPECTED

Upon completion of this chapter, you will have:

1. Examined evidence of and trends in the "Silent Revolution."
2. Developed a definition of entrepreneurship and looked at its practical, intellectual, and policy agenda.
3. Determined how successful entrepreneurs define and measure success.
4. Looked at the failure rule and examined why there are exceptions to the failure rule and the types of new businesses that succeed.
5. Discussed briefly a framework for analyzing new ventures.
6. Analyzed the proposed start-up of Outdoor Scene, Inc.
7. Conducted an interview with a successful entrepreneur.

THE SILENT REVOLUTION

The American Dream

We are in the midst of what can be called the *Silent Revolution*. It is entirely possible that the Silent Revolution will affect the 21st century as much as, and probably more than, the Industrial Revolution affected the 20th.[1]

Among the adult working population in the United States, which in 1993 numbered 124 million, more than one in seven is self-employed, and it can be said that the dream of working for oneself exists in the minds of millions of other Americans. Compared to managers and those working for others, as many as three times more plan never to retire.[2]

And it is no wonder that so many have the dream—a dream of walking the breathtaking highlands of success mentioned in the opening quotation.[3] The self-employed feel good about themselves, about their work lives, and about the economic rewards they earn. Uniformly, the self-employed report the highest levels of personal satisfaction, challenge, pride, and remuneration. They seem to love the entrepreneurial game for its own sake. They love their work because it is invigorating, energizing, and meaningful.

[1] Jeffry A Timmons, *The Entrepreneurial Mind* (Acton, MA: Brick House Publishing, 1989).

[2] Howard H Stevenson, "Who are the Harvard Self-Employed?" in *Frontiers of Entrepreneur Research: 1983,* ed J A Hornaday et al. (Babson Park, MA: Babson College, 1983), p. 233.

[3] From an interview with his father, an entrepreneur, conducted by Gian Perotti, Babson College, class of 1984.

Entrepreneurs are critical contributors to our economy, and their contributions include: leadership; management, economic, and social renewal; innovation; research and development effectiveness; job creation; competitiveness and productivity; the formation of new industries; and regional economic development. Charles Handy, a visiting professor at the London School of Economics, describes a time full of change where

> the future, in so many areas, is there to be shaped, by us and for us—a time when the only prediction that will hold true is that no predictions will hold true; a time, therefore, for bold imaginings in private life as well as public, for thinking the unlikely and doing the unreasonable.[4]

At the same time, society looks to those who are answering the management, economic, and social questions of the present which shape the future. What are people thinking about today that could change your life in the future? When Handy asked a group of young executives about the year 2000, they proposed such changes as *cordless telephones*, whereby "a telephone will then belong to a person, not a place,"[5] or *the transgenic pig*, which could make organs available on demand because pigs and humans are biologically similar.[6] Recent research on innovation and research and development effectiveness supports the assumption that these wild ideas will, in fact, change our lives. The National Science Foundation and the Department of Commerce have reported that entrepreneurial firms are responsible for 95 percent of the radical innovations since World War II, while claiming 50 percent of all innovations. These inventions not only contribute products and services, but they also create jobs for our economy as a whole. Among the 4.6 million US companies with 500 or fewer employees, the Small Business Administration reported that 14.6 million people are employed. In 1990 the Fortune 500 firms accounted for a mere 7 percent of the total US employment, and the reduction has continued in 1991 with a loss of 450,000 jobs.[7] Competitively, the entrepreneurial "gazelles" have left America's largest companies in the dust. Additionally, entrepreneurs have created a number of multibillion dollar industries. A few examples: semiconductors, mini- and microcomputers, telecommunications, cellular telephones, and biotechnology. In terms of regional economic development, one does not have to look very far from East Cambridge, Massachusetts, because, within a single square mile, some 636 new companies have formed since 1949—which employ 300,000 people and contribute $10 billion in new wages and salaries.[8] How does President Clinton plan to create more jobs while establishing economic stability in the nation's cities? He hopes to draw upon the revolutionary Shorebank model, an entrepreneurial bank that promotes economic renewal in a previously underserved community.[9]

The vast majority of the nearly 2 million millionaires in the United States in 1993 accumulated their wealth through entrepreneurial acts.

What may be more surprising is that even graduates of the Harvard Business School, which has long been thought of as the West Point for the Fortune 500, thrive on this entrepreneurial dream. About one-third end up working for themselves, and the vast majority of all graduates 10 years after graduation work for smaller companies employing

[4] Charles Handy, *The Age of Unreason* (Boston: Harvard Business School Press, 1990), p. 5.

[5] Ibid., p. 18.

[6] Ibid., p. 19.

[7] Compiled from various sources, including D Birch, EFER Conference, Berlin, 1991; Department of Commerce; and the Small Business Administration.

[8] Compiled from various sources, including Bank of Boston Study, Venture Economics, and the Small Business Administration.

[9] Christine C Remey and J Gregory Dees, "Shorebank Corporation," HBS Case 393-096, Harvard Business School, 1992.

fewer than 1,000 persons. Ninety percent of the second-year MBA candidates say they want to work for themselves.[10] What may surprise many is that 59 percent of Harvard Business School's class of 1967, at their 25th reunion, reported they were self-employed.

The entrepreneurial wave has also spread to communities, universities, colleges, and high schools in recent years. Surveys claim that between 600 and 1,000 American colleges and universities offer courses in starting new ventures and entrepreneurship, compared to as few as 50 in 1975. A 1987 Roper survey showed that 46 percent of all college freshmen surveyed felt that owning one's own business was an attractive career alternative. Programs like the National Foundation for Teaching Entrepreneurship to Handicapped and Disadvantaged Youth, Inc., are currently working in high schools "to promote entrepreneurial literacy in America's inner cities and to help each one start his/her own business."[11] Steve Mariotti, the founder of NFTE, reported in 1993 that "over the last six years, we've had 3,800 inner-city graduates of our course, most in the 9th through 12th grades. About 14 percent of our graduates have some type of business after 80 hours of instruction . . . [The other 86 percent] may start businesses sometime in the future and thereby create jobs for themselves and others. They're certainly more likely to get jobs because they are economically literate."[12] Ewing M. Kauffman's Center for Entrepreneurial Leadership introduces students in kindergarten through grade 12 to entrepreneurship and provides training and support for adult entrepreneurs as well.[13]

The entrepreneurial wave in America in the past decade has brought unprecedented benefits, not just to individuals, but to society as a whole. Entrepreneurs, it turns out, are the fuel, engine, and throttle for the economic engine of the country. Consider the following:

- Over 1 million *enterprises,* from one-person operations on up, were launched in the United States in 1991. By the year 2000, demographers estimate there will be 30 million firms in the United States, up significantly from the 18 million firms in existence in 1988.[14]
- Virtually all of the net new jobs created in this country come from these *new and expanding firms* – not from large, established companies. In fact, according to census data, small business accounted for 68 percent of new job growth – 11.3 million of the 16.5 million net gain in jobs. "More recently, from 1988 to 1990, small firms have created all of the new jobs in the economy and most of this growth has occurred in firms with fewer than 20 employees."[15]
- In the United States, 36 million jobs have been created in the last 20 years, whereas in Europe there has been a net loss.
- Since World War II, 50 percent of all innovations, and 95 percent of all radical innovations, have come from *new and smaller firms.* These have included, for example, the microcomputer, the pacemaker, overnight express packages, the quick oil change, fast food, oral contraceptives, the X-ray machine, and so forth.[16]
- The companies of the 53 individual entrepreneurs who were inducted into the Babson College Academy of Distinguished Entrepreneurs from 1977 to 1993 have combined

[10] Stevenson, "Who Are the Harvard Self-Employed?"

[11] Alice Oberfield and J Gregory Dees, *Steve Mariotti and NFTE* (HBS Case 9-391-169), p. 3.

[12] "Interview with an Entrepreneur: Starting a Business Can Motivate Students to Do Better," *Education Today*, January 1993, p. 4.

[13] "A Good Word About Profit," *INC.* July 1992, p. 12.

[14] Frank Swain, Office of Advocacy, Small Business Administration, Washington, DC (speech in Dallas at Ernst & Whinney's Privately Owned and Emerging Businesses, "Current Matters," October 6, 1988).

[15] *The State of Small Business: A Report of the President, Transmitted to Congress, 1992* (Washington, DC: Small Business Administration, 1992).

[16] Several studies by the United States Department of Commerce.

sales in 1993 equalling the GNP of the *16th largest country in the world.*[17] Many of these entrepreneurs built their companies from nothing, and their names include entrepreneurial legends,[18] as well as others with equal deeds but less public familiarity. Since 1988, many founder-entrepreneurs have been added to the list, including Alan Bond of Dallhold Investments; Amar G. Bose of Bose Corporation; Paul Fireman of Reebok International Ltd.; John R. Furman of Furman Lumber; Kazuo Inamori of Kycera Corporation; Sandra L. Kurtzig of ASK Computer Systems; Edward Lowe of Edward Lowe Industries; Patrick J. McGovern of International Data Group; William G. McGowan of MCI Communications Corporation; Michael W. J. Smurfit of Jefferson Smurfit Group; John C. Merritt of Van Kampen Merritt Holdings Corp., Inc.; Leslie H. Wexner of the Limited, Inc.; Anita Roddick of the Body Shop; Ewing Marion Kauffman of Marion Merrell Dow, Inc.; Jacob Stoft-Nielsen, Jr., of Stoft Tankers and Terminals; and Robert A. Swanson of Genetech, Inc.

- Between $60 billion and $80 billion of informal risk capital exists in our economy in 1993, and another $35 billion of venture capital funds are available from professional sources seeking to back small-company entrepreneurs.
- In the United States, a national survey by the Yankalovich organization found two significant trends: (1) Women are questioning the traditional world of work and seeking alternatives to it by exploring opportunities for *entrepreneurship* and (2) people in their 50s and 60s are not planning to retire but rather to pursue second careers in smaller, more *entrepreneurial settings.*
- In the United States, women own over 5 million companies.[19] Recently, the Small Business Administration reported that "women owned about 32 percent of the nation's sole proprietorships in 1990, up from 26 percent in 1980. . . . [Furthermore, it is expected that women will] form businesses 1.5 times faster than men during the 1990s.[20] Thus, by the year 2000, "it is projected that 40 to 50 percent of all businesses will be owned by women."[21]
- There were at least 1 million minority-owned businesses in 1990, based on conservative estimates.[22] According to the Small Business Administration, for every 1,000 small businesses in 1990, 1.3 were owned by African-Americans, 1.7 were owned by Hispanic-Americans, and 5.5 were owned by Asian-Americans.
- *Entrepreneurship is not just the domain of new and small firms.* It can also happen in older and larger companies (although it is seen far less frequently); in slower growing and even troubled companies; in nonprofit organizations; and in Eastern, Western, and developing economies.

[17] Compiled by John Marthinsen, Professor, Babson College.

[18] Royal Little of Textron, Inc.; An Wang, Wang Laboratories, Inc.; Frank Purdue, Purdue Farms, Inc.; Ken Olsen, Digital Equipment Corporation; Sochio Honda, Honda Motor Company, Ltd.; Ray Kroc, McDonald's Corporation; Fred Smith, Federal Express Corporation; Nolan Bushnell, Pizza Time Theatre, Inc.; Trammel Crow, Trammel Crow Company; J Willard Marriott, Jr., The Marriott Corporation; Ed Lowe, Ed Lowe Enterprises (The Kitty-Litter Company); Wally Amos, The Famous Amos Chocolate Chip Cookie Corporation; HR Bloch, H & R Block, Inc.; Don Burr, People Express; John Cullinane, Cullinet Software, Inc.; Rupert Murdoch, New America Publishing, Inc.; Peter Sprague, National Semiconductor Corporation; and John Templeton, The Templeton Funds.

[19] Country Price and Dick Fleming, "Four-Year Study of Colorado Entrepreneurship with Minority and Women Business Owners," in *Frontiers of Entrepreneurship Research: 1991*, ed. Neil C Churchill et al. (Babson Park, MA: Babson College, 1991), p. 49.

[20] Sue Shellenbarger: "Work & Family: Women Start Younger at Own Businesses," *The Wall Street Journal*, March 15, 1993, p. B1.

[21] Joline Godfrey, *Our Wildest Dreams* (New York: Harper Business, 1992), p. xx.

[22] Rudolph Winston, Jr., "The Status of Minority Enterprise," in *Minority Enterprise in the 90s: A Questionable Future?*, ed. Rudy Winston (Cambridge, MA: Rudolph Winston, Jr., 1991), p. 47.

Dawn of a New Era

This source of economic progress is now being discovered worldwide, and there exists the unprecedented promise of a sustained global entrepreneurial effort. Again, lighting the flame of the entrepreneurial spirit empowers nations and people who, as Mark Twain said, know "the difference between lightning and a lightning bug."

Consider the following global trends in entrepreneurship:

- For the first time in June and July of 1987, 46 senior policy makers, researchers, entrepreneurs, and executives from 26 countries met in Salzburg, Austria, for an eight-day seminar in *entrepreneurship*.[23]
- In 1988 the newly organized European Foundation for Entrepreneurship Research held its first annual conference of researchers and practicers at IMEDE in Lausanne, Switzerland.
- The European Commission began the European Seed Capital Fund Network in 1988, which offered support and financial incentives to seed capital funds. By late 1992, close to 80 investments had been made by 24 funds.[24]
- Despite the lack of formal venture capital sources outside the United States in the 1980s, "by 1990 over half of all the $80 billion of venture capital under management worldwide was outside of the United States."[25] Today, the availability of such funds is a worldwide phenomenon occurring in the United Kingdom, Western Europe, Scandinavia, Kenya, Spain, Brazil, Australia, the Philippines, Japan, Korea, and elsewhere.

WHAT IS ENTREPRENEURSHIP?

A Definition

Entrepreneurship is creating and building something of value from practically nothing. That is, entrepreneurship is the process of creating or seizing an opportunity and pursuing it regardless of the resources currently controlled.[26] Entrepreneurship involves the definition, creation, and distribution of value and benefits to individuals, groups, organizations, and society. Entrepreneurship is very rarely a get-rich-quick proposition; rather, it is one of building long-term value and durable cash flow streams.

Fundamentally, entrepreneurship is a human creative act. It involves finding personal energy by initiating and building an enterprise or organization, rather than by just watching, analyzing, or describing one. Entrepreneurship usually requires a vision and the passion, commitment, and motivation to transmit this vision to other stakeholders, such as partners, customers, suppliers, employees, and financial backers. It also requires a willingness to take calculated risks—both personal and financial—and then doing everything possible to influence the odds.

Entrepreneurship involves building a team of people with complementary skills and talents; of sensing an opportunity where others see chaos, contradiction, and confusion; and of finding, marshalling, and controlling resources (often owned by others) to pursue the

[23] Led by the author and Howard H Stevenson, Sarofim-Rock Professor, Harvard Business School.

[24] Audrey Choi, "Seed-Capital Funds Play Growing Role in Helping European Firms Get Started," *The Wall Street Journal*, November 10, 1992.

[25] William D Bygrave and Jeffry A Timmons, *Venture Capital at the Crossroads* (Boston: Harvard Business School Press, 1992), p. 67.

[26] The definition of entrepreneurship has evolved over the past few years from work done at the Harvard Business School and at Babson College. Particular credit is due to Howard H Stevenson of the Harvard Business School. Credit is also due to other colleagues of the author at the Harvard Business School and at Babson College.

opportunity. And, entrepreneurship involves making sure the venture does not run out of money when it needs money most.

The Stark Urgency of Entrepreneurship

Entrepreneurship has been likened to athletics or medicine, where the entrepreneur is to business what a decathlete is to the Olympics or a surgeon is to an operation. In all, winning strategies require intense, active, and creative involvement. There are challenges, uncertainty, calculated risk taking, and risk minimizing. And disaster can pounce with unexpected suddenness.

Entrepreneurship can be compared to the Boston Marathon, a race with an especially punishing series of long hills, called in the marathon Heart Break Hill. Or the successful entrepreneurial act is reminiscent of the improvisation and resourcefulness of a downhill ski racer speeding like a projectile. A downhill ski racer is always at the edge of disaster but just as close to victory, and the balance shifts to victory if his or her talents and abilities exceed those of the competition and if split-second judgments and mental calculations result in actions that keep the racer pointed toward victory. And, as with the racer, disaster for an entrepreneur can pounce unexpectedly. Just ask Adam Osborne, who in 1981 developed and marketed the first portable minicomputer. By 1985, Osborne Computer, having made the wrong move at the wrong time, was displaced by another firm, Compaq, and went out of business.

Still others have likened entrepreneurship to a symphony orchestra, where people with diverse skills and personalities are so blended by the conductor, with mastery and balance, that the whole is greater than the sum of the parts. Or it has been compared to juggling—because of adroitness under stress and pressure, the skillful juggler can keep many balls in the air at once and recover quickly from the slightest miscast.

Entrepreneurship parallels other activities having similar demands and unknowns. Take, for instance, the unknowns and urgency to act faced by the first pilot to break the sound barrier, the legendary Chuck Yeager, as documented in *The Right Stuff:*

> In the thin air at the edge of space, where the stars and the moon came out at noon, in an atmosphere so thin that the ordinary laws of aerodynamics no longer applied and a plane could skid into a flat spin like a cereal bowl on a waxed Formica counter and then start tumbling, end over end like a brick . . . you had to be "afraid to panic." In the skids, the tumbles, the spins there was only one thing you could let yourself think about: What do I do next?[27]

All the acts above are artistic and creative. Their outcomes also tend to be either highly rewarding successes or painful and visible misses. And common to all is that stark urgency—What do I do next?

The Practical Agenda

Entrepreneurship is holistic and integrated; that is, entrepreneurship concerns the business and its managers/founders in their entirety, not just piecemeal. Thus, entrepreneurship is akin to the problem-solving task of constructing a jigsaw puzzle. In the process of creating the puzzle, pieces will invariably be missing or obscure, and the trick is to see and anticipate patterns—before others do. The educational focus of the practical agenda centers on this question: *What are the concepts, skills, know-how and know-who, information, attitudes, alternatives, and resources that entrepreneurs and entrepreneurial managers need?*

[27] Tom Wolfe, *The Right Stuff* (New York: Bantam Books, 1980), pp. 51–52.

The Intellectual and Policy Agenda

The study of entrepreneurship also seeks to understand a rich, complex, and challenging intellectual agenda. A provocative intellectual question, which has important policy implications, is, *Why does entrepreneurship occur—and fail to occur—in new firms and old; in small firms and large; in fast- and slow-growing firms; in the private and public sectors; and in the East, the West, and developing economies?*

As was suggested by the working definition earlier, entrepreneurship is not just the domain of new and emerging businesses. The intellectual and policy agenda addresses at least the following issues:

- Recognition, creation, and pursuit of opportunity in new and existing firms.
- Building, survival, and renewal of companies.
- Financing of new, emerging, and submerging organizations.
- Entrepreneurship's role in larger organizations.
- Public policy.

As the intellectual and policy domain gains importance in the decade ahead, entrepreneurs need to preserve and enhance a favorable climate for future entrepreneurs. Such a climate might have the following attributes: "A culture that prizes entrepreneurship, an imperative to educate our population so that our entrepreneurial potential is second to none; and a government that generously supports pure and applied science, fosters entrepreneurship with enlightened policies, and enables schools to produce the best educated students in the world."[28]

THE PROBLEM OF SURVIVAL

Failure Rule

An extraordinary variety of people, opportunities, and strategies characterize the approximately 20 million corporations, partnerships, and proprietorships in this United States.[29] There has been an unprecedented number of new company formations in the United States in the past few years. In 1992, for example, 1.1 million new businesses were started, according to government estimates.

Not only can almost anyone start a business, but a great many succeed. While it certainly helps, a person does not have to be a genius to create a successful business. As Nolan Bushnell has asserted, "If you are not a millionaire or bankrupt by the time you are thirty, you are not really trying."[30]

While its rigors may favor the young, age is no barrier to entry. One study showed that nearly 21 percent of the founders were over 40 when they embarked on their entrepreneurial careers, the majority were in their 30s, and just over one-quarter did so by the time they were 25. Further, numerous examples exist of founders who were over 60. Take, for instance, Colonel Sanders of Kentucky Fried Chicken. Another example, although perhaps less well known, is that of Stanley Rich, who is over 70 years old and has started at least seven businesses since the age of 60.[31]

Discussed above in the definition of entrepreneurship is the idea of value creation and distribution, not just for the owners but also for other stakeholders, such as partners,

[28] Jeffry A Timmons, Testimony before the Subcommittee on Technology, Environment, and Aviation, HR 820: The Civilian Technology Development Act of 1993, February 16, 1993.

[29] Only nonfarm businesses are included in the figure. See *The State of Small Business 1992*, Table 1.1.

[30] In response to a question from a student at Founder's Day, Babson College, 1983.

[31] A Price–Babson College Fellow, Stanley Rich is a founder of the MIT Enterprise Forum[SM].

customers, suppliers, employees, and backers. Even for those businesses which survive, realizing a capital gain or at least deriving sufficient income from the business is decidedly more difficult.

This ability to generate sufficient income or potential for capital gain is a critical measure of success and separates those businesses which fail or which merely survive as a job substitute from those which succeed.

For the vast majority of new businesses in the country, the odds of survival definitely are not in their favor. While government data, research, and business mortality statisticians may not agree on the precise failure and survival figures for new businesses, they do agree that failure is the rule, not the exception.

Exhibit 1.1
Overall New Business Failure Rates

Time to Fail
The following percentages of small businesses are dissolved within two, four, and six years:

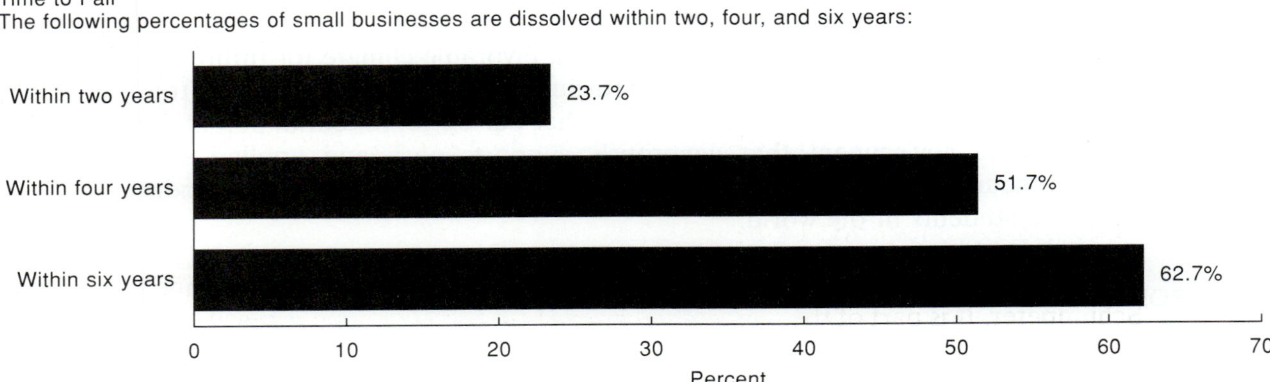

Reasons for Failure
A breakdown of why businesses fail:

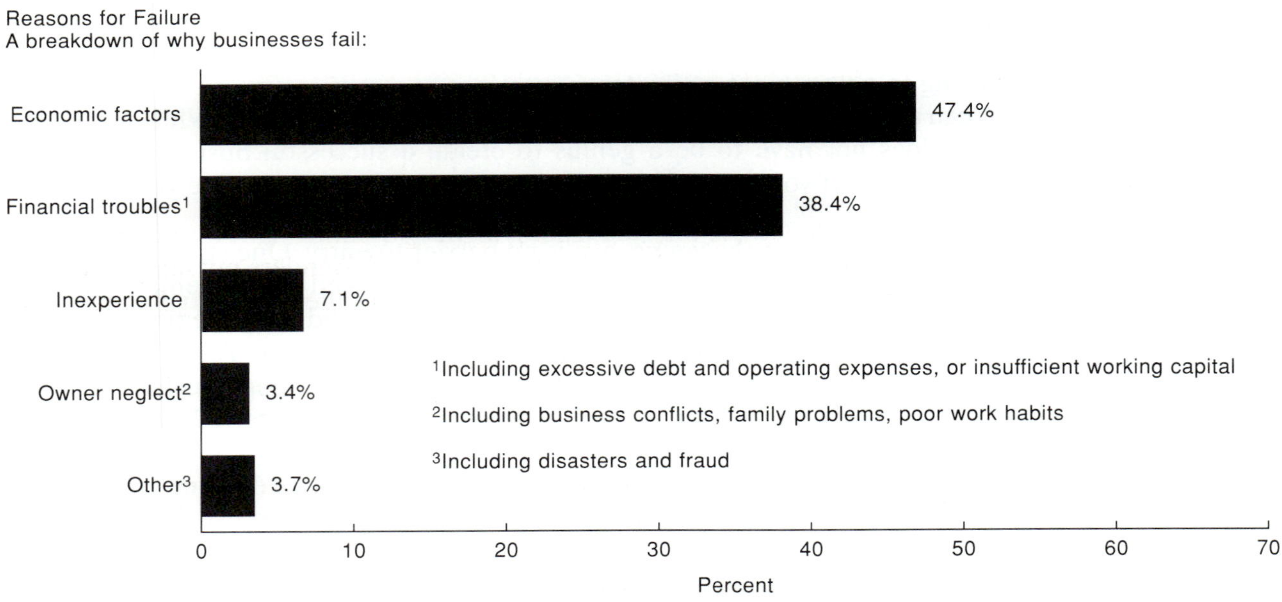

Note: A "dissolved" business includes those that are voluntarily shut down as well as those forced to file for bankruptcy.
Source: *The Wall Street Journal,* October 16, 1992, p. R7.

Complicating efforts to obtain precise figures is the fact that it is not easy to define and identify failures, and reliable statistics and databases just are not available. However, the Small Business Administration estimated in 1983 that, for every three new businesses formed, two close their doors.[32]

There is also wide variation in failure rates across industries. In 1991, for instance, even though retail and services accounted for two of nine categories reported in *The State of Small Business*, they accounted for 61 percent of all failures and bankruptcies in that year.[33]

Exhibit 1.1 is a distillation of a number of studies of failure rates over the last 50 years. Illustrated are the facts that (1) failure rates are high and (2) although the majority of the failures occur in the first two to five years, it may take considerably longer for some to fail. This picture is supported by the findings of several different studies.[34]

Another study of business failures and bankruptcies found that for those businesses which failed, over 53 percent of the failures occurred in the first 5 years; nearly 30 percent occurred in years 6 through 10; and the remaining 17 percent involved firms in existence more than 10 years.[35]

To make matters worse, most people think that the failure rates are actually much higher. Since most would argue that actions are governed, more often than not, by perceptions rather than facts alone, this perception of failure, in addition to the dismal record, can be a serious obstacle to aspiring entrepreneurs.

Innovation, Economic Renewal, and Learning

A certain level of failure is part of "creative self-destruction" described by Joseph Schumpeter. It is part of the dynamics of innovation and economic renewal, a process which requires both births and deaths.

More important, it is also part of the learning process inherent in gaining an entrepreneurial apprenticeship. If a business fails, no other country in the world has laws, institutions, and social norms that are more forgiving. Firms go out of existence, but entrepreneurs do not.

EXCEPTIONS TO THE FAILURE RULE

Higher Potential Ventures

Success, rather than failure, is the rule among higher potential ventures and attractive small companies. They are driven by talented and experienced founders pursuing attractive opportunities who are able to attract both the right people and the necessary financial and other resources to make the venture work.

[32] *The State of Small Business: A Report of the President, Transmitted to the Congress, March 1983* (Washington, DC: Small Business Administration, 1983).

[33] *The State of Small Business 1992, p. 128..*

[34] Summaries of these are reported by Albert N Shapero and Joseph Giglierano, "Exits and Entries: A Study in Yellow Pages Journalism," in *Frontiers of Entrepreneurship Research: 1982*, ed. K Vesper et al. (Babson Park, MA: Babson College, 1982), pp. 113–41; and Arnold C Cooper, William C Dunkelberg, and Carolyn Y Woo, "Survival and Failure: A Longitudinal Study," in *Frontiers of Entrepreneurship Research: 1988*, ed. B Kirchhoff et al. (Babson Park, MA: Babson College), pp. 225–37.

[35] Dun & Bradstreet, Business Economics Division, *The Business Failure Record, 1980* (New York, 1982), p. 10.

Types of Ventures

A majority of businesses started each year are traditional, very small businesses employing one or two people who are willing to sacrifice income for the lifestyle they are afforded. These firms are called mom-and-pop businesses, marginal firms, or lifestyle firms. Remember, however, that the idea of value creation and distribution is implicit in the definition of entrepreneurship; thus, lifestyle firms are not entrepreneurs according to our definition. If we separate lifestyle firms from the pool of new businesses, two other types of firms remain: foundation firms or attractive small companies, which generate enough income to compensate fully those involved.

High Potential Ventures. The remaining firms are those that have the potential for significant capital gain. These higher potential ventures have sales of at least $500,000 to $1 million and grow at a rate of at least 10 percent per year. Recently, a study summarized the characteristics of high potential ventures as follows:

Management—better able to retain key personnel. *Venture and strategy*—higher gross margin; superior product quality; faster response to opportunity; market entry via regulation change, marketing innovation, niche strategy, favored customer purchasing agreements; greater marketing expense as a percentage of sales; more extensive experience with key suppliers; fewer changes in written business plans. *Market*—larger attainable market share; faster growing industry.[36]

Threshold Concept

There appears to be a minimum threshold size of at least 5 to 10 employees—and 20 is even better—and of sales of at least $1 million. *Exhibit 1.2* shows that based on a cross section of all new firms, one-year survival rates for new firms jump from approximately 78 percent for firms having up to 9 employees to approximately 95 percent for firms with between 20 and 99 employees.

A 1991 study found that "empirical evidence supports the liability of newness and liability of smallness arguments and suggests that newness and small size make survival problematic"; the authors inferred that "perceived satisfaction, cooperation, and trust between the customer and the organization [are] important for the continuation of the relationship. High levels of satisfaction, cooperation, and trust represent a stock of goodwill and positive beliefs which are critical assets that influence the commitment of the two parties to the relationship."[37] It is interesting that the authors of this study noted that "smaller organizations are found to be more responsive, while larger organizations are found to provide greater depth of service. . . . The entrepreneurial task is to find a way to either direct the arena of competition away from the areas where you are at a competitive disadvantage, or find some creative way to develop the required competency.[38]

After four years, as shown in *Exhibit 1.3*, the survival rate jumps from approximately 37 percent for firms with less than 19 employees to about 54 percent for firms with 20 to 49 employees.

Although any estimates based on sales per employee vary considerably from industry to industry, this minimum threshold translates roughly to a threshold of $50,000 to $100,000

[36] Harry J Sapienza, "Comets and Duds: Characteristics Distinguishing High and Low Performing High Potential Ventures," in *Frontiers of Entrepreneurial Research: 1991*, p. 124.

[37] S Venkataraman and Murray B Low, "On the Nature of Critical Relationships: A Test of the Liabilities and Size Hypothesis," in *Frontiers of Entrepreneurial Research: 1991*, p. 97.

[38] Ibid., p. 105–6.

Exhibit 1.2
One-Year Survival Rates by Firm Size

Firm Size (employees)	*Survival Percent*
0–9	77.8%
10–19	85.5
20–99	95.3
100–249	95.2
250+	100.0

Source: Michael B Teitz et al., "Small Business and Employment Growth in California," Working Paper No. 348, University of California at Berkeley, March 1981, p. 42.

Exhibit 1.3
Four-Year Survival Rates by Firm Size

Firm Size (employees)	*D&B Study (1969–76)*	*California Study (1976–80)*
0–19	37.4%	49.9%
20–49	53.6	66.9
50–99	55.7	66.9
100–499	67.7	70.0

Sources: David L Birch, *MIT Studies, 1979–1980;* and Michael B Teitz et al., "Small Business and Employment Growth in California," Working Paper No. 348, University of California at Berkeley, March 1981, table 5, p. 22.

of sales per employee annually. But highly successful firms can generate much higher sales per employee.

Promise of Growth

The definition of entrepreneurship implies the promise of expansion and the building of long-term value and durable cash flow streams as well.

But, as will be discussed later, it takes a long time for new companies to become established and grow. A Small Business Administration study, summarized in *Exhibit 1.4*, covering the period from 1976 to 1986, found that two of every five small firms founded survived six or more years but that few achieved growth during the first four years.[39] The study also found that survival rates more than double for firms which grow, and the earlier in the life of the business that growth occurs, the higher the chance of survival.[40]

Other data also confirm this exception. A study done by *INC.* shows that, between 1982 and 1987, the average growth in sales of the INC. 500 was 96 percent per year. The study also finds that, of the 7 million corporations in the United States, approximately 7 percent (just under 500,000 firms) grew over 20 percent per year and just over 1 percent (approximately 80,000 firms) grew 50 percent per year.

Some of the true excitement of entrepreneurship lies in conceiving, launching, and building firms such as these.

[39] Bruce D Phillips and Bruce A Kirchhoff, "An Analysis of New Firm Survival and Growth," in *Frontiers in Entrepreneurship Research: 1988*, p. 266–67.

[40] This confirms this exception to the failure rule noted above and in the original edition of this book in 1977.

Exhibit 1.4
Percentage of New Small Firms Surviving Six or More Years*

Industry	All Classes (percent)	Zero Growth 0%	Low Growth 1–4%	Medium Growth 5–9%	High Growth +10%
Total, All Industries	39.8%	27.5%	66.3%	75.5%	78.4%
Agriculture, Forestry, Fishing	43.1	35.0	74.7	80.7	82.8
Mining	39.1	27.1	67.8	61.5	57.0
Construction	35.3	24.1	65.0	72.2	74.3
Manufacturing	46.9	27.0	66.9	73.5	76.0
Transportation, Utilities, Communications	39.7	25.7	68.5	72.4	75.6
Wholesale Trade	44.3	28.3	66.5	74.9	77.2
Retail Trade	38.4	27.1	62.7	74.4	76.8
Finance, Insurance, Real Estate	38.6	28.7	68.7	76.4	78.5
Services	40.9	28.7	69.1	79.4	83.5

* Ranked by number of jobs created from 1976–86.
Source: U.S. Small Business Administration, August 29, 1988; B D Phillips and B A Kirchhoff, "An Analysis of New Firm Survival and Growth," *Frontiers in Entrepreneurship Research: 1988,* ed. B Kirchhoff et al., pp. 266–67.

Venture Capital Backing

Another notable pattern of exception to the failure rule is found for businesses which have attracted start-up financing from successful private venture capital companies. Instead of the 70 percent to 90 percent failure rate shown when all types of new firms are considered, these new ventures enjoy a *survival* rate nearly that high.

Studies of success rates of venture capital portfolios, summarized in *Exhibit 1.5*, show that in the portfolios of experienced professional venture capital firms, typically about 15 percent to 20 percent of the companies will result in total loss of the original investments and, further, that it is unusual for the loss rates for portfolios of experienced venture capital firms to exceed 30 percent to 35 percent and for the loss rates to fall below 10 percent.[41]

According to *Venture Economics* (1988), more than one-third of 383 investments made by 13 firms between 1969 and 1985 resulted in an absolute loss. More than two-thirds of the individual investments made by these same firms resulted in capital returns of less than double the original cost. Nevertheless, the returns on a few investments have more than offset these disappointments. *Venture Economics* (1988) reports, for example, that 6.8 percent of the investments resulted in payoffs greater than 10 times cost and yielded 49.9 percent of the ending value of the aggregate portfolio (61.4 percent of the profits).[42] Even higher returns have been achieved by such spectacular successes as Apple Computer, Lotus, Digital Equipment, Intel, Compaq, and the like.

It is clear that venture capital is not essential to a start-up, nor is it a guarantee of success, as is evident in the following statistics: only 5 percent of the INC. 500 have venture funding and merely 1 percent of all new companies have venture funding. Consider, for instance, that "in 1987—a banner year—venture capitalists financed a grand total of 1,729

[41] J A Timmons et al., *New Venture Creation* (Homewood, IL: Richard D Irwin, 1977), pp. 10–11; E B Roberts, "How to Succeed in a New Technology Enterprise," *Technology Review* 2, no. 2 (1970); C Taylor, "Starting-Up in the High Technology Industries in California," commissioned by the Wells Fargo Investment Company, 1969; R B Faucett, "The Management of Venture Capital Investment Companies," Sloan School master's thesis, MIT, 1971; and R B Faucett, "Venture Capital: Fact and Myth," Foothill Group, 1972.

[42] Cited in W A Sahlman, "Structure of Venture-Capital Organizations," *Journal of Financial Economics* 27 (1990), p. 483.

Exhibit 1.5
Studies of Success Rates of Venture Capital Portfolios

	Success Rates (percent)
Venture Capital Journal survey (1983)—232 portfolio companies and 32 venture capital firms	85%
International venture capital firm results (1972–88)—$60 million funds in US, UK, Canada, and Belgium	85
Wells Fargo Bank study (1972)—279 high-technology firms	65
Studies by MIT and other studies	80–82

companies, of which 112 were seed financings and 232 were start-ups. In that same year, 631,000 new businesses incorporations were recorded.[43]

This compelling data has led some to conclude that there is a threshold core of 10 percent to 15 percent of new companies which will become the winners in terms of size, job creation, profitability, innovation, and potential for harvesting (and thereby realizing a capital gain). Eventually, from among these 10 percent to 15 percent of all new firms emerge the "winning performers."[44] As shown in *Exhibit 1.6*, the top 25 percent among all medium-sized companies achieved records of growth from 1978 to 1983 that exceeded the growth of the top quarter of the economy, the top quarter of the Fortune 500, and firms classified as "excellent companies."

AN ANALYTICAL FRAMEWORK

Driving Forces

What is going on here? What do these talented entrepreneurs and companies backed by venture capital do differently? What is accounting for this exceptional record? Are there some lessons here for aspiring entrepreneurs?

The conclusion is this: Some central, fundamental forces drive the entrepreneurial process and account for these success rates. Granted, there are almost as many different approaches, philosophies, and nuances to the art and craft of new venture creation as there are entrepreneurs, private investors, and venture capital companies. Yet, time and again, central themes rise to the surface.

Professional venture capital investors follow a unique approach in their businesses, and successful entrepreneurs who grow multimillion-dollar firms, often from scratch and sometimes with little money, also understand that *entrepreneurial achievement is driven by people who search for and shape superior opportunities*.

Most important, an understanding of these fundamental forces is not the monopoly of venture capitalists or the entrepreneurs they back. Thousands of examples confirm the universal nature of the forces driving the entrepreneurial process.

Take, for example, the following:

- Tony Harnett came to this country from his native Ireland as a young high school dropout. He had a lot of ambition and was in search of opportunity. In 1976, he and his wife, Susan, bought a small natural foods store in Brookline, Massachusetts, with annual sales of a

[43] Amar Bhide, "Bootstrap Finance: The Art of Start-Ups," *Harvard Business Review* (November–December 1992), p. 110.

[44] Donald K Clifford, Jr., and Richard E Cavanagh, *The Winning Performance* (New York: Bantam Books, 1985), p. 3.

Exhibit 1.6
Compound Annual Growth Rates, 1978–83

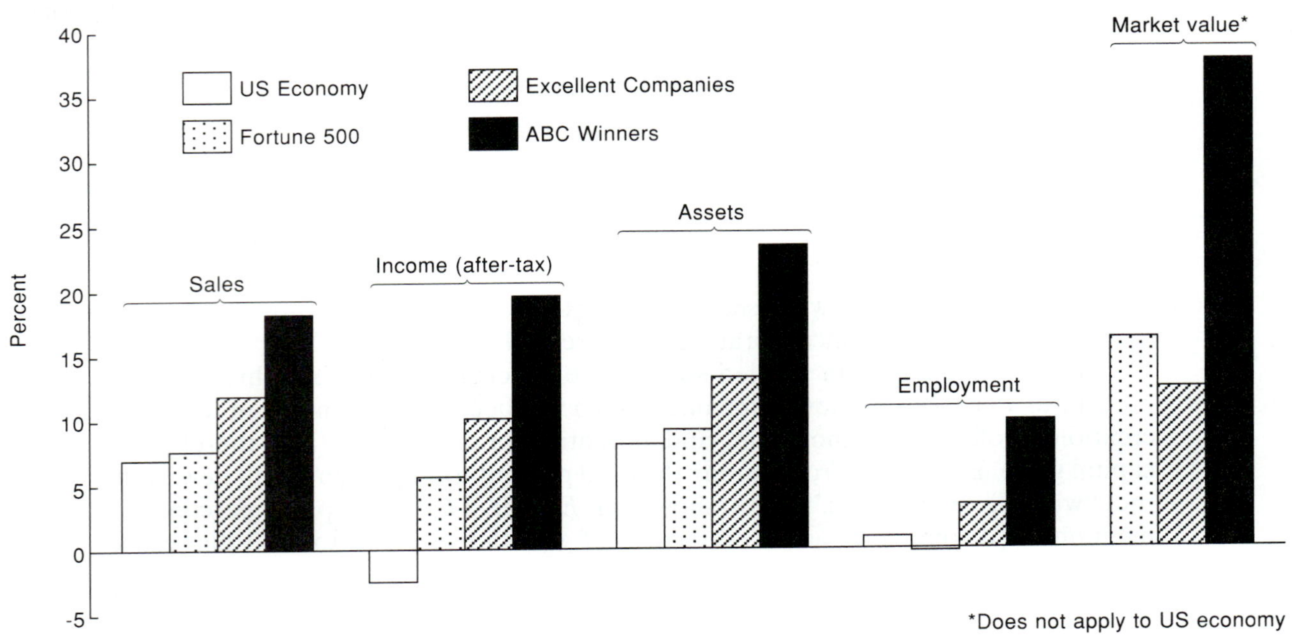

Growth Rates, 1978–83 (percent)

Performance Measure	*US Economy*	*Fortune 500*	*Excellent Companies*	*ABC Winners*
Sales	7.1%	7.9%	12.0%	18.4%
After-tax income	−2.7	5.9	10.4	19.7
Assets	8.3	9.5	13.5	23.6
Employment	1.0	−0.5	3.6	10.0
Market value	NA	16.3	12.5	37.8

Source: Donald K Clifford, Jr., and Richard E Cavanagh, *The Winning Performance* (New York: Bantam Books, 1985).

meager $110,000 per year. By paying a lot of attention to the critical driving forces, those that venture capitalists also seem to concentrate on, they have built Bread and Circus into a multistore venture whose annual sales in 1988 exceeded $35 million. Interestingly, they did this without having to raise a dime of venture capital. Recently, Tony and Susan Harnett sold Bread and Circus for close to $30 million.

- Another entrepreneur started and built a small company, without venture capital, which became the leading firm manufacturing and selling metal picture frames. By 1983, the company had about 70 percent of the North American market, yet did only $15 million in very profitable sales. The company was acquired by a European firm for over $20 million in cash.

In analyzing the entrepreneurial process, you will find that, relying only on traditional models, such as a psychological model or a competitive strategy model, to analyze new ventures is not useful. First, any unidimensional model that attempts to distill the common basis for the collective successes of entrepreneurial ventures can tell only part of the story. Second, systematic research into the characteristics of successful ventures

Exhibit 1.7
Real-World Environmental Context and Central Driving Forces of Entrepreneurship

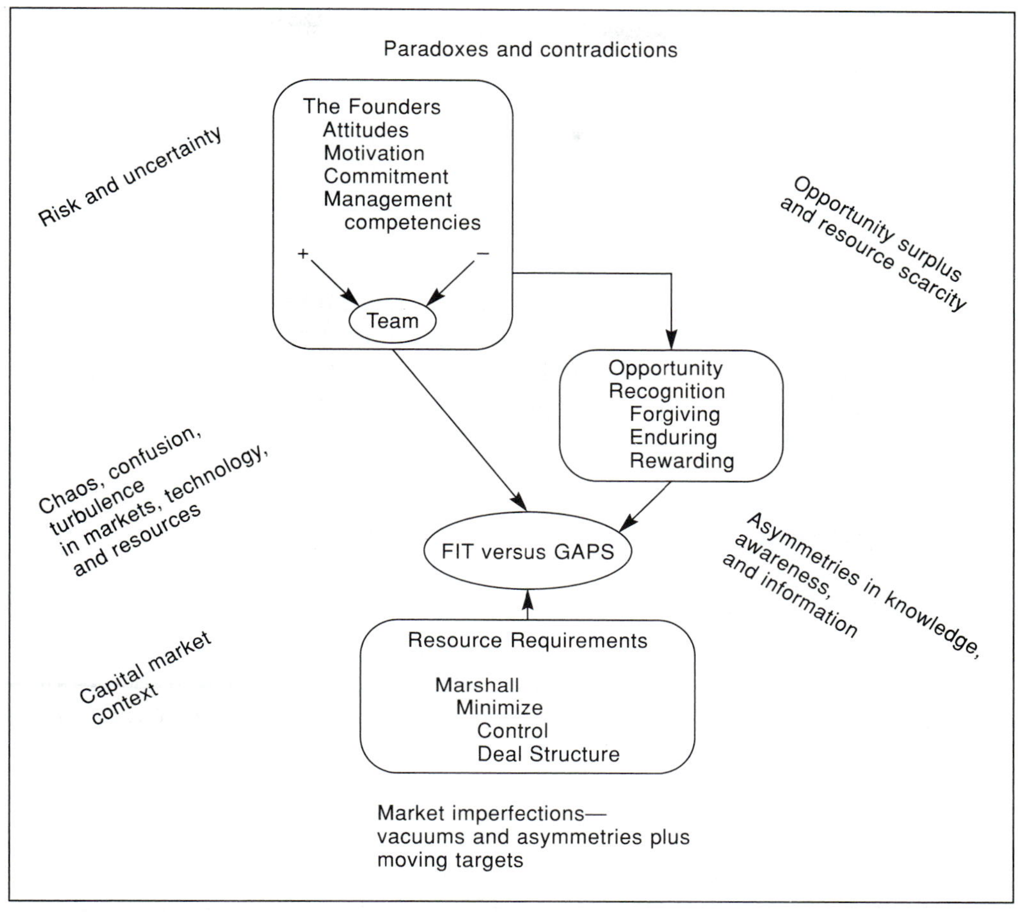

is a new and inexact science, and research in economics and strategic management has barely begun to focus on new venture development and performance. Third, entrepreneurship typically occurs in a real-world environment that lacks certainty, predictability, stability, and smoothness. Risk and uncertainty, paradoxes and contradictions, market imperfections, and asymmetries and vacuums are the rules, rather than the exceptions. Consequently, business as usual includes confusing and often chaotic change and turbulence in markets, technology, and availability of resources. (It is no wonder that large, multilayered organizations have such a dismal record competing and innovating in this domain.)

Instead, the analytical framework, illustrated in *Exhibit 1.7*, isolates the three primary driving forces behind new venture creation: the founders, opportunity recognition, and resource requirements. Experience shows that these forces can be assessed and influenced to improve the chances of succeeding. The key to success in new venture creation is a continual, careful, and realistic assessment of these driving forces and the real time in which they are occurring.

The Importance of Fit

Throughout, it is a trial-and-error iterative process of finding out what it takes, the gaps faced as the venture unfolds, and how to shape a good fit. Not surprisingly, this approach seems to work well for a lot of innovative undertakings. After all, the Wright brothers flew over 1,000 glider flights, in the effort to find out what worked, before attaching a motor-driven propeller to their airplane.

The key elements of successful new ventures (i.e., founders, opportunity, and resources) fit one another—rarely perfectly, but reasonably so—in the real world. The potential of the venture will depend on fit of the lead entrepreneur with his or her management team and of the lead entrepreneur and his or her management team with the opportunity.

A question which should be answered, then, is: For whom is the opportunity desirable? It should be recognized that the personal values and lifestyles of the founders enter heavily into whether there is a fit. In turn, the lead entrepreneur, the management team, and the opportunity must fit with the ability to marshall and control the necessary resources. Thus, realistically evaluating the merits and deficiencies of each element and accurately judging the potential fit of each element are essential.

The Importance of Timing

Every entrepreneurial event occurs in *real time,* where the clock can be enemy or friend, or both.

Thus, timing is crucial in every entrepreneurial situation. Recognizing and seizing an opportunity is often a precarious race with an hourglass—when the disappearing sand is the cash running out.

The Founders

Lead Entrepreneur and the Management Team

Several studies, including one that considered the 50 most active venture capital firms in the United States, have confirmed the view that one of the central forces driving the entrepreneurial process is the founders.[45] Research on high-technology companies formed in this country since 1967—highly innovative technological ventures, where one would expect the elegance of the technology to have special importance—shows that the founders are more important than the technology.[46] Of course, the high-tech game cannot be won without innovative technology; but venture capitalists, who are among the most active and prominent investors in the country in this area, still insist that they place greatest weight and emphasis on the quality and proven track record of the management team.

Thus, at times, investors are captivated "by the creative brilliance of a company's lead entrepreneur: a Mitch Kapor, a Steve Jobs, or a Fred Smith. . . . other times, investors bet on the superb track records of the management team working as a group."[47] This argument was validated further by Alan Grant, of Babson College, who examined what makes entrepreneurs successful by interviewing 25 senior US venture capitalists. The Entrepre-

[45] J A Timmons and D E Gumpert, "Discard Many Old Rules for Raising Venture Capital," *Harvard Business Review*, January–February 1982.

[46] Jeffry A Timmons, Norman D Fast, and William D Bygrave, "The Flow of Venture Capital to Highly Innovative Technological Ventures," in *Frontiers of Entrepreneurship Research: 1983*, p. 316.

[47] William D Bygrave and Jeffry A Timmons, *Venture Capital at the Crossroads* (Boston: Harvard Business School Press, 1992), p. 8.

neurial Leadership Paradigm that evolved was divided into three clusters: the lead entrepreneur, the venture team, and external influences.[48]

That the team is a driving force of the entrepreneurial process is demonstrated in the responses of venture capitalists when they are asked to list the five most important factors which determine if a new venture will be successful. Venture capitalists state plainly and simply:

- The lead entrepreneur and the quality of the team.
- The lead entrepreneur and the quality of the team.
- The lead entrepreneur and the quality of the team.
- The lead entrepreneur and the quality of the team.
- Market potential.

A good example of this is the philosophy of Burr Egan Deleage & Company of Boston, one of the largest and most successful venture capital firms, with over $200 million under management and investments in over 100 emerging companies. Partner Bill Egan, who has been centrally involved in such successes as Continental Cablevision, Federal Express, and Tandon, states his strong preference for high-quality management this way:

> The management team must have quality, depth and maturity. It must be experienced in the industry in which the company competes. The top manager should have had prior profit center responsibility. Management must possess intimate knowledge of the market for its products and have a well thought out strategy for the penetration of this market. The strength of the management team is the most important consideration in the investment decision.

Ideally, having a top-notch idea or innovation and a first-rate entrepreneurial team is the best of all worlds. But this does not happen very often. General Georges Doriot, the founder of American Research & Development Corporation and father of the American venture capital industry, is often quoted for his insistence that he preferred a Grade A entrepreneurial team with a Grade B idea to a Grade B team with a Grade A idea.[49] This view has become one of the standard operating axioms of the venture capital industry today.[50]

Another famous entrepreneur who expressed such a position is Arthur Rock, founder of a firm that was the lead capital investor in such new ventures as Fairchild Semiconductor, Teledyne, Scientific Data Systems, Intel, and Apple Computer. He put it this way: "If you can find good people, they can always change the product. Nearly every mistake I've made has been [that] I picked the wrong people, not the wrong idea."[51]

Further, the management team is critically important to the chances of survival and expansion of new ventures, whether or not they are candidates for venture capital. As was seen earlier, those firms that grew beyond 20 employees and roughly $1 million in sales were most likely to survive and prosper. In a majority of cases, it is quite difficult to do this without a team of at least two key contributors.

[48] Alan J Grant, "The Development of an Entrepreneurial Leadership Paradigm for Enhancing New Venture Success," doctoral dissertation, 1992.

[49] In 1946, General Doriot, a retired Harvard Business School professor noted for encouraging entrepreneurship among his students, founded American Research & Development Corporation in Boston, the first institutional US venture capital firm. The company put venture capital on the map when its investment of about $70,000 in 1957 in four young MIT engineers with an idea for a new computer grew to about $350 million—as shares in Digital Equipment Corporation, today America's second largest computer firm.

[50] J A Timmons, N D Fast, S E Pratt, and W D Bygrave, "Venture Capital Investing in Highly Innovative Technological Ventures," published by *Venture Economics*, Needham, MA, March 1984, for the National Science Foundation.

[51] Arthur Rock, "Strategy vs. Tactics from a Venture Capitalist," *Harvard Business Review*, November–December 1987, pp. 63–67.

A Word about Solo Entrepreneurs

A substantial amount of research, as well as practical experience, confirms that a team grows a business while a solo entrepreneur makes a living. If an entrepreneur's aspirations include growing a business large and profitable enough to realize a capital gain, then he or she needs to think team. But teams are not for everyone. Numerous examples exist of solo entrepreneurs carving out small niches for themselves, earning substantial six-figure incomes, and building wealth by wise financial planning and investing.[52] In these instances, the fundamental driving forces are at work without a team.

Opportunity Recognition

Ideas Are Not Necessarily Opportunities

If there is any single spark that ignites an entrepreneurial explosion, it is the opportunity.[53] There certainly does not seem to be a lack of ideas for new or improved products or services. Entrepreneurs, inventors, innovators, and college students abound with new ideas. However, there are far more ideas than good business opportunities. This is because—and it cannot be repeated enough—*an idea is not necessarily an opportunity.*[54] While at the center of an opportunity is always an idea, not all ideas are opportunities.

In understanding the difference between an opportunity and just another idea, you must understand that entrepreneurship is a market-driven process.

An opportunity is attractive, durable, and timely, and it is anchored in a product or service that creates or adds value for its buyer or end user. Opportunities are created because of changing circumstances, inconsistencies, chaos, lags or leads, information gaps, and a variety of other vacuums, and because entrepreneurs can recognize and seize them. Successful new ventures are invariably anchored in opportunities with rewarding, forgiving, and durable gross margins and profits.

The challenge, then, is recognizing an opportunity buried in often contradictory data, signals, and the inevitable noise and chaos of the marketplace. Since the more *imperfect* the market (i.e., the greater the gaps, asymmetries, and inconsistencies of knowledge and information), the more abundant the opportunities, a skillful entrepreneur can shape and create an opportunity where others see little or nothing—or see it too early or too late.

After all, if recognizing and seizing an opportunity were simply a matter of using available techniques, checklists, and other screening and evaluation methods, we might have far more than the one-in-five businesses that had sales in 1990 of over $2 million. After all, the literature on techniques for screening and evaluating ideas indicates that over 200 such methods have been developed and documented.

[52] Sources of information about solo entrepreneurs and small enterprises include the following magazines: *Entrepreneur*, *In-Business*, and *Home-Based Business*.

[53] Opportunity recognition was originally identified as a driving force in new venture creation in the 1977 edition of this text. The conceptual framework developed by Howard H Stevenson, at the Harvard Business School, and his helpful suggestions have reinforced and refocused this identification of opportunity recognition as central. See also Howard H Stevenson, "A New Paradigm for Entrepreneurial Management," in *Entrepreneurship: What It Is and How to Teach It*, ed. John J Kao and Howard H Stevenson (Boston: Harvard Business School, 1984). Empirical research bearing on the question of opportunity screening and evaluation and any common characteristics of successful entrepreneurial ventures is documented in a paper by Jeffry A Timmons, Daniel F Muzyka, Howard H Stevenson, and William D Bygrave, "Opportunity Recognition: The Core of Entrepreneurship," in *Frontiers of Entrepreneurship Research: 1987*, ed. Neil Churchill et al. (Babson Park, MA: Babson College, 1987), p. 409.

[54] See Jeffry A Timmons, *New Business Opportunities* (Acton, MA: Brick House Publishing, 1989).

Another Look at Fit, Timing, and Context

Recent work has lent even further support to the hypothesis that an opportunity is quite situational and depends on the mix and match of the key players and on how promising and forgiving the opportunity is, given the team's strengths, advantages, and shortcomings. Further, the vast majority of those founding new businesses run out of money *before* they find enough customers for their good ideas. Thus, for entrepreneurs, timing can be everything.

Another critical question therefore is: If there really is a business opportunity, rather than just a product or two, is there time to seize the opportunity? If there is an opportunity, whether an entrepreneur can seize it in time depends on movements in technology and competitors' thrusts, among other factors. Thus, an opportunity is also a constantly moving target for which there exists a "window of opportunity."

Resource Requirements

Control of Minimum Resources

Identifying, attracting, and managing the resources required to execute the opportunity, both inside and outside the business, is the third driving force in entrepreneurship.[55]

Entrepreneurs have a quite different mentality when it comes to resources. First, entrepreneurs manage to get more out of less; that is, their approach often is to find ways to push ahead with *minimum resources.* To accomplish this, they often invest "sweat equity" and use customer advances, barter, and other bootstrapping techniques.

Also, successful entrepreneurs know that they can get the odds in their favor and even improve the chances of attaining their business plan if they utilize resources differently. They position themselves to commit and decommit quickly, thereby avoiding commitment to future resources until necessary.

Thus, entrepreneurs seek to *control resources* rather than own them. They would rather borrow, rent, or lease these resources. For example, finding and properly using outside resources, such as bankers, CPAs, lawyers, informal advisors, board members, and other experts, is one way of controlling, rather than owning, resources and one of the most easily overlooked challenges entrepreneurs face.

You can minimize the risk and required capital by reducing the required resources to a minimum and controlling, rather than owning, those resources.

Financial Resources

When initially asked to name the most critical ingredients needed to successfully launch a new company, most people include money among the top three items. No doubt about it, a venture cannot go far without it. But, in truth, the capacity to raise money is a result of having the other parts of the act together. Financing *follows* from identifying good people to pursue a good opportunity who demonstrate that they clearly grasp the driving forces that will govern success.

In fact, it seems that one of the worst things that can happen to an entrepreneur is having *too much money too early.* Take, for instance, Howard Head's approach to developing the very first metal ski. He left his job at a large aircraft manufacturer after World War II, and working out of his own garage with his savings on a shoe string, he began to develop his metal ski. It took over 40 iterations before he finally developed a marketable metal ski. Head feels that had he insisted on having all the right talent and financing in place before he started

[55] The role of outside resources as a key success factor was contributed early by Patrick R Liles, doctoral dissertation, Harvard Business School, 1970.

to develop the product, he would have failed by wasting them prematurely. Head Ski subsequently dominated the international ski industry through the late 1960s and was sold to AMF.[56]

Implementation

The real work and challenge begin in the implementation. In this regard, a business plan is a key tool in the process of identifying gaps and fits, pulling the vision together, and transmitting the passion to others.

However, having a superbly prepared document describing a timely opportunity may be a necessary condition for launching and building a successful venture, but it is far from sufficient. The lead entrepreneur and the management team must be able to implement it. Arthur Rock has said:

> Most entrepreneurs have no problem coming up with a good strategy . . . but they usually need all the help they can get in developing and implementing the tactics that will make them successful in the long run.[57]

Creation of Value

Creation of value is the end product of the entrepreneurial process for an entrepreneur, his or her backers, and the other stakeholders (i.e., partners, employees, customers, suppliers, and service providers). Clearly, harvesting value is a nonissue until something begins to sprout.

Starting a venture, growing a venture, and then harvesting a venture successfully are not the same. In that respect, we are reminded of the comment by George Bernard Shaw, taken from a different context: "Any darned fool can start a love affair, but it takes a real genius to end one successfully."

MYTHS AND REALITIES

Folklore and stereotypes about entrepreneurs and entrepreneurial success are remarkably durable, even in these informed and sophisticated times. More is known about the founders and the process of entrepreneurship than ever before.

However, certain myths enjoy recurring attention and popularity. Part of the problem is that while generalities may apply to certain types of entrepreneurs and particular situations, the great variety of founders tend to defy generalization. *Exhibit 1.8* shows myths about entrepreneurs that have persisted and realities that are supported by research.

Studies have indicated that 90 percent or more of founders start their companies in the same marketplace, technology, or industry they have been working in.[58] Others have found that founders are likely to have from 8 to 10 years of experience, and they are likely to be well educated. It also appears that successful entrepreneurs have wide experience in products/markets and across functional areas.[59]

Studies also have shown that most successful entrepreneurs start companies in their 30s.

[56] Howard Head subsequently followed the same approach in developing the Prince tennis racket, which he sold in 1982.

[57] Rock, "Strategy vs. Tactics from a Venture Capitalist," pp. 63–67.

[58] A good summary of some of these studies is provided by Robert H Brockhaus, "The Psychology of the Entrepreneur," in *Encyclopedia of Entrepreneurship*, ed. C Kent, D Sexton, and K Vesper (Englewood Cliffs, NJ: Prentice-Hall, 1982), pp. 50–55.

[59] Over 65 studies in this area have been reported in *Frontiers of Entrepreneurship Research* (Babson Park, MA: Babson College) for the years 1981 through 1993.

Exhibit 1.8
Myths about Entrepreneurs

Myth 1—Entrepreneurs are born, not made.

Reality—While entrepreneurs are born with certain native intelligence, a flair for creating, and energy, these talents by themselves are like unmolded clay or an unpainted canvas. The making of an entrepreneur occurs by accumulating the relevant skills, know-how, experiences, and contacts over a period of years and includes large doses of self-development. The creative capacity to envision and then pursue an opportunity is a direct descendent of at least 10 or more years of experience that lead to pattern recognition.

Myth 2—Anyone can start a business.

Reality—Entrepreneurs who recognize the difference between an idea and an opportunity, and who think big enough, start businesses that have a better chance of succeeding. Luck, to the extent it is involved, requires good preparation. And the easiest part is starting up. What is hardest is surviving, sustaining, and building a venture so its founders can realize a harvest. Perhaps only one in 10 to 20 new businesses that survive five years or more results in a capital gain for the founders.

Myth 3—Entrepreneurs are gamblers.

Reality—Successful entrepreneurs take very careful, calculated risks. They try to influence the odds, often by getting others to share risk with them and by avoiding or minimizing risks if they have the choice. Often they slice up the risk into smaller, quite digestible pieces; only then do they commit the time or resources to determine if that piece will work. They do not deliberately seek to take more risk or to take unnecessary risk, nor do they shy away from unavoidable risk.

Myth 4—Entrepreneurs want the whole show to themselves.

Reality—Owning and running the whole show effectively puts a ceiling on growth. Solo entrepreneurs usually make a living. It is extremely difficult to grow a higher potential venture by working single-handedly. Higher potential entrepreneurs build a team, an organization, and a company. Besides, 100 percent of nothing is nothing, so rather than taking a large piece of the pie, they work to make the pie bigger.

Myth 5—Entrepreneurs are their own bosses and completely independent.

Reality—Entrepreneurs are far from independent and have to serve many masters and constituencies, including partners, investors, customers, suppliers, creditors, employees, families, and those involved in social and community obligations. Entrepreneurs, however, can make free choices of whether, when, and what they care to respond to. Moreover, it is extremely difficult, and rare, to build a business beyond $1 million to $2 million in sales single-handedly.

Myth 6—Entrepreneurs work longer and harder than managers in big companies.

Reality—There is no evidence that all entrepreneurs work more than their corporate counterparts. Some do, some do not. Some actually report that they work less.

Myth 7—Entrepreneurs experience a great deal of stress and pay a high price.

Reality—No doubt about it: Being an entrepreneur is stressful and demanding. But there is no evidence that it is any more stressful than numerous other highly demanding professional roles, and entrepreneurs find their jobs very satisfying. They have a high sense of accomplishment, are healthier, and are much less likely to retire than those who work for others. Three times as many entrepreneurs as corporate managers say they plan never to retire.

Myth 8—Starting a business is risky and often ends in failure.

Reality —Talented and experienced entrepreneurs—because they pursue attractive opportunities and are able to attract the right people and necessary financial and other resources to make the venture work—often head successful ventures. Further, businesses fail, but entrepreneurs do not. Failure is often the fire that tempers the steel of an entrepreneur's learning experience and street savvy.

Myth 9—Money is the most important start-up ingredient.

Reality—If the other pieces and talents are there, the money will follow, but it does not follow that an entrepreneur will succeed if he or she has enough money. Money is one of the least important ingredients in new venture success. Money is to the entrepreneur what the paint and brush are to the artist—an inert tool which, in the right hands, can create marvels. Money is also a way of keeping score, rather than just an end in itself. Entrepreneurs thrive on the thrill of the chase; and, time and again, even after an entrepreneur has made a few million dollars or more, he or she will work incessantly on a new vision to build another company.

Myth 10—Entrepreneurs should be young and energetic.

Reality—While these qualities may help, age is no barrier. The average age of entrepreneurs starting high potential businesses is in the mid-30s, and there are numerous examples of entrepreneurs starting businesses in their 60s. What is critical is possessing the relevant know-how, experience, and contacts that greatly facilitate recognizing and pursuing an opportunity.

Myth 11—Entrepreneurs are motivated solely by the quest for the almighty dollar.

Reality—Entrepreneurs seeking high potential ventures are more driven by building enterprises and realizing long-term capital gains than by instant gratification through high salaries and perks. A sense of personal achievement and accomplishment, feeling in control of their own destinies, and realizing their vision and dreams are also powerful motivators. Money is viewed as a tool and a way of keeping score.

(Continued)

Exhibit 1.8 *(concluded)*

Myth 12—Entrepreneurs seek power and control over others.

Reality—Successful entrepreneurs are driven by the quest for responsibility, achievement, and results, rather than for power for its own sake. They thrive on a sense of accomplishment and of outperforming the competition, rather than a personal need for power expressed by dominating and controlling others. By virtue of their accomplishments, they may be powerful and influential, but these are more the by-products of the entrepreneurial process than a driving force behind it.

Myth 13—If an entrepreneur is talented, success will happen in a year or two.

Reality—An old maxim among venture capitalists says it all: The lemons ripen in two and a half years, but the pearls take seven or eight. Rarely is a new business established solidly in less than three or four years.

Myth 14—Any entrepreneur with a good idea can raise venture capital.

Reality—Of the ventures of entrepreneurs with good ideas who seek out venture capital, only 1 to 3 out of 100 are funded.

Myth 15—If an entrepreneur has enough start-up capital, he or she can't miss.

Reality—The opposite is often true; that is, too much money at the outset often creates euphoria and a spoiled-child syndrome. The accompanying lack of discipline and impulsive spending usually lead to serious problems and failure.

One study of founders of high-tech companies on Route 128 in Boston from 1982 to 1984 showed that the average age of the founders was 40.

It has been found that entrepreneurs work both more and less than their counterparts in large organizations, that they have high degrees of satisfaction with their jobs, and that they are healthier.[60] Another study showed that nearly 21 percent of the founders were over 40 when they embarked on their entrepreneurial career, the majority were in their 30s, and just over one quarter did so by the time they were 25.

THE ENTREPRENEURIAL MIND[61]

What Successful Entrepreneurs Do

Most research about entrepreneurs has focused on the influences of genes, family, education, career experience, and so forth, but no psychological model has been supported. Successful entrepreneurs seem to be of both sexes and in every imaginable size, shape, color, and description. Perhaps one Price–Babson College fellow phrased it best when he said, "One does not want to overdo the personality stuff, but there is a certain ring to it."[62]

However, the real question is, *What do successful entrepreneurs do?* That is, how do they think, what actions do they initiate, and how do they go about starting and building businesses? The result is what counts, and by understanding the attitudes, behaviors, management competencies, experience, and know-how that contribute to entrepreneurial success, one has some useful benchmarks for gauging what to do and what to do differently.

Successful entrepreneurs share common attitudes and behaviors. They work hard and are driven by an intense commitment and determined perseverance; they see the cup half full, rather than half empty; they strive for integrity; they burn with the competitive desire to excel and win; they are dissatisfied with the status quo and seek opportunities to improve almost any situation they encounter; they use failure as a tool for learning and eschew perfection in favor of effectiveness; and they believe they can personally make an enormous difference in the final outcome of their ventures and their lives.

[60] Stevenson, "Who Are the Harvard Self-Employed?" p. 233.

[61] See Timmons, *The Entrepreneurial Mind*.

[62] Comment made during a presentation at the June 1987 Price–Babson College Fellows Program by Jerry W Gustafson, Coleman–Fannie May Candies Professor of Entrepreneurship, Beloit College, at Babson College.

Exhibit 1.9
Who Is the Entrepreneur?

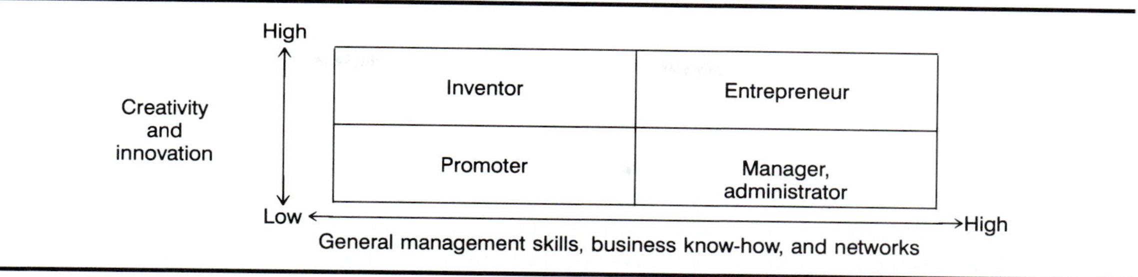

Those who have succeeded speak of these attitudes and behaviors time and again.[63] For example, two famous entrepreneurs have captured the intense commitment and determined perseverance of entrepreneurs. Wally Amos, famous for his chocolate chip cookies, said, "You can do anything you want to do."[64] And John Johnson of Johnson Publishing Company (publisher of *Ebony*) expressed it this way: "You need to think yourself out of a corner, meet needs, and never, never accept no for an answer."[65]

It seems that entrepreneurs who succeed possess not only a creative and innovative flair and other attitudes and behaviors but also solid general management skills, business know-how, and sufficient contacts. *Exhibit 1.9* demonstrates this relationship. Inventors, noted for their creativity, often lack the necessary management skills and business know-how. Promoters usually lack serious general management and business skills and true creativity. Administrators govern, police, and ensure the smooth operation of the status quo; their management skills, while high, are tuned to efficiency as well, and creativity is usually not required. Although the management skills of the manager and the entrepreneur overlap, the manager is more driven by conservation of resources and the entrepreneur is more opportunity-driven.[66]

Apprenticeship: Acquiring the 50,000 Chunks

During the past several years, studies about entrepreneurs have tended to confirm what practitioners have known all along: that some attitudes, behaviors, and know-how can in fact be acquired and that some of these attributes are more desirable than others.[67]

Increasingly, evidence from research about the career paths of entrepreneurs and the self-employed suggests that the role of experience and know-how is central in successful venture creation.[68] Evidence also suggests that success is linked to thoughtful preparation and planning.[69] This is what getting the 50,000 chunks of experience is all about.

Most successful entrepreneurs follow a pattern of apprenticeship, where they prepare for becoming entrepreneurs by gaining the relevant business experiences from parents who

[63] See the excellent summary of a study of the first 21 inductees into Babson College's Academy of Distinguished Entrepreneurs by John A Hornaday and Nancy Tieken, "Capturing Twenty-One Heffalumps," in *Frontiers of Entrepreneurship Research: 1983*, pp. 23–50.

[64] Made during a speech at his induction in 1982 into the Academy of Distinguished Entrepreneurs, Babson College.

[65] Made during a speech at his induction in 1979 into the Academy of Distinguished Entrepreneurs, Babson College.

[66] Timmons, Muzyka, Stevenson, and Bygrave, "Opportunity Recognition: The Core of Entrepreneurship," pp. 42–49.

[67] See studies cited in footnote 59.

[68] Karl H Vesper, "New Venture Ideas: Don't Overlook the Experience Factor," *Harvard Business Review*, reprinted in *Growing Concerns: Building and Managing the Smaller Business*, ed D E Gumpert (New York: John Wiley & Sons, 1984), pp. 28–55.

[69] See Robert Ronstadt's and Howard Stevenson's studies reported in *Frontiers of Entrepreneurship Research: 1983*.

are self-employed or through job experiences. They do not leave acquisition of experience to accident or osmosis. As entrepreneur Harvey "Chet" Krentzman has said, "Know what you know and what you *don't* know."

Role Models

Further, there is no more powerful teacher than a good example. Numerous studies show a strong connection between the presence of role models and the emergence of entrepreneurs. For instance, one recent study showed that over half of those starting new businesses had parents who owned businesses.[70] The authors summarized it this way:

> People who start companies are more likely to come from families in which their parents or close relatives were in business for themselves. These older people were examples, or "models," for the children. Whether they were successful or not probably didn't matter. However, for the children growing up in such a family, the action of starting a new business seems possible – something they can do.

CASE – OUTDOOR SCENE, INC.*

Preparation Questions

1. What are the strengths and weaknesses of the entrepreneurs, individually and as a team?
2. What is the opportunity?
3. Would you invest in the entrepreneurs if you were convinced that the opportunity was sound? Why or why not?
4. What are the critical skills and resources necessary to succeed in the business?
5. What should the entrepreneurs do and why?

OUTDOOR SCENE, INC.

In early 1993, at age 31, J. C. Egnew was employed as vice president of manufacturing by Wilderness Products, Inc., a large tent producer. He was responsible for the overall planning and administration of the company's manufacturing operations. The company's sales were about $12 million per year, and it employed over 350 people at three plants. Although the company was growing, Egnew began to encounter basic differences of opinion and philosophy with the owners and top management of the company, particularly over issues of new product development and expansion. Prompted by these differences, Egnew became increasingly intrigued with the possibility of starting his own tent-manufacturing company. He discussed his ideas with a co-worker, John F. Moore, the sales service manager.

Wilderness Products had experienced substantial growth in unit volume and dollar sales, but Egnew was troubled about its apparent lack of concern for profits. Drawing from his business school training, he also observed other problems in the company:

> There is not one page of formal planning. There is no real organization – everyone is just doing his own thing. And the techniques being used to manage the company aren't keeping up with the rate of growth. They may be appropriate for a $3–6 million tent manufacturer, but not one doing $36 million.

[70] A Cooper and W Dunkelberg, *A New Look at Business Entry* (San Mateo, CA: National Federation of Independent Businesses, March 1984).

There were still other problems with the way the company was being managed. As Egnew put it:

> If I ask the production manager, the sales manager, and the president what our capacity is and for a sales forecast, I get three very different answers. The company is very sales oriented in a seller's market. So we fill up with orders which require too much overtime to produce, and we end up with missed delivery schedules and unprofitable sales. It has gotten to the point where I honestly feel that something is way out of balance.

During the three years since joining Wilderness Products, Egnew had gained experience in, and knowledge of, the tent-manufacturing industry. He felt that there was a substantial national market for tents and that his current employer was not competing as effectively as it could. In particular, he felt that there was significant potential to manufacture and market a line of camping tents and accessories having broad-based consumer appeal. He felt that such trends as more discretionary income and more leisure time were favorably affecting consumer demand for tents. Two-thirds of heads of households surveyed by the University of Michigan agreed that camping is the best vacation a family can take. The US Travel Data Center reported that camping was the nation's second most popular vacation activity in 1991. Hiking was first.[1]

Egnew's operating experience in the industry was confirming the impact of these trends. During the previous four years, for example, the six major tent manufacturers had been continually delinquent to customers because they were unable to keep pace with the growing market. Poor deliveries prevailed in this period, while production by the "big six" was expanding at an annual rate of 20 percent. Egnew also knew that strong retail demand had led to a severe erosion of product quality as a result of haphazard industry expansion.

In response to the situation, Egnew decided to try to convince the management that a coordinated plan was needed to pull the business together and make it profitable. During evenings and weekends he and Moore drew up what they considered a sensible long-range plan, and Egnew then discussed the plan with his employer. "I got them to agree to it, but in six months it all went out the window." He concluded: "I didn't have what it takes to convince them to run the business the way I wanted to."

This left him with what he felt were three principal alternatives:

1. Quit and get another job.
2. Get the president fired.
3. Start his own tent manufacturing company.

Egnew had little net worth and only three years in the business. He was married and had a son. His salary of $78,000 per year provided him with a comfortable standard of living. He wondered whether he wasn't kidding himself, whether it was realistic to go out on his own, and how he might pursue the idea since he had never started a company previously.

Determined to resolve their future, Egnew and Moore agreed to meet again for an entire weekend to decide on a strategy.

Personal Backgrounds

J. C. Egnew. J. C. Egnew was born and raised in Indiana. He recalled some of his attitudes, which he attributed to his upbringing:

> My dad was a teacher, but a farmer at heart. I remember his thoroughness—"If you're going to do something, do it well." He believed in sticking with things. Both my parents developed in me a high regard for my individual freedom.

[1] Tom Huggler, camping editor. "The *Compleat* Camper," *Outdoor Life*, June 1993, p. 59.

This independence apparently also included emancipation from the classroom and attraction to the world of work and basketball. By the time Egnew was 16 he was working full-time after school. He noted: "I learned a sense of self-responsibility and how to support myself. I made most of my own decisions concerning school and other things. I found work a lot more interesting than school."

In addition to working full-time in high school, Egnew also played basketball. His schoolwork suffered. "I always did what I had to do to get by, and I wasn't sure I wanted to go to college." He graduated from high school 401st in a class of 439 students.

Following graduation from high school, Egnew entered the University of Evansville, where he received his bachelor of science in mechanical engineering in 1984. He described himself as a loner during college, without a large circle of friends. He became very interested in the cooperative education program, which allowed students to alternate between full-time schooling and work. During co-op he worked for NASA in Huntsville, Alabama, rising from the rank of GS-3 to GS-5 in two years. He graduated in the lower third of his class after an erratic academic performance that included both dean's list and probation. He summed it up: "I hated to take tests, and I was not a crammer."

After graduation he joined NASA in Huntsville as a flight systems test engineer, GS-7, and rose to GS-9 by July 1986. He served as lead test engineer responsible for the conduct of hardware development test programs. This included coordinating and directing about 20 engineers and technicians in formulating, conducting, and evaluating tests and test results. In July 1986, he was promoted to production test manager for NASA and moved to Bay St. Louis, Mississippi. His responsibilities included the supervision of flight vehicle tests. By August 1989, he had risen to GS-13. He commented on his work:

> I enjoyed getting involved in things where there was no established solution. I liked to find the solutions. I especially liked the new position since it involved work that hadn't been done before. But in about two years most of the problems were solved and it got boring. So I decided to return to school for my master's in industrial management at the University of Tennessee, Knoxville.

John F. Moore. John Moore was born and raised in Columbus, Ohio, one of two sons of a navy career officer who had worked his way up through the ranks. Though his father ran the house "like the commander of a ship," he was quite permissive with his two sons. "He taught us right from wrong. But what he really gave me was the motivation to do things on my own."

In high school John Moore was captain of the swimming, baseball, and football teams. At the same time he worked about 15 hours a week after school in a shoe store, and each summer he worked full-time paving driveways. He graduated in the lower third of his high school class, noting that "I did what I had to do to stay eligible and graduate." His considerable athletic promise earned him a full baseball scholarship to Ohio State University. The lure of fraternity life, particularly its social activities, detracted further from his less-than-enthusiastic interest in academics. Repeated academic probation caused him to lose his scholarship, so he entered the navy in April 1982. He was honorably discharged in April 1986.

In July 1986, Moore joined North American Rockwell Corporation as a materials requirements analyst, and in early 1989 he became supervisor in the Support Operations Division. In September 1989, he returned to college and met with greater academic success: "Once I went back, I got A's and B's and even won an honors medal in physics."

Upon graduating in June 1991 with a BS in industrial management from the University of Tennessee, Knoxville, Moore returned to North American Rockwell for three months as logistics staff assistant in Bay St. Louis, Mississippi. In October 1991, after much urging by J. C. Egnew, he joined Wilderness Products, Inc., as sales service manager.

At Wilderness, he was responsible for customer service, inventory control, transportation, and warehouse activities. This included factory sales to key "house accounts," developing product mix and initiating marketing plans, supervising 30 employees in office areas and transportation and warehousing facilities, and purchasing some accessory products and equipment.

Discussions between Egnew and Moore

In early 1993, Egnew and Moore began a series of thoughtful discussions about what their future might hold. The first topic they raised was a very basic one: the reasons that each of them had for wanting to start his own business. Egnew felt that

> as long as my professional talents are being challenged, I have an opportunity to grow, and the rewards for my contributions are commensurate with the marketplace, I'm happy. Everybody likes to have their future tied to a winner. Nobody likes to be in a losing operation. I have begun to look at alternatives. I see tremendous opportunities in the tent business that aren't being properly taken care of. I feel that there is room for another firm. Now I'm trying to decide what to do next.
>
> I never really think about the chance to make a big killing. If I'm on target in 5, 8, or 10 years, at the end of that time I'll be able to do what I want to do. I'll have a new sense of freedom, a sense of independence to do my own thing. Ownership and growth will provide the real rewards. We all dream about making something happen. If you succeed in building your own business, there's no question about who's responsible.

Moore shared similar views:

> J. C. is the only one at Wilderness doing anything with any principles in mind or using what we learned in school instead of just shooting from the hip. If we could get organized, we could do it. I feel that I have been exposed to the business. It is dynamic, something new every day, and I like this. I am excited by the challenge of doing it ourselves. I keep thinking to myself, we can do it!

In addition to the challenge, both men appreciated the need to make a total commitment to the business if it was to be a success. Egnew believed that

> the commitment to go into business is made when you sever whatever ties you have and say "my livelihood is dependent on this enterprise"—that's when the commitment is made. If the two or three people aren't willing to use most of their key assets for the business, then I wouldn't touch them. So the commitment is also shown when you get everybody to put their bucks in. That's when it all starts.

He also believed that starting salaries were a useful measure of commitment and that investors were right to expect personal and financial commitment from the key team members:

> Starting salaries should be lean. A new business needs every possible advantage it can find. If key personnel won't make sacrifices up front, then they won't make them when it gets tough. You should be prepared to make a substantial personal commitment to your business if you haven't already done so. I would be naive to think, "Well, I have this fine educational background, and I have some pretty relevant experience—after all, I'm putting my professional reputation on the line here. What else can you ask for?" "But if the milk turns sour," an investor would point out, "all you have to do is move to some place as far away as southwest Texas and get a 10 percent or 20 percent salary increase in a new job and you're off and running again, while we're sitting here holding all the empty baskets." That's when it really hit me. If I were investing money in a new business and the two or three key people weren't able to make a significant commitment based on their personal assets, then I sure wouldn't be willing to commit a dime to them. That's the commitment that makes you work a little bit harder and makes you determined that you're going to find a way to succeed. Any investor with sense is going to look for this kind of commitment.

Risks and Rewards

Next, Egnew and Moore discussed their attitudes about risks and rewards in starting a new business. Egnew began:

> If we were to start our own business, I wouldn't waste much time thinking about "What if it doesn't work out?" My thinking is positive. If we can ever afford to blow something, now is the time—we are young and have no heavy debts. The idea or dream of having your own business is one many people have, and here is our opportunity. We are frustrated with the way things are going at Wilderness, the opportunity for a better way to do things looks real, and we have a chance to build something.

Moore's comments reflected his confidence in Egnew's optimism:

> If we decide to go ahead, I won't have time to worry or think about not making it. I don't feel that it's that much of a risk when we sit here talking about it, I am so hyped up thinking it could work. I guess if we'd both been fired from Wilderness and had to start our own company, I would do a bit more worrying. Whenever I am ready to throw in the towel, J. C. keeps the momentum going. It looks like an opportunity to make a lot of money. Wilderness went public in 1972, and one owner with 7 percent of the stock made $1,800,000. I feel J. C. has it all together, more than any other person I've ever met. I have tremendous respect for him. I am willing to gamble on a good guy, and therefore I feel it is a good gamble.

Taking the Plunge—Or Not

By spring 1993, J. C. Egnew and John F. Moore had continued to investigate the idea of starting their own tent-manufacturing business. Recognizing the difficulties of starting a new venture and their own inexperience in business, they began to assess their entrepreneurial and management strengths and weaknesses, and to analyze the feasibility of the new business idea. Time was also becoming a serious factor and Egnew and Moore were faced with a serious dilemma: how to start their business in time to take advantage of the 1994 spring market.

From their previous business training, both Egnew and Moore were aware of the high failure rates of new businesses. Egnew expressed his opinions on this issue:

> Most new companies begin with an idea for a new product or service. Few of them survive, and rarely, if ever, does one excel on the strength of the product alone. You have to put it all together. You can't just have a great idea that's better than anything on the market and have a winner. You also need an organization and a plan. Getting the movement going is the hardest thing. That's what makes a start-up so risky. All these things have to get moving at the same time—it's like the inertia of a large train. You've got to devote a lot of energy just to get things going.

Part of the process of taking the plunge included assessing the opportunity. Although committed to the venture psychologically, they did not want to launch a venture that had a poor chance of succeeding. A principal aim of their initial work was to determine whether any major flaws existed in their idea and to decide whether the business was worth pursuing. *Exhibit A* summarizes the industry and financial data Egnew and Moore have gathered to investigate the potential for their new tent-manufacturing business.

More Dilemmas

Their preliminary investigation provided Egnew and Moore with a substantial amount of data. Since they began their investigation, several more weeks had passed. They wondered whether their idea was worth pursuing.

Certain developments, previously unknown to them, emerged from their investigations. First, they found that the industry was closed to outsiders, making it very difficult to get useful market information. Second, they found that the sales of the major canvas suppliers for tents had been declining steadily in recent years, as synthetic fabrics, such as nylon and polyester, became the material of choice. Third, they discovered, to their surprise, that no new US firms had entered the tent business in the past five to six years, in spite of what they estimated as a growing, seller's market. Further, they learned that a handful of small tent manufacturers had actually failed and gone out of business during this period. There had also been significant inroads by offshore manufacturers who imported into the United States.

The Entrepreneurial Process

If Egnew and Moore did start this tent company, what would make them successful? Between the two of them there seemed to be the basic know-how of the business, but was that enough? Were they missing an important element of the business? Or several key competencies? Would there be a need for a third or fourth founder? Who should make up their board? These were constant concerns of both Egnew and Moore as they commuted, worked, and relaxed after work.

At times both Egnew's and Moore's thoughts wandered off into the pursuit of the dream, but there were so many issues they had to confront first. For instance, how would the management of Wilderness react to their resignations? If there was a negative reaction, then they wondered if Wilderness would be an obstacle to their company. After all, Wilderness did have established supplier relationships, lines of distribution, and recognition in the marketplace. With all these attributes, Wilderness could be a valuable ally or a large destructive competitor.

Additionally, questions were emerging as Egnew and Moore wrote Sara Reed, their advisor (see *Exhibit A*). How much money did they need to get this business off the ground? How much more money would they need to operate the business, until it was self-sustaining? When would their tent company be self-sustaining? Where should they be looking for investors? Who would be likely to invest? Were Egnew and Moore willing to give up some equity? Were there assets they could use to secure bank loans? So many things had to be decided on quickly, because the 1994 spring market was quickly approaching.

Exhibit A

To: Sara Reed June 10, 1993

From: J. C. Egnew
John Moore

Re: Feasibility Information for a New Tent Manufacturing Company

The Industry

The significant tent-producing companies in the continental United States are ranked below, based on 1993 sales:

Kellwood Company:	
Sears	30,000,000
Wentzel	24,000,000
	54,000,000
Hettrick (Olin Corporation)	45,000,000
Wilderness Products	30,000,000
National Canvas Products	21,000,000
Coleman	12,000,000
Eureka Tent and Awning	9,000,000
Other	9,000,000
Total	180,000,000

The Thomas Register lists a good many other firms in the tent business. Most of these firms are small mom-and-pop operations consisting of those who custom produce (make to order) awnings and tents and other canvas items such as show tents and circus-type carnival tents. Others are primarily in the repair business. Some of these have a national market, while others have a regional market only.

Approximately 10 percent of this total tent market consists of tents designed for specific uses (e.g., mountain climbing and backpacking). This factor will limit the general tent market potential for the coming year to $162 million (not accounting for an anticipated 1994 growth factor of 20 percent in the market as a whole).

Following is an estimated geographic breakdown of the national tent market that is based on observed industry sales patterns:

	Percent	
New England states	22%	
Metropolitan New York City	13	
Mideast (New York, Pennsylvania)	8	
Midwest (Corn Belt, Plains)	26	
Central Atlantic Coast	4	
Southeast	9	
Southwest	6	
Far West (Coastal)	8	
Other	4	
Total	100%	($180,000,000)

It has been an industry practice for retailers to start taking deliveries of tents after January 1 since tents are not usually Christmas items. To encourage early order commitments and deliveries, the industry has been allowing "net April 1st" payment terms on tents delivered prior to April. Because delivery service has been poor in the past, it is not unusual for customers to place orders in October and November for tents desired in March or April. Projected sales trends by month for the total tent market follow:

Month	*Percent of Annual Sales*
January	16%
February	21
March	15
April	11
May	10
June	6

July	4
August	2
September	3
October	3
November	4
December	5
Total	100%

The Competition

Listed below is a comparison of prices among three of the industry leaders for some of the main types of tents available to the consumer. Profit margins do not vary significantly from one type of tent to another.

Prices of the Major Products for Three Competitors (1993 published prices)

Style	*Size*	*Wilderness*	*Hettrick*	*National*
Cabin	7 × 7	$ 90.80	$ NA	$ 99.60
	8 × 10	120.00	142.05	151.74
	9 × 12	143.85	167.25	175.44
	10 × 16	167.85	197.70	NA
Cabin-screen	10 × 16	209.25	230.40	NA
Umbrella	7 × 7	65.70	63.00	71.46
	9 × 9	96.75	110.40	123.36
Canopy	10 × 10	38.25	NA	45.51
	12 × 12	46.35	47.25	55.20
Screenhouse	10 × 10	86.85	100.95	NA
Pup tent	5 × 7	14.25	13.35	15.54
	5 × 7	32.40	31.50	30.00
Jvc. umbrella	7 × 7	26.25	27.75	33.48
Tri. awning	8 × 10	41.25	47.40	51.60
	8 × 12	49.05	54.60	55.80

NA means not offered by that competitor.
All prices listed are for the season and are expected to increase from 10 % to 12 % on the average for the upcoming season.

The next table presents a comparison of the number of models of each type of tent produced by some of the leading manufacturers.

Comparison of the Number of Models* Offered by Five Major Tent Producers

Company	*Cabin*	*Umbrella*	*Play*	*Canopy and Screen*	*Awnings*	*Nylon*	*Other*
Wilderness:							
Regular	20	4	5	8	9	6	2
Special	32	3	2	9	2	—	—
Hettrick:							
Regular	12	4	9	7	10	2	6
National	9	6	17	6	14	1	4
Coleman	18	2	2	3	—	1	13
Eureka	9	9	14	11	31	7	13

* Includes ice tents, "flies," wind curtains, etc.

Financial Considerations

The following is a summary of industry practices relating to the manufacture and sale of tents.

Accounts receivable:	75% of all sales prior to April 1 billing. Further, 50% of the accounts will be paid on or before April 1, 35% will be 30 days past due, 10% will be 60 days past due, and 5% will be 90 or more days past due when paid.
Inventories:	Monthly inventories will peak in February and be at a minimum level in June.
Work in process:	20% of monthly production.
Finished goods:	9.3% of monthly sales.
Accounts payable:	80% of monthly purchases.
Cost of goods sold:	76% of sales.
Gross profit:	24% of sales.
General, selling, and administration:	Industry average is 15% of sales.

EXERCISE—A VISIT WITH AN ENTREPRENEUR

Over the years, students have found it valuable to interview entrepreneurs who have, within the past 5 to 10 years, started firms whose sales now exceed $1 million and which are profitable. Through such an interview, you can gain insight into an entrepreneur's reasons, strategies, approaches, and motivations for starting and owning a business. Gathering information through interviewing is a valuable skill to practice. You can learn a great deal in a short time through interviewing if you prepare thoughtfully and thoroughly.

The Visit With an Entrepreneur Exercise has been used by students to interview successful entrepreneurs. While there is no right way to structure an interview, the interview in the exercise has merit because it is chronological and it has been tested successfully on many occasions. A breakfast, lunch, or dinner meeting is an excellent vehicle.

EXERCISE
A VISIT WITH AN ENTREPRENEUR

STEP 1: CONTACT THE PERSON YOU HAVE SELECTED AND MAKE AN APPOINTMENT. Be sure to explain why you want the appointment and to give a realistic estimate of how much time you will need.

STEP 2: IDENTIFY SPECIFIC QUESTIONS YOU WOULD LIKE TO HAVE ANSWERED AND THE GENERAL AREAS ABOUT WHICH YOU WOULD LIKE INFORMATION. (SEE SUGGESTED INTERVIEW IN **STEP 3.**) Using a combination of open-ended questions, such as general questions about how the entrepreneur got started, what happened next, and so forth, and closed-ended questions, such as specific questions about what his or her goals were, if he or she had to find partners, and so forth, will help to keep the interview focused and yet allow for unexpected comments and insights.

STEP 3: CONDUCT THE INTERVIEW. Recording the interview on audiotape can be very helpful to you later and is recommended unless you or the person being interviewed objects to being recorded. Remember, too, that you most likely will learn more if you are an interested listener.

Interview

Questions for Gathering Information

- Would you tell me about yourself before you started your first venture?

  Were your parents, relatives, or close friends entrepreneurial? How so?

  Did you have any other role models?

  What was your education/military experience? In hindsight, was it helpful? In what specific ways?

  What was your previous work experience? Was it helpful? What particular "chunks of experience" were especially valuable or irrelevant?

  Did you have a business or self-employment during your youth?

  In particular, did you have any sales or marketing experience? How important was it or a lack of it to starting your company?

- How did you start your venture?

  How did you spot the opportunity? How did it surface?

  What were your goals? What were your lifestyle needs or other personal requirements? How did you fit these together?

  How did you evaluate the opportunity in terms of the critical elements for success? The competition? The market? Did you have specific criteria you wanted to meet?

  Did you find or have partners? What kind of planning did you do? What kind of financing did you have?

  Did you have a start-up business plan of any kind? Please tell me about it.

  How much time did it take from conception to the first day of business? How many hours a day did you spend working on it?

(Continued)

How much capital did it take? How long did it take to reach a positive cash flow and break-even sales volume? If you did not have enough money at the time, what were some ways in which you bootstrapped the venture (bartering, borrowing, and the like). Tell me about the pressures and crises during that early survival period.

What outside help did you get? Did you have experienced advisors? Lawyers? Accountants? Tax experts? Patent experts? How did you develop these networks and how long did it take?

How did any outside advisors make a difference in your company?

What was your family situation at the time?

What did you perceive to be your own strengths? Weaknesses?

What did you perceive to be the strengths of your venture? Weaknesses?

What was your most triumphant moment? Your worst moment?

Did you want to have partners or do it solo? Why?

- Once you got going:

  What were the most difficult gaps to fill and problems to solve as you began to grow rapidly?

  When you looked for key people as partners, advisors, or managers, were there any personal attributes or attitudes you were especially seeking because you knew they would fit with you and were important to success? How did you find them?

  Are there any attributes among partners and advisors that you would definitely try to avoid?

  Have things become more predictable? Or less?

  Do you spend more time, the same amount of time, or less time with your business now than in the early years?

  Do you feel more managerial and less entrepreneurial now?

  In terms of the future, do you plan to harvest? To maintain? To expand?

  In your ideal world, how many days a year would you want to work? Please explain.

  Do you plan ever to retire? Would you explain.

  Have your goals changed? Have you met them?

  Has your family situation changed?

  What do you learn from both success and failure?

Questions for Concluding

- What do you consider your most valuable asset—the thing that enabled you to make it?
- If you had it to do over again, would you do it again, in the same way?

- As you look back, what do you feel are the most critical concepts, skills, attitudes, and know-how you needed to get your company started and grown to where it is today? What will be needed for the next five years? To what extent can any of these be learned?
- Some people say there is a lot of stress being an entrepreneur. What have you experienced? How would you say it compares with other "hot seat" jobs, such as the head of a big company or a partner in a large law firm or accounting firm?
- What things do you find personally rewarding and satisfying as an entrepreneur? What have been the rewards, risks, and trade-offs?
- Who should try to be an entrepreneur? And who should not? Can you give me any ideas there?
- What advice would you give an aspiring entrepreneur? Could you suggest the three most important lessons you have learned? How can I learn them while minimizing the tuition?
- Would you suggest any other entrepreneur I should talk to?

STEP 4: EVALUATE WHAT YOU HAVE LEARNED. Write down the information you have gathered in some form that will be helpful to you later on. Be as specific as you can. Jotting down direct quotes is more effective than statements such as "highly motivated individual." And be sure to make a note of what you did *not* find out.

STEP 5: WRITE A THANK YOU NOTE. This is more than a courtesy; it will also help the entrepreneur to remember you favorably should you want to follow up on the interview.

New Venture Ideas

2

Nothing is more dangerous than an idea, when it's the only one we have.

Alain Emile Chartier

RESULTS EXPECTED

At the conclusion of the chapter, you will have:

1. Examined the role of ideas in entrepreneurship.
2. Discussed the creative process and how experience and trial-and-error iteration can aid in pattern recognition.
3. Examined ways to enhance creativity and its role in the development of ideas.
4. Identified some source for locating new business ideas.
5. Analyzed the PC-Build case.
6. Generated some new venture ideas using the Idea Generation exercise.

THE ROLE OF IDEAS

Ideas As Tools

It is worth emphasizing again that *a good idea is nothing more than a tool in the hands of an entrepreneur.* Finding a good idea is the *first* step in the task of converting an entrepreneur's creativity into an opportunity.

The importance of the idea is most often overrated, usually at the expense of underemphasizing the need for products or services, or both, which can be sold in enough quantity to real customers.

Further, the new business that simply bursts from a flash of brilliance is rare. What is usually necessary is a series of trial-and-error iterations, or repetitions, before a crude and promising product or service fits with what the customer is really willing to pay for. After all, Howard Head made 40 different metal skis before he finally made the model that worked consistently. In fact, with surprising frequency, major businesses are built around totally different products than those originally envisioned. Consider these examples:

- F. Leland Strange, the founder and president of Quadram, a maker of graphics and communications boards and other boards for microcomputers, told the story of how he developed his marketing idea into a company with $100 million in sales in three years.[1] He stated that he had developed a business plan to launch his company, and the company

[1] Keynote address at the 1984 Babson Entrepreneurship Research Conference, cosponsored by the School of Management, Georgia Institute of Technology, April 23–25, 1984, Atlanta, Georgia.

even hit projected revenues for the first two years. He noted, however, that success was achieved with completely *different* products than those in the original plan.

- Polaroid Corporation was founded with a product based on the principle of polarizing light waves, a discovery by Dr. Land that he patented. Polarized head lamps, it was reasoned, would have the compelling safety feature of reducing head-on collisions caused at night by the "blinding" by oncoming lights. Conceivably, such polarized lamps could be installed by car manufacturers in every vehicle manufactured. However, the company grew to its present $2 billion-plus size through a quite different application of the original technology—instant photography.
- IBM began in the wire and cable business and later expanded to time clocks. Sales in the 1920s were only a few million dollars a year. Its successful mainframe computer business and then its successful personal computer business emerged much later.

As one entrepreneur expressed it:

> Perhaps the existence of business plans and the language of business give a misleading impression of business building as a rational process. But, as any entrepreneur can confirm, starting a business is very much a series of fits and starts, brainstorms and barriers. Creating a business is a round of chance encounters that leads to new opportunities and ideas, mistakes that turn into miracles.[2]

The Great Mousetrap Fallacy

Perhaps no one did a greater disservice to generations of would-be entrepreneurs than Ralph Waldo Emerson in his oft-quoted line: "If a man can make a better mousetrap than his neighbor, though he builds his house in the woods the world will make a beaten path to his door."

What can be called the great mousetrap fallacy was thus spawned. Indeed, it is often assumed that success is possible if an entrepreneur can just come up with a new idea. And, in today's changing world, if the idea has anything to do with technology, success is certain—or so it would seem.

The truth of the matter is that ideas are inert and, for all practical purposes, worthless. Further, the flow of ideas is really quite phenomenal. Venture capital investors, for instance, during the investing boom of the 1980s, received as many as 100 to 200 proposals and business plans each month. Only 1 to 3 percent of these actually received financing, however.

Yet the fallacy persists despite the lessons of practical experience noted long ago in the insightful reply to Emerson by O. B. Winters: "The manufacturer who waits for the world to beat a path to his door is a great optimist. But the manufacturer who shows this 'mousetrap' to the world keeps the smoke coming out his chimney."

Contributors to the Fallacy

One cannot blame it all on Ralph Waldo Emerson. There are several reasons for the perpetuation of the fallacy. One is the portrayal in oversimplified accounts of the ease and genius with which such ventures as Xerox, IBM, and Polaroid have made their founders wealthy. Unfortunately, these exceptions do not provide a useful rule to guide aspiring entrepreneurs.

Another is that inventors seem particularly prone to mousetrap myopia. Perhaps, like Emerson, they are substantially sheltered in viewpoint and experience from the tough, competitive realities of the business world. Consequently, they may underestimate, if not

[2] Joline Godfrey, *Our Wildest Dreams: Women Entrepreneurs, Making Money, Having Fun, Doing Good* (New York: Harper Business, 1992), p. 27.

seriously downgrade, the importance of what it takes to make a business succeed. Frankly, inventing and brainstorming may be a lot more fun than the careful and diligent observation, investigation, and nurturing of customers that are often required to sell a product or service.

Contributing also to the great mousetrap fallacy is the tremendous psychological ownership attached to an invention or, later, to a new product. This attachment is different from attachment to a business. The intense and highly involved personal identity and commitment to an invention or new widget tends to weaken or preclude entirely realistic assessment of the other crucial aspects of the business. While an intense level of psychological ownership and involvement is certainly a prerequisite for creating a new business, the fatal flaw in attachment to an invention or product is the narrowness of its focus. The focal point needs to be the building of the business, rather than just one aspect of it, the idea.

Another source of mousetrap myopia lies in a technical and scientific orientation, that is, a desire to do it better. A good illustration of this is the experience of a Canadian entrepreneur who founded, with his brother, a company to manufacture truck seats. The entrepreneur's brother had developed a new seat for trucks that was a definite improvement over other seats. The entrepreneur knew he could profitably sell the seat his brother had designed, and they did so. When they needed more manufacturing capacity, one brother was not as interested in manufacturing more of the first seat, but he had several ideas on how to improve the seat. The first brother stated: "If I had listened to him, we probably would be a small custom shop today, or out of business. Instead, we concentrated on making seats that would sell at a profit, rather than just making a better and better seat. Our company has several million dollars of sales today and is profitable."

The Best Idea

Consider the following examples, which drive the point home that having the best technology or idea by itself often does not make the critical difference in success:

- UNIVAC had the early elegance and technology lead over IBM in computers, but it was never able to seize the emerging, significant opportunities in the computer industry.
- In 1967 and 1968, a lead investor, Fred Adler, received over 50 business plans from entrepreneurs who proposed to start minicomputer firms. Several minicomputer companies were started at that time, and several of the firms actually had a better idea in the form of more advanced technology than the one that most attracted Adler's attention. Data General's lead entrepreneur and his team had an entrepreneurial flair and market focus, which Adler bet on.[3] In 1988, the company had sales of $1.3 billion.
- In 1969, the then-fledgling Cullinet, Inc., raised $500,000 in the then-hot new issues market. Two years later, the firm had spent this initial capital, and according to its founder, John Cullinane, still had a payroll of $8,500 to meet. Cullinane said the money had been spent unwisely through "programmer anarchy." He turned the company around by firing his programmers since, he said, they did not understand what happiness was. "Happiness," Cullinane said, "is a satisfied customer."[4] He then developed customer-anchored software products and a plan for growth that led to a substantial venture capital investment during a lean time for venture capital.
- Finally, Lotus and its product, Lotus 1-2-3, the first integrated package for the personal computer to include spreadsheet, graphics, and database management capabilities, is a good example. Critics and reviewers have since reported that some new software products

[3] The story of the entrepreneurial culture at Data General was told in a best-seller by Tracy Kidder, *The Soul of a New Machine* (Boston: Little, Brown, 1981).

[4] Speaking at his induction in 1984 into the Babson College Academy of Distinguished Entrepreneurs.

are indeed more elegant and sophisticated than Lotus 1-2-3, but new entrants probably require $5 million and up to fund the marketing necessary to launch new software products and gain attention and distribution in this tumultuous marketplace.

Being There First

Further, having the best idea first by no means is a guarantee of success. Again, just ask Adam Osborne, or Dan Bricklin, who was first with the spreadsheet software VisiCalc.

Also, unless having the best idea first also includes the capacity to preempt other competitors by capturing a significant share of the market or by erecting insurmountable barriers to entry, being there first can mean proving for the competition that the market exists to be snared.

PATTERN RECOGNITION

The Experience Factor

Since ideas are building tools, one cannot build a successful business without them, as one could not build a house without a hammer. In this regard, experience is vital in looking at new venture ideas. Those with experience have been there before.

Time after time, experienced entrepreneurs exhibit an ability to recognize quickly a pattern—and an opportunity—while it is still taking shape. Herbert Simon, of the Department of Psychology at Carnegie-Mellon University, described the recognizing of patterns as a creative process that is not simply logical, linear, and additive. He says that the process often is intuitive and inductive, involving the creative linking, or cross-association, of two or more in-depth "chunks" of experience, know-how, and contacts.[5] Simon contends that it takes 10 years or more for people to accumulate what he calls the "50,000 chunks" of experience, and so forth, that enable them to be highly creative and recognize patterns—familiar circumstances that can be translated from one place to another.

Thus, the process of sorting through ideas and recognizing a pattern also can be compared to the process of fitting pieces into a three-dimensional jigsaw puzzle. It is impossible to assemble such a puzzle by looking at it as a whole unit. Rather, one needs to see the relationships between, and be able to fit together, seemingly unrelated pieces before the whole is visible.

Recognizing ideas which can become entrepreneurial opportunities stems from a capacity to see what others do not—that one plus one equals three, or more. Consider the following examples of the common thread of pattern recognition and creating new businesses by linking knowledge in one field or marketplace with quite different technical, business, or marketing know-how:

- A middle manager employed by a larger company was on a plant tour of a small machinery manufacturer, a customer, in the Midwest. A machinist was mechanically cutting metal during a demonstration of a particular fabricating operation. Shockingly, the machinist accidentally sliced his hand in the cutting machine, removing two fingers. Instantly, the manager recognized that the application of new laser technology for this cutting operation was a significant business opportunity which would make it possible to eliminate such horrible accidents as he had just witnessed. He subsequently launched and built a multimillion-dollar company. Here linking the knowledge of the capabilities of lasers to an old, injury-prone metal-cutting technology yielded an opportunity.

[5] Described in a working paper by Herbert A Simon, "What We Know About the Creative Process," Carnegie-Mellon University, 1984.

- During travel throughout Europe, the eventual founders of Crate & Barrel frequently saw stylish and innovative products for the kitchen and home that were not yet available in the United States. When they returned home, the founders created Crate & Barrel to offer these products, for which market research had, in a sense, already been conducted in Europe. This knowledge of consumer buying habits in one geographical region, Europe, was applied to a previously untapped consumer market in another country, the United States.
- Howard Head had been an aeronautical design engineer working with new light metal alloys to build more efficient airfoils during World War II. Head transferred knowledge of metal bonding technology from the aircraft manufacturing business to a consumer product, metal skis, and then to another, tennis rackets. In the first case, although he had limited skiing experience, he had concluded that if he could make a metal ski, there would be a significant market as a result of the limitations of wooden skis. His company dominated the ski industry for many years. In talking about his decision to develop the oversized Prince tennis racket after he saw a need for ball control among players learning tennis, Head said, "I saw the pattern again that had worked at Head Ski. . . . I had proven to myself before that you can take different technology and know-how and apply it to a solution in a new area."[6] He had set about learning enough about the physics of tennis rackets and surfaces and developed the Prince racket.
- In Texas, a young entrepreneur launched a modular home sales business in the late 1970s. First, he parlayed experience as a loan officer with a large New York City bank into a job with a manufacturer of mobile and modular homes in Texas. This enabled him, over a three-year period, to learn the business and to understand the market opportunity. He then opened a sales location in a growing suburb about 25 miles from booming larger cities. By studying his competitors and conducting an analysis of how customers actually went about purchasing new modular homes, he spotted a pattern that meant opportunity. Customers usually shopped at three different locations, where they could see different models and price ranges, before making a purchase decision. Since his market analysis showed there was room in the city for three or four such businesses, he opened two additional sites, each with a different name and with different but complementary lines. Within two years, despite record high interest rates, his business had nearly tripled to $17 million in annual sales, and his only competitor was planning to move.

Enhancing Creative Thinking

The creative thinking described above is of great value in recognizing opportunities, as well as other aspects of entrepreneurship. The notion that creativity can be learned or enhanced holds important implications for entrepreneurs who need to be creative in their thinking. Most people can certainly spot creative flair. Children seem to have it, and many seem to lose it. Several studies suggest that creativity actually peaks around the first grade because a person's life tends to become increasingly structured and defined by others and by institutions. Further, the development in school of intellectual discipline and rigor in thinking takes on greater importance than during the formative years, and most of our education beyond grade school stresses a logical, rational mode of orderly reasoning and thinking. Finally, social pressures may tend to be a taming influence on creativity.

There is evidence that one can enhance creative thinking in later years. Take, for instance, a group called Synectics of Cambridge, Massachusetts, one of the first organizations in the early 1950s to investigate systematically the process of creative thinking and to conduct

[6] Keynote address at the first annual Entrepreneur's Night of UCLA Graduate School of Business, April 18, 1984, Westwood, California.

training sessions in applying creative thinking to business. Underlying the Synectics approach to developing creativity were the following theories:[7]

- The efficiency of a person's creative process can be markedly increased if he or she understands the psychological process by which the process operates.
- The emotional component in the creative process is more important than the intellectual, and the irrational more important than the rational.
- The emotional, irrational elements need to be understood in order to increase the probability of success in a problem-solving situation.

The author participated in one of these training sessions, and it became evident during the sessions that the methods did unlock the thinking process and yielded very imaginative solutions.

Approaches to Unleashing Creativity

Since the 1950s, a good deal has been learned about the workings of the human brain. Today, there is general agreement that the two sides of the brain process information in quite different ways. The left side performs rational, logical functions, while the right side operates the intuitive and nonrational modes of thought. A person uses both sides, actually shifting from one mode to the other (see Exhibit 2.1). How to control modes of thought is of interest to entrepreneurs and they can, perhaps, draw on two interesting approaches.

More recently, professors have focused on the creativity process. For instance, Michael Gordon stressed the importance of creativity and the need for brainstorming in a recent presentation on the Elements of Personal Power. He suggested that creative visualization could be enhanced by using the following 10 brainstorming rules:[8]

1. Define your purpose.
2. Choose participants.
3. Choose a facilitator.
4. Brainstorm spontaneously, copiously.
5. No criticism, no negatives.
6. Record ideas in full view.
7. Invent to the "void."
8. Resist becoming committed to one idea.
9. Identify the most promising ideas.
10. Refine and prioritize.

Team Creativity

It seems teams of people can generate creativity that may not exist in a single individual. Continually, the creativity of a team of people is impressive, and comparable or better creative solutions to problems evolving from the collective interaction of a small group of people have been observed.

A good example of the creativity generated by using more than one head is that of a company founded by a Babson College graduate with little technical training. He teamed up with a talented inventor, and the entrepreneurial and business know-how of the founder

[7] William J J Gordon, *Synectics* (New York: Harper & Row, 1961), p. 6.

[8] Michael Gordon, "Why Personal Power?" Presented at the Price-Babson Reflect, May 1992. Reprinted with permission from Michael Gordon.

Exhibit 2.1
Comparison of Left-Mode and Right-Mode Characteristics

L-Mode	*R-Mode*
Verbal: Using words to name, describe, and define.	*Nonverbal:* Awareness of things, but minimal connection with words.
Analytic: Figuring things out step-by-step and part-by-part.	*Synthetic:* Putting things together to form wholes.
Symbolic: Using a symbol to *stand for* something. For example, the sign + stands for the process of addition.	*Concrete:* Relating to things as they are at the present moment.
Abstract: Taking out a small bit of information and using it to represent the whole thing.	*Analogic:* Seeing likenesses between things; understanding metaphoric relationships.
Temporal: Keeping track of time, sequencing one thing after another, doing first things first, second things second, etc.	*Nontemporal:* Without a sense of time.
Rational: Drawing conclusions based on *reason* and *facts.*	*Nonrational:* Not requiring a basis of reason or facts; willingness to suspend judgment.
Digital: Using numbers as in counting.	*Spatial:* Seeing where things are in relation to other things, and how parts go together to form a whole.
Logical: Drawing conclusions based on logic; one thing following another in logical order—for example, a mathematical theorem or a well-stated argument.	*Intuitive:* Making leaps of insight, often based on incomplete patterns, hunches, feelings, or visual images.
Linear: Thinking in terms of linked ideas, one thought directly following another, often leading to a convergent conclusion.	*Holistic:* Seeing whole things all at once; perceiving the overall patterns and structures, often leading to divergent conclusions.

Source: Betty Edwards, *Drawing on the Right Side of the Brain* (Boston, MA: Houghton Mifflin, 1979), p. 40.

Table 2.1
Sources of Opportunities

Source	*Percent of Companies*
Work activity	47%
Improving an existing product/service	15
Identifying an unfilled niche	11
Other sources	16

Source: Adapted from John Case, "The Origins of Entrepreneurship," INC., June 1989, p. 54. The survey involved 500 of the fastest growing companies.

complemented the creative and technical skills of the inventor. The result has been a rapidly growing multimillion-dollar venture in the field of video-based surgical equipment.

Students interested in exploring this further may want at this time to do the Creative Squares exercise at the end of the chapter.

FINDING IDEAS

If over half of the ideas for successful companies come from work place experiences, as *Table 2.1* suggests, why haven't more new ventures come out of existing businesses? Furthermore, Karl H. Vesper suggests that many opportunities were ready prior to the founding of a company, for instance, hot-air corn poppers, aseptic packaging of US foods, just-in-time inventory control, and fiberglass skis.[9] These factors suggest that it takes the right person, in the right place, at the right time—so, how can you increase your chances of being

[9] Karl H Vesper, *New Venture Mechanics* (Englewood Cliffs, NJ: Prentice-Hall, 1993), p. 3.

the next Anita Roddick of The Body Shop? There are numerous sources of information and available opportunities:[10]

- ***Existing businesses.*** Purchasing an on-going business is an excellent way to find a new business idea. Such a route to a new venture can save time and money and can reduce risk as well. Investment bankers and business brokers are knowledgeable about businesses for sale, as are trust officers. It is worth noting, however, that the very best private businesses for sale are not advertised by brokers, and the real gems are usually bought by individuals or firms closest to them, such as management, directors, customers, suppliers, or financial backers. Bankruptcy judges have a continual flow of ventures in serious trouble. There can be some excellent opportunities buried beneath all the financial debris of a bankrupt firm.
- ***Franchises.*** Franchising is another way to enter an industry, by either starting a franchise operation or becoming a franchisee. This is a fertile area. The number of franchisors nationally now stands at over 2,000, according to the International Franchise Association and the Department of Commerce, and franchisors account for well over $300 billion in sales annually and nearly one-third of all retail sales.[11] The following sources can provide a useful start for a search in this field:
  - *Franchise Opportunity Handbook,* US Department of Commerce.
  - *The Franchise Annual Handbook and Directory,* edited by Edward L. Dixon.
  - *Franchising: Proven Techniques for Rapid Company Expansion and Market Dominance,* by David Seltz.
  - *Franchising World,* published by the International Franchise Association.
  - *Franchising Today,* published by Franchise Technologies.
  - Listings of opportunities and ads in such publications as *INC., Venture,* and *The Wall Street Journal.*
  - *International Franchise Handbook.*
  - Databases, such as Dialog and CompuServe.
- ***Patents.*** Patent brokers specialize in marketing patents that are owned by individual inventors, corporations, universities, or other research organizations to those seeking new commercially viable products. Some brokers specialize in international product licensing, and, occasionally, a patent broker will purchase an invention and then resell it. Although, over the years, the patent broker's image has been tarnished by a few unscrupulous brokers, acquisitions effected by reputable brokers have resulted in significant new products. Notable among these was Bausch & Lomb's acquisition, through the National Patent Development Corporation, of the United States rights to hydron, a material used in contact lenses. Some patent brokers are:
  - MGA Technology, Inc., Chicago, Illinois.
  - New Product Development Services, Inc., Kansas City, Missouri.
  - University Patents, Chicago, Illinois.
  - Research Corporation, New York, New York.
  - Pegasus Corporation, New York, New York.
  - National Patent Development Corporation, New York, New York.
- ***Product licensing.*** A good way to obtain exposure to a large number of product ideas available from universities, corporations, and independent investors is to subscribe to information services, such as the *American Bulletin of International Technology, Selected*

[10]See also David E Gumpert and Jeffry A Timmons, *The Encyclopedia of Small Business Resources* (New York: Harper & Row, 1984).

[11]Ibid., p. 177

Business Ventures (published by General Electric Company), *Technology Mart, Patent Licensing Gazette,* and the National Technical Information Service. In addition, corporations, not-for-profit research institutes, and universities are sources of ideas:

Corporations. Corporations engaged in research and development develop inventions or services that they do not exploit commercially. These inventions either do not fit existing product lines or marketing programs or do not represent sufficiently large markets to be interesting to large corporations. A good number of corporations license these kinds of inventions, either through patent brokers, product-licensing information services, or their own patent-marketing efforts. Directly contacting a corporation with a licensing program may prove fruitful. Among the major corporations known to have active internal patent-marketing efforts are the following:

- Gulf and Western Invention Development Corporation.
- Kraft Corporation, Research and Development.
- Pillsbury Company, Research and Development Laboratories.
- Union Carbide Corporation, Nuclear Division.
- RCA Corporation, Domestic Licensing.
- TRW Corporation, Systems Group.
- Lockheed Corporation, Patent Licensing.

Not-for-profit research institutes. These nonprofit organizations do research and development under contract to the government and private industry as well as some internally sponsored research and development of new products and processes that can be licensed to private corporations for further development, manufacturing, and marketing. Perhaps the most famous example of how this works is Battelle Memorial Institute's participation in the development of xerography and the subsequent license of the technology to the Haloid Corporation, now Xerox Corporation. Some nonprofit research institutes with active licensing programs are:

- Battelle Memorial Institute.
- ITT Research Institute.
- Stanford Research Institute.
- Southwest Research Institute.

Universities. A number of universities are active in research in the physical sciences and seek to license inventions that result from this research, either directly or through an associated research foundation that administers its patent program. Massachusetts Institute of Technology and the California Institute of Technology publish periodic reports containing abstracts of inventions they own which are available for licensing. In addition, since a number of very good ideas developed in universities never reach formal licensing outlets, another way to find these ideas is to become familiar with the work of researchers in an area of interest. Among universities that have active licensing programs are:

- Massachusetts Institute of Technology.
- California Institute of Technology.
- University of Wisconsin.
- Iowa State University.
- Purdue University.
- University of California.
- University of Oregon.

- ***Industry and Trade Contacts.***

  Trade shows and association meetings. Trade shows and association meetings in an industry can be an excellent way to examine the products of many potential competitors, meet distributors and sales representatives, learn of product and market trends, and identify potential products. The American Electronics Association is a good example of an association which holds such seminars and meetings.

  Customers. Contacting potential customers of a certain type of product can help determine what their needs are and where existing products are deficient or inadequate. For example, discussions with doctors who head medical services at leading hospitals might lead to product ideas in the biomedical equipment business.

  Distributors and wholesalers. Contacting people who distribute a certain type of product can yield extensive information about the strengths and weaknesses of existing products and the kinds of product improvements and new products that are needed by customers.

  Competitors. Examining products offered by companies competing in an industry can show whether an existing design is protected by patent and whether it can be improved or imitated.
- ***Former employers.*** A number of businesses are started with products or services, or both, based on technology and ideas developed by entrepreneurs while they were employed by others. In some cases, research laboratories were not interested in commercial exploitation of technology, or the previous employer was not interested in the ideas for new products, and the rights were given up or sold. In others, the ideas were developed under government contract and were in the public domain. In addition, some companies will help entrepreneurs set up companies in return for equity.
- ***Professional contacts.*** Ideas can also be found by contacting such professionals as patent attorneys, accountants, commercial bankers, and venture capitalists who come into contact with those seeking to license patents or to start a business using patented products or processes.
- ***Consulting.*** A method for obtaining ideas that has been successful for technically trained entrepreneurs is to provide consulting and one-of-a-kind engineering designs for people in fields of interest. For example, an entrepreneur wanting to establish a medical equipment company can do consulting or can design experimental equipment for medical researchers. These kinds of activities often lead to prototypes that can be turned into products needed by a number of researchers. For example, this approach was used in establishing a company to produce psychological testing equipment that evolved from consulting done at the Massachusetts General Hospital and, again, in a company to design and manufacture oceanographic instruments which were developed from consulting done for an oceanographic research institute.
- ***Networking.*** Networks can be a stimulant and source of new ideas, as well as a source of valuable contacts with people. Much of this requires personal initiative on an informal basis; but around the country, organized networks can facilitate and accelerate the process of making contacts and finding new business ideas. Consider, for example, in the Boston area, a high-density area of exceptional entrepreneurial activity, several networks have emerged in recent years, including the Babson Entrepreneurial Exchange, the Smaller Business Association of New England (SBANE), the MIT Enterprise Forum, the 128 Venture Group, and the Boston Computer Society. Similar organizations can be found in all of the United States, for example, the American

Women's Economic Development Corporation in New York City; the Association of Women Entrepreneurs; the Entrepreneur's Roundtable of the UCLA Graduate Student Association; and the Association of Collegiate Entrepreneurs at Wichita State University.

CASE—PC-BUILD, INC.*

Preparation Questions

1. Evaluate the PC-Build™ business plan and the opportunity.[1]
2. Should Michael Healey and Robert Lofblad start the business?
3. Would you invest in the business? Join the venture?
4. What should the founders do?

PC-BUILD, INC.

"We won!" Elation flooded Mike Healey's head with the announcement that he, Bob Lofblad, and their team had won the 1992 MBA Douglass Prize at Babson College for the best proposed business among dozens of business plans submitted to the competition. It was not the $5,000 award plus the engraved watch that were most important. Was this award the confirmation of nearly a year-long effort to determine whether PC-Build was a serious business opportunity or just another good idea? After all, the panel of judges was made up of experienced and successful entrepreneurs who thought that PC-Build was the best idea of the lot. Mike and Bob wondered if the panel's support was a positive indicator of how the market would assess PC-Build's potential.

Graduation was less than a month away, May 1992. Mike thought it was a bit scary: Should we really try to launch this business? Most people say starting a business right out of school is too risky. While most classmates were headed for regular jobs, Mike had not spent time at the placement office. He wondered if this was the right time and place to take the plunge. He was confident about the idea, the market potential, and his team—but some major issues still needed to be resolved. Among them, how much capital would be required to get started? As Mike thought about the capital requirements, he commented to Bob, "I do not think that this venture will require that much capital, because the only thing we plan to buy new is lunch!" Yet, he continued to wonder: How could he raise money and on what terms? Who might invest in the company? If everything worked out, the upside was not hard to figure out. But what if it did not work out? Could he get another job? What would his family and friends think? How would he handle all that? What follows is the original business plan for PC-Build Computer Kits.

*Research Associate Christine C Remey prepared this case, under the supervision of Professor Jeffry A Timmons, as the basis for class discussion rather than to illustrate either effective or ineffective handling of an administrative situation. Reprinted with permission from Michael Healey and Robert Lofblad.

[1]PC-Build™ is a registered trademark of Discovery Curve, Inc.

PC-BUILD COMPUTER KITS—BUSINESS PLAN

A DIVISION OF DISCOVERY CURVE, INC.

Table of Contents

EXECUTIVE SUMMARY....Page 51
THE INDUSTRY AND THE COMPANY AND ITS PRODUCT....Page 51
- Opportunity Rationale
- The Company
- The Product

MARKET RESEARCH AND ANALYSIS....Page 56
- Estimated Market Share and Sales
- Market Trends
- Competition
- Ongoing Market Evaluation

THE ECONOMICS OF THE BUSINESS....Page 59
- Supplier Selection Criteria

MARKETING PLAN....Page 64
- Overall Marketing Strategy
- Pricing
- Sales Tactics
- Service and Warranty Policies
- Advertising and Promotion
- Distribution

DESIGN AND DEVELOPMENT PLANS....Page 66
- Future Products
- Proprietary Issues

MANUFACTURING AND OPERATIONS PLAN....Page 67
- Manufacturing Policy
- Operating Cycle

MANAGEMENT TEAM....Page 69
- Future Team Members
- Board of Directors

OVERALL PROJECT SCHEDULE....Page 70
CRITICAL RISKS, PROBLEMS, AND ASSUMPTIONS....Page 70
THE FINANCIAL PLAN....Page 73
- Break-even Analysis
- Balance Sheet
- Income Statement
- Cash Flows

PROPOSED COMPANY OFFERING....Page 77

EXECUTIVE SUMMARY

Discovery Curve Corporation was formed in October 1991 and incorporated in Massachusetts in February 1992. Discovery Curve's primary line of business is the manufacture and sale of IBM-compatible personal computer kits, sold as PC-Build Computer Kits. These kits are targeted at the home hobbyist and educational institutions, such as computer camps and adult continuing education. This market niche targets the computer users who "want to get their hands dirty." There are similar kits for a variety of industries, including stereo equipment and automobiles. The founders believe an opportunity exists in the personal computer (PC) industry for four main reasons:

- Technological standardization.
- Changing consumer attitudes toward PCs.
- Definite market opportunity.
- Sleepy competitors.

As a result of these conditions, there is a unique opportunity to provide high-quality PC kits at affordable prices.

The Company differentiates itself from its direct competition by being a full-service provider of an integrated learning experience. PC-Build kits will be far more than the "box of parts" favored by our competition. Competitors target users whose primary goal is saving money. We target those who love to experiment and learn.

The total market size for build-it-yourself computers in 1991 was estimated to be $70 million, roughly 66,000 units. PC-Build's Year 1 projected sales volume is 1,500 units, about $1.2 million. This represents a very conservative 1.43 percent market share. The company's break-even volume is 749 units of its lowest priced kit. Gross margins are 28–35 percent.

Initial market research has been encouraging. The company has 10 education proposals under review and has received orders from several individuals. Preliminary supplier selection is complete, and the company has secured production/administrative facilities in Wellesley, Massachusetts.

Management has done exhaustive research into the industry, the product, and the market. The company is proceeding according to schedule. Discovery Curve, Inc., is seeking $100,000 to implement the plans described herein. The 3,000 shares of common stock offered for $33 per share will represent 30 percent of PC-Build.

THE INDUSTRY AND THE COMPANY AND ITS PRODUCT

The personal computer (PC) industry has undergone tremendous growth in the last 10 years. Advances in microprocessor technology have put mainframe power in the price range of the individual. The acceptance of PCs has been fueled by a boom in available software. As a result, PCs have become commonplace in the office, at school, and at home. Worldwide sales of PCs were 24 million units ($10.4 billion) in 1990.

In the late 1970s and early 1980s, a large number of PC kits were available. As industry sales grew, the kits died off. Profitability for the manufacturer came from volume production. Kits were a low-volume niche product. Many PC makers, notably Apple and Dell, switched from selling kits to selling finished products because the margins and volumes were higher. As of today, there are only two national manufacturers of complete PC kits.

The industry can be split into two general product segments, IBM compatible and Apple. *IBM compatible* refers to all MS-DOS–based PCs that are 100 percent compatible with IBM. This group accounts for over 80 percent of industry sales; the rest go to Apple and some smaller segments.

The IBM-compatible segment has developed a unique pecking order. Any major technological change is usually released by a major player, such as IBM or Intel. Within weeks, all major clone makers follow suit. The result is that previous versions of hardware are bumped down and begin to drop in price. This pecking order is not limited to fully assembled PCs. The same pattern is evident in components such as hard disks and monitors.

Opportunity Rationale

There are three main reasons why an opportunity exists for PC-Build: Technological standardization, changing consumer attitudes, and an identified neglected market segment.

Technological Standardization. All IBM compatibles are based on Intel's microprocessor technology. Intel has become the dominant producer of central processing units (CPUs). The clones also use the same standard layout for their main circuit boards. By doing so they can claim 100 percent compatibility and easily accommodate any add-in hardware, such as a modem.

Standardization has created machines that are relatively simple to assemble. All complex engineering is done on the board. Boards simply plug into a slot. A typical PC is made up of only 11 major components. A working PC can be easily assembled by an ordinary individual. This ease can be enhanced by making some structural changes to the typical PC chassis and by creating detailing assembly instructions.

Common circuit board designs have given rise to a booming original equipment manufacturing (OEM) business. Most PC manufacturers, including IBM, do not build all their components in house. Most components are subcontracted out, leaving the PC maker the task of assembly and testing. PC-Build will be able to pick and choose suppliers based on their price, quality, warranty and delivery terms.

PC-Build also gains a "free-engineering" factor because of this standardization and pecking order of new releases. PC-Build kits will not be the leading edge in PC technology. Instead, they will lag one generation behind. For example, PC-Build will be marketing a 286 PC as its low-end product. This computer is not leading edge, but is standard in the market. By waiting until a standard develops in the marketplace, PC-Build has its systems engineered for free. (Please refer to the "Technological Surfing" section on p. 55 for a detailed explanation of this logic.)

Changing Consumer Attitudes. PCs are everywhere—in the home, the office, and at school. The number of different distribution channels available underscores PCs' acceptability. Even the *Home Shopping Channel* sells PCs.

Changing consumer attitudes affect PC-Build in two ways. First, consumers are no longer loyal to brand names. Buying a big name is no longer an issue. Second, the PC itself is no longer a mystery. This second change can best be seen by examining recent trends with add-in hardware. This area used to be a major contributor to a retail computer store's profits. People would bring their PCs into the store to have the component added by a technician. The volume of this business has been steadily declining. Many consumers are simply buying the add-in and installing it themselves.

Market Opportunity. After considerable reseach and analysis the founders of PC-Build are convinced that the kit segment of the PC market is being inadequately served. The market leader offers an overpriced, low-quality product. The entire industry ignored the educational learning aspect of a "Do It Yourself" (DIY) computer. All competitors treat kits in one of two ways:

- *Minor side business*: These companies' main line of business is selling assembled PCs. Kits represent a side business that merits no serious investment.
- *Cash cow*: The main competitor, Heathkit, is a small subsidiary of Bull, the French

conglomerate. The company puts minimal effort into the product in terms of quality and marketing support.

The Company

The opportunity for a new manufacturer to enter the personal computer kit industry was conceived in February 1991. The company will begin operations in 1992, with the first product available in May 1992. Initially, the company intends to sell all products directly, eventually expanding to retail DIY electronics stores.

The Product

A full line of 100 percent IBM-compatible, MS-DOS–based personal computer kits will be produced. These kits are designed for a nontechnical individual who possesses some knowledge of computers. No soldering or wiring is required. All an individual needs is a few basic tools and a desire to learn.

The computer kit will be supplemented with a fully illustrated instruction manual and video cassette. Both will be fully integrated, designed to walk the customer through the assembly. The instruction manual will also explain the basics of how a computer works.

All kits will come with a 30-day money-back guarantee and a one-year warranty on parts. Customers will be given access to PC-Build's toll-free technical support line, available Monday through Friday 9:00 AM to 5:00 PM EST. Each kit comes complete with MS-DOS 5.0 and PC-Build's proprietary DOS starter program, Quickstart™.[2]

Quickstart is an interactive program designed to configure and test the assembled computer. Quickstart automatically tests the assembly, configures the hard disk, and loads MS-DOS. It also contains an interactive tutorial that explains the basics of Microsoft's MS-DOS.

Product Line. The Company will initially offer three main products. These products are intended to appeal to a broad range of home hobbyists and computer users.

- *B2000 Basic Kit.* Designed for the budget conscious consumer who wants a simple, inexpensive kit. Ideal for the head of household who wants to build a computer as a family experience. Priced at $699. Kit includes:

80286-based motherboard (16 MHz).	1 MB Ram.
20 MB hard disk.	5¼-inch and 3½-inch floppy disk drives.
Floppy/hard disk controller.	Parallel/serial/game port card.
Keyboard.	VGA monitor card.
Cabinet and power supply.	MS-DOS 5.0
Instruction manual and video.	*Monitor not included.*

Note: The 286 motherboard may be replaced with a 386SX/16 board by May.

- *SX3000 Super Kit.* Designed for the more computer literate customer who wants a technically superior machine. This is ideal for the individual who understands the basics of computers and wants to "get his/her hands dirty." Priced at $899. Kit includes:

80386/SX-based motherboard (20 MHz).	2 MB RAM.
44 MB hard disk.	5¼-inch and 3½-inch floppy disk drives.
Floppy/hard disk controller.	Parallel/serial/game card.
Keyboard.	VGA monitor card.
Cabinet and power supply.	MS-DOS 5.0.
Instruction manual and video.	*Monitor not included.*

[2]Quickstart™ is a registered trademark of Discovery Curve, Inc.

- *SX4000 Deluxe Kit.* Designed for the power computer customer who wants a big machine. This is ideal for the individual who understands and uses computers frequently, and wants to build a "rocket." Priced at $1,500. Kit includes:

80486/SX-based motherboard (20 MHz).	4 MB RAM.
120 MB hard disk.	5¼-inch and 3½-inch floppy disk drives.
Floppy/hard disk controller.	Parallel/serial/game card.
Keyboard.	VGA monitor card.
Cabinet and power supply.	MS-DOS 5.0
Instruction manual and video.	*Monitor not included.*

- *Custom Kit.* This option is designed for consumers having an in-depth understanding of the various PC components who seek to build a custom kit. PC-Build has designed its components and manufacturing operations in such a way that customer orders can be processed economically. All custom kits include MS-DOS 5.50, 5¼-inch and 3½-inch floppy disk drives, disk controller card, keyboard, cabinet, power supply, parallel/serial/game card, instruction manual and video. Individuals can choose their own:
  Motherboard (286, 386, or 486 based, various MHz speeds).
  Amount of RAM (1–8 MB).
  Hard disk size (20–110 MB).
  Monitor (monochrome, VGA black and white, VGA color, or Super VGA).
- *Monitors.* The company will offer a full line of monitors. All monitors are VGA based and are compatible with the aforementioned kits. Models and prices are as follows:

Black and white VGA (800 × 600 resolution)	$125
Color VGA (800 × 600 resolution)	275
Super color VGA (1024 × 768 resolution)	400

Computer Education Service. The company will offer additional service to the computer education market. Training materials designed to supplement the instructional manual will be available as part of our education services. In addition, the company will offer the service of original equipment manufacturer (OEM)-certified instructors for $200 per session. The company will waive this fee for volume purchases.

Additional Business. Discovery Curve's founders will continue to offer services in programming, consulting, and documentation development. Both founders have excellent industry reputations and have established consulting arrangements with several companies. The exact amount of this additional income is difficult to predict, but is estimated in the range of $25,000 to $35,000 annually.

Competitive Advantages. PC-Build will strive to offer the best quality kit on the market. No other competitor has its combination of design, service, and instruction. This gives the company four main competitive advantages:

- *Quality.* All components are from recognized suppliers, such as Intel and Seagate. An unconditional one-year warranty covers all parts.
- *User friendliness.* PC-Build kits have been designed with the customer in mind. The instruction manual will have complete instructions on assembly and computer operations. PC-Build is the only company to offer a video that details the assembly process.
- *Service.* No other competitor offers a 30-day money back guarantee and access to a toll-free technical support line. Our custom product line gives an individual the ability to design the exact kit he or she wants.
- *Affordability.* PC-Build's prices are 10–15 percent below a comparable fully assembled PC. This creates a perception of true savings.

Technological Surfing. PC-Build kits will not be the leading edge in PC technology. The company will follow a policy of always lagging one generation behind. This gives the company four main advantages:

- Proven hardware.
- Easy access to suppliers.
- A recognizable standard.
- Lower cost components.

Please note that PC-Build is fully aware of the fact that by not offering a leading edge kit, we are eliminating a segment of the home hobbyist market. However, we feel this loss is outweighed by the savings in engineering, warranties, and material costs.

The primary reason an individual buys a kit is the desire to build and learn about computers, not to buy the most expensive leading-edge technology. New technologies will be introduced based upon our new technology screening system (see "Future Products" section on p. 66).

Entry and Growth Strategy. The company will begin selling to educational institutions first. The first target will be computer education camps in operation throughout the United States. PC-Build plans to offer its products beginning in June 1992. There are several reasons why this market was chosen first:

- No competition.
- High volume.
- Proven customer interest.
- Minimal up-front marketing costs.

No competitors are offering PC kits to computer education camps. Initial contacts with these camps have been encouraging. Several camps are considering purchases. Personal selling will continue to be the main marketing approach. PC-Build has identified all the potential customers in this category and can contact them directly.

Another key reason for targeting this market first is the fact that a product can be developed and introduced relatively quickly. A video instruction tape is unnecessary for computer camps. The initial product and instructional manual will be production ready by June (See "Overall Project Schedule" section on p. 70).

PC-Build will target the home hobbyist market in November. PC-Build has chosen the direct marketing channel to reach the home market. We feel this channel is important because it gives us a greater degree of control over pricing, quality, and volume. PC-Build will advertise in publications that our target market members read, such as *Popular Electronics.* The intent of these advertisements is to provoke them to call our toll-free sales line for more information. Our telemarketing staff can then personally sell the product.

Eventually, PC-Build will expand to retail outlets, specifically do-it-yourself (DIY) stores. There are over 500 such stores in the United States (excluding Radio Shack). Radio Shack (Tandy Corporation) has stated that they will not offer a kit through their retail outlets. They feel it will cannibalize assembled PC sales.

We feel that by going direct first we achieve two main goals: (1) establishing the PC-Build name and (2) creating a direct marketing organization. Experience in the PC industry has shown that companies have successfully expanded from direct marketing into retail, but not the reverse.

Expansion Opportunities. The most natural expansion route for the company is add-on sales. As soon as a significant customer base is developed, the company will begin offering add-in boards, such as modems and sound cards. Our customers are perfect prospects for these types of products; they are comfortable with PCs and have a proven track record of purchasing high tech toys.

MARKET RESEARCH AND ANALYSIS

As indicated above, PC-Build will have two primary target segments, the home hobbyist PC user and educational institutions. The following is a description of the major characteristics of each:

The *home computer user* is somewhat price sensitive but concerned about quality and service. Home computers are typically purchased at a computer store or a department store. However, a substantial percentage is sold through nontraditional channels such as mail order. Currently 15 percent of all personal computers sold for home use were purchased through mail order. This percentage is expected to increase over the coming years. Buyers are overwhelmingly male. Home computers are mainly used for word processing, computer games, education, and database management/filing. The age groups, listed in order of dominance: 35–44, 25–34, 45–55, and 18–24. Our targeted customers are predominantly male and fall into the 18 to 44 age group. Thus, PC-Build's customers range from college-aged kids to dads wanting to build PCs as a family product.

Educational institutions refer to schools, colleges, or businesses that specialize in computer training. The most promising segment is the computer camp. There are 252 accredited summer camps offering computer learning programs. Over 90 percent of these camps are run during the summer months. The camps offer courses on programming, computer games, microelectronics, and so on. Students pay a flat fee for the camp. Fees range from $700 to $2,000 per week. A PC kit is a natural extension of their program. Camps will have the option of incorporating the cost of the kit into their tuition, or charging an additional fee. The following camps are potential customers:

- TIC Computer Camps, Washington, DC.
- High Tech Educational Camps, Woburn, Massachusetts.
- FutureKids, Franchised throughout the United States.

The education market also includes all vocational schools, technical colleges, and other tertiary educational institutes that offer computer-training programs, workshops, and courses. There are over 10,000 such institutions in the United States. Approximately 10 percent of them offer computer assembly training. The company is currently negotiating with:

- Computer Learning Centers, Somerville, Massachusetts.
- MIT-Lowell Institute School, Cambridge, Massachusetts.
- UMass, Lowell, Amherst, and Boston, Massachusetts.
- PRA Computer Training Center, Marlboro, Massachusetts.

Educational institutions can be thought of as a distribution channel. They funnel our products to the end user. The value-added they provide is personal instruction. PC-Build will offer volume discounts to these institutions, as well as access to trainers and teaching materials.

Whether they are a channel or customer is a minor point; they are an untapped market. Many institutions we spoke to had considered the concept, but could not find a product. Until now.

Market Size. 1990 Total US sales of products that can be considered kits are estimated at $70 million. The company derived this estimate by analyzing total personal computer sales, direct competitor sales, and indirect competitor sales.

Worldwide sales of all types of personal computers in 1990 are 24 million units. Most forecasts project 8–10 percent annual growth for the next several years. The US home market is a small portion of this total market, with 5.5 million units sold in 1990. This segment is expected to grow faster than the overall industry growth rates, with industry sources projecting 15–30 percent growth rates.

Direct competitor sales in 1990 were approximately $20 million. Indirect competitor sales were $50 million. Indirect competition refers to companies that offer all the components needed to build a PC, but not as a kit, and limited instructions.

Estimated Market Share and Sales

PC-Build's estimated market share and sales volumes are presented in *Exhibit 1*. The first year's sales figure is based on bulk sales of 200 units to the education market during summer (i.e., summer camps) and 250 units sold during the Christmas season. The remainder of the volume is spread out throughout the year. Given these assumptions, our market share (of total amount of kits and pseudo kits sold) will be less than 2 percent of the entire market. This market share is projected to increase to 4 percent by 1996. Sales growth is estimated to be 20 percent per annum after the second year.

Market Trends

It is estimated that the home market consists of 94 million households; penetration of the home market therefore reached 5.6 percent in 1990. The inherent potential for growth within this segment is revealed by the low level of market penetration. This growth potential applies to PC-Build since our kits are targeted toward the home users.

Given the increased computer literacy, the introduction of user friendly software, and the increased usage of computers for business and education, the home market is expected to continue growing. Sales projections for 1994 reach 7.4 million units for this segment. In the long run the viability of the PC is dependent upon factors such as the development of:

Exhibit 1
PC-Build: Market Analysis

	1991	*1992*	*1993*	*1994*	*1995*	*1996*
Unit sales (in 000s):						
Total PCs	10,500	11,400	12,400	13,400	14,600	15,900
PCs for home use	5,500	6,000	6,500	7,000	7,700	8,300
PCs sold as kits and pseudokits	61	66	72	77	85	91
Dollar sales (in millions):						
Total PCs	$31,800	$34,500	$37,500	$40,700	$44,200	$48,000
PCs for home use	$16,700	$18,100	$19,700	$21,300	$23,200	$25,200
PCs sold as kits and pseudokits	$ 65	$ 70	$ 75	$ 81	$ 88	$ 96
PC-Build sales forecasts:						
Units		1,200	2,200	2,600	3,200	3,800
Dollars (in millions)		$1.0	$2.0	$2.5	$3.0	$3.6
PC-Build market share:						
Units		1.82%	3.08%	3.38%	3.78%	4.16%
Dollars		1.43%	2.67%	3.09%	3.41%	3.75%

Notes: Total market growth expected at 8% per year.
Home Sales represent approximately 50% total market sales. Kits sales were estimated by looking at total market sales and competitor sales (both direct and indirect competitors).

- Software programs.
- Multimedia applications.
- On-line information systems and personal service systems.
- Integrated home management networks controlling, for example, communications and security systems.

Competition

Two PC kits are available nationally. Atlanta Technical Specialists builds an Apple-based kit that retails complete for $1,100 to $2,000. Heathkit sells an IBM-compatible PC that retails for $1,000 to $1,800.

Some regional companies manufacture IBM kits as a side business. The quality is poor in terms of both the hardware and the instruction materials. Also, a large number of companies do not sell all components needed to build a PC. *Table A* is a breakdown of our major competitors.

Direct Competitors. The largest competitor is Heathkit. The company was one of the pioneers in the PC industry in the 1970s. They subsequently became part of Zenith Data Systems in the early 1980s. Both are now wholly owned subsidiaries of the French conglomerate Groupe Bull. The Groupe Bull purchase has been a disaster for Zenith Data Systems. Revenues are down by more than $1 billion. Heathkit is a small fraction of Bull's business and has been ignored. The products are high priced and offer limited options. Custom models are not offered. Heathkit's main strength is its market leader position. However, its main weakness is its apathy toward the market. The company no longer advertises nationally and its direct sales offices only sell Zenith systems.

Atlanta Technical Specialists (ATS) is a relatively new player in the market. They began offering their Apple-based kits only two years ago and have seen their kits sales climb to $3 million in that time period. The company markets kits which are high quality and high priced. The high prices reflect the relatively higher cost of Apple computers versus IBM. The company's main strength is the quality of its kits. They supply Apple with some of their components and developed kits as an expansion in that business. ATS's main weakness is their reliance on Apple. Apple machines constitute only 10 percent of the over-the-counter market; IBM compatibles are the recognized standard.

Indirect Competition. These companies merit special attention for two main reasons. First, the sheer volume of the component sales is an indication of the size of this neglected market. Second, their product offerings are often poor in quality and are not user-friendly. Instruction manuals are nonexistent; customers are often left to fend for themselves. Often these companies are unaware they are even serving the do-it-yourself PC segment. For

Table A
Major Competitors

Competitor Type	*Annual Sales*	*Pricing Strategy*	*Market Share*	*Distribution Channel*	*Major Strength/Weakness*
Heathkit, direct	$ 10 million	Highest	15%	Direct	Size & name; ignored market changes
ATS, direct	3 million	High	5	Direct	Only Apple kit; side business
Microtech, direct	1 million	Low	1	Retail	Custom service; side business
DTK, indirect	15 million	Medium	23	Retail	Supplier to local PC makers
JDR, indirect	5–6 million	Medium	10	Direct	Established PC maker; no complete kit
Jameco, indirect	5–6 million	High	10	Direct	Poor quality PCs disguised as kits
Microlabs, indirect	5 million	Low	5	Both	Good quality parts; no complete kit

Table B
Competitor Product Analysis

Company	Product	Price	Warranty	Technical Support	30 day guarantee	Manual	Video
PC-Build	286 Standard	$ 825	One year	Yes	Yes	Yes	Yes
	386 Super	999	One year	Yes	Yes	Yes	Yes
	Custom kits	1,200	One year	Yes	Yes	Yes	Yes
Heathkit	286-based kit	929	One year	Yes	No	Yes	No
	386-based kit	1,200	One year	Yes	No	Yes	No
Microtech	386-based kit	1,149	Six months	Yes	Yes	No	No
ATS	Mac-based kit	1,699	One year	Yes	No	Yes	No
DTK	Parts only	850	One year	Yes	No	No	No
Jameco	Parts Sales	779	Limited	Yes	No	No	No

example, DTK manufactures a variety of computer components, including motherboards, video cards, and disk controllers. According to the company, their main customers are local manufacturers who assemble and sell their systems complete. (See *Table B* for product comparisons.)

However, we discovered several local manufacturers who market DTK components as a kit, offering a bare-bones shell (consisting of a case, power supply, and motherboard) plus a selection of components. These companies advertise a "customer kit you can build yourself." PC-Build adds significant value over the competition by offering a complete kit, with superior quality and service. Our kits are priced competitively, further accenting our value for the dollar.

Ongoing Market Evaluation

Continuous market evaluation is crucial to the long-term viability of the company. New product introduction by industry leaders and sales levels of existing technologies will be monitored closely. These figures form the basis of PC-Build's pricing and technology decisions. We are a niche player, receiving our cues from the market leaders. Competitors' products and market strategies will naturally be under close scrutiny. The company will subscribe to all industry periodicals and associations, and will make extensive use of board members and personal contacts.

THE ECONOMICS OF THE BUSINESS

The continuing trend in PC price reduction is expected to continue for the next several years. The actual downward pressure on prices stems from two main forces: competitive price pressure and declining material costs. The combination of these factors has reduced industry margins, down from an average of 35 percent in 1985 to under 30 percent today. PC-Build has a projected gross margin of 28–35 percent.

Our higher margins are due to labor savings. Labor generally is 20 percent of the total product cost. PC-Build computers have relatively low levels of labor. Only a portion of this savings is passed on to the consumer, the rest goes to PC-Build. A PC-Build kit is priced 10–20 percent below a comparable assembled PC. Refer to the marketing section for a detailed explanation of pricing logic. For a detailed breakdown of actual unit cost for the basic kit, see *Table C*. These costs are based on volume purchases from our suppliers.

One of the key elements to PC-Build's continued profitability is our ability to purchase quality components at the lowest possible cost. To increase our relative bargaining position,

Table C
Cost Estimates

Component	*Unit Cost*
Chasis	$ 30.00
Power supply	31.00
Motherboard	58.00
MB RAM memory	10.00
I/O Port	9.00
Monitor card	35.00
Monitor	86.00
Keyboard	21.00
Floppy drives	88.00
Hard drive	140.00
Disk controller	9.00
Software cost	40.00
Video cost	7.00
Documentation	5.00
Shipping/handling	0.00
Total cost	$569.00

Note: Cost estimates include supplier quantity breaks.

PC-Build will have at least three alternative suppliers for all components, except the operating system.

PC-Build has a master license agreement with Microsoft Corporation. Microsoft is paid a flat fee ($32) for every MS-DOS–based system we sell. In return, PC-Build can incorporate DOS into its proprietary software programs.

We fully expect downward pressure on our prices. As overall PCs prices continue to fall, kits will be expected to follow suit. By selling directly, we will have a greater degree of control over when we reduce prices and by how much. Suppliers will be expected to follow suit with component price reductions. Overhead will be kept at a minimum via the following:

- Operations management.
- Free engineering factor.
- Extensive use of subcontractors.
- Early automation.

PC-Build does not assemble PCs in house; therefore, fixed costs are naturally lower. Our operations are mainly for packing and shipping. The main fixed costs will be for rented space.

As mentioned, PC-Build will make extensive use of its suppliers. In the beginning, all components will be sources outside the company; no internal manufacturing will be done. There is an abundance of component suppliers in the marketplace. PC-Build has developed a supplier certification process to ensure good supplier selection. *Table D* outlines our supplier selection criteria. By waiting until a new standard develops in the marketplace, PC-Build gets its systems engineered for free. Suppliers have developed expertise with the new technology and it has been market tested.

PC-Build's entire operations will be computerized from the beginning. Order processing, manufacturing, accounting, and purchasing will be automated. The toll-free phone network will be managed by a voice messaging service. By automating in the initial stages of the corporation PC-Build can grow without significant additions to administrative overhead.

Exhibit 2 lists first-year fixed costs and details the PC-Build break-even point. Under the most conservative scenario, the company will break even after selling 1,300 units, with an average gross profit of 30 percent. This projection is *very* conservative. It assumes that all sales

Table D
Supplier Selection Criteria

Criterion	*Specific Target*	*Description*
Price	10–15% less than industry average	Suppliers must offer prices that are less than industry standard. This standard will be calculated based on public sources.
Discounts	Quality based	PC-Build will strive for high-volume purchases. Suppliers are required to offer additional discounts at quantities of 100, 250, and 500 units.
Quality	Zero defect target	Each supplier must embrace some type of quality management program. Annual defects cannot exceed 2% of purchases.
Delivery	Same week delivery	Average order-processing time should range from one to two weeks.
Expandability	N/A	Suppliers who can easily meet orders of up to 1,000 units will be given priority.
Technology	N/A	PC-Build will be expanding to EDI* ordering within two years. All suppliers should have or be planning EDI.
Terms	30 days	PC-Build expects credit terms from all suppliers.
Obsolete stock	Negotiable	Suppliers should have some type of buyback provision for obsolete components.
Warranty	One year	All suppliers *must* offer a one-year warranty.

*EDI stands for electronic data interchange.

Exhibit 2
PC-Build: Cost Analysis and Break-Even Levels

	Cost Analysis			
		Fixed and Semivariable Costs		*Fixed Costs Only*
	Start-up	*Six Month*	*One Year*	*One Year*
Office	$ 0	$ 3,000	$ 6,000	$ 6,000
Inventory	15,000	15,000	15,000	15,000
Advertising	15,000	40,000	61,500	50,000
Wages	0	45,000	105,000	80,000
Phone	1,550	4,525	6,800	3,000
Equipment	4,300	4,300	4,300	4,300
Insurance	1,333	8,000	8,000	8,000
Software	1,700	9,700	9,700	9,700
Video	5,500	5,500	5,500	5,500
Printing	4,500	4,500	6,500	4,500
Other	1,700	4,700	7,700	1,700
Total	$50,583	$144,225	$236,000	$187,700

Break-Even Points—First Year, Conservative Scenario

Costs	*Units*
Fixed Only	733
Fixed and Semivariable	922
Varied Product Sales	
Fixed Only	430
Fixed and Semivariable	540

Note: Conservative scenario is low-priced-product sales only. Varied sales mix is split evenly between models.

are for the B2000, and no higher priced kits are included. Based on our sales forecast, we should break even within the first 10 months of operations.

The company produces a positive cash flow from operations within two months, but returns to negative cash flows two months later. (See *Exhibit 3* for pro forma cash flow statement.) This is due to the highly cyclical nature of sales to computer education camps. The company will be spending a minimum amount on advertising, development, and salaries, yet can achieve significant unit sales.

Exhibit 3
PC-Build: Pro Forma Monthly Cash Flow—Year 1

	Start-up	Month 1 Jul. 1992	Month 2 Aug. 1992	Month 3 Sept. 1992	Month 4 Oct. 1992	Month 5 Nov. 1992	Month 6 Dec. 1992	Month 7 Jan. 1993	Month 8 Feb. 1993	Month 9 Mar. 1993	Month 10 Apr. 1993	Month 11 May 1993	Month 12 June 1993
Sales	$ 0	$ 61,875	$ 82,500	$ 82,500	$ 123,750	$ 165,000	$103,125	$ 61,875	$ 61,875	$ 61,875	$ 61,875	$ 82,500	$123,750
Units		75	100	100	150	200	125	75	75	75	75	100	150
Purchases	15,000	41,775	55,700	55,700	83,550	111,400	69,625	41,775	41,775	41,775	41,775	55,700	83,550
A/R collections	0	0	60,328	80,438	80,438	120,656	160,875	100,547	60,328	60,328	60,328	60,328	80,438
A/P payments	7,500	7,500	41,775	55,700	55,700	83,550	111,400	69,625	41,775	41,775	41,775	41,775	55,700
Office	0	500	500	500	500	500	500	500	500	500	500	500	500
Advertising/promo	15,000	1,500	1,500	5,000	5,000	7,000	5,000	1,500	1,500	5,000	7,000	5,000	1,500
Wages	0	5,000	5,000	7,000	9,000	9,000	10,000	9,000	9,000	9,000	10,000	11,000	12,000
Commissions	0	0	0	0	0	3,506	0	0	0	3,919	0	0	0
Utilities	0	500	500	500	500	500	550	550	550	550	550	550	550
Phone	1,750	338	400	400	525	650	463	338	338	338	338	400	525
Equipment	4,300	0	0	0	0	0	0	0	0	0	0	0	0
Insurance	6,000	0	0	0	0	0	2,000	0	0	0	0	0	0
Software	9,700	0	0	0	0	0	0	0	0	0	0	200	0
Video	5,500	0	0	0	0	0	0	0	0	0	0	3,500	0
Warranty exp.	0	0	50	50	50	50	50	50	50	50	50	50	50
Printing	4,500	0	0	0	0	0	0	0	0	0	0	4,000	0
Other	1,700	500	500	500	500	500	500	500	500	500	500	500	500
Cash needs	−55,950	−15,838	10,103	10,788	8,663	15,400	30,413	18,484	6,116	−1,303	−384	−7,147	9,113
+ Carry over	90,000	34,050	18,213	28,316	39,103	47,766	63,166	93,578	112,063	118,178	116,875	116,491	109,344
Ending cash	$ 34,050	$ 18,213	$ 28,316	$ 39,103	$ 47,766	$ 63,166	$ 93,578	$112,063	$118,178	$116,875	$116,491	$109,344	$118,456
Cash flow from operations	−55,950	−71,788	−61,684	−50,897	−42,234	−26,834	3,578	22,063	28,178	26,875	26,491	19,344	28,456

(Continued)

Exhibit 3 (*concluded*)
Pro Forma Monthly Cash Flow—Year 2

	Month 1 Jul. 1993	*Month 2 Aug. 1993*	*Month 3 Sept. 1993*	*Month 4 Oct. 1993*	*Month 5 Nov. 1993*	*Month 6 Dec. 1993*	*Month 7 Jan. 1994*	*Month 8 Feb. 1994*	*Month 9 Mar. 1994*	*Month 10 Apr. 1994*	*Month 11 May 1994*	*Month 12 June 1994*
Sales	$165,000	$247,500	$123,750	$206,250	$247,500	$247,500	$123,750	$ 82,500	$103,125	$165,000	$165,000	$185,625
Units	200	300	150	250	300	300	150	100	125	200	200	225
Purchases	111,400	167,100	83,550	139,250	167,100	167,100	83,550	55,700	69,625	111,400	111,400	125,325
A/R collections	120,656	160,875	241,313	120,656	201,094	241,313	241,313	120,656	80,438	100,547	160,875	160,875
A/P payments	83,550	111,400	167,100	83,550	139,250	167,100	167,100	83,550	55,700	69,625	111,400	111,400
Office	833	833	833	833	833	833	833	833	833	833	833	833
Advertising/ promo	3,000	5,000	7,000	8,000	9,000	8,000	3,000	3,000	5,000	7,000	8,000	3,000
Wages	12,000	14,000	15,000	15,000	16,000	17,000	14,000	14,000	14,000	14,000	14,000	14,000
Commissions	3,300	0	0	0	7,425	0	0	0	7,013	0	0	0
Utilities	600	600	600	600	600	600	600	600	600	600	600	600
Phone	650	900	525	775	900	900	525	400	463	650	650	713
Equipment	0	0	0	0	0	0	0	0	0	0	0	0
Insurance	6,000	0	0	0	0	2,000	0	0	0	0	0	0
Software	0	0	0	0	0	0	2,500	0	0	0	0	0
Video	0	0	2,000	0	0	2,000	0	0	2,000	0	0	2,000
Warranty exp.	50	50	50	50	50	50	75	75	75	75	75	100
Printing	0	0	2,000	0	0	2,000	0	0	2,000	0	0	2,000
Other	500	500	500	500	500	500	500	500	500	500	500	500
Cash needs	10,173	27,592	45,704	11,348	26,535	40,329	52,179	17,698	−7,746	7,264	24,817	25,729
+ Carryover	118,456	128,629	156,221	201,925	213,273	239,808	280,138	332,317	350,015	342,269	349,532	374,349
Ending cash	$128,629	$158,221	$201,925	$213,273	$239,808	$280,138	$332,317	$350,015	$342,269	$349,532	$374,349	$400,078
Cash flow from operations	38,629	66,221	111,925	123,273	149,808	190,138	242,317	260,015	252,269	259,532	284,349	310,078

Notes: 30-day collection on all receivables (ignores MC/Visa payment).
30-day collection on all payables.
Start-up funds are detailed in business plan.
To be conservative, all sales are forecasted as low-end products (Basic kit w/B&W VGA).
One-half of initial inventory will be purchased on cash terms.
Cyclical sales indicated by surges before Christmas and summer.
A/R collections reflect 2.5% discount for MC/VISA purchases.
Payroll reflects additional hirings per schedule.
Phone charges are minimum of $150 per month plus $2.50 per sale.
Initial software/video/manual production will be 1,000 units.
Minimum $15,000 cash balance is added for unforeseen expenses.
Warranty costs include postage and handling of replacement parts.
Commissions are 1% of sales and are paid quarterly.

However, camp sales are highly cyclical, occurring only during the summer months. As the summer ends, the initial marketing effort toward the home hobbyist begins. Home sales will also be cyclical, peaking during Christmas and late spring (graduation, beginning of summer). The company will have continuous positive cash flow from the operations after the seventh month.

MARKETING PLAN

Overall Marketing Strategy

The company's overall marketing strategy will be to appeal to our target markets' demonstrated desire to experiment and learn. PC-Build will be the company of reference for personal computer kits on the MS-DOS platform. The company will establish this position by means of a two-pronged marketing attack:

- Heavy personal selling and advertising in the education channel. This means high-school level computer science curricula and computer camps. Penetration of this market segment has already begun and will be the primary focus of the company's early efforts. This segment will provide the volume needed to fund the early stages of the product adoption phase in the home hobby market.
- The home hobby market is represented by single-unit sales to end users either directly or through a distribution channel.

PC-Build will differentiate itself by emphasizing the user-friendly, high-quality service and documentation approach that marks the success of our corporate cousins in the ready-to-serve PC market.

Pricing

Prices start at $699 for the basic 286-based kit and vary according to central processing unit (CPU), options, and quantities ordered. Prices will be in the low-average range for the content (CPU, options) category, but margins will be above average because of our sourcing and the absence of labor cost for assembly. The price will play a role in positioning the product as a premium value kit. This means that the company's customers will not consider us to be low-budget; rather, they will perceive that they paid a fair price for value received.

"Clone makers" have traditionally gone after market share on the basis of price competitiveness. By purchasing cheap parts in quantity, achieving efficiencies in mass assembly, and distributing in the less-expensive mail-order channel, they have been able to arrive at a cost structure that allows them to undercut the major PC players. The early entrants to this market cycle have been successful, but with low barriers to entry this market is getting crowded. Margins are shrinking as players cut their prices to maintain the gaps between their offerings and those of the major players. Thus, the business is poised on the brink of a shakeout—commodity pricing is putting the clone makers in a hard-to-win situation.

Sales Tactics

Personal selling will be the method of choice for sales to our multiple unit educational and camp customers. This sales effort will be effected by the president and the vice president for product development. An in-house telemarketing staff (one person initially) will close sales and manage inquiries generated by advertisements in general and specialty magazines.

Service and Warranty Policies

The company will include in the price of the kit a 30-day money-back guarantee, and a one-year parts replacement warranty. These types of guarantee mechanisms have become standard in the larger mail-order clone industry, but 30-day money-back guarantees are not standard among our direct competition in PC kits. The components used in the kits are covered by manufacturers' warranties and are tested prior to leaving the factory. Statistically, failure rates of these types of electro-mechanical components have been fairly low, around 3 percent. The company forecasts a much lower (1 percent) component failure rate for the kits because of the following:

- Standard, tested technology.
- Supplier certification process screens for high quality suppliers.
- In-house total quality management program.

Advertising and Promotion

Advertising and promotion strategy is linked directly to the channel being targeted. End-user sales will be sought with print advertisements in several periodicals. The choice of periodical is very important to the success of the advertising campaign because of the specialty nature of our product. While mainstream computer magazines may be a part of our customers' reading "diet," hobbyists have their own subculture and sources of information in which we must appear to gain acceptance by the early adopter and hard-core hobbyists. See *Table E* for a list of magazines which the company feels adequately reach our target audience. The print campaign will have two primary focuses driving it:

- Create awareness of the company and its products.
- Sell boxes.

The company will endeavor to obtain low-cost or free promotion in the form of news reports or endorsements from industry luminaries. Press releases will be distributed regularly, as will copies of the instruction video and a video of young campers having fun putting together the standard kit.

Distribution

As time progresses and unit volume grows, the company's main channel of distribution will evolve from direct sales to retail. As a small, unknown company, we would have limited leverage with retailers and be forced to accept lower margins. Further, research has shown

Table E
First-Year Advertising Budget

Publication	*Circulation*	*Ad Price*	*Number of Ads*	*Total*
Popular Electronics	152,000	$2,200	4	$ 8,800
Popular Science	750,000	6,200	4	24,800
Discover	450,000	5,400	2	10,800
Electronic Learning	87,000	2,325	2	4,650
PC Home Journal	500,000	5,500	2	11,000
Computer Buyer's	Special Issue	3,000	1	3,000
	Total advertising			$63,050
	Initial press releases			2,000
	Trade shows			5,000
	Grand total			$70,050

that the competition and the early mail-order PC success stories have gone direct first and retail later and not vice versa. Dell, for example, made its mark as a high-quality mail-order supplier and then began selling through retailers. On the flip side, industry giant IBM abandoned its plans.

The move to retail will come when the company's market position is such that it can sustain itself in that realm. Among the factors contributing to the decision to make the move will be sales volume (demand), the financing situation and other company economics, and the existence of a suitable strategic partner to be the primary retail distributor.

DESIGN AND DEVELOPMENT PLANS

The development process is ongoing. To date, an initial prototype has been completed and is fully functional. The Quickstart program is complete and operational. Several key development tasks still must be completed:

- Final system specification.
- Final prototype production.
- Video production.
- Supplier selection/certification.
- Manual development.

These items are not mutually exclusive. The order in which they are listed is the order in which they must be completed. A certain amount of work can be done concurrently, but the system specifications must be completed before any other work can be finished. *Table F* is a general breakdown of time and money required for each task.

Please note: PC-Build kits will be FCC Class B certified. FCC certification means the product is suitable for home use. We have located several suppliers who have Class B certification for the cabinet/motherboard configurations. In addition, all suppliers' components must be Class B certified.

Future Products

PC-Build will upgrade its kits based on a predefined technology-screening system. This system can best be illustrated by applying it to the next level of Intel chip, the 486DX. This system will be applied to all new technologies, not just to Intel chips. PC-Build will begin offering 486DX-based kits when the following criteria have been met:

1. *Demonstrated market acceptance*. The new chip should account for at least 20 percent of new PC sales before it will be considered by PC-Build. This 20 percent hurdle ensures market acceptance and significant volume to push unit costs within PC-Build's customer's price range. 486DX sales only account for 10 percent of current unit volume.

Table F
Development Plans

Task	*Money Required*	*Time*
System specifications	0	Eight weeks
Supplier selection	$ 500	Four weeks
Prototype production	1,500	Two weeks
Manual development	4,000	Six weeks
Video production	5,500	Six weeks

2. *Reliable supplier base.* All new motherboard suppliers must meet supplier certification requirements. Existing suppliers will be reevaluated with respect to their new motherboard. A limited number of 486DX suppliers meet PC-Build's selection criteria.
3. *Unit cost decreases.* The price difference between the new technology versus PC-Build's current technology must not exceed 30 percent. Currently, 486DX-based motherboards are 85 percent more expensive than 486SX-based boards.

Proprietary Issues

The company is seeking and is in the process of copyrighting the following:

- Instructional video.
- Instructional manual.
- Computer set-up program.
- Advertising copy.

The company name, logo, model names, and Quickstart program will all be registered trademarks of the corporation.

MANUFACTURING AND OPERATIONS PLAN

PC-Build has located its main facilities in Wellesley, Massachusetts. This location was chosen for three main reasons: (1) cost, (2) location, and (3) expandability. Discovery Curve has signed a 14-month lease for 1,500 square feet at $1,000 a month. This includes heat, electricity, furniture, and the use of an existing phone system.

Actual production is relatively simple. PC-Build's operations are essentially for packing and shipping; all other production is subcontracted. No major fixed investment in manufacturing is required other than for assembly, storage, and staging equipment. The initial 1,500 square feet can support production of up to 500 units per month. A bigger storage area and extra shipping bays will be needed if capacity exceeds this level.

Manufacturing Policy

Manufacturing will be done using a multipurpose assembly line. All three products can be produced quickly using the same line. Inventory will be located at multiple points along the assembly line. (See *Exhibit 4.*) Operations seek to leverage the standardization of PC-Build's production lines. Actual production and ordering will be controlled by integrated software. (*Exhibit 5* details actual work flow.)

Production and inventory control will follow the basic principle of materials requirements planning. The company will strive to develop and maintain a zero defect rate for its products. This philosophy will be extended to our suppliers. Total quality management is essential to our business. A rejected part will result in an unfinished kit, hence an angry customer.

Operating Cycle

Because PC-Build sells direct, the operating cycle is fairly short. (See *Exhibit 6.*) In the best-case scenario, cash is converted within three days after purchase payment. This would be the case if we had a massive demand surge and were producing for back orders. In the

Exhibit 4
PC-Build: Operations Flow

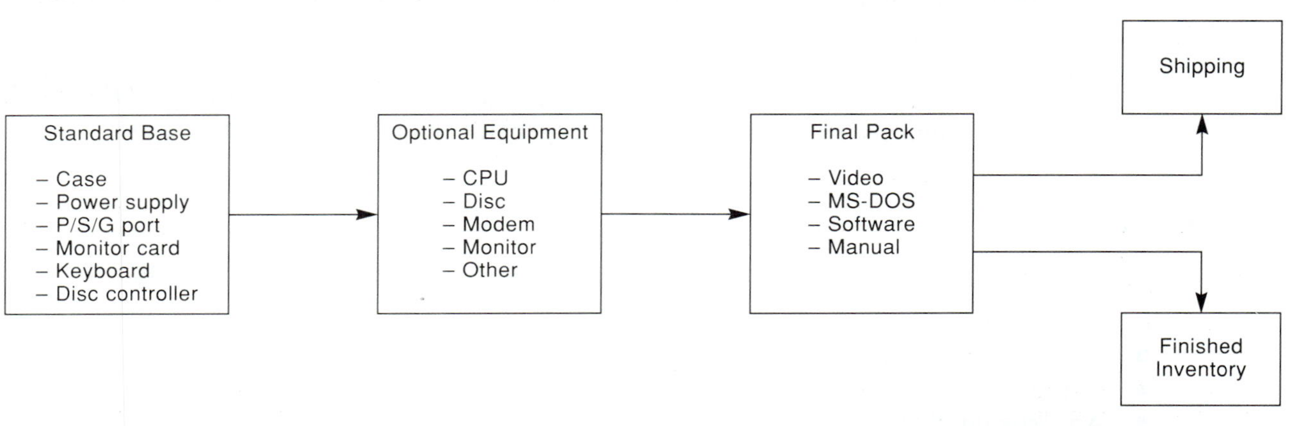

Exhibit 5
PC-Build: Work Flow

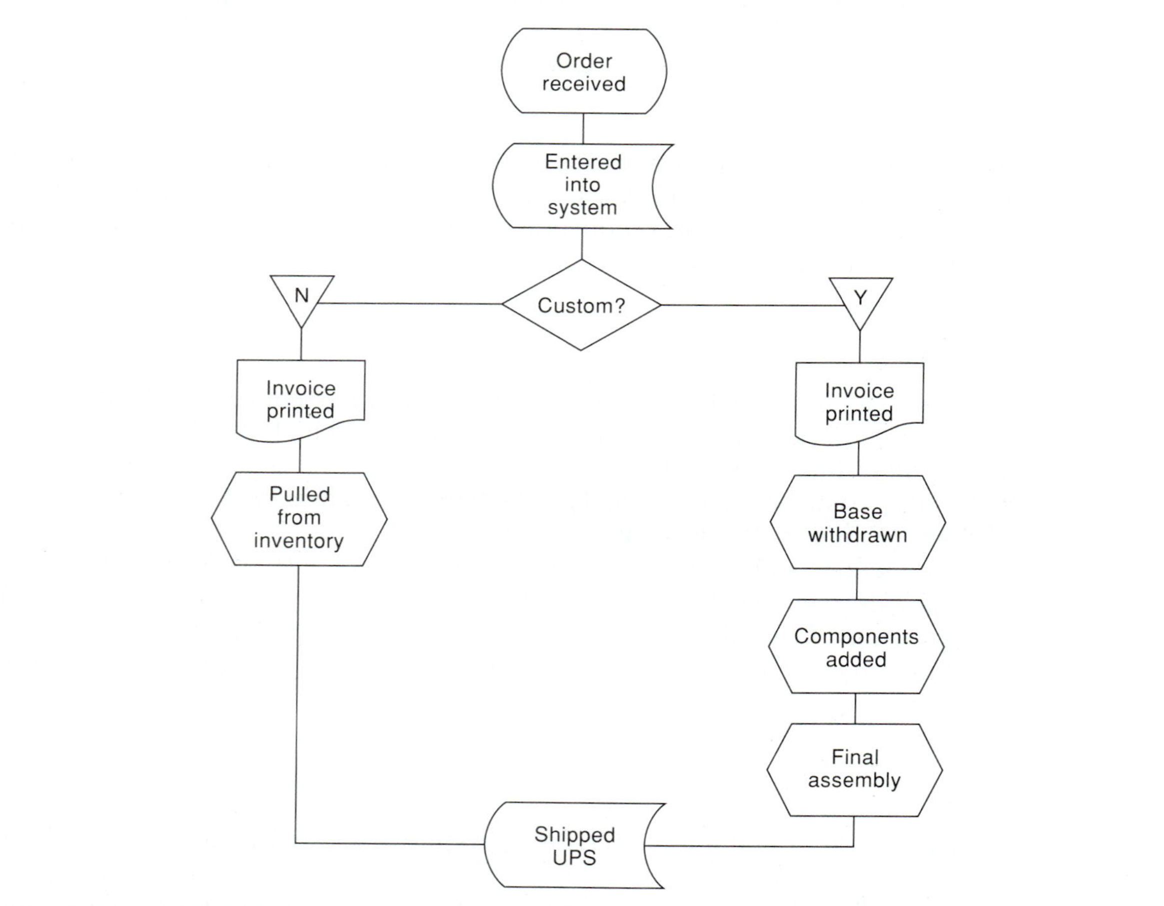

Exhibit 6
PC-Build: Cash Conversion

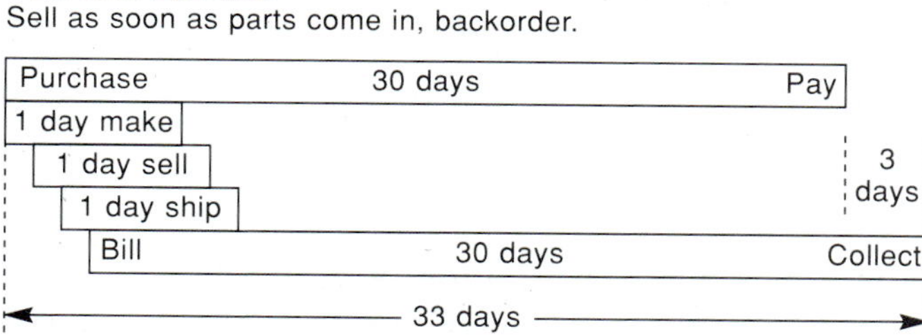

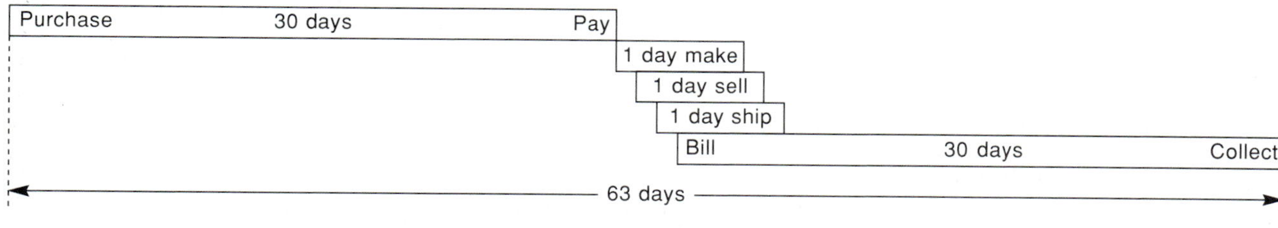

conservative scenario, cash is converted within 33 days of initial purchase payment. This is the most likely scenario, since PC-Build is expecting to hold some inventory to meet unexpected demand.

MANAGEMENT TEAM

Michael Healey, President. Mr. Healey has several years of experience in manufacturing and computer systems. He has served as a project manager for large-scale automation projects. At Automatic Data Processing (ADP) Corporation, he managed new customer implementation of Distribution 2000, ADP's business application software. At Nixdorf Computer Corporation, as an international business consultant, he was the US contact for all activities related to COMET, Nixdorf's worldwide business application software. He successfully developed a series of training materials for the product and has taught both software and hardware courses. He has built several personal computers for customers in the Boston area. Mr. Healey received his master of business administration degree in international business from Babson Graduate School of Business in May 1992. He received his bachelor's degree in management from the University of Massachusetts School of Management in 1986.

Robert P. Lofblad, Vice President, Development and Support. Mr. Lofblad has over 10 years of experience working with personal computers. He has written programs for a variety of applications, from financial analysis to computer games. At Bank Leu in Zurich, he designed an automated system for tracking client positions in derivative securities. At the Boston Company in Boston, he was marketing systems liaison and designed the user interface for the company's telemarketing control system. He has performed systems analysis and

Table G
Compensation/Ownership

Name	Annual Salary	Percent Ownership
Robert Lofblad	$30,000	25%
Michael Healey	30,000	40

design for several local companies, including TBC Funds Distributor, W. A. Wilde Co., Eight Oars, and Corob Corporation. Mr. Lofblad received his master of business administration degree in high-technology marketing from Babson Graduate School of Business in May 1992. He received his bachelor's degree in management information systems from Providence College in 1986.

Mr. Healey and Mr. Lofblad will each receive a year-end bonus, based on pre-tax earnings. This bonus will be based on percentage ownership. (See *Table G* for ownership percentages.)

Future Team Members

In addition to the two principals, one other key person has committed to PC-Build's program. John Healey will oversee the development and implementation of all educational materials for the education segment. Mr. Healey will also serve on the review committee for the manual development. Mr. Healey has a BS in mathematics and computer science and a masters in education from the University of Lowell. Due to the seasonal nature of educational camp sales, Mr. Healey will continue his full-time teaching position at Trinity Catholic in Newton.

Board of Directors

PC-Build currently has plans for a board of directors of four to seven members. Current members: Kevin Glynn, vice president of sales and marketing, Glynn Electronics; Robert Lofblad, PC-Build; Michael Healey, PC-Build; Paul Storiale, former president, Omni Bank of Connecticut; and one directorship is reserved for representation of equity investors.

Supporting Professional Staff. PC-Build is represented by James Dangora, of Dangora Associates, as general counsel.

OVERALL PROJECT SCHEDULE

See *Table H.*

CRITICAL RISKS, PROBLEMS, AND ASSUMPTIONS

- *Educational sales fail to materialize:*

  Evaluation: Given the size of the educational market (summer camps) and the interest already expressed in this regard, it is unlikely that sales to this segment of the education market will fail to materialize.

  Contingency: PC-Build's survival is not contingent upon the highly cyclical sales of this market. The company aims to derive its main income from the steady demand from

Table H
Overall Schedule

Dates:	Dec	Jan	Feb	Mar	Apr	May	Jun	Jul	Aug	Sep	Oct
General											
Incorporation	>>>>>										
Investor presentation	>>>>>	>>>>>	>>>>>	>>>>>							
Initial funding				>>>>>							
Establish bank relations				>>>>>							
Facility											
Site selection				>>>>>							
Equipment purchase						>>>>>					
Development											
System specification			>>>>>	>>>>>							
Supplier selection				>>>	>>>>>						
Prototype production					>>>						
Testing						>>>>>					
Manual development				>>>>>	>>>>>						
Video production					>>>>>	>>>>					
Production											
Order materials						>>>>>					
Production							>>>>>	>>>>>	>>>>>	>>>>>	>>>>>
Marketing											
Brochure printing				>>>>>							
First camp sales						>>>>>					
Advertising								>>>>>	>>>>>	>>>>>	>>>>>
First home sales										>>>>>	

home hobbyists. If this market produces no sales at all in the first year, the company can still be profitable.

- *Price cutting continues in market:*

  Evaluation: Price cutting has become commonplace in the PC industry. Older technologies often become commodities. Companies that simply compete on price are constantly seeing margins erode. However, as end user prices of older technologies drop, suppliers follow suit.

  PC-Build has a differentiated product and will therefore not engage in the price wars of the commodity sellers. However, the company realizes that the declining price of the technology does affect PC-Build. The price of our products is partly based on projected labor savings. Our product must be priced below the market price of fully assembled machines. (See *Table I.*)

  Contingency: PC-Build has developed a pricing policy regarding model price reductions. We will reduce prices when the price differential between our kits and a fully assembled substitute drops to 15 percent. PC-Build can sustain price cuts of up to 15 percent on its current prices and still remain in our target gross margin range, 30–40 percent.

Table I
Pricing Sensitivity Analysis

Markup Levels	*Price*	*Percentage of Sales*		
20% margin	$711.25	Basic kit with B&W VGA monitor:		
25% margin	758.67	Target price	$825.00	
30% margin	812.86	Unit cost	569.00	69.97%
35% margin	875.38	Gross margin	256.00	31.03
40% margin	948.33			

- *Swift response from competition (particularly Heathkit):*

  Evaluation: response to our product offering will come from other niche players such as Heathkit. Given the recent purchase of Zenith Data systems by Groupe Bull and the financial difficulties of the former, it is unlikely that Zenith will embrace and support this minuscule and poorly run fraction of Bull's business.

  Contingency: PC-Build will have an established lead over any competitor, seeking to introduce video-aided education or sales to education institutions. The market entry strategy intentionally avoids direct confrontation with competitors. Within a short time span, our product will be complete and our sales network established. The company will be in a strong position within two years. However, if there is a massive response from a number of large competitors, PC-Build could consider using our strong position as the basis for a quick harvest.

- *Higher-than-expected sales volume:*

  Evaluation: The educational institution is a new channel. There is no market data on the potential sales of computer kits to this segment. We have used extremely conservative figures for this market. Higher-than-expected sales volume is a real possibility.

  Contingency: The company should financially be able to meet any unexpected demand from the education market. Computer camps will place orders after they receive applications from new campers. The company can secure interim financing based on these orders. Main capacity is 500 units. The real challenge will be for our suppliers, getting large orders to us in a short period of time. One of the key elements of our supplier selection criteria is the ability to meet demand quickly.

- *Lower-than-expected sales volumes:*

  Evaluation: Given the size of our market, the superiority of our product, and our conservative approach in determining our market share, it is unlikely that our actual sales volume will be substantially less than the volumes estimated.

  Contingency: The company already has a low break-even point of 749 units per year. This figure was calculated by using our lowest selling product only. The super and custom kits have approximately the same gross margin percent as the basic kit, but contribute significantly more dollars. A large portion of first-year fixed costs, such as hirings, are based upon our sales projection. If sales fail to materialize, the company can cut back on non-essential fixed costs. This reduces our break-even point to 521 units. Sales can be less than half of the current forecast (1,200 units) and the company will still make money.

- *Shut out of supplier network:*

  Evaluation: The standardization of the layout of circuit boards has led to a booming OEM business. Entry is easy, and small firms can stay competitive by providing service and support and by pricing competitively. Several manufacturers supply industry giants such as IBM and Compaq, yet few exclusive supply arrangements exist. OEMs benefit from having multiple customers in that demand risk is dispersed and product life is extended. The relative bargaining power of customer groups also remains less threatening. Additionally, overseas suppliers are marketing their products more aggressively in the United States. The industry trend toward less concentration and more internationalization is expected to continue as worldwide competition increases. Being shut out of the supplier network is highly unlikely.

  Contingency: If a shutout occurs, PC-Build can source components from non-US-based manufacturers interested in breaking into the US market. Another option would be to license older technologies and manufacture components in-house. The viability of this alternative depends on the circumstances then at hand.

- *Delays in design or manufacturing:*

  Evaluation: Several key development tasks must still be completed. The execution of the first phase of our planned entry strategy depends on the completion of the following key development tasks:
  —Final system specification.
  —Final prototype production.
  —Video production.
  —Supplier selection/certification.
  —Manual development.
  These tasks must be completed in the order listed. The estimated time frame for completion is 14 weeks. Currently 24 weeks remain before the planned roll-out in June 1992. Allowing for double the planned normal production lead-time, 22 weeks remain. A buffer of eight weeks thus remains in the event of manufacturing delays. A delay is not anticipated.

  Contingency: In the event of a delay extending beyond this period, PC-Build will be rolled out in November of 1992 in accordance with its planned entry into the home hobbyist market. The final development tasks necessary to enter this market can be completed simultaneously and will take up to a maximum of 12 weeks. This leaves us with an additional 16 weeks to complete the initial tasks. Since the company's survival is not dependent upon the education market, a delay, however disappointing, will not be fatal.

THE FINANCIAL PLAN

Detailed financial forecasts for the first several years of operations have been created utilizing figures from sales forecasts, pricing strategy, detailed cost estimates, overhead budgets and hiring schedules. (See *Table J* and *Exhibits 7–10* for these forecasts.) All projections are based in 1991 dollars. PC-Build's fiscal year is from July 1 to June 30.

Table J
Initial Capital Equipment

Capital Equipment	*Cost*
Three personal computers	$ 1,800
Two printers	500
Fax machine	450
Phone system	1,000
Phone lines	300
Production equipment	2,000
Software	8,000
Total equipment	$14,050
Other Expenses	*Cost*
Brochure printing	$ 500
Documentation printing	4,000
Software production	1,500
Software copying	200
Video production	3,500
Video copying	2,000
Prototype system	2,000
Initial inventory	15,000
Initial advertising	15,000
Travel/entertainment	5,000
Other	2,250
Total	$50,950
Additional working capital estimate: (derived by examining sales forecast cash conversion cycle, and desired minimum cash balance of $15,000)	34,000
Total funds needed	$99,000

Break-even Analysis

The worst-case scenario break-even point for the company is 1,300 units. We felt this is a very conservative figure. This figure was calculated by using the dollar contribution of our lowest priced product only.

The SX3000, SX4000, and custom kits have approximately the same gross margin percent as the basic kit, but contribute significantly more dollars. The actual sales mix does not affect fixed costs; therefore, to be conservative we used the lowest contributor. If PC-Build simply achieves an even sales mix of all three products, the break-even point drops to 521 units. (See *Exhibit 8*.)

Balance Sheet

PC-Build's proposed financial plan provides excellent financial strength and liquidity. Company operations are designed to be lean and to reflect this in the balance sheet. (See *Exhibit 9*.) Accounts receivable payments do not represent a significant risk for the company; most payments will be made using Visa or Mastercard (MC).

The company has intentionally set high working capital requirements as a buffer against unforeseen contingencies. Balance sheet assumptions are:

- 30 day terms on receivables and payables.
- Accounts receivable reflect a 2% payment of MC/Visa.
- No significant debt financing.
- Inventories turn 6–12 times per year.

Exhibit 7
Pro Forma Income Statement, Years 1–5

	Year 1	*Percent*	*Year 2*	*Percent*	*Year 3*	*Percent*	*Year 4*	*Percent*	*Year 5*	*Percent*
Gross sales	$1,237,500	100.00%	$2,000,000	100.00%	$2,500,000	100.00%	$3,000,000	100.00%	$3,600,000	100.00%
Less discounts	49,500	4.00	80,000	4.00	100,000	4.00	120,000	4.00	144,000	4.00
Net sales	1,188,000	96.00	1,920,000	96.00	2,400,000	96.00	2,880,000	96.00	3,456,000	96.00
COGS	853,500	68.97	1,379,394	68.97	1,724,242	68.97	2,069,091	68.97	2,482,909	68.97
Gross profit	334,500	27.03	540,606	27.03	675,758	27.03	810,909	27.03	973,091	27.03
Office	6,000	0.48	10,000	0.50	12,000	0.48	12,000	0.40	12,000	0.33
Advertising	61,500	4.97	69,000	3.45	100,000	4.00	110,000	3.67	120,000	3.33
Wages	105,000	8.48	173,000	8.65	198,950	7.96	238,740	7.96	286,488	7.96
Commissions	11,880	0.96	19,200	0.96	24,000	0.96	28,800	0.96	34,560	0.96
Utilities	6,350	0.51	7,200	0.36	9,000	0.36	10,800	0.36	12,960	0.36
Phone	6,800	0.55	8,050	0.40	10,063	0.40	12,075	0.40	14,490	0.40
Depreciation	2,679	0.22	3,250	0.16	4,107	0.16	4,800	0.16	5,760	0.16
Insurance	8,000	0.65	8,000	0.40	8,800	0.35	9,400	0.31	10,000	0.28
R&D	1,700	0.14	2,500	0.13	3,500	0.14	5,000	0.17	5,000	0.14
Travel/ entertainment	5,700	0.46	8,000	0.40	10,000	0.40	12,000	0.40	14,000	0.39
Printing	5,500	0.44	6,500	0.33	7,500	0.30	8,500	0.28	9,500	0.26
Other	7,700	0.62	6,000	0.30	5,000	0.20	6,000	0.20	7,200	0.20
EBT	105,691	8.54	219,906	11.00	282,838	11.31	352,794	11.76	441,133	12.25
Income tax	31,707	2.56	65,972	3.30	84,851	3.39	105,838	3.53	132,340	3.68
Projected net profit	$ 73,984	5.98%	$ 153,934	7.70%	$ 197,987	7.92%	$ 246,956	8.23%	$ 308,793	8.58%

Note: All figures are displayed before management bonuses/profit sharing (see "Compensation and Dividends" section).

Exhibit 8
PC-Build: Break-Even Analysis (1 Year)

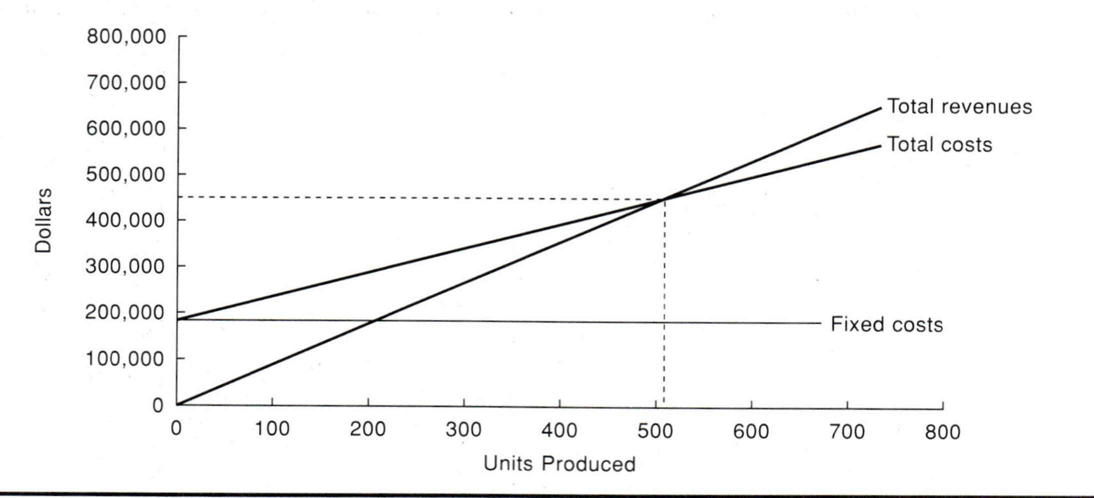

Exhibit 9
Pro Forma Balance Sheets

	Fiscal Years Ended June 30, 1992–1994					
	1992	*Percent*	*1993*	*Percent*	*1994*	*Percent*
Current Assets						
Cash	$118,456	33.82%	$310,078	49.83%	$400,000	46.48%
Accounts Receivable	123,750	35.33	185,625	29.83	235,000	27.31
Inventory	92,000	26.26	107,040	17.20	195,000	22.66
Total Current Assets	334,206	95.41	602,743	96.87	830,000	96.44
Fixed Assets						
Computer system	14,000	4.00	14,000	2.25	25,000	2.90
Manufacturing equipment	2,000	0.57	4,000	0.64	5,000	0.58
Furnitures/fixtures	2,750	0.79	4,750	0.76	5,750	0.67
Less: Depreciation	(2,679)	−0.76	(3,250)	−0.52	(5,107)	−0.59
Net Fixed Assets	16,071	4.59	19,500	3.13	30,643	3.56
Total Assets	$350,278	100.00%	$622,243	100.00%	$860,643	100.00%
Current Liabilities						
Accounts Payable	$ 83,550	23.85%	$125,325	20.14%	$154,916	18.00%
Accrued Expenses	83,744	23.91	160,000	25.71	170,823	19.85
Total Current Liabilities	$167,294	47.76%	$285,325	45.85%	$325,739	37.85%
Equity						
Capital stock	$ 10,000	2.85%	10,000	1.61%	10,000	1.16%
Paid-in surplus	99,000	28.26	99,000	15.91	99,000	11.50
Retained earnings	73,984	21.12	227,918	36.63	425,905	49.49
Total equity	182,984	52.24	336,918	54.15	534,905	62.15
Total liabilities and equity	$350,278	100.00%	$622,243	100.00%	$860,643	100.00%

Income Statement

Company sales are forecast to increase from $1.2 million in 1992 to $3.6 million by 1996. First-year net profit is only $93,014, which represents 8.5 percent of sales. This figure is expected to climb steadily over the next five years, mainly through realization of economies of scale with respect to direct marketing, operations, and product development. Net profit margins are 14 percent by 1996.

Cash Flows

Equity capital raised at start-up should be enough to finance PC-Build's operations. The company expects positive cash flow from operations after seven months of operations. However month-to-month cash flows are subject to cyclical swings, particularly during the off months, January–March. The company intends to limit expenditures during this time period, minimizing the negative impact on cash balances.

PROPOSED COMPANY OFFERING

PC-Build was incorporated in February 1992, with 20,000 shares of common voting stock authorized. The company issued 6,500 shares to the founders in exchange for their initial contributions.

The company is planning to issue an additional 3,000 shares to outside investors at $33 per share. The common stock sold will represent 30 percent of the outstanding stock. Any future stock issues will be offered to current shareholders first.

Offering: All partners and the outside investor receive common stock in return for effort and investments in the proportions described in *Table K.*

Dividend Payments. The company will pay dividends during the first profitable year. Dividends will be paid on a quarterly basis, and will be equal to 25 percent of projected after-tax profits.

Table K
Proposed Offering

Name	*Percent Ownership*	*Number of Shares*
Robert Lofblad	25%	2,500
Michael Healey	40	4,000
Board Members	3	300
Outside Investors	30	3,000

Note: The shares being offered to all the investors are restricted securities and may not be sold readily.

Exhibit 10
Hiring Schedule

	Responsibilities	*Hire Dates*
Initial staff:		
M. Healey	President	Start-up
B. Lofblad	Tech support/ development	Start-up
Part-time telemarketer	Sales/sales support	Start-up
Variable staff:		
Trainers	Computer camp training	Seasonal
Sales and marketing:		
Unknown	Director sales/ marketing	January 1993
Telemarketer (2)	Sales/sales support	November 1992
Outside sales	Sales	March 1993
Technical/ administrative support:		
B. Batra	Production/ development	Part-time
Tech Support		April 1993
Secretary		June 1993
Operations:		
Assembly		December 1992
Shipping		May 1993

Note: Projections are based on sales forecasts in cash flow. The company will adjust hiring based on actual sales.

EXERCISE—CREATIVE SQUARES

The Creative Squares Exercise can show group creativity in action.

EXERCISE
CREATIVE SQUARES

STEP 1: DIVIDE YOUR GROUP BY (1) SEPARATING INTO A NUMBER OF GROUPS OF THREE OR MORE PERSONS EACH AND (2) HAVING AT LEAST FIVE INDIVIDUALS WORK ALONE.

STEP 2: SHOW THE FOLLOWING FIGURE TO EVERYONE AND ASK THE GROUPS AND THE INDIVIDUALS TO COUNT THE TOTAL NUMBER OF SQUARES IN THE FIGURE. Assume that the figure is a square box on a single flat plane. In counting, angles of any square must be right angles, and the sides must be of equal length.

STEP 3: DISCUSS THE CREATIVE PROCESS BY WHICH THE GROUPS AND THE INDIVIDUALS REACHED THEIR ANSWERS.

EXERCISE – IDEA GENERATION GUIDE

Before beginning the process of generating ideas for new ventures, it is useful to reflect on an old German proverb that says, "Every beginning is hard." If you allow yourself to think creatively, you will be surprised at the number of interesting ideas you can generate once you begin.

The Idea Generation Guide is an exercise in generating ideas. The aim is for you to generate as many interesting ideas as possible. *While generating your ideas, do not evaluate them or worry about their implementation.* Discussion and exercises in the rest of the book will allow you to evaluate these ideas to see if they are opportunities and to consider your own personal entrepreneurial strategy.

And remember – in any creative endeavor there are no right answers.

EXERCISE
IDEA GENERATION GUIDE

NAME:

DATE:

STEP 1: GENERATE A LIST OF AS MANY NEW VENTURE IDEAS AS POSSIBLE. Thinking about any unmet or poorly filled customer needs you know of that have resulted from regulatory changes, technological changes, knowledge and information gaps, lags, asymmetries, inconsistencies, and so forth, will help you generate such a list. Also, think about various products and services (and their substitutes) and the providers of these products or services. If you know of any weaknesses or vulnerabilities, you may discover new venture ideas.

STEP 2: EXPAND YOUR LIST IF POSSIBLE. Think about your personal interests, your desired lifestyle, your values, what you feel you are likely to do very well, and contributions you would like to make.

STEP 3: ASK AT LEAST THREE PEOPLE WHO KNOW YOU WELL TO LOOK AT YOUR LIST, AND REVISE YOUR LIST TO REFLECT ANY NEW IDEAS EMERGING FROM THIS EXCHANGE. See discussion about getting feedback in Chapter 19.

STEP 4: JOT DOWN INSIGHTS, OBSERVATIONS, AND CONCLUSIONS THAT HAVE EMERGED ABOUT YOUR BUSINESS IDEAS OR YOUR PERSONAL PREFERENCES:

Opportunity Recognition

3

I was seldom able to see an opportunity until it had ceased to be one.

Mark Twain

RESULTS EXPECTED

At the conclusion of the chapter, you will have:

1. Defined the differences between an idea and an opportunity.
2. Examined opportunity in the context of the real world and real time and how opportunity fits within a framework for analysis.
3. Examined criteria used by successful entrepreneurs and investors to evaluate opportunities.
4. Looked at some personal criteria that can be used in evaluating opportunities.
5. Identified how to find information that can be used in screening opportunities.

RECOGNIZING OPPORTUNITIES

Good Ideas Are Not Necessarily Good Opportunities

If an idea is not an opportunity, what is an opportunity?[1] *An opportunity has the qualities of being attractive, durable, and timely and is anchored in a product or service which creates or adds value for its buyer or end user.*

For an opportunity to have these qualities, the "window of opportunity" is opening and remains open long enough. Further, entry into a market with the right characteristics is feasible and the management team is able to achieve it. The venture has or is able to achieve a competitive advantage (i.e., to achieve leverage). Finally, the economics of the venture are rewarding and forgiving and allow significant profit and growth potential.

To repeat, opportunities that have the qualities named above are anchored in a product or service that creates or adds value for its buyer or end user. The most successful entrepreneurs, venture capitalists, and private investors are opportunity-focused; that is, they start with what customers and the marketplace want and do not lose sight of this.

The Real World

Opportunities are created, or built, using ideas and entrepreneurial creativity. Yet, while the image of a carpenter or mason at work is useful, in reality the process is more like the collision of particles in the process of a nuclear reaction or like the spawning of hurri-

[1] See Jeffry A Timmons, *New Business Opportunities* (Acton, MA: Brick House Publishing, 1989).

canes over the ocean. Ideas interact with real-world conditions and entrepreneurial creativity at a point in time. The product of this interaction is an opportunity around which a new venture can be created.

The business environment in which an entrepreneur launches his or her venture is usually given and cannot be altered significantly. Despite the assumptions individuals make about social and nonprofit organizations, they too are subject to market forces and economic constraints. Consider, for instance, what would happen to donations if it were perceived that a nonprofit organization was not reinvesting its surplus returns, but instead was paying management excessive salaries. Or what if a socially oriented organization, like the Body Shop, concentrated all its efforts on the social mission, while neglecting profits? Clearly, dealing with suppliers, production costs, labor, and distribution are critical to the health of these social corporations. Thus, social and nonprofit organizations are just as concerned with positive cash flow and generating sufficient cash flows, even though they operate in a different type of market than for-profit organizations. For-profit businesses operate in a free enterprise system characterized by private ownership and profits.

In a free enterprise system, *opportunities* are spawned when there are changing circumstances, chaos, confusion, inconsistencies, lags or leads, knowledge and information gaps, and a variety of other vacuums in an industry or market.

Changes in the business environment and, therefore, anticipation of these changes, are so critical in entrepreneurship that constant vigilance for changes is a valuable habit. It is thus that an entrepreneur with credibility, creativity, and decisiveness can seize an opportunity while others study it.

Opportunities are situational. Some conditions under which opportunities are spawned are entirely idiosyncratic, while, at other times, they are generalizable and can be applied to other industries, products, or services. In this way, cross-association can trigger in the entrepreneurial mind the crude recognition of existing or impending opportunities. It is often assumed that a marketplace dominated by large, multibillion-dollar players is impenetrable by smaller, entrepreneurial companies. After all, how can you possibly compete with entrenched, resource-rich, established companies? The opposite can be true for several reasons. A number of research projects have shown that it can take six years or more for a large company to change its strategy, and even longer to implement the new strategy since it can take 10 years and more to change the culture enough to operate differently. For a new or small company 10 or more years is forever. When Cellular One was launched in Boston, giant NYNEX was the sole competitor. From all estimates they built twice as many towers (at $500,00 each), spent two to three times as much on advertising and marketing, in addition to having a larger head-count. Yet, Cellular One grew from scratch to $100 million in sales in five years and won three customers for every one that NYNEX won. What made this substantial difference? An entrepreneurial management team at Cellular One.

Some of the most exciting opportunities have actually come from fields the conventional wisdom said are the domain of big business: technological innovation. The performance of smaller firms in technological innovation is remarkable—95 percent of the radical innovations since World War II have come from new and small firms, not the giants. In fact, another study from the National Science Foundation found that smaller firms generated *24 times as many innovations* per research and development dollar versus firms with 10,000 or more employees.

There can be exciting opportunities in plain vanilla businesses that might never get the attention of venture capital investors. The revolution in microcomputers, management information systems (MIS), and computer networking has had a profound impact on a number of businesses that had changed little in decades. Take, for instance, the used-auto-wreck and used-auto-parts business, which has not changed in decades. Yet, Pintendre Auto, Inc., saw a new opportunity in this field by applying the latest computer and information technology to a traditional business that relied on crude, manual methods to track inventory and find parts for customers.[2] In just three years, he built a business with $16 million in sales.

Other regulatory and technology changes can radically alter the way you think about the opportunities because of the economics of sales and distribution for many customer products, from fishing lures to books to cosmetics to sporting goods. By the mid-1990s, there will be 500 or so cable television channels in America versus 40 to 50 for most markets in 1993. A number of new companies up to $100 million in sales have already been built using "infomercials." A 30-minute program can be produced for $50,000 to $150,000 and a half hour of air time can be purchased today for about $20,000 in Los Angeles or for about $4,000 in smaller cities. Compare that with a $25,000+ cost of a full-page advertisement in a monthly magazine. With a large increase in the number of channels, the cost and market focus will undoubtedly improve. Traditional channels of distribution through distributors, wholesalers, specialty stores, and retailers will be completely leapfrogged. Entrepreneurs will find ways to convert those funds previously spent on the profit margin that went to the distribution channel (30 to 50+ percent) to their informercial marketing budget and to an increased gross margin for their business.

Consider the following broad range of examples that illustrate the phenomenon of vacuums in which opportunities are spawned:

- Deregulation of telecommunications and airlines led to the formation of tens of thousands of new firms in the 1980s, including Cellular One and Federal Express.
- Microcomputer hardware in the early 1980s far outpaced the development of software. The development of the industry was highly dependent on the development of software, leading to aggressive efforts by IBM, Apple, and others to encourage software entrepreneurs to close this gap.
- Many opportunities exist in fragmented, traditional industries that may have a craft or mom-and-pop character and where there is little appreciation or know-how in marketing and finance. Consider such possibilities as fishing lodges, inns, and hotels; cleaners/laundries; hardware stores; pharmacies; waste management plants; flower shops; nurseries; tents; and auto repairs.
- In our service-dominated economy (where 70 percent of businesses are service businesses, versus 30 percent just 25 years ago), customer service, rather than the product itself, can be the critical success factor. One study by the Forum Corporation in Boston showed that 70 percent of customers leave because of poor service and only 15 percent because of price or quality. Can you think of your last "wow" experience with exceptional customer service?
- Sometimes existing competitors cannot, or will not, increase capacity as quickly as the market is moving. For example, the tent industry, as seen in the Outdoor Scene case earlier, was characterized by this capacity stickiness in the mid-1970s. In the late-1970s, some steel firms had a 90-week delivery lag, with the price to be determined, and foreign competitors certainly took notice.
- The tremendous shift to off-shore manufacturing of labor-intensive and transportation-insensitive products in Asia, Eastern Europe, and Mexico, such as computer-related and microprocessor-driven consumer products, is an excellent example.
- In a wide variety of industries, entrepreneurs sometimes find they are the only ones who can perform. Such fields as consulting, software design, financial services, process engineering, and technical and medical products and services abound with examples

[2] Barrie McKenna, "More than the Sum of its Parts," *The Globe and Mail*, February 23, 1993, p. B24.

of know-how monopolies. Sometimes a management team is simply the best in an industry and irreplaceable in the near term, just as is seen with great coaches with winning records.

Big Opportunities with Little Capital

Within the dynamic free enterprise system, opportunities are apparent to a limited number of individuals—and not just to the individuals with financial resources. Ironically, successful entrepreneurs like Howard Head attribute their success to the discipline of limited capital resources. Thus, in the 1990s, many entrepreneurs have been learning the key to success is in the art of bootstrapping, which "in a start-up is like zero inventory in a just-in-time system: It reveals hidden problems and forces the company to solve them."[3] Consider the following:

- A 1991 study revealed that of the 110 start-ups researched, 77 percent had been launched with $50,000 or less; 46 percent were started with $10,000 or less as seed capital. Further, the primary source of capital was, overwhelmingly, personal savings (74 percent), rather than outside investors with deep pockets.[4]
- In the 1930s, Josephine Esther Mentzer assisted her uncle by selling skin care balm and quickly created her own products with $100 initial investment. After convincing the department stores rather than the drug stores to carry her products, Estee Lauder was on its way to a $3 billion corporation.[5]
- Putting their talents (cartooning and finance) together, Roy and Walt Disney moved to California and started their own film studio—with $290 in 1923. Today, the Walt Disney Co. has a market value exceeding $16 billion.[6]
- While working for a Chicago insurance company, a 24-year-old sent out 20,000 inquiries for a black newsletter. With 3,000 positive responses and $500, John Harold Johnson published *Jet* for the first time in 1942. In the 1990s, Johnson Publishing publishes various magazines, including *Ebony*.[7]
- With $100, Nicholas Graham, age 24, went to a local fabric store, picked out some patterns, and made $100 worth of ties. Having sold the ties to specialty shops, Graham was approached by Macy's to place his patterns on men's underwear. So Joe Boxer Corporation was born and "six months into Joe Boxer's second year, sales had already topped $1 million."[8]

Real Time

Opportunities exist or are created in real time and have what is called a window of opportunity. For an entrepreneur to seize an opportunity requires that the window be opening, not closing, and that it remain open long enough.

Exhibit 3.1 illustrates a window of opportunity for a generalized market. Markets grow at different rates over time and as a market quickly becomes larger, more and more opportunities are possible. As the market becomes larger and established, conditions are not

[3] Amar Bhide, "Bootstrap Finance," *Harvard Business Review*, November–December 1992, p. 112.

[4] Edward B Roberts, *Entrepreneurs in High Technology: Lessons from MIT and Beyond* (New York: Oxford University Press, 1991), p. 144, Table 5–2.

[5] Teri Lammers and Annie Longsworth, "Guess Who? Ten Big-Timers Launched from Scratch," *Inc.*, September 1991, p. 69. © 1991 by Goldhirsh Group, Inc., 38 Commercial Wharf, Boston, MA 02110.

[6] Ibid.

[7] Ibid.

[8] Robert A Mamis, "The Secrets of Bootstrapping," *INC.*, September 1991, p. 54.

Exhibit 3.1
Changes in the Placement of the Window of Opportunity

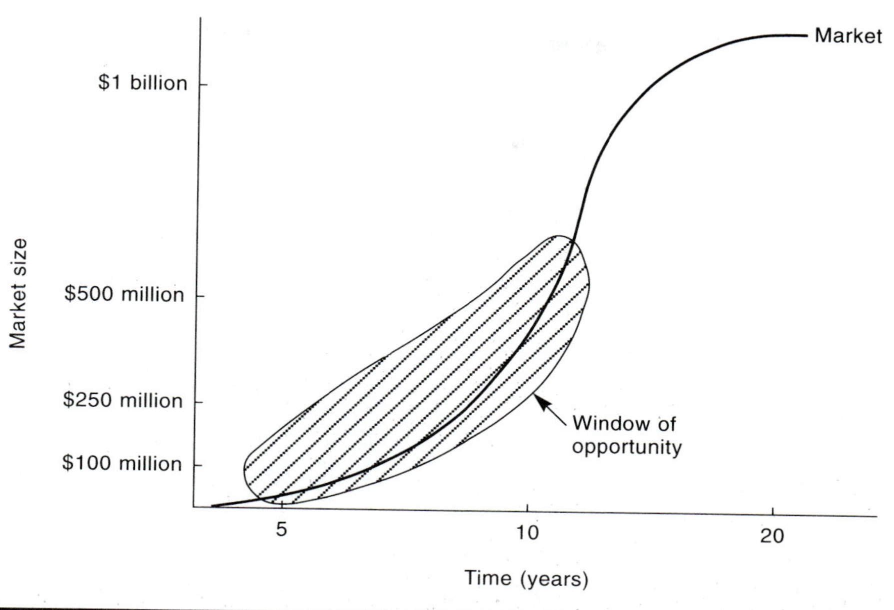

as favorable. Thus, at the point where a market starts to become sufficiently large and structured (e.g., at 5 years in *Exhibit 3.1*), the window opens; the window begins to close as the market matures (e.g., at 15 years in the exhibit).

The curve shown describes the rapid growth pattern typical of such new industries as microcomputers and software, cellular car phones, quick oil changes, and biotechnology. For example, in the cellular car phone industry, most major cities began service between 1983 and 1984 for the very first time. By 1989, there were over 2 million subscribers in the United States, and the industry continued to experience significant growth. In other industries, such as a mature industry, where growth is not so rapid, the slope of a curve would be less steep and the possibilities for opportunities fewer.

Finally, in considering the window of opportunity, the length of time the window will be open is important. It takes a considerable length of time to determine whether a new venture is a success or a failure. And, if it is to be a success, the benefits of that success need to be harvested.

Exhibit 3.2 shows that for venture-capital-backed firms, the lemons (i.e., the losers) ripen in about two and a half years, while the pearls (i.e., the winners) take seven or eight years. An extreme example of the length of time it can take for a pearl to be harvested is the experience of a Silicon Valley venture capital firm that invested in a new firm in 1966 and was finally able to realize a capital gain in early 1984.

Another way to think of the process of creating and seizing an opportunity in real time is to think of it as a process of selecting objects (opportunities) from a conveyor belt moving through an open window, the window of opportunity. The speed of the conveyor belt changes, and the window through which it moves is constantly opening and closing. That the window is continually opening and closing and that the speed of the conveyor belt is constantly changing represent the volatile nature of the marketplace and the importance of timing. For an opportunity to be created and seized, it needs to be selected from the conveyor belt before the window closes.

Exhibit 3.2
Lemons and Pearls

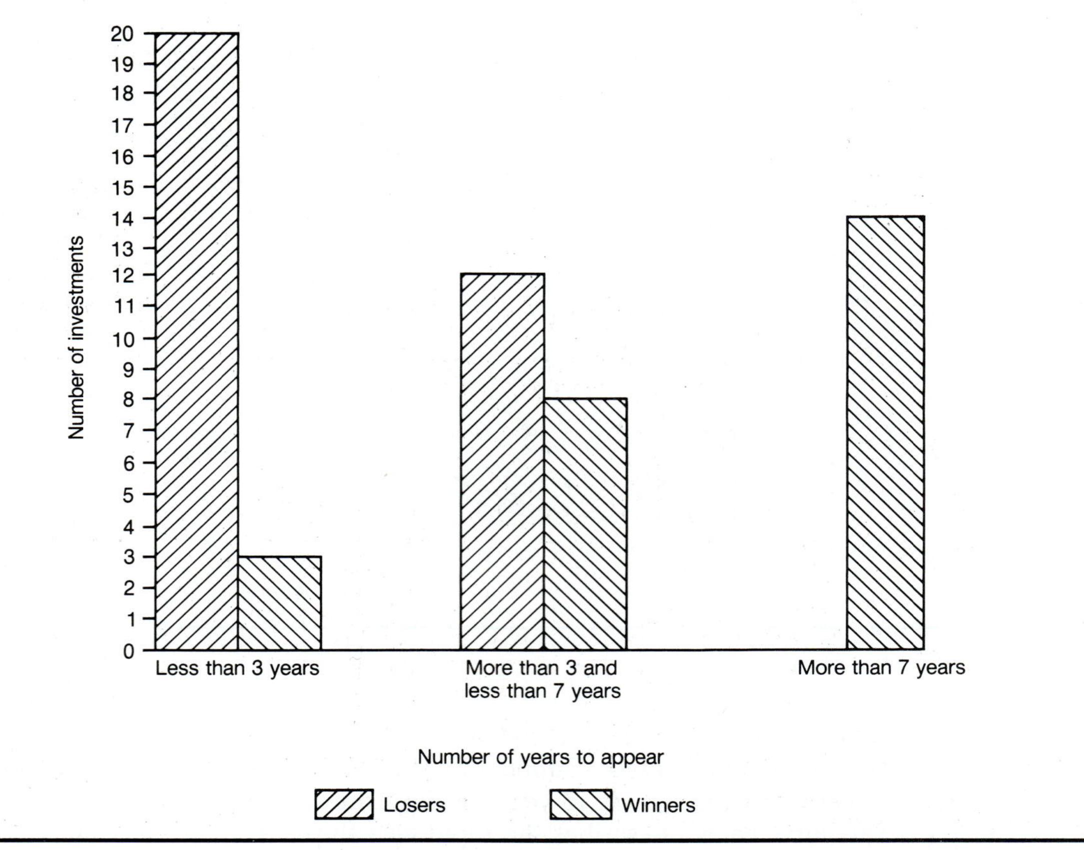

The ability to recognize a potential opportunity when it appears and the sense of timing to seize it as the window is opening, rather than slamming shut, are critical. That opportunities are a function of real time is illustrated in a statement made by Ken Olsen, the president and founder of Digital Equipment Corporation, in 1977: "There is no reason for any individual to have a computer in their home." Nor is it so easy for even the world's leading experts to predict just which innovative ideas and concepts for new business will evolve into the major industries of tomorrow. This is vividly illustrated by several quotations from very famous innovators. In 1901, two years before the famous flight, Wilbur Wright said, "Man will not fly for 50 years." In 1910, Thomas Edison said, "The nickel-iron battery will put the gasoline buggy . . . out of existence in no time." And in 1932, Albert Einstein made it clear: "There is not the slightest indication that nuclear energy will ever be obtainable. It would mean that the atom would have to be shattered at will."

Relation to the Framework of Analysis

It is also important to remember that successful opportunities, once recognized, fit with the other forces of new venture creation. This iterative process of assessing and reassessing the fit among the central driving forces in the creation of a new venture was shown in *Exhibit 1.7* in Chapter 1. Of utmost importance when talking of opportunity recognition is the fit of the lead entrepreneur and the management team with an opportunity. Good opportunities are both *desirable* to and *attainable* by those on the team using the resources that are available.

In order to understand how the entrepreneurial vision relates to the analytical framework, it may be useful to look at an opportunity as a three-dimensional relief map with its valleys, mountains, and so on, all represented. Each opportunity has three or four critical factors (e.g., proprietary license, patented innovation, sole distribution rights, an all-star management team, breakthrough technology). These elements pop out at the observer; they indicate huge possibilities where others might see obstacles. Thus, it is easy to see why there are thousands of exceptional opportunities that will fit with a wide variety of entrepreneurs, but that might not fit neatly into the framework outlined in *Exhibit 3.3*.

Exhibit 3.3
Criteria for Evaluating Venture Opportunities

	Attractiveness	
Criteria	*Highest Potential*	*Lowest Potential*
Industry and market	Changes way people live and work	Incremental improvement only
Market:	Market driven; identified; recurring revenue niche	Unfocused; one-time revenue
Customers	Reachable; purchase orders	Loyal to others or unreachable
User benefits	Less than one-year payback	Three years plus payback
Value added	High; advance payments	Low; minimal impact on market
Product life	Durable	Perishable
Market structure	Imperfect, fragmented competition or emerging industry	Highly concentrated or mature or declining industry
Market size	100+ million to $1 billion sales potential	Unknown, less than $20 million or multibillion sales
Growth rate	Growth at 30–50% or more	Contracting or less than 10%
Market capacity	At or near full capacity	Undercapacity
Market share attainable (Year 5)	20% or more; leader	Less than 5%
Cost structure	Low-cost provider; cost advantages	Declining cost
Economics		
Time to breakeven/positive cash flow	Under 1½–2 years	More than 4 years
ROI potential	25% or more; high value	Less than 15–20%; low value
Capital requirements	Low to moderate; fundable	Very high; unfundable
Internal rate of return potential	25% or more per year	Less than 15% per year
Free cash flow characteristics:	Favorable; sustainable; 20–30% or more of sales	Less than 10% of sales
Sales growth	Moderate to high (+15% to +20%)	Less than 10%
Asset intensity	Low/sales $	High
Spontaneous working capital	Low, incremental requirements	High requirements
R&D/capital expenditures	Low requirements	High requirements
Gross margins	Exceeding 40% and durable	Under 20%
After-tax profits	High; greater than 10%; durable	Low
Time to break-even profit and loss	Less than two years; breakeven not creeping	Greater than four years; breakeven creeping up
Harvest issues		
Value-added potential	High strategic value	Low strategic value
Valuation multiples and comparables	Price/earnings = $20+x_\$$; $8–10+x_\$$ EBIT; $1.5–2+x_\$$revenue: free cash flow $8–10 + x_\$$	Price/earnings ≤ 5x, EBIT ≤ 3–4x; revenue ≤ .4
Exit mechanism and strategy	Present or envisioned options	Undefined; illiquid investment
Capital market context	Favorable valuations, timing, capital available; realizable liquidity	Unfavorable; credit crunch
Competitive advantage issues		
Fixed and variable costs	Lowest; high operating leverage	Highest
Control over costs, prices, and distribution	Moderate to strong	Weak
Barriers to entry:		
Proprietary protection	Have or can gain	None
Response/lead time	Competition slow; napping	Unable to gain edge

(Continued)

Exhibit 3.3 (*concluded*)

Criteria	*Attractiveness* — *Highest Potential*	*Lowest Potential*
Legal, contractual advantage	Proprietary or exclusivity	None
Contracts and networks	Well-developed; accessible	Crude; limited
Key people	Top talent; an A team	B or C team
Management team		
Entrepreneurial team	All-star combination; free agents	Weak or solo entrepreneur
Industry and technical experience	Top of the field; super track-record	Underdeveloped
Integrity	Highest standards	Questionable
Intellectual honesty	Know what they do not know	Do not want to know what they do not know
Fatal-flaw issue	Non-existent	One or more
Personal criteria		
Goals and fit	Getting what you want; but wanting what you get.	Surprises, as in *The Crying Game*
Upside/downside issues	Attainable success/limited risks	Linear; on same continuum
Opportunity costs	Acceptable cuts in salary, etc.	Comfortable with status quo
Desirability	Fits with lifestyle	Simply pursuing big money
Risk/reward tolerance	Calculated risk; low risk/reward ratio	Risk averse or gambler
Stress tolerance	Thrives under pressure	Cracks under pressure
Strategic differentiation		
Degree of fit	High	Low
Team	Best in class; excellent free agents	B team; no free agents
Service management	Superior service concept	Perceived as unimportant
Timing	Rowing with the tide	Rowing against the tide
Technology	Groundbreaking; one of a kind	Many substitutes or competitors
Flexibility	Able to adapt; commit and decommit quickly	Slow; stubborn
Opportunity orientation	Always searching for opportunities	Operating in a vacuum; napping
Pricing	At or near leader	Undercut competitor; low prices
Distribution channels	Accessible; networks in place	Unknown; inaccessible
Room for error	Forgiving strategy	Unforgiving, rigid strategy

SCREENING OPPORTUNITIES

Opportunity Focus

Opportunity focus is also the most fruitful point of departure for screening opportunities. The screening process should not begin with strategy (which derives from the nature of the opportunity), with financial and spreadsheet analysis (which flow from the former), or with estimations of how much the company is worth and who will own what shares.[9]

These starting points, and others, usually place the cart before the horse. Perhaps the best evidence of this phenomenon comes from the tens of thousands of tax-sheltered investments that turned sour in the mid-1980s. Also, as has been noted, a good number of entrepreneurs who start businesses—particularly those for whom the ventures are their first—run out of cash at a faster rate than they bring in customers and profitable sales. There are lots of reasons why this happens, but one thing is certain: These entrepreneurs have not focused on the right opportunity.

Over the years, those with experience in business and in specific market areas have developed rules of thumb to guide them in screening opportunities. For example, one such

[9] See J A Timmons, D F Muzyka, H H Stevenson, and W D Bygrave, "Opportunity Recognition: The Core of Entrepreneurship," in *Frontiers of Entrepreneurship Research: 1987*, ed. Neil Churchill et al. (Babson Park, MA: Babson College, 1987), p. 409.

rule of thumb was used by a firm with approximately $1 billion in sales in evaluating start-ups in the minicomputer industry in the mid-1980s. This firm believed, based on an analysis of performance data relating to 60 computer-related start-ups in the United States from 1975 to 1984, that one leading indicator of the progress of new firms and a good boundary measure of positive performance and a healthy start was sales per employee of $75,000 or more. To this firm, sales of less than $50,000 per employee signaled serious trouble. While there is always the risk of oversimplification in using rules of thumb, it is true also that one can miss the fundamentals while searching for subtleties.

Screening Criteria: The Characteristics of High-Potential Ventures

Venture capitalists, savvy entrepreneurs, and investors also use this concept of boundaries in screening ventures. *Exhibit 3.3* summarizes criteria used by venture capitalists to evaluate opportunities. These criteria are used by this group to evaluate a select group of opportunities that tend to have a high-technology bias. As will be seen later, venture capital investors reject 60–70 percent of the new ventures presented to them very early in the review process, based on how the entrepreneurs satisfy these criteria.

However, these criteria are not the exclusive domain of venture capitalists. The criteria are based on plain good business sense that is used by successful entrepreneurs, private investors, and venture capitalists. Consider the following examples of great little companies built without a dime of professional venture capital.

- Paul Tobin, who built Cellular One in eastern Massachusetts from ground zero to $100 million in revenue in five years, has started Roamer Plus with less than $300,000 of internally generated funds from other ventures. Within two years, it grew to a $15 million annual sales rate and was very profitable.
- Another entrepreneur started a small specialty publishing company with minimal capital and grew it to over $12 million in highly profitable sales by 1987. While looking for acquisitions, he discovered that valuations were at an all-time high. Instead of buying, he decided to sell. In 1988, he sold his small firm for over $70 million.
- Morris Alper & Sons was a third-generation, small, traditional food brokerage business with around 40 employees when the founder's grandson joined the firm in the early 1970's. By 1993, financed entirely by internally generated cash flow, they have grown to nearly 350 employees. The company has become an integrated marketing services firm whose clients are 70 of the largest consumer food product companies in North America.
- In 1983, Charlie Butcher, at age 66, had to decide whether to buy out an equal partner in his 100-year-old industrial polish and wax business with less than $10 million in sales. This niche business had high gross margins, very low working capital and fixed-asset requirements for increased sales, substantial steady growth of over 18 percent per year, and excellent products. The result was a business with very high free cash flow and potential for growth. He acquired the company with a bank loan and seller financing, and then he increased sales to over $50 million by 1993. The company continues to be highly profitable. Charlie vows never to utilize venture capital money or to take the company public.

The point of departure here is opportunity and, implicitly, the customer, the marketplace, and the industry. *Exhibit 3.3* shows how higher and lower potential opportunities can be placed along an attractiveness scale. The criteria provide some quantitative way in which an entrepreneur can make judgments about industry and market issues, competitive advantage issues, economic and harvest issues, management team issues, and fatal flaw issues and whether these add up to a compelling opportunity. For example, *dominant* strength in any one of these criteria can readily translate into a winning entry, whereas a flaw in any one can be fatal.

Entrepreneurs contemplating opportunities that will yield attractive companies, not high-potential ventures, can also benefit from paying attention to these criteria. These entrepreneurs will then be in a better position to decide how these criteria can be compromised. As outlined in *Exhibit 3.3,* business opportunities with the greatest potential will possess many of the following, or they will so dominate in one or a few that the competition cannot come close:

- ***Industry and market issues***

  Market. *Higher potential* businesses can identify a market niche for a product or service that meets an important customer need and provides high value-added or value-created benefits to customers. Customers are reachable and receptive to the product or service, with no brand or other loyalties. The potential payback to the user or customer of a given product or service through cost savings or other value-added or value-created properties is one year or less and is identifiable, repeatable, and verifiable. Further, the life of the product or service exists beyond the time needed to recover the investment, plus a profit. And the company is able to expand beyond a one-product company. Take, for example, the growing success of cellular car phone service. At prevailing rates, one can talk for about $25 an hour, and many providers of professional services can readily bill more than the $25 an hour for what would otherwise be unused time. If benefits to customers cannot be calculated in such dollar terms, then the market potential is far more difficult and risky to ascertain.

  Lower potential opportunities are unfocused regarding customer need, and customers are unreachable and/or have brand or other loyalties to others. A payback to the user of more than three years and a low value-added or value-created also makes an opportunity unattractive. Being unable to expand beyond a one-product company also can make for a lower potential opportunity. The failure of one of the first portable computer companies, Osborne Computer, is a good example of this.

  Market structure. Market structure, such as evidenced by the number of sellers, size distribution of sellers, whether products are differentiated, conditions of entry and exit, number of buyers, cost conditions, and sensitivity of demand to changes in price, is significant.

  A fragmented, imperfect market or emerging industry often contains vacuums and asymmetries that create unfilled market niches—for example, markets where resource ownership, cost advantages, and the like can be achieved. In addition, those where information or knowledge gaps exist and where competition is profitable, but not so strong as to be overwhelming, are attractive. An example of a market with an information gap is that of the experience a Boston entrepreneur encountered with a large New York company that wanted to dispose of a small, old office building in downtown Boston. This office building, because its book value was about $200,000, was viewed by the financially oriented firm as a low-value asset, and the company wanted to dispose of it so the resulting cash could be put to work for a higher return. The buyer, who had done more homework than the out-of-town sellers, bought the building for $200,000 and resold it in less than six months for over $8 million.

  Industries that are highly concentrated, that are perfectly competitive, or that are mature or declining industries are typically unattractive. The capital requirements and costs to achieve distribution and marketing presence can be prohibitive, and such behavior as price cutting and other competitive strategies in highly concentrated markets can be a significant barrier to entry. (The most blatant example is organized crime and its life-threatening actions when territories are invaded.) Yet, revenge by normal competitors who are well-positioned through product strategy, legal tactics, and the like, also can be punishing to the pocketbook.

The airline industry, after deregulation, is an example of a perfectly competitive market and one where many of the recent entrants will have difficulty. The unattractiveness of perfectly competitive industries is captured by the comment of prominent Boston venture capitalist William Egan, who put it this way: "I want to be in a nonauction market."[10]

Market size. An attractive new venture sells to a market that is large and growing (i.e., one where capturing a small market share can represent significant and increasing sales volume). A minimum market size of over $100 million in sales is attractive. Such a market size means it is possible to achieve significant sales by capturing roughly 5 percent or less and thus not threatening competitors. For example, to achieve a sales level of $1 million in a $100 million market requires capturing only 1 percent of the market. Thus, a recreational equipment manufacturer entered a $60 million market that was expected to grow at 20 percent per year to over $100 million by the third year. The founders were able to create a substantial smaller company without obtaining a major market share and possibly incurring the wrath of existing competitors.

However, such a market can be too large. A multibillion-dollar market may be too mature and stable, and such a level of certainty can translate into competition from Fortune 500 firms and, if highly competitive, into lower margins and profitability. Further, an unknown market or one that is less than $10 million in sales also is unattractive. To understand the disadvantage of a large, more mature market, consider the entry of a firm into the microcomputer industry today versus the entry of Apple Computer into that market in 1975.

Growth rate. An attractive market is large and growing (i.e., one where capturing a good share of the increase is less threatening to competitors and where a small market share can represent significant and increasing sales volume). An annual growth rate of 30–50 percent creates new niches for new entrants, and such a market is a thriving and expansive one, rather than a stable or contracting one, where competitors are scrambling for the same niches. Thus, for example, a $100 million market growing at 50 percent per year has the potential to become a $1 billion industry in a few years, and if a new venture is able to capture just 2 percent of sales in the first year, it can attain sales in the first year of $1 million. If it just maintains its market share over the next few years, sales will grow significantly.

Market capacity. Another signal of the existence of an opportunity in a market is a market at full capacity in a growth situation—in other words, a demand that the existing suppliers cannot meet. This situation was precisely the case for Outdoor Scene, the company profiled in Chapter 1. Not only was there a 20 percent growth rate, but the other manufacturers were at full capacity. Timing is of vital concern in such a situation, which means the entrepreneur should be asking himself or herself, Can a new entrant fill that demand before the other players can decide to and then actually increase capacity?

Market share attainable. The potential to be a leader in the market and capture at least a 20 percent share of the market is important. The potential to be a leader in the market and capture at least 20 percent can create a very high value for a company that might otherwise be worth not much more than book value. For example, one such firm, with less than $15 million in sales, became the dominant factor in its small market niche with a 70 percent market share. The company was acquired for $23 million in cash.

[10] Comments made during a presentation at Babson College, May 1985.

A firm that will be able to capture less than 5 percent of a market is unattractive in the eyes of most investors seeking a higher potential company.

Cost structure. A firm that can become the low-cost provider is attractive, but a firm that continually faces declining cost conditions is less so. Attractive opportunities exist in industries where economies of scale are insignificant (or work to the advantage of the new venture). Attractive opportunities boast of low costs of learning by doing. Where costs per unit are high when small amounts of the product are sold, existing firms that have low promotion costs can face attractive market opportunities.

For instance, consider the operating leverage of Johnsonville Sausage. Their variable costs were 6 percent labor and 94 percent materials. What aggressive incentives could management put in place for the 6 percent to manage and to control the 94 percent? Imagine the disasters that would occur if the scenario were reversed!

A word of caution from Scott W. Kunkel and Charles W. Hofer, who observed that

> Overall, industry structure . . . had a much smaller impact on new venture performance than has previously been suggested in the literature. This finding could be the result of one of several possibilities:
>
> 1. Industry structure impacts the performance of established firms, but does NOT have a significant impact on new venture performance.
> 2. The most important industry structural variables influencing new ventures are different from those which impact established firms and thus research has yet to identify the industry structural variables that are most important in the new venture environment.
> 3. Industry structure does NOT have a significant DIRECT impact on firm performance, as hypothesized by scholars in the three fields of study. Instead, the impact of industry structure is strongly mitigated by other factors, including the strategy selected for entry.[11]

- ***Economics:***

  Profits after tax. High and durable gross margins usually translate into strong and durable after-tax profits. Attractive opportunities have potential for durable profits of at least 10–15 percent, and often 15–20 percent or more. Those generating after-tax profits of less than 5 percent are quite fragile.

  Time to breakeven and positive cash flow. As mentioned above, breakeven and positive cash flow for attractive companies are possible within two years. Once the time to breakeven and positive cash flow is greater than three years, the attractiveness of the opportunity diminishes accordingly.

  ROI potential. An important corollary to forgiving economics is reward. Very attractive opportunities have the potential to yield a return on investment of 25 percent or more per year. After all, during the 1980s, many venture capital funds achieved only single-digit returns on investment. High and durable gross margins and high and durable after-tax profits usually yield high earnings per share and high return on stockholders' equity, thus generating a satisfactory "harvest" price for a company. This is most likely true whether the company is sold through an initial public offering or privately or whether it is acquired. Given the risk typically involved, a return on investment potential of less than 15–20 percent per year is unattractive.

  Capital requirements. Ventures that can be funded and have capital requirements that are low to moderate are attractive. Realistically, most higher potential businesses need significant amounts of cash—several hundred thousand dollars and up—to get started. However, a business that can be started with little or no capital is rare, but they do exist. One such venture was launched in Boston in 1971 with $7,500 of the founder's

[11] Scott W Kunkel and Charles W Hofer, "The Impact of Industry Structure on New Venture Performance," *Frontiers of Entrepreneurship Research: 1993.* Reproduced with permission.

capital and grew to over $30 million in sales by 1989. In today's venture capital market, the first round of financing is typically $1 million to $2 million or more for a start-up.[12] Some higher potential ventures, such as those in the service sector or "cash sales" businesses, have lower capital requirements than do high-technology manufacturing firms with continual large research and development expenditures.

If the venture needs too much money or cannot be funded, it is unattractive. An extreme example is a venture that a team of students recently proposed to repair satellites. The students believed that the required start-up capital was in the $50 million to $200 million range. Projects of this magnitude are in the domain of the government and the very large corporation, rather than that of entrepreneurs and venture capitalists.

Internal rate of return potential. Is the risk reward relationship attractive enough? The response to this question can be quite personal, but the most attractive opportunities often have the promise of—and deliver—a very substantial upside of 5 to 10 times the original investment in 5 to 10 years. Of course, the extraordinary successes can yield 50 to 100 times or more, but these truly are exceptions. A 25 percent or more annual compound rate of return is considered very healthy. In the early 1990s, those investments considered basically risk free had yields of 3 to 8 percent.

Free cash flow characteristics.[13] Free cash flow is a way of understanding a number of crucial financial dimensions of any business: the robustness of its economics; its capital requirements, both working and fixed assets; its capacity to service external debt and equity claims; and its capacity to sustain growth. We define unlevered free cash flow (FCF) as earnings before interest but after taxes (EBIAT) *plus* amortization (A) and depreciation (D) *less* spontaneous working capital requirements (WC) *less* capital expenditures (CAPex), or $FCF = EBIAT + [A + D] - [+ \text{ or } - \ WC] - CAPex$. EBIAT is driven by sales, profitability, and asset intensity. Low-asset-intensive, high-margin businesses generate the highest profits and sustainable growth.[14]

Gross margins. The potential for high and durable gross margins (i.e., the unit selling price less all direct and variable costs) is important. Gross margins exceeding 40–50 percent provide a tremendous built-in cushion that allows for more error and more flexibility to learn from mistakes than do gross margins of 20 percent or less. High and durable gross margins, in turn, mean that a venture can reach breakeven earlier, an event that preferably occurs within the first two years. Thus, for example, if gross margins are just 20 percent, for every $1 increase in fixed costs (e.g., insurance, salaries, rent, and utilities), sales need to increase $5 just to stay even. If gross margins are 75 percent, however, a $1 increase in fixed costs requires a sales increase of just $1.33. An example of the cushion provided by high and durable gross margins is provided by an entrepreneur who built the international division of an emerging software company to $17 million in highly profitable sales in just five years (when he was 25 years of age). He stresses there is simply no substitute for outrageous gross margins, by saying, "It allows you to make all kinds of mistakes that would kill a normal company. And we made them all. But our high gross margins covered all the learning tuition and still left a good profit."[15] Gross margins of less than 20 percent, particularly if they are fragile, are unattractive.

[12] J A Timmons, W Bygrave, and N Fast, "The Flow of Venture Capital to Highly Innovative Technological Ventures," a study for the National Science Foundation, reprinted in *Frontiers of Entrepreneurship Research: 1984*, ed J A Hornaday et al. (Babson Park, MA: Babson College, 1984).

[13] For a more detailed description of free cash flow, see "Note on Free Cash Flow Valuation Models: Identifying the Critical Factors that Affect Value," HBS 288-023, Harvard Business School, 1987.

[14] William A Sahlman, "Sustainable Growth Analysis," HBS 9-284-059, Harvard Business School, 1984.

[15] R Douglas Kahn, president, Interactive Images, Inc., speaking at Babson College about his experiences as international marketing director at McCormack & Dodge from 1978 through 1983.

Time to breakeven—cash flow and profit and loss (P&L). New businesses which can quickly achieve a positive cash flow and become self-sustaining are highly desirable. It is often the second year before this is possible, but the sooner the better. Obviously, simply having a longer window does not mean that the business will be lousy. Two great companies illustrate that a higher potential business can have a longer window. For instance, Pilkington Brothers, an English firm that developed plate glass technology, ran huge losses for over two and a half years before it was regarded as a great company. Similarly, Federal Express went through an early period of enormous negative cash flows of $1 million a month.

- ***Harvest issues:***

Value-added potential. New ventures that are based on strategic value in an industry, such as valuable technology, are attractive, while those with low or no strategic value are less attractive. For example, most observers contend, a product technology of compelling strategic value to Xerox was owned, in the mid-1980s, by a small company with about $10 million in sales and showing a prior-year loss of $1.5 million. Xerox purchased the company for $56 million. Opportunities with extremely large capital commitments, whose value on exit can be severely eroded by unanticipated circumstances, are less attractive. An example would be nuclear power.

Thus, one characteristic of businesses that command a premium price is that they have high value-added strategic importance to their acquirer: distribution, customer base, geographic coverage, proprietary technology, contractual rights, and the like. To illustrate, such companies might be valued at four, five, even six times (or more) last year's *sales*, whereas perhaps 60 to 80 percent of companies might be purchased at .75 to 1.25 times sales.

Valuation multiples and comparables. Consistent with the above point, there is a large spread in the value the capital markets place on private and public companies. Part of your analysis is to identify some of the historical boundaries for the valuations placed on companies in the market/industry/technology area you intend to pursue. The rules of thumb outlined in *Exhibit 3.3* are variable and should be thought of as a boundary and a point of departure.

Exit mechanism and strategy. Businesses that are eventually sold—privately or to the public—or acquired usually are started and grown with a harvest objective in mind. Attractive companies that realize capital gains from the sale of their businesses have, or envision, a harvest or exit mechanism. Unattractive opportunities do not have an exit mechanism in mind. Planning is critical because, as is often said, it is much harder to get out of a business than to get into it. Giving some serious thought to the options and likelihood that the company can eventually be harvested is an important initial and ongoing aspect of the entrepreneurial process.

Capital market context. The context in which the sale or acquisition of the company takes place is largely driven by the capital market context at that particular point in time. Timing can be a critical component of the exit mechanism because, as one study indicated, since World War II, the average bull market on Wall Street has lasted just six months. For a keener appreciation of the critical difference the capital markets can make, one only has to recall the stock market crash of October 19, 1987, or the bank credit crunch of 1990–1992. In fact, by the end of 1987, the valuation of the Venture Capital 100 index dropped 43 percent and private company valuations followed. Initial public offerings are especially vulnerable to the vicissitudes of the capital markets; here the timing is vital. Some of the most successful companies seem to have been launched when debt and equity capital were most available and relatively cheap.

- ***Competitive advantages issues:***

Variable and fixed costs. An attractive opportunity has the potential for being the lowest-cost producer and for having the lowest costs of marketing and distribution. For example, Bowmar was unable to remain competitive in the market for electronic calculators after the producers of large-scale integrated circuits, such as Hewlett-Packard, entered the business. Being unable to achieve and sustain a position as a low-cost producer shortens the life expectancy of a new venture.

Degree of control. Attractive opportunities have potential for moderate-to-strong degree of control over prices, costs, and channels of distribution. Fragmented markets where there is no dominant competitor—no IBM—have this potential. These markets usually have a market leader with a 20 percent market share *or less.* For example, sole control of the source of supply of a critical component for a product or of channels of distribution can give a new venture market dominance even if other areas are weak.

Lack of control over such factors as product development and component prices can make an opportunity unattractive. For example, in the case of Viatron, its suppliers were unable to produce several of the semiconductors that the company needed at low enough prices to permit Viatron to make the inexpensive computer terminal that it had publicized extensively.

A market where a major competitor has a market share of 40 percent, 50 percent, or, especially, 60 percent usually implies a market where power and influence over suppliers, customers, and pricing create a serious barrier and risk for a new firm. Such a firm will have few degrees of freedom. However, if a dominant competitor is at full capacity, is slow to innovate or to add capacity in a large and growing market, or routinely ignores or abuses the customer (remember "Ma Bell"), there may be an entry opportunity. However, entrepreneurs usually do not find such sleepy competition in dynamic, emerging industries dense with opportunity.

Entry barriers. Having a favorable window of opportunity is important. Having or being able to gain proprietary protection, regulatory advantage, or other legal or contractual advantage, such as exclusive rights to a market or with a distributor, is attractive. Having or being able to gain an advantage in response/lead times is important since these can create barriers to entry or expansion by others. For example, advantages in response/lead times in technology, product innovation, market innovation, people, location, resources, or capacity make an opportunity attractive. Possession of well-developed, high-quality, accessible contacts that are the products of years of building a top-notch reputation and that cannot be acquired quickly is also advantageous. In fact, there are times when this competitive advantage may be so strong as to provide dominance in the marketplace, even though many of the other factors are weak or average. An example of how quickly the joys of start-up may fade if others cannot be kept out is the experience of firms in the hard disk drive industry that were unable to erect entry barriers in the United States in the early to mid-1980s. By the end of 1983, some 90 hard disk drive companies were launched, and severe price competition led to a major industry shakeout.

If a firm cannot keep others out or if it faces already existing entry barriers, it is unattractive. An easily overlooked issue is a firm's capacity to gain distribution of its product. As simple as it may sound, even venture-capital-backed companies fall victim to this market issue. Air Florida apparently assembled all the right ingredients, including substantial financing, yet was unable to secure sufficient gate space for its airplanes.

Even though it sold passenger seats, it had no place to pick the passengers up or drop them off.

- ***Management team issues:***

  Entrepreneurial team. Attractive opportunities have teams which are existing and strong and contain industry superstars. The team has proven profit and loss experience in the same technology, market, and service area, and members have complementary and compatible skills. An unattractive opportunity does not have such a team in place or has no team.

  Industry and technical experience. A management track record of significant accomplishment in the industry, with the technology, and in the market area, with a proven profit, and lots of achievements where the venture will compete is highly desirable. A top-notch management team can become the most important strategic competitive advantage in an industry. Imagine relocating the Chicago Bulls or the Phoenix Suns to Halifax, Nova Scotia; do you think you would have a winning competitor in the National Basketball Association?

  Integrity. Trust and integrity are the oil and glue that make economic interdependence possible. Having an unquestioned reputation in this regard is a major long-term advantage for entrepreneurs and should be sought in all personnel and backers. A shady past or record of questionable integrity is for B team players only.

  Intellectual honesty. There is a fundamental issue of whether the founders know what they do and do not know, as well as whether they know what to do about shortcomings or gaps in the team and the enterprise.

- ***Fatal-flaw issues.*** Basically, attractive ventures have no fatal flaws; an opportunity is rendered unattractive if it suffers from one or more fatal flaws. Usually, these relate to one of the above criteria, and examples abound of markets which are too small, which have overpowering competition, where the cost of entry is too high, where an entrant is unable to produce at a competitive price, and so on. An example of an entry barrier's being a fatal flaw was Air Florida's inability to get its flights listed on reservation computers.

- ***Personal criteria:***

  Goals and fit. Is there a good match between the requirements of business and what the founders want out of it? A very wise woman, Dorothy Stevenson, pinpointed the crux of it with this powerful insight: "Success is *getting* what you want. Happiness is *wanting* what you get."

  Upside/downside issues. An attractive opportunity does not have excessive downside risk. The upside and the downside of pursuing an opportunity are not linear, nor are they on the same continuum. The upside is easy, and it has been said that success has a thousand sires. The downside is quite another matter, since it has also been said that failure is an orphan. An entrepreneur needs to be able to absorb the financial downside in such a way that he or she can rebound, without becoming indentured to debt obligations. If an entrepreneur's financial exposure in launching the venture is greater than his or her net worth – the resources he or she can reasonably draw upon, and his or her alternative disposable earnings stream if it does not work out – the deal may be too big. While today's bankruptcy laws are extremely generous, the psychological burdens of living through such an ordeal are infinitely more painful than the financial consequences. An existing business needs to consider if a failure will be too demeaning to the firm's reputation and future credibility, aside from the obvious financial consequences.[16]

  Opportunity cost. In pursuing any venture opportunity, there are also opportunity costs. An entrepreneur who is skilled enough to grow a successful, multimillion-dollar

[16] This point was made by J Willard Marriott, Jr., at Founder's Day, Babson College, 1988.

venture has talents that are highly valued by medium- to large-sized firms as well. While assessing benefits that may accrue in pursuing an opportunity, an entrepreneur needs to take a serious look at other alternatives, including potential "golden handcuffs," and account honestly for any cut in salary that may be involved in pursuing a certain opportunity.

Further, pursuing an opportunity can shape an entrepreneur in ways that are hard to imagine. An entrepreneur will probably have time to execute between two to four multimillion-dollar ventures between the ages of 25 and 50. Each of these experiences will position him or her, *for better or for worse,* for the next opportunity. Since it is important for an entrepreneur, in his or her early years, to gain relevant management experience and since building a venture (either one that works out or one that does not) takes a lot more time than is commonly believed, it is important to consider alternatives while assessing an opportunity.

Desirability. A good opportunity is not only attractive but also desirable (i.e., a good opportunity fits). An example of an intensely personal criterion would be the desire for a certain lifestyle. This desire may preclude pursuing certain opportunities (i.e., certain opportunities may be opportunities for someone else). The founder of a major high-technology venture in the Boston area was asked why the headquarters of his firm were located in downtown Boston, while those of other such firms were located on the famous Route 128 outside of the city. His reply was that he wanted to live in Boston because he loved the city and wanted to be able to walk to work. He said, "The rest did not matter."

Risk/reward tolerance. Successful entrepreneurs take calculated risks or avoid risks they do not need to take; as a country western song put it: "You have to know when to hold 'em, know when to fold 'em, know when to walk away, and know when to run." This is not to suggest that all entrepreneurs have the same risk tolerance; some are quite conservative while others actually seem to get a kick out of the inherent danger and thrill in higher risk and higher stake games. The real issue is fit—recognizing that gamblers and overly risk averse entrepreneurs are unlikely to sustain any long-term successes.

Stress tolerance. Another important dimension of the fit concept is the stressful requirements of a fast-growth high-stakes venture. Or as President Harry Truman said so well: "If you can't stand the heat, then stay out of the kitchen."

- ***Strategic differentiation:***

Degree of fit. To what extent is there a good fit among the driving forces (founders and team, opportunity and resource requirements) and the timing given the external environment?

Team. There is no substitute for an A quality team, since the execution and the ability to adapt and to devise constantly new strategies is so vital to survival and success. A team is nearly unstoppable if it can inculcate into the venture a philosophy and culture of superior learning, as well as teaching skills, an ethic of high standards, delivery of results, and constant improvement. Are they free agents—clear of employment, noncompete, proprietary rights, and trade secret agreements—who are able to pursue the opportunity?

Service management. A few years ago, the Forum Corporation of Boston conducted research across a wide range of industries with several hundred companies to determine why customers stopped buying these companies' products. The results were surprising; 15 percent of the customers defected because of quality and 70 percent stopped using a product or service because of bad customer service. Having a "turbo-service" concept that can be delivered consistently can be a major competitive weapon against small and large competitors alike. Home Depot, in the home supply business, and Lexus, in the auto industry, have set an entirely new standard of service for their industries.

Timing. From business to historic military battles to political campaigns, timing is often the one element that can make a significant difference. Time can be an enemy or a friend; being too early or too late can be fatal. The crux is to row with the tide, not against it. Strategically, ignoring this principle is perilous.

Technology. A breakthrough, proprietary product is no guarantee of success, but it certainly creates a formidable competitive advantage (see *Exhibit 3.4*).

Flexibility. Maintaining the capacity to commit and decommit quickly, to adapt, and to abandon if necessary is a major strategic weapon, particularly when competing with larger organizations. Larger firms can typically take six years or more to change basic strategy and 10 to 20 years or more to change the culture.

Opportunity orientation. To what extent is there a constant alertness to the marketplace? A continual search for opportunities? As one insightful entrepreneur put it, "Any opportunity that just comes in the door to us, we do not consider an opportunity. And we do not have a strategy until we are saying no to lots of opportunities."

Pricing. One of the most common mistakes of new companies, with high-value-added products or services in a growing market, is to underprice. A price slightly below to as much as 20 percent below competitors is rationalized as necessary to gain market entry. In a 30 percent gross margin business a 10 percent price increase results in a 20–36 percent increase in gross margin and will lower the break-even sales level for a company with $900,000 in fixed costs to $2.5 million from $3 million. At the $3 million sales level, the company would realize an extra $180,000 in pre-tax profits.

Distribution channels. Having access to the distribution channels is sometimes overlooked or taken for granted. New channels of distribution can leapfrog and demolish traditional channels; take for instance, direct mail, home shopping networks, infomercials, and the coming revolution in interactive television in your own home.

Room for error. How forgiving is the business and the financial strategy? How wrong can the team be in estimates of revenue, costs, cash flow, timing, and capital requirements? How bad can things get, yet be able to survive? If some single engine planes are more prone to accidents, by 10 or more times, which plane do you want to fly in? High leverage, lower gross margins, and lower operating margins are the signals in a small company of these flights destined for fatality.

Exhibit 3.4
Major Inventions by US Small Firms in the 20th Century

Acoustical suspension speakers
Aerosol can
Air conditioning
Airplane
Artificial skin
Assembly line
Automatic fabric cutting
Automatic transfer equipment
Bakelite
Biosynthetic insulin
Catalytic petroleum cracking
Continuous casting
Cotton picker
Fluid flow meter
Fosin fire airinguisher
Geodesic dome
Gyrocompass
Heart valve
Heat sensor
Helicopter
Heterodyne radio
High capacity computer
Hydraulic brake
Learning machine
Link trainer
Nuclear magnetic resonance
Piezo electronic devices
Polaroid camera
Prefabricated housing
Pressure-sensitive cellophane
Quick frozen foods
Rotary oil drilling bit
Safety razor
Six-axis robot arm
Soft contact lens
Sonar fish monitoring
Spectographic gird
Stereographic image sensoring

Source: Small Business Association.

GATHERING INFORMATION

The data available about market characteristics, competitors, and so on, is frequently inversely related to the real potential of an opportunity; that is, if market data are readily available and if the data clearly show significant potential, then a large number of competitors will enter the market and the opportunities will diminish.

The good news: Most data will be incomplete, inaccurate, and contradictory, and their meaning will be ambiguous. For entrepreneurs, gathering the necessary information and seeing possibilities and making linkages where others see only chaos are essential.

Leonard Fuld defined competitor intelligence as highly specific and timely information about a corporation.[17] Finding out about competitors' sales plans, key elements of their corporate strategies, the capacity of their plants and the technology used in them, who their principal suppliers and customers are, and a good bit about the new products that rivals have under development is difficult, but not impossible, even in emerging industries, when talking to intelligence sources.[18]

Using published resources is one source of such information. Interviewing people and analyzing data also is critical. Fuld believes that since business transactions generate information which flows into the public domain, one can locate intelligence sources by understanding the transaction and how intelligence behaves and flows.[19]

This can be done legally and ethically. There are, of course, less-than-ethical tactics, which include conducting phony job interviews, getting customers to put out phony bid requests, and lying, cheating, and stealing. Entrepreneurs need to be very careful to avoid such practices and are advised to consult an attorney when in doubt.

Note that the sources of information given below are just a start. Much creativity, work, and analysis will be involved to find intelligence and to extend the information obtained into useful form. For example, a competitor's income statement and balance sheet will rarely be handed out. Rather, they most likely must be derived from information in public filings or news articles or from credit reports, financial ratios, and interviews.[20]

Published Sources

The first step is a complete search of material in libraries. You can find a huge amount of published information, databases, and other sources about industry, market, competitor, and personnel information. Some of this information will have been uncovered in searching for ideas (see the list of sources in Chapter 2). Listed below are additional sources for gathering information to help you get started.

- ***Guides and company information.*** Information is available in special issues of *Forbes* and *Fortune* and in the following:
  - *Thomas Register.*
  - *Directory of Corporate Affiliations.*
  - *Standard & Poor's Register of Corporations, Directors and Executives.*
  - *Standard & Poor's Corporation Records.*
  - *Dun & Bradstreet Million Dollar Directory.*

[17] Leonard M Fuld, *Competitor Intelligence: How to Get It; How to Use It* (New York: John Wiley & Sons, 1985), p. 9.

[18] An excellent resource is Fuld, *Competitor Intelligence.* See also David E Gumpert and Jeffry A Timmons, *The Encyclopedia of Small Business Resources* (New York: Harper & Row, 1984); *Fortune*, "How to Snoop on Your Competitors," May 14, 1984, pp. 28–33; and information published by accounting firms, such as *Sources of Industry Data*, published by Ernst and Whinney.

[19] Fuld, *Competitor Intelligence*, pp. 12–17.

[20] Ibid., p. 325.

- *Dun & Bradstreet Billion Dollar Directory; America's Corporate Families.*
- *Dun & Bradstreet Principal International Businesses.*
- *Dun & Bradstreet Business Information Reports.*
- *Moody's Manuals.*
- *World Almanac.*
- *Encyclopedia of Business Information Sources,* edited by Paul Wasserman.
- *Business Information Sources,* by Lorna Daniels.
- *Directory of Industry Data Sources,* by Harfax.
- *Business Information,* by Michael Lavin.
- *Financial Analyst's Handbook,* by Sumner Levine.
- *Value Line Investment Survey.*
- *Encyclopedia of Small Business Resources,* by David E. Gumpert and Jeffry A. Timmons.

- ***Overviews and general industry information.*** Overviews of American industries, such as:
  - *Moody's Investors Industrial Review.*
  - *Standard & Poor's Industry Surveys.*
  - *US Industrial Outlook,* US Department of Commerce.
  - *Current Industrial Reports,* US Department of Commerce.
  - Census Information from the US Department of Commerce.
  - *County Business Patterns,* US Department of Commerce.
  - *Industry Surveys,* Standard & Poor's.
  - *Forbes Annual Report on American Industry.*
  - *The Wall Street Transcript.*
  - *Inside US Business,* by Philip Mattera.
- ***Statistics and financial and operating ratios.*** Industry statistics listed under the subject heading *statistics* in library catalogs, and under Standard Industrial Classification (SIC) code numbers in publications (see the *Standard Industrial Classification Manual*). Such information also can be obtained from trade associations. There are also guides to statistics, general collections of industry statistics, and sources of composite financial and operating ratios, such as:
  - *Statistical Abstract of the United States,* US Bureau of the Census.
  - *Encyclopedia of Business Information Sources,* edited by Paul Wasserman.
  - *Economic Indicators.*
  - *Statistical Reference Index.*
  - *American Statistics Index.*
  - *Statistics Sources.*
  - *Basebook,* Predicasts.
  - *Statistical Service,* Standard & Poor's.
  - *County Business Patterns,* US Bureau of the Census.
  - US Bureau of the Census publications on certain industries.
  - Competitive assessments of certain industries in the United States by the US International Trade Administration.
  - *Summary of Trade and Tariff Information,* US International Trade Administration.
  - Studies of media and markets by Simmons Market Research Bureau, Inc.
  - *Industry Norms and Key Business Ratios,* Dun & Bradstreet.
  - *Annual Statement Studies,* Robert Morris Associates.
  - *Analysts Handbook,* Standard & Poor's.
  - *Almanac of Business and Industrial Financial Ratios,* published by Prentice-Hall.
- ***Projections and forecasts.*** Projections and forecasts listed under the subject heading in library catalogs and publications, such as:

- *Predicasts Forecasts.*
- *Predicasts F&S Index.*

- ***Market data.*** An overall guide to sources of data on consumer and industrial markets can be found in such publications as:
  - *Data Sources for Business & Market Analysis,* Scarecrow Press.
  - *Basebook,* Predicasts.
  - *US Industrial Outlook Handbook.*
  - *Findex* (Find/SVP).
- ***Consumer expenditures.*** Data on consumer expenditures can be found in such publications as:
  - *Editor & Publisher Market Guide.*
  - *US Census Reports* (*Business, Housing,* etc.).
  - *Survey of Buying Power,* published by Sales Management, Inc.
- ***Market studies.*** Market studies of particular industries and products available from such companies as:
  - Predicasts (Cleveland, Ohio).
  - Simmons Market Research Bureau (New York, New York).
  - Arthur D. Little, Inc. (Cambridge, Massachusetts).
  - Business Communications Company (Stamford, Connecticut).
  - Frost & Sullivan, Inc. (New York, New York).
  - Morton Research Corporation (Merrick, New York).
  - Theta Technology Corporation (Wethersfield, Connecticut).
- ***Data services.*** A listing of on-line databases appeared in the June 1984 *Personal Software.* Data services and databases, such as:[21]
  - Dialog Information Service, Inc. (Knight-Ridder, Inc.).
  - CompuServe Information Service Company (H&R Block, Inc.).
  - Dow Jones News/Retrieval Service (Dow Jones & Company).
  - *Lexis, Nexis, Mesis* (Mead Corporation).
  - The Information Bank (Parsipanny, New Jersey).
  - Information Data Search, Inc. (Brookline, Massachusetts).
  - Economic Information Systems (New York, New York).
- ***Articles.*** Magazine and newspaper articles published by trade associations, government agencies, and commercial publishers. Lists can be found by consulting periodical indexes and directories, such as:
  - *The Directory of Directories.*
  - *Predicasts F&S Index.*
  - *Business Periodicals Index.*
  - *Guide to Special Issues and Indexes of Periodicals.*
  - *Public Affairs Information Service Bulletin.*
  - *Applied Science and Technology Index.*
  - *The Wall Street Journal Index.*
  - *New York Times Index.*
  - *Encyclopedia of Business Information Sources.*
  - *Standard Periodical Directory.*
  - Library directories of current periodical publications.
- ***Other sources:***
  - *Wall Street Transcript.*
  - *CIRR: Company & Industry Research Reports.*

[21] Gumpert and Timmons, *The Encyclopedia of Small Business Resources*, pp. 376–79.

- *Encyclopedia of Associations.*
- *National Trade and Professional Associations of the United States and Canada and Labor Unions.*
- *Ayer Directory of Newspapers, Magazines, and Trade Publications.*
- Brokerage house reports.
- Trade association material.
- Books and other material listed in library catalogues under the name of the industry.
- NASA Industrial Applications Centers and several universities, such as Southeastern Oklahoma State University, the University of New Mexico, the University of Southern California, and the University of Pittsburgh provide technically oriented reports, studies, and literature searches.
- Company annual reports.

■ ***Biographical:***
- *Standard & Poor's Register of Corporations, Directors and Executives.*
- *Dun & Bradstreet Reference Book of Corporation Managements.*
- *Who's Who* directories.

Other Intelligence

Everything entrepreneurs need to know will not be found in libraries, since this information needs to be "highly specific" and "current." This information is most likely available from people—industry experts, suppliers, and the like.

Summarized below are some useful sources of intelligence.

- ***Trade associations.*** Trade associations, especially the editors of their publications and information officers, are good sources of information.[22] Especially, trade shows and conferences are prime places to discover the latest activities of competitors.
- ***Employees.*** Employees who have left a competitor's company often can provide information about the competitor, especially if the employee departed on bad terms. Also, a firm can hire people away from a competitor. While consideration of ethics in this situation is important, certainly the number of experienced people in any industry is limited, and competitors must prove that a company hired a person intentionally to get specific trade secrets in order to challenge any hiring legally. Students who have worked for competitors are another source of information.
- ***Consulting firms.*** Consulting firms frequently conduct industry studies and then make this information available. Frequently, in such fields as computers or software, competitors use the same design consultants, and these consultants can be sources of information.
- ***Market research firms.*** Firms doing the market studies, such as those listed under published sources above, can be sources of intelligence.
- ***Key customers, manufacturers, suppliers, distributors, and buyers.*** These groups are often a prime source of information.
- ***Public filings.*** Federal, state, and local filings, such as filings with the Securities and Exchange Commission (SEC) or Freedom-of-Information Act filings, can reveal a surprising amount of information. There are companies that process inquiries of this type.
- ***Reverse engineering.*** Reverse engineering can be used to determine costs of production and sometimes even manufacturing methods. An example of this practice is the exper-

[22] Ibid., pp. 46 and 48.

ience of Advanced Energy Technology, Inc., of Boulder, Colorado, which learned first-hand about such tactics. No sooner had it announced a new product, which was patented, when it received 50 orders, half of which were from competitors asking for only one or two of the items.

- ***Networks.*** The networks mentioned in Chapter 2 as sources of new venture ideas also can be sources of competitor intelligence.
- ***Other.*** Classified ads, buyers guides, labor unions, real estate agents, courts, local reporters, and so on, can provide clues.[23]

CASE—FIBERCOM APPLICATIONS, INC.

Preparation Questions

1. Evaluate the business opportunity, the business plan, and the start-up strategy. How would you improve the business plan?
2. What should Smith and McCormack do now?
3. What fund-raising strategy and sources of financing should they consider and not consider? Why?
4. As a private investor, what valuation would you accept, and what would your position be in negotiating with Fibercom? As a venture capitalist?

FIBERCOM APPLICATIONS, INC.

In late January 1985, Gary Smith contacted his former professor to seek some advice on his and his partners' efforts to launch a company in the rapidly emerging fiber optics industry. After catching up on the prior 10 years, Smith summarized their situation:

> "My partner, Tom McCormack, and I had worked together at BIW Cable for several years, and had *often* talked about the idea of starting our own company. After BIW went public in 1983 the place seemed to slide into a fat 'n' happy approach to the business. It was difficult to get top management interested in some niches in the market that Tom and I believed existed.
>
> So last spring, we decided to put a business plan together, raise $750,000, and do it. Tom actually resigned in May of 1984 and began concentrating on this full-time. The plan was for me to stay on until we raised the money. Tom, myself, and four other partners put up about $100,000 of seed money to enable us to raise the rest."

"When will you run out of cash?" the professor queried. After a considerable silence, and some modest clearing of the throat, Smith reckoned, with his eyes now glued to an apparent object on the floor, "We are about out now." He continued to explain that no other money was in sight, because

> Raising money has turned out to be more challenging than we had anticipated. We have sent the business plan to 35 venture capital firms in the Boston area, as well to 30 New York venture capital firms. Not one of these 65 firms has shown any interest—which has been shocking to me. Why is it so difficult? What do you suggest that we do at this point?

"If I had a look at your business plan, I might have an idea or two," responded the professor. Smith reached into his pocket and handed the professor the latest version of the

[23] Fuld, *Competitor Intelligence,* pp. 369–418.

business plan, conspicuously dated January 1985. Attached is a copy of Fibercom Applications, Inc., business plan.

Fibercom Applications, Inc., Business Plan, January, 1985

Company
Fibercom Applications, Inc.
1625 Aero Drive
Raleigh, NC 27623
919-555-8200

Contact
Mr. Thomas J. McCormack, President

Business

Fibercom Applications was formed in May 1984 to manufacture fiber optic cables and cable assemblies for the data communication, process control, and other specialty markets.

Sales are forecast to grow to $50,000,000 within five years.

Manufacturing fiber optic cables requires special equipment and highly skilled, competent, and experienced design, production, and management personnel. Fibercom Applications has proprietary knowledge of the design, manufacture, and marketing of fiber optic cables.

The company will make use of unique materials to custom design fiber optic cables for use by specific market segments. By choosing these segments, the management's experience is that the company can sell its products at higher margins than those available in other parts of the fiber optic cable market.

Only a small number of competitors are serving the company's target industries. The company will compete with these firms by offering a variety of cable types and by possessing an in-depth knowledge of its customers' requirements. Because of the experience and specialized skills necessary to produce fiber optic cables it is difficult for other companies to readily enter the fiber optic cable business.

Selected Financial Data
Dollars are in thousands:

Year	*1*	*2*	*3*	*4*	*5*
Sales	1,750	3,500	10,000	25,000	50,000
Earnings	(25)	244	1,017	3,507	7,394

Management

The company has three key managers. Together, they sold and produced more than $2,000,000 of specialty fiber optic cable in 1983, representing about 10 percent of the available market in that year. The management is exceptionally experienced in manufacturing specialty fiber optic cables.

Thomas J. McCormack, founder and president, has more than six years experience in specialty cable manufacturing, including four years in fiber optics. He has been general manager of the Fiber Optics Division of BIW Cable Systems, a specialty cable manufacturer, where he started their fiber optic efforts. He has sold to, and produced cable for, all of the company's targeted markets.

Gary A. Smith, vice president of sales and marketing, has more than four years experience in the sales and marketing of specialty cables, including fiber optic cable. He has sold to all of the company's targeted markets. In 1983, at BIW Cable Systems, he was the top-ranked sales manager in the country, increasing his territory's sales by 21 percent, to $7.1 million.

Clint M. Owens, vice president of engineering, has 20 years experience with wire and cable, including 6 years with fiber optics. He started the fiber optics group at Brand Rex Company, and directed the growth of his division to more than $2,000,000 in 1984. He has extensive experience in selling to, and producing fiber optic cables for, the company's targeted markets.

Funds Required

Fibercom Applications requires $750,000 of additional funding to begin operations. The company proposes to issue 300,000 shares of common stock, representing 10.7 percent ownership, for this funding. Alternate structuring will be considered.

Use of Funds

The funds will be used as follows:

Capital equipment	$530,000
Working capital	220,000

Business Plan—Table of Contents

Title	Section
Summary	1
Financing Requirements	2
Business	3
Market Size and Competition	4
Sales Projections	5
Capital Equipment	6
Year 0 Operations	7
Years 1–5 Operations	8
Risk Factors	9
Appendix A: Financial Projections	10
Appendix B: Management Résumés	11

1. Summary

Fibercom Applications (the "company") will design, manufacture, and market fiber optic cables and cable assemblies. Fiber optic cables use hair-thin flexible glass fibers to transmit information as light pulses or as a modulated beam of light. Fiber optic cable assemblies have fiber optic connectors attached to the ends of the cable.

The company will serve selected segments of the rapidly growing fiber optic market. The company's targeted market segments are the computer interconnection/local area network and process control areas. These emerging market niches are not being adequately served by current suppliers and provide the best opportunities for highly profitable sales of the company's unique and proprietary cables.

Manufacturing fiber optic cables requires special equipment, along with highly skilled, competent, and experienced design, manufacturing, and management personnel. Fibercom Applications has extensive experience in and possesses proprietary knowledge of the design, manufacture, and marketing of fiber optic cables.

Fibercom Applications will manufacture fiber optic cables for specialty applications. By providing custom engineered products, Fibercom Applications will be recognized as the technical expert in each market. Through its technical superiority, the company will be better able to anticipate market needs, to identify potential market niches, and to sell at premium margins.

The management of the company is exceptionally experienced in providing fiber optic cables to these markets. The company's three key employees have combined experience of more than 15 years in the design, manufacture, marketing, and selling of fiber optic cables to the target markets. Two of the key employees have previous experience in starting up a specialty fiber optic cable manufacturing operation. In 1983, the three key employees sold more than $2,000,000 of specialty fiber optic cables, representing about 10 percent of the available market.

The company will have a limited number of competitors in its target industries (see "Market Size and Competition," Section 4). Some of these competitors are larger than the company and have access to more financial resources than the company. Others, while having current sales in excess of the company's, do not possess the technical and marketing skills of Fibercom Applications. Because manufacturing fiber optic cables requires special equipment and unique skills, it is very difficult for new manufacturers, including existing electrical wire and cable companies, to enter the market. The management of the company believes it can successfully compete with both existing and possible future manufacturers in its targeted markets on the basis of superior technology and variety of fiber products, and by providing outstanding service to its customers.

The company's sales are forecast to grow to $50 million in Year 5. To permit operations as outlined herein, $750,000 of capital is required immediately. This capital will be used for the following:

A. Purchase of equipment	$530,000
B. Working capital	220,000
Total	$750,000

This capital will fund the company's operations for 18 months, when additional capital will be required. This additional capital may have to be raised by selling additional equity.

2. Financing Requirements

Fibercom Applications has completed seed financing totaling $150,000 and requires additional equity capital of $750,000. The company will use short-term debt, provided by commercial banks, to meet cash flow requirements.

Fibercom Applications, a Delaware corporation, was incorporated in May 1984. The company has an authorized level of 2,000 shares of common stock, of which 1,250 shares are currently issued and outstanding and 110 shares are reserved for sale under existing warrant and option agreements.

Existing ownership of the company is as follows:

Shareholder	*Number of Shares*
Thomas J. McCormack	325
Gary A. Smith	325
Clint M. Owens	100
All others (total = 6 people)	500
Reserved for issue	110
Total	1,360

Prior to raising the additional capital, the company intends to split its stock at a ratio of 2,000 new shares for each currently existing share, to reserve 250,000 shares for an incentive stock plan for future employees, and to raise the company's authorized level of stock to 5 million shares.

The company proposes to raise $750,000 by selling 300,000 shares of newly issued common stock at a price of $2.50 per share. After issuing these shares, the company's capitalization will be:

2.8 million shares of common stock, issued and outstanding:		
Par value, $0.01 per share		$ 28,000
Additional paid-in capital		827,000
Total capital		$900,000
The ownership of the company will then be:		
Existing shareholders	2,500,000	$150,000
New shareholders	300,000	750,000
Total	2,800,000	$900,000

3. Business

Fibercom Applications designs, manufactures, and markets fiber optic cables to a select number of market segments. In the broadest sense, fiber optic cables are used by two distinct markets—the telephone industry and specialty markets. These two areas are different, both technically and commercially. While cables for the telephone industry offer state-of-the-art optical performance, the cables are sold as a commodity at low margins. In the specialty market, the cables may have less-stringent optical requirements, but other performance needs must be met. Fibercom Applications will serve selected areas of the specialty market. The company will treat each market niche independently, both in terms of cable design and in selling techniques. Fibercom Applications will be recognized as the expert in each segment, will be able to anticipate market needs, and will identify and participate in the profitable niches of each.

Communication technology has rapidly changed in the last decade. The increasing use of telephone systems, computers, and other systems that utilize low-power digital signals, in place of systems where high-power analog signals convey information, has imposed stringent new requirements on the communication media.

For these modern systems, conventional electrical interconnections may not be satisfactory without extensive equipment modification or costly installation changes, or both. The low-power digital signals are particularly susceptible to electromagnetic interference. Further, all electronic equipment radiates electromagnetic noise, and the US government has recently established strict limits on the amount of radiation that can be emitted from electronic equipment. Electrical interconnecting cables accentuate this emission problem. Fiber optic communication systems overcome this and other problems associated with electrical equipment.

Fiber optics is a relatively new technology offering a number of advantages over the traditional electrical method of transmitting information. Fiber optic systems (see "Fiber Optic Systems," below) can carry more information than electrical systems and are immune to electromagnetic and radio frequency interference. Fiber optic cables do not radiate electromagnetic signals as electrical cables do. Fiber optic cables are smaller and lighter than electrical cables, thereby reducing installation costs. Fiber optic cables also have lower losses than the electrical cables they replace, and can therefore transmit signals of a given strength over longer distances than electrical cables.

Fiber Optic Markets

The market for fiber optic cables is expected to grow to $1 billion by 1990 (see "Market Size and Competition," Section 4). Fibercom Applications has divided the total market into four segments.

1. Telecommunications. The telecommunications market may be subdivided into two areas.

*(a) **Long-Haul Communications.*** This market segment is characterized by high-capacity, high-fiber-count cables. These cables usually contain over 24 signal mode fibers. The cables are installed with long distances between terminals, so the cables must be produced in the longest practical lengths, 2 km or more. Optical performance of these cables is state-of-the-art, and cable performance is the most important evaluation criterion.

*(b) **Subscriber Loop.*** This part of the telephone market uses cables with relatively high fiber counts, ranging from 6 to 24 fibers per cable. The cables contain either single mode or high performance graded index fibers. These applications are growing rapidly as terminal equipment, connecting devices, and splicing equipment become more readily available.

The telephone market segment is by far the largest, accounting for up to 75 percent of the total market. There are seven suppliers to this market area, and the company does not intend to capture a significant part of this market. It is likely that the company will have limited sales to the telephone industry, in those applications where special performance is needed, or where a special design is required.

2. Computer Interconnection/Local Area Networks. The interconnection of mainframe, minicomputers, microcomputers, and peripherals by local area networks is predicted to grow explosively in the next few years. The success of the "office of the future" depends upon reliable, secure, and high-speed transmission of data between the CPU and peripheral devices.

Electrical interconnections are limited in their ability to meet these criteria. Electrical cable is limited in the amount of data that can be carried and in the distance the data can be sent without amplification. The data also is subject to error from interference picked up by the cable, and the cables themselves radiate electromagnetic noise. Fiber optics eliminates these problems.

The cables for this market have relatively low fiber counts, ranging from 2 to 12 fibers per cable, and are installed in a wide variety of environments. The cables typically use larger core fibers than the telecommunications products.

The management of Fibercom Applications has experience in serving this market area. The company has designed and developed a unique product for interoffice connections and intends to aggressively promote this product to the computer interconnection market. The company intends to fully serve this market. Competitors and market size are discussed in Section 4.

3. Process Control. With the expanding use of microprocessor-based control systems and programmable controllers in factory and plant environments, fiber optics is making significant inroads into the process control industry primarily because of its noise immunity and high data transfer capacity.

The cables for this market usually have low fiber counts, from 1 to 12 fibers per cable, and must be custom designed for each application. For example, a process control system may have a basic requirement for a two-channel cable. If the control system is being installed in a nuclear generating station, the cable must be radiation resistant, while if the control system is being installed in a chemical refinery, the cable may have to withstand exposure to hazardous vapors. While the same basic design may be used for each cable, different materials may have to be used in each application to meet the specific environmental requirements.

The management of Fibercom Applications has extensive experience in serving many different parts of the process control industry. Using its specialized knowledge of materials and constructions, the company has designed a number of unique cables for use in industrial environments. The company will supply a significant portion of the fiber optic cable used in this market.

The size and competition in this market segment are discussed in Section 4.

4. Military. The military market presents a variety of applications. The cables are characterized by low fiber counts, 1 to 12 fibers, and frequently use special radiation-resistant large-core fibers. The cables are subject to stringent performance requirements, including low temperature, severe bending and twisting, and fungus attack.

The company intends to serve the military market where special performance is needed. The company will provide extremely rugged, gas- and/or water-blocked cables, and cables suitable for performance over a wide temperature range. Competition and market size are discussed in Section 4.

In each of its target markets, the company's management has successful prior experience in designing, manufacturing, and selling cables. The target markets are growing rapidly, as shown in Section 4. In the target markets, the management's experience is that higher gross margins are available, and that the company's extensive knowledge of special materials and cable design can be sold at a premium.

Fiber Optics Systems

Fiber optic cable is one part of an overall fiber optic system. Fiber optic communications requires a system consisting of three parts—an optical transmitter, an optical fiber cable, and an optical receiver. The transmitter takes incoming electrical signals and converts them to optical pulses. The fiber optic cable carries the light pulses from the transmitter to the receiver. The receiver reverses the process, converting the optical pulses back to electrical signals. Operational failure of any one part of the system is catastrophic. Any individual part is useless unless the other parts are functional. Transmitters and receivers with outstanding reliability are now commercially available at low cost. Cable technology, however, has not been highly developed for nontelephone applications. Fibercom Applications will provide the highly reliable cables that will assure high system reliability.

Great progress has been made in designing and manufacturing optical fiber, the primary component of the cable. Cost reductions of 90 percent and more have been made over the last three years, while, during the same time, quality and performance of the fiber has improved.

Because of their delicate structure, optical fibers cannot be used without the protection of properly designed cable. Fiber optic cable development efforts have been limited to cables used for long-distance telecommunications. The design of cables containing optical fibers for specialty market applications has not progressed.

The designer of cables for use in the specialty markets must consider many parameters, including installation conditions, environmental temperatures, flame retardancy, radiation resistance, water resistance, and chemical resistance. In fact, to maximize cable reliability, specific and unique cables must be designed for each application.

The lack of properly designed cables has impeded the use of fiber optics in the nontelephone market. For instance, local area networking of computers is an application that can benefit from using fiber optics. In recognition of this need, the American National Standards Committee has formed a working group to write a standard for fiber optics in the local area network (LAN). This committee is of national stature, and its work will accelerate the use of fiber in LANs. In reporting on the committee's work, the *Electronic Engineering Times*, of May 14, 1984, quotes the committee as saying "the lack of satisfactory commercially available fiber optic cable" is the main reason for slow implementation of fiber optics in this application.

Once a suitable cable has been developed, it may not be usable for all applications in a market. In one system the fiber optic cable may be installed beneath carpets, in air-handling ducts, in walls, in conduits, in cable trays, and under floors. The cable design must be tailored to make the cable suitable for each application. This entails selecting alternative materials, changing the relative position of the fibers, or varying the strength characteristics.

Fiber Optic Cable Design

The design of fiber optic cables is similar to that of electrical cables, but with several significant differences. In most electrical cables no consideration is given to the physical strength of the cable, since the electrical conductor provides sufficient strength. Electrical cables are simply designed to provide a dielectric covering over the conductor by using an insulating material applied to the conductor, by physically separating the conductors, or by combining both methods.

In comparison, many factors must be considered when designing a fiber optic cable. The glass optical fiber has little inherent strength and is easily damaged by external forces. Therefore, a fiber optic cable must be designed to maximize the protection of the fiber. Excessive coiling or stretching will damage the fiber. Thermal expansion and contraction of the other cable materials relative to the optical fiber may damage the fiber. Materials must be selected in view of their physical and thermal performance, and the fiber must be precisely located in the cable to achieve maximum isolation from its environment.

Fibercom Applications has designed cables with a variety of materials that are thermally compatible with the optical fiber and that provide a high level of protection to the fiber. These designs provide a higher level of protection than that provided by our competitors' cables.

Fibercom Applications will custom design fiber optic cables to meet its customers' service requirements. The company will provide features in its products that are unavailable from its competitors, including:

1. Unique Applications of Materials

Fibercom Applications will manufacture cables using the widest variety of materials available in the fiber optic market.

Every material must be processed in a different manner, and small variations in processing will cause scrap. Process development for each material is both costly and time-consuming and requires considerable experience both in extrusion and in fiber optics. For this reason, most companies do not offer a wide range of materials.

The management of Fibercom Applications has extensive experience in processing a variety of materials. The company is experienced in developing methods and techniques to utilize many materials in fiber optic cables, and the company will continue to develop these processes. Where practical, the company will seek to protect its processes with patents.

2. Heavy-Wall Loose Tubes

The company's targeted markets demand cables that are extremely rugged and highly reliable.

To provide these features, Fibercom Applications will manufacture fiber optic cables that have a thick, loose tube protecting the fiber. Extruding thick, loose tubes over optical fibers is very difficult and requires careful attention to processing. All the residual stress in the materials must be eliminated, and the loose tubes must be made under precise and controlled conditions. Moreover, the company will manufacture these tubes in a variety of materials.

The heavy-wall loose-tube feature makes the cable slightly more expensive to build, but its higher reliability permits it to be sold at a higher price.

The management of the company has experience in designing and building cables with heavy-wall loose tubes. This experience will be used to efficiently produce this product with little or no scrap.

3. Flame Retardancy

Many of the company's target markets demand cables with a high degree of flame retardancy. The company will manufacture highly flame-retardant cables for "plenum" use at a lower cost than its competition. The company, therefore, can achieve a higher profit margin on this product.

Fibercom Applications also will manufacture cables that meet the stringent flame test requirements for Type TC cable, allowing the company's product to be used in the same way as electrical cables and without the extra costs associated with installing a separate cable mounting system.

Other companies produce flame-retardant fiber optic cables. However, their choice of materials is very limited. To differentiate its products, Fibercom Applications will work with the customer to select a material that achieves all the customer's needs and will try to persuade the customer to specify the company's unique materials for its cables.

4. Specialization in Large-Core Fibers

Fibercom Applications will manufacture cables with large-core optical fibers. Large-core fibers are used extensively in short-distance applications typical of many of the company's targeted markets. Large-core fibers are very susceptible to damage from handling; therefore, manufacturing cables incorporating these fibers is more difficult than making cables with small-core fibers. Because of the manufacturing difficulties, many manufacturers of fiber optic cables do not offer cables with large-core fibers.

The management of Fibercom Applications has extensive experience in successfully building cables with large-core fibers. The company is experienced with these fibers and in selecting machinery and processes compatible with them. By choosing the proper equipment, and specializing in making these cables, the company will be more efficient than others and therefore more profitable.

Fibercom Applications will also provide many other features in its products. The company's management has many years of experience in designing and manufacturing fiber optic cables. The company has already designed cables that consider these properties for specific applications, and it has perfected techniques to economically manufacture the cables. These products include:

1. *Undercarpet cables.* The company has designed and built a fiber optic cable for use in undercarpet office applications. This special design uses a unique material and construction that has been successfully tested by a major supplier of undercarpet systems.
2. *Molded cable assemblies.* The company has designed an assembly with connectors molded to the end of the cable that promises to be more rugged, durable, and reliable

than existing assemblies. The company believes this product will have great acceptance in the computer interconnection market and in the process control industry.

3. *Plenum cables.* The company has designed a series of plenum cables using less-expensive materials than other cables of this type. Prototype cables must be built and tested to make this product commercial.

Manufacturing

Fiber optic cable manufacturing differs significantly from making electrical cables. Because the fiber is delicate and cannot be reclaimed if damaged, properly designed, operated, and maintained equipment must be used in making fiber optic cables. This equipment must have precise tension controls, along with other sensitive control mechanisms, to achieve a high-quality thermally stable covering over the fiber. Profitability depends upon error-free manufacturing with little scrap.

Satisfactory performance of the finished cable depends upon achieving a uniform material over the optical fiber. The uniformity of the material depends on many factors, but of primary importance is the proper extrusion process. Control of the entire extrusion process is critical. Extrusion tool design must be tailored to the material and its dimensions. Temperature of the melting extrudate must be precisely controlled to avoid residual stress. Cooling characteristics must be tailored to each material. These controls are not normally imposed or needed for electrical cable manufacturing.

Fiber optic cables must be manufactured in a cleaner environment than electrical cables. Moreover, fiber optic cables cannot be made in the same area with electrical cables. Any airborne contaminants that come in contact with the optical fiber may damage it, with resulting scrap.

The company has developed a unique method of manufacturing one- and two-channel optical cables more efficiently than its competitors. Both cable types are widely used in many of the company's targeted markets, and the company expects to capture a large portion of this business.

Fibercom Applications will only manufacture fiber optic cables. The company will be expert in the handling of optical fiber. It will enforce housekeeping and cleanliness standards that could not be enforced in a plant making both electrical and optical cables.

The management of the company has combined experience of more than 10 years in building fiber optic cables and in designing and installing the proper equipment to make them efficiently. The company's specialization, experience, and efficiency will be its competitive advantage.

Marketing and Sales

Fibercom Applications will market its products primarily on the basis of technical superiority. The company will establish a reputation of supplying a high-quality product that is delivered on time.

A major goal of the company's marketing plan is to produce the company's products as specified by its customers. To accomplish this, it will identify specific customers in each target market area and work closely with each customer's engineers in preparing performance specifications for their cables.

Repeat orders from a customer are an important part of the company's growth philosophy. To promote goodwill and allegiance and, thereby, to obtain repeat orders, the company will organize and direct its efforts to provide outstanding service to its customers.

To achieve brand recognition, the company will actively promote its products through advertising and trade show participation. The company plans regular mailings of informational literature to its customers.

Fibercom Applications will sell its products through an integrated network of direct salespeople, manufacturers' agents, and distributors.

The company will hire direct salespeople to serve several areas where the use of agents and distributors is impractical. They will be responsible for sales to computer manufacturers (IBM, DEC, Wang), to process control manufacturers (Honeywell, Foxboro), and to other large customers (architect-engineers, electric utilities).

Manufacturers' agents will sell to all of our other accounts, particularly those that buy smaller quantities of cable and those that do not require continuous technical sales efforts. The vice president of sales and marketing will supervise these agents and monitor their progress. The company expects that it will take at least a year to complete a representative network.

The company also will support distributor sales to those industries that prefer to buy in this way.

The company does not intend to serve all the targeted markets at once. The company will concentrate its efforts in the process control and computer markets. These markets promise the fastest returns on the sales efforts, for several reasons. First, the company's management has extensive experience in selling to both the process control and computer markets. Second, both areas are currently purchasing sufficient volumes of cable to permit the company's revenue targets to be met. Third, the markets are not being adequately served by the existing suppliers.

4. Market Size and Competition

Fibercom Applications will serve selected areas of the market for specialty fiber optic cable assemblies. The company's target markets include the computer interconnection, process control, military, and broadband markets.

All areas of the fiber optic cable market are experiencing extremely high growth rates that are expected by many market research firms to continue for the next decade. Several market research organizations (Kessler Marketing Intelligence, Gnostic Concepts, A. D. Little, Frost and Sullivan) have made predictions about the growth. These studies estimate that the total market for fiber optic cables in 1984 was about $240 million. The studies also indicate that the telephone industry accounted for about 80 percent of the 1984 market and that the market for the company's products was between $40 and $60 million in 1983.

The company believes that in 1984 the market for its products was approximately $48 million, up 85 percent from 1983. The company's estimate was determined by consolidating internal estimates with the published figures of several sources. The internal estimates were made by personal knowledge of the market, evaluating competitors' size, and discussions with fiber manufacturers.

The market for fiber optic cables is growing at a rapid pace. Published growth rates range from 40–65 percent per year. The company's own estimate is on the conservative end of this range; Fibercom Applications estimates that its targeted markets will grow at an annual rate of 40 percent. The size of the company's market is shown in *Table 4–A*.

Competition

Fibercom Applications will have several competitors for the nontelephone market. The three largest competitors are Siecor, Belden, and ITT.

Siecor. Siecor is a joint venture of Corning Glass Works and the Siemens Corporation. Corning is the second largest supplier of optical fiber in the United States (after AT&T Technologies) and Siemens is a German-based cable manufacturer. With the exception of AT&T Technologies, Siecor is the largest manufacturer of fiber optic cables in the United States.

Siecor concentrates its efforts in the telephone business, but with excess cable capacity to date, it is also the largest supplier of nontelephone cables. The explosive growth of sales

Table 4–A
Projected Size of the Company's Market

Year	Estimated Target Market
1983	$ 26,000,000
1984	48,000,000
1985	70,000,000
1986	100,000,000
1987	160,000,000
1988	220,000,000
1989	300,000,000
1990	400,000,000

to the telephone market, however, has impaired Siecor's ability to serve the specialty market and opens this part of their business to invasion by other manufacturers.

Siecor offers a variety of cables and currently competes in many of Fibercom's targeted markets. Siecor builds both loose and tight buffered cables and uses a relatively large number of materials in its cables. However, Fibercom Applications believes it can compete with Siecor on the basis of customer service and delivery.

Belden. Belden is a unit of Cooper Industries. It does not manufacture fiber optic cables for the telephone industry but concentrates its efforts in markets similar to Fibercom's. Belden's fiber optic sales in 1984 were between $5 million and $8 million. Belden is well-known in the fiber optic cable business.

Belden produces both tight and loose buffered cables but uses only a small number of materials. Therefore, it is at a disadvantage when competing with Fibercom Applications. It has an established sales and distribution network, which will help it in competing with Fibercom.

ITT. ITT acquired Valtec Corporation, which was a division of US Philips, in September 1984. Combined with its own fiber optic cable business, ITT became a major supplier of fiber optic cable. Valtec concentrates its major sales efforts in the telephone industry, with lesser efforts in the military and computer interconnection markets. Prior to its acquisition, Valtec had several ownership changes in the last few years, and the continuity of management, necessary in the specialty business, has been difficult to maintain. Fibercom Applications estimates Valtec's total sales in 1984 to be $15 million, with nontelephone sales of between $4 million and $6 million. ITT had nontelephone sales of between $1 million and $2 million in 1984, so the combined company has nontelephone sales of between $5 million and $8 million.

ITT will concentrate its efforts in the long-distance telecommunications field, with a lesser effort in the military area. Fibercom Applications does not expect to compete directly against ITT in the data communications or process control markets.

Other Competitors. Several other companies sell fiber optic cables to the company's targeted markets. These companies include Times Fiber Communications, Phalo (a division of Transitron), Mohawk (a division of Conductron), BIW Cable Systems, Brand Rex, Pirelli, General Cable, Anaconda-Ericcson, Optical Cable Corporation, and Whitmore. While the exact size of each company is unknown, Fibercom's estimates of 1984 sales for each are shown in *Table 4–B.* Based on this analysis, the total size of the company's targeted nontelephone markets was between $37 million and $59 million.

Of these companies, General Cable and Anaconda-Ericcson continue to concentrate their sales efforts in the telephone industry and will play ever smaller roles in the specialty markets. Fibercom's superior market knowledge and variety of materials will be used in competing with these companies. Brand Rex, BIW Cable Systems, Phalo, Mohawk, and

Table 4–B
Sales to the Nontelephone Markets

Company	1984 Estimated Sales Low	1984 Estimated Sales High
Siecor	$15,000,000	$20,000,000
ITT-Valtec	5,000,000	8,000,000
Belden	5,000,000	8,000,000
General Cable	2,000,000	4,000,000
Times Fiber	2,000,000	3,000,000
Brand Rex	1,500,000	2,000,000
Phalo	1,000,000	2,500,000
Mohawk	1,000,000	2,000,000
Maxlight	1,000,000	2,000,000
Pirelli	1,000,000	2,000,000
Anaconda-Ericcson	1,000,000	2,000,000
Optical Cable	750,000	1,500,000
BIW Cable	250,000	500,000
Whitmore	250,000	500,000
Others	500,000	1,000,000
Total	$37,250,000	$59,000,000

Whitmore have not made the commitment of manufacturing and engineering resources that is necessary to compete in the fiber optic market. Brand Rex and BIW have extensive skills in processing many materials. However, unless they make major investments in plant and personnel for the fiber optic business, they will not be able to challenge Fibercom on a performance basis. Of the other companies, Phalo and Whitmore do not possess the technical or material processing skills of the company. Mohawk has withdrawn from the fiber optic business. Fibercom Applications will use its knowledge and experience in fiber optics to compete against these companies.

Optical Cable Corporation (OCC) is a relatively new company, formed in 1983, and by virtue of its specialization in fiber optics, it will be a factor in Fibercom's markets. The management of Fibercom Applications has more experience in the company's target markets, however, and their specialized marketing skills will be used in competition with OCC.

At the present time, the company is aware of only three other potential competitors, Madison Wire and Cable, Berk-Tek, and Celwave Technologies. The company anticipates that one or more of these companies could become a major competitor.

5. Sales Projections

Fibercom Applications has established the following five-year sales forecast (see *Table 5–A*):

Table 5–A
Sales Forecast

Year	Fibercom Applications Forecast
1	$ 1,750,000
2	3,500,000
3	10,000,000
4	25,000,000
5	50,000,000

This is a compound annual growth rate of more than 130 percent and requires substantial investment in plant, the hiring of extremely talented personnel, and an effective sales effort.

The sales projections result in a Year 5 market penetration of more than 10 percent. This market share can be achieved within the company's marketing and manufacturing resources. The availability of trained design engineers and qualified sales personnel may make it difficult to attain higher growth rates in the specialty markets.

The company's potential customers range from large industrial and utility companies with multibillion-dollar revenues, to small privately owned companies with sales under $1 million. These potential customers will be contacted through an integrated marketing and sales campaign, including space advertising, trade show participation, and direct sales contact. More information concerning the company's marketing and sales efforts are in Section 3.

6. Capital Equipment Requirements

Special equipment must be employed to produce the highest-quality fiber optic cables. Of particular importance, tension controls must be present on all fiber handling equipment to avoid damaging the fiber.

Fibercom Applications has extensive capital equipment requirements. Initial capital expenditures include the following:

1. A small plastic extrusion line, approximately 1.5 inches, for the primary application of buffering material over the fiber. The extruder must be able to process high-temperature fluoropolymer materials. Support equipment includes a water bath, fiber payoff and tensioning equipment, extrusion tools, pullout equipment, and a traversing take-up.
2. A medium-size plastic extrusion line for secondary extrusion of cable jackets. This equipment also must be able to handle fluoropolymer resins, plus conventional jacketing materials. Support equipment similar to that on item 1 is required.
3. A fiber optic cabler, capable of stranding 18 fibers in one operation. Each payout bay must have precise tension controls. The line also will include taping equipment to apply both metallic and nonmetallic coverings over the cable's core.
4. A serving head, for use in the cabling machine or in the extrusion lines, to apply strength members to the cable.
5. Test equipment for performing bandwidth, attenuation, numerical aperture, and pulse dispersion measurements on optical fiber. Mechanical testing equipment, to test both cables and cable materials, and an optical time domain reflectometer are also needed.

The primary extrusion equipment (item 1, above) and test equipment (item 5, above) will be purchased as new equipment. Used equipment suitable for these purposes is not available. A used jacket extrusion line and cabler will be purchased for the initial operations.

The lead time for the equipment ranges from one to four months. The first equipment that must be installed is the small, primary extrusion line. After this line is installed, the secondary extrusion line and the fiber optic cabler will be installed.

With the use of overtime and multiple shifts, the initial equipment will support shipments through Year 1. To support the projected sales in Years 2 through 5, additional equipment is needed.

7. Year 0 Operations

The company's initial year (ending July 31, 1985) is an organizational year. Because of the high growth rates the company will experience, it is essential that proper systems and procedures be implemented immediately to achieve the financial goals that have been established. Efforts in this year will be concentrated in seven key areas:

1. Obtaining capital.
2. Recruiting key personnel.
3. Locating manufacturing space.
4. Purchasing and installing equipment.
5. Manufacturing trial products for internal and external evaluation.
6. Designing and executing an advertising campaign.
7. Obtaining initial production orders.

Meeting the sales forecast depends upon meeting several milestones in the initial year, shown in *Table 7–A*. Failure to meet these milestones may have an adverse effect on later operations.

Initial sales of the company will be produced by other manufacturers on a private-label basis. These sales will generate cash flow and establish Fibercom Applications in the marketplace. However, because others will be manufacturing the product, none of the company's proprietary cables can be sold at this time.

Year 0 operating expenses are in four areas:

1. Salaries of executive officers.
2. Design and implementation of an advertising campaign.
3. Salaries of start-up production and test personnel.
4. Materials used in product trial manufacturing.

Pro forma financial statements for Year 0 are included in Section 10.

8. Years 1–5 Operations and Organization

Section 10 contains pro forma financial statements for Years 1 through 5. These projections have been made using the assumptions outlined below.

A. Cost of Goods Sold

The actual material costs for the assumed product mix were calculated. Also from the product mix, machine loadings were calculated and the labor necessary to operate the machinery was determined.

B. Operating Expenses

Engineering. Engineering and R&D are the responsibility of, and under the direction of, the vice president of engineering.

The vice president of engineering is responsible for all technical operations of the company and fulfills five functions. First, he or she maintains contact with chemical, compound, and other raw material suppliers to be aware of new materials as they become available. Second, he or she is responsible for all cable designs. Third, he or she recruits, trains, and supervises all application and process engineers. Fourth, he or

Table 7–A
1985 Milestones (Year 0)

Date	*Milestone*
March 1	Receive start-up capital
March 1	Begin advertising campaign
May 1	Install primary extruder
June 1	Begin trial extrusions
June 30	Produce initial production orders

she recruits, trains, and supervises all test personnel. Last, because the marketing of the company's products will be technically oriented, he or she has extensive customer contact.

The company initially will employ an experienced process engineer. He or she will report to the vice president of engineering and be responsible for all process development. This person must be highly skilled, with a strong technical background in plastic extrusion and possess hands-on experience with extrusion equipment. He or she also will participate in the company's development efforts to evaluate new materials and their applicability to fiber optic cables.

Test personnel and application engineers will be added as needed to support the production and sales efforts. By Year 5, the company expects to employ 56 engineers and technicians.

Sales. The vice president—sales and marketing is responsible for the sales, marketing, and customer service operations of the company.

The vice president of sales and marketing is technically knowledgeable about fiber optics and is experienced with the sales and marketing of products by manufacturers' agents, direct sales personnel, and distributors.

The vice president recruits and trains all sales personnel. He or she plans and directs the company's marketing plan, including an aggressive advertising campaign. He or she writes sales literature, prepares technical and commercial proposals, and sets price levels.

The company's initial sales efforts will be made through a network of manufacturers' agents, directed and coordinated by the vice president. The vice president is directly responsible for sales to the larger customers until a direct sales force is put in place.

Advertising and trade show participation are important parts of the company's sales efforts. Brand recognition will be gained by regular advertising in user-oriented industrial trade publications and by participation in trade shows.

The company will employ direct salespeople as quickly as possible. The vice president will coordinate the efforts of both the direct salespeople and the manufacturer's agents. Inside sales efforts will be organized and staffed to complement the outside sales efforts.

By Year 5, the company expects to employ 35 people in sales and have a national network of manufacturer's agents.

Administrative. Administrative overhead includes manufacturing management, accounting, bookkeeping, purchasing, and production coordination.

Initially, the president will directly supervise the administrative and manufacturing efforts. A vice president of manufacturing is added to the company in Year 1, who will be responsible for all manufacturing operations.

Additional overhead expenses include telephone and telex service, office expenses (copying, postage, stationery, etc.), legal and accounting services, and insurance costs.

Depreciation. Depreciation is calculated on a five-year, straight-line basis.

9. Risk Factors

There are several risk factors to consider in making an investment in the company.

No Operating History

Fibercom Applications is a start-up company and has no operating history. All financial statements presented herein are estimates of future operations. If anticipated revenues are not received, if actual costs exceed projections, or if delays are encountered in developing the company's products, additional financing may be necessary.

To minimize this risk, strict controls will be imposed over material costs, labor costs, inventories, and other costs. Operations will be managed to maximize cash flow.

Limited Management Experience

The management of the company, while experienced in the manufacturing and sales of fiber optic cables, has no experience in organizing and starting up a new venture.

Mr. McCormack's experience with his former employer, where he started a fiber optics division, and Mr. Owens's experience with his former employer, where he started a fiber optics manufacturing operation, will be used to offset this risk. Both of these people have extensive contacts in the fiber optics and cable manufacturing business, and this experience will be used to the company's benefit. Additionally, outside directors and advisors will be sought to provide management guidance and assistance.

Market Growth

The success of the company depends on the projected growth of the overall market for fiber optic systems.

To minimize this risk, the company has based its projections on the low end of the projected growth of the industry. If this growth level is not achieved, a higher level of market share, sales to other markets, and sales of other specialty cables will be sought.

Raw Material Availability

The company will depend on outside sources for its major raw material, optical fiber. Disruption of this supply will adversely affect the company's ability to produce its products.

The company will attempt to negotiate annual supply contracts for optical fiber with one or more suppliers. There is no assurance that these contracts can be negotiated, or that they can be made on terms favorable to the company. Alternatively, significant additional investments will have to be made in both equipment and personnel to manufacture optical fiber.

Dependence upon Key Employees

The success of the company depends upon the continued employment of Messrs. McCormack, Smith, and Owens. Employment and noncompetition agreements will be negotiated with each to assure this continuity.

Other key employees must be hired, and the company will offer favorable compensation programs to attract and retain these employees.

10. Appendix A: Financial Projections

The financial projections were made using the following assumptions:

Income Statement

Sales. Sales projections were made based upon the company's estimate of the current market size and its growth projections. Conservative estimates were made of the company's market share.

Cost of Goods. Cost of goods was calculated from actual cable constructions. Material costs were determined from suppliers of these materials. Labor costs were estimated at current labor rates, increased at 5 percent per year to represent a real increase. Inflation has not been considered.

Operating Expenses. The actual staffing needed to produce the estimated sales was determined, and actual labor costs were used to determine expenses in each category. Labor costs were escalated at 5 percent per year, as above.

Depreciation. Depreciation on all equipment was calculated on a five-year, straight-line basis.

Interest Income. Interest income was calculated at 5 percent of the previous year's cash balance.

Taxes. Taxes were calculated at 46 percent of pre-tax income, less investment tax credits and operating loss carryforwards.

Projected Income Statement
Seven Months Ending July 31, 1985

	Jan.	*Feb.*	*March*	*April*	*May*	*June*	*July*
Sales	$ 3,500	$ 7,500	$ 13,500	$ 28,500	$ 23,500	$ 20,000	$ 50,000
Cost of goods sold:							
Fiber						2,000	10,000
Other material						540	2,698
Direct labor						1,517	1,517
Indirect labor					1,750	4,250	4,250
Space	3,000	3,000	3,000	3,000	3,000	3,000	3,000
Benefits					350	1,153	1,153
Purchased products	0	3,600	9,000	22,500	18,000	13,500	22,500
Total cost of goods sold	3,000	6,600	12,000	25,500	23,100	25,960	45,118
Gross profit	500	900	1,500	3,000	400	(5,960)	4,882
Operating expenses:							
Engineering	4,525	4,525	4,525	4,525	4,525	4,575	4,775
Sales	5,888	5,888	5,888	5,888	5,888	6,438	6,638
Lease costs	0	0	0	0	0	0	5,018
Administration	8,850	10,850	10,850	10,850	12,500	12,500	12,500
Depreciation	83	83	83	5,292	5,292	5,292	5,500
Total operating expenses	19,346	21,346	21,346	26,555	28,205	28,805	34,431
Operating profit	(18,846)	(20,446)	(19,846)	(23,555)	(27,805)	(34,765)	(29,549)
Interest expense (income)	(350)	(309)	(278)	(4,028)	(2,545)	(2,236)	(1,919)
Net income before taxes	(18,496)	(20,137)	(19,568)	(19,527)	(25,260)	(32,529)	(27,630)
Taxes	0	0	0	0	0	0	0
Net income after taxes	$(18,496)	$(20,137)	$(19,568)	$(19,527)	$(25,260)	$(32,529)	$(27,630)

Projected Cash Flow
Seven Months Ending July 31, 1985

	Jan.	*Feb.*	*March*	*April*	*May*	*June*	*July*
Sources of cash:							
Increase in equity	$ 0	$ 0	$750,000	$ 0	$ 0	$ 0	$ 0
Increase in debt	0	0	0	0	0	0	0
Net income	(18,496)	(20,137)	(19,568)	(19,527)	(25,260)	(32,529)	(27,630)
Depreciation	83	83	83	5,292	5,292	5,292	5,500
Increase in current liabilities	10,250	13,851	19,250	33,385	(22,792)	17,794	37,897
Total sources	(8,163)	(6,203)	749,765	19,150	(42,760)	(9,443)	15,767
Uses of cash:							
Capital expenditures	0	0	0	312,500	0	0	12,500
Increase in accounts receivable	0	0	0	0	0	5,000	25,000
Increase in inventory	0	0	0	1,270	7,619	16,508	25,397
Total uses	0	0	0	313,770	7,619	21,508	62,897
Cash flow	(8,163)	(6,203)	749,765	(294,620)	(50,379)	(30,951)	(47,130)
Beginning cash	70,000	61,837	55,635	805,400	510,780	460,401	429,450
Ending cash	$ 61,837	$ 55,634	$805,400	$ 510,780	$460,401	$429,450	$382,320

Projected Balance Sheet
Seven Months Ending July 31, 1985

	Jan.	*Feb.*	*Mar.*	*Apr.*	*May*	*June*	*Jul.*
				Assets			
Current assets:							
Cash	$ 61,837	$ 55,635	$ 805,400	$ 510,780	$ 460,401	$ 429,450	$ 382,320
Accounts receivable						5,000	30,000
Inventory				1,270	8,889	25,397	50,794
Total current assets	61,837	55,635	805,400	512,050	469,290	459,847	463,114
Property, plant, and equipment:							
At cost	5,000	5,000	5,000	317,500	317,500	317,500	330,000
Less accumulated depreciation	83	167	250	5,542	10,834	16,125	21,625
	4,917	4,833	4,750	311,958	306,666	301,375	308,375
Total assets	$ 66,754	$ 60,468	$ 810,150	$ 824,008	$ 775,956	$ 761,222	$ 771,489
				Liabilities and Shareholders' Equity			
Current liabilities:							
Accounts payable	$	$ 3,600	$ 12,600	$ 35,100	$ 49,500	$ 56,540	$ 69,238
Accrued expenses							
Accrued salaries	10,250	20,500	30,750	41,000			
Short-term debt				635	4,444	15,198	40,397
Total current liabilities	10,250	24,100	43,350	76,735	53,944	71,738	109,635
Shareholders' equity:							
Contributed capital	120,000	120,000	870,000	870,000	870,000	870,000	870,000
Retained earnings	(63,496)	(83,632)	(103,200)	(122,727)	(147,988)	(180,516)	(208,146)
Total shareholders' equity	56,504	36,368	766,800	747,273	722,012	689,484	661,854
Total liabilities and shareholders' equity	$ 66,754	$ 60,468	$ 810,150	$ 824,008	$ 775,956	$ 761,222	$ 771,489

Projected Income Statement
Twelve Months Ending July 31, 1986

	Aug.	*Sept.*	*Oct.*	*Nov.*	*Dec.*	*Jan.*	*Feb.*	*Mar.*	*Apr.*	*May*	*June*	*Jul.*
Sales	$ 50,000	$100,000	$150,000	$150,000	$150,000	$150,000	$165,000	$165,000	$170,000	$165,000	$165,000	$170,000
Cost of goods sold:												
Fiber	16,667	33,333	50,000	50,000	50,000	50,000	55,000	55,000	56,667	55,000	55,000	56,667
Other materials	4,497	8,995	13,492	13,492	13,492	13,492	14,842	14,842	15,291	14,842	14,842	15,291
Direct labor	2,687	5,373	10,053	10,053	10,053	10,053	10,053	10,053	11,093	10,053	10,053	11,093
Indirect labor	4,250	4,250	4,250	4,250	4,250	4,250	4,250	4,250	4,250	4,250	4,250	4,250
Space	3,333	3,333	3,333	3,333	3,333	3,333	3,333	3,333	3,333	3,333	3,333	3,333
Benefits	1,387	1,925	2,861	2,861	2,861	2,861	2,861	2,861	3,069	2,861	2,861	3,069
Total cost of goods sold	32,821	57,209	83,989	83,989	83,989	83,989	90,339	90,339	93,703	90,339	90,339	93,703
Gross profit	17,179	42,791	66,011	66,011	66,011	66,011	74,661	74,661	76,297	74,661	74,661	76,297
Operating expenses:												
Engineering	11,330	11,829	13,767	13,766	13,766	13,766	13,916	13,916	13,966	13,915	13,915	13,966
Sales	9,618	12,889	18,660	18,910	19,160	19,410	19,810	20,060	20,360	20,560	20,810	21,110
Administration	15,484	17,984	18,484	18,484	18,484	18,484	18,634	18,634	18,684	18,634	18,634	18,657
Lease cost	5,018	5,018	5,018	5,018	5,018	5,018	5,018	5,018	5,018	5,018	5,018	5,018
Depreciation	8,208	8,208	8,208	8,417	8,417	8,417	8,625	8,625	8,625	8,834	8,834	8,834
Total operating expenses	49,658	55,928	64,137	64,595	64,845	65,095	66,003	66,253	66,653	66,961	67,211	67,585
Operating profit	(32,479)	(13,137)	1,874	1,416	1,166	916	8,658	8,508	9,644	7,700	7,450	8,712
Interest expense (income)	(1,012)	340	1,147	2,461	3,275	3,669	3,704	3,827	3,891	3,955	3,965	3,935
Net income before taxes	(31,467)	(13,477)	727	(1,045)	(2,109)	(2,753)	4,954	4,581	5,753	3,745	3,485	4,777
Taxes	0	0	0	0	0	0	0	0	0	0	0	0
Net income after taxes	$(31,467)	$ (13,477)	$ 727	$ (1,045)	$ (2,109)	$ (2,753)	$ 4,954	$ 4,581	$ 5,753	$ 3,745	$ 3,485	$ 4,777

Projected Cash Flow
Twelve Months Ending July 31, 1986

	Aug.	Sept.	Oct.	Nov.	Dec.	Jan.	Feb.	Mar.	Apr.	May	June	Jul.
Sources of cash:												
Increase in equity	$ 0	$ 0	$ 0	$ 0	$ 0	$ 0	$ 0	$ 0	$ 0	$ 0	$ 0	$ 0
Increase in debt	0	0	0	0	0	0	0	0	0	0	0	0
Net income	(31,467)	(13,477)	727	(1,045)	(2,109)	(2,753)	4,954	4,581	5,753	3,745	3,485	4,777
Depreciation	8,208	8,208	8,208	8,417	8,417	8,417	8,625	8,625	8,625	8,834	8,834	8,834
Increase in current liabilities	39,804	71,870	103,294	92,328	47,752	3,174	14,378	14,378	17,407	528	1,587	2,116
Total sources	16,545	66,601	112,229	99,700	54,060	8,838	27,957	27,584	31,785	13,107	13,906	15,727
Uses of cash:												
Capital expenditures	162,500	0	0	12,500	0	0	12,500	0	0	12,500	0	0
Increase in accts. rec.	50,000	70,000	150,000	100,000	50,000	0	15,000	15,000	20,000	0	0	0
Increase in inventory	23,279	21,164	0	0	3,175	6,349	1,058	1,058	(2,116)	1,058	3,175	4,233
Total uses	235,779	91,164	150,000	112,500	53,175	6,349	28,558	16,058	17,884	13,558	3,175	4,233
Cash flow	(219,234)	(24,563)	(37,771)	(12,800)	885	2,489	(601)	11,526	13,901	(451)	10,731	11,494
Beginning cash	382,320	163,086	138,523	100,752	87,952	88,837	91,326	90,725	102,251	116,152	115,701	126,432
Ending cash	$ 163,086	$138,523	$100,752	$ 87,952	$88,837	$91,326	$90,725	$102,251	$116,152	$115,701	$126,432	$137,926

Projected Balance Sheet
Twelve Months Ending July 31, 1986

	Aug.	Sept.	Oct.	Nov.	Dec.	Jan.	Feb.	Mar.	Apr.	May	June	Jul.
Assets												
Current assets:												
Cash	$ 163,086	$ 138,523	$ 100,752	$ 87,952	$ 88,837	$ 91,326	$ 90,725	$ 102,251	$ 116,153	$ 115,702	$ 126,433	$ 137,927
Accounts receivable	80,000	150,000	300,000	400,000	450,000	450,000	465,000	480,000	500,000	500,000	500,000	500,000
Inventory	74,073	95,238	95,238	95,238	98,413	104,762	105,820	106,878	104,763	105,820	108,995	113,228
Total current assets	317,159	383,761	495,990	583,190	637,250	646,088	661,545	689,129	720,916	721,522	735,428	751,155
Property, plant, and equipment:												
At cost	492,500	492,500	492,500	505,000	505,000	505,000	517,500	517,500	517,500	530,000	530,000	530,000
Less accumulated depreciation	29,833	38,042	46,250	54,667	63,084	71,501	80,126	88,751	97,377	106,210	115,044	123,877
	462,667	454,458	446,250	450,333	441,916	433,499	437,374	428,749	420,123	423,790	414,956	406,123
Total assets	$ 779,826	$ 838,219	$ 924,240	$1,033,523	$1,079,166	$1,079,587	$1,098,919	$1,117,878	$1,141,039	$1,145,312	$1,150,384	$1,157,278
Liabilities and Shareholders' Equity												
Current liabilities:												
Accounts payable	$ 72,402	$ 98,690	$ 126,984	$ 169,312	$ 190,477	$ 190,476	$ 196,825	$ 203,175	$ 211,640	$ 211,640	$ 211,640	$ 211,640
Accrued expenses	0	0	0	0	0	0	0	0	0	0	0	0
Short-term debt	77,037	122,619	197,619	247,619	274,206	277,381	285,410	293,439	302,381	302,910	304,497	306,614
Total current liabs.	149,439	221,309	324,603	416,931	464,683	467,857	482,235	496,614	514,021	514,550	516,137	518,254
Shareholders' equity:												
Contributed capital	870,000	870,000	870,000	870,000	870,000	870,000	870,000	870,000	870,000	870,000	870,000	870,000
Retained earnings	(239,613)	(253,090)	(252,363)	(253,408)	(255,517)	(258,270)	(253,316)	(248,736)	(242,982)	(239,238)	(235,753)	(230,976)
Total equity	630,387	616,910	617,637	616,592	614,483	611,730	616,684	621,264	627,018	630,762	634,247	639,024
Total liabilities and shareholders' equity	$ 779,826	$ 838,219	$ 942,240	$1,033,523	$1,079,166	$1,079,587	$1,098,919	$1,117,878	$1,141,039	$1,145,312	$1,150,384	$1,157,278

11. Appendix B: Management Résumés

Thomas J. McCormack

Professional Experience

BIW Cable Systems, Inc.

July 1983–May 1984

General Manager, Fiber Optics Division

Promoted to general manager—Fiber Optics Division in July 1983. Managed all efforts of the company in fiber optics. Prepared and executed a business plan that saw sales grow from less than $150,000 in 1982 to over $400,000 in 1983. Purchased and supervised the installation of initial extrusion lines and cabling equipment. Hired and trained test technician and production personnel. Managed all engineering, marketing, and sales activities of the company's fiber optic products. Developed new product for interoffice data communications.

Worked closely with the national sales manager, vice president—marketing, and marketing managers to set sales targets and direct the sales efforts.

Had full P&L responsibility beginning in January 1984. Prior to this time, I had complete control over the fiber optics operations, but the division operations were not separately stated. I worked closely with the controller in determining and instituting procedures to define the division operation.

In this position, I worked closely with major fiber suppliers to determine acceptable products. Met with major foreign manufacturers to determine potential license arrangements.

1978–1983

Marketing Manager, Utility and Fiber Optic Products

Responsible for all marketing activities of the company for both electrical products to electric utility companies and for fiber optic products to all of the company's customers.

Utility Products

Doubled the company's sales of all products to electric utility companies, while at the same time increasing the gross margin from 30 percent to over 50 percent. Responsible for developing and executing yearly marketing plans, setting five-year sales goals, outlining new product needs, producing sales literature, setting price levels, supervising application engineering activities, monitoring development of new materials and products, preparing quotations, and administering contracts. Introduced three major lines of new products, including standard cables that came to account for 50 percent of utility sales. Decreased utility related overhead by 25 percent. Expanded customer base from only architect-engineers to include direct sales to major utilities. Negotiated the largest contract in the company's history. As a matrix organization, participated with manufacturing in production planning for both short- and long-term needs. Supervised the utility sales efforts of 10 district sales managers.

Fiber Optic Products

Participated in company task force in 1979–80 to determine potential involvement with fiber optic products. Recommended to president to proceed with fiber optic business on a limited basis. The recommendation was accepted and I was designated to spend part-time in continuing investigation, and to secure limited initial orders. Sold first fiber optic cable in 1981. Recommended increased marketing activities in 1982 and planned initial capital expenditures made in 1982. Wrote company's first marketing plan in 1982, identifying target markets and setting five-year sales projections. Supervised the engineering and development efforts in fiber optics. Directed the sales activities of district sales managers. Made direct sales presentations to all categories of customers—process control, television networks, electric utilities, computer OEMs, and so on. Prepared sales literature, set price levels, and wrote sales quotations. Had production, sales, marketing, and engineering people reporting to me on a matrix basis.

Public Service Electric and Gas Company
1970–1978

Senior Staff Engineer, Systems Engineering Group

Worked in Systems Engineering for a large, integrated utility company. Varied technical responsibilities, including:

Wire and Cable

Determined acceptable materials and construction for all low-voltage cables used in power generating stations. Acted as consultant to operating division to investigate problems or service failures. Performed engineering studies related to cable materials and design features (ampacity, temperature rating, environmental qualification). Prepared specifications for purchase.

Determined acceptable vendors and evaluated bids. Purchased materials worth approximately $5 million per year.

Worked closely with purchasing, legal, and construction departments within the company, and with manufacturers, other utilities, and architect-engineers outside the company.

Major accomplishments included expansion of acceptable vendors list, with an estimated cost savings of over $1 million in 1976–77, and qualified alternate constructions with estimated cost savings of over $500,000 per year.

Power Transformers

Similar duties and responsibilities as for wire and cable. Performed engineering studies to determine acceptable parameters and designs. Prepared specifications and evaluated manufacturer's proposals. Worked closely with operating departments regarding field service problems, and with the construction department on installation of large transformers.

Purchased and installed more than $10 million of power transformers per year.

Major accomplishments included the expansion of the acceptable vendors list, with subsequent savings of over $1 million per year. Specified and purchased the largest power transformers installed in the United States.

Other Responsibilities

Prepared general construction specifications for labor and materials. Prepared the general terms and conditions required for purchase of all engineered equipment. Performed special studies regarding power system operations.

Education

Rensselaer Polytechnic Institute, Troy, New York
Master of Electrical Engineering, 1970
Philip Sporn Fellowship
Bachelor of Science, Electrical Engineering, 1969
Eta Kappa Nu

Personal

Member—IEEE
—IEEE Power Engineering Society
—IEEE Industry Applications Society
—IEEE Communications Society
Voting Member—IEEE PES Insulated Conductors Committee
Chairman—IEEE Working Group 12-32
—IEEE Standard 383
—Qualification of Nuclear Power Plant Cables
Chairman—IEEE Working Group 14-2
—Fiber Optics in Power Plants

Gary A. Smith

Professional Experience

BIW Cable Systems
Manufacturing, Boston, Massachusetts

May 1982–present

District Sales Manager

Reporting to the vice president of sales and marketing, responsible for sales of all product lines in seven-state region, including New England and New York State (1983 sales $7.1 million). Direct interface with target markets and accounts. Establish forecasts, set key accounts, and formulate overall strategy for various product classes in territory. Supervise and manage three representative agencies (nine field salespeople).

March 1980–May 1982

Inside Sales Manager, Utility and Fiber Optic Products

Complete responsibility for proposals, contract administration, and customer service for market segment with $6–7 million in annual sales.

Supervise support personnel with dotted-line responsibility for customer service department.

Review proposals, establish pricing levels and directions. Establish programs for major contracts and monitor performance of various internal disciplines until completion. Interface with customers on all contract-related matters and advise and direct engineering, manufacturing, and quality assurance departments.

RCA Corporation, Automated Systems Division
Manufacturing, Burlington, MA

January 1979–March 1980

Senior Level Product Specialist

Responsible for procuring of $1–2 million annually of highly specialized optical and precision fabricated components for combat and field support devices.

Texas Instruments Inc.
Manufacturing, Attleboro, MA

June 1976–January 1979

Buyer

Responsible for procuring $4–5 million annually of contracted services for Facilities Group, electromechanical components and capital equipment. Direct interaction with engineering and manufacturing. Preparation of technical specifications. Responsible for vendor selection and development, contract negotiation, quality and delivery assurance, and cost reduction programs.

Education

Northeastern University, Boston, Massachusetts
  Master of Business Administration/Finance awarded June 1976
Bucknell University, Lewisburg, Pennsylvania
  Bachelor of Science in Civil Engineering awarded June 1974

Clint M. Owens

Qualifications in Brief

Successful development and marketing of new Fiber Optic products. Successfully managed the production scale-up of new ideas developed in the laboratory.

Extensive experience in solving engineering problems in high temperature wire and cable, including Kapton and Teflon insulations.

Employment

1975–1984

Brand Rex Company
Willimantic, Connecticut

1975–1976

R&D Engineer—Responsible for new-product development, principally high-temperature wire and cable.

1976–1982

Senior Product Engineer—Developed new products, principally for the military market. During this time, products developed accounted for an increase in sales from $1 million to $10 million per year.

1978–1982

Fiber Optics
Product Engineer—Was the company leader in their entry into fiber optics. Planned, had funds authorized, purchased equipment, and set up the fiber optics operations. Designed and sold fiber optic cables for the data communications industry. Current annual sales over $2 million. Hold a patent for transmission cable aimed at the computer market.

1982–1984

New Product Marketing Manager, Fiber Optics—Promoted to marketing manager while retaining my engineering responsibilities. Work closely with customers in new designs, determine if new products can be made. Thrust is toward proprietary products. Designed and marketed a major new product for LAN use.

1972–1975

Hitemp Wires, Inc.,
Happauge, New York

Director, Technical Services—Principally charged with maintaining an accurate material usage versus estimated costs. Established cost accounting, manufacturing engineering specifications, and departmental procedures. Twenty-five percent of the time was spent with sales, reporting to the vice president of sales and engineering. My sales experience involved working closely with customers on new products. Developed many new products, including Power Buss Assembly (extruded Tefzel bonded to flat cable), Shurheat Heater Cable, Fire Alarm Cable (NY Law 5), and Ullage Cable (Tefzel insulated cable for measuring amount of oil in tankers).

Experience in screw extrusion, cabling, cable assembly, braiding, and quality control.

1972

Dor-Flex Electronics of California
Santa Ana, California

Director of Engineering—Designed new equipment for maximum efficiency for polyimide dispersions, taping, sealing, and etching. Maintained liaison with equipment manufacturers and production group to maximize production output. Dor-Flex purchased Carolina Wire and Cable in December 1971.

1969–1971

Carolina Wire and Cable, Inc.
Santa Ana, California

Wire & Cable Engineer—Developed new Teflon dispersion, high-speed Liquid II applications, new taping methods, and instituted new QC test methods. Designed the power cable system for the Grumman F-14. Also developed the cables used by Sperry Flight Systems and TRW on the Pioneer spacecraft. All polyimide insulations used by General Dynamics, Fort Worth, Texas, for Aerojet (GTR-22) were my developments.

1965–1969

E. I. Dupont de Nemours & Co., Inc.
Wilmington, Delaware

Senior Technical Assistant—Worked directly for Dr. Lewis on the development and testing of Kapton. The airframe wiring used by Lockheed on the L-1011 was the primary project. I performed all testing for the "Orange" report. Developed new splice methods for Kapton. Also worked on electrical applications of films, including Mylar, polypropylene, fluorocarbons, and so on.

Education
Penn Morton College
Completed two and one-half years of general engineering

EXERCISE—VENTURE OPPORTUNITY SCREENING GUIDE

The Venture Opportunity Screening Guide (VOSG) is based on the screening criteria discussed in Chapter 3.

As you proceed through the VOSG, you will come to checkpoints. At each checkpoint, you can evaluate whether to proceed with your evaluation, change the definition of your opportunity in some way, or abandon it. When you pass all checkpoints in the VOSG, the extent of your opportunity's attractiveness should be much more apparent. Rarely is it simply cut and dried, however. Most of the time, there will be considerable uncertainty and numerous unknowns and risk involved even at this point. What the process can do is help you to understand those uncertainties and risks in making your decision and to devise ways to make them acceptable for you. If they cannot be made acceptable, then you keep searching.

Deciding where your opportunity falls will take a considerable amount of work. Plan to spend at least 20–30 hours in completing the VOSG. Depending upon the nature of your opportunity and your knowledge and access to critical information, completing the VOSG may require more effort, but probably not less. While this time commitment may seem large, the amount of time ultimately consumed in evaluating an opportunity by trial and error is almost always greater, and the tuition is much higher.

Every venture is unique. Operations, marketing, cash flow cycles, and so forth, vary a good bit from company to company, from industry to industry, and from region to region or country to country. As a result, you may find that not every issue pertinent to your venture will be covered in the VOSG or that some questions are irrelevant. Here and there, you may have to add to the VOSG or tailor it to your particular circumstances.

We suggest that you and each of the members of your team should fill out a VOSG.

As with other exercises in the book, feel free to make as many Xerox copies of the VOSG as you need.

EXERCISE
VENTURE OPPORTUNITY SCREENING GUIDE

Name:

Venture:

Date:

STEP 1: BRIEFLY DESCRIBE YOUR OPPORTUNITY CONCEPT WITHOUT MENTIONING THE SPECIFIC PRODUCT(S) OR SERVICE(S). An example of an opportunity concept would be the one seen by the founders of Outdoor Scene via delivery, quality, and service in the leisure-time industry. Such a summary will usually be between 50 and 100 words in length and include what compelling conditions and circumstances are propelling the opportunity and why the opportunity exists, now, for you. Most concepts begin in a fuzzy, ill-defined way, which is normal and acceptable. Once you have completed the remaining sections of the guide, you can return to this summary and refine it.

STEP 2: FILL IN THE VENTURE OPPORTUNITY PROFILE BELOW BY INDICATING FOR EACH INDIVIDUAL CRITERION WHERE YOUR VENTURE IS LOCATED ON THE *POTENTIAL* CONTINUUM. Make an *x* to indicate your best estimate of where your idea stacks up. Be as specific as possible. (If you have trouble, relevant trade magazines and newsletters, other entrepreneurs, trade shows, fairs, or other sources can help.)

Criterion	Venture Opportunity Profile: *Highest Potential*	*Lowest Potential*
Industry and Market		
Market: Need	Market driven; identified; recurring revenue niche	Unfocused; one-time revenue
Customers	Reachable; purchase orders	Loyal to others or unreachable
User benefits	Less than one year payback	Three years plus payback
Value added	High; advance payments	Low; minimal impact on market
Product life	Durable	Perishable
Market structure	Imperfect, fragmented competition or emerging industry	Highly concentrated or mature or declining industry
Market size	\$100+ million to \$1 billion sales potential	Unknown, less than \$20 million or multibillion sales
Growth rate	Growth at 30 to 50% or more	Contracting or less than 10%
Market capacity	At near or full capacity	Undercapacity
Market share attainable (Year 5)	20% or more; leader	Less than 5%
Cost structure	Low-cost provider; cost advantages	Declining cost
Economics		
Profits after tax	10–15% or more; durable	Less than 15%; fragile

Criteria	Highest Potential	Lowest Potential
ROI potential	25% or more; high value	Less than 15 to 20%; low value
Capital requirements	Low to moderate; fundable	Very high; unfundable
Internal rate of return potential	25% or more per year	Less than 15% per year
Free cash flow characteristics	Favorable; sustainable; 20–30+% of sales	Less than 10% of sales
Sales growth	Moderate to high (15+% to 20+%)	Less than 10%
Asset intensity	Low/sales $	High
Spontaneous working capital	Low, incremental requirements	High requirements
R&D/capital expenditures	Low requirements	High requirements
Gross margins	Exceeding 40% and durable	Under 20%
Time to breakeven—cash flow	Less than 2 years; breakeven not creeping	Greater than 4 years; breakeven creeping up
Time to breakeven—P&L	Less than 2 years; breakeven not creeping	Greater than 4 years; breakeven creeping up
Harvest Issues		
Value-added potential	High strategic value	Low strategic value
Valuation multiples and comparables	p/e 20+ ×; 8–10+ × EBIT; 1.5–2+ × revenue free cash flow 8–10+ ×	p/e = 5×, EBIT = 3–4×; revenue = .4

(Continued)

Criterion	Highest Potential	Lowest Potential
Exit mechanism and strategy	Present or envisioned options	Undefined; illiquid investment
Capital market context	Favorable valuations, timing, capital available; realizable liquidity	Unfavorable; credit crunch
Competitive Advantage Issues		
Fixed and variable costs	Lowest; high operating leverage	Highest
Control over costs, prices, and distribution	Moderate to strong	Weak
Barriers to entry: Proprietary protection	Have or can gain	None
Response/lead time	Competition slow; napping	Unable to gain edge
Legal, contractual advantage	Proprietary or exclusivity	None
Contacts and networks	Well-developed; accessible	Crude; limited
Key people	Top talent; an A team	B or C team
Management Team		
Entrepreneurial team	All-star combination; free agents	Weak or solo entrepreneur
Industry and technical experience	Top of the field; super track record	Underdeveloped
Integrity	Highest standards	Questionable
Intellectual honesty	Know what they do not know	Do not want to know what they do not know
Fatal-Flaw Issue	Non-existent	One or more
Personal Criteria		
Goals and fit	Getting what you want; but wanting what you get	Surprises, as in *The Crying Game*

Upside/downside issues	Attainable success/limited risks	Linear; on same continuum
Opportunity costs	Acceptable cuts in salary, etc.	Comfortable with status quo
Desirability	Fits with lifestyle	Simply pursuing big money
Risk/reward tolerance	Calculated risk; low R/R ratio	Risk averse or gambler
Stress tolerance	Thrives under pressure	Cracks under pressure
Strategic Differentiation		
Degree of fit	High	Low
Team	Best in class; excellent free agents	B team; no free agents
Service management	Superior service concept	Perceived as unimportant
Timing	Rowing with the tide	Rowing against the tide
Technology	Groundbreaking; one-of-a-kind	Many substitutes or competitors
Flexibility	Able to adapt; commit and decommit quickly	Slow; stubborn
Opportunity orientation	Always searching for opportunities	Operating in a vacuum; napping
Pricing	At or near leader	Undercut competitor; low prices
Distribution channels	Accessible; networks in place	Unknown; inaccessible
Room for error	Forgiving strategy	Unforgiving, rigid strategy

STEP 3: ASSESS THE EXTERNAL ENVIRONMENT SURROUNDING YOUR VENTURE OPPORTUNITY. Include the following:

- An assessment of the characteristics of the opportunity window, including its perishability:

- A statement of what entry strategy suits the opportunity, and why:

- A statement of evidence of and/or reasoning behind your belief that external environment and the forces creating your opportunity, described in **Step 1** and in the Venture Opportunity Profile, fit:

- A statement of your exit strategy and an assessment of the prospects that this strategy can be met, including a consideration of whether the risks, rewards, and trade-offs are acceptable:

CHECKPOINT: BEFORE YOU PROCEED, BE SURE THE OPPORTUNITY YOU HAVE OUTLINED IS COMPELLING AND YOU CAN ANSWER THE QUESTION, WHY DOES THE OPPORTUNITY EXIST NOW? IT IS JUST POSSIBLE YOU OUGHT TO ABANDON OR ALTER THE PRODUCT OR SERVICE IDEA BEHIND YOUR VENTURE AT THIS POINT. THE AMOUNT OF MONEY AND TIME NEEDED TO GET THE PRODUCT OR SERVICE TO MARKET, AND TO BE OPEN FOR BUSINESS, MAY BE BEYOND YOUR LIMITS. REMEMBER, EVEN IN THE ABUNDANT VENTURE CAPITAL MARKET OF THE MID-1980S, ONLY 1–3 PERCENT OF ALL VENTURES RECEIVED FUNDING. REMEMBER, ALSO, THAT THE FIRST ROUND OF FINANCING IS TYPICALLY IN THE $1 MILLION TO $2 MILLION RANGE AND, TO RAISE OVER $5 MILLION, YOU NEED A TRULY EXCEPTIONAL MANAGEMENT TEAM AND A CONCEPT WHOSE POTENTIAL REWARDS ARE LARGE COMPARED TO THE RISKS AND VULNERABILITIES TO OBSOLESCENCE AND COMPETITION.

STEP 4: ASSESS THE ATTRACTIVENESS OF YOUR VENTURE OPPORTUNITY BY APPLYING SCREENING CRITERIA. Include the following:

- A brief description of the market(s) or market niche(s) you want to enter:

- An exact description of the product(s) or service(s) to be sold and, if a product, its eventual end use(s). (If your product(s) or service(s) are already commercially available or exist as prototypes, attach specifications, photographs, samples of work, etc.)

- An estimate of how perishable the product(s) or service(s) are, including if it is likely to become obsolete and when:

- An assessment of whether there are substitutes for the product(s) or services(s):

- An assessment of the status of development and an estimate of how much time and money will be required to complete development, test the product(s) or service(s), and then introduce the product(s) or service(s) to the market:

Development Tasks		
Development Task	$ Required	Months to Complete

- An assessment of any major difficulties in manufacturing the product(s) or delivering the service(s) and how much time and money will be required to resolve them:

- A description of the necessary customer support, such as warranty service, repair service, and training of technicians, salespeople, service people, or others:

- An assessment of the strengths and weaknesses, relative to the competition, of the product(s) or service(s) in meeting customer need, including a description of payback of and value added by the product(s) or service(s):

- An assessment of your primary customer group:
  - A description of the main reasons why your primary group of customers will buy your product or service, including whether customers in this group are reachable and receptive and how your product or service will add or create value, and what this means for your entry or expansion strategy:

– A list of 5 to 10 crucial questions you need to have answered and other information you need to know to identify good customer prospects:

– An indication of how customers buy products or services (e.g., from direct sales, either wholesale or retail; through manufacturers' representatives or brokers; through catalogs; via direct mail; etc.):

– A description of the purchasing process (i.e., where it occurs and who is ultimately responsible for approving expenditures; what and who influence the sale; how long does it take from first contact to a close, to delivery, and to cash receipt; and your conclusions about the competitive advantages you can achieve and how your product or service can add or create value):

- An assessment of the market potential for your venture's product or service, the competition, and what is required to bring and sell the product or service to the customer. (Such an analysis need not be precise or comprehensive but should serve to eliminate from further consideration those ventures that have obvious market difficulties.) Include the following information:
  - An estimate, for the past, present, and future, of the *approximate* size of the *total* potential market, as measured in units and in dollars or number of customers. In making your estimates, use available market data to estimate *ranges* of values and to identify the area (country, region, locality, etc.) and data for each segment if the market is segmented:

	Total Market Size				
	Year				
	19	19	19	19	19
Sales of Units/ Number of Customers					
Sales in Dollars					

Sources of Data:

Researcher:

Confidence in Data:

– An assessment of the type of market in terms of price, quality, and service; degree of control, and so on; and your conclusions about what approaches are necessary to enter, survive, and win:

- An assessment, based on a survey of customers, of how your customers do business, and of what investigative steps are needed next:

	Customer Survey		
	Customer		
	No. 1	No. 2	No. 3
Nature of Customers			
Business or Role			
Reactions: Positive Negative Questions			

Specific Needs/Uses			
Acceptable Terms—Price, Support, Etc.			
Basis of Purchase Decisions: Time Frame Who Makes Decision Dollar Limits			
Substitutes/Competitive Products or Services Used			

Names of Competitors			
Competitive Products			
Substitute Products			

Customers Surveyed	
No.	Name

- An assessment of how your product or service will be positioned in the market, including:
  - A statement of any proprietary protection, such as patents, copyrights, or trade secrets, and what this means in the way of a competitive advantage:

– An assessment of any competitive advantages you can achieve in the level of quality, service, and so forth, including an objective description of any strengths (and weaknesses) of the product or service:

– An assessment of your pricing strategy versus those of competitors:

	Pricing Strategy		
	Highest Price	Average Price	Lowest Price
Retail			
Wholesale			
Distributor			
Other Channel			
Manufacturing			

– An assessment of where competitors in your industry or market niche are in terms of price versus performance/benefits/value added:

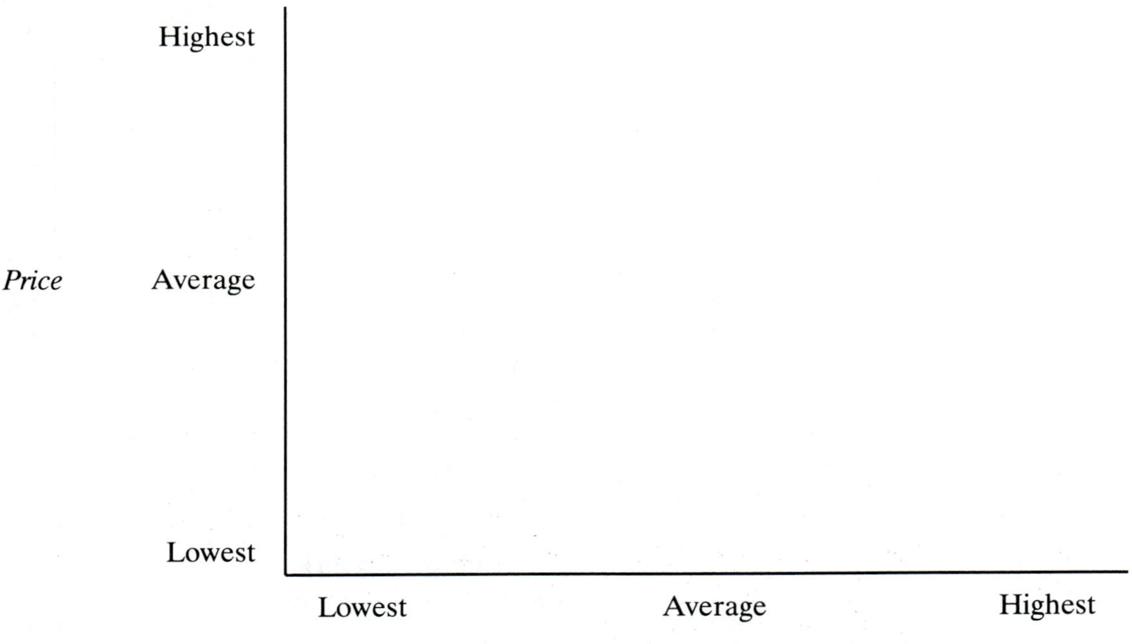

– An indication of how you plan to distribute and sell your product or services (e.g., through direct sales, mail order, manufacturers' representatives, etc.) and the likely sales, marketing, and advertising/trade promotion costs:

– A distribution plan for your product(s) or service(s), including any special requirements, such as refrigeration, and how much distribution costs will be as a percent of sales and of total costs:

- Map the value chain for your product or service (i.e., indicate how your product or service will get to the end user or consumer, the portion of the final selling price realized in each step, and the dollar and percentage markup and the dollar and percentage gross margin per unit).

  (Note that the value chain below is constructed for a generalized consumer product and needs to be modified for your particular product or service.)

Value Chain

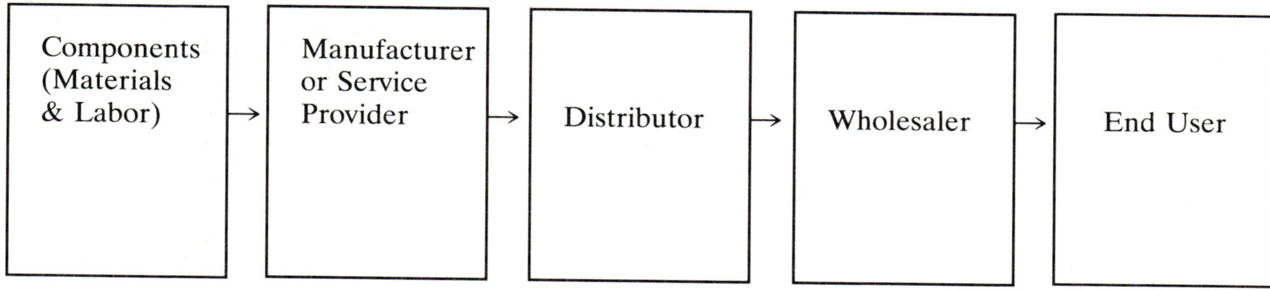

Price/Unit:
Dollars
Percent

Markup/Unit:
Dollars
Percent

Gross Margin:
Dollars
Percent

- An assessment of the costs and profitability of your product or service:

Product/Service Costs and Profitability

Product/Service:

Sales Price:

Sales Level:

	$/Unit	Percent of Sales Price/Unit
Production Costs (i.e., labor and material costs) or Purchase Costs		
Gross Margin		
Fixed Costs		
Profit before Taxes		
Profit after Taxes		

- An assessment of the minimum resources required to "get the doors open and revenue coming in," the costs, dates required, alternative means of gaining control of (but not necessarily owning) these, and what this information tells you:

Resource Needs

	Minimum Needed	Cost ($)	Date Required	Probable Source
Plant, Equipment, and Facilities				
Product/Service Development				
Market Research				
Setup of Sales and Distribution (e.g., brochures, demos, and mailers)				
One-Time Expenditures (e.g., legal costs)				
Lease Deposits and Other Prepayments (e.g., utilities)				

Overhead (e.g., salaries, rent, and insurance)				
Sales Costs (e.g., trips to trade shows)				
Other Start-up Costs				
TOTAL				
COMMENTS				

- A rough estimate of requirements for manufacturing and/or staff, operations, facilities, including:
  - An assessment of the major difficulties for such items as equipment, labor skills and training, and quality standards in the manufacture of your product(s) or the delivery of your service(s):

– An estimate of the number of people who will be required to launch the business and the key tasks they will perform:

– An assessment of how you will deal with these difficulties and your estimate of the time and money needed to resolve them and begin saleable production:

- An identification of the cash flow and cash conversion cycle for your business over the first 15 months (including a consideration of leads/lags in getting sales, producing your product or service, delivering your product or service, and billing and collecting cash). Show as a bar chart the timing and duration of each activity below:

Cash Flow, Conversion Cycle, and Timing of Key Operational Activities

Development of Forecasts

Manufacturing

Sales Orders

Billing:

Invoice

Collect

Selling Season

1 2 3 4 5 6 7 8 9 10 11 12 13 14 15

Months

- A preliminary, estimated cash flow statement for the first year, including considerations of resources needed for start-up and your cash conversion cycle:

- An estimation of (1) the total amount of asset and working capital needed and peak months and (2) the amount of money needed to reach positive cash flow and the amount of money needed to reach breakeven, and an indication of the months when each will occur:

- Create a break-even chart similar to the following:

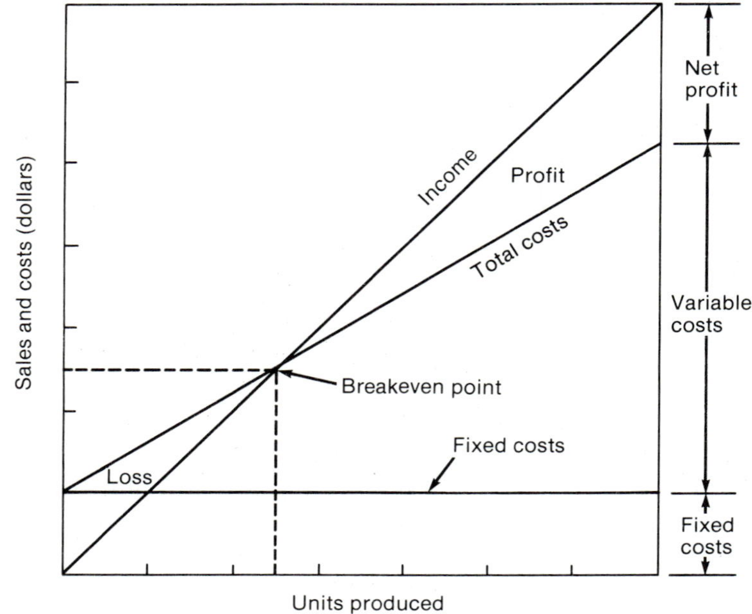

- An estimate of the capital required for asset additions and operating needs (and the months in which these will occur) to attain the sales level projected in five years:

- A statement of how you intend to raise capital, including all types (e.g., venture capital, financing raised through asset lenders, financing against inventory, receivables, equipment, and real estate), when, and from whom:

- A statement of whether you intend to harvest your venture, how and when this might occur, and the prospects. (If you do not intend to harvest the venture, include instead a statement of the prospects that profits will be both durable and large enough to be attractive.)

- An assessment of the sources of value, such as strategic, to another firm already in the market or one contemplating entry and an indication if there is a logical buyer(s) of your venture:

- An assessment of how much it would take to liquidate the venture if you decided to exit and whether this is high:

CHECKPOINT: RECONSIDER IF YOUR VENTURE OPPORTUNITY IS ATTRACTIVE. BEWARE OF COMPROMISING ON WHETHER YOUR OPPORTUNITY HAS FORGIVING AND REWARDING ECONOMICS. FOR EXAMPLE, ARE YOU CONVINCED THAT THE AMOUNT YOU NEED TO RAISE IS REASONABLE WITH RESPECT TO THE VENTURE'S POTENTIAL AND RISK? ARE OTHERS CONVINCED? IF THEY ARE NOT, WHAT DO YOU KNOW THAT THEY DO NOT (AND VICE VERSA)? MOST START-UPS RUN OUT OF CASH BEFORE THEY SECURE ENOUGH PROFITABLE CUSTOMERS TO SUSTAIN A POSITIVE CASH FLOW. YOUR PRELIMINARY ESTIMATES OF FINANCIAL REQUIREMENTS NEED TO BE WITHIN THE AMOUNT THAT AN INVESTOR, VENTURE CAPITALIST, OR OTHER LENDER IS WILLING TO COMMIT TO A SINGLE VENTURE OR THAT YOU CAN PERSONALLY RAISE. EVEN IF YOUR IDEA IS NOT A CANDIDATE FOR VENTURE CAPITAL FINANCING, IT IS WORTH LOOKING AT YOUR VENTURE IN THIS WAY.

- An assessment of competitors in the market, including those selling substitute products:

Competitor No.	Name	Products/Services That Compete Directly	Substitutes

- A profile of the competition:

Competitor Profile

	Competitor No.			
	1	2	3	4
Estimated Sales/Year ($)				
Estimated Market Share (%)				
Description of Sales Force				

Marketing Tactics: Selling Terms Advertising/Promotion Distribution Channel Service/Training/Support Pricing				
Major Strengths				
Major Weaknesses				

- A ranking of major competitors by market share:

No.	Competitor	Estimated Market Share

- A Robert Morris Associates statement study:

RMA Study

RMA Data for Period Ending	*Estimates for Proposed Venture*				
Asset Size	*Under $250M*	*$250M and Less than $1MM*	*$1MM and Less than $10MM*	*$10MM and Less than $50MM*	*All Sizes*
Number of Statements					
Assets: Cash Marketable securities Receivables net Inventory net All other current Total current Fixed assets net All other noncurrent Total	%	%	%	%	%
Liabilities: Due to banks—short-term Due to trade Income taxes Current maturities long-term debt All other current Total current debt Noncurrent debt, unsubordinated Total unsubordinated debt Subordinated debt Tangible net worth Total					
Income data: Net sales Cost of sales Gross profit All other expense net Profit before taxes					
Ratios: Quick Current Fixed/worth Debt/worth Unsubordinated debt/capital funds Sales/receivables Cost sales/inventory Sales/working capital Sales/worth Percent profit before taxes/worth Percent profit before taxes/total assets Net sales/total assets					

M = thousand.
MM = million.

- An assessment of whether there are economies of scale in production and/or cost advantages in marketing and distribution:

- An assessment, for *each* competitor's product or service, of its costs and profitability:

	Competitor Costs and Profitability			
Product/Service				
Sales Price				
Sales Level				

For Each:

	Dollars/Unit	Percent of Sales Price/Unit
Production Costs (i.e., labor and material costs) or Purchase Costs		
Gross Margin		
Fixed Costs		
Profit before Taxes		
Profit after Taxes		

- An assessment of the history and projections of competitors' profits and industry averages:

Competitor Profits—Historical and Projected

	Industry Average	Competitor 1	Competitor 2	Competitor 3	Competitor 4
Profits (percent of sales)					
Past Two Years					
Current Year					
Projected Next Two Years					
Sales/Employee					
Profit/Employee					

- A ranking of competitors in terms of cost:

No.	Competitor

- A profile for the current year of your competitors in terms of price and quality and of market share and profitability. Place competitors (using small circles identified by names) in the appropriate locations in the boxes below:

Array of Competitors

Price

Highest

Lowest

Last

Leader

Quality

Market Share

Largest

Smallest

Lowest

Highest

Profitability

- An assessment of the degree of control in the market (including that over prices, costs, and channels of distribution and by suppliers, buyers, etc.) and the extent to which you can influence these or will be subject to influence by others:

- An assessment of current lead times for changes in technology, capacity, product and market innovation, and so forth:

- An assessment of whether your venture will enjoy cost advantages or disadvantages in production and in marketing and distribution, and an indication of whether your venture will have the lowest, average, or highest costs of production, marketing, and distribution:

- An assessment of other competitive advantages which you have or can gain, how you would secure these, and what time and money is required, including:
  - An indication of whether your product or service will benefit from, or be subject to, any regulations and of the status of any copyrights, trade secrets, or patents or licenses and distribution or franchise agreements:

– An indication if you enjoy advantages in response and lead times for technology, capacity changes, product and market innovation, and so forth:

– An indication if you enjoy other unfair advantage, such as a strategic advantage, people advantage, resource advantage, location advantage, and so on:

– An assessment of whether you think you can be price competitive and make a profit, or other ways, such as product differentiation, in which you can compete:

- A ranking of your venture in terms of price and quality and of market share and profitability relative to your competitors. Add your venture to the Arrays of Competitors above:

- An assessment of whether any competitors enjoy competitive advantages, such as legal or contractual advantages:

- An assessment of whether any competitors are vulnerable, the time period of this vulnerability, and the impact on market structure of their succumbing to vulnerabilities:

CHECKPOINT: DO YOU HAVE SUFFICIENT COMPETITIVE ADVANTAGE? REMEMBER, A SUCCESSFUL COMPANY SELLS TO A MARKET THAT IS LARGE AND GROWING, WHERE CAPTURING A SMALL MARKET SHARE CAN BRING SIGNIFICANT SALES VOLUME, WHERE IT DOES NOT FACE SIGNIFICANT BARRIERS TO ENTRY, AND WHERE ITS COMPETITION IS PROFITABLE BUT NOT SO STRONG AS TO BE OVERWHELMING. FURTHER, A SUCCESSFUL COMPANY HAS A PRODUCT OR SERVICE THAT SOLVES SIGNIFICANT PROBLEMS THAT CUSTOMERS HAVE WITH COMPETITIVE PRODUCTS, SUCH AS POOR QUALITY, POOR SERVICE, POOR DELIVERY, ETC., AND A SALES PRICE THAT WILL ENABLE IT TO PENETRATE THE MARKET.

- An assessment of your partners and/or management team, including:
  - An evaluation of whether the founders and/or the management team are sufficiently committed to the opportunity and how much they are personally willing to invest in time, money, personal guarantees, and so forth:

  - An assessment of whether the founders and/or the management team possess the industry knowledge, experience, know-how, and skills required for the venture's success; if additional personnel is necessary and if these can be attracted to the venture; and if anyone on the team has managed previously what you are trying to undertake:

  - An assessment of whether the founders and/or management team have the necessary vision and entrepreneurial zest and whether they will be able to inspire this in others:

- An assessment of the level of trust felt among the founders and/or management team:

- A statement about who will do what—roles, responsibilities, and tasks:

- A statement about the contributions each founder and team member is expected to make:

- A statement about who will get what salary, what benefits, and what ownership share:

CHECKPOINT:	CAN DO? REMEMBER, THE TEAM IS A PRIMARY FORCE DRIVING SUCCESSFUL ENTREPRENEURIAL VENTURES. IT IS IMPORTANT TO QUESTION THE ASSUMPTIONS ON WHICH YOUR TEAM HAS BEEN SHAPED; FOR EXAMPLE, EQUAL SALARIES AND STOCK OWNERSHIP CAN INDICATE THAT ASSUMPTIONS AS TO TASKS, ROLES, AND RESPONSIBILITIES ARE NAIVE. SOMEONE ON YOUR TEAM NEEDS TO BE EXPERIENCED AND COMPETENT IN THESE AREAS, OR THE TEAM NEEDS TO BE ABLE TO ATTRACT SOMEONE WHO IS.

STEP 5: INCLUDE ANY OTHER VITAL ISSUES OR CONSIDERATIONS THAT ARE UNIQUE TO YOUR VENTURE OPPORTUNITY AND THAT HAVE NOT BEEN COVERED IN THE VOSG. For example, a location analysis is necessary for retail establishments or real estate:

STEP 6: ASSESS WHETHER YOUR VENTURE OPPORTUNITY HAS ANY FATAL FLAWS:

STEP 7: LIST SIGNIFICANT ASSUMPTIONS (ASSUMPTIONS ABOUT CUSTOMER ORDERS, SALES PROJECTIONS, ETC.), INCLUDING:

- A consideration of significant trade-offs that you have made:

- A consideration of the major risks (unreliability of customer orders; overoptimistic sales projections; inability to achieve cost and time estimates; underestimating the magnitude, intensity, and vindictiveness of competitors' responses; etc.):

STEP 8: RANK ASSUMPTIONS ACCORDING TO IMPORTANCE:

STEP 9: EVALUATE THE DOWNSIDE CONSEQUENCES, IF ANY, WHEN YOUR ASSUMPTIONS ARE PROVED INVALID; HOW SEVERE THE IMPACT WOULD BE; AND IF AND HOW THESE CAN BE MINIMIZED, INCLUDING:

- The cost and consequences of (1) lost growth opportunities and (2) liquidation or bankruptcy to the company, to you, and to other stakeholders:

STEP 10: RATE THE RISK OF THE VENTURE AS HIGH, MEDIUM, OR LOW:

STEP 11: LIST CHRONOLOGICALLY THE 10 TO 15 MOST CRITICAL ACTIONS YOU NEED TO TAKE DURING THE NEXT SIX MONTHS AND THE HURDLES THAT NEED TO BE OVERCOME IN ORDER TO CONVERT YOUR IDEA INTO A REAL OPPORTUNITY. It is a good idea to have another person review what you have listed and adjust the list, if warranted.

Date	Action

STEP 12: MAKE A WEEK-BY-WEEK SCHEDULE OF KEY TASKS TO BE PERFORMED, WHEN THEY ARE TO BE PERFORMED, AND BY WHOM. Break larger tasks into their smallest possible components. Be alert for conflicts.

Week No.	Task	Date Completed	Person Responsible

CHECKPOINT: IT IS IMPORTANT TO TAKE A HARD LOOK AT THE ASSUMPTIONS YOU HAVE MADE, BOTH IMPLICIT AND EXPLICIT, AND TO ASSESS THE RISK OF THE VENTURE. TIME AND AGAIN, FIRST-TIME ENTREPRENEURS OVERESTIMATE SALES AND DELIVERY DATES AND UNDERESTIMATE COSTS, EFFORT, AND TIME REQUIRED TO EXECUTE THE OPPORTUNITY AND TO REACH A POSITIVE CASH FLOW. ALSO, WHILE EACH NEW BUSINESS HAS ITS RISKS AND PROBLEMS, AS WELL AS ITS OPPORTUNITIES, DIFFICULTIES NEED TO BE IDENTIFIED AS SOON AS POSSIBLE SO THEY CAN BE AVOIDED OR ELIMINATED OR THEIR IMPACT MINIMIZED.

STEP 13: RETURN TO **STEPS 1** AND **2** TO REFINE YOUR OPPORTUNITY SUMMARY AND MAKE ANY ADJUSTMENTS TO YOUR VENTURE OPPORTUNITY PROFILE. Attach to your VOSG a list of the names, addresses, and phone numbers of relevant sources of industry and market data.

CHECKPOINT: YOUR RESPONSES TO THE "VENTURE OPPORTUNITY SCREENING GUIDE" WILL HELP YOU TO DETERMINE WHETHER YOU WANT TO CONTINUE WITH YOUR VENTURE AND DEVELOP A COMPLETE BUSINESS PLAN. IF YOUR VENTURE HAS PASSED, A CRUCIAL QUESTION TO CONSIDER BEFORE PROCEEDING, IS, WHAT DO I WANT TO GET OUT OF THE BUSINESS? YOU WILL WANT TO THINK TWICE ABOUT WHETHER THE VENTURE PROVIDES A STRONG FIT WITH YOUR PERSONAL GOALS, VALUES, AND NEEDS, IS WHAT GIVES YOU ENERGY, LEADS YOU DOWN THE PATH YOU WANT TO BE ON AND TO FURTHER AND EVEN BETTER OPPORTUNITIES. REMEMBER, YOU ARE WHAT YOU DO. IF YOU HAVE BEEN ABLE TO COMPLETE THE GUIDE, ARE SATISFIED THAT MOST OF THE RESULTS ARE POSITIVE, AND IF THE ANSWERS TO THE PERSONAL ISSUES ARE YES (SEE PART VI), THEN *GO FOR IT*.

THE FOUNDERS

PART II

Survival odds for a venture go up once sales of at least $1 million are reached and employees exceed approximately 20. Launching or acquiring and then building a business that will exceed 20 employees is more fun and more challenging than being involved in the vast majority of small one- or two-person operations. But perhaps most important, a business of this magnitude achieves the critical mass necessary to attract good people, and as a result, the prospects of realizing a harvest are significantly enhanced.

A leader who thinks and acts with an "entrepreneurial mind" can make a critical difference as to whether a business is destined to be a traditional very small lifestyle firm, a stagnant or declining large one, or a higher potential venture. Practicing certain mental attitudes and actions in a certain way can stimulate, motivate, and reinforce the kind of zest and entrepreneurial culture whose self-fulfilling prophecy is success.

It is almost impossible to take a number of people, give them a single test, and determine who possess entrepreneurial minds and who do not. Rather, it is useful for would-be entrepreneurs and others involved in entrepreneurship to study how successful entrepreneurs think, feel, and respond and how those factors that are significant can be developed and strengthened—as a decathlete develops and strengthens certain muscles to compete at a certain level.

Entrepreneurs who create or recognize opportunities and then seize and shape them into higher potential ventures *think and do things differently.* They operate in an entrepreneurial domain, a place governed by certain modes of action and dominated by certain principal driving forces.

External and internal pressures mandate that the entrepreneur be a manager as his or her venture grows beyond being founder-driven and dominated by the need to survive. The development of competencies as an entrepreneurial manager is critical. Thus, not only do acquired skills and relevant experience position entrepreneurs to see opportunities that others do not see or cannot grasp, these acquired skills and experience are key to achieving longer-term sustained growth and an eventual harvest.

It makes a lot of sense for entrepreneurs to pay particular attention to picking partners, key business associates, and managers with an eye for complementing their own weaknesses and strengths and the needs of the venture. As will be seen, they seek people who *fit.* The reason for this is that not only can a weakness be an Achilles' heel for new ventures, but also the whole is almost always greater than the sum of its parts. For example, Ken Fisher joined Prime Computer in 1975 as president when the company had sales of just $7 million and employed 150 people. In six years the company grew to $365 million in sales and 4,500 employees. Sales grew at a compounded annual rate of 88 percent and net income by 108 percent, while return on shareholders' equity reached a high of 48.8 percent and topped 35.0 percent for four consecutive years. During his stay, Prime's share price increased 126 times to its 1981 high, just prior to his resignation. He subsequently formed Encore Computer Corporation with two industry leaders. In talking about his experiences, Fisher said a lead entrepreneur has need for "an ego that sustains and drives a person to achieve, stress tolerance, controlled empathy, ability to resolve conflicts, keeping everything in perspective between the business and personal life, and least important of all these, intelligence."

Finally, ethics are terribly important in entrepreneurship. In highly unpredictable and fragile situations, ethical issues cannot be handled according to such simplistic notions as "always tell the truth."

The Entrepreneurial Mind in Thought and Action

5

Nothing that sends you to the grave with a smile on your face comes easy. Work hard doing what you love. Find out what gives you energy and improve on it.

Betty Coster, Entrepreneur

RESULTS EXPECTED

Upon completion of this chapter, you will have:

1. Examined ways to help you discover whether being an entrepreneur gives you sustaining energy, rather than takes it away.
2. Explored the entrepreneurial mind—the strategies, approaches, attitudes, and behaviors that work for entrepreneurs who build higher potential ventures.[1]
3. Developed concepts for evaluating a personal entrepreneurial strategy and an apprenticeship.
4. Developed an entrepreneur's "creed."
5. Analyzed a case: Kevin Mooney.
6. Crafted a personal entrepreneurial strategy.

THE SEARCH FOR UNDERSTANDING

As was noted in Chapter 1, there is much more behind "walking the breathtaking highlands of success." The lead entrepreneurs who find and seize opportunities and grow higher potential ventures *do* things differently. Recall from *Exhibit 1.9* and the discussion in Chapter 1 that entrepreneurs—in thought and action—are anchored by certain attitudes and behaviors and by the "chunks" of experience, skills, know-how, and contacts they possess. They are thus positioned to see what others do not and seize opportunities and grow higher potential ventures.

Two Principles for Achieving Entrepreneurial Greatness

One of the most extraordinary entrepreneurial success stories of our time is that of the late Ewing Marion Kauffman, who founded and built Marion Labs, a company with $2.5 billion in sales. Kauffman started his pharmaceutical company, now one of the leading companies in the world, in 1950 with $5,000—in the basement of his Kansas City home. Previously, he had been very successful at another company. Kauffman (or "Mr. K" as he preferred) recalled that "the president first cut back my sales commission, then he cut back my territory. So, I quit and created Marion Labs."

[1] Jeffry A Timmons, *The Entrepreneurial Mind* (Acton, MA: Brick House Publishing, 1989).

By 1989, after acquiring Merrell-Dow in 1989 (now Marion, Merrell Dow, Inc.), over 300 people had become millionaires. Thirteen foundations have been created by former Marion associates, and the Ewing Marion Kauffman Foundation is one of only a dozen or so foundations in America with assets of over $1 billion. The two-pronged mission of the foundation is to make a lasting difference in helping youths at risk and encouraging leadership in all areas of American life.

Having had the great privilege and honor, since 1991, of working with Mr. K and his management team at Marion Labs, I have come to know and appreciate more each passing year the two core principles that are the cornerstone of the values, philosophy, and culture of Marion Labs and now of the Kauffman Foundation.

- Treat others as you would want to be treated.
- Share the wealth that is created with all those who have contributed to it at all levels.

As simple as these may be, ask yourself the number of organizations you have visited and been a part of that truly, sincerely, and consistently practice these principles. It takes a lot more than lip-service or a stand-alone profit-sharing plan to create this entrepreneurial culture. Consider the following unique characteristics at Marion Labs and the Ewing Marion Kauffman Foundation:

- No one is an employee; they are all associates.
- Even at $2.5 billion in sales, there are no formal organizational charts.
- Everyone who meets or exceeds high performance goals participates in a companywide bonus, profit-sharing, and stock option plan.
- Benefit programs treat all associates the same, even top management.
- Managers who attempt to develop a new product and fail are not punished with lateral promotions or geographic relocation to Timbuktu, nor were they ostracized. Failures were gateways to learning and continual improvement.
- Those who will not or cannot practice these two core principles are not tolerated.

The ultimate message is clear: Great companies can be built upon simple but elegant principles, and all the capital, technology, service management, and latest information technology available cannot substitute for these principles, nor will they cause such a culture to happen. These ideals are at the very heart of the difference between good and great companies.

Leadership and Human Behavior

A single psychological model of entrepreneurship has not been supported by research. However, behavioral scientists, venture capitalists, investors, and entrepreneurs share the opinion that the eventual success of a new venture will depend a great deal upon the talent and behavior of the lead entrepreneur and of his or her team.

The first chapter mentioned that a number of myths persist about entrepreneurs. Foremost among these myths is the belief that leaders are born, not made. The roots of much of this thinking reflect the assumptions and biases of an earlier era, when rulers were royal and leadership was the prerogative of the aristocracy. Fortunately, such notions have not withstood the tests of time or the inquisitiveness of researchers of leadership and management. Consider recent research, which distinguishes managers from leaders, as summarized in *Exhibit 5.1.* It is widely accepted today that leadership is an extraordinarily complex subject, depending more on the interconnections among the leader, the task, the situation, and those being led than on inborn or inherited characteristics alone.

There are numerous ways of analyzing human behavior and so, too, of trying to understand the entrepreneurial mind. The many theories of human behavior have im-

Exhibit 5.1
Comparing Management and Leadership

	Management	*Leadership*
Creating an agenda	Planning and budgeting—establishing detailed steps and timetables for achieving needed results, and then allocating the resources necessary to achieve these results	Establishing direction—developing a vision of the future, often the distant future, and strategies for producing the changes needed to achieve that vision
Developing a human network for achieving the agenda	Organizing and staffing—establishing some structure for accomplishing plan requirements, staffing that structure with individuals, delegating responsibility and authority for carrying out the plan, providing policies and procedures to help guide people, and creating methods or systems to monitor implementation	Aligning people—communicating the direction by words and deeds to all those whose cooperation may be needed to influence the creation of teams and coalitions that understand the vision and strategies, and accept their validity
Execution	Controlling and problem solving—monitoring results versus plan in some detail, identifying deviations, and then planning and organizing to solve these problems	Motivating and inspiring—energizing people to overcome major political, bureaucratic, and resource barriers to change by satisfying very basic, often unfulfilled human needs
Outcomes	Produces a degree of predictability and order, and has the potential of consistently producing key results expected by various stakeholders	Produces change, often to a dramatic degree, and has the potential of producing extremely useful change

Source: Reprinted with the permission of The Free Press, a Division of Macmillan, Inc. from *A Force for Change: How Leadership Differs from Management* by John P. Kotter. Copyright © 1990 by John P. Kotter, Inc.

plications in the study of entrepreneurship. For example, for over 35 years Dr. David C. McClelland of Harvard University and Dr. John W. Atkinson of the University of Michigan and their colleagues have sought to understand individual motivation.[2] Their theory of psychological motivation is a generally accepted part of the literature on entrepreneurial behavior and has been used to a considerable extent in actual research, evaluation, and training efforts.

The theory states that people are motivated by three principal needs: (1) the need for achievement, (2) the need for power, and (3) the need for affiliation. The *need for achievement* is the need to excel and for measurable personal accomplishment. A person competes against a self-imposed standard that does not involve competition with others. The individual sets realistic and challenging goals and likes to get feedback on how well he or she is doing in order to improve performance. The *need for power* is the need to influence others and to achieve an "influence goal" (i.e., the goal of outperforming someone else or establishing a reputation or position according to an externally derived and oriented standard). While it is sometimes easier to see the negative aspects of power motivation, bear in mind that socialized and civilized power needs have played an important role in influencing people and institutions. The *need for affiliation* is the need to attain an "affiliation goal" (i.e., the goal to build a warm relationship with someone else and/or to enjoy mutual friendship).

Research

Other research focused on the common attitudes and behaviors of entrepreneurs. A 1983 study found a relationship between attitudes and behaviors of successful entrepreneurs and various stages of company development.[3] A year later, another study found that

[2] See John W Atkinson, *An Introduction to Motivation* (Princeton, NJ: van Nostrand, 1964); J W Atkinson, *Motives in Fantasy, Action and Society* (Princeton, NJ: van Nostrand, 1958); D C McClelland, *The Achieving Society* (Princeton, NJ: van Nostrand, 1961); J W Atkinson and N T Feather, eds., *A Theory of Achievement Motivation* (New York: John Wiley & Sons, 1966); and D C McClelland and D G Winter, *Motivating Economic Achievement* (New York: Free Press, 1969).

[3] Neil Churchill, "Entrepreneurs and Their Enterprises: A Stage Model," *Frontiers of Entrepreneurship Research: 1983*, ed. J A Hornaday et al. (Babson Park, MA: Babson College, 1983), pp. 1–22.

entrepreneurs were unique individuals; for instance, this study found that "what is characteristic is not so much an overall type as a successful, growth-oriented entrepreneurial type. . . . It is the company builders who are distinctive."[4] More recently, a study of 118 entrepreneurs revealed that "those who like to plan are much more likely to be in the survival group than those who do not."[5] Clearly, the get-rich-quick entrepreneurs are not the company builders, nor are they the planners of successful ventures. Rather it is the visionary who participates in the day-to-day routine to achieve a long-term objective and who is generally passionate and not exclusively profit-oriented.

Academics have continued to characterize the special qualities of entrepreneurs. (See *Exhibit 5.2* for a summary of the research.) As a participant in this quest to understand the entrepreneurial mind, in January 1983, Howard H. Stevenson and I spoke with 60 practicing entrepreneurs.[6] One finding was that entrepreneurs felt they had to concentrate on certain fundamentals: responsiveness, resiliency, and adaptiveness in seizing new opportunities.

These entrepreneurs spoke of other attitudes, including an ability "to activate vision" and a willingness to learn about and invest in new techniques, to be adaptable, to have a professional attitude, and to have patience. They talked about the importance of "enjoying and being interested in business," as well as the business as "a way of life."

Many respondents recognized and endorsed the importance of human resource management; one entrepreneur said that one of the most challenging tasks was playing "a leadership role in attracting high-quality people, imparting your vision to them, and holding and motivating them."

Many focused on the importance of building an organization and teamwork. For example, the head of a manufacturing firm with $10 million in sales said, "Understanding people and how to pull them together toward a basic goal will be my main challenge in five years." The head of a clothing manufacturing business with 225 employees and $6 million in sales shared a view of many that one of the most critical areas where an entrepreneur has leverage and long-term impact is in managing employees. He said, "Treating people honestly and letting them know when they do well goes a long way."

A number of respondents felt that the ability to conceptualize their business and do strategic planning would be of growing importance, particularly when thinking five years ahead. Other attitudes they spoke of included a willingness to learn about and invest in new techniques, to be adaptable, to have a professional attitude, and to have patience. They talked about the importance of "enjoying and being interested in business" and also of the business "as a way of life." They mentioned an ability to "activate vision."

Similarly, the ageless importance of sensitivity to and respect for employees was stressed by a chief executive officer of a firm with $40 million in sales and 400 employees: "It is essential that the separation between management and the average employee should be eliminated. Students should be taught to respect employees all the way down to the janitor and accept them as knowledgeable and able persons." At least one company has taken this concept to heart; Ben & Jerry's Homemade Ice Cream Inc. began operations with a covenant that "no boss got more than five times the compensation, including both pay and benefits, of the lowest-paid worker with at least one year at the company."[7] Since its inception, the

[4] N R Smith and John B Miner, "Motivational Considerations in the Success of Technologically Innovative Entrepreneurs," in *Frontiers of Entrepreneurship Research: 1984,* ed. J Hornaday et al. (Babson Park, MA: Babson College, 1984), pp. 448–95.

[5] John B Miller, Norman R Smith, and Jeffrey S Bracker, "Entrepreneur Motivation and Firm Survival among Technologically Innovative Companies," ed. Neil C Churchill et al., *Frontiers of Entrepreneurship Research: 1991* (Babson Park, MA: Babson College, 1992), p. 31.

[6] J A Timmons and H H Stevenson, "Entrepreneurship Education in the 80s: What Entrepreneurs Say," in *Entrepreneurship: What It Is and How to Teach It,* ed. J Kao and H H Stevenson (Boston: Harvard Business School, 1985), pp. 115–34.

[7] Floyd Norris, "Low-Fat Problem At Ben & Jerry's," *The New York Times*, September 9, 1992, p. D6.

Exhibit 5.2
Characteristics of Entrepreneurs

Date	*Author(s)*	*Characteristics*	*Normative*	*Empirical*
1848	Mill	Risk-bearing	X	
1917	Weber	Source of formal authority	X	
1934	Schumpeter	Innovation; initiative	X	
1954	Sutton	Desire for responsibility	X	
1959	Hartman	Source of formal authority	X	
1961	McClelland	Risk-taking; need for achievement		X
1963	Davids	Ambition; desire for independence, responsibility; self-confidence		X
1964	Pickle	Drive/mental; human relations; communication ability; technical knowledge		X
1971	Palmer	Risk measurement		X
1971	Hornaday and Aboud	Need for achievement; autonomy; aggression; power; recognition; innovative/independent		X
1973	Winter	Need for power	X	
1974	Borland	Internal locus of control		X
1974	Liles	Need for achievement		X
1977	Gasse	Personal value orientation		X
1978	Timmons	Drive/self-confidence; goal-oriented; moderate risk-taker; locus of control; creativity/innovation	X	X
1980	Sexton	Energetic/ambitious; positive setbacks		X
1981	Welsh and White	Need to control; responsibility seeker; self-confidence/drive; challenge taker; moderate risk taker		X
1982	Dunkelberg and Cooper	Growth oriented; independence oriented; craftsman oriented		X
1982	Hoy and Hellriegel	Preference for technical versus managerial tasks		X
1983	Pavett and Lau	Conceptual, human, and political competence; technical familiarity in a specialized field	X	
1985	MacMillan, Siegel, and SubbaNarisimha	Familiarity with the market; a capacity for intense effort; leadership ability	X	
1986	Ibrahim and Goodwin	Ability to delegate, manage customer and employee relations; interpersonal skills	X	
1987	Aldrich and Zimmer	Networking with people who control important resources and who have relevant skills and abilities	X	
1987	Hofer and Sandberg	Drive to see firm creation through to fruition; ability to clearly communicate goals; ability to motivate others to behave in synergistic manner		X
1987	Schein	Strong management skills with high levels of responsibility and authority; specialist versus general manager		X
1987	Timmons, Muzyka, Stevenson, and Bygrave	Ability to recognize and envision taking advantage of opportunity		X
1989	Wheelen and Hunger	Ability to implement strategy with programs, procedures, budgets, evaluations, etc.		X
1992	Chandler and Jansen	Self-assessed ability to recognize opportunity	X	
1992	McGrath, MacMillan, and Scheinberg*	High individualism; poor distance; uncertainty avoidance; and masculinity		X

Source: James W Carland, Frank Hoy, William R Boulton, and Jo Ann C Carland, "Differentiating Entrepreneurs from Small Business Owners: A Conceptualization," *Academy of Management Review* 9, no. 2 (1984), p. 356; Gaylen N. Chandler and Erik Jansen, "The Founder's Self-Assessed Competence and Venture Performance," *Journal of Business Venturing* 7, pp. 233–36.

*V McGrath et al., "Elitists, Risktakers, and Rugged Individualists? An Exploratory Analysis of Cultural Differences between Entrepreneurs and Non-Entrepreneurs," *Journal of Business Venturing* 7, pp. 115–35.

covenant has been modified to seven to one, while the company reported $63.2 million in revenue in the first half of 1992.[8]

A consulting study by McKinsey of medium-size growth companies (i.e., companies with sales between $25 million and $1 billion and with sales or profit growth of more than 15 percent annually over five years) confirms that the chief executive officers of winning companies were notable for three common traits: perseverance, a builder's mentality, and a strong propensity for taking calculated risks.[9]

CONVERGING ON THE ENTREPRENEURIAL MIND

Desirable and Acquirable Attitudes and Behaviors

Many successful entrepreneurs have emphasized that while successful entrepreneurs have initiative and take charge, are determined and persevere, and are resilient and able to adapt, it is not just a matter of their personalities, *it is what they do.*[10]

While there is an undeniable core of such inborn characteristics as energy and raw intelligence, which an entrepreneur either has or does not, it is becoming apparent that possession of these characteristics does not necessarily an entrepreneur make. There is also a good deal of evidence that entrepreneurs are born and made better and that certain attitudes and behaviors can be acquired, developed, practiced, and refined—through a combination of experience and study.[11]

While not all attitudes and behaviors can be acquired by everyone at the same pace and with the same proficiency, entrepreneurs are able to significantly improve their odds of success by concentrating on those that work, by nurturing and practicing them, and by eliminating, or at least mitigating, the rest. Painstaking effort may be required, and much will depend upon the motivation of an individual to grow, but it seems people have an astounding capacity to change and learn if they are motivated and committed to do so.

Testimony given by successful entrepreneurs also confirms there are attitudes and behaviors that successful entrepreneurs have in common. Take, for instance, the first 21 inductees into Babson College's Academy of Distinguished Entrepreneurs, including such well-known entrepreneurs as Ken Olsen of DEC, An Wang of Wang Computers, Wally Amos of Famous Amos' Chocolate Chip Cookies, Bill Norris of Control Data, Sochiro Honda of Honda Motors, and the late Ray Kroc of McDonald's. All 21 of the inductees mentioned the possession of three attributes as the principal reasons for their successes: (1) the ability to respond positively to challenges and learn from mistakes, (2) taking personal initiative, and (3) great perseverance and determination.[12] In the 1990s, the following entrepreneurs were inducted into the Academy of Distinguished Entrepreneurs because of their success and by making a world of difference through their work for social change and human development: Paul Fireman of Reebok International Ltd., Sandra L. Kurtzig of ASK Computer Systems, Inc., Amar G. Bose of Bose Corporation, John R. Furman of Furman Lumber, Inc., and William G. McGowan of MCI Communications Corporation, Ewing Marion Kauffman of

[8] Ibid.

[9] Donald K Clifford, Jr., and Richard E Cavanagh, *The Winning Performance* (New York: Bantam Books, 1985), p. 3.

[10] Determining the attitudes and behaviors in entrepreneurs that are "acquirable and desirable" represents the synthesis of over 50 research studies compiled for the first and second editions of this book. See extensive references in J A Timmons, L E Smollen, and A L M Dingee, Jr., *New Venture Creation,* 2nd ed. (Homewood, Ill.: Richard D Irwin, 1985 pp. 139–69).

[11] David C McClelland, "Achievement Motivation Can Be Developed," *Harvard Business Review,* November–December 1965; David C McClelland and David G Winter, *Motivating Economic Achievement* (New York: Free Press, 1969); and Jeffry A Timmons, "Black Is Beautiful—Is It Bountiful?" *Harvard Business Review,* November–December 1971, p. 81.

[12] John A Hornaday and Nancy B Tieken, "Capturing Twenty-One Heffalumps," in *Frontiers of Entrepreneurship Research: 1983,* ed. J A Hornaday et al. (Babson Park, MA: Babson College, 1983), pp. 23–50.

Marion Merrell Dow, Inc., John C. Merritt of Van Kampen Merritt Holding Corp., Inc., Anita Roddick of the Body Shop, and Leslie H. Wexner of the Limited, Inc.

There are "themes" that have emerged from what successful entrepreneurs do and how they perform. In discussing these themes, it is important to emphasize there are undoubtedly many attitudes and behaviors characterizing the entrepreneurial mind and there is no single set of attitudes and behaviors that every entrepreneur must have for every venture opportunity. Further, the *fit* concept argues that what is required in each situation depends on the mix and match of the key players and how promising and forgiving the opportunity is, given the founders' strengths and shortcomings. And, a team might collectively show many of the desired strengths. Even then, there is no such thing as a perfect entrepreneur—as yet.

Six Dominant Themes

A consensus has emerged around six dominant themes, shown in *Exhibit 5.3:*

- *Commitment and determination.* Commitment and determination are seen as more important than any other factor. With commitment and determination, an entrepreneur can overcome incredible obstacles and also compensate enormously for other weaknesses.

Exhibit 5.3
Six Themes—Desirable and Acquirable Attitudes and Behaviors

Theme	*Attitude or Behavior*
Commitment and Determination	Tenacity and decisiveness, able to decommit/commit quickly
	Discipline
	Persistence in solving problems
	Willingness to undertake personal sacrifice
	Total immersion
Leadership	Self-starter; high standards but not perfectionist
	Team builder and hero maker; inspires others
	Treat others as you want to be treated
	Share the wealth with all the people who helped to create it
	Integrity and reliability; builder of trust; practices fairness
	Not a lone wolf
	Superior learner and teacher
	Patience and urgency
Opportunity Obsession	Having intimate knowledge of customers' needs
	Market driven
	Obsessed with value creation and enhancement
Tolerance of Risk, Ambiguity, and Uncertainty	Calculated risk taker
	Risk minimizer
	Risk sharer
	Manages paradoxes and contradictions
	Tolerance of uncertainty and lack of structure
	Tolerance of stress and conflict
	Ability to resolve problems and integrate solutions
Creativity, Self-reliance, and Ability to Adapt	Nonconventional, open-minded, lateral thinker
	Restlessness with status quo
	Ability to adapt and change; creative problem solver
	Ability to learn quickly
	Lack of fear of failure
	Ability to conceptualize and "sweat details" (helicopter mind)
Motivation to Excel	Goal-and-results orientation; high but realistic goals
	Drive to achieve and grow
	Low need for status and power
	Interpersonally supporting (versus competitive)
	Aware of weaknesses and strengths
	Having perspective and sense of humor

As President Calvin Coolidge stated:

> Nothing in the world can take the place of persistence. Talent will not; nothing is more common than unsuccessful men with talent. Genius will not; unrewarded genius is almost a proverb. Education will not; the world is full of educated derelicts. Persistence and determination alone are omnipotent. The slogan "Press on" has solved and solved and always will solve the problems of the human race.

All of the distinguished entrepreneurs referred to earlier said these attitudes were critical. Carl Sontheimer, president and founder of Cuisinarts, Inc., said: "Entrepreneurs come in all flavors, personalities, degrees of ethics, but one thing they have in common is they never give up." Franklin P. Purdue, president of Purdue Farms, Inc., said: "Nothing, absolutely nothing, replaces the willingness to work. You have to be willing to pay the price."

Total commitment is required by almost all entrepreneurial ventures. Almost without exception, entrepreneurs live under huge, constant pressures—first for their firms to survive start-up, then for them to stay alive, and finally for them to grow. A new venture demands top priority for the entrepreneur's time, emotions, and loyalty. Thus, being involved in commitment and determination is usually personal sacrifice. An entrepreneur's commitment can be measured in several ways—through willingness to invest a substantial portion of his or her net worth in the venture, through willingness to take a cut in pay since he or she will own a major piece of the venture, and through other major sacrifices in lifestyle and family circumstances.

Entrepreneurs who successfully build new enterprises desire to overcome hurdles, solve problems, and complete the job; they are disciplined, tenacious, and persistent in solving problems and in performing other tasks. They are able to commit and decommit quickly. They are not intimidated by difficult situations; in fact, they seem to think that the impossible just takes a little longer. However, they are neither aimless nor foolhardy in their relentless attack on a problem or obstacle that can impede their business. If a task is unsolvable, an entrepreneur actually will give up sooner than others. Most researchers share the opinion that while entrepreneurs are extremely persistent, they are also realistic in recognizing what they can and cannot do, and where they can get help to solve a very difficult but necessary task.

- *Leadership.* Successful entrepreneurs are experienced, including having intimate knowledge of the technology and marketplace in which they will compete, have sound general management skills, and have a proven track record. They are self-starters and have an internal locus of control with high standards.

  They are patient leaders, capable of installing tangible visions and managing for the longer-haul. The entrepreneur is at once a learner and a teacher, a doer and a visionary. The vision of building a substantial enterprise that will contribute something lasting and relevant to the world while realizing a capital gain requires the patience to stick to the task for 5 to 10 years or more.

  Recent work by Alan Grant lends significant support to the fundamental "driving forces" theory of entrepreneurship articulated in *Exhibit 1.7.* Grant surveyed 25 senior venture capitalists to develop an entrepreneurial leadership paradigm. Three clear areas evolved from his study: the lead entrepreneur, the venture team, and the external environment influences, which are outlined in further detail in *Exhibit 5.4.* Furthermore, Grant suggested that to truly understand this paradigm, it should be "metaphorically associated with a *troika*, a Russian vehicle pulled by three horses of *equal* strength. Each

Exhibit 5.4
The Entrepreneurial Leadership Paradigm

The Lead Entrepreneur	
Self concept	Has a realist's attitude rather than one of invincibility.
Intellectually honest	Trustworthy, his/her word is her/her contract.
	Admits what and when he/she does not know.
Pace maker	Displays a high energy level and a sense of urgency.
Courage	Capable of making hard decisions; setting and beating high goals.
Communication skills	Maintains an effective dialogue with the venture team, in the marketplace, and with other venture constituents.
Team player	Competent in people management and team-building skills.
The Venture Team	
Organizational style	The lead entrepreneur and the venture team blend their skills to operate in a participative environment.
Ethical behavior	Practices strong adherence to ethical business practices.
Faithfulness	Stretched commitments are consistently met or bettered.
Focus	Long-term venture strategies are kept in focus but tactics are varied in order to achieve them.
Performance/reward	High standards of performance are created and superior performance is rewarded fairly and equitably.
Adaptability	Responsive to rapid changes in product/technological cycles.
External Environmental Influences	
Constituent needs	Organization needs are satisfied, in parallel with those of the other publics the enterprise serves.
Prior experiences	Extensive prior experiences are effectively applied.
Mentoring	The competencies of others are sought and used.
Problem resolution	New problems are immediately solved or prioritized.
Value creation	High commitment is placed on long-term value creation for backers, customers, employees, and other stakeholders.
Skill emphasis	Marketing skills are stressed over technical ones.

Source: Adapted from Alan Grant, "The Development of the Entrepreneurial Leadership Paradigm," unpublished manuscript, Babson College, 1993, Table 4, p. 11.

horse represents a cluster of the success factors. The troika was driven toward success by the *visions* and *dreams* of the founding entrepreneurs."[13]

There is among successful entrepreneurs a well-developed capacity to exert influence *without* formal power. These people are adept at conflict resolution. They know when to use logic and when to persuade, when to make a concession, and when to exact one. To run a successful venture, an entrepreneur learns to get along with many different constituencies, often with conflicting aims—the customer, the supplier, the financial backer, the creditor, as well as the partners and others on the inside. Success comes when the entrepreneur is a mediator, a negotiator rather than a dictator.

Successful entrepreneurs are interpersonally supporting and nurturing—not interpersonally competitive. When a strong need to control, influence, and gain power over others characterizes the lead entrepreneur, or where he or she has an insatiable appetite for putting an associate down, more often than not the venture gets into trouble. Entrepreneurs should treat others as they want to be treated; they should share the wealth with those who contributed. A dictatorial, adversarial, and domineering management style makes it very difficult to attract and keep people who thrive on a thirst for achievement, responsibility, and results. Compliant partners and managers often are chosen. Destructive conflicts often erupt over who has the final say, who is right, and whose prerogatives are what.

[13] Alan Grant, "The Development of an Entrepreneurial Leadership Paradigm for Enhancing New Venture Success," *Frontiers of Entrepreneurship Research: 1992.*

Entrepreneurs who create and build substantial enterprises are not lone wolves and super-independent. They do not need to collect all the credit for the effort. They not only recognize the reality that it is rarely possible to build a substantial business working all alone, but they actively build a team. They have an uncanny ability to make heroes out of the people they attract to the venture by giving responsibility and sharing credit for accomplishments.

In the corporate setting, this "hero-making" ability is identified as an essential attribute of successful entrepreneurial managers.[14] These hero-makers, of both the independent and corporate varieties, try to make the pie bigger and better, rather than jealously clutching and hoarding a tiny pie that is all theirs. They have a capacity for objective interpersonal relationships as well, which enables them to smooth out individual differences of opinion by keeping attention focused on the common goal to be achieved.[15]

- *Opportunity obsession.* Successful entrepreneurs are obsessed—with opportunity. They are oriented to the goal of pursuing and executing an opportunity for accumulating resources or money per se. Much has been said about opportunity in the first chapters of this book. The obsession of entrepreneurs is manifested in total immersion in the opportunity. They are discriminating, realizing that ideas are a dime a dozen. They are intimately familiar with their industries, customers, and competition. This obsession with opportunity is what guides how an entrepreneur deals with important issues. It is noteworthy that the Chinese characters for crisis and problem, when combined, mean opportunity.
- *Tolerance of risk, ambiguity, and uncertainty.* Since high rates of change and high levels of risk, ambiguity, and uncertainty are almost a given, successful entrepreneurs tolerate risk, ambiguity, and uncertainty. They manage paradoxes and contradictions.

  Entrepreneurs risk money and much more than that—reputation. Successful entrepreneurs are not gamblers; they take calculated risks. Like the parachutist, they are willing to take a risk; however, in deciding to take a risk, they calculate the risk carefully and thoroughly and do everything possible to get the odds in their favor. Entrepreneurs get others to share inherent financial and business risks with them. Partners put up money and put their reputations on the line, and investors do likewise. Creditors also join the party, as do customers who advance payments and suppliers who advance credit. For example, one researcher studied three very successful entrepreneurs in California who initiated and orchestrated actions that had risk consequences.[16] It was found that while they shunned risk, they sustained their courage by the clarity and optimism with which they saw the future. They limited the risks they initiated by carefully defining and strategizing their ends and by controlling and monitoring their means—and by tailoring them both to what they saw the future to be. Further, they managed risk by transferring it to others.

  More recently, in 1990, John B. Miner proposed his concept of motivation–organizational fit, within which he contrasted a hierarchic (managerial) role with a task (entrepreneurial) role.[17] This study of motivational patterns showed that those who are

[14] David L Bradford and Allan R Cohen, *Managing for Excellence: The Guide to Developing High Performance in Contemporary Organizations* (New York: John Wiley & Sons, 1984).

[15] Churchill, "Entrepreneurs and Their Enterprises: A Stage Model," pp. 1–22.

[16] Daryl Mitton, "No Money, Know-How, Know-Who: Formula for Managing Venture Success and Personal Wealth," *Frontiers of Entrepreneurship Research: 1984*, ed J. Hornaday et al. (Babson Park, Mass.: Babson College, 1984), p. 427.

[17] John B Miner, "Entrepreneurs, High Growth Entrepreneurs and Managers: Contrasting and Overlapping Motivational Patterns," *Journal of Business Venturing* 5, p. 224.

task oriented (i.e., entrepreneurs) opt for the following roles because of the corresponding motivations:

Role	Motivation
1. Individual achievement.	A desire to achieve through one's own efforts and to attribute success to personal causation.
2. Risk avoidance.	A desire to avoid risk and leave little to chance.
3. Seeking results of behavior.	A desire for feedback.
4. Personal innovation.	A desire to introduce innovative solutions.
5. Planning and goals setting.	A desire to think about the future and anticipate future possibilities.

Entrepreneurs also tolerate ambiguity and uncertainty and are comfortable with conflict. Ask someone working in a large company how sure they are about receiving a paycheck this month, in two months, in six months, and next year. Invariably, they will say that it is virtually certain and will muse at the question. Start-up entrepreneurs face just the opposite situation; there may be no revenue at the beginning, and if there is, a 90-day backlog in orders would be quite an exception. To make matters worse, lack of organization, structure, and order is a way of life. Constant changes introduce ambiguity and stress into every part of the enterprise. Jobs are undefined and changing continually, customers are new, co-workers are new, and setbacks and surprises are inevitable. And there never seems to be enough time.

Successful entrepreneurs maximize the good "higher performance" results of stress and minimize the negative reactions of exhaustion and frustration. Two surveys have suggested that very high levels of both satisfaction and stress characterize founders, to a greater degree than managers, regardless of the success of their ventures.[18]

- *Creativity, self-reliance, and ability to adapt.* The high levels of uncertainty and very rapid rates of change that characterize new ventures require fluid and highly adaptive forms of organization. An organization that can respond quickly and effectively is a must.

  Successful entrepreneurs believe in themselves. They believe that their accomplishments (and setbacks) lie within their own control and influence and that they can affect the outcome. Successful entrepreneurs have the ability to see and "sweat the details" and also to conceptualize (i.e., they have "helicopter minds"). They are dissatisfied with the status quo and are restless initiators.

  The entrepreneur has historically been viewed as an independent, a highly self-reliant innovator, and the champion (and occasional villain) of the free enterprise economy. More modern research and investigation have refined considerably the ways of focusing on this self-reliance. There is considerable agreement among researchers and practitioners alike that effective entrepreneurs actively seek and take initiative. They willingly put themselves in situations where they are personally responsible for the success or failure of the operation. They like to take the initiative to solve a problem or fill a vacuum where no leadership exists. They also like situations where personal impact on problems can be measured. Again, this is the action-oriented nature of the entrepreneur expressing itself.

  Successful entrepreneurs are adaptive and resilient. They have an insatiable desire to know how well they are performing. They realize that to know how well they are doing

[18] D Boyd and D E Gumpert, "Loneliness of the Start-Up Entrepreneur," in *Frontiers of Entrepreneurship Research: 1982 and 1983*, ed J A Hornaday et al. (Babson Park, MA: Babson College, 1983), pp. 478–87.

and how to improve their performance, they need to actively seek out and use feedback. Seeking and using feedback is also central to the habit of learning from mistakes and setbacks, and of responding to the unexpected. For the same reasons, these entrepreneurs often are described as excellent listeners and quick learners.

Entrepreneurs are not afraid of failing; rather, they are more intent on succeeding, counting on the fact that "success covers a multitude of blunders,"[19] as George Bernard Shaw eloquently stated. People who fear failure will neutralize whatever achievement motivation they may possess. They will tend to engage in a very easy task, where there is little chance of failure, or in a very difficult situation, where they cannot be held personally responsible if they do not succeed.

Further, successful entrepreneurs have the ability to use failure experiences as a way of learning. They better understand not only their roles but also the roles of others in causing the failure, and thus are able to avoid similar problems in the future. There is an old saying to the effect that the cowboy who has never been thrown from a horse undoubtedly has not ridden too many! The iterative, trial-and-error nature of becoming a successful entrepreneur makes serious setbacks and disappointments an integral part of the learning process.

- *Motivation to excel.* Successful entrepreneurs are motivated to excel. Entrepreneurs are self-starters who appear driven internally by a strong desire to compete against their own self-imposed standards and to pursue and attain challenging goals. This need to achieve has been well established in the literature on entrepreneurs since the pioneering work of McClelland and Atkinson on motivation in the 1950s and 1960s. Seeking out the challenge inherent in a start-up and responding in a positive way, noted by the distinguished entrepreneurs mentioned above, is achievement motivation in action.

Conversely, these entrepreneurs have a low need for status and power, and they derive personal motivation from the challenge and excitement of creating and building enterprises. They are driven by a thirst for achievement, rather than by status and power. Ironically, their accomplishments, especially if they are very successful, give them power. But it is important to recognize that power and status are a result of their activities.

Setting high but attainable goals enables entrepreneurs to focus their energies, be very selective in sorting out opportunities, and know what to say no to. Having goals and direction also helps define priorities and provides measures of how well they are performing. Having an objective way of keeping score, such as changes in profits, sales, or stock price, is also important. Thus, money is seen as a tool, and a way of keeping score, rather than the object of the game by itself.

Successful entrepreneurs insist on the highest personal standards of integrity and reliability. They do what they say they are going to do, and they pull for the long-haul. These high personal standards are the glue and fiber that binds successful personal and business relationships and makes them endure. A study involving 130 members of the Small Company Management Program at Harvard Business School confirmed how important this issue is. Most simply said it was the single most important factor in their *long-term* successes.[20]

The best entrepreneurs have a keen awareness of their own strengths and weaknesses and those of their partners and of the competitive and other environments surrounding and influencing them. They are coldly realistic about what they can and cannot do and do not delude themselves; that is, they have "veridical awareness" or "optimistic realism." It also is worth noting that successful entrepreneurs believe in

[19] Cited in Royal Little, *How to Lose $100,000,000 and Other Valuable Advice* (Boston: Little, Brown and Company, 1979), p. 72.

[20] Timmons and Stevenson, "Entrepreneurship Education in the 80s: What Entrepreneurs Say," pp. 115–34.

themselves. They do not believe the success or failure of their venture will be governed by fate, luck, or other powerful, external forces. They believe that they personally can affect the outcome. This attribute is also consistent with achievement motivation, which is the desire to take personal responsibility, and self-confidence.

This veridical awareness often is accompanied by other valuable entrepreneurial traits—perspective and a sense of humor. The ability to retain a sense of perspective, and to "know thyself" in both strengths and weaknesses, makes it possible for an entrepreneur to laugh, to ease tensions, and—frequently—to get an unfavorable situation set in a more profitable direction.

Other Desirable (but Not So Acquirable) Attitudes and Behaviors

The list of characteristics that most experts and observers would argue are more innate than acquired is, fortunately, much shorter. Even here researchers debate extensively whether these can be learned or nurtured to some degree. A friend who is a pediatrician provided a very appropriate explanation of the extent to which certain aspects of our personalities and makeup can be changed. It is like working with fine sandpaper on a large and very hard piece of wood. The surface of the wood can be modified by smoothing and refining it, but to alter its shape is an enormous undertaking.

The following five areas are of this nature. While these, too, are highly desirable givens for any aspiring entrepreneur with which to begin, it is possible to find quite successful entrepreneurs that may be lacking some or possess only a modest degree of each of these. Once again, few entrepreneurs—or others—have exceptional capacities in each of these areas. If these describe a particular entrepreneur's innate talents, then he or she possesses a tremendous potential to be harnessed.

- *Energy, health, and emotional stability.* The extraordinary work loads and stressful demands faced by entrepreneurs place a premium on energy and on physical and emotional health. While each has strong genetic roots, they can also be fine-tuned and preserved by careful attention to eating and drinking habits, exercise, and relaxation.
- *Creativity and innovativeness.* Creativity once was thought of as an exclusively inherited capacity, and most would agree that its roots are strongly genetic. But that may be a surprisingly culture-bound notion, judging by the level of creativity and innovation in the United States, compared with other equally sophisticated cultures that are not as creative and innovative. As noted in Chapter 2, a growing school of thought believes that creativity can actually be learned.
- *Intelligence.* Intelligence and conceptual ability are great advantages for an entrepreneur. There is most likely no successful higher potential venture whose founder would be described as dumb or even of average intelligence. But street smarts (i.e., a nose for business), the entrepreneur's gut feel and instincts, and "ratlike cunning"[21] are special kinds of intelligence. Also, there are many examples of school dropouts who go on to become truly extraordinary entrepreneurs.

  Take, for instance, the late Colonel Sanders of Kentucky Fried Chicken fame. He has been quoted as saying, "When I got to the point in school where they said *X* equals the unknown quantity *Y,* I decided I had learned as much as I could, and decided I needed to quit school and go to work!" Needless to say, this is not intended to encourage anyone to leave school. The point is that an individual may have a kind of intelligence that will serve him or her well as an entrepreneur but not so well in some other situations.

[21] The author thanks Phillip Thurston of Harvard Business School for this insightful term.

- *Capacity to inspire.* Vision is that natural leadership quality that is charismatic, bold, and inspirational. All great leaders through the ages share vision, as do many truly extraordinary entrepreneurs. It is difficult to get anyone to argue that such exceptional personal qualities are other than inborn. Yet, though an entrepreneur's charisma quotient may be low, he or she is still the leader, and his or her vision is conveyed by the style of leadership. The entrepreneur's goals and values will establish the atmosphere within which all subsequent activity will unfold, and his or her inspiration, regardless of the form it takes, will shape the venture.
- *Values.* Personal and ethical values seem to reflect the environments and backgrounds from which entrepreneurs have come and are developed early in life. These values are an integral part of an individual.

A Look at the Nonentrepreneurial Mind

There also appears to be a nonentrepreneurial mind that spells trouble for a new venture, or can be fatal. There is apparently no research on this topic, other than broad-brush abstractions about "management as the leading cause of failure."

Findings about hazardous thought patterns of pilots that may contribute to bad judgment are intriguing.[22] There may well be some parallels between the piloting task and leading an emerging company. Such feelings as invulnerability, being macho, being antiauthoritarian, being impulsive, and having outer control have been shown by researchers to be hazardous to pilots. To this list have been added three others—being a perfectionist, being a know-it-all, and being counter-dependent.

- *Invulnerability.* This is a thought pattern of people who feel nothing disastrous could happen to them. They are likely to take unnecessary chances and unwise risks. This behavior obviously has severe implications when flying an airplane or launching a company.
- *Being macho.* This describes people who try to prove they are better than others and can beat them. They may try to prove themselves by taking large risks, and they may try to impress others by exposing themselves to danger (i.e., they are adrenaline junkies). While it is associated with overconfidence, this thought pattern goes beyond that definition. Foolish head-to-head competition and irrational takeover battles may be good examples of this behavior.
- *Being antiauthoritarian.* Some people resent control of their actions by any outside authority. Their approach is summed up by the following: "Do not tell me what to do. No one can tell me what to do!" Contrast this thought pattern with the tendency of successful entrepreneurs to seek and use feedback to attain their goals and to improve their performance, and with their propensity to seek team members and other necessary resources to execute an opportunity.
- *Impulsivity.* Facing a moment of decision, certain people feel they must do something, do anything, and do it quickly. They fail to explore the implications of their actions and do not review alternatives before acting.
- *Outer control.* This is the opposite of the internal locus of control characteristic of successful entrepreneurs. People with the outer-control trait feel they can do little, if anything, to control what happens to them. If things go well, they attribute it to good luck, and vice versa.
- *Perfectionist.* Time and again, perfectionism is the enemy of the entrepreneur. The time and cost implications of attaining perfection invariably result in the opportunity window's

[22] Berl Brechner, "A Question of Judgment," *Flying*, May 1981, pp. 47–52.

being slammed shut by a more decisive and nimble competitor, or disappearing altogether by a leapfrog in technology. (Being a perfectionist and having high standards are not the same, however.)

- *Know it all.* Entrepreneurs who think they have all the answers usually have very few. To make matters worse, they often fail to recognize what they do *not* know. Good people find good opportunities in other ways.
- *Counterdependency.* An extreme and severe case of independence can be a limiting mind-set for entrepreneurs. Bound and determined to accomplish things all by themselves, without a particle of help from anyone, these entrepreneurs often end up accomplishing very little. But it is all theirs to claim.

THE CONCEPT OF APPRENTICESHIP

Shaping and Managing an Apprenticeship

When one looks at successful entrepreneurs, one sees profiles of careers rich in experience. Time and again there is a pattern among successful entrepreneurs. They have all acquired 10 or more years of substantial experience, built contacts, possess the know-how, and established a track record in the industry, market, and technology niche within which they eventually launch, acquire, or build a business. Frequently, they have acquired intimate knowledge of the customer, distribution channels, and market through direct sales and marketing experience. The more successful ones have made money for their employer before doing it for themselves. Consider the following examples:

- Apple Computer founders Steve Jobs and Steve Wozniak were computer enthusiasts as preteens and had accumulated a *relatively* lengthy amount of experience by the time they started the company in their mid-20s. In entirely new industries such as microcomputers, a few years can be a large amount of experience.
- Paul Tobin had no prior cellular phone experience when he was picked up by John Kluge to launch Cellular One of eastern Massachusetts—but neither did anyone else! He had had six years of experience at Satellite Business Systems in marketing and had previously spent over five years launching and building his own company in a nontechnology business. His learning curves as an entrepreneur were invaluable in the next start-up.
- Jeff Parker had worked for 10 years in the bond-trading business at three major investment banks; he had sold, managed, and built a substantial trading business at one of the investment banks. His technical and computer background enabled him to write programs to assist bond traders on the first Apple Computers. He launched Technical Data Corporation with $100,000 in 1981 and built the first on-line computer system for bond traders. A few years later, his company was sold to Telerate for over $20 million.[23]

There are tens of thousands of similar examples. There are always exceptions to any such pattern, but if you want the odds in your favor get the experience first. As was shown in Chapter 1, successful entrepreneurs are likely to be older and to have at least 8 to 10 years of experience. They are likely to have accumulated enough net worth to contribute to funding the venture or to have a track record impressive enough to give investors and creditors the necessary confidence. Finally, they usually have found and nurtured relevant business and other contacts and networks that ultimately contribute to the success of their ventures.

It is fair to say that the first 10 or so years after leaving school can make or break an entrepreneur's career in terms of how well he or she is prepared for serious entrepreneuring.

[23] This example is drawn from "Technical Data Corporation," HBS Cases 283-072, 283-073, Harvard Business School, 1987.

Evidence suggests that the most durable entrepreneurial careers, those found to last 25 years or more, were begun across a broad age spectrum, but after the person selected prior work or a career to prepare specifically for an entrepreneurial career.

Having relevant experience, know-how, attitudes, behaviors, and skills appropriate for a particular venture opportunity can dramatically improve the odds for success. The other side of the coin is that if an entrepreneur does not have these, then he or she will have to learn them while launching and growing the business. The tuition for such an approach is often greater than most entrepreneurs can afford.

Since entrepreneurs frequently evolve from an entrepreneurial heritage or are shaped and nurtured by their closeness to entrepreneurs and others, the concept of an apprenticeship can be a useful one. And there's no doubt that a lot of what an entrepreneur needs to know about entrepreneuring comes from learning by doing. Knowing for what to prepare, where the windows for acquiring the relevant exposure lie, how to anticipate these, where to position oneself, and when to move on can be quite useful.

As Howard Stevenson of the Harvard Business School has said:

> You have to approach the world as an equal. There is no such thing as being supplicant. You are trying to work and create a better solution by creating action among a series of people who are relatively equal. We destroy potential entrepreneurs by putting them in a velvet-lined rut, by giving them jobs that pay too much, and by telling them they are too good, before they get adequate intelligence, experience, and responsibility.

Windows of Apprenticeship

Exhibit 5.5 summarizes the key elements of an apprenticeship and experience curve and relates these to age windows.[24] Age windows are especially important because of the inevitable time it takes to create and build a successful activity, whether it is a new venture or within another organization.

There is the saying in the venture capital business that the "lemons," or losers, in a portfolio ripen in about two and one half years and that the "pearls," or winners, on the other hand, usually take seven or eight years to come to fruition (see *Exhibit 3.2*). Therefore, seven years is a realistic time frame to expect to grow a higher potential business to a point where a capital gain can be realized. Interestingly, seven years is often described by presidents of large corporations, presidents of colleges, and self-employed professionals as the time it takes to do something significant.

The implications of this are quite provocative. First, time is precious. Assume an entrepreneur spends the first five years after college or graduate school gaining relevant experience. He or she will be 25 to 30 years of age (or maybe as old as 35) when launching a new venture. By the age of 50, there will have been time for starting, at most, three successful new ventures. What's more, entrepreneurs commonly go through false starts or even a failure at first in the trial-and-error process of learning the entrepreneurial ropes. As a result, the first venture may not be launched until later (i.e., in the entrepreneur's mid- to late-30s). This would leave time to grow the current venture and maybe one more. (There is, of course, always the possibility of staying with a venture and growing it to a larger company of $50 million or more in sales.)

Reflecting on *Exhibit 5.5* will reveal some other paradoxes and dilemmas. For one thing, just when an entrepreneur's drive, energy, and ambition are at a peak, the necessary relevant

[24] The author wishes to acknowledge the contributions to his thinking by Mr. Harvey "Chet" Krentzman, entrepreneur, lecturer, author, and nurturer of at least three dozen growth-minded ventures over the past 20 years.

Exhibit 5.5
Windows of the Entrepreneurial Apprenticeship

Elements of the Apprenticeship and Experience Curve	*Age Window* 20s	30s	40s	50s
1. Relevant business experience.	Low	Moderate to high	Higher	Highest
2. Management skills and know-how.	Low to moderate	Moderate to high	High	High
3. Entrepreneurial goals and commitment.	Varies widely	Focused high	High	High
4. Drive and energy.	Highest	High	Moderate	Lowest
5. Wisdom and judgment.	Lowest	Higher	Higher	Highest
6. Focus of apprenticeship.	Discussing what you enjoy; key is learning business, sales, marketing; profit and loss responsibility.	General management Division management Founder	Growing and harvesting	Reinvesting
7. Dominant life-stage issues*	Realizing your dream of adolescence and young adulthood.	Personal growth and new directions and ventures.	Renewal, regeneration, reinvesting in the system.	

*Adapted from Daniel J Levinson et al., *The Seasons of a Man's Life* (New York: Alfred A. Knopf, 1978).

business experience and management skills are least developed, and those critical elements wisdom and judgment are in their infancy. Later on, when an entrepreneur has gained the necessary experience in the "deep, dark canyons of uncertainty" and has thereby gained wisdom and judgment, mother nature has begun to recall the vast energy and drive that got him or her so far. Also, patience and perseverance to relentlessly pursue a long-term vision need to be balanced with the urgency and realism to make it happen. Flexibility to stick with the moving opportunity targets and to abandon some and shift to others is also required. However, flexibility and the ability to act with urgency disappear as the other commitments of life are assumed.

A Personal Strategy

An apprenticeship can be an integral part of the process of shaping an entrepreneurial career. One principal task is to determine what kind of an entrepreneur he or she is likely to become, based on background, experience, and drive. Through an apprenticeship, an entrepreneur can shape a strategy and action plan to make it happen. Part VI addresses this issue more fully.

Despite all the work involved in becoming an entrepreneur, the bottom line is revealing. Evidence about the careers and job satisfaction of entrepreneurs all points to the same conclusion: If they had to do it over, not only would more of them become entrepreneurs again, but they would do it sooner.[25] And, they would also do it earlier in their careers.[26] They report higher personal satisfaction with their lives and their careers than their managerial counterparts. Nearly three times as many say they plan never to retire, according to Stevenson, than do managers. Numerous other studies show that the satisfaction from independence and living and working where and how they want to is a source of great

[25] Stevenson, "Who Are the Harvard Self-Employed?" *Frontiers of Entrepreneurship Research: 1983*, ed. J A Hornaday et al. (Babson Park, MA: Babson College, 1983), pp. 233–54.

[26] Boyd and Gumpert, "Loneliness of the Start-Up Entrepreneur," p. 486.

Immediately after graduation Kevin married his high school sweetheart and enrolled in Stanford Business School. He recalled his decision to enroll:

Stanford advised students entering directly from undergraduate school to work for several years before beginning the MBA. I figured that most of the younger students probably followed Stanford's advice. So I decided to enroll right away, learn from *their* work experiences, and save myself some time!

During his two years at Stanford Kevin chose courses he thought would help him run a small business of his own. Then, before job interviews began, Kevin and his wife decided that the Pacific Northwest was the place they wanted to live; he planned his company interviews accordingly. (See *Exhibit A.*)

Price Waterhouse was interviewing students interested in working in its newly created small business division in Seattle. Although Kevin never planned to be an accountant, the location appealed to him and he thought the job would give him the opportunity to get to

Exhibit A
Kevin Mooney's Résumé

KEVIN MOONEY
Blackwelder 5–G
Stanford, California 94305
(555) 321–6877

JOB OBJECTIVE:	To secure a consulting or staff position in corporate or financial planning.
EDUCATION:	
1974–1976	STANFORD GRADUATE SCHOOL OF BUSINESS Candidate for MBA degree in June 1976. Concentration in finance. Selected to represent the Stanford Graduate School of Business on the Journey for Perspective Foundation 1975 international study program abroad. Traveled to Eastern and Western Europe for seminars with business and political leaders. Member of Investment Club and Business Development Association.
1970–1974	CORNELL UNIVERSITY, Ithaca, New York BS degree in Industrial Engineering and Operations Research in June 1974. Dean's list. Chairman of Cornell Student Finance Commission. Responsibilities included financial planning for more than 100 organizations, allocation of $130,000 of student fees, hiring and directing office staff, and administration of accounts. President of Quill & Dagger Society (senior honorary).
BUSINESS EXPERIENCE:	
Summer 1975	PEAT, MARWICK, MITCHELL & CO., San Francisco, California Management Consultant. Performed conceptual design and implementation of a centralized purchase order system. Developed complete cost accounting system and contributed in formulating approach and preparing written proposal for a consulting engagement.
Summer 1974	CORNELL UNIVERSITY, Ithaca, New York Summer Conference Coordinator. Administrative responsibility for summer conference programs. Duties included computer information system development and implementation, personnel administration, and coordination of university departments and facilities.
Summers 1972, 1973	DECISION DATA COMPUTER CORPORATION, Horsham, Pennsylvania Manufacturing Engineer. Responsibilities included plant layout, tool design, and writing manufacturing instructions.
Additional Information	Married. Private pilot, currently pursuing additional ratings. Other interests include skiing, photography, swimming, and bicycling.
References	Personal references are on file with the Placement Office and will be forwarded upon request.

know the region's business community. He took the job, and within three months he was generating all his own work, often attending business breakfasts to drum up prospective clients. During the first year he brought five new clients to the firm.

Softcorp, Inc.

One of his many clients was Softcorp, Inc. Founded in 1969 by two men who had worked together at Hewlett-Packard, the company was just beginning to build a reasonable customer base. In the beginning the two founders, Joe Hegarty and Bob Wilson, designed the company's accounting applications packages themselves. Accounts Payable and Fixed Asset Accounting were the company's flagship products and contributed about 90 percent of Softcorp's revenue. Entirely internally funded except for a small line of credit at the bank, Softcorp dedicated its efforts to product development, marketing, and customer support and training. By 1976, it had 29 employees and sales of $1.2 million. (See *Exhibit B.*)

Hegarty and Wilson first came to Price Waterhouse for help in enhancing their fixed-asset system to incorporate the latest IRS depreciation rules. After three years and no solution, Softcorp's executives were understandably frustrated. Kevin Mooney took over their account and resolved the outstanding problems within three months. Mooney's manner and competence impressed the two men, and their relationship thrived. Then, in late 1977, Hegarty and Wilson approached Kevin about the job as director of international marketing.

The Job Negotiations

The offer intrigued Mooney. He saw the opportunities inherent in this small company. He knew little about the general markets for software packages and even less about the international markets. Softcorp was small and undercapitalized, and Kevin wondered what resources would be available to him to launch an international marketing effort.

Kevin worked well with the two founders. He and his wife had been guests at Hegarty's home. In December 1977, Kevin Mooney met with Hegarty and Wilson to discuss the details of the job.

I remember asking them if they knew of any international customers out there who wanted their products. Hegarty just shrugged his shoulders and said, "If there are, we know you'll find them."

I reminded them that I didn't have any operating experience, but that didn't seem to bother them. They seemed very impressed with my competence and my education. Frankly, I don't think I would have hired me!

They offered me a nice salary (a 20 percent increase over what I was making at PW) plus a bonus which would be tied to performance. I raised the question of equity participation. Both men were reluctant to give me any equity up front. They cited examples of two employees who had been given stock, but only after each had demonstrated his commitment and loyalty to the company. They told me that once I had done the same, equity would be a possibility.

Exhibit B
Softcorp, Inc., Performance, 1974–1976 ($000)

	1974	*1975*	*1976*
Annual revenue	$357	$734	$1,217
Installations (cumulative)	383	449	530
Total employees	11	23	29

The elevator stopped at the lobby. Kevin had just had a last meeting with his boss, Bob Baker. His mentor at Price Waterhouse was disappointed that Kevin would throw away his promising future at Price Waterhouse.

Baker reminded Kevin that promotions would be announced in a few months, and he thought Kevin had a very good shot at being promoted to manager. Baker asked him several questions he couldn't answer: What resources would Softcorp make available to build the international division? How were they planning to measure his performance? What would constitute success or failure?

When the meeting ended, Baker shook Kevin Mooney's hand and said, "Do you realize if you go to Softcorp, you are probably going to fail? Are you prepared for that?" Mooney left the building with Baker's questions running through his mind. Softcorp's offer letter and nondisclosure agreement were in his briefcase, ready for his signature. He had two weeks to make his decision.

EXERCISE (OPTIONAL)

If desired, the Personal Entrepreneurial Strategy Exercises in Chapter 21, Part VI, may be done at this point. Before proceeding with the exercises, however, be sure to read the material on planning and obtaining feedback in Chapter 11.

The Entrepreneurial Manager 6

It's rare to find a leader who can carry a growing company through all its phases. When you get into the $1- to $2-billion range, then you may find leaders with entrepreneurial tendencies; but, in addition, they have real management and people skills.

Peter J. Sprague,
Chairman of the Board,
National Semiconductor Corporation

RESULTS EXPECTED

Upon completion of this chapter, you will have:

1. Studied different views about entrepreneurial managers and discovered that an individual can be both an entrepreneur and a manager.
2. Identified the stages of growth entrepreneurial ventures go through, the domain occupied, the venture modes characteristic of the entrepreneurial domain, and the principal forces acting in the domain.
3. Identified specific skills entrepreneurs need to know in order to manage start-up, survival, and growth.
4. Analyzed the case of PMI, Inc.
5. Evaluated your own skills and developed an action plan.

THE ENTREPRENEURIAL DOMAIN

Converging on the Entrepreneurial Manager

There are convergent pressures on being an entrepreneur and being a manager as a venture accelerates and grows beyond founder-driven and founder-dominated survival. Key to achieving longer-term sustained growth, and an eventual harvest, is the ability of an entrepreneur to have or develop competencies as an entrepreneurial manager.

In the past, those studying entrepreneurship and others active in starting new ventures, such as venture capitalists, professors, and researchers, have generally felt that the kind of person with the entrepreneurial spirit required to propel a new venture through start-up to a multimillion-dollar annual sales level is different from the kind of person who has the capacity to manage the new firm as it grows from $5 million to $20 million or $30 million in sales. Further, it has long been thought that the entrepreneur who clings to the lead role too long during the maturation process will subsequently limit company growth, if not seriously retard it.

As John Kenneth Galbraith explained in 1971, "The great entrepreneur must, in fact, be compared in life with the male 'apis mellifera.' He accomplishes his act of conception at the price of his own extinction."[1]

In short, 'conventional wisdom' stated that a good entrepreneur is usually not a good manager, since he or she lacks the necessary management skill and experience. Likewise, it

[1] John Kenneth Galbraith, *The New Industrial State* (Boston: Houghton Mifflin, 1971).

is assumed that a manager is not an entrepreneur, since he or she lacks some intense personal qualities and the orientation required to launch a business from ground zero.

Increasingly, however, evidence suggests that new ventures that flourish beyond start-up and grow to become substantial, successful enterprises can be headed by entrepreneurs who are also effective managers. For instance, a 1983 survey by *INC.* magazine of the heads of the top 100 new ventures showed that the majority of these companies had founders who were still chief executive officers after several years and after their companies had attained sales of at least $10 million (and some as much as $50 million or more). Testing conventional wisdom, two researchers empirically studied the tenure of 54 Fortune 1,000 corporations' founders. They assumed that there are three reasons why founders have to adapt: (1) shift from creation to exploitation, (2) shift from passionate commitment to dispassionate objectivity, and (3) shift from direct personal control over organizational actions to indirect impersonal control. Taking into account the growth rate, the timing of the initial public offering, the founder's age, education, and other factors, this 1990 study found the following:

1. "If the firm grows relatively slowly, and the founder is capable of some adaptation, then the firm can apparently become quite large."
2. "Founders with scientific or engineering backgrounds remain in control of the companies they found for shorter periods than do founders whose academic focus was business."
3. "The founder's tenure will typically be longer in family dominated firms."[2]

More recently, researchers "observed that many founders can and do manage growth successfully. The applicability of conventional wisdom regarding the 'leadership crisis' in rapid-growth entrepreneurial firms may no longer be valid, if, in fact, it ever was."[3]

These and other data seem to defy the notion that entrepreneurs can start but cannot manage growing companies. While the truth is probably somewhere in between, one thing is apparent: Growing a higher potential venture requires management skills.

Clearly, a complex set of factors goes into making someone a successful entrepreneurial manager. Launching a new venture and then managing rapid growth involves managerial roles and tasks not found in most mature or stable environments. Further, one of the greatest strengths of successful entrepreneurs is that they know what they do and do not know. They have disciplined intellectual honesty, which prevents their optimism from becoming myopic delusion and their dreams from becoming blind ambition. No individual has all these skills, nor does the presence or absence of any single skill guarantee success or failure. That an entrepreneur knows that he or she needs a certain skill and knows where to get it is clearly as valuable as knowing whether he or she already has it.

Principal Forces and Venture Modes

Companies, whether they are new, growing, or mature, occupy a place in either an administrative or an entrepreneurial domain, an area influenced by certain principal forces and characterized by ways of acting, called venture modes. *Exhibits 6.1* and *6.2* illustrate the entrepreneurial and administrative domains and the dynamic of the principal forces acting in the domains and the dominant venture modes which result.

In the exhibits, the four cells are defined by the stage of the venture (upper axis), the extent of change and uncertainty accompanying it (right axis), and the degree to which a venture is administrative (bottom axis) or entrepreneurial (left axis). Clearly, the entrepreneurial domain is the two upper cells in both exhibits, and the domains are functions both of the change and uncertainty facing a venture and the stage of growth of the venture.

[2] George C Rubenson and Anil K Gupta, "The Founder's Disease: A Critical Reexamination," *Frontiers of Entrepreneurship Research: 1990*, ed. Neil Churchill et al. (Babson Park, MA: Babson College, 1990), pp. 177–78.

[3] Gary E Willard, David A Krueger, and Henry R Feeser, "In Order to Grow, Must the Founder Go: A Comparison of Performance Between Founder and Non-Founder Managed High-Growth Manufacturing Firms," *Journal of Business Venturing* 7, p. 190.

Exhibit 6.1
Dominant Venture Modes

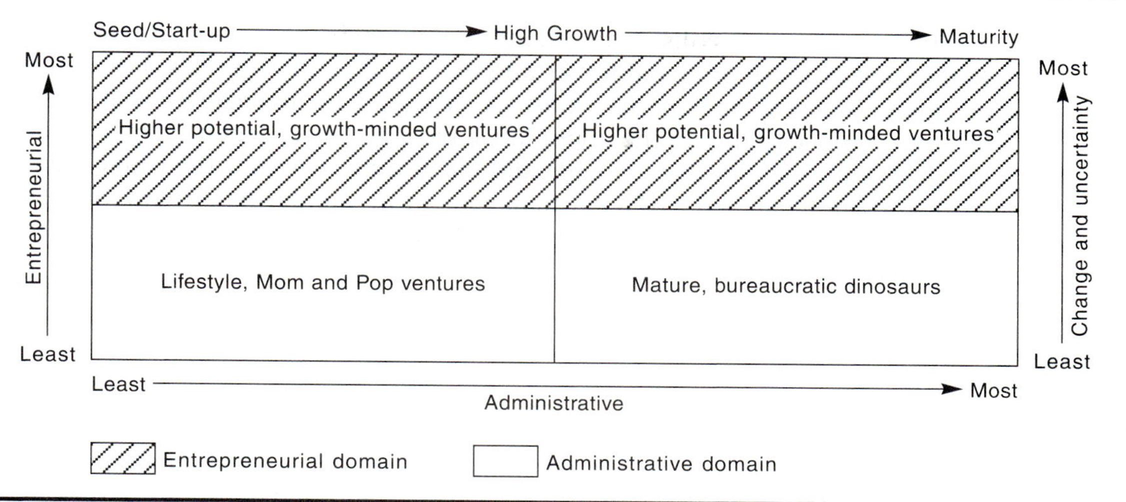

Exhibit 6.2
Principal Driving Forces

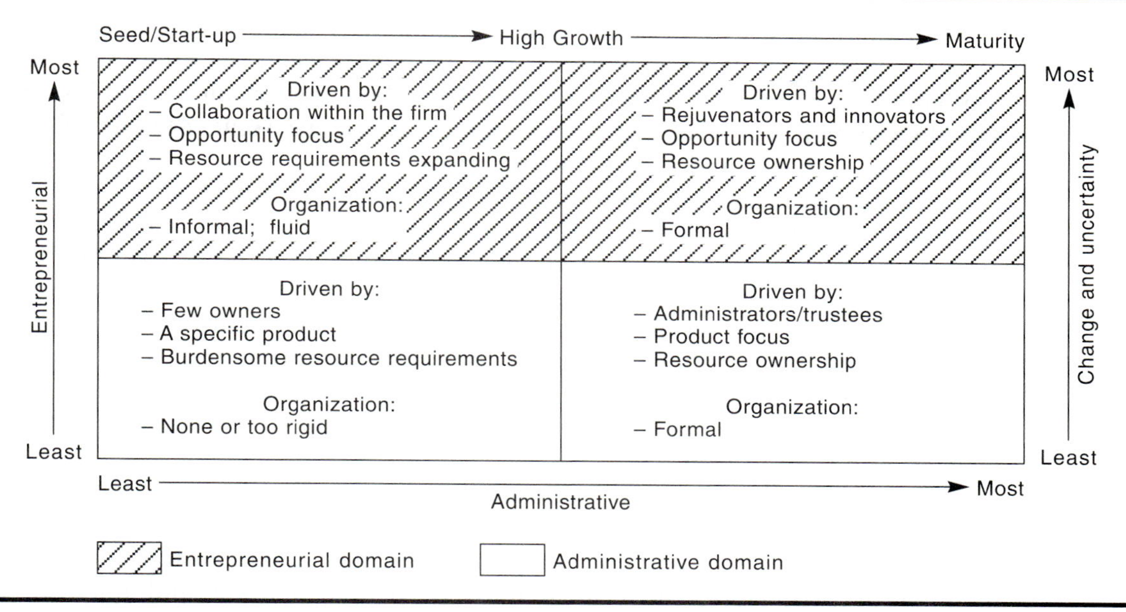

Source: These exhibits are built on work by Timmons and Stevenson: See Howard H Stevenson, "A New Paradigm for Entrepreneurial Management," in *Entrepreneurship: What It Is and How to Teach It* (Boston: Harvard Business School, 1985), pp. 30–61; and Jeffry A Timmons and Howard H Stevenson, "Entrepreneurship Education in the 80s: What Entrepreneurs Say," in *Entrepreneurship: What It Is and How to Teach It,* pp. 115–34.

Each venture mode (i.e., ways of acting) for firms in each cell is driven by certain principal forces. These forces are shown in *Exhibit 6.1.* Shown in *Exhibit 6.2* are dominant venture modes characteristic of firms in each cell. Organizations at different stages are characterized by differing degrees of change and uncertainty and are therefore more or less entrepreneurial or more or less administrative. Thus, for example, a new venture in the seed/start-up stage, which is characterized by high change and uncertainty, is most entrepreneurial. These firms will be new, innovative, or backbone ventures; will be led by a team; will be driven by their founders' goals, values, commitment, and perceptions of the opportunities; and will minimize the use of resources. At the other extreme is a mature firm, one which is in the maturity stage and characterized by low change and uncertainty, one

Exhibit 6.4
Entrepreneurial Transitions

Modes/Stages	*Doing*	*Managing*	*Managing Managers*
Sales	0 to $3 million	$3 to 10 million	$10 million or more
Employees	0 to 30	30 to 75	75 and up
Transitions	Characteristics: Founder-driven creativity Constant change, ambiguity and uncertainty Time compression Informal communicatins Counterintuitive decision making and structure Relative inexperience	Probable crises: Erosion of creativity of founders Confusion over ambiguous roles, responsibilities, and goals Desire for delegation versus autonomy and control	Probable crises: Failure to clone founders Specialization/eroding of collaboration versus practice of power, information, and influence Need for operating controls and mechanisms Conflict among founders

influence are derived not only from achieving one's own goals but also from contributing to the achievements of others as well. Influence also is derived from keeping the overall goals in mind, from resolving differences, and from developing a reputation as a person who gets results, can manage others, and grows managerial talent as well.

Thus, among successful entrepreneurs and entrepreneurial managers, there is a well-developed capacity to exert influence *without* formal power. These people are adept at conflict resolution. They know when to use logic and when to persuade, when to make a concession and when to exact one. To run a successful venture, an entrepreneur learns to get along with many different constituencies, often with conflicting aims—the customer, the supplier, the financial backer, and the creditor, as well as the partners and others on the inside. Similarly, an entrepreneurial manager must operate in a world that is increasingly interdependent. Attempting to advise managers on how to exert "influence without authority," Allan R. Cohen and David L. Bradford assert that "if you are a manager, you not only need to exercise influence skills with your peers and your own boss, but also to help the people who work for you learn to be effective influencers—even of you—since that will free you to spend more of your time seeking new opportunities and working the organization above and around you."[7]

Whereas successful entrepreneurs are interpersonally supporting and nurturing—not interpersonally competitive—successful entrepreneurial managers understand their interdependencies and have learned to incorporate mutual respect, openness, trust, and mutual benefit into their management style. Fundamental to this progressive style of management is the awareness and practice of reciprocity for mutual gain.[8] When a strong need to control, influence, and gain power over others characterizes the lead entrepreneur or the entrepreneurial manager or when he or she has an insatiable appetite for putting an associate down, more often than not the venture gets into trouble. A dictatorial, adversarial, and dominating management style makes it very difficult to attract and keep people who thrive on a thirst for achievement, responsibility, and results. Compliant partners and managers are often chosen. Destructive conflicts often erupt over who has the final say, who is right, and whose prerogatives are what.

In the corporate setting, the "hero-making" ability is identified as an essential attribute of successful entrepreneurial managers.[9] These hero-makers try to make the pie bigger and better, rather than jealously clutching and hoarding a tiny pie that is all theirs. They have a

[7] Allan R Cohen and David L Bradford, *Influence Without Authority* (New York: John Wiley & Sons, 1990), p. 17.

[8] Ibid.

[9] David L Bradford and Allan R Cohen, *Managing for Excellence: The Guide to Developing High Performance in Contemporary Organizations* (New York: John Wiley & Sons, 1984).

capacity for objective interpersonal relationships as well, which enables them to smooth out individual differences of opinion by keeping attention focused on the common goal to be achieved.[10]

Exhibit 6.4 characterizes probable crises that growing ventures will face, including erosion of creativity by founders and team; confusion or resentment, or both, over ambiguous roles, responsibilities, and goals; failure to be able to clone founders; specialization and eroding of collaboration; desire for autonomy and control; need for operating mechanisms and controls; and conflict and divorce among founders and members of team. It further delineates issues that confront entrepreneurial managers.

- *Compounding of time and change.* In the high-growth stage, change, ambiguity, and uncertainty seem to be the only things that remain constant. Change, which is constant, creates higher levels of uncertainty, ambiguity, and risk, which, in turn, compound to shrink time, an already precious commodity. One result of change is a series of shock waves rolling through a new and growing venture by way of new customers, new technologies, new competitors, new markets, and new people. In industries characterized by galloping technological change, with relatively miniscule lead and lag times in bringing new products to market and in weathering the storms of rapid obsolescence, the effects of change and time are extreme. For example, the president of a rapidly growing, small computer company said, "In our business it takes 6 to 12 months to develop a new computer, ready to bring to the market, and product technology obsolescence is running about 9 to 12 months." This time compression has been seen in such industries as electronics and aerospace in the 1960s; small computers, integrated circuits, and silicon chips in the 1970s; microcomputers in the 1980s; and telecommunications and biotechnology in the 1990s.
- *Nonlinear and nonparametric events.* Entrepreneurial management is characterized by nonlinear and nonparametric events. Just as the television did not come about by a succession of improvements in the radio and the jet plane did not emerge from engineers' and scientists' attempting to develop a better and better piston engine plane, so too within firms, events do not follow straight lines, progress arithmetically, or even appear related. Rather, they occur in bunches and in step-wise leaps. For example, a firm may double its sales forces in 15 months, rather than over eight years, while another may triple its manufacturing capacity and adopt a new materials resource planning system immediately, rather than utilizing existing capacity by increasing overtime, then adding a third shift nine months later, and finally adding a new plant three years hence.
- *Relative inexperience.* In addition, the management team may be relatively inexperienced. The explosive birth and growth of these firms are usually unique events that cannot be replicated, and most of the pieces in the puzzle—the technology, applications, customers, the people, the firm itself—are usually new. Take Prime Computer as an example. Sales of this manufacturer of minicomputers grew rapidly in five years from $100 million per year to nearly $1.2 billion per year. The average age of all employees in the company was less than 29 years, and the firm was barely 10 years old.
- *Counterintuitive, unconventional decision making.* Yet another characteristic of rapidly growing ventures in the entrepreneurial domain is counterintuitive, unconventional patterns of decision making. For example, a computer firm needed to decide what approach to take in developing and introducing three new products in an uncertain, risky marketplace. Each proposed new product appeared to be aimed at the same end-user market, and the person heading each project was similarly enthusiastic, confident, and determined about succeeding. A traditional approach to such a problem would have been to determine the size and growth rates of each market segment; evaluate the probabilistic

[10] Neil C Churchill, "Entrepreneurs and Their Enterprises: A Stage Model," in *Frontiers of Entrepreneurship Research: 1983*, ed J A Hornaday et al. (Babson Park, MA: Babson College, 1983), pp. 1–22.

estimates of future revenue costs and capital requirements for their accuracy; compare the discounted, present-value cash flow streams that will emerge from each project; and select the project with the highest yield versus the required internal rate of return. Such an analysis sometimes overlooks the fact that most rapid growth companies have many excellent alternatives and, more commonly, the newness of technology, the immaturity of the marketplace, and the rapid discovery of further applications make it virtually impossible to know which of any product proposals is best. The computer firm decided to support all three new products at once, and a significant new business was built around each one. New market niches were discovered simultaneously and the unconventional approach paid off.

- *Fluid structures and procedures.* Most rapid-growth ventures also defy conventional organizational patterns and structures. It is common to find a firm that has grown $25 million, $50 million, or even $150 million per year in sales and that still has no formal organizational chart. If an organizational chart does exist, it usually has three distinguishing features: First, it is inevitably out of date. Second, it changes frequently. For example, one firm had eight major reorganizations in its first five years as it grew to $5 million. Third, the organizational structure is usually flat (i.e., it has few management layers), and there is easy accessibility to the top decision makers. But the informality and fluidity of organization structures and procedures do not mean casualness or sloppiness when it comes to goals, standards, or clarity of direction and purpose. Rather, it translates into responsiveness and readiness to absorb and assimilate rapid changes while maintaining financial and operational cohesion.
- *Entrepreneurial culture.* There exists in growing new ventures a common value system, which is difficult to articulate, which is even more elusive to measure, and which is evident in behavior and attitudes. There is a belief in and commitment to growth, achievement, improvement, and success and a sense among members of the team that they are "in this thing together." Goals and the market determine priorities, rather than whose territory or whose prerogatives are being challenged. Managers appear unconcerned about status, power, and personal control. They are more concerned about making sure that tasks, goals, and roles are clear than whether the organizational chart is current or whether their office and rug reflect their current status. Likewise, they are more concerned about the evidence, competence, knowledge, and logic of arguments affecting a decision than the status given by a title or the formal position of the individual doing the arguing. Contrast this with a multibillion-dollar—but stagnant—firm in England. Reportedly, 29 different makes and models of automobiles are used in the firm to signify one's position.

This entrepreneurial climate, or culture, exists in larger firms also. Such a climate attracts and encourages the entrepreneurial achievers, and it helps perpetuate the intensity and pace so characteristic of high-growth firms. *Exhibit 6.5* shows how five companies studied by Rosabeth Moss Kanter range from most to least entrepreneurial. Continuing to study "intrapreneurship" throughout the 1980s, Kanter asserted that the global economy was experiencing the postentrepreneurial revolution which "takes entrepreneurship a step further, applying entrepreneurial principles to the traditional corporation, creating a marriage between entrepreneurial creativity and corporate discipline, cooperation, and teamwork."[11] This revolution has not made managing any easier; in fact, Kanter suggests that "this constitutes the ultimate corporate balancing act. Cut back and grow. Trim down and build. Accomplish more, and do it in new areas, with fewer resources."[12] Clearly, some corporations will embrace these challenges with more

[11] Rosabeth Moss Kanter, *When Giants Learn to Dance* (New York: Simon & Schuster, 1989), pp. 9–10.

[12] Ibid., p. 31.

Exhibit 6.5
Characteristics of Five Companies, Ranging from Most to Least Entrepreneurial

	Companies Studied				
	CHIPCO	*RADCO*	*MEDCO*	*FINCO*	*UTICO*
Percent of effective managers with entrepreneurial accomplishments	71%	69%	67%	47%	33%
Economic trend	Steadily up	Trend up but now down	Upward trend	Mixed	Downward trend
Change issues	Change normal; constant change in product generation; proliferating staff and units.	Change normal in products, technologies; changeover to second management generation with new focus.	Reorganized 2–3 years ago to install matrix; normal product and technology changes.	Change a shock; new top-management group from outside reorganizing and trying to add competitive market posture.	Change a shock; undergoing reorganization to install matrix and add competitive market posture and reducing staff.
Organization structure	Matrix	Matrix in some areas; product lines act as quasi divisions.	Matrix in some areas.	Divisional; unitary hierarchy within division; some central officers.	Functional organization; currently overlaying matrix of regions and markets.
Information flow	Decentralized	Mixed	Mixed	Centralized	Centralized
Communication emphasis	Free Horizontal	Free Horizontal	Moderately free Horizontal	Constricted Vertical	Constricted Vertical
Culture	Clear, consistent; favors individual initiative.	Clear, though in transition from invention emphasis to routinization and systems.	Clear; pride in company; belief that talent will be rewarded.	Idiosyncratic; depends on boss and area.	Clear but undergoing changes; favors security, maintenance, and protection.
Emotional climate	Pride in company, team feeling, some burnout.	Uncertainty regarding changes.	Pride in company; team feeling.	Low trust; high uncertainty.	High uncertainty, confusion.
Rewards	Abundant; visibility, chance to do more challenging work in the future, and get bigger budget projects.	Abundant; visibility, chance to do more challenging work in the future, and get bigger budget projects.	Moderately abundant; conventional.	Scarce; primarily monetary.	Scarce; promotion and salary freeze; recognition by peers grudging.

Source: Adapted from Rosabeth Moss Kanter, "Middle Managers as Innovators," *Harvard Business Review,* July–August 1982, p. 103.

success than others; the following section will shed some light on how "giants learn to dance."[13]

What Entrepreneurial Managers Need to Know

Much of business education traditionally has emphasized and prepared students for life in the administrative domain. There is nothing wrong with that, but education preparing students to start and manage vibrant, growing new ventures cannot afford to emphasize administrative efficiency, maintenance tasks, resource ownership, and institutional formalization. Rather, such a program needs to emphasize skills necessary for life in the entrepreneurial domain. For example, effective entrepreneurial managers need to be especially skillful at managing conflict, resolving differences, balancing multiple viewpoints and demands, and building teamwork and consensus. These skills are particularly difficult when working with others outside one's immediate formal chain of command.

In talking of larger firms, Kanter identifies power and persuasion skills, skill in managing problems accompanying team and employee participation, and skill in understanding how change is designed and constructed in an organization as necessary. Kanter notes:

> In short, individuals do not have to be doing "big things" in order to have their cumulative accomplishments eventually result in big performance for the company. . . . They are only rarely the inventors of the "breakthrough" system. They are only rarely doing something that is totally unique or that no one, in any organization, ever thought of before. Instead, they are often applying ideas that have proved themselves elsewhere, or they are rearranging parts to create a better result, or they are noting a potential problem before it turns into a catastrophe and mobilizing the actions to anticipate and solve it.[14]

A recent study of mid-sized-growth companies having sales between $25 million and $1 billion and a sales or profit growth of more than 15 percent annually over five years confirms the importance of many of these same fundamentals of entrepreneurial management.[15] For one thing, these companies practiced opportunity-driven management. According to the study, they achieved their first success with a unique product or distinctive way of doing business and often became leaders in market niches by delivering superior value to customers, rather than through low prices. They are highly committed to serving customers and pay very close attention to them. For another thing, these firms put great emphasis on financial control and managing every element of the business.

In a book that follows up on the implementation issues of how one gets middle managers to pursue and practice entrepreneurial excellence (first made famous in *In Search of Excellence* by Tom Peters and Bob Waterman), two authors note that some of the important fundamentals practiced by team-builder entrepreneurs—who are more intent on getting results than just getting their own way—also are emulated by effective middle managers.[16] Or as John Sculley, of Apple Computers, explained:

> The heroic style—the lone cowboy on horseback—is not the figure we worship anymore at Apple. In the new corporation, heroes won't personify any single set of achievements. Instead, they personify the process. They might be thought of as gatekeepers, information carriers, and teams. Originally

[13] Ibid.

[14] Rosabeth Moss Kanter, *The Change Masters* (New York: Simon & Schuster, 1983), pp. 354–55.

[15] The study was done by McKinsey & Company. See "How Growth Companies Succeed," reported in *Small Business Report*, July 1984, p. 9.

[16] David L Bradford and Allan R Cohen, *Managing for Excellence* (New York: John Wiley & Sons, 1984), pp. 3–4.

heros at Apple were the hackers and engineers who created the products. Now, more teams are heros.[17]

MANAGEMENT COMPETENCIES

Entrepreneurs who build substantial companies that grow to over $10 million in sales and over 75 to 100 employees are good entrepreneurs *and* good managers. Typically, they will have developed a solid base and a wide breadth of management skills and know-how over a number of years working in different areas (e.g., sales, marketing, manufacturing, and finance). It would be unusual for any single entrepreneur to be outstanding in all areas. More likely, a single entrepreneur will have strengths in one area, such as strong people management, conceptual and creative problem-solving skills, and marketing know-how, as well as some significant weaknesses. While it is risky to generalize, often entrepreneurs whose background is technical are weak in marketing, finance, and general management. Entrepreneurs who do not have a technical background are, as you might expect, often weakest in the technical or engineering aspects, manufacturing, and finance.

What has been stressed throughout this book is the concept of fit. What's important is having a management team whose skills are complementary, not the possession by an individual of a single, absolute set of skills or a profile. The art and craft of entrepreneuring involves recognizing the skills and know-how needed to succeed in a venture, knowing what each team member does or does not know, and then compensating for shortcomings, either by getting key people on board to fill voids or by an individual's accumulating the additional "chunks" before he or she takes the plunge.

Skills in Building an Entrepreneurial Culture

Managers of entrepreneurial firms need to recognize and cope with innovation, taking risks, and responding quickly, as well as with absorbing major setbacks. The most effective managers seem to thrive on the hectic, and at times chaotic, pace and find it challenging and stimulating, rather than frustrating or overwhelming. They use a consensus approach to build a motivated and committed team, they balance conflicting demands and priorities, and they manage conflicts especially adroitly.

These managers thus need interpersonal/team work skills that involve (1) the ability to create, through management, a climate and spirit conducive to high performance, including pressing for performance while rewarding work well done and encouraging innovation, initiative, and calculated risk taking; (2) the ability to understand the relationships among tasks and between the leader and followers; and (3) the ability to lead in those situations where it is appropriate, including a willingness to manage actively, supervise and control activities of others through directions, suggestions, and the like.

These interpersonal skills can be called entrepreneurial influence skills, since they have a great deal to do with the way these managers exact influence over others:

- *Leadership/vision/influence.* These managers are skillful in creating clarity out of confusion, ambiguity, and uncertainty. These entrepreneurial managers are able to define adroitly and gain agreement on who has what responsibility and authority. Further, they do this in a way that builds motivation and commitment to cross-departmental and

[17] John Sculley with John Byrne, *Odyssey: Pepsi to Apple . . . A Journey of Adventures, Ideas, and The Future.* New York: HarperCollins Publishers Inc., 1987, p. 321.

corporate goals, not just parochial interests. But this is not perceived by other managers as an effort to jealously carve out and guard personal turf and prerogatives. Rather, it is seen as a genuine effort to clarify roles, tasks, and responsibilities, and to make sure there is accountability and appropriate approvals. This does not work unless the manager is seen as willing to relinquish his or her priorities and power in the interest of an overall goal. It also requires skill in making sure the appropriate people are included in setting cross-functional or cross-departmental goals and in making decisions. When things do not go as smoothly as was hoped, the most effective managers work them through to an agreement. Managers who are accustomed to traditional line/staff or functional chains of command are often baffled and frustrated in their new role. While some may be quite effective in dealing with their own subordinates, it is an entirely new task to manage and work with peers, the subordinates of others, and even superiors outside one's chain of command.

- *Helping/coaching and conflict management.* The most effective managers are very creative and skillful in handling conflicts, generating consensus decisions, and sharing their power and information. They are able to get people to open up, instead of clamming up; they get problems out on the table, instead of under the rug; and they do not become defensive when others disagree with their views. They seem to know that high-quality decisions require a rapid flow of information in all directions and that knowledge, competence, logic, and evidence need to prevail over official status or formal rank in the organization. The way they manage and resolve conflicts is intriguing. For one thing, they are able to get potential adversaries to be creative and to collaborate by seeking a reconciliation of viewpoints. Rather than emphasizing differences and playing the role of hard-nose negotiator or devil's advocate to force their own solution, they blend ideas. They are more willing to risk personal vulnerability in this process—often by giving up their own power and resources—than are less-effective managers. The trade-offs are not easy: At the outset, such an approach involves more managers, takes more time, often appears to yield few immediate results, and seems like a more painful way to manage. Later on, however, the gains from the motivation, commitment, and teamwork anchored in consensus are striking. For one thing, there is swiftness and decisiveness in actions and follow through, since the negotiating, compromising, and accepting of priorities is history. For another, new disagreements that emerge do not generally bring progress to a halt, since there is both high clarity and broad acceptance of the overall goals and underlying priorities. Without this consensus, each new problem or disagreement often necessitates a time-consuming and painful confrontation and renegotiation simply because it was not done initially. Apparently, the Japanese understand this quite well.
- *Teamwork and people management.* Another form of entrepreneurial influence has to do with encouraging creativity and innovation, and with taking calculated risks. Simply stated, entrepreneurial managers build confidence by encouraging innovation and calculated risk taking, rather than by punishing or criticizing whatever is less than perfect. They breed independent, entrepreneurial thinking by expecting and encouraging others to find and correct their own errors and to solve their own problems. This does not mean they follow a throw-them-to-the-wolves approach. Rather, they are perceived by their peers and other managers as accessible and willing to help when needed, and they provide the necessary resources to enable others to do the job. When it is appropriate, they go to bat for their peers and subordinates, even when they know they cannot always win. An ability to make heroes out of other team members and contributors and to make sure others are in the limelight, rather than accept these things oneself, is another critical skill.

The capacity to generate trust—the glue that binds an organization or relationship together—is critical. The most effective managers are perceived as trustworthy; they behave in ways that create trust. How do they do this? For one thing, they are straightforward: They do what they say they are going to do. They are not the corporate rumor carriers. They are open and spontaneous, rather than guarded and cautious with each word. And they are perceived as being honest and direct. Also, it is easy to envision the kind of track record and reputation these entrepreneurial managers build for themselves. They have a reputation of getting results, because they understand that the task of managing in a rapid-growth company usually goes well beyond one's immediate chain of command. They become known as the creative problem solvers who have a knack for blending and balancing multiple views and demands. Their calculated risk taking works out more often than it fails. And they have a reputation for developing human capital (i.e., they groom other effective growth managers by their example and their mentoring).

Other Management Competencies

Entrepreneurial managers need a sound foundation in what are considered traditional management skills. Interestingly, in the study of practicing entrepreneurs mentioned earlier, no one assigned much importance to capital asset-pricing models, beta coefficients, linear programming, and so forth, the prevailing and highly touted "new management techniques."[18]

The list below is divided into two cross-functional areas (administration and law and taxation) and four key functional areas (marketing, finance, production and operations, and microcomputers). Technical skills unique to each venture are also necessary.

- ***Administration***
  - *Problem solving.* Ability to anticipate potential problems; ability to gather facts about problems, analyze them for *real* causes, and plan effective action to solve them; and ability to be very thorough in dealing with details of particular problems and to follow through.
  - *Communications.* Ability to communicate effectively and clearly—orally and in writing—to media, public, customers, peers, and subordinates.
  - *Planning.* Ability to set realistic and attainable goals, identify obstacles to achieving the goals, and develop detailed action plans to achieve those goals, and the ability to schedule personal time very systematically.
  - *Decision making.* Ability to make decisions on the best analysis of incomplete data, when the decisions need to be made.
  - *Project management.* Skills in organizing project teams, setting project goals, defining project tasks, and monitoring task completion in the face of problems and cost/quality constraints.
  - *Negotiating.* Ability to work effectively in negotiations, and the ability to balance quickly value given and value received. Recognizing one-time versus continuing on-going relationships.
  - *Managing outside professionals.* Ability to identify, manage, and guide appropriate legal, financial, banking, accounting, consulting, and other necessary outside advisors.
  - *Personnel administration.* Ability to set up payroll, hiring, compensation, and training functions.

[18] Timmons and Stevenson, "Entrepreneurship Education in the 80s: What Entrepreneurs Say," pp. 115–34.

- ***Law and taxes:***
  - *Corporate and securities law.* Familiarity with the uniform commercial code, including forms of organization and the rights and obligations of officers, shareholders, and directors; and familiarity with Security and Exchange Commission, state, and other regulations concerning the securities of your firm, both registered and unregistered, and the advantages and disadvantages of different instruments.
  - *Contract law.* Familiarity with contract procedures and requirements of government and commercial contracts, licenses, leases, and other agreements, particularly employment agreements and agreements governing the vesting rights of shareholders and founders.
  - *Law relating to patent and proprietary rights.* Skills in preparation and revision of patent applications and the ability to recognize a strong patent, trademark, copyright, and privileged information claims, including familiarity with claim requirements, such as to intellectual property.
  - *Tax law.* Familiarity with state and federal reporting requirements, including specific requirements of a particular form of organization, of profit and other pension plans, and the like.
  - *Real estate law.* Familiarity with leases, purchase offers, purchase and sale agreements, and so on, necessary for the rental or purchase and sale of property.
  - *Bankruptcy law.* Knowledge of bankruptcy law, options, and the forgivable and nonforgivable liabilities of founders, officers and directors.
- ***Marketing:***
  - *Market research and evaluation.* Ability to analyze and interpret market research study results, including knowing how to design and conduct studies and to find and interpret industry and competitor information, and a familiarity with questionnaire design and sampling techniques. One successful entrepreneur stated that what is vital "is knowing where the competitive threats are and where the opportunities are and an ability to see the customers' needs."
  - *Marketing planning.* Planning skills in planning overall sales, advertising, and promotion programs and in deciding on effective distributor or sales representative systems and setting them up.
  - *Product pricing.* Ability to determine competitive pricing and margin structures and to position products in terms of price and ability to develop pricing policies that maximize profits.
  - *Sales management.* Ability to organize, supervise, and motivate a direct sales force, and the ability to analyze territory and account sales potential and to manage a sales force to obtain maximum share of market.
  - *Direct selling.* Skills in identifying, meeting, and developing new customers and in closing sales. Without orders for a product or service, a company does not really have a business.
  - *Service management.* Ability to perceive service needs of particular products and to determine service and spare-part requirements, handle customer complaints, and create and manage an effective service organization.
  - *Distribution management.* Ability to organize and manage the flow of product from manufacturing through distribution channels to ultimate customer, including familiarity with shipping costs, scheduling techniques, and so on.
  - *Product management.* Ability to integrate market information, perceived needs, research and development, and advertising into a rational product plan, and the ability to understand market penetration and breakeven.

  - *New-product planning.* Skills in introducing new products, including marketing testing, prototype testing, and development of price/sales/merchandising and distribution plans for new products.
- ***Operations/production:***
  - *Manufacturing management.* Knowledge of the production process, machines, manpower, and space required to produce a product and the skill in managing production to produce products within time, cost, and quality constraints.
  - *Inventory control.* Familiarity with techniques of controlling in-process and finished goods inventories of materials.
  - *Cost analysis and control.* Ability to calculate labor and materials costs, develop standard cost systems, conduct variance analyses, calculate overtime labor needs, and manage/control costs.
  - *Quality control.* Ability to set up inspection systems and standards for effective control of quality of incoming, in-process, and finished materials. Benchmarking continuous improvement.
  - *Production scheduling and flow.* Ability to analyze work flow and to plan and manage production processes, the ability to manage work flow, and the ability to calculate schedules and flows for rising sales levels.
  - *Purchasing.* Ability to identify appropriate sources of supply, to negotiate supplier contracts, and to manage the incoming flow of material into inventory, and familiarity with order quantities and discount advantages.
  - *Job evaluation.* Ability to analyze worker productivity and needs for additional help, and the ability to calculate cost-saving aspects of temporary versus permanent help.
- ***Finance:***
  - *Raising capital.* Ability to decide how best to acquire funds for start-up and growth; ability to forecast funds needs and to prepare budgets; and familiarity with sources and vehicles of short- and long-term financing, formal and informal.
  - *Managing cash flow.* Ability to project cash requirements, set up cash controls, and manage the firm's cash position, and the ability in identifying how much capital is needed, when and where you will run out of cash, and breakeven.
  - *Credit and collection management.* Ability to develop credit policies and screening criteria, and to age receivables and payables, and an understanding of the use of collection agencies and when to start legal action.
  - *Short-term financing alternatives.* Understanding of payables management and the use of interim financing, such as bank loans, factoring of receivables, pledging and selling notes and contracts, bills of lading, and bank acceptance; and familiarity with financial statements and budgeting/profit planning.
  - *Public and private offerings.* Ability to develop a business plan and an offering memo that can be used to raise capital, a familiarity with the legal requirements of public and private stock offerings, and the ability to manage shareholder relations and to negotiate with financial sources.
  - *Bookkeeping, accounting, and control.* Ability to determine appropriate bookkeeping and accounting systems as the company starts and grows, including various ledgers and accounts and possible insurance needs.
  - *Other specific skills.* Ability to read and prepare an income statement and balance sheet, and the ability to do cash flow analysis and planning, including break-even analysis, contribution analysis, profit and loss analysis, and balance sheet management.

Exhibit A *(concluded)*

The last point to be covered is that of equity participation in the company. Both Joe and I are open-minded with regard to stockholder expansion. The issue itself is open for discussion in any performance review that occurs after you have joined the company. Specifically, Kevin, when we recognize that a significant and continuing contribution is being made to the basic strength of the company itself, we would be of a frame of mind to structure an equity position for the individual responsible for that contribution.

We hope you will accept the position that we have offered, because we feel that the company can truly benefit from the talents and skills that you would bring to bear on the outlined function. We also feel that this position offers you an outstanding opportunity for personal and professional growth.

Please be in touch if you have any questions.

Sincerely,

Robert W. Wilson

Robert W. Wilson
President

Once he had learned what marketing areas were important to Wilson, he didn't tamper with them. Several months later, it was Kevin's turn to invite Wilson to lunch. The lunch was very pleasant; Wilson was surprised and pleased with how much better the US marketing picture looked and complimented Kevin on his job.

Although Kevin Mooney had succeeded in smoothing the relationship between himself and the vice president, he did not spend much time working on building relationships with the other managers at his peer level. He enjoyed his job and liked watching his department succeed, but he didn't like the interdepartmental politics that some of the managers seemed to thrive on.

Personalities

Lack of leadership from both Hegarty and Wilson contributed significantly to the role that politics played. Hegarty, the president, was the creative thinker. Personable and charming, he was the idea generator and was comfortable dealing with the big picture, always avoiding the details. Bob Wilson's personality complemented Hegarty's. He was the detail man and very good at making Hegarty's ideas work. Wilson's leadership style was not to issue clear directives to his managers. Instead, he worked to get a consensus, preferring that his managers work out their differences among themselves. Kevin recalled:

> Wilson's problem-solving style really was pretty ineffective. Split fights began to occur between the international and domestic divisions. Splits happen when two or more departments have to split a sales commission. I never had any problem splitting commission within my department, and I don't think the VP of domestic had any problem within his. But there was always trouble when we had to split it between us. I just got frustrated, sat down and wrote a memo to Wilson suggesting ideas for ways to alleviate the problem. I didn't think my solution was the only one, but I felt it was a start. Instead of getting back to me with his reaction, Wilson sent my memo on to the domestic VP. And nothing was ever resolved!

Employment Agreement

This agreement dated 3-13-78 between Softcorp, Inc., a Washington Corporation, having its principal place of business at 381 East Street, Seattle, Washington (hereinafter called the "Company"), and Kevin Mooney, residing at 560 Hillside Avenue, Seattle, Washington 98115 (hereinafter called the "Employee").

In consideration of the mutual covenants herein contained, the parties agree as follows:

Section 1: The Company will employ the Employee and the Employee will serve the Company upon the terms and conditions provided herein, unless terminated as provided herein.

Section 2: During the term of employment hereunder the Employee shall devote his full time during business hours and use his best efforts in furtherance of the business of the Company.

Section 3: At the Company's request, the Employee agrees to assist the Company in every proper way to obtain for its or their own benefit patents for discoveries, inventions, or improvements thereof in any and all countries and all discoveries, inventions, or improvements are to remain the property of the Company whether patented or not.

Section 4: The Employee shall not divulge or communicate to any person or entity other than customers of the Company without the express written consent of the Company any trade secrets, trade knowledge, discoveries, inventions, innovations, computer programs, and other information obtained or conceived by the Company along all lines of work of said Company. During the term of employment hereunder and for a period of two years after the termination of this agreement by any means whatsoever, the Employee shall not within the territorial limits of the United States of America engage in business dealings competitive with the business of the Company with any persons, corporations, or associations and shall not engage as an Employee, Officer, Director, Partner, or Consultant in any business competitive with that of the Company. In the event that this section shall be determined by any court of competent jurisdiction to be unenforceable by reason of its extending for too great a period of time or over too large a geographic area or over too great a range of activities, it shall be interpreted to extend only over the maximum period of time, geographic area, or range of activities as to which it may be enforceable.

Section 5: Any and all notices under this agreement shall be in writing.

Section 6: This agreement supersedes all prior agreements written or oral between the Employee and the Company as of the date of the commencement of employment hereunder and shall constitute the only agreement between the parties for the period of employment hereunder. No provisions of this agreement shall be changed or modified nor shall this agreement be discharged in whole or in part except by an agreement in writing signed by the party against whom such change, modification, or discharge is claimed or sought to be enforced.

Section 7: This agreement shall inure to the benefit of and be binding upon the Company or its successors and assigns. All obligations of the Employee arising under this agreement shall survive the termination of this agreement and shall be binding upon his heirs, executors, and administrators.

Section 8: In the event the Employee leaves the Company voluntarily or is discharged by the Company, this agreement will be terminated except that Section 4 hereof shall survive such termination.

Softcorp, Inc.	Employee
By Robert W. Wilson	By Kevin Mooney

The International Department

Although Kevin Mooney was not inclined to interact with the other vice presidents, he did have the skills needed to build an international customer base. From the first day, he built the department brick by brick. By early 1979, he had signed the first two agent agreements (companies appointed to represent Softcorp in foreign countries) in England and Australia. Kevin selected companies, which he called affiliates, already established in the computer service industry. By year-end the international division revenues accounted for almost 100 percent of Softcorp's profits.

By 1980, Scandinavia and Mexico were added to the list of international customers. Kevin Mooney recalled:

> We were 120 percent over our plan for the year. I felt that I had demonstrated my commitment to the company and went to Hegarty to see about my getting some equity participation. I was surprised that he didn't remember our conversation about equity during the interview process.
>
> Several weeks later I was flying to Dallas with Bob Wilson. Luckily, I had dug out the letter they had sent me. I showed Bob the letter and told him that I didn't want to pressure him, that the company certainly didn't have to give me any equity, but if that was their decision, Softcorp wasn't the place I wanted to work.

Seeing the letter was apparently quite significant for Wilson. Kevin Mooney was given 1 percent stock participation in Softcorp. (*Exhibit C* is a letter Mooney sent to Hegarty and Wilson.)

In 1981, Mooney was promoted to vice president; Wilson moved to president of Softcorp, and Hegarty to chairman. By 1982, the international division had grown to include South Africa, Southeast Asia, and Venezuela; by 1983, new countries included New Zealand, France, Brazil, and Argentina. (See *Exhibit D.*)

The Acquisition

Since 1980, Softcorp had considered the idea of going public. Each year, however, these plans were scratched because the company profile was never good enough to attract a market. It lacked timely financial statements, its profits weren't very good, and its performance was erratic. In 1983, however, Softcorp received a bona fide offer from a Fortune 500 firm, Prentiss-McGraw, Inc. (PMI). The firm thought Softcorp fitted well into its portfolio of companies; it saw Softcorp as a growth company with little need to generate healthy profits each year. Furthermore, its deal promised a hands-off approach. It was content to let the founders continue to manage the company. The purchase price was a range between $50 million and $80 million, depending on the company's performance over the next three years. The acquisition, however, had different harvest implications for several members of the management committee, as shown by the equity distribution among the eight management committee members. (See *Exhibit E.*) Kevin Mooney said:

> As a part of the deal, the buyer asked all of us—Hegarty, Wilson, and the six vice presidents—to sign a noncompete agreement and an employment contract guaranteeing that we would work for them for three years. They explained that the employment contract was designed to protect us and that the noncompete agreement was meant to protect them. Everyone but me seemed very ready to sign. One of the VPs wanted the contract to be for five years!
>
> Three of the vice presidents had received their stock options just eight months before the offer, and they weren't entitled to the capital gains tax treatment. PMI promised to provide them with additional compensation because their options would be taxed as ordinary income.

Exhibit C

Joseph Hegarty
381 East Street
Seattle, Washington 98115

3-17-80
Personal

Dear Joe,

It's 12:45 AM, and I'm at 30,000 feet en route to San Francisco. I'll attend our seminar there tomorrow and then on to Australia. This flight has been a long one (and I've just started the journey), but it's given me a chance to think about SOFTCORP and the opportunities I've had here.

Let me first thank you sincerely for putting into place the equity plan that Bob described to me last week. Obviously, I appreciate it from a financial standpoint, but equally important, I appreciate the confidence you must have in me to justify such a program.

As you know, equity is something I have felt strongly about since I joined SOFTCORP, and I believe the plan you are implementing is well designed to meet both your objectives and mine. The quantity of stock is sufficient to meet my personal goals as long as we continue our tremendous growth over the next few years. Obviously, this provides strong motivation for me to dedicate my best talents and efforts to this pursuit.

This is also a good opportunity to thank you for the confidence you and Bob have shown in me over the past few years. The experience I've had has been terrific. I hope you've been as satisfied with my performance as I've been with the job. It's been a lot of hard work, but I can't imagine a better place to have done it. I hope the next few years can be as interesting, challenging, and successful as the past few. I'm confident that the international division will continue to grow and prosper and that there's still lots of room for improvement in the U.S. marketing activities.

Thank you for the opportunities you've provided and once again, thank you for the "precious" equity.

Kevin

P.S. I've sent a similar letter to Bob.

Exhibit D
Softcorp, Inc., Performance, 1977–1983 ($ millions)

	1977	*1978*	*1979*	*1980*	*1981*	*1982*	*1983*
Total sales	$1.7	$3.1	$7.5	$15.6	$26.2	$39.0	$56.0
Profit	$0.048	$0.221	$0.775	$0.910	$1.02	$2.1	$3.6
International			$0.75	$1.5	$3.7	$8.7	$17.0
Employees	57	85	138	251	350	400	640

Exhibit E
Softcorp, Inc., Distribution of Equity

Joe Hegarty, chairman	25% stock
Bob Wilson, president	25% stock
Dave Cassidy, VP, operations	8% stock
Jonathan Latham, VP, research and development	8% stock
Richard White, VP, marketing	0.8% stock (options)
Roger Fineman, VP, sales	0.8% stock (options)
Stephen Marx, VP, finance and treasurer	0.8% stock (options)
Kevin Mooney, VP, international	0.8% stock

The other two VPs, who owned 8 percent each in the form of stock, and Hegarty and Wilson were set for life. There I was, standing alone with my 1 percent, now diluted to 0.8 percent, stock, certainly not enough to retire on.

Exhibits F and *G* are the employment and noncompete agreements drawn up by PMI's attorneys for execution by Softcorp's executives.

Kevin Mooney's Dilemma

Kevin knew that he was pretty much alone in his reluctance to sign. But he had to consider what was most important to him. He was a young man with a young family. Right now, his job required lots of travel and he wasn't sure he wanted to continue traveling so much. In addition, he loved the job because he could be his own boss and run his own show. He had no idea how PMI's presence would affect that. Whether or not to sign the contract weighed heavily on Kevin's mind.

I thought I had better see a lawyer if for no other reason than to be able to use him as "the bad guy" in all of this. He confirmed my feelings about signing. He told me that I had built a good reputation in the industry and that I could leverage that reputation elsewhere. He told me, "Unless they give you something, don't sign."

Then, at a sales meeting in Hawaii, Wilson cornered me, referring to my reluctance to sign as "the Mooney problem." He told me I was ruining it for the rest of them—that the deal wouldn't go through without my signature.

Kevin wondered how he should proceed.

EXERCISE—MANAGERIAL SKILLS AND KNOW-HOW ASSESSMENT

The purposes of the Management Skills and Know-How Assessment are three.

First, the assessment is intended to introduce important management competencies and skills in more detail. However, a complete treatment of traditional management skills is outside the scope of this book, and there are many excellent texts covering each fundamental area.

The second purpose of the assessment is that of enabling a lead entrepreneur or member of a management team to so evaluate his or her strengths and weaknesses and those of potential team members that the needs in a venture can be evaluated.

Another important purpose is to enable an entrepreneur to diagnose his or her deficiencies in certain areas of management, to assess his or her strengths, and to begin to develop an agenda for learning. This self-knowledge is vital, whether an individual is to be a lead entrepreneur or whether he or she is considering becoming a member of an entre-

Shaw & Cartwright
Counselors at Law
60 City Square, N.W.
Seattle, Washington 98100
(206) 227-9740

March 25, 1983

Hand Delivered

R. Kevin Mooney, Vice President
Softcorp, Inc.
381 East Street
Seattle, WA 98115

Dear Kevin:

As promised earlier this week, I am enclosing copies of the following documents, which constitute *all* of the documents to be signed by senior Softcorp officers in connection with the Prentiss-McGraw, Inc., acquisition:

1. *Sellers Agreement.* This has already been signed by the seven senior officers. It contains a covenant not to compete, on page 5, with a reference to Appendix A, which lists the termination dates of the covenant for each senior officer.

2. *Sellers' Agent Agreement.* I believe you have not yet seen this agreement, which also has already been signed by all senior officers. Basically, it constitutes a power of attorney granted to Bob and Joe to act on behalf of all sellers throughout the mechanics of the closing, distribution of cash proceeds, etc. and the earn-out period over the next three years. It grants no authority to negotiate or amend individual employment agreements whatsoever.

3. *Employment Agreement.* This has not yet been signed by anyone, but it is proposed that on or immediately before the closing (approximately April 26), all individuals in "tier two" would sign an employment agreement in the form of Exhibit 7, with individual treatment for salaries only. You will especially want to note Section 2 providing for a term of the Agreement through December 31, 1985, and Section 6*(c)* containing another covenant not to compete continuing for four months after such termination date (i.e., until April 30, 1986).

I would be pleased to attempt to answer any questions you may have regarding any of the above three agreements. If it appears likely that you may be signing any one or more of them, then you will undoubtedly want to secure your personal attorney's views.

I expect to be talking with you next week.

Very truly yours,

John J. Marshall

John J. Marshall

JJM:akl
Enclosures

Employment Agreement

This AGREEMENT, dated as of May 4, 1983, between Softcorp, Inc. ("Company") and R. Kevin Mooney ("Executive").

Witnesseth:

Whereas, the Company, the Prentiss-McGraw, Inc. ("Buyer"), P&M Merger Corporation, a wholly owned subsidiary of Buyer ("Merger Corp."), and Robert W. Wilson and Joseph M. Hegarty, collectively as agent ("Sellers' Agent") for holders, including Executive, of the outstanding shares of capital stock and options to purchase capital stock of the Company ("Sellers"), have entered into an Agreement and Plan of Merger, dated as of March 21, 1983 (the "Merger Agreement"), pursuant to which Buyer will acquire the Company as a result of the merger of the Merger Corp. with and into the Company (the "Merger");

Whereas, Executive is and has been employed by the Company for more than five years and is currently Vice President—International of the Company;

Whereas, Executive possesses an intimate knowledge of the business and affairs of the Company, its policies, methods, personnel, and problems;

Whereas, the Board of Directors of the Company recognizes that Executive's contribution to the growth and success of the Company has been substantial and desires to assure the Company of Executive's continued employment and to compensate him therefor;

Whereas, Executive desires to be so employed by the Company, on the terms and conditions herein set forth;

Now, therefore, in consideration of the premises and the terms hereinafter set forth, but subject to the consummation of the Merger under the aforesaid Merger Agreement, the parties agree as follows:

1. *Employment.* After the Effective Date, as that term is defined in the Merger Agreement (the "Effective Date"), the Company shall employ Executive pursuant to the terms of this Agreement. Executive shall hold the office of Vice President—International and, in addition to the duties prescribed for such office, shall have such other duties, responsibilities, and powers as shall be consistent with such office and as may be prescribed from time to time. Executive shall devote substantially all of his business time and attention to the business of the Company. Executive hereby accepts said employment and agrees faithfully to perform said duties in compliance with the policies and procedures applicable to Executive's positions and to render said services for the term of his employment. During the term of this Agreement, Company shall not require Executive to change his current domicile to another state.

2. *Term.* The term of this Agreement shall commence as of the Effective Date and shall continue until December 31, 1985 (the "Termination Date"), unless sooner terminated pursuant to Paragraph 5 hereof. The provisions of Executive's previous employment arrangements with the Company shall continue in effect until the Effective Date, at which time such employment arrangements shall terminate.

3. *Compensation.*

(a) During the term of this Agreement, Executive shall be paid, as compensation for his services under this Agreement, as follows:

(i) Salary at the rate of $100,000 per annum, payable by check not less often than monthly and not later than the fifteenth day following the expiraton of the month in which services are rendered hereunder; and

(ii) Bonus, payable within three (3) months after the end of each year, and based upon the Company's Compensation and Bonus Plan in effect from year to year.

(iii) All salaries and bonuses hereunder shall be reviewed by the Company annually, which reviews shall not result in any reduction of the salaries hereunder.

(b) Executive shall be entitled to four weeks' vacation during each calendar year of this Agreement.

(c) As an employee of the Company, Executive shall be entitled to the employee welfare benefit, pension, and other benefit plans available to the employees of the Company, which shall not be less than those presently enjoyed by Executive.

4. *Confidential Information.* In the course of his employment with the Company prior to the date hereof Executive had, and in the course of his employment hereunder Executive will have, access to confidential information and records, data, formulas, specifications, and other trade secrets of the Company, Buyer, and Buyer's affiliates. During and after his employment by the Company, Buyer, or any of Buyer's affiliates, Executive shall not directly or indirectly disclose such information to any person or use any such information, except as required in the course of such employment. All records, files, drawings, documents, models, equipment, and the like relating to the Company's, Buyer's, or any of Buyer's affiliates' business, which Executive shall prepare or use or come in contact with, shall be and remain such company's sole property and shall not be removed from such company's premises without its written consent, except as required in the course of such employment.

5. *Termination.*

(a) Termination for Cause. The Company may terminate this Agreement for cause at any time without notice, and thereby cancel all rights and obligations of the parties hereto, except those set forth in Paragraphs 4 and 6*(c)* hereof. For purposes of this Agreement, "cause" shall mean action by Executive involving material breach of the terms of this Agreement which shall not have ceased within ten (10) days after written notice thereof, dishonesty, moral turpitude, or gross obstruction of business operations. If, however, Executive shall dispute whether he was discharged for "cause," then such dispute shall promptly be referred for final determination to binding arbitration in Seattle, Washington, in accordance with the rules and regulations of the American Arbitration Association. Pending such final determination of such dispute, Executive shall continue to participate in the employee welfare benefit, pension, and other benefit plans available to the employees of the Company to the extent that such continued participation is permitted under such plans and applicable law, and all compensation which would have been payable to Executive under Paragraph 3 hereof if the Agreement had not been terminated for cause by the Company shall be deposited as it would have become payable in an interest-bearing bank account in any commercial bank doing business in the City of Seattle, Washington, to be held by such bank as escrowee pending such final determination and to be released (together with any interest earned thereon) in accordance with the instructions set forth in such final determination.

(b) Termination upon Disability. If, during the term of this Agreement, Executive shall become incapable of fulfilling his obligations hereunder because of injury or physical or mental illness, and such incapacity shall exist or may reasonably be expected upon competent medical opinion to exist for more than six (6) months in the aggregate during any period of twelve (12) consecutive months, the Company may, upon at least thirty (30) days' prior written notice to Executive, terminate all rights and obligations of the parties hereto, except those set forth in Paragraphs 4 and 6*(c)* and except as to payment of compensation in accordance with the terms of the Agreement for a period of at least six (6) months after the commencement of such injury or physical or mental illness.

(c) Termination by Death. If Executive dies during the term of his employment hereunder, this Agreement shall terminate immediately and any payments due Executive hereunder shall be paid to his legal representative.

6. *General Provisions.*

(a) Assignability. The rights and duties of the parties hereunder shall not be assignable, except that this Agreement and all rights and obligations hereunder may be assigned by the Company to, and assumed by, any corporation or other business entity which succeeds to all or substantially all of the business of the Company through merger, consolidation, acquisition of assets, or other transaction, upon condition that such assignee or successor assumes all of the obligations of the Company hereunder.

(Continued)

(b) Integration. This Agreement contains the entire agreement among the parties regarding the employment of Executive and supersedes all prior agreements and undertakings whether oral or written. No amendment to this Agreement may be made except by a writing signed by the party to be bound.

(c) Noncompetition; Specific Enforcement. Executive agrees that, prior to the applicable date set forth below, he will not directly or indirectly (as a director, officer, partner, employee, manager, consultant, independent contractor, advisor, or otherwise) engage in competition with, own any interest in, provide any financing for, or perform any service for any business or organization which directly or indirectly engages in competition with any business conducted by the Company or any subsidiary or division of the Company in any area where such business is then conducted:

(i) if Executive's employment with the Company terminates on or after the Termination Date, four months after such date of termination;

(ii) if Executive's employment with the Company either terminates for "cause" or by voluntary termination prior to the Termination Date, the later of (A) the Termination Date or (B) four months after such date of termination.

The foregoing provisions shall not prohibit Executive's ownership of not more than 1 percent of the outstanding shares of any publicly held corporation or not more than 3 percent of the outstanding shares of any privately held corporation, partnership, or other business entity. In the event of a breach of the provisions of this subparagraph, Executive agrees that the remedy at law may be inadequate and that the Company, in addition to any other remedies, shall be entitled to temporary or permanent injunctive or mandatory relief without the necessity of proving damages. Notwithstanding any of the foregoing to the contrary, if Executive shall be discharged without "cause," there shall immediately upon such termination be no restrictions whatsoever upon the freedom of Executive to engage in competition with the business of the Company.

(d) Waiver. The waiver by any party of a breach of any provision of this Agreement shall not operate or be construed as a waiver of any subsequent breach of the same provision or of any other provision of this Agreement.

(e) Notices. Any notice to the Company or Executive hereunder shall be given in writing either by personal delivery or by registered or certified mail, postage prepaid, return receipt requested, addressed to the Company at its principal place of business or to Executive at his home address as then shown on the records of the Company. For purposes of determining compliance with any time limit herein, notice shall be deemed given when personally delivered or on the third business day after the day of such mailing.

(f) Severability. If, for any reason whatsoever, any one or more of the provisions of this Agreement shall be finally determined to be inoperative, unenforceable, or invalid, by a court of competent jurisdiction, in a particular case or in all cases, such determination shall not render such provision invalid in any other case or render any of the other provisions of this Agreement inoperative, unenforceable, or invalid.

(g) Applicable Law. The exercise, validity, construction, operation, and effect of the terms and provisions of this Agreement shall be determined in accordance with the laws of the State of Washington.

(h) Captions. The captions to the paragraphs of this Agreement are for convenience only and shall not be considered or referred to in resolving questions of interpretation.

(i) Counterparts. This Agreement may be executed in one or more counterparts, each of which shall be deemed an original, but all of which together shall constitute one and the same agreement.

In witness whereof, the parties have executed this Agreement as of the date first above written.

Softcorp, Inc.

Robert W. Wilson ______________ By: ______________

Executive

preneurial management team now or in the future. In this regard, the assessment can be seen as an integral part of developing a personal entrepreneurial strategy and of the Personal Strategy Exercises in Chapter 19, Part VI.

The assessment is arranged as a list of management skills, divided into key areas, those requiring functional skills (i.e., marketing, finance, production and operations, and computers) plus areas requiring cross-functional skills (i.e., administration and law and taxation). The individual is asked to decide if he or she has thorough knowledge of the specific skills, some knowledge and experience, or no knowledge or experience.

As with any other decision process, the process of assessing management skills, whether a person's own or those of others, is most productive when it is done with the benefit of the most complete information available.

An assumption behind the format of the assessment is that a systematic recording and analysis of experiences can help an individual see where he or she has been and provide some direction for the future. Once the assessment has been completed, a determination can be made of whether a particular skill is required and when. In any case, the job of assessment is iterative in nature and requires continual review and adjustment.

Finally, a complex set of factors clearly goes into making someone a successful entrepreneur. As with personal qualities, attitudes, and behaviors described in the last chapter, no individual has all the managerial skills defined in the exercise. The presence or absence of any one does not guarantee success or failure as an entrepreneur. Again, for an entrepreneur to know that he or she does not have a certain skill and to know how to acquire it are clearly as valuable as knowing that you already have a skill.

	Competency Inventory				
	Rank	Thorough Knowledge & Experience (Done Well)	Some Knowledge & Experience (So-so)	No Knowledge or Experience (New Ground)	Importance (1–3 Years)
MARKETING					
Market Research and Evaluation *Finding and interpreting industry and competitor information; designing and conducting market research studies; analyzing and interpreting market research data; etc.*					
Market Planning *Planning overall sales, advertising, and promotion programs; planning and setting up effective distributor or sales representative systems; etc.*					

Product Pricing *Determining competitive pricing and margin structures and break-even analysis; positioning products in terms of price; etc.*					
Sales Management *Organizing, supervising, and motivating a direct sales force; analyzing territory and account sales potential; managing sales force; etc.*					
Direct Selling *Identifying, meeting, and developing new customers; closing sales; etc.*					
Direct Mail/ Catalog Selling *Identifying and developing appropriate direct mail and catalog sales and related distribution; etc.*					

Telemarketing *Identifying, planning, implementing appropriate telemarketing programs; etc.*					
Customer Service *Determining customer service needs and spare-part requirements; managing a service organization and warranties; training; technical back-up; etc.*					
Distribution Management *Organizing and managing the flow of product from manufacturing through distribution channels to customer, etc.*					
Product Management *Integrating market information, perceived needs, research and development, and advertising into a rational product plan; etc.*					

New Product Planning *Planning the introduction of new products, including marketing testing, prototype testing, and development of price, sales, merchandising, and distribution plans; etc.*					
OPERATIONS/ PRODUCTION					
Manufacturing Management *Managing production to produce products within time, cost, and quality constraints; knowledge of Manufacturing Resource Planning; etc.*					
Inventory Control *Using techniques of controlling in-process and finished goods inventories, etc.*					

Cost Analysis and Control *Calculating labor and materials costs; developing standard cost systems; conducting variance analyses; calculating overtime labor needs; managing and controlling costs; etc.*					
Quality Control *Setting up inspection systems and standards for effective control of quality in incoming, in-process, and finished goods; etc.*					
Production Scheduling and Flow *Analyzing work flow; planning and managing production processes; managing work flow; calculating schedules and flows for rising sales levels; etc.*					

Purchasing *Identifying appropriate sources of supply; negotiating supplier contracts; managing the incoming flow of material into inventory, etc.*					
Job Evaluation *Analyzing worker productivity and needs for additional help; calculating cost-saving aspects of temporary versus permanent help; etc.*					
FINANCE					
Accounting *Determining appropriate bookkeeping and accounting systems; preparing and using income statements and balance sheets; analyzing cash flow, breakeven, contribution, and profit and loss; etc.*					

Capital Budgeting *Preparing budgets; deciding how best to acquire funds for start-up and growth; forecasting funds needs; etc.*					
Cash Flow Management *Managing cash position, including projecting cash requirements; etc.*					
Credit and Collection Management *Developing credit policies and screening criteria, etc.*					
Short-Term Financing *Managing payables and receivables; using interim financing alternatives; etc.*					

Public and Private Offering Skills *Developing a business plan and offering memo; managing shareholder relations; negotiating with financial sources; etc.*					
ADMINISTRATION					
Problem Solving *Anticipating problems and planning to avoid them; analyzing and solving probems, etc.*					
Communications *Communicating effectively and clearly, both orally and in writing, to customers, peers, subordinates, and outsiders; etc.*					

Planning *Ability to set realistic and attainable goals, identify obstacles to achieving the goals, and develop detailed action plans to achieve those goals.*					
Decision Making *Making decisions based on the analysis of incomplete data, etc.*					
Project Management *Organizing project teams; setting project goals; defining project tasks; monitoring task completion in the face of problems and cost/quality constraints; etc.*					
Negotiating *Working effectively in negotiations; etc.*					

Personnel Administration *Setting up payroll, hiring, compensation, and training functions; identifying, managing, and guiding appropriate outside advisors; etc.*					
Management Information Systems *Knowledge of relevant management information systems available and appropriate for growth plans; etc.*					
Computer *Using spreadsheet, word processing, and other relevant software; using electronic mail; etc.*					

INTERPERSONAL/ TEAM					
Leadership/ Vision/Influence *Actively leading, instilling vision and passion in others, and managing activities of others; creating a climate and spirit conducive to high performance; etc.*					
Helping *Determining when assistance is warranted and asking for or providing such assistance.*					
Feedback *Providing effective feedback or receiving it; etc.*					
Conflict Management *Confronting differences openly and obtaining resolution; using evidence and logic; etc.*					

Teamwork and People Management *Working with others to achieve common goals; delegating responsibility and coaching subordinates, etc.*					
LAW					
Corporations *Understanding the uniform commercial code, including that regarding forms of organization and the rights and obligations of officers, shareholders, and directors; etc.*					
Contracts *Understanding the requirements of government and commercial contracts, licenses, leases, and other agreements; etc.*					

Taxes *Understanding state and federal reporting requirements; understanding tax shelters, estate planning, fringe benefits, and so forth; etc.*					
Securities *Understanding regulations of Security and Exchange Commission and state agencies concerning the securities, both registered and unregistered; etc.*					
Patents and Proprietary Rights *Understanding the preparation and revision of patent applications; recognizing strong patent, trademark, copyright, and privileged information claims; etc.*					

Real Estate *Understanding agreements necessary for the rental or purchase and sale of property; etc.*					
Bankruptcy *Understanding options and the forgivable and nonforgivable liabilities of founders, officers, directors, and so forth; etc.*					
UNIQUE SKILLS					
Unique competencies required.					

PART II—MANAGERIAL ASSESSMENT

Part II involves assessing management strengths and weaknesses, deciding which areas of competence are most critical, and developing a plan to overcome or compensate for any weaknesses and to capitalize on management strengths.

STEP 1: ASSESS MANAGEMENT STRENGTHS AND WEAKNESSES:

– Which management skills are particularly strong?

– Which skills are particularly weak?

– What patterns are evident?

STEP 2: CIRCLE THE AREAS OF COMPETENCE MOST CRITICAL TO THE SUCCESS OF THE VENTURE, AND CROSS OUT THOSE THAT ARE IRRELEVANT.

STEP 3: CONSIDER THE IMPLICATIONS FOR YOU AND FOR THE VENTURE:

- What are the implications of this particular constellation of management strengths and weaknesses?

- What specific actions can overcome or compensate for each critical weakness?

- What specific actions can be taken on critical strengths?

- What are the time implications of the above actions?

- What areas need to be explored further?

STEP 4: OBTAIN FEEDBACK. If you are evaluating your management competencies as part of the development of a personal entrepreneurial strategy and planning your apprenticeship, it is recommended you read Chapter 19 and complete the management assessment and feedback exercises in Part VI at this time.

The New Venture Team

7

Behind every truly successful entrepreneur I know of, there stands an organization equipped to help convert ideas into purposeful action, to help accomplish the mission the entrepreneur has set for his enterprise, to help implement his strategy.

Gustavo A. Cisneros
Organizacion Diego Cisneros

RESULTS EXPECTED

Upon completion of the chapter, you will have:

1. Identified and examined the role and significance of teams in building successful new ventures.
2. Examined successful entrepreneurial philosophies and attitudes which can anchor vision in forming and developing effective new venture teams.
3. Identified the critical issues and hurdles, including common pitfalls, faced by entrepreneurs in forming and building new venture teams.
4. Examined issues of reward that new teams face in slicing the equity pie.
5. Analyzed the "Setting the Stage" case.
6. Developed a reward system for your own venture.

THE IMPORTANCE OF THE TEAM

The Connection to Success

Entrepreneurial team building is addressed in light of both the author's experience and recent research that has brought some facts and thoughtful analysis to this least understood aspect of new venture creation.

Accumulating evidence suggests that a management team can make quite a difference in venture success. There is a strong connection between the growth potential of a new venture (and its ability to attract capital beyond the founder's resources from private and venture capital backers) and the quality of its management team.

The existence of a quality management team is one of the major differences between a firm that provides its founder simply a job substitute and the ability to employ perhaps a few family members and others and a higher potential venture. The lone-wolf entrepreneur may make a living, but the team builder creates an organization and a company—a company where substantial value, and harvest options, are created.

Ventures that do not have teams are not necessarily predestined for the new venture graveyard. Yet, building a higher potential venture without a team is extremely difficult. It is true that some entrepreneurs have acquired a distaste for partners and that some lead entrepreneurs can be happy only if they are in complete control; that is, they want employees, not partners, either internally or in outside investors. Take, for instance, an entrepreneur who founded a high-technology firm that grew steadily, but slowly, over 10 years to nearly $2 million in sales. As new patents and technological advances in fiber optics drew much interest from venture capitalists, he had more than one offer of up to $5 million of funding, which he turned down because the investors wanted to own 51 percent or more of his venture. Plainly and simply, he said, "I do not want to give up control of what I have worked so long and hard to create." While clearly the exception to the rule, this entrepreneur has managed to grow his business to more than $20 million in sales.

As was noted in the first chapter, a lot of evidence suggests the team can make quite a difference in venture success.[1] The studies cited indicated that venture capitalists believe teams are important, that the survival rate among venture capital-backed firms was the inverse of national averages, and that returns on these investments were high. A study of 104 high-technology ventures launched in the 1960s reported that 83.3 percent of high-growth companies, which achieved sales of $5 million or more annually, were launched by teams, while only 53.8 percent of the 73 discontinued companies had several founders.[2] This pattern is apparent from an even more recent study of the "Route 128 One Hundred" (i.e., the top firms comprising the new venture phenomenon in the greater Boston area along Route 128).[3] Typically, these firms averaged impressive annual sales of $16 million for ventures up to 5 years old, $49 million for those 6 to 10 years old, and several hundred million for more mature firms. It was found that *70 percent* of these had multiple founders. Among 86 firms, 38 percent actually had three or more founders, 17 percent had four or more, and 9 percent had five or more. One firm was launched by a team of eight.

Not only is the existence of a team important, but so too is the quality of the team. Because of this, venture capital investors have become even more active in helping to shape, and reshape, management teams. One recent study showed a significant shift toward this activity during the boom period in venture capital in the 1980s in contrast with practices in the 1970s.[4] Another study, examining the nature of venture capital investing in highly innovative technical ventures, revealed this role can be quite active.[5]

There is, then, a valuable role that the right partner(s) can play in a venture. In addition, mounting evidence suggests that entrepreneurs face loneliness, stress, and other pressures.[6] At the very least, finding the right partner can serve to mitigate these pressures. The key is identifying and working with the right partner or partners. Getting the right partners and working with them successfully usually involves anticipating and dealing with some very critical issues and hurdles, when it is neither too early nor too late.

FORMING/BUILDING TEAMS

Anchoring Vision in Team Philosophy and Attitudes

The most successful entrepreneurs seem to anchor their vision of the future in certain entrepreneurial philosophies and attitudes (i.e., attitudes about what a team is, what its mission is, and how it will be rewarded). The soul of this vision concerns what the founder or founders

[1] Jeffry A Timmons, "Careful Self-Analysis and Team Assessment Can Aid Entrepreneurs," in *Growing Concerns,* ed. D E Gumpert (New York: John Wiley & Sons, 1984), pp. 43–52.

[2] Arnold C Cooper and Albert V Bruno, "Success among High Technology Firms," *Business Horizons,* April 1977, p. 20.

[3] Jeffry A Timmons and Susan Skinner, research assistant, "The Route 128 One Hundred," working paper, Babson College, Wellesley, MA, 1984.

[4] Jeffry A Timmons, "Discard Many Old Rules about Raising Venture Capital," in *Growing Concerns,* ed. D E Gumpert (New York: John Wiley & Sons, 1984), pp. 273–80.

[5] Jeffry A Timmons, "Venture Capital: More than Money?" in *Pratt's Guide to Venture Capital Sources,* 8th ed. (Wellesley Hills, MA: Venture Economics, 1984), pp. 39–43.

[6] David Boyd and David Gumpert, "The Loneliness of the Start-up Entrepreneur," in *Frontiers of Entrepreneurship Research, 1982* ed. J A Hornaday et al. (Babson Park, MA: Babson College), pp. 478–87.

are trying to accomplish and the unwritten ground rules that become the fabric, character, and purpose guiding how a team will work together, succeed and make mistakes together, and realize a harvest together. The rewards, compensation, and incentive structures rest on this philosophy and attitudes.

This fundamental mind-set is often evident in later success. The anchoring of this vision goes beyond all the critical nuts-and-bolts issues covered in the chapters and cases on the opportunity, the business plan, financing, and so forth. Each of these issues is vital, but each by itself may not lead to success. A single factor rarely, if ever, does.

The capacity of the lead entrepreneur to craft a vision, and then to lead, inspire, persuade, and cajole key people to sign up for and deliver the dream makes an enormous difference between success and failure, between loss and profit, and between substantial harvest and "turning over the keys" to get out from under large personal guarantees of debt. Instilling a vision, and the passion to win, occurs very early on, often during informal discussions, and seems to trigger a series of self-fulfilling prophecies that lead to success, rather than to "almosts" or to failure.

Thus, lead entrepreneurs and team members who understand team building and teamwork have a secret weapon. Many with outstanding technical or other relevant skills, educational credentials, and so on, will be at once prisoners and victims of the highly individualistic competitiveness that got them to where they are. They may be fantastic lone achievers, and some may even "talk a good team game." But when it comes to how they behave and perform, their egos can rarely fit inside an airplane hangar. They simply do not have the team mentality.

What are these team philosophies and attitudes that the best entrepreneurs have and are able to identify or instill in prospective partners and team members? These can be traced to the entrepreneurial mind-set discussed in Chapter 5—a mind-set that can be seen actively at work around the team-building challenge. While there are innumerable blends and variations, most likely the teams of those firms that succeed in growing up big will share in common many of the following:

- *Cohesion.* Members of a team believe they are all in this together, and if the company wins, everyone wins. Members believe that no one can win unless everyone wins and, conversely, if anyone loses, everyone loses. Rewards, compensation, and incentive structures rest on building company value and return on capital invested, no matter how small or sizable.
- *Teamwork.* A team that works as a team, rather than one where individual heroes are created, may be the single most distinguishing feature of the higher-potential company. Thus, on these teams, efforts are made to make others' jobs easier, to make heroes out of partners and key people, and to motivate people by celebrating their successes. As Harold J. Seigle, the highly successful, now retired, president and chief executive officer of the Sunmark Companies, likes to put it, "High performance breeds strong friendships!"
- *Integrity.* Hard choices and trade-offs are made regarding what is good for the customer, the company, and value creation, rather than being based on purely utilitarian or Machiavellian ethics or narrow personal or departmental needs and concerns. There is a belief in and commitment to the notion of getting the job done without sacrificing quality, health, or personal standards.
- *Commitment to the long haul.* Like most organizations, new ventures thrive or wither according to the level of commitment of their teams. Members of a committed team believe they are playing for the long haul and that the venture is not a get-rich-quick drill. Rather, the venture is viewed as a delayed—not instant—gratification game in which it can take 5, 7, or even 10 or more years to realize a harvest. *No one gets a windfall profit*

by signing up now but bailing out early or when the going gets tough. Stock vesting agreements reflect this commitment. For example, stock will usually be so vested over five or seven years that anyone who leaves early, for whatever reasons, can keep stock earned to date, but he or she is required to sell the remaining shares back to the company at the price originally paid. Of course, such a vesting agreement usually provides that if the company is unexpectedly sold or if a public offering is made long before the five- or seven-year vesting period is up, then stock is 100 percent vested automatically with that event.

- *Harvest mind-set.* A successful harvest is the name of the game. This means that eventual capital gain is viewed as the scorecard, rather than the size of a monthly paycheck, the location and size of an office, a certain car, or the like.
- *Commitment to value creation.* Team members are committed to value creation—making the pie bigger for everyone, including adding value for customers, enabling suppliers to win as the team succeeds, and making money for the team's constituencies and various stakeholders.
- *Equal inequality.* In successful emerging companies, democracy and blind equality generally do not work very well, and diligent efforts are made to determine who has what responsibility for the key tasks. The president is the one to set the ground rules and to shape the climate and culture of the venture. Bill Foster, founder and president of Stratus Computer, was asked if he and his partners were all equal. He said, "Yes, we are, except I get paid the most and I own the most stock."[7] For example, stock is usually not divided equally among the founders and key managers. In one company of four key people, stock was split as follows: 34 percent for the president, 23 percent each for the marketing and technical vice presidents, and 6 percent for the controller. The remainder went to outside directors and advisors. In another company, seven founders split the company as follows: 22 percent for the president, 15 percent for each of the four vice presidents, and 9 percent for each of the two other contributors. An example of how failure to differentiate in terms of ownership impacts a business is seen in a third firm, where four owners each had equal share. Yet, two of the owners contributed virtually everything, while the other two actually detracted from the business. Because of this unresolved problem, the company could not attract venture capital and never was able to grow dramatically.
- *Fairness.* Rewards for key employees and stock ownership are based on contribution, performance, and results *over time.* Since these can only be roughly estimated in advance, and since there will invariably be surprises and inequities, both positive and negative, as time goes on, adjustments are made. One good example is a company that achieved spectacular results in the rather short time period of two years in the cellular car phone business. When the company was sold, it was evident that two of the six team members had contributed more than was reflected in their stock ownership position. To remedy this, another team member gave one of the two team members stock worth several hundred thousand dollars. Since the team was involved in another venture, the president made adjustments in the various ownership positions in the new venture, with each member's concurrence, to adjust for past inequities. In addition, it was decided to set aside 10 percent of the next venture to provide some discretion in making future adjustments for unanticipated contributions to ultimate success.
- *Sharing of the harvest.* This sense of fairness and justness seems to be extended by the more successful entrepreneurs to the harvest of a company, even when there is no legal or ethical obligation whatsoever to do so. For example, as much as 10 percent to 20 percent of the "winnings" is frequently set aside to distribute to key employees. In one such recent harvest, employees were startled and awash with glee when informed they would each receive a year's salary after the company was sold. However, this is not always

[7] Remarks made at a Babson College Venture Capital Conference, June 1985.

the case. In another firm, 90 percent of which was owned by an entrepreneur and his family, the president, who was the single person most responsible for the firm's success and spectacular valuation, needed to expend considerable effort to get the owners to agree to give bonuses to other key employees of around $3 million, an amount just over 1 percent of the $250 million sale price. (It is worth considering how this sense of fairness, or lack of it, affects future flows of quality people and opportunities from which these entrepreneurs can choose new ventures.)

A Process of Evolution

An entrepreneur considering issues of team formation will rarely discover black-and-white, bulletproof answers that hold up over time. Nor is it being suggested that an entrepreneur needs answers to *all* questions concerning what the opportunity requires, and when, before moving ahead. Emphasis on the importance of new venture teams also does not mean every new venture must start with a *full* team that plunges into the business. It may take some time for the team to come together as a firm grows, and there will also always be some doubt, a hope for more than a prospective partner can deliver, and a constant recalibration. Again, creative acts, such as running a marathon or entrepreneuring, will be full of unknowns, new ground, and surprises. Preparation is an insurance policy, and thinking through these team issues and team building concepts in advance is very inexpensive insurance.

The combination of the right team of people and a right venture opportunity can be a most powerful one. The whole is, in such instances, greater than the sum of the parts. However, the odds for highly successful venture teams are rather thin. Even if a venture survives, the turnover among team members during the early years probably exceeds the national divorce rate. Studies of new venture teams seeking venture capital show many never get off the ground. These usually exhaust their own resources and their commitment prior to raising the venture capital necessary to launch their ventures. Of those that are funded, about 1 in 20 will become very successful in three to five years, in that they will return in excess of five times the original investment in realizable capital gains.

The formation and development of new venture teams seems to be idiosyncratic, and there seems to be a multitude of ways in which venture partners come together. Some teams form by accidents of geography, common interest, or working together. Perhaps the common interest is simply that the team members want to start a business, while in other cases the interest is an idea that members believe responds to a market need. Others form teams by virtue of past friendships. For example, roommates or close friendships in college or graduate school frequently lead to business partnerships. This was the case with two of the author's classmates in the MBA program at the Harvard Business School. Concluding that they would eventually go into business together after rooming together for a week, Leslie Charm and Carl Youngman have been partners for over 20 years as owners of three national franchise companies, Doktor Pet Centers, Command Performance, and Eye-Natural.

In the evolution of venture teams, two distinct patterns are identifiable. In the first, one person has an idea (or simply wants to start a business), and then three or four associates join the team over the next one to three years as the venture takes form. Alternatively, an entire team forms at the outset based on such factors as a shared idea, a friendship, an experience, and so forth.

Filling the Gaps

There is no simple cookbook solution to team formation; rather, there are as many approaches to forming teams as there are ventures with multiple founders.

Successful entrepreneurs search out people and form and build a team based on what the opportunity requires, and when.[8] Team members will contribute high value to a venture if they complement and balance the lead entrepreneur—and each other. Yet, ironically, while a substantial amount of thought usually accompanies the decision of people to go into business together, an overabundance of the thinking, particularly among the less experienced, can focus on less-critical issues, such as titles, corporate name, letterhead, or what kind of lawyer or accountant is needed. Thus, teams are often ill-conceived from the outset and can easily plunge headlong into unanticipated and unplanned responses to crises, conflicts, and changes.

A team starts with a lead entrepreneur. In a start-up situation, the lead entrepreneur usually wears many hats. Beyond that, comparison of the nature and demands of the venture and the capabilities, motivations, and interests of the lead entrepreneur will signal gaps that exist and that need to be filled by other team members or by accessing other outside resources, such as a board of directors, consultants, lawyers, accountants, and so on.

Thus, for example, if the strengths of the lead entrepreneur or a team member are technical in nature, other team members, or outside resources, need to fill voids in marketing, finance, and such. Realistically, there will be an overlapping and sharing of responsibilities, but team members need to complement, not duplicate, the lead entrepreneur's capabilities and those of other team members.

Note that a by-product of forming a team may be alteration of an entry strategy if a critical gap cannot be filled. For example, a firm may find that it simply cannot assault a certain market because it cannot hire the right marketing person. (But it may find it could attract a top-notch person to exploit another niche with a modified product or service.)

Most important, the process of evaluating and deciding who is needed, and when, is dynamic and is not a one-time event. What know-how, skills, and expertise are required? What key tasks and action steps need to be taken? What are the requisites for success? What is the firm's distinctive competence? What external contacts are required? How extensive and how critical are the gaps? How much can the venture afford to pay? Will the venture gain access to the expertise it needs through additions to its board of directors or outside consultants? Questions such as these determine when and how these needs could be filled. And answers to such questions will change over time.

The following, organized around the analytical framework shown in *Exhibit 1.7,* can guide the formation of new venture teams:

- ***The founder.*** What kind of team is needed depends upon the nature of the opportunity and what the lead entrepreneur brings to the game. One key step in forming a team is for the lead entrepreneur to assess his or her entrepreneurial strategy. (The personal entrepreneurial strategy exercise in Chapter 19 is a valuable input in approaching these issues.) Thus, the lead entrepreneur needs to first consider whether the team is desirable or necessary and whether he or she wants to grow a higher potential company. He or she then needs to assess what talents, know-how, skills, track record, contacts, and resources are being brought to the table; that is, what "chunks" have been acquired. (See the "Managerial Skills and Know-How" assessment in Chapter 6.) Once this is determined, the lead entrepreneur needs to consider what the venture has to have to succeed, who is needed to complement him or her, and when. The best entrepreneurs are optimistic realists and have a real desire to improve their performance. They work at knowing what they do and do not know and are honest with themselves. The lead entrepreneur needs to consider issues such as:
  – What relevant industry, market, and technological know-how and experience are needed to win, and do I bring these to the venture?

[8] See J A Timmons, "The Entrepreneurial Team," *Journal of Small Business Management,* October 1975, pp. 36–37.

- Are my personal and business strengths in those specific areas that are critical to success in the proposed business?
- Do I have the contacts and networks needed (and will the ones I have make a competitive difference), or do I look to partners in this area?
- Can I attract a "first team" of all-star partners, and can I manage these people and other team members effectively?
- Why did I decide to pursue this particular opportunity now, and what do I want out of the business (i.e., what are my goals and my income and harvest aspirations)?
- Do I know what the sacrifices and commitment will be, and am I prepared to make these?
- What are the risks involved, am I comfortable with them, and do I look for someone with a different risk-taking orientation?

■ ***The opportunity.*** The need for team members is something an entrepreneur constantly thinks about, especially in the idea stage before start-up. What is needed in the way of a team depends on the match-up between the lead entrepreneur and the opportunity, and how fast and aggressively he or she plans to proceed. (See the "Venture Opportunity Screening Guide" in Chapter 4.) While most new ventures plan to bootstrap it and bring on additional team members only as the company can afford them, the Catch-22 is that if a venture is looking for venture capital or serious private investors, the more it has the team in place in advance, the higher will be its valuation and the smaller the ownership share that will have to be parted with. Some questions which need to be considered are:

- Have I clearly defined the value added and the economics of the business? Have I considered how (and with whom) the venture can make money in this business? For instance, whether a company is selling razors or razor blades makes a difference in the need for different team members.
- What are the critical success variables in the business I want to start, and what (or who) is needed to influence these variables positively?
- Do I have, or have access to, the critical external relationships with investors, lawyers, bankers, customers, suppliers, regulatory agencies, and so forth, that are necessary to pursue my opportunity? Do I need help in this area?
- What competitive advantage and strategy should I focus on? What people are necessary to pursue this strategy or advantage?

■ ***Outside resources.*** Gaps can be filled by accessing outside resources, such as boards of directors, accountants, lawyers, consultants, and so forth.[9] Usually, tax and legal expertise can best be obtained initially on a part-time basis. Other expertise (e.g., expertise required to design an inventory control system) is specialized and needed only once. Generally, if the resource is a one-time or periodic effort, or if the need is peripheral to the key tasks, goals, and activities required by the business, then an alternative such as using consultants makes sense. However, if the expertise is a must for the venture at the outset and the lead entrepreneur cannot provide it or learn it quickly, then one or more people will have to be acquired. Some questions are:

- Is the need for specialized, one-time or part-time expertise peripheral or on the critical path?
- Will trade secrets be compromised if I obtain this expertise externally?

[9] See William A Sahlman and Howard H Stevenson, "Choosing Small Company Advisors," *Harvard Business Review*, March–April 1987.

Additional Considerations

Forming and building a team is, like marriage, a rather unscientific, occasionally unpredictable, and frequently surprising exercise—no matter how hard one may try to make it otherwise! The analogy of marriage and family, with all the accompanying complexities and consequences, is a particularly useful one. Forming a team has many of the characteristics of the courtship and marriage ritual, involving decisions based in part on emotion. There may well be a certain infatuation among team members and an aura of admiration, respect, and often fierce loyalty. Similarly, the complex psychological joys, frustrations, and uncertainties that accompany the birth and raising of children (here, the product or service) are experienced in entrepreneurial teams as well.

Thus, the following additional issues need to be considered:

- ***Values, goals, and commitment.*** It is critical that a team be well anchored in terms of values and goals. In any new venture the participants establish psychological contracts and climates. While these are most often set when the lead entrepreneur encourages standards of excellence and respect for team members' contributions, selection of team members whose goals and values are in agreement can greatly facilitate establishment of a psychological contract and an entrepreneurial climate. In successful companies, the personal goals and values of team members align well, and the goals of the company are championed by team members as well. While this alignment may be less exact in large publicly owned corporations and greatest in small closely held firms, significant overlapping of a team member's goals with those of other team members and the overlap of corporate goals and team members' goals is desirable. Practically speaking, these evaluations of team members are some of the most difficult to make.
- ***Definition of roles.*** A diligent effort needs to be made to determine who is comfortable with and who has what responsibility for, the key tasks so duplication of capabilities or responsibilities is minimized. Roles cannot be pinned down precisely for all tasks, since some key tasks and problems simply cannot be anticipated and since contributions are not always made by people originally expected to make them. Indeed, maintaining a loose, flexible, flat structure with shared responsibility and information is desirable for utilizing individual strengths, flexibility, rapid learning, and responsive decision making.
- ***Peer groups.*** The support and approval of family, friends, and co-workers can be helpful, especially when adversity strikes. Reference group approval can be a significant source of positive reinforcement for a person's career choice and, thus, his or her entire self-image and identity.[10] Ideally, peer group support for each team member should be there. (If it is not, the lead entrepreneur may have to accept the additional burden of encouragement and support in hard times—one which can be sizable.) Therefore, questions of whether a prospective team member's spouse is solidly in favor of his or her decision to pursue an entrepreneurial career and the "sweat equity" required and of whether the team member's close friends will be a source of support and encouragement or of detraction or negativism need to be considered.

Common Pitfalls

There can be difficulties in the practical implementation of these philosophies and attitudes, irrespective of the venture opportunity and the people involved. The company then may come unglued before it gets started, may experience infant mortality, or may live

[10] Reference groups—groups consisting of individuals with whom there is frequent interaction (such as family, friends, and co-workers), with whom values and interests are shared, and from whom support and approval for activities are derived—have long been known for their influence on behavior. See John W Thibault and Harold H Kelley, *The Social Psychology of Groups* (New York: John Wiley & Sons, 1966).

perpetually immersed in nasty divisive conflicts and power struggles that will certainly cripple its potential, even if they do not eventually kill the company.

Often, a team lacks skill and experience in dealing with such difficult start-up issues, does not take the time to go through an extended "mating dance" among potential partners during the moonlighting phase prior to actually launching the venture, or does not seek the advice of competent advisors. As a result, such a team may be unable to deal with such sensitive issues as who gets how much ownership, who will commit what time and money or other resources, how disagreements will be resolved, and how a team member can leave or be let go. Thus, crucial early discussions among team members sometimes lead to a premature disbanding of promising teams with sound business ideas. Or in the rush to get going, or because the funds to pay for help in these areas are lacking, a team may stay together but not work through, even in a rough way, many of these issues. Such teams do not take advantage of the moonlighting phase to test the commitment and contribution made by team members. For example, to build a substantial business, a partner needs to be totally committed to the venture. The success of the venture is the partner's most important goal, and other priorities, including his or her family, come second.[11] Another advantage of using such a shakedown period effectively is that the risks inherent in such factors as premature commitment to permanent decisions regarding salary and stock are lower.

The common approach to forming a new venture team also can be a common pitfall for new venture teams. Here, two to four entrepreneurs, usually friends or work acquaintances, decide to demonstrate their equality with such democratic trimmings as equal stock ownership, equal salaries, equal office space and cars, and other items symbolizing their peer status. Left unanswered are questions of who is in charge, who makes the final decisions, and how real differences of opinion are resolved. While some overlapping of roles and a sharing in and negotiating of decisions are desirable in new venture teams, too much looseness is debilitating. Even sophisticated buy-sell agreements among partners often fail to resolve the conflicts.

Another pitfall is a belief that there are no deficiencies in the lead entrepreneur or the management team. Or a team is overly fascinated with or overcommitted to a product idea. For example, a lead entrepreneur who is unwilling or unable to identify his or her own deficiencies and weaknesses and to add appropriate team members to compensate for these, and who further lacks an understanding of what is really needed to make a new venture grow into a successful business, has fallen into this pitfall.[12]

Failing to recognize that creating and building a new venture is a dynamic process is a problem for some teams. Therefore, such teams fail to realize that initial agreements are likely not to reflect actual contributions of team members over time, regardless of how much time one devotes to team-building tasks and regardless of the agreements team members make before start-up. In addition, they fail to consider that teams are likely to change in composition over time. Richard Testa, a leading attorney whose firm has dealt with such ventures as Lotus Development Corporation and with numerous venture capital firms, recently startled those attending a seminar on raising venture capital by saying:

> The only thing that I can tell you with great certainty about this start-up business has to do with you and your partners. I can virtually guarantee you, based on our decade plus of experience, that five years from now at least one of the founders will have left every company represented here today.[13]

[11] This has been shown, for example, by Edgar H Schein's research about entrepreneurs, general managers, and technical managers who are MIT alumni. See the *Proceedings* of the Eastern Academy of Management meeting, May 1972, Boston.

[12] J A Timmons presented a discussion of these entrepreneurial characteristics at the First International Conference on Entrepreneurship. See "Entrepreneurial Behavior," *Proceedings,* First International Conference on Entrepreneurship, Center for Entrepreneurial Studies, Toronto, November 1973.

[13] The seminar, held at Babson College, was called "Raising Venture Capital," and was cosponsored by *Venture Capital Journal* and Coopers & Lybrand, 1985.

Such a team, therefore, fails to put in place mechanisms that will facilitate and help structure graceful divorces and that will provide for the internal adjustments required as the venture grows.

Destructive motivations in investors, prospective team members, or the lead entrepreneur spell trouble. Teams suffer if they are not alert to signs of potentially destructive motivations, such as an early concern for power and control by a team member.

Finally, new venture teams may take trust for granted. Integrity is important in long-term business success, and the world is full of high-quality, ethical people; yet the real world also is inhabited by predators, crooks, sharks, frauds, and imposters. It is paradoxical that an entrepreneur cannot succeed without trust, but he or she probably cannot succeed with blind trust either. Trust is something that is earned, usually slowly, for it requires a lot of patience and a lot of testing in the real world. This is undoubtedly a major reason why investors prefer to see teams that have worked closely together. In the area of trust, a little cynicism goes a long way, and teams that do not pay attention to detail, such as performing due diligence with respect to a person or firm, fall into this pit.

REWARDS AND INCENTIVES

The Reward System

John L. Hayes and the late Brian Haslett of Venture Founders Corporation have made a major contribution in the area of reward systems, and the following is based on their work.

The reward system of a new venture includes both the financial rewards of a venture—such as stock, salary, and fringe benefits—*and* the chance to realize personal growth and goals, exercise autonomy, and develop skills in particular venture roles. Also, what is perceived as a reward by any single team member will vary. This perception will depend very much upon personal values, goals, and aspirations. Some may seek long-range capital gains while others desire more short-term security and income.

The reward system established for a new venture team should facilitate the interface of the venture opportunity and the management team. It needs to flow from team formation and enhance the entrepreneurial climate of the venture and the building of an effective team. For example, being able to attract and keep high-quality team members depends, to a great extent, on financial and psychological rewards given. The skills, experience, commitment, risk, concern, and so forth, of these team members are secured through these rewards.

The rewards available to an entrepreneurial team vary somewhat over the life of a venture. While intangible rewards, such as opportunity for self-development and realization, may be available throughout, some of the financial rewards are more or less appropriate at different stages of the venture's development.

Because these rewards are so important and because, in its early stages, a venture is limited in the rewards it can offer, the *total* reward system over the life of the venture needs to be thought through very carefully and efforts be made to assure that the venture's capacity to reward is not limited as levels of contribution change or as new personnel are added.

External issues also have an impact on the reward system created for a new venture. It is important to realize that the division of equity between the venture and external investors will affect how much equity is available to team members. Further, the way a venture deals with these questions also will determine its credibility with investors and others, because these people will look to the reward system for signs of commitment by the venture team.

Critical Issues

It is an early critical task for the lead entrepreneur to lead in dividing ownership among the founding team, based on the philosophy and vision discussed earlier. Investors may provide advice but will, more often than not, dump the issue squarely back in the lap of the lead entrepreneur, since whether and how these delicate ownership decisions are resolved often is seen by investors as an important litmus test.

Also, the process by which a reward system is decided and the commitment of each team member to deal with problems in a way which will assure that rewards continue to reflect performance are of utmost importance. Each key team member needs to be committed to working out solutions that reflect the commitments, risks, and anticipated relative contributions of team members as fairly as possible.

A good reward system reflects the goals of the particular venture and is in tune with valuations. If a venture is not seeking outside capital, outside owners need not be considered; but the same issues need to be resolved. For example, if a goal is to realize a substantial capital gain from the venture in the next 5 to 10 years, then the reward system needs to be aimed at reinforcing this goal and encouraging the long-term commitment required for its attainment.

No time-tested formulas or simple answers exist to cover all questions of how distributions should be made. However, the following issues should be considered:

- *Differentiation.* The democracy approach can work, but it involves higher risk and more pitfalls than a system that differentiates based on the value of contributions by team members. As a rule, different team members rarely contribute the same amount to the venture, and the reward system needs to recognize these differences.
- *Performance.* Reward needs to be a function of performance (as opposed to effort) during the early life of the venture and not during only one part of this period. Many ventures have been torn apart when the relative contributions of the team members changed dramatically several years after start-up without a significant change in rewards. (Vesting goes a long way toward dealing with this issue.)
- *Flexibility.* Regardless of the contribution of any team member at any given time, the probability is high that this will change over time. The performance of a team member may be substantially more or less than anticipated. Further, a team member may have to be replaced and someone may have to be recruited and added to the existing team. Flexibility in the reward system, including such mechanisms as vesting and setting aside a portion of stock for future adjustments, can help to provide a sense of justice.

Considerations of Timing

Division of rewards, such as the split of stock between the members of the entrepreneurial team, will most likely be made very early in the life of the venture. Rewards may be a way of attracting significant early contribution; however, it is performance over the life of the venture that needs to be rewarded.

For example, regarding equity, once the allocation of stock is decided, changes in the relative stock positions of team members will be infrequent. New team members or external investors may dilute each member's position, but the relative positions will probably remain unchanged.

However, one or more events may occur during the early years of a venture. First, a team member who has a substantial portion of stock may not perform and need to be replaced early in the venture. Or a key team member may find a better opportunity and quit. Or a key team member could die in an accident. In each of these cases, the team will then be faced with the question of what will happen to the stock held by the team member. In each case, stock was intended as a reward for performance by the team member during the first several years of the venture, but the team member will not perform over this time period.

In the case of equity, several mechanisms are available to a venture when the initial stock split is so made that the loss or freezing of equity can be avoided. To illustrate, a venture can retain an option of returning stock to its treasury at the price at which it was purchased in certain cases, such as when a team member needs to be replaced. A buyback agreement is a mechanism to achieve this purpose.

To guard against the event that some portion of the stock has been earned and some portion will remain unearned, as when a team member quits or dies, the venture can place stock purchased by team members in escrow to be released over a two- or three-year period. Such a mechanism is called a stock-vesting agreement, and such an agreement can foster longer-term commitment to the success of the venture, while at the same time, providing a method for a civilized no-fault corporate divorce if things do not work out. Such a stock-vesting agreement is attached as a restriction on the stock certificate. Typically, the vesting agreement establishes a period of years, often four or more. During this period, the founding stockholders can "earn out" their shares. If a founder decides to leave the company prior to completion of the four-year vesting period, he or she may be required to sell the stock back to the company for the price originally paid for it, usually nothing. The departing shareholder, in this instance, would not own any stock after the departure. Nor would any capital gain windfall be realized by the departing founder. In other cases, founders may vest a certain portion each year, so they have some shares even if they leave. Such vesting can be weighted toward the last year or two of the vesting period. Other restrictions can give management and the board control over the disposition of stock, whether the stockholder stays or leaves the company. In essence, a mechanism such as a stock-vesting agreement confronts team members with the reality that "this is not a get-rich-quick exercise."

Other rewards, such as salary, stock options, bonuses, and fringe benefits, can be manipulated more readily to reflect changes in performance. But the ability to manipulate these is also somewhat dependent upon the stage of development of the venture. In the case of cash rewards, there is a trade-off between giving cash and the growth of the venture. Thus, in the early months of a venture, salaries will necessarily be low or nonexistent, and bonuses and other fringe benefits usually will be out of the question. Salaries, bonuses, and fringe benefits all drain cash, and until profitability is achieved, cash can always be put to use for operations. After profitability is achieved, cash payments will still limit growth. Salaries can become competitive once the venture has passed breakeven, but bonuses and fringe benefits should probably be kept at a minimum until several years of profitability have been demonstrated.

Considerations of Value

Of course, the contributions of team members will vary in nature, extent, and timing. In developing the reward system, and particularly the distribution of stock, contributions in certain areas are of particular value to a venture, as follows:

- *Idea.* In this area, the originator of the idea, particularly if trade secrets or special technology for a prototype was developed or if product or market research was done, needs to be considered.
- *Business plan preparation.* Preparing an acceptable business plan, in terms of dollars and hours expended, needs to be considered.
- *Commitment and risk.* A team member may invest a large percentage of his or her net worth in the company, be at risk if the company fails, have to make personal sacrifices,

put in long hours and major effort, risk his or her reputation, accept reduced salary, or already have spent a large amount of time on behalf of the venture. This commitment and risk need to be considered.

- *Skills, experience, track record, or contacts.* A team member may bring to the venture skills, experience, track record, or contacts in such areas as marketing, finance, and technology. If these are of critical importance to the new venture and are not readily available, these need to be considered.
- *Responsibility.* The importance of a team member's role to the success of the venture needs to be considered.

Being the originator of the idea or expending a great amount of time or money in preparing the business plan is frequently overvalued. If these factors are evaluated in terms of the real success of the venture down the road, it is difficult to justify much more than 15 percent to 20 percent of equity for them. Commitment and risk, skills, experience, and responsibility contribute more by far to producing success of a venture.

The above list is valuable in attempting to weigh fairly the relative contributions of each team member. Contributions in each of these areas have some value; it is up to a team to agree on how to assign value to contributions and, further, to leave enough flexibility to allow for changes.

CASE—SETTING THE STAGE*

Preparation Questions

1. Evaluate the situation at Morris Alper & Sons, Inc.
2. How should family companies handle the problem of succession?
3. What should Frederic M. Alper do?

MORRIS ALPER & SONS, INC.

A. SETTING THE STAGE[1]

In December 1979, Frederic M. Alper, president of Morris Alper & Sons, Inc. (MAS), was beginning to think about long-term succession. At that time, Fred was 40 years old and had been president for seven years. Reviewing his own succession, he analyzed what was done right and what could have been done better. Heavy on his mind were the numerous implications over a broad range. The personal as well as economic consequences of the transition process were tremendous; after all, the company accounted for nearly all of the net worth of the Alper family. The company itself was like a second family to Fred. Employees had shown pride and loyalty to MAS, and Fred felt a profound personal obligation to these people. Continuity of the business was something he took very seriously.

There were three backup prospects: Edward J. Downey, Jay W. Hughes, and Victor R. Del Regno. (See *Exhibit A,* management profiles, and *Exhibit B,* organizational chart.) Ed,

* Research Associate Christine C Remey wrote this case under the supervision of Professor Jeffry A Timmons. Harvard Business School case 294-019 (revised 7/23/93).

[1] The authors would like to convey our deepest thanks to Frederic M Alper, Victor R Del Regno, and many others at Morris Alper for their endless generosity. Throughout the hours and days of interviews and revisions, Fred and Vic approached very difficult issues openly with the intent to share with others the specific challenges of succession. There is a significant amount of risk involved in this type of openness; after all, the food brokerage business is a service business and Morris Alper is a private company. The manner in which Fred and Vic have contributed to this effort reveals a strong sense of confidence in themselves and in their company. We applaud their efforts, as the reader should.

Exhibit A
Management Profiles (December 1979)

Frederic M. Alper

President

Fred, at age 40, had been with Morris Alper & Sons for nine years and president for seven years. Previously, he worked for Bumble Bee Seafoods and IBEC. Education: Phi Beta Kappa and magna cum laude graduate of Brown University, a master of arts in philosophy from the University of Washington and a master of business administration from Harvard Business School.

Edward J. Downey

Executive Vice President

Ed, at the age of 49, had been with Morris Alper & Sons for 20 years. He worked in retail and direct sales in the Connecticut branch and headed sales for that branch from 1970 to 1973. In 1973, he was promoted to New England sales manager. One year later, he was again promoted to vice president, sales. In 1975, he was promoted to executive vice president. Education: Fairfield University.

Jay W. Hughes

Vice President, Grocery Sales

Jay, at the age of 47, had been with Morris Alper & Sons for six years. After three years, he was promoted to his current position. He had been with the Campbell Soup Company for 16 years, where he worked in a number of management positions, including assistant to the president of sales. Education: Boston College bachelor of science in business and master of business administration.

Victor R. Del Regno

Vice President, Frozen/Dairy Sales

Vic, at the age of 31, joined Morris Alper & Sons in January of 1979. Previously at Standard Brands, Vic had been vice president, sales and planning, of the Planter's division and vice president of the western division. Education: Pace University bachelor of business administration—marketing.

a long-time employee and executive vice president, seemed to be the most logical choice if something happened to Fred unexpectedly. Ed was eight years older than Fred and was not a planned successor. Within MAS, there had been an unspoken understanding that Ed was next in line. Jay understood this better than anyone. This assumption was also validated in conversations between Fred and Vic, before and after Vic was hired in early 1979.

Suddenly Fred was interrupted by the phone; it was one of their large clients. (These clients were the manufacturers MAS represented; they were referred to as principals.) Thoughts of succession would have to be postponed for the moment, but how long should Fred wait to begin the process of planning backup and long-term succession?

Exhibit B
Organizational Chart (1979)

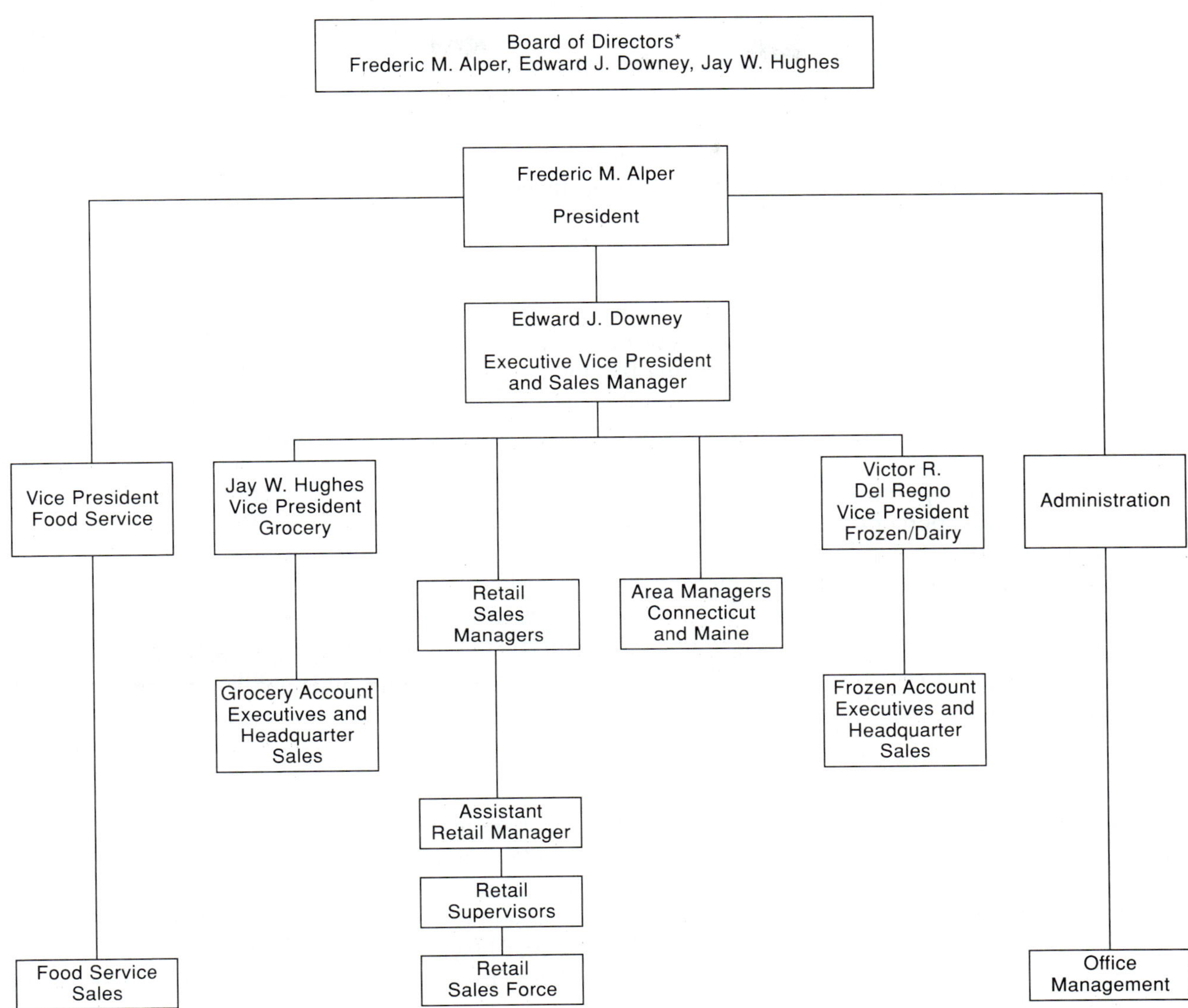

*In late 1979, Victor R. Del Regno had just been elected to the Board of Directors.

BACKGROUND

Industry Context[2]

Traditionally, a food brokerage company was an independent sales agency that sold noncompeting food and nonfood products on behalf of a manufacturer (called a principal). The main services food brokers provided for manufacturers were headquarter and retail

[2]Unless otherwise noted, information from this section was drawn from Benson P Shapiro and Jeffrey J Sherman, "Morris Alper & Sons, Inc.," HBS Case 581-098, Harvard Business School, 1982.

selling, as well as merchandising. A brokerage company handled products from 6 to 60 principals. Brokers assumed no credit liability, nor did they warehouse or physically distribute products. Brokers were paid a commission on net sales, generally in the range of 3 to 5 percent, depending on the principal and the products. Contracts usually included 30-day termination notice. The brokerage business required little in the way of assets, and brokers characterized themselves as "living by our wits, our know-how, and our relationships."

The three main functions of a food broker were distribution, department, and promotion. *Distribution* entailed acquiring an agreement from a customer/grocery account to stock the product on a regular basis. Most grocery chains and independent stores were controlled by a central buying staff and local store managers. How products were merchandised on the shelf was referred to as *department*. Checking the number of facings, rotating the stock, checking the shelf tags, and obtaining the most desirable shelf location were all duties carried out by retail representatives. Finally, *promotion* encompassed retailers' advertising and displaying products.

Fred Alper explained that "our industry is like a three-legged stool: principals who pay us, the customers to whom we sell, and our people who perform the services." Some principals considered brokers a necessary evil, tolerated only until sales of a product had grown to a point where principals could afford their own direct sales force, though in recent years this perception had been changing. There were over 2,300 food brokers in the United States in 1979. Barriers to entry were low. With principal contacts and/or marketing experience, individuals had successfully established their own firms. Competition was fierce. Since there were many brokers and only 30-day contracts, principals could quickly reassign business. However, principals had a vested interest in developing long-standing relationships with high-performing food brokers, as a widening gulf was developing between modern, progressive food brokers and all the rest.

Morris Alper & Sons, Inc.

In 1932, MAS was founded as a flour brokerage business by Morris Alper and his son, David. Through the Depression, MAS expanded the business into various other commodities. MAS began to represent branded products in 1945. Welch's was one of the first manufacturers of branded products to be represented by MAS. One of the conditions to this business relationship was the understanding that David Alper would take over as president. Morris Alper commented, "What an honor it was to be told that my son was ready to succeed me." Yet, privately, Morris told his son that nothing was going to change.

Despite his father's comment, David Alper was 38 years old when, in 1945, he succeeded his father. Dave focused on this question: "Once you have established that you can make a living, the key question is what kind of a life do you want to lead?" Dave's business philosophy was based on democracy, whereby there was little status differences between MAS management and employees. For instance, when a new principal was added to the MAS list of principals, everyone was consulted, including secretaries, middle management, and senior executives. Virtually all of the employees drove the same kind of cars and there were no assigned parking spaces. Almost every day at their coffee breaks, Dave would be at the center of a social gathering, where there was much social conversation, including some joking around. Each employee was valued as an individual. This democratic culture was enhanced by an open and nonpolitical work environment. The structure, attitudes, and organization of the company had always been somewhat unconventional; classic big company thinking was foreign to MAS. There was very little formal supervision in the company. Even in the early days of MAS, there was some employee ownership; in addition, all employees felt that they were sharing in the company both financially and psychologically. MAS even instituted profit sharing, which was innovative in the food brokerage industry and very leading edge for its day.

Sadly, in 1967 Dave was struck with an illness which forced him to retire as president of MAS. George Edwards, age 60, was named as the transitional president; he had a retailer background and had been with MAS just a few years. Dave remained involved as treasurer and as an informal advisor well into the 1970s. However, he was not active in running the business after 1967.

Three years after his father stepped down, Frederic M. Alper joined MAS, with a clear aspiration to succeed George Edwards. Fred had not planned on joining the family business and had pursued a career outside of MAS. By 1970, Fred had established himself both professionally and academically. Fred's recollection was that he consciously chose to join MAS in 1970 when he was in the process of making a career change, although he recognized that there might have been some unconscious things going on that drew him to the business.

In 1972, at the age of 33, Fred became president. He was thrust into the presidency because George Edwards, the president, was in his mid-sixties and a change was needed. Fred had been in the business for only two years and was not really ready to assume the presidency. He had to contend with a rival, Jack Quilty, who was an ambitious, talented man hired as the heir apparent, in the 1960s, when it appeared that Fred was not going to enter the business. Jack had incredible analytical skills, but very questionable people skills. In 1973, a year after Fred became president, Jack sought to buy the company. When he failed, Jack left MAS and took some key people with him to another broker, which is no longer in business.

Under Fred's direction, the company focused on expanding the business derived from existing principals. Better controls and systems were put into place by Fred to manage MAS's growth. Fred originated a no-nepotism policy. No longer solely owned by the family, MAS stock was held by many key employees. MAS had widespread employee ownership, and each stockholder, including Fred, maintained a minority position. Other brokers viewed MAS as a proactive organization intent on building a solid reputation through its people and the product lines it represented. MAS was an organization which "invested in its employees, rather than making the family wealthy." MAS had an excellent reputation within the industry. It was well represented in trade magazines, conferences, and associations.

Progress at MAS was steady. The number of employees had increased from 40 in 1970 to over 108 by December of 1979 (see *Table 1*). The number of principals MAS represented went from 6 to 12 (12 was considered relatively few principals). These 12 principals generated $155 million in sales of product lines that MAS represented.

Philosophy and Culture

MAS strived to be a leader in all the important areas of the business. "Using the phrase 'having arrived' was not appropriate for MAS," Michael Cirincione, a sales manager, explained, "because you cannot grow if you define yourself as 'having arrived'. We were

Table 1
The Number of MAS Employees (1970 to 1980)

1970	40
1972	48
1974	61
1976	74
1978	89
1980	108

always trying to outdo ourselves." The company culture was based primarily on people, with special emphasis on reputation, pride, and intensity.

Reputation. Building an impeccable reputation in the industry and within the company was a constant priority. Dave Alper had developed criteria for principal representation:

1. Must have quality products which we believe in.
2. Must have No. 1 products in their categories or a willingness to make them No. 1.
3. Must be growth oriented.
4. Must be willing to advertise, promote, and market aggressively.
5. Must be good people to work with.

Dave vowed that MAS would "not represent more principals than the company's organization was capable of handling at a given time."

Fred continued this policy, reasoning that "it was no accident that certain brokers represented certain principals. Like brokers and manufacturers tend to be attracted to one another." In one instance, a vice president of an unprofitable department became excited about the prospect of representing a principal whose account represented at least $100,000 of new business. The vice president had recently joined MAS, and this was an opportunity to get his department in the black. He called a meeting with Jay, Vic, Fred, and another vice president to prepare for the first interview and to analyze the principal's products. Before the preparations were even discussed, a vote was taken on whether or not MAS should present themselves to this principal. The vote was four to one—not to interview. The vice president was the only one excited about this new prospect. "I must be missing something," he exclaimed. "Why wouldn't we want this business?" The group explained that this principal had a history of hiring a broker one year, then switching to direct sales, then to another broker, which was designed to build short-term sales volume. This principal would not be hiring MAS to build long-term sales volume and to establish itself as a leader. It did not meet the standards of an MAS principal. An area manager stated that "whereas more is usually better, at MAS better is more."

Morris Alper Pride. Fred summarized the fundamental purpose at MAS:

Pride, "Morris Alper pride." That is everything. That is the one thing that is unique to this company and people feel it. There is pride in all that we do from the selection of sales people [see *Table 2*], to the way that we sell and merchandise. There are many ways to spend a manufacturer's money, but there is pride in doing it right. Some brokers would spend more to get the order, but we do it on an equitable and fair basis. People here take pride in doing it right. This is sometimes contrary to the nature of a salesman, which is to get the order at all costs.

Table 2
Published Criteria for a MAS Salesperson

Consistent performer	Hard worker
Honest and inspires mutual trust	Team player
Creative	Has a sense of urgency
Has a sense of pride and confidence	Enthusiastic
Professional	Cares about the company
Happy	Growth oriented

Remember: "*Quality people are almost always associated with quality products.*"

Individuals at MAS took pride in being the first to a reset and the last to go.[3] From the retail level throughout the organization, individuals "raised the high bar" to exceed the expectations of MAS management and of the principals. For instance, several years in a row, MAS had been recognized in one department as the most outstanding broker in the country. MAS employees saw this award as a benchmark and worked late during the week and on weekends to keep winning it each year. One senior manager commented, "Our people have a commitment of not just winning championships, but of defending them as well." The reputation of MAS was quality products and quality people.

Virtually all MAS employees wore a pin that symbolized their shared pride in the company. Wearing the pin indicated that the person subscribed to the criteria of a MAS salesperson.

Intensity. Fred felt "that part of the specialness of our company is reading big significance into details. Sometimes people accuse us of being really nit-picking, but we are always probing and questioning. We read big significance and patterns into little things. This is a large part of the company." As a result there was always a lot of focus on what some would consider "little things."

Donald King, vice president/area manager in Maine, added:

> We are recognized because of our accomplishments as the best in the business. We are looked up to in the trade by our customers, our competition, and our principals. Keeping with the standard of always striving to be better, after every meeting with a customer or principal, we meet afterward to ask, What did we miss? What could we have done differently? At MAS, Fred has always said that there is a lot of learning involved in asking and answering these questions.

People-based Philosophy. MAS emphasized the development of the company through the growth of the employees. "What can we do better?" was a question that constantly resurfaced throughout the company. Constructive criticism was constant and all employees had to accept that everything, from writing a letter to drafting a marketing plan, always could be improved on. MAS was a living organism that was constantly evolving through the growth of its employees. It was not only a work place; it was "Alper University," where teaching and learning were part of every task of every day.

The compensation system was designed to enhance the focus on personal growth. Fred explained this unique aspect of a sales business:

> We do not have only quantitative objectives, such that if you make this number, then you will make this amount of money—nowhere in our company. It could be argued that we are at odds with the sales business, because you can quantify what you sell and what you get paid. Here, it is "enlightened subjectivity;" as we judge people qualitatively as well as quantitatively. We want to foster a team atmosphere. We believe that many things influence how one performs and many of them are out of one's control. A lot of sales organizations do not recognize that fact. We would rather trust our own enlightened judgment with some objectivity than have our people get a feast or famine that they do not deserve.

Donald King, Maine's vice president, elaborated on the ownership attitude of MAS:

> We are a subchapter S corporation. As employees, we all have a job to do and there are owners at many levels within the company who have that ownership mentality. It follows that we are looking for the best-qualified people, with the knowledge that they are just not born, they are developed. Those who know Fred and who have come to know the company preach people development, talk about it, let others know about it, and they tell someone, and so on. It does not matter where you are—in New York, on Long Island, or in the most northern part of Maine—it is the same culture with the intensity

[3] A *reset* refers to how products are reorganized on supermarket shelves. Brokers are responsible for obtaining the given amount of space and correct positioning for their principals' products.

and the pride. We have all been "Alperized." Although there are only 35 owners, the ownership mentality pervades in the organization in terms of pride, recognition, and compensation.

The prevailing philosophy was that future success of MAS depended on a blend of "street" and "strategy." "Street" is necessary to get the job done day to day. Where MAS stood out was doing that and always looking at strategy as well. In order to get individuals to contribute to the long-term growth of the company, the MAS philosophy had always stressed the need for decisions that focused on the future and not on the short-term reward. MAS was committed to longevity, and in order to translate intentions into results, everyone had to buy into the commitment. Fred expanded:

> Where brokers usually are deficient is with their own people, because there is not much short-term leverage in nurturing that leg of the stool. The biggest leverage is getting a new principal. There is also a lot of leverage in putting your time on a present manufacturer to assure a continuity of relationship and on customers to get the order. Those are no-brainers, but your own people are captive. They often do not get treated with the same kind of respect because it takes time and it is difficult. You need to nurture people. Doing this whole people-oriented thing is tough, but in the long term, doing it well is crucial.

MAS invested in its people. Nurturing and developing good people was a basic tenet.

ANTICIPATING SUCCESSION

David Alper's Succession Principles

Dave thought of MAS in a thoughtful long-term perspective, never taking for granted the importance of the early culture and strategy. Dave's thoughts on succession were as follows:

- Preference for MAS to remain a family business.

Starting the company and working closely with his own father, Dave hoped that the Alper family would continue to play a significant role in the company. He had devoted time and energy to create a workplace that was not only profitable but enjoyable. In 1967, when he was taken ill, Dave offered the presidency to his brother Mark Alper, who declined. If the ability and interest were there, Dave ideally wanted one of his sons to take over MAS.

- Commitment to the longevity of MAS.

Employee ownership and promotions from within were indicators of the investment the company was willing to make in its people. Dave believed that the return on this investment was invaluable to the longevity of MAS. Planning for his own succession, he hired a key person in 1967. He was the best he could find. It was critical for the president to plan for the future growth and succession of the company, and thereby find the most capable people to manage the company.

- Realism about the business.

He stressed the need to have capable people, while recognizing changes in the business and the need for more systems, accountability, and a results orientation.

- Emphasis on company values.

Dave cared about the MAS culture as much as he did about economic prosperity. He had represented only those principals that were absolutely blue-chip. Dave continually stressed in his interaction with employees, principals, and customers that people were an end in themselves. Dedicated, loyal, hard-working people profited personally and economically from their association with MAS.

Fred's Perspective

In late 1979, Fred related his feeling on the need for a successor:

Theoretically, I believe that 8 to 10 years is the maximum amount of time that an individual should run a company. It is like a presidential term of 8 years—just the right amount of time to get the job done. But after that it is really hard to ferment change from within. You get locked into your own systems.

I was somewhat captive of certain ideas and had loyalties to people. I was not really tired, I was not bored, and I was not burned out. I was running at a ferocious pace. It was not the hours; it was the intensity of the problems with the three legged stool. They compound and there are always 8 to 10 issues backed up at one time.

Fred reflected on his transition:

When I was a new president, I wanted advice from my dad, but often had a short fuse. The more insecure I was, the shorter the fuse. My dad was basically hands-off, with an occasional lapse. George Edwards was hanging on with ego needs to be involved and did not have trust or confidence in younger people to run the company. As a result of this, I was determined, when I turned the company over, to let go, not to make decisions, not to confuse who is the boss, and to be active in promoting the succession—but while doing all of the above, not necessarily committed to being passive and not involved.

Further, Fred had learned the following things from his own succession:

- I had empathy for a new president in a successful company, because I knew that it was a scary job. There is a lot more downside risk than upside potential. If you are successful, then people perceive that you were merely perpetuating the previous leader's objectives. However, if you are a failure, then you have wrecked a good thing.
- I understood that there was a need for planning. More readiness was desirable.
- A lot of difficulty surrounds a power transition. As an example, I recall an incident in which a large principal was unhappy with MAS, and George Edwards, then president, responded, "Not to worry; Dave and I are still around." That was the last thing the principal wanted to hear. George failed to recognize that new people were on center stage.
- It is hard to determine if the predecessor is acting out of his own ego needs, lacks confidence in you, or is thinking about the company's needs—in any case it is tough for the new president.
- As the new president, you want your own team to put your own stamp on things. You inherit some decay, which you have to deal with. Some of it can be subtle and has been building slowly for a long time. You also find that the former regime has developed some friendships and relationships that overshadow business needs and you have to live with that.
- The first year of presidency is devoted to establishing your leadership and placing your own imprint. The real changes and the best ones begin in a year or two.
- If a company is successful, there is a need to respect and recognize past policies and philosophies while still evolving them. There are obligations and expectations that are inherited.

Thus, Fred would not compromise on the following criteria for his successor: integrity, work ethic, appropriate toughness, strong relationships outside the company, respect within the company, attention to detail, a sense of urgency, personal strength, an ability to deal with the highs and lows of the business, and a commitment to personal and professional growth. Fred was looking for an individual who had respect for, and who took pride in, the traditions of the company, recognizing that they were important, meaningful, and contributing to success, while being modern enough to make significant changes and to be progressive.

The Three Backup Prospects. Fred had not decided on a succession plan. After all, he was only 40. He observed his key managers in day-to-day situations, to see how they reacted and with what results. When he mentored them, he watched to see whether they learned and grew. He felt that you could tell a lot about a manager by observing the way he or she responded to mentoring and constructive criticism. Ideally, Fred would have liked to have three to four stars to see who would emerge. Edward J. Downey moved up through MAS and was second in command. Jay W. Hughes had been with MAS since 1974 and had grown to be a key member of the management team. Victor R. Del Regno had been at MAS for close to a year, and while he had adapted quickly to the brokerage business, he still faced a lot of adjustment to the company and its culture. At this point, Vic was not sure that the brokerage business was right for him. Though Ed was the most likely person to be interim president in case of a calamity, Vic had an edge because he was new, young, and ambitious. Yet, Fred knew that it would be presumptuous to assume that Vic would evolve into a candidate, even though the company's confidence level in Vic was high enough to have just elected him a member of the board of directors.

There were certain areas in which Vic needed to grow. Fred discussed them:

> Vic appeared very intense and I worried about that even though I was highly intense too. I recognize that people need room to breathe to do their job well, to be creative, and to grow with the company. You do not develop personal trust by discussing solely business; it is more in the personal discussions. Vic was too much business, which was inhibiting his abilities to nurture trust and build relationships with some individuals in the company.
>
> For instance, although the days of the coffee breaks were long gone, when Vic joined the company in 1979, many of the executives often went to lunch together. Business was not necessarily discussed. But Vic usually did not take the time to leave the office for lunch; he either skipped lunch or would have a sandwich brought in. One day, Vic called a meeting during lunch, which bothered a few people. He ordered sandwiches for the group to be paid for by the company since this was going to be a working lunch. As the sandwiches were being brought into the meeting room, the bookkeeper, who had been there when Dave Alper was president, commented that "we do not do things like this here." Vic's response was, "Well, things are going to change then."
>
> I also wondered whether it would be a good fit long-term. Vic was in frozen foods, which was a fast, ever-changing, competitive business with a lot of young people in it; Jay was in grocery, which was more slow moving, inflexible, and unchanging. Vic was a guy who was great in frozen—it was almost like an actor who played a certain part so well that you had a temptation to cast him as a one-role actor. Could he do the grocery act and beyond?
>
> Finally, as a member of the board of directors, I was concerned about how Vic spent money and how it was perceived by Jay and Ed. Spending conservatively and always watching things was my style. Vic's style was to spend big here and find other places to save. We came to the same amount, but the methodology getting there was different.

All of these concerns were mixed blessings for the company. Vic's intensity fit with the culture and raised the high bar a notch, yet it was hard for some individuals to trust him. Similarly, his performance in frozen foods exhibited Vic's abilities, while at the same time characterizing him too narrowly. Finally, changing the traditional ways of the company often produced both results and unsolicited criticism. Vic never took criticism well at the time it was given, but usually reflected on it, absorbed it, learned, and grew from it. He was strong and independent, which was refreshing but quite frustrating to deal with at times. Fred had to consider these concerns as he pondered Vic's future growth and the company's anticipated needs.

Victor R. Del Regno. Vic described his thought process when he joined MAS:

> In January 1979, I headed up the frozen food department. I came from Standard Brands, where I was a vice president and where I had held several jobs in grocery. With the MAS culture and coming in from the outside, Fred argued that for the good of the company that I join as a department head and

not as a vice president, although I had been a vice president at Standard Brands. Fred's sensitivity puzzled me. Fred said you really ought to come in and prove yourself to the organization. I said that I'm making a major career change here and have proven myself already. We worked our way through it and I joined as a vice president.

Fred reviewed his early impressions:

Vic was ambitious. He had a style that to some degree clashed with the culture of the company. One of the things that we have always tried to do with the people that come from outside is, not only to have them marry our culture, but also to have them change our culture as well. But do not try to change us too much, because we are pretty damn successful and we do not need to totally change. We want to get pulled and yanked in this area or that area, but 90 percent of us is where we wanted to be.

During Vic's first week, there were two issues: car washes and weekly sales figures. First, in regard to washing one's car, I said "We are a small company and not eager to incur costs like this." Vic exclaimed: "I do not agree. It is important that our cars are clean for our customers and principals. It is a reflection on the people and MAS." I suggested that we revisit it in nine months. It never came up again and our employees still pay for car washes. The second issue was weekly sales figures. Vic could not understand how you can operate without weekly sales figures. I said that this thing moves so fast, you are not going to be able to look at weekly sales figures. The point is that here was a guy who came with ideas. He wanted to change things. He did not want to change the company culture. He was molding it to fit his own standard. Even from the very beginning he married the culture, but he never lost the need to put his personal imprint on it. He was a good manager with his own independence.

Vic remembered asking Fred about the succession plan in an early interview. Vic recalled the reply,

Fred said that there was a plan and Ed was the logical successor, if something should happen to him. This worried me a little bit. Although I respected Ed's stature, I did not see in Ed a young contemporary mind.

When asked about his aspirations to become president of the company, Vic responded:

Honestly, I recall that I aspired to do more than to be vice president of frozen. I was used to being on a fast track at a large company. Jay made it clear, even in the interview, when I talked about growth and about Ed's job, that I should not even aspire to it: Ed had a lock on that and no one was ever going to dethrone Ed Downey. I aspired to grow; I never really thought about the presidency. I just wanted to continue to grow both personally and professionally. I had always worked hard and had results. The right things would happen. Fred said you will grow with the company and I believed him.

Fred hung up the phone with the principal. His thoughts returned to the issues surrounding succession: What did he need to do to prepare himself, MAS, their principals and customers for a change? When would it be best to pass the baton? To whom should the baton be passed?

EXERCISE—REWARDS

The following exercise can help an entrepreneur devise a reward system for a new venture. In proceeding with the exercise, it is helpful to pretend to look at these issues from an investor's point of view and to imagine that the venture is in the process of seeking capital from an investor group to which a presentation was made several weeks ago and which is favorably impressed by the team and its plan for the new venture. Imagine then that this investor group would like a brief presentation (of 10 to 15 minutes) about how the team plans to reward its members and other key contributors.

EXERCISE
REWARDS

Name:

Venture:

Date:

PART I

Part I is to be completed by each individual team member—*alone.*

STEP 1: INDICATE WHO WILL DO WHAT DURING THE FIRST YEAR OR TWO OF YOUR VENTURE, WHAT CONTRIBUTIONS EACH HAS MADE OR WILL MAKE TO CREATING A BUSINESS PLAN, THE COMMITMENT AND RISK INVOLVED FOR EACH, AND WHAT UNIQUE CRITICAL SKILLS, EXPERIENCE, CONTACTS, AND SO FORTH, EACH BRINGS TO THE VENTURE. Try to be as specific as possible, and be sure to include yourself.

Team Member	Responsibility	Title	Contribution to Business Plan	Commitment and Risk	Unique/Critical Skills, Etc.

STEP 2: INDICATE BELOW THE APPROXIMATE SALARY AND SHARES OF STOCK (AS A PERCENT) EACH MEMBER SHOULD HAVE UPON CLOSING THE FINANCING OF YOUR NEW VENTURE.

Team Member	Salary	Shares of Stock (%)

STEP 3: INDICATE BELOW WHAT FRINGE BENEFITS YOU BELIEVE THE COMPANY SHOULD PROVIDE DURING THE FIRST YEAR OR TWO.

Team Member	Vacation	Holidays	Health/Life Insurance	Retirement Plan	Other

STEP 4: LIST OTHER KEY CONTRIBUTORS, SUCH AS MEMBERS OF THE BOARD OF DIRECTORS, AND INDICATE HOW THEY WILL BE REWARDED.

Name	Expertise/ Contribution	Salary	Shares of Stock (%)	Other

PART II

Part II involves meeting as a team to reach consensus on the responsibilities of each team member and how each will be rewarded. In addition to devising a reward system for the team and other key contributors, the team will examine how consensus was reached.

STEP 1: MEET AS A TEAM AND REACH CONSENSUS ON THE ABOVE TEAM ISSUES AND INDICATE THE CONSENSUS SOLUTION BELOW.

Responsibilities/Contributions

Team Member	Responsibility	Contribution to Business Plan	Commitment and Risk	Unique/Critical Skills, Etc.

Rewards

Team Member	Salary	Shares of Stock (%)

Rewards (continued)

Team Member	Title	Vacation	Holidays	Health/Life Insurance	Retirement Plan	Other

STEP 2: MEET AS A TEAM AND REACH CONSENSUS ON ISSUES INVOLVING OTHER KEY CONTRIBUTORS AND INDICATE THE CONSENSUS SOLUTION BELOW.

Name	Expertise/ Contribution	Salary	Shares of Stock (%)	Other

STEP 3: DISCUSS AS A TEAM THE FOLLOWING ISSUES AND INDICATE ANY IMPORTANT LESSONS AND IMPLICATIONS:

– What patterns emerged in the approaches taken by each team? What are the differences and similarities?

– How difficult or easy was it to reach agreement among team members? Did any issues bog down?

– If salaries or stock were equal for all team members, why was this so? What risks or problems might such an approach create?

– What criteria, either implicit or explicit, were used to arrive at a decision concerning salaries and stock? Why?

The Family Venture 8

Daring as it is to investigate the unknown, even more so it is to question the known.

Kaspar

RESULTS EXPECTED

Upon completion of the chapter, you will have:

1. Identified and examined the role and significance of the family in building a venture.
2. Analyzed some of the important problems associated with new venture teams that involve immediate family members.
3. Considered ways of managing problems of control, credibility, family dynamics, and succession.
4. Analyzed and developed courses of action to deal with a family business crisis.
5. Analyzed a case, "Passing the Baton."

POPULAR AND NUMEROUS

Family businesses are very popular today, and there has been an influx of young talent into family-owned businesses for several reasons. As the editors of *Business Week* stated: "All over the country, the bright young types who formerly opted for management consulting or the fast track at blue-chip corporations are eagerly joining family businesses. . . . Changed attitudes and a changing economy account for this turnabout."[1] It seems that people are tired of bureaucracy and have turned to family ventures in hopes of success, security, and humanistic work values.

Historically, involvement by families in business ventures has been the least understood aspect of new venture creation. Yet, of the more than 18 million businesses in the United States, 9 out of 10 are family dominated.[2] Family firms range in size from small local stores to such large multinational corporations as Mars, S. C. Johnson & Sons, and McDonnell Douglas. They employ half of the nation's work force and produce half the gross national product.

This chapter was written by Wendy C Handler, DBA. Dr. Handler teaches family business management at Babson College and conducts research on succession in family firms from the perspective of next-generation family members.

[1] *Business Week*, July 1, 1985. Reprinted with permission. © 1993 McGraw-Hill, Inc.

[2] R Beckhard and W G Dyer, Jr., "Managing Continuity in the Family-owned Business," *Organizational Dynamics*, Summer 1983, pp. 5–12.

THE IMPACT OF GOALS

Three Types of Firms

In successful businesses, the goals of the firm and the goals of the owners or managers, or both, overlap to some degree. Family businesses are unique in structure and purpose. They are unlike public corporations and closely held nonfamily firms, because of the existence of family members in business and the function of family goals. *Exhibit 8.1* shows how corporate goals and the goals of owners/managers, and for family firms, those of family members, overlap.

As can be seen in *Exhibit 8.1,* in *publicly owned corporations,* the overlap between corporate goals and the personal goals of managers is limited. Corporate and institutional goals supersede personal, especially nonbusiness, goals.

In *closely held corporations* that are nonfamily, this common area, or area of overlap, is usually greater, because the corporate goals are personally determined by those who own and operate the corporation, as shown in *Exhibit 8.1.*

Exhibit 8.1
Relationship of Goals in Three Types of Firms

Publicly Owned Corporations

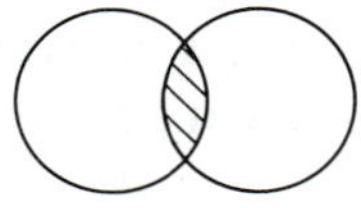

Closely Held Firms (nonfamily)

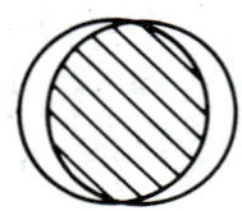

Family Firms

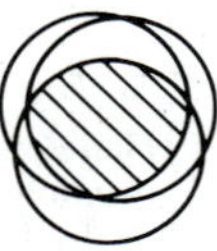

Finally, in *family owned or controlled firms,* there is an additional set of goals or values determined by the family in charge. These values associated with the family influence the development of corporate goals. They also interact with the personal goals of managers in the determination of day-to-day business decisions and longer-term business strategy. Often, the overlap is much greater than in publicly owned or closely held corporations. One direct consequence is a much greater degree of potential conflicts and complications in balancing and achieving these goals. The interaction of the three sets of goals also is shown in *Exhibit 8.1.*

In family firms, the presence of the family can provide opportunities for collaboration, trust, and team effort. In these optimal cases, there is general agreement or synergy between the goals of the corporation, the family, and the owner/managers, who are typically family members. For example, the daughter of the founder of a successful New York–based real estate development firm talked about how working with her father and other family members was special because of the team spirit. She described one afternoon when three family members walked down Park Avenue. "We looked at buildings we have owned and pointed out different aspects of other buildings and . . . felt like the three of us were so in tune and learning from each other," she said.

In this case, values concerning *family togetherness, sharing, and closeness* were being met, as were corporate values associated with *profit making and equity building,* and personal goals associated with *individual growth and learning.*

Convergent/Divergent Goals in Family Firms

On the other hand, personal goals or corporate goals may differ or clash with family goals, producing tension, conflict, and heated arguments in the context of the family firm. An example is in the Bingham family of Louisville, Kentucky, where personal goals concerning ownership conflicted with corporate and family goals leading to the downfall and sale of the $400 million media empire.

In other words, as *Exhibit 8.2* illustrates, it is possible for the overlapping of goals to become greater, or for goals which had overlapped to begin to diverge at some time.

The implications are profound. There are more subtleties and complications, and there is a greater need for participants to pay attention to, and devise strategies that take into account the nature of, family relationships. For investors, lenders, suppliers, and customers, the additional family ownership dimension introduces a dilemma beyond the normal expo-

Exhibit 8.2
Shared or Divergent Goals in Family Firms

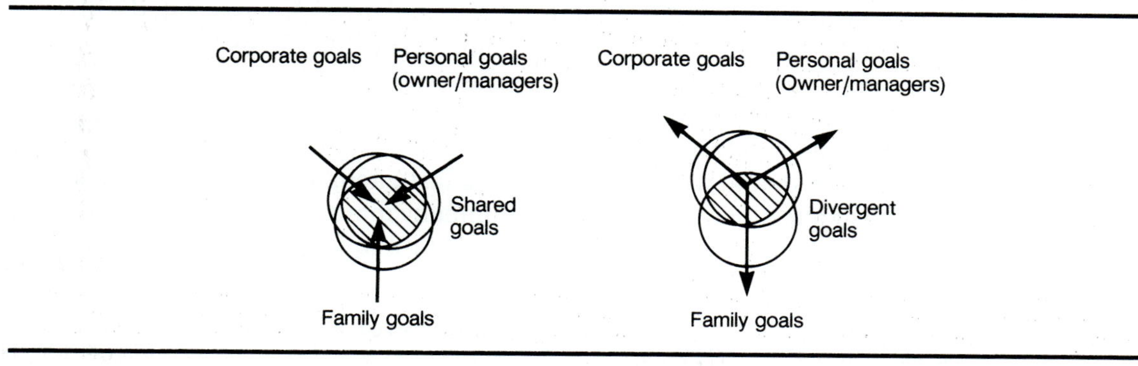

sure to risk in a nonfamily enterprise, and that is, Will the family ownership enhance the vigor and potential upside, or introduce a potential future risk through the eruption of conflicts, the development of problems in managing succession, and the resulting stagnation or demise of the firm? The same dilemma is faced also by anyone considering joining the family firm.

Timing

Family members may become involved in ventures at all stages of growth; each possibility has its own advantages and risks.

- *Start-up.* A family member may become involved from start-up (or buyout) as a partner or member of an entrepreneurial team. The advantages are (1) initial costs and early losses may be more easily shared, (2) later success benefits the family as a whole, (3) the family can be together, and (4) trust is deepened. To illustrate, one of the major reasons married couples choose to go into business with one another is that they can be together, and this form of partnership gained in popularity in the 1980s.[3] Family members also may trust one another more than they do people outside the family. For example, the issue of trust is paramount in the wholesale diamond business. As one member of a family firm in that industry explained, "Dealing with diamonds is basically a family business, because you're dealing with these small things that are very expensive, and you must have a lot of trust in whomever you work with. So you don't hire [nonfamily] salesmen."
- *Early growth.* A family member may join a recently launched family venture early in its operation. In this instance, the lead entrepreneur already has declared himself or herself and presumably has identified the areas in which the venture needs the help of potential family partners, employees, and backers. A family member may welcome the opportunity to help the business, because his or her working benefits the family and he or she may enjoy working together with other family members. Furthermore, a family member is typically seen as more trustworthy or responsible than outsiders and, thus, needs less close supervision, resulting in less bureaucracy.
- *High growth/maturity.* A family member may join a family business at any time during the life of the organization as a second- or third-generation member. Advantages to joining the venture as a next-generation family member include opportunities to gain experience and to expand the venture or to find a niche in a rapidly expanding environment. In addition, a family member can help the family and experience personal job security, flexibility, and growth. For example, Thomas Watson, Jr., "got his job from his father, but built IBM into a colossus big enough to satisfy even the wildest of the old man's dreams."[4] Similarly, J. Willard Marriott, Jr., built the Marriott Corporation from a $750 million company in 1966 to a $7.5 billion company in 1989.

A significant number of the potential risks and problems associated with family ventures stem from the involvement of the family. They include problems of control, credibility, family dynamics, and succession. These issues as well as strategies for minimizing them are discussed later in the chapter.

As with other ventures, success within the family business will depend to a great extent on company growth and whether it's growing fast enough to accommodate new ideas or new divisions. Such questions as whether the company matured and stabilized at its present level of sales or if the management style permits latitude are also important. *Exhibit 8.3* shows characteristics of companies at various stages of growth.

[3] For more on couples in business, see Frank and Sharon Barnett, *Working Together: Entrepreneurial Couples* (Berkeley, CA: Ten Speed Press, 1988); and Sharon Nelton, *In Love and In Business* (New York: John Wiley & Sons, 1986).

[4] "The Greatest Capitalist in History," *Fortune,* August 31, 1987.

Exhibit 8.3
Characteristics of Company Growth

Organizational Characteristic	*Patterns of the First Stage*	*Patterns of the Second Stage*	*Patterns of the Third Stage*
Core problem	Survival	Management of growth	Managerial control and allocation of resources
Central function	Fusion of diverse talents and purposes into a unified company	Fission of general authority into specialized functions	Fusion of independent units into an interdependent union of companies
Control systems	Personal (inside); survival in marketplace (outside)	Cost centers and policy formulation (inside); growth potential (outside)	Profit centers and abstract performance criteria (inside); capital expansion potential (outside)
Reward and motivation	Ownership, membership in the family	Salary opportunities and problems of growth	Salary performance bonus, stock options, peer prestige
Management style	Individualistic; direct management	Integrating specialists; collaborative management	Integrating generalists; collection management
Organization:			
Structure	Informal	Functional specialists	Division organizations
CEO's primary task	Direct supervision of employees	Managing specialized managers	Managing generalist managers
Levels of management	Two	At least three	At least four

Source: L B Barnes and S A Hershon, "Transferring Power in the Family Business," *Harvard Business Review,* July–August 1976, p. 145.

Types of Involvement

Individuals join family businesses for many reasons. Research indicates that next-generation family members seek (1) to meet their *career interests,* (2) to develop their *personal identity,* and (3) to satisfy their needs associated with their *life stage* in the context of the family firm.[5]

In this regard, individuals in their early 20s are concerned with *exploration* of life's options, while *advancement* is critical in one's late 20s and 30s, and *balance* between work and other activities is the concern for individuals in their 40s. The degree to which each of these life-stage needs can be met in the context of the family firm is critical to the quality of the individual's experience.

The involvement of family members falls into three categories:

- *Helper.* The helper is the individual who joins to help the family in the organization for an uncertain period of time. Often the helper joins at the early stages of the firm's development, when family members may need to be relied on for flexible work hours and pay. The helper may stay to learn the business from the bottom up, in which case he or she usually does not have a regular title or position, but is expected to be a *factotum*—someone who does all kinds of work.

  For the helper, the family firm can serve as a safety net and security blanket. If the helper is a son, daughter, or other relative, he or she may have one or more limitations: timidness; lack of confidence to seek work beyond the protective cover of the family; sheer lack of business power, creativity, and talent; or lack of ambition. The individual may choose to enter and remain in the family firm, because of the security it provides, as well

[5] Wendy C Handler, "Managing the Family Firm Succession Process: The Next Generation Family Member's Experience," doctoral dissertation, Boston University School of Management, Department of Organizational Behavior, 1989.

as a potential shelter from having to address his or her own apparent weaknesses. One of the hardest things for parents, sisters, brothers, aunts, and uncles to face up to is this harsh reality.

One well-known example of the timid and dutiful helper is Edsel Ford, only son of the original Henry Ford and father of Henry Ford II, who, even as president of Ford Motor Company, found himself overshadowed by his father, the real power in the company. For example, when his father told him to shut up when Edsel made a recommendation to a large group of executives, he took it because, "one, he was a loyal son. He loved his father. Two, he was a Ford, with that awful burden on his shoulders."[6]

- *Apprentice.* Some individuals use the family firm as a stepping stone on a career path. They are interested in it as a convenient career opportunity—a launching pad to other job choices. For example, two sons of restauranteur Anthony Anthanas, owner of Anthony's Pier 4 in Boston, set up a seafood supply company in Maine, with the intent of having their father be one of their most loyal customers. Another example: Ira Riklis, son of conglomerate Meshulam Riklis, of Rapid-American Corporation, worked for his father for one year, developing an ulcer and the conviction that the role was not for him. However, the contacts he made enabled him to start a successful company of his own.
- *Socialized successor.* This individual joins and becomes socialized into the family business, with the strong likelihood of becoming the next-generation president. One notable example is the Bechtel Corporation, begun by Warren Bechtel to build railroads. His son, Steve, Sr., directed the firm in construction of pipelines and nuclear power plants. Today, Steve, Jr., heads the $3 billion company, which has further diversified.

THE FAMILY VENTURE TEAM

Everything that has been said about choosing entrepreneurial teams and practicing teamwork applies to new family ventures.

Family partnerships can work well, particularly when the partners have abilities and responsibilities that complement each other, like brothers Ernest and Julio Gallo of Gallo Vineyards. Ernest was chairman and in charge of marketing, sales, and distribution. Julio was president and oversaw production. Julio described himself as a farmer at heart, who likes to "walk in the fields with the old-timers." Ernest's office, on the other hand, was cluttered with mementos from selling. The brothers mesh well: Julio's goal was to make more wine than Ernest could sell. Ernest's goal was to sell more wine than Julio could make.[7]

Critical Issues

Many individuals find that the complexities of putting together a venture team are compounded when immediate family members or other relatives, or both, become involved. Often family members fail to realize that they are entering a business relationship, and they make the assumption that these issues are understood because "it's all in the family."

As with other entrepreneurial teams—perhaps even more so—it is important to have a clear understanding about the following issues:

- Who (if anyone) the lead entrepreneur is.
- What the backgrounds of each member of the team in business are.

[6] B Herndon, *Ford: An Unconventional Biography of the Men and Their Times.*

[7] J Fierman, "How Gallo Crushes the Competition," *Fortune,* September 1, 1986.

- What the specific strengths and weaknesses of each member of the team are; what and how each will contribute to the building of the business; and what skills and talents does the venture really need to succeed during its next phase.
- What the specific responsibilities of each will be.
- How much money each will put up, and how equity will be divided.
- Under what circumstances and on what terms nonfamily will be brought into the venture.
- What compensation each will receive—that is, what salary, bonuses, equity shares, or mixture of the above each will receive.
- What will be done in the event of a disagreement, or if one family member is not pulling his or her weight, and what mechanisms exist to facilitate and structure a graceful divorce.
- What the ante is, and whether it can be redeemed if the joining family member changes his or her mind.

Unique Problems

Members of family ventures can experience problems of control, credibility, family dynamics, and succession during the course of the firm's operation.

- *Control, fairness, and equity.* Problems of control, fairness, and equity are common. Conflicts over control result when each partner has a different idea of how to run the business, and both are unwilling to compromise. Issues of fairness and equity arise over division of work and how much each partner is contributing to profit. Also, while keeping a venture strictly in the family ensures complete control, this approach also may limit growth by discouraging able and potential partners from joining, if the inner circle is closed to them. It also may discourage potential investors, lenders, vendors, and customers who may question the growth potential of a tightly held operation.
- *Credibility.* A related issue is establishing credibility. Founding parents often have difficulty believing that their children ever grow up. They may push their children to enter the business but then fail to give them responsibility or encouragement. Few next-generation family members appear to be given direct positive feedback about their performance. Often, they must find out from others if the parent thinks they are doing a good job.

  Gaining credibility is typically a slow, gradual dance between parent and child. Generally, the parent (particularly the founder) has worked hard and expects the child to do the same. Family members often have higher expectations of other family members in the firm. One implication is that *because* they are family, they do not have to praise their work.

  Alternatively, it also is possible for there to be "credibility inflation" or overkill. This occurs when there is a "pet child" or other family member who can do no wrong. A family or parental myopia contributes to a grossly exaggerated level of credit and praise for the family member, which can be demoralizing to other high-performing family members as well as to nonfamily members.
- *Family dynamics.* A third complication of entering a family business is family dynamics. When there are no boundaries between family life and the business, tensions from one may spill over into the other. *Family strains* occur when business issues pervade family discussions and interactions outside the business. *Business strains* occur due to excessive family emotionality, conflict, unrealistic expectations, and arbitrary policies for family members within the context of the business.

  For example, in the case of siblings and relatives—especially if they are close in age and of the same gender—rivalry and jealousy may crop up if the relationship is not carefully managed. In addition, the relationship between predecessor and next-generation family member can have a critical effect within the business. In one extreme case, the leadership of the organization was in limbo because of the relationship between the father and the heir apparent. Despite the father's alcoholism, the family auto dealership had been very successful under his control. However, he had never given his son adequate recognition, because he sought attention for himself. The son, who is now in charge, doubts his own abilities, because his father has given him and continues to give so many bad messages. His father will not give up control or the presidency, even though he no longer has any real responsibilities in the organization.

Furthermore, an entrepreneur employing a parent may experience role reversal, which can be awkward. In addition, the parent may be resentful if the work is unrewarding, tedious, or difficult.

Even more extreme are cases of outright hostilities, such as family businesses that have been nearly destroyed by family feuds. Cesare Mondavi, founder of Mondavi Vineyards, before he died, mediated disputes between his two sons over running the family's Charles Krug Winery. The sons, Robert and Peter, had been known for fist-fights at their grape-shipping plant. By 1972, Robert was suing Peter for his investment in Krug and being countersued for trying to monopolize the Napa Valley wine industry. In 1978, a California Superior Court judge ordered that Krug be sold. One month before the sale, Peter bought out Robert's share and saved the business from the auction block.[8]

In a business run by a couple, difficulties in the personal relationship may undermine the business. For example, Esprit, the billion-dollar international clothing company, has experienced plummeting sales, largely blamed on founder-owners Doug and Susie Tompkins being "at each other's throat," according to *Newsweek* magazine (May 23, 1988). They have moved into separate buildings on their estate overlooking San Francisco Bay. They disagree as well about the future direction of the company. She wants to produce more mature clothes for the aging baby boomers, while he insists on sticking with the youth market. In May 1988, to placate concerned stockholders, the couple agreed to reorganize the company and have given up some of their personal control of it.

- *Succession.* *Exhibit 8.4* indicates the evolution of the relationship between the owner of a family firm and a next-generation family member in succession. This evolution is typically a slow, subtle process of transition.[9]

As the exhibit shows, the roles of both individuals evolve over time and also interact with one another. Central to succession is the disengagement of the owner and the

Exhibit 8.4
Evolution of Relationship between the Owner/Manager and Next-Generation in Succession

Owner/Manager

Sole operator → Monarch → Overseer/Delegator → Consultant

Interacts with

Next-Generation Family Member

Ambiguous role → Helper → Manager → Leader/Chief decision maker

[8] E Topolnicki, "Family Firms Can Leave the Feuds Behind,"*Money,* July 1983.

[9] Handler, "Managing the Family Firm Succession Process: The Next-Generation Family Member's Experience."

corresponding increased level of responsibility of the next-generation family member. However, often the owner has difficulty moving beyond his or her role as *monarch* with preeminent power over other family members. This is the classic problem of the owner who cannot let go. To many founders, the company is child and lover. The founder cannot stand to relinquish any part of it and will often deny the successor the training necessary to qualify to take it over.

For the next-generation family member to gain leadership responsibilities, the founder or owner must become first the *overseer and delegator* of management tasks, and then the *consultant* to the next generation. This involves giving up some control; otherwise the next-generation family member can become a permanent person-in-waiting.

This was the case for Stanley Marcus, who was son of Herbert Marcus, the founder of the Dallas-based retail store Neiman-Marcus. He described the greatest single disappointment in his life as his father's failure to name him president before his 40th birthday.

> He had completed high school at 16 and college at 20 so that assuming a business presidency while still in his 30s would have completed his track record. Even when his health began to fail, Herbert Marcus remained in control; to promote his son at that time would have been recognition of his declining physical capacity, something which no founder-father wants to admit.[10]

A seasoned observer has summarized the dilemma facing such owner/managers:

> Dad's successor is an entrepreneur in training. He's expected to be the trail blazer when Dad passes on his machete. He's expected to be independent, yet he is forced to work for one of the most domineering bosses in existence, a successful business owner. To make it worse, this "boss" is also the successor's father.[11]

Furthermore, as a well-known family business consultant has explained, the practice of choosing a successor is "an organizationally hazardous activity that might better be abolished."[12] Unconsciously, owner/managers may want to prove no one can fill their shoes. Successors appear to be aware of this dynamic. One, for example, is still trying to come to grips with his father's words: "If anything happens to me, don't think for one minute that you could ever run this business without me."

STRATEGIES FOR SUCCESS

Managing the family in the family venture means dealing with problems of control, credibility, dynamics, and succession. While there are no absolute prescriptions, problems of control, fairness, and equity can be mitigated by the following four strategies:

- *Expression of interest.* As a next-generation family member, it is important to express interest in the family business and to discuss goals if one is interested. It should not be assumed that family members know of them. Next-generation family members should be direct and forthright about the responsibility they want and what they are capable of. Research clearly indicates that they are more likely to achieve for themselves and the business when they are clear about their needs and communicate them directly to the owner in charge.
- *Acquisition of experience.* It is recommended that a family member acquire practical business experience outside the family business, particularly if one is uncertain about a

[10] P Alcorn, *Success and Survival in the Family-owned Business* (New York: McGraw-Hill, 1982), p. 152.

[11] L Danco, *Inside the Family Business* (Cleveland: Center for Family Business, 1980), p. 131.

[12] H Levinson, "Don't Choose Your Own Successor," *Harvard Business Review,* March–April 1971.

career in the family business. This helps increase knowledge, experience, and confidence. It is also the single most effective way to enhance credibility with employees in a family business, who may be skeptical about the qualifications of family members.

A son of the founder of a software marketing and consulting company in New York was adamant about gaining experience elsewhere:

> I think it gives you a very narrow perspective on life to go at age 21 into your family business and be there for the rest of your life. I think it limits your exposure; I don't think you can become as broad and as developed an individual if you're involved in one thing for your entire life.

- *Acceptance of responsibility.* Family members should take responsibility for their own development and consider how—or if—personal goals are to be met by the family business. They should ask themselves:
  - Am I cultivating an entrepreneurial mind (i.e., attitudes and behaviors discussed in Chapter 5)?
  - What are the critical skills and know-how required in the business now and in the immediate future?
  - In what ways will my personal needs be satisfied through the family venture?
  - If we plan to double the size of the business in the next 3, 5, or 10 years, what are the likely requirements?
  - What do I bring to the team now, and later?
  - What are my strengths, and what do I need to work on?
  - What additional relevant "chunks" of experience do I need, and how can I get them?
  - What other aspects of the business do I need to learn?
  - Do I have the qualities to be a leader?
  - Am I happy working in the business, and does it give me energy?
  - Is there anything else I need to be doing to meet my goals?

  As part of one's responsibility, individuals who hope to become head of the business should learn as much about the business as they can. A leading family business expert suggests an initial learning stage to understand the business better, followed by a specialization stage to acquire a specific skill. He then suggests becoming a generalist and learning to manage.[13] How appropriate these steps are, however, depends on the nature, complexity, and size of the business.
- *Establishment of networks.* It is recommended that individuals cultivate relationships with mentors, peers, and family members who can act as coaches, protectors, role models, counselors, or friends. Next-generation family members often try to manage their own development without seeking help or advice. They desire a sense of independence and tend to be ambivalent about having their parents serve as mentors. Actually, it may be unwise to turn to parents for mentoring, because of the possible inherent conflict of interest. Parents play many roles with children; for example, as has been mentioned, they may not want them to grow up and may have subconscious difficulty accepting this reality. Looking to respected individuals outside the family for counseling and long-term development support is a good strategy.

  Becoming involved in a peer network is also highly recommended for family entrepreneurs. There are a variety of national and regional organizations for individuals involved in family ventures. Through the Family Firm Institute, the Small Business

[13] S Nelton, "Making Sure the Business Outlasts You," *Nation's Business,* January 1986.

Association, the American Management Association, or the National Family Business Council, one can become affiliated with local professionals and personal support groups. In addition, the Young Presidents Association is geared to presidents of entrepreneurial and family businesses. Whatever issues a member of a family new venture team might be struggling with, it is likely that others have confronted them, or know someone who has. Sharing experiences can be useful and therapeutic for people involved in family ventures.

In addition, there are three ways to minimize problems of family dynamics:

- *Definition of responsibility.* One is to define different responsibilities clearly and with minimum overlap and assign them according to personal capabilities and interests. In most well-managed family businesses, this approach is used. On the other hand, in family businesses plagued with conflict, siblings typically perform similar jobs, competing with each other and vying for attention from parents and other family members.
- *Emphasis on issues.* Family members, if they fight, should fight over issues, not emotions. As a woman whose husband entered and then quit her father's business explained:

  > Two years ago, my husband was determined to make my father see the importance of expanding. After plotting and pushing, he got the OK. But this was the beginning of almost daily confrontations. He and my father began to fight over people hired and money being spent. If they had discussed plans for company expansion rationally, before my husband began working for my father, much of this could have been resolved.[14]

- *Establishment of mechanisms.* Establishing various mechanisms to enhance communication (both informal sessions for sharing and formal means for family planning and exchange) is advised. The development of a family council also is advised, one composed of all family members key to the future of the business, such as the founder, spouse, and children, as well as other relatives who have a significant interest in the business.[15] Having regular family meetings allows the airing of problems or differences that might otherwise be ignored—but that will not go away. A family council helps establish open communication, understanding, and trust. It also serves as a forum for planning the future of the family and the business.

Since it is entirely possible that the chemistry of the family simply does not work and family history involves deep scars, resentment, hostility, and other complex emotional feelings that may not be easily mended, family members should realize it is all right, if not preferable, to recognize that reality and seek their fortunes elsewhere.

CASE—PASSING THE BATON*

Preparation Questions

1. Evaluate the new management and organization of Morris Alper & Sons, Inc.
2. Analyze *Exhibits C* and *D*. If you are Fred, what do these assignments mean? If you are Vic? Key employees at MAS? Customers?
3. What will happen in the succession process at Morris Alper & Sons?
4. What should Vic and Fred do?

[14] M Crane, "How to Keep Families from Feuding," *INC.*, February 1982.

[15] I Lansberg, "The Succession Conspiracy," *Family Business Review*, Summer 1988.

*Research Associate Christine C Remey wrote this case under the supervision of Professor Jeffry A Timmons as the basis for class discussion, rather than to illustrate either effective or ineffective handling of an administrative situation.

MORRIS ALPER & SONS, INC.

B. PASSING THE BATON[1]

External forces will never cause this company to explode, because of the talent you have here. Your greatest threat is implosion from within.

Edward J. Downey, at his retirement dinner, late November 1990

In early November 1990, the new president of Morris Alper & Sons (MAS), Victor R. Del Regno, paced around his new office surveying the items on the walls, on the desk, and in the bookcase—all of which symbolized some aspect of the business and the MAS philosophy. He paused and focused on the poster entitled *VISION: An obstacle is not the end; it's a new beginning.* Vic was searching for an appropriate action plan for the December 1990 brokers' convention, the largest and most important annual meeting in the brokerage industry. How should Vic and Fred Alper, the past president and now the chairman, decide which meetings to attend? On the one hand, Vic wanted to be sensitive to Fred, who had for over 17 years represented MAS to the major clients or manufacturers (referred to in the trade as principals). In the eyes of some of the principals, Fred was MAS. Vic had to establish himself as the president and the convention was the perfect opportunity for sending clear signals.

Meanwhile in the same building, just down the hall, Fred thought about how to respond to the question, What are you going to tell people you do now? Fred thought of all the friends and colleagues he would see at the brokers' convention, and he pondered how he would explain his new role as chairman. He did not want to fade completely into the background; he was still active in the company. However, Fred very much wanted to demonstrate that Vic was running the show.

THE DECADE OF TRANSITION

In the early 1980s, Fred demonstrated the commitment of MAS to the food brokerage business by erecting a new office building. The building illustrated the investment MAS had made in the past and would continue to make in the future. Systems, accountability, and a results orientation were all at the forefront of Fred's agenda. Under his leadership, MAS enjoyed tremendous growth. The number of employees increased from 48 in 1972 to 330 in 1989, while the number of principals represented increased significantly as well.

Anticipating the 1990s

Fred and Vic knew that the business was undergoing tremendous change. MAS needed a president equipped to embrace and adapt to the new environment. The new president also had to be able to anticipate appropriately how some of these changes could impact their business. Fred stated that "it is no longer just about selling cases. It is about survival." The challenges facing the next president would require the combination of a tough, decisive leader as well as a team player who could inspire management. As mergers and consolidations created more conflicts within the industry and the pace quickened, the environment was tending to become more impersonal. The more progressive food brokerage firms had allowed an unprecedented number of young people to assume more responsibility. During this dawn of an era of sophisticated technologies, pressures focused on short-term performance. The new president had to be able to deal with a number of different people, including principals, customers, and employees, and he needed a committed and capable

[1]The authors would like to credit Richard E Vancil for his symbolic title, *Passing the Baton* (Boston: Harvard Business School Press, 1987).

team of executives to help him handle the new size and complexity of the business. To be successful as the president of MAS, Vic would have to manage all this in the short term, while planning for the long term. Fred commented that "there are very few people in senior management who can handle the difficult problems that present themselves to the president of a large food brokerage company." Fred felt that Vic had the capacity and foresight to accept these challenges of the 1990s. They talked formally and casually about the future of the industry and MAS. Together they were able to pick apart a problem, analyze it, discuss alternative solutions, and ultimately reach a resolution. Fred said: "We both knew that we were an unbeatable team together. Vic was somewhat more operational, and I was somewhat more strategic, but we were both very much 'street and strategy.' "

Fred and Vic agreed fundamentally on the direction of the industry and they envisioned a similar future. Their vision was to grow beyond the traditional food broker role – beyond moving cases of products – to becoming a fully integrated marketing service. Principals had been delegating more trade promotion funds to the field and had started to earmark some consumer budgets over to promote sales. MAS needed to acquire or to develop more sophisticated promotional capabilities. Information usage was a key to survival in the 1990s. Collecting, analyzing, and interpreting data into results at the local-market level would enable brokers to add value. Developing strategic alliances with principals and customers was time-consuming and difficult. If brokers were able to document efficiencies and effectiveness, they would help assure an important place for themselves in the future. Understanding brand and category objectives while contributing to the principal's strategic and marketing plans would be essential tasks for brokers. Overall, brokers had to increase volume that was profitable for all parties.

Victor R. Del Regno as Executive Vice President

Based on their shared vision and relationship, Fred had promoted Vic to executive vice president in 1986, which sent a signal throughout the company and the industry. Fred admitted that

> there was some opposition within the management ranks to Vic's ascending to executive vice president because he was ambitious and had a style that to some degree clashed with those who had a more conservative style. For instance, in a particular meeting, Vic orchestrated a skit to add some levity and fun to the business; the older guys on the board resented it. But what I saw was somebody trying to get creativity, excitement, and some bubbling into the company. Vic knew that he had my support and that eventually things were going to change. The future was exciting and we were no longer going to do things the way that we always had.
>
> I believe that if you have a company where the management is too old – not chronologically old but old in attitudes – then you have a slow decay. If your management is too young, you will have a series of short-term disasters. The ideal balance is somewhere in between, neither crazy ups and downs nor a slow decay. But if you have to choose between the two extremes, I'll pick the young, immature stuff anytime. I was philosophically embracing the change, yet there was some resistance to his ideas, his personality, and ambition.

Since Vic joined the company in 1979, he had learned more about himself, while growing and contributing to the continued success of MAS. One of Vic's lessons was that he was a *tell* rather than *sell* person. Vic began to see that intense people who come on strong often get misconstrued as having bad intentions. He commented that "I was really learning. I could decipher the hills to go around and the hills to die on." Observing the changes in Vic, Fred commented that "Vic was putting his hand over the stove. It burned and burned and burned and at a certain point he had to adjust his hand." When a goal was identified, Vic wanted to attack it head-on right away, while Fred wanted to analyze it longer. Their

Exhibit A
Organizational Chart (1986)

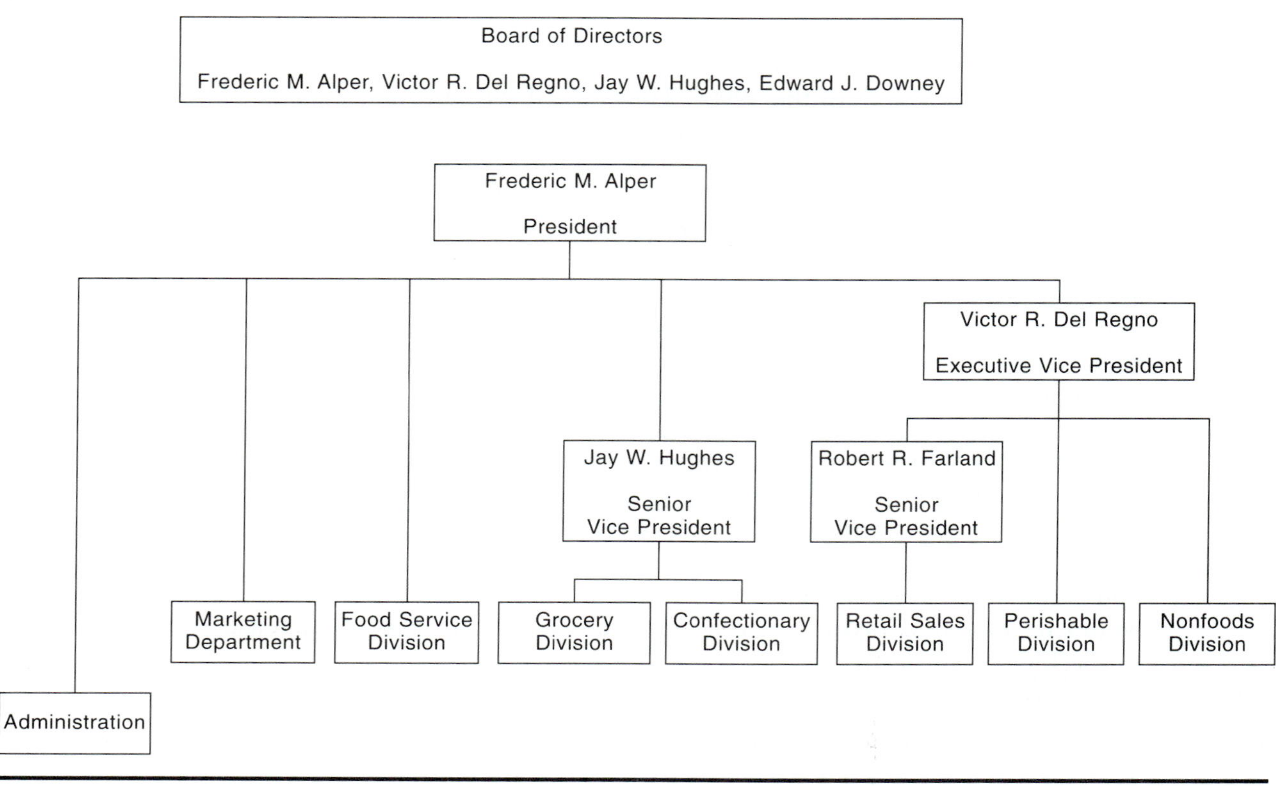

resolutions were close to perfect because of the balance between Vic's decisiveness and Fred's probing. The two worked very closely together, engaging in small and large matters with much give and take. Although there were differences between them, Fred and Vic shared the same high standards, a need for constructive criticism, and intense involvement in the business. Although the outside world perceived that Fred was the boss, there was little status differentiation between the two when they made decisions.

When Vic became executive vice president, as shown in *Exhibit A*, "Organizational Chart (1986)," perishable, nonfoods, and retail sales reported to him, while grocery and confectionery divisions reported to Jay. By this time, Vic had been more accepted by Jay and Ed. Their hesitations were addressed out in the open. Vic, Jay, and Ed had gone to lunch together many times to discuss the transition and to assess Vic's readiness. Having gained an appreciation of Vic's talents, Jay felt that "the tension was not over my desire to be the next president but over my desire to let Fred make the decision without any undue pressure. Once I saw how comfortable Fred was with the progression of the succession plan, I did an about-face and supported Vic."

PLANNING FOR THE TRANSITION (1988–1990)

As discussions about the succession plan progressed, Jay recalled that

> if there was a specific plan to make Vic the next president, Fred did not share it with us. All we knew was that Vic was the heir apparent, which made sense in terms of Vic's age. He was nine years younger

Exhibit B
Organizational Chart (1989)

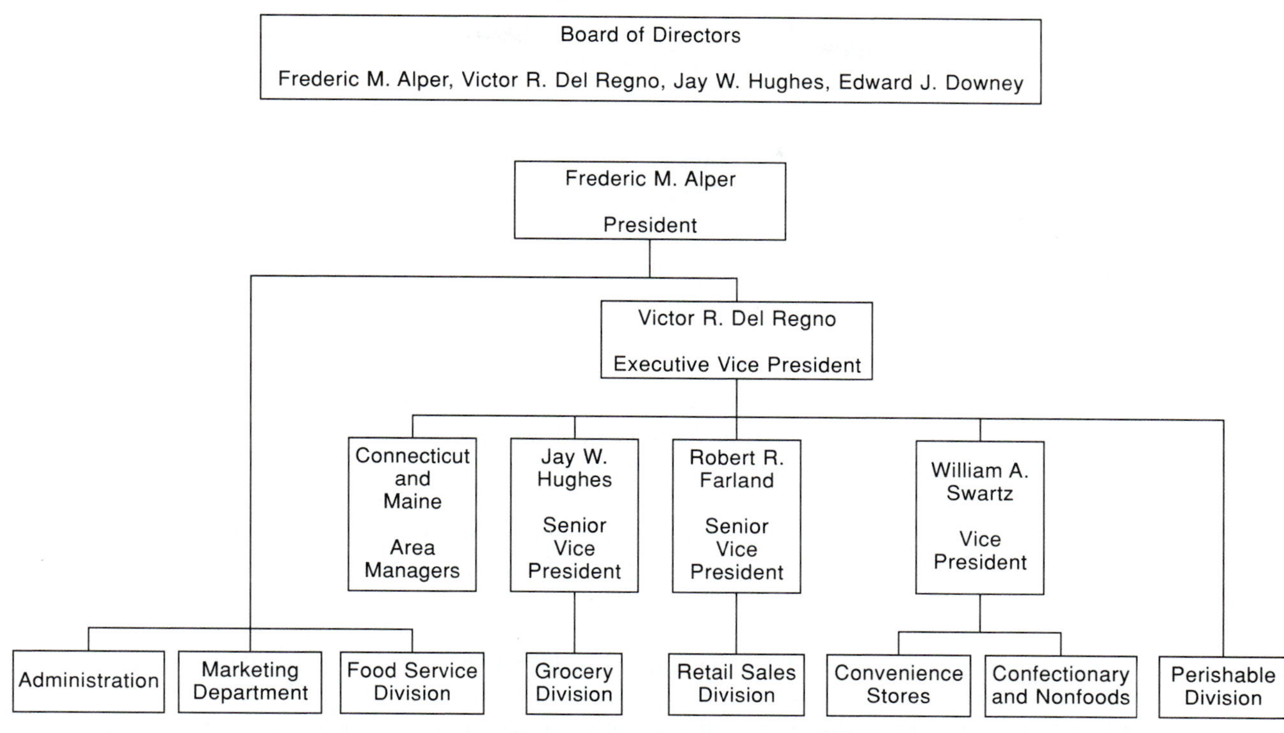

than Fred. But there were a few times when we were not sure if there was undue pressure on Fred or if Fred really felt that Vic was ready. Vic was a very ambitious, very bright, hard-working guy. A few years before, when Vic and I were at the same level, I recall Vic was often recommending that we have a clean-cut succession plan. How much of this was based on his philosophy and how much was personal ambition, no one could be sure. Everyone on the board knew Vic was to be the next president sometime in the future. Yet, there were times when Ed and I felt strongly that Vic was not ready for the presidency. In retrospect I think that we felt that Fred was not ready to step down.

Fred responded to these perceptions:

Vic never said that he wanted it, but I always felt that he was deserving and at some point he would be unsatisfied at MAS. He needed the opportunity to run something; it was his nature. He deserved a shot at it. He had been with the company for almost 10 years, knew all the areas of it, shared in the culture, and was a lot like me. Yet, he was a different person with the appropriate skills for facing the 1990s. He was not afraid of the job—he was afraid of me not being ready to really relinquish the reins.

A food broker told me years ago, "If you have good people, they are constantly professionally trying to push you out." It is not negative. It is just saying, I want more, I can do more. If you do not have people who are working toward expansion and change, but who are happy with the status quo, you are not going to be a growth company. Vic was looking to grow with the company, but not in a way that made me uncomfortable. I saw the future as Vic taking over.

By 1989, all six product divisions were reporting directly to Vic. Administrative services, marketing, and food service were reporting to Fred, as shown in *Exhibit B*, "Organizational Chart (1989)." The succession process was well established and Vic felt comfortable with things as they stood. "If you have a visionary with good strategic skills combined with a good operational guy who has a vision, boy, is that a dynamic team!" Vic said.

Vic also resisted further progress on the succession plans, for the same reason Jay had mentioned—Fred should not step down at this time; it was too early. But Fred felt that his term as president should come to a close soon for the betterment of the company. He explained:

> I certainly was not stale, but I was well beyond the 8-to-10 year window, which was the amount of time anyone should be president of a company. It was compounded by the fact that I was having some irregular heartbeats, which were not a serious health risk, but scary nonetheless. I just knew that it was not right for me to continue, for several reasons. First, because of the years that I had done it; second, because of the signals that my body were giving me; and finally, because of a desire to get free of all the details. The only unique factor was that I wanted to stay semiactive. I was only 49 years old and not ready to retire.

Fred's urgency and desire to step down were incomprehensible to Vic at the time. Vic asked: "Why do we have to change? Everyone is happy this way." Vic knew the succession plan was established and thought that in the next 8 to 10 years it might be executed. He would be in his late 40s or early 50s and Fred in his late 50s to early 60s. This timetable made more sense to Vic, who rationalized that Fred was speeding up the plans because of his health concerns. Over the course of the next few years, Fred had to convince Vic that he was serious about executing his plan. Fred said:

> Vic was ready and deserving. I felt he wanted it, although he did not articulate any desire to be president. He was more appropriate for the times than I was. Additionally, I believe that people relate best to people who are within a 10-year span of their age because they are at the same stage in life. Younger people were assuming more and more responsibility than in past years. I felt that someone younger was needed.

New Roles and Titles

After Fred had convinced Vic that he was serious about effecting the transition, the two started to explore their new roles, how they would relate to each other, and what their titles would be. Neither was opposed to exploring and considering unique and/or different titles and roles. As an example, Fred had hoped that one of the roles that he would play would be a kind of assistant to Vic on some pressing problems to fulfill both Fred's personal needs and to provide continuity of the communications between the two, which had worked so well for so long. Fred knew that this was very unorthodox, but he thought it was desirable and could work. Vic was always uncomfortable with this because he felt "it was like having two head chefs in the kitchen—it does not work. There are numerous examples in the animal kingdom where only one leader ultimately takes over."

Fred went through the entire food brokers' directory, looking at all the food brokerage firms in the country, and reviewing the different title arrangements. Co-presidents, managing partners, president, chairman, or chief operating officer were all considered. Which of these titles fit MAS? At one point Vic suggested that Fred be the chairman and the chief executive officer. Fred responded: "Vic, you need to operate with authority. I am no longer in charge. If I have a chairman/CEO title, you would not be considered the boss. The CEO title was not appropriate for this company." The idea of co-presidents was rejected for a similar reason. Fred felt that "the company had never been hung up on titles, and decisions were always made on the reasonableness of ideas rather than the status of the managers."

After much discussion about different titles, they decided that Vic would assume the presidency and Fred would be the chairman. Vic associated the role of the chairman with "infinite wisdom, strategies, vision, being there for counsel, but not involved in the day-to-day." With the industry reputation that Fred had he would be out in the field presenting industry papers, delivering speeches, and playing a larger role in the National Food Brokers Association (NFBA). The food service division was the only part of the company that would operationally report to Fred. Food service, which was selling products to restaurants, institutions, prisons, hospitals, and schools, was autonomous and represented 10 percent of the business.

The Honeymoon Begins

In the summer of 1990, a few months before the official transition date, Fred was proactive in explaining the transition. When a principal would call to discuss a specific account, he would refer the principal to Vic. Vic felt that Fred went out of his way to make it a smooth transition. There were no surprises for the principals. "There was virtually not a wrinkle," Fred recalled.

New Offices

The only physical change was moving to new offices. Fred insisted that Vic take his office. Vic was the president and was entitled to the president's office. It was symbolic of the change. Fred moved into a smaller office, not a corner office. Fred wanted to be "not too close, and not too far away." Fred's selection was similar to that of his father, when he stepped down from the presidency to be the treasurer. Dave Alper moved into a smaller and inconspicuous office. Fred's selection of a small office upset Vic, who commented, "I wanted him to have a nicer office with new furniture. I had changed the carpeting, moved my desk in, picked up a few new pieces, and made it my office. I wanted Fred to do the same."

Fred felt that it was important to do just the opposite. He explained: "I like to go the other way to prove a point to myself and to others that the office location and size do not matter to me. People probably think that I do not know the difference, but I certainly do. My move to a small office was definitely planned."

Although the official transition date was October 1, 1990, over the summer, Vic was acting as president. All the decisions came from him and he consulted Fred on some issues. Both Fred and Vic felt that things were moving as expected and they were very comfortable with their new roles. Therefore, October 1 was business as usual.

ADAPTING TO THEIR NEW ROLES

Fred talked about his role as chairman:

> I wanted to be strategic, nonoperational, futuristic, and big picture. In addition, I was going to take some time off. I was going to be freer. I wanted to be more industry involved if it would help the company. I did not feel that our relationship had to be structured. I would be involved on certain projects that might be operational. People would not be reporting to me. I did not want people to think that I was still running the show or second guessing Vic. But, I wanted to be part of the process, one of the gang, and involved in some of the action.

Vic remembered a situation in the fall of 1990:

> I was in Chicago at a food broker share group meeting, an organization made up of 16 noncompeting food brokerage presidents from around the country. We were having cocktails; everything was going

well; I felt confident. Someone asked, "How is Fred?" I responded, "He is doing well." They pressed further: "What is he doing?" I said, "He is going to be involved in strategic issues and food service. He is also going to be more involved in NFBA and other industry associations. I think that he is planning some travel—a chance to smell the roses." They said, Yeah, right! You are dreaming. We know Fred Alper and it will never work.

In the back of his mind, Vic had other concerns during this transition. He wondered, "Was Fred ready to relinquish power?" After all, Fred was heavily invested in MAS both financially and psychologically. A lot of tradition existed. And on top of it all, his name was on the door. The fact that Fred was an Alper and Vic was not made Vic wonder, Would things ever change? Would he ever really be able to operate as a president? Additionally, he was concerned that Fred would look at him as being like Jack Quilty, who tried to purchase the company from the Alper family and whom Fred did not trust. Vic could not live with being a figurehead who deferred decisions to Fred. During the transition, Fred was busy in the food service division, which had enough of the operational issues to keep him in the action, while being involved in overall strategy and industry work. Fred commented that "everyone was waiting for us to argue and were surprised that it was going well."

Voice Mail

A few issues were brewing. For instance, an MAS executive left a voice mail message for Vic and Fred. An important principal was coming to Boston and a dinner meeting needed to be set up. It was clear that this executive had not adapted to the transition as he was posting both Fred and Vic to be present at what was to be a purely operational meeting. After hearing the message, Fred knew that this would be irritating to Vic. Vic heard the voice mail message and got very upset. He sent a voice mail to Fred: "If this is the way that it is going to be, then I do not want to be president! I think that we should have done a co-presidents thing to avoid situations like this." In retrospect both Fred and Vic admit that they knew things like this would happen. A few people would revert to the way things were. They were breaking habits that principals, employees, and customers had had for 17 years. The fact was that virtually everyone accepted Vic as the successor. The transition had been gradual, which helped people adjust to the changes.

Internally, there was an issue about the reporting of marketing and administration. Both of the people running these divisions were important. They were staff, which did not classify them clearly in Fred's strategic sphere, nor in Vic's operational sphere. At the time of the transition, Fred's desire to be involved and Vic's desire to take charge created strife between Fred and Vic—not to mention confusion for the executives of marketing and administration because both Vic and Fred were heavily involved in these areas at this time. It was soon resolved that both of these divisions would report to Vic. This was to be the plan all along, but the timetable was moved up to relieve the tension it was causing for everybody.

Ed Downey's Farewell Dinner

After thirty years at MAS, Ed Downey planned to retire on December 31, 1990. All of management agreed that a going away/retirement party would be appropriate. Vic talked to Fred about orchestrating the party. In their discussion, Fred was concerned about Vic's role because it was Ed's special night, and there was not a warm relationship between Vic and Ed. On the other hand, Vic was the new president and it was important for him to have a significant part in planning the party and being part of the program. Vic talked to Ed and told him to think about how he wanted the party handled. Vic recalled that

> it was important to show harmony within the company. I was worried that his early retirement would be associated with my becoming president. I knew that Ed had opposed my ascension in the company. It was important to me personally that Ed be recognized for his contributions and leave MAS in good standing. When we got into planning speeches and toasts, I felt that I would be conspicuous by my absence if not included. I had worked with Ed for almost 12 years. I sensed from Fred that my insistence created tension.

The retirement party took place in late November, shortly after Vic became president. Vic made a short speech and presented a ring to Ed. Ed's son spoke about Dave Alper.

The words of Ed Downey—"External forces will never cause this company to explode because of the talent we have here; your greatest threat is implosion from within"—stayed with Vic for a long time after that dinner. Vic felt that "that comment was the biggest thing that Ed left me. I had just become the president. Ed and I were having these little rubs. There was tension. I felt that Ed threw this cutting comment at me." Fred did not see it that way. Fred saw it in the same light as Eisenhower's address concerning the threat of the military-industrial complex; this was the biggest thing that the nation had to work on. Similarly, these internal forces were the thing that MAS had to worry about. Vic elaborated on his perception of this statement: "It might have been meant that way but I thought, we had all this growth under Fred. Then there was some tension; I was going into Fred's shoes. Ed was leaving early and he started talking about internal decay. Who else could it be?"

The 1990 National Food Brokers Convention

In December every year, MAS participated in the largest, single most important convention for food brokers, the National Food Brokers Convention. It was organized by the NFBA, which had over 1,600 members nationwide at that time. Principals hosted meetings, cocktail parties, dinners, and awards dinners. The previous year, MAS sent a dozen executives to the convention. With a very busy schedule and a number of major principals at the convention, all the MAS executives were running from one meeting to a cocktail party to an awards dinner. (See *Exhibit C*, "The 1989 National Food Brokers Convention.")

These few days were very intense, political, and important for maintaining and developing relationships with principals. In fact, simply missing a certain principal's event could create some real sensitivity. Vic explained that

> about 15,000 people attend this annual convention. It is both an exciting and a grueling event. During the day, you'd jump from hotel to hotel, attending meetings and presentations, and then the same process started all over in the evenings with several cocktail parties hosted by your principals. If you did not make a certain meeting or cocktail party, then the manufacturer might say, "We are not important enough for them." It was all very exciting but also very stressful.

In early November, Vic had begun thinking about the convention, planning the accommodations, and selecting who would be representing the company. In his regular staff meetings he had reminded the senior vice presidents to keep the convention in the back of their minds. The discussions were casual. Now, as Vic set the agenda for the next staff meeting, he thought about how to involve Fred in the formal planning. There was an unspoken set of expectations between them—Vic would tell Fred where he wanted Fred involved, and Fred would communicate to Vic what he wanted to do. Vic had received the official list of the participants and the 1990 schedule. (See *Exhibit D*, "The 1990 National Food Brokers Convention.") Should the senior vice presidents invite Fred to specific meetings, meals, and presentations? If so, which ones? Vic wanted to be sure not to slight Fred, but he also wanted to paint a clear picture of MAS with himself as the president.

Exhibit C
The 1989 National Food Brokers Convention

Thursday, November 30, 1989	
NFBA* (education and training, trustees)	FMA
Campbell Sales Company	**FMA**
Broker Meeting	VRD
Campbell Sales Company (social event)	**FMA**
Friday, December 1, 1989	
NFBA (general session)	FMA/VRD
Gravymaster	FMA/VRD
Charms/Tootsie Roll (social event)	FMA/VRD
Tyson Foods Inc. (social event)	**FMA/VRD**
Pillsbury Company (social event)	
Presentation, Broker of the Year	**FMA/VRD**
Bumble Bee (dinner)	**FMA/VRD**
Saturday, December 2, 1989	
Sundance (Breakfast)	FMA
Pillsbury Company	**VRD**
Block Household	FMA
Pillsbury Company	**VRD**
Welch's (luncheon) Awards Presentation	**FMA**
Chicopee (food service)	FMA
James River/Dixie	**VRD**
Dole	**FMA**
Heinz Pet Products (social event)	FMA/VRD
Tyson Foods, Inc.	**FMA/VRD**
Ore-Ida	FMA/VRD
Schering	**FMA**
Dole Dried Fruit & Nuts	**FMA/VRD**
Mrs. Smith (dinner) 25 Year Anniversary	FMA/VRD
Sunday, December 3, 1989	
Block Household (breakfast)	FMA/VRD
Tetley, Inc. (social event) Broker of the Year	FMA/VRD
Bumble Bee Seafoods (social event)	**FMA/VRD**
Jerome Foods	VRD
3M Personal Care	FMA
On-Cor Foods, Inc.	FMA/VRD
Designer Foods, Inc. (new principal)	FMA/VRD
Allergan	FMA
Heinz	**FMA/VRD**
All American Gourmet (social event)	FMA/VRD
Pet Inc. (dinner)	FMA/VRD
Monday, December 4, 1989	
Drumstick (breakfast)	FMA/VRD
Sioux Honey	FMA
Chelsea Milling	FMA
Pet Inc. (social event)	FMA

Key: Bold = large principal; VRD = Victor R. Del Regno; FMA = Frederic M. Alper.

*National Food Brokers Association.

Exhibit D
The 1990 National Food Brokers Convention

Friday, December 7, 1990

NFBA (breakfast and board meeting)
Ore-Ida Foods, Inc. (luncheon)
Campbell Soup Company
Colgate-Palmolive (food service)
Campbell Soup Company
Charms/Tootsie Roll (social event)
Pillsbury Company
Chicopee (dinner) (food service)
Mott's (dinner)

Saturday, December 8, 1990

NFBA (Dry Grocery Steering Committee and General Session)
On-Cor Foods, Inc.
Whitman's
James River/Dixie (lunch)
Block Drug Company (social event)
Green Giant
Mrs. Smith/Eggo (social event)
Swift-Eckrich (social event)
Tyson Foods, inc. (social event)
Block Drug Company (Dinner)

Sunday, December 9, 1990

Block Drug Company (Breakfast)
Tetley (Breakfast)
Schering-Plough
Mott's USA
3M Personal Care
Welch's (meeting and luncheon)
Sara Lee
Chicopee (food service)
Mott's USA
Dole Dried Fruit & Nuts
Mrs. Smith/Eggo (social event)
Mr. Coffee, Inc.
NFBA (VIP reception)
All American Gourmet Co. (social event)
H.J. Heinz Company (social event)
James River/Dixie (social event)

Monday, December 10, 1990

Sargento
Sioux Honey
Mr. Coffee, Inc.
E. R. Squibb
Block Drug Company
On-Cor Foods, Inc. (social event)
Pet/Progresso (social event)
Sundance (social event)
Dole

Personal Ethics and the Entrepreneur 9

If you gain financial success at the expense of your integrity, you are not a success at all.

John Cullinane
Founder of Cullinet, Inc., and 1984 Inductee,
Babson Academy of Distinguished Entrepreneurs

RESULTS EXPECTED

Upon completion of this chapter, you will have:

1. Made decisions involving ethical issues and identified and analyzed your reasons for deciding as you did.
2. Discussed with others the ethical implications of the decisions you made and identified how they might affect you, your partners, your customers, and your competitors in the contexts described.
3. Acquired a background, based on history, philosophy, and research, about the nature of business ethics and a context for thinking about ethical behavior.
4. Gained an awareness of the importance of ethical awareness and high standards in an entrepreneurial career.
5. Analyzed "When the Party's Over."

EXERCISE—ETHICS

In the "Ethics" exercise, decisions will be made in ethically ambiguous situations and then analyzed. As in the real world, all the background information on each situation will not be available, and assumptions will need to be made in order to decide.

*It is recommended that the "Ethics" exercise be completed first—**before** reading the following material.*

bankruptcy. And if you delay the shipment or inform the customer of these problems, you may lose the order and also go bankrupt. What would you do?

_______ *(a)* I would not ship the order and place my firm in voluntary bankruptcy.
_______ *(b)* I would inform the customer and declare voluntary bankruptcy.
_______ *(c)* I would ship the order and inform the customer, after I received payment.
_______ *(d)* I would ship the order and not inform the customer.

Situation 4. You are the cofounder and president of a new venture, manufacturing products for the recreational market. Five months after launching the business, one of your suppliers informs you it can no longer supply you with a critical raw material since you are not a large-quantity user. Without the raw material the business cannot continue. What would you do?

_______ *(a)* I would grossly overstate my requirements to another supplier to make the supplier think I am a much larger potential customer in order to secure the raw material from that supplier, even though this would mean the supplier will no longer be able to supply another, noncompeting small manufacturer who may thus be forced out of business.
_______ *(b)* I would steal raw material from another firm (noncompeting) where I am aware of a sizable stockpile.
_______ *(c)* I would pay off the supplier, since I have reason to believe that the supplier could be persuaded to meet my needs with a sizable under-the-table payoff that my company could afford.
_______ *(d)* I would declare voluntary bankruptcy.

Situation 5. You are on a marketing trip for your new venture for the purpose of calling on the purchasing agent of a major prospective client. Your company is manufacturing an electronic system that you hope the purchasing agent will buy. During the course of your conversation, you notice on the cluttered desk of the purchasing agent several copies of a cost proposal for a system from one of your direct competitors. This purchasing agent has previously reported mislaying several of your own company's proposals and has asked for additional copies. The purchasing agent leaves the room momentarily to get you a cup of coffee, leaving you alone with your competitor's proposals less than an arm's length away. What would you do?

_______ *(a)* I would do nothing but await the man's return.
_______ *(b)* I would sneak a quick peek at the proposal, looking for bottom-line numbers.
_______ *(c)* I would put the copy of the proposal in my briefcase.
_______ *(d)* I would wait until the man returns and ask his permission to see the copy.

PART II

STEP 1: BASED ON THE CRITERIA YOU USED, PLACE YOUR ANSWERS TO EACH OF THE ABOVE SITUATIONS ALONG THE CONTINUUM OF BEHAVIOR SHOWN BELOW:

	Duty	Contractual	Utilitarian	Situational
Situation 1				
Situation 2				
Situation 3				
Situation 4				
Situation 5				

STEP 2: AFTER SEPARATING INTO TEAMS OF FIVE TO SIX PEOPLE, RECORD THE ANSWERS MADE BY EACH INDIVIDUAL MEMBER OF YOUR TEAM ON THE FORM BELOW. Record the answer of each team member in each box and the team's solution in the column on the far right.

Member Name | | | | | | Team Answer

Situation 1						
Situation 2						
Situation 3						
Situation 4						
Situation 5						

STEP 3: REACH A CONSENSUS DECISION IN EACH SITUATION (IF POSSIBLE) AND RECORD THE CONSENSUS WHICH YOUR TEAM HAS REACHED ABOVE. Allow 20 to 30 minutes.

STEP 4: REPORT TO THE ENTIRE GROUP YOUR TEAM'S CONCLUSIONS AND DISCUSS WITH THEM HOW THE CONSENSUS, IF ANY, WAS REACHED. The discussion should focus on the following questions:

- Was a consensus reached by each group?
- Was this consensus difficult or easy to achieve and why?
- What kinds of ethical issues emerged?
- How were conflicts, if any, resolved, or were they left unresolved?

STEP 5: DISCUSS WITH THE GROUP THE FOLLOWING ISSUES:

- What role do ethical issues play and how important are they in the formation of a new venture management team?
- What role do ethical issues play and how important are they in obtaining venture capital? That is, how do investors feel about ethics and how important are they to them?
- What feelings bother participants most about the discussion and consensus reached? For example, if a participant believes that his or her own conduct was considered ethically less than perfect, does he or she feel a loss of self-respect or a sense of inferiority? Does he or she fear others' judgment, and so on?

STEP 6: DEFINE EACH GROUP MEMBER'S GENERAL ETHICAL POSITION AND NOTE WHETHER HIS OR HER ETHICAL POSITION IS SIMILAR TO OR DIFFERENT FROM YOURS:

Member	Position	Different/ Similar

STEP 7: DECIDE WHOM YOU WOULD AND WOULD NOT WANT AS A BUSINESS PARTNER BASED ON THEIR ETHICAL POSITIONS:

Would Want	Would Not Want

OVERVIEW OF ETHICS

A good number of successful entrepreneurs believe that high ethical standards and integrity are exceptionally important to long-term success. For example, the author and his colleague, Howard H. Stevenson, conducted a study among 128 presidents/founders attending the Harvard Business School's Owner/President Management program (OPM) in 1983.[1] Their firms typically had sales of $40 million, and sales ranged from $5 million to $200 million. These entrepreneurs were also very experienced, with the average age in the mid-40s, and about half had founded their companies. They were asked to name the most critical concepts, skills, and know-how for success at their companies at the time and what they would be in five years. The answer to this question was startling enough that the Sunday *New York Times* reported the findings: 72 percent of the presidents responding stated that high ethical standards were the single most important factor in long-term success.

Conventional ethical disciplines have been accused of dealing with the business mode by narrowing and defining the scope of inquiry so as to avoid floundering. One author, for instance, *assumed* that "competitors are ethical and engaged in business, rather than jungle warfare."[2]

However, what is ethical and what is not often is not obvious; rather, situations involving ethical issues are often ambiguous. Today, as throughout much of this century, students, business people, and others have received many conflicting signals, as "first artists and intellectuals, then broader segments of the society, challenged every convention, every prohibition, every regulation that cramped the human spirit or blocked its appetites and ambitions."[3]

This discussion has generated also a lot of controversy. As an example, a provocative and controversial article published in the *Harvard Business Review* asserted that the ethics of business were not those of society but rather those of the poker game.[4] The author of the article argued that "most businessmen are not indifferent to ethics in their private lives, everyone will agree. My point is that in their office lives they cease to be private citizens; they become game players who must be guided by a somewhat different set of ethical standards." The author further argued that personal ethics and business ethics are often not in harmony, and either by negotiation or compromise, a resolution must be reached. The article provoked a storm of response.

Another story that attracted attention was reported by *INC.* magazine in 1989; an interview with Phillippe Kahn of Borland International revealed the following:

INC.: The story goes that Borland was launched by a single ad, without which we wouldn't be sitting here talking about the company. How much of that is apocryphal?
Kahn: It's true; one full-page ad in the November issue of *BYTE* magazine got the company running. If it had failed, I would have had nowhere else to go.
INC.: If you were so broke, how did you pay for the ad?
Kahn: Let's put it that we convinced the salesman to give us terms. We wanted to appear only in *BYTE*—not any of the other microcomputer magazines—because *BYTE* is for programmers, and that's who we wanted to reach. But we couldn't afford it. We figured the only way was somehow to convince them to extend us credit terms.
INC.: And they did?

[1] Jeffry A Timmons and Howard H Stevenson, "Entrepreneurship Education in the 1980s," presented at the 75th Anniversary Entrepreneurship Symposium, Harvard Business School, Boston, 1983. *Proceedings,* pp. 115–34.

[2] Thomas Garrett, *Business Ethics* (New York: Appleton-Century-Crofts, 1966), pp. 149–50.

[3] Derek Bok, "Ethics, the University, & Society," *Harvard Magazine,* May–June 1988, p. 39.

[4] Reprinted by permission of *Harvard Business Review*. An Excerpt from "Is Business Bluffing Ethical?" by Albert Z Carr, January-February 1968, pp. 145–52. Copyright © 1967 by the President and Fellows of Harvard College.

Kahn: Well, they didn't *offer*. What we did was, before the ad salesman came in—we existed in two small rooms, but I had hired extra people so we would look like a busy, venture-backed company—we prepared a chart with what we pretended was our media plan for the computer magazines. On the chart we had *BYTE* crossed out. When the salesman arrived, we made sure the phones were ringing and the extras were scurrying about. Here was this chart he thought he wasn't supposed to see, so I pushed it out of the way. He said, "Hold on, can we get you in *BYTE*?" I said, "We don't really have to be in your book, it's not the right audience for us." "You've got to try," he pleaded. I said, "Frankly, our media plan is done, and we can't afford it." So he offered good terms, if only we'd let him run it just once. We expected we'd sell maybe $20,000 of software and at least pay for the ad. We sold $150,000 worth. Looking back now, it's a funny story, then it was a big risk.[5]

Commenting on this article, Howard H. Stevenson and Amar Bhide noted that this incident of "early deceit is remembered, if at all, as an amusing prank."[6] But the question remains, How are business people supposed to operate in this capitalist system?

In addition, the law, which one might expect to be black and white, is full of thorny issues. Laws not only have authority but also limitations. In the first place, laws are made with forethought and with the deliberate purpose of ensuring justice. They are therefore ethical in intent and deserve respect. However, laws are made in legislatures, not in heaven. They do not anticipate new conditions; they do not always have the effect they were intended to have; they sometimes conflict with one another; and they are, as they stand, incapable of making judgments where multiple ethical considerations hang in the balance or seem actually to war with one another. Thus, from the beginnings of recorded history in Egypt and the Middle East, a code of laws was always accompanied by a human interpreter of laws, a judge, to decide when breaking the letter of the law did not violate the spirit or situation that the law was intended to cover. Great moments in history, religion, philosophy, and literature focus on the legal/ethical dilemma, and debating teams would wither away if the dilemma were to disappear.

ETHICAL STEREOTYPES

The 1990s ushered in the "New Era of Entrepreneurship" worldwide. The United States, now as in the past, is seen as providing an inviting and nurturing climate for those wishing to start their own enterprises and reap the rewards. In part, this is because the federal government has encouraged, to a greater degree than in any other country, an atmosphere under which free market forces, private initiative, and individual responsibility and freedom can flourish. Legislation such as antitrust laws, laws regulating labor, and the graduated income tax has not hampered the growth of entrepreneurship in America.

These laws, enacted in response to society's changing perceptions of what constitutes ethical business practices, have had the equally desirable effect of encouraging those in many industries to develop codes of ethics—in large part because they wished to have the freedom to set their own rules, rather than to have rules imposed on them by Congress.

As the ethical climate of business has changed, so has the image of the entrepreneur. The *good* stereotype is personified by Horatio Alger. The *ruthless* stereotype is represented by entrepreneurs doing business in the unfettered economic climate in the 19th century—the era of the Robber Barons, where acts of industrial sabotage, which today we would not condone, were common. The battles of James Hill and Edward Harriman over the rights of

[5] "Management by Necessity," *INC.*, March 1989, p. 33. Reprinted with permission. Copyright © 1989 by Goldhirsh Group, Inc., 38 Commercial Wharf, Boston, MA 02110.

[6] Howard H Stevenson and Amar Bhide, "Why Be Honest, If Honesty Does Not Pay?" *Harvard Business Review*, September–October 1990, p. 123.

railroads, the alleged sabotage by John D. Rockefeller of his competitors' oil refineries, the exploitation of child labor in New England's textile mills and of black labor in the southern cotton plantations, and the promoting of "snake oil" and Lydia Pinkham's tonics leave an unsavory aftertaste in the minds of today's more ethically conscious entrepreneurs.

Yet, thoughtful historians of American entrepreneurship will also recall that regardless of standards by which they are judged or of the motivations attributed to them, certain American entrepreneurs gave back to society such institutions as the Morgan Library and the Rockefeller Foundation. The extraordinary legacy of Andrew Carnegie is another example. (And, of course, these scholars are much more inclined to examine and dissect the ethical behavior of the business sector, rather than that of the clergy, or even of academia itself. In many comparisons, the behavior of the business sector would look quite pure.)

Carnegie's case is also interesting because he described the total change of attitude that came over him after he had amassed his fortune. Carnegie was the son of a Scots weaver and was able personally to amass $300 million in the production of crude steel between 1873 and 1901. As Carnegie himself described, he believed that competition "insures the survival of the fittest in every department." Carnegie also felt that "the fact that this talent for organization and management is rare among men is proved by the fact that it invariably secures enormous rewards for its possessor."[7] So apparently satisfied was Carnegie with the correctness of his view, he did not try to reconcile it with the fact that British steel rails were effectively excluded by a protective tariff equaling over half the production price of each ton of steel rails.[8] That Carnegie's mind was not easy over his fortune, however, is evident from his statement that "I would as soon give my son a curse as the almighty dollar."[9] After 1901, when he sold Carnegie Steel to United States Steel under pressure from a combine headed by J. P. Morgan, Carnegie personally supervised the giving in the United States and Great Britain of more than $300 million—an amount which is equivalent to many billions in today's dollars. Among his gifts to humanity were over 2,800 libraries, an Endowment for International Peace, and the Carnegie Institute of Pittsburgh.

From today's perspective, the entrepreneurs above might be described as acting in enlightened self-interest. However, when the same sort of entrepreneurial generosity is demonstrated today by such people as Armand Hammer of Occidental Petroleum and An Wang of Wang Laboratories and Arnold Hiatt of the Stride Rite Corporation, we are more likely to speak of their acts as philanthropy than as fulfilling their social contract.

Yet, a touch of suspicion still tinges entrepreneurial activity, and the word *entrepreneur* may still connote to some a person who belongs to a ruthless, scheming group located a good deal lower than the angels. In 1975, *Time* suggested that a businessman might make the best-qualified candidate for US president but noted the "deep-rooted American suspicion of businessmen's motives."[10] Quoting John T. Conner, chairman of Allied Chemical and former head of Merck and Company, *Time*'s editors added: "Anyone with previous business experience becomes immediately suspect. Certain segments think he can't make a decision in the public interest."[11]

However, in 1988, the prophecy of *Time* was fulfilled when George Bush, an oil entrepreneur, was elected as president of the United States, a revealing conclusion to America's most entrepreneurial decade.

[7] "Introduction to Contemporary Civilization in the West," *the Gospel of Wealth* (New York: Century, 1900), p. 620.

[8] W E Woodward, *A New American History* (Garden City, N.Y.: Garden City Publishing, 1938), p. 704.

[9] Ibid., p. 622.

[10] "Time Essay: New Places to Look for Presidents," *Time*, December 15, 1975, p. 19.

[11] Ibid., p. 19.

SHOULD ETHICS BE TAUGHT?

Just as the 1990s ushered in a new era of worldwide entrepreneurship, the world of business ethics has redefined itself, according to Andrew Stark. Stark asserts that

> advocates of the new business ethics can be identified by their acceptance of two fundamental principles. While they agree with their colleagues that ethics and interest can conflict, they take that observation as the starting point, not the ending point, of an ethicist's analytical task. . . . Second, the new perspective reflects an awareness and acceptance of the messy world of mixed motives.[12]

The challenge facing this new group of business ethicists is to bridge the gap between the moral philosophers and the managers. The business ethicists talk of "moderation, pragmatism, minimalism"[13] in their attempt to "converse with real managers in a language relevant to the world they inhabit and the problems they face."[14] With this focus on the practical side of decision making, courses on ethics can be useful to entrepreneurs and all managers.

Ethics Can and Should Be Taught

In an article that examines the ancient tradition of moral education, the decline of moral instruction beginning in the 19th century, and the renaissance of interest in ethics in the 1960s, Derek Bok, president of Harvard University, argues that ethics can and should be taught by educational institutions and that this teaching is both necessary and of value:

> Precisely because its community is so diverse, set in a society so divided and confused over its values, a university that pays little attention to moral development may find that many of its students grow bewildered, convinced that ethical dilemmas are simply matters of personal opinion beyond external judgment or careful analysis.
>
> Nothing could be more unfortunate or more unnecessary. Although moral issues sometimes lack convincing answers, that is often not the case. Besides, universities should be the last institutions to discourage belief in the value of reasoned argument and carefully considered evidence in analyzing even the hardest of human problems.[15]

It is noteworthy that John Shad, a former chairman of the New York Stock Exchange, gave over $20 million to the Harvard Business School to help develop a way to include ethics in the MBA curriculum. Beginning in the fall of 1988, first-year students at the Harvard Business School are required to attend a three-week, nongraded ethics module called Decision Making and Ethical Values. The cases discussed range from insider trading at Salomon Brothers to discrimination in employee promotions to locating a US manufacturing unit in Mexico. Thomas R. Piper, associate dean, emphasizes that the role of the course is "not converting sinners . . . but we're taking young people who have a sense of integrity and trying to get them to connect ethics with business decisions."[16] J. Gregory Dees, another ethics professor at Harvard, stresses that the "primary objective of the course is to get people thinking about issues that are easy to avoid . . . What we want people to leave DMEV with is a commitment to raising these issues in other settings, other courses, and on the job, with [an acceptable] comfort level in doing so."[17]

[12] Andrew Stark, "What's the Matter with Business Ethics?" *Harvard Business Review*, May–June 1993, p. 46.

[13] Ibid., p. 48.

[14] Ibid.

[15] Derek Bok, "Is Dishonesty Good for Business?" *Business & Society Review*, Summer 1979, p. 50.

[16] John A. Byrne, "Can Ethics Be Taught? Harvard Gives It The Old College Try," *Business Week* (April 6, 1992), p. 34.

[17] Chitra Nayak, "Why Ethics DMEV under The Microscope," *The Harbus*.

Since John Shad made his contribution three second-year electives (Moral Dilemmas of Management, Managing Information in a Competitive Context, and Profits, Markets, and Values) have been added to Harvard's ethics program. The Wharton School has a similar course required of first-year MBA students, *Leadership Skills*, which is a year-long, graded course with a four-week ethics module. The Wharton faculty are hoping to introduce the core literature of business ethics and corporate responsibility, to expose students to discussions, and to stimulate the students to address these moral issues in their other courses. These two programs are part of a larger effort to incorporate ethics, as

> over 500 business-ethics courses are currently taught on American campuses; fully 90 percent of the nation's business schools now provide some kind of training in the area. There are more than 25 textbooks in the field and three academic journals dedicated to the topic. At least 16 business-ethics research centers are now in operation, and endowed chairs in business ethics have been established at Georgetown, Virginia, Minnesota, and a number of other prominent business schools.[18]

The Usefulness of Academic Ethics

The study of ethics does seem to have the advantage of making students more aware of the pervasiveness of ethical situations in business settings, of bringing perspective to ethical situations from a distance, and of providing a framework for understanding ethical problems when they arise. Further, the study of ethics has been shown to affect, to some degree, both beliefs and behavior. For example, in a study of whether ethics courses affect student values, value changes in business school students who had taken a course in business ethics and those who did not were examined closely and were plotted across the multiple stages.[19]

The study used a sequence of stages, called the Kohlberg construct, developed by Kohlberg in 1967. These stages are presented in *Exhibit 9.1.* In the Kohlberg construct, being moral in *Stage 1* is synonymous with being obedient, and the motivation is to avoid condemnation. In *Stage 2,* the individual seeks advantage. Gain is the primary purpose, and interaction does not result in binding personal relationships. The orientation of *Stage 3* is toward pleasing others and winning approval. Proper roles are defined by stereotyped images of majority behavior. Such reciprocity is confined to primary group relations. In *Stage 4,* cooperation is viewed in the context of society as a whole. External laws serve to coordinate moral schemes, and the individual feels committed to the social order. One thus subscribes to formal punishment by police or the courts. In *Stage 5,* there is acknowledgement that reciprocity can be inequitable. New laws and social arrangements now may be invoked as corrective mechanisms. All citizens are assured of fundamental safety and equality. Cognitive

Exhibit 9.1
Classification of Moral Judgment into Stages of Development

Stage	*Orientation*	*Theme*
1	Punishment and obedience	Morality of obedience
2	Instrumental relativism	Simple exchange
3	Interpersonal concordance	Reciprocal role taking
4	Law and order	Formal justice
5	Legitimate social contract	Procedural justice
6	Universal ethical principle	Individual conscience

Source: Adapted from Kohlberg (1967).

[18] Andrew Stark, "What's the Matter with Business Ethics?" *Harvard Business Review*, May–June 1993, p. 38.

[19] David P Boyd, "Enhancing Ethical Development by an Intervention Program," unpublished manuscript, Northeastern University, 1980.

structures at the *Stage 6* level automatically reject credos and actions that the individual considers morally reprehensible, and the referent is a person's own moral framework, rather than stereotyped group behavior. Because most of one's fellows endorse a law does not guarantee its moral validity. When confronting social dilemmas, the individual is guided by internal principles that may transcend the legal system. Although these convictions are personal, they are also universal since they have worth and utility apart from the individual espousing them. Kohlberg's final stage thus represents more than mere conformity with state, teacher, or institutional criteria. Rather, it indicates one's capacity for decision making and problem solving in the context of personal ethical standards. In the study, those who took a course in business ethics showed a progression up the ethical scale, while those who had not taken a course did not progress.

Entrepreneurs' Perspectives

Most entrepreneurs also believe ethics should be taught. In the research project mentioned on page 313, entrepreneurs and chief executive officers attending the Owner/President Management (OPM) program at the Harvard Business School were asked the question: Is there a role for ethics in business education for entrepreneurs? Of those responding, 72 percent said ethics can and should be taught as part of the curriculum. (Only 20 percent said it should not, and two respondents were not sure.)

The most prominently cited reason for including ethics was that ethical behavior is at the core of long-term business success, because it provides the glue that binds enduring successful business and personal relationships together. In addition, the responses reflected a serious and thoughtful awareness of the fragile but vital role of ethics in entrepreneurial attainment and of the long-term consequences of ethical behavior for a business. Typical comments were:

- If the free enterprise system is to survive, the business schools better start paying attention to teaching ethics. They should know that business is built on trust, which depends upon honesty and sincerity. BS comes out quickly in a small company.
- If our society is going to move forward, it won't be based on how much money is accumulated in any one person or group. Our society will move forward when all people are treated fairly—that's my simple definition of ethics. I know of several managers, presidents, etc., who you would not want to get between them and their wallets or ambitions.
- In my experience the business world is by and large the most ethical and law-abiding part of our society.
- Ethics should be addressed, considered and thoroughly examined; it should be an inherent part of each class and course . . .; instead of crusading with ethics, it is much more effective to make high ethics an inherent part of business—and it is.

However, these views were not universally held. One entrepreneur who helped to found a large company with international operations warned: "For God's sake, don't forget that 90 percent of the businessman's efforts consist of just plain hard work."

There is also some cynicism. The 40-year-old head of a real estate and construction firm in the Northeast with 300 employees and $75 million in annual sales said: "There is so much hypocrisy in today's world that even totally ethical behavior is questioned since many people think it is some new negotiating technique."

It would be unfortunate if the entrepreneur did not realize his or her potential for combining action with ethical purpose because of the suspicion that the two are unrelated or inimical. There is no reason why they need be considered generically opposed. Nevertheless, in analyzing ethics, the individual can expect no substitute for his or her own effort and intelligence.

THORNY ISSUES FOR ENTREPRENEURS

Although the majority of entrepreneurs take ethics seriously, researchers in this area are still responding to David McClelland's call for inquiry: "We do not know at the present time what makes an entrepreneur more or less ethical in his dealings, but obviously there are few problems of greater importance for future research."[20] In a recent article, the topics for research were outlined (see *Exhibit 9.2*). Clearly, an opportunity for further research still exists.

Action under Pressure

During an entrepreneurial career, an entrepreneur will have to act on issues under pressure of time and when struggling for survival. In addition, the entrepreneur will most likely decide ethical questions that involve obligations on many sides—to customers, employees, stockholders, family, partners, himself, or a combination of these. Walking the tightrope and balancing common sense with an ethical framework is precarious.

As a way to cope with the inevitable conflicts an entrepreneur will encounter, a first step is developing an awareness of his or her own explicit and implicit ethical beliefs, those of his or her team and investors, and those of the milieu within which the company competes for survival. As the successful entrepreneurs quoted above believe, in the long run, succumbing to the temptations of situational ethics will, in all likelihood, result in a tumble into the quicksand, not a safety net—just ask Ivan Boesky.

Exhibit 9.2
Selected Ethical Dilemmas of Entrepreneurial Management

Dilemma: Elements	*Issues That may arise*
Promoter: Entrepreneurial euphoria Impression management Pragmatic versus moral considerations	What does honesty mean when promoting an innovation? Does it require complete disclosure of the risks and uncertainties? Does it require a dispassionate analysis of the situation, with equal time given to the downside as well as the upside? What sorts of influence tactics cross the line from encouragement and inducement to manipulation and coercion?
Relationship: Conflicts of interest and roles Transactional ethics Guerilla tactics	Tension between perceived obligations and moral expectations. Changes in roles and relationships: pre versus post venture status. Decisions based on affiliative concerns rather than on task-based concerns. Transition from a trust-based work environment to one that is more controlled.
Innovator: "Frankenstein's problem" New types of ethical problems Ethic of change	Side effects and negative externalities force a social reconsideration of norms and values. Heightened concern about the future impact of unknown harms. Who is responsible for the assessment of risk? Inventor? Government? Market? Breaking down traditions and creating new models.
Other dilemmas: Finders-keepers ethic Conflict between personal values and business goals Unsavory industry practices	Is there a fair way to divide profits when they are the result of cooperative efforts? Should the entrepreneur take all the gains that are not explicitly contracted away? Managing an intimate connection between personal choices and professional decisions. Coping with ethical pressures with creative solutions and integrity. Seeking industry recognition while not giving into peer pressure to conform.

Source: Adapted from J Gregory Dees and Jennifer A Starr, "Entrepreneurship through an Ethical Lens," in *The State of the Art of Entrepreneurship*, ed. Donald L Sexton and John D Kasarda (Boston: PWS-Kent Publishing Company, 1992), p. 96.

[20] David McClelland, *Achieving Society* (New York: Van Nostrand, 1961), p. 331.

An appreciation of this state of affairs is succinctly stated by Fred T. Allen, chairman and president of Pitney-Bowes:

> As businessmen we must learn to weigh short-term interests against long-term possibilities. We must learn to sacrifice what is immediate, what is expedient, if the moral price is too high. What we stand to gain is precious little compared to what we can ultimately lose.[21]

Different Views

Different reactions to what is ethical may explain why some aspects of venture creation go wrong, both during start-up and in the heat of the battle, for no apparent reason. Innumerable examples can be cited to illustrate that broken partnerships often can be traced to apparent differences in the personal ethics among the members of a management team. So, too, with investors. While the experienced venture capital investor seeks entrepreneurs with a reputation for integrity, honesty, and ethical behavior, the definition is necessarily subjective and depends in part on the beliefs of the investor himself and in part on the prevailing ethical climate in the industry sector in which the venture is involved.

Problems of Law

For entrepreneurs, there are increasingly frequent situations where one law directly conflicts with another. For example, a small-business investment company in New York City became involved in serious financial trouble. The Small Business Administration stated that the company should begin to liquidate its investments, because it would otherwise be in defiance of its agreement with the SBA. However, the Securities and Exchange Commission stated that this liquidation would constitute unfair treatment of stockholders, due to resulting imbalance in their portfolios. After a year and a half of agonizing negotiation, the company was able to satisfy all the parties, but compromises had to be made on both sides.

Another example of conflicting legal demands involves conflicts between procedures of the Civil Service code and the Fair Employment Practice Acts. The code states that hiring will include adherence to certain standards, a principle that was introduced in the last century to curb the patronage abuses in public service. Recently, however, the problem of encouraging and aiding minorities has led to Fair Employment Practice Acts, which require the same public agencies that are guided by Civil Service standards to hire without prejudice, and without the requirement that a given test shall serve as the criterion of selection. Both these laws are based on valid ethical intent, but the resolution of such conflicts is no simple matter.

Further, unlike the international laws governing commercial airline transportation, there is no international code of business ethics. When doing business abroad, entrepreneurs may find that those with whom they wish to do business have little in common with them – no common language, no common historical context for conducting business, and no common set of ethical beliefs about right and wrong and everything in between. For example, in the United States, bribing a high official to obtain a favor is considered both ethically and legally unacceptable; in parts of the Middle East, it is the only way to get things done. What we see as a bribe, those in parts of the Middle East see as a tip, like what you might give the headwaiter at a fancy restaurant in New York for a good table.

"When in Rome . . ." is one approach to this problem. Consulting a lawyer with expertise in international business before doing anything is another. Assuming that the object of an entrepreneur's international business venture is to make money, he or she needs to

[21] Letter to the Editor, *The Wall Street Journal*, October 17, 1975.

figure out some way that is legally tolerable under the codes of laws that do apply and that is ethically tolerable personally.

Examples of the Ends-and-Means Issue

A central question in any ethical discussion concerns the extent to which a noble end may justify ignoble means—or whether using unethical means for assumed ethical ends may not subvert the aim in some way. As an example of a noble end, consider the case of a university agricultural extension service whose goal was to aid small farmers to increase their crop productivity. The end was economically constructive and profit oriented only in the sense that the farmers might prosper from better crop yields. However, to continue being funded, the extension service was required to provide predictions of the annual increase in crop yield it could achieve, estimates it could not provide at the required level of specificity. Further, unless it could show substantial increases in crop yields, its funding might be heavily reduced. In this case, the extension service decided, if need be, to fudge the figures since it was felt that even though the presentation of overly optimistic predictions was unethical, the objectives of the persons running the organization were highly ethical and even the unethical aspects could be condoned within the context of the inability of the various groups involved to speak each other's language clearly. The fact that the funding source finally backed down in its demand ameliorated the immediate problem. But if it had not, certainly a danger existed that the individuals in this organization, altruistic though their intentions were, would begin to think that falsification was the norm and would forget that actions that run contrary to one's ethical feelings gradually would build a debilitating cynicism.

Another example is given in the case of a merger of a small rental-service business with a middle-sized conglomerate, where a law's intent was in direct opposition to what would occur if the law was literally enforced. In this case, a partner in the rental firm, shortly before the merger, had become involved in a severe automobile accident, suffered multiple injuries, and was seemingly unable to return to work. The partner also knew that the outlook for his health in the immediate future was unpredictable. Under these circumstances, he was eager, for the sake of his family, to seek some of the stock acquired in the merger and make a large portion of his assets liquid. However, federal law does not allow quick profit taking from mergers and therefore did not allow such a sale. The partner consulted the president and officers of the larger company, and they acquiesced in his plans to sell portions of his stock and stated their conviction that no adverse effect on the stock would result. Still unsure, the man then checked with his lawyer and found that the federal law in question had almost never been prosecuted. Having ascertained the risk and having probed the rationale of the law as it applied to his case, the man then sold some of the stock acquired in the merger in order to provide security for his family in the possible event of his incapacitation or death. Although he subsequently recovered completely, this could not have been foreseen.

In this instance, the partner decided that a consideration of the intrinsic purpose of the law allowed him to act as he did. In addition, he made as thorough a check as possible of the risks involved in his action. He was not satisfied with the decision he made, but he felt that it was the best he could do at the time. One can see in this example the enormous ethical tugs-of-war that go with the territory of entrepreneurship.

An Example of Integrity

That entrepreneurial decisions are complicated also is illustrated in the following example. At age 27, an entrepreneur joined a new computer software firm with sales of $1.5 million as vice president of international marketing of a new division. His principal goal was to establish profitable distribution for the company's products in the major industrialized nations. Stock incentives and a highly leveraged bonus plan placed clear emphasis on profitability, rather than on volume. In one European country, the choice of distributors was narrowed to 1 from a field of over 20. The potential distributor was a top firm, with an excellent track record and management, and the chemistry was right. In fact, the distributor was so anxious to do business with the entrepreneur's company that it was willing to accept a 10 percent commission, rather than the normal 15 percent royalty. The other terms of the deal were acceptable to both parties. In this actual case, the young vice president decided to give the distributor the full 15 percent commission, in spite of the fact that it would have settled for much less. This approach was apparently quite successful because, in five years, this international division grew from zero to $18 million in very profitable sales, and the venture was acquired by a large firm for $80 million. In describing his reasoning, the entrepreneur said his main goal was to create a sense of long-term integrity. He said further:

> I knew what it would take for them to succeed in gaining the kind of market penetration we were after. I also knew that the economics of their business definitely needed the larger margins from the 15 percent, rather than the smaller royalty. So I figured that if I offered them the full royalty, they would realize I was on their side, and that would create such goodwill that when we did have some serious problems down the road—and you always have them—then we would be able to work together to solve them. And that's exactly what happened. If I had exploited their eagerness to be our distributor, then it only would have come back to haunt me later on.

ETHICS EXERCISE REVISITED

The following statements are often made, even by practicing entrepreneurs: "How can we think about ethics when we haven't enough time even to think about running our venture?" "Entrepreneurs are doers, not thinkers—and ethics is too abstract a concept to have any bearing on business realities." "When you're struggling to survive, you're not worried about the means you use—you're fighting for one thing: survival."

However, the contemplation of ethical behavior is not unlike poetry—emotion recollected in tranquility. This chapter is intended to provide one such tranquil opportunity.

Through the decisions actually made, or not made, an individual could become more aware of his or her own value system and how making ethical decisions can be affected by the climate in which these decisions are made. However, in the exercise, participants were asked only to answer questions. They were not being asked to carry out an action. Between intent and action lies a large gap, which can only be filled by confronting and acting in a number of ambiguous situations.

CASE—WHEN THE PARTY'S OVER

Preparation Questions

1. What has happened at MAS and why? Compare the 1989 and 1990 exhibits of the NFBC. Why was Fred so upset?
2. What should Fred and Vic say and do now? How should they go about this?
3. What has to happen and why? What will happen?

MORRIS ALPER & SONS, INC.

C. WHEN THE PARTY'S OVER*

If the two of us agree on everything, then one of us is not necessary.

Victor R. Del Regno

It had been over a year since Victor R. Del Regno succeeded Frederic M. Alper as president of Morris Alper & Sons, Inc. (MAS), yet loose ends remained. Echoing in Vic's mind was the question, Are we ever going to get this transition tension behind us? Today, October 21, 1991, it was something new. In addition to planning the 1991 National Food Brokers Convention, Vic was pondering an ethical dilemma. Jay W. Hughes, a senior vice president, had brought the issue to Vic and Fred. This dilemma had dominated their thoughts and discussions for the past few days. It was not an everyday operating matter; it involved serious policy and ethical considerations and was quite complex.

Fred and Vic had discussed the issue a few days before, and Fred had convinced Vic of a course of action. Now, as Vic was preparing to go to an important meeting, Fred reopened the discussion and wanted to reassess the decision. Vic was very uncomfortable with this vacillation and was anxious to reach a course of action and stay with it.

THE 1990 NATIONAL FOOD BROKERS CONVENTION

Almost a year earlier, recognizing the sensitivity surrounding the 1990 National Food Brokers Convention, Vic had said to Fred: "I know that this is going to be a sensitive time for you. You are probably going to be uncomfortable. You are going to feel that the change is really occurring." Fred responded, "You tell me what you want me involved in and I will let you know what I want to do."

In the fall of 1990, the staff meetings served as the forum for developing a plan for the 1990 convention. Usually, these meetings were discussions of operational issues. All of the senior vice presidents and Vic shared their problems, concerns, and ideas. At one of the staff meetings, Vic moved to address the convention schedule and stressed Fred's participation. It was up to the senior vice presidents to request Fred's involvement. After some discussion, the schedule was planned and circulated, so that any conflicts could be resolved and changes made. (See *Exhibit A*, "The 1990 National Food Brokers Convention.") The schedule passed through management without any major changes. The convention was held in early December. Vic expressed his recollections:

> Our people handled things well and the principals seemed to have accepted the changing of the guard. The Morris Alper pride really showed. We ran around like crazy. With 15 of our people there out of 15,000, our paths did not cross often. Everyone does not go to the same meetings. I could tell that things were not going well for Fred. I thought that it was natural for Fred to feel a sense of loss. The bottom line was that MAS's role at the convention was another great success.

*Research Assistant Christine C Remey wrote this case under the supervision of Professor Jeffry A Timmons as the basis for class discussion, rather than to illustrate either effective or ineffective handling of an administrative situation. Harvard Business School case 294-021 (revised 7/23/93).

Exhibit A
The 1990 National Food Brokers Convention

Friday, December 7, 1990	
NFBA (breakfast and board meeting)	FMA
Ore-Ida Foods, Inc. (luncheon)	VRD
Campbell Soup Company	**VRD**
Colgate-Palmolive (food service)	FMA
Campbell Soup Company	**VRD**
Charms/Tootsie Roll (social event)	FMA/VRD
Pillsbury Company (social event)	**FMA/VRD**
Chicopee (dinner) (food service)	FMA/VRD
Mott's (dinner)	**VRD**
Saturday, December 8, 1990	
NFBA (dry grocery steering committee and general session)	VRD
On-Cor Food, Inc.	FMA
Whitman's	VRD
James River/Dixie (lunch)	**VRD**
Block Drug Company (social event)	VRD
Green Giant	**VRD**
Mrs. Smith/Eggo (social event)	**FMA/VRD**
Swift-Eckrich (social event)	FMA/VRD
Tyson Foods, Inc. (social event)	**FMA/VRD**
Block Drug Company (dinner)	VRD
Sunday, December 9, 1990	
Block Drug Company (breakfast)	VRD
Tetley (breakfast)	FMA/VRD
Schering-Plough	**VRD**
Mott's USA	**VRD**
3M Personal Care	FMA
Welch's (meeting & luncheon)	**FMA/VRD**
Sara Lee	**VRD**
Chicopee (food service)	FMA
Mott's USA	**FMA/VRD**
Dole Dried Fruit & Nut	**VRD**
Mrs. Smith/Eggo (social event)	**FMA/VRD**
Mr. Coffee, Inc.	VRD
NFBA (VIP reception)	FMA
All American Gourmet Co. (social event)	FMA/VRD
H.J. Heinz Company (social event)	**FMA/VRD**
James River/Dixie (social event)	**FMA/VRD**
Monday, December 10, 1990	
Sargento	**VRD**
Sioux Honey	FMA
Mr. Coffee, Inc.	VRD
E. R. Squibb	VRD
Block Drug Company	VRD
On-Cor Food, Inc. (social event)	VRD
Pet/Progresso (social event)	**VRD**
Sundance (social event)	VRD
Dole	**VRD**

Key: Bold = large principal; VRD = Victor R. Del Regno; FMA = Frederic M. Alper.

The Honeymoon is Over

Despite Vic's sensitivity to Fred, Fred had another perspective:

I was very much reconciled to the fact that I would play a much changed and reduced role at the convention. The last thing that I wanted to do was to be perceived as still very much at the forefront of operational meetings, or even to be present at them.

Exhibit B
Organizational Chart (December 1990)

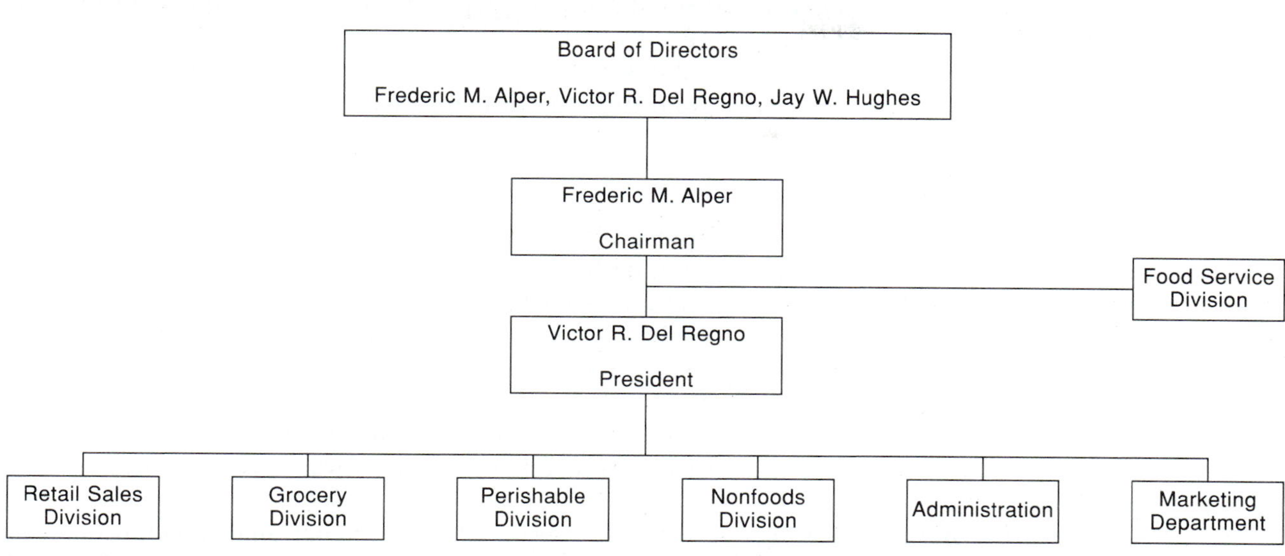

Vic felt that "he had the convention under control; the people were orchestrated; things were done right. I had been adequately sensitive to Fred, while communicating the change to the principals."

One of the senior vice presidents, when presented with the option of involving Fred, felt that he needed to help make the changes clear. No one in the staff meetings wanted to hinder the changes that needed to be communicated. The upcoming 1990 convention seemed like an opportune time to show the world the new management structure of MAS. (See *Exhibit B*, Organizational Chart (December 1990).)

After months of harboring his feelings, Fred put it this way:

> I wanted an involvement where I could be helpful, but really had the feeling that Vic did not really want me involved at all. I felt that his total preoccupation was in establishing the new regime and that my sensitivities were not much considered, nor were the legitimate areas where my presence would be helpful. I understood Vic's need to establish operational control. He was the president and had to be "the man" at the key meetings, without my being present. I wanted, not to violate Vic's role, but to be present with smaller principals, where Vic could not make all of the meetings, and to be at social gatherings. It was not that I was excluded; I just felt that Vic did not really want me involved.
>
> I felt that any important involvement, and particularly success on my part was perceived by Vic to diminish him, and on occasion, I reacted by feeling like that toward him also. It was like a see-saw, in which both of us could not rise and grow. I had to keep growing, albeit in new ways, because I was not ready to retire.
>
> He might have said that he did not object to having Fred attend those meetings, but the senior vice presidents did not invite me to meetings. They sensed that it was not the right move on their part to disrupt the changes and to counter the wishes of the new president. At the time, the senior vice presidents confirmed to me the legitimacy of my feelings; later, I came to learn that they were all "working both sides of the street," since they validated Vic's concerns when they talked to him.

Vic conceded that "the senior vice presidents wanted to make sure that they were going the way the wind was blowing. I believe that they were wrestling with divided loyalties and confusion. But I will go to my grave knowing that I did everything in my power to involve Fred in the convention."

The 1990 convention revealed some problems with the new structure concerning the relationship between Vic and Fred. Fred's feelings had been hurt at the convention and he had harbored his emotions. Vic sensed that they were walking around each other on pins and needles, but he was not sure how to address the discomfort.

"WALKING ON EGG SHELLS"

Communicating. During this time, Vic and Fred continued to keep each other up to date on their business activities. The strength of their partnership in the past had been their ability to resolve issues by pulling them apart, analyzing them, and proposing alternative solutions. One indicator of their inability to communicate was their use of voice mail. Vic remembered "retaping messages two or three times and listening to them back to say 'what could Fred read into that?'" Similarly, Fred would send a message, then call back to cancel it in a halting, tentative tone. Both admitted that there were many instances where they would think about qualifying their statements. Fred felt that "there was a real sickness in our relationship."

The All-Company Meeting. Early in the spring of 1991, the national economy entered a recession. Prior to this, MAS had enjoyed double-digit growth for several years. MAS had planned for the recession, and the financial viability of the company was not at risk, but in regular meetings concerns were being raised. At a staff meeting, the senior vice presidents and Vic decided that the company needed a good old-fashioned company sales meeting. Throughout the company, people were having department meetings and issues were being heard, but management felt that a morale-building, all-company sales meeting was the boost people were seeking. It was to be a big and special event—the first event of its type under Vic's presidency.

Vic set the date of the meeting for June of 1991. Fred first heard about the event through the office grapevine and knew that he had planned a vacation out of the country at that time. Fred felt that

> when the meeting was set up, Vic did not discuss it with me. From the beginning, I had no feeling of ownership, or participation. I knew that this event fell into that gray area between operations and strategy, but I thought on something as big as an all-company sales meeting, it might have been nice to talk it over.

After the meeting, Vic commented:

> It was fantastic! I was so proud of our people. The day broke new ground for MAS. We had put together a state of the art, multimedia presentation that was upbeat and inspirational. It was right after the Persian Gulf War, so we set the whole thing to the song "Proud to be an American." We had an outside speaker. We gave away our longevity awards to commemorate the commitment our people had made to MAS.
>
> I wanted Fred to be there. I referred to him at the meeting. I was saying something like, "Even in this tough time, we are still working toward Fred Alper's vision." We had some fun and displayed a photo of Fred showing off our CouponaRama™ insert to a turtle while vacationing.[1] Word got back to me shortly after the meeting that Fred was upset about the display of his picture. I did not know what had upset him. I felt that he had a sense of humor; everyone here does. What was the big deal with calling a meeting? After all, I was the president.

[1] CouponaRama™, a registered trademark of MAS, was a free-standing insert of several different coupons of the brands of various principals MAS represents. It was distributed in Sunday newspapers.

From Fred's point of view, he was upset because

> displaying the turtle picture was a surprise. Also, because of the growth in the company, there were a lot of people I did not know in the company, so I was concerned about being portrayed in this way. Even though I knew that Vic's intentions were good, in my new role, I was very sensitive, and felt that the displaying of the photo was not very sensitive.

Victor R. Del Regno as President. Vic described the events of 1991, "The recession, the Persian Gulf war, gas prices were going to the moon, the operating costs were in the stratosphere, and the company had the first downsizing in its history. I was feeling all this on my shoulders along with the problems with Fred. I kept thinking, Why is this happening? We need each other." In fact, 1991 was one of the best profit years for MAS. Fred observed growth in Vic. "His being placed on important broker advisory councils brought further industry recognition to Vic and to our company. There was positive feedback from the principals. I sensed that Vic had an excellent grasp of the company. He was feeling good about himself."

THE DISCOVERY OF A CRISIS

An ethical dilemma had come to the attention of Jay Hughes, who immediately spoke with both Fred and Vic. There was no question about it, this issue was not operational; it involved both policy and philosophical issues. Jay, Vic, and Fred all agreed that a timely response was essential. Fred said, "It was a very complex issue. We did not know what to do." Vic felt that at the board meeting "we threw out all the alternatives. We peeled back the artichoke."

Over the next few days, they had come up with a resolution, but Fred revisited and reflected on their discussion. Fred could not help but think that their solution should be rethought. So he went in to talk with Vic, who was getting ready to go on a business trip. Fred recalled that

> Vic was hassled, getting ready for meetings, and preparing for the trip. I caught him and began trying to rethink what we had agreed on earlier. Vic got very upset with me.
>
> I said, "Vic, you are drawing new lines in the sand. This is an issue for the board of directors; this is not operational." I was really upset with him. This was more than mucking around at the bottom. We had gone off the bottom to a new bottom.

Thoughts of Leaving

Fred and Vic each felt that the whole situation would be better off if he was not part of the company. Fred's feeling was that he needed to leave MAS. But that would have to wait because it could be disastrous for the company image. Fred told Vic, "I won't be sad to leave, believe me." Vic did not want to be the bad guy, the Jack Quilty of the company, so he thought it would be best if he left the company. He was not an Alper. He would be the one to leave. Staring at each other, attempting to reconcile the ethical issue, Fred and Vic wondered if all of this pain and struggle were worth it. Even if they could get over this obstacle, what problems could they expect to surface in connection with the next convention? (See *Exhibit C*, "The 1991 National Food Brokers Convention.")

Exhibit C
The 1991 National Food Brokers Convention

Thursday, December 5, 1991

Mott's (dinner)

Friday, December 6, 1991

NFBA (education foundation: breakfast and meeting)
NFBA (business development presentation)
Schering-Plough Health Products
Clairol
NFBA (board of directors meeting)
Campbell Soup Company
Charm's
Ore-Ida
Campbell's General Session (broker of the year presentation)
Charm's (social event)
Bumble Bee
Pillsbury (awards ceremony and social event)
Green Giant
Pet/Progresso

Saturday, December 7, 1991

Basic American (breakfast)
Swift-Eckrich
NFBA (luncheon)
Block Household
Green Giant
Mrs. Smith's (social event)
NFBA (board of directors meeting)
Block Drug Company
Swift-Eckrich
Dole Packaged Foods
Bumble Bee
Clairol, Drackett, & Bristol Myers Products
Block Drug Company (dinner)

Sunday, December 8, 1991

Block Drug Company (breakfast)
Chelsea Milling
Gravymaster
James River/Dixie
Pillsbury
Pet Inc.
Sara Lee
Mrs. Smith's
Nestle/Contadina (Broker of the Year presentation and dinner)
Dole Food Service
NFBA VIP reception
Bumble Bee (social event)
Tyson, Inc. (social event)
All American Gourmet (social event)
Dole Dried Fruit & Nut (social event)
Mauna Loa Corporation (social event)
H.J. Heinz Company (social event)
Bumble Bee (dinner)

Monday, December 9, 1991

Mauna Loa
On-Cor Foods, Inc.
Sargento
Kikkoman International
Dole Packaged Foods (dinner)
Kikkoman International (social event)

Tuesday, December 10, 1991

Sargento (social event)
NFBA Dry Grocery Meeting
Nestle Dairy Systems (meeting and lunch)

RESOURCE REQUIREMENTS

PART III

Resources to the entrepreneur are like the paint and the brush to the artist. They remain inert until the creative flair engages them with the canvas. There are special attitudes, strategies, and techniques used by successful entrepreneurs in *gaining control over the minimal resources* necessary to pursue an opportunity. Ownership of these resources is not the key. What is vital is control and influence over OPR (other people's resources)—both monetary and nonmonetary. The latter are often far more important than is commonly thought.

Identifying the necessary financial requirements of a start-up or emerging firm is a primary task. This includes knowing how much cash the venture will need, when, and where to raise it. Developing the appropriate financial statements "without the pain" is something every entrepreneur would like to accomplish. An exercise in Chapter 10 will help entrepreneurs get started. Another significant task is identifying and utilizing effectively various outside resources—directors, advisors, accountants, attorneys, bankers, and the like. It is important to know where and how the best outsiders can be found, and what needs to be known about selecting, compensating, and working with them.

If the resources are the paint and brush, then the concept of the business plan is the canvas. By itself, it is sterile and bland. What's critical is knowing why, whether, and how to turn one's idea, a team, and resources into an artistic feat in the form of a first-rate business plan that can be used to raise money and resources and to grow the business.

Finally, what do entrepreneurs do when the pace is so quick that there is simply not enough time to prepare a complete business plan? This can happen to an entrepreneur seeking to acquire a business, a license, a franchise, or other rights in a hot seller's market. Knowing what to do and how to develop quickly a "dehydrated" business plan can make the difference between success and disappointment.

Resource Requirements

10

When it comes to control of resources . . . all I need from a source is the ability to use [the resource]. There are people who describe the ideal business as a post office box to which people send cash.

Howard H. Stevenson
Harvard Business School

RESULTS EXPECTED

Upon completion of the chapter, you will have:

1. Examined the successful entrepreneur's unique attitudes about and approaches to resources—people, capital, and other assets.
2. Identified the important issues in the selection and effective utilization of outside professionals, such as members of a board of directors, lawyers, accountants, and consultants.
3. Examined decisions about financial resources.
4. Analyzed the Fenchel Lampshade case.
5. Created simple cash flow and income statements and a balance sheet.
6. Discovered the ways in which entrepreneurs turn less into more.

THE ENTREPRENEURIAL APPROACH TO RESOURCES

Resources include (1) people, such as the management team, the board of directors, lawyers, accountants, and consultants; (2) financial resources; (3) assets, such as plant and equipment; and (4) a business plan. Successful entrepreneurs view the need for and the ownership and management of these resources in the pursuit of opportunities differently from the way managers in many large organizations view them. This different way of looking at resources is reflected in the definition of entrepreneurship given in Chapter 1—the process of creating or seizing an opportunity and pursuing it *regardless of the resources currently controlled.*[1]

Howard H. Stevenson has contributed to understanding the unique approach to resources of successful entrepreneurs. The decisions on what resources are needed, when they are needed, and how to acquire them are strategic decisions that fit with the other driving forces of entrepreneurship. Further, Stevenson has pointed out that entrepreneurs seek to use the minimum possible amount of all types of resources at each stage in their ventures' growth. Rather than own the resources they need, they seek to control them.

[1] This definition was developed by Howard H Stevenson and colleagues at the Harvard Business School. His work on a paradigm for entrepreneurial management has contributed greatly to this area of entrepreneurship. See Howard H Stevenson, "A New Paradigm for Entrepreneurial Management," in *Proceedings from the 7th Anniversary Symposium on Entrepreneurship, July 1983* (Boston: Harvard Business School, 1984).

Entrepreneurs with this approach reduce some of the risk in pursuing opportunities:

- *Capital.* The amount of capital required is simply smaller, thereby reducing the financial exposure and the dilution of the founder's equity.
- *Flexibility.* Entrepreneurs who do not own a resource are in a better position to commit and decommit quickly.[2] One price of ownership of resources is an inherent inflexibility. With the rapidly fluctuating conditions and uncertainty with which most entrepreneurial ventures have to contend, inflexibility can be a serious curse. Response times need to be short if a firm is to be competitive. Decision windows are most of the time small and elusive. And it is extremely difficult to predict accurately the resources which will be necessary to execute the opportunity. In addition, the entrepreneurial approach to resources permits iterations or strategic experiments in the venture process—that is, ideas can be tried and tested without committing to the ownership of all assets and resources in the business, to markets and technology which change rapidly, and so forth. For example, Howard Head says that if he had raised all the money he needed at the outset, he would have failed by spending it all too early on the wrong version of his metal ski. Consider also, for example, the inflexibility of a company that commits permanently to a certain technology, software, or management system.
- *Low sunk cost.* In addition, sunk costs are lower if the firm exercises the option to abort the venture at any point. Consider, instead, the enormous up-front capital commitment of a nuclear power plant and the cost of abandoning such a project.
- *Costs.* Fixed costs are lowered, thus favorably affecting breakeven. Of course, the other side of the coin is that variable costs may rise. If the entrepreneur has found an opportunity with forgiving and rewarding economics, then there still will most likely be ample gross margins in the venture to absorb this rise.
- *Reduced risk.* In addition to reducing total exposure, other risks, such as the risk of obsolescence of the resource, are also lower. For example, it is no wonder that venture leasing has been used by biotechnology companies as a way to supplement sources of equity financing.

While some might scoff at the practice, assuming erroneously that the firm cannot afford to buy a resource, the truth of the matter is that not owning one provides advantages and options. This is not to say that these decisions are not extremely complex, involving consideration of such details as the tax implications of leasing versus buying, and so forth.

Marshalling and Minimizing Resources

Minimizing resources is referred to in colloquial terms as bootstrapping it or, more formally, as a lack of resource intensity, defined as a multistage commitment of resources with a minimum commitment at each stage or decision point.[3] Thus, to persevere, entrepreneurs ask at every step how they can accomplish a little more with a little less and pursue the opportunity. Or as Amar Bhide explained, "For the great majority of would-be founders, the biggest challenge is not raising money but having the wits and hustle to do without it."[4]

As was outlined in *Exhibit 6.2,* just the opposite attitude is often evident in large institutions that usually are characterized by a trustee or custodial viewpoint. Managers in larger institutions seek to have not only enough committed resources for the task at hand but also a cushion against the tough times.

[2] Howard H Stevenson, Michael J Roberts, and H Irving Grousbeck, *New Business Ventures and the Entreprenuer* (Homewood, IL: Richard D. Irwin, 1985).

[3] Ibid.

[4] Amar Bhide, "Bootstrap Finance: The Art of Start-Ups," *Harvard Business Review,* November–December 1992, p. 110.

Using Other People's Resources (OPR)

Obtaining the use of other people's resources, particularly in the start-up and early-growth stages of a venture, is an important approach for entrepreneurs. In contrast, large firms assume that virtually all resources have to be owned to control their use, and decisions center around how these resources will be acquired and financed—not so with entrepreneurs.

What is key is having the use of the resource and being able to control or influence the deployment of the resource. The quote at the beginning of the chapter illustrates this mind-set perfectly.

Other people's resources can include, for example, money invested or loaned by friends, relatives, business associates, or other investors. Or resources can include people, space, equipment, or other material loaned, provided inexpensively or free by customers or suppliers, or secured by bartering future services, opportunities, and the like. In fact, using other people's resources can be as simple as benefiting from free booklets and pamphlets, such as those published by many of the Big Six accounting firms, or making use of low-cost educational programs or of government-funded management assistance programs.

How can you as an entrepreneur begin to tap into these resources? Howard H. Stevenson and William H. Sahlman suggest that you have to do "two seemingly contradictory things: seek out the best advisors—specialists if you have to—and involve them more thoroughly, and at an earlier stage, than you have in the past. At the same time, be more skeptical of their credentials and their advice."[5] In addition to networking with family, friends, classmates, and advisors, Stevenson and Sahlman suggest that the human touch enhances the relationship between the entrepreneur and the advisors to the venture.[6] Jennifer A. Starr and Ian C. MacMillian tested their hypothesis that "some entrepreneurs and intrapreneurs employ social assets, such as friendship, liking, trust, obligation, and gratitude to secure resources at prices far lower than the market price, to the significant benefit of their ventures."[7] Yet another group of researchers, Paola Dubini and Howard Aldrich, have contributed to the growing body of knowledge about how these "social assets" may in fact benefit the bottom line of a new venture; see *Exhibit 10.1* for the strategic principals they have identified. However, entrepreneurs should be cautioned that another study "found no evidence . . . that the size of an entrepreneur's personal network or the amount of time invested in developing and maintaining a network affect business survival or performance."[8]

There are many examples of controlling people resources, rather than owning them. In real estate, even the largest firms do not employ top architects full-time but, rather, secure them on a project basis. Most smaller firms do not employ lawyers but obtain legal assistance as needed. Technical consultants, design engineers, and programmers are other examples.

An example of this approach is a company that grew to $20 million in sales in about 10 years with $7,500 cash, a liberal use of credit cards, reduced income for the founders, and hard work and long hours. This company has not had to raise any additional equity capital.

An example of the opposite point of view is a proposed new venture in the minicomputer software industry. The business plan called for about $300,000, an amount which would pay for only the development of the first products. The first priority in the deployment of the company's financial resources outlined in the business plan was to

[5] Howard H Stevenson and William H Sahlman, "How Small Companies Should Handle Advisors," in *The Entrepreneurial Venture* (Boston: Harvard Business School, 1992), p. 296. See also a *Harvard Business Review* reprint series called "Boards of Directors: Part I" and "Board of Directors: Part II" (Boston: Harvard Business Review, 1976).

[6] Ibid., p. 301.

[7] Jennifer A Starr and Ian C MacMillan, "Resource Corporation Via Social Contracting: Resource Acquisition Strategies For New Ventures," *Strategic Management Journal* 2 (1990).

[8] Howard E Aldrich and Pat Ray Reese, "Does Networking Pay Off?" (Forthcoming).

Exhibit 10.1
Hypotheses Concerning Networks and Entrepreneurial Effectiveness

Effective entrepreneurs are more likely than others to systematically plan and monitor network activities.
- Effective entrepreneurs are able to *chart their present network* and to discriminate between production and symbolic ties.
- Effective entrepreneurs are able to *view effective networks as a crucial aspect for ensuring the success of their company.*
- Effective entrepreneurs are able to *stabilize and maintain networks,* in order to increase their effectiveness and their efficiency.

Effective entrepreneurs are more likely than others to undertake actions toward increasing their network density and diversity.
- Effective entrepreneurs set aside time for purely random activities—things done with no specific problem in mind.
- Effective entrepreneurs are able to *check network density,* so as to avoid too many overlaps (because they affect network efficiency) while still attaining solidarity and cohesiveness.
- Effective entrepreneurs multiply, through extending the reachability of their networks, the stimuli for better and faster adaptation to change.

Source: Adapted from Paola Dubini and Howard Aldrich, "Executive Forum: Personal and Extended Networks Are Central to the Entrepreneurial Process," *Journal of Business Venturing* 6, no. 5., (September 1991), pp. 310–12.

buy outright a computer costing approximately $150,000. The founders refused to consider other options, such as leasing the computer or leasing computer time. The company was unable to attract venture capital, even though, otherwise, it had an excellent business plan. The $150,000 raised from informal private investors was not enough money to execute the opportunity, and the founders decided to give it back and abandon the venture. Would not a more entrepreneurial team have figured out a way to keep going under these circumstances?

OUTSIDE PEOPLE RESOURCES

Board of Directors

Initial work in evaluating the need for people resources is done in the process of forming a new venture team (see Chapter 7). Once resource needs have been determined and a team has been selected, it will usually be necessary to obtain additional resources outside of the venture, in the start-up stage and during other stages of growth as well.

The decision of whether to have a board of directors and, if the answer is yes, the process of choosing and finding the people who will sit on the board are troublesome for new ventures.[9]

The Decision

The decision of whether to have a board of directors is influenced first by the form of organization chosen for the firm. If the new venture is organized as a corporation, it must have a board of directors, which must be elected by the shareholders. There is flexibility with other forms of organization.

In addition, certain investors will require a board of directors. Venture capitalists almost always require boards of directors and that they be represented on the boards.

Beyond that, deciding to involve outsiders is worth careful thought. This decision starts with the identification of missing relevant experience, know-how, and networks, and of what the venture needs at this stage of its development, that can be provided by outside directors. Their probable contributions then can be balanced against the fact that having a board of directors will necessitate greater disclosure to outsiders of plans for operating and financing the business. It also is worth noting that one of the responsibilities of a board of directors

[9] The author is indebted to Howard H Stevenson of the Harvard Business School, and to Leslie Charm and Karl Youngman of Doktor Pet Centers and Command Performance hair salons, respectively, for insights into and knowledge of boards of directors.

is to elect officers for the firm, so the decision also is tied to decisions about financing and the ownership of the voting shares in the company.

A survey of entrepreneurial firms showed that one-fourth of the companies responding had no outside directors and 16 percent had only one.[10] Of those who did have outside directors, these companies valued them most for their objectivity. Among the respondents, 93 percent had sales under $25 million, while 58 percent had annual revenues of less than $2 million. Eighty-three percent reported they were profitable. Sixty-four percent said the lead entrepreneur owned a controlling equity interest. This might account for a somewhat more sanguine view in the survey results.

Recently, when Art Spinner of Hambro International was interviewed by *INC.*, he explained that

> entrepreneurs worry about the wrong thing . . . that the boards are going to steal their companies or take them over. Though entrepreneurs have many reasons to worry, that's not one of them. It almost never happens. In truth, boards don't even have much power. They are less well equipped to police entrepreneurs than to advise them.[11]

As Spinner suggests, the expertise that members of a board can bring to a venture, at a price it can afford, can far outweigh any of the negative factors mentioned above. In one venture, for instance, a venture capitalist who first invested in the company sat on the board of directors through the first years of highly successful growth. He made vital contributions in helping to recruit key top management, in giving the firm credibility with potential customers, in being a sounding board and devil's advocate, and in stimulating strategic thinking at a critical time—two years earlier than would have been done otherwise. The director served until it was evident that another kind of contribution was needed—that is, someone who could be valuable in helping in a public offering.[12]

Selection Criteria: Add Value with Know-How and Contacts

Once the decision to have a board of directors has been made, finding the appropriate people for the board is a challenge. It is important to select people who are known to be trustworthy and to be objective. Most ventures typically look to personal acquaintances of the lead entrepreneur or the team or to their lawyers, bankers, accountants, or consultants for their first outside directors. While such a choice might be the right one for a venture, the process also involves finding the right people to fill the gaps discovered in the process of forming the management team.

This issue of filling in the gaps relates back to one of the criteria of a successful management team, intellectual honesty, that is, knowing what you know and what you need to know (see *Exhibit 3.3*). In a recent study of boards and specifically venture capitalists' contribution to them, entrepreneurs seemed to value operating experience over the financial expertise.[13] In addition, the study reported that "those CEOs with a top-20 venture capital firm as the lead investor, on average did rate the value of the advice from their venture capital board members significantly higher—but not outstandingly higher—than the advice from other outside board members."[14]

Defining expectations and minimum requirements for board members might be a good way to get the most out of a board of directors.

[10] "The *Venture* Survey: Who Sits on Your Board?" *Venture*, April 1984, p. 32.

[11] "Confessions of a Director: Hambro International's Art Spinner Says Most CEOs Don't Know How to Make Good Use of Boards. Here He Tells You How," *INC.*, April 1991, p. 19.

[12] Jeffry A Timmons and Harry J Sapienza, "Venture Capital: More Than Money?" in *Pratt's Guide to Venture Capital Sources* (New York: Venture Economics Publishing, 1993), p. 47–53.

[13] Joseph Rosenstein, Albert V Bruno, William D Bygrave, and Natalie T Taylor, "The CEO, Venture Capitalist, and the Board," *Journal of Business Venturing* 8 (1988), pp. 99–113.

[14] Ibid., pp. 99–100.

A top-notch outside director usually spends *at least* 9 to 10 days per year on his or her responsibilities. Four days per year are spent for quarterly meetings, a day of preparation for each meeting, a day for another meeting to cope with an unanticipated issue, plus up to a day or more for various phone calls. Yearly fees are usually paid for such a commitment.

Quality directors become involved for the learning and professional development opportunities, and so forth, rather than for the money. Compensation to board members varies widely. Fees can range from as little as $500 to $1,000 for a half- or full-day meeting to $10,000 to $30,000 per year for four to six full-day to day-and-a-half meetings, plus accessibility on a continuous basis. Directors are also usually reimbursed for their expenses incurred in preparing for and attending meetings. Stock in a start-up company, often 2 percent to 5 percent, or options, for 5,000 to 50,000 shares, are common incentives to attract and reward directors.

Additionally, Art Spinner, a director of 11 companies and an advisor to two other companies suggested the following as a simple set of rules to guide you toward a productive relationship with your board:

- Treat your directors as individual resources.
- Always be honest with your directors.
- Set up a compensation committee.
- Set up an audit committee.
- Never set up an executive committee.[15]

New ventures are finding that for a variety of reasons, people who could be potential board members are increasingly cautious about getting involved:

- *Liability.* Directors of a company can be held personally liable for its actions and those of its officers, and, worse, a climate of litigation exists in many areas. For example, some specific grounds of liability of a director have included voting a dividend that renders the corporation insolvent, voting to authorize a loan out of corporate assets to a director or an officer who ultimately defaults, and signing a false corporate document or report. Courts have held that if a director acts in good faith, he or she is excused for his or her involvement. The problem is, however, that for a director to *prove* that he or she has acted in good faith, especially in a start-up situation, is no easy matter. This proof is complicated by several factors, including possibly an inexperienced management team, the financial weaknesses and cash crises that occur and demand solution, and the lack of good and complete information and records, which are necessary as the basis for action. In recent years, many states have passed what is known as the "Dumb Director Law." In effect, the law allows that directors are normal human beings who can make mistakes and misjudgments; it goes a long way in taking the sting out of potential lawsuits that are urged by ambulance chasers.
- *Harassment.* Outside stockholders, who may have acquired stock through a private placement or through the over-the-counter market, can have unrealistic expectations about the risk involved in a new venture, the speed at which a return can be realized, as well as the size of the return. Such stockholders are a source of continual annoyance for boards and for their companies.
- *Time and risk.* Experienced directors know that often it takes more time and intense involvement to work with an early-stage venture with sales of $10 million or less than with one having sales of $25 million to $50 million or more, and the former is riskier.

One solution to liability concerns is for the firm to purchase indemnity insurance for its directors. But this insurance is expensive. Despite the liability problems noted above, the

[15] "Confessions of a Director," *INC.*, April 1991, p. 119. Reprinted with permission. © 1991 by Goldhirsh Group, Inc. 38 Commercial Wharf, Boston, MA 02110.

survey mentioned found that just 11 percent of the respondents reported difficulty in recruiting board members.[16] In dealing with this issue, new ventures will want to examine a possible director's attitude toward risk in general and evaluate whether this is the type of attitude the team needs to have represented.

Alternatives to a Formal Board

The use of advisors and quasi boards can be a useful alternative to having a formal board of directors.[17] A firm can solicit objective observations and feedback for these advisors. Such informal boards can bring needed expertise to bear, without the legal entanglements and formalities of a regular board. Also, the possible embarrassment of having to remove someone who is not serving a useful role can be avoided. Informal advisors are usually much less expensive, with honorariums of $500 to $1,000 per meeting common. It should perhaps be noted that the level of involvement of these advisors probably will be less than members of a formal board. The firm also does not enjoy the protection of law, which defines the obligations and responsibilities of board members of a formal board.

An informal group of advisors can also be a good mechanism through which a new venture can observe a number of people in action and select one or two as regular directors. The entrepreneur gains the advantages of counsel and advice from outsiders without being legally bound by their decisions.

Attorneys

The Decision

Almost all companies need and use the services of attorneys, and entrepreneurial ventures perhaps more so.[18] *INC.* magazine recently conducted a readership poll of approximately 5,000 subscribers and 5,000 lawyers. The typical subscribing company reported it had sales of $5.1 million, with 62 employees. Of these companies, 94 percent reported that they regularly relied on outside legal counsel. In addition, 88 percent of the attorneys who responded considered small business clients important to their practices.[19]

Indeed, it may be necessary for entrepreneurs to possess extensive knowledge of the law in addition to selecting good attorneys. John Van Slyke, a consultant who has also taught at Harvard Business School, thinks it may be wise for entrepreneurs to pursue a law degree, either instead of or in addition to an MBA.[20] He believes that students of entrepreneurship have remained novices about the law and are not aware they are vulnerable. He says:

> While lawyers are currently in abundant supply, quality in the profession is so thinly spread that our students are told repeatedly by guest speakers in class that it is vital to *find a good lawyer.* Yet experienced businessmen and women know that legal advice is in fact another form of outside expertise which must be managed effectively. To manage relationships with lawyers effectively, entrepreneurs must know what lawyers do and how they think. Prudent businessmen and women do not delegate wholesale all important legal matters to their lawyers, nor do they allow their lawyers to make many decisions for them. After all, the important signatures on contracts, tax forms, and other legal documents are those of the principals, not the lawyers.[21]

[16] "The *Venture* Survey: Who Sits on Your Board?" p. 32.

[17] See the article by Harold W Fox, "Quasi Boards: Useful Small Business Confidants," in *Growing Concerns*, ed. David E Gumpert (New York: John Wiley & Sons and *Harvard Business Review*, 1984), pp. 307–16.

[18] The author wishes to acknowledge the input provided by Gerald Feigen of the Center for Entrepreneurial Studies, University of Maryland, from a course on entrepreneurship and the law he has developed and teaches at George Washington University Law School; also John Van Slyke of Alta Research.

[19] Bradford W Ketchum, Jr., "You and Your Attorney," *INC.*, June 1982, pp. 51-56.

[20] John R Van Slyke, "What Should We Teach Entrepreneurs about the Law," *Entrepreneurship: What It Is and How to Teach It* (Boston, MA: Harvard Business School, 1985), p. 135.

[21] Ibid., p. 139.

Exhibit 10.2
How Attorneys Are Used

	Annual Company Sales (percent of respondents)				
Legal Service Used (ranked by total mentions)	*Under $1 Million*	*$1–2.9 Million*	*$3–4.9 Million*	*$5–24.9 Million*	*$25 Million or More*
Contracts and agreements	70%	74%	69%	84%	85%
Personal needs of top management	46	58	56	53	38
Formal litigation	34	50	63	61	91
Real estate and insurance matters	32	35	50	51	56
Incorporation	45	34	39	33	24
Estate planning	23	42	48	44	17
Delinquent accounts	20	33	39	34	21
Liability protection	20	17	22	33	41
Copyrights, trademarks, and patents	21	19	24	28	38
Mergers and acquisitions	12	14	29	32	47
Employee benefit plans	10	26	19	27	27
Tax planning and review	13	17	22	17	12
Employee stock ownership plans	9	15	10	18	21
Franchising and licensing	13	11	14	14	12
Government-required reports	8	6	6	10	12
Prospectus for public offering	2	1	5	2	18
Labor relations	1	2	2	3	3

The need for legal counsel is obvious when it comes to contracts and lawsuits. But the *INC.* survey shows that small business managers also rely on company attorneys for personal problems ranging from tax matters to divorce and estate probate. As company size increases, so does the need for advice in such areas as liability, mergers, and benefit plans.

Just how attorneys are used by entrepreneurial ventures depends on the needs of the venture at its particular stage. Size is also a factor. *Exhibit 10.2* summarizes the findings of a survey by *INC.* magazine. Apparently, firms with sales under $1 million use attorneys mostly for contracts and agreements. These companies also use a substantial amount of their attorneys' time for the personal needs of top management, matters surrounding incorporation, and formal litigation. As company size increases, so does the need for advice in such areas as liability, mergers, and benefit plans. It is also noteworthy that contracts and agreements were almost uniformly the predominant use, regardless of the size of the venture.

The following are areas of the law that entrepreneurs will most likely need to get assistance with:

- *Incorporation.* Issues, such as the forgivable and nonforgivable liabilities of founders, officers, and directors or the form of organization chosen for a new venture are important. As tax laws and other circumstances change, they are important for more-established firms as well. How important this area can be is illustrated by the case of a founder who nearly lost control of his company as a result of the legal maneuvering of the clerk and another shareholder. The clerk and the shareholder controlled votes on the board of directors, while the founder had controlling interest in the stock of the company. The shareholder tried to call a directors' meeting and not re-elect the founder president. The founder found out about the plot and adroitly managed to call a stockholders' meeting to remove the directors first.
- *Franchising and licensing.* Innumerable issues concerning future rights, obligations, and what happens in the event of nonperformance by either a franchisee or lessee or a franchisor or lessor require specialized legal advice.
- *Contracts and agreements.* Firms need assistance with contracts, licenses, leases, and other such agreements as noncompete employment agreements and those governing the vesting rights of shareholders.

- *Formal litigation, liability protection, and so on.* In today's litigious climate, sooner or later most entrepreneurs will find themselves as defendants in lawsuits and require counsel.
- *Real estate, insurance, and other matters.* It is hard to imagine an entrepreneur who, at one time or another, will not be involved in various kinds of real estate transactions, from rentals to the purchase and sale of property, and require the services of an attorney.
- *Copyrights, trademarks, patents, and intellectual property protection.* Products are hard to protect. But, pushing ahead with development of products, such as software, before ample protection from the law is provided can be expedient in the short term but disastrous in the long term. For example, an entrepreneur—facing the loss of a $2.5 million sale of his business and uncollected fees of over $200,000 if his software was not protected—obtained an expert on the sale, leasing, and licensing of software products. The lawyer devised subtle but powerful protections, such as internal clocks in the software that shut down the software if they were not changed.
- *Employee plans.* Benefit and stock ownership plans have become complicated to use effectively and to administer. They require the special know-how of lawyers so common pitfalls can be avoided.
- *Tax planning and review.* Here, a word of caution is in order. All too frequently the tail of the accountant's tax avoidance advice wags the dog of good business sense. Entrepreneurs who worry more about finding good opportunities to make money, rather than tax shelters, are infinitely better off.
- *Federal, state, and other regulations and reports.* Understanding the impact of and complying with regulations often is not easy. Violations of federal, state, and other regulations often can have serious consequences.
- *Mergers and acquisitions.* There is specialized legal know-how in buying or selling a company. Unless an entrepreneur is highly experienced and has highly qualified legal advisors in these transactions, he or she can either lose the deal or end up having to live with legal obligations that may be costly.
- *Bankruptcy law.* Many people have heard tales of entrepreneurs who did not make deposits to pay various federal and state taxes in order to use that cash in their business. It is likely that these entrepreneurs falsely assumed that if their companies went bankrupt, the government was out of luck, just like the banks and other creditors. They were wrong. In fact, the owners, officers, and often the directors are held personally liable for those obligations.
- *Other matters.* These matters can range from assistance with collecting delinquent accounts to labor relations.
- *Personal needs.* As entrepreneurs accumulate net worth (i.e., property and other assets), legal advice in estate, tax, and financial planning is important.

Selection Criteria: Add Value with Know-How and Contacts

In a survey of the factors that enter into the selection of a law firm or an attorney, 54 percent of the respondents said personal contact with a member of the firm was the main factor.[22] Reputation was a factor for 40 percent, and a prior relationship with the firm, 26 percent. Equally revealing was the fact that fees were mentioned by only 3 percent.

In many areas of the country are attorneys who specialize in new ventures and in firms with higher growth potential. The best place to start is with acquaintances of the lead entrepreneur, of members of the management team, or of directors. Recommendations from accountants, bankers, and associates also are useful. Other sources are partners in venture capital firms, partners of a Big Six accounting firm (those who have privately owned and

[22] Ketchum, "You and Your Attorney," p. 52.

emerging company groups), a bar association, or the *Martindale-Hubbell Law Directory* (a listing of lawyers).

An attorney, to be effective, needs to have the experience and expertise to deal with specific issues facing a venture. Stevenson and Sahlman state that

> hooking up with the vast resources of a large law firm or Big Six accounting firm may be the best course, but we do not necessarily advise that strategy. You can usually get reasonable tax or estate-planning advice from a big law firm merely by picking up a telephone. The trade-off is that, if you are a small company and they have a dozen General Electrics as clients, you may get short shrift. One- to two-person firms can have an excellent network of specialists to refer to for problems outside their bailiwick. The point is, you'd better use the specialist when you have to.[23]

For example, one entrepreneur who relocated his business to new office space—in a renovated historical building that was being converted into office condominiums—did not use the two attorneys who handled his other business and personal affairs because neither had specific experience in office condominium deals involving historical properties and the complicated tax and multiple ownership issues involved. Moreover, as with members of the management team, directors, and investors, the chemistry also is important.

Finally, advice to be highly selective and to expect to get what you pay for is sound. It is also important to realize that lawyers are not business people and that they do not usually make *business* judgments. Rather, they seek to provide perfect or fail-safe protection.

Most attorneys are paid on an hourly basis. Retainers and flat fees are sometimes paid, usually by larger ventures. The amount a venture pays for legal services expectedly rises as the firm grows. Many law firms will agree to defer charges or initially to provide services at a lower than normal rate in order to obtain a firm's business. According to the *Massachusetts Lawyers Weekly*, legal fees fall into the following ranges: partners' hourly rates, from $195 to $400; associates' hourly rates, from $80 to $245; and paralegals' rates are between $45 and $165.

Bankers and Other Lenders

The Decision

Deciding whether to have a banker or another lender usually involves decisions about how to finance certain needs (see Part IV). It appears that most companies will need the services of a banker or other lender at some time in this respect. The decision also can involve how a banker or other lender can serve as an advisor.

As with other advisors, the banker or other lender needs to be a partner, not a difficult minority shareholder. First and foremost, therefore, an entrepreneur will be well advised to pick the *right banker or lender,* rather than to pick just a bank or a financial institution, although picking the bank or institution is also important. Different bankers and lenders have reputations ranging from "excellent" to "just OK" to "not OK" in how they work with entrepreneurial companies. Their institutions also have reputations for how well they work with entrepreneurial companies. Ideally, an entrepreneur needs an excellent banker or lender with an excellent bank or financial institution, although an excellent banker or lender with a just OK bank or institution is preferable to a just OK banker or lender with an excellent bank or financial institution.

For an entrepreneur to know clearly what he or she needs from a lender is an important starting point. Some will have needs that are asset-based, such as money for equipment, facilities, or inventory. Others may need working capital to fund short-term operating needs.

[23] Stevenson and Sahlman, "How Small Companies Should Handle Advisers," p. 297.

Having a business plan is invaluable preparation for selecting and working with a lender. Also, since a banker or other lender is a "partner," it is important to invite him or her to see the company in operation, to avoid late financial statements (as well as late payments and overdrafts), and to be honest and straightforward in sharing information.

Selection Criteria: Add value with Know-How and Contracts

Bankers and other lenders are known to other entrepreneurs, lawyers, accountants that provide general business advisory services, and venture capitalists. Starting with their recommendations is ideal. From among four to seven or so possibilities, an entrepreneur will find the right lender and the right institution.

Today's banking and financial services marketplace is much more competitive than in the past. There are more choices, and it is worth the time and effort to shop around.

Accountants

The Decision

The accounting profession has come a long way from the "green eyeshades" stereotype one hears reference to occasionally. Today, virtually all of the larger accounting firms have discovered the enormous client potential of new and entrepreneurial ventures, and a significant part of their business strategy is to cater specifically to these firms. In the Boston area, for instance, leading Big Six accounting firms have located new offices for their small business groups on Route 128 in the heart of entrepreneurs' country.

Accountants often are unfairly maligned. As one author put it:

> It is hard for entrepreneurs to fully appreciate accounting and what it can do for them. In fact, many tend to view the accountant as a bean counter, a sort of scorekeeper sitting on the sidelines, rather than as a player on the first team. This is a great mistake.[24]

Accountants who are experienced as advisors to emerging companies can provide, in addition to audits and taxation, other valuable services. An experienced general business advisor can be invaluable in helping to think through strategy, in helping to find and raise debt and equity capital, in mergers and acquisitions, in locating directors, and in helping to balance business decisions with important personal needs and goals. For a listing of how five small companies use their accountants, see *Exhibit 10.3*.

Selection Criteria: Add Value with Know-How and Contacts

In selecting accountants, the first step is for the venture to decide whether to go with a smaller local firm, a regional firm, or one of the Big Six accounting firms. Although each company should make its own decision, it is noteworthy that in an informal survey of companies with sales between $4 million and $20 million, "More than 85 percent of the CEOs preferred working with smaller regional accounting firms, rather than the Big Six, because of lower costs and what they perceived as better personal attention."[25] In making this decision, you will need to address several factors:[26]

- *Service.* Levels of service offered and the attention likely to be provided need to be evaluated. Chances are, for most start-ups, both will be higher in a small firm than a large one. But, if an entrepreneur of a higher potential firm seeking venture capital or a strategic partner has aspirations to go public, a Big Six firm is a good place to start.

[24] Gordon Baty, *Entrepreneurship for the 80s* (Reston, VA: Reston Publishing, 1982), p. 107.

[25] Susan Greco and Christopher Caggiano, "Advisors: How Do You Use Your CPA?" *INC.*, September 1991.

[26] Neil C Churchill and Louis A Werbaneth, Jr., "Choosing and Evaluating Your Accountant," in *Growing Concerns*, ed. David E Gumpert (New York: John Wiley & Sons and *Harvard Business Review*, 1984), p. 265.

Exhibit 10.3
How Do You Use Your CPA?

Company	*How Often Does CEO Consult CPA?*	*What's CEO Looking for in a CPA?*	*How Often Has Company Switched CPAs?*
Coastal Production Service; operates oil and gas platforms	Once a month	Audit proficiency, so CEO chose a firm that employs a former IRS auditor.	Twice
UniLink Software; software developer	Weekly	Computer literacy, since CEO especially tailors his cash flow and other statements.	Never
Pro-Tec Industries; manufacturer of truck parts	Quarterly	Ability to analyze numbers quickly, especially during expansion activities.	Never
Vance International; protective services	Quarterly	Red-flag warnings on issues like insurance costs or financial ratios.	Twice
Roadshow Services; theatrical-transportation management	Once every two months	Reality checks to keep fast-growing company's profit and other margins in line.	Twice

Source: Adapted from Susan Greco and Christopher Caggiano, "Advisors: How Do You Use Your CPA?" *INC.*, September 1991, p. 136.

- *Needs.* Needs, both current and future, have to be weighed against the capabilities of the firm. Larger firms are more equipped to handle highly complex or technical problems, while smaller firms may be preferable for general management advice and assistance because the principals are more likely to be involved in handling the account. However, if the goal of the firm is to go public, a series of audits from one of the larger firms is preferable.
- *Cost.* Most Big Six firms will offer very cost-competitive services to start-ups with significant growth and profit potential. If a venture needs the attention of a partner in a larger firm, services of the larger firm are more expensive. However, if the firm requires extensive technical knowledge, a larger firm may have more experience and therefore be cheaper.
- *Chemistry.* Always, chemistry is an important consideration.

Of course, the right accountant is competent, as evidenced by the fact that he or she does not always adopt the government's point of view on tax matters, does not need to look up information often, and seems interested and informed on managerial issues.[27] Sources of reference for good attorneys are also sources of reference for accountants, and trade groups are also valuable sources.

Once a firm has reached any significant size, it will have many choices. The founders of one firm, which had grown to about $5 million in sales and had a strong potential to reach $20 million in sales in the next five years and eventually go public, put together a brief summary of the firm, including its background and track record, and a statement of needs for both banking and accounting services. The founders were quite startled at the time at the aggressive response they received from several banks and Big Six accounting firms.

The accounting profession is straightforward enough. Whether the firm is small or large, they sell time, usually by the hour. In a 1990 survey, the hourly partner rates were reported to be between $235, for one of the Big Six firms, to $117, for a small, local firm.[28]

[27] Ibid., p. 263.

[28] Survey was conducted by *Accounting Today* (New York, 1990) and published in *INC.* (November 1991), p. 196.

Consultants

The Decision[29]

Consultants are hired to solve particular problems and to fill gaps not filled by the management team. There are many skilled consultants who can be of invaluable assistance and a great source of "other people's resources." Advice needed can be quite technical and specific or quite general or far ranging. Problems and needs also vary widely, depending upon whether the venture is just starting up or is an existing business.

Start-ups usually require help with critical one-time tasks and decisions that will have lasting impact on the business. In a recent study of how consultants are used and their impact on venture formation, Karl Bayer, of Germany's Institute for Systems and Innovation Research of the Fraunhofer-Society, interviewed 315 firms. He found that 96 used consultants and that consultants are employed by start-ups for the following reasons:

1. To compensate for a lower level of professional experience.
2. To target a wide market segment (possibly to do market research for a consumer goods firm).
3. To undertake projects which require a large start-up investment in equipment.[30]

These tasks and decisions might include assessing business sites, evaluating lease and rental agreements, setting up record- and bookkeeping systems, finding business partners, obtaining start-up capital, and formulating initial marketing plans.

Existing businesses face ongoing issues resulting from growth. Many of these issues are so specialized that rarely is this expertise available on the management team. Issues of obtaining market research, evaluating when and how to go about computerizing business tasks, whether to lease or buy major pieces of equipment, and whether to change inventory valuation methods can be involved.

While it is not always possible to pinpoint the exact nature of a problem and sometimes simply an unbiased and fresh view is needed, a new venture is usually well advised to try to determine the broad nature of its concern, such as whether it involves a personnel problem, manufacturing problem, or marketing problem, for example. Observations in the *Harvard Business Review* by a consultant are revealing:

> Management consultants are generally hired for the wrong reasons. Once hired, they are generally poorly employed and loosely supervised. The result is, more often than not, a final report that decorates an executive's bookshelf with as much usefulness as "The Life and Mores of the Pluvius Aegiptus" would decorate his coffee table—and at considerably more expense.[31]

Confirming these observations, Bayer reported that the use of consultants had a negative effect on sales three to five years later. Additionally, his surveys overwhelmingly reported (two-thirds of the 96) that "the work delivered by the consultants . . . [was] inadequate for the task."[32] So how can entrepreneurs fill gaps and solve problems? Bayer suggests that the entrepreneur can find and adequately prepare a consultant, so that the firm benefits in the long run. His advice includes:

- Use a coentrepreneurial approach with a high degree of interaction between entrepreneur and consultant.

[29] The following is excerpted in part from David E Gumpert and Jeffry A Timmons, *The Encyclopedia of Small Business Resources* (New York: Harper & Row, 1984), pp. 48–51.

[30] Karl Bayer, "The Impact of Using Consultants during Venture Formation on Venture Performance," in *Frontiers of Entrepreneurship Research 1991*, ed. Neil H Churchill et al. (Babson Park, MA: Babson College, 1991), pp. 298–99.

[31] Jean Pierre Frankenhuis, "How to Get a Good Consultant," *Harvard Business Review*, November–December 1977, p. 133.

[32] Bayer, "The Impact of Using Consultants," p. 301.

- Make sure the consultant states the results of his or her work in terms easily accessible to the founder.
- Insist that the consultant demonstrate a readiness to check the plausibility of the entrepreneur's statements and to inform the entrepreneur if those statements and assumptions are not correct.[33]

Selection Criteria: Add Value with Know-How and Contacts

Unfortunately, nowhere are the options so numerous, the quality so variable, and the costs so unpredictable as in the area of consulting. The number of people calling themselves management consultants is large and growing steadily. By 1989, there were an estimated 50,000 to 60,000 private management consultants around the country. It is estimated that approximately 2,000 or more are added annually. Further, somewhat more than half the consultants were found to work on their own, while the remainder work for firms. In addition, government agencies (primarily the Small Business Administration) employ consultants to work with businesses; various private and nonprofit organizations provide management assistance to help entrepreneurs; and others, such as professors, engineers, and so forth, provide consulting services part time. Such assistance also may be provided by other professionals, such as accountants and bankers.

Again, the right chemistry is critical. One company president who was asked what he had learned from talking to clients of the consultant he finally hired said, "They couldn't really pinpoint one thing, but they all said they would not consider starting and growing a company without him!"

As unwieldy and risky as the consulting situation might appear, there are ways of limiting the choices. For one thing, consultants tend to have specialties; while some consultants claim wide expertise, most will indicate the kinds of situations they feel most comfortable with and skillful in handling. Some of the desirable qualities in a consulting firm are summarized below:[34]

- A shirtsleeve approach to the problems.
- An understanding attitude toward the feelings of managers and their subordinates.
- A modest and truthful offer of services and an ability to produce results.
- A reasonable and realistic charge for services.
- A willingness to maintain a continuous relationship.

Three or more potential consultants can be interviewed about their expertise and approach and their references checked. Candidates who pass this initial screening then can be asked to prepare specific proposals.

A written agreement, specifying the consultant's responsibilities and objectives of the assignment, the length of time the project will take, and the type and amount of compensation, is highly recommended. Some consultants work on an hourly basis, some on a fixed-fee basis, and some on a retainer-fee basis. Huge variations in consulting costs for the same services exist. At one end of the spectrum is the Small Business Administration, which provides consultants to small businesses without charge. At the other end of the spectrum are well-known consulting firms that may charge large amounts for minimal marketing studies or technical feasibility studies.

While the quality of many products roughly correlates with their price, this is not so with consulting services. The point is that it is difficult to judge consultants solely on the basis of the fees they charge.

[33] Bayer, "The Impact of Using Consultants," pp. 302–3.

[34] Harvey C Krentzman and John N Samaras, "Can Small Business Use Consultants," in *Growing Concerns*, ed. David E Gumpert (New York: John Wiley & Sons and *Harvard Business Review*, 1984), pp. 243–62.

FINANCIAL RESOURCES

Analyzing Financial Requirements

Once the opportunity has been assessed, once a new venture team has been formed, and once all resources needs have been identified, *then* is the time for a new venture to evaluate what financial resources are required and when. (Sources of financing and how to obtain funding are covered in detail in Part IV.)

As has been noted before, there is a temptation, in this area particularly, to place the cart before the horse. Entrepreneurs are tempted to begin their evaluation of business opportunities—and particularly their thinking about formal business plans—by analyzing spreadsheets, rather than focusing first on defining the opportunity, deciding how to seize it, and then preparing the financial estimates of what is required.

However, when the time comes to analyze financial requirements, it is important to realize that cash is the life's blood of a venture. As James Stancill, professor of finance at the University of Southern California's business school, has said: "Any company, no matter how big or small, moves on cash, not profits. You can't pay bills with profits, only cash. You can't pay employees with profits, only cash."[35] Financial resources are almost always limited, and important and significant trade-offs need to be made in evaluating a company's needs and the timing of those needs.

Spreadsheets

Computers and spreadsheet programs are tools that save time and increase productivity and creativity enormously. Spreadsheets are nothing more than pieces of accounting paper adapted for use with a computer. *Exhibit 10.4* shows a sample spreadsheet analysis done using Lotus 1-2-3 and Robert Morris Associates (RMA) data. (See Appendix I for information on using RMA data.)

The origins of the first spreadsheet program, VisiCalc, reveal its potential relevance for entrepreneurs. It was devised by an MBA student[36] while he was attending Harvard Business School. The student was faced with analyzing pro forma income statements and balance sheets, cash flows, and breakeven for his cases. The question "*What if* you assumed such and such?" was inevitably asked.

The major advantage of using spreadsheets to analyze capital requirements is having the ability to answer what-if questions. This takes on particular relevance also when one considers, as James Stancill points out:

> Usual measures of cash flow—net income plus depreciation (NIPD) or earnings before interest and taxes (EBIT)—give a realistic indication of a company's cash position only during a period of steady sales.[37]

Take cash flow projections. For example, an entrepreneur could answer a question such as, What if sales grow at just 5 percent, instead of 15 percent, and what if only 50 percent, instead of 65 percent, of amounts billed are paid in 30 days? The impact on cash flow of changes in these projections can be seen.

The same what-if process also can be applied to pro forma income statements and balance sheets, budgeting, and break-even calculations. To illustrate, by so altering assumptions about revenues and costs that cash reaches zero, breakeven can be analyzed. Thus, for example, RMA assumptions could be used as comparative boundaries for testing assumptions about a venture.

[35] Reprinted by permission of *Harvard Business Review*. An excerpt from "When Is There Cash in Cash Flow?" by James M. Stancill, March-April 1987, p. 38. Copyright © 1987 by the President and Fellows of Harvard College.

[36] Dan Bricklin.

[37] Stancill, "When Is There Cash in Cash Flow?" p. 38.

Exhibit 10.4
Sample Spreadsheet Analysis

OUTPUT GENERATED:

##################
Cash Budget
##################

	Months											
	1	2	3	4	5	6	7	8	9	10	11	12
CASH BALANCE (Opening)	$50,000	$31,235	$9,073	($18,917)	($50,811)	($85,583)	($122,252)	($173,852)	($228,743)	($293,067)	($359,823)	($431,361)
Plus RECEIPTS: Sales Collections	$2,725	$6,000	$9,675	$13,350	$17,025	$20,700	$24,375	$28,050	$34,350	$38,775	$42,750	$46,425
Other Proceeds	$0	$0	$2,000	$0	$2,000	$5,000	$0	$4,000	$0	$0	$0	$0
Total	$2,725	$6,000	$11,675	$13,350	$19,025	$25,700	$24,375	$32,050	$34,350	$38,775	$42,750	$46,425
Less DISBURSEMENTS: Raw Material Payables	$16,875	$20,625	$26,260	$31,875	$37,500	$43,125	$50,625	$60,000	$67,500	$71,250	$76,875	$82,500
Other Expenses (Accruals)	$4,494	$6,806	$9,169	$11,531	$13,894	$16,256	$19,313	$22,369	$25,706	$28,069	$30,431	$32,794
Fixed Asset Additions	$0	$0	$3,000	$0	$0	$0	$2,400	$0	$0	$0	$0	$0
Lease Expense	$0	$80	$80	$80	$80	$80	$80	$80	$80	$80	$80	$80
Long Term Debt Payments	$5	$5	$5	$5	$5	$5	$5	$5	$5	$5	$5	$5
Other Expenses (Itemized)	$0	$30	$0	$60	$20	$0	$0	$500	$0	$0	$0	$0
"Other Asset" Additions	$0	$0	$10	$0	$0	$0	$0	$0	$0	$0	$0	$0
Federal Taxes (Operations)	$238	$645	$1,048	$1,430	$1,863	$2,285	$2,678	$2,840	$3,915	$4,328	$4,740	$5,153
Total	$21,611	$28,191	$39,561	$44,981	$53,361	$61,751	$75,100	$85,794	$97,206	$103,731	$112,131	$120,531
Net Cash Gain (Loss)	($18,886)	($22,191)	($27,886)	($31,631)	($34,336)	($36,051)	($50,725)	($53,744)	($62,856)	($64,956)	($69,381)	($74,106)
Cumulative Cash Balance	$31,114	$9,044	($18,813)	($50,548)	($85,147)	($121,634)	($172,977)	($227,595)	($291,599)	($358,023)	($429,205)	($505,467)
Financial Income (Expense), net of tax	$121	$29	($104)	($263)	($436)	($618)	($875)	($1,148)	($1,468)	($1,800)	($2,156)	($2,537)
ENDING CASH BALANCE	$31,235	$9,073	($18,917)	($50,811)	($85,583)	($122,252)	($173,852)	($228,743)	($293,067)	($359,823)	($431,361)	($508,004)
Desired Cash Level	$2,000	$2,000	$2,000	$2,000	$2,000	$2,000	$2,000	$2,000	$2,000	$2,000	$2,000	$2,000
Loan Required to Maintain Minimum Cash Level	$0	$0	$20,813	$52,548	$87,147	$123,634	$174,977	$229,595	$293,599	$360,023	$431,205	$507,467
Cash Surplus	$29,114	$7,044	$0	$0	$0	$0	$0	$0	$0	$0	$0	$0

Exhibit 10.4
(continued)

OUTPUT GENERATED:

################## # Income Statement # ##################	Months											
	1	2	3	4	5	6	7	8	9	10	11	12
NET SALES	$5,000	$10,000	$15,000	$20,000	$25,000	$30,000	$35,000	$40,000	$50,000	$55,000	$60,000	$65,000
Allowance for Slippage of Sales Forecast	$1,250	$2,500	$3,750	$5,000	$6,250	$7,500	$8,750	$10,000	$12,500	$13,750	$15,000	$16,250
GROSS SALES	$3,750	$7,500	$11,250	$15,000	$18,750	$22,500	$26,250	$30,000	$37,500	$41,250	$45,000	$48,750
Less: Materials Used	$1,875	$3,750	$5,625	$7,500	$9,375	$11,250	$13,125	$15,000	$18,750	$20,625	$22,500	$24,375
Direct Labor	$375	$750	$1,125	$1,500	$1,875	$2,250	$2,625	$3,000	$3,750	$4,125	$4,500	$4,875
Other Manufacturing Expense	$159	$319	$478	$638	$797	$956	$1,116	$1,275	$1,594	$1,753	$1,913	$2,072
Indirect Labor	$159	$319	$479	$638	$797	$956	$1,116	$1,275	$1,594	$1,753	$1,913	$2,072
COST OF GOODS SOLD	$2,569	$5,138	$7,706	$10,275	$12,844	$15,413	$17,981	$20,550	$25,688	$28,256	$30,825	$33,394
GROSS PROFIT	$1,181	$2,363	$3,544	$4,725	$5,906	$7,088	$8,269	$9,450	$11,813	$12,994	$14,175	$15,356
Less: Sales Expense	$188	$375	$563	$750	$938	$1,125	$1,313	$1,500	$1,875	$2,063	$2,250	$2,438
General and Administrative Expense	$94	$188	$281	$375	$469	$563	$656	$750	$938	$1,031	$1,125	$1,219
Bad Debt Expense	$75	$150	$225	$300	$375	$450	$525	$600	$750	$825	$900	$975
Depreciation Expense, Fixed Assets	$250	$250	$300	$300	$300	$300	$340	$340	$340	$340	$340	$340
Lease Expense	$0	$80	$80	$80	$80	$80	$80	$80	$80	$80	$80	$80
Other Expenses (Itemized Above)	$0	$30	$0	$60	$20	$0	$0	$500	$0	$0	$0	$0
OPERATING PROFIT	$575	$1,290	$2,095	$2,860	$3,725	$4,570	$5,355	$5,680	$7,830	$8,655	$9,480	$10,305
Income Taxes on Operations	$238	$645	$1,048	$1,430	$1,863	$2,285	$2,678	$2,840	$3,915	$4,328	$4,740	$5,153
OTHER FINANCIAL REVENUE (EXPENSE)	$243	$59	($208)	($525)	($871)	($1,236)	($1,750)	($2,296)	($2,936)	($3,600)	($4,312)	($5,075)
Income Tax Provision	$121	$29	($104)	($263)	($436)	($618)	($875)	($1,148)	($1,468)	($1,800)	($2,156)	($2,537)
NET PROFIT	$459	$674	$944	$1,167	$1,427	$1,667	$1,803	$1,692	$2,447	$2,528	$2,584	$2,615

(Continued)

Exhibit 10.4
(continued)

LIST OF ASSUMPTIONS:

Months	1	2	3	4	5	6	7	8	9	10	11
Net Sales $	$5,000	$10,000	$15,000	$20,000	$25,000	$30,000	$35,000	$40,000	$50,000	$55,000	$60,000
Projected Sales, net of slippage	$3,750	$7,500	$11,250	$15,000	$18,750	$22,500	$26,250	$30,000	$37,500	$41,250	$45,000

YEAR	1984	1985	1986	1987	1988
Slippage of Sales Forecast, % of sales . . . What if?	25.0%	15.0%	10.0%	10.0%	5.0%
Material Costs, as % of sales	50.0%	48.0%	46.0%	45.0%	45.0%
Direct Labor, as % of sales	10.0%	10.0%	9.0%	9.0%	9.0%
Other expense (overhead, etc., but exclude depreciation), as % of sales	4.3%	4.3%	4.3%	4.3%	4.3%
Indirect Labor, as % of sales	4.3%	4.3%	4.3%	4.3%	4.3%
Sales expense, as % of sales	5.0%	4.0%	4.0%	4.0%	4.0%
General and administrative, $	2.5%	2.5%	2.5%	2.5%	2.5%
Federal income tax rate, % of Profit before Tax	50.0%				
What month does this analysis begin? (1-12)	1				
What is the present year?	1984				
Schedule B – Accounts Receivable Aging					
% Collections 0-30 Days	70%	70%	70%	80%	80%
% Collections 30-60 Days	20%	20%	20%	19%	19%
% Collections 60-90 Days	8%	8%	8%	0%	0%
% Uncollectable – Bad Debts	2%	2%	2%	1%	1%
Schedule C – Accounts Payable Aging (Raw Materials)					
% Payments 0-30 Days	100%	100%	80%	80%	80%
% Payments 30-60 Days	0%	0%	20%	20%	20%
% Payments 60-90 Days	0%	0%	0%	0%	0%
Schedule E – Direct Labor, Indirect Labor, M'fg Expense, Selling and G & A Expense, Accruals Aging					
% Payments 0-30 Days	100%	100%	90%	90%	90%
% Payments 30-60 Days	0%	0%	10%	10%	10%
Schedule F – Inventory Assumptions					
What is desired cash level? ($)	$2,000	$5,000	$7,000	$10,000	$10,000
How many months of finished goods inventory on hand?	2	2	3	3	3
How many months of raw materials inventory on hand?	3	3	4	4	4
Schedule G – Finanical Revenue and Term Debt Assumptions					
What interest is paid on outstanding loans to maintain desired cash level?	12%	12%	12%	15%	15%
What is your return on a cash surplus?	10%	10%	10%	11%	11%

Exhibit 10.4
(continued)

Schedule H—Beginning Balances, period one

ASSETS:	
Cash Balance	$50,000
Accounts Receivable	$100
Raw Materials Inventory	$100
Finished Goods Inventory	$300
Fixed Assets, Depreciable	$3,000
Accumulated Depreciation	$50
Other Assets, net	$200
Total Assets	$53,650

LIABILITIES:	
Raw Materials Payable	$100
Accruals Payable	$50
Notes Payable—Banks	$100
Long-Term Debt	$100
Contributed Capital	$500
Retained Earnings	$52,800
Total Liabilities + Equity	$53,650

Other—Present Loss Carryforward (−)	($100)

Schedule I—Cash Budget, Income Statement Monthly Changes $$

Months	1	2	3	4	5	6	7	8	9	10	11	12
Receipts (Cash Basis):												
Other Proceeds (LTD)	$0	$0	$2,000	$0	$2,000	$0	$0	$4,000	$0	$0	$0	$0
Contributed Capital Additions	$0	$0	$0	$0	$0	$5,000	$0	$0	$0	$0	$0	$0
Disbursements (Cash Basis):												
Long-Term Debt Payments	$5	$5	$5	$5	$5	$5	$5	$5	$5	$5	$5	$5
Other Expenses	$0	$30	$0	$60	$20	$0	$0	$500	$0	$0	$0	$0
"Other Asset" Additions, non-depreciable	$0	$0	$10	$0	$0	$0	$0	$0	$0	$0	$0	$0

Schedule J—Fixed Asset Additions	Asset 1	Asset 2	Asset 3
	-------	-------	-------
CURRENT ASSETS:			
Amount	$3,000		
Depreciation Period	1		
YEAR 1:			
Amount	$2,400	$3,000	$2,400
Month Bought (1-12)	2	3	7
Depreciation Period or Lease Term	3	5	5
Cash Basis = 1 / Lease = 2	2	1	1
YEAR 2:			
Amount	$3,600	$3,600	$3,600
Month Bought (1-12)	1	6	6
Depreciation Period or Lease Term	5	5	5
Cash Basis = 1 / Lease = 2	1	1	1
YEAR 3:			
Amount	$4,000	$4,000	$5,000
Date Bought	2	3	2
Depreciation Period or Lease Term	3	3	3
Cash Basis = 1 / Lease = 2	2	2	1

NOTE : YEARS FOUR AND FIVE ASSUMPTIONS SAME AS ABOVE

(Continued)

While it was exhilarating to think that they would be able to buy Fenchel, Steve and Michele were also painfully aware of the risks. Steve would have to resign from his consulting job at Bain & Company, in Boston, and Michele would have to leave her job in the admissions office at Harvard Business School. They and their two small children would have to move from Boston to Chicago, where Michele would find a new full-time job and Steve would take over responsibility for managing Fenchel. They had no illusions about what it would mean to own and run a small company, one that would be highly leveraged after the deal. On the other hand, that is what they had always wanted to do, and now, it seemed, it would finally be possible.

Background

The search for a business to own had begun for Steve and Michele Rogers while Steve was still in his first year in the MBA program at Harvard Business School (HBS). After careful study, he had decided that he should try to buy a McDonald's franchise. McDonald's was actively seeking African-American owners for the Boston area and Steve felt he could find an attractive opportunity with McDonald's help. At the beginning of his second year at HBS, he enrolled in a mandatory McDonald's training program for people interested in owning a franchise. While his classmates ate at the Charles Hotel or flew to New York for meals at Cote Basque, Steve spent 20 hours a week training at a McDonald's store in Lynn, Massachusetts. He did everything from cooking hamburgers to cleaning the lavatories.

After graduating from HBS in June 1985, Steve took a job as a research associate for the Production and Operations Management course at Harvard Business School. Michele, who was pregnant with their second child, was entering her second year at HBS. Steve continued his duties at the McDonald's restaurant. The work was hard and not very glamorous but Steve was committed to the program. Owning a McDonald's franchise and ultimately owning a number of stores would be a lucrative and demanding outcome. In the spring of 1986, Steve began serious negotiations with McDonald's about which store he might be able to buy and the terms. Each McDonald's franchise was priced according to its potential sales volume.

McDonald's suggested that Steve buy a franchise in downtown Boston. After considerable investigation, however, Steve became concerned that the opportunity was not very attractive. The price was too high—on the order of $650,000 for a store with sales of approximately $1 million—given what Steve perceived to be the prospects of the location. McDonald's asking price was based on what Steve thought to be unrealistically optimistic assumptions about what the store could do in the future. After exploring several other store possibilities, and after sometimes heated discussions with McDonald's, Steve finally decided to abandon his two years of training and the related plan to buy a McDonald's franchise.

In the summer of 1986, Steve decided to join Bain & Company, a major international consulting company with headquarters in Boston. After graduation from the MBA program, Michele stayed on at Harvard Business School in the admissions area. Though both were making a lot of money and enjoyed their work, they still wanted to own their own business.

A number of Steve's consulting assignments with Bain took him to the Midwest, where he and Michele had grown up. Steve started the process of trying to find a company to buy in that area. He contacted a number of business brokers, commercial bankers, accountants, and law firms in Chicago, and also began to subscribe to the Chicago papers. Over time he began to receive proposals from his contacts. On his frequent visits to the area, he would meet with representatives of the sellers or visit the company. In total, he saw some 25 companies in early 1987. Discouragingly, none was particularly attractive.

The Fenchel Lampshade Company

In May 1987, Steve was contacted by a business broker about the possibility that a lampshade manufacturing company might be for sale. He had already seen one lampshade company, which he had rejected because it focused on the highly competitive low end of the market, had terrible management, and was egregiously overpriced. But Fenchel sounded different. They were a manufacturer of premium lampshades with total sales volume of about $1 million.

Steve flew to Chicago to meet the broker representing the owners and was favorably impressed by what he heard. The company was managed by 65-year-old Kenneth Fenchel, whose father and uncle had founded the company in 1926. The company was owned by Kenneth and his uncle and aunt, who had assumed control when Kenneth's father passed away. Kenneth's uncle was 88 years old and was effectively retired from the business. The company was profitable and had provided the owners with an attractive income stream for many years.

It was also apparent to Steve that the business had not been very aggressively managed. Sales growth had been modest, and Steve was convinced that he could improve the operations of the company.

While Steve's original meeting with the broker representing the Fenchel family was positive, it soon became clear that the Fenchel family was not totally committed to selling the business. Each year they owned Fenchel Lampshades, income was very high. Aside from a desire to retire and concerns about health, there was no real pressure to sell.

Also, the Fenchels had placed an $800,000 total value on the company and had insisted that all of the money be paid up front. They were unwilling to consider any kind of seller financing. For Steve and Michele Rogers, this was an unacceptable demand, given the inevitable uncertainties associated with taking over any business. Without seller financing, also, it might be much more difficult to arrange other elements of the financing plan.

Steve's hope of working out a mutually acceptable deal was dashed on December 7, 1987, when Ken Fenchel called to say that he had decided not to sell, and that he intended to take the company off the market. This call came exactly one week after Steve, Ken, and their respective lawyers and accountants had met for over nine hours to finalize the terms of a letter of intent.

While disappointed, Steve and Michele were more committed than ever to buying a company. Moreover, they had decided that Fenchel was perfect for their plans. The company was profitable, generated attractive cash flows, and was affordable. Their conversations with the business broker representing the Fenchels had suggested that there might be another opportunity to buy the company if they were patient. As a result, Steve and Michele suspended their active search for another company.

At the same time, they decided to move to Chicago regardless of the outcome at Fenchel. Steve believed that he would be able to continue his work as a consultant for Bain, which was considering opening a Chicago office, and Michele had arranged to work for James Lowry & Co., a Chicago-based consulting company. They planned to move in mid-summer of 1988.

Back on Track

In April, Steve received a call from the broker representing the Fenchels, who said that it made sense to talk. Ken Fenchel was considering selling the company again. However, a preliminary meeting in May revealed that Ken's uncle was still adamantly opposed to seller financing.

Steve proceeded to line up various potential sources of capital on the assumption that he could work out a reasonable solution to the impasse with the Fenchel family. Steve was convinced that he could get the Fenchel family to take a $75,000 note back for part of the agreed-upon $745,000 purchase price. He and Michele were prepared to invest $50,000 of their own money as a starting point. With respect to the other capital, there were a number of options.

First, Fenchel had certain assets that could be pledged as collateral. Steve intended to apply for a Small Business Administration loan. Under this program, banks agreed to lend money to small businesses and up to 85 percent of the principal amount of the loan was guaranteed by the US government. Thus, at least some of the risk was passed off on the government, which resulted in significantly lower interest costs.

Steve hoped to gain access to other debt financing by going to certain state and local programs that had been set up to make investments in local businesses. The City of Chicago had such a program from which Steve hoped to raise $100,000. An additional $50,000 would hopefully come from a State of Illinois loan program.

With respect to the remaining capital required, Steve knew that he would have to gain access to some equitylike financing. There were no other assets to pledge, and every lender would insist on some equity base before loaning the money.

One possibility was to go to a MESBIC (Minority Enterprise Small Business Investment Corporation). The MESBIC program was established by the Small Business Administration in 1969 for the purpose of providing long-term financing and management assistance to new ventures started by minorities. MESBICs were private companies that raised equity from individuals or institutions (often commercial banks) and were able to leverage their equity through government guarantees of loans. Under existing regulations, MESBICs could borrow up to four times their equity capital using government guarantees.

The next step was to turn possibilities into realities. The loan request documentation and related business plan prepared by Steve and Michele Rogers is included as Appendix A.

Remaining Issues

Steve and Michele had debated for hours about how much they should pay for Fenchel, how they should get access to the required capital, and what they should do if they were able to buy the company. Now it seemed that they were finally close. That was very exciting, but it was also slightly frightening. As Steve had discovered more than once during his search for a company to buy, being a Harvard MBA was not an automatic ticket to success. In his more cynical moments, he asked himself what he thought a snot-nosed 31 year old Harvard MBA knew about running a business. On the other hand, he was ready to find out.

APPENDIX A

Fenchel Lampshade Company
Loan Request

Table of Contents	*Section*	*Page*
Loan Request Summary	I	355
Business Plan Summary	II	355
Business Plan	III	356–364
Historical Financial Statements	IV	364–365
Projected Financial Statements	V	366–367
Sources and Uses of Funds Tables	VI	368

SECTION I: LOAN REQUEST SUMMARY

- Loan type: SBA loan.
- Amount: $300,000.
- Borrower: Steven and Michele Rogers.
- Purpose of loan: To purchase Fenchel Lampshade Company.
- Total cost of project: $745,000—does not include working capital.
- Other potential funding sources:
  - —The Chicago Capital Fund.
  - —The Neighborhood Fund.
  - —State of Illinois.
- Collateral: Assets of Fenchel Lampshade Company and personal guarantees of company's new owners, Steven and Michele Rogers.

SECTION II: BUSINESS PLAN SUMMARY

Steven and Michele Rogers are attempting to buy Fenchel Lampshade Company. Michele will serve as a consultant to the company while Steve works as a full-time owner/operator.

Fenchel is recognized as a leading manufacturer of premium-quality lampshades in the midwest. The company has annual sales in excess of $1 million with annual cash flow margins of 15–30 percent. The company is over 61 years old and is owned by Kenneth Fenchel, age 65, and his 88-year-old uncle and 73-year-old aunt. They are selling the business in order to retire.

In 1986, the lampshade industry had total sales of $70 million, a figure that has been growing at a rate of 5 percent since 1972. There are four identifiable segments in the industry. Fenchel operates in the premium-quality segment (approximately $20 million in 1986 volume) and sells to lamp specialty shops and upscale department stores.

Fenchel sells hard-back and fabric lampshades. All of the lampshades are hand made and have wholesale prices of $5 to $35. The company has 65 accounts. Marshall Field's is the company's largest customer, accounting for 10 percent of sales in 1986.

While there are 34 lampshade manufacturers in the country, competition in the industry is generally restricted to geographical regions due to the extremely high cost of transportation. Most manufacturers are in New York or New Jersey.

The acquirers are both graduates of the Harvard Business School. Steven was born and raised on Chicago's south side where he attended Lewis Champlin grammar school and Englewood high school. He has work experience as a manager, business analyst, and consultant. As the supervisor of customer services with Cummins, he managed eight unionized employees. He also has negotiating and financial analysis experience as a result of working as a purchasing agent with Consolidated Diesel Company and as a business analyst with UNC Venture Capital Company. Finally, his work with Bain as a general management consultant has enhanced his ability to solve business problems through the use of analytical tools and has trained him to be an effective task force leader.

Michele has a strong work history in personnel administration. She has worked for Cummins Engine Company in personnel administration and labor relations, Harvard University in development, and Harvard Business School in admissions. Michele will be employed full-time with James Lowry and Associates, a Chicago-based consulting firm, but will be available for consultation at Fenchel.

John Smith, who has been with Fenchel for 15 years, will continue his position as the supervisor of production. Gerri Wandall, who has been the office manager for the past five years, will also continue in her present position.

The diversified labor force at Fenchel will remain after the acquisition. Of the 18 employees, 15 are female, 13 are Black, 2 Hispanic, 2 White, and 1 Asian. Their length of employment with Fenchel ranges from 1 to 21 years.

This combination of characteristics—a loyal and diversified customer base, an experienced and dedicated labor force, and strong cash flow that can meet debt service requirements—makes Fenchel an ideal acquisition candidate.

SECTION III: BUSINESS PLAN

The Company

Fenchel Lampshade Company is a manufacturer of premium-quality rayon, acetate, and hard back–covered lampshades for the replacement market. In addition to diverse materials, Fenchel lampshades vary by style, shape, and color. All of the lampshades are made in response to customer orders, with delivery commitments ranging from 4 to 6 weeks.

Fenchel's customers include department stores, independent lamp and shade retail stores, lighting showrooms, and a few (about 2 percent) lamp manufacturers. Of the company's sales, 80 percent are made to customers in the midwest.

The name *Fenchel* is well regarded in the industry because of the company's strong reputation for high-quality products. To take advantage of Fenchel's strong customer name recognition, customers, such as Gatelys and Marshall Field's, regularly use the name in their advertisements.

In 1926 Herbert Fenchel (born in 1900) incorporated the company in Chicago. The corporation became a partnership in 1947 when Herbert's wife, Lois Fenchel (born in 1915), joined the company. That same year, Herbert's nephew, I. Kenneth Fenchel (born in 1923), began working for the company as a salesman. In 1957 Kenneth became an equal partner with Herbert and Lois.

For the past five years Kenneth has operated the company alone; Herbert and Lois have been silent partners. For health reasons Herbert and Lois live in Florida six months each year.

The Industry

The domestic lampshade industry has total annual volume of approximately $70 million spread over 34 manufacturers. The manufacturers are located in seven states; over half of them are in the New York/New Jersey area. The typical manufacturer is a family-owned business with over 25 years of experience in the industry. Since 1972 the industry's compounded annual growth rate has been 5 percent (*Exhibit A*).

The lampshade industry is seasonal. The slow season is summer, when people usually spend most of their time outdoors and are not making internal home improvements. Less than 15 percent of all sales will be made during the months of June, July, and August. The best sales period occurs through the remaining nine months when people typically spend more time aside. The strongest months for sales are before holidays such as Thanksgiving, Christmas, and Easter.

There are four categories of lampshade manufacturing: lamp manufacturing companies (e.g., Alsy and Stiffel) with internal lampshade production, independent lampshade manufacturers that sell primarily to lamp manufacturers, low- to medium-quality lampshade manufacturers (e.g., Lampshade, Inc.) with discount stores as their primary customers, and premium-quality lampshade manufacturers that sell to lamp specialty shops and upscale department stores. The latter category, which includes Fenchel, is a market of approximately $20 million.

Exhibit A
Historical Lampshade Sales

Year	Lampshade Sales*
1972	$36,900,000
1973	42,800,000
1974	43,300,000
1975	41,500,000
1976	37,800,000
1977	51,400,000
1978	55,400,000
1979	58,900,000
1980	53,400,000
1981	59,100,000
1982	41,800,000
1983	45,300,000
1984	65,400,000
1985	70,100,000

*Does not include metal, plastic, or glass lampshades.

Source: Census Bureau Annual Survey of Manufacturing Value of Product Shipments.

Product Description

Fenchel's products serve the premium-quality segment of the market. Every lampshade is completely handmade, with all stages of production carefully supervised and inspected. All fabrics are sewn to the frames, not glued. All frames are rust resistant. The trims and folds are bonded to the shade to ensure hand washability. In addition, the lampshades are wrinkle resistant, glare free, and shadow free. In fact, Fenchel advertises itself as the industry leader of shadow-free lampshades. All of these characteristics in one lampshade are very rare, thereby giving Fenchel a reputation for high quality and workmanship. Only two other manufacturers, Silk-o-Lite and Diane, in the New York/New Jersey area, produce lampshades of similar quality.

Fenchel's lampshades can be divided into two categories, fabric and hard back. Fabric lampshades are manufactured using various fabrics on the exterior with satin internal backings. Fenchel sells fabric lampshades in six different styles, 16 shapes, six materials, four colors, and seven trims. These lampshades have historically accounted for 63 percent to 74 percent of the company's sales and 64 percent to 76 percent of the company's profits.

Hard-back shades have various fabrics on the exterior and laminated or vinyl internal backings. Fenchel's hard-back lampshades are distinctive because, unlike competitive products, they are made with more material, which leads to better defined pleats. In addition, Fenchel's products are made with thicker vinyl or laminated backing and heavier frames than competitive products. The end result is a more durable and beautiful lampshade. The company's hard-back lampshades are sold in two different styles and five shapes. These lampshades have historically accounted for 26 percent to 37 percent of the company's sales and 24 percent to 36 percent of profits.

The wholesale price range of Fenchel lampshades is $5 to $35. The average selling price is $15. These shades will ultimately be sold by a retailer at prices from $20 to $65.

Fenchel's average wholesale price of $15 compares to $6 for a lampshade from a low- to medium-quality manufacturer such as Lampshades, Inc., which sells primarily to discount department stores.

In addition to producing a standard line of lampshades highlighted in its catalog (*Exhibit B*), Fenchel accepts custom work. The company will manufacture lampshades to a

Exhibit B
Description of Fenchel Lampshades

It is with great pride that we introduce our first catalog. Its purposes are to simplify and facilitate your ordering and to show, in detail, the wide scope of the Fenchel lamp shade line.

For more than 50 years, Fenchel Lamp Shade Company has built a reputation for value and workmanship.

All fabrics are sewn—not glued—to assure beauty and quality. A wide array of materials is available.
All rust-resistant frames are offered in an extensive variety of shapes and sizes.
We lead the industry in shadow-free shades.
Trims and folds are bonded to the shade to insure washability.
All stages of production are carefully supervised and inspected.

We hope you find this catalog convenient, and that you continue to avail yourselves of Fenchel lamp shades, and the high standards of excellence they represent.

Fenchel
Lamp Shades

customer's specifications or even design an exclusive line for a customer (e.g., Marshall Field's).

Customers

As a manufacturer of premium-quality lampshades, Fenchel has a stable and loyal customer base. Over 60 percent of their annual sales are to upscale department stores such as Marshall Field's, headquartered in Chicago; the May Company, headquartered in St. Louis; and Lazarus, headquartered in Indianapolis. The only lampshades sold by these stores are Fenchel's. (In fact, the Marshall Field's State Street store in Chicago has an area on the fourth floor, approximately 12 feet by 12 feet, dedicated entirely to Fenchel lampshades). The balance of sales are to independent retail stores, lighting showrooms, and lamp manufacturers.

Fifty of Fenchel's 65 customer accounts are located in the midwest. Some 45 customers account for 80 percent of total sales. The largest customer is Marshall Field's, which operates 25 stores in metropolitan Chicago, Texas, and Wisconsin and accounts for 10 percent of total sales.

Typical orders are \$10,000 to \$25,000 from department stores and \$400 to \$2,000 from independent retail stores.

Unlike customers for low- to medium-quality lampshades, Fenchel's customers do not base their purchase decisions on price alone. These customers view product quality and delivery to be just as important as price. Thus, Fenchel's reputation for impeccable quality and service for over 50 years has resulted in a very loyal customer base. For example, Marshall Field's has been a Fenchel customer for 20 years.

Exhibit C
American Lampshade Manufacturers

Lampshade Manufacturer	*Location*
1. ABC Lampshade Company.	New York
2. Artemis Studios.	New York
3. Diane Studios.	New York
4. Edwards Lamp and Shade Company.	California
5. Else Lamp and Shade Studio.	New York
6. Elite Lamp Shade Manufacturing.	California
7. Gold-Ray Shades.	New Jersey
8. H. Grabell and Sons.	New Jersey
9. Grabell Industries.	California
10. Hamilton Corporation.	Illinois
11. Hirks Lane Lamp Parts.	Pennsylvania
12. Lake Shore Studios.	Mississippi
13. Lampshades, Inc.	Illinois
14. Loumel Corporation.	New Jersey
15. MSWV, Inc.	Illinois
16. Natalie Lamp and Shade Company.	New Jersey
17. Paladin Lampshade.	Pennsylvania
18. Penn Shade Crafters.	Pennsylvania
19. Queen Anne Lampshades.	New Jersey
20. RLR Industries.	New York
21. Robinson Lamp Parts.	New York
22. Roseart Lampshades.	New York
23. Saxe lampshade.	Pennsylvania
24. Silk-O-Lite.	New Jersey
25. Springel Sales.	Pennsylvania
26. Standard Shade.	New York
27. Stiffel.	New York
28. William B. Venit.	Illinois
29. Versaponents.	New York
30. Frederick Cooper.	Illinois
31. Foss.	California
32. Style Craft.	New York
33. Rod International.	Florida
34. Fenchel.	Illinois

Source: Lamp and Shade Institute of America.

Competition

Although there are 34 American lampshade manufacturers (*Exhibit C*), competition in the industry is regional due to extremely high transportation costs. Lampshades are bulky but light in weight, which creates strong regional barriers to entry. Those premium-quality lampshade manufacturers located in the New York/New Jersey area find it cost prohibitive to enter the midwest region.

The five other lampshade manufacturers in the midwest are not competitors of Fenchel because their product focus is the low/medium market.

Silk-o-Lite, a 60-year-old New Jersey firm with sales in excess of $2 million, is Fenchel's closest competitor.

Fenchel's strong reputation for quality and service, combined with prohibitive shipping costs, make it very difficult for a competitor outside of the midwest to take away any of Fenchel's market without engaging in predatory pricing.

Marketing and Sales Plan

Fenchel had a 1.3 percent compound annual growth rate in sales from 1983 to 1986. This minuscule rate of growth reflected Kenneth Fenchel's choice not to aggressively market the company's products. He did not want sales to grow because it would require more of his time, which he did not want to give at this stage of his life. The business cash flow of approximately $140,000 annually was more than enough to satisfy him, his uncle, and his aunt.

By taking a more aggressive approach in marketing and sales, the company can grow at $100,000 to $500,000 annually. Steven's strategy for growing the company will include a continuation of Fenchel's present marketing practices, such as maintaining the co-op advertising program with 20 department stores, the annual product catalog that is mailed to 200 prospective customers, attending the two annual lamp and lampshade trade shows (Kenneth will attend one with Steven), and advertising in lamp and lampshade journals (*Exhibit D*). Steven will also continue the practice of employing manufacturing representatives, which is common throughout the industry. Fenchel's representatives account for 33 percent of sales. Finally, Steven will service the same 20 in-house accounts that are presently being

Exhibit D
Fenchel Trade Journal Advertising

Fenchel

lamp shade co.

NOT INC

612 SOUTH CLINTON • CHICAGO, ILLINOIS 60607
(312) 922-6454-55-56 • 1-800-345-1456

WE'RE OVER 64 YRS. YOUNG

And We Thank You For Your
Continued Support And Confidence

We know the needs of the consumer and provide you with the quality, fashion, value and service to meet their demands.

Why tie your money up in inventory carrying costs?
We have outstanding delivery!

We welcome your visit in Dallas
World Trade Center — Room 10015
where you'll see many exciting
new additions to our lines

certain territories available for
experienced reps

managed by the owner. Kenneth will visit each of the accounts with Steven for introductory purposes and to assure the customers that product quality and service will be maintained.

In addition, Steven will make several changes. First, he will do a thorough analysis of each form of advertising to gauge effectiveness. The data from this analysis will tell him where advertising dollars should be spent in order to achieve a higher return on investment. Next, he will hire and train more manufacturing representatives in an attempt to increase the number of customers in the independent lamp and lampshade retail stores and lighting showrooms. Both of these potential customer groups are ideal for Fenchel lampshades and are experiencing significant growth in affluent suburban areas.

The addition of more manufacturing representatives will be a variable cost since they are entirely compensated via commissions. The present commission system gives a representative 10 percent of any revenues generated. The commission is paid on the 10th of each month following product delivery. Such a system does not encourage the opening of new accounts since the representative gets the same percentage for a new account order as for an order from an existing customer. Therefore, the third change that Steven will make is to give a one-time bonus for new account orders.

Fourth, he will personally market Fenchel's lampshades to the premium-quality lamp manufacturers. Opportunities are definitely available in this market, based on the statement of Peter Gershanov, vice president of Frederick Cooper, to Steven that only two lamp manufacturers, Frederick Cooper and Stiffel, make their own lampshades while the others purchase them from an outside manufacturer. This industry, with sales in excess of $2 billion, is too large to continue to ignore.

He will also seek to increase sales by pursuing untapped accounts in the midwest, such as Ehr's Lamp Shade Shoppe in Waukesha, Wisconsin, which carries Silk-o-Lite, but not Fenchel, lampshades.

Other opportunities will come from new kinds of customers not presently served by Fenchel. These potential customers include interior decorating companies, mail-order catalogs, upscale hotels, hospitals, colleges, upscale convalescent homes, and the government.

As a minority-owned company, Steven anticipates opportunities to increase revenue by selling to local, state, and federal government agencies through the 8(a) Set Aside Program (*Exhibit E*).

As a former purchasing agent, minority supplier coordinator, and member of the National Minority Purchasing Council, Steven is aware that many private corporations have minority supplier programs where buyers actively search to buy from minority-owned businesses. He intends to take advantage of such opportunities.

The opportunity to increase sales in upscale department stores will also present itself because of the presence of minority vendor programs in stores such as Bloomingdale's, I. Magnin, and Lazarus (*Exhibit F*). Steven's ability to take advantage of such programs will be enhanced by the efforts of organizations such as the Black Retailers Action Group (BRAG). One of the group's goals, as explained by Mr. J. Thomas, the president of BRAG and also a vice president of Bloomingdale's, "is to increase the volume of dollars spent by major retailers with minority-owned manufacturers." Thus, with Fenchel's excellent reputation it should not be difficult to take advantage of such opportunities.

Another department store opportunity should come from Marshall Field's expansion. On September 18, 1987, the *Chicago Tribune* newspaper reported that "a new Marshall Field's store will open in Columbus, Ohio, next year as the start of an expansion campaign in the midwest." Hopefully, as they expand, their demand for Fenchel lampshades will increase.

The most important thing about Fenchel's future marketing and sales efforts is that an increase in revenues will occur from selling to customers interested in Fenchel's premium-quality products. The Fenchel reputation for quality, service, and value will not be compromised or sacrificed to increase short-term sales through price discounting.

Exhibit G
Selected Data on the Fenchel Work force

Number of Employees	*Years With Fenchel*
10	1–2
4	4
1	11
2	15
1	22
Number of Employees	*Age*
3	20–30 years old
3	31–40 years old
2	41–50 years old
10	51–60 years old

Steven will be intimately involved in the operations of Fenchel. His work experience (*Exhibit H*) includes general management duties with Cummins Engine Company, financial analysis with UNC Venture Capital Ltd., and business analysis and problem solving with Bain Consulting, Ltd. Along with this diverse work background, he has a master of business administration degree from Harvard Business School.

With the assistance of Kenneth for three months, Steven plans to immerse himself in learning the lampshade business and nurturing relationships with customers and employees. His functional responsibilities will include marketing, sales, and purchasing. Finally, his main objective will be to bring in enough revenue to meet payroll, service debt, and maintain and expand the business.

While Steven will oversee the entire operation, the office manager and production supervisor will continue to manage their respective areas. This strategy will minimize disruptions and make the transfer of ownership as smooth as possible.

Gerri, the office manager for the past five years, will continue her present duties of order processing and bookkeeping. Her work in these areas will be enhanced by the introduction of a personal computer.

John, the 53-year-old production supervisor for the past 15 years, will also continue his present duties of managing production operations.

The skills and personalities of this group will complement each other and continue to result in an effective management team. The goals and objectives of the management team will be consistent on-time product delivery, improved product quality, reduced operating costs, labor productivity gains, increased sales and profits, and a happy labor force.

Potential Risks

While Fenchel has a long history of success in the lampshade business, there are several risks, which can all be managed proactively. The threat of department store consolidation is quite prevalent today. Thus, there is a chance that Fenchel could lose an account such as the May Company if May was purchased by another department store that wanted to stock its stores with lampshades from a company other than Fenchel. To minimize this risk, Steven will continue to keep the customer base diversified and not become too dependent on department stores, in general, or on any specific store. Steven believes it is safe to have the largest customer account be no more than 15 percent of total sales.

Exhibit H
Resume of Steven Rogers

STEVEN ROGERS

Education 1983–1985	**HARVARD GRADUATE SCHOOL OF BUSINESS ADMINISTRATION** **BOSTON, MA** Master in Business Administration, general management curriculum. Member of Venture Capital Club and the Afro-American Student Union. COGME Fellow. Resident Director of Wellesley High School "A Better Chance" program.
1975–1979	**WILLIAMS COLLEGE** **WILLIAMSTOWN, MA** Bachelor of Arts. Liberal arts program with a major in history. Deans List. Recipient of Lehman Scholarship, Black Student Leadership Award, and Belvedere Brooks Memorial Medal. Varsity Football. Member of ECAC Division II All-Star Football Team. Treasurer of Black Student Union. Resident Tutor of Mount Greylock High School "A Better Chance" program. Tutor at Monroe State Prison.
Employment Experience 1986–Present	**BAIN AND COMPANY** Consultant. Case team member on consulting assignments for Fortune 500 corporations in the health care, glassware, electronics, and manufacturing industries. Researched and analyzed financial, market, and productivity data for use in developing and implementing performance improvement strategies. Managed client task forces and teams.
1985–1986	**HARVARD BUSINESS SCHOOL** Research Associate. Wrote and published business school case studies concerning various manufacturing businesses. Collected data through statistical analyses, field work, interviews, and library research. Subjects included rubber products, health care, and communications industries.
Summer 1984	**UNC VENTURES, INC.** **BOSTON, MA** Summer Associate. Assessed the market and return potential of proposals for venture capital financing. Performed detailed investigation of selected ventures; analyzed proposed strategy, market conditions, management qualifications, valuation, and pricing terms. Completed legal synopses, business overviews, and internal rate of return and investment recovery analyses for portfolio companies. Attended UNC Ventures Board of Directors meeting. Visited portfolio companies. Reported directly to the President.
1981–1983	**CONSOLIDATED DIESEL COMPANY** **WHITAKERS, NC** Original member of company's start-up team on $450MM project. Commodity Manager of direct and indirect materials. Responsible for $15MM in purchases annually. Negotiated long-term commodity and service contracts. Initiated source selection and approval. Implemented engineering changes. Controlled price increases. Purchased material from foreign suppliers. Consolidated Minority Supplier Program. Interfaced with manufacturing, accounting, finance, engineering, quality, transportation, and marketing. Completed 75% of examinations for National Certified Purchasing Manager certification.
1979–1981	**CUMMINS ENGINE COMPANY** **COLUMBUS, IN** Supervisor of Customer Services Parts Department. Trained and supervised eight employees responsible for entering, administering, and expediting parts ordered by distributors. Developed an order entry presentation for visitor orientation program. Coordinated distributor ownership transfers. Supported Marketing's $100MM special parts program.
Personal Background	Head coach, PAL Football team, "A Better Chance" student at Radnor High School in Pennsylvania. Raised in Chicago, Illinois. Guardian of 11-year-old sister for six years. Married with two daughters. NACEL host family. Interests include traveling, reading, and participating in all sports.

Another risk is the threat of a competitor locating in Chicago or the midwest. The Fenchel reputation will be a very difficult obstacle for any new competitor to overcome. But Steven will not rely solely on Fenchel's name. He will maintain close relationships with customers to ensure that Fenchel's lampshades completely meet their quality and delivery expectations. He will also manage costs in order to provide the customer with a product that is competitively priced without discounting. Therefore, Fenchel will be able to maintain and grow market share by emphasizing customer service as it relates to quality, delivery, and costs.

Balance Sheet (best-case scenario)

	1988	*1989*	*1990*
Assets			
Current assets:			
Cash	$ 20,000	$ 25,000	$ 30,000
Accounts receivable	135,000	180,000	225,000
Allowance for uncollectibles	(8,000)	(8,000)	(8,000)
Merchandise inventories	105,000	140,000	175,000
Prepaid rent	4,250	4,250	4,250
Total current assets	256,250	341,250	426,250
Machinery, furniture, and fixtures at cost	50,000	50,000	50,000
Total assets	$316,250	$391,250	$476,250
Liabilities and Equity			
Current liabilities:			
Accounts payable	$105,000	$140,000	$175,000
Other expenses	75,000	100,000	125,000
Total current liabilities	180,000	240,000	300,000
Long-term debt	550,000	440,000	330,000
Total liabilities	$730,000	$680,000	$630,000

Income Statement (worst-case scenario)

	1988	*1989*	*1990*
Net sales	$1,100,000	$1,200,000	$1,300,000
Cost of sales:			
Materials	407,000	444,000	481,000
Direct labor	143,000	156,000	169,000
Other costs	44,000	48,000	52,000
Total costs	594,000	648,000	702,000
Gross profit	506,000	552,000	598,000
Operating expenses:			
Factory	154,000	168,000	182,000
Selling	110,000	120,000	130,000
Administrative	33,000	36,000	39,000
Total expenses	297,000	324,000	351,000
Income before owners' salary	209,000	228,000	247,000
Owners' salary	50,000	60,000	70,000
Income before debt payments	$ 159,000	$ 168,000	$ 177,000

Balance Sheet (worst-case scenario)

	1988	*1989*	*1990*
Assets			
Current assets:			
Cash	$ 11,000	$ 12,000	$ 13,000
Accounts receivable	99,000	108,000	117,000
Allowance for uncollectibles	(8,000)	(8,000)	(8,000)
Merchandise inventories	77,000	84,000	91,000
Prepaid rent	4,250	4,250	4,250
Total current assets	183,250	200,250	217,250
Machinery, furniture, and fixtures at cost	50,000	50,000	50,000
Total assets	$233,250	$250,250	$267,250
Liabilities and Equity			
Current liabilities:			
Accounts payable	$105,000	$110,000	$115,000
Other expenses	55,000	60,000	65,000
Total current liabilities	160,000	170,000	180,000
Long-term debt	550,000	440,000	330,000
Total liabilities	$710,000	$610,000	$510,000

SECTION VI: SOURCES AND USES OF FUNDS TABLES

Table 1
Proposed Sources and Uses of Funds, 1988

Sources of funds:	
Bank (SBA loan)	$300,000
Fenchel trade debt	105,000
City of Chicago	100,000
MESBIC/SBIC	115,000
Fenchel family	75,000
State of Illinois	50,000
Steven and Michele Rogers	50,000
Total sources of funds	$795,000
Use of funds:	
Accounts receivable	$120,000
Inventory	125,000
Machinery, equipment, and patterns	100,000
Noncompete clause (five years)	400,000
Working capital	50,000
Total uses of funds	$795,000

Table 2
Terms of Sources of Funds

Source	*Amount*	*Form*	*Terms*
1. Bank Loan.	$300,000	Senior debt	Prime plus 2%
2. City of Chicago.	$100,000	Subordinated debt (second position)	75% of prime 60 monthly payments
3. State of Illinois.	$ 50,000	Subordinated debt (third position)	5% 60 monthly payments
4. Fenchel family.	$ 75,000	Subordinated debt (fourth position)	10% 60 monthly payments of $1,592.95
5. Fenchel trade debt.	$105,000		Normal terms of invoices
6. MESBIC/SBIC.	$115,000	Equity (15-25%); Preferred stock	9% cumulative dividend of $2,600 paid quarterly Redeem preferred stock at beginning of Year 4

EXERCISE—FINANCIAL STATEMENTS

For most entrepreneurs, preparing financial statements is a pain. To help make the preparation of financial statements easier, William D. Bygrave, professor in entrepreneurial studies at Babson College, prepared a guide for students at Babson College. The Financial Statements Exercise is based on this guide and will help you get *started.* See also information in Appendices I and II.

Entrepreneurs use the following basic financial statements:

- Income statements, monthly for the first two years and then quarterly for the next three years.
- Cash flow statements, monthly for the first two years and then quarterly for the next three years.
- Balance sheets, yearly for five years.

Exhibit 10.5
Balance Sheet

BYGRAVE & SCHUMAN, INC.
Balance Sheet
Years Ending December 31
($1,000)

	1989	*1990*	*1991*	*1992*	*1993*
ASSETS					
Current:					
Cash	$255				
A/R*	100				
Inventory	49				
Rent deposit	9				
Utilities dep.	2				
Total	$415				
LIABILITIES					
Current:					
A/P†	$ 15				
Bank loan	60				
Long-term:					
Bank loan	240				
Equity pd.-in	20				
Ret. earnings	80				
Total	$415				

* A/R means Accounts Receivable.
† A/P means Accounts Payable.

Exhibit 10.6
Assumptions for Financial Statements

(1) Wages and salaries are paid in month they are earned (i.e., no accruals).
(2) Material is paid for one month after purchase.
(3) Finished goods are shipped and booked as sales in the month after they were manufactured.
(4) Payment terms are net 30 days; so A/R equals revenue in the prior month.
(5) There are prepaid deposits for rent and utilities.
(6) Insurance is paid quarterly.
(7) Income tax is paid in the current month (i.e., no accruals or deferrals). (It is a crude approximation.)
(8) Loan is to be repaid in Years 2 through 6.
(9) Ending inventory is the cost of goods sold (CGS) in the following month (i.e., the goods manufactured in the current month are sold next month).

The "Financial Statements" exercise will help you generate financial statements like those shown in *Exhibit 10.5* through *Exhibit 10.7.* These financial statements were created for a fictional company, Bygrave & Schuman, Inc., a start-up business that manufactures alternative lifestyle bicycles. In the exercise, the fiscal year is the calendar year.

The exercise is a guide to get you started, and it is based on a very simple example. Accounting in your venture will most likely be more complicated. For example, you could use LIFO (last in/first out) or FIFO (first in/first out) in accounting for inventory, you may have fixed assets and need to choose from different methods of depreciation, and so forth. There are excellent texts available. It also is recommended that you consult an accountant.

Exhibit 10.7
Income and Cash Flow Statements

BYGRAVE & SCHUMAN, INC.
Income Statement
($1,000)

	1989 Jan.	*Feb.*	*Mar.*	*Apr.*	*May*	*June*	*July*	*Aug.*	*Sept.*	*Oct.*	*Nov.*	*Dec.*	*1989 Total Year*
Revenues	$ 0	$100	$150	$200	$200	$150	$100	$ 50	$100	$100	$200	$100	$1,450
Material	0	15	23	30	30	23	15	8	15	15	30	15	218
Labor	0	30	45	60	60	45	30	15	30	30	60	30	435
Bldg. rent	0	2	2	2	2	2	2	2	2	2	2	2	22
Equip. rent	0	2	2	2	2	2	2	2	2	2	2	2	22
Total CGS	0	49	72	94	94	72	49	27	49	49	94	49	697
Gross income	$ 0	$ 51	$ 79	$106	$106	$ 79	$ 51	$ 24	$ 51	$ 51	$106	$ 51	$ 754
Salaries	20	20	20	20	20	20	20	20	20	20	20	20	240
Marketing	20	20	20	20	20	20	5	5	20	20	20	20	210
Utilities	5	5	5	5	5	5	5	5	5	5	5	5	60
Insurance	4	4	4	4	4	4	4	4	4	4	4	4	48
Office rent	1	1	1	1	1	1	1	1	1	1	1	1	12
Automobiles	1	1	1	1	1	1	1	1	1	1	1	1	12
Travel	2	2	2	2	2	2	2	2	2	2	2	2	24
Entertainment	1	1	1	1	1	1	1	1	1	1	1	1	12
Total GA&S	54	54	54	54	54	54	39	39	54	54	54	54	618
Interest	3	3	3	3	3	3	3	3	3	3	3	3	36
Income tax	0	0	0	0	8	5	2	0	0	0	5	0	$ 20
Net income	$ (57)	$ (6)	$ 22	$ 49	$ 41	$ 17	$ 7	$ (19)	$ (6)	$ (6)	$ 44	$ (6)	$ 80
						Cash flow ($1,000)							
Begin cash	$ 0	$210	$ 93	$ 54	$ 45	$105	$190	$254	$275	$223	$179	$157	
Bank loan	300												
Equity pd. in	20												
Revenue	0	0	100	150	200	200	150	100	50	100	100	200	
Total cash in	$320	$ 0	$100	$150	$200	$200	$150	$100	$ 50	$100	$100	$200	
Material	0	15	23	30	30	23	15	8	15	15	30	15	
Labor	30	45	60	60	45	30	15	30	30	60	30	30	
Bldg. rent	8	2	2	2	2	2	2	2	2	2	2	2	
Equip. rent	2	2	2	2	2	2	2	2	2	2	2	2	
Salaries	20	20	20	20	20	20	20	20	20	20	20	20	
Marketing	20	20	20	20	20	20	5	5	20	20	20	20	
Utilities	7	5	5	5	5	5	5	5	5	5	5	5	
Insurance	12			12			12			12			
Office rent	4	1	1	1	1	1	1	1	1	1	1	1	
Automobiles	1	1	1	1	1	1	1	1	1	1	1	1	
Travel	2	2	2	2	2	2	2	2	2	2	2	2	
Entertainment	1	1	1	1	1	1	1	1	1	1	1	1	
Interest	3	3	3	3	3	3	3	3	3	3	3	3	
Income tax	0	0	0	0	8	5	2	0	0	0	5	0	
Tot. cash out	100	177	140	159	140	115	86	80	102	144	122	102	
Ending cash	$210	$ 93	$ 54	$ 45	$105	$190	$254	$275	$223	$179	$157	$255	

EXERCISE

FINANCIAL STATEMENTS

STEP 1: CREATE YOUR INCOME STATEMENT, EXCEPT FOR INTEREST, PROFIT BEFORE TAXES, TAXES, AND PROFIT AFTER TAXES. Use a cash basis, rather than an accrual basis.

- Determine your sales revenue on a monthly basis. Remember this is actual revenue received.
- Determine cost of goods sold. Remember that the cost of goods sold in any period is the cost of the goods that actually were sold in the period, not the cost of goods that were manufactured but not sold.
- Determine overhead costs. Do not include interest at this point because until you have made cash flow projections, you do not know how much money you will need. And do not fool with income tax at this point.

STEP 2: CREATE A CASH FLOW STATEMENT, EXCEPT FOR INTEREST AND TAXES. You will be creating a real-time cash flow statement, not a sources and uses of funds statement (although you can do that later), so use a cash basis, rather than an accrual basis, in accounting for income and expenses.

- Start with beginning cash of $0 and add to it any equity paid in at the start of the company. Do not include any loans at this point, since any debt will be determined from the initial cash flow projections.
- Determine, month by month, when the company will receive payments for goods and/or services; and when the company will pay wages, bills, interest, taxes, and so on, as follows:
  a. Add any revenue that the company expects to receive in that month. Remember, this is actual cash received, not accounts receivable.
  b. Subtract cash that flows out. Remember, this is not accounts payable or wages payable; rather, payments are recognized when the cash leaves the company. Recognize payroll taxes and corporate income taxes in the month they become due (a conservative approach). Do not include interest and income taxes at this point, because you do not yet know how much money you need to borrow.
  c. Use ending cash for the period as beginning cash for the next period.

STEP 3: DETERMINE HOW MUCH MONEY YOU NEED TO BORROW, THE INTEREST, AND THE INCOME TAXES.

- Determine the amount you need to borrow by looking at the maximum cash shortfall and estimating the amount needed for contingencies.
- Determine interest and income taxes. Be sure to carry forward losses from period to period.
- Since interest and income taxes will change the amount of the maximum shortfall, adjust, as needed, the amount you need to borrow.
- Go through as many iterations of the income and cash flow statements as necessary to determine the amounts.

STEP 4: COMPLETE YOUR INCOME STATEMENT.

- Determine monthly interest payments.
- Determine profit before taxes.
- Determine corporate income taxes.
- Determine profit after taxes.

STEP 5: COMPLETE YOUR CASH FLOW STATEMENT.

- Determine interest and income tax payments.

STEP 6: CREATE YOUR BALANCE SHEET.

- Determine current assets. It is assumed there are no fixed assets.
  - *a.* Determine cash, the ending cash balance on December 31.
  - *b.* Determine accounts receivable on December 31.
  - *c.* Determine inventory on December 31.
  - *d.* Determine other assets, such as a rent deposit or a deposit with the telephone company.
- Determine current liabilities:
  - *a.* Determine accounts payable on December 31.
  - *b.* Determine the amount of your bank loan that is due in the next 12 months.
- Determine long-term liabilities:
  - *a.* Determine the amount of the bank loan that is due after the next 12 months.
  - *b.* Determine paid-in equity (i.e., total equity paid in by the stockholders).
  - *c.* Determine retained earnings (or losses)—that is, accumulated earnings (or losses) from the inception of the company through the date of the balance sheet.

STEP 7: WRITE FOOTNOTES DETAILING IMPORTANT ASSUMPTIONS USED.

EXERCISE—HOW ENTREPRENEURS TURN LESS INTO MORE

Entrepreneurs are often creative and ingenious in bootstrapping their ventures and in getting a great deal out of very limited resources. This assignment can be done alone, in pairs or in trios. Identify at least two or three entrepreneurs whose companies exceed $3 million in sales and are less than 10 years old and who have started their companies with less than $25,000 to $50,000 of initial seed capital. Interview them with a focus on their strategies and tactics which minimize and control (not necessarily own) the necessary resources.

1. What methods, sources, and techniques did they devise to acquire resources?
2. Why were they able to do so much with so little?
3. What assumptions, attitudes, and mind sets seemed to enable them to think and function in this manner?
4. What patterns, similarities, and differences exist among the entrepreneurs you interviewed?
5. What impact did these minimizing bootstrapping approaches have on their abilities to conserve cash and equity and to create future options or choices to pursue other opportunities?
6. How did they devise unique incentive structures in the deals and arrangements with their people, suppliers, and other resource providers (their first office space or facility, brochures, etc.)?
7. In lieu of money, what other forms of currency did they use, such as bartering for space, equipment, or people or giving an extra day off or an extra week's vacation?
8. Can they think of examples of how they acquired (gained control of) a resource which they could afford to pay for with real money and did not?
9. Many experienced entrepreneurs say that for first-time entrepreneurs it can be worse to start with too much money rather than too little. How do you see this and why?
10. Some of the strongest new companies are started during an economic recession, among tight credit and capital markets. It is invaluable to develop a lean-and-mean, make-do, less-is-more philosophy and sense of frugality and budgetary discipline. Can you think of any examples of this? Do you agree or disagree? Can you think of opposite examples, such as companies started at or near the peak of the 1980s economic boom with more capital and credit than they needed?

You will find as very useful background reading the feature articles on bootstrapping, in *INC.* magazine.

The What, Whether, and Why of the Business Plan

11

Madame, enclosed please find the novel you commissioned. It is in two volumes. If I had had more time I could have written it in one.

Voltaire

RESULTS EXPECTED

Upon completion of this chapter, you will have:

1. Identified what a business plan is, whether a business plan needs to be prepared, who needs to prepare it, and why.
2. Examined requirements of effective business plans.
3. Looked at common pitfalls of planning.
4. Studied how to write a business plan, including learning the difference between opportunity screening and writing a business plan, who develops the business plan, how to develop the action steps necessary, and some do's and don'ts in planning.
5. Analyzed a classic business plan written by entrepreneurs to raise capital for an actual company.
6. Looked at the differences between thinking about and screening opportunities and writing a business plan.
7. Written a business plan for a new venture.

PLANNING AND THE BUSINESS PLAN

The What

Planning is a way of thinking about the future of a venture—of deciding where a firm needs to go and how fast, how to get there, and what to do along the way to reduce the uncertainty and to manage risk and change. Effective planning is a *process* of setting goals and deciding how to attain them. Planning occurs in start-up situations, in growing enterprises, and in very large firms. In some sense, most successful ventures plan. One author writing in the *Harvard Business Review* observed that

> the smaller companies weathering the current difficult economic times seem to be those following an idea—call it a no-frills, down-to-earth, but clear plan—of how to take advantage of the environment and how to allocate resources.[1]

[1] Phillip Thurston, "Should Smaller Companies Make Formal Plans?" *Harvard Business Review,* September–October 1983, p. 184.

This observation has recently been substantiated by research that concluded "growth-oriented, high-performing leaders can influence change through their involvement in intentional efforts to prepare and plan for significant shifts in structure, systems, culture or key processes."[2]

A business plan is one type of planning document that results from the process of planning. A business plan is a written document that (1) summarizes a business opportunity (i.e., why the opportunity exists and why the management team has what it takes to execute the plan) and (2) defines and articulates how the management team expects to seize and execute the opportunity identified.[3]

A complete business plan usually is of considerable length. In recent years, however—particularly in business based on certain technologies, products, or services, where there is turbulence, greater-than-usual unpredictability, and rapid change—an alternative to a complete full-blown business plan has become acceptable. This can be called a "dehydrated" business plan. Dehydrated business plans serve most often as trial balloons for prospective investors and are launched before a decision is made to undertake a complete business plan.

In any case, creating a business plan is more a process than simply a product, and the resulting plan is not immutable. By the same token, the business plan for a business is not itself the business. A business plan is analogous to a pilot's cross-country flight plan, in that it defines the most desired, most timely, and least-hazardous route to a given destination. Yet, innumerable factors, such as unexpected weather and traffic, can significantly alter the course of the actual flight. Similarly, for new companies, it is common for the actual course of the business to diverge from what was originally developed in a business plan. As was said in the first century, BC, "It is a bad plan that admits of no modification."[4]

The Why

Business plans are used primarily (1) for raising capital and (2) as a means of guiding growth. The decision whether to plan, and ultimately whether to write a business plan, involves the following:

- Whether the venture needs to raise capital, and whether a business plan is valuable for this purpose.
- Whether the planning process itself will be valuable enough to the venture in terms of defining and anticipating potential risks, problems, and trade-offs to justify the time spent.

For ventures seeking to raise venture capital or other equity in today's highly competitive environment, a quality business plan is a must. As William Egan, founding partner of one of the nation's largest and most successful venture capital funds, Burr, Egan & Deleage, put it:

> Ten to 15 years ago, a high-quality business plan really stood out and gave the entrepreneur a competitive edge in getting our attention. Today, you have to have a high-quality plan as a given—without it you're dead—but since everyone coming to us for money has a highly professional plan, the plan won't give you much of an edge by itself.

As a vehicle for raising capital, a business plan convinces investors that the new venture has identified an opportunity, has the entrepreneurial and management talent to exploit that

[2] Debora S Humphreys and Judith W Harley, "Leading Planned Change in Small Firms: Process and Involvement," in *Frontiers of Entrepreneurship Research: 1990*, ed. Neil C Churchill et al. (Babson Park, MA: Babson College, 1990), p. 83.

[3] See J A Timmons, "A Business Plan is More than a Financing Device," *Harvard Business Review*, March–April 1980.

[4] Said by Publilius Syrus.

opportunity, and has a rational, coherent, and believable program for achieving revenue and expense targets on time. If the business plan passes the initial screening, the plan will be given a more detailed evaluation, and it will become a prime measure of the abilities of those involved to define and analyze opportunities and problems and to identify and plan actions to deal with them.

A business plan can be particularly helpful after start-up as a tool to understand and as a means of guiding growth. One can think of developing a business plan as using a flight simulator. The consequences of different strategies and tactics and the human and financial requirements for launching and building the venture can be determined and worked through without the risk and cost of working these out in real time. The learning necessary to start a company can thus be accelerated. As Nolan Bushnell responded when asked by a student if he should prepare a business plan: "That's exactly what you have to do. There is no way around it; you're doing the best thing. Every time you prepare a business plan, you become a better entrepreneur—I really believe that."[5]

The founder/president of one venture that grew to sales of $14 million in seven years said that

> once you are in the business, you realize that everyone, including the founders, is learning his or her job. If you have a thoughtful and complete business plan, you have a lot more confidence in your decisions. You have a reference already there to say, "Well I have already run the numbers on inventory or cost of goods, and this is what will happen."

For example, a business plan can be valuable in the important areas, such as product pricing. The initial strategy of one of the founders of a new venture was to price products below the competition even though the venture's products were based on a superior product innovation and could compete in a growing market. In the process of writing a business plan, the founders were persuaded, as a result of vigorously arguing about the pricing strategy with their venture investors, to set prices 10 percent above those of the competition. By its second year, the new company enjoyed pretax profits of $850,000, based on about $9 million in sales. Through the detailed analysis of the industry and competition for the marketing section of the business plan, the wisdom of a different pricing strategy became evident.

A business plan also can help in refining strategy and in making difficult decisions. An entrepreneur in Nova Scotia, who built commercial fishing boats, decided to raise his prices by more than 40 percent, based on an outside analysis and a critique of his business plan. Of five original orders, he knew he would lose two orders, but he also knew he would make more profit on the remaining three orders than he did on all five at the old price. His delivery time would be cut in half as well, and the shortened delivery time would lead to additional sales at the higher margins. He also decided to require progress payments. These payments would eliminate the need to raise outside equity capital.

The process also can clarify the venture's financial requirements. For example, an entrepreneur in Kentucky, with a three-year-old $1 million-plus business erecting coal-loading sites, believed he needed $350,000 in expansion capital. After reflecting on a detailed critique of his presentation of his business plan, he concluded: "The worst thing I could do right now is put more money into the business. The first thing I should do is get my own backyard more in order. But I will be back in two or three years." True to his prediction, he returned two and a half years later. His company then approached $3 million in sales and had a business plan for expansion that resulted in a $400,000 debt capital investment without relinquishing any ownership.

[5] Taken from comments Nolan Bushnell, founder of Atari, Pizza Time Theaters, and a venture capital firm, made at a seminar during his induction in 1983 into the Babson College Academy of Distinguished Entrepreneurs.

The Whether

Phillip Thurston of the Harvard Business School identified dimensions that are unique to each venture and management team. Understanding where a venture sits along these dimensions can help it decide whether to plan:[6]

- *Administrative style and ability.* Whether to plan depends on the ability of the lead entrepreneur or chief executive officer to grasp multiple and interrelated aspects of the business, keep all that is necessary in his or her head, and retrieve it in an orderly fashion. Further, whether to plan depends on the lead entrepreneur's management style.
- *Wishes of the management team.* Whether and how to plan depend on the wishes of the management team. Some management teams want to participate in the planning process, and others do not.
- *Complexity of the business.* The complexity of a business will determine whether to plan.
- *Strength of competition.* Strength of the competition is a factor. Some ventures compete in highly competitive environments where there is a need to be lean and tightly disciplined to survive, while others are more insulated and have a larger margin for error.
- *Level of uncertainty.* Whether to plan depends also on the level of uncertainty the venture faces. Some ventures face a quite volatile, rapidly changing environment and must be prepared for contingencies, while some enter stable, fairly predictable industries where precipitous actions are not warranted.

In addition, ventures have to face different constituencies, both external and internal, including creditors, shareholders, regulators, customers, community groups, employee groups, and the like. The more of these a firm has to contend with and respond to, the greater the potential payoff in some form of organized and disciplined planning.

Among existing firms, especially those backed by venture capital, the harvest issue is especially important. A business plan for an ongoing business can significantly enhance its harvest potential. Such a document can focus and articulate why there is a major opportunity for a prospective buyer in much the same way a business plan does for a venture that is starting up and seeking investors. For firms not backed by professional investors, planning is important because they do not have such a backer as the prime motivator and a driving force to realize a harvest or easy access to the skills, know-how, and networks of such a backer.

In addition, an existing firm contemplating launching a venture opportunity internally needs to consider a business plan and may already have formal planning processes in place. Take, for instance, one of the founders of a firm that had grown to $20 million in sales in about a dozen years. He used a business plan to present to his partners and to his board a statement of an opportunity for internal expansion—essentially a new business from within.

Other reasons commonly cited for planning are:[7]

- *Working smarter.* Planning helps a management team to work smarter (i.e., come up with a better way by considering alternatives), rather than simply harder. Planning enables a management team to understand and clarify the risks and, in turn, to devise ways to manage those risks and reduce them.
- *Future orientation.* Planning necessitates an orientation to the future. Thinking ahead helps a team anticipate and thus be more alert for and responsive to problems, opportunities, and changes.
- *Testing ideas.* Planning helps management to develop and then to update strategy by testing the sensibility of its ideas and approaches.

[6] Thurston, "Should Smaller Companies Make Formal Plans?" pp. 162–88.

[7] Ibid.

- *Results orientation.* Goal setting also gives a team a results orientation (i.e., a concern for accomplishment and progress).[8] Developing and stating a specific goal, which is measurable and phased over time, enables performance to be evaluated.
- *Stress management.* Establishing realistic goals can help in managing and coping with what is by nature a stressful situation.
- *Motivation.* A more subtle consequence of planning is the effect that setting realistic goals has on motivation. Inherent in any goal is some level of effort required to attain it, and this level of effort, once made clear, can be judged in terms of its ease of attainment. Research has shown that individuals pursuing challenging but attainable goals are more motivated to work toward that goal than are individuals pursuing goals that are either too easy or too difficult.

Problems with Planning

Planning is not for everyone. Commonly cited problems, which often result in decisions not to plan, are the following:

- *Currency.* A plan, such as a business plan, can be out of date as soon as, or even before, it is written. For example, in highly volatile and turbulent technologies and rapidly changing market niches, planning tends to be ad hoc and spontaneous and any plans are often obsolete before they get printed.
- *Inflexibility.* It sometimes is undesirable to commit under uncertainty since the future cannot be predicted. Planning requires setting goals, making choices, and setting priorities. Inherent in this process is the possibility that future or yet unknown options, which actually might be more attractive than the one chosen, may be lost or excluded.
- *Inability to plan.* Invariably, an event entirely beyond the control of a management team, such as the Arab oil crisis in the 1970s, may boost or sink its best-laid plans. No planning process can foresee such developments.
- *Time problems.* During the demanding early survival stages of a new company, whose life expectancy at times may be estimated in weeks or months, major allocations of time and effort to planning for next year may not make sense.[9]
- *Sales jeopardy.* A potentially fatal problem for entrepreneurs occurs when planning is substituted for action in getting orders.

While these are usually rationalizations, there may be times when they are valid. An example would be when the window of an attractive opportunity is closing faster than a business plan can be developed. (However, usually an opportunity that is attractive, as defined in Chapter 3, does not have such an extremely small window that all planning needs to be jettisoned.)

PITFALLS OF EFFECTIVE PLANNING

What Can Go Wrong

Finally, there are pitfalls in planning itself (see below). Most important, the process of planning can be carried to extreme. One author warns of the excesses of "planning systems."[10] Excessive detail, analysis, and bureaucratic tendencies toward red tape and

[8] Peter R Drucker, *Managing for Results* (New York: Harper & Row, 1964).

[9] For a discussion of some approaches to this dilemma, see George A Steiner, "Approaches to Long-Range Planning for Small Business," *California Management Review*, Fall 1967, pp. 3–16.

[10] Thurston, "Should Smaller Companies Make Formal Plans?" pp. 162–88.

"checkups" can detract from the purpose of planning, which needs to be the accomplishment of goals and implementation.

This is one reason why large companies have a difficult time developing new, entrepreneurial business from within. Take, for example, an entrepreneur who headed up a new business venture for a Fortune 500 company. At a conference at the Harvard Business School in early 1989, she described how the "financial overseers" had insisted on 13 very detailed budget reviews, and defenses, during the start-up's first year. The entrepreneurs in attendance, and the author, were astounded at such a mentality and were even more delighted to discover how the competition was approaching the start-up process!

Perhaps there is no greater frustration for entrepreneurs and managers than to experience failure with plans seemingly well prepared and well intended. Not only is it frustrating and consumes precious hours, but it is downright demoralizing when a plan does not work initially. The planning process goes awry for some of the following reasons:

- *Wrong emphasis.* Planning is ineffective if the *process* itself is overlooked and planning is viewed as an end in itself. If a plan does not seem to work immediately, the lead entrepreneur and his or her team often retreat to the familiar and fall back on an activity-oriented routine or crisis management, which lacks or confuses priorities, has no longer-term purpose, and is not aimed at the attainment of particular objectives.
- *Rigidity.* Planning fails when the process becomes too rigid and is performed in a lock-step, immutable order. Entrepreneurs need to be very certain that if their strategies and plans define directions which have irreversible consequences, they are certain they wind up where they want to be and can live with the consequences.
- *Misunderstanding of the function of a business plan.* Marketability, for example, generally outweighs technical elegance in the success equation, and it usually is necessary to plan to achieve a good fit. Yet some entrepreneurs place more faith, ofttimes unwarranted, in a product or invention, especially if it is patented. Readers will recognize the better mousetrap fallacy in this attitude. Even those who understand the value of marketing and business acumen, and who have done a great deal of thinking about how to execute an opportunity, ignore the function of planning in identifying problems, testing the soundness of their ideas internally and with knowledgeable outside sources, and so forth.
- *Misunderstanding of the process of raising capital.* There is a misconception that a business plan is solely a selling and negotiating tool for raising money. Indeed, more than one entrepreneur has been heard to comment that the plan is "destined for the circular file" once the funds are in the bank. Such a view is wrong for several reasons. First, to prospective partners, investors, or suppliers, such an attitude communicates a shallow understanding of the requirements for creating a successful business. It also can signal to these people a promotional attitude – a search for fast money and a hope for an early sellout – and create mistrust. In addition, entrepreneurs do not understand that business plans are used, in addition to being the basis of investment decisions, to screen investments. Thus, relying on raising money as an indication that an idea is sound is a cart-before-the-horse approach, which usually results in rejection.

Exhibit 11.1 summarizes some of the ailments of effective planning listed below, which, if not cured, can cause the death of the planning for an organization:

- *Lack of commitment.* It is quite easy to obtain only a lip service commitment and not a commitment to and ownership of a plan. Commitment is critical to the success of any plan because it provides the motivation for critical people to see a plan through to completion. Commitment seems to stem from involving critical people in the process of

Exhibit 11.1
Planning: Its Ailments, Symptoms, and Cures

Planning	*Symptoms*	*Cure*
1. No real goals.	Goals are vague, general. Goals not specific, measurable, or time-phased. No subgoals or action steps. Activity-oriented, not goal-oriented.	Set specific, time-phased, measurable goals, subgoals, and action steps. Keep the overall aim in mind. Be opportunistic in pursuing goals.
2. Failure to anticipate obstacles.	Excessive optimism. No alternative strategies. No conflicts recognized. "Don't worry, I had thought of that." Missed meeting delivery date. Missed lead time forecasts. Didn't get support when needed. Crises prevail.	Be flexible in planning and anticipating as far as possible obstacles and how to overcome them. Face unanticipated obstacles with confidence—there'll always be some. Ask someone else to brainstorm with you, "What could go wrong or get in our way?" Realism is key.
3. Lack of milestones and progress reviews.	"It can wait." "I can remember that." "I'll know how we're doing when we get there—let's play it by ear." Don't really know how you are doing. Short-term orientation. Can't recall when we last reviewed how we are doing. No recent revisions of plan.	Set specific task milestones and progress review dates; stick to them and revise when needed. Ask each day, "What did I accomplish today toward reaching my goal?" Ask each day, "What have I learned that will help me to make more rapid progress?"
4. Lack of commitment.	"I told you it wouldn't work—it wasn't *my* plan!" Procrastination. Focus on routine, daily activities. Failure to meet goals, milestones. Failure to develop specific action steps to meet goals. Lack of priorities. Missed meetings, appointments.	Set goals mutually; utilize *joint* review, negotiation, compromise, and data sharing. Meet periodically, and track progress. Encourage informal discussion with team members, both to test and to renew commitment. Keep team members informed about results obtained. Recognize and reward performance that meets your high standards.
5. Failure to revise goals.	Plan never changes, lacks resiliency. Inflexible or stubborn in face of feedback dictating change. Goals not met or exceeded greatly. Unresponsive to changing situation. Help not sought when needed. Wasted time or unproductive tasks or activities. Activities don't match goal priorities.	Meet periodically to review goals and progress and to assess the situation. Change emphasis and approach as appropriate. Create a climate that is tolerant of bad news and invites constructive critiques and feedback.
6. Failure to learn from experience.	Lost sight of goals. Mistake is repeated. Feedback is ignored or denied. Same routine—same crises as previously. Unwillingness to change way of doing things. Not asking, "What do we learn from this experience?"	Set improvement and learning objectives. Use milestones, and reassess periodically. Collaborate more frequently in tracking progress and learning. Document at end of one project/plan lessons, benchmarks, guidelines that have emerged. What was learned? Be adaptive, flexible, and responsive to unfolding events. A new venture start-up is full of surprises. Concentrate on producing results, not on reports for their own sake.

planning and developing goals from the outset, since this involvement generates their interest, inputs, and more importantly, ownership in the plan.

- *Performance expectations.* It is easy to overlook clarity in expectations. Performance expectations need to be made clear and a win/win situation created for critical people.
- *Undefined goals.* Admirable missions, such as "improving performance," "pursuing growth," or "increasing business" are not concrete goals, and plans centered around these undefined goals are unlikely to work. Specific, measurable, time-phased, and

Before proceeding, however, it is essential to reiterate that effective planning is goal-oriented, rather than activity-oriented. *Action steps are devised through effective goal setting.*

Goals are not dreams, fantasies, or the product of wishful thinking, nor are they mere predictions or guesses about future outcomes. A goal is a decision or choice about future outcomes. Once set, goals should not become static targets. Goal setting is not a task but a process, a way of dealing with the world that is repeated over and over as conditions change.

There are numerous ways of actually going about goal setting and planning. Most of these approaches have in common a balanced emphasis on both the process by which goals are set and the results they seek. Research and practical experience have shown that certain ingredients are common to almost all successful planning efforts:

- Establishment of goals that are:
  - Specific and concrete.
  - Measurable.
  - Related to time (i.e., specific about what will be accomplished over a certain time period).
  - Realistic and attainable.
  - Capable of being modified and adapted.
  - Certain to make a significant difference.
- Establishment of priorities and identification of conflicts and how to resolve them.
- Identification of problems and obstacles.
- Specification of necessary tasks and actions steps.
- Indication of how results will be measured.
- Establishment of progress milestones, especially revenue, expense, and cash targets, deadlines, and dates.
- Identification of risks involved and alternatives for coping with possible contingencies.
- Identification of outside help and resources that need to be marshalled and controlled.
- Periodic review of progress and revision of goals as factors such as the changing competitive situation require.

In the process of establishing goals and priorities, a planner needs a sense of perspective. The general wisdom is that 80 percent of a task usually is accomplished using the first 20 percent of the effort. Therefore, one needs to focus first on what will result in 80 percent of the accomplishments. Often, there will not be time to do otherwise.

Who Develops the Business Plan

Consideration often is given to hiring an outside professional to prepare the business plan, so the management team can use its time to obtain financing and start the business.

There are two good reasons why it is *not* a good idea to hire outside professionals. First, in the process of planning and of writing the business plan, the consequences of different strategies and tactics and the human and financial requirements for launching and building the venture can be examined, before it is too late. For example, one entrepreneur discovered, while preparing his business plan, that the major market for his biomedical product was in nursing homes, rather than in hospital emergency rooms, as he and his physician partner had previously assumed. This realization changed the focus of the entire marketing effort. Had he left the preparation to an outsider, this might not have been discovered, or, at the very least, it is unlikely he would have had the same sense of confidence and commitment to the new strategy.

Further, if a venture intends to use the business plan to raise capital, it is important for the team to do the planning and write the plan itself. Investors attach great importance to the quality of the management team *and* to their complete understanding of the business they are preparing to enter. Thus, investors want to be sure that what they see is what they get—that is, the team's analysis and understanding of the venture opportunity and its commitment to it. They are going to invest in a team and a leader, not in a consultant. Nothing less will do, and anything less is usually obvious.

Segmenting and Integrating Information

In the task of planning and writing a business plan, it is necessary to organize information in a way that it can be managed and that is useful.

An effective way to organize information with the idea of developing a business plan is to segment the information into sections, such as one about the target market, a section about the industry, one about competition, one about the financial plan, and so on, and then integrate the information into a business plan.

This process works best if sections are discrete and the information within them digestible. Then the order in which sections are developed can vary, and different sections can be developed simultaneously. For example, since the heart and soul of a plan lies in the analysis of the market opportunity, of the competition, and of a resultant competitive strategy that can win, it is a good idea to start with these sections and integrate information along the way. Since the financial and operations aspects of the venture will be driven by the rate of growth and the magnitude and specific substance of the market revenue plans, these can be developed later.

The information is then further integrated into the business plan. For example, the executive summary is prepared last.

Establishing Action Steps

The following steps, centered around actions to be taken, outline the process by which a business plan is written. Note these action steps are then presented in an exercise, "The Business Plan Guide."

- *Segmenting information.* An overall plan for the project, by section, needs to be devised and needs to include priorities, who is responsible for each section, the due date of a first draft, and the due date of a final draft.
- *Creating an overall schedule.* A list of specific tasks, their priorities, who is responsible for them, when they will be started, and when they will be completed needs to be made. This list needs to be as specific and detailed as possible. Tasks need to be broken down into the smallest possible component (e.g., a series of phone calls may be necessary before a trip). The list then needs to be examined for conflicts and lack of reality in time estimates. Peers and business associates can be asked to review the list for realism, timing, and priorities.
- *Creating an action calendar.* Tasks on the *do* list then need to be placed on a calendar. When the calendar is complete, the calendar needs again to be examined for conflicts or lack of realism.
- *Doing the work and writing the plan.* The necessary work needs to be done and the plan written. Adjustments need to be made to the *do* list and the calendar, as necessary. As part of this process, it is important to have a plan reviewed by an attorney to make sure that it contains no misleading statements and unnecessary information and caveats, and

also reviewed by an objective outsider, such as an entrepreneurially minded executive who has significant profit and loss responsibility, or a venture capitalist who would not be a potential investor. No matter how good the lead entrepreneur and his or her team are in planning, there will be issues that they will overlook and certain aspects of the presentation that are inadequate or less than clear. Few entrepreneurs are good at both planning and communication. A good reviewer also can act as a sounding board in the process of developing alternative solutions to problems and answers to questions investors are likely to ask.

CASE—FAX INTERNATIONAL, INC.*

Preparation Questions

1. Evaluate the opportunity and the FAX International business plan.
2. What fund-raising and financial strategy should Douglas Ranalli pursue?
3. What should Doug do?

FAX INTERNATIONAL, INC. BUSINESS PLAN

EXECUTIVE SUMMARY

FAX International, Inc., was founded in June 1990 by Mr. Douglas J. Ranalli and Dr. Thomas P. Sosnowski, PhD. The goal of the company is to build an international communications network that will be seven times more efficient at transmitting fax documents than the switched voice networks of AT&T, MCI, and Sprint. The company's year-long design and development effort has been extremely successful. As a result the network will be ready for demonstration by the end of July 1991, and ready for full-scale implementation during October 1991. The opportunity now exists to offer business customers a vastly superior facsimile transmission service between the United States and major international city centers like Tokyo, London, Paris, and so on. Service is superior because it is both easier to use than direct-dial service from AT&T and 50 percent less expensive. For example, customers currently paying an average of $1.40/minute for service to Tokyo will pay only $.69 with FAX International, Inc. The FAX International network is so efficient that it will provide business customers 50 percent savings over current rates while earning 50 percent gross margins on the service once a minimum efficient volume level has been achieved.

The international telecommunications market has historically been closed to competition due to the presence of monopoly carriers in almost every country. The regulatory situation, however, is changing rapidly as countries all over the world look for ways to make their telecommunications industries more competitive. In June 1990, the European Commission directed members of the European Economic Community to begin deregulating all enhanced telecommunications services. Similarly, the United States and Japan negotiated the International Value Added Network Services (IVANS) agreement, which guarantees US value-added network service providers like FAX International fair and equal access to the Japanese market. The actions of the European Commission and the signing of the IVANS agreement between the United States and Japan have created an opportunity for a variety of international enhanced-communications services between the United States, Europe, and Japan. The opportunities have yet to be exploited due to the time required for companies to understand the recent regulatory changes and to develop appropriate technologies. An

*Reprinted with the permission of Douglas J Ranalli, Founder and President of FAX International.

article in the June 15 issue of *EMMS* (Electronic Mail and Micro Systems) summed up the opportunity as follows:

What is the magic formula for success in enhanced fax service? Whoever figures it out may turn out to be the William McGowan (MCI) success story of the 1990s. . . . Conceivably, a fax from [the United States] could travel via private lines to Tokyo, or London and be delivered with a local call—completely eliminating the need for the international switched network. The economic incentive is so strong that over the next two to three years, hundreds of millions of dollars/year of international facsimile traffic are likely to migrate from the switched voice networks of AT&T, MCI, and Sprint to dedicated facsimile networks.

FAX International, Inc., is prepared with the technology, the management team, and the regulatory approvals necessary to capitalize on this exciting international opportunity.

FAX International's initial objective is to establish a leadership position in the United States-to-Tokyo market during the first 12 months of operation. Expansion into two more markets, London to the United States and Paris to the United States, will follow soon afterwards. The United States–Tokyo market has been targeted first for three reasons:

1. It is the highest-volume international facsimile route in the world (390 million fax minutes/year in both directions between the United States and Japan in 1990; 175 million fax minutes/year in one direction from just the United States to Tokyo). See "Market Size."
2. It is the fastest growing route (growth rate projected at over 30 percent/year).
3. Potential customers are highly concentrated in a few major US city centers and are easy to identify. Of the 9,000 Japanese affiliated firms operating in the United States, over 50 percent are located in Los Angeles, San Francisco, and New York.

FAX International has succeeded in assembling the technology, the business support systems, and the management team necessary to provide a full scale service between the United States, Tokyo, and other major international city centers. The next step is to complete a second round of financing which will be used to install the network and bring the company to a cash-positive position within the first 12 months of operations. An equity investment of $1,000,000 combined with equipment lease loans representing assets worth $1,500,000 will be required to achieve the following projected financial results:

	Year 1	*Year 2*	*Year 3*
Revenue:	$2,200,000	$8,800,000	$14,800,000
EBIT:	$ (950,000)	$1,950,000	$ 4,200,000

TABLE OF CONTENTS

I. Market Development Strategy
II. Market Size
III. How the Network Works
IV. Network Economics
V. Technology
VI. Sales Strategy
VII. Price Comparisons
VIII. Sales Expectations
IX. Competition

X. FAX International Team
XI. FAX International Advisory Board
XII. Financial Projections
XIII. Revenue and Expense Assumptions

MARKET DEVELOPMENT STRATEGY

FAX International's market development strategy is based on expanding into one international market at a time and building traffic to an efficient economy of scale before moving into the next market. FAX International has chosen this conservative strategy based on an analysis of the economic, regulatory, and competitive environments the company is likely to encounter over the next several years. The company's board of advisors has played an instrumental role in providing detailed market and competitive information during the formulation of this strategy.

- *Economics.* The economics of the store-and-forward facsimile business are driven by the need to achieve substantial traffic volume along each selected international route (i.e., the United States to Tokyo, or the United States to London). This economic environment results from the high cost of setting up a digital circuit between two points and the low cost of carrying additional traffic on an already established circuit. Efficient operation of FAX International's network results from carrying 7,000,000 minutes of traffic/year on any given route. For example, variable costs on the United States-Tokyo route drop from $.61/minute to $.31/minute as traffic volume grows from 0 minutes/year to 7,000,000 minutes/year. (See "Market Size" and "Network Economics.") The economics of this industry heavily favor a strategy focused on achieving high traffic volume on each individual route.
- *Regulatory Complexity.* The international regulatory environment has eased dramatically in the last two years. However, the regulatory issues associated with carrying international telecommunications traffic are still complex, cumbersome, and specific to each international market. Each new market represents a commitment of time, money, and management resources to a process that is fraught with uncertainty and delays.
- *Competition.* FAX International anticipates the emergence of a large number of small competitors in the international store-and-forward business as the market develops. The world market for this type of service is large enough to support dozens of small niche players operating on the multiple international routes. In the long run, however, the economics of the industry dictate that the only competitive companies will be those that reach the minimum required economy of scale along a given route. Consolidation is almost guaranteed to occur since increasing volume leads to decreasing variable costs. Those firms which fail to achieve the minimum scale will be faced with an increasingly competitive environment and an inferior cost structure.

In summary, FAX International's analysis reveals that although the opportunity exists to launch a service in multiple markets, the fastest and most conservative route to profitability lies in concentrating on one market at a time. FAX International has decided to address the markets in the order outlined below based on an analysis of each market's size, growth rate, cost of entry, cost of customer acquisition, and short- and long-term profit potential.

- United States to Tokyo.
- Tokyo to the United States.
- London and Paris to the United States.

Market Entry Strategy: The United States to Tokyo

FAX International will utilize a low-price, fast-growth strategy to enter the United States–Tokyo market. This strategy was chosen based on FAX International's analysis of the US telecommunications market and an analysis of MCI's success against AT&T in a similar competitive situation.

The objective is to reach 7,000,000 minutes of traffic per year from the United States to Tokyo as quickly as possible. FCC statistics show that fax traffic on the United States–Japan route has been growing at 30 percent per year and reached 250 million minutes per year in 1990. Traffic on the United States-to-Tokyo route alone is estimated at 175 million minutes per year. FAX International's business plan is based on winning just 4 percent of this clearly defined and highly focused United States–Tokyo market segment (source: FCC Statistics, "International Message Telephone Service between the United States and Selected Countries, 1957–1989").

MCI successfully proved that business customers in the United States are willing to test new telecommunications services if the cost savings are attractive enough. MCI started in the United States as an unknown and unproven company but their aggressive offer of 30 percent to 50 percent discounts prompted potential customers to take a chance. MCI's low-price, fast-growth strategy allowed it to quickly capture the market share necessary to reach an efficient scale of operations. FAX International will apply a nearly identical strategy in entering the facsimile transmission market.

The FAX International network has been designed from the ground up to meet the needs of US-based customers identified through market research and field interviews. Potential customers have stated they will test and utilize the service if it can deliver the following features:

- 40–60 percent cost savings for business customers of all sizes on calls from the United States to Tokyo.
- No risk trial offer:
  - No installation fees or up-front costs.
  - No change in long-distance carrier required.
  - No employee training needed to use the service.
  - No change in fax equipment required.
  - Free 100-minute test period for every potential customer.

The recessionary economic environment in the United States is the ideal time for FAX International to launch a low-price, fast-growth strategy. The facsimile market between the United States and Tokyo is huge and growing at 30 percent per year. Breaking into a new market is never easy, but the opportunity is clear, the cost savings are clear, the customers are easy to identify, and the timing is perfect.

Japanese Market Entry Strategy

The Japanese telecommunications market is completely different than the US market in terms of customer willingness to test a service from a new and unproven competitor. Japanese customers prefer to work with established Japanese organizations. Breaking into the Japanese market as a small US company has proven over and over again to be almost impossible.

FAX International's strategy for breaking into the Japanese market is to enter into a joint venture agreement with a large Japanese firm that already has access to the target customers in Japan. FAX International is in a position to offer an extremely attractive joint venture opportunity because the network has been designed to carry traffic in both directions simultaneously between the United States and Japan. Once a steady flow of traffic has been developed from the United States to Tokyo, return traffic can be carried at an extremely low variable cost ($.13/minute). By succeeding in the United States–Tokyo market first, FAX International will be in a position to provide a Japanese firm with a complete franchiselike opportunity for carrying fax traffic from Tokyo back to the United States. The Japanese partner will be responsible for marketing the service in Tokyo and providing all customer support. Business customers in Tokyo currently pay $1.20 to $1.60 per minute for facsimile transmission service to the United States. FAX International's current plan is to offer the Japanese partner an opportunity to carry traffic on the network at a cost of just $.35/minute. At this rate, the Japanese partner will be in a position to mark up their cost of goods sold by 100 percent and still offer customers a 40–60 percent savings. At a rate of $.35/minute, FAX International will earn 60 percent gross margins on all return traffic from Tokyo. The profit opportunity is extremely attractive for all parties involved.

FAX International will begin searching for a joint venture partner in early 1992 once the network has been successfully established between the United States and Tokyo. Several options for identifying joint venture partners have already been presented. One option under serious consideration is to hire Mr. Douglas Fine to negotiate and manage the joint venture. Doug Fine has had specific experience in negotiating joint ventures for US firms interested in entering the Japanese market while working for the venture capital arm of Nomura Securities in Tokyo. Doug holds a BS and master's degree in electrical engineering from Stanford University, is a graduate of the Harvard Business School, and is fluent in Japanese.

FAX International's activities in Japan to date have been coordinated through two key relationships that have developed over the past year:

- *Coopers & Lybrand.* The consulting office of Coopers & Lybrand in Tokyo has been responsible for working with FAX International personnel to secure the necessary operating licenses for the company in Japan.
- *KDD.* KDD is Japan's largest international telecommunications carrier. KDD has been selected to provide FAX International's digital communications lines between the United States and Japan in coordination with AT&T. In addition, FAX International's network equipment will be housed in Tokyo within the KDD facilities. The KDD facility provides FAX International with 24-hour network monitoring, 24-hour security, climate control, guaranteed power backup, and other emergency control measures.

London/Paris Market Strategy

FAX International anticipates an opportunity to enter the London and Paris markets simultaneously with a low-price, fast-growth approach identical to the strategy employed in the United States. The geographic proximity of London and Paris will allow these two major markets to be serviced from a single business support office located in London. International facsimile traffic in and out of Great Britain and France is highly concentrated within London and Paris. Rough estimates provided by the consulates of each country show 70 percent or more of each country's international traffic tied to these two cities. Each city will have its own sales office and customer support office, but will share a common business systems office providing billing, accounting, and network management services.

The economic opportunity in both London and Paris is extremely attractive.

In addition to carrying traffic from London and Paris to the United States, the network will be capable of carrying traffic in all directions between London, Paris, and Tokyo. The

	London	Paris
Current business rates to United States:	$1.08/minute	$1.58/minute
FAX International variable cost:	$0.30*	$0.30*
FAX International rate/minute:	$0.60	$0.60
Customer savings:	44%	62%

*Variable costs based on traffic volume of $5 million/year from each city.

economic opportunity along all of these routes is equally attractive to the opportunity outlined above.

MARKET SIZE

The Federal Communications Commission keeps track of the number of direct dial international calls placed every year over the public switched networks. (AT&T, MCI, Sprint, etc.) An analysis of the statistics shows the following trends:

1. Switched international voice traffic is growing at 15–20 percent per year worldwide.
2. Switched international facsimile traffic is growing at more than twice the pace of voice traffic (30–40 percent).
3. Facsimile traffic already accounts for up to 70 percent of the calls on the United States/Japan route and 33 percent on the US/United Kingdom route. These statistics are estimates and are unavailable for most international routes.
4. International traffic is highly concentrated between major US city centers and major international city centers. For example, Tokyo represents almost 70 percent of the traffic in and out of Japan. Similar traffic concentrations exist in London, Paris, Hong Kong, and so forth.

International Direct Dial Calls—Voice and Fax 1990

	Voice and Fax Traffic	Percent Fax	Fax Market
US/Japan (both directions)	560 million minutes/year	70%	390 million
US/Great Britain	1,150 million minutes/year	33	380 million
US/France	390 million minutes/year	N/A	N/A
US/West Germany	700 million minutes/year	N/A	N/A

N/A = not available.
Note: Unlike most telecommunications equipment, the FAX International network has been designed to meet the regulatory requirements of every international phone system. The opportunity exists to expand the service to all of the countries listed above plus many others.
Sources: FCC and June 15, 1990 issue of *EMMS* (Electronic Mail and Micro Systems)

HOW THE NETWORK WORKS

The FAX International network can be broken down into four functional components:

1. Interface with the customer.
2. Collect and distribute documents within a country.
3. Transmit documents to a foreign country.
4. Monitor the status of every document on the network.

Customer Interface

The goal of the customer interface is to allow customers to utilize the FAX International network without changing their current behavior. The expectations of the 100 customers interviewed to date were clear and straightforward. Customers want to dial a phone number into their fax machine and know that the document is going to reach its destination. If the document is destined for Tokyo, then it should be invisibly routed over the FAX International network. If the document is destined for a city not served by FAX International then it should be transmitted via the customer's primary long-distance carrier (AT&T, MCI, Sprint, etc.). FAX International has achieved this goal of invisible performance by incorporating an intelligent auto-dialer into the system. Every fax machine that is signed onto the network will have a programmable auto-dialer attached to the back of the machine. The auto-dialer will determine which fax calls should be routed over FAX International. For example, if a customer enters a phone number destined for Tokyo, the dialer will intercept the call, dial an access number to reach FAX International, and then pass along the following information:

- Customer account number.
- Password.
- Other control information.
- Phone number entered by the customer.

The network will read in the information from the auto-dialer, check to make sure the customer is authorized to use the network, and then issue a fax receive tone to the customer's fax machine. The document will be received into the FAX International network and then forwarded to the appropriate destination country. The auto-dialer is able to perform the tasks outlined above in less time than it takes AT&T to connect an average international call. The customer experiences no delay as a result of the auto-dialer's activities.

Collect and Distribute Documents within a Country

Customers located anywhere in the United States will be able to access the FAX International network. The capability has been built in to send or receive a document from any fax machine in the United States, but over time the communications assets utilized to accomplish the task will change.

1. *Initial approach*. FAX International will start with a single network node (central node) located in Boston. When a customer in New York City dials a number destined for Japan, the auto-dialer attached to the customer's fax machine will reach FAX International by dialing an 800 number. This type of 800 number access will cost FAX International $.15/minute on average.
2. *Network expansion*. Once the volume of traffic in and out of a given city like New York exceeds 500 minutes per day, a separate network node will be installed in that city. The auto-dialers located in New York City will then be reprogrammed to access FAX International by dialing a local call in New York to reach the network. The document will be received into the New York City node and then transmitted to the central node in Boston over a high-speed digital line. The cost of collecting a document from New York City will then drop to only $.05/minute.

Over time, FAX International will expand the network to include remote nodes all over the country. The same type of expansion will take place in Japan thus allowing the company to reach customers more efficiently. Since the auto-dialers installed at the customer sites can be programmed remotely, customers will not be affected as the network configuration changes and grows.

Transmit Documents to a Foreign Country

Once a document has reached the central node in the United States it will be transmitted to its foreign destination over a dedicated high speed digital line. Dedicated fiber optic based circuits between the United States and Tokyo can be leased from a variety of international carriers, including AT&T, MCI, and Sprint. These lines are billed on a flat monthly charge basis. The line will be dedicated to FAX International and available for simultaneous use in both directions 24 hours a day. The average cost of sending a fax document from the United States to Tokyo over one of these lines depends on two factors:

1. *Size of the fiber optic lines*. Substantial economies of scale result from leasing high-volume lines known as full T1 circuits. A full T1 circuit consists of 24 smaller channels which can be leased one at a time. The first channel between the United States and Tokyo costs $14,500/month to lease. The cost per channel drops consistently as channels are added until the average cost per channel reaches $5,000/month on a full T1 circuit. A traffic volume of 7 million minutes/year is required to efficiently utilize a full T1 circuit between any two points.
2. *Utilization of the T1 line in each direction*. The international T1 circuit utilized by FAX International can carry traffic in both directions simultaneously. The average cost per minute of traffic carried on the circuit will depend on the volume of traffic flowing in each direction. In order to be conservative, the FAX International business plan is based on the full cost of the circuit being covered by traffic running from the United States to Tokyo.

Monitor the Status of Every Document on the Network

Customers demand perfectly accurate, up-to-the-minute information on the status of their documents as they move through the network. The FAX International network has been designed to provide a status update on every document once every five minutes. The information will be used to provide high-quality customer service and to provide customers with up-to-the-minute status on all of the documents entered into the network.

Document status information will be collected at the central node in the United States and forwarded to the company's customer service office. The customer service office can be located anywhere in the United States. Initially it will be located in the Boston area, but if necessity dictates a move to a different location, the operation can be easily relocated.

NETWORK ECONOMICS

The economics of the FAX International network are based on two issues, hardware costs and communications costs. Outlined below is an introduction to the variables which drive these two cost centers. Surprisingly, the network hardware is quite inexpensive when measured by the revenue it produces. The financial plan will show that hardware lease costs end up representing less than 5 percent of gross revenue once the network achieves an efficient operating volume. Communications costs on the other hand are quite expensive since they represent the network's cost of goods sold. Variable communications costs will eventually stabilize to represent 50 percent or less of gross revenue. The hardware costs and communications costs are connected to the extent that the deployment of hardware assets has a direct bearing on the cost of collecting or distributing a fax document within the United States or Japan.

Hardware Costs

The network hardware can be broken into three pieces:

- Fixed/core network hardware and software.
- Variable network hardware and software.
- Customer-based auto-dialers.

The hardware block diagram provides a graphic representation of the central processing nodes that will be installed in both the United States and Tokyo (see *Exhibit A*). All of the equipment shown will be leased rather than purchased by FAX International. The company is currently working with a leasing operation located in Boston called TLP Leasing Programs, Inc.

Exhibit A
Central Node: Hardware Block Diagram

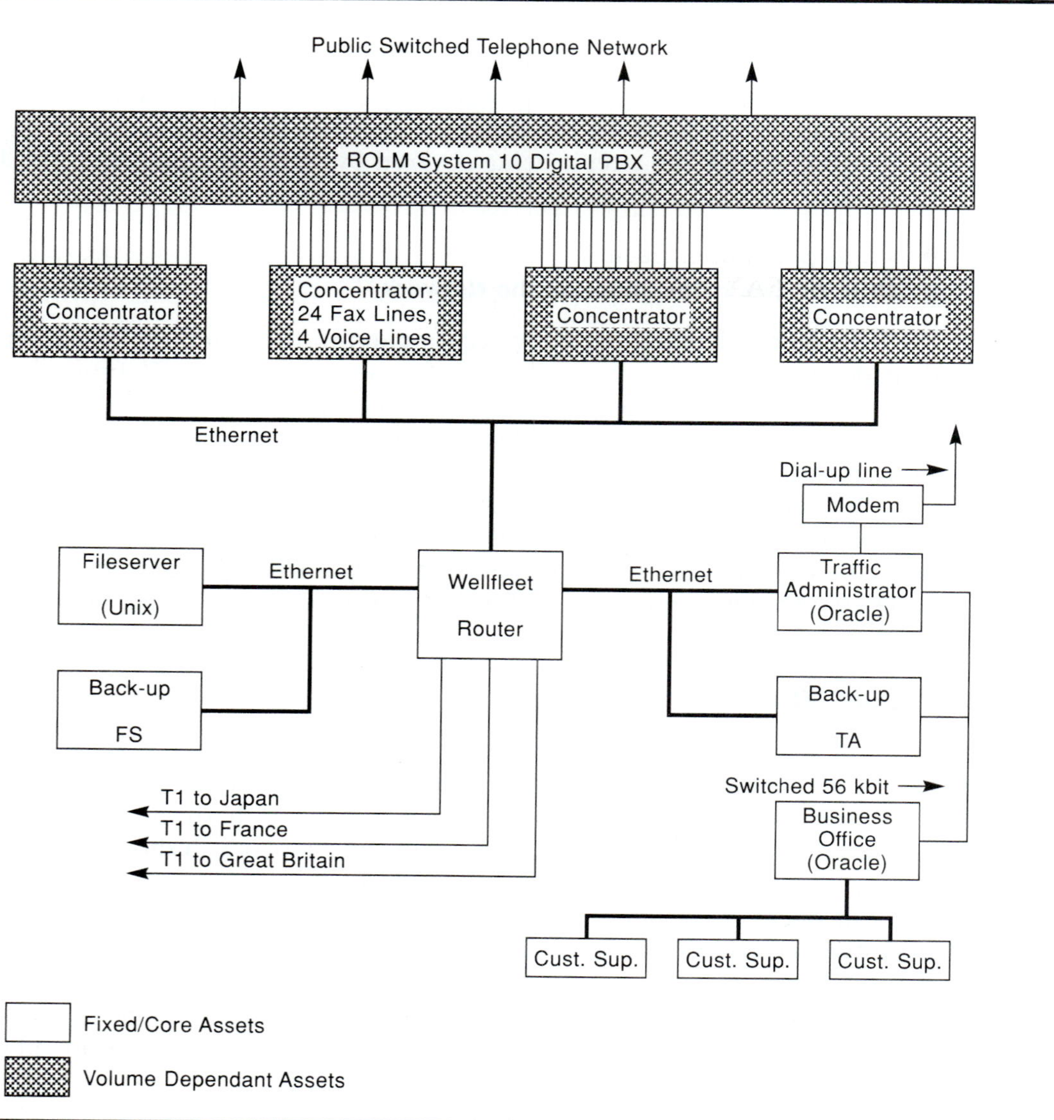

Fixed Network Hardware/Software

A fixed core investment is required to allow the company to function properly. The core system includes all of the hardware and software necessary to provide the following system features:

- Efficient document transmission.
- Critical asset redundancy.
- Customer service and support system.
- Sales support and Customer Installation system.
- Network management system.
- Business management software (includes automated billing).
- Core system investment: $300,000.

Variable Network Hardware

The second component of the network varies depending on the volume of traffic carried daily. As traffic volume increases, additional fax lines will be added to the central node and to the remote city nodes around the United States and Japan. Additional capacity can be added in units of 5,000 traffic minutes per day.

- Additional investment required for each additional 5,000 minutes/day: $45,000.

Customer Site Auto-dialers

FAX International will be using programmable auto-dialers produced by MITEL Electronics. Purchased in volume, they cost $125/dialer. The auto-dialers provide the following capabilities:

- *Fraud prevention*. Each auto-dialer will be given a unique password to use when dialing into the FAX International network.
- *Invisible access to the network*. The auto-dialer will allow customers to utilize the FAX International network without changing their current routine. A customer simply dials a destination phone number on a fax machine and hits the start button. Documents destined for Tokyo will be intercepted by the auto-dialer and passed on to the FAX International network automatically. The process is completely invisible to the customer.

Customers will be provided with a certain number of free auto-dialers based on their average daily volume of traffic. A free auto-dialer will be provided for every 10 minutes of traffic per day. This policy is designed to deter customers from asking FAX International to install auto-dialers on fax machines that are rarely used for international transmissions. At the customer's request, additional auto-dialers will be provided for a rental fee rate of $10/month per auto-dialer. For planning purposes, the company has planned to provide a free auto-dialer for every 10 minutes/day of additional traffic that is signed onto the network.

Auto-dialers will be purchased in units of 500 dialers. If each dialer represents 10 minutes per day of traffic and costs $125 then the following cost structure results.

- Auto-dialer Investment for each 5,000 minutes/day of traffic: $62,500.

Hardware Utilization Analysis

Each additional 5,000 minutes per day of traffic that is added to the FAX International network requires a hardware investment of $45,000 in network hardware and $62,500 in customer auto-dialers, for a total investment of $107,500. At an average rate of $.74 per minute to Tokyo, 5,000 minutes of traffic per day represents $890,000 per year of revenue, assuming 20 business days per month.

An investment of $107,500 in hardware and software that has a useful life of at least three years will generate $890,000 per year in incremental revenue. The asset intensity of this network is extremely low.

Communications Costs

FAX International has the option to purchase its fiber optic communications lines from a variety of common carriers, including AT&T, MCI, Sprint, Cable & Wireless, and many other less well-known carriers. Transmitting a document between the United States and Tokyo involves three types of communications costs:

1. Local reception or delivery in the United States:
   a. Minimum $.09/minute.
   b. Maximum $.15/minute.
   c. Average cost will drop as volume grows.
2. Transmission from the United States to Tokyo:
   a. Minimum $.20/minute.
   b. Maximum $.43/minute.
   c. Average cost will drop as volume grows.
3. Local reception or delivery in Tokyo: Average $.03/minute regardless of volume.

Substantial economies of scale result from reaching a minimum volume of 7 million minutes of traffic/year on the network. A company operating in this market at a low volume (less than 1 million minutes/year) will be faced with variable costs of $.61/minute. Alternatively, a company operating at a volume of 7 million minutes per year will face a variable cost of just $.31/minute. These variable cost figures are based on carrying traffic in one direction only. The international leased circuit between the United States and Tokyo is capable of carrying traffic in two directions simultaneously. As a result, once traffic has been developed in one direction, the network is capable of carrying return traffic at very low variable cost.

The following *Table 1* and *Table 2* summarize the variable cost structure that FAX International will face at different levels of traffic volume.

Table 1
Variable Costs—United States to Tokyo

Traffic Volume	*US Reception*	*Transmit to Tokyo*	*Local Delivery in Tokyo*	*Total*
<500,000 min/yr	$.15	$.43	$.03	$.61
<1,000,000	$.15	$.34	$.03	$.52
<3,000,000	$.09	$.28	$.03	$.40
<5,000,000	$.09	$.24	$.03	$.36
<7,000,000	$.09	$.20	$.03	$.32

Table 2
Return Traffic Variable Costs—Tokyo to the United States

Traffic Volume	*Tokyo Reception*	*Transmit to the United States*	*Local Delivery in the United States*	*Total*
<500,000 min/yr	Free	Free	$.14	$.14
<1,000,000	Free	Free	$.13	$.13
<3,000,000	Free	Free	$.13	$.13
<5,000,000	Free	Free	$.13	$.13
<7,000,000	Free	Free	$.13	$.13

TECHNOLOGY

Dr. Thomas P. Sosnowski, PhD, is responsible for the network design and development effort. Dr. Sosnowski (Tom), age 54, has worked his entire career in telecommunications development, including 13 years at AT&T's Bell Labs.

Network Systems

The following network systems are currently under development at FAX International:

1. *Communications network.* A fiber optic based network that can move a fax document between the United States and any foreign country seven times as efficiently as the AT&T switched voice network.
2. *Customer interface.* A system that will allow FAX International to invisibly route specific documents from a customer's fax machine onto the network. The goal is to ensure that the process of using the FAX International network is completely invisible to a customer sending a fax to Tokyo.
3. *Sales support.* A sales rep support system based on a portable PC platform that will dramatically increase the efficiency of the field sales force.
   a. Lead management and tracking software.
   b. Automated customer installation system.
   c. Automated proposal generation.
4. *Customer service.* A system that will automatically identify service problems, suggest solutions, and assist service reps in contacting the affected customers before the customer even knows a problem exists.
5. *Network management.* A system to allow an operator to sit at a terminal in Boston and monitor the behavior of every piece of network equipment worldwide.
6. *Business management.* A system to provide the FAX International management team with access to the following information on a daily basis:
   a. Network asset utilization.
   b. Customer behavior statistics.
   c. Sales rep productivity.
   d. Customer service rep productivity.
   e. Billing/accounting data.
7. *Integrated billing and accounting system.* A system to automate the entire billing and accounting cycle under the ORACLE relational database management program. Customer bills will be generated automatically by the network and entered into the integrated accounting system.

Development Philosophy

Tom Sosnowski and his development team are dedicated to producing a network that is capable of meeting the full range of business objectives set out for FAX International. Outlined below are some of the design tenets that have been used to guide the development process:

1. Utilize standard off-the-shelf technology wherever possible. Never make what you can buy.
2. Efficient technical development results from extensive planning. Project costs are projected based on an average of 80 percent planning and 20 percent implementation.
3. The design and construction of the network should be focused on meeting the specific needs of the customers, the sales force, and the customer service reps, not on potential technological capabilities.

4. Develop a hardware and software architecture that can incorporate frequent changes in customer demands.
5. Build the network in a modular fashion so that it can grow as quickly as the business requires.

SALES STRATEGY

The FAX International sales strategy has been designed around one primary goal:

Make it easy for customers of all sizes to say yes to a free test of the service. Once customers have tested the network, they will sign up for the service if it successfully provides the following features and benefits:

- High quality, reliable service.
- 40 percent to 60 percent savings.
- No up front fees.
- No training or change in behavior.
- No change in equipment.
- No change in long-distance carrier.

The FAX International sales organization will be based around a sales force of six field sales reps located in Los Angeles, San Francisco, and New York City. Although the FAX International sales presentation is simple enough to be delivered via a telemarketing operation, a field sales force approach has been selected for the following reasons:

1. *On-site installations required*. Signing up a customer to use the network involves attaching auto-dialers to each of the customer's fax machines and entering information about each user into the FAX International database. Gathering accurate information during the installation process is crucial to the efficient operation of the business. FAX International explored several opportunities to use third-party organizations for installation work but opted against this approach.
2. *Highly concentrated customer base*. FAX International sales reps will be pursuing leads provided by a directory, *Japanese Affiliated Companies in the US*, published by the Japanese External Trade Organization. This directory list 9,000 Japanese-affiliated firms in the United States. Over half of these leads are located in New York City, Los Angeles, and San Francisco. FAX International further estimates that over 80 percent of the decision makers for the 9,000 listed organizations are located in these three cities. The definition of a Japanese-affiliated firm is one that is at least 10 percent owned by a Japanese firm.

Convincing customers to accept a free, no-risk test of the network is the primary job of the field sales organization. Once a customer has agreed to a free test, the network will sell itself based on the performance of the system. Convincing customers to test the service is dependent on FAX International's cutting through the confusion and clutter created by the intense competition in the United States between MCI, Sprint, and AT&T.

FAX International is not offering a typical long-distance service, and the company cannot afford to let customers categorize the service as being similar to MCI, Sprint, and so on. FAX International is offering a totally different service concept which offers customers both superior service and superior price with no risk to the customer's organization. FAX International's sales presentation and promotional material have been designed to transmit the following five points:

1. *Totally different communications concept*. The FAX International network is seven times more efficient at transmitting a fax document than the voice network of AT&T, MCI,

or Sprint. Comparing a highly specialized service like FAX International to AT&T, MCI, or Sprint is like comparing Federal Express to the US Post Office.

2. *Better service*. The FAX International network has been designed to simplify life for heavy fax users:
   – Automatic redialing of busy numbers.
   – Delayed delivery and priority delivery options.
   – Broadcast distribution.
   – Enhanced billing functions.
3. *Better price*. FAX International's introductory offer of $.69 per minute to Tokyo represents a 40–60 percent cost savings for customers of all sizes. AT&T, MCI, Sprint, and others charge between $1.80 and $2.75 for the first minute of a call to Tokyo and $.90 to $1.15 for each additional minute during business hours.
4. *No-risk decision*. FAX International customers do not have to change their primary long-distance carrier. Only those fax calls destined for Tokyo or other cities serviced by FAX International will be routed over the network. All other fax calls will be transmitted by the customer's primary long-distance carrier. In most situations the customer's primary long-distance carrier won't even know that FAX International exists.
5. *Free test opportunity for qualified customers*. Customer interviews have shown that the biggest barrier to accepting the service is a fear that the network will not function as advertised. To combat this primary objection, FAX International will offer customers 100 free minutes of digital fax service to Tokyo from a single fax machine, with no strings attached.

PRICE COMPARISON

FAX International, Inc. pricing structure:

- *Small customers* (below $500/month): $.79/minute (billed in six-second increments).
- *Large customers* (above $500/month): $.69/minute.
- *Auto-dialer rental fee:* Customers will receive a free auto-dialer for every fax machine that transmits an average of 10 minutes of traffic/business day over the network. Additional auto-dialers will be provided at a rental rate of $10/month. Note: Auto-dialers cost FAX International $125/unit.

Price/minute comparison for an average three-minute fax call to Tokyo:

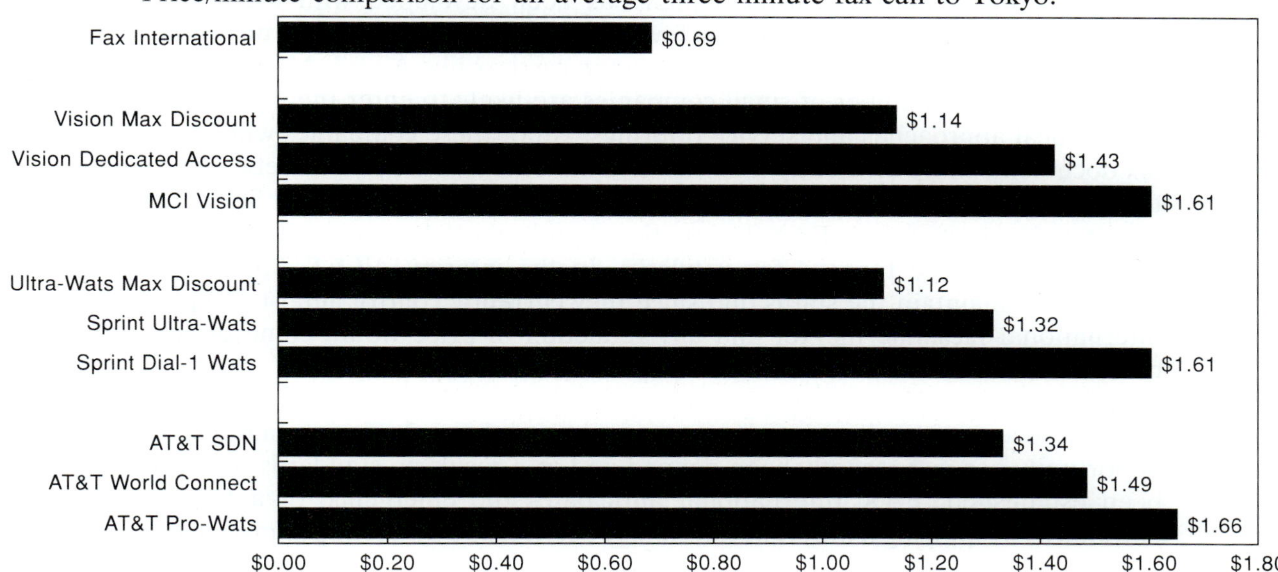

SALES EXPECTATIONS

FAX International field sales reps will be responsible for qualifying accounts, setting up network demonstrations, installing free tests, and closing sales. The sales cycle is short and clearly defined. The profile of an ideal sales rep for FAX International is a young, successful sales person who has proven abilities to qualify accounts, set up meetings, and close sales. Top performers in the telecommunications industry in similar sales environments earn $40,000, including bonuses and commissions. FAX International's goal is to take six of these superior performers and offer them a base salary of $36,000 with an opportunity to earn $60,000 or more.

Monthly sales goals have been set with the following expectations in mind:

1. *5 to 10 new accounts per month*. The definition of an account is a single customer location that sends at least 25 minutes of traffic per day to Tokyo. Most of the customers contacted by FAX International will operate out of multiple offices in the United States. As a result, each sales presentation has the potential to result in sales to multiple locations.
2. *350 minutes/day of new traffic each month*. An average customer office location is expected to generate between 35 and 70 minutes of traffic per day. Interviews with 100 customers showed a range of 10 to 500 minutes of traffic per day from a single customer location.
3. *$700,000 in net new business per year*. The aggregate goal for the year is to sign up at least 4,000 minutes/day of new traffic. The potential exists to sign-up a single customer that represents 1,000 minutes/day or more from a combination of multiple locations. For example, Nippon Express is one of the companies that has expressed great interest in testing the service. The Boston office of Nippon Express sends 125 pages per day to Tokyo and they reperesent just 1 of 17 US offices.

Field sales reps will be responsible for working with accounts located within driving distance of their assigned metropolitan area. All sales contacts made outside of the assigned area will be passed on to corporate headquarters. Installations at remote customer sites will be handled by a sales rep working out of the Boston office and travelling around the country.

COMPETITION

FAX International's business plan has been developed with the assumption that competition will develop over the next few years from two sources: small niche players similar to FAX International and full-service common carriers like AT&T, MCI, and Sprint. In the near term a large number of small companies are likely to enter the market with a variety of technical approaches and service offerings. All of these companies will be able to move fax documents more efficiently than the international switched voice networks, and most of these competitors will succeed in winning customers. AT&T, MCI, and Sprint are expected to enter the market once FAX International and others have proven that a large market exists for store and forward fax networks. In the interim, AT&T, MCI, and Sprint are expected to maintain the status quo since they currently control almost 100 percent of the international facsimile market and any reduction in price would come directly off their bottom lines.

Niche players: The international store and forward fax market has the potential to support dozens of small niche players operating on the multiple international routes. The opportunity has just recently been defined and as a result no standards of excellence have been established. FAX International anticipates the emergence of a large number of entrants each applying a different technology, service, and marketing approach in an attempt to find out what the customers are willing to buy. A limited number of these companies will enjoy great success and as a result will define standards for the industry. Success will be based on how well the networks function, how closely the service offerings meet the needs of the customers, and the efficiency of the sales/marketing approach applied. FAX International has designed a network and series of business support systems that will allow the company to refine its approach quickly to meet the needs of the market.

AT&T, MCI, and Sprint: All three of these companies have the technology and resources required to dominate this new market, but none of these companies has the incentive. All three companies know that if one enters the market the other two will follow immediately. The result will be a quick drop in revenue for all three companies with no change in market share or competitive advantage. FAX International anticipates that all three competitors will prepare the necessary technology to compete in the market but will avoid entry until FAX International and several other players develop the market and capture substantial market share.

AT&T, MCI, and Sprint represent both a threat and an opportunity to FAX International. Once FAX International reaches 7,000,000 minutes ($5,000,000) of traffic/year on the United States–Tokyo route, the company will be in a position to operate profitably no matter who enters the market. FAX International expects to grow far beyond this minimum required level in several markets before any major competitor presents a competing offer. If AT&T, MCI, and Sprint enter the market, a furious fight for market share is likely to ensue. All of those niche players that failed to reach the minimum required economy of scale will be forced out of the market. FAX International on the other hand should be in the enviable position of being able to sell out at a premium to one of several companies eager to build market share quickly.

FAX INTERNATIONAL TEAM

- *Douglas J. Ranalli*: president/founder, age 30. Mr. Ranalli brings a combination of marketing, entrepreneurial, and engineering skills to the organization. Past experience includes five years as the Founder/Publisher of *Student Life* magazine. Mr. Ranalli built *Student Life* to a national circulation of 1,200,000 copies per issue before selling to Time, Inc., in 1987 for a multiple of 1.3 times revenue. Educational background: MBA, Harvard Business School (Baker Scholar); BS, Cornell University, industrial engineering.
- *Dr. Thomas P. Sosnowski*: vice president and director of engineering, age 54. Dr. Sosnowski is an engineering project management and product development specialist in the communications industry. Tom's background in telecommunications includes 13 years in R&D at Bell Laboratories.
- *Steven Lanzilla*: US sales manager, age 37. Mr. Lanzilla brings 17 years of sales experience in telecommunications to the FAX International team. In particular, Steven's experience includes four years of sales, sales management, and product development experience at US Sprint. Currently Steven is a telecommunications consultant in Boston.
- *Steven Orr*: UNIX system designer, age 38. Mr. Orr is a UNIX systems development consultant on PC platforms. Steve is responsible for system design, testing, and redundancy analysis.
- *Tom Flaherty*: database development and administration, age 32. Mr. Flaherty is a relational database programming expert specializing in the ORACLE RDMS. Tom is responsible for all database management, which includes information for billing, accounting, customer service, network management, and sales support.
- *Michael Landino*: database development, age 26. Michael is an ORACLE programmer specializing in SQL Forms 3.0 development.

- *Bradlee T. Howe*: chief financial officer (CFO), age 50. Mr. Howe is the president of Financial Managers Trust of Cambridge, Massachusetts, a company which serves as the part-time CFO for high-tech start-ups and smaller corporations.
- *James O. Jacoby, Jr.*: finance consultant, age 28. Mr. Jacoby is employed full-time by the Corporate Finance Department of Chemical Bank in New York City. Jim will be assisting FAX International in the two critical areas of fund-raising and bank relationship management. Jim's background includes a finance degree from Notre Dame and an MBA from Harvard.
- *Barry Nearhos:* accountant, Coopers & Lybrand. Mr. Nearhos is a partner in the Emerging Business Group in the C&L Boston office.
- *Steve Snyder*: lawyer. Mr. Snyder is a partner at O'Connor, Broude, and Snyder in Waltham, Massachusetts, specializing in high-tech start-ups.

FAX INTERNATIONAL ADVISORY BOARD

- *Mike Williams*: age 53. Mr. Williams retired from AT&T in 1990 after a 29-year career and now resides in Tucson, Arizona. Recent positions within AT&T included President of the AT&T—Americas subsidiary, and chief negotiator for AT&T's first joint venture in Japan.
- *Kurt Weidenhaupt*: age 52. Mr. Weidenhaupt is a German national and President of AEG of North America, a subsidiary of Daimler-Benz. Mr. Weidenhaupt's career has encompassed numerous international assignments, including 13 years in London.
- *Robert Casale*: age 52. Mr. Casale's career has included senior executive positions in both the communications and financial services industry. Currently, Mr. Casale is the president of ADP's Brokerage Information Services Group in Journal Square, New Jersey.
- *Jerry Johnson*: age 54. A retired AT&T mergers and acquisitions executive, Mr. Johnson is now managing partner of the MJI consulting firm in Stamford, Connecticut. MJI specializes in forming strategic alliances within the telecommunications industry.
- *Bob Petzinger*: age 51. Mr. Petzinger retired from AT&T in 1990 and now resides in Naples, Florida. Mr. Petzinger's most recent position was as director of AT&T's operations in the United Kingdom.

FINANCIAL PROJECTIONS

Year 1 Statement of Operations

	1991 *Aug.*	*Sept.*	*Oct.*	*Nov.*	*Dec.*	*1992* *Jan.*	*Feb.*	*Mar.*	*Apr.*	*May*	*June*	*Jul.*	*Total year*
Net sales	$0	$0	$0	$73,260	$114,286	$155,311	$196,337	$237,362	$278,388	$319,414	$377,939	$431,215	$2,183,512
Operating expenses:													
Cost of communications	500	1,000	2,000	64,500	85,680	107,060	129,490	127,120	143,800	158,680	182,010	197,815	1,199,655
Administrative expenses	38,850	10,050	10,050	10,100	10,100	10,150	10,200	10,250	10,250	10,300	10,300	10,350	150,950
Billing and accounting expenses	500	5,520	5,520	7,487	7,580	8,023	13,067	13,660	13,753	13,847	13,940	14,033	116,930
Sales expenses	11,750	64,500	50,500	54,163	56,214	58,266	60,317	62,368	64,419	66,471	68,522	70,573	688,063
Japanese J/V expenses	0	0	0	0	0	10,000	0	10,000	20,000	10,000	10,000	10,000	70,000
Customer service	2,500	2,500	2,500	5,000	5,000	7,500	9,000	10,500	10,500	12,000	12,000	13,500	92,500
Lease expense	1,656	31,356	13,967	24,498	17,942	24,047	26,461	23,596	29,700	32,114	34,529	36,943	296,809
Technical expenses	21,700	21,700	143,200	33,200	33,200	34,700	39,700	36,200	36,200	36,200	36,200	36,200	508,400
Total expenses	77,456	136,626	227,737	198,947	215,717	259,746	288,235	293,694	328,623	339,612	367,501	389,415	3,123,307
EBITDA	(77,456)	(136,626)	(227,737)	(125,687)	(101,431)	(104,434)	(91,898)	(56,331)	(50,235)	(20,198)	10,438	41,800	(939,796)
Depreciation/amortization	0	0	0	0	0	0	0	0	0	0	0	0	0
Corporate expenses	0	0	0	0	0	0	0	0	0	0	0	0	0
EBIT	(77,456)	(136,626)	(227,737)	(125,687)	(101,431)	(104,434)	(91,898)	(56,331)	(50,235)	(20,198)	10,438	41,800	(939,796)
Other income (expense):													
Cash interest income	0	0	0	0	0	0	0	0	0	0	0	0	0
Revolver interest (11%)	0	0	0	0	0	0	0	0	(14)	(567)	(847)	(904)	(2,332)
Extraordinary items	0	0	0	0	0	0	0	0	0	0	0	0	0
Other (expenses) income	0	0	0	0	0	0	0	0	0	0	0	0	0
Total other income (expenses)	0	0	0	0	0	0	0	0	(14)	(567)	(847)	(904)	(2,332)
EBT	(77,456)	(136,626)	(227,737)	(125,687)	(101,431)	(104,434)	(91,898)	(56,331)	(50,249)	(20,765)	9,591	40,896	(942,128)
Income taxes	0	0	0	0	0	0	0	0	0	0	0	0	0
Net income	($77,456)	($136,626)	($227,737)	($125,687)	($101,431)	($104,434)	($91,898)	($56,331)	($50,249)	($20,765)	$9,591	$40,896	($942,128)
Cumulative NOLs	(77,456)	(214,083)	(441,819)	(567,507)	(668,938)	(773,372)	(865,270)	(921,601)	(971,849)	(992,615)	(983,024)	(942,128)	

EBITDA = earnings before interest, tax, depreciation, and amortization; EBIT = earnings before interest and tax; NOL = net operating loss.

Year 1 Balance Sheet

	1991 Aug.	Sept.	Oct.	Nov.	Dec.	1992 Jan.	Feb.	Mar.	Apr.	May	June	Jul.
Assets												
Current assets:												
Cash	$923,037	$786,904	$560,153	$427,516	$312,226	$196,181	$95,759	$10,000	$10,000	$10,000	$10,000	$10,000
Invested cash	0	0	0	0	0	0	0	0	0	0	0	0
Accounts receivable	0	0	0	72,256	112,720	153,184	193,647	234,111	274,574	315,038	372,762	425,308
Total current assets	923,037	786,904	560,153	499,773	424,946	349,364	289,406	244,111	284,574	325,038	382,762	435,308
Long-term assets:												
Capital leases costs, net	0	0	0	0	0	0	0	0	0	0	0	0
Net property, plant, and equipment	0	0	0	0	0	0	0	0	0	0	0	0
Intangibles	0	0	0	0	0	0	0	0	0	0	0	0
Organizational expenses	150,000	150,000	150,000	150,000	150,000	150,000	150,000	150,000	150,000	150,000	150,000	150,000
Total assets	$1,073,037	$936,904	$710,153	$649,773	$574,946	$499,364	$439,406	$394,111	$434,574	$475,038	$532,762	$585,308
Liabilities												
Accounts payable	$493	$986	$1,973	$63,616	$84,506	$105,593	$127,716	$125,379	$141,830	$156,506	$179,517	$195,105
Accrued expenses	0	0	0	3,663	9,377	17,143	26,960	38,828	52,747	68,718	87,615	109,176
Revolving facility	0	0	0	0	0	0	0	1,505	61,847	92,429	98,654	73,155
Other current/CMLTD	0	0	0	0	0	0	0	0	0	0	0	0
Total current liabilities	493	986	1,973	67,279	93,884	122,376	154,676	165,712	256,424	317,653	365,785	377,436
Total liabilities	$493	$986	$1,973	$67,279	$93,884	$122,736	$154,676	$165,712	$256,424	$317,653	$365,785	$377,436
Shareholders' equity												
Founders' invested capital	150,000	150,000	150,000	150,000	150,000	150,000	150,000	150,000	150,000	150,000	150,000	150,000
Additional paid-in capital	1,000,000	1,000,000	1,000,000	1,000,000	1,000,000	1,000,000	1,000,000	1,000,000	1,000,000	1,000,000	1,000,000	1,000,000
Retained earnings	(77,456)	(214,083)	(441,819)	(567,507)	(668,938)	(773,372)	(865,270)	(921,601)	(971,849)	(992,615)	(983,024)	(942,128)
Total shareholders' equity	1,072,544	935,918	708,181	582,493	481,062	376,628	284,730	228,399	178,151	157,385	166,976	207,872
Total liabilities and shareholders' equity	$1,073,037	$936,904	$710,153	$649,773	$574,946	$499,364	$439,406	$394,111	$434,574	$475,038	$532,762	$585,308

Year 1 Statement of Cash Flow

	1991 Aug.	Sept.	Oct.	Nov.	Dec.	1992 Jan.	Feb.	Mar.	Apr.	May	June	Jul.	Total Year
Net income	($77,456)	($136,626)	($227,737)	($125,687)	($101,431)	($104,434)	($91,898)	($56,331)	($50,249)	($20,765)	$9,591	$40,896	($942,128)
Depreciation/amortization	0	0	0	0	0	0	0	0	0	0	0	0	0
Other adjustments	0	0	0	0	0	0	0	0	0	0	0	0	0
Gross cash flow	(77,456)	(136,626)	(227,737)	(125,687)	(101,431)	(104,434)	(91,898)	(56,331)	(50,249)	(20,765)	9,591	40,896	(942,128)
Changes in working capital													
Accounts receivable	0	0	0	(72,256)	(40,464)	(40,464)	(40,464)	(40,464)	(40,464)	(40,464)	(57,724)	(52,546)	(425,308)
Accounts payable	493	493	986	61,644	20,890	21,087	22,123	(2,338)	16,452	14,676	23,010	15,588	195,105
Accrued commissions	0	0	0	3,663	5,714	7,766	9,817	11,868	13,919	15,971	18,897	21,561	109,176
Other current liabilities	0	0	0	0	0	0	0	0	0	0	0	0	0
Cash flow from operations	(76,963)	(136,133)	(226,750)	(132,637)	(115,290)	(116,045)	(100,422)	(87,264)	(60,341)	(30,582)	(6,225)	25,499	(1,063,155)
Capital expenditures	0	0	0	0	0	0	0	0	0	0	0	0	0
Operating cash flow	(76,963)	(136,133)	(226,750)	(132,637)	(115,290)	(116,045)	(100,422)	(87,264)	(60,341)	(30,582)	(6,225)	25,499	(1,063,155)
Changes in nonoperations items													
Change in capital stock	1,000,000	0	0	0	0	0	0	0	0	0	0	0	1,000,000
Cash available	$923,037	($136,133)	($226,750)	($132,637)	($115,290)	($116,045)	($100,422)	($87,264)	($60,341)	($30,582)	($6,225)	$25,499	($63,155)
Cumulative cash	923,037	786,904	560,153	427,516	312,226	196,181	95,759	8,495	(51,847)	(82,429)	(88,654)	(63,155)	
Maintenance cash level	10,000	10,000	10,000	10,000	10,000	10,000	10,000	10,000	10,000	10,000	10,000	10,000	

Year 1 Assumptions and Ratios

	1991 Aug.	Sept.	Oct.	Nov.	Dec.	1992 Jan.	Feb.	Mar.	Apr.	May	June	Jul.
Income statement:												
Net monthly sales growth				N/A	56%	36%	26%	21%	17%	15%	18%	14%
Current gross margin				12%	25%	31%	34%	46%	48%	50%	52%	54%
Current EBITDA margin				−172%	−89%	−67%	−47%	−24%	−18%	−6%	3%	10%
Communication as percentage of sales				88%	75%	69%	66%	54%	52%	50%	48%	46%
Administrative as percentage of sales				14%	9%	7%	5%	4%	4%	3%	3%	2%
Sales expense as percentage of sales				74%	49%	38%	31%	26%	23%	21%	18%	16%
Customer service as percentage of sales				7%	4%	5%	5%	4%	4%	4%	3%	3%
Leases as percentage of sales				33%	16%	15%	13%	10%	11%	10%	9%	9%
Technical costs as percentage of sales				45%	29%	22%	20%	15%	13%	11%	10%	8%
Balance sheet:												
A/R days	30.0	30.0	30.0	30.0	30.0	30.0	30.0	30.0	30.0	30.0	30.0	30.0
A/P days	30.0	30.0	30.0	30.0	30.0	30.0	30.0	30.0	30.0	30.0	30.0	30.0
Revolver as percentage of receivable base				0.00%	0.00%	0.00%	0.00%	0.64%	22.52%	29.34%	26.47%	17.20%

Year 1 Revenue Breakdown

	1991 Aug.	Sept.	Oct.	Nov.	Dec.	1992 Jan.	Feb.	Mar.	Apr.	May	June	Jul.	Total Year
United States:													
Avg price/minute	$0.74												
Monthly growth rate	350 minutes/salesrep												
Free minutes/day	0	0	0	1,000	1,000	1,000	1,000	1,000	1,000	1,000	1,000	1,000	
Net new minutes/day	0	0	0	5,000	2,800	2,800	2,800	2,800	2,800	2,800	2,800	2,800	
Total paid minutes/day	0	0	0	5,000	7,800	10,600	13,400	16,200	19,000	21,800	24,600	27,400	
Total minutes/month (20 days)	0	0	0	100,000	156,000	212,000	268,000	324,000	380,000	436,000	492,000	548,000	2,916,000
Monthly gross revenue	0	0	0	74,000	115,440	156,880	198,320	239,760	281,200	322,640	364,080	405,520	2,157,840
Uncollectables (1%)	0	0	0	740	1,154	1,569	1,983	2,398	2,812	3,226	3,641	4,055	21,578
Net monthly US revenue	$0	$0	$0	$73,260	$114,286	$155,311	$196,337	$237,362	$278,388	$319,414	$360,439	$401,465	2,138,262
Japan joint venture:													
Avg price/minute	$0.35												
Total minutes/month	0	0	0	0	0	0	0	0	0	0	50,000	85,000	135,000
Net Japanese revenue	$0	$0	$0	$0	$0	$0	$0	$0	$0	$0	$17,500	$29,750	47,250
Total US/Japan revenues	$0	$0	$0	$73,260	$114,286	$155,311	$196,337	$237,362	$278,388	$319,414	$377,939	$431,215	$2,183,512

Year 1 Expense Breakdown

	1991 *Aug.*	*Sept.*	*Oct.*	*Nov.*	*Dec.*	*1992* *Jan.*	*Feb.*	*Mar.*	*Apr.*	*May*	*June*	*Jul.*	*Total* *Year*
Technical development:													
Dr. Tom Sosnowski	$6,000	$6,000	$6,000	$6,000	$6,000	$6,000	$6,000	$6,000	$6,000	$6,000	$6,000	$6,000	$72,000
Tom Flaherty (Oracle)	4,200	4,200	4,200	4,200	4,200	4,200	4,200	4,200	4,200	4,200	4,200	4,200	50,400
Steve Orr (UNIX)	6,000	6,000	6,000	6,000	6,000	7,500	7,500	7,500	7,500	7,500	7,500	7,500	82,500
Michael Landino (Oracle)	3,500	3,500	3,500	3,500	3,500	3,500	3,500	3,500	3,500	3,500	3,500	3,500	42,000
Contract programmers	0	0	0	0	0	0	0	0	0	0	0	0	0
Tokyo engineer	0	0	1,500	1,500	1,500	1,500	1,500	1,500	1,500	1,500	1,500	1,500	15,000
Equipment housing expenses	0	0	0	10,000	10,000	10,000	10,000	11,500	11,500	11,500	11,5000	11,500	97,500
Installation expenses	0	0	120,000	0	0	0	5,000	0	0	0	0	0	125,000
Other expenses	2,000	2,000	2,000	2,000	2,000	2,000	2,000	2,000	2,000	2,000	2,000	2,000	24,000
Subtotal	21,700	21,700	143,200	33,200	33,200	34,700	39,700	36,200	36,200	36,200	36,200	36,200	508,400
Sales expenses:													
Doug Ranalli	0	5,000	5,000	5,000	5,000	5,000	5,000	5,000	5,000	5,000	5,000	5,000	55,000
Steve Lanzilla – VP sales	5,000	5,000	5,000	5,000	5,000	5,000	5,000	5,000	5,000	5,000	5,000	5,000	60,000
LA sales reps (2)	0	6,000	6,000	6,000	6,000	6,000	6,000	6,000	6,000	6,000	6,000	6,000	66,000
San Francisco reps (2)	0	6,000	6,000	6,000	6,000	6,000	6,000	6,000	6,000	6,000	6,000	6,000	66,000
NYC sales reps (2)	0	6,000	6,000	6,000	6,000	6,000	6,000	6,000	6,000	6,000	6,000	6,000	66,000
National accounts sales rep	0	3,000	3,000	3,000	3,000	3,000	3,000	3,000	3,000	3,000	3,000	3,000	33,000
Sales commissions (5%)	0	0	0	3,663	5,714	7,766	9,817	11,868	13,919	15,971	18,022	20,073	106,813
Sales office space	750	4,500	4,500	4,500	4,500	4,500	4,500	4,500	4,500	4,500	4,500	4,500	50,250
Sales expenses	6,000	14,000	14,000	14,000	14,000	14,000	14,000	14,000	14,000	14,000	14,000	14,000	160,000
Marketing/office supplies	0	5,000	1,000	1,000	1,000	1,000	1,000	1,000	1,000	1,000	1,000	1,000	15,000
Headhunter fees	0	10,000	0	0	0	0	0	0	0	0	0	0	10,000
Total sales personnel	1	8	8	8	8	8	8	8	8	8	8	8	
Subtotal	11,750	64,500	50,500	54,163	56,214	58,266	60,317	62,368	64,419	66,471	68,522	70,573	688,063
Japanese joint venture:													
Doug Fine	0	0	0	0	0	0	0	5,000	5,000	5,000	5,000	5,000	25,000
Chuo Coopers & Lybrand	0	0	0	0	0	10,000	0	0	10,000	0	0	0	20,000
Performance Bonuses	0	0	0	0	0	0	0	0	0	0	0	0	0
Expenses	0	0	0	0	0	0	0	5,000	5,000	5,000	5,000	5,000	25,000
Subtotal	0	0	0	0	0	10,000	0	10,000	20,000	10,000	10,000	10,000	70,000
Network assets:													
Network hardware lease	1,500	9,600	9,600	12,480	12,480	13,920	15,360	15,360	16,800	18,240	18,240	19,680	163,260
Japanese J/V hardware	0	0	0	0	0	0	0	0	0	0	1,440	1,440	2,880
Auto-dialer lease	0	0	1,600	2,347	3,093	3,840	4,587	5,333	6,080	6,827	7,573	8,320	49,600
Up-front lease deposits	0	8,100	1,600	3,627	747	2,187	2,187	747	2,187	2,187	2,187	2,187	27,940
Extended service contract	117	750	875	1,158	1,217	1,388	1,558	1,617	1,788	1,958	2,129	2,300	16,855
Import duties	0	12,656	0	4,500	0	2,250	2,250	0	2,250	2,250	2,250	2,250	30,656
Equipment insurance	39	250	292	386	406	463	519	539	596	653	710	767	5,618
Operating leases	1,656	31,356	13,967	24,498	17,942	24,047	26,461	23,596	29,700	32,114	34,529	36,943	296,809
Network asset value	46,875	300,000	350,000	463,333	486,667	555,000	623,333	646,667	715,000	783,333	851,667	920,000	

	1991 Aug.	Sept.	Oct.	Nov.	Dec.	1992 Jan.	Feb.	Mar.	Apr.	May	June	Jul.	Total Year
Communications expenses:													
Network Demonstrations	$500	$1,000	$2,000	$0	$0	$0	$0	$0	$0	$0	$0	$0	$3,500
Avg Variable Cost/Min	$0.18	$0.18	$0.18	$0.18	$0.18	$0.18	$0.18	$0.13	$0.13	$0.13	$0.13	$0.13	
Monthly U.S. Variable Costs	0	0	0	21,600	31,680	41,760	51,840	44,720	52,000	59,280	66,560	73,840	443,280
Monthly Japanese JV Costs	0	0	0	0	0	0	0	0	0	0	6,750	11,475	18,225
Number of 64kbps Channels	0	0	0	4	6	8	10	11	13	15	17	18	
Fractional T1	0	0	0	30,400	41,800	52,250	64,600	69,350	77,900	85,500	93,100	96,900	611,800
Switched Digital Service	0	0	0	4,800	4,800	4,800	4,800	4,800	4,800	4,800	4,800	4,800	43,200
Local Loop Service	0	0	0	4,700	6,400	7,250	7,250	7,250	8,100	8,100	9,800	9,800	68,650
Installation Expenses	0	0	0	3,000	1,000	1,000	1,000	1,000	1,000	1,000	1,000	1,000	11,000
Subtotal	500	1,000	2,000	64,500	85,680	107,060	129,490	127,120	143,800	158,680	182,010	197,815	1,199,655
Customer Service:													
Carla Ferrara (CSR)	2,000	2,000	2,000	2,000	2,000	2,000	2,000	2,000	2,000	2,000	2,000	2,000	24,000
Add'l full-time reps	0	0	0	0	0	2,000	2,000	2,000	2,000	2,000	2,000	2,000	14,000
Peak period service reps	0	0	0	0	0	0	1,000	2,000	2,000	3,000	3,000	4,000	15,000
Evening service rep	0	0	0	2,000	2,000	2,000	2,000	2,000	2,000	2,000	2,000	2,000	18,000
Expenses	500	500	500	1,000	1,000	1,500	2,000	2,500	2,500	3,000	3,000	3,500	21,500
Number of service personnel	1	1	1	2	2	3	4	5	5	6	6	7	
Subtotal	2,500	2,500	2,500	5,000	5,000	7,500	9,000	10,500	10,500	12,000	12,000	13,500	92,500
Administrative expenses:													
Headquarters office space	350	2,550	2,550	2,600	2,600	2,650	2,700	2,750	2,750	2,800	2,800	2,850	29,950
Furniture lease	0	1,000	1,000	1,000	1,000	1,000	1,000	1,000	1,000	1,000	1,000	1,000	11,000
Legal and accounting consultants	30,000	2,000	2,000	2,000	2,000	2,000	2,000	2,000	2,000	2,000	2,000	2,000	52,000
Financial consulting	2,000	2,000	2,000	2,000	2,000	2,000	2,000	2,000	2,000	2,000	2,000	2,000	24,000
Office supplies, etc.	5,000	1,000	1,000	1,000	1,000	1,000	1,000	1,000	1,000	1,000	1,000	1,000	16,000
Other expenses	1,500	1,500	1,500	1,500	1,500	1,500	1,500	1,500	1,500	1,500	1,500	1,500	18,000
Subtotal	38,850	10,050	10,050	10,100	10,100	10,150	10,200	10,250	10,250	10,300	10,300	10,350	150,950
Billing and accounting													
Payroll expenses	0	5,020	5,020	5,320	5,320	5,670	6,120	6,620	6,620	6,620	6,620	6,620	65,570
Bookkeeper	500	500	500	1,500	1,500	1,500	3,000	3,000	3,000	3,000	3,000	3,000	24,000
Credit/collections person	0	0	0	0	0	0	3,000	3,000	3,000	3,000	3,000	3,000	18,000
Bill preparation/mailing	0	0	0	167	260	353	447	540	633	727	820	913	4,860
Errors/omissions insurance	0	0	0	500	500	500	500	500	500	500	500	500	4,500
Subtotal	500	5,520	5,520	7,487	7,580	8,023	13,067	13,660	13,753	13,847	13,940	14,033	116,930
Total expenses	$77,456	$136,626	$227,737	$198,947	$215,717	$259,746	$288,235	$293,694	$328,623	$339,612	$367,501	$389,415	3,123,307

Year 2 Statement of Operations

	1992 Aug.	Sept.	Oct.	Nov.	Dec.	1993 Jan.	Feb.	Mar.	Apr.	May	June	Jul.	Total Year
Net sales	$454,592	$505,096	$555,600	$606,103	$656,607	$707,110	$757,614	$808,118	$858,621	$909,125	$959,628	$1,010,132	$8,788,340
Operating expenses:													
Cost of communications	222,970	240,675	259,130	278,185	302,340	324,145	346,950	366,055	389,760	411,615	431,670	447,275	4,020,770
Administrative expenses	15,350	15,400	15,450	15,450	15,500	15,500	15,550	15,600	15,600	15,650	15,650	15,700	186,400
Billing and accounting expenses	15,547	15,640	15,733	15,827	15,920	16,013	16,107	16,200	16,293	16,387	16,480	16,573	192,720
Sales expenses	77,130	75,042	75,684	75,684	75,684	75,684	75,684	75,684	75,684	75,684	75,684	75,684	909,012
Japanese J/V expenses	14,463	12,713	13,325	13,938	14,550	15,163	15,775	16,388	17,000	17,613	18,225	18,838	187,988
Customer service	14,100	15,600	17,100	17,100	18,600	18,600	20,100	21,600	21,600	23,100	23,100	24,600	235,200
Lease expense	39,358	41,772	49,467	42,911	49,016	56,710	50,154	61,539	54,983	61,088	68,782	62,227	638,007
Technical expenses	40,300	40,300	40,300	40,300	40,300	40,300	40,300	40,300	40,300	40,300	40,300	40,300	483,600
Total operating expenses	439,217	457,142	486,189	499,394	531,910	562,115	580,620	613,365	631,221	661,436	689,891	701,197	6,853,696
EBITDA	15,376	47,954	69,411	106,709	124,697	144,996	176,994	194,752	227,401	247,689	269,737	308,935	1,934,650
Depreciation/amortization	0	0	0	0	0	0	0	0	0	0	0	0	0
Corporate expenses	0	0	0	0	0	0	0	0	0	0	0	0	0
EBIT	15,376	47,954	69,411	106,709	124,697	144,996	176,994	194,752	227,401	247,689	269,737	308,935	1,934,650
Other income (expense):													
Cash interest income	0	0	0	0	0	0	0	0	0	0	0	0	0
Revolver interest (11%)	(671)	(311)	0	(1,034)	(349)	0	0	0	0	0	0	0	(2,365)
Extraordinary items	0	0	0	0	0	0	0	0	0	0	0	0	0
Other (expenses) income	0	0	0	0	0	0	0	0	0	0	0	0	0
Total other income (expense)	(671)	(311)	0	(1,034)	(349)	0	0	0	0	0	0	0	(2,365)
EBT	14,705	47,643	69,411	105,675	124,348	144,996	176,994	194,752	227,401	247,689	269,737	308,935	1,932,285
Income taxes	0	0	0	0	0	0	0	0	55,691	84,214	91,711	105,038	336,653
Net income	$14,705	$47,643	$69,411	$105,675	$124,348	$144,996	$176,994	$194,752	$171,710	$163,475	$178,027	$203,897	$1,595,632
Cumulative NOL's	(927,423)	(879,780)	(810,370)	(704,694)	(580,347)	(435,351)	(258,357)	(63,605)	0	0	0	0	0

EBITDA = earnings before interest, tax, depreciation, and amortization; EBIT = earnings before interest and tax; NOL = net operating loss.

Year 2 Balance Sheet

	1992 Aug.	Sept.	Oct.	Nov.	Dec.	1993 Jan.	Feb.	Mar.	Apr.	May	June	Jul.
Assets												
Current Assets:												
Cash	$10,000	$16,581	$10,000	$10,000	$70,240	$186,930	$336,604	$500,388	$645,667	$780,885	$928,880	$1,098,357
Invested cash	0	0	0	0	0	0	0	0	0	0	0	0
Accounts receivable	448,365	498,177	547,989	597,800	647,612	697,424	747,236	797,047	846,859	896,671	946,483	996,295
Total current assets	458,365	514,758	557,989	607,800	717,852	884,354	1,083,840	1,297,436	1,492,526	1,677,556	1,875,363	2,094,652
Long-term assets:												
Capital leases, costs, net	0	0	0	0	0	0	0	0	0	0	0	0
Net property, Plant, and equipment	0	0	0	0	0	0	0	0	0	0	0	0
Intangibles	0	0	0	0	0	0	0	0	0	0	0	0
Organizational expenses	150,000	150,000	150,000	150,000	150,000	150,000	150,000	150,000	150,000	150,000	150,000	150,000
Total assets	$608,365	$664,758	$707,989	$757,800	$867,852	$1,034,354	$1,233,840	$1,447,436	$1,642,526	$1,827,556	$2,025,363	$2,244,652
Liabilities												
Accounts payable	$219,916	$237,378	$255,580	$274,374	$298,198	$319,705	$342,197	$361,041	$384,421	$405,976	$425,757	$441,148
Accrued expenses	131,905	157,160	0	0	0	0	0	0	0	0	0	0
Revolving facility	33,967	0	112,778	38,121	0	0	0	0	0	0	0	0
Other current/CMLTD	0	0	0	0	0	0	0	0	0	0	0	0
Total current liabilities	385,788	394,538	368,358	312,495	298,198	319,705	342,197	361,041	384,421	405,976	425,757	441,148
Total liabilities	$385,788	$394,538	$368,358	$312,495	$298,198	$319,705	$342,197	$361,041	$384,421	$405,976	$425,757	$441,148
Shareholders' equity												
Founders' invested capital	150,000	150,000	150,000	150,000	150,000	150,000	150,000	150,000	150,000	150,000	150,000	150,000
Additional paid-in capital	1,000,000	1,000,000	1,000,000	1,000,000	1,000,000	1,000,000	1,000,000	1,000,000	1,000,000	1,000,000	1,000,000	1,000,000
Retained earnings	(927,423)	(879,780)	(810,370)	(704,694)	(580,347)	(435,351)	(258,357)	(63,605)	108,105	271,580	449,606	653,504
Total shareholders' equity	222,577	270,220	339,630	445,306	569,653	714,649	891,643	1,086,395	1,258,105	1,421,580	1,599,606	1,803,504
Total liabilities and shareholders' equity	$608,365	$664,758	$707,989	$757,800	$867,852	$1,034,354	$1,233,840	$1,447,436	$1,642,526	$1,827,556	$2,025,363	$2,244,652

Year 2 Statement of Cash Flow

	1992 Aug.	Sept.	Oct.	Nov.	Dec.	1993 Jan.	Feb.	Mar.	Apr.	May	June	Jul.	Total Year
Net income	$ 14,705	$ 47,643	$ 69,411	$105,675	$124,348	$144,996	$176,994	$194,752	$171,710	$163,475	$178,027	$ 203,897	$1,595,632
Depreciation/amortization	0	0	0	0	0	0	0	0	0	0	0	0	0
Other adjustments	0	0	0	0	0	0	0	0	0	0	0	0	0
Gross cash flow	14,705	47,643	69,411	105,675	124,348	144,996	176,994	194,752	171,710	163,475	178,027	203,897	1,595,632
Changes in working capital:													
Accounts receivable	(23,057)	(49,812)	(49,812)	(49,812)	(49,812)	(49,812)	(49,812)	(49,812)	(49,812)	(49,812)	(49,812)	(49,812)	(570,987)
Accounts payable	24,810	17,462	18,202	18,794	23,824	21,506	22,493	18,843	23,380	21,556	19,780	15,391	246,043
Accrued commissions	22,730	25,255	(157,160)	0	0	0	0	0	0	0	0	0	(109,176)
Other current liabs	0	0	0	0	0	0	0	0	0	0	0	0	0
Cash flow from operations	39,188	40,548	(119,359)	74,657	98,360	116,690	149,675	163,784	145,279	135,218	147,995	169,477	1,161,512
Capital expenditures	0	0	0	0	0	0	0	0	0	0	0	0	0
Operating cash flow	39,188	40,548	(119,359)	74,657	98,360	116,690	149,675	163,784	145,279	135,218	147,995	169,477	1,161,512
Changes in non-operating items													
Change in capital stock	0	0	0	0	0	0	0	0	0	0	0	0	0
Cash available	$ 39,188	$ 40,548	($ 119,359)	$ 74,657	$ 98,360	$116,690	$149,675	$163,784	$145,279	$135,218	$147,995	$ 169,477	$1,161,512
Cumulative cash	(23,967)	16,581	(102,778)	(28,121)	70,240	186,930	336,604	500,388	645,667	780,885	928,880	1,098,357	
Maintenance cash level	10,000	10,000	10,000	10,000	10,000	10,000	10,000	10,000	10,000	10,000	10,000	10,000	

Year 2 Assumptions and Ratios

	1992 Aug.	Sept.	Oct.	Nov.	Dec.	1993 Jan.	Feb.	Mar.	Apr.	May	June	Jul.
Income statement:												
Net monthly sales growth	5%	11%	10%	9%	8%	8%	7%	7%	6%	6%	6%	5%
Current gross margin	51%	52%	53%	54%	54%	54%	54%	55%	55%	55%	55%	56%
Current EBITDA margin	3%	9%	12%	18%	19%	21%	23%	24%	26%	27%	28%	31%
Communication as percentage of sales	49%	48%	47%	46%	46%	46%	46%	45%	45%	45%	45%	44%
Administrative as percentage of sales	3%	3%	3%	3%	2%	2%	2%	2%	2%	2%	2%	2%
Sales expense as percentage of sales	17%	15%	14%	12%	12%	11%	10%	9%	9%	8%	8%	7%
Customer service as percentage of sales	3%	3%	3%	3%	3%	3%	3%	3%	3%	3%	2%	2%
Leases as percentage of sales	9%	8%	9%	7%	7%	8%	7%	8%	6%	7%	7%	6%
Technical costs as percentage of sales	9%	8%	7%	7%	6%	6%	5%	5%	5%	4%	4%	4%
Balance sheet:												
A/R days	30.0	30.0	30.0	30.0	30.0	30.0	30.0	30.0	30.0	30.0	30.0	30.0
A/P days	30.0	30.0	30.0	30.0	30.0	30.0	30.0	30.0	30.0	30.0	30.0	30.0
Revolver as percentage receivable base	7.58%	0.00%	20.58%	6.38%	0.00%	0.00%	0.00%	0.00%	0.00%	0.00%	0.00%	0.00%

Year 2 Revenue Breakdown

	1992 Aug.	Sept.	Oct.	Nov.	Dec.	1993 Jan.	Feb.	Mar.	Apr.	May	June	Jul.	Total Year
United States:													
Avg price/minute	$0.69												
Monthly Growth Rate	350 Minutes/rep												
Free minutes/day	1,000	1,000	1,000	1,000	1,000	1,000	1,000	1,000	1,000	1,000	1,000	1,000	
Net new minutes/day	2,800	2,800	2,800	2,800	2,800	2,800	2,800	2,800	2,800	2,800	2,800	2,800	
Total paid minutes/day	30,200	33,000	35,800	38,600	41,400	44,200	47,000	49,800	52,600	55,400	58,200	61,000	
Total minutes/month (20 days)	604,000	660,000	716,000	772,000	828,000	884,000	940,000	996,000	1,052,000	1,108,000	1,164,000	1,220,000	10,944,000
Monthly gross revenue	416,760	455,400	494,040	532,680	571,320	609,960	648,600	687,240	725,880	764,520	803,160	841,800	7,551,360
Uncollectables (1%)	4,168	4,554	4,940	5,327	5,713	6,100	6,486	6,872	7,259	7,645	8,032	8,418	75,514
Net monthly US revenue	$412,592	$450,846	$489,100	$527,353	$565,607	$603,860	$642,114	$680,368	$718,621	$756,875	$795,128	$833,382	7,475,846
Japan joint venture:													
Avg price/minute	$0.35												
	35,000												
Total minutes/month	120,000	155,000	190,000	225,000	260,000	295,000	330,000	365,000	400,000	435,000	470,000	505,000	3,750,000
Net Japanese Revenue	$42,000	$54,250	$66,500	$78,750	$91,000	$103,250	$115,500	$127,750	$140,000	$152,250	$164,500	$176,750	$1,312,500
Total US/Japan revenues	$454,592	$505,096	$555,600	$606,103	$656,607	$707,110	$757,614	$808,118	$858,621	$909,125	$959,628	$1,010,132	$8,788,346

Year 2 Expense Breakdown

	1992 Aug.	Sept.	Oct.	Nov.	Dec.	1993 Jan.	Feb.	Mar.	Apr.	May	June	Jul.	Total Year
Technical development:													
Dr. Tom Sosnowski	$7,000	$7,000	$7,000	$7,000	$7,000	$7,000	$7,000	$7,000	$7,000	$7,000	$7,000	$7,000	$84,000
Tom Flaherty (Oracle)	4,800	4,800	4,800	4,800	4,800	4,800	4,800	4,800	4,800	4,800	4,800	4,800	57,600
Steve Orr (UNIX)	7,500	7,500	7,500	7,500	7,500	7,500	7,500	7,500	7,500	7,500	7,500	7,500	90,000
Michael Landino (Oracle)	4,000	4,000	4,000	4,000	4,000	4,000	4,000	4,000	4,000	4,000	4,000	4,000	48,000
Contract programmers	2,000	2,000	2,000	2,000	2,000	2,000	2,000	2,000	2,000	2,000	2,000	2,000	24,000
Tokyo engineer	1,500	1,500	1,500	1,500	1,500	1,500	1,500	1,500	1,500	1,500	1,500	1,500	18,000
Equipment housing expenses	11,500	11,500	11,500	11,500	11,500	11,500	11,500	11,500	11,500	11,500	11,500	11,500	138,000
Installation expenses	0	0	0	0	0	0	0	0	0	0	0	0	0
Other expenses	2,000	2,000	2,000	2,000	2,000	2,000	2,000	2,000	2,000	2,000	2,000	2,000	24,000
Subtotal	40,300	40,300	40,300	40,300	40,300	40,300	40,300	40,300	40,300	40,300	40,300	40,300	483,600
Sales expenses:													
Doug Ranalli	7,000	7,000	7,000	7,000	7,000	7,000	7,000	7,000	7,000	7,000	7,000	7,000	84,000
Steve Lanzilla-VP Sales	5,000	5,000	5,000	5,000	5,000	5,000	5,000	5,000	5,000	5,000	5,000	5,000	60,000
LA sales reps (2)	6,000	6,000	6,000	6,000	6,000	6,000	6,000	6,000	6,000	6,000	6,000	6,000	72,000
San Francisco reps (2)	6,000	6,000	6,000	6,000	6,000	6,000	6,000	6,000	6,000	6,000	6,000	6,000	72,000
NYC sales reps (2)	6,000	6,000	6,000	6,000	6,000	6,000	6,000	6,000	6,000	6,000	6,000	6,000	72,000
National accounts sales rep	3,000	3,000	3,000	3,000	3,000	3,000	3,000	3,000	3,000	3,000	3,000	3,000	36,000
Sales commissions (5%)	20,630	22,542	23,184	23,184	23,184	23,184	23,184	23,184	23,184	23,184	23,184	23,184	275,012
Sales office space	4,500	4,500	4,500	4,500	4,500	4,500	4,500	4,500	4,500	4,500	4,500	4,500	54,000
Sales expenses	14,000	14,000	14,000	14,000	14,000	14,000	14,000	14,000	14,000	14,000	14,000	14,000	168,000
Marketing/office supplies	5,000	1,000	1,000	1,000	1,000	1,000	1,000	1,000	1,000	1,000	1,000	1,000	16,000
Headhunter fees	0	0	0	0	0	0	0	0	0	0	0	0	0
Total sales personnel	8	8	8	8	8	8	8	8	8	8	8	8	
Subtotal	77,130	75,042	75,684	75,684	75,684	75,684	75,684	75,684	75,684	75,684	75,684	75,684	909,012
Japanese joint venture:													
Doug Fine	5,000	5,000	5,000	5,000	5,000	5,000	5,000	5,000	5,000	5,000	5,000	5,000	60,000
Chuo Coopers & Lybrand													
Performance bonuses	4,463	2,713	3,325	3,938	4,550	5,163	5,775	6,388	7,000	7,613	8,225	8,838	67,988
Expenses	5,000	5,000	5,000	5,000	5,000	5,000	5,000	5,000	5,000	5,000	5,000	5,000	60,000
Subtotal	14,463	12,713	13,325	13,938	14,550	15,163	15,775	16,388	17,000	17,613	18,225	18,838	187,988
Network assets:													
Network Hardware Lease	19,680	21,120	22,560	22,560	24,000	25,440	25,440	26,880	26,880	28,320	29,760	29,760	302,400
Japanese J/V Hardware	2,880	2,880	4,320	4,320	4,320	5,760	5,760	7,200	7,200	7,200	8,640	8,640	69,120
Auto-dialer Lease	9,067	9,813	10,560	11,307	12,053	12,800	13,547	14,293	15,040	15,787	16,533	17,280	158,080
Up-front Lease Deposits	2,187	2,187	3,627	747	2,187	3,627	747	3,627	747	2,187	3,627	747	26,240
Extended Service Contract	2,471	2,642	2,925	2,983	3,154	3,438	3,496	3,779	3,838	4,008	4,292	4,350	41,375
Import Duties	2,250	2,250	4,500	0	2,250	4,500	0	4,500	0	2,250	4,500	0	27,000
Equipment Insurance	824	881	975	994	1,051	1,146	1,165	1,260	1,279	1,336	1,431	1,450	13,792
Operating leases	39,358	41,772	49,467	42,911	49,016	56,710	50,154	61,539	54,983	61,088	68,782	62,227	638,007
Network asset value	988,333	1,056,667	1,170,000	1,193,333	1,261,667	1,375,000	1,398,333	1,511,667	1,535,000	1,603,333	1,716,667	1,740,000	

(Continued)

Year 2 Expense Breakdown *(concluded)*

	1992 Aug.	Sept.	Oct.	Nov.	Dec.	1993 Jan.	Feb.	Mar.	Apr.	May	June	Jul.	Total Year
Communications expenses:													
Network demonstrations	$0	$0	$0	$0	$0	$0	$0	$0	$0	$0	$0	$0	$0
Avg variable cost/min	$0.13	$0.13	$0.13	$0.13	$0.13	$0.13	$0.13	$0.13	$0.13	$0.13	$0.13	$0.13	
Monthly U.S. variable costs	81,120	88,400	95,680	102,960	110,240	117,520	124,800	132,080	139,360	146,640	153,920	161,200	1,453,920
Monthly Japanese JV costs	16,200	20,925	25,650	30,375	35,100	39,825	44,550	49,275	54,000	58,725	63,450	68,175	506,250
Number of 64kbps channels	20	22	24	25	27	29	31	32	34	36	38	39	
Fractional T1	103,550	109,250	114,000	121,050	133,200	141,300	152,100	157,500	169,200	178,200	185,400	189,000	1,753,750
Switched digital service	9,600	9,600	9,600	9,600	9,600	9,600	9,600	9,600	9,600	9,600	9,600	9,600	115,200
Local loop service	11,500	11,500	13,200	13,200	13,200	14,900	14,900	16,600	16,600	17,450	18,300	18,300	179,650
Installation expenses	1,000	1,000	1,000	1,000	1,000	1,000	1,000	1,000	1,000	1,000	1,000	1,000	12,000
Subtotal	222,970	240,675	259,130	278,185	302,340	324,145	346,950	366,055	389,760	411,615	431,670	447,275	4,020,770
Customer service:													
Carla Ferrara (CSR)	2,200	2,200	2,200	2,200	2,200	2,200	2,200	2,200	2,200	2,200	2,200	2,200	26,400
Add'l full-time reps	2,200	2,200	2,200	2,200	2,200	2,200	2,200	2,200	2,200	2,200	2,200	2,200	26,400
Peak period service reps	4,000	5,000	6,000	6,000	7,000	7,000	8,000	9,000	9,000	10,000	10,000	11,000	92,000
Evening service rep	2,200	2,200	2,200	2,200	2,200	2,200	2,200	2,200	2,200	2,200	2,200	2,200	26,400
Expenses	3,500	4,000	4,500	4,500	5,000	5,000	5,500	6,000	6,000	6,500	6,500	7,000	64,000
Number of service personnel	7	8	9	9	10	10	11	12	12	13	13	14	
Subtotal	14,100	15,600	17,100	17,100	18,600	18,600	20,100	21,600	21,600	23,100	23,100	24,600	235,200
Administrative expenses:													
Headquarters office space	2,850	2,900	2,950	2,950	3,000	3,000	3,050	3,100	3,100	3,150	3,150	3,200	36,400
Furniture lease	1,000	1,000	1,000	1,000	1,000	1,000	1,000	1,000	1,000	1,000	1,000	1,000	12,000
Legal and accounting consultants	2,000	2,000	2,000	2,000	2,000	2,000	2,000	2,000	2,000	2,000	2,000	2,000	24,000
Financial consulting	7,000	7,000	7,000	7,000	7,000	7,000	7,000	7,000	7,000	7,000	7,000	7,000	84,000
Office supplies, etc.	1,000	1,000	1,000	1,000	1,000	1,000	1,000	1,000	1,000	1,000	1,000	1,000	12,000
Other expenses	1,500	1,500	1,500	1,500	1,500	1,500	1,500	1,500	1,500	1,500	1,500	1,500	18,000
Subtotal	15,350	15,400	15,450	15,450	15,500	15,500	15,550	15,600	15,600	15,650	15,650	15,700	186,400
Billing and accounting:													
Payroll expenses	7,790	7,790	7,790	7,790	7,790	7,790	7,790	7,790	7,790	7,790	7,790	7,790	93,480
Bookkeeper	3,000	3,000	3,000	3,000	3,000	3,000	3,000	3,000	3,000	3,000	3,000	3,000	36,000
Credit/collections person	3,000	3,000	3,000	3,000	3,000	3,000	3,000	3,000	3,000	3,000	3,000	3,000	36,000
Bill preparation/mailing	1,007	1,100	1,193	1,287	1,380	1,473	1,567	1,660	1,753	1,847	1,940	2,033	18,240
Errors/omissions insurance	750	750	750	750	750	750	750	750	750	750	750	750	9,000
Subtotal	15,547	15,640	15,733	15,827	15,920	16,013	16,107	16,200	16,293	16,387	16,480	16,573	192,720
Total expenses	$439,217	$457,142	$486,189	$499,394	$531,910	$562,115	$580,620	$613,365	$631,221	$661,436	$689,891	$701,197	6,853,696

REVENUE AND EXPENSE ASSUMPTIONS

Detailed Revenues

United States:

Average price/minute:

- *Year 1*: The average price assumes that new account traffic will be split evenly between large and small accounts. Accounts billing over $500/month will be billed at $.69/minute. Small accounts will be billed at $.79/minute.
- *Year 2 and Year 3*: Average price is projected to drop to $.69/minute in Year 2 and $.62/minute in Year 3 as the percentage of large customers increases and as competition enters the market.

Monthly growth rate: Each sales rep is expected to generate 350 new minutes/day of traffic each month. A detailed explanation of this item is provided in the business plan under "Sales Expectations."

Free minutes/day: Sales reps are expected to give away 100 free minutes of service to three times as many accounts as they are expected to close.

Net new minutes/day: Multiplication of the number of sales reps times the monthly growth rate figure addressed above.

Uncollectible accounts: One percent uncollectibles based on statistics generated by AT&T.

Japan joint venture:

Average price/minute: Average price per minute charged to the Japanese partner for use of the network is a combination of $.30/minute to cover transmission costs and $.05/minute to cover the equipment dedicated to the Japanese joint venture.

Total minutes/month: Aggregate number of minutes transmitted by the Japanese partner each month. Traffic growth rate is estimated to be 60% of the rate achieved by the US sales force. The 60% number was selected with the intention of being conservative. Initial sales from Japan are not scheduled to begin until six months after a list of qualified joint venture partners has been developed. Initial sales volume from Japan will be bolstered by the actions of US sales reps introducing the return service to Japanese companies already using FAX International in the United States.

Detailed Expenses

Technical development:

Personnel: All salary figures reflect actual agreements for full-time employment. All four full-time network development personnel are tied into three-year stock vesting programs. Dr. Sosnowski and Steve Orr have each accepted salary reductions equal to $6,000/month in return for their stock positions.

Contract programmers: No additional consulting work is anticipated in Year 1. A small budget has been set aside for Years 2 and 3 to deal with intermittent needs.

Tokyo engineer: Ministry of Post and Telecommunications (MPT) in Japan requires that FAX International employ a certified senior telecommunications engineer to be responsible for meeting all regulatory approvals.

Equipment housing expenses: FAX International's network hardware will be housed at KDD's main international switching facility in Tokyo. All hardware and communications lines will be monitored and maintained on a 24-hour basis. Similar arrangements have been negotiated in the U.S. with Teleport Communications in Boston and New York, and M.F.S. in Los Angeles and San Francisco.

Installation expenses: Budget for installation of all network hardware and communications lines in Tokyo and Boston. The majority of the cost will go towards custom installation work performed by KDD to provide security, 24-hour maintenance, earthquake protection, guaranteed back-up power supply, and so on.

Sales expenses:

Sales office space: Field sales reps in Los Angeles, New York, and San Francisco will share an office in an executive office suite. The budget for each shared office has been set at $1,500/month. Offices will include furniture, limited secretarial support, answering service, voice mail, copy facilities, mail facilities, and so on.

Sales expenses: Field sales reps will be responsible for covering all accounts within driving distance of their assigned metropolitan area. Expenses for each field sales rep are projected at $500/month to cover local travel expenses and local phone expenses. An additional $10,000/month has been allocated to cover travel expenses and long distance phone expense for Ranalli, Lanzilla, and the national accounts installation rep.

Japanese joint venture:

Chuo Coopers & Lybrand: C&L has submitted a proposal for a $20,000 three-month project to identify and prequalify a list of joint venture candidates. No decision has been made but a budget has been set aside beginning in January 1992.

Network assets:

Network hardware lease: All lease payments are based on three-year contracts at a monthly lease rate of 3.2% per month calculated on the purchase price of the assets. The lease rate assumption is based on the current rates being paid by FAX International.

Japanese J/V hardware: Hardware purchased specifically to handle return traffic from Japan.

Import duties: 10 percent import duty paid on all network hardware equipment purchased in the United States and shipped to Japan for use in the Tokyo network node.

Communications expenses:

Network demonstrations: FAX International sales reps will be able to provide full-function network demonstrations to potential customers before the system is actually installed between the United States and Tokyo. Expenses cover the cost of placing international telephone calls to Tokyo to deliver the demonstration documents.

(Continued)

REVENUE AND EXPENSE ASSUMPTIONS (*concluded*)

Average variable cost per minute: Combination of $.15/minute to collect a document in the United States via an 800 number and $.03/minute to deliver a document via a local call in Tokyo. Average variable cost drops to $.13 in March once the US network is expanded to include remote collection nodes in Los Angeles, San Francisco, and New York City. Documents received at a remote collection node cost only $.05/minute to collect. Business plan assumes half of all documents will always be received via an 800 number.

Monthly Japanese JV costs: Documents received from the Japanese partner will be delivered in the United States via a long-distance call from Boston to the destination fax machine. Average cost per minute will be a maximum of $.135.

Number of 64kbps channels: Calculation of the total bandwidth required on the international private line between Boston and Tokyo.

Fractional T1: Monthly fee for an international private line with the number of active channels shown in the row above.

Local loop service: Cost of fiber optic communications access from the FAX International network nodes in the United States and Tokyo into the AT&T and KDD facilities.

Installation expenses: Fees paid for adding capacity to the communications facilities outlined above.

Customer service: FAX International will employ both full-time customer service reps (CSR) and part-time reps to cover peak demand periods. CSR staffing levels are based on the assumption that 5% of all documents handled by the network will require special handling by a CSR. Each CSR is expected to be able to handle a maximum of 20 problem documents per hour. Note: Research conducted by Cable & Wireless shows that 98% of all fax documents get delivered within three attempts.

Administrative expenses:

Legal and accounting consulting: $30,000 charge in the first month of operations is an estimate of the cost to negotiate and close a deal for the second round of financing. Monthly budget of $2,000 is intended to cover all ongoing legal and accounting consulting fees.

PREPARING A BUSINESS PLAN

A Complete Business Plan

It may seem to an entrepreneur who has completed the Opportunity Screening Guide in Chapter 4 and who has spent hours of thinking and planning informally that all that now needs to be done is to jot down a few things. *However, there is a great difference between screening an opportunity and developing a business plan.*

There are two important differences in the way these issues need to be addressed. First, a business plan can have two uses: (1) inducing someone to part with maybe $500,000 to $2 million, or even more, and (2) guiding the policies and actions of the firm over a number of years. Therefore, strategies and statements made need to be well thought out, unambiguous, and capable of being supported.

Another difference is that more detail is needed. (The exception to this is the "Dehydrated Business Plan" discussed later in this chapter.) This means that the team needs to spend more time in gathering detailed data, in interpreting it, and in presenting it clearly. For example, for the purpose of screening an opportunity, it may be all right to note (if one cannot do any better) that the target market for a product is in the $30–$60 million range and the market is growing over 10 percent per year. For purposes of planning to launch an actual new enterprise, determine strategy, and so forth, this level of detail would not get by. The size range would need to be narrowed considerably; if it were not narrowed, those reading or using the plan would have little confidence in this critical number. And saying the target market is growing at over 10 percent is too vague. Does that mean the market grew at the stated rate between last year and the year before, or does it mean that the market grew on average by this amount over the past three years? Also, a statement phrased in terms of "over 10 percent" smacks of imprecision. The actual growth rate needs to be known and needs to be stated. Whether the rate will or will not remain the same, and why, needs to be explained also.

Preparing an effective business plan for a start-up can easily take 200 to 300 hours. Squeezing that amount of time into evenings and weekends can make the process stretch over 3 to 12 months.

A business plan for a business planning expansion or for a situation such as a leveraged buyout typically can take half this effort. The reason is that the knowns about the business, including the market, its competition, financial and accounting information, and so on, at this point are greater.

Exhibit 11.3 is a sample table of contents for a business plan. The information shown is included in most effective business plans. The way information is presented in this exhibit is a good framework to follow. First, organizing the material into sections makes dealing with the information more manageable. Second, while the amount of detail and the order of presentation may vary for a particular venture according to its particular circumstances, most effective business plans contain this information in some form. (Note that the amount of detail and the order in which information is presented is important. These can vary for each particular situation, and will depend upon the purpose of the plan and the age and stage of the venture, among other factors.)

The Dehydrated Business Plan

A dehydrated business plan usually runs from 4 to 10 pages, but rarely more. It covers key points, such as those suggested for the executive summary in the Business Planning Guide that follows. Essentially, such a plan documents the analysis of and information about the heart of the business opportunity, competitive advantages the company will enjoy, and *creative insights* that an entrepreneur often has.

Since it can usually be prepared in a few hours, it is preferred by entrepreneurs who find it difficult to find enough slack time while operating a business to write a complete plan. In many instances investors prefer a dehydrated plan in the initial screening phase.

It is important to note that such a plan is not intended to be used exclusively in the process of raising or borrowing money, and it is not useful in guiding the operations of a business over time.

EXERCISE—THE BUSINESS PLAN GUIDE

The Business Plan Guide follows the order of *presentation* outlined in *Exhibit 11.3.* Based on a guide originally developed at Venture Founders Corporation by Leonard E. Smollen and the late Brian Haslett, and on over 20 years of observing and working with entrepreneurs and actually preparing and evaluating hundreds of plans, it is intended to make this challenging task easier.

Certainly, there is no single best way to write a business plan, and there are many ways to approach the preparation for and writing of a business plan. It is recommended that you begin with the market research and analysis sections. In the final analysis, the task will evolve in a way that suits you and your situation.

In writing your plan, you should remember that although one of the important functions of a business plan is to influence investors, rather than preparing a fancy presentation, you and your team need to prove to yourselves and others that your opportunity is worth pursuing, and to construct the means by which you will do it. Gathering information, making hard decisions, and developing plans come first.

The plan guide that follows shows how to present information succinctly and in a format acceptable to investors. While it is useful to keep in mind who your audience is, and that information not clearly presented will most likely not be used, it also is important not to be concerned *just* with format.

In the Business Plan Guide, issues are indicated. The intent is to show you what needs to be included in a business plan and why.

Exhibit 11.3
Business Plan

Table of Contents

- I. EXECUTIVE SUMMARY
  - A. Description of the Business Concept and the Business.
  - B. The Opportunity and Strategy.
  - C. The Target Market and Projections.
  - D. The Competitive Advantages.
  - E. The Economics, Profitability, and Harvest Potential.
  - F. The Team.
  - G. The Offering.
- II. THE INDUSTRY AND THE COMPANY AND ITS PRODUCT(S) OR SERVICE(S)
  - A. The Industry.
  - B. The Company and the Concept.
  - C. The Product(s) or Service(s).
  - D. Entry and Growth Strategy.
- III. MARKET RESEARCH AND ANALYSIS
  - A. Customers.
  - B. Market Size and Trends.
  - C. Competition and Competitive Edges.
  - D. Estimated Market Share and Sales.
  - E. Ongoing Market Evaluation.
- IV. THE ECONOMICS OF THE BUSINESS
  - A. Gross and Operating Margins.
  - B. Profit Potential and Durability.
  - C. Fixed, Variable, and Semivariable Costs.
  - D. Months to Breakeven.
  - E. Months to Reach Positive Cash Flow.
- V. MARKETING PLAN
  - A. Overall Marketing Strategy.
  - B. Pricing.
  - C. Sales Tactics.
  - D. Service and Warranty Policies.
  - E. Advertising and Promotion.
  - F. Distribution.
- VI. DESIGN AND DEVELOPMENT PLANS
  - A. Development Status and Tasks.
  - B. Difficulties and Risks.
  - C. Product Improvement and New Products.
  - D. Costs.
  - E. Proprietary Issues.
- VII. MANUFACTURING AND OPERATIONS PLAN
  - A. Operating Cycle.
  - B. Geographical Location.
  - C. Facilities and Improvements.
  - D. Strategy and Plans.
  - E. Regulatory and Legal Issues.
- VIII. MANAGEMENT TEAM
  - A. Organization.
  - B. Key Management Personnel.
  - C. Management Compensation and Ownership.
  - D. Other Investors.
  - E. Employment and Other Agreements and Stock Option and Bonus Plans.
  - F. Board of Directors.
  - G. Other Shareholders, Rights, and Restrictions.
  - H. Supporting Professional Advisors and Services.
- IX. OVERALL SCHEDULE
- X. CRITICAL RISKS, PROBLEMS, AND ASSUMPTIONS
- XI. THE FINANCIAL PLAN
  - A. Actual Income Statements and Balance Sheets.
  - B. Pro Forma Income Statements.
  - C. Pro Forma Balance Sheets.
  - D. Pro Forma Cash Flow Analysis.
  - E. Breakeven Chart and Calculation.
  - F. Cost Control.
  - G. Highlights.
- XII. PROPOSED COMPANY OFFERING
  - A. Desired Financing.
  - B. Offering.
  - C. Capitalization.
  - D. Use of Funds.
  - E. Investors' Return.
- XIII. APPENDIXES

Further, you may feel as though you have seen much of this before. You should. The guide is based on the analytical framework described in the book and builds upon the Opportunity Screening Guide in Chapter 4. If you have not completed the Opportunity Screening Guide, it will help you to do so before proceeding. It is assumed in the Business Plan Guide that you will be able to draw on data and analysis developed in the Opportunity Screening Guide to help you prepare your business plan.

As you proceed through the Business Plan Guide, remember that statements need to be supported with data where possible. Note also that it is sometimes easier to present data in tabular form. Include the source of all data, the methods and/or assumptions used, and the credentials of people doing research. If data on which a statement is based is available elsewhere in the plan, be sure to indicate where it can be found.

Finally, it is important to remember that the Business Plan Guide is just that—a guide. It is intended to be applicable to a wide range of product and service businesses. For any particular industry or market, certain critical issues are unique to that industry or market. In the chemical industry, for example, some special issues of significance currently exist, such as increasingly strict regulations at all levels of government covering the use of chemical products and the operation of processes, diminishing viability of the high-capital-cost special-purpose chemical processing plants serving a narrow market, and long delivery times of processing equipment. In the electronics industry, the special issues may be the future availability and price of new kinds of large-scale integrated circuits.

Common sense should rule in applying the guide to your specific venture.

STEP 3: COMBINE THE LIST OF SEGMENTS AND THE LIST OF TASKS AND CREATE A CALENDAR. In combining your list, consider if anything has been omitted and whether you have been realistic in what people can do, when they can do it, what needs to be done, and so forth. To create your calendar, place an *X* in the week when the task is to be started and an *X* in the week it is to be completed and then connect the *X*s. When you have placed all tasks on the calendar, look carefully again for conflicts or lack of realism. In particular, evaluate if team members are overscheduled.

Task	Week														
	1	2	3	4	5	6	7	8	9	10	11	12	13	14	15

STEP 4: DEVELOP AND WRITE A BUSINESS PLAN USING THE FOLLOWING AS A FRAMEWORK. As has been discussed, the framework follows the order of presentation of the table of contents shown in *Exhibit 11.3*. While preparing your own plan, you will most likely want to consider sections in a different order from the one presented in *Exhibit 11.3*. (Also, when you integrate your sections into your final plan, you may choose to present material somewhat differently.)

Cover

The cover page includes the name of company, its address, its telephone number, the date, and the securities offered. Usually, the name, address, telephone number, and the date are centered at the top of the page and the securities offered are listed at the bottom. Also suggested on the cover page at the bottom is the following text:

This business plan has been submitted on a confidential basis solely for the benefit of selected, highly qualified investors in connection with the private placement of the above securities and is not for use by any other persons. Neither may it be reproduced, stored, or copied in any form. By accepting delivery of this plan, the recipient agrees to return this copy to the corporation at the address listed above if the recipient does not undertake to subscribe to the offering. Do not copy, fax, reproduce, or distribute without permission.

Table of Contents

Included in the table of contents is a list of the sections, any appendices, and any other information and the pages on which they can be found. (See *Exhibit 11.3.)*

I. Executive Summary

The first section in the body of the business plan is usually an executive summary. The summary is usually short and concise (one or two pages). The summary articulates what the opportunity conditions are and why they exist, who will execute the opportunity and why they are capable of doing so, how the firm will gain entry and market penetration, and so on. Essentially, the summary for your venture needs to mirror the criteria shown in *Exhibit 3.3* and the Venture Opportunity Screening Guide.

The summary is usually prepared after the other sections of the business plan are completed. It is therefore helpful, as the other sections are drafted, to note one or two key sentences, and some key facts and numbers from each.

The summary is important for those ventures trying to raise or borrow money. Many investors, bankers, managers, and other readers use the summary to determine quickly whether the venture the plan describes is of interest. Therefore, unless the summary is appealing and compelling, it may be the only section read, and you may never get the chance to make a presentation or discuss your business in person.

Therefore, leave plenty of time to prepare the summary. (Successful public speakers have been known to spend an hour of preparation for each minute of their speech.)

The executive summary usually contains a paragraph or two covering each of the following:

A. *Description of the business concept and the business.* Describe the business concept for the business you are or will be in. For example, Outdoor Scene, Inc. (see Chapter 1), wanted to produce tents, but the concept was "to become a leader in providing quality, service, and on-time delivery in outdoor leisure products." Be sure the description of your concept explains how your product or service will fundamentally change the way customers currently do certain things. For example, Arthur Rock, the lead investor in Apple Computer and Intel, has stated that he focuses on concepts that will change the way people live and/or work. You need to identify when the company was formed, what it will do, what is special or proprietary about its product, service, or technology, and so forth. Include summary information about any proprietary technology, trade secrets, or unique capabilities that give you an edge in the marketplace. If the company has existed for a few years, a brief summary of its size and progress is in order. Try to make your description 25 words or less, and mention the specific product or service.

B. *The opportunity and strategy.* Summarize what the opportunity is, why it is compelling, and the entry strategy planned to exploit it. This information may be presented as an outline of the key facts, conditions, competitors' vulnerabilities ("sleepiness", sluggishness, poor service, etc.), industry trends, and other evidence and logic that define the opportunity. Note plans for growth and expansion beyond the entry products or services and into other market segments (such as international markets) as appropriate.

C. *The target market and projections.* Identify and briefly explain the industry and market, who the primary customer groups are, how the product(s) or service(s) will be positioned, and how you plan to reach and service these groups. Include information about the structure of the market, the size and growth rate for the market segments or niches you are seeking, your unit and dollar sales estimates, your anticipated market share, the payback period for your customers, and your pricing strategy (including price versus performance/value/benefits considerations).

D. *The competitive advantages.* Indicate the significant competitive edges you enjoy or can create as a result of your innovative product, service, and strategy; advantages in lead time; competitors' weaknesses and vulnerabilities; and other industry conditions.

E. *The economics, profitability, and harvest potential.* Summarize the nature of the "forgiving and rewarding" economics of the venture (e.g., gross and operating margins, expected profitability and durability of those profits); the relevant time frames to attain breakeven and positive cash flow; key financial projections; the expected return on investment; and so on. Be sure to include a brief discussion of your contribution analysis and the underlying operating and cash conversion cycle. Use key numbers whenever possible.

F. *The team.* Summarize the relevant knowledge, experience, know-how, and skills of the lead entrepreneur and any team members, noting previous accomplishments, especially those involving profit and loss responsibility and general management and people management experience. Include significant information, such as the size of a division, project, or prior business with which the lead entrepreneur or a team member was the driving force.

G. *The offering.* Briefly indicate the dollar amount of equity and/or debt financing needed, how much of the company you are prepared to offer for that financing, what principal use will be made of the capital, and how the targeted investor, lender, or strategic partner will achieve its desired rate of return.

II. The Industry and the Company and Its Product(s) or Service(s)

A major area of consideration is the company, its concept for its product(s) and service(s), and its interface with the industry in which it will be competing. This is the context into which the marketing information, for example, fits. Information needs to include a description of the industry, a description of the concept, a description of your company, and a description of the product(s) or service(s) you will offer, the proprietary position of these product(s) or service(s), their potential advantages, and entry and growth strategy for the product(s) or service(s).

A. *The industry:*

- Present the current status and prospects for the industry in which the proposed business will operate. Be sure to consider industry structure.
- Discuss briefly market size, growth trends, and competitors.

- Discuss any new products or developments, new markets and customers, new requirements, new entrants and exits, and any other national or economic trends and factors that could affect the venture's business positively or negatively.

B. *The company and the concept:*

- Describe generally the concept of the business, what business your company is in or intends to enter, what product(s) or service(s) it will offer, and who are or will be its principal customers.
- By way of background, give the date your venture was incorporated and describe the identification and development of its products and the involvement of the company's principals in that development.
- If your company has been in business for several years and is seeking expansion financing, review its history and cite its prior sales and profit performance, and if your company has had setbacks or losses in prior years, discuss these and emphasize current and future efforts to prevent a recurrence of these difficulties and to improve your company's performance.

C. *The product(s) or service(s):*

- Describe in some detail each product or service to be sold.
- Discuss the application of the product or service and describe the primary end use as well as any significant secondary applications.
- Emphasize any unique features of the product or service and how these will create or add significant value; also, highlight any differences between what is currently on the market and what you will offer that will account for your market penetration. Be sure to describe how value will be added and the payback period to the customer—that is, discuss how many months it will take for the customer to cover the initial purchase price of the product or service as a result of its time, cost, or productivity improvements.
- Include a description of any possible drawbacks (including problems with obsolescence) of the product or service.
- Define the present state of development of the product or service and how much time and money will be required to fully develop, test, and introduce the product or service. Provide a summary of the functional specifications and photographs, if available, of the product.
- Discuss any head start you might have that would enable you to achieve a favored or entrenched position in the industry.
- Describe any features of the product or service that give it an "unfair" advantage over the competition. Describe any patents, trade secrets, or other proprietary features of the product or service.
- Discuss any opportunities for the expansion of the product line or the development of related products or services. (Emphasize opportunities and explain how you will take advantage of them.)

D. *Entry and growth strategy:*

- Indicate key success variables in your marketing plan (e.g., an innovative product, timing advantage, or marketing approach) and your pricing, distribution, advertising, and promotion plans.
- Summarize how fast you intend to grow and to what size during the first five years and your plans for growth beyond your initial product or service.
- Show how the entry and growth strategy is derived from the opportunity and value-added or other competitive advantages, such as the weakness of competitors.

III. Market Research and Analysis

Because of the importance of market analysis and the critical dependence of other parts of the plan on this information, you are advised to prepare this section of the business plan before any other. Take enough time to do this section very well and to check alternative sources of market data.

Information in this section needs to support the assertion that the venture can capture a substantial market in a growing industry in the face of competition.

This section of the business plan is one of the most difficult to prepare, yet it is one of the most important. Other sections of the business plan depend on the market research and analysis presented here. For example, the predicted sales levels directly influence such factors as the size of the manufacturing operation, the marketing plan, and the amount of debt and equity capital you will require. Yet most entrepreneurs seem to have great difficulty preparing and presenting market research and analyses that show that their ventures' sales estimates are sound and attainable.

A. *Customers:*

- Discuss who the customers for the product(s) or service(s) are or will be. Note that potential customers need to be classified by relatively homogeneous groups having common, identifiable characteristics (e.g., by major market segment). For example, an automotive part might be sold to manufacturers and to parts distributors supplying the replacement market, so the discussion needs to reflect two market segments.
- Show who and where the major purchasers for the product(s) or service(s) are in each market segment. Include regional and foreign countries, as appropriate.
- Indicate whether customers are easily reached and receptive, how customers buy (wholesale, through manufacturers' representatives, etc.), where in their organizations such buying decisions are made, and how long such decisions take. Describe customers' purchasing processes, including the bases on which they make purchase decisions (e.g., price, quality, timing, delivery, training, service, personal contacts, or political pressures) and why they might change current purchasing decisions.
- List any orders, contracts, or letters of commitment that you have in hand. These are far and away *the most powerful data* you can provide. List also any potential customers who have expressed an interest in the product(s) or service(s) and indicate why; also list any potential customers who have shown no interest in the proposed product or service and explain why they are not interested and explain what you will do to overcome negative customer reaction. Indicate how fast you believe your product or service will be accepted in the market.
- If you have an existing business, list your principal current customers and discuss the trends in your sales to them.

B. *Market size and trends:*

- Show for five years the size of the current total market and the share you will have, by market segment and/or by region and/or country, for the product or service you will offer, in units, dollars, and potential profitability.
- Describe also the potential annual growth for at least three years of the total market for your product(s) or service(s) for each major customer group, region, or country, as appropriate.
- Discuss the major factors affecting market growth (e.g., industry trends, socioeconomic trends, government policy, and population shifts) and review previous trends in the market. Any differences between past and projected annual growth rates need to be explained.

C. *Competition and competitive edges:*

- Make a realistic assessment of the strengths and weaknesses of competitors. Assess the substitute and/or alternative products and services and list the companies that supply them, both domestic and foreign, as appropriate.
- Compare competing and substitute products or services on the basis of market share, quality, price, performance, delivery, timing, service, warranties, and other pertinent features.
- Compare the fundamental value that is added or created by your product or service, in terms of economic benefits to the customer and to your competitors.
- Discuss the current advantages and disadvantages of these products and services and say why they are not meeting customer needs.
- Indicate any knowledge of competitors' actions that could lead you to new or improved products and an advantageous position. For example, discuss whether competitors are simply sluggish or nonresponsive or are asleep at the switch.
- Review the strengths and weaknesses of the competing companies and determine and discuss the share of the market of each competitor, its sales, its distribution methods, and its production capabilities.
- Review also the financial position, resources, costs, and profitability of the competition and their profit trend. Note that you can utilize Robert Morris Associates data for comparison (see Appendix I).
- Indicate who are the service, pricing, performance, cost, and quality leaders. Discuss why any companies have entered or dropped out of the market in recent years.
- Discuss the three or four key competitors and why customers buy from them, and determine and discuss why customers *leave* them.
- From what you know about the competitors' operations, explain why you think that they are vulnerable and you can capture a share of their business. Discuss what makes you think it will be easy or difficult to compete with them. Discuss, in particular, your competitive advantages gained through such "unfair" advantage as patents.

D. *Estimated market share and sales:*

- Summarize what it is about your product(s) or service(s) that will make it saleable in the face of current and potential competition. Mention, especially, the fundamental value added or created by the product(s) or service(s).
- Identify any major customers (including international customers) who are willing to make, or who have already made, purchase commitments, and indicate the extent of those commitments and why they were made, and discuss which customers could be major purchasers in future years and why.
- Based on your assessment of the advantages of your product or service, the market size and trends, customers, the competition and their products, and the trends of sales in prior years, estimate the share of the market and the sales in units and dollars that you will acquire in each of the next three years. Remember to show assumptions used.
- Show how the growth of the company sales in units and its estimated market share are related to the growth of its industry and customers and the strengths and weaknesses of competitors. Remember, the assumptions used to estimate market share and sales need to be clearly stated.
- If yours is an existing business, also indicate the total market, your market share, and sales for two prior years.

E. *Ongoing market evaluation:*

- Explain how you will continue to evaluate your target markets so as to assess customer needs and service and to guide product-improvement programs and new-product programs, plan for expansions of your production facility, and guide product/service pricing.

IV. The Economics of the Business

The economic and financial characteristics, including the apparent magnitude and durability of margins and profits generated, need to support the fundamental attractiveness of the opportunity. The underlying operating and cash conversion cycle of the business, the value chain, and so forth, need to make sense in terms of the opportunity and strategies planned.

A. *Gross and operating margins:*
- Describe the magnitude of the gross margins (i.e., selling price less variable costs) and the operating margins for each of the product(s) and/or service(s) you are selling in the market niche(s) you plan to attack. Include results of your contribution analysis.

B. *Profit potential and durability:*
- Describe the magnitude and expected durability of the profit stream the business will generate—before and after taxes—and reference appropriate industry benchmarks, other competitive intelligence, or your own relevant experience.
- Address the issue of how perishable or durable the profit stream appears to be, and why, such as barriers to entry you can create, your technological and market lead time, and so on.

C. *Fixed, variable, and semivariable costs:*
- Provide a detailed summary of fixed, variable, and semivariable costs, in dollars and as percentages of total cost as appropriate, for the product or service you offer and the volume of purchases and sales upon which these are based.
- Show relevant industry benchmarks.

D. *Months to breakeven:*
- Given your entry strategy, marketing plan, and proposed financing, show how long it will take to reach a unit breakeven sales level.
- Note any significant stepwise changes in your breakeven that will occur as you grow and add substantial capacity.

E. *Months to reach positive cash flow:*
- Given the above strategy and assumptions, show when the venture will attain a positive cash flow.
- Show if and when you will run out of cash. Note where the detailed assumptions can be found.
- Note any significant stepwise changes in cash flow that will occur as you grow and add capacity.

V. Marketing Plan

The marketing plan describes how the sales projections will be attained. The marketing plan needs to detail the overall marketing strategy that will exploit the opportunity and your competitive advantages. Include a discussion of sales and service policies; pricing, distribution, promotion, and advertising strategies; and sales projections. The marketing plan needs to describe *what* is to be done, *how* it will be done, *when* it will be done, and *who* will do it.

A. *Overall marketing strategy:*
- Describe the specific marketing philosophy and strategy of the company, given the value chain and channels of distribution in the market niche(s) you are pursuing. Include, for example, a discussion of the kinds of customer groups that you already have orders from or that will be targeted for initial intensive selling effort and those

targeted for later selling efforts; how specific potential customers in these groups will be identified and how will they be contacted; what features of the product or service, such as service, quality, price, delivery, warranty, or training, will be emphasized to generate sales; if any innovative or unusual marketing concepts will enhance customer acceptance, such as leasing where only sales were previously attempted; and so forth.

– Indicate whether the product(s) or service(s) will initially be introduced internationally, nationally, or regionally; explain why; and if appropriate, indicate any plans for extending sales at a later date.
– Discuss any seasonal trends that underlie the cash conversion cycle in the industry and what can be done to promote sales out of season.
– Describe any plans to obtain government contracts as a means of supporting product development costs and overhead.

B. *Pricing:*

– Discuss pricing strategy, including the prices to be charged for your product and service, and compare your pricing policy with those of your major competitors, including a brief discussion of payback (in months) to the customer.
– Discuss the gross profit margin between manufacturing and ultimate sales costs and indicate whether this margin is large enough to allow for distribution and sales, warranty, training, service, amortization of development and equipment costs, price competition, and so forth—and still allow a profit.
– Explain how the price you set will enable you (1) to get the product or service accepted, (2) to maintain and increase your market share in the face of competition, and (3) to produce profits.
– Justify your pricing strategy and differences between your prices and those for competitive or substitute products or services in terms of economic payback to the customer and value added through newness, quality, warranty, timing, performance, service, cost savings, efficiency, and the like.
– If your product is to be priced lower than those of the competition, explain how you will do this and maintain profitability (e.g., through greater value added via effectiveness in manufacturing and distribution, lower labor costs, lower material costs, lower overhead, or other component of cost).
– Discuss your pricing policy, including a discussion of the relationship of price, market share, and profits. For example, a higher price may reduce volume but result in a higher gross profit.
– Describe any discount allowance for prompt payment or volume purchases.

C. *Sales tactics:*

– Describe the methods (e.g., own sales force, sales representatives, ready-made manufacturers' sales organizations, direct mail, or distributors) that will be used to make sales and distribute the product or service and both the initial plans and longer-range plans for a sales force. Include a discussion of any special requirements (e.g., refrigeration).
– Discuss the value chain and the resulting margins to be given to retailers, distributors, wholesalers, and salespeople and any special policies regarding discounts, exclusive distribution rights, and so on, given to distributors or sales representatives and compare these to those given by your competition. (See the Venture Opportunity Screening Guide.)
– Describe how distributors or sales representatives, if they are used, will be selected, when they will start to represent you, the areas they will cover and the build-up (a head count) of dealers and representatives by month, and the expected sales to be made by each.

- If a direct sales force is to be used, indicate how it will be structured and at what rate (a head count) it will be built up; indicate if it is to replace a dealer or representative organization and, if so, when and how.
- If direct mail, magazine, newspaper, or other media, telemarketing, or catalog sales are to be used, indicate the specific channels or vehicles, costs (per 1,000), and expected response rates and yield (as percentage) from the various media, and so on, used. Discuss how these will be built up.
- Show the sales expected per salesperson per year and what commission, incentive, and/or salary they are slated to receive, and compare these figures to the average for your industry.
- Present a selling schedule and a sales budget that includes all marketing promotion and service costs.

D. *Service and warranty policies:*

- If your company will offer a product that will require service, warranties, or training, indicate the importance of these to the customers' purchasing decisions and discuss your method of handling service problems.
- Describe the kind and term of any warranties to be offered, whether service will be handled by company servicepeople, agencies, dealers and distributors, or returns to the factory.
- Indicate the proposed charge for service calls and whether service will be a profitable or break-even operation.
- Compare your service, warranty, and customer training policies and practices to those of your principal competitors.

E. *Advertising and promotion:*

- Describe the approaches the company will use to bring its product or service to the attention of prospective purchasers.
- For original equipment manufacturers and for manufacturers of industrial products, indicate the plans for trade show participation, trade magazine advertisements, direct mailings, the preparation of product sheets and promotional literature, and use of advertising agencies.
- For consumer products, indicate what kind of advertising and promotional campaign is contemplated to introduce the product and what kind of sales aids will be provided to dealers, what trade shows, and so forth, are required.
- Present a schedule and approximate costs of promotion and advertising (direct mail, telemarketing, catalogs, etc.), and discuss how these costs will be incurred.

F. *Distribution:*

- Describe the methods and channels of distribution you will employ.
- Indicate how sensitive shipping cost is as a percent of the selling price.
- Note any special issues or problems that need to be resolved, or present potential vulnerabilities.
- If international sales are involved, note how these sales will be handled, including distribution, shipping, insurance, credit, and collections.

VI. Design and Development Plans

The nature and extent of any design and development work and the time and money required before a product or service is marketable need to be considered in detail. (Note that design and development costs are often underestimated.) Such design and development might be the engineering work necessary to convert a laboratory prototype to a finished product; the design of special tooling; the work of an industrial designer to make a product more attractive and salable; or the identification and organization of employees, equipment, and special techniques, such as the equipment, new computer software, and skills required for computerized credit checking, to implement a service business.

A. *Development status and tasks:*
- Describe the current status of each product or service and explain what remains to be done to make it marketable.
- Describe briefly the competence or expertise that your company has or will require to complete this development.
- List any customers or end users who are participating in the development, design, and/or testing of the product or service. Indicate results to date or when results are expected.

B. *Difficulties and risks:*
- Identify any major anticipated design and development problems and approaches to their solution.
- Discuss the possible effect on the cost of design and development, on the time to market introduction, and so forth, of such problems.

C. *Product improvement and new products:* In addition to describing the development of the initial products, discuss any ongoing design and development work that is planned to keep product(s) or service(s) competitive and to develop new related product(s) or service(s) that can be sold to the same group of customers. Discuss customers who have participated in these efforts and their reactions, and include any evidence that you may have.

D. *Costs:*
- Present and discuss the design and development budget, including costs of labor, materials, consulting fees, and so on.
- Discuss the impact on cash flow projections of underestimating this budget, including the impact of a 15 to 30 percent contingency.

E. *Proprietary issues:*
- Describe any patent, trademark, copyright, or intellectual property rights you own or are seeking.
- Describe any contractual rights or agreements that give you exclusivity or proprietary rights.
- Discuss the impact of any unresolved issues or existing or possible actions pending, such as disputed rights of ownership, relating to proprietary rights on timing and on any competitive edge you have assumed.

VII. Manufacturing and Operations Plan

The manufacturing and operations plan needs to include such factors as plant location, the type of facilities needed, space requirements, capital equipment requirements, and labor force (both full- and part-time) requirements. For a manufacturing business, the manufacturing and operations plan needs to include policies on inventory control, purchasing, production control, and which parts of the product will be purchased and which operations will be performed by your workforce (called make-or-buy decisions). A service business may require particular attention to location (proximity to customers is generally a must), minimizing overhead, and obtaining competitive productivity from a labor force.

A. *Operating cycle:*
- Describe the lead/lag times that characterize the fundamental operating cycle in your business. (Include a graph similar to the one found in the Venture Opportunity Screening Guide.)
- Explain how any seasonal production loads will be handled without severe dislocation (e.g., by building to inventory or using part-time help in peak periods).

B. *Geographical location:*
- Describe the planned geographical location of the business. Include any location analysis, and so on, that you have done.
- Discuss any advantages or disadvantages of the site location in terms of such factors as labor (including labor availability, whether workers are unionized, and wage rates), closeness to customers and/or suppliers, access to transportation, state and local taxes and laws (including zoning regulations), access to utilities, and so forth.

C. *Facilities and improvements:*
- For an existing business, describe the facilities, including plant and office space, storage and land areas, special tooling, machinery, and other capital equipment currently used to conduct the company's business, and discuss whether these facilities are adequate. Discuss any economies to scale.
- For a start-up, describe how and when the necessary facilities to start production will be acquired.
- Discuss whether equipment and space will be leased or acquired (new or used) and indicate the costs and timing of such actions and how much of the proposed financing will be devoted to plant and equipment.
- Explain future equipment needs in the next three years.
- Discuss how and when, in the next three years, plant space and equipment will be expanded to the capacities required by future sales projections and any plans to improve or add to existing plant space or move the facility; indicate the timing and cost of such acquisitions.

D. *Strategy and plans:*
- Describe the manufacturing processes involved in production of your product(s) and any decisions with respect to subcontracting of component parts, rather than complete in-house manufacture.
- Justify your proposed make-or-buy policy in terms of inventory financing, available labor skills, and other nontechnical questions, as well as production, cost, and capability issues.
- Discuss who potential subcontractors and/or suppliers are likely to be and any information about, or any surveys which have been made of, these subcontractors and suppliers.
- Present a production plan that shows cost/volume information at various sales levels of operation with breakdowns of applicable material, labor, purchased components, and factory overhead, and that shows the inventory required at various sales levels.
- Describe your approach to quality control, production control, inventory control, and explain what quality control and inspection procedures the company will use to minimize service problems and associated customer dissatisfaction.

E. *Regulatory and legal issues:*
- Discuss here any relevant state, federal, or foreign regulatory requirements unique to your product, process, or service, such as laws or other regulatory compliance unique to your business and any licenses, zoning permits, health permits, environmental approvals, and the like, necessary to begin operation.
- Note any pending regulatory changes that can affect the nature of your opportunity and its timing.
- Discuss any legal or contractual obligations that are pertinent as well.

VIII. Management Team

This section of the business plan includes a description of the functions that will need to be filled, a description of the key management personnel and their primary duties, an outline of the organizational structure for the venture, a description of the board of directors, a description of the ownership position of any other investors, and so forth. You need to present indications of commitment, such as the willingness of team members to initially accept modest salaries, and of the existence of the proper balance of technical, managerial, and business skills and experience in doing what is proposed.

A. *Organization:*
- Present the key management roles in the company and the individuals who will fill each position. (If the company is established and of sufficient size, an organization chart needs to be appended.)
- If it is not possible to fill each executive role with a full-time person without adding excessive overhead, indicate how these functions will be performed (e.g., using part-time specialists or consultants to perform some functions), who will perform them, and when they will be replaced by a full-time staff member.
- If any key individuals will not be on board at the start of the venture, indicate when they will join the company.
- Discuss any current or past situations where key management people have worked together that could indicate how their skills complement each other and result in an effective management team.

B. *Key management personnel:*
- For each key person, describe in detail career highlights, particularly relevant know-how, skills, and track record of accomplishments, that demonstrate his or her ability to perform the assigned role. Include in your description sales and profitability achievements (budget size, numbers of subordinates, new product introductions, etc.) and other prior entrepreneurial or general management results.
- Describe the exact duties and responsibilities of each of the key members of the management team.
- Complete resumes for each key management member need to be included here or as an exhibit and need to stress relevant training, experience, and concrete accomplishments, such as profit and sales improvement, labor management success, manufacturing or technical achievements, and meeting of budgets and schedules.

C. *Management compensation and ownership:*
- State the salary to be paid, the stock ownership planned, and the amount of their equity investment (if any) of each key member of the management team.
- Compare the compensation of each key member to the salary he or she received at his or her last independent job.

D. *Other investors:*
- Describe here any other investors in your venture, the number and percentage of outstanding shares they own, when they were acquired, and at what price.

E. *Employment and other agreements and stock option and bonus plans:*
- Describe any existing or contemplated employment or other agreements with key members.
- Indicate any restrictions on stock and vesting that affect ownership and disposition of stock.
- Describe any performance-dependent stock option or bonus plans that are contemplated.
- Summarize any incentive stock option or other stock ownership plans planned or in effect for key people and employees.

F. *Board of directors:*
- Discuss the company's philosophy about the size and composition of the board.
- Identify any proposed board members and include a one- or two-sentence statement of the member's background that shows what he or she can bring to the company.

G. *Other shareholders, rights, and restrictions:*

- Indicate any other shareholders in your company and any rights and restrictions or obligations, such as notes or guarantees, associated with these. (If they have all been accounted for above, simply note that there are no others.)

H. *Supporting professional advisors and services:*

- Indicate the supporting services that will be required.
- Indicate the names and affiliations of the legal, accounting, advertising, consulting, and banking advisors selected for your venture and the services each will provide.

IX. Overall Schedule

A schedule that shows the timing and interrelationship of the major events necessary to launch the venture and realize its objectives is an essential part of a business plan. The underlying cash conversion and operating cycle of the business will provide key inputs for the schedule. In addition to being a planning aid, by showing deadlines critical to a venture's success, a well-presented schedule can be extremely valuable in convincing potential investors that the management team is able to plan for venture growth in a way that recognizes obstacles and minimizes investor risk. Since the time to do things tends to be underestimated in most business plans, it is important to demonstrate that you have correctly estimated these amounts in determining the schedule. Create your schedule as follows:

Step 1: Lay out (use a bar chart) the cash conversion cycle in the business to capture for each product or service expected the lead and elapsed times from an order to the purchase of raw materials or inventory to shipping and collection.

Step 2: Prepare a month-by-month schedule that shows the timing of such activities as product development, market planning, sales programs, production, and operations, and that includes sufficient detail to show the timing of the primary tasks required to accomplish an activity.

Step 3: Show on the schedule the deadlines or milestones critical to the venture's success, such as:

- Incorporation of the venture.
- Completion of design and development.
- Completion of prototypes.
- Obtaining of sales representatives.
- Obtaining product display at trade shows.
- Signing up of distributors and dealers.
- Ordering of materials in production quantities.
- Starting of production or operation.
- Receipt of first orders.
- Delivery on first sale.
- Receiving the first payment on accounts receivable.

Step 4: Show on the schedule the "ramp up" of the number of management personnel, the number of production and operations personnel, and plant or equipment and their relation to the development of the business.

Step 5: Discuss in a general way the activities most likely to cause a schedule slippage, what steps will be taken to correct such slippages, and the impact of schedule slippages on the venture's operation, especially its potential viability and capital needs.

X. Critical Risks, Problems, and Assumptions

The development of a business has risks and problems, and the business plan invariably contains some implicit assumptions about them. You need to include a description of the risks and the consequences of adverse outcomes relating to your industry, your company and its personnel, your product's market appeal, and the timing and financing of your start-up. Be sure to discuss assumptions concerning sales projections, customer orders, and so forth.

If the venture has anything that could be considered a fatal flaw, discuss why it is not. The discovery of any unstated negative factors by potential investors can undermine the credibility of the venture and endanger its financing. Be aware that most investors will read the section describing the management team first and then this section.

It is recommended that you *not omit* this section. If you do, the reader will most likely come to one or more of the following conclusions:

1. You think he or she is incredibly naive or stupid, or both.
2. You hope to pull the wool over his or her eyes.
3. You do not have enough objectivity to recognize and deal with assumptions and problems.

Identifying and discussing the risks in your venture demonstrate your skills as a manager and increase the credibility of you and your venture with a venture capital investor or a private investor. Taking the initiative on the identification and discussion of risks helps you to demonstrate to the investor that you have thought about them and can handle them. Risks then tend not to loom as large black clouds in the investor's thinking about your venture.

1. Discuss assumptions and risks implicit in your plan.
2. Identify and discuss any major problems and other risks, such as:
   - Running out of cash *before* orders are secured.
   - Potential price cutting by competitors.
   - Any potentially unfavorable industrywide trends.
   - Design or manufacturing costs in excess of estimates.
   - Sales projections not achieved.
   - An unmet product development schedule.
   - Difficulties or long lead times encountered in the procurement of parts or raw materials.
   - Difficulties encountered in obtaining needed bank credit.
   - Larger-than-expected innovation and development costs.
   - Running out of cash *after* orders pour in.
3. Indicate what assumptions or potential problems and risks are most critical to the success of the venture, and describe your plans for minimizing the impact of unfavorable developments in each case.

XI. The Financial Plan

The financial plan is basic to the evaluation of an investment opportunity and needs to represent your best estimates of financial requirements. The purpose of the financial plan is to indicate the venture's potential and to present a timetable for financial viability. It also can serve as an operating plan for financial management using financial benchmarks. In preparing the financial plan, you need to look creatively at your venture and consider alternative ways of launching or financing it.

As part of the financial plan, financial exhibits need to be prepared. To estimate *cash flow needs,* use cash-based, rather than an accrual-based, accounting (i.e., use a real-time cash flow analysis of expected receipts and disbursements). This analysis needs to cover three years. Included also are current- and prior-year income statements and balance sheets, if applicable; profit and loss forecasts for three years; pro forma income statements and balance sheets; and a break-even chart. On the appropriate exhibits, or in an attachment, assumptions behind such items as sales levels and growth, collections and payables periods, inventory requirements, cash balances, cost of goods, and so forth, need to be specified. Your analysis of the operating and cash conversion cycle in the business will enable you to identify these critical assumptions.

Pro forma income statements are the plan-for-profit part of financial management and can indicate the potential financial feasibility of a new venture. Since usually the level of profits, particularly during the start-up years of a venture, will not be sufficient to finance operating asset needs, and since actual cash inflows do not always match the actual cash outflows on a short-term basis, a cash flow forecast that will indicate these conditions and enable management to plan cash needs is recommended. Further, pro forma balance sheets are used to detail the assets required to support the projected level of operations and, through liabilities, to show how these assets are to be financed. The projected balance sheets can indicate if debt-to-equity ratios, working capital, current ratios, inventory turnover, and the like are within the acceptable limits required to justify future financings that are projected for the venture. Finally, a break-even chart showing the level of sales and production that will cover all costs, including those costs that vary with production level and those that do not, is very useful.

A. *Actual income statements and balance sheets.* For an existing business, prepare income statements and balance sheets for the current year and for the prior two years.

B. *Pro forma income statements:*

- Using sales forecasts and the accompanying production or operations costs, prepare pro forma income statements for at least the first three years.
- Fully discuss assumptions (e.g., the amount allowed for bad debts and discounts, or any assumptions made with respect to sales expenses or general and administrative costs being a fixed percentage of costs or sales) made in preparing the pro forma income statement and document them.
- Draw on Section X of the business plan and highlight any major risks, such as the effect of a 20 percent reduction in sales from those projected or the adverse impact of having to climb a learning curve on the level of productivity over time, that could prevent the venture's sales and profit goals from being attained, plus the sensitivity of profits to these risks.

C. *Pro forma balance sheets:* Prepare pro forma balance sheets semiannually in the first year and at the end of each of the first three years of operation.

D. *Pro forma cash flow analysis:*

- Project cash flows monthly for the first year of operation and quarterly for at least the next two years, detailing the amount and timing of expected cash inflows and outflows; determine the need for and timing of additional financing and indicate peak requirements for working capital; and indicate how needed additional financing is to be obtained, such as through the equity financing, through bank loans, or through short-term lines of credit from banks, on what terms, and how it is to be repaid. Remember they are based on cash, not accrual, accounting.
- Discuss assumptions, such as those made on the timing of collection of receivables, trade discounts given, terms of payments to vendors, planned salary and wage increases, anticipated increases in any operating expenses, seasonality characteristics of the business as they affect inventory requirements, inventory turnovers per year, capital equipment purchases, and so forth. Again, these are real time (i.e., cash), not accrual.
- Discuss cash flow sensitivity to a variety of assumptions about business factors (e.g., possible changes in such crucial assumptions as an increase in the receivable collection period or a sales level lower than that forecasted).

E. *Break-even chart:*

- Calculate breakeven and prepare a chart that shows when breakeven will be reached and any stepwise changes in breakeven which may occur.

- Discuss the breakeven shown for your venture and whether it will be easy or difficult to attain breakeven, including a discussion of the size of break-even sales volume relative to projected total sales, the size of gross margins and price sensitivity, and how the break-even point might be lowered in case the venture falls short of sales projections.

F. *Cost control.* Describe how you will obtain information about report costs and how often, who will be responsible for the control of various cost elements, and how you will take action on budget overruns.

G. *Highlights:*

- Highlight the important conclusions, such as what the maximum amount of cash required is and when it will be required, the amount of debt and equity needed, how fast any debts can be repaid, etc., that can be drawn.

XII. Proposed Company Offering

The purpose of this section of the plan is to indicate the amount of any money that is being sought, the nature and amount of the securities offered to the investor, a brief description of the uses that will be made of the capital raised, and a summary of how the investor is expected to achieve its targeted rate of return. It is recommended that you read the discussion about financing in Part IV.

It is important to realize the terms for financing your company that you propose here are the *first step* in the negotiation process with those interested in investing, and it is very possible that your financing will involve different kinds of securities than originally proposed.

A. *Desired financing.* Based on your real-time cash flow projections and your estimate of how much money is required over the next three years to carry out the development and/or expansion of your business as described, indicate how much of this capital requirement will be obtained by this offering and how much will be obtained via term loans and lines of credit.

B. *Offering:*

- Describe the type (e.g., common stock, convertible debentures, debt with warrants, debt plus stock), unit price, and total amount of securities to be sold in this offering. If securities are not just common stock, indicate by type, interest, maturity, and conversion conditions.
- Show the percentage of the company that the investors of this offering will hold after it is completed or after exercise of any stock conversion or purchase rights in the case of convertible debentures or warrants.
- Securities sold through a private placement and that therefore are exempt from SEC registration should include the following statement in this part of the plan:

> The shares being sold pursuant to this offering are restricted securities and may not be resold readily. The prospective investor should recognize that such securities might be restricted as to resale for an indefinite period of time. Each purchaser will be required to execute a Non-Distribution Agreement satisfactory in form to corporate counsel.

C. *Capitalization:*

- Present in tabular form the current and proposed (postoffering) number of outstanding shares of common stock. Indicate any shares offered by key management people and show the number of shares that they will hold after completion of the proposed financing.
- Indicate how many shares of your company's common stock will remain authorized but unissued after the offering and how many of these will be reserved for stock options for future key employees.

D. *Use of funds.* Investors like to know how their money is going to be spent. Provide a brief description of how the capital raised will be used. Summarize as specifically as possible what amount will be used for such things as product design and development, capital equipment, marketing, and general working capital needs.

E. *Investors' return.* Indicate how your valuation and proposed ownership shares will result in the desired rate of return for the investors you have targeted and what the likely harvest or exit mechanism (IPO, outright sale, merger, MBO, etc.) will be.

XIII. Appendixes

Include pertinent information here that is too extensive for the body of the business plan but which is necessary (product specs or photos; lists of references; suppliers of critical components; special location factors, facilities, or technical analyses; reports from consultants or technical experts; and copies of any critical regulatory approval, licenses, etc).

STEP 5: INTEGRATE YOUR DISCRETE SECTIONS INTO A COHERENT AND LOGICAL BUSINESS PLAN, THAT CAN BE USED FOR THE PURPOSE FOR WHICH IT IS CREATED.

STEP 6: GET FEEDBACK; IF YOUR PLAN IS TO BE SUBMITTED TO OUTSIDE INVESTORS, HAVE YOUR PLAN REVIEWED BY YOUR ATTORNEY. Once written, it is recommended that you get the plan reviewed. No matter how good you and your team are, you will most likely overlook issues and treat aspects of your venture in a manner that is less than clear. A good reviewer can give you the benefit of an outside objective evaluation. Your attorney can make sure that there are no misleading statements in your plan and that it contains all the caveats and the like.

FINANCING ENTREPRENEURIAL VENTURES

PART IV

A financing strategy should be driven by corporate and personal goals, by resulting financial requirements, and ultimately by the available alternatives. In the final analysis, these alternatives are governed by the entrepreneur's relative bargaining power and skill in managing and orchestrating the fund-raising moves. In turn, that bargaining power is governed to a large extent by the cruelty of *real time.* It is governed by when the company will run out of cash given its current cash burn rate.

There are more numerous alternatives for financing a company than ever before. Many contend that money remains plentiful for well-managed emerging firms with the promise of profitable growth. Yet, savvy entrepreneurs remain vigilant for the warnings noted here to avoid the myopic temptation to "take the money and run."

While some of these alternatives look distinct and separate, a financing strategy probably will encompass a combination of both debt and equity capital.

In considering which financial alternatives are best for a venture at any particular growth stage, it is important to draw on the experience of others who have already been there. This includes other entrepreneurs, professional investors, lenders, accountants, and other professionals.

In their search for either debt or equity capital, it is important that entrepreneurs take a professional approach to selecting and presenting their ventures to investors and lenders.

Entrepreneurial Finance

12

Happiness to an entrepreneur is a positive cash flow.

Fred Adler
Venture Capitalist

RESULTS EXPECTED

Upon completion of this chapter, you will have:

1. Examined critical issues in financing new ventures.
2. Studied the difference between entrepreneurial finance and conventional administrative or corporate finance.
3. Examined the process of crafting financial and fund-raising strategies and the critical variables involved, including identifying the financial life cycles of new ventures, a financial strategy framework, and investor preferences.
4. Analyzed the issues and approaches utilized by Douglas Ranalli.

VENTURE FINANCING: THE ENTREPRENEUR'S ACHILLES' HEEL[1]

There are three core principles of entrepreneurial finance: (1) more cash is preferred to less cash, (2) cash sooner is preferred to cash later, and (3) less risky cash is preferred to more risky cash. While these principles seem simple enough, entrepreneurs, chief executive officers, and division managers often seem to ignore them. To these individuals, financial analysis seems intimidating, regardless of the size of the company. Even management teams, comfortable with the financial issues, may not be adept at linking strategic and financial decisions to their companies' challenges and choices. Take, for example, the following predicaments:

- Reviewing the year-end results just handed to you by your chief financial officer, you see no surprises—except that the company loss is even larger than you had projected three months earlier. Therefore, for the fourth year in a row, you will have to walk into the boardroom and deliver bad news. A family owned business since 1945, the company has survived and prospered with average annual sales growth of 17 percent. In fact, the company's market share has actually increased during the recent years despite the losses. With the annual growth rate in the industry averaging less than 5 percent, your mature markets offer few opportunities for sustaining higher growth. How can this be happening? Where do you and your company go from here? How do you explain to the board that for four years you have increased sales and market share, but produced losses? How will you propose to turn the situation around?

[1] This section is drawn from Jeffry A Timmons, "Financial Management Breakthrough for Entrepreneurs."

- During the past 20 years, your cable television company has experienced rapid growth through the expansion of existing properties and numerous acquisitions. By 1978, your net wealth reached $25 million. The next decade of expansion was fueled by the high leverage common in the cable industry and valuations soared. By 1988, your company had a market value in the $500 million range. You had a mere $300 million in debt, and you owned 100 percent of the company. By 1990, just two years later, your $200 million net worth is an astonishing zero! Additionally, you now face the personally exhausting and financially punishing restructuring battle to survive; personal bankruptcy is a very real possibility. How could this happen? Can the company be salvaged?[2]
- From 1986 through 1988, your company was the industry leader, meeting as well as exceeding the 1986 business plan targets for annual sales, profitability, and new stores. Exceeding these targets while doubling sales and profitability each year has propelled your stock price from $15 at the initial public offering to the mid $30s. Meanwhile, you still own a large chunk of the company. Then the shocker—in 1989, your company loses $78 million on just over $90 million in sales! The value of your stock plummets. A brutal restructuring follows in which the stock is stripped from the original management team, including you, and you are ousted from the company you founded and loved. Why did the company spin out of control? Why couldn't you as the founder have anticipated its demise? Could you have saved the company in time?
- As the chairman of a rapidly growing telecommunications firm, you are convening your first board meeting after a successful public stock offering. As you think about the agenda, your plans are to grow the company to $15 million in sales in the next three years, which is comfortable given the $5 million in sales last year, the $3.5 million of cash in the bank, and no debt on the balance sheet. Early in the meeting one of the two outside directors asks the controller and the chief financial officer his favorite question, "When will you run out of cash?" The chief financial officer is puzzled at first, then he is indignant, if not outraged, by what he considers to be an irrelevant question. After all he reasoned, our company has plenty of cash and we won't need to use our bank line. However, 16 months later, without warning from the chief financial officer, the company is out of cash and has overdrawn its $1 million credit line by $700,000 and the hemorrhaging may get worse. The board fires the president, the chief financial officer, and the senior audit partner from a a major accounting firm. The chairman has to take over the helm and must personally invest half a million dollars in the collapsing company to keep it afloat. At this point, it's the bank that is indignant and outraged. You have to devise an emergency battle plan to get on top of the financial crisis. How can this be done?

Financial Management Myopia: It Can't Happen to Me

All of these situations have three things in common. First, they are real companies and these events actually happened. Second, each of these companies was led by successful entrepreneurs who knew enough to prepare audited financial statements.[3] Third, in each example, the Achilles' heel was financial management myopia, a combination of self-delusion and just plain not understanding the *complex dynamics* and *interplay between financial management and business strategy.* Why is this so?

Getting beyond "Collect Early, Pay Late." During my 25 years as an educator, author, director, founder, and investor in entrepreneurial companies, I have met a few thousand entrepreneurs and managers, including executives participating in an executive MBA

[2] For more detail, see Burton C Hurlock and William A Sahlman, "Star Cablevision Group: Harvesting in a Bull Market," HBS Case 293-036, Harvard Business School, 1992.

[3] Their outcomes as of this writing have ranged from demise to moderate success to radical downsizing followed by dramatic recovery to still being in the midst of a turnaround.

program, MBA students, company founders, presidents, members of the Young Presidents Organization, and the chief executive officers of middle-market companies. By their own admission, they felt uniformly uncomfortable if not downright intimidated and terrified, by their lack of expertise in financial analysis and its relationship to management and strategy. No doubt about it, the vast majority of entrepreneurs and nonfinancial managers are disadvantaged. Beyond "collect early, pay late," there is precious little sophistication and an enormous level of discomfort when it comes to these complex and dynamic financial interrelationships. Even good managers who are reveling in major sales increases and profit increases often fail to realize until it's too late the impact increased sales have on the cash flow required to finance the increased receivables and inventory.

The Spreadsheet Mirage. It is hard to imagine any entrepreneur who would not want ready answers to many financial vigilance questions. (See *Exhibit 12.1.*) Until now, however, getting the answers to these questions was a rarity. If the capacity and information are there to do the necessary analysis (and all too often they are not), it can take up to several weeks to get a response. In this era of spreadsheet mania, more often than not, the answers will come in the form of a lengthy report with innumerable scenarios, pages of numbers, backup exhibits, and possibly a stand-up presentation by a staff financial analyst, controller, or chief financial officer.

Yet, all too often the barrage of spreadsheet exhibits is really a *mirage*. What is missing? Traditional spreadsheets can only report and manipulate the data. The numbers may be there, the trends may be identified, but the connections and interdependencies between financial structure and business decisions inherent in key financial questions may be missed. As a result, gaining true insights and getting to creative alternatives and new solutions may be painfully slow, if not interminable. By themselves, spreadsheets cannot model the more complex financial and strategic interrelationships that entrepreneurs need to grasp. And for the board of directors, failure to get this information would be fatal and any delay would mean too little and too late. Such a weakness in financial know-how becomes life-threatening for entrepreneurs such as those noted earlier, when it comes to anticipating the financial and

Exhibit 12.1
The Crux of It: Anticipation and Financial Vigilance

To avoid some of the great tar pits like the ones described earlier, entrepreneurs need answers to questions that link strategic business decisions to financial plans and choices. The crux of it is anticipation: *What is most likely to happen? When? What can go right along the way? What can go wrong? What has to happen to achieve our business objectives and to increase or to preserve our options?* Financially savvy entrepreneurs know that such questions trigger a process that can lead to creative solutions to their financial challenges and problems. At a practical level financially astute entrepreneurs and managers maintain vigilance over numerous key strategic and financial questions:

- What are the financial consequences and implications of crucial business decisions such as pricing, volume, and policy changes affecting the balance sheet? How will these change over time?
- How can we measure and monitor changes in our financial strategy and structure from a management, not just a GAAP, perspective?
- What does it mean to grow too fast in our industry? How fast can we grow without requiring outside debt or equity? How much capital is required if we increase or decrease our growth by X percent?
- What will happen to our cash flow, profitability, return on assets, and shareholder equity if we grow faster or slower by X percent?
- How much capital will this require? How much can be financed internally and how much will have to come from external sources? What is a reasonable mix of debt and equity?
- What if we are 20% less profitable than our plan calls for?
- What should be our focus and priorities? What are the cash flow and net income break-even points for each of our product lines? For our company? For our business unit?
- What about our pricing, our volume, and costs? How sensitive is our cash flow and net income to increases or decreases in price, variable costs, or volume? What price/volume mix will enable us to achieve the same cash flow and net income?
- How will these changes in pricing, costs and volume affect our key financial ratios and how will we stack up against others in our industry? How will our lenders view this?
- At each stage—start-up, rapidly growing, stagnating, or mature company—how should we be thinking about these questions and issues?

see a recent MBA or investment banking firm alumnus or alumna show up with an HP-12C calculator or the latest laptop personal computer and then proceed to develop "the 10-year discounted cash flow stream." The assumptions normally made and the mind-set behind them are irrelevant or grossly misleading for valuation of smaller private firms.

- *Convential financial ratios.* Current financial ratios are misleading when applied to most private entrepreneurial companies. For one thing, entrepreneurs often own more than one company at once and move cash and assets from one to another. For example, an entrepreneur may own real estate and equipment in one entity and lease it to another company. Use of different fiscal years compounds the difficulty of interpreting what the balance sheet really means and the possibilities for aggressive tax avoidance. Further, many of the most important value and equity builders in the business are off-balance-sheet or hidden assets: the excellent management team; the best scientist, technician, or designer; or know-how and business relationships that cannot be bought or sold, let alone valued for the balance sheet.
- *Goals.* Creating value over the long term, rather than maximizing quarterly earnings, is a prevalent mind-set and strategy among highly successful entrepreneurs. Since profit is more than just the bottom line, financial strategies are geared to build value, often at the expense of short-term earnings. The growth required to build value often is heavily self-financed, thereby eroding possible accounting earnings.

DETERMINING CAPITAL REQUIREMENTS

How much money does my venture need? When is it needed? How long will it last? Where and from whom can it be raised? How should this process be orchestrated and managed? These are vital questions to any entrepreneur at any stage in the development of a company. In the next two sections these questions are answered.

Financial Strategy Framework

The financial strategy framework shown in *Exhibit 12.4* is a way to begin the crafting of financial and fund-raising strategies.[8] The exhibit provides a flow and logic with which an otherwise confusing, if not befuddling task, can be attacked. *The opportunity leads and drives the business strategy, which in turn drives the financial requirements, the sources and deal structures, and the financial strategy.* (Again, unless and until this part of the exercise is well-defined, developing spreadsheets and "playing with the numbers" is just that—playing.)

Once the core of the market opportunity and the strategy for seizing it are well defined as well as possible (of course, these may well change, even dramatically), an entrepreneur can then begin to examine the financial requirements in terms of (1) operating needs (i.e., working capital for operations) and (2) asset needs (for start-up or for expansion facilities, equipment, research and development, and other apparently one-time expenditures). This framework leaves ample room for crafting a financial strategy, for creatively identifying sources, for devising a fund-raising plan, and for structuring deals.

Each *fund-raising strategy*, along with its accompanying deal structure, commits the company to actions that incur actual and real-time costs and may enhance or inhibit future financing options. Similarly, each *source* has particular requirements and costs—both

[8] This framework was developed for the course, Financing Entrepreneurial Ventures, at Babson College and is used in the Entrepreneurial Finance course at the Harvard Business School.

Exhibit 12.4
Financial Strategy Framework

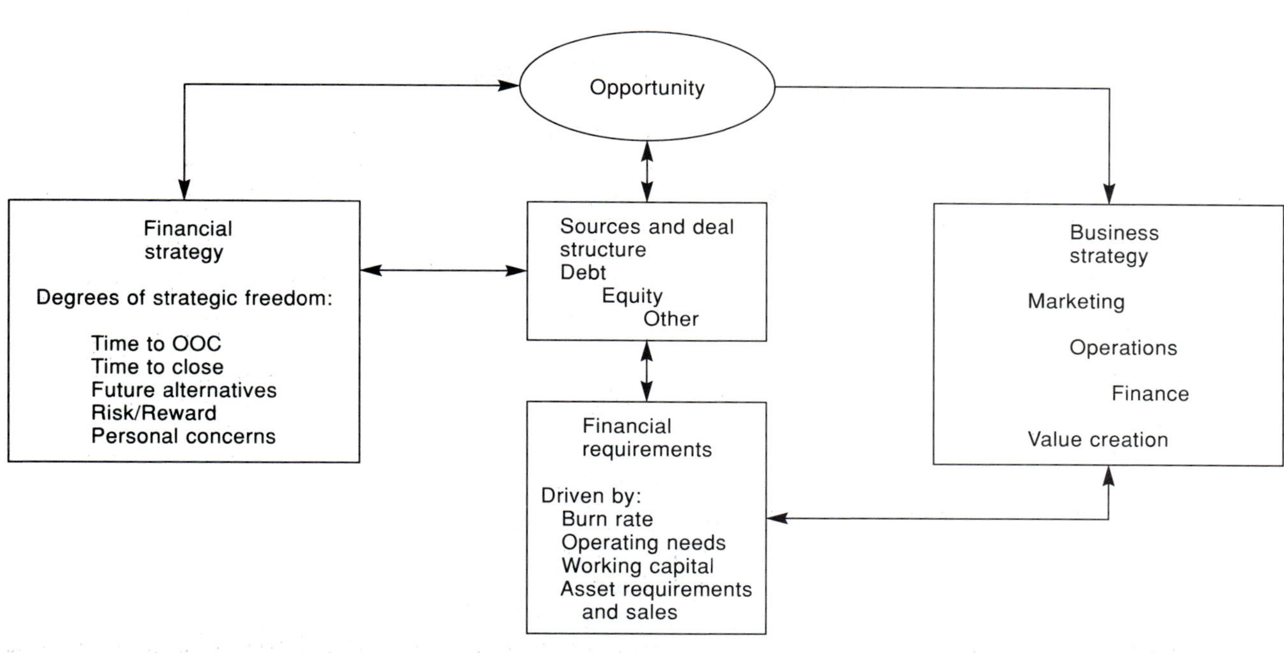

apparent and hidden—that carry implications for both financial strategy and financial requirements. The premise is that successful entrepreneurs are aware of potentially punishing situations, and that they are careful to "sweat the details" and proceed with a certain degree of wariness as they evaluate, select, negotiate, and craft business relationships with potential funding sources. In doing so, they are more likely to find the right sources, at the right time, and on the right terms and conditions. They are also more likely to avoid potential mismatches, costly sidetracking for the wrong sources, and the disastrous marriage to these sources that might follow.

Certain changes in the financial climate, such as the aftershocks felt after October 1987, can cause repercussions across financial markets and institutions serving smaller companies. These take the form of greater caution by lenders and investors alike as they seek to increase their protection against risk. When the financial climate becomes harsher, an entrepreneur's capacity to devise financing strategies and to effectively deal with financing sources can be stretched to the limit and beyond. Also, certain lures of cash that come in unsuspecting ways turn out to be a punch in the wallet. (The next chapter covers some of these potentially fatal lures and some of the issues and considerations needed to recognize and avoid these traps while devising a fund-raising strategy and evaluating and negotiating with different sources.)

Free Cash Flow: Burn Rate, OOC, and TTC

The core concept in determining the external financing requirements of the venture is free cash flow. Three vital corollaries are the *burn rate* (projected or actual), time to *OOC* (when will the company be out of cash), and *TTC*, or the time required to close the financing—and have the check clear! These are critical since they have major impact on the

Exhibit 12.5
Entrepreneur's Bargaining Power Based on Time to OOC

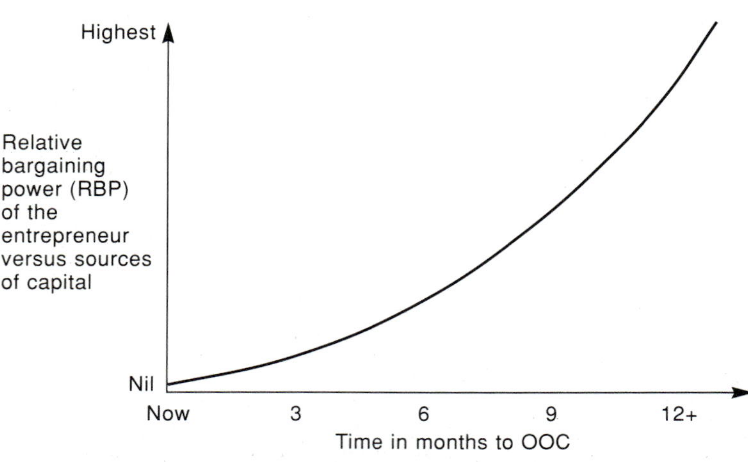

entrepreneur's choices and relative bargaining power with various sources of equity and debt capital, which is represented in *Exhibit 12.5*. Chapter 14, "The Deal: Valuation, Structure, and Negotiation," addresses the details of deal structuring, terms, conditions, and covenants.

The message is clear: If you are out of cash in 90 days or less, you are at a major disadvantage. OOC even in six months is perilously soon. But if you have a year or more, the options, terms, price, and covenants that you will be able to negotiate will improve dramatically. The implication is clear: Ideally, raise money when you do not need it.

The cash flow generated by a company or project is defined as follows:

	Earnings before interest and taxes (EBIT)
Less	Tax exposure (tax rate times EBIT)
Plus	Depreciation and other noncash charges
Less	Increase in operating working capital
Less	Capital expenditures

Economists call this figure free cash flow. The definition takes into account the benefits of investing, the income generated, *and* the cost of investing, the amount of investment in working capital and plant and equipment required to generate a given level of sales and net income.

The definition can fruitfully be refined further. Operating working capital is defined as:

	Transactions cash balances
Plus	Accounts receivable
Plus	Inventory
Plus	Other operating current assets (e.g., prepaid expenses)
Less	Accounts payable
Less	Taxes payable
Less	Other operating current liabilities (e.g., accrued expenses)

Finally, this expanded definition can be collapsed into a simpler one:[9]

	Earnings *before interest* but *after taxes* (EBIAT)
Less	Increase in net total operating capital (FA + WC)

where the increase in net total operating capital is defined as:

	Increase in operating working capital
Plus	Increase in net fixed assets

CRAFTING FINANCIAL AND FUND-RAISING STRATEGIES

Critical Variables

When financing is needed, a number of factors affect the availability of the various types of financing, and their suitability and cost:

- Accomplishments and performance to date.
- Investor's perceived risk.
- Industry and technology.
- Venture upside potential and anticipated exit timing.
- Venture anticipated growth rate.
- Venture age and stage of development.
- Investor's required rate of return or internal rate of return.
- Amount of capital required and prior valuations of the venture.
- Founders' goals regarding growth, control, liquidity, and harvesting.
- Relative bargaining positions.
- Investor's required terms and covenants.

Certainly, numerous other factors, especially an investor's or lender's view of the quality of a business opportunity and the management team, will also play a part in a decision to invest in or lend to a firm.

Generally speaking, a company's operations can be financed through debt and through some form of equity financing.[10] Moreover, it is generally believed that a new or existing business needs to obtain both equity and debt financing if it is to have a sound financial foundation for growth without excessive dilution of the entrepreneur's equity.

Usually, short-term debt (i.e., debt incurred for one year or less) is used by a business for working capital and is repaid out of the proceeds of its sales. Longer-term borrowings (i.e., term loans of one to five years or long-term loans maturing in more than five years) are used for working capital and/or to finance the purchase of property or equipment that serve as collateral for the loan. Equity financing is used to fill the nonbankable gaps, preserve ownership, and lower the risk of loan defaults.

However, a new venture just starting operations will have difficulty obtaining either short-term or longer-term bank debt without a substantial cushion of equity financing or

[9] This section is drawn directly from "Note on Free Cash Flow Valuation Models," HBS 288-023, p. 2–3.

[10] In addition to the purchase of common stock, equity financing is meant to include the purchase of both stock and subordinated debt, or subordinated debt with stock conversion features or warrants to purchase stock.

long-term debt that is subordinated or junior to all bank debt.[11] As far as a lender is concerned, a start-up has little proven capability to generate sales, profits, and cash to pay off short-term debt and even less ability to sustain profitable operations over a number of years and retire long-term debt. Even the underlying protection provided by a venture's assets used as loan collateral may be insufficient to obtain bank loans. Asset values can erode with time; in the absence of adequate equity capital and good management, they may provide little real loan security to a bank.[12]

A bank may loan money to a start-up to some maximum debt-to-equity ratio. As a rough rule of thumb, a start-up *may* be able to obtain debt for working capital purposes that is equal to its equity and subordinated debt. A start-up can also obtain loans through such avenues as the Small Business Administration, manufacturers and suppliers, or through leasing.

An existing business seeking expansion capital or funds for a temporary use has a much easier job obtaining both debt and equity. Sources like banks, professional investors, and leasing and finance companies often will seek out such companies and regard them as important customers for secured and unsecured short and term loans or as good investment prospects. Furthermore, an existing and expanding business will find it easier to raise equity capital from private or institutional sources and to raise it on better terms than the start-up.

A key message from the above is that awareness of criteria used by various sources of financing—whether for debt, equity, or some combination of the two—that are available for a particular situation is central to devise a time-effective and cost-effective search for capital.

Financial Life Cycles

One useful way to begin the process of identifying equity financing alternatives, and when and if certain alternatives are available, is to consider what can be called the financial life cycle of firms. *Exhibit 12.6* shows the types of capital available over time for different types of firms at different stages of development (i.e., as indicated by different sales levels).[13] It also summarizes, at different stages of development (research and development, start-up, early growth, rapid growth, and exit), the principal sources of risk capital and costs of risk capital.

As can be seen in the exhibit, sources have different preferences and practices, including how much money they will provide, when in a company's life cycle they will invest, and the cost of the capital or expected annual rate of return they are seeking. The available sources of capital change dramatically for companies at different stages and rates of growth, and there will be variations in different parts of the country.

Thus, one can see that many of the sources of equity are not available until a company progresses beyond the earlier stages of its growth. Conversely, some of the sources available to early-stage companies, especially personal sources, friends, and other informal investors or angels, will be insufficient to meet the financing requirements generated in later stages, if the company continues to grow successfully.

One also can see that another key factor affecting the availability of financing is the upside potential of a company. Recall that of the 1.2 million new businesses of all kinds

[11] For lending purposes, commercial banks regard such subordinated debt as equity. Venture capital investors normally subordinate their business loans to the loans provided by the bank or other financial institutions.

[12] The bank loan defaults by the real estate investment trusts (REITs) in 1975 are examples of the failure of assets to provide protection in the absence of sound management and adequate equity capital.

[13] William H Wetzel, Jr., of the University of New Hampshire, originally showed the different types of equity capital that are available to three types of companies. The exhibit is based on a chart by Wetzel, which the author has taken the liberty of updating and modifying. See William H Wetzel, Jr., "The Cost of Availability of Credit and Risk Capital in New England," in *A Region's Struggling Savior: Small Business in New England*, ed. J A Timmons and D E Gumpert (Waltham, MA: Small Business Foundation of America, 1979).

Exhibit 12.6
Financing Life Cycles

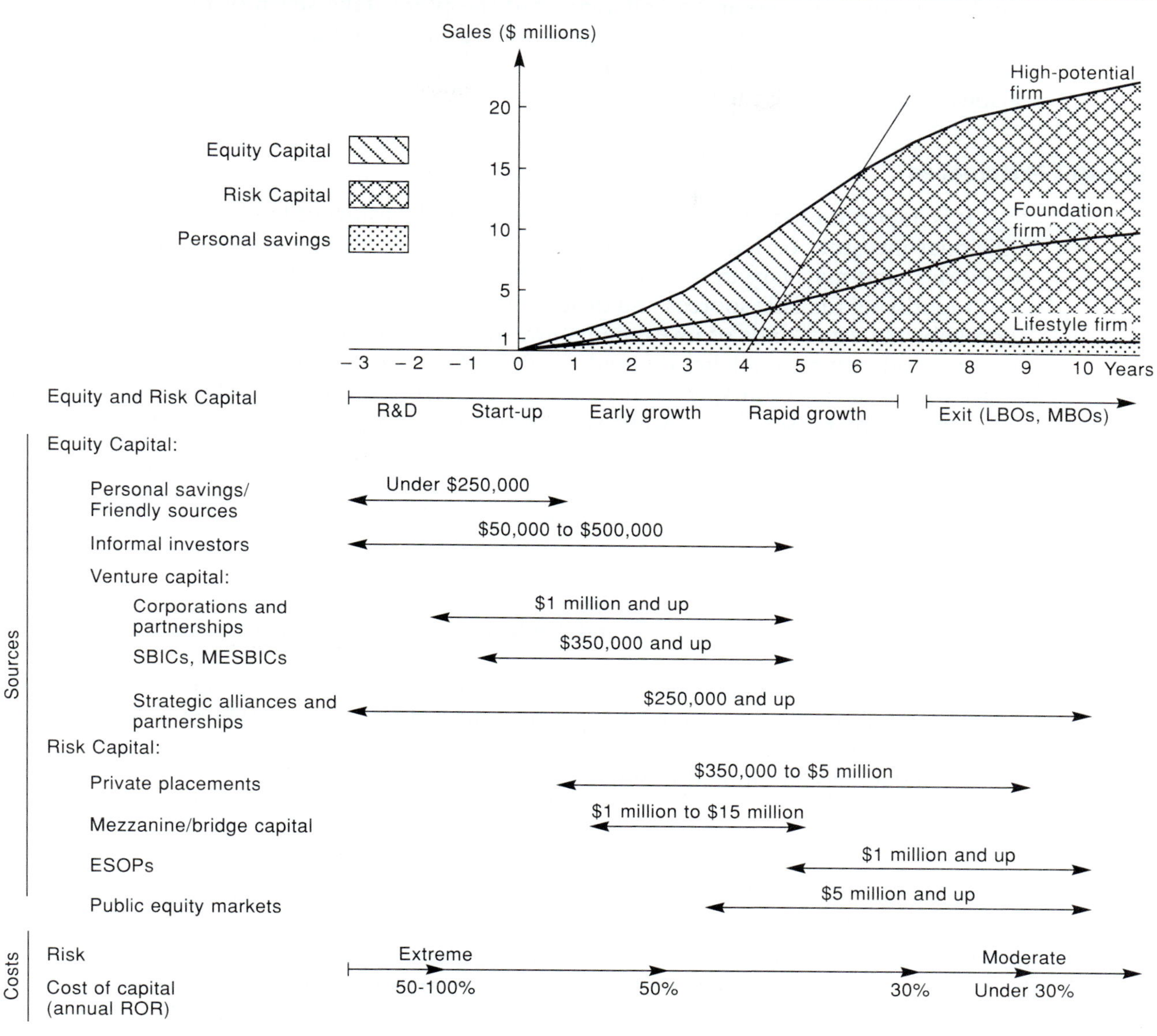

Source: Adapted from W H Wetzel, Jr., "The Cost of Availability of Credit and Risk Capital in New England," in *A Region's Struggling Savior: Small Business in New England*, ed. J A Timmons and D E Gumpert (Waltham, MA: Small Business Foundation of America, 1979), p. 175.

expected to be launched in the United States in 1994, for example, probably 5 percent or less of these will achieve the growth and sales levels of high-potential firms. Foundation firms will total around 8–12 percent of all new firms, which will grow more slowly but exceed $1 million in sales and may grow to $5 million to $15 million. Remaining are the traditional, stable lifestyle firms. What have been called high-potential firms (those that grow rapidly and are likely to exceed $20 million to $25 million or more in sales) are strong prospects for a public offering and have the widest array of financing alternatives, including combinations of debt and equity and other alternatives (which are noted later on), while foundation firms have fewer, and lifestyle firms are limited to the personal resources of their founders and whatever net worth or collateral they can accumulate.

In general, investors believe the younger the company, the more risky the investment. This is a variation of the old saying in the venture capital business that has been seen before: The lemons ripen in two and a half years, but the plums take seven or eight.

While the time line and dollar limits shown are only guidelines, they do reflect how these money sources view the riskiness, and thus the required rate of return, of companies at various stages of development.

Investor Preferences

It is important to realize that precise practices of investors or lenders may vary between individual investors or lenders in a given category, may change with the current market conditions, and may vary in different areas of the country from time to time.

Identifying realistic sources and developing a fund-raising strategy to tap them depend upon knowing what kinds of investments investors or lenders are seeking. While the stage, amount, and return guidelines noted in *Exhibit 12.6* can help, doing the appropriate homework in advance on specific investor or lender preferences can save months of wild goose chases and personal cash, while significantly increasing the odds of successfully raising funds on acceptable terms.

CASE—DOUGLAS J. RANALLI*

Preparation Questions

1. Evaluate the opportunity and FAX International's performance and financing requirements.
2. What financing strategies and capital structure should FAX International pursue?
3. What would you recommend to Ranalli for a deal proposal? The minimum number of shares and share price Ranalli should accept?
4. What should Doug do? Why?

DOUGLAS J. RANALLI

As he left the office March 23, 1992, Doug Ranalli, founder and president of FAX International (FI), said goodnight to the engineers and salespeople that were working late again. It was the end of another long and exhausting day. He began the 20-minute drive from his Burlington, Massachusetts, office to his home in Cambridge with a lot on his mind. Ranalli knew he had some important decisions to make and soon. He had to decide whether or not to launch the FI service, now several weeks overdue, with its imperfections. He also needed to decide how much money to raise and under what terms.

Ranalli had begun building FI some 18 months earlier after he came up with the idea of starting a private telecommunications network exclusively for facsimile traffic between the United States and Tokyo. The last year had been spent assembling the management team, designing and building the network, and recruiting and training the sales and service groups. After more than two months of identifying potential customers, the sales force had finally commenced selling the service on March 9, promising the customers a start date during the next week to 10 days.

However, the network, originally scheduled for a February 1 start date, was still experiencing technical difficulties and thus was not yet operational. Certain bugs in the

*Benjamin Campbell (MBA 1992) prepared this case under the supervision of Professor Jeffry A Timmons as the basis for class discussion, rather than to illustrate either effective or ineffective handling of an administrative situation.

software and in the vendor hardware were causing periodic shutdowns and the loss of test documents. The customers who had been sold in the first week had now waited two weeks for the network to go online and the sales force was running out of excuses. To make matters worse, due to the length of this unexpected delay, FI was out of money. The private investors Ranalli had lined up for the next round of financing were all waiting for an operational network before they invested.

Ranalli was faced with a serious dilemma. On the one hand, he could bring the imperfect network online to get the much needed cash infusion, yet he ran the risk of losing customers and demoralizing the sales and service people if the system experienced shutdowns. On the other hand, he could wait until the system was fully debugged before going online, which could take weeks. And he was already running on fumes financially. The costs in lost momentum would be tremendous if he had to slow or stop operations due to lack of funds.

In addition, Ranalli wondered how much money he should raise in this round of financing and at what price. The sales in minutes of traffic/day seemed to be holding at twice the projected business plan assumptions. (See *Exhibits A* through *D* for pro forma assumptions.) If this kept up, FI would be able to finance operations from internally generated funds sooner than expected. In fact, Ranalli hoped that this would be the last financing round FI would need before he expanded to other international locations later in the year.

Company History

Ranalli started his first business, *Student Life* magazine, while studying industrial engineering at Cornell University. After selling *Student Life* to Time, Inc., in 1987, he worked at Time, Inc., for one year, after which he entered the Harvard Business School (HBS). While at HBS he searched for new business ideas to pursue upon graduation. Given the fast pace of growth in information technology industries and his background in engineering, he decided to focus on areas involving information technology. Ranalli firmly believed that he could start a successful entrepreneurial venture in an area in which he had little or no experience, as long as he researched the industry and the idea thoroughly.

Throughout his second year at HBS, Ranalli tried to think of ideas and either prove or disprove their viability by researching them in his spare time. He came up with eight possible ventures that he thought were worthy of pursuit but proceeded to discard each of them. In his last semester (spring 1990) he completed an independent research report on his most promising idea to date, only to conclude at the end of the study that it, too, was not viable.

Ranalli graduated as a Baker Scholar with the HBS class of 1990 and still had no business to pursue. He had spent the summer after his first year working for a prominent consulting firm that had given him a very lucrative employment offer. Determined to launch an entrepreneurial venture, Ranalli decided to dedicate the summer to finding a viable business idea. He informed the firm that he would begin work in September if he was unsuccessful. The firm was supportive, due in part to their skepticism regarding his chances of success.

In late July, while reading through an AT&T technology journal, Ranalli believed he had found the concept he had been searching for. The article described the different types of information that people were sending over telephone lines. It explained that the phone companies had no idea whether the open line was being used for voice or data. More importantly, it revealed that data travels on a phone line seven times more efficiently than voice traffic. Thus, when a fax is sent over the telephone line, only one-seventh of the line is being used, yet the phone company must dedicate an entire line to the call since it has no idea whether voice or data traffic is on the line. The business, in its most basic form, was born. Ranalli knew that if he could build a network exclusively for facsimile traffic, then he could,

Exhibit A

From the Original Business Plan (December 1991) Pro Forma Revenue/Expense Breakdown (Year 1)

	1992 Jan.	Feb.	Mar.	Apr.	May	June	Jul.	Aug.	Sept.	Oct.	Nov.	Dec.	Total Year
Detailed Revenue													
United States:													
Average price/minute	$0.75												
Monthly growth rate	500 minutes/sales rep												
Free minutes/day	0	1,000	1,000	1,000	1,000	1,000	1,000	1,000	1,000	1,000	1,000	1,000	
Net new minutes/day	0	500	1,500	2,000	2,500	2,500	2,500	2,500	2,500	2,500	2,500	2,500	
Total paid minutes/day	0	500	2,000	4,000	6,5000	9,000	11,500	14,000	16,500	19,000	21,500	24,000	
Total minutes/month (month = 20 days)	0	10,000	40,000	80,000	130,000	180,000	230,000	280,000	330,000	380,000	430,000	480,000	2,570,000
Monthly traffic revenue	0	$7,500	$30,000	$60,000	$97,500	$135,000	$172,500	$210,000	$247,500	$285,000	$322,500	$360,000	$1,927,500
Uncollectibles (1%)	0	(75)	(300)	(600)	(975)	(1,350)	(1,725)	(2,100)	(2,475)	(2,850)	(3,225)	(3,600)	(19,275)
Autodialer rental revenue	0	333	1,333	2,667	4,333	6,000	7,667	9,333	11,000	12,667	14,333	16,000	85,667
Net monthly US revenue	0	$7,758	$31,033	$62,067	$100,858	$139,650	$178,442	$217,233	$256,025	$294,817	$333,608	$372,400	$1,993,892
Japan joint venture:													
Average price/minute:	$0.35												
Monthly growth rate:	1,500 minutes/day												
Total paid minutes/day	0	0	0	0	0	0	0	500	2,000	3,500	5,000	6,500	
Total minutes/month	0	0	0	0	0	0	0	10,000	40,000	70,000	100,000	130,000	350,000
Net Japanese revenue	0	0	0	0	0	0	0	3,500	14,000	24,500	35,000	45,500	122,500
Total US/Japan revenues	0	$7,758	$31,033	$62,067	$100,858	$139,650	$178,442	$220,733	$270,025	$319,317	$368,608	$417,900	$2,116,392

*The Japan joint venture was part of Ranalli's original plan to have a partner in Japan to sell traffic from Japan to the United States. As of September 1992, a joint venture partner had not been found.

Exhibit A *(continued)*

Detailed Expenses	*1992* *Jan.*	*Feb.*	*Mar.*	*Apr.*	*May*	*June*	*Jul.*	*Aug.*	*Sept.*	*Oct.*	*Nov.*	*Dec.*	*Total Year*
Technical development:													
Salaries	$30,000	$30,000	$30,000	$30,000	$30,000	$30,000	$30,000	$30,000	$30,000	$30,000	$30,000	$30,000	$360,000
Other expenses	2,000	2,000	2,000	2,000	2,000	2,000	2,000	2,000	2,000	2,000	2,000	2,000	24,000
Subtotal:	$32,000	$32,000	$32,000	$32,000	$32,000	$32,000	$32,000	$32,000	$32,000	$32,000	$32,000	$32,000	$384,000
Sales expenses:													
Douglas Ranalli	5,000	5,000	5,000	5,000	5,000	5,000	5,000	5,000	5,000	5,000	5,000	5,000	60,000
Number of sales reps	5	5	5	5	5	5	5	5	5	5	5	5	
Base salaries	15,000	15,000	15,000	15,000	15,000	15,000	15,000	15,000	15,000	15,000	15,000	15,000	180,000
Sales commissions	0	388	1,552	3,103	5,043	6,983	8,922	10,862	12,801	14,741	16,680	18,620	99,695
Sales expenses	6,000	10,500	10,500	10,500	10,500	10,500	10,500	10,500	10,500	10,500	10,500	10,500	121,500
Office supplies	5,000	1,000	1,000	1,000	1,000	1,000	1,000	1,000	1,000	1,000	1,000	1,000	16,000
Headhunter fees	8,000	0	0	0	0	0	0	0	0	0	0	0	8,000
Subtotal:	$39,005	$31,893	$33,057	$34,608	$36,548	$38,488	$40,427	$42,367	$44,306	$46,246	$48,185	$50,125	$485,255
Japanese joint venture:													
Country manager	0	0	0	0	0	0	0	0	0	0	0	0	0
Chuo Coopers & Lybrand	2,500	2,500	2,500	2,500	2,500	2,500	2,500	2,500	2,500	2,500	2,500	2,500	30,000
Subtotal:	$2,500	$2,500	$2,500	$2,500	$2,500	$2,500	$2,500	$2,500	$2,500	$2,500	$2,500	$2,500	$30,000
Network hardware:													
Network hardware lease	12,800	14,240	14,240	15,680	15,680	17,120	17,120	18,560	18,560	20,000	21,440	21,440	206,880
Japanese J/V hardware	0	0	0	0	0	0	0	1,440	1,440	1,440	2,880	2,880	10,080
Auto-dialer lease	2,000	2,000	2,000	2,080	2,773	3,467	4,160	4,853	5,547	6,240	6,933	7,627	49,680
Tokyo engineer	1,000	1,000	1,000	1,000	1,000	1,000	1,000	1,000	1,000	1,000	1,000	1,000	12,000
Equipment housing	0	6,500	6,500	6,500	10,000	10,000	10,000	10,000	10,000	10,000	10,000	10,000	99,500
Installation	25,000	0	0	0	10,000	0	45,000	0	0	25,000	0	0	105,000
Up-front deposits	0	1,440	0	1,520	693	2,133	693	3,573	693	2,133	3,573	693	17,147
Extended service contract	1,156	1,269	1,269	1,388	1,442	1,608	1,663	1,942	1,996	2,163	2,442	2,496	20,831
Equipment insurance	385	423	423	463	481	536	554	647	665	721	814	832	6,944
Subtotal:	$42,342	$26,872	$25,432	$28,630	$42,069	$35,864	$80,190	$42,016	$39,901	$68,697	$49,082	$46,968	$528,062
Network asset value	$462,500	$507,500	$507,500	$555,000	$576,667	$643,333	$665,000	$776,667	$798,333	$865,000	$976,667	$998,333	

(Continued)

Exhibit A ***(concluded)***

	1992 Jan.	Feb.	Mar.	Apr.	May	June	Jul.	Aug.	Sept.	Oct.	Nov.	Dec.	Total Year
Communications:													
Average variable cost (per minute)	$0.18	$0.18	$0.18	$0.18	$0.13	$0.13	$0.13	$0.13	$0.13	$0.13	$0.13	$0.13	
US variable costs	0	5,400	10,800	18,000	19,500	26,000	32,500	39,000	45,500	52,000	58,500	65,000	372,200
Japanese JV costs	0	0	0	0	0	0	0	1,350	5,400	9,450	13,500	17,550	47,250
Number of kbps channels	0	1	2	4	5	7	8	10	11	13	15	16	
Fractional T1	0	9,700	15,400	23,800	31,150	37,750	49,800	49,800	58,800	58,800	58,000	58,000	431,550
Digital service	1,500	1,200	2,400	4,800	4,800	4,800	4,800	4,800	4,800	4,800	4,800	4,800	48,300
Local loop service	2,100	2,100	2,100	3,100	3,100	3,100	4,100	5,300	5,300	6,300	7,500	8,500	52,600
Installation	1,000	500	500	500	500	500	500	500	500	500	500	500	6,500
Subtotal	$4,600	$18,900	$31,200	$50,200	$59,050	$72,650	$79,650	$100,750	$111,300	$131,850	$143,600	$155,150	$958,400
Account management:													
VP account management	3,500	3,500	3,500	3,500	3,500	3,500	3,500	3,500	3,500	3,500	3,500	3,500	42,000
Full-time AMs	2,000	4,000	4,000	4,000	4,000	4,000	4,000	4,000	4,000	4,000	4,400	4,400	46,800
Peak period reps	0	0	0	0	0	0	1,000	1,000	2,000	2,000	3,000	3,000	12,000
Evening AM	0	2,000	2,000	2,000	2,000	2,000	2,000	2,000	2,000	2,000	2,000	2,000	22,000
Other expenses	2,000	4,000	4,000	4,000	4,000	4,000	5,000	5,000	6,000	6,000	7,000	7,000	58,000
Number of AMs	2	4	4	4	4	4	5	5	6	6	7	7	
Subtotal	4,000	10,000	10,000	10,000	10,000	10,000	12,000	12,000	14,000	14,000	16,400	16,400	138,800
Administrative:													
Headquarters office	2,500	5,500	5,500	5,500	5,500	5,500	5,500	5,500	5,500	5,500	5,500	5,500	63,000
Furniture lease	1,000	1,000	1,000	1,000	1,000	1,000	1,000	1,000	1,000	1,000	1,000	1,000	12,000
Legal and accounting	2,000	2,000	2,000	2,000	2,000	2,000	2,000	2,000	2,000	2,000	2,000	2,000	24,000
Financial consulting	2,000	2,000	2,000	2,000	2,000	2,000	2,000	2,000	2,000	2,000	2,000	2,000	24,000
Office supplies, etc.	5,000	1,000	1,000	1,000	1,000	1,000	1,000	1,000	1,000	1,000	1,000	1,000	16,000
Other expenses	1,500	1,500	1,500	1,500	1,500	1,500	1,500	1,500	1,500	1,500	1,500	1,500	18,000
Subtotal	14,000	13,000	13,000	13,000	13,000	13,000	13,000	13,000	13,000	13,000	13,000	13,000	157,000
Billing and accounting:													
Payroll expenses	5,720	6,300	6,300	6,300	6,300	6,300	6,600	6,600	6,600	6,600	6,640	6,640	76,900
Bookkeeper	1,700	3,500	3,500	3,500	3,500	3,500	3,500	3,500	3,500	3,500	3,500	3,500	40,200
Credit/collections	0	0	0	0	0	0	3,000	3,000	3,000	3,000	3,000	3,000	18,000
Bills/mailings	0	25	100	200	325	450	575	700	825	950	1,075	1,200	6,425
Omissions Insurance	500	500	500	500	500	500	500	500	500	500	500	500	6,000
Subtotal	7,920	10,325	10,400	10,500	10,625	10,750	14,175	14,300	14,425	14,550	14,715	14,840	147,525
Total expenses	$146,367	$145,490	$157,588	$181,438	$205,792	$214,752	$273,942	$258,932	$271,432	$322,843	$319,483	$330,983	$2,829,041
Net cash result	$(147,367)	$(137,731)	$(126,555)	$(119,372)	$(104,933)	$(75,102)	$(95,500)	$(41,699)	$(15,407)	($28,026)	$14,126	$41,417	$(835,150)
Total cash loss	$(890,693)												

Exhibit B
From the Original Business Plan (December 1991) Pro Forma Statement of Income (Year 1)

	1992 Jan.	Feb.	Mar.	Apr.	May	June	Jul.	Aug.	Sept.	Oct.	Nov.	Dec.	Total Year
Net sales	$ 0	$ 7,758	$ 31,033	$ 62,067	$ 100,858	$ 139,650	$ 178,442	$ 220,733	$ 270,025	$ 319,317	$ 368,608	$417,900	$2,116,392
Operating expenses:													
Communications	4,600	18,900	31,200	50,200	59,050	72,150	79,650	100,750	111,300	131,850	143,600	155,150	958,400
Administrative	14,000	13,000	13,000	13,000	13,000	13,000	13,000	13,000	13,000	13,000	13,000	13,000	157,000
Billing and accounting	7,920	10,325	10,400	10,500	10,625	10,750	14,175	14,300	14,425	14,550	14,715	14,840	147,525
Sales expenses	39,005	31,893	33,057	34,608	36,548	38,488	40,427	42,367	44,306	46,246	48,185	50,125	485,255
Japanese J/V	2,500	2,500	2,500	2,500	2,500	2,500	2,500	2,500	2,500	2,500	2,500	2,500	30,000
Customer service	4,000	10,000	10,000	10,000	10,000	10,000	12,000	12,000	14,000	14,000	16,400	16,400	138,800
Network expenses	42,342	26,872	25,432	28,630	42,069	35,864	80,190	42,016	39,901	68,697	49,082	46,968	528,062
Technical expenses	32,000	32,000	32,000	32,000	32,000	32,000	32,000	32,000	32,000	32,000	32,000	32,000	384,000
Operating expenses	$ 146,367	$ 145,490	$ 157,588	$ 181,438	$ 205,792	$ 214,752	$ 273,942	$ 258,932	$ 271,432	$ 322,843	$ 319,483	$330,983	$2,829,041
EBIT	(146,367)	(137,731)	(126,555)	(119,372)	(104,933)	(75,102)	(95,500)	(38,199)	(1,407)	(3,526)	49,126	86,917	(712,650)
Other income:													
Cash interest	0	0	0	0	0	0	0	0	0	0	0	0	0
Revolver interest	0	0	0	0	0	0	0	0	(284)	(872)	(1,395)	(1,520)	(4,071)
Extraordinary items	0	0	0	0	0	0	0	0	0	0	0	0	0
Other income	0	0	0	0	0	0	0	0	0	0	0	0	0
Other income	$ 0	$ 0	$ 0	$ 0	$ 0	$ 0	$ 0	$ 0	$ (284)	$ (872)	$ (1,395)	$ (1,520)	$ (4,071)
EBT	(146,367)	(137,731)	(126,555)	(119,372)	(104,933)	(75,102)	(95,500)	(38,199)	(1,691)	(4,398)	47,730	85,397	(716,721)
Income taxes	0	0	0	0	0	0	0	0	(284)	(872)	(1,395)	(1,520)	(4,071)
Net income	$(146,367)	$(137,731)	$(126,555)	$(119,372)	$(104,933)	$ (75,102)	$ (95,500)	$ (38,199)	$ (1,691)	$ (4,398)	$ 47,730	$ 85,397	$ (716,721)
Cumulative NOL's	$(146,367)	$(284,098)	$(410,653)	$(530,025)	$(634,958)	$(710,060)	$(805,560)	$(845,450)	$(849,849)	$(802,118)	$(716,721)		

Exhibit C

From the Original Business Plan (December 1991) Pro Forma Balance Sheet (Year 1)

	1992 Jan.	Feb.	Mar.	Apr.	May	June	Jul.	Aug.	Sept.	Oct.	Nov.	Dec.
Assets												
Current assets:												
Cash	$158,170	$23,065	$624,207	$477,663	$324,068	$204,496	$59,003	$10,000	$10,000	$10,000	$10,000	$10,000
Invested cash	0	0	0	0	0	0	0	0	0	0	0	0
Accounts receivable	0	11,478	45,912	91,825	149,215	206,605	263,996	326,564	399,489	472,414	545,338	618,263
Total current assets	$158,170	$34,543	$670,120	$569,488	$473,283	$411,102	$322,998	$336,564	$409,489	$482,414	$555,338	$628,263
Long-term assets:												
Capital leases costs	0	0	0	0	0	0	0	0	0	0	0	0
Net property and equipment	0	0	0	0	0	0	0	0	0	0	0	0
Intangibles	0	0	0	0	0	0	0	0	0	0	0	0
Organizational expense	450,000	450,000	450,000	450,000	450,000	450,000	450,000	450,000	450,000	450,000	450,000	450,000
Total assets	$608,170	$484,543	$1,120,120	$1,019,488	$923,283	$861,102	$772,998	$786,564	$859,489	$932,414	$1,005,338	$1,078,263
Liabilities												
Accounts payable	4,537	18,641	30,773	49,512	58,241	71,162	78,558	99,370	109,775	130,044	141,633	153,025
Revolving facility	0	0	0	0	0	0	0	30,954	95,164	152,218	165,824	141,959
Other current/CML TD	0	0	0	0	0	0	0	0	0	0	0	0
Total current liabilities	$4,537	$18,641	$30,773	$49,512	$58,241	$71,162	$78,558	$130,324	$204,939	$282,262	$307,457	$294,984
Total liabilities	4,537	18,641	30,773	49,512	58,241	71,162	78,558	130,324	204,939	282,262	307,457	294,984
Shareholders' Equity												
Founders' capital	150,000	150,000	150,000	150,000	150,000	150,000	150,000	150,000	150,000	150,000	150,000	150,000
Add'l paid-in capital	600,000	600,000	1,350,000	1,350,000	1,350,000	1,350,000	1,350,000	1,350,000	1,350,000	1,350,000	1,350,000	1,350,000
Retained earnings	(146,367)	(284,098)	(410,653)	(530,025)	(634,958)	(710,060)	(805,560)	(843,759)	(845,450)	(849,849)	(802,118)	(716,721)
Total shareholders' equity	$603,633	$465,902	$1,089,347	$969,975	$865,042	$789,940	$694,440	$656,241	$654,550	$650,151	$697,882	$783,279
Total liabilities and shareholders' equity	$608,170	$484,543	$1,120,120	$1,019,488	$923,283	$861,102	$772,998	$786,564	$859,489	$932,414	$1,005,338	$1,078,263

Exhibit C ***(concluded)***

Assumptions and Ratios

	1992 Feb.	Mar.	Apr.	May	June	Jul.	Aug.	Sept.	Oct.	Nov.	Dec.
Income statement:											
Net monthly sales growth	N/A	300%	100%	63%	38%	28%	24%	22%	18%	15%	13%
Current gross margin	−144%	−1	19	41	48	55	54	59	59	61	63
Current EBITDA margin	−1775	−408	−192	−104	−54	−54	−17	−1	−1	13	21
Communication as percent of sales	244	101	81	59	52	45	46	41	41	39	37
Administration as percent of sales	168	42	21	13	9	7	6	5	4	4	4
Sales expense as percent of sales	411	107	56	36	28	23	19	16	14	13	12
Account management as percent of sales	129	32	16	10	7	7	5	5	4	4	4
Equipment lease as percent of sales	346	82	46	42	26	45	19	15	22	13	11
Technical costs as percent of sales	412	103	52	32	23	18	14	12	10	9	8
Revolver as percent of receivable base	0	0	0	0	0	0	9	24	32	30	23

Exhibit D
From the Original Business Plan (December 1991) Pro Forma Statement of Cash Flow (Year 1)

	1992 Jan.	*Feb.*	*Mar.*	*Apr.*	*May*	*June*	*Jul.*	*Aug.*	*Sept.*	*Oct.*	*Nov.*	*Dec.*	*Total Year*
Net income	$(146,367)	(137,731)	(126,555)	(119,372)	(104,933)	(75,102)	(95,500)	(38,199)	(1,691)	(4,398)	47,730	85,397	(716,721)
Gross cash flow	(146,367)	(137,731)	(126,555)	(119,372)	(104,933)	(75,102)	(95,500)	(38,199)	(1,691)	(4,398)	47,730	85,397	(716,721)
Changes in working capital:													
Accounts receivable	0	(11,478)	(34,434)	(45,912)	(57,390)	(57,390)	(57,390)	(62,568)	(72,925)	(72,925)	(72,925)	(72,925)	(618,263)
Accounts payable	4,537	14,104	12,132	18,740	8,729	12,921	7,397	20,811	10,405	20,268	11,589	11,392	153,025
Other current liabilities	0	0	0	0	0	0	0	0	0	0	0	0	0
Cash flow from operations	$(141,830)	$(135,105)	$(148,858)	$(146,544)	$(153,595)	$(119,572)	$(145,494)	$(79,956)	$(64,210)	$(57,054)	$(13,605)	$23,864	$(1,181,959)
Operating cash flow	(141,830)	(135,105)	(148,858)	(146,544)	(153,595)	(119,572)	(145,494)	(79,956)	(64,210)	(57,054)	(13,605)	23,864	(1,181,959)
Changes in non-operating items:													
Change in capital	300,000	0	750,000	0	0	0	0	0	0	0	0	0	
Cash available	$158,170	$(135,105)	$601,142	$(146,544)	$(153,595)	$(119,572)	$(145,494)	$(79,956)	$(64,210)	$(57,054)	$(13,605)	$23,864	
Cumulative cash	158,170	23,065	624,207	477,663	324,068	204,496	59,003	(20,954)	(85,164)	(142,218)	(155,824)	(131,959)	
Maintenance cash level	10,000	10,000	10,000	10,000	10,000	10,000	10,000	10,000	10,000	10,000	10,000	10,000	

with the right equipment, send seven times the amount of data that a normal fax machine could send in a given time period. A quick phone call to the author of the article verified his assumption about the fundamental viability of such a business.

Ranalli spent the next several days calling the valuable contacts he had made in the industry while researching ideas over the past year and a half. His initial questions were very simple. Will the idea work? Is anyone else already doing it? Are there any regulations against it?

Over the course of the next month, Ranalli was able to work out enough of the basic details, including the decision to focus on high-cost international traffic, to feel comfortable turning down the consulting offer and pursuing FAX International. He recalled:

Before I felt comfortable writing a business plan or asking anyone to invest, I needed to know a lot more and I needed a director of engineering. I searched for three months before I found someone. I soon discovered I was mistaken and had to fire him after only a month. That was a very difficult decision. It was not until the next February [1991] that I found Tom Sosnowski.

At age 52, Tom Sosnowski, PhD, the new vice president and director of engineering, had spent most of his adult life in either engineering project management or product development, including 12 years at AT&T Bell Labs and 4 years at GTE. He had been an engineering management consultant for the last six years prior to joining Ranalli at FI. (*Exhibit E* contains Ranalli's and Sosnowski's resumes.) Sosnowski was a true expert in this field. Ranalli commented later:

It was a very difficult decision for me. Although I don't feel comfortable discussing the details, let's just say I had to give up more of the company than I had originally intended in order to get him. But in the end, I knew that he could get the job done. I knew that I needed his expertise. I knew that he shared the vision. And I knew that he was a good man and that we would get along well.

It just doesn't pay to be greedy. Sure, I could have fought tooth and nail and held on to a few extra percent of the company, but what's a few extra percent of nothing if the business doesn't fly because I was too focused on the money and not on getting the job done?

In hindsight, one of the best decisions I made during the early stages of the business was to tie the entire engineering group into the company with three-year stock vesting agreements.

Reflecting on this period, Sosnowski commented:

Doug initially wanted me to consult for the company but he couldn't afford my rates so I told him that I'd let him take me to lunch when he needed to bounce his ideas off someone. Eventually, I did do some consulting for him. And after his first head of engineering did not work out, he asked me to come on full-time.

Virtually every company I consulted for had asked me to join them full-time. Doug's offer was the first I even considered. The reason I decided to accept goes beyond the obvious opportunity I saw in the Fax International concept. It had to do with how I felt about Doug and his philosophy of treating people. I believe that there is an enormous gulf in our society between what is known about how people should be treated and the way most managers actually treat people in practice. Doug and I see eye to eye on the importance of treating and rewarding people fairly. One doesn't find that kind of match very often.

When I first met Doug, I don't think he fully appreciated the importance or the worth of the engineering side of this business. This value was more clear to me, not just from my years in the industry but from the fees I charged in my private consulting practice. We had many discussions about it and I think we are much more in agreement today.

In some industries, once a product is designed and built, the engineers can just go home. That's not the case here. The engineering side of this business is an ongoing thing in a big way. The operation

Exhibit E
Resumes of Douglas J. Ranalli and Thomas J. Sosnowski

DOUGLAS J. RANALLI

Education

1988–1990 **HARVARD GRADUATE SCHOOL OF BUSINESS ADMINISTRATION** — **BOSTON, MA**
Candidate for Master in Business Administration degree, June 1990. General management curriculum.

1979–1983 **CORNELL UNIVERSITY** — **ITHACA, NY**
Awarded Bachelor of Science in Operations Research and Industrial Engineering, *with distinction*, in May 1983. Member Tau Beta Pi National Engineering Honor Society. Elected President of Cornell University Senior Class, and President of the 1983 Alumni Class. Member Phi Sigma Kappa social fraternity. Elected social chairman 1981.

Experience

1987–1988 **TIME INC.** — **NEW YORK, NY**
Publisher, *Student Life* magazine

Student Life is a national publication for college students delivered twice a year, by direct mail, to 1,200,000 students living on 600 campuses nationwide. Founded *Student Life* in 1981, published it independently for six years, and sold it to Time, Inc. in 1987. (Details below)

1983–1987 ***Student Life* Magazine** — **UPPER SADDLE RIVER, NJ**
Founder and President

Launched *Student Life* in 1981 as an undergraduate at Cornell. Raised $200,000 in equity/loan financing after graduating in 1983 to fund national development. Expanded circulation to over 1,000,000 per issue within four years. Negotiated the sale of *Student Life* to Time, Inc., in January 1987 for a multiple of 17 times earnings. Continued as publisher at the request of Time, Inc.

Experiences and accomplishments include:

- Personally sold $250,000 of advertising in the first national issue published Sept. 1984. Clients included: AT&T, Ford, Revlon, General Foods, Anheuser-Busch, US Army, Marines, etc. Increased sales to a maximum of $750,000/issue by September 1987.
- Hired and trained full-time staff including: Editor, Circulation Director, Sales Director, and salespeople. All art, photography, and production positions managed on a contract basis.
- Negotiated printing and production contracts worth $600,000 per year.
- Managed media/public relations. Quoted or featured in: *The Wall Street Journal, Venture, Entrepreneur, Advertising Age, Ad Week, Marketing and Media Decisions, Manhattan Inc.*

Summers

1982 **AT&T COMMUNICATIONS** — **NEW YORK, NY**
Summer management development program.

1981 **COMEX Futures Exchange** — **NEW YORK, NY**
Runner on commodities exchange for Continental Grain.

Personal Married. Favorite activities include golf, skiing, and tennis.

November, 1988

of the network, as well as the design, assembly, and expansion of it, is and will continue to be very engineering intensive.

Commenting on the period following Sosnowski's hiring, Ranalli explained:

Even with Tom's expertise it still took us five to six more months to find the other five members of the engineering team, transfer the vision, find a suitable headquarters, and get moving. Only then was I comfortable enough about what we knew and where we were headed to write a business plan and ask people to give me their money. [*Exhibit F* contains excerpts from the business plan "Executive Summary."]

It was funny—when I first thought of the idea, I actually believed I could get a working prototype up between August and the end of 1990. As it turned out, it was almost a full year later [the following June] before I felt knowledgeable enough about what I was doing even to sit down and write the plan. Planning and budgeting are very difficult in an entrepreneurial venture. And it changes daily in the early stages. No matter how closely you try to calculate a timetable, it always takes longer than you think. There are just too many unknowns.

Exhibit E *(continued)*

THOMAS P. SOSNOWSKI

SUMMARY

Senior manager with experience spanning basic research through product development. Thorough understanding of the role of research in the product development process. Expertise in strategic and tactical planning, project analysis, allocation of resources, program proposal review and evaluation, manufacturability, negotiation with subcontractors and vendors, and policy development. Substantial knowledge of a broad range of technologies, including telephone switching and terminal systems, gas lasers, holography, optical waveguides, and microcomputer-based systems.

SELECTED PROFESSIONAL HIGHLIGHTS

As a consultant, aided numerous companies in restructuring their engineering organizations. Clients include Fortune 100 companies but the majority are small entrepreneurial organizations. As part of the restructuring, often assume control of the engineering organization and assist in the selection of new engineering management. Products involved range from sophisticated microcomputer-controlled optical systems to high-volume automotive components in which manufacturability and reliability are paramount concerns.

Organized the commercial engineering section of a small high-tech company; oversaw expansion to over 50 professional and support staff with a $3.8 million annualized budget in less than two years. Structured interfaces with marketing to assure proper product configuration and with manufacturing to provide smooth transition into production. Created policies and procedures which established the orderly development of new products. Initiated and directed redesign of product lines; results included reduction in product costs while increasing functionality, quality, and aesthetic design.

Created, staffed, and managed a new department to research new products and services for telecommunications. Initiated construction of an image processing facility to explore new services. Demonstrated the utility of several new communication systems including an innovative visual telephone system for use by the deaf. Research efforts in local area networks contributed to the specialized voice and data networks required to meet future business objectives.

Conceived and implemented many new devices and system concepts, including: An interactive visual communication system which used standard voice-grade telephone lines for interconnection, one of the first systems to contain a microcomputer for system control and signal processing; a mechanism to implement voice conferencing using digital technology, which served as the basis for experimental PABX systems and was later incorporated into toll telephone switches; several new techniques to control light in optical waveguides; mechanisms to improve He-Cd gas lasers, allowing for the first time continuous wave operation in the ultraviolet; new holographic devices including a means to improve single tube color television cameras.

(Continued)

Financing

As with his approach toward finding a venture, Ranalli's approach toward raising money was unconventional. His initial position was reasonably secure due to the fact that he had saved most of the money from the sale of his first business. However, he was determined to use no more than half of this nest egg. His attitude throughout the financing was that if he could not convince people to invest in the company, then either the idea was simply not viable or he had not yet earned the right to use their money.

Initially Ranalli tried to follow the advice he had heard at HBS, "Raise as much as you can up front." Yet, as hard as he tried, Ranalli found this to be impossible. Several venture capital companies were interested but each insisted on taking the majority of the company. Ranalli was unwilling to do this as long as he thought he could raise the money through private investors. The problem he encountered was that no wealthy individuals were willing to invest in the seed round. They all seemed interested but were not willing to take the risk at the embryonic stage. They wanted to see more than just the idea. It soon became clear to Ranalli that he was not going to be able to raise the money he needed up front. If he wanted to keep the company, he would have to use his own and the management team's money as seed capital. They would have to take all the up-front risk alone. No one else was willing to share it yet. Ranalli commented:

I decided that the only way I was going to succeed at raising the money on my own was to structure the first round (after the seed round) financing in stages. I figured if I could lay out the start-up process in definite stages where each would be complete once a hurdle was met (such as working prototype completed or certain government approval received), then I could convince investors to invest more in each subsequent stage if I had proven to them that I was able to achieve the preestablished goal.

Exhibit E *(concluded)*

T. P. Sosnowski (Cont.)

EXPERIENCE

Management and Engineering Consultant (Jan 1986–Present)
Self-Employed

Director of Product Development (Jan 1984–Jan 1986)
Elkonix Corporation, Bedford, MA

Department Manager (Jun 1980–Jan 1984)
Advanced Communication Techniques
GTE Laboratories, Waltham, MA

Team Leader, Member of Technical Staff (Feb 1968–Jun 1980)
Computer Systems Research
Bell Telephone Laboratories, Holmdel, NJ

SKILLS

Management – Highly creative yet pragmatic problem solver and decision maker. Known for logical, practical, and cost-effective project planning and implementation strategies. Exceptional ability to evaluate projects. Good negotiator. Excellent verbal and written communication skills. A thorough understanding of the innovation process, including the transition of ideas from research into product development; a highly developed sense for recognizing the time to terminate development and finalize engineering design. Participative management style. Regarded as a team player with an ability to attract high-quality staff.

Technical – Excellent understanding of a wide range of technical disciplines. Broad experience with devices and systems, hardware and software. A hands-on individual with an exceptional ability to "make things work." Highly creative with superior conceptual skills. Author of 22 publications in reviewed technical journals; holds nine patents with one pending.

EDUCATION

PhD Engineering, Case-Western Reserve University 1967
MS Engineering, Case-Western Reserve University 1965
BS Engineering Science, Penn. State University 1962

PROFESSIONAL ASSOCIATIONS

Senior Member, IEEE
Member, IEEE Management Society
Former Officer, IEEE Multimedia Services and Terminals Committee
Listed in *American Men and Women in Science*
Adjunct Professor of Management Science, Wentworth Institute of Technology

I told them point-blank that if I cannot reach this goal, then I have not earned the right to your money. Thus, it was only as the project became less risky that I was able to gradually find investors to share in the risk. I know I was taking a chance by raising money in this manner, but the way I see it is that I had no choice. I did not want to scrap the idea and I did not want to give the company away. So I took it as I could get it.

Ranalli found raising the money easier and easier as he got closer to actually turning on the network. (*Exhibit G* summarizes the financing rounds.) Once he was able to actually set a date to close the first round, then most of the investors that had been undecided made up their minds to invest, due mostly to the fact that the price per share was scheduled to increase the day the network became operational. In February 1992, Ranalli commented:

People are as afraid of missing an opportunity to make money as they are of losing money. Once you have delivered on your promises and once you've convinced them that the odds are reasonably good that your concept really will work, then raising money is less of a problem.

Ranalli conceded that the resulting business had become a much larger and more expensive enterprise than he had originally envisioned. By the time he had finished hiring the initial sales team (February 1992), FI was rapidly running out of money. (See *Table 1.*)

Exhibit F
The Business Plan (Excerpts from the "Executive Summary," dated December 1991)

FAX International, Inc., was founded in June 1990 by Mr. Douglas J. Ranalli and Dr. Thomas P. Sosnowski. The goal of the company is to build an international communications network that is six times more efficient at transmitting fax documents than the switched voice networks of AT&T, MCI, and US Sprint.

FAX International's tremendous efficiency results from designing a network with special technology for transmitting fax documents only. A standard international telephone circuit is capable of transmitting data at 64 kbps (kilo bits per second). A standard fax machine however is only capable of transmitting data at 9.6 kbps. Since AT&T and the other major carriers don't know in advance whether a customer is going to place a voice or fax call when they pick up the phone, each call is allocated a full 64 kbps channel. The result is that each fax call utilizes less than 1/6th of the capability of the circuit. FAX International knows in advance that every call carried by the network is a fax call and hence the network has been designed to carry six fax calls on the same circuit that AT&T, MCI, and Sprint currently use to transmit a single fax call.

FAX International's year-long design and development effort has been extremely successful. As a result, the network went into full-scale testing in November 1991, and is scheduled for installation in January 1992. The opportunity now exists to offer business customers a vastly superior facsimile transmission service between the United States and major international city centers like Tokyo, London, Paris, and so on. Superior because it is just as easy to use as direct dial service from AT&T, MCI, or Sprint at half the price. For example, business customers who are currently paying an average of $1.50/minute for service to Tokyo will pay only $.75 with FAX International, Inc. The FAX International network is so efficient that it will provide business customers with 50 percent savings over current rates while earning 50 percent gross margins on the service once a minimum efficient volume level has been achieved.

Minimum efficient volume is defined by FAX International as the traffic volume necessary to utilize a full T1 circuit between the United States and any single international city center. (A T1 circuit is equivalent to 24 standard 64 kbps voice circuits.) Seven million minutes of traffic per year are required to efficiently utilize a T1 circuit. To reach this minimum volume on FAX International's first route between the United States and Tokyo, the company will have to win 3 percent of market for fax calls in one direction from the United States to Tokyo.

The international telecommunications market has historically been closed to competition due to the presence of monopoly carriers in almost every country. But, the regulatory situation is changing rapidly as countries all over the world look for ways to make their telecommunications industries more competitive. In June 1990, the European Commission directed members of the European Economic Community to begin deregulating all enhanced telecommunications services. Similarly, the United States and Japan negotiated an agreement known as the International Value Added Network Services (IVANS) agreement which guarantees US value-added network service providers like FAX International fair and equal access to the Japanese market. The actions of the European Commission coupled with the signing of the IVANS agreement between the United States and Japan have created an opportunity for a variety of international enhanced communication services between the United States, Europe, and Japan. The opportunities have yet to be exploited due to the time required for companies to understand the recent regulatory changes and the time required to develop appropriate technologies. An article in the June 15 issue of *EMMS* (Electronic Mail and Micro Systems) summed up the opportunity as follows:

What is the magic formula for success in enhanced fax service? Whoever figures it out may turn out to be the William McGowan (MCI) success story of the 1990s. . . . Conceivably, a fax from the United States could travel via private lines to Tokyo or London and be delivered with a local call—completely eliminating the need for the international switched network.

FAX International, Inc., is prepared with the technology, the management team, and the regulatory approvals necessary to capitalize on this exciting international opportunity.

Exhibit G
Capitalization

Round	*Percentage of Total Ownership Fully Diluted*	*Number of Shares CS*	*Number of Shares Convertible Pref. @ $1/share*	*Debt @ 12% ($)*	*Total $ Raised*
Seed financing (Ranalli, Sosnowski, management team)	71.3%	3,250,000		$200,000	$ 335,000
Reserved shares for future directors/ employees	3.3	150,000			
First round—closed February 1992 (private investors)	14.4		655,500		655,500
Second round—proposed to close May 1992 (private investors)	11		500,000	500,000	1,000,000
Total	100%	3,400,000	1,155,500	$700,000	2,010,500

Table 1
Monthly Burn-Rate (000)

Salaries	$ 60
Asset expenses	16
Office operating expenses	15
Expenses in Japan	20
Fixed communication expenses	25
Miscellaneous start-up expenses (lawyers, network installation, equipment, travel)	39
Total	$175

The FI Network

A user-friendly, bug-free system was a critical factor in determining the success or failure of the venture. User-friendly in this case meant invisible. The less the customer had to change his or her current fax habits, the more likely they would be to use the service. Thus, the concept of the auto-dialer (called FAXLINK) was born. The Sosnowski team designed a device which could be easily plugged into a fax machine, exactly as an answering machine plugs into a telephone line, which would scan every outgoing call. The FAXLINK would reroute only those calls destined for Tokyo over the FI network. (See *Exhibit H* for a FAXLINK diagram.) The call would first go over regular phone lines to the FI node in San Francisco. There it would wait (five-minute maximum) to be sent on the international leg of its journey simultaneously with other faxes bound for Tokyo. Once received in Tokyo, the faxes would be sent to their local destinations over regular telephone lines again. (See *Exhibit I* for a description of the FI network.)

Everyone involved understood the importance of the network functioning properly. If the system was not fully debugged by start-up time, many of the customers trying the service for the trial period would probably become discouraged and decide not to join the network. It was this factor that had delayed the start-up from February 1 to late March after the appearance of last-minute minor glitches in the software. In the last week of February Sosnowski commented:

> I have never told anyone this . . . but it wasn't until just about a week ago that I really started to believe that this monster was really actually going to work the way we designed it. I knew that it would send faxes as we wanted . . . but it had to be error-free. Up until last week, when we found that burned-out card in the switch at the San Francisco node, we were running tests with failure rates of 30 percent. If we were not able to get them down below 1 or 2 percent then I knew we were out of business. For a while there I was really worried. Now we're running it with almost zero errors and I've shifted my worry to whether or not we'll be able to sell it.

Customer Service

Ranalli understood the importance of outstanding service to FI's survival. It was with this in mind that the network was designed as a total service concept and not just as a discount alternative alone. To aid them in this critical area, Ranalli made yet another move that many would consider unconventional. In February 1992, he hired his wife Shae, also an engineer from Cornell, to design and run their service department. Ranalli spoke candidly about this decision.

> Shae had worked closely with me in my first business, *Student Life* magazine. Not only did I find that she was extremely capable but we didn't experience any of the problems that many couples seem to encounter in similar situations. With respect to Fax International, I knew that I would have to search

Exhibit H
FAXLINK diagram

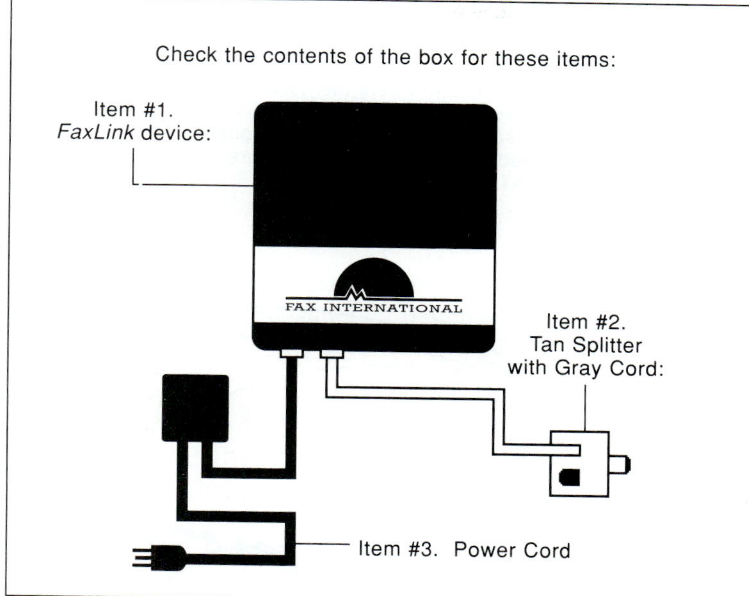

Installing the *FaxLink* Device

1. Fax International has arranged for an Account Manager to assist you in connecting the *FaxLink* device. Before you call your Account Manager, please go to your fax machine, locate the phone line and follow this line to the phone jack on the wall. This is where your *FaxLink* will be located.
2. When you can set aside ten to fifteen minutes to complete connecting *FaxLink*, please call your Account Manager.
3. Prior to contacting your Account Manager, please do not unplug anything from your fax machine.

Note: Hold on to the Federal Express box in case *FaxLink* needs to be returned.

Drawing of Installed *FaxLink*

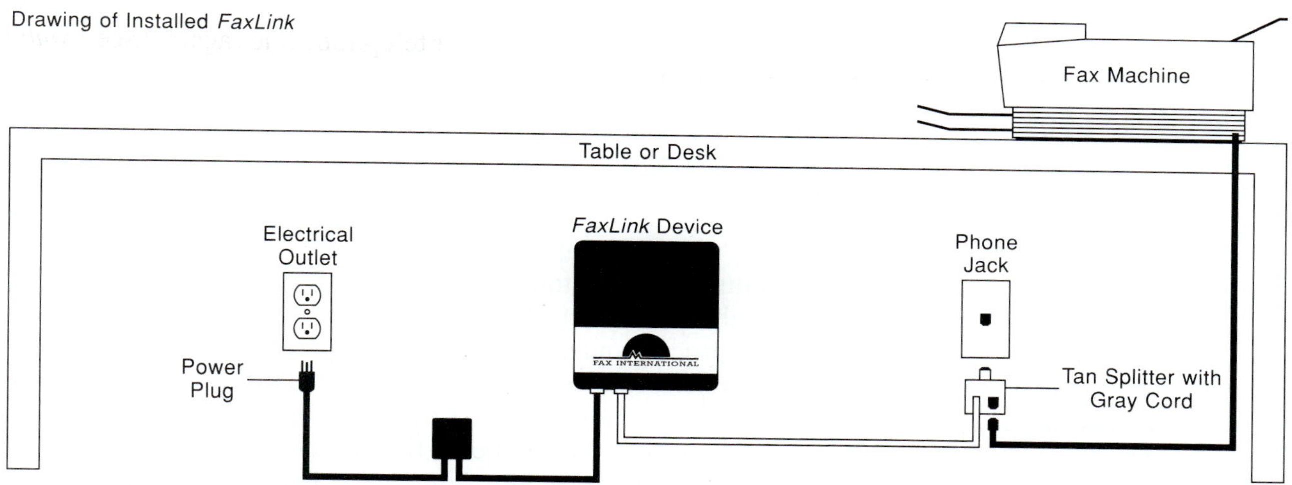

months in order to find anyone as qualified. Even then it would take months more still before they understood the business or the vision the way she already did.

I found that having her in the business gave us another added advantage—better communication with the other employees. No matter how open I try to be with everyone here, there would always be things that the employees would be reluctant to tell the boss. Shae was very close with everyone. And they all knew that if something was bothering them they could share it with her and that it would get back to me right away. This was very helpful in terms of keeping the culture and the communication open and understanding.

Shae's first action in building the service department was to create the position of (24 hr) account manager (AM). She designed the role of the AM as the focal point of FI's

Exhibit I
The FAX International Network

HOW ARE THESE SAVINGS POSSIBLE?

Documents are received into the Fax International network at one of six network nodes within the United States. Once a document enters the network it is converted from the standard fax transmission speed of 9.6 kbps to 64 kbps. This six-fold increase in the transmission speed allows Fax International to use its communications link between the United States and Tokyo far more efficiently than the switched networks of AT&T, MCI, or Sprint.

"Technology is available to build networks that are far more efficient at serving high volume international communications routes. Fax International is dedicated to utilizing this new technology to dramatically lower the cost of international fax communication."

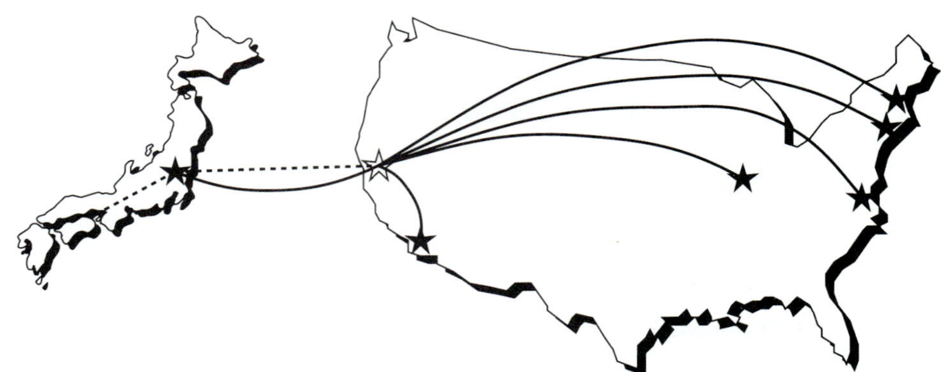

No change in long-distance carrier or the way you currently operate your fax machine is required. Once a fax machine is registered with the network, all documents destined for Tokyo will be automatically routed to the Fax International network. All other documents will continue to be handled by your company's standard long-distance carrier.

strategy to compete by offering outstanding customer service. The AMs were responsible for notifying customers of nondeliverable documents. In addition, they were in charge of walking customers through the installation process and monitoring customer accounts for any sudden decline in usage. Furthermore, in an effort to achieve the idea of total service, the FI system was designed so that a user could send a fax on the first try every time. Never again would a customer have to wait by the machine until the number at the other end was no longer busy. Every customer had a choice as to the length of time that would be allowed to pass before they were to be notified that a fax was undeliverable due to a wrong or busy number, or a broken machine at the final destination. The network would store the fax and attempt delivery continuously until it was either successful or the predetermined time had elapsed, at which time a 24 hour AM would notify the sender and request additional instructions.

Sales

Considering that FI was a new concept, Ranalli found himself faced with the question of how and where to look for customers. He decided early on that he did not want to spend large sums of money on an advertising campaign. First, he did not have a great deal of faith in the effectiveness of such an approach for this concept. Second, he did not want to alert the world and would-be competitors to the idea any sooner than he had to, especially considering the infant state of the company.

Exhibit J
Marketing Material for FAX International

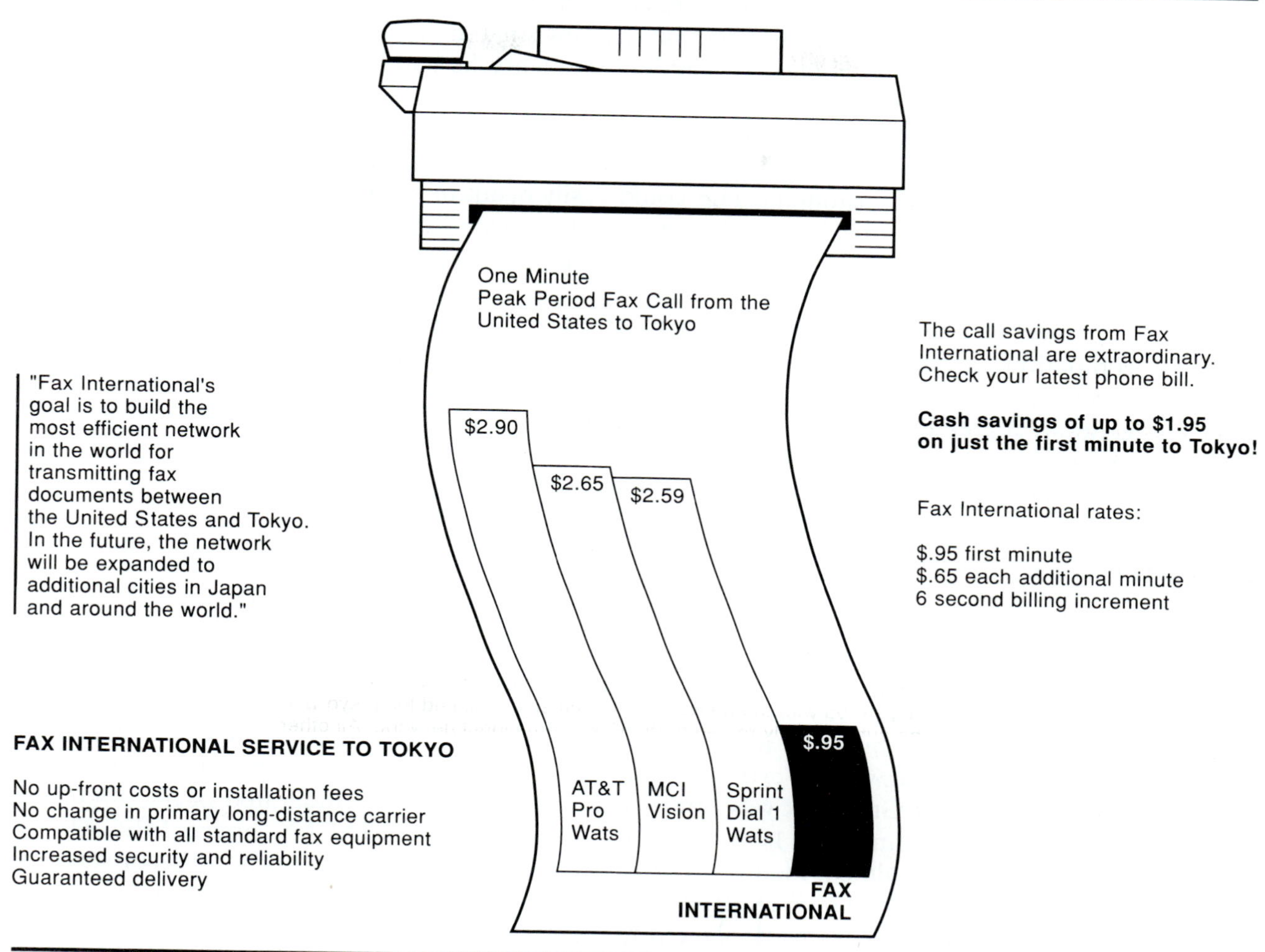

Ranalli believed that the service could be sold over the phone via telemarketers. To qualify as a lead, a company had to send a minimum of 10 pages per day. In December 1991, approximately three months before the network was scheduled to become operational, two members of the sales team conducted a day-long test to determine the usefulness of the *Directory of Japanese-Affiliated US Companies* as a lead generator. They called 100 of the companies listed in the directory to ascertain the number of pages faxed to Tokyo per day and the key decision maker with respect to long-distance service. Forty percent of the companies called faxed at least the minimum 10 pages daily to Tokyo; many were faxing over 100.

Great care was taken to teach the salespeople to position the service as a fax network only, a totally new concept with a two-week/unlimited-usage free trial. They wanted to completely dissociate themselves in the customer's mind from the long-distance carrier wars that were currently raging. It was decided early on that the service would be priced 50 percent less than the average discount package offered by any of the big three carriers. (See *Exhibit J* for the FI marketing material which compared AT&T, MCI, and Sprint to FI.)

Ranalli found himself facing a variety of strategic issues on several different fronts. As mentioned, one issue was rate of growth. A decision as to how fast he could safely grow would clearly affect strategy in a variety of areas. He had to decide whether or not to focus on just high-volume accounts for fast growth or on many small to medium-sized accounts for better entrenchment. His initial impulse told him that since he had no proprietary technology, he should grow as fast as possible in order to gain scale economies early and enhance his competitive position. On the other hand, if he grew too fast, he could run into two very real problems. The first was the risk of being noticed by, and angering, AT&T or MCI for taking too many big customers. This could easily result in predatory pricing and the loss of critical volume in a very short period of time. The second was the danger of overloading the capacity of the entire operation before new capital could be raised to finance the necessary expansion.

Overall, the primary strategic concern was creating barriers to entry and a strong competitive advantage. Ranalli intended to do this by providing outstanding service through a very user-friendly system and a very efficient service department. This in turn should generate a greater customer base that would allow him to achieve further scale economies on which to compete. What he did not know was how the competition would react to his entry in the marketplace, particularly with respect to FI's ultra-low price.

Competition

Unfortunately, Ranalli was not the first to think of this concept. There were already three direct competitors, each backed by powerful companies, offering almost exactly the same service.

Graphnet, Inc., was a Global Telecommunications company that started in the messaging services business in the late 1960s. In 1979 they received FCC authorization to compete directly with Western Union in the public record message services business. By the late 1980s Graphnet was offering text fax services and integrated packet switched services to its customers. In 1991 they began offering the MEGAFAX service. MEGAFAX was a fax network almost identical to FI in concept. In addition to each of the FI services mentioned above, MEGAFAX offered a voice prompted user menu, document broadcast capability (to send the same document to many different locations), a fax mailbox feature that allowed customers receiving faxes to store them in a confidential mailbox and retrieve them all at once at their discretion, and a special user phone number that allowed customers away from home to retrieve their faxes from any telephone in the world. Furthermore, unlike FI, MEGAFAX did not transmit exclusively to Tokyo. Their worldwide network covered all major US cities for domestic transmissions, as well as four major European cities, three major South American cities, the Philippines, Seoul, South Korea, and Osaka, Japan. The savings offered by MEGAFAX over the big three carriers ranged from 33 percent to 45 percent. (See *Exhibit K* for a comparison of direct competitor prices versus FI.)

K-NET was owned by a consortium of major companies (mostly Japanese) such as Matsushita Electric, Mitsubishi, Nippon Life Insurance, Sumitomo, and British Telecom. The K-NET service was called SUPERFax and was essentially a network identical to that of FI. The only significant service differences were a broadcast function and a mailbox feature, both similar to MEGAFAX. However, SUPERFax was different from the others in that it offered a range of prices depending on the time of day, much like the three time periods offered by the big three long-distance carriers. In addition, SUPERFax charged a monthly subscription charge of $15 per terminal and a per-page add-on price for most of their service options that came standard with the other competitors. SUPERFax savings over the big three carriers ranged from 30 percent to 57 percent.

Exhibit K
Comparison of Direct Competitor Prices

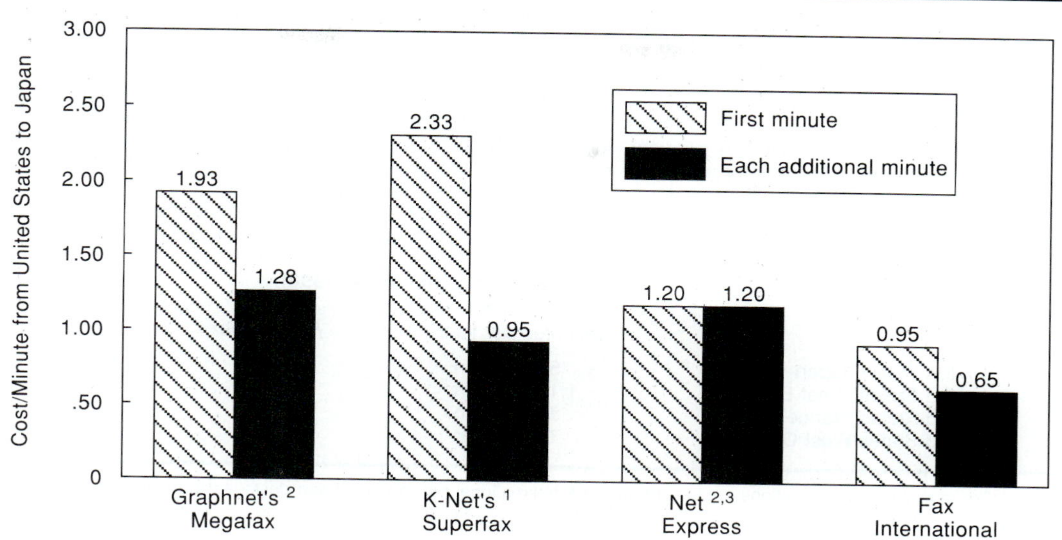

[1] Rate during standard business hours.

[2] Company charges by the page.
Per minute price calculated using industry average of 40 seconds per page.

[3] Net Express charges a $250 per month minimum usage fee.

Net Express, Inc., was founded in 1982 by two entrepreneurs in association with DHL worldwide express and Canon, Inc. DHL, as a major international courier, and Canon, as a major maker of fax machines, each had obvious reasons for being interested in this market. NetExpress was slightly different in the way it functioned. The user had to first dial a special phone number with each fax sent in order to access the network. Other than this, the services offered were roughly the same as the other FI competitors. However, the network could send documents to virtually every country in the world. The rate per page varied depending on country of destination, but estimates put savings over the Big Three ranging between 30 percent and 75 percent.

Ranalli was uncertain as to how these different and powerful competitors would react as FI tried to enter the market. (See business plan estimate of market size, *Exhibit L*.)

Current Situation

By March 1992, Ranalli had succeeded in raising close to $1 million in the seed and first private placement round of financing. His biggest concern, based on the current and projected sales figures, was not whether or not he was going to meet the plan but by how much was he going to exceed the plan. He had been conservative in his projections. Now he was concerned that the possibility of explosive growth was very real. What would this mean in terms of his financial needs? Would the $1 million second round be enough?

On March 24, 1992, Ranalli and Sosnowski made the decision to "light the fuse" and bring the network online. Customers were informed that their service had been installed, and

Exhibit L
Market Size Estimate

The Federal Communications Commission keeps track of the number of direct-dial international calls placed every year over the public switched networks (AT&T, MCI, Sprint, etc.). An analysis of the statistics shows the following trends:

1. Switched international voice traffic is growing at 15–20% per year worldwide.
2. Switched international facsimile traffic is growing at more than twice the pace of voice traffic (30–40% per year). During the past five years annual traffic growth for all types of international direct dial calls has grown an average of 20%. Japan in particular has averaged growth rates of almost 25% per year while Great Britain has averaged close to 15% per year.
3. Facsimile traffic already accounts for up to 70% of the calls on the United States/Japan route and 33% on the United States/United Kingdom route. These statistics were not found for any other international routes.
4. International traffic is highly concentrated between major US city centers and major international city centers. For example, Tokyo represents almost 70% of the traffic in and out of Japan. Similar traffic concentrations exist in London, Paris, Hong Kong, etc.

International Direct Dial Calls (1990)

	Voice and Fax Traffic (minutes per year)	*Percent Fax*	*Fax Market (minutes per year)*
United States/Japan	560 million	70%	392 million
United States/Great Britain	1,150 million	33%	380 million
United States/France	390 million	N/A	N/A
United States/West Germany	700 million	N/A	N/A

Note: Unlike most telecommunications equipment, the FAX International network has been designed to meet the regulatory requirements of every international phone system. The opportunity exists to expand the service to all of the countries listed above plus many others.

Sources: Adapted from FCC and *Electronic Mail and Micro Systems*, June 15, 1990.

traffic flowed without incident for the remainder of the day. The next morning, March 25, the network experienced a total shutdown. Fortunately, the system was designed so that all FAXLINKs automatically deactivate during a shutdown. This means that customers' fax transmissions were simply carried over their normal long-distance carrier rather than being routed over the FI network. However, the service department was flooded with calls from customers wondering why their machines indicated AT&T and MCI had carried the calls rather than the far less expensive FI network. The FI account managers assured the customers that it was only a routine "software enhancement" procedure and that service would be back on shortly.

The FI engineers worked all through the night and finally discovered that the failure had come from a defect in the leased line and not the FI system. The next morning the system was back on and the company was back to business as usual. The most important lesson had actually been a positive one. The network worked properly in terms of deactivating the FAXLINKs so that not a single customer's fax was lost.

Ranalli believed he had cleared a major hurdle. The network was now operational and working properly. The possibility of a shutdown was still very real but he felt that any damage that could be caused was survivable. It was time to turn his full attention to his desperate financial situation. He had a host of investors waiting only for the network to come online to write their checks. Therefore, Ranalli immediately issued an "investor update" (see *Exhibit M*) and opened the next round of financing.

Only days after this announcement, Ranalli was introduced to Jeff Parker, a successful entrepreneur Ranalli had read about in several HBS cases. At a lunch meeting the following day, much to Ranalli's surprise, Parker, along with a large family investment fund (Family A) led by Mr. Gulee Arshad, expressed an interest in investing the full $1 million for the coming round. Of course they would want a slightly better deal than the proposed $500,000 in debt and 500,000 shares of convertible preferred stock. They would also need a seat on the FI board of directors.

Exhibit M
Investor Update (March 1992)

I. Network Start Date

FAX International officially began marketing its service between the United States and Tokyo on March 9th and began carrying traffic between the United States and Tokyo on March 24, 1992. A list of the customers who began using the service on March 24th is attached. The sales organization has done an outstanding job over the past two weeks of bringing on a large number of highly desirable Japanese customers. Based on the initial customer response, it appears that the sales organization will substantially exceed the growth rate projected in the Business Plan, dated December 1991. The first two weeks of selling experience seem to indicate that the potential customer base is much larger and more receptive to the service offering than originally anticipated.

II. Financing

February 28, 1992: FAX International closed its Series A preferred stock financing offer after substantially exceeding the original goal of $600,000. The Series A offer finished $125,000 oversubscribed. Many thanks to all of the investors who have helped to make FAX International's vision a reality.

March 10, 1992: TLP Leasing Programs, Inc. provided FAX International with the final installment of a $450,000 equipment lease package. The TLP lease combined with a $130,000 loan from Douglas Ranalli has allowed FAX International to install sufficient network capacity to meet the growth needs of the company for a period of three to six months.

March 24, 1992: FAX International announced a $1,000,000 Series B preferred stock offering. The initial closing date for the offering has been set at April 10, 1992. The company has been preparing for this round of financing since November and we expect the round to proceed smoothly. Funds will be raised from accredited investors in units of $50,000. Each Unit is comprised of 25,000 shares of convertible preferred stock and a $25,000 subordinated two-year debenture paying 12% cumulative annual interest. At the conclusion of this round of financing the company will have approximately 4,600,000 shares of common and convertible preferred stock outstanding. Series B investors will own approximately 11% of the fully diluted shares of the company.

III. Japanese Approval Process

On January 23, 1992, FAX International received its license from the Ministry of Post and Telecommunications in Japan to operate as a Special Type II International Telecommunications Carrier. FAX International is the first American firm which was not an existing telecommunications carrier to receive this license.

IV. Key Indicators to Watch

In order to simplify the process of tracking FAX International's progress, each investor will receive a bimonthly growth rate report during 1992. The report will contain a growth rate chart which will present information in the format outlined below. The numbers shown represent the section of the Business Plan under Year 1 Detailed Revenues. Please note that the Business Plan shows the company starting on February 1. For simplicity and clarity, all future analysis will be presented with a start date of April 1, 1992.

	April Month 1	*May Month 2*	*June Month 3*	*July Month 4*	. . .
Business plan	500*	1,500	2,000	2,500	
New projections	1,000	3,000	(to be projected one month in advance)		
Actual results	(provided at the end of each month)				

*Net new minutes per day

Ranalli felt he was faced with yet another dilemma; the trade-offs were relatively obvious. On the one hand, one single, very sophisticated investor would make the fund-raising simple and quick. He could be back doing the important job of running the company and planning the future in a much shorter period of time with fewer headaches than he would encounter dealing with a dozen or more smaller investors. Yet, even though Parker seemed a perfectly reasonable individual at their first meeting, he couldn't help but remember the cases he had read concerning a few of Parker's earlier investments. Were Ranalli to accept this investment offer, then Parker would clearly be the most powerful private investor in the company. How much would Parker want? What should Ranalli do about the other investors waiting to write their checks? How much should he raise? He wanted to be sure that they had enough not to have to worry about returning to the well. Yet, he did not want to unnecessarily dilute the value of the stock either. He wanted to be sure to consider all his options. (See *Exhibit N* for information on the capital market environment.) One thing was clear—FI was out of cash. He would have to make a decision soon.

Once the *need* for additional capital has been identified and quantified, the management team must consider the desirability of an equity investment. As was mentioned in Chapter 10, bootstrapping continues to be an attractive source of financing. For instance, *INC.* magazine suggested that entrepreneurs in certain industries "tap vendors"[2] by getting them to extend credit.

Other entrepreneurs interviewed by *INC.* suggested getting "customers to pay fast."[3] These options, and others, exist if the management team members feel that a loss of equity would adversely impact the company and their ability to manage it effectively. An equity investment requires that the management team firmly believe that investors can and will add value to the venture. With this belief, the team can begin to identify those investors who bring expertise to the venture.

Deciding *who* should invest is a process more than a decision. The management team has a number of sources to consider. There are both informal and formal investors, private and public markets. The single most important criterion for selecting an investor is what they can contribute to the value of the venture—beyond just capital. Angels or wealthy individuals are often sought because the amount needed may be less than the minimum investment required by formal investors (i.e. venture capitalists and private placements). Whether a venture capitalist would be interested in investing can be determined by the amount needed and the required rate of return expected.

Recently, as classic venture capitalists apparently are becoming a rare breed and as the banks exercise serious credit restraint, syndicated private offerings are meeting the needs of younger companies.[4] Take Symbus Technology, for instance. When this Massachusetts-based software company was in need of cash, their options were limited. The *Boston Globe* reported that a bank loan was out of the question. Venture capital meant the loss of both equity and control, and the public markets would not have responded to Symbus Technology's $2 million in 1992 revenue.[5] Thus, a syndicated private offering was pursued by Richard Tabor, the president and chief executive officer. The company successfully raised $3.1 million in August 1992. Yet, entrepreneurs should be cautioned that "only 30 to 40 percent of the companies seeking private equity actually wind up getting it at the end of the process."[6] Additionally, the fees due the investment bankers and attorneys involved in writing up the prospectus and other legal documents must be paid whether or not the company raises capital.

Timing

Timing is also critical. It is important that a venture not delay looking for capital until it has a serious cash shortage. For a start-up, especially one with no experience or success in raising money, it is unwise to delay looking for capital since it is likely to take six months or more to raise money. In addition to the problems with cash flow, the lack of planning implicit in waiting until there is a cash shortage can undermine the credibility of a venture's management team and negatively impact its ability to negotiate with investors; recall *Exhibit 12.5*.

[2] Robert A Mamis, "The Secrets of Bootstrapping," *INC.*, September 1992, p. 72.

[3] Ibid., p. 76.

[4] Andrew D Myers, "Syndicated Private Offerings Add Equity to Emerging Companies," *Corporate Cashflow*, December 1992, p. 47.

[5] Judy Temes, "When the venture capital dries up . . . small firms look to private placement," *Boston Globe*, May 16, 1993, pp. 76–77.

[6] Ibid.

On the other hand, if a venture tries to obtain equity capital too early, the equity position of the founders may be unnecessarily diluted and the discipline instilled by financial leanness may be eroded inadvertently.

ANGELS AND INFORMAL INVESTORS

Who They Are

Wealthy individuals are probably the single most important source of capital for start-up and emerging businesses in America today.[7] According to William Wetzel, there are 250,000 or more such wealthy individuals, or "angels," in the United States, 100,000 of whom are active.[8] In total, Wetzel believes angels invest $5 billion to $10 billion annually in 20,000 to 30,000 companies, an amount which is staggering in comparison to the 3,000 to 3,500 investments made each year by the United States venture capital industry. Typical investments are in the $20,000–$50,000 range, with 36 percent involving less than $10,000 and 24 percent over $50,000. These amounts are usually too small for professional venture capital sources.

Wetzel has found that these angels are mainly American self-made entrepreneur millionaires. They have made it on their own, have substantial business and financial experience, and are likely to be in their 40s or 50s. They are also well educated; 95 percent hold college degrees from four-year colleges, and 51 percent have graduate degrees. Of the graduate degrees, 44 percent are in a technical field and 35 percent are in business or economics.

Since the typical informal investor will invest from $10,000 to $50,000 in any one venture, informal investors are particularly appropriate for the following:[9]

- Ventures with capital requirements of between $50,000 and $500,000.
- Ventures with sales potential of between $2 million and $20 million within 5 to 10 years.
- Small, established, privately held ventures with sales and profit growth of 10 percent to 20 percent per year, a rate which is not rapid enough to be attractive to a professional investor, such as a venture capital firm.
- Special situations, such as very early financing of high-technology inventors who have not developed a prototype.

These investors may invest alone or in syndication with other wealthy individuals, may demand considerable equity for their interests, or may try to dominate ventures. They also can get very impatient when sales and profits do not grow as they expected.

Usually, these informal investors will be knowledgeable and experienced in the market and technology areas they invest in. If the right angel is found, he or she will add a lot more to a business than just money. As an advisor or director, his or her savvy, know-how, and contacts that come from having "made it" can be far more valuable than the $20,000 to $50,000 invested. Generally, the evaluations of potential investments by such wealthy investors tend to be less thorough than those undertaken by organized venture capital groups, and such noneconomic factors as the desire to be involved with entrepreneurship may

[7] G Baty, *Initial Financing of the New Research Based Enterprise in New England*, Federal Reserve Bank of Boston research Report No. 25, Boston, MA, 1964; and G Baty, *Entrepreneurship: Play to Win* (Reston, VA: Reston Publishing, 1974), p. 97.

[8] William H Wetzel, Jr., "Angels and Risk Capital," *Sloan Management Review* 24, no. 4 (Summer 1984), pp. 23–34. The information in the text about angels is based on Wetzel's work.

[9] William H Wetzel, Jr., "Informal Investors—When and Where to Look," in *Pratt's Guide to Venture Capital Sources*, 6th ed., ed. Stanley E Pratt (Wellesley Hills, MA: Capital Publishing, 1982), p. 22.

be important to their investment decisions. For example, a successful entrepreneur may want to help other entrepreneurs get started, or a wealthy individual may want to help build new businesses in his or her community.

Finding Informal Investors

Finding these backers is not easy. One expert noted: "Informal investors, essentially individuals of means and successful entrepreneurs, are a diverse and dispersed group with a preference for anonymity. Creative techniques are required to identify and reach them."[10]

Invariably, they are found by tapping an entrepreneur's own network of business associates and other contacts. Other successful entrepreneurs know them, as do many tax attorneys, accountants, bankers, and other professionals. Apart from serendipity, the best way to find informal investors is to seek referrals from attorneys, accountants, business associates, university faculty, and entrepreneurs who deal with new ventures and are likely to know such people. Since such investors learn of investment opportunities from their business associates, fellow entrepreneurs, and friends, and since many informal investors invest together, more or less regularly, in a number of new venture situations, one informal investor contact can lead the entrepreneur to contacts with others.

In most larger cities, there are law firms and private placement firms that syndicate investment packages as Regulation D offerings to networks of private investors. They may raise from several hundred thousand dollars to several million. Directories of these firms are published annually by *Venture* magazine and are written about in magazines such as *INC.*

Contacting Investors

If an entrepreneur has obtained a referral, he or she needs to get permission to use the name of the person making a referral when the investor is contacted. A meeting with the potential investor then can be arranged. At this meeting, the entrepreneur needs to make a concise presentation of the key features of the proposed venture.

However, entrepreneurs need to avoid meeting with more than one informal investor at the same time. Meeting with more than one investor often results in any negative viewpoints raised by one investor being reinforced by another. It is also easier to deal with negative reactions and questions from only one investor at a time. Like a wolf on the hunt, if an entrepreneur isolates one target "prey" and then concentrates on closure, he or she will increase the odds of success.

Whether or not the outcome of such a meeting is continued investment interest, the entrepreneur needs to try to obtain the names of other potential investors from this meeting. If this can be done, the entrepreneur will develop a growing list of potential investors and will find his or her way into one or more networks of informal investors.

If the outcome is positive, often the participation of one investor who is knowledgeable about the product and its market will trigger the participation of other investors.

Evaluation Process

An informal investor will want to review a business plan, meet the full management team, see any product prototype or design that may exist, and so forth. The investor will conduct background checks on the venture team and its product potential, usually through someone he or she knows who knows the entrepreneur and the product. The process is not

[10] Ibid.

dissimilar to the due diligence of the professional investors (see below) but may be less formal and structured.

The new venture entrepreneur, if given a choice, would be wise to select an informal investor who can be a useful advisor and whose objectives are consistent with those of the entrepreneur.

The Decision

If the investor decides to invest, he or she will have some sort of investment agreement drafted by an attorney. This agreement may be somewhat simpler than those used by professional investors, such as venture capital firms. All the cautions and advice about investors and investment agreements that are discussed later on in the chapter apply here as well.

Most likely, the investment agreement with an informal investor will include some form of a "put," whereby the investor has the right to require the venture to repurchase his or her stock after a specified number of years at a specified price. If the venture is not harvested, this put will provide an investor with a cash return.

VENTURE CAPITAL: GOLD MINES AND TAR PITS

There are only two classes of investors in new and young private companies: value-added investors and all the rest. If all you receive from an investor, especially a venture capitalist or a substantial private investor, is money, then you may not be getting much of a bargain at all. One of the keys to raising risk capital is to seek investors who will truly add value to the venture well beyond the money. Research and practice show that investors may add or detract value in a young company. Therefore, carefully screening potential investors to determine how specifically they might fill in some gaps in the founders' know-how and networks can yield significant results.

A young founder of an international telecommunications venture landed a private investor who also served as an advisor. The following are examples of how this private investor provided critical assistance: introduced the founder to other private investors, to foreign executives (who became investors and helped in a strategic alliance), to the appropriate legal and accounting firms; served as a sounding board in crafting and negotiating early rounds of investments; identified potential directors and other advisors familiar with the technology and relationships with foreign investors and cross-cultural strategic alliances.

Numerous other examples exist of venture capitalists' being instrumental in opening doors to key accounts and vendors that otherwise might not take a new company very seriously. They may also provide valuable help in such tasks as negotiating OEM agreements, licensing or royalty agreements, making key contacts with banks and leasing companies, finding key people to build the team, helping to revise or to craft a strategy. It is always tempting for an entrepreneur desperately in need of cash to go after the money that is available, rather than wait for the value-added investor. These quick solutions to the cash problem usually come back to haunt the venture.

What is Venture Capital?[11]

The word *venture* suggests that this type of capital involves a degree of risk and even something of a gamble. Specifically, "the venture capital industry supplies capital and other

[11] Unless otherwise noted, this section is drawn from William D Bygrave and Jeffry A Timmons, *Venture Capital at the Crossroads* (Boston: Harvard Business School Press, 1992.), pp. 13–14. Copyright © 1992 by William D Bygrave and Jeffry A Timmons.

Exhibit 13.1
Classic Venture Capital Investing Process

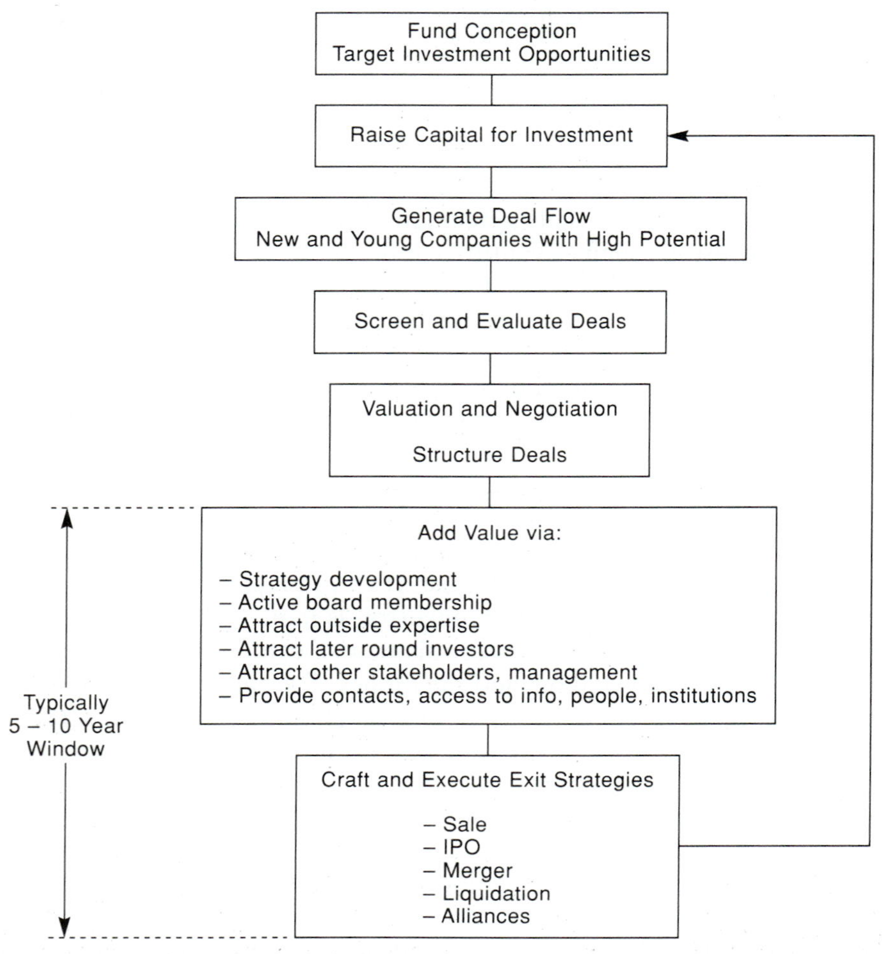

Source: William D Bygrave and Jeffry A Timmons, *Venture Capital at the Crossroads* (Boston: Harvard Business School Press, 1992), Figure 1–4.

resources to entrepreneurs in business with high growth potential in hopes of achieving a high rate of return on invested funds."[12] The whole investing process involves many stages, which are represented in *Exhibit 13.1.* Throughout the investing process, venture capital firms seek to add value in several ways: identifying and evaluating business opportunities, including management, entry, or growth strategies; negotiating and closing the investment; tracking and coaching the company; providing technical and management assistance; and attracting additional capital, directors, management, suppliers, and other key stake holders and resources. The process begins with the conception of a target investment opportunity or class of opportunities, which leads to a written proposal or prospectus to raise a venture capital fund. Once the money is raised, the value creation process moves from generating deals to crafting and executing harvest strategies and back to raising another fund. The process usually takes up to 10 years to unfold, but exceptions in both directions often occur. (See *Exhibit 13.2.*)

[12] "Note on the Venture Capital Industry (1981)," HBS Case 285-096, Harvard Business School, 1982, p. 1.

Exhibit 13.2 (A)
Venture Capital Industry

Estimated Capital Under Management and Disbursements
(Millions of Dollars)
1969 to 1992

Year	*New Capital Committed to Independent Private Venture Capital Firms Only*	*Total Venture Capital Under Management**	*Disbursements to Portfolio Companies*
1992	$2,550	$ 31,074	$2,540
1991	1,388	32,870	1,348
1990	1,800	35,950	1,922
1989	2,400	34,430	3,395
1988	2,900	31,100	3,847
1987	4,200	29,000	3,977
1986	3,300	24,100	3,242
1985	2,300	19,600	2,681
1984	3,200	16,300	2,771
1983	3,400	12,100	2,581
1982	1,400	7,600	1,454
1981	867	5,800	1,155
1980	661	4,500	608
1979	170	3,800	457
1978	216	3,500	288
1977	—	2,500-3,000	159
1976	—		107
1975	—		92
1974	—		100
1973	—		201
1972	—		128
1971	—		134
1970	—		83
1969	—	2,500-3,000	not available

*Total venture capital under management remained static from 1969 through 1977 at approximately $2.5 to $3.0 billion with new funding more or less equal to withdrawals (Venture Economics' policy is to withdraw dollars invested in the industry after eight years).

NOTE: Some numbers may be affected by rounding.

Source: Venture Economics National Venture Capital Association Annual Report

(Continued)

The Venture Capital Industry[13]

Although the roots of venture capital can be traced from investments made by wealthy families in the 1920s and 1930s, most industry observers credit Ralph E. Flanders, then president of the Federal Reserve Bank of Boston, with the idea. In 1946, Flanders joined a top-ranked team to found American Research and Development Corporation, the first firm, as opposed to individuals, to provide risk capital for new and rapidly growing firms, most of which were manufacturing and technology oriented.

Despite the success of American Research & Development, the venture capital industry did not experience a growth spurt until the 1980s, when the industry "went ballistic." See *Exhibit 13.3* for the capital commitments between 1969 and 1990. Before 1980, venture capital investing activities could be called dormant; just $460 million was invested in 375 companies in 1979. But at its peak in 1987, the industry had ballooned to more than 700 venture capital firms, which invested $3.94 billion in 1,729 portfolio companies. The sleepy, cottage industry of the 1970s was transformed into a vibrant, at times frenetic, occasionally myopic, and dynamic market for private risk and equity capital in the 1980s. "After shrinking by an average of 25 percent a year for four years, new venture capital raised in 1992 more than

[13] Bygrave and Timmons, *Venture Capital at the Crossroads*, pp. 16–28.

Exhibit 13.2 (B)
Total Venture Capital Under Management

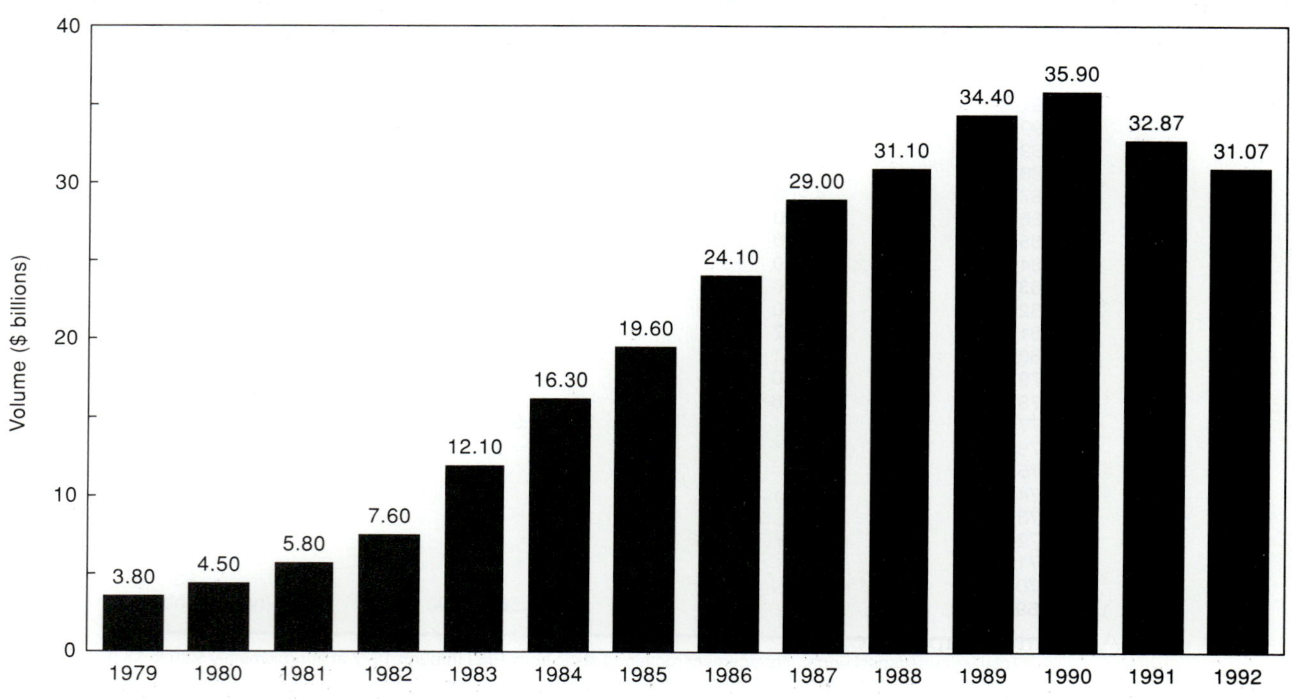

Source: Venture Economics.

Exhibit 13.3
United States Commitments (1969–1992)

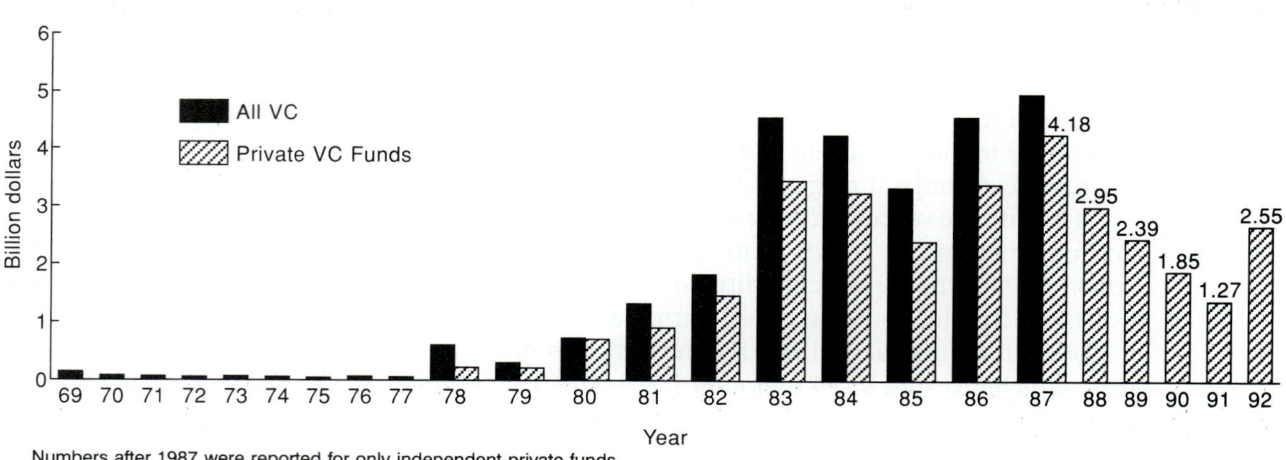

Numbers after 1987 were reported for only independent private funds.

Source: Venture Economics Publishing, *Venture Capital Journal*, January 1993, p. 32.

doubled over 1991."[14] Yet, industry observers attributed the increase to "repeat fund raisers assembling partnerships of more than $100 million."[15]

By the late 1980s, not only had the commitments changed, but there a new structure was emerging, increasingly specialized and focused. See *Exhibit 13.4*. This chart summarized some of the important changes in the industry, which have implications for entrepreneurs seeking money and for those investing it.

The Venture Capital Process

Exhibit 13.5 represents the core activities of the venture capital process. At the heart of this dynamic flow is the collision of entrepreneurs, opportunities, investors, and capital.[16] Because the venture capitalist brings, in addition to money, experience, networks, and industry contacts, a professional venture capitalist can be very attractive to a new venture. Moreover, a venture capital firm has deep pockets and contacts with other groups that can facilitate the raising of money as the venture develops.

The venture capital process occurs in the context of mostly private, quite imperfect capital markets for new, emerging, and middle-market companies (i.e., those companies with $5 million to $100 million in sales). The availability and cost of this capital depend on a number of factors:

- Perceived risk, in view of the quality of the management team and the opportunity.
- Industry, market, attractiveness of the technology, and fit.
- Upside potential and downside exposure.
- Anticipated growth rate.
- Age and stage of development.
- Amount of capital required.
- Founders' goals for growth, control, liquidity, and harvest.
- Fit with investors' goals and strategy.
- Relative bargaining positions of investors and founders.

However, no more than 2 to 4 percent of the ventures contacting venture capital firms receive financing from them; see *Exhibit 13.6* for the number of companies and the types of investments made. Despite the increase in funds in 1992, observers comment that the repeat fund-raisers "stay away from seed and early-stage investments largely because those deals tend to require relatively small amounts of capital and the megafunds, with $100 million-plus to invest, like to make larger commitments."[17] Further, an entrepreneur may give up 25 to 75 percent of his or her equity for seed/start-up financing. Thus, after several rounds of venture financing have been completed, an entrepreneur may own no more than 10 to 20 percent of the venture.

It is the venture capitalists' stringent criteria for their investments that limit the number of companies receiving venture capital money. Venture capital investors look for ventures with very high growth potential where they can quintuple their investment in five years; they place a very high premium on the quality of management in a venture; and they like to see a management team with complementary business skills headed by someone who has previous entrepreneurial or profit-and-loss (P&L) management experience. In fact, these investors are searching for the "superdeal." Superdeals meet the investment criteria outlined in *Exhibit 13.7*.

[14] Michael Vachon, "Venture Capital Reborn," *Venture Capital Journal*, January 1993, p. 32.

[15] Ibid.

[16] Bygrave and Timmons, *Venture Capital at the Crossroads*, p. 11.

[17] Vachon, "Venture Capital Reborn," p. 35.

Exhibit 13.4
New Heterogeneous Structure of the Venture Capital Industry

	Megafunds	*Mainstream*	*Second Tier*	*Specialists and Niche Funds*	*Corporate Financial and Corporate Industrial*
Estimated number and type (1988)	89 Predominately private, independent funds	100–125+ Predominately private and independent; some large institutional SBICs and corporate funds	150–175 Mostly SBICs; some private independent funds	40–50 Private, independent	85 and 84, respectively
Size of funds under management	$100M+	$25–$99M	Below $25M	$3–$15M	$25-$50M+
Typical invest. (1st round)	$1M–$3M+	$750K–$1M	$500K–$750K	$50K–$200K	Larger $10M–$15M deals possible
Stage of investment	Later expansion, LBOs, start-ups	Later expansion, LBOs, some starts; mezzanine	Later stages; few starts; specialized areas	Seed and start-up Technology or market focus	Later
Strategic focus	Technology; national and international markets; capital gains; broad focus	Technology and manufacturing; national and regional markets; capital gains; more specialized focus	Eclectic—more regional than national; capital gains, current income; service business	High-technology national and international links; "feeder funds" capital gains	Windows on technology; direct investment in new markets and suppliers; diversification; strategic partners; capital gains
Balance of equity and debt	Predominately equity	Predominately equity; convertible preferred	Predominately debt; about 91 SBICs do equity principally	Predominately equity	Mixed
Principal sources of capital	Mature national and international institutions; own funds; insurance company and pension funds; institutions and wealthy individuals; foreign corporation and pension funds; universities		Wealthy individuals; some smaller institutions	Institutions and foreign companies; wealthy individuals	Internal funds
Main investing role	Active lead or colead; frequent syndications; board seat	Less coinvesting with some solo investing	Initial or lead investor; outreach; shirtsleeves involvement	Later stages, rarely start-ups; direct investor in funds and portfolio companies	

Note: Target rates of return vary considerably, depending on stage and market conditions. Seed and start-up investors may seek compounded after-tax rates of return in excess of 50 to 100 percent; in mature, later stage investments they seek returns in the 30–40 percent range. The rule of thumb of realizing gains of 5 to 10 times the original investment in 5 to 10 years is a common investor expectation.

The author is most appreciative of the assistance of Jane Morris, editor, *Venture Capital Journal*, in providing some of the data for this table.

Exhibit 13.5
Flows of Venture Capital

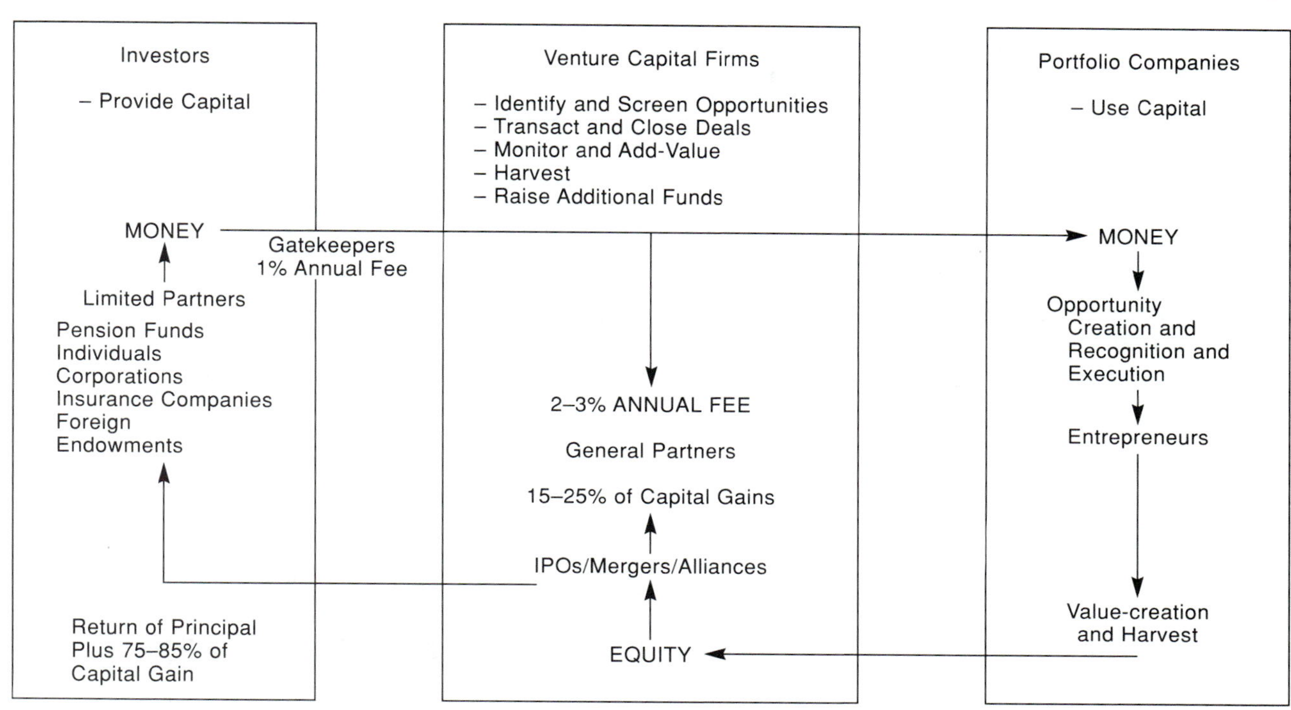

Source: William D Bygrave and Jeffry A Timmons, *Venture Capital at the Crossroads* (Boston: Harvard Business School Press, 1992), Figure 1–3.

Exhibit 13.6
USA Venture Capital Investment by Year (1979–1989)

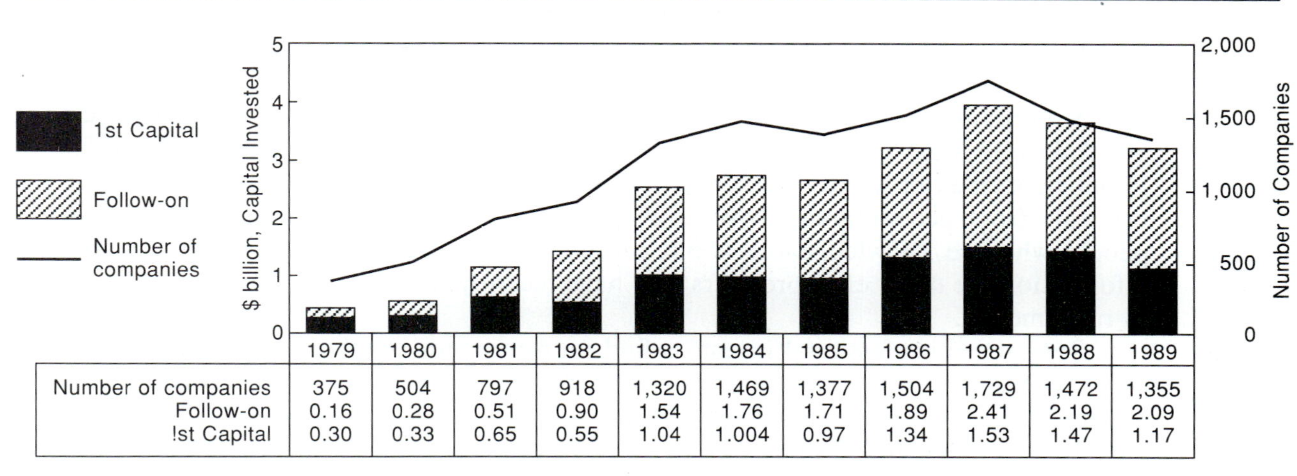

	1979	1980	1981	1982	1983	1984	1985	1986	1987	1988	1989
Number of companies	375	504	797	918	1,320	1,469	1,377	1,504	1,729	1,472	1,355
Follow-on	0.16	0.28	0.51	0.90	1.54	1.76	1.71	1.89	2.41	2.19	2.09
!st Capital	0.30	0.33	0.65	0.55	1.04	1.004	0.97	1.34	1.53	1.47	1.17

Source: *Venture Capital Journal*, July 1990, p. 14.

Exhibit 13.7
Characteristics of the Classic Superdeal from the Investor's Perspective

Mission
- Build a highly profitable and industry-dominant company.
- Go public or merge within four to seven years at a high price-earnings (P/E) multiple.

Complete Management Team
- Led by industry "superstar."
- Possess proven entrepreneurial, general management, and P&L experience in the business.
- Have leading innovator or technologies/marketing head.
- Possess complementary and compatible skills.
- Have unusual tenacity, imagination, and commitment.
- Possess reputation for high integrity.

Proprietary Product
- Has significant competitive lead and "unfair" advantages.
- Has product or service with high value-added properties resulting in early payback to user.
- Has or can gain exclusive contractual or legal rights.

Large and Rapidly Growing Market
- Will accommodate a $50 million entrant in five years.
- Has sales currently at $100 million, and more, and growing at 25% per year.
- Has no dominant competitor now.
- Has clearly identified customers and distribution channels.
- Possesses forgiving and rewarding economics, such as:
  - Gross margins of 40% to 50%, or more.
  - 10 percent or more profit after tax.
  - Early positive cash flow and break-even sales.

Deal Valuation and ROR
- Has "digestible" first-round capital requirements (i.e., greater than $1 million and less than $10 million).
- Able to return 10 times original investment in five years at P/E of 15 times or more.
- Has possibility of additional rounds of financing at substantial markup.
- Has antidilution and IPO subscription rights.

Source: William D Bygrave and Jeffry A Timmons, *Venture Capital at the Crossroads* (Boston: Harvard Business School Press, 1992), Figure 1–2.

Identifying Venture Capital Investors

Venture capital corporations or partners have an established capital base and professional management. Their investment policies cover a range of preferences in investment size and the maturity, location, and industry of a venture. Capital for these investments can be provided by one or more wealthy families, one or more financial institutions (e.g., insurance companies or pension funds), and wealthy individuals. Most are organized as limited partnerships, in which the fund managers are the general partners and the investors are the limited partners. Today, most of these funds prefer to invest from $500,000 to $1 million or more. Although some of the smaller funds will invest less, most of their investments are in the range of $500,000 to $1.5 million. Some of the so-called megafunds with upwards of $100 million to invest do not consider investments of less than $1 million to $2 million. The investigation and evaluation of potential investments by venture capital corporations and partnerships are thorough and professional. Most of their investments are in high-technology businesses, but a good number will consider investments in other areas.

Sources and Guides. If an entrepreneur is searching for a venture capital investor, a good place to start is with *Pratt's Guide to Venture Capital Sources*, published by Venture Economics, one of several directories of venture capital firms. Entrepreneurs also can seek referrals from accountants, lawyers, investment and commercial bankers, and business people who are knowledgeable about professional investors. Especially good sources of information are other entrepreneurs who have recently tried, successfully or unsuccessfully, to raise money.

Sometimes professional investors find entrepreneurs. Rather than wait for a deal to come to them, a venture capital investor may decide on a product or technology it wishes to commercialize and then put its own deal together. Kleiner Perkins used this approach to launch Genentech and Tandem Computer Corporation, as did Greylock and J. H. Whitney in starting MassComp.

What to Look For. Entrepreneurs are well advised to screen prospective investors to determine the appetites of such investors for the stage, industry, technology, and capital requirements proposed. It is also useful to determine which investors have money to invest, which are actively seeking deals, and which have the time and people to investigate new deals. Depending on its size and investment strategy, a fund which is a year or two old will generally be in an active investing mode.

Early-stage entrepreneurs need to seek investors who (1) are considering new financing proposals and can provide the required level of capital; (2) are interested in companies at the particular stage of growth; (3) understand and have a preference for investments in the particular industry (i.e., market, product, technology, or service focus); (4) can provide good business advice, moral support, and contacts in the business and financial community; (5) are reputable and ethical and with whom the entrepreneur gets along; and (6) have successful track records of 10 years or more advising and building smaller companies.[18]

Entrepreneurs can expect a number of value-added services from an investor. Ideally, the investor should define his or her role as a coach, thoroughly involved, but not a player. In terms of support, investors should have both patience and bravery. The entrepreneur should be able to go to the investor when he or she needs a sounding board, counseling, or an objective, detached perspective. Investors should be helpful with future negotiations, financing, private and public offerings, as well as in relationship building with key contacts.

What to Look Out For. There are also some things to be wary of in finding investors. These warning signs are worth avoiding unless an entrepreneur is so desperate that he or she has no real alternatives:

- *Attitude.* Entrepreneurs need to be wary if they cannot get through to a general partner in an investment firm and keep getting handed off to a junior associate, or if the investor thinks he or she can run the business better than the lead entrepreneur or the management team.
- *Overcommitment.* Entrepreneurs need to be wary of lead investors who indicate they will be active directors but who also sit on the boards of six to eight other start-up and early-stage companies or are in the midst of raising money for a new fund.
- *Inexperience.* Entrepreneurs need to be wary of dealing with venture capitalists who have an MBA; are under 30 years of age; have worked only on Wall Street or as a consultant; have no operating, hands-on experience in new and growing companies; *and* have a predominantly financial focus.
- *Unfavorable reputation.* Entrepreneurs need to be wary of funds that have a reputation for early and frequent replacement of the founders or those where over one-fourth of the portfolio companies are in trouble or failing to meet projections in their business plans.

Dealing with Venture Capitalists[19]

It is important to keep in mind that venture capitalists see lots of business plans and proposals, sometimes one hundred or more a month. Typically, they invest in only one to three of these. The following suggestions may be helpful in working with them.

If possible, obtain a personal introduction from someone that is well-known to the investors (a director or founder of one of their portfolio companies, a limited partner in their fund, a lawyer or accountant who has worked with them on deals) and who knows you well. After identifying the best targets, you should create a market for your company by marketing it. Have several prospects. Be vague about who else you are talking with. The problem is, you can end up with a rejection from everyone if the other firms know who was the first firm that

[18] For more specifics see Harry A Sapienza and Jeffry A Timmons, "Launching and Building Entrepreneurial Companies: Do the Venture Capitalists Build Value?" in *Proceedings of the Babson Entrepreneurship Research Conference, May 1989,* Babson Park, MA. See also Jeffry A Timmons, "Venture Capital: More than Money," in *Pratt's Guide to Venture Capital Sources*, 13th ed., ed. Jane Morris (Needham, MA: Venture Economics, 1989), p. 71.

[19] The author expresses appreciation to Mr. Thomas Huseby, CEO of Innova Corporation, Seattle, WA, for his valuable insights in the following two sections.

turned you down. It is also much harder to get a yes than to get a no. You can waste an enormous amount of time before getting there.

Most investors who have serious interest will have some clear ideas about how to improve your strategy, product line, positioning, and a variety of other areas. This is one of the ways they can add value—if they are right. Consequently, you need to be prepared for them to take apart your business plan and to put it back together. They are likely to have their own format and their own financial models. Working with them on this is a good way to get to know them.

Never lie. As one entrepreneur put it, "You have to market the truth, but do not lie." Do not stop selling until the money is in the bank. Let the facts speak for themselves. Be able to deliver on the claims, statements, and promises you make or imply in your business plan and presentations. Tom Huseby adds some final wisdom: "It's much harder than you ever thought it could be. You can last much longer than you ever thought you could. They have to do this for the rest of their lives!" Finally, never say no to an offer price. There is an old saying that your first offer may be your best offer.

Due Diligence: A Two-Way Street

It usually takes several weeks or months to complete the due diligence on a start-up, although if the investors know the entrepreneurs, it can go much more quickly. The verification of facts, backgrounds, and reputations of key people, market estimates, technical capabilities of the product, proprietary rights, and the like, is a painstaking investigation for investors. They will want to talk with your directors, advisors, former bosses, and previous partners. Make it as easy as possible for them by having very detailed resumes, lists of 10 to 20 references (with phone numbers and addresses) such as former customers, bankers, vendors, and so on, who can attest to your accomplishments. Prepare extra copies of published articles, reports, studies, market research, contract, or purchase orders, technical specifications, and the like, that can support your claims.

While all this is going on, do your own due diligence on the venture fund. Ask for the names and phone numbers of some of their successful deals, some that did not work out, and the names of any presidents they ended up replacing. Who are their legal and accounting advisors? What footprint have they left in the sand vis-à-vis their quality, reputation, and record in truly adding value to the companies in which they invest? Finally, the chemistry between the management team and the general partner that will have responsibility for the investment and, in all likelihood, a board seat is crucial. If you do not have a financial partner you respect and can work closely with, then you are likely to regret ever having accepted the money.

OTHER EQUITY SOURCES

Small Business Administration's 7(a) Guaranteed Business Loan Program

Promoting small businesses by guaranteeing long-term loans, the Small Business Administration's 7(a) Guaranteed Business Loan Program has been supporting start-up and high-potential ventures since 1953. Between 1980 and 1991, the SBA guaranteed $31 billion[20] in loans through the 7(a) program. The 7(a) program is almost exclusively a guarantee program, but under this program the Small Business Administration also makes direct loans to the handicapped, veterans, and Minority Enterprise Small Business Investment Companies (MESBICs). Eligible activities under 7(a) include acquisition of

[20] "SBA Loans Spur Start-Up Growth," *INC.*, November 1992, p. 66.

borrower-occupied real estate, fixed assets such as machinery and equipment, and working capital for items such as inventory or to meet cashflow needs.[21]

The $500,000 guarantees, the largest of all the SBA's programs, have helped many entrepreneurs start, stay in, expand, or purchase a business. In fact, a recent Price Waterhouse study found that "the SBA-backed companies showed a higher survival rate than the nonrecipients. Four years after receiving the loans, more than three-quarters of the SBA recipients were still in business, versus fewer than two-thirds of the comparison group."[22]

Small Business Investment Companies[23]

SBICs (small business investment companies) are licensed by the SBA and can obtain from it debt capital—four dollars in loans for each dollar of private equity. An SBIC's equity capital is generally supplied by one or more commercial banks, wealthy individuals, and the investing public. In 1990, there were about 450 SBICs in the United States, of which about 137 had active venture capital rather than just loan programs; some of these SBICs are affiliates of venture capital firms.

SBICs are limited by law to taking minority shareholder positions and can invest no more than 20 percent of their equity capital in any one situation. Because SBICs borrow much of their capital from the SBA and must service this debt, they prefer to make some form of interest-bearing investment.

Four common forms of financing are long-term loans with options to buy stock, convertible debenture, straight loans, and in some cases, preferred stock. A typical financing is in the range of $100,000 to $300,000. Also, because of their SBA debt, SBICs tend not to finance start-ups and early-stage companies but to make investments in more mature companies. SBICs have been an important small business financing source and in over 20 years have invested $3 billion in more than 50,000 businesses. At this writing, major changes are being proposed to improve the operating regulations and structure of the SBIC program.

Mezzanine Capital[24]

At the point where the company has overcome many of the early-stage risks, it may be ready for mezzanine capital. The term *mezzanine financing* refers to capital that is between senior debt financing and common stock. In some cases it takes the form of redeemable preferred stock, but in most cases it is subordinated debt which carries an equity "kicker" consisting of warrants or a conversion feature into common stock. This subordinated-debt capital has many characteristics of debt but also can serve as equity to underpin senior debt. It is generally unsecured, with a fixed coupon and maturity of 5 to 10 years. A number of variables are involved in structuring such a loan: the interest rate, the amount and form of the equity, exercise/conversion price, maturity, call features, sinking fund, covenants, and put/call options. These variables provide for a wide range of possible structures to suit the needs of both the issuer and the investor.

Offsetting these advantages are a few disadvantages to mezzanine capital compared to equity capital. As debt, the interest is payable on a regular basis, and the principal must be repaid, if not converted into equity. This is a large claim against cash and can be burdensome

[21] Daniel R Garner, Robert R Owen, and Robert P Conway, *The Ernst & Young Guide to Raising Capital* (New York: John Wiley & Sons, 1991), pp. 165–66.

[22] "SBA Loans Spur Start-Up Growth," p. 66.

[23] This section was drawn from Jeffry A Timmons, *Planning and Financing the New Venture* (Acton, MA: Brick House Publishing Company, 1990), pp. 49–50.

[24] This section was drawn from Donald P Remey, "Mezzanine Financing: A Flexible Source of Growth Capital," in *Pratt's Guide to Venture Capital Sources*, ed D Schutt (New York: Venture Economics Publishing, 1993), pp. 84–86.

if the expected growth and/or profitability does not materialize and cash becomes tight. In addition, the subordinated debt often contains covenants relating to net worth, debt, and dividends.

Mezzanine investors generally look for companies that have a demonstrated performance record, with revenues approaching $10 million or more. Since the financing will involve paying interest, the investor will carefully examine existing and future cash flow and projections.

Mezzanine financing is utilized in a wide variety of industries, ranging from basic manufacturing to high technology. As the name implies, however, it focuses more on the broad middle spectrum of business, rather than on high-tech, high-growth companies. Specialty retailing, broadcasting, communications, environmental services, distributors, and consumer or business service industries are more attractive to mezzanine investors.

Private Placements

Private placements are an attractive source of equity capital for a private company that for whatever reason has ruled out the possibility of going public. If the goal of the company is to raise a specific amount of capital in a short period of time, this equity source may be the answer. In this transaction, the company offers stock to a few private investors, rather than to the public as in a public offering. A private placement requires little paperwork compared to a public offering, in addition to the fact that this private transaction can take a small amount of time.

If the company's management team knows of enough investors, then the private placement could be distributed among a small group of friends, family, relatives, or acquaintances. Or the company may decide to have a broker circulating the proposal among a few investors who have expressed an interest in small companies. The following four groups of investors might be interested in a private placement:[25]

1. Let us say you manufacture a product and sell to dealers, franchisors, or wholesalers. These are the people who know and respect your company. Moreover, they depend on you to supply the product they sell. They might consider it to be in their own self-interest to buy your stock if they believe it will help assure continuation of product supply, and perhaps give them favored treatment if you bring out a new product or product improvement. One problem is when one dealer invests and another does not; can you treat both fairly in the future? Another problem is that a customer who invests might ask for exclusive rights to market your product in a particular geographical area, and you might find it hard to refuse.
2. A second group of prospective buyers for your stock are those professional investors who are always on the lookout to buy a good, small company in its formative years, and ride it to success. Very often, these sophisticated investors choose an industry and a particular product or service in that industry they believe will become hot and then focus 99 percent of their attention on the caliber of the management. If your management, or one key individual, has earned a high reputation as a star in management, technology, or marketing, these risk-minded investors tend to flock to that person. (The high-tech industry is an obvious example.) Whether your operation meets their tests for stardom as a hot field may determine whether they find your private placement a risk to their liking.

[25] The following examples are drawn directly from Daniel R Garner, Robert R Owen, and Robert P Conway, *The Ernst & Young Guide to Raising Capital* (New York: John Wiley & Sons, 1991), pp. 51–52.

3. Other investors are searching for opportunities to buy shares of smaller growth companies in the expectation that the company will soon go public and they will benefit as new investors bid the price up, as often happens. For such investors, news of a private placement is a tip-off that a company is on the move and worth investigating, always with an eye on the possibility of its going public. These investors usually have no fear of losing control or suffering their interference.
4. Private placements also often attract venture capitalists who hope to benefit when the company goes public or when the company is sold. To help assure that happy development, these investors get seriously active at the level of the board of directors, where their skill and experience can help the company reach its potential.

Initial Public Stock Offerings

Commonly referred to as an IPO, an initial public offering raises capital through federally registered and underwritten sales of the company's shares. Numerous federal and state securities laws and regulations govern these offerings; thus, it is important that management consult with lawyers and accountants who are intimately familiar with the current regulations.

In the past, such as during the strong bull market for new issues that occurred in 1983, 1986, and 1992, it was possible to raise money for an early-growth venture or even for a start-up. These boom markets are easy to identify because the number of new issues jumped from 281 in 1980 to an astounding 888 in 1983, representing a jump from $1.4 billion in 1980 to about three times that figure in 1983 (see *Exhibit 13.8*). Another boom came three years later, in 1986, when the number of new issues reached 727. While in 1992, the number of new

Exhibit 13.8
Initial Public Offerings (1980–1992)

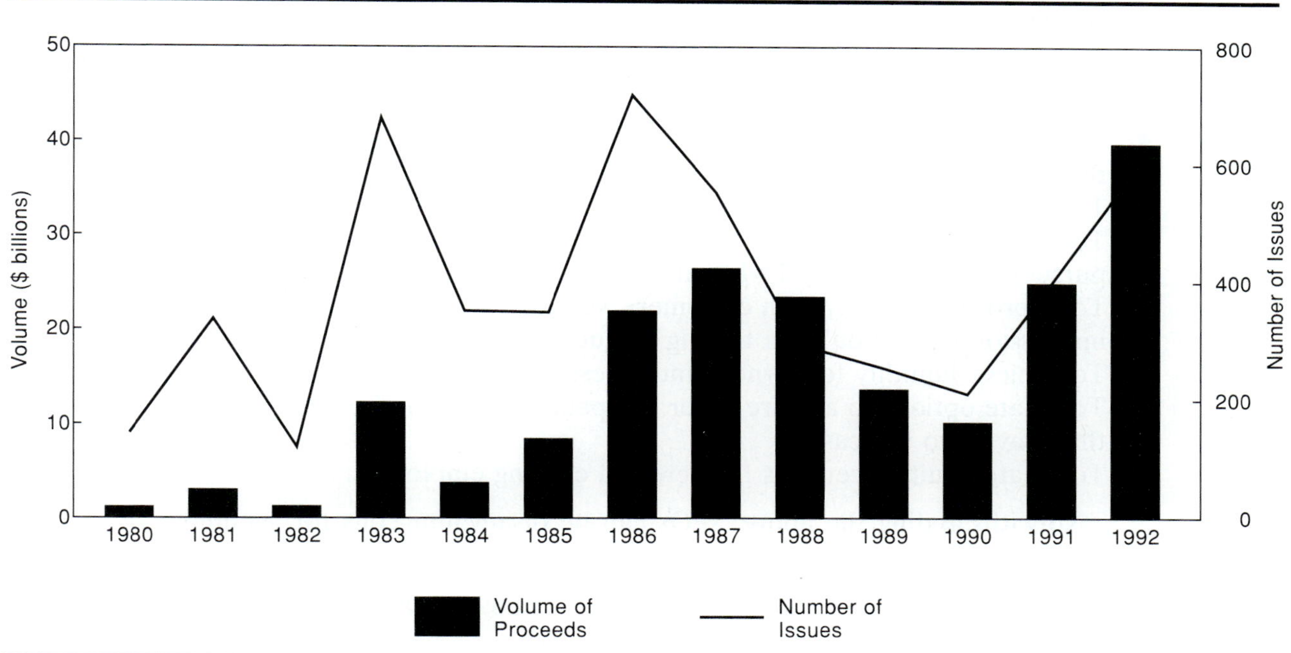

Source: Securities Data Corporation.

issues (595) did not exceed the 1986 record, a record $39.4 billion was raised in IPOs.[26] Accounting for this reduction in the number of new issues and the increase in the amounts raised, one observer commented that "the average size of each 1983 deal was a quarter of the $70 million average for the deals done."[27]

In other, more difficult financial environments, most dramatically, following the stock market crash on October 19, 1987, the new-issues market became very quiet for entrepreneurial companies, especially compared to the hot market of 1986. As a result, exit opportunities were limited. In addition, it was very difficult to raise money for early-growth or even more mature companies from the public market. The following examples are typical:

An entrepreneur spent a dozen years building a firm in the industrial mowing equipment business from scratch to $50 million in sales. The firm had a solid record of profitable growth in recent years. Although the firm is still small by Fortune 500 standards, it was the dominant firm in the business in mid-1987. Given the firm's plans for continued growth, the entrepreneur, the backers, and the directors decided the timing was right for an IPO, and the underwriters agreed. By early 1987, everything was on schedule and the "road show," which was to present the company to the various offices of the underwriter, was scheduled to begin in November. The rest is history. Nearly two years later, the IPO was still on hold.

In 1991, as the IPO market began to heat up, a Cambridge-based biotech firm was convinced by its investors and investment bankers to take the company public. In the spring, the IPO window opened as medical and biotechnology stocks were the best performing of all industry groups. By May, they had the book together; in June, the road show started in Japan, went through Europe and ended in the United States in mid-July. As the scheduled IPO date approached, so did the United Nations deadline for Saddam Hussein. After US involvement, the new issues market turned downward, as the management of the biotech company watched their share price decline from $14 to $9 per share.[28]

The more mature a company is when it makes a public offering, the better the terms of the offering. A higher valuation can be placed on the company, and less equity will be given up by the founders for the required capital.

There are also a number of reasons why an entrepreneurial company would want to go public. The following are some of the advantages

- To raise more capital with less dilution than occurs with private placements or venture capital.
- To improve the balance sheet and/or to reduce or to eliminate debt, thereby enhancing the company's net worth.
- To obtain cash for pursuing opportunities that would otherwise be unaffordable.
- To access other suppliers of capital and to increase bargaining power, as the company pursues additional capital when it needs it least.
- To improve credibility with customers, vendors, key people, and prospects. To give the impression that "You're in the big leagues now."
- To achieve liquidity for owners and investors.
- To create options to acquire other companies with a tax-free exchange of stock, rather than having to use cash.
- To create equity incentives for new and existing employees.

Notwithstanding the above, IPOs can be disadvantageous for a number of reasons:

- The legal, accounting, and administrative costs of raising money via a public offering are more disadvantageous than other ways of raising money.

[26] Sara Calian, "IPOs Raise Record $39.4 Billion for '92," *The Wall Street Journal*, January 4, 1993, p. C1.

[27] Thomas N Cochran, "IPOs Everywhere: New Issues Hit a Record in the First Quarter," *Barrons*, April 19, 1993, p. 14.

[28] This synopsis is drawn from "Rational Drug Design Corporation," HBS Case 293-102, Harvard Business School, 1992.

- A large amount of management effort, time, and expense are required to comply with SEC regulations and reporting requirements and to maintain the status of a public company. This diversion of management's time and energy from the tasks of running the company can adversely affect its performance and growth.
- Management can become more interested in maintaining the price of the company's stock and computing capital gains than in running the company. Short-term activities to maintain or increase a current year's earnings can take precedence over longer-term programs to build the company and increase its earnings.
- The liquidity of a company's stock achieved through a public offering may be more apparent than real. Without a sufficient number of shares outstanding and a strong "market maker," there may be no real market for the stock and, thus, no liquidity.
- The investment banking firms willing to take a new or unseasoned company public may not be the ones with whom the company would like to do business and establish a long-term relationship.

Private Placement After Going Public[29]

Sometimes a company goes public and then, for any number of reasons that add up to bad luck, the high expectations that attracted lots of investors in the first place turn sour. Your financial picture worsens; there is a cash crisis; down goes the price of your stock in the public marketplace. You find that you need new funds to work your way out of difficulties, but public investors are disillusioned and not likely to cooperate if you bring out a new issue.

Still, other investors are sophisticated enough to see beyond today's problems; they know the company's fundamentals are sound. While the public has turned its back on you, these investors may well be receptive if you offer a private placement to tide you over. In such circumstances, you may use a wide variety of securities—common stock, convertible preferred stock, convertible debentures. There are several types of exempt offerings. They are usually described by reference to the securities regulation that applies to them.

Regulation D is the result of the first cooperative effort by the SEC and the state securities associations to develop a uniform exemption from registration for small issuers. A significant number of states allow for qualification under state law in coordination with the qualification under Regulation D. Heavily regulated states, such as California, are notable exceptions. However, even in California, the applicable exemption is fairly consistent with the Regulation D concept.

Although Regulation D outlines procedures for exempt offerings, there is a requirement to file certain information (Form D), with the SEC. Form D is a relatively short form that asks for certain general information about the issuer and the securities being issued, as well as some specific data about the expenses of the offering and the intended use of the proceeds.

Regulation D provides exemptions from registration when securities are being sold in certain circumstances. The various circumstances are commonly referred to by the applicable Regulation D rule number. The rules and their application are as follows:

Rule 504. Issuers that are not subject to the reporting obligations of the Securities Exchange Act of 1934 (nonpublic companies) and that are not investment companies may sell up to $1,000,000 worth of securities over a 12-month period to an unlimited number of investors.

Rule 505. Issuers that are not investment companies may sell up to $5 million worth of securities over a 12-month period to no more than 35 nonaccredited purchasers, and to an unlimited number of accredited investors. Such issuers may be eligible for this exemption even though they are public companies (subject to the reporting requirements of the 1934 Act).

[29] Garner, Owen, and Conway, *The Ernst & Young Guide to Raising Capital*, pp. 52–54.

Rule 506. Issuers may sell an unlimited amount of securities to no more than 35 unaccredited but sophisticated purchasers, and to an unlimited number of accredited purchasers. Public companies may be eligible for this exemption.

Employee Stock Option Plans (ESOPs)

ESOPs are another potential source of funding used by existing companies that have high confidence in the stability of their future earnings and cash flow. An ESOP is a program in which the employees become investors in the company, thereby creating an internal source of funding. An ESOP is a tax-qualified retirement benefit plan. In essence, an ESOP borrows money, usually from a bank or insurance company, and uses the cash proceeds to buy the company's stock (usually from the owners or the treasury). The stock then becomes collateral for the bank note, while the owners or treasury have cash that can be used for a variety of purposes. For the lender, 50 percent of the interest earned on the loan to the ESOP is tax exempt. The company makes annual tax-deductible contributions—of *both* interest and principal—to the ESOP in an amount needed to service the bank loan. "The combination of being able to invest in employer stock and to benefit from its many tax advantages make the ESOP an attractive tool."[30]

Keeping Current about Capital Markets

One picture is vivid from all this: Capital markets, especially for closely held, private companies right through the initial public offering, are very dynamic, volatile, asymmetrical, and imperfect. Keeping abreast of what is happening in the capital markets in the 6 to 12 months prior to a major capital infusion can save invaluable time and hundreds of thousands and occasionally millions of dollars. Below are listed the best sources currently available to keep you informed:

- William D. Bygrave and Jeffry A. Timmons, *Venture Capital at the Crossroads* (Boston: Harvard Business School Press, 1992).
- Daniel R. Garner, Robert R. Owen, and Robert P. Conway, *The Ernst & Young Guide to Raising Capital* (New York: John Wiley & Sons, 1991).
- David Schutt ed., *Pratt's Guide to Venture Capital Sources* (New York: Venture Economics Publishing, 1993).
- *Venture Capital Journal* (published monthly by Venture Economics Publishing).
- *Venture Finance.*
- *IPO Reporter.*
- *INC.*

CASE—HINDMAN & COMPANY

Preparation Questions

1. Evaluate the business opportunity for the franchisee and the franchisor. How do they make money in this business?
2. Evaluate the company's growth and financial strategy. What have been the consequences?
3. Evaluate the current strategy, both for growth and for financing. How much money is needed and when?
4. What should Hindman do?

[30] Ibid., p. 281.

HINDMAN & COMPANY

Dismal Friday

It is March 10, 1983, another "Dismal Friday" for Jiffy Lube, Inc., and Jim Hindman, president and founder. Today's layoffs are the latest in a series of cutbacks that have reduced Jiffy Lube's payroll by over 40 percent since the beginning of February. The layoffs and other cost reductions are painful, but Hindman realizes that things can still get worse.

Jim Hindman founded Jiffy Lube in 1979. Now, in March 1983, it is the largest franchisor of quick oil change and lubrication service centers in the United States. Jiffy Lube service centers perform a "14 point fluid maintenance program" on automobiles in approximately 10 minutes. Customers pay $18–$20 for the basic service (optional services also are provided for an additional charge).

Background

After graduating from the University of Minnesota with a master's degree in health care administration, Hindman worked 10 years as a hospital administrator. In 1967, he started his own health care business, Hindman & Associates. The company built 32 nursing homes and eventually diversified into several unrelated businesses. By the mid-1970s, Hindman's ownership interests in these ventures were worth several million dollars, and he was bored and looking for new challenges.

In the early 1970s, Hindman began coaching football in his free time, eventually taking over as head coach of Western Maryland College in 1977. By 1979, Hindman was again restless and looking for new business opportunities. One of the factors that prompted Hindman to start another business was a comment made by one of his students, who claimed that: "There are no opportunities left. You couldn't make a million dollars in America today."

"I was really perplexed at how in the hell he could come away from college believing that," recalls Hindman. "That really was a major, triggering, emotional event that caused me to start looking around for a new business." Joining him were Ed Kelley and Steve Spinelli. Kelley had worked for Hindman in the health care business and was an assistant coach at Western Maryland.

The fast oil change business quickly caught Hindman's attention. Research revealed that in the prior 10 years, the number of full-service gas stations had been reduced by almost half. Most had been replaced by self-service stations, which didn't do oil changes or other minor maintenance. Hindman's brother-in-law knew a man who operated a "Jiffy Lube" franchise (part of a chain of oil change centers headquartered in Utah). After several meetings with Jiffy Lube's owner in Utah, Hindman purchased the Jiffy Lube trademark and the rights to seven franchises.

Early Strategy

Jim Hindman describes Jiffy Lube's early progress after acquiring the first seven units in May 1979:

> We spent most of the first year putting together a formal policy and procedure manual for the franchises and developing a standard design for the service centers. E&W assisted us in the development of our franchise audit program and in setting up our accounting system. We also did a complete market study; we were trying to develop a system that would be responsive to the customer.

Jiffy Lube's early strategy is summarized in excerpts from a business plan prepared in the first year of operation (see *Exhibit A*).

Exhibit A
Business Plan

Over 100 Jiffy Lube Service centers will be in operation by the end of 1982. Expansion will be accomplished through:
1. Sales of new franchises.
2. Acquisition of existing service centers or small franchise chains which meet the company's specifications.

Franchising will be used as the primary means of expanding the Jiffy Lube network. Franchising will attract qualified managers to each individual center because of the ownership opportunity offered them. Franchising will also accelerate growth because it eliminates many of the managerial and financial requirements that would be necessary to develop and maintain a large network of company-operated centers.

Franchises will be positioned to create blocks of service centers in targeted cities. "Clustering" these centers in large blocks will build name recognition and make advertising cost-effective.

The overall image of Jiffy Lube is not yet at the point where all franchisees will be willing to pay up front the $250K–$300K required to purchase land and develop a new center. In many situations it may be necessary for Jiffy Lube to provide the real estate development financing.

Reaching 100 units by the end of 1982 will require the sale of 40 to 60 new franchises (depending on the number of units acquired from existing chains). The company may find it necessary to provide real estate financing for half, or 20 to 30, of these units. Based on a cost of $300K per unit, Jiffy Lube will need to obtain real estate financing of $6 million to $9 million to achieve the projected level of new franchise sales.

Ed Kelley sums up their early strategy:

> Our goal was to get to 100 units as quickly as possible. We were trying to reach a level of respectability. That would allow us to go out and do some of the things we needed to do, which was primarily to attract capital, and attract people to buy our franchises.

Expansion . . . and Losses

The Jiffy Lube network of service centers has grown rapidly from its original seven units (*Exhibit B*). The growth has come from the acquisition of four small chains of service centers (approximately 30 units in total), the acquisition of individual centers, and the sale of new franchises.

Jiffy Lube has successfully expanded its network of service centers, but it has incurred cumulative losses of more than $5 million since inception (*Exhibit C*). The entire network of service centers is projected to generate over $15 million in sales for fiscal 1983. However, as the franchisor, Jiffy Lube shares in only a portion of this total. Jiffy Lube's revenues are made up of the following:

- Royalty fees from franchisees (approximately 5 percent of each franchisee's gross sales).
- Rental income on property leased or subleased to franchisees.
- Initial fees from new franchises (approximately $20,000 per new service center).
- Sales by company-owned centers (however, as described in a later section, all company-owned centers were disposed of in fiscal 1983).

The majority of franchisees are individuals who operate one or two franchises.

Early Financing

Jiffy Lube was financed during its start-up and first several years of growth largely through Jim Hindman's personal resources. During the first three years of operation Hindman contributed over $1.5 million in the form of cash, assumptions of debt, and forgiveness of personal loans made to Jiffy Lube. Hindman also personally guaranteed certain transactions Jiffy Lube entered into, including lines of credit with banks, loans relating to the purchase or development of service centers, and real estate lease obligations.

Exhibit B
Jiffy Lube Service Center Network (includes statistics for both franchised and company-owned centers)

	Year Ending March 31			
	1980	*1981*	*1982*	*1983 (projected)*
Total gross sales for network (millions)	$1.5	$2.5	$7.1	$15.6
Total centers in operation:				
Franchised	7	19	40	96
Company owned	1	10	30	0

Exhibit C
Jiffy Lube, Inc., Operating Results

	Year Ended March 31 (in millions)			
	1980	*1981*	*1982*	*1983 (projected)*
Revenues	$ .2	$ 2.0	$ 3.5	$ 5.5
Net loss	$(0.4)	$(0.7)	$(1.4)	$(2.6)

See *Exhibit G* for projected 1983 financial statements.

Ernst & Whinney provided introductions to several banks and, at Hindman's request, participated in key meetings with the bankers.

Financing also was obtained through the sale of stock to directors, officers, employees, and other investors. The most significant sale was a private placement of $530K in preferred stock, the majority of which was sold to a small group of Midwest investors. In addition, Jiffy Lube used its common stock in several acquisitions, the largest being the purchase of Speedy Lube, a franchisor and operator of seven oil change centers.

In addition to the above, the need for real estate financing outlined in Jiffy Lube's business plan resulted in the company's most significant financing transaction to date, its 1981 agreement with Pennzoil.

Pennzoil Agreement

In December 1980, Hindman and Kelley attended a trade meeting put on by Pennzoil for its regional sales people and major distributors. Pennzoil was the oil supplier for the majority of Jiffy Lube centers and believed that the quick oil change business could become a new major distribution channel for oil products. Pennzoil saw the quick change industry as an opportunity to gain market share from Quaker State, the leading oil distributor in the eastern United States. Pennzoil's national sales manager told Hindman that the oil company planned on building 100 quick oil change centers in the East.

Hindman spent the night writing a proposal to convince Pennzoil to work with Jiffy Lube, rather than compete against it. In October 1981, the two companies signed an agreement (*Exhibit D*). For $1 million Jiffy Lube sold convertible preferred stock representing 29 percent of the company to Pennzoil. The agreement allowed Pennzoil to place four members on Jiffy Lube's board of directors. Pennzoil agreed to guarantee $6.3 million of real estate financing. Service centers developed with the financing guaranteed by Pennzoil were required to purchase the majority of their oil products from Pennzoil.

Pennzoil's financing allowed Jiffy Lube to initiate its aggressive expansion plan. The agreement also strengthened Jiffy Lube's financial credibility, and enabled it to increase its bank line of credit from $300K to over $1.2 million.

Exhibit D
Pennzoil Agreement

Pennzoil will purchase 10,000 shares of Jiffy Lube Convertible Preferred Stock for $1,000,000.

Cumulative dividends of $12 per preferred share are payable quarterly. Any deficiency must be paid or declared before setting aside any funds for any junior stock. These shares are redeemable by Jiffy Lube at any time after November 17, 1985, upon payment in cash of $110 per share plus an amount equal to all accrued dividends. They can be converted at the option of Pennzoil into common stock at a conversion price of $0.553 per share of each $1.00 Preferred Stock value.

Pennzoil shall have the option of electing the greater of 3 or 30 percent of the members of the board of directors of Jiffy Lube.

Jiffy Lube agrees to furnish Pennzoil certain financial information, including audited financial statements within 150 days after the close of each fiscal year, and unaudited statements within 45 days after the close of the first three fiscal quarters.

Jim Hindman, and then Jiffy Lube, shall have the right of first refusal should Pennzoil desire to sell any of its shares of Jiffy Lube stock. Pennzoil has the right of first refusal should Jim Hindman decide to sell any of his shares of Jiffy Lube stock.

Pennzoil agrees to issue a commitment to guarantee $6,250,000 worth of indebtedness to be incurred in connection with the financing of real estate site acquisition and construction cost in connection with the erection of Jiffy Lube centers. These units are to be built east of the Mississippi River and generally along the eastern seaboard.

Pennzoil agrees to guarantee an additional $1,000,000 in order to finance Jiffy Lube's purchase from Pennzoil of four units which Pennzoil has financed under its "Build to Suit" program.

Any units built using financing guaranteed by Pennzoil will be required to enter into a Lube Center Sales Agreement and to execute a Pennzoil Sign Agreement. Pennzoil will have the right to approve the selection of new sites to be financed under this agreement.

The relationship with Pennzoil was far from perfect, however. The two companies apparently had different objectives, which resulted in different strategies for Jiffy Lube's expansion. Jiffy Lube's business plan emphasized "clustering" and "franchising"; Pennzoil advocated "wide coverage" and "assured distribution channel" (company-owned service centers).

Jiffy Lube quickly discovered that Pennzoil's "right to approve the selection of new sites" as outlined in the agreement really meant that the oil company would select the new sites. Pennzoil used a "scattergun" approach to site selection. To create maximum exposure for the Pennzoil name, the oil company wanted service centers to be developed in as many markets as possible. "It seemed like we had one center in every major city from Miami to Boston," recalls Hindman.

In addition, Pennzoil did not believe that franchising should be relied on to provide all of the growth. Jim Hindman:

> As soon as we signed the agreement and walked out of their corporate offices, they took me by the hand and got us involved in the acquisition of service centers which we were to operate. This was despite the fact that our business plan specifically stated that we were going to go out and franchise.

Under Pennzoil's direction, Jiffy Lube acquired three chains of oil change centers (23 units in total) in late 1981 and early 1982. Hindman felt that Pennzoil's strategy ran counter to Jiffy Lube's own strategy and that "our business plan had been trashed. We were not capitalized to operate these centers, and we didn't have the management team." Why did Jiffy Lube go along? "They were supplying the money. I felt that we just got married to these guys; we've got to go along to get along."

The acquired stores quickly became a burden to Jiffy Lube. By the end of fiscal 1982, 30 of the 70 Jiffy Lube centers were owned and operated by the company. These required a large commitment of Jiffy Lube's managerial and financial resources and resulted in significant overhead costs. And sales at many of the new centers were not growing as fast as expected. "Every market where we had just one unit we were dying," recalls Hindman. Jiffy Lube lost $1.4 million in the year ended March 31, 1982, and was expected to lose $2.6 million for fiscal 1983.

By April 1982 Hindman made three major decisions:

1. All company-owned centers would be sold to franchisees.
2. Hindman was going to buy Pennzoil's Jiffy Lube stock.
3. Jiffy Lube would have to find other sources of financing to continue its growth plans.

Between May 1982 and February 1983, Jiffy Lube sold all of its company-owned centers to franchisees. In most cases, to expedite the sale, Jiffy Lube retained ownership of the service center's real estate and sold only the rights to operate the franchise. The real estate was then leased to the franchisee.

Hindman had also tried to resolve the conflict with Pennzoil:

> We tried to convince Pennzoil that (1) we had to cluster and (2) we had to have a different relationship. They were a giant and they took too long. They had 10 committees, and everything required 10 sign-offs. We needed to move fast to get back to our original strategy. Our only solution was to buy them out. We had to move carefully, though. We wanted to end up with a good relationship with Pennzoil. Even if they sold us the stock back, they were still our largest supplier, and had guaranteed over $5 million in real estate financing for us.
>
> From October 1982 to February 1983, I didn't put any money into the company even though we were hurting. I knew that if I started putting money in, it would just give Pennzoil an incentive to want to keep their stock. So we let our payables build up and let a large part of our staff go.

In February 1983, Pennzoil agreed to sell Hindman its stock for $435K. Jiffy Lube's worsening financial status during fiscal 1983 made it easier for Hindman to buy out Pennzoil: "They wanted out. Maybe they thought we were going bankrupt, and they could pick up the service centers after we went under."

The split with Pennzoil was reasonably amicable. Hindman:

> They recognized that the arrangement wasn't working. Pennzoil still believed in the concept of quick oil change centers, though. They believed that regardless of whether we survived or not, a large amount of oil was going to be sold through the quick change centers. Pennzoil kept their real estate guarantees in place.

Current Situation: 1983

Now, in 1983, Jiffy Lube feels that it is well positioned for the future, despite the past losses and current cash crises. Jiffy Lube has 96 units and is the largest franchisor of quick oil change centers in the United States. The company has reached a respectable size and feels it can take advantage of the name recognition being generated in some areas.

In addition, the company has gotten back to its original strategy of franchising, rather than operating service centers. The sale of all company-owned stores has cut costs and freed management to spend more time selecting and selling new franchise sites. The company expects to open at least 25 new franchises in the coming year. Jiffy Lube also expects improvements in the units it recently sold, as franchised centers have historically outperformed the company-owned centers. *Exhibit E* summarizes the financial characteristics of the typical franchise.

Fiscal 1983 is coming to a close, and projected financial statements have been prepared based on the first 11 months of operation (*Exhibits G, H, I,* and *J*). Jiffy Lube is now dependent on franchise royalties and rental income, because of the sale of the company stores. Management's analysis of future operations is also included (see *Exhibit F*).

Because of its dependence on franchise royalties, Jiffy Lube needs to quickly increase the number of franchises. Much of the growth to date has come through the acquisition of existing chains. Franchise agreements for new units are typically made with individuals for

Exhibit E
Financial Characteristics of Typical Jiffy Lube Franchise

Real estate requirements	15,000 square feet of land (building interior covers 2,500 square feet)
Cost of land and building	$300,000
Start-up costs (equipment, etc.)	$100,000
Monthly fixed costs	$8,000
Variable costs	57% of sales
Breakeven car count/day	28–35 cars
Typical months to breakeven	7–8 months

A "typical" mature unit (approximately two years old) will service between 60–70 cars per day, producing annual revenues of about $400,000–$500,000 and $75,000–$100,000 of pretax income.

Depending on whether the franchisee owns or leases the real estate, the monthly fixed costs include a charge for either:

1. Rent ($3,000–$4,000) paid to Jiffy Lube or to a 3rd party lessor, or
2. A similar charge for mortgage interest.

The 96 franchises currently in operation have the following real estate arrangements:

Real estate owned by Jiffy Lube and rented to the franchisee	20
Real estate owned by Jiffy Lube and subleased to the franchisee	4
Real estate owned or leased by the franchisee. (Approximately 30 of these were part of chains to which Jiffy Lube acquired the franchise rights. In these cases the franchisees already had their own real estate arrangements before Jiffy Lube became involved.)	72

Exhibit F
Management's Analysis of Future Operations

Management has made the following projections of future operations:

	Service Centers in Operation		
Fiscal Year	*At Year End*	*On Average during the Year*	*Total Gross Sales for Network*
1983	96	83	$16 million
	(based on 11 months of actual operations)		
1984	125	111	$28 million
1985	200	163	$49 million
1986	300	250	$75 million

In addition to projecting the future revenues, management has reviewed current expenditures and made the following prognosis for the upcoming year:

1. All expenses related to the company-operated centers have been eliminated.
2. Management believes that because of the recent restructuring, selling, general, and administrative expenses can be held to approximately $2.1 million during fiscal 1984. To achieve the growth projected for fiscal 1985 and 1986, it is anticipated that selling, general, and administrative (S, G, & A) expenses will have to increase to $2.6 million and $3.1 million respectively.
3. The only other significant expenses expected are interest on the outstanding debt and real estate lease commitments.

Exhibit G
Projected Statement of Operations and Balance Sheet

Projected Statement of Operations

	Year Ended March 31, 1983 (projected)
Revenues:	
Sales by company-operated units	$ 3,877,000
Initial franchise fees	685,000
Franchise royalties	542,000
Rental income from franchisees	276,000
Net gain on sales of company-operated units	40,000
Miscellaneous	41,000
Total revenues	5,461,000
Expenses:	
Company-operated units:	
Cost of products sold	1,300,000
Salaries and wages	1,090,000
Depreciation and amortization	180,000
Interest	258,000
Rent	308,000
Other	1,250,000
Total units expenses	4,386,000
Commissions	136,000
Selling, general, and administrative expenses	2,749,000
Interest expense	762,000
Total expenses	8,033,000
Net loss	$(2,572,000)

(Continued)

one or two service centers. Experience to date has proven that the sale and development of new franchises can be accelerated when Jiffy Lube offers to provide or arrange for real estate and construction financing.

Possible Alternatives

Hindman has already used the majority of his liquid assets in his prior contributions to Jiffy Lube and in the purchase of the Pennzoil stock. His major remaining assets are his interests in W. James Hindman, Ltd. (75 percent ownership), and several other nursing home partnerships (these might be worth as much as $3 million).

Hindman has considered disposing of his partnership interests to provide cash for Jiffy Lube. However, Hindman's tax basis in these (approximately $200K) is far less than the current market value, and he views the outright sale of them as a last resort because of the tax consequences. Several other investors in W. James Hindman, Ltd., are also shareholders in Jiffy Lube and seem willing to use their investments to raise cash for Jiffy Lube.

Another source Jiffy Lube has considered is a second private placement with existing shareholders. Specific terms haven't been discussed, and it is unknown how much these investors would be willing to contribute.

Exhibit G *(concluded)*

Projected Balance Sheet

	March 31, 1983 (projected)
Assets	
Current assets:	
Cash	$ 139,000
Accounts receivable	962,000
Prepaid expenses	23,000
Total current assets	1,124,000
Accounts receivable from future franchises	636,000
Property and equipment:	
Land	2,372,000
Buildings and improvements	3,913,000
Automobiles, furniture, and equipment	255,000
Construction in progress	682,000
	7,222,000
Less allowances for depreciation	203,000
	7,019,000
Intangible assets—trademarks, franchise rights, and deferred finance costs	815,000
Deferred franchise costs	199,000
Other assets	103,000
Total assets	$ 9,896,000
Liabilities and Stockholders' Equity	
Current liabilities:	
Accounts payable and accrued expenses	$ 1,252,000
Due to officers, directors, and employees	696,000
Notes payable	2,211,000
Current portion of long-term debt	86,000
Current portion of capital lease obligations	4,000
Total current liabilities	4,249,000
Long-term debt, less current portion	6,577,000
Capital lease obligations, less current portion	359,000
Deferred franchise fees	1,143,000
Stockholders' equity:	
Series A 12% cumulative convertible preferred stock	1,307,000
$12.00 cumulative convertible preferred stock	1,000,000
Common stock	166,000
Capital in excess of par value	880,000
Retained-earnings deficit	(5,238,000)
	(1,885,000)
Less cost of common stock held in treasury	(547,000)
Total stockholders' equity	(2,432,000)
Total liabilities and stockholders' equity	$ 9,896,000

Exhibit H
Long-Term Debt/Rent Commitments at March 1983

Description	*March 1983 Balance*	*Interest Rate*	*Payment Terms/ Comments*
Construction loans:			
NA mortgage	$5,372,000	16.5%	Monthly payments of approximately $75,000 are required in fiscal 1984. Requires increasing monthly payments for interest and maturity through February 1994. Guaranteed by Pennzoil.
Maryland National Bank	524,000	Prime	Monthly payments of approximately $7,000, varying based on the prime interest rate.
Notes relating to acquisitions of service center chains:			
Benchmark/Archeo	250,000	Prime + 1%	Due 6/85
Browns Quick Lube	117,000	13%	Due 2/87
Joe Wilkerson	117,000	13%	Due 2/87
Stock repurchase—John Lindholm	104,000	Prime	Annual payments of approximately $50,000.
Others	179,000	Vary from 12% to 18%	Mature at various times through 1987.
	$6,663,000		
Rent commitments:			
Fiscal 1984 commitments *payable* under capital and operating leases ($150K represents real estate subleased to franchisees; the remainder is office building, etc., included in S, G & A)	$ 230,000		
Rentals *receivable* in fiscal 1984 from franchises already in operation, land, buildings, and improvements rented to franchisees	$ 775,000		

Exhibit I
Notes Payable and Amounts Due to Officers, Directors, and Employees at March 1983

Description	*March 1983 Balance*	*Interest Rate*	*Payment Terms/Comments*
Notes payable:			
Bank lines of credit:			
Maryland National Bank	$ 499,000	Prime + 1%	Minimum interest rate of 12%. The notes become payable at various times between 6/83 and 3/84. Jiffy Lube has drawn the full amount of each line.
Savings Bank	500,000	Prime + 1%	
1st National	250,000	Prime + 1%	
Jiffy Lube International Partnership #1	675,000	Prime + ½%	Due on demand. Hindman owns 27% of partnership. Another 56% is owned by four individuals who are directors (or former directors) of Jiffy Lube.
Notes to four accounts payable vendors	287,000	0-10%	All due by 6/83.
	$2,211,000		
Due to officers, directors, and employees:			
Jim Hindman	$ 550,000	Prime + 1%	Due on demand.
Others	146,000	Majority are noninterest-bearing demand notes to J. Hindman.	
	$ 696,000		

Exhibit J
Ownership at March 1983

	Shares	*Percent*
Common stock:		
Jim Hindman, president/CEO	2,133,333	69%
Gilbert Campbell, director	285,710	9
Others (less than 5%)	675,775	22
	3,094,818	100%
Series A 12% cumulative preferred stock:		
Jim Hindman	7,255	66%
Others (less than 5%)	5,815	44
	13,070	100%
(Convertible at the option of the holders into approximately 1,568,000 shares of common stock.)		
$12.00 cumulative convertible preferred stock:		
Jim Hindman	10,000	100%
(Convertible at the option of the holders into approximately 1,808,000 shares of common stock.)		

The Deal: Valuation, Structure, and Negotiation

14

Always assume the deal will not close and keep several alternatives alive.

James Hindman
Founder, Chief Executive Officer, and Chairman
Jiffy Lube International

RESULTS EXPECTED

Upon completion of this chapter, you will have:

1. Determined methodologies used by venture capitalists and professional investors to estimate the value of a company.
2. Examined how equity proportions are allocated to investors.
3. Examined how deals are structured, including critical terms, conditions, and covenants.
4. Examined key aspects of negotiating and closing deals.
5. Characterized good versus bad deals and identified some of the sand traps entrepreneurs face in venture financing.
6. Analyzed an actual deal presented to an entrepreneur in the Bridge Capital Investors case.

THE ART AND CRAFT OF VALUATION

Entrepreneurial Value versus Corporate Finance Value[1]

Entrepreneurial finance differs from corporate finance in a number of dimensions. First the players and markets that are explored are different; corporate finance deals primarily with decisions confronting chief financial officers of publicly traded companies. Entrepreneurial finance deals primarily with decisions confronting the chief executive officer of private companies. The suppliers of capital to each are very different. Also, the nature of the contracts between suppliers and users of capital is very different. Finally, the typical projects, companies, industries, and stages of development are very different. Corporate finance deals with more mature situations than entrepreneurial finance; in the latter, the context of decision making is more often characterized by rapid change and great uncertainty.

Determinants of Value

The message here is simple. The criteria and methods applied in corporate finance to value companies traded publicly in the capital markets, when cavalierly applied to entrepreneurial companies, have severe limitations. The ingredients to the entrepreneurial valuation are cash, time, and risk. In Chapter 12 you determined the burn rate, OOC, and

[1] The following paragraph is adapted from "Entrepreneurial Finance—Course Introduction," by William A. Sahlman. HBS Note 9-288-004, Harvard Business School, 1988, p. 6. Copyright © 1988 by the President and Fellows of Harvard College.

Exhibit 14.1
Risk versus Rate of Return

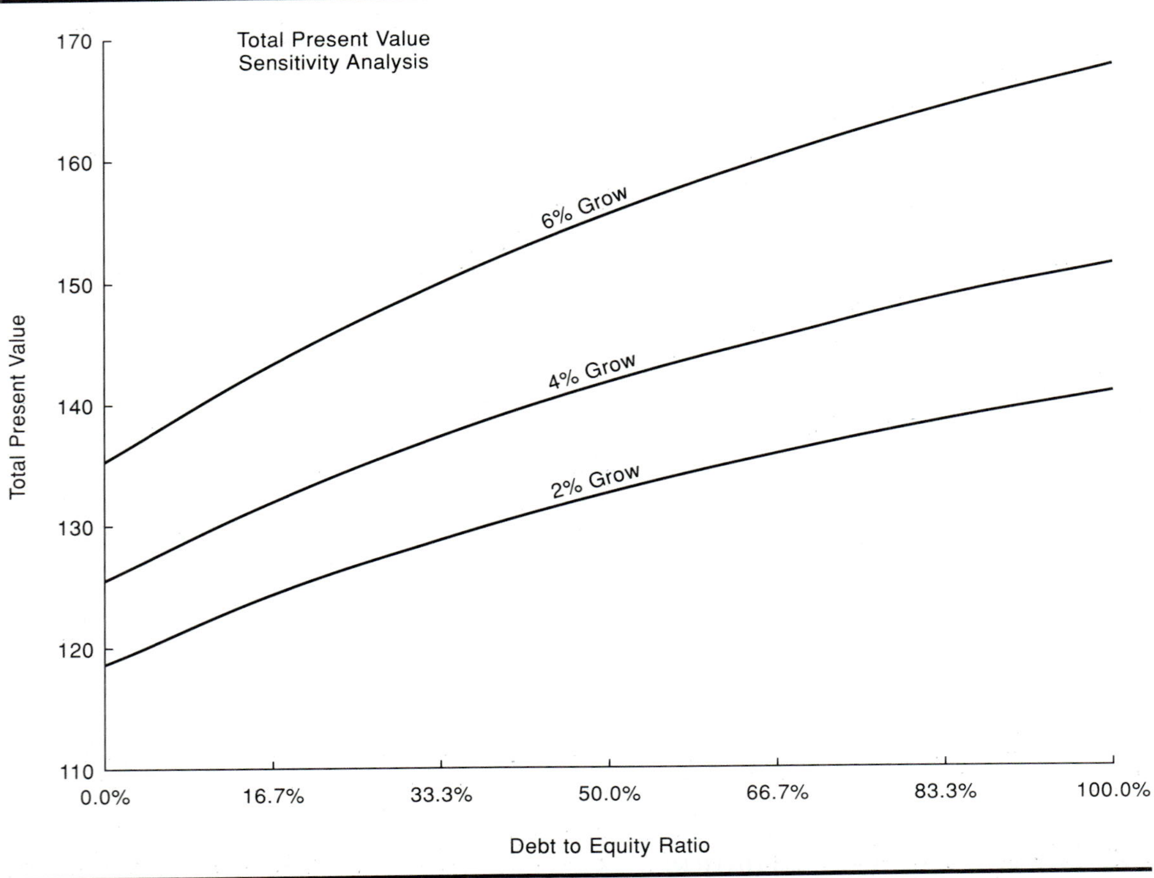

Source: "Note on Free Cash Flow Valuation Models" by William A Sahlman, 1987, page 13, Harvard Business School Press, Boston, MA 02163.

the TTC for your venture, so it is not hard to infer that the amount of cash available and the cash generated will play an important role in valuation. Similarly, if you recall *Exhibit 12.5*, "The Entrepreneur's Bargaining Power Based on Time to OOC," you'll remember that time also plays an influential role. Finally, risk or perception of risk contributes to the determination of value. The old adage "The greater the risk, the greater the reward" plays a considerable role in how investors size up the venture. A useful theoretical way of understanding how risk levels are perceived by the capital markets is shown in *Exhibit 14.1*. Consider for a moment that you are thinking about investing $1,000 and your options are to invest in a start-up company or in a mutual fund. Where would you expect the greater return? Why?

Long-Term Value Creation versus Quarterly Earnings

The core mission of the entrepreneur is to build the best company possible and, if possible, a great company. This is the single surest way of generating long-term value for all the stakeholders and society. Such a mission has quite different strategic imperatives than one aimed solely at maximizing quarterly earnings in order to attain the highest share price possible given price/earnings ratios at the time. More will be said about this in Chapter 18, "The Harvest and Beyond."

Psychological Factors Determining Value

Time after time companies are valued at preposterous multiples of any sane price/earnings or sales ratios. In the best years, for example, the 1992–93 bull market, the New York Stock Exchange Index was trading at nearly 20 times earnings; it sank to around 8 after the stock market crash of October 19, 1987. Even 12 to 15 would be considered good in many years. In contrast, consider a recent survey of the top one hundred public companies in Massachusetts. The stocks of many of these companies were being traded at 50 or more times earnings and several were at 95 to 100 times earnings and six to seven times sales!

Often what is behind extraordinarily high valuations is a psychological wave, a combination of euphoric enthusiasm for a fine company, exacerbated by greed and fear – of missing the run up. The same psychology can also drive prices to undreamed of heights in private companies. In the late 1960s, for instance, Xerox bought Scientific Data Systems, then at $100 million in sales and earning $10 million after taxes, for $1 billion: 10 times sales and 100 times earnings! Value is also in the eye of the beholder.

A Theoretical Perspective

Establishing Boundaries and Ranges, Rather than Calculating a Number. Valuation is much more than science, as can be seen from the examples just noted. As will be seen shortly, there are at least a dozen different ways of determining the value of a private company. A lot of assumptions and a lot of judgment calls are made in every valuation exercise. In one case, for example, the entrepreneur consulted 13 different experts to determine how much he should bid for the other half of a $10 million in sales company. The answers ranged from $1 million to $6 million. He subsequently acquired the other half for $3.5 million.

It can be a serious mistake, therefore, to approach the valuation task in hopes of arriving at a single number or even a quite narrow range. All you can realistically expect is a range of values with boundaries driven by the different methods and underlying assumptions for each. Within that range the buyer and the seller need to determine the comfort zone of each. At what point are you basically indifferent to buying and selling? Determining your point of indifference can be an invaluable aid in preparing you for negotiations to buy or sell.

Investor's Required Rate of Return (IRR)

Various investors will require a different rate of return (ROR) for investments in different stages of development and will expect holding periods of various lengths. For example, *Exhibit 14.2* summarizes, as ranges, the annual rates of return that venture capital investors seek on investments in firms by stage of development and how long they expect to hold these investments. Several factors underlie the required ROR on a venture capital investment, including premium for systemic risk, illiquidity, and value added. Of course, these can be expected to vary regionally and from time to time as market conditions change, because these investments are in what are decidedly imperfect capital market niches to begin with.

Exhibit 14.2
Rates of Return Sought by Venture Capital Investors

Stage	*Annual ROR%*	*Typical Expected Holding Period (years)*
Seed and start-up	50–100% or more	More than 10
First stage	40–60	5–10
Second stage	30–40	4–7
Expansion	20–30	3–5
Bridge and mezzanine	20–30	1–3
LBOs	30–50	3–5
Turnarounds	50+	3–5

Exhibit 14.3
Investor's Required Share of Ownership under Various ROR Objectives

Assumptions:
Amount of initial start-up investment = \$1 million
Holding period = 5 years
Required rate of return = 50%
Year 5 after-tax profit = \$1 million
Year 5 Price/earnings ratio = 15

Calculating the required share of ownership:

Price/Earnings Ratio	**Investor's Return Objective Percent/Year Compounded**			
	30%	*40%*	*50%*	*60%*
10 X	37%	54	76	106
15 X	25	36	51	70
20 X	19	27	38	52
25 X	15	22	30	42

Investor's Required Share of Ownership

The rate of return required by the investor determines the investor's required share of the ownership, as *Exhibit 14.3* illustrates. The future value of our \$1 million investment at 50 percent compounded is \$1 million $\times$ $(1.5)^5$ = \$1 million $\times$ 7.59 = 7.59 million. The future value of the company in Year 5 is profit after tax $\times$ price/earnings ratio = \$1 million $\times$ 15 = \$15 million. Thus, the share of ownership required in year five is:

$$\frac{\text{Future value of the investment}}{\text{Future value of the company}} = \frac{\$7.59 \text{ million}}{\$15.00 \text{ million}} = 51\%$$

As a final note, one can readily see that by changing any of the key variables, the results will change accordingly.

If the venture capitalists require the RORs mentioned earlier, the ownership they also require is determined as follows: In the start-up stage, 25–75 percent for investing all of the required funds; beyond the start-up stage, 10–40 percent, depending on the amount invested, maturity, and track record of the venture; in a seasoned venture in the later rounds of investment, 10–30 percent to supply the additional funds needed to sustain its growth.

Valuation Methods

The Venture Capital Method.[2] This method is appropriate for investments in a company with negative cash flows at the time of the investment, but which in a number of years is projected to generate significant earnings. As discussed in Chapter 13, venture capitalists are the most likely professional investors to partake in this type of an investment, thus the reference to the venture capital method. The steps involved in this method are as follows:

1. Estimate the company's *net income* in a number of years, at which time the investor plans on harvesting. This estimate will be based on the sales and margin projections presented by the entrepreneur in his or her business plan.
2. Determine the appropriate *price-to-earnings ratio*, or P/E ratio. The appropriate P/E ratio can be determined by studying current multiples for companies with similar economic characteristics.
3. Calculate the projected *terminal value* by multiplying net income and the P/E ratio.
4. The terminal value can then be discounted to find the *present value* of the investment. Venture capitalists use discount rates ranging from 35 percent to 80 percent, because of the risk involved in these types of investments.
5. To determine the investor's *required percentage of ownership*, based on their initial investment, the initial investment is divided by the estimated present value.

To summarize the above steps the following formula can be used:

$$\text{Final ownership required} = \frac{\text{Required future value (investment)}}{\text{Total terminal value}}$$

$$= \frac{(1 + \text{IRR})^{\text{years}}\ (\text{investment})}{\text{P/E ratio (terminal net income)}}$$

6. Finally, the number of shares and the share price must be calculated by using the following formula:

$$\text{New shares} = \frac{\text{Percentage of ownership required by investor}}{1 - (\text{Percentage ownership required by investor} \times \text{Old shares})}$$

By definition, the share price equals the price paid divided by the number of shares.

This method is commonly used by venture capitalists because they make equity investments in industries often requiring a large initial investment with significant projected revenues; in addition to the fact that in the negotiations, the percentage of ownership is a key issue.

The Fundamental Method. This method is simply the present value of the future earnings stream (see *Exhibit 14.4*).

The First Chicago Method.[3] Another alternative valuation method, developed at First Chicago Corporation's venture capital group, employs a lower discount rate, but applies it to an *expected* cash flow. That expected cash flow is the average of three possible scenarios,

[2] The venture capital method of valuation is adapted from William A Sahlman, "A Method for Valuing High-Risk, Long-Term Investments: The "Venture Capital Method," Note 9-288-006, Harvard Business School, 1988, pp. 2–4. Copyright © 1988 by the President and Fellows of Harvard College.

[3] This paragraph is adapted from Sahlman, "A Method for Valuing High-Risk, Long-Term Investments: The Venture Capital Method," p. 56.

Exhibit 14.4
Example of the Fundamental Method

HITECH, INC.

Year	*Percentage growth of revenue*	*Revenue (millions)*	*After-Tax Margin*	*After-Tax Profit (millions)*	*Present Value Factor*	*PV of Each Year's Earnings (millions)*
1	50%	$ 3.00	-0-	-0-	1.400	-0-
2	50	4.50	4.0%	$+0.18	1.960	$0.09
3	50	6.75	7.0	0.47	2.744	0.17
4	50	10.13	9.0	0.91	3.842	0.24
5	50	15.19	11.0	1.67	5.378	0.31
6	40	21.26	11.5	2.45	7.530	0.33
7	30	27.64	12.0	3.32	10.541	0.32
8	20	33.17	12.0	3.98	14.758	0.27
9	15	38.15	12.0	4.58	20.661	0.22
10	10	41.96	12.0	5.04	28.926	0.17
Total present value of earnings in the supergrowth period						$2.12
Residual future value of earnings stream				$ 63.00	28.926	2.18
Total present value of company						$4.30

Source: QED.

Exhibit 14.5
Example of the First Chicago Method

	Success	*Sideways survival*	*Failure*
1. Revenue growth rate (from base of $2 million)	60%	15%	0%
2. Revenue level after 3 years	$8.19 million	$3.04 million (liquidation)	$2 million
3. Revenue level after 5 years	$20.97 million (IPO)	$4.02 million	
4. Revenue level after 7 years		$5.32 million (acquisition)	
5. After-tax profit margin and earnings at liquidity	15% $3.15 million	7% $.37 million	
6. Price-earnings ratio at liquidity	17	7	
7. Value of company liquidity	$53.55 million	$2.61 million	$.69 million
8. Present value of company using discount rate of 40%	$9.96 million	$.25 million	$.25 million
9. Probability of each scenario	.4	.4	.2
10. Expected present value of the company under each scenario	$3.98 million	$.10 million	$.05 million
11. Expected present value of the company		$4.13 million	
12. Percentage ownership required to invest $2.5 million		60.5%	

with each scenario weighted according to its perceived probability. The equation to determine the investor's required final ownership is:

$$\text{Required final ownership} = \frac{\text{Future value of investment} - \text{Future value of non-IPO cash flow}}{\text{Probability (Success) (Forecast terminal value)}}$$

This formula[4] differs from the original basic venture capital formula in two ways: (1) the basic formula assumes that there are no cash flows between the investment and the harvest in Year 5. The future value of the immediate cash flows is subtracted from the future value of the investment because the difference between them is what must be made up for out of the terminal value; (2) the basic formula does not distinguish between the *forecast* terminal value and the *expected* terminal value. The traditional method uses the forecast terminal value, which is adjusted through the use of a high discount rate. The formula employs the expected value of the terminal value. *Exhibit 14.5* is an example of using this method.

[4] Ibid., pp. 58–59.

Exhibit 14.6
Example of a Three-Stage Financing

HI-POTENT, INC. (000)

	Year 0 1989	*Year 1* 1990	*Year 2* 1991	*Year 3* 1992	*Year 4* 1993	*Year 5* 1994
Revenues	500	1,250	2,500	5,000	8,000	12,800
Net income	(250)	(62)	250	750	1,360	2,500
Working capital @ 20%	100	250	500	1,000	1,600	2,560
Fixed assets @ 40%	200	500	1,000	2,000	3,200	5,120
Free cash flow	(550)	(512)	(500)	(750)	(440)	(380)
Cumulative external financial need	500	1,653	1,543	2,313	2,753	3,133
Equity issues	1,500	0	1,000	0	1,000	0
Equity outstanding	1,500	1,500	2,500	2,500	3,500	3,500
Cash balance	950	436	938	188	748	368
Assume: long-term IRR required each round by investors	50%	45%	40%	30%	25%	20%

Source: William A Sahlman, "A Method for Valuing High-Risk, Long-Term Investments," Harvard Business School Note 288-006, Exhibit 9, p. 45.

Ownership Dilution.[5] The previous example is unrealistic because in most cases, several rounds of investments are necessary to finance a high-potential venture. Take for instance the pricing worksheet presented in *Exhibit 14.6*, in which three financing rounds are expected. In addition to estimating the appropriate discount rate for the current round, the first-round venture capitalist must now estimate the discount rates that are most likely to be applied in the following rounds, which are projected for Years 2 and 4. Although a 50 percent rate is still appropriate for Year 0, it is estimated that investors in HI-Potent, Inc., will demand a 40 percent return in Year 2, and a 25 percent return in Year 4. The final ownership that each investor must be left with, given a terminal price/earnings ratio of 15, can be calculated using the basic valuation formula:

Round 1:

$$\frac{\text{Future value (Investment)}}{\text{Terminal value (Company)}} = \frac{1.50^5 \times \$1.5 \text{ million}}{15 \times \$2.5 \text{ million}} = 30.4\% \text{ ownership}$$

Round 2:

$$(1.40^3 \times 1 \text{ million}) \,/\, (15 \times \$2.5 \text{ million}) = 7.3\%$$

Round 3:

$$(1.25^1 \times \$1 \text{ million}) \,/\, (15 \times \$1.5 \text{ million}) = 3.3\%$$

Discounted Cash Flow. In a simple discounted cash flow method, three time periods are defined: (1) Years 1–5, (2) Years 6–10, and (3) Years 11–infinity.[6] The necessary operating assumptions for each period are initial sales, growth rates, EBIAT/sales, and (net fixed assets + operating working capital)/sales. While using this method, one should also note relationships and trade-offs. With these assumptions, the discount rate can be applied to the weighted average cost of capital (WACC).[7] Then the value for free cash flow (Years 1–10) is added to the terminal value. This terminal value is the growth perpetuity.

Other Rule-of-Thumb Valuation Methods. Several other valuation methods are also employed to estimate the value of a company. Many of these are based on similar most recent transactions of similar firms, established by a sale of the company, or a prior investment. Such

[5] Ibid., p. 24.

[6] Jeffry A Timmons, "Valuation Methods and Raising Capital," lecture, Harvard Business School, March 2, 1993.

[7] Note that it is WACC, not free cash flow, because of the tax factor.

comparables may look at several different multiples, such as earnings, free cash flow, revenue, EBIT, and book value. Knowledgeable investment bankers and venture capitalists make it their business to know the activity on the current market place for private capital and how deals are being priced. These methods are used most often to value an existing company, rather than a start-up, since there are so many more knowns about the company and its financial performance.

Tar Pits Facing Entrepreneurs

Inherent Conflicts Between Users and Suppliers of Capital.[8] There are several inherent conflicts between entrepreneurs or the users of capital and investors or the suppliers of capital. Whereas the entrepreneur wants to have as much time as possible for the financing, the investors want to supply capital just in time or to invest only when the company needs the money. Entrepreneurs should be thinking of raising money when they do not need it, while preserving the option to find another source of capital.

Similarly, users of capital want to raise as much money as possible, while the investors want to supply just enough capital in staged capital commitments. The investors, such as venture capitalists, use staged capital commitments to manage their risk exposure over 6- to 12-month increments of investing.

In the negotiations of a deal, the entrepreneur sometimes becomes attracted to a high valuation with the sentiment "My price, your terms." The investors will generally attempt to change this opinion, because after all it is their capital. The investors will thus focus on a low valuation, with the sentiment, "My price *and* my terms."

This tension applies not only to financial transactions but to the styles of the users versus the styles of the suppliers of capital. The users value their independence and treasure the flexibility their own venture has brought them. However, the investors are hoping to preserve their options as well. These options usually include both reinvesting and abandoning the venture.

These points of view also clash in the composition of the board of directors, where the entrepreneur seeks control and independence, and the investors want the right to control the board if the company does not perform as well as was expected. This sense of control is an emotional issue for most entrepreneurs, who want to be in charge of their own destiny. Prizing their autonomy and self-determination, many of these users of capital would agree with the passion Walt Disney conveyed in this statement: "I don't make movies to make money. I make *money* to make movies." The investors may believe in the passions of these users of capital, but they still want to protect themselves with first refusals, initial public offering rights, and various other exit options.

The long-term goals of the users and suppliers of capital may also be contradictory. The entrepreneurs may be content with the progress of their venture and happy with a single or double. It is their venture, their baby; if it is moderately successful, many entrepreneurs feel that they have accomplished a lot. Yet, the investors will not be quite as content with moderate success, but instead want their capital to produce extraordinary returns—they want a home run from the entrepreneur. Thus, the pressures put on the entrepreneur may seem unwarranted to the entrepreneur, yet necessary for the investor.

These strategies contradict each other when they are manifested in the management styles of the users and providers of capital. When the entrepreneur is willing to take a calculated risk or is working to minimize and avoid unnecessary risks, the investor has bet on the art of the exceptional and thus is willing to bet the farm everyday.

Entrepreneurs possess the ability to see opportunities and, more importantly, to seize those opportunities. They possess an instinctual desire to change, to adapt, or to decommit

[8] Jeffry A Timmons, "Deals and Deal Structuring," lecture, Harvard Business School February 23, 1993.

in order to seize new opportunities. Yet, the investors are looking for clear steady progress, as projected in the business plan, which leaves little room for surprises.

Finally, the final goals may differ. As the entrepreneur who continues to build his or her company may find operating a company enjoyable. At this point, the definition of success both personally and for the company may involve long-term company building, such that a sustainable institution is created. But the investors will want to cash out in two to five years, so that they can reinvest their capital in another venture.

Staged Capital Commitments[9]

Venture capitalists rarely, if ever, invest all the external capital that a company will require to accomplish its business plan; instead, they invest in companies at distinct stages in their development. As a result, each company begins life knowing that it has only enough capital to reach the next stage. By staging capital, the venture capitalists preserve the right to abandon a project whose prospects look dim. The right to abandon is essential because an entrepreneur will almost never stop investing in a failing project as long as others are providing capital.

Staging the capital also provides incentives to the entrepreneurial team. Capital is a scarce and expensive resource for individual ventures. Misuse of capital is very costly to venture capitalists but not necessarily to management. To encourage managers to conserve capital, venture capital firms apply strong sanctions if it is misused. These sanctions ordinarily take two basic forms. First, increased capital requirements invariably dilute management's equity share at an increasingly punitive rate. Second, the staged investment process enables venture capital firms to shut down operations completely. The credible threat to abandon a venture, even when the firm might be economically viable, is the key to the relationship between the entrepreneur and the venture capitalist. By denying capital, the venture capitalist also signals other capital suppliers that the company in question is a bad investment risk.

Short of denying the company capital, venture capitalists can discipline wayward managers by firing or demoting them. Other elements of the stock purchase agreement then come into play. For example, the company typically has the right to repurchase shares from departing managers, often at prices below market value, and vesting schedules limit the number of shares employees are entitled to if they leave prematurely. Finally, noncompete clauses can impose strong penalties on those who leave, particularly if their human capital is closely linked to the industry in which the venture is active.

Entrepreneurs accept the staged capital process because they usually have great confidence in their own abilities to meet targets. They understand that if they meet those goals, they will end up owning a significantly larger share of the company than if they had insisted on receiving all of the capital up front.

STRUCTURING THE DEAL

What Is a Deal?[10]

Deals are defined as economic agreements between at least two parties. In the context of entrepreneurial finance, most deals involve the allocation of cash flow streams (with respect to both amount and timing), the allocation of risk, and hence the allocation of value

[9] The following section was adapted from W A Sahlman, "Structure of Venture Capital Organizations," *Journal of Financial Economics* 27(1990), pp. 506–7. Reprinted with permission.

[10] The following paragraph was adapted from "Note on Financial Contracting: Deals," by William A. Sahlman. HBS Note 288-014, Harvard Business School, 1988, p. 1. Copyright © 1988 by the President and Fellows of Harvard College.

investment provisions also apply (vesting, employment agreements, etc.). The venture capital firm has the right of first refusal on all future rounds and other deals management may find.

– Deal B: Another venture capital firm will lead a $4 million investment. Management will invest nothing. The future gains are to be split 75 percent for the venture capital firm and 25 percent for management on a side-by-side basis. Until the venture achieves positive cash flow, this venture capital firm has the right of first refusal on future financing and deals management may find.

- A group of very talented money managers is given $40 million in capital to manage. The contract calls for the managers to receive 20 percent of the excess return on the portfolio over the Treasury bond return. The contract runs for five years. The managers cannot take out any of their share of the gains until the last day of the contract (except to pay taxes).

While reading and considering these deals, try to identify the underlying assumptions, motivations, and beliefs of the individuals proposing the deals. These are some questions that may help in identifying the bets of the players:

- What is the bet?
- Who is it for?
- Who is taking the risk? Who receives the rewards?
- Who should be making these bets?
- What will happen if the entrepreneurs exceed the venture capitalists' expectations? If they fall short?
- What are the incentives for the money managers? Consequences of their success or failure to perform?
- How will the money managers behave? What will be their investing strategy?

Some of the Lessons Learned: The Dog in the Suitcase

A few years ago a friend, living in a New York City high-rise, called in great distress. Her beloved barkless dog had died in the middle of the night. She wanted a decent burial for the dog, but since it was the dead of winter, she did not know what to do. It was suggested that she contact a pet cemetery on Long Island and take the dog there. It would be frozen until spring, at which time it would be properly buried. After all, such things are common in the Big Apple!

She gathered her courage, placed the dog in a suitcase, and headed down the elevator to the outdoors. As she struggled toward the nearest intersection a block away to catch a cab, a young man noticed her struggle and offered to help. Puffing by now, she sized up the young man quickly and accepted his offer to carry the bag. In no time, she turned to find the young man sprinting down the street with her suitcase. Now, imagine the look on the faces of the young man and his buddies when they opened the suitcase and discovered the loot!

The moral of this story is that raising capital can have all the surprises of a dog in the suitcase for the entrepreneur. The following tips may help to minimize many of these surprises:

1. Raise money when you do not need it.
2. Learn as much about the process and how to manage it as you can.
3. Know your relative bargaining position.
4. If all you get is money, you are not getting much.
5. Assume the deal will never close.

6. Always have a backup source of capital.
7. The legal and other experts can blow it—sweat the details yourself.
8. Users of capital are invariably at a disadvantage in dealing with suppliers of capital.
9. If you are out of cash when you seek to raise capital, suppliers of capital will eat your lunch.
10. Start-up entrepreneurs are raising capital for the first time; suppliers of capital have done it many times, everyday, for a living.

NEGOTIATIONS

Negotiations have been defined by many experts in a variety of ways, as the following examples demonstrate. Herb Cohen, the author of *You Can Negotiate Anything*, defines negotiations as "a field of knowledge and endeavor that focuses on gaining the favor of people from whom we want things"[14] or, similarly, as "the use of information and power to affect behavior within a 'web of tension.' "[15] Other experts in the field of negotiations, Roger Fisher and William Ury, assert that negotiations are a "back-and-forth communication designed to reach an agreement when you and the other side have some interests that are shared and others that are opposed."[16]

What Is Negotiable?

Far more is negotiable than entrepreneurs think.[17] For instance, a normal ploy of the attorney representing the investors is to insist, matter of factly, that "this is our boilerplate" and that the entrepreneur should take it or leave it. Yet, it is possible for an entrepreneur, in a number of cases, to negotiate and craft an agreement that is responsive to his or her needs and requirements.

During the negotiation, the investors will be evaluating the negotiating skills, intelligence, and maturity of the entrepreneur. The entrepreneur has precisely the same opportunity to size up his or her investor. If the investors see anything that shakes their confidence or trust, they probably will withdraw from the deal. Similarly, if an investor turns out to be arrogant, hot-tempered, unwilling to see the other side's needs and to compromise, and seems bent on getting every last ounce out of the deal by locking an entrepreneur into as many of the "burdensome clauses" as is possible, the entrepreneur might well want to withdraw.

Throughout the negotiations, entrepreneurs need to bear in mind that a successful negotiation is one in which both sides believe that they have made a fair deal. The best deals are those in which neither party wins and neither loses, and such deals are possible to negotiate. This approach is further articulated in the works of Roger Fisher and William Ury, who have focused neither on soft nor hard negotiation tactics, but rather on principled negotiation, a method developed at the Harvard Negotiation Project. This method asserts that the purpose of negotiations is "to decide issues on their merits rather than through a haggling process focused on what each side says it will and won't do. It suggests that you look for mutual gains wherever possible, and that where your interests conflict, you should insist that the result be based on some fair standards independent of the will

[14] Herb Cohen, *You Can Negotiate Anything* (New York: Bantam Books, 1982), p. 15.

[15] Ibid., p. 16.

[16] Roger Fisher and William Ury, *Getting to Yes* (New York: Penguin Books, 1991), p. xvii.

[17] See, for example, H M Hoffman and J Blakey, "You Can Negotiate with Venture Capitalists," *Harvard Business Review*, March–April 1987, pp. 16–24.

of either side."[18] They continue to describe principled negotiations in the following four points:

- *People*: Separate the people from the problem.
- *Interests*: Focus on interests, not positions.
- *Options*: Generate a variety of possibilities before deciding what to do.
- *Criteria*: Insist that the result be based on some objective standard.

Others have spoken of this method of principled negotiation, for example, Bob Woolf of Bob Woolf Associates, a Boston-based firm that represents everyone from Larry Bird to Gene Shalit. Woolf states simply that "you want the other side to be reasonable, not defensive—to work *with* you. You'll have a better chance of getting what you want. Treat someone the way that you would like to be treated, and you'll be successful most of the time."[19]

The Specific Issues Entrepreneurs Typically Face[20]

Whatever method you choose in your negotiations, chances are that the primary focus will be on how much the entrepreneur's equity is worth and how much is to be purchased by the investor's investment. Even so, numerous other issues involving legal and financial control of the company and the rights and obligations of various investors and the entrepreneur in various situations may be as important as valuation and ownership share. Not the least of which is the value behind money—such as contacts and helpful expertise, additional financing when and if required, and patience and interest in the long-term development of the company—that a particular investor can bring to the venture. The following are some of the most critical aspects of a deal that go beyond "just the money":

- Number, type, and mix of stocks (and perhaps of stock and debt) and various features that may go with them (such as puts) which affect the investor's rate of return.
- The amounts and timing of takedowns, conversions, and the like.
- Interest rate in debt or preferred shares.
- The number of seats, and who actually will represent investors, on the board of directors.
- Possible changes in the management team and in the composition of the board of directors.
- Registration rights for investor's stock (in case of a registered public offering).
- Right of first refusal granted to the investor on subsequent private or initial public stock offerings.
- Stock vesting schedule and agreements.
- Employment, noncompete, and proprietary rights agreements.
- The payment of legal, accounting, consulting, or other fees connected with putting the deal together.

Entrepreneurs may find some subtle but highly significant issues negotiated. If they, or their attorneys, are not familiar with these, they may be missed as just boilerplate when, in fact, they have crucial future implications for the ownership, control, and financing of the business. Some issues that can be proven burdensome for entrepreneurs are:

- *Cosale provision.* This is a provision by which investors can tender their shares of their stock before an initial public offering. It protects the first-round investors but can

[18] Fisher and Ury, p. xviii.

[19] Quoted in Paul B Brown and Michael S Hopkins, "How to Negotiate Practically Anything." Reprinted with permission. *Inc.* magazine, (February 1989) p. 35. Copyright © 1989 by Goldhirsh Group, Inc. 38 Commercial Wharf, Boston, MA 02110.

[20] Jeffry A Timmons, from Deals and Valuation lecture, Feb. 1993.

cause conflicts with investors in later rounds and can inhibit an entrepreneur's ability to cash out.

- *Ratchet antidilution protection.* This enables the lead investors to get for free additional common stock if subsequent shares are ever sold at a price lower than originally paid. This protection can create a "dog-in-the-manger syndrome," whereby first-round investors can prevent the company from raising additional necessary funds during a period of adversity for the company. While nice from the investors' perspective, it ignores the reality that in distress situations, the last money calls the shots on price and deal structure.
- *Washout financing.* This is a strategy of last resort, which wipes out all previously issued stock when existing preferred shareholders will not commit additional funds, thus diluting everyone.
- *Forced buyout.* Under this provision, if management does not find a buyer or cannot take the company public by a certain date, then the investors can proceed to find a buyer at terms they agree upon.
- *Demand registration rights.* Here, investors can demand at least one IPO in three to five years. In reality, such clauses are hard to invoke since the market for new public stock issues, rather than the terms of an agreement, ultimately governs the timing of such events.
- *Piggyback registration rights.* These grant to the investors (and to the entrepreneur, if he or she insists) rights to sell stock at the IPO. Since the underwriters usually make this decision, the clause normally is not enforceable.
- *Mandatory redemption of preferred stock.* Under mandatory redemption, the company is required to buy out investors if an IPO fails to occur. However, if a company is not attractive enough to go public, it will most likely be attractive enough to raise other cash for a buyout.
- *Key-person insurance.* This requires the company to obtain life insurance on key people. The named beneficiary of the insurance can be either the company or the preferred shareholders.

SAND TRAPS[21]

Strategic Circumference

Each fund-raising strategy sets in motion some actions and commitments by management that will eventually *scribe a strategic circumference* around the company in terms of its current and future financing choices. These future choices will permit varying degrees of freedom as a result of the previous actions. Those who fail to think through the consequences of a fund-raising strategy and the effect on their degrees of freedom fall into this trap.

While it is impossible to avoid strategic circumference completely, and while in some cases scribing a strategic circumference is clearly intentional, others may be unintended and, unfortunately, unexpected. For example, a company that plans to remain private or plans to maintain a 1.5 to 1.0 debt-to-equity ratio has intentionally created a strategic circumference.

Legal Circumference

Many have an aversion to becoming involved in the minutia of the legal or accounting details. Many believe that since they pay sizeable professional fees, their advisors should and will pay attention to the details.

[21] Copyright © 1990 by Jeffry A Timmons.

Legal documentation spells out the terms, conditions, responsibilities, and rights of the parties to a transaction. Since different sources have different ways of structuring deals, and since these legal and contractual details come at the *end* of the fund-raising process, an entrepreneur may arrive at a point of no return, facing some very onerous conditions and covenants that are not only very difficult to live with but also create tight limitations and constraints—legal circumference—on future choices that are potentially disastrous. Entrepreneurs cannot rely on attorneys and advisors to protect them in this vital matter.

To avoid this trap, entrepreneurs need to have a fundamental precept: "The devil is in the details." It is very risky for an entrepreneur *not* to carefully read final documents and very risky to use a lawyer who is *not* experienced and competent. It also is helpful to keep a few options alive and to conserve cash. This also can keep the other side of the table more conciliatory and flexible.

Attraction to Status and Size

It seems there is a cultural attraction to higher status and larger size, even when it comes to raising capital. Simply targeting the largest or the best-known or most-prestigious firms is a trap entrepreneurs often fall into.

These are often the most visible firms because of their size and investing activity and because they have been around a long time. Yet, as the venture capital industry has become more heterogeneous, as well as for other reasons, such firms may or may not be a good fit.

Take, for example, an entrepreneur who had a patented, innovative device that was ready for use by manufacturers of semiconductors. He was running out of cash from an earlier round of venture capital investment and needed more money for his device to be placed in test sites and then, presumably, into production. Although lab tests had been successful, his prior backers would not invest further since he was nearly two years behind the schedule in his business plan. For a year, he concentrated his efforts on many of the largest and most well-known firms and celebrities in the venture capital business, but to no avail. With the help of outside advice, he then decided to pursue an alternative fund-raising strategy. First, he listed those firms that were mostly likely prospects as customers for the device. Next, he sought to identify investors who already had investments in this potential customer base, because it was thought that these would be the most likely potential backers, since they would be the most informed about his technology, its potential value-added properties, and any potential competitive advantages the company could achieve. Less than a dozen venture capital firms were identified (from among a pool of over 700), and none had been contacted previously by this entrepreneur. In fact, many were virtually unknown to him, even though they were very active investors in the industry. In less than three months, offers were on the table from three of them and the financing was closed.

It is best to avoid this trap by looking for financial backers, whether debt or equity, who have intimate knowledge and first-hand experience with the technology, marketplace, and networks of expertise and intelligence in the competitive arena and to focus on the relevant know-how that would characterize a good match.

Unknown Territory

Venturing into unknown territory is another problem. Entrepreneurs need to know the terrain in sufficient detail, particularly the requirements and alternatives of various equity sources. If they do not, they may make critical strategic blunders and waste time.

For example, a venture that is not a "mainstream venture capital deal" may be overvalued and directed to investors who are not a realistic match, rather than being realistically valued and directed to small and more specialized funds, private investors, or potential strategic partners. The example is a real one. The founders went through nearly $100,000 of their own funds, strained their relationship to the limit, and nearly had to abandon the project.

Another illustration of a fund-raising strategy that was ill conceived and, effectively, a lottery—rather than a well-thought-out and focused search—is a company in the fiberoptics industry called Opti-Com.[22] Opti-Com was a spin-off as a start-up from a well-known public company in the industry. The management team was entirely credible but members were not considered superstars. The business plan suggested the company could achieve the magical $50 million in sales in five years, which the entrepreneurs were told by an outside advisor was the minimum size that venture capital investors would consider. The plan proposed to raise $750,000 for about 10 percent of the common stock of the company. Realistically, since the firm was a custom supplier for special applications, rather than a provider of a new technology advance with a significant proprietary advantage, a sales estimate of $10 million to $15 million in five years would have been more plausible. The same advisor urged that their business plan be submitted to 16 blue-ribbon mainstream venture capital firms in the Boston area. Four months later they had received 16 rejections. The entrepreneurs then were told to "go see the same quality of venture capital firms in New York." A year later, the founders were nearly out of money and had been unsuccessful in their search for capital. When redirected away from mainstream venture capitalists to a more suitable source, a small fund specifically created in Massachusetts—to provide risk capital for emerging firms that might not be robust enough to attract conventional venture capital but would be a welcome addition to the economic renewal of the state—the fit was right. Opti-Com raised the necessary capital, but at a valuation much more in line with the market for start-up deals.

Opportunity Cost

The lure of money often leads to a most common trap—the opportunity cost trap. After all, an entrepreneur's optimism leads him or her to the conclusion that with good people and products (or services), there has to be a lot of money out there with "our name on it!" In the process, entrepreneurs tend to grossly underestimate the real costs of getting the cash in the bank. Further, entrepreneurs also underestimate the real time, effort, and creative energy required. Indeed, the degree of effort fund-raising requires is perhaps the least appreciated aspect in obtaining capital. In both these cases, there are opportunity costs in expending these resources in a particular direction when both the clock and the calendar are moving.

For a start-up company, for instance, founders can devote nearly all of their available time for months to seeking out investors and telling their story. It may take six months or more to get a yes and up to a year for a no. In the meantime, a considerable amount of cash and human capital has been flowing out, rather than in, and this cash and capital might have been better spent elsewhere.

One such start-up began its search for venture capital in 1984. A year later the founders had exhausted $100,000 of their own seed money and had quit their jobs to devote full time to the effort. Yet, they were unsuccessful after approaching over 35 sources of capital. The opportunity costs are clear.

There are opportunity costs, too, in existing emerging companies. In terms of human capital, it is common for top management to devote as much as half of its time trying to raise a major amount of outside capital. Again, this requires a tremendous amount of emotional and physical energy as well, of which there is a finite amount to devote to the daily operating demands of the enterprise. The effect on near-term performance is invariably negative. In

[22] This is a fictional name for an actual company.

Lube collected a 6 percent royalty after the franchise had been operating for one year. Jiffy Lube also achieved some vertical integration in its business by acquiring its major supplier of automotive supplies, Heritage Merchandising.

Jiffy Lube's goals and strategy for the future are summarized in this excerpt from its business plan prepared in the late summer of 1985:

> The company's goal is to become the nation's dominant supplier of fast oil changes, with approximately 1,300 service centers by 1990. Its strategy for achieving this goal is to cluster centers in the 30 major metropolitan markets, thereby realizing economies of scale in operations, advertising, and the distribution of auto supplies. As the company becomes a nationwide firm and undertakes national advertising and promotional campaigns, it should be able to capture an increasingly large market share.

Jim Hindman summarized Jiffy Lube's plan with the following comparison: "We will become the 'McDonald's' of the quick oil change business." With approximately 270 service centers currently open in late 1985, these goals require the opening of over 1,000 new centers by 1990.

Construction Financing

Jiffy Lube's growth and the sale of the large area development rights increased the need for real estate financing. Purchasing real estate today for a new center generally costs between $100K and $275K, while construction typically costs an additional $225K. Even with more sophisticated investors, it is often necessary to provide real estate and construction financing to speed the development of the new franchises (approximately 50 percent of the franchisees have required assistance with their real estate and construction financing). Jiffy Lube funds real estate purchases and construction costs through two main sources.

"Permanent real estate financing" consists of mortgages on properties owned by the company and rented to franchisees. The mortgage payments are offset by rental income received from the franchisees. The other source is "construction financing," used to develop centers to be sold to franchisees. Upon sale of the centers, Jiffy Lube uses the proceeds to retire the debt, while the franchisees obtain their own permanent financing.

In 1983, Jiffy Lube signed an agreement with Old Court Savings & Loan to provide $16 million in construction financing for the purchase and development of 37 new centers (see *Exhibit B*). In addition, Old Court agreed to supply permanent financing to a partnership purchasing these centers from Jiffy Lube.

By May 1985, other projects were also in process, and the company had 60 new service centers in various stages of development. Jiffy Lube determined that its growth pace would require additional capital, and it researched the possibility of a private placement. Management hoped to raise up to $10 million and began working with Shearson Lehman Brothers in April 1985 to organize a deal.

May 1985: Crisis

In May 1985, as the morning headlines announced, the state declared Old Court Savings & Loan insolvent and appointed a conservator. The state had been investigating the S&L since early in the year, but there had been no warning that the situation was this serious and Jiffy Lube's management was caught off guard. All loan activity was halted, including the funding on Jiffy Lube's development projects. Before the collapse, partial financing (approximately $6.3 million) on only 25 of the 37 service centers had been provided.

Exhibit B
Old Court Savings & Loan Master Commitment

OLD COURT SAVINGS AND LOAN

May 24, 1983

Jiffy Lube, Inc.

RE: Various Sites—Jiffy Lube—Master Commitment

Gentlemen:

Please be advised that Old Court Savings & Loan, Inc., will provide construction funds, on various sites, for buildings to be built by your company. As your request draws on specific sites Old Court will issue individual commitments to you. The following is a general outline of our understanding of your request and Old Court's commitment to you:

BORROWER:	Jiffy Lube, Inc.
TOTAL COMMITMENT AMOUNT:	Not to exceed sixteen million ($16,000,000) dollars.
INTEREST RATE:	Two (2%) percent over Union Trust prime.
TERM OF EACH INDIVIDUAL LOAN:	Six (6) months after closing, with one six month extension.
LOAN FEES:	One and one-half (1½) points for first (1st) six (6) months, one (1%) percent additional if additional six month extension is used.

SPECIAL CONDITIONS:
1. Subject to satisfactory appraisal on each site.
2. Subject to satisfactory financial statements, to be updated from time to time.
3. Review and approval of all loan documents by Old Court's attorney.
4. Subject to availability of funds for loan.

Please indicate your acceptance of this general outline of terms and conditions by signing the bottom of this letter and returning it to me.

Sincerely,

David Falco
Executive Vice-President

Jiffy Lube quickly found that obtaining substitute financing from another lender was unlikely. Old Court had liens on the partially funded properties; because of the existing liens, no lenders were willing to fund the completion of these units.

As Jim Hindman describes:

> Whatever could go wrong, did go wrong. We had one bank lined up who seemed ready to continue the financing. On Monday, we went down to Old Court to show the bank the records detailing the loans, property liens, and so forth. During the weekend, the state had moved some of Old Court's records to another location, and lost all the Jiffy Lube documents! The bank we had lined up got nervous and said "see you later." (The records were eventually located.)

In late May, Shearson Lehman also backed away and progress on the private placement stopped. "It was a case of guilt by association," notes Hindman. The state's investigation had turned up allegations of improprieties at Old Court, including charges of falsified appraisals on certain loans. Although Jiffy Lube was not involved or implicated in any of the allegations, the shadow of Old Court appeared to scare off potential backers.

Another investment banker, Alex Brown & Sons, proposed raising $10 million in equity for a real estate partnership. The partnership would then obtain $40 million in debt from a savings and loan. The money would be used to replace Old Court and fund the development of Jiffy Lube centers.

Hindman was confident that the deal would go through, but Alex Brown's final review committee turned down the proposal. The Ernst & Whinney CSE phoned a contact at Alex Brown and determined that the deal had been rejected because of the Old Court situation. Old Court's key officers were under investigation for improper activities and "no one wanted to touch anything Old Court has been involved with."

Short-Term Solutions

Management decided immediately after the May 6 announcement of Old Court's collapse that Jiffy Lube could not wait for funding from the S&L to resume (particularly since this did not appear to be a likely possibility). Development of the service centers involved a series of events which could not be put on hold. Jiffy Lube would default on a number of real estate purchases if cash payments were not made by specified dates. Contractors were lined up, and individuals expecting to earn their livelihood operating franchises were depending on the service centers' being completed.

In addition, significant delays would damage the company's strategy. Jim Hindman:

> I really believe that the guy that gets his distribution system in place first is going to have the chance of being the "McDonald's" of the industry. Speed is the most critical element; we have to get out there before anyone else does. It's like Patton's rush across Europe in World War II; go until you run out of fuel. Once you take territory, you never have to give it back.
>
> There have been many times when we could have pulled back and been just a regional company. A couple of our directors have always pushed for us to slow down and concentrate more on short-term profits. Look at what is happening now, though. The small firms are being snapped up—like all of the local chains we've bought. And now Minit Lube has been acquired by Quaker State. If we maintain our growth, we will be the only independent company in the industry with the ability to go on national television, and the smaller chains will see their car counts go down.

Jiffy Lube decided to proceed with construction of the centers and to fund the costs itself out of its limited operating capital. Construction draws required approximately \$150K–\$200K per week, and Jiffy Lube's cash reserves were quickly used up. Hindman lent Jiffy Lube \$865K.

Franchisees also rallied behind Jiffy Lube. Jiffy Lube had recognized from the start that the franchisees were the parties responsible for actually selling and providing the quick lube service to consumers. They were the key link to the success or failure of Jiffy Lube. Acknowledging their importance, Jiffy Lube had worked hard to create a "partnership" relationship between it and the franchisees. Shortly after the crises began, franchisees combined with employees to make \$1.2 million in short-term unsecured loans to Jiffy Lube.

The cash drain continued, however, and by July Jiffy Lube was again out of cash. John Sasser, the CFO, walked into Hindman's office on a Wednesday and told him that they needed a million dollars by Monday if Jiffy Lube was to meet all its commitments. With no apparent sources of cash immediately available, Hindman consulted with his attorney, Jacques Schlenger, about the options available, including the potential benefits of filing Chapter 11.

Schlenger happened to represent two entrepreneurs who had recently cashed out of a business. Schlenger set up a 45-minute meeting between Hindman and one of the men on Thursday. By Monday, Jiffy Lube had a loan for the \$1 million it needed.

In the late summer of 1985, the state of Maryland determined that Old Court was not salvageable and placed the S&L in receivership for the purpose of liquidation. Ed Kelley, senior vice president, describes the decision Jiffy Lube had to make:

> We didn't know if we should join the bandwagon and threaten suits against Old Court and the state, or try diplomacy. We decided that the best approach was to be nice guys, and told them, "Look, we

understand you've got a problem and we want to cooperate with you to work it out. We want to pay you back everything that we've borrowed, but we can't do that until these units are completed."

In September, the receiver of Old Court agreed to allow the S&L to extend a $4 million line of credit to Jiffy Lube for temporary construction financing on the units Jiffy Lube could not complete on its own (16 units). The key points of this agreement are summarized in *Exhibit C*.

Decision-making Time: Long-Term Alternatives

By late summer, Shearson Lehman became convinced that Jiffy Lube was not going to suffer any more fallout as a result of the Old Court disaster, and again became interested in putting together a private placement. At the same time a number of major oil companies demonstrated an interest in Jiffy Lube.

The environment Jiffy Lube faced in late 1985 is summarized in the excerpts from the company's business plan: (see *Exhibit D*):

Since the Old Court collapse, Jiffy Lube has followed through on its business strategy by using a variety of the short-term financing sources available to it. The new agreement with

Exhibit C
Old Court Savings & Loan: Amended Master Commitment

On September 12, 1985, Jiffy Lube signed an agreement with Old Court Savings and Loan:

> *Amended Master Commitment for Real Estate Acquisition and Construction Financing on Sixteen (16) Jiffy Lube Locations*

The agreement is summarized in the excerpts below:

> *Financing shall consist of no more than sixteen (16) loans (collectively the "loan," and individually, the "individual loan"). Proceeds of each loan to be used to defray a portion of the acquisition and construction costs for the purchase of each individual property.*

Terms and conditions:

> Loan Amount. *On each individual loan the amount of the total advance shall be equal to eighty percent (80%) of the appraised fair market value of the real estate, including the improvements to be constructed thereon. In no event, however, shall the amount of the loan exceed the sum of four million dollars ($4,000,000).*
>
> Interest Rate. *A floating rate two percent (2%) over the prime rate charged by the Union Trust Company of Maryland, but in no event shall the rate be less than thirteen percent (13%) per annum.*
>
> Interest Payments. *Interest only is payable on the first (1st) day of each month following closing and upon payment in full of each individual loan.*
>
> Maturity. *Each individual loan shall mature on the first (1st) day of the seventh (7th) calendar month following closing. Borrower shall have the option to extend the maturity of each individual loan to the first (1st) day of the tenth (10th) calendar month following closing.*

Special Conditions:

> *This commitment letter supersedes the May 24, 1983, master commitment. Borrower releases and holds harmless the Bank for any claims arising out of the master agreement or any alleged defaults by the bank thereunder.*
>
> *All existing notes and mortgages will be modified to provide for payment in full on the first (1st) day of the seventh (7th) month following execution of this commitment letter. Borrower will have the right, upon payment of an extension fee equal to one (1%) percent of the loan amount, to extend the maturity date of the loans to first day of the thirteenth (13th) month following the date of the commitment.*
>
> *Bank's obligation to perform hereunder is expressly conditioned upon:*
>
> > *(i) the delivery by Borrower to Bank a letter from Shearson Lehman Brothers wherein Shearson agrees that it will use its best efforts to market not less than nine million dollars ($9,000,000) of subordinated notes with warrants of Jiffy Lube International, Inc., of which two and one-half million dollars ($2,500,000) will be paid to Bank within five days of Borrower's closing under its agreement with Shearson.*
> >
> > *(ii) the delivery by Borrower to Bank a letter from Reality Income Corporation (RIC) wherein RIC agrees that it will purchase eighteen (18) Jiffy Lube locations which are secured by mortgages to Bank.*
>
> (Note: Both letters referred to above were delivered to the bank at the time the agreement was signed.)

Exhibit D
Industry Trends and Current Developments

Fast oil change specialists currently perform approximately 3.5 percent of the 367 million oil changes estimated annually for automobiles and light trucks. The company believes the market share should grow rapidly due to the decline in the number of full-service gas stations. According to the 1985 National Petroleum News Factbook Annual Issue, the number of gas stations offering oil changes decreased to fewer than 137,000 in 1985 from 226,000 in 1973. A recent Pennzoil study concluded that quick oil change centers would become one of the major distribution channels for oil lubrication products by the early 1990s.

The company currently has approximately 270 service centers operating, and estimates that the other major fast oil change operators have the following numbers of centers:

Minit Lube	90
Grease Monkey	45
Rapid Oil Change	26
Kwik Change	19
McQuick Oilube	16
Lube Pit Stop	14

On August 1, 1985, Quaker State Oil Refining Corporation announced that it had signed a letter of intent to acquire Arctic Circle, Inc., for $35 million in stock. Arctic Circle, Inc., is the parent company of Minit Lube, and holds over 100 Arctic Circle restaurants in addition to the oil change centers.

Exhibit E
Debt Outstanding at September 30, 1985

Description	*September 30, 1985, Balance (000's)*	*Interest Rate*	*Payment Terms/Comments*
Financing for centers under construction:			
Old Court Savings & Loan	$ 6,300	Prime + 2%	See "Amended Master Commitment" (*Exhibit C*)
James McDonagh and Robert Vogel	1,000	11%	Due 8/86.
Jim Hindman	865	15%	Five notes, maturing between 9/85 and 1/86.
Other directors, employees, and franchisees	1,185	15%	Due 3/86.
	9,350		
Permanent real estate financing:			
INA Mortgage	5,250	16.5%	Requires increasing monthly payment through 2/94. Current payments are approximately $80,000.
Other mortgages	2,052	Prime + 1 to 2%	Monthly payments of approximately $40,000. All mature by 1993.
	7,302		
Funds borrowed to acquire companies or assets:			
Pennzoil	1,800	14.25%	Due 2/86.
Maryland National Bank	1,300	Prime + 1%	Borrowed under line of credit agreement and due on demand. Under an oral agreement with the bank, the loan can be paid over five years, beginning in 12/85, if necessary.
Others (included notes payable to selling shareholders of chains acquired, and debts assumed in acquisitions)	2,900	8%–18%	Mature over the next four years.
	6,000		
Total at September 30, 1985	$22,652		

Exhibit F
Jiffy Lube, Inc., Projected Operations

	1986	*1987*	*1988*	*1989*	*1990*	*1991*
Revenue:						
Sales by company-operated units	$ 7,683	$10,169	$14,218	$18,840	$ 22,210	$ 23,954
Initial franchise fees	3,630	4,527	4,735	5,048	5,215	2,706
Area development fees	2,000	500				
Franchise royalties	5,280	9,946	16,062	23,405	32,162	41,014
Sales of automotive products	8,880	15,789	24,489	34,623	46,169	56,561
Rental income from franchisees	2,328	3,010	3,701	4,440	5,137	5,442
Total revenues	29,801	43,941	63,205	86,356	110,893	129,677
Costs and expenses:						
Company-operated units	6,377	8,440	11,801	15,637	18,434	19,882
Cost of sales of automotive products	7,548	13,420	20,816	29,429	39,243	48,077
Expenses related to rental properties, including interest	1,711	1,546	1,502	1,433	1,341	1,332
Selling, general, and administrative expenses	8,880	14,399	20,341	26,163	31,694	35,221
Total costs and expenses	24,516	37,805	54,460	72,662	90,712	104,512
Income from operations	5,285	6,136	8,745	13,694	20,181	25,165
Other income (expense):						
Interest expense	(2,798)	(3,423)	(2,650)	(2,827)	(2,883)	(2,259)
Other	315	324	97	68	439	1,286
Income before income taxes	2,802	3,037	6,192	10,935	17,737	24,192
Income tax expense	951	1,518	3,096	5,465	8,868	12,096
Net income	$ 1,851	$ 1,518	$ 3,096	$ 5,467	$ 8,868	$ 12,096
Service centers in operation:						
Franchised	361	578	805	1,047	1,297	1,427
Company-operated	23	31	39	47	47	47

These projections were prepared assuming that Jiffy Lube obtains $10 million in debt financing.

Old Court, though, requires Jiffy Lube to quickly pay off $2.5 million of the $6.3 million construction loans outstanding. Jiffy Lube has committed to paying this amount with the proceeds from the private placement proposed by Shearson or through other means.

Personal loans and other short-term borrowings are also coming due (see *Exhibit E* for a summary of the outstanding debt). And, additional financing is needed if the company is to execute its long-term growth plan. Jiffy Lube, with the assistance of Ernst & Whinney, prepared a projection of its operations for fiscal 1986 and for the five years following. A summary of the projections is included in *Exhibit F*.

NOVEMBER 1985 ALTERNATIVES

Bridge Capital Investors

As the Old Court episode cooled down toward the end of August, Shearson Lehman again proposed putting together a private placement. Shearson worked through the rest of August and September searching for parties interested in a $10 million private debt placement. By early October 1985, Shearson had identified four interested parties, and key management from Jiffy Lube flew to New York to meet with each of them.

One of the four, Bridge Capital Investors, expressed an immediate interest in Jiffy Lube. Bridge Capital Investors, a mezzanine capital partnership, proposed providing financing through the purchase of $10 million in subordinated notes with warrants attached to purchase 10 percent of Jiffy Lube. The proposed terms are summarized in *Exhibit G*.

Exhibit G
Bridge Capital Investors: Proposed Private Placement

12% Senior Subordinated Notes Due 1992 with Warrants

NOTES

Amount	$10,000,000
Issue price	97.254%
Maturity	December 15, 1992 (7 years)
Interest rate	12%, payable quarterly

Mandatory sinking fund

Beginning during the fourth year, the Company will make eight equal semiannual payments of $1,250,000.

In the event of an initial public offering of $20 million or more, the Company shall prepay at par 50% of the Notes from the proceeds of the offering.

Subordination

The notes will be subordinate in payment of principal and interest to senior debt, and senior to all subsequent subordinated debt.

WARRANTS

Amount

549,218 warrants to purchase 10% of the fully diluted, pro forma shares of common stock. After six months there will be an adjustment for any new shares or warrants issued to maintain 10%.

Issue price	$0.50 per warrant
Exercise price	$6 per share
Term	Seven years

Put Provision

If during five years from issuance, the Company's common stock has not traded publicly at levels set forth in the table that follows, the Purchasers may put the warrants and/or underlying stock to the Company. The price will be determined by the calculation of the amount necessary to result in a 30% per annum internal rate of return to the Purchasers on that proportion of warrants not previously sold, taking into account all interest premium and principal repayment on the proportionately related notes.

If (i) the Company completes one or more public offerings of common stock with aggregate proceeds to the Company of at least $15 million and (ii) the average closing price for 60 consecutive trading days exceeds:

6 months ending 6/88—$17.50
6 months ending 12/88—$20.00
6 months ending 6/89—$25.00
6 months ending 12/89—$30.00
6 months ending 6/90—$35.00
6 months ending 12/90—$40.00

then the put provision will expire.

In the event the Company is unable to pay the amount due, the Purchasers have the right to nominate a majority of the Board of Directors.

Merger/Sale

If prior to December 21, 1987, the Company is sold or merged into another company the Purchasers shall be entitled to not less than $15 per warrant share.

BOARD OF DIRECTORS

Donald P. Remey to be elected as Director.

Don Remey, general partner, described Bridge Capital as a "$50 million partnership financed by pension funds and insurance companies. We specialize in financing growing companies, using debt with equity kickers." Remey also indicated that "unlike venture capital, we do not seek control or a major share of ownership." The personal chemistry between Hindman and Remey was positive from the first meeting on.

Quaker State

The president of Quaker State called in August and said, "Look, we just bought Minit Lube and I think we should talk." After some preliminary meetings, Jiffy Lube agreed to let Quaker State perform "due diligence" on the company as a prelude to a possible purchase offer. In September, Quaker State made an offer to purchase Jiffy Lube. The purchase price is contingent on future earnings as described in the purchase offer summarized in *Exhibit H*.

Details of Quaker State's Arctic Circle/Minit Lube acquisition are now available (these were outlined in the S-14 filing related to the transaction and in the company's September 30, 1985, 10-Q). The shareholders of Arctic Circle received 1,425,000 shares of Quaker State common stock; the stock was trading at $24⅞ at the time of the transaction; Arctic Circle had sales and net income of $31 million and $1.4 million, respectively, for the year ended March 31, 1985. Minit Lube accounted for 47 percent and 57 percent of the sales and net income, respectively.

Financial details of debt and operation are in *Exhibits I* and *J*; Jiffy Lube's master agreement for real estate and construction is in *Exhibit K*.

Pennzoil

Jiffy Lube had maintained a good relationship with Pennzoil despite Hindman's repurchase of the oil company's investment. Pennzoil was Jiffy Lube's largest supplier of oil products, and it had arranged financing for the development and acquisition of some Jiffy Lube centers. Jiffy Lube was a major channel of distribution, and Pennzoil had much to lose if Jiffy Lube was acquired by another oil company.

Pennzoil told Hindman: "We don't think we should buy you. You don't want to be owned by a large oil company. Your biggest need is for real estate financing. Let's cut a deal whereby we can arrange a financing vehicle that will allow you to grow. With enough money for real estate development you can attract equity on your own." The two parties agreed to continue to discuss this possibility.

Other Options

In the summer, Ashland Oil (the makers of Valvoline) contacted Jiffy Lube to see if the two companies had any interest in each other (e.g., investment, joint venture, purchase). A team of Ashland executives and attorneys came out to do their own due diligence on Jiffy Lube, but the talks have not yet moved beyond the conceptual stage.

Exxon also expressed an interest because of surplus properties it was holding. No serious discussions have been held.

Working for Amoco, Boston Consulting Group had tried to put together a deal whereby Amoco would acquire both Jiffy Lube and Minit Lube. Now, after Quaker State's purchase of Minit Lube, Boston Consulting was working on a proposal for Amoco to purchase Jiffy Lube. No serious discussions have been held yet.

Exhibit H
Quaker State Purchase Offer

PURCHASE PRICE

Quaker State will purchase the outstanding shares of Jiffy Lube for $13 per share, contingent on Jiffy Lube's meeting the earnings requirements detailed below. The total potential purchase price is as follows:

Total shares (shares outstanding, warrants, and options)	4,144,681
Purchase price per share	× $13
Total	$53,880,853

$5 million will be paid in cash at closing, the remainder is payable June 30, 1989, based on Jiffy Lube's net income for the three years ending March 31, 1989 (in aggregate):

Aggregate Net Income for 3 Years Ending March 31, 1989	**Purchase Price** *Per Share*	*Total*
Exceeding $10 million	$13.0	$53,880,853
8	10.4	43,104,682
6	7.8	32,328,512
4	5.2	21,552,341
2	2.6	10,776,171
$2 million or less	1.2	5,000,000

An additional $25 million will be paid to management as bonuses based on Jiffy Lube's net income for the five years ending March 31, 1991 (in aggregate):

Aggregate Net Income for 5 Years Ending March 31, 1991	*Total Bonus*
Exceeding $25 million	$25 million
20	20
15	15
10	10
5	5
$5 million or less	0

TRANSACTIONS PRIOR TO CLOSE OF SALE

Upon signing of a contract of sales, Quaker State will loan Jiffy Lube $10 million. If negotiations break down or are stopped for antitrust reasons, Jiffy Lube will repay the debt one year after the formal break off of negotiations.

Jiffy Lube management will be independent of Quaker State from signing until closing except that no new stock, warrants, or options shall be issued until the deal is closed, canceled, or one year passes.

ORGANIZATION AND CONTINUING OPERATIONS

Jiffy Lube will operate as a separate subsidiary, reporting directly to the President or CEO of Quaker State. Jiffy Lube will have a separate board composed of Jiffy Lube and Quaker State management.

The name "Jiffy Lube" shall be maintained on all units in the system.

In any market where Jiffy Lube has sold the exclusive area rights or where Jiffy Lube units and Minit Lube units have conflicting franchise or territorial rights, the Minit Lube system must be kept separate until an agreement is reached between the Jiffy Lube and Minit Lube franchises.

REAL ESTATE FINANCING

Quaker State commits to provide at least $50 million of real estate financing to Jiffy Lube per year for the next four (4) years at competitive rates. Such debt will be used to build quick lubrication centers, all of which will, as a condition of the lease, use at least 80 percent of their motor oil from Quaker State.

INA debt guaranteed by Pennzoil is to be repaid or assumed.

Exhibit I
Consolidated Balance Sheet

	March 31	
	1985	*1984*
Assets		
Current assets:		
Cash	$ 1,476,889	$ 510,282
Accounts receivable, less allowance of $164,800 in 1985 and $47,000 in 1984	1,933,576	1,181,396
Current portion of fees receivable from franchises in development	1,311,000	143,500
Current portion of loans and notes receivable and net investment in direct financing leases	1,215,825	628,824
Current portion of loans and notes receivable from related parties	411,221	219,177
Inventory	985,554	467,351
Real estate held for resale	6,510,781	1,516,492
Prepaid expenses	122,178	181,449
Total current assets	13,967,024	4,848,471
Fees receivable from franchises in development	1,232,500	975,000
Loans and notes receivable, less current portion	898,805	642,876
Loans and notes receivable from related parties, less current portion		261,000
Net investment in direct financing leases	1,006,057	
Investments in and advances to affiliates	306,204	
Property and equipment:		
Land	2,854,344	2,371,679
Buildings and improvements	6,868,768	3,998,741
Automobiles, furniture, and equipment	1,205,801	335,600
	10,928,913	6,706,020
Less allowances for depreciation	761,455	433,686
Intangible assets, less accumulated amortization:		
Franchise rights	5,246,583	461,918
Other	913,628	549,185
	6,160,211	1,011,103
Deferred franchise costs	335,050	144,780
Other assets	206,870	23,374
Total assets	$34,280,179	$14,178,938
Liabilities and Stockholders' Equity		
Current liabilities:		
Accounts payable and accrued expenses	$ 5,129,510	$ 1,387,460
Notes payable	1,679,470	300,000
Construction advances for real estate held for resale	5,936,682	1,506,015
Current portion of long-term debt and capital lease obligations	864,312	165,506
Total current liabilities	13,609,974	3,358,981
Long-term debt, less current portion	10,196,905	5,639,701
Capital lease obligations, less current portion	2,341,217	417,353
Deferred franchise fees	3,595,250	1,302,500
Minority interest	36,498	
Stockholders' equity:		
Common stock, par value $0.05:		
Authorized—5,000,000 shares		
Issued—3,499,521 shares in 1985		
—3,243,996 shares in 1984	174,974	162,198
Capital in excess of par value	9,648,965	8,875,764
Retained-earnings deficit	(4,427,524)	(5,030,730)
Less: Cost of common stock held in treasury—22,808 shares	546,829	546,829
Due from officers for purchase of common stock	349,251	
Total stockholders' equity	4,500,335	3,460,403
Total liabilities and stockholders' equity	$34,280,179	$14,178,938

Exhibit J
Consolidated Statement of Operations

	Year Ended March 31	
	1985	*1984*
Revenue:		
Sales by company-operated units	$ 2,037,325	$ 80,118
Initial franchise fees	1,177,875	672,500
Area development fees	2,208,125	1,219,500
Franchise royalties	2,141,600	1,294,617
Sales of automotive products	5,811,421	1,839,270
Rental income from franchisees	1,108,852	909,597
Total revenues	14,485,198	6,015,602
Costs and expenses:		
Company-operated units	1,714,645	59,585
Cost of sales of automotive production	4,985,386	1,779,658
Costs and expenses related to rental properties, including interest of $966,894 in 1985 and $928,974 in 1984	1,413,794	1,250,485
Selling, general, and administrative expenses	5,908,195	2,821,181
Total costs and expenses	14,022,020	5,910,909
Income (loss) from operations	463,178	104,693
Other income (expense):		
Other income	339,663	203,810
Interest expense	(212,702)	(304,062)
Minority interest in loss of subsidiary	13,067	
Income (loss) before income taxes	603,206	4,441
Income tax expense	301,603	
Income (loss) before disposal of partnership interests and extraordinary item	301,603	4,441
Income from operations and disposition of partnership interests, net of tax of $115,906		190,933
Income (loss) before extraordinary item	301,603	195,374
Extraordinary reduction of income tax expense arising from the utilization of prior year's net operating losses	301,603	115,906
Net income (loss)	$ 603,206	$ 311,280

Opportunities or "Vultures"?

In Ed Kelley's words, Jiffy Lube is in the middle of a "feeding frenzy." Management has little time to do anything other than contend with the parties interested in arranging a deal with the company.

Jiffy Lube is an enigma; it is the largest quick lube franchisor in the United States but is continually fighting for survival. Hindman feels that the oil companies, especially Quaker State, are "playing hardball" because they don't expect Jiffy Lube to last much longer on its own. Sometimes it seems like Jiffy Lube is surrounded by vultures waiting to pick up the pieces.

Exhibit K
Old Court Savings & Loan: Amended Master Commitment

On September 12, 1985, Jiffy Lube signed an agreement with Old Court Savings and Loan:

Amended Master Commitment for Real Estate Acquisition and Construction Financing on Sixteen (16) Jiffy Lube Locations

The agreement is summarized in the excerpts below:

Financing shall consist of no more than sixteen (16) loans (collectively the "Loan," and individually, the "Individual Loan."). Proceeds of each loan to be used to defray a portion of the acquisition and construction costs for the purchase of each individual property.

Terms and conditions:

Loan Amount. *On each individual Loan the amount of the total advance shall be equal to eighty percent (80%) of the appraised fair market value of the real estate, including the improvements to be constructed thereon. In no event, however, shall the amount of the loan exceed the sum of Four Million Dollars ($4,000,000).*

Interest Rate. *A floating rate two percent (2%) over the prime rate charged by the Union Trust Company of Maryland, but in no event shall the rate be less than thirteen percent (13%) per annum.*

Interest Payments. *Interest only is payable on the first (1st) day of each month following closing and upon payment in full of each Individual Loan.*

Maturity. *Each Individual Loan shall mature on the first (1st) day of the seventh (7th) calendar month following closing. Borrower shall have the option to extend the maturity of each individual loan to the first (1st) day of the tenth (10th) calendar month following closing.*

Special Conditions:

This commitment letter supersedes the May 24, 1983, Master Commitment. Borrower releases and holds harmless the Bank for any claims arising out of the Master agreement or any alleged defaults by the bank thereunder.

All existing notes and mortgages will be modified to provide for payment in full on the first (1st) day of the seventh (7th) month following execution of this commitment letter. Borrower will have the right, upon payment of an extension fee equal to one (1%) percent of the loan amount, to extend the maturity date of the loans to first day of the thirteenth (13th) month following the date of the commitment.

Bank's obligation to perform hereunder is expressly conditioned upon:

(i) the delivery by Borrower to Bank a letter from Shearson Lehman Brothers wherein Shearson agrees that it will use its best efforts to market not less than Nine Million Dollars ($9,000,000) of subordinated notes with warrants of Jiffy Lube International, Inc., of which Two and One-half Million Dollars ($2,500,000) will be paid to Bank within five days of Borrower's closing under its agreement with Shearson.

(ii) the delivery by Borrower to Bank a letter from Reality Income Corporation (RIC) wherein RIC agrees that it will purchase eighteen (18) Jiffy Lube locations which are secured by mortgages to Bank.

(Note: Both letters referred to above were delivered to the bank at the time the agreement was signed.)

Obtaining Debt Capital

15

Leveraging a company is like driving your car with a sharp stick pointed at your heart through the steering wheel. As long as the road is smooth it works fine. But hit one bump in the road and you may be dead.

Warren Buffet

RESULTS EXPECTED

The 1990s ushered in a new era in credit availability—or lack thereof—for emerging companies. Many old rules disappeared and a newer, harsher banking climate has evolved. This chapter is aimed at preparing you to cope better with the new realities in the debt capital markets. Upon completion of this chapter, you will have:

1. Identified sources of debt and how to access them in the 1990s capital markets.
2. Examined the lender's perspective and criteria in making loans, how to prepare a loan proposal, and how to negotiate a loan.
3. Gained a knowledge to help you in managing and orchestrating the acquisition of debt capital.
4. Determined how lenders estimate the debt capacity of a company.
5. Identified some tar pits entrepreneurs need to avoid in considering debt.
6. Analyzed a case involving the purchase of a small company and the use of banking financing by Michigan Lighting, Inc.

THE 1990s: THE NEW CREDIT ENVIRONMENT

Few entrepreneurs and bankers can recall such sudden crisis as the major, nationwide credit crunch which occurred following the savings and loan crisis of the late 1980s. In a paniclike reaction, bank regulators sent a series of shock waves through the capital markets resulting in not just stricter lending polices but—for tens of thousands of younger companies—a shut-down of bank credit. In a matter of weeks and months after mid-1989, banks simply stopped making loans. Policy makers began to lower the Federal discount rate in hopes of resuscitating the economy, but the real problem was the lending institution. Bruised and bloodied by the savings and loan fiasco and its aftermath, they simply curtailed their lending and began to regroup.

To make matters worse, in mid-1990, the regulators began to sternly warn banks against making loans that could be described as highly leveraged transactions (HLTs). Deals greater than $20 million should not have a debt to equity ratio greater than one. The effect on business transactions, such as new investments in companies where the use of debt was common, was catastrophic. For example, the valuations (i.e., selling prices) of cable television, radio, and television properties plummeted from 11 to 13 times cash flow to as low as 6 to 8 in less than a year. Lenders would not provide debt capital at prices higher than this. Worse yet, few, if any, loans were made; nearly all transactions were on hold, thereby creating enormous uncertainty and fear, and a downward spiral of prices and activity. Even at this writing, the nation is still suffering from these policies and the havoc they caused and has yet to recover.

New Rules in a New Game

One consequence for entrepreneurs is a new set of rules in the new credit game of the 1990s. For one thing, personal guarantees are back. Even the most creditworthy companies with enviable records for timely repayment of interest and principal have been asked to provide personal guarantees by the owners. As if this were not onerous enough, there has been a second phenomenon which can only be called a perversion of the debt capital markets. As the credit crunch became more severe, banks faced their own illiquidity and insolvency problems, resulting in the failure of many banks, including such giants as the venerable Bank of New England. To cope with their own balance sheet dissipation, banks would commonly *call the best loan first!* Thousands of high-quality smaller companies were stunned and debilitated by such actions. After all, given their excellent credit records, it was easy for them to assume their loans would not be terminated. Yet, a bank can run out of cash too and have few choices when its own survival is at stake. The net effect of this credit crunch is a massive reduction of balance sheets in the 1990s. Debt reduction has become a dominant financial strategy of small and large companies alike.

The Lender's Perspective

Lenders have always been wary capital providers. Understandably, since banks may earn a 1 percent net profit on total assets, they are especially sensitive to the possibility of a loss. Imagine writing off a $1 million loan to a small company. The bank has to turn around and write an incremental $100 million in profitable loans just to recover the loss. Additionally, given the mayhem of the decade, they are even more sensitive.

Yet, they are businesses and seek to grow and improve profitability as well. They can do this only if they find and bet on successful, young, growing companies. Historically, points and fees charged for making the loan have been a major contributor to bank profitability. The opportunity to entice banks to make loans by offering various sweeteners may be reviving. Take, for instance, a recent lending proposal for a company seeking a $15 million five-year-term loan. In addition to the up-front origination fees and points, the bank further proposed a YES, or yield enhancement security, as a part of the loan. This additional requirement would entitle the bank to receive an additional $3 million payment from the company once its sales exceeded $10 million and it was profitable, or if it was sold, merged, or taken public. The loan was closed in mid-1993, and management and existing investors were happy and would have been willing to pay more.

SOURCES OF DEBT CAPITAL[1]

The principal sources[2] of borrowed capital for new and young businesses are trade credit, commercial banks, finance companies, factors, and leasing companies. Admittedly, start-ups have more difficulty borrowing money than existing businesses. Nevertheless, start-ups managed by an entrepreneur with a track record and with significant equity in the business who can present a sound business plan can borrow money from one or more

[1] This section is drawn from Jeffry A Timmons, *Financing and Planning the New Venture* (Acton, MA: Brick House Publishing Company, 1990).

[2] Ibid., p. 68.

sources. But if little equity or collateral exists, the start-up won't have much success with banks.

The availability of such debt depends, in part, on where the business is located. Debt and leases as well as equity capital are more available to start-up companies in such hotbeds of entrepreneurial activity as eastern Massachusetts and Silicon Valley in California than, say, in the Midwest. Also, in the hotbed areas there is close contact between venture capital firms and the high-technology lending officers of banks. This contact tends to make it easier for start-ups and early-stage companies to borrow money.

The advantages and disadvantages[3] of these sources, summarized in *Exhibit 15.1*, are basically determined by such obvious dimensions as the interest rate or cost of capital, the key terms, conditions and covenants, and the fit with the owner's situation and the company's needs at the time. How good a deal you can strike is a function of your relative bargaining position and the competitiveness among the alternatives.

What is ultimately most important, given a deal at or above an acceptable threshold, is the person you will be dealing with, rather than the amount, terms, or institution. In other words, you will be better off seeking the right banker (or other provider of capital) than just the right bank. Once again, the industry and market characteristics, stage and health of the firm in terms of cash flow, debt coverage, and collateral are central to the evaluation process. *Exhibit 15.2* summarizes the term of financing available from these different sources. Note the difficulty in finding sources for more than one year of financing.

[3] Ibid., p. 33.

Exhibit 15.1
Debt Financing Sources for Types of Business

Source	*Start-Up Company*	*Existing Company*
Trade credit	Yes	Yes
Commercial banks	Occasionally, with strong equity	Yes
Finance companies	Rare (if assets are available)	Yes
Factors	Rare	Yes
Leasing companies	Difficult, except for start-ups with venture capital	Yes
Mutual savings banks and savings & loans	Rare	Real estate and other asset based companies
Insurance companies	Rare, except alongside venture capital	Yes

Source: Jeffry A Timmons, *Financing and Planning the New Venture* (Acton, MA: Brick House Publishing Company, 1990), p. 34.

Exhibit 15.2
Debt Financing Sources by Term of Financing

	Term of Financing		
Source	*Short*	*Medium*	*Long*
Trade credit	Yes	Yes	Possible
Commercial banks	Most frequently	Yes (asset-based)	Rare (depends on asset)
Factors	Most frequently	Rare	No
Leasing companies	No	Most frequently	Some
Mutual savings banks, savings & loans	No	No	Real estate and other asset-based companies
Insurance companies	Rare	Most frequently	Yes

Source: Jeffry A Timmons, *Financing and Planning the New Venture* (Acton, MA: Brick House Publishing Company, 1990), Table 3, p. 34.

Exhibit 15.3
What Is Bankable? Specific Lending Criteria

Security	*Credit Capacity*
Accounts receivable	70%–80% of those less than 90 days
Inventory	40%–60% depending on obsolescence risk
Equipment	70%–80% of market value (less if specialized)
Chattel mortgage	100%–150% or more of auction appraisal value
Conditional sales contract	60%–70% or more of purchase price
Plant improvement loan	60%–80% of appraised value or cost

Source: Jeffry A Timmons, *Financing and Planning the New Venture* (Acton, MA: Brick House Publishing Company, 1990), Table I, p. 33.

Finally, an enduring question entrepreneurs ask is, What is bankable? How much money can I expect to borrow based on my balance sheet? *Exhibit 15.3* summarizes some general guidelines in answer to this question. Since most loans and lines of credit are asset-based loans, knowing the guidelines employed by lenders to determine how much to lend the company is very important. When you observe the percentages of key balance sheet assets that are often allowable as collateral, note that these are only ranges and will vary from region to region and for different types of businesses. For instance, nonperishable consumer goods versus technical products that may have considerable risk of obsolescence would be treated very differently in making a loan collateral computation. If the company already has significant debt and has pledged all of its assets, there may not be a lot of room for negotiations. A bank with full collateral in hand for a company having cash flow problems is unlikely to give up such a position in order to enable the company to attract another lender, even though the collateral is more than enough to meet these guidelines.

Trade Credit[4]

Trade credit is a major source of short-term funds for small businesses. In fact, trade credit represents 30–40 percent of the current liabilities of nonfinancial companies, with generally higher percentages in smaller companies. Trade credit is reflected on the balance sheets as accounts payable.

If a small business is able to buy goods and services and be given, or take, 30, 60, or 90 days to pay for them, that business has essentially obtained a loan of 30 to 90 days. Many small and new businesses are able to obtain such trade credit when no other form of debt financing is available to them. Suppliers offer trade credit as a way of getting new customers, and often build the bad debt risk into their prices.

The ability of a new business to obtain trade credit depends on the quality and reputation of its management and the relationships it establishes with its suppliers. A word of warning: continued late payment or nonpayment may cause suppliers to cut off shipments or ship only on a COD basis. Also, the real cost of using trade credit can be very high, for example, the loss of discounts for prompt payment. Because the cost of trade credit is seldom expressed as an annual amount, it should be analyzed carefully, and a new business should shop for the best terms.

Trade credit may take some of the following forms: extended credit terms; special or seasonal datings, where a supplier ships goods in advance of the purchaser's peak selling season and accepts payment 90–120 days later during the season; inventory on consignment, not requiring payment until sold; and loan or lease of equipment.

[4] Ibid., pp. 68–80.

Commercial Bank Financing

Commercial banks prefer to lend to existing businesses that have a track record of sales, profits, satisfied customers, and a current backlog. Their concern about the high failure rates in new businesses can make them less than enthusiastic about making loans to such firms. They like to be no-risk lenders. For their protection, they look first to positive cash flow and then to collateral, and in new and young businesses they are likely to require personal guarantees of the owners' business. Like equity investors, they place great weight on the quality of the management team.

Notwithstanding these factors, banks do not make loans to start-ups or young businesses that have strong equity financings from venture capital firms. This is especially true in such centers of entrepreneurial and venture capital activity as Silicon Valley, Boston, and Los Angeles.

Commercial banks are the primary source of debt capital for existing (not new) small and medium-sized businesses, those with less than $5 million in sales. Small business loans may be handled by a bank's small business loan department. Larger loans may require the approval of a loan committee. If a loan exceeds the limits of a local bank, part or all of the loan will be offered to "correspondent" banks in neighboring communities and nearby financial centers. This correspondent network enables the smaller banks in rural areas to handle loans that otherwise could not be made.

Most of the loans made by commercial banks are for one year or less. Some of these loans are unsecured and others are secured by receivables, inventories, or other assets. Commercial banks also make a large number of intermediate-term loans (or term loans) with a maturity of one to five years. On about 90 percent of these term loans, the banks require collateral, generally consisting of stocks, machinery, equipment, and real estate. Most term loans are retired by systematic payments over the life of the loan. Apart from real estate mortgages and loans guaranteed by the SBA or a similar organization, commercial banks make few loans with maturities greater than five years.

Banks also offer a number of services to the small business, such as computerized payroll preparation, letters of credit, international services, lease financing, and money market accounts.

There are almost 14,000 commercial banks in the United States. A complete listing of these banks can be found, arranged by states, in the *American Bank Directory* (McFadden Business Publications), published semiannually.

Line of Credit Loans

A line of credit is a formal or informal agreement between a bank and a borrower concerning the maximum loan balance a bank will allow the borrower for a one-year period. Often the bank will charge a fee of a certain percent of the line of credit for a definite commitment to make the loan when requested.

Line of credit funds are used for such seasonal financings as inventory buildup and receivable financing. It is general practice to repay these loans from the sales and liquidation of short-term assets that they financed. Lines of credit can be unsecured, but often a bank will require a pledge of inventory, receivables, equipment, or other acceptable assets. Unsecured lines of credit have no lien on any asset of the borrower and no priority over any trade creditor, but the banks do require that all debt to the principals and stockholders of the company be subordinated to the line of credit debt.

The line of credit is executed through a series of renewable 90-day notes or through an installment loan to be paid within the year. The renewable 90-day note is the more common practice, and the bank will expect the borrower to pay off his or her open loan within a year and to hold a zero loan balance for one to two months. This is known as "resting the line." Commercial banks may also generally require that a borrower maintain a checking account at the bank with a minimum ("compensating") balance of 15 to 20 percent of the outstanding loan.

For a large, financially sound company, the interest rates for a "prime risk" line of credit will be quoted at about 1 to 2 percent over the rediscount rate charges by the Federal Reserve. A small firm may be required to pay a higher rate. It should be noted that the true rate of interest will depend on the method of charging interest. If the bank deducts interest in advance (discounts the loan) or the loan is prepaid in installments, the effective rate of interest will be higher than the quoted figure. Any compensating-balance or resting-the-line requirements will also increase effective interest rates.

Accounts Receivable Financing

Accounts receivable financing is short-term financing that involves either the pledge of receivables as collateral for a loan or the sale of receivables (factoring). Accounts receivable loans are made by commercial finance companies and factoring concerns. Only a very limited number of banks do factoring.

Accounts receivable bank loans are made on a discounted value of the receivables pledged. Invoices that do not meet the bank's credit standard will not be accepted as collateral. (Receivables more than 90 days old are not normally accepted.) A bank may inform the purchaser of goods that the account has been assigned to the bank, and payments are made directly to the bank, which credits them to the borrower's account. This is called a notification plan. Alternatively, the borrower may collect the accounts as usual and pay off the bank loan; this is a nonnotification plan.

Accounts receivable loans can make it possible for a company to secure a loan that it might not otherwise get. The loan can be increased as sales and receivables grow. However, receivables loans do have drawbacks. They can be expensive, and receivable financing is sometimes regarded by trade creditors as evidence of a company in financial difficulty.

Time-Sales Finance

Many dealers or manufacturers who offer installment payment terms to purchasers of their equipment cannot themselves finance installment or conditional sales contracts. In such situations, they sell and assign the installment contract to a bank or sales finance company. (Some very large manufacturers do their own financing through captive finance companies. Most very small retailers merely refer their customer installment contracts to sales finance companies, which provide much of this financing, and on more flexible terms.)

From the manufacturer's or dealer's point of view, time-sales finance is, in effect, a way of obtaining short-term financing from long-term installment accounts receivable. From the purchaser's point of view, it is a way of financing the purchase of new equipment.

Under time-sales financing, the bank purchases installment contracts at a discount from their full value and takes as security an assignment of the manufacturer/dealer's interest in the conditional sales contract. In addition, the bank's financing of installment note receivables includes recourse to the seller in the event of loan default by the purchaser. Thus, the bank has the payment obligation of the equipment purchaser, the manufacturer/dealer's security interest in the equipment purchased, and recourse to the manufacturer/dealer in the event of default. The bank also withholds a portion of the payment (5 percent or more) as a dealer reserve until the note is paid. Since the reserve becomes an increasing percentage of the note as the contract is paid off, an arrangement is often made when multiple contracts are financed to ensure that the reserve against all contracts will not exceed 20 percent or so.

The purchase price of equipment under a sales financing arrangement includes a "time-sales price differential" (e.g., an increase to cover the discount, typically 6–10 percent) taken by the bank that does the financing. Collection of the installments may be made directly by the bank or indirectly through the manufacturer/dealer.

Unsecured Term Loans

Bank term loans are generally made for periods of from one to five years, and may be unsecured or secured. Most of the basic features of bank term loans are the same for secured and unsecured loans. Secured term loans are described below under chattel mortgages and collateral loans.

Term loans provide needed growth capital to companies that could not obtain such capital from the sale of stock. They are also a substitute for a series of short-term loans made with the anticipation of renewal by both the borrower and the lender.

Term loans have three distinguishing features: They are made by banks for periods of up to five years (and occasionally more). Periodic repayment is required. Term loan agreements are designed to fit the special needs and requirements of the borrower (e.g., payments can be smaller at the beginning of a loan term and larger at the end).

Because term loans do not mature for a number of years, during which time there could be a significant change in the situation and fortunes of the borrower, the bank must carefully evaluate the prospects and management of the borrowing company. Even the protection afforded by initially strong assets can be wiped out by several years of heavy losses. Term lenders place particular stress on the entrepreneurial and managerial abilities of the borrowing company. The bank will also carefully consider such things as the long-range prospects of the company and its industry, its present and projected profitability, and its ability to generate the cash required to meet the loan payments.

To lessen the risks involved in term loans, a bank will require some restrictive covenants in the loan agreement. These covenants might prohibit additional borrowing, merger of the company, payment of dividends, sales of assets, and the like.

Chattel Mortgages and Equipment Loans

Assigning an appropriate possession (chattel) as security is a common way of making secured term loans. The chattel is any machinery, equipment, or business property that is made the collateral of a loan in the same way as a mortgage on real estate. The chattel remains with the borrower unless there is default, in which case the chattel goes to the bank. Generally, credit against machinery and equipment is restricted primarily to new or highly serviceable and salable used items.

It should be noted that in many states, loans that used to be chattel mortgages are now executed through the security agreement forms of the Uniform Commercial Code (UCC). However, chattel mortgages are still used in many places, and from custom, many lenders continue to use that term even though the loans are executed through the UCC's security agreements. The term *chattel mortgage* is typically from one to five years; some are longer-term.

Conditional Sales Contracts

Conditional sales contracts are used to finance a substantial portion of the new equipment purchased by businesses. Under a sales contract, the buyer agrees to purchase a piece of equipment, makes a nominal down payment, and pays the balance in installments over a period of from one to five years. Until the payment is complete, the seller holds title to the equipment. Hence, the sale is conditional upon the buyer's completing the payments.

A sales contract is financed by a bank that has recourse to the seller should the purchaser default the loan. This makes it more difficult to finance a purchase of a good piece of used equipment at an auction. No recourse to the seller is available if the equipment is purchased at an auction; the bank would have to sell the equipment if the loan goes bad. Occasionally, a firm seeking financing on existing and new equipment will sell some of its equipment to a dealer and repurchase it, together with new equipment, in order to get a conditional sales contract financed by a bank.

The effective rate of interest on a conditional sales contract is high, running to as much as 15–18 percent if the effect of installment features is considered. The purchaser/borrower should thus make sure that the interest payment is covered by increased productivity and profitability resulting from the new equipment.

Plant Improvement Loans

Loans made to finance improvements to business properties and plants are called plant improvement loans. They can be intermediate- and long-term and are generally secured by a first mortgage on that part of the property or plant that is being improved.

Commercial Finance Companies

The commercial bank is generally the lender of choice for a business. From whom does a business seek loans when the bank says no? Commercial finance companies, which aggressively seek borrowers. They frequently loan money to companies that do not have positive cash flow—although they will not make loans to companies unless they consider them viable.

The primary factors in a bank's loan decision are the continuing successful operation of a business, and its generation of more than enough cash to repay a loan. By contrast, commercial finance companies lend against the liquidation value of assets (receivables, inventory, equipment) that it understands, knows how and where to sell, and whose liquidation value is sufficient to repay the loan.

In the case of inventories or equipment, liquidation value is the amount that could be realized from an auction or quick sale. Finance companies will generally *not* lend against receivables more than 90 days old, federal or state government agency receivables (because they are slow payers), or any receivables whose collection is contingent on the performance of a delivered product.

Because of the liquidation criteria, finance companies prefer readily salable inventory items such as electronic components, or metal in such commodity forms as billets or standard shapes. Generally, a finance company will not accept inventory as collateral unless it also has receivables. As for equipment loans, these are made only by certain finance companies and against such standard equipment as lathes, milling machines, and the like.

How much of the value of collateral will a finance company lend? Generally, 70–80 percent of acceptable receivables under 90 days old, 42–50 percent of the liquidation value of raw materials and/or finished goods inventory that are not obsolete or damaged, and 60–70 percent of the liquidation value of equipment, as determined by an appraiser. Receivables and inventory loans are for one year, while equipment loans are for three to seven years.

All of these loans have tough prepayment penalties: Finance companies do not want to be immediately replaced by banks when a borrower has improved its credit image.

The data required for a loan from a finance company includes all that would be provided to a bank, plus additional details for the assets being used as collateral. For receivables financing this includes detailed aging of receivables (and payables) and historical data on sales, returns, and collections.

For inventory financing, it includes details on the items in inventory, how long they have been there and their rate of turnover. Requests for equipment loans should be accompanied by details on the date of purchase, cost of each equipment item, and appraisals, if available. If not, the finance company will have such an appraisal made.

The advantage of dealing with a commercial finance company is that it will make loans that banks will not, and it can be flexible in lending arrangements. The price a finance company exacts for this is an interest rate anywhere from 2 to 6 percent over that charged by a bank, prepayment penalties, and in the case of receivables loans recourse to the borrower for unpaid collateralized receivables.

Because of their greater risk taking and asset-based lending, finance companies usually place a larger reporting and monitoring burden on the borrowing firm in order to stay on top of the receivables and inventory serving as loan collateral. Personal guarantees will generally be required from the principals of the business. The finance company will generally reserve the right to reduce the percentage of the value lent against receivables or inventory if it gets nervous about the borrower's survivability.

Factoring

Factoring is a form of accounts receivable financing. However, instead of borrowing and using receivables as collateral, the receivables are sold, at a discounted value, to a factor. Some commercial finance companies do factoring. The factor provides receivables financing for the company unable to obtain such financing from a bank.

In a standard factoring arrangement, the factor buys the client's receivables outright, without recourse, as soon as the client creates them by shipment of goods to customers. Although the factor has recourse to the borrowers for returns, errors in pricing, and so on, the factor assumes the risk of bad debt losses that develop from receivables it approves and purchases.

Cash is made available to the client as soon as proof is provided (old-line factoring) or on the average due date of the invoices (maturity factoring). With maturity factoring, the company can often obtain a loan of about 90 percent of the money a factor has agreed to pay on a maturity date. Most factoring arrangements are for one year.

Factoring fits some businesses better than others. For a business that has annual sales volume in excess of $300,000 and a net worth over $50,000 that sells on normal credit terms to a customer base that is 75 percent credit rated, factoring is a real option. Factoring has become almost traditional in such industries as textiles, furniture manufacturing, clothing manufacturing, toys, shoes, and plastics.

The same data required from a business for a receivable loan from a bank is required by a factor. Because a factor is buying receivables with no recourse, it will carefully analyze the quality and value of a prospective client's receivables. It will want a detailed aging of receivables plus historical data on bad debts, return, and allowances. It will also investigate the credit history of customers to whom its client sells and establish credit limits for each customer. The business client can receive factoring of customer receivables only up to the limits so set.

The cost of financing receivables through factoring is higher than that of borrowing from a bank or a finance company. The factor is assuming the credit risk, doing credit investigations and collections, and advancing funds. A factor generally charges up to 2 percent of the total sales factored as a service charge.

There is also an interest charge for money advanced to a business, usually 2–6 percent above prime. A larger, established business borrowing large sums will command a better interest rate than the small borrower with a one-time, short-term need. Finally, factors withhold a reserve of 5 to 10 percent of the receivables purchased.

Factoring is not the cheapest way to obtain capital, but it does quickly turn receivables into cash. Moreover, although more expensive than accounts receivable financing, factoring saves its users credit agency fees, salaries of credit and collection personnel, and bad debt write-offs.

Leasing Companies

The leasing industry has grown substantially in recent years, and lease financing has become an important source of medium-term financing for businesses. There are about 700 to 800 leasing companies in the United States. In addition, many commercial banks and finance companies have leasing departments. Some leasing companies handle a wide variety of equipment, while others specialize in certain types of equipment—machine tools, electronic test equipment, and the like.

Common and readily resalable items such as automobiles and trucks, typewriters and office furniture can be leased by both new and existing businesses. However, the start-up will find it difficult to lease other kinds of industrial, computer, or business equipment without providing a certificate of deposit to secure the lease or personal guarantees from the founders or from a wealthy third party.

An exception to this condition is high-technology start-ups that have received substantial venture capital. Some of these ventures have received large amounts of lease financing for rather special equipment from equity-oriented lessors, who receive some form of stock purchase rights in return for providing the start-up's lease line. Two companies doing this sort of venture leasing are Equitec of Oakland, California, with offices in Boston, New York, and Dallas, and Intertec of Mill Valley, California.

Generally, industrial equipment leases have a term of three to five years, but in some cases may run longer. There can also be lease renewal options for 3 to 5 percent per year of the original equipment value. Leases are usually structured to return the entire cost of the leased equipment plus finance charges to the lessor, although some so-called operating leases do not, over their term, produce revenues equal to or greater than the price of the leased equipment.

Typically, an up-front payment is required of about 10 percent of the value of the item being leased. The interest rate on equipment leasing may be more or less than other forms of financing, depending on the equipment leased, the credit of the lessee, and the time of year.

Leasing credit criteria are very similar to the criteria used by commercial banks for equipment loans. Primary considerations are the value of the equipment leased, the justification of the lease, and the lessee's projected cash flow over the lease term.

Should a business lease equipment? Leasing has certain advantages. It enables a young or growing company to conserve cash, and can reduce its requirements for equity capital. Leasing can also be a tax advantage, because payments can be deducted over a shorter period than depreciation.

Finally, leasing provides the flexibility of returning equipment after the lease period if it is no longer needed or if it has become technologically obsolete. This can be a particular advantage to companies in high-technology industries.

Leasing no longer improves a company's balance sheet, because accounting practice now requires that the value of the equipment leased be capitalized and a lease liability shown.

MANAGING AND ORCHESTRATING THE BANKING RELATIONSHIP

Before the Loan Decision[5]

Choosing a bank and, more specifically, a banker is one of the more important decisions a new or young business will make. (See *Exhibit 15.4.*) A good lender relationship can sometimes mean the difference between the life and death of a business during difficult times. There have been cases where, other things being equal, one bank has called its loans to a struggling business, causing it to go under, and another bank has stayed with its loans and helped a business to survive and prosper. (Although I refer specifically to banks and banking relationships, much of what follows on lending practices and decisions applies as well to commercial finance company lenders.)

Some banks and bankers will make loans to start-ups and early-stage ventures and others will not. Those that will not generally cite the lack of operating track record as the reason for turning down a loan. Lenders that make such loans usually do so for previously successful entrepreneurs of means or for firms backed by investors with whom they have had prior relationships and whose judgment they trust—established venture capital firms, for example.

In centers of high technology and venture capital, the main officers of the major banks will have one or more high-technology lending officers who specialize in making loans to early-stage, high-technology ventures. Through much experience, these bankers have come to understand the market and operating idiosyncrasies, problems, and opportunities of such

Exhibit 15.4
What to Look for in a Bank

Banking Knowledge: Few bankers will intentionally lead you astray. But Dan Lang, co-owner of Nature's Warehouse, a $6 million baked-goods business in Sacramento, recently discovered that some bankers have a tighter grip than others on what's possible on a given situation. Lang and his partner recently met with lending officers at several banks to try to get $1 million in financing to help buy Nature's Warehouse. But only one, the lending officer at Sacramento Commercial Bank, "said right away he could do it as a 10-year SBA loan. Without hesitating, he knew what he could and couldn't do."

Sense of Urgency: "Banker's hours" may be a fading notion, but a CEO's and a banker's ideas of a "quick turnaround" are often days, even weeks, apart. Tom Kinder, co-owner of Pure Patience, a bedding-products mail-order business in Sharon, Vermont, found that his bankers at Vermont National Bank were able—and extremely willing—to meet his compressed timetable for a recent $100,000 loan. Kinder says he even got calls during evening at home, updating him on the progress.

Teaching Talent: Many bankers can't—or don't want to—articulate what they expect from customers and how the bank makes its decisions. But Dwight Mulch, president of three-year-old Preferred Products Corp., a building-materials distributor in Burlington, Iowa, says he gets both types of information from his leading officer at First Star Bank and has benefitted greatly. "When I was starting," says Mulch, "he practically led me around by the nose. He showed me what to put in the plan, and he still tells me how the system works."

Industry Knowledge: Whatever industry you're in, it helps to have a banker who has had some exposure to your type of business, says Dave Sanger, president of Resource Solution Group, a computer-consulting business in Southfield, Michigan. Sanger's lending officer at Manufacturer's Bank in Detroit "knows we don't have the same kind of assets as a retailer or a manufacturer," Sanger says, "and she knows the terminology."

Financial Stability: Given a choice, Kevin Whalen, chief financial adviser of Twin Modal, Inc., a Minneapolis transportation-brokerage firm, didn't pick the bank that was offering the most aggressive deal. And it's a good thing too, he says: "that bank has had real problems with regulators and has pulled way back." Before selecting Marquette Bank, in 1989, Whalen, a former banker himself, did spreadsheet comparisons of several banks, comparing returns on assets, capital-to-asset ratios, and so on. "I felt that in the long run, we'd be better off with the most conservative bank around."

Manager with Backbone: Banks have policies, notes Mike Walker, president of Walker Communications Inc., a public relations firm in Scottsdale, Arizona. "But you want to have a manager with the courage to override them if it makes sense to do so." Walker's branch manager at First Interstate Bank of Arizona, for instance, allows him to draw on checks immediately after they're deposited and often acts as a troubleshooter for him within the bank. "I don't know what the manual says," offers Walker, "but I think you need somebody who can take a stand."

Source: Karen E Carney and Phaedra Hise, "What to Look For in a Bank." Reprinted with permission, *Inc.* magazine, (July 1992), p. 88. Copyright © 1992 by Goldhirsh Group, Inc., 38 Commercial Wharf, Boston, MA 02110.

[5] Ibid., pp. 81–82.

Exhibit 15.5
Key Steps in Obtaining a Loan

Before choosing and approaching a banker or other lender, the entrepreneur and his or her management team should go through the following steps in preparing to ask for a loan.

- Decide how much growth they want, and how fast they want to grow, observing the dictum that financing *follows* strategy.
- Determine how much money they require, and when they need to have it. To this end, they must:
  —Develop a schedule of operating and asset needs.
  —Prepare a real-time cash flow projection.
  —Decide how much capital they need.
  —Specify how they will use the funds they borrow.
- Revise and update the "corporate profile" in their business plan. This should consist of:
  —The core ingredients of the plan in the form of an executive summary.
  —A history of the firm (as appropriate).
  —Summaries of the financial results of the past three years.
  —Succinct descriptions of their markets and products.
  —A description of their operations.
  —Statements of cash flow and financial requirements.
  —Descriptions of the key managers, owners, and directors.
  —A rundown of the key strategies, facts and logic that guide them in growing the corporation.
- Identify potential sources for the type of debt they seek, and the *amount, rate, terms, and conditions* they seek.
- Select a bank or other lending institution, solicit interest, and prepare a presentation.
- Prepare a *written loan request.*
- Present their case, negotiate, and then close the deal.
- After the loan is granted, it is important that the borrowers maintain an effective relationship with the lending officer.

Source: Jeffry A Timmons, *Financing and Planning the New Venture* (Acton, MA: Brick Housing Publishing Co., 1990), pp. 82–83. Also see Bruce G Posner,"The One-Page Loan Proposal," *INC.*, September 1991.

ventures. They generally have close ties to venture capital firms and will refer entrepreneurs to such firms for possible equity financing. The venture capital firms, in turn, will refer their portfolio ventures to the bankers for debt financing.

What should an entrepreneur consider in choosing a lender? What is important in a lending decision? How should entrepreneurs relate to their lenders on an ongoing basis? In many ways, the lender's decision is similar to that of the venture capitalist. The goal is to make money for his or her company, through interest earned on good loans. The lender fears losing money by making bad loans to companies that default on their loans. To this end, he or she avoids risk by building in every conceivable safeguard. The lender is concerned with the client company's loan coverage, its ability to repay, and the collateral it can offer. Finally, but most important, he or she must judge the character and quality of the key managers of the company to whom the loan is being made. *Exhibit 15.5* outlines the key steps.

Choosing a Value-added Banker

Because of the importance of a banking relationship, an entrepreneur should shop around before making a choice. The criteria for selecting a bank should be based on more than just loan interest rates. Equally important, entrepreneurs should not wait until they have a dire need for funds to try to establish a banking relationship. The choice of a bank and the development of a banking relationship should begin when you do not urgently need the money. When an entrepreneur faces a near-term financial crisis, the venture's financial statements are at their worst and the banker has good cause to wonder about management's financial and planning skills—all to the detriment of the entrepreneur's chances of getting a loan.

G. B. Baty and J. M. Stancill describe some of the factors that are especially important to an entrepreneur in selecting a bank.[6]

[6] G B Baty, *Entrepreneurship: Playing to Win* (Reston, VA: Reston Publishing Company, 1974); J M Stancill, "Getting the Most from Your Banking Relationship," *Harvard Business Review*, March–April 1980.

- The bank selected should be big enough to service a venture's foreseeable loans but not so large as to be relatively indifferent to your business.
- Banks differ greatly in their desire and capacity to work with small firms. Some banks have special small business loan officers and regard new and early-stage ventures as the seeds of very large future accounts. Other banks see such new ventures loans as merely bad risks.
- Does the bank tend to call or reduce its loans to small businesses that have problems? When they have less capital to lend will they cut back on small business loans and favor their older, more solid customers?
- Are they imaginative, creative, and helpful when a venture has a problem? To quote Baty, "Do they just look at your balance sheet and faint or do they try to suggest constructive financial alternatives?"
- Has the bank had lending experience in your industry, especially with young, developing companies? If they have, your chances of getting a loan are better, and the bank will be more tolerant of problems and better able to help you exploit your opportunities.
- Is there good personal chemistry between you and your prospective lending officer? Remember, the person you talk to and deal with is the bank. Does this person know your industry and competition? Can this officer competently explain your business, technology, and uniqueness to other loan officers? Is he or she experienced in administering loans to smaller firms? Can you count on this person consistently? Does he or she have a good track record? Does his or her lending authority meet or exceed your needs? Does he or she have a reputation for being reasonable, creative, and willing to take a sound risk?

How does an entrepreneur go about evaluating a bank? First, the entrepreneur should consult accountants, attorneys, and other entrepreneurs who have had dealings with the bank. The advice of entrepreneurs who have dealt with a bank through good and bad times can be especially useful. Second, the entrepreneur should meet with loan officers at several banks and systematically explore their attitudes and approaches to their business borrowers. Who meets with you, for how long, and with how many interruptions can be useful measures of a bank's interest in your account. Finally, ask for small business references from their list of borrowers and talk to the entrepreneurs of those firms. Throughout all of these contacts and discussions, check out particular loan officers as well as the viability of the bank itself; they are a major determinant of how the bank will deal with you and your venture.

Approaching and Meeting the Banker

Obtaining a loan is a sales job. Many borrowers tend to forget this. An entrepreneur with an early-stage venture must sell himself or herself as well as the viability and potential of the business to the banker. This is much the same situation that the early-stage entrepreneur faces with a venture capitalist.

The initial contact with a lender will likely be by telephone. The entrepreneur should be prepared to describe quickly the nature, age, and prospects of the venture; the amount of equity financing and who provided it; the prior financial performance of the business; the entrepreneur's experience and background; and the sort of bank financing desired. A referral from a venture capital firm or a business associate who knows the banker can be very helpful.

If the loan officer agrees to a meeting, he or she may well ask that a summary loan proposal, business plan, and financial statements be sent ahead of time. A well-prepared business plan and a reasonable amount of equity financing should pique a banker's interest—even for a start-up venture.

The first meeting with a loan officer will likely be at the venture's place of business. The banker will be interested in meeting the management team, seeing how they relate to the entrepreneur, and getting a sense of the financial controls and reporting used and how well things seem to be run. The banker may also want to meet one or more of the venture's equity investors. Most of all, the banker is using this meeting to evaluate the integrity and business acumen of those who will ultimately be responsible for the repayment of the loan.

Throughout meetings with potential bankers, the entrepreneur must convey an air of self-confidence and an optimistic but realistic view of the venture's prospects. If the banker is favorably impressed by what has been seen and read, he or she will ask for further documents and references and begin to discuss the amount and timing of funds that the bank might lend to the business.

What the Banker Wants to Know[7]

What are you going to do with the money? Does the use of the loan make business sense? Should some or all of the money required be equity capital rather than debt? For new and young businesses, lenders do not like to see total debt-to-equity ratios greater than one. The answers to this question will also determine the type of loan (e.g., line of credit or term).

How much do you need? You must be prepared to justify the amount requested and describe how the debt fits into an overall plan for financing and developing the business. (See *Exhibit 15.6.*) Further, the amount of the loan should have enough cushion to allow for unexpected developments.

When and how will you pay it back? This is an important question. Short-term loans for seasonal inventory build-ups or for financing receivables are easier to obtain than long term loans, especially for early-stage businesses. How the loan will be repaid is the bottom-line question. Presumably you are borrowing money to finance activity that will throw off enough cash to repay the loan. What is your contingency plan if things go wrong? Can you describe such risks and indicate how you will deal with them? Is there a secondary source of repayment, a guarantor of means?

When do you need the money? If you need the money tomorrow, forget it. You are a poor planner and manager. On the other hand, if you need the money next month or the month after, you have demonstrated an ability to plan ahead, and you have given the banker time to investigate and process a loan application. Typically, a lending decision can be made in one to three weeks.

One of the best ways for all entrepreneurs to answer these questions is by providing the bankers with a well-prepared business plan. This plan should contain projections of cash flow, profit and loss, and balance sheets that will demonstrate the need for a loan and how it can be repaid.

A well-prepared business plan is vital for the start-up seeking loans. Particular attention will be given by the lender to such financial ratios as current assets to current liabilities, gross margins, net worth to debt, accounts receivable and payable periods, inventory turns, and net profit to sales. The ratios for the borrower's venture will be compared to averages for competing firms to see how the potential borrower measures up to them.

For an existing business, the lender will want to review financial statements from prior years prepared or audited by a CPA, a list of aged receivables and payables, the turnover of inventory, and lists of key customers and creditors. The lender will also want to know that all tax payments are current. Finally, he or she will need to know details of fixed assets and any liens on receivables, inventory, or fixed assets.

[7] Timmons, *Financing and Planning the New Venture*, pp. 85–88.

Exhibit 15.6
Sample of a Summary Loan Proposal

Date of request:	May 30, 1994	
Borrower:	Curtis-Palmer & Company, Inc.	
Amount:	$4,200,000	
Use of proceeds:	A/R, up to	$1,600,000
	Inventory, up to	824,000
	WIP, up to	525,000
	Marketing, up to	255,000
	Ski show specials	105,000
	Contingencies	50,000
	Officer loans dues	841,000
		$4,200,000
Type of loan:	Seasonal revolving line of credit	
Closing date:	June 15, 1994	
Term:	One year	
Rate:	Prime + 1 percent, no compensating balances, no points or origination fees.	
Takedown:	$500,000 at closing	
	1,500,000 on August 1, 1994	
	1,500,000 on October 1, 1994	
	700,000 on November 1, 1994	
Collateral:	70 percent of A/R	
	50 percent of inventory	
Guarantees:	None	
Repayment schedule:	$4,200,000 or balance on anniversary of note	
Source of funds for repayment:	*a.* Excess cash from operations (see cash flow).	
	b. Renewable and increase of line if growth is profitable.	
	c. Conversion to three-year note.	
Contingency source:	*a.* Sale and leaseback of equipment	
	b. Officer's loans.	

Source: Jeffry A Timmons, *Financing and Planning the New Venture* (Acton, MA: Brick House Publishing Co., 1990), p. 86.

The entrepreneur-borrower should regard his or her contacts with the bank as a sales mission and provide data that are required promptly and in a form that can be readily understood. The better the material entrepreneurs can supply to demonstrate their business credibility, the easier and faster it will be to obtain a positive lending decision.

The Lending Decision

One of the significant changes in today's lending environment is the centralized lending decision. Traditionally, loan officers might have up to several million dollars of lending authority and could make loans to small companies. Besides the company's creditworthiness as determined by analysis of its past results via the balance sheet, income statement, cash flow, and collateral, the lender's assessment of the character and reputation of the entrepreneur was central to the decision. As loan decisions are made increasingly by loan committees, this face-to-face part of the decision process has given way to deeper analysis of the company's business plan, cash flow drivers and dissipators, competitive environment, and the cushion for loan recovery given the firm's game plan and financial structure.

The implication for entrepreneurs is a demanding one: You can no longer rely on your salesmanship and good relationship with your loan officer alone to continue to get favorable lending decisions. You, or the key team member, needs to be able to prepare the necessary analysis and documentation to convince people you may never meet that the loan is a good one. You also need to know the financial ratios and criteria used to compare your loan request with industry norms and to defend the analysis. Such a presentation can make it easier and faster to obtain approval of a loan.

candid with the banker or that management does not have the business under the proper control. Either conclusion by a banker is damaging to the relationship.

If a future loan payment cannot be met, entrepreneurs should not panic and avoid their bankers. On the contrary, they should visit their banks and explain why the loan payment cannot be made and say when it will be made. If this is done before the payment due date and the entrepreneur–banker relationship is good, the banker will go along. After all, what else can he or she do? If an entrepreneur has convinced a banker of the viability and future growth of a business, the banker really does not want to call a loan and cause bankruptcy. The real key to communicating with a banker is candidly to inform but not to scare. In other words, entrepreneurs must indicate that they are aware of adverse events and have a way of dealing with them.

To build credibility with bankers further, entrepreneurs should borrow before they need to and then repay the loan. This will establish a track record of borrowing and reliable repayment. Entrepreneurs should also make every effort to meet the financial targets they set for themselves and have discussed with their banker. If this cannot be done, there will be an erosion of the credibility of the entrepreneur, even if the business is growing.

Bankers have a right to expect an entrepreneur to continue to use them as the business grows and prospers, and not to go shopping for a better interest rate. In return, entrepreneurs have the right to expect that their bank will continue to provide them with needed loans, particularly during difficult times when a vacillating loan policy could be dangerous for businesses' survival.

The TLC of a Banker or Other Lender

1. Your banker is your partner, not a difficult minority shareholder.
2. Be honest and straightforward in sharing information.
3. Invite the banker to see your business in operation.
4. Always avoid overdrafts, late payments, and late financial statements.
5. Answer questions frankly and honesty. *Tell the truth.* Lying is illegal and undoubtedly violates loan covenants.

What to Do When the Bank Says No

What do you do if the bank turns you down for a loan? Regroup, and review the following questions.

1. Does the company really need to borrow now? Can cash be generated elsewhere? Tighten the belt. Are some expenditures not really necessary? Sharpen the financial pencil: Be lean and mean.
2. What does the balance sheet say? Are you growing too fast? Compare yourself to published industry ratios to see if you are on target.
3. Does the bank have a clear and comprehensive understanding of your needs? Did you *really* get to know your loan officer? Did you do enough homework on the bank's criteria and their likes and dislikes? Was your loan officer too busy to give your borrowing package proper consideration? A loan officer may have 50 to as many as 200 accounts. Is your relationship with the bank on a proper track?
4. Was your written loan proposal realistic? Was it a normal request, or something that differed from the types of proposals the bank usually sees? Did you make a verbal request for a loan, without presenting any written backup?
5. Do you need a new loan officer, or a new bank? If your answers to the above questions put you in the clear, and your written proposal was realistic, call the head of the commercial loan department and arrange a meeting. Sit down and discuss the history of your loan effort, the facts, and the bank's reasons for turning you down.

TAR PITS: ENTREPRENEURS BEWARE

Modern corporate financial theory has preached the virtues of zero cash balances and the use of leverage to enhance return on equity. Such thinking applied to closely held companies whose dream is to last forever can be extremely destructive. If you judge by the 1980s, the excessive leverage used by so many larger companies apparently simply is not worth the risk: Two-thirds of the LBOs done in the 1980s have ended up in serious trouble, and the jury is still out on others. It is no accident that the serious erosion of IBM began about the same time as the company acquired debt on its balance sheet for the very first time, in the early 1980s.

Beware of Leverage: The ROE Mirage

According to the theory, one can significantly improve return on equity (ROE) by utilizing debt. Thus, the present value of a company would also increase significantly as the company went from a zero debt-to-equity ratio to 100 percent, as shown in *Exhibit 15.7*. On closer examination, however, such an increase in debt only improves the present value, given the 2 percent to 8 percent growth rates, shown by 17 to 26 percent. If the company gets into any trouble at all—and the odds of that happening sooner or later are very high—its options and flexibility become very seriously constrained by the covenants of the senior lenders. Leverage creates an unforgiving capital structure and the potential additional ROI often is not worth the risk. If the upside is worth risking the loss of the entire company should adversity strike, then go ahead. This is easier said than survived, however.

Ask any entrepreneur who has had to deal with the workout specialists in a bank and you will get a sobering, if not frightening, message: It is hell and you will not want to do it again.

Exhibit 15.7
Total Present Value

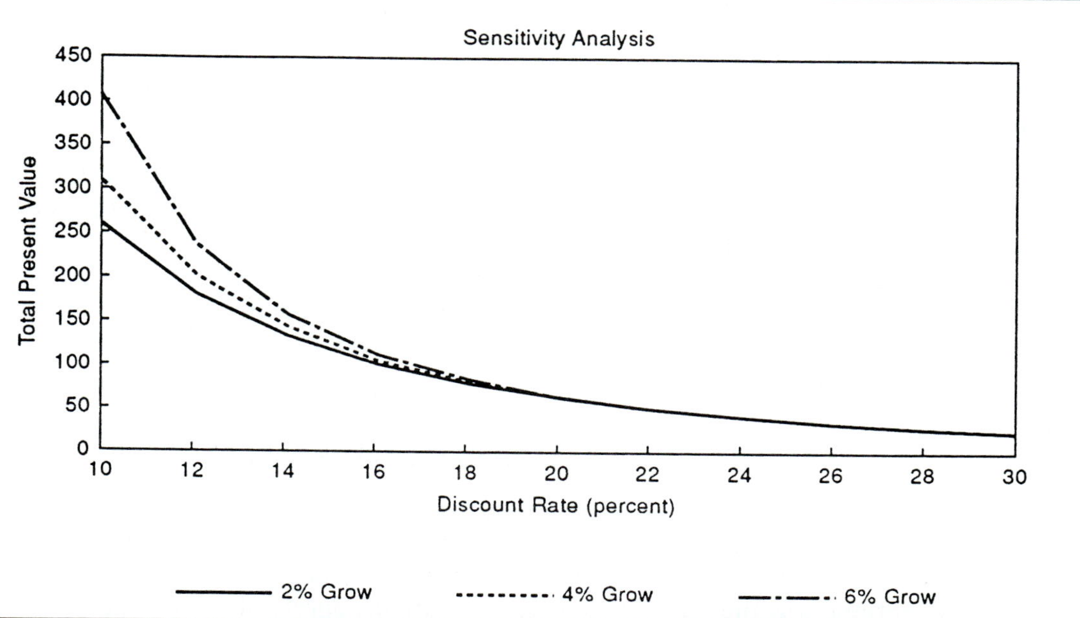

Source: William A Sahlman, "Note on Free Cash Flow Valuation Models," HBS Note 288–023, Figure 1.

IRS: Time Bomb for Personal Disaster

There is a much lesser known tar pit that entrepreneurs need to be aware of when considering leveraging their companies. Once the company gets into serious financial trouble, a subsequent restructuring of debt is often part of the survival and recovery plan. The problem becomes, in such a restructuring, principal and interest due to lenders may be forgiven in exchange for warrants, direct equity, or other considerations. Unfortunately, such forgiven debt becomes *taxable income* for the entrepreneur who owns the company and who has personally had to guarantee the loans. In one restructuring of a mid-western cable television company, the founder at one point faced a possible $12 million personal tax liability, which would have forced him into personal bankruptcy, and possibly worse. In this case, fortunately, the creative deal restructuring enabled him to avoid such a calamitous outcome, but many other overleveraged entrepreneurs from the 1980s have not fared as well.

Neither a Lender Nor a Borrower Be, But if You Must . . .

In Garrison Keillor's radio program, "A Prairie Home Companion," he describes the mythical town of Lake Wobegon, Minnesota. Inscribed in granite over the entrance to the Bank of Lake Wobegon is the motto Neither a Lender Nor a Borrower Be, which is actually very good advice for early-stage entrepreneurs. Thus, the following may serve as useful tips if you must borrow:

1. Borrow when you do not need it (which is the surest way to accomplish No. 2).
2. Avoid personal guarantees, put caps and time limits on the amounts based on performance milestones, such as achieving certain cash flow, working capital, and equity levels.
3. The devil is in the details. Read each loan covenant and requirement carefully—only the owner can truly appreciate their consequences.
4. Do not accept so-called hair-trigger covenants, such as: If there is any change or event of any kind that can have any material adverse effect on the future of the company, the loan shall become due and payable.
5. Be conservative and prudent.

CASE—MICHIGAN LIGHTING, INC.

Preparation Questions

1. Evaluate the company. How much do you believe the company is worth? Bring to class a written bid of how much you would pay for it if you were Scott and Peterson.
2. What should they do to resolve the ownership situation?
3. How would you finance the purchase of the company?
4. Assume you do purchase the company: What specific actions would you plan to take on the first day? By the end of the first week? By the end of six months? Explain how and why.

MICHIGAN LIGHTING, INC.

Jack Peterson was discouraged by the continuing conflicts with his partner, David Scott, and had sought advice on how to remedy the situation from friends and associates as early as 1976. In 1984, Jack was beginning to believe that he and David had just grown too far apart to continue together. Jack had to find a mutually agreeable way to accomplish a separation. One alternative was for one partner to buy the other out, but they would first have to agree on this and find an acceptable method. David seemed to have no interest in such an arrangement.

During 1984, the differences between the partners grew. The vacillations in leadership were disruptive to the operation and made the employees very uncomfortable.

By early 1985, the situation was growing unbearable. Jack recalled the executive committee's annual planning meeting in January:

> It was a total disaster. There were loud arguments and violent disagreements. It was so bad that no one wanted to ever participate in another meeting. We were all miserable.
>
> What was so difficult was that each of us truly thought he was right. On various occasions other people in the company would support each of our positions. These were normally honest differences of opinion, but politics also started to enter in.

Company Description

Michigan Lighting, Inc. (MLI), manufactures custom-engineered fluorescent lighting fixtures used for commercial and institutional applications. Sales in 1985 were approximately $4.4 million with profits of $115,000.

Most sales are for standard items within the nine major lines of products designed and offered by the company. Ten percent of sales are completely custom-designed or custom-built fixtures, and 15 percent of orders are for slightly modified versions of a standard product. In 1985, CFI shipped 66,000 fixtures. Although individual orders range from one unit to over 2,000 units, the average order size is approximately 15–20 fixtures. Modified and custom-designed fixtures average about 25 per order. Jack Peterson, MLI president, describes their market position:

> Our product-marketing strategy is to try to solve lighting problems for architects and engineers. We design products which are architecturally styled for specific types of building constructions. If an architect has an unusual lighting problem, we design a special fixture to fit his needs. Or if he designs a lighting fixture, we build it to his specifications. We try to find products that satisfy particular lighting needs that are not filled by the giant fixture manufacturers. We look for niches in the marketplace.
>
> Having the right product to fit the architect's particular needs is the most important thing to our customer. Second is the relationship that the architect, the consulting engineer, or the lighting designer has with the people who are representing us. The construction business is such that the architect, engineer, contractor, distributor, and manufacturer all have to work as a team together on a specified project to ensure its successful completion. The architect makes a lot of mistakes in every building he designs, unless he just designs the same one over and over. Consequently, there's a lot of trading that goes on during the construction of a building, and everybody's got to give and take a little to get the job done. Then the owner usually gets a satisfactory job and the contractors and manufacturers make a fair profit. It requires a cooperative effort.
>
> Most of our bids for orders are probably compared with bids from half a dozen other firms across the country. Since a higher percentage of our orders are for premium-priced products, we are not as price sensitive as producers of more commonplace lighting fixtures. It is difficult for a small firm to compete in that market. As many as 30 companies might bid on one standard fixture job.

MLI owns its own modern manufacturing facility, located outside Pontiac, Michigan. Production consists of stamping, cutting, and forming sheet metal; painting; and assembling the fixture with the electrical components which are purchased from outside suppliers. The company employs a total of 104 workers, with 34 people in sales, engineering, and administration, and another 70 in production and assembly.

The company sells nationwide through regional distributors to contractors and architects for new buildings and renovations. Prior to 1983, MLI sold primarily to a regional

Exhibit A
Historical Performance

Year	*Net Sales*	*Profit after Tax*	*No. of Fixtures Shipped*	*Total Employees*	*Hourly Employees*
1985	$4,412,191	$115,209	66,000	104	70
1984	3,573,579	101,013	58,000	94	58
1983	2,973,780	106,528	52,000	82	52
1982	2,935,721	63,416	54,000	82	50

market. At that time, marketing activities were broadened geographically. This is the primary reason that sales have been increasing over the last few years even during a weak construction market. (See *Exhibit A* for historical sales, earnings, unit sales, and employment.)

Background

Michigan Lighting, Inc., was formed in Flint, Michigan, in 1936 by Daniel Peterson and Julian Walters. Each owned one-half of the company. Peterson was responsible for finance and engineering and Walters for sales and design. They subcontracted all manufacturing for the lighting systems they sold.

After several years, differences in personal work habits led Peterson to buy out Walters' interest. Daniel Peterson then brought in Richard Scott as his new partner. Scott had been one of his sheet metal subcontractors. Richard Scott became president and Daniel Peterson treasurer. Ownership was split so that Peterson retained a few shares more than half and all voting control because of his prior experience with the company.

In 1940, MLI began manufacturing and moved its operations to a multifloor 50,000-square-foot plant also located in Flint. The company grew and was quite profitable during the war years and during the following boom in construction of the early 1950s. Peterson and Scott were quite satisfied with the earnings they had amassed during this period and were content to let the company remain at a steady level of about $1 million in sales and about $15,000 in profit after taxes.

Daniel Peterson's son, Jack, joined MLI as a salesman in 1963 after graduating from MIT and then Colorado Business School. Richard Scott's son, David, who was a graduate of Trinity College, became an MLI salesman in 1964 when he was discharged from the service. The two sons were acquaintances from occasional gatherings as they were growing up but had not been close friends.

In 1966, Daniel Peterson had a heart attack and withdrew from management of the business. Although he remained an interested observer and sometime advisor to his son, Daniel was inactive in company affairs after this time. Richard Scott assumed overall responsibility for the management of the company.

Jack Peterson moved inside to learn about other parts of the company in 1967. His first work assignments were in manufacturing and sales service. David Scott joined his father in the manufacturing area a year later. Jack Peterson became sales manager, David Scott became manufacturing manager, and, at Richard Scott's suggestion, another person was added as financial manager. These three shared responsibility for running the company and worked well together, but major decisions were still reserved for Richard Scott, who spent less and less time in the office.

As the new group began revitalizing the company, a number of employees who had not been productive and were not responding to change were given early retirement or asked to leave. When the man who had been Richard Scott's chief aide could not work with the three younger managers, they ultimately decided he had to be discharged. Richard Scott became so angry that he rarely entered the plant again.

For several years the three managers guided the company as a team. However, there were some spirited discussions over the basic strategic view of the company. As sales manager, Jack Peterson pressed for responding to special customer needs. This, he felt, would be their strongest market niche. David Scott argued for smooth production flows and less disruption. He felt they could compete well in the "semistandard" market.

In 1968, Jack Peterson began to work with an individual in forming a company in the computer field. The company rented extra space from MLI, and MLI provided management and administrative support, helping the new company with bidding and keeping track of contracts. Although David Scott was not active in this company, Jack split his partial ownership in this new company with David because they were partners, and because Jack was spending time away from MLI with the computer company.

In 1969, the fathers moved to restructure the company's ownership to reflect the de facto changes in management. The fathers converted their ownership to nonvoting class A stock, and then each transferred 44 percent of their nonvoting stock to their sons. Daniel Peterson decided to relinquish his voting control at this time in an effort to help things work as the new generation took over. Accordingly, Jack Peterson and David Scott were each issued 50 percent of the class B voting shares.

Due to the demands associated with the start-up of the computer company, this new effort began to weaken the relationship between Jack and David. At the same time, David and the financial manager began to have strong disagreements. These seemed to arise primarily from errors in cost analysis, which led the financial manager to question some of David's decisions. There were also differences of opinion over relations with the workforce and consistency of policy. David preferred to control the manufacturing operation in his own way. Jack felt David could be more consistent, less arbitrary, and more supportive of the workforce. When the computer company was sold in 1975, the financial manager joined it as treasurer and resigned from MLI.

Growing Conflict

The departure of the financial manager led to a worsening of the relationship between Jack and David. Jack had been made company president in 1970. Jack recalled the decision:

> "Richard Scott had resigned as president and the three of us were sitting around talking about who should be president. David Scott finally said, 'I think you should be it.' And I said, 'Okay.' "

Yet even after Jack became president, the three managers had really operated together as a team for major decisions. Now, Jack was upset that they had lost an excellent financial manager, someone critical to the operation (partially due, in his opinion, to the disagreements with David). Also, there was no longer a third opinion to help resolve conflicts. Although the financial manager was replaced with an old classmate of David's, the new manager became one of several middle-level managers who had been hired as the company grew.

The pressure of growth created more strains between Jack and David. Sales had reached $1.8 million and had begun to tax MLI's manufacturing capacity. Jack felt that some of the problems could be alleviated if David would change methods that had been acceptable during slacker periods but hindered intense production efforts. David had different views. Both, however, agreed to look for additional space.

The transition to a new factory outside Pontiac, Michigan, in 1977 eased the stresses between the partners. A major corporation had purchased an indirect competitor to obtain its product lines and sold MLI the 135,000-square-foot plant. MLI also entered into an agreement to manufacture some of the other company's light fixtures as a subcontractor. The plant was in poor condition, and David Scott took over the project of renovating it and continuing production of the other company's lines.

Jack Peterson remained in Flint running the MLI operation alone until such time as it became possible to consolidate the entire operation in Pontiac. Jack described this interlude:

> The next year was a sort of cooling-off period. David was immersed in the project with the new factory and I was busy with the continuing operation. David had always enjoyed projects of this sort and was quite satisfied with this arrangement.
>
> Then, in 1978, we hired a plant manager to run the Pontiac plant and David came back to work in Flint. By that time, of course, a lot of things had changed. All of Flint had been reporting to me. I had somewhat reshaped the operation and the people had gotten used to my management style, which was different from David's.
>
> David's reaction was to work primarily with the design and engineering people, but he really wasn't involved very much with the daily manufacturing anymore. He developed a lot of outside interests, business and recreation, that took up much of his time.
>
> I was very happy with the arrangement because it lessened the number of conflicts. But when he did come back, the disagreements that did rise would be worse. I guess I resented his attempts to change things when he only spent a small amount of his time in the company.
>
> Then, in 1980, we made the decision to sell the Flint plant and put the whole company in Pontiac. We were both involved in that. Most of the key people went with us. David and I were very active in pulling together the two groups, and in integrating the operations.
>
> That began a fairly good time. I was spending my time with the sales manager trying to change the company from a regional company to a national one and was helping to find new representatives all over the country. David Scott spent his time in the engineering, design, and manufacturing areas. There was plenty of extra capacity in the new plant, so things went quite smoothly. In particular, David did an excellent job in upgrading the quality standards of the production force we had acquired with the plant. This was critical for our line of products and our quality reputation.
>
> This move really absorbed us for almost two years. It just took us a long time to get people working together and to produce at the quality level and rate we wanted. We had purchased the plant for an excellent price with a lot of new equipment and had started deleting marginal product lines as we expanded nationally. The company became much more profitable.

During the company's expansion, a group of six people formed the operating team. David Scott concentrated on applications engineering for custom fixtures and new product design. In addition, there was a sales manager, financial manager, engineering manager, the plant manufacturing manager, and Jack Peterson. Disagreements began again. Jack recounted the problems:

> Our operating group would meet on a weekly or biweekly basis, whatever was necessary. Then we would have monthly executive committee meetings for broader planning issues. These became a disaster. David had reached the point where he didn't like much of anything that was going on in the company and was becoming very critical. I disagreed with him, as did the other managers on most occasions. Tempers often flared and David became more and more isolated.
>
> He and I also began to disagree over which topics we should discuss with the group. I felt that some areas were best discussed between the two of us, particularly matters concerning personnel, and that other matters should be left for stockholders meetings. The committee meetings were becoming real battles.

In 1977, Richard Scott died. Although he had remained chairman of the board, he had generally been inactive in the company since 1968. Daniel and Jack Peterson and David Scott remained as the only directors.

Search for a Solution

When Jack Peterson returned from a summer vacation in August 1985, he was greeted by a string of complaints from several of MLI's sales agents and also from some managers. Jack decided that the problem had to be resolved. Jack sought an intermediary:

I knew that David and I weren't communicating and that I had to find a mediator David trusted. I had discussed this before with Allen Burke, our accountant. He was actually far more than our accountant. Allen is a partner with a Big Six accounting firm and is active in working with smaller companies. Allen was a boyhood friend who had grown up with David. I felt he had very high integrity and was very smart. David trusted him totally and Allen was probably one of David's major advisors about things.

When I first talked to Burke in March, he basically said, "Well, you have problems in a marriage and you make it work. Go make it work, Jack." He wasn't going to listen much.

Then in early September, I went back to say that it wasn't going to work anymore. I asked him for his help. Allen said that David had also seen him to complain about the problems, so Allen knew that the situation had become intolerable.

Both directly and through Burke, Jack pressured David to agree to a meeting to resolve the situation. Although David was also unhappy about their conflicts, he was hesitant to meet until he had thought through his options.

Jack felt that there were several principal reasons for David's reluctance to meet. Since they couldn't seem to solve their differences, the alternative of having one of them leave the company or become a silent partner glared as a possibility. Jack knew that David's only work experience was with MLI and was limited primarily to managing manufacturing operations he had known for years. Second, Jack thought that David was very uncertain about financial analysis, in which he had little training. Because he had not been directly involved in the financial operations, he was not aware of all the financial implications of his decisions. Jack felt that this made David's task of weighing the pros and cons of alternative courses of action much more difficult. Finally, there was the emotional tie to the company and the desire to avoid such a momentous decision.

As discussion began to result in the possibility that the partners would sell the company, David's reluctance waxed and waned. Just before Thanksgiving, David called Jack, who was sick at home, and said he had decided to fire the financial manager and become the treasurer of the company. David wanted to look at the figures for a year or so, and then he would be able to make a better decision. Jack felt that the financial manager was essential and could not be discharged. He thought that this was really more of an attempt to buy time. After some discussion, Jack convinced David that the financial manager should be retained.

After another month of give and take, Jack and David realized that they had no estimate of the value of the company if it were to be sold. Both felt that this might alter the attractiveness of the alternatives that each was considering.

Valuing the Company

Before making his decision, Jack reviewed the thinking he had done since first considering the idea of buying or selling the company. He began with the company's current position. With the serious discussions going on about the buyout agreement, preparation of the financial statements for 1985 had been accelerated and they were already completed. (These are shown, together with the results of 1984 and 1983, as *Exhibits B* and *C*.)

Jack had also begun developing the bank support he might need to fund a buyout. The company's banker indicated that he would loan Jack funds secured by his other personal

Exhibit B
Financial Statements

Statement of Earnings

	Year Ended December 31		
	1985	*1984*	*1983*
Net sales	$4,412,191	$3,573,579	$2,973,780
Costs of goods sold:			
Inventories at beginning of year	742,907	593,185	416,512
Purchases	1,599,426	1,275,665	1,109,781
Freight in	19,520	26,595	20,966
Direct labor	430,154	360,568	328,487
Manufacturing expenses	977,229	802,172	673,643
	3,769,236	3,058,185	2,549,389
Inventories at end of year	826,228	742,907	593,185
	2,943,008	2,315,278	1,956,204
Gross profit	1,469,183	1,285,301	1,017,576
Product development expenses	131,746	128,809	102,299
Selling and administrative expenses	1,112,542	915,140	740,801
	1,244,288	1,043,949	843,100
Operating income	224,895	214,352	174,476
Other expense (income):			
Interest expense	56,259	37,790	32,416
Payments to retired employee	10,000	10,000	20,000
Miscellaneous	(923)	(1,551)	(6,193)
	65,336	46,239	46,223
Earnings before income taxes	159,559	168,113	128,253
Provision for income taxes	44,350	67,100	49,000
Earnings before extraordinary income	115,209	101,013	79,253
Extraordinary income—life insurance proceeds in excess of cash surrender value			27,275
Net earnings	$115,209	$101,013	$106,528
Earnings per share of common stock	$19.15	$16.79	$13.17

assets if Jack was the buyer, but that since he had not worked with David, the bank would decline to finance an acquisition with David as the buyer. In addition, the bank would continue the company's existing line of credit, which was secured by MLI's cash and accounts receivable. The maximum which could be borrowed with this line was an amount equal to 100 percent of cash plus 75 percent of receivables. Both types of borrowing would be at one percent over the prime rate (then about 9 percent).

Jack worked with the financial manager to develop financial projections and valuation assessments. To be conservative, Jack had made the sales projections about 10 percent lower each year than he really thought they would achieve. Because fixed costs would not rise appreciably with modest increases in sales, any improvements in sales volume would directly increase profits. He felt he should consider how these various changes would impact his financing requirements and his assessment.

Jack also had sought out common valuation techniques. By looking through business periodicals and talking to friends, he found that these methods were not necessarily precise. Private manufacturing companies were most often valued at between 5 and 10 times after tax earnings. Book net asset value also helped establish business worth, but was often adjusted to reflect differences between the market value of assets and the carrying values

Exhibit B *(continued)*

	December 31		
	1985	*1984*	*1983*
Assets			
Current assets:			
Cash	$51,248	$3,778	$70,520
Accounts receivable:			
Customers	600,361	430,750	318,356
Refundable income taxes	23,001		
Other		2,276	5,289
	623,362	433,026	323,645
Less allowance for doubtful receivables	3,500	3,500	3,500
	619,862	429,526	320,145
Inventories:			
Raw materials	291,790	259,550	277,072
Work in progress	534,438	483,357	316,113
	826,228	742,907	593,185
Prepaid insurance and other	14,208	20,134	26,070
Total current assets	1,511,366	1,196,345	1,009,920
Property, plant, and equipment:			
Buildings and improvements	341,426	325,686	295,130
Machinery and equipment	210,493	173,073	135,419
Motor vehicles	32,578	32,578	29,421
Office equipment	42,866	43,905	36,949
	627,363	575,242	496,919
Less accumulated depreciation	273,284	233,444	185,215
	354,079	341,798	311,704
Land	11,101	11,101	11,101
	365,180	352,899	322,805
Other assets:			
Cash surrender value of life insurance policies (less loans of $19,478 in 1985, $19,590 in 1984, and $19,432 in 1983)	81,978	77,215	72,569
Total assets	$1,958,524	$1,626,459	$1,405,294

(Continued)

shown on balance sheets. For MLI, this was significant because they had obtained their new plant at an excellent price. Jack felt that it alone was probably worth $200,000 more than the stated book value.

To Jack, the variations in worth suggested by these different methods not only reflected the uncertainty of financial valuation techniques but also showed that a business had different values to different people. His estimate would have to incorporate other, more personal and subjective elements.

Personal Financial Considerations

One important consideration was what amount of personal resource each could and should put at risk. Both Jack and David were financially very conservative. Neither of them had ever had any personal long-term debt—even for a house. Jack could gather a maximum of $650,000 of assets outside of MLI that could be pledged to secure borrowing. His bank had already confirmed that he could borrow against those assets. However, for him to put his entire worth at risk to purchase David's share of the company, he would want to be very comfortable that the price was a reasonable one. Jack described his feelings: "You get very

Exhibit B ***(continued)***

	December 31		
	1985	*1984*	*1983*
Liabilities and Stockholders' Equity			
Current liabilities:			
Current maturities of long-term debt	$12,184	$10,558	$9,000
Note payable—bank	325,000	200,000	
Note payable—officer		30,000	39,000
Accounts payable	389,582	295,208	313,203
Amount due for purchase of treasury stock			75,000
Accrued liabilities	154,590	116,134	88,957
Total current liabilities	881,356	651,900	525,160
Long-term debt	176,522	189,122	195,710
Stockholders' Equity			
Contributed capital:			
6% cumulative preferred stock—authorized 10,000 shares of $10 per value; issued 2,000 shares	20,000	20,000	20,000
Common stock:			
Class A (nonvoting):			
Authorized 15,000 shares of $10 par value; issued 8,305 shares	83,050	83,050	83,050
Class B (voting):			
Authorized 5,000 shares of $10 par value; issued and outstanding 20 shares	200	200	200
	103,250	103,250	103,250
Retained earnings	892,396	777,187	676,174
	995,646	880,437	779,424
Less shares reacquired and held in treasury—at cost:			
2,000 shares 6% cumulative preferred stock	20,000	20,000	20,000
2,308 shares Class A common stock	75,000	75,000	75,000
	95000	95,000	95,000
	900,646	785,437	684,424
Total liabilities and stockholders' equity	$1,958,524	$1,626,459	$1,405,294

protective about what you have outside the company. The problem you always have with a small company is that most of your worth is tied up in it and you may have very little to fall back on if something goes sour. We both have never been big leverage buyers or anything like that."

Besides the element of increased financial risk, there were several other considerations that tempered Jack's willingness to pay a very high price. Since they had moved to the plant in Pontiac, the one-hour commute to work had been a bit burdensome. It would be nice not to have that drive. Jack also felt that he had good experience in the overall management of a business and his engineering undergraduate degree and MBA gave him a certain amount of flexibility in the job market. This was important because, for both financial and personal reasons, he felt he would still have to work if he was no longer associated with MLI.

On the other hand, some factors encouraged Jack to be aggressive. His father cautioned him to be reasonable, but Jack knew his father would be very disappointed if he lost the company, and Jack himself had strong emotional ties to MLI. Jack also developed a point of view that in some ways he was buying the entire company, rather than just half: "I'm sitting here with a company that I have no control over because of our disagreements. If I buy the other half share, I'm buying the whole company—I'm buying peace of mind, I could do what

Exhibit B *(concluded)*

Statement of Changes in Financial Position

	Year Ended December 31		
	1985	*1984*	*1983*
Working capital provided:			
From operations:			
Earnings before extraordinary income	$115,209	$101,013	$ 79,253
Add depreciation not requiring outlay of working capital	55,978	50,658	44,267
Working capital provided from operation	171,187	151,671	123,520
Extraordinary income from life insurance proceeds			27,275
Capitalized equipment lease obligation		5,295	
Proceeds from cash surrender value of life insurance policies			51,877
Total working capital provided	171,187	156,966	202,672
Working capital applied:			
Additions to property, plant, and equipment	68,259	80,752	47,107
Increase in cash surrender value of life insurance policies—net of loans	4,763	4,646	5,954
Reduction of long-term debt	12,600	11,883	8,995
Purchase of 2,308 shares of nonvoting Class A stock			75,000
Total working capital applied	85,622	97,281	137,057
Increase in working capital	$ 85,565	$ 59,685	$ 65,615
Net change in working capital consists of:			
Increase (decrease) in current assets:			
Cash	$ 47,470	$(66,742)	$ 64,854
Accounts receivable—net	190,336	109,381	(3,548)
Inventories	83,321	149,722	176,673
Prepaid expenses	(6,106)	(5,936)	(4,980)
	315,021	186,425	232,999
Increase (decrease) in current liabilities:			
Current portion of long-term debt	1,626	1,558	500
Note payable to bank	125,000	200,000	
Note payable to officer	(30,000)	(9,000)	
Accounts payable	94,374	(17,995)	104,083
Amount due for purchase of treasury stock		(75,000)	75,000
Contribution to profit-sharing trust			(20,000)
Accrued liabilities	38,456	27,177	7,801
Total	229,456	126,740	167,384
Increase in working capital	85,565	59,685	65,615
Working capital at beginning of year	544,445	484,760	419,145
Working capital at end of year	$630,010	$544,445	$484,760

I want, I wouldn't have to argue. So I'd buy a 'whole peace of mind' if I bought the other half of the company."

Finally, Jack considered his competitive position versus David. Although David had not accumulated the personal resources that Jack had, he had a brother-in-law with a private company that Jack knew had the ability to match Jack's resources and might be willing to back David financially. The brother-in-law would also be giving David financial advice in evaluating his alternatives and setting a value for the company. David also probably had fewer job prospects if he sold out. His undergraduate study was in liberal arts and his entire experience was within MLI. Jack also thought David might have some doubts abut his ability to manage the company on his own.

Exhibit C
Pro Forma Financial Statements

Income Statement Projections (prepared by Jack Peterson)

Historical Percentages			*Projected Percentages*				*Thousands of Dollars*		
1983	*1984*	*1985*	*1986*	*1987*	*1988*		*1986*	*1987*	*1988*
100.00	100.00	100.00	100.0	100.0	100.0	Net sales	$4,800	$5,100	$5,400
65.80	64.79	66.70	67.0	67.0	67.0	Cost of goods sold	3,216	3,417	3,618
34.22	35.21	33.30	33.0	33.0	33.0	Gross income	1,584	1,683	1,782
28.61	29.28	28.25	28.0*	28.0	28.0	Operating, general, and admin.	1,344	1,428	1,512
5.61	5.93	5.05	5.0	5.0	5.0	Profit before taxes	240	255	270
38.20	39.90	27.80	39.0†	39.0	39.0	Taxes	94	99	105
						Net earnings	$ 146	$ 156	$ 165

*Projected percentages reflect an assumption that one partner will leave the company, and include a $25,000 cost reduction for the reduced salary requirements of a replacement.

†Effective tax rate.

The Meeting

After another conversation with Allen Burke, David Scott called Jack Peterson at home one evening: "Jack, I realize that you're right—I can't live in this tense environment any longer. I've spoken with Allen, and he has agreed to meet with both of us to discuss our situation, and to attempt to identify some possible solutions. Would Friday at 9:00 be convenient for you?"

PART V
START-UP AND AFTER

Under conditions of rapid growth, entrepreneurs face unusual paradoxes and challenges as their companies grow and the management modes required by these companies change.

Whether they have the adaptability and resiliency in the face of swift developments to grow fast enough as managers and whether they have enough courage, wisdom, and discipline to balance growing fast enough to keep pace with the competition and lightninglike industry movements and turbulence will become crystal clear.

There are enormous pressures and physical and emotional wear and tear that entrepreneurs will face during the rapid growth of their companies. It goes with the territory. Entrepreneurs after start-up find that "it" has to be done now, that there is no room to falter, and that there are no "runners up." Clearly, those who have a personal entrepreneurial strategy, who are healthy, who have their lives in order, and who know what they are signing up for fare better than those who do not.

Among all the stimulating and exceedingly difficult challenges entrepreneurs face—and can meet successfully—none is more liberating and exhilarating than a harvest. Perhaps the point is made best in one of the final lines of the play *Oliver*: "In the end all that counts, is in the bank, in large amounts!"

Obviously, money is not the only thing, or everything. But money is the vehicle that can ensure both independence and autonomy to do what you want to do, mostly on your terms, and can significantly increase the options and opportunities at your discretion. In effect, for entrepreneurs, net worth is the final score card of the value creation process.

Various life cycle models, and our previous discussion, depicted the life cycle of a growing firm as a smooth curve with rapidly ascending sales and profits and a leveling off toward the peak and then dipping toward decline.

In truth, however, very very few, if any, new and growing firms experience such smooth and linear phases of growth. By and large, if the actual growth curves of new companies are plotted over their first 10 years, the curves will look far more like the ups and downs of a roller-coaster ride than the smooth progressions usually depicted. Over the life of a typical growing firm, there are periods of jerks, bumps, hiccups, indigestion, and renewal interspersed with periods of smooth sailing. Sometimes there is continual upward progress through all this, but with others, there are periods where the firms seem near collapse or at least in considerable peril.

Core Management Mode

As was noted earlier, changes in several critical variables determine just how frantic or easy transitions from one stage to the next will be. As a result, it is possible to make some generalizations about the main management challenges and transitions that will be encountered as the company grows. The core management mode is influenced by the number of employees a firm has, which is in turn related to its dollar sales.[1]

Recall that, in *Exhibit 6.4* in Chapter 6, until sales reach approximately $3 million and employees number 30, the core management mode is one of *doing.* Between $3 million and $10 million in sales and 30 to 75 employees, the core management mode is *managing.* When sales exceed $10 million and employees number over 75, the core management mode is *managing managers.* Obviously, these revenue and employment figures are broad generalities. The number of people is a better indicator of the increasing complexity of the management task, and suggest a new wall to be scaled, rather than a precise point. To illustrate just how widely sales per employee can vary, consider *Exhibit 16.1*. Typically, in 1992, established firms generated $125,000 to $175,000 in sales, but Reebok's $671,000 (due to having relatively few employees because of a great deal of subcontracting of shoe manufacture) was nearly 35

Exhibit 16.1
1992 Sales Per Employee

Company	*(000)*
Raytheon Company	$141.8
Digital Equipment Corporation	138.7
Data General Corporation	159.5
Stratus Computer, Inc.	185.5
Wang Laboratories, Inc.	164.8
Well Fleet Communications	226.9
Lotus Development Corporation	204.6
Gillette	167.6
Biogen, Inc.	309.4
Genetic Institute	158.1
Picture Tel Corporation	199.2
Augat, Inc.	92.7
Ground Round Restaurants	23.4
Sonesta International Hotels	19.7
Mediplex Group, Inc.	40.8
Neiman Marcus Group	170.0
Stop & Shop Company	118.5
Reebok International Ltd.	691.7

Source: *Boston Globe*, June 8, 1993, p. 60.

[1] Harvey "Chet" Krentzman described this phenomenon to the author many years ago. The principle still applies.

times larger than Sonesta International Hotel's $19,700. Thus, these numbers are boundaries, constantly moving as a result of inflation and competitive dynamics.

The central issue facing entrepreneurs in all sorts of businesses is this: as the size of the firm increases, the core management mode likewise *changes from doing to managing to managing managers.*

During each of the stages of growth of a firm, there are entrepreneurial crises, or hurdles, that most firms will confront. *Exhibit 16.2,* as well as the following discussion, considers by stage some indications of crisis.[2] As the exhibit shows, for each fundamental driving force of entrepreneurship, there are a number of "signals" that crises are imminent. While the list is long, these are not the only indicators of crises new ventures can and most likely will see—only the most common. Of course, each of these signals does not necessarily

Exhibit 16.2
Crises and Symptoms

Pre-Start-Up (Years −3 to −1)

Entrepreneurs:
- *Focus.* Is the founder really an entrepreneur, bent on building a company, or an inventor, technical dilettante, or the like?
- *Selling.* Does the team have the necessary selling and closing skills to bring in the business and make the plan—on time?
- *Management.* Does the team have the necessary management skills and relevant experience, or is it overloaded in one or two areas (e.g., the financial or technical areas)?
- *Ownership.* Have the critical decisions about ownership and equity splits been resolved, and are the members committed to these?

Opportunity:
- *Focus.* Is the business really user- , customer- , and market-driven (by a need), or is it driven by an invention of a desire to create?
- *Customers.* Have customers been identified with specific names, addresses, and phone numbers, and have purchase levels been estimated, or is the business still only at the concept stage?
- *Supply.* Are costs, margins, and lead times to acquire supplies, components, and key people known?
- *Strategy.* Is the entry plan a shotgun and cherry-picking strategy, or is it a rifle shot at a well-focused niche?

Resources:
- *Resources.* Have the required capital resources been identified?
- *Cash.* Are the founders already out of cash (OOC) and their own resources?
- *Business plan.* Is there a business plan, or is the team "hoofing it"?

Start-Up and Survival (Years 0 to 3)

Entrepreneurs:
- *Leadership.* Has a top leader been accepted, or are founders vying for the decision role or insist on equality in all decisions?
- *Goals.* Do the founders share and have compatible goals and work styles, or are these starting to conflict and diverge once the enterprise is underway and pressures mount?
- *Management.* Are the founders anticipating and preparing for a shift from doing to managing and letting go—of decisions and control—that will be required to make the plan on time?

Opportunity:
- *Economics.* Are the economic benefits and payback to the customer actually being achieved, and on time?
- *Strategy.* Is the company a one-product company with no encore in sight?
- *Competition.* Have previously unknown competitors or substitutes appeared in the marketplace?
- *Distribution.* Are there surprises and difficulties in actually achieving planned channels of distribution on time?

Resources:
- *Cash.* Is the company facing a cash crunch early as a result of not having a business plan (and a financial plan)? That is, is it facing a crunch because no one is asking: When will we run out of cash? Are the owners' pocketbooks exhausted?
- *Schedule.* Is the company experiencing serious deviations from projections and time estimates in the business plan? Is the company able to marshall resources according to plan and on time?

(Continued)

[2] The crises discussed here are the ones the author considers particularly critical. Usually, failure to overcome even a few can seriously imperil a venture at a given stage. There are, however, many more, but a complete treatment of all of them is outside the scope of this book.

Exhibit 16.2 *(concluded)*

Early Growth (Years 4–10)

Entrepreneurs:

- *Doing or managing.* Are the founders still just *doing,* or are they managing for results by a plan? Have the founders begun to delegate and let go of critical decisions, or do they maintain veto power over all significant decisions?
- *Focus.* Is the mind-set of the founders operational only, or is there some serious strategic thinking going on as well?

Opportunity:

- *Market.* Are repeat sales and sales to new customers being achieved on time, according to plan, and because of interaction with customers, or are these coming from the engineering, R&D, or planning group? Is the company shifting to a marketing orientation without losing its killer instinct for closing sales?
- *Competition.* Are price and quality being blamed for loss of customers or for an inability to achieve targets in the sales plan, while customer service is rarely mentioned?
- *Economics.* Are gross margins beginning to erode?

Resources:

- *Financial control.* Are accounting and information systems and control (purchasing orders, inventory, billing, collections, cost and profit analysis, cash management, etc.) keeping pace with growth and being there when they are needed?
- *Cash.* Is the company always out of cash—or nearly OOC, and is no one asking when it will run out or is sure why or what to do about it?
- *Contacts.* Has the company developed the outside networks (directors, contacts, etc.) it needs to continue growth?

Maturity (Years 10–15 plus)

Entrepreneurs:

- *Goals.* Are the partners in conflict over control, goals, or underlying ethics or values?
- *Health.* Are there signs that the founders' marriages, health, or emotional stability are coming apart (i.e., are there extramarital affairs, drug and/or alcohol abuse, or fights and temper tantrums with partners or spouses)?
- *Teamwork.* Is there a sense of team building for a "greater purpose," with the founders now managing managers, or is there conflict over control of the company and disintegration?

Opportunity:

- *Economics/competition.* Are the products and/or services that have gotten the company this far experiencing unforgiving economics as a result of perishability, competitor blind sides, new technology, or off-shore competition, and is there a plan to respond?
- *Product encore.* Has a major new product introduction been a failure?
- *Strategy.* Has the company continued to cherry-pick in fast-growth markets, with a resulting lack of strategic definition (which opportunities to say no to)?

Resources:

- *Cash.* Is the firm OOC again?
- *Development/information.* Has growth gotten out of control, with systems, training, and development of new managers failing to keep pace?
- *Financial control.* Have systems continued to lag behind sales?

Harvest/Stability (Years 15–20 plus)

Entrepreneurs:

- *Succession/ownership.* Are there mechanisms in place to provide for management succession and the handling of very tricky ownership issues (especially family)?
- *Goals.* Have the partners' personal and financial goals and priorities begun to conflict and diverge? Are any of the founders simply bored or burned out, and are they seeking a change of view and activities?
- *Entrepreneurial passion.* Has there been an erosion of the passion for creating value through the recognition and pursuit of opportunity, or are turf-building, acquiring status and power symbols, and gaining control favored?

Opportunity:

- *Strategy.* Is there a spirit of innovation and renewal in the firm (e.g., a goal that half the company's sales come from products or services less than five years old), or has lethargy set in?
- *Economics.* Have the core economics and durability of the opportunity eroded so far that profitability and return on investment are nearly as low as that for the Fortune 500?

Resources:

- *Cash.* Has OOC been solved by increasing bank debt and leverage because the founders do not want—or cannot agree—to give up equity?
- *Accounting.* Have accounting and legal issues, especially their relevance for wealth building and estate and tax planning, been anticipated and addressed? Has a harvest concept been part of the long-range planning process?

indicate that particular crises will happen to every company at each stage; but when the signals are there, serious difficulties cannot be too far behind.

The Problem in Rate of Growth

Difficulties in anticipating these shifts by recognizing signals and developing management approaches are compounded by rate of growth itself. The faster the rate of growth, the greater the potential for difficulty; this is because of the various pressures, chaos, confusion, and loss of control. It is not an exaggeration to say that these pressures and demands increase geometrically, rather than in a linear way (see discussion in Chapter 6).

Growth rates affect all aspects of a business. Thus, as sales increase, as more people are hired, and as inventory increases, sales outpace manufacturing capacity. Facilities are then increased, people are moved between buildings, accounting systems and controls cannot keep up, and so on. The cash burn rate accelerates, and such acceleration continues. Learning curves do the same. Worst of all, cash collections lag behind, as shown in *Exhibit 16.3.*

For example, distinctive issues caused by rapid growth were considered at seminars at Babson College with the founders and presidents of rapidly growing companies—companies with sales of at least $1 million and growing in excess of 30 percent per year.[3] These founders and presidents pointed to the following:

- *Opportunity overload.* Rather than lacking enough sales or new market opportunities, a classic concern in mature companies, these firms faced an abundance. Choosing from among these was a problem.
- *Abundance of capital.* While most stable or established smaller or medium-sized firms often have difficulties obtaining equity and debt financing, most of the rapidly growing

[3] These seminars were held at Babson College near Boston in 1985 and 1986. A good number of the firms represented had sales over $1 million, and a good number were growing at greater than 100 percent per year.

Exhibit 16.3
Spend-Rate/Orders/Collection Leads and Lags

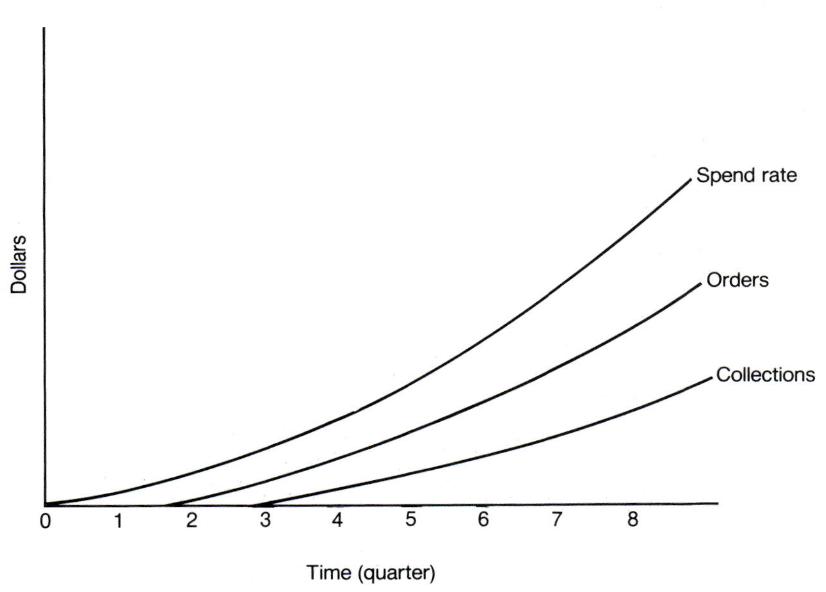

firms were not constrained by this. The problem was, rather, how to evaluate investors as "partners" and the terms of the deals with which they were presented.

- *Misalignment of cash burn and collection rates.* These firms all pointed to problems of cash burn rates racing ahead of collections. They found that unless effective integrated accounting, inventory, purchasing, shipping, and invoicing systems and controls are in place, this misalignment can lead to chaos and collapse. One firm, for example, had tripled its sales in three years from $5 million to $16 million. Suddenly, its president resigned, insisting that, with the systems which were in place, the company would be able to grow to $100 million. However, the computer system was disastrously inadequate, which compounded other management weaknesses. The generation of any believable financial and accounting information that could be relied upon was not possible for many months. Losses of more than $1 million annually mounted, and the company's lenders panicked. To make matters worse, the auditors failed to stay on top of the situation until it was too late and were replaced. While the company has survived, it has had to restructure its business and has shrunk to $6 million in sales, to pay off bank debt and to avoid bankruptcy. Fortunately, it is in the process of recovering.
- *Decision making.* Many of the firms succeeded because they executed functional day-to-day and week-to-week decisions, rather than strategizing. Strategy had to take a back seat. Many of the representatives of these firms argued that in conditions of rapid growth it was only about 10 percent of the story.
- *Surprises and the like.* Expansion of space or facilities is a problem and one of the most disrupting events during the early explosive growth of a company. Managers of many of these firms were not prepared for the surprises, delays, organizational difficulties, and system interruptions that are spawned by such expansion.

Industry Turbulence

The problems just discussed are compounded by the amount of industry turbulence surrounding the venture. Firms with higher growth rates usually are found in industries that are also developing rapidly. In addition, there are often many new entrants, both with competing products or services and with substitutes.

The effects are many: Often, prices fluctuate. The turbulence in the semiconductor industry in the 1980s is a good example. From June 1984 to June 1985, the price to original equipment manufacturers (OEMs) of 64K memory chips fell from $2.50 each to 50 cents. The price to OEMs of 256K chips fell from $15 to $3. The disruption this caused in marketing and sales projections, in financial planning and cash forecasting, and the like, for firms in the industry can be imagined. Often, too, there are rapid shifts in cost and experience curves.

THE IMPORTANCE OF CULTURE AND ORGANIZATIONAL CLIMATE

Six Dimensions

The organizational culture and climate, either of a new venture or of an existing organization, are critical in how well the organization will deal with growth. A number of studies of performance in large business organizations that used the concept of organizational climate (i.e., the perceptions of people about the kind of place it is to work in) have led to two general conclusions.[4] First, the climate of an organization can

[4] See Jeffry A Timmons, "The Entrepreneurial Team: Formation and Development," a paper presented at the Academy of Management, annual meeting, Boston, August 1973.

have significant impact on performance. Further, climate is created both by the expectations people bring to the organization and the practices and attitudes of the key managers.

The climate notion has relevance for new ventures, as well as for entrepreneurial efforts in large organizations. An entrepreneur's style and priorities—particularly, how he or she manages tasks and people—is well-known by the people being managed and affects performance. Recall the entrepreneurial climate described by Enrico of Pepsi, where the critical factors included setting high-performance standards by developing short-run objectives that do not sacrifice long-run results, providing responsive personal leadership, encouraging individual initiative, helping others to succeed, developing individual networks for success, and so forth. Or listen to the tale of Gerald H. Langeler, the president of the systems group of Mentor Graphics Corporation, who explained what the "vision trap" was.[5] Langeler described the vision of his company's entrepreneurial climate as simply to "Build Something People Will Buy."[6] The culture of Mentor Graphics was definitely shaped by the founders' styles because "there were perhaps 15 of us at the time—we could not only share information very quickly, we could also create a sense of urgency and purpose without the help of an articulated vision."[7]

Evidence suggests that superior teams operate differently in terms of setting priorities, in resolving leadership issues, in what and how roles are performed by team members, in attitudes toward listening and participation, and in dealing with disagreements. Further, evidence suggests that specific approaches to management can impact the climate of a growing organization. For example, gains from the motivation, commitment, and teamwork, which are anchored in a consensus approach to management, while not immediately apparent, are striking later on. At that time there is swiftness and decisiveness in actions and in follow-through, since the negotiating, compromising, and accepting of priorities are history. Also, new disagreements that emerge generally do not bring progress to a halt, since there is both high clarity and broad acceptance of overall goals and underlying priorities. Without this consensus, each new problem or disagreement often necessitates a time-consuming and painful confrontation and renegotiation simply because it was not done initially.

Organizational climate can be described along six basic dimensions:

- *Clarity.* The degree of organizational clarity in terms of being well organized, concise, and efficient in the way that tasks, procedures, and assignments are made and accomplished.
- *Standards.* The degree to which management expects and puts pressure on employees for high standards and excellent performance.
- *Commitment.* The extent to which employees feel committed to the goals and objectives of the organization.
- *Responsibility.* The extent to which members of the organization feel individual responsibility for accomplishing their goals without being constantly monitored and second-guessed.
- *Recognition.* The extent to which employees feel they are recognized and rewarded (nonmonetarily) for a job well done, instead of only being punished for mistakes or errors.
- *Esprit de corps.* The extent to which employees feel a sense of cohesion and team spirit, of working well together.

[5] Gerald H Langeler, "The Vision Trap," *Harvard Business Review*, March–April 1992 reprint 92204.

[6] Ibid., p. 4.

[7] Ibid., p. 5.

Approaches to Management

In achieving the entrepreneurial culture and climate described above, certain approaches to management (also discussed in Chapter 6) are common across core management modes.

Leadership

No single leadership pattern seems to characterize successful ventures. Leadership may be shared, or informal, or a "natural leader" may guide a task. Common, however, is the pattern whereby a manager defines and gains agreements on who has what responsibility and authority and who does what with and to whom. Roles, tasks, responsibilities, accountabilities, and appropriate approvals are defined.

There is no competition for leadership in these organizations, and leadership is based on expertise, not authority. Emphasis is placed on performing task-oriented roles, but someone invariably provides for "maintenance" and group cohesion by good humor and wit. Further, the leader does not force his or her own solution on the team or exclude the involvement of potential resources. Instead, the leader understands the relationships among tasks and between the leader and his or her followers and is able to lead in those situations where it is appropriate, including managing actively the activities of others through directions, suggestions, and so forth.

This approach is in direct contrast to the "commune approach," where two to four entrepreneurs, usually friends or work acquaintances, leave unanswered such questions as who is in charge, who makes the final decisions, and how real differences of opinion are resolved. While some overlapping of roles and a sharing in and negotiating of decisions are desirable in a new venture, too much looseness is debilitating.

This approach also contrasts with situations where a self-appointed leader takes over, where there is competition for leadership, or where one task takes precedence over other tasks.

Consensus Building

Leaders of most successful new ventures define authority and responsibility in a way that builds motivation and commitment to cross-departmental and corporate goals. Using a consensus approach to management requires managing and working with peers and with the subordinates of others (or with superiors) outside formal chains of command and balancing multiple viewpoints and demands.

In the consensus approach, the manager is seen as willing to relinquish his or her priorities and power in the interests of an overall goal, and the appropriate people are included in setting cross-functional or cross-departmental goals and in making decisions. Participation and listening are emphasized.

The most effective managers, in addition, are committed to dealing with problems and working problems through to agreement by seeking a reconciliation of viewpoints, rather than emphasizing differences, and by blending ideas, rather than playing the role of hard-nose negotiator or devil's advocate to force their own solution. There is open confrontation of differences of opinion and a willingness to talk out differences, assumptions, reasons, and inferences. Logic and reason tend to prevail, and there is a willingness to change opinions based on consensus.

Communication

The most effective managers share information and are willing to alter individual views. Listening and participation are facilitated by such methods as circular seating arrangements, few interruptions or side conversations, and calm discussion versus many interruptions, loud or separate conversations, and so forth, in meetings.

Encouragement

Successful managers build confidence by encouraging innovation and calculated risk-taking, rather than by punishing or criticizing what is less than perfect, and by expecting and encouraging others to find and correct their own errors and to solve their own problems. They are perceived by their peers and others as accessible and willing to help when needed, and they provide the necessary resources to enable others to do the job. When it is appropriate, they go to bat for their peers and subordinates, even when they know they can't always win. Further, differences are recognized and performance is rewarded.

Trust

The most effective managers are perceived as trustworthy and straightforward. They do what they say they are going to do; they are not the corporate rumor carriers; they are more open and spontaneous, rather than guarded and cautious with each word; and they are perceived as being honest and direct. They have a reputation of getting results and become known as the creative problemsolvers who have a knack for blending and balancing multiple views and demands.

Development

Effective managers have a reputation for developing human capital (i.e., they groom and grow other effective managers by their example and their mentoring). As noted in Chapter 6, Bradford and Cohen distinguish between the "heroic manager," whose need to be in control in many instances actually may stifle cooperation, and the "postheroic manager," a developer who actually brings about excellence in organizations by developing entrepreneurial middle management. If a company puts off developing middle management until price competition appears and its margins erode, the organization may come unraveled. Linking a plan to grow human capital at the middle management and the supervisory levels with the business strategy is an essential first step.

ENTREPRENEURIAL MANAGEMENT FOR THE 21ST CENTURY: THREE BREAKTHROUGHS

Three extraordinary companies have been built or revolutionized in the past two decades: Marion Labs, Inc., of Kansas City, Johnsonville Sausage of Cheybogan, Wisconsin, and Springfield Remanufacturing Corporation of Springfield, Missouri. Independently and unbeknownst to each other, these companies created what I describe as "High Standard, Perpetual Learning Cultures," which create and foster a "Chain of Greatness." The lessons from these three great companies provide a blueprint for entrepreneurial management in the twenty-first century. They set the standard and provide a tangible vision of what is possible. Not surprisingly, the most exciting, faster growing, and profitable companies in America today have striking similarities to these firms.

Ewing Marion Kauffman and Marion Labs

As described in Chapter 1, Marion Labs, founded in Ewing Marion Kauffman's garage in 1950, had reached $2.5 billion in sales by the time it merged with Dow-Merrel in 1989. Its market capitalization was $6.5 billion. Over 300 millionaires and 13 foundations were created from the builders of the company, including the Ewing Marion Kauffman Foundation. In sharp contrast, RJR Nabisco, about 10 times larger than Marion Labs at the time of the KKR leveraged buyout, generated only 20 millionaires. Clearly, these were very different companies. What was central to this phenomenal success story was the combination of a high potential opportunity with management execution based on core values and management philosophy ahead of its time. These principles are simple enough, but difficult to inculcate and sustain through good times and bad:

1. Treat everyone as you would want to be treated.
2. Share the wealth with those who have created it.
3. Pursue the highest standards of performance and ethics.

As noted earlier the company had no organizational chart, referred to all its people as associates, not employees, and had widespread profit-sharing and stock participation plans. Having worked for a few years now with "Mr. K" and the top management that built Marion Labs and that now runs the foundation, I can say that they are genuine and serious about these principles. They also have fun while succeeding, but they are highly dedicated to the practice of these core philosophies and values.

Jack Stack and Springfield Remanufacturing Corporation

The truly remarkable sage of this revolution in management is captured in Jack's book, *The Great Game of Business*, which is a must read for any entrepreneur. In 1983, Stack and a dozen colleagues acquired a tractor engine remanufacturing plant from the failing International Harvester Corporation. With an 89-to-1 debt-to-equity ratio and 21 percent interest, they acquired the company for 10 cents a share. In 1993, the company's shares were valued near $20 for the employee stock option plan (ESOP), and the company had completely turned around with sales approaching $100 million. What had happened?

Like Ewing Marion Kauffman, Jack Stack created and implemented some management approaches and values radically opposite to the top-down, hierarchical, custodial management commonly found in large manufacturing enterprises. At the heart of his leadership was creating a vision. *The Big Picture: Think and act like owners, be the best we can be, and be perpetual learners. Build teamwork as the key by learning from each other, open the books to everyone, and educate everyone so they can become responsible and accountable for the numbers, both short- and long-term.* Stack puts it this way:

> We try to take ignorance out of the workplace and force people to get involved, not with threats and intimidation but with education. In the process, we are trying to close the biggest gaps in American business—the gap between workers and managers. We're developing a system that allows everyone to get together and work toward the same goals. To do that, you have to knock down the barriers that separate people, that keep people from coming together as a team.[8]

At Springfield Remanufacturing Corporation, everyone learns to read and interpret all the financial statements, including an income statement, balance sheet, and cash flow, and how his or her job affects each line item. This open-book management style is linked with pushing responsibility downward and outward, and to understanding both wealth creation (i.e., shareholder value) and wealth sharing through short-term bonuses and long-term equity participation. Jack describes the value of this approach thus: "The payoff comes from getting the people who create the numbers to understand the numbers. When that happens, the communication between the bottom and the top of the organization is just phenomenal."[9] The results he has achieved in 10 years are nothing short of astounding. What is more amazing is that he has found the time to share this approach with others. To date, over 150 companies have participated in seminars that have enabled them to adopt this approach.

[8] Jack Stack, *The Great Game of Business* (New York: Currency/Doubleday Books, 1991), p. 5.

[9] Ibid., p. 93.

Ralph Stayer and Johnsonville Sausage Company[10]

In 1975, Johnsonville Sausage was a small company with about $5 million in sales and a fairly traditional, hierarchical, and somewhat custodial management. In just a few years, Ralph Stayer, the owner's son, created a radical transformation of the company, a management revolution whose values, culture, and philosophy are remarkably similar to the principles of Ewing Marion Kauffman and Jack Stack.

The results are astonishing: By 1980 the company had reached $15 million in sales; by 1985, $50 million; and by 1990, $150 million. At the heart of the changes he created was the concept of *total learning culture: everyone is a learner, seeking to improve constantly, finding better ways. High performance standards accompanied by an investment in training, and performance measures that made it possible to reward fairly both short- and long-term results* were critical to the transition. Responsibility and accountability was spread downward and outward. For example, instead of forwarding complaint letters to the marketing department, where they are filed and the standard response is sent, they go directly to the front-line sausage stuffer responsible for the product's taste. They are the ones who respond to customer complaints now. Another example is the interviewing, hiring, and training process for new people. A newly hired woman pointed out numerous shortcomings with the existing process and proposed ways to improve it. As a result, the entire responsibility was shifted from the traditional human resources/personnel group to the front line, with superb results.

As one would guess, such radical changes do not come easily. After all, how do such changes ever become initiated in the first place? Consider Ralph's insight:

> In 1980, I began looking for a recipe for change. I started by searching for a book that would tell me how to get people to care about their jobs and their company. Not surprisingly, the search was fruitless. No one could tell me how to wake up my own workforce; I would have to figure it out for myself. . . . The most important question any manager can ask is: "In the best of all possible worlds what would I really want to happen?"[11]

Even having taken such a giant step, Jack was ready to take the next, equally perilous steps:

> Acting on instinct, I ordered a change. "From now on," I announced to my management team, "you're all responsible for making your own decision." . . . I went from authoritarian control to authoritarian abdication. No one had asked for more responsibility; I had forced it down their throats.[12]

Further insight into just how challenging it is to transform a company like Johnsonville Sausage is revealed in another Stayer quote:

> I spent those two years pursuing another mirage as well—detailed strategic and tactical plans that would realize my goals of Johnsonville as the world's greatest sausage maker. We tried to plan organizational structure two to three years before it would be needed. . . . Later I realized that these structural changes had to grow from day-to-day working realities; no one could dictate them from above, and certainly not in advance.[13]

Exhibit 16.4 summarizes the key steps in the transformation of Johnsonville Sausage over several years. Such a picture undoubtedly oversimplifies the process and understates the extraordinary commitment and effort required to pull it off, but it does show how the central elements weave together.

[10] For an excellent discussion of this transformation, see "The Johnsonville Sausage Company," HBS Case 387-103, rev. June 27, 1990. Copyright © 1990 by the President and Fellows of Harvard College. See also Ralph Stayer, "How I Learned to Let My Workers Lead," *Harvard Business Review*, November–December 1990. Copyright © 1990 by the President and Fellows of Harvard College.

[11] Stayer, "How I Learned to Let My Workers Lead," p. 1.

[12] Ibid., pp. 3–4.

[13] Ibid., p. 4.

Exhibit 16.4
Summary of the Johnsonville Sausage Company

The critical aspects of the transition:

1. Started at the top: Ralph Stayer recognized that he was the heart of the problem and recognized the need to change—the most difficult step.
2. Vision was anchored in human resource management and in a particular idea of the company's culture:
   - Continuous learning organization.
   - Team concept—change players.
   - New model of jobs (Ralph Stayer's role and decision making).
   - Performance- and results-based compensation and rewards.
3. Stayer decided to push responsibility and accountability downward to the front-line decision makers:
   - Front-liners are closest to customer and the problem.
   - Define the whole task.
   - Invest in training and selection.
   - Job criteria and feedback = development tool.
4. Controls and mechanisms make it work:
   - Measure performance, not behavior, activities, and the like.
   - Emphasize learning and development, not allocation of blame.
   - Customize to you and the company.
   - Decentralize and minimize staff.

Exhibit 16.5
The Chain of Greatness

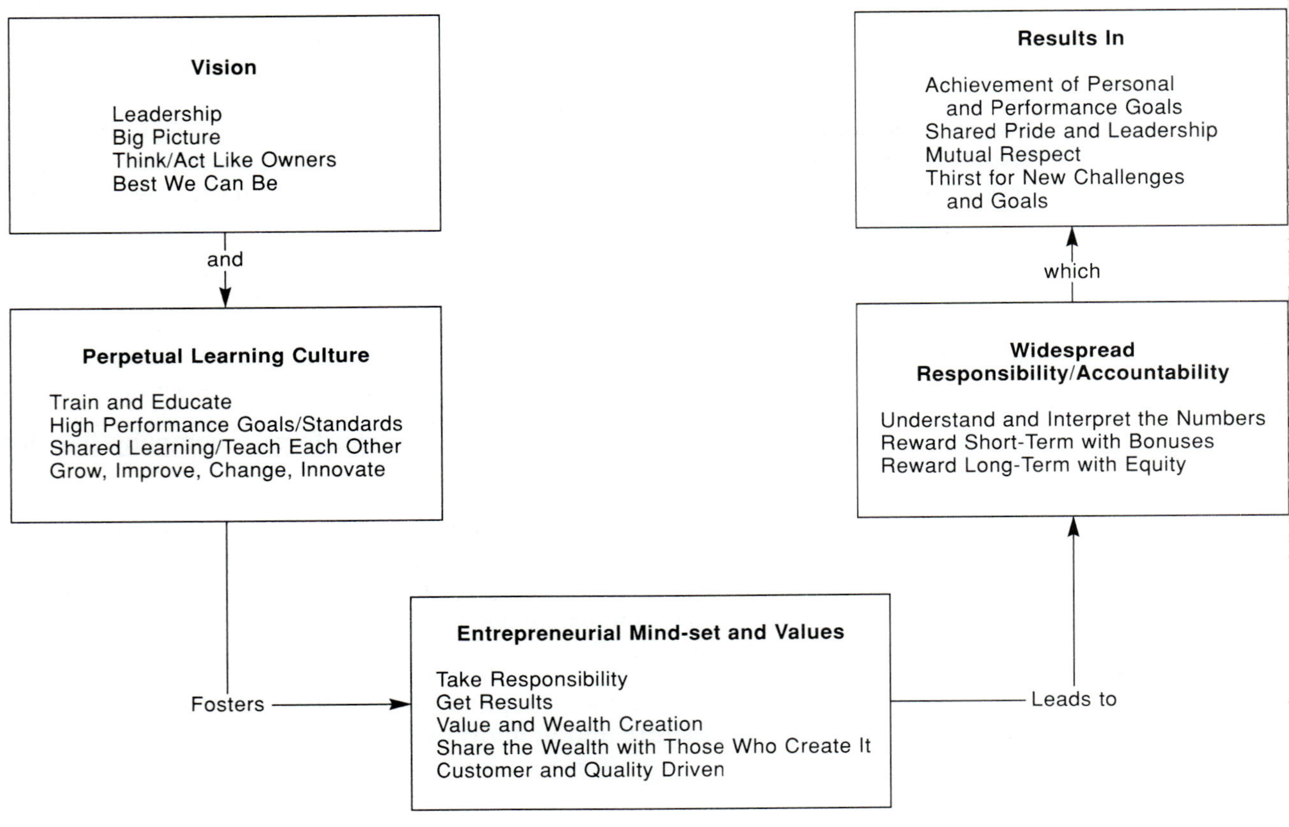

The Chain of Greatness

As we reflect on these three great companies, we can see that there is clearly a pattern here, with some common denominators in both the ingredients and the process. This "Chain of Greatness" becomes reinforcing and perpetuating (see *Exhibit 16.5*). Leadership that instills across the company a vision of greatness and an owner's mentality is a common beginning. A philosophy of perpetual learning throughout the organization accompanied by high standards of performance is key to the value-creating entrepreneurial cultures at the three firms. A culture that teaches and rewards teamwork, improvement, and respect for each other provides the oil and glue to make things work. Finally, a fair and generous short- and long-term reward system, as well as the necessary education to make sure that everyone knows and can use the numbers, creates a mechanism for sharing the wealth with those who contributed to it. The results speak for themselves: extraordinary levels of personal, professional, and financial achievement.

CASE—JIFFY LUBE INTERNATIONAL, INC.

Preparation Questions

1. Evaluate Jiffy Lube International's performance, opportunities, and financial strategy.
2. What should Hindman do now?
3. What should Don Remey do in order to realize his investment objectives?
4. As a new outside director to Jiffy Lube International, what questions would you raise and what recommendations would you offer to management?

JIFFY LUBE INTERNATIONAL, INC.

In the summer of 1987, Jiffy Lube International, Inc., faced some of the most critical issues in its young life. Preparing for a strategy meeting with some board members, management, and franchisees, Jim Hindman paced the room in the same way he had paced the locker room before a football game. Booz, Allen & Hamilton had recently completed a study of the quicklube industry; their findings indicated a fragmented, rapidly growing market. These market findings encouraged Hindman, who had projected a market of 6,000 units by 1990. The study indicated demand for 12,000 units. Additionally, the study revealed that Jiffy Lube International had a competitive advantage with a large number of mature units and the resources to sustain a national promotional campaign.

Jim Hindman and Jiffy Lube International (JLI) had come a long way from the acquisition of seven centers in Utah in 1979. By 1987 JLI had exceeded its projections for the last four years. (See *Exhibits G, H,* and *I.*) The company's growth included a larger management team and a more formal relationship with franchisees.

Hindman went over the agenda for the meeting. He wanted to review JLI's progress and to evaluate the operational and financial strategy going forward. He wondered about the credibility of Booz, Allen & Hamilton's findings. Was JLI taking enough risk to capture the potentially huge reward that Booz, Allen & Hamilton envisioned, or was the company on the verge of overextending itself?

THE QUICKLUBE INDUSTRY

Since 1979, the quicklube market had legitimized itself, as many Americans changed how they maintain their automobiles. As Jim Hindman stated:

> The "quicklube" industry was the fastest growing in the automotive aftermarket, due in part to the way more and more Americans live today. Because both spouses are employed in the majority of families, car dependency is higher than ever. Women are now faced with more of the responsibility in seeking car service, too. Greater work demands have created the need for prompt attention

to car care matters. Leaving the car for a day at a typical car care facility becomes a serious time strain for many. People are also keeping cars longer these days. While many drivers understand the importance of frequent oil changes, more are coming to appreciate the importance of complete fluid maintenance.

Additionally, JLI conservatively estimated that the number of passenger cars and small trucks on the road would grow at a rate of 1 to 2 percent annually. Also, the smaller engines in automobiles would require more frequent oil changes. The combined effects of these factors suggested, at the very least, a 2 percent increase in the quicklube market annually. (See *Exhibit A*.) Indeed, according to investment banker Alex Brown & Sons, "as consumer awareness and service availability improve, there was no reason why market share in new areas could not approach the [20 percent market share] level reached in Salt Lake City."[1]

Within the quicklube industry, this growth opportunity attracted competition. (See *Exhibit B*.) Major oil companies invested in the quicklube market to increase their market share, to increase brand awareness, and to take advantage of this growing distribution channel. In the summer of 1985, Quaker State became a major competitor, having purchased Minit Lube for $29 million. In 1986, Valvoline purchased Rapid Lube and also planned to develop centers in the quicklube market. In addition, many small, local, and regional, chains were being developed by entrepreneurs.

Exhibit A
Automobile Oil Change and Lubrication Market

	1985 Actual	*1990 Estimated*
Number of oil changes (millions)	360	397
Average price:	$ 19.00	$ 22.00
Subtotal ($ millions)	$6,840	$8,734
Related supplies ($ millions)	821	1,048
Total ($ millions)	$7,661	$9,782
Quicklube market share	4.6%	11.5%
Quicklube sales ($ millions)	$ 352	$1,125
Number of centers	2,000	5,500

Sources: Jiffy Lube and Alex Brown & Sons estimates

Exhibit B
Major Quicklube Center Operators (October 1986)

	Number of Centers in Operation				
Operator	*Company*	*Franchised*	*Total*	*Market Share*	*Ownership*
Jiffy Lube	21	401	422	63%	Private
Minit Lube	70	63	133	20%	Quaker State
Grease Monkey	0	75	75	11%	Public
Rapid Oil	42	0	42	6%	Valvoline
			672		

Source: Alex Brown & Sons, Industry Report (October 30, 1986)

[1]Alex Brown & Sons, "Industry Note," October 30, 1986.

JLI's Financial Strategy

In December 1985, Bridge Capital Investors (BCI) led a private placement group that invested $10 million in JLI. The investment fueled the effort to build out rapidly and for JLI to be the first quicklube company to advertise nationally. Capital contributed to expenses, new franchisees, and acquisitions. (See *Exhibit C.*)

Pennzoil and Jiffy Lube shared a mutually beneficial relationship. JLI was the largest purchaser of Pennzoil oil; Pennzoil provided the necessary financial backing for JLI to acquire real estate and to develop centers. In December 1985, the $100 million Pennzoil/Jiffy Lube Real Estate Partnership was established. Each party contributed $15 million in cash or properties valued at actual cost incurred over the next three years, with an additional $70 million in seven-year notes. The agreement provided for the development of 325 units over the next three years. Additionally, all the independent quicklubes affiliated with Pennzoil were to be converted into Jiffy Lube centers.

Jiffy Lube pursued its strategy by acquiring independent quicklube centers. In March 1985, JLI acquired 26 centers from Chicago's BW Oil Change chain and 5 centers from Indiana's Pit Stop '500 chain. The Chicago centers were franchised and the Indiana centers were operated by the new Company Operated Stores division. At the same time, on the franchisee level, JLI offered a "growth-oriented real estate program, targeting individual locations with third-party landowners. 'We are interested in talking to anyone who's interested in us,' Hindman said."[2] Expansion was not limited to the United States. In 1986, Jiffy Lube began to investigate international markets in Canada, Great Britain, and France.

In the United States, internal operations were developed to meet the challenges that accompany growth. As units were added, some organizational structure was needed to establish communication avenues for both the franchisee and the franchisor. Franchisees were organized into three geographic locations, with regional presidents for each area. The Association of Franchisees, of which all franchisees were a part, increased its prestige within the national organization by securing a seat on the board of directors. The president of the Association of Franchisees worked as a liaison between JLI management, the board, and the franchisees.

At the board's recommendation, Hindman brought in a professional manager as president. Bringing someone into JLI from the outside was not an easy transition for Hindman.

Exhibit C
Financial Characteristics of Typical Jiffy Lube Franchise

Real estate requirements	15,000 square feet of land
Cost of land and building	$300,000
Start-up costs (equipment, etc.)	$100,000
Monthly fixed costs	$8,000
Variable costs	57% of sales
Break-even car count/day	28–35 cars
Typical Months to breakeven	7–8 months

A typical mature unit (approximately two years old) will service between 60 and 70 cars per day, producing annual revenues of about $400,000–$500,000 and $75,000–$100,000 of pre-tax income.

Depending on whether the franchisee owns or leases the real estate, the monthly fixed costs include a charge for either:

1. Rent ($3,000–$4,000) paid to Jiffy Lube or to a third party lessor.
2. A similar charge for mortgage interest.

Source: Jiffy Lube International, Inc., annual reports, 1985–1987.

[2] "Jiffy Lube Buyouts Bolster Market Lead," *National Petroleum News*, March 1985, p. 35.

He remembered his response to their request: "Some of these Wall Street types, the first thing that they wanted to do was to get a search committee to get someone to run this business. I thought: What am I doing so terribly wrong? I am telling you—I took that request personally."

In April 1986, J. Richard Breen was appointed president and chief operating officer. Hindman found Breen himself and had confidence in his appointment based on Breen's experience as the executive vice president of international for Tenneco Automotive, a $500 million business, and as executive vice president of Fram Corporation, where he was in charge of the sales of Autolite Spark Plug Corporation and the Bentrix Brake.

GOING PUBLIC

With the put provision on the $10 million private placement by BCI in December 1985 and the need for more capital for expansion, an initial public offering (IPO) was inevitable. As Stephen Spinelli, the president of the Association of Franchisees, recalled:

> From the first meeting, Don Remey of BCI said, "When we go public. . . "—he never allowed any alternative to be introduced. He got everyone to naturally believe that we were going public. Negotiations focused on when we were going public and what the return would be on the put. [See *Exhibit D*.)

In addition to BCI's incentive to achieve liquidity, other members of the board and investors wanted to see JLI go public. Prior investors wanted cash or a cash equivalent. The management of JLI had obligations to meet and wanted to reduce debt. In 1986, the Old Court Savings and Loan financing for the construction of centers would finally be paid. Pennzoil's earlier investment of $1.6 million was also due. Management realized that the company was highly leveraged and that the proceeds of an offering would reduce the large interest and principal obligations.

Hindman saw the IPO as a chance to attract a large amount of capital, possibly JLI's largest investment ever, at a cheap price. Beyond the lower cost of money the IPO offered, Hindman felt that the IPO would generate name recognition. As a public company, Hindman believed that the units would profit from added publicity, advertising, and credibility. The

Exhibit D
Excerpt from Bridge Capital Investors: Private Placement

12% Senior Subordinated Notes Due 1992 with Warrants

Put Provision
If during five years from issuance, the Company's Common Stock has not traded publicly at levels set forth in the table that follows, the Purchase may put the warrants and/or underlying stock to the Company. The price will be determined by the calculation of the amount necessary to result in a 30% per annum internal rate of return to the Purchasers on that proportion of warrants not previously sold, taking into account all interest premium and principal repayment on the proportionately related Notes.

If (i) the Company completes one or more public offerings of Common Stock with the aggregate proceeds to the Company of at least $15 million and (ii) the average closing price for 60 consecutive trading days exceeds:

6 months ending 6/88—$17.50
6 months ending 12/88—$20.00
6 months ending 6/89—$25.00
6 months ending 12/89—$30.00
6 months ending 6/90—$35.00
6 months ending 12/90—$40.00

then the put provision will expire.
In the event the Company is unable to pay the amount due, the Purchasers have the right to nominate a majority of the Board of Directors.

parent company, JLI, would be more visible as a public company, which would help the franchisees in obtaining real estate financing. Acquisitions would also benefit because stock, rather than cash, could be used to purchase independent units and chains.

A major pressure on Hindman was the put, which compounded at a 30 percent internal rate of return. Depending on the timing of a public offering or a sale of the company, the put represented a major obligation of $9.1 million to $17.1 million. (See *Exhibit E*.)

Hindman had begun discussing the possibility of a public offering shortly after the closing of the $10 million private placement. By the spring of 1986, Alex Brown & Sons, a major Baltimore-based investment banker, indicated that a public offering might be possible later that year. They were impressed by the company's recent success and the growth opportunity for quicklubes. Shearson Lehman Hutton, which had acted as the agent on the $10 million private offering, was also supportive of an IPO. Preliminary pricing was discussed in the $8 to $12 per share range which was over 30 times estimated 1986 earnings per share. Hindman worked hard to produce company results and to develop underwriters' interest for an IPO.

The company filed a registration statement to sell 2,030,000 shares, in July 1986. The IPO market was increasingly receptive and the offering generated significant retail investor demand. The "road show" meetings in 10 cities in the United States and Canada gave Hindman and John Sasser, the chief financial officer, the opportunity to share their enthusiasm with hundreds of prospective investors.

> The investment bankers priced the issue at $10 to $12 per share, or more than 30 times fiscal 1986 earnings per share. Interest created by the road show pushed the actual price to $15. And when Jiffy Lube finished its first day on the ticker—carrying the stock ticker JLUB—it had risen to $21.25.[3]

In its final review of the registration statement, the Securities and Exchange Commission ruled that the put could be a significant claim against future stockholders' equity. BCI and the other investors agreed, just prior to the offering, to give up the put, in consideration for the pending stock offering at $15 versus their warrants at $6. The IPO was over subscribed by 300 percent and the aftermarket was very robust.

Exhibit E
Possible outcomes of the put

Likelihood of Reaching Minimum Stock Prices as Outlined in the BCI proposal

	FY 1988	*FY 1989*	*FY 1990*
Projected Net Income	$3,096	$5,467	$8,868
Earnings Per Share	$.56	$.99	$1.61
Minimum Market Price	$17.5	$25	$35
Price/Earnings Ratio	31x	25x	22x

Potential Amounts due under the Put Option

Three Possible Scenarios	*Amount Payable*
No public offering, notes are outstanding for entire term	$17.1 million
Public offering after two years, $5 million worth of notes are prepared	$13.1 million
Entire $10 million of notes are prepaid after two years	$ 9.1 million

FY = fiscal year.

[3]Michael Yockel, "Striking It Rich: Fast Oil Changes Have Made Jim Hindman and Jiffy Lube a Nice Piece of Change: Is This the McDonald's of the Oil Industry?" *Baltimore Business Monthly*, October 1988, p. 89.

Further Expansion

The $28 million of IPO proceeds fueled JLI's continued expansion. Hindman was convinced that Jiffy Lube would "*never* be 'just another company.' " The IPO investors had shown their confidence in the company. In fiscal 1987, ending in March, the average number of cars serviced was 42 daily, with 5.4 million customers serviced annually. Hindman attributed the success of the individual units to the JLI philosophy: Integrity. Intensity. And Intimacy. The number of Jiffy Lube centers increased from 348 in 1986 to 561 in 1987, and 54 service centers had been acquired by JLI. "An internal acquisitions team had been formed and was headed by an acquisition manager,"[4] according to John Sasser, chief financial officer. Neal D. Borden, the executive vice president and secretary, added that JLI

> represented, by virtue of our acquisitions and conversions, not just Jiffy Lube but also a lot of the pioneers in this business. We were far ahead of our competition and we wouldn't let them catch us. Our goal was to maintain rapid growth, to stay ahead. We were getting close to 600 stores. Our nearest competitor only had around 200.[5]

Not only had JLI covered 29 out of 30 media markets in the United States, international agreements for development had been secured in England and France.

At the same time, JLI broadened the scope of services to the franchisees. Training and maintenance of company programs and policies were high priorities. (See *Exhibit F*.) A certification program for technicians was developed and run by JLI. Formal procedures were established for employee selection. To ensure that individual centers were following company procedures, a "mystery shopper" paid surprise visits to the units. John Sasser

Exhibit F
Jiffy Lube International, Inc., Franchisee Agreement (1986)

"A company is only as strong as its weakest link. At Jiffy Lube, our links are our franchisees. They are the people doing the ultimate selling and are indispensable, invaluable company representatives." (Jiffy Lube International, Inc., Annual Report, 1986, p. 10)

Area Development Fee

Franchisee purchased the exclusive right to develop and operate a number of centers within a geographic location for an initial, nonrefundable area development fee. Fees varied based on the number of centers to be developed, the difficulty of development, and the demographics of the area.

Franchisee signed a master license agreement. Licensees were obligated to find the site, to finance the real estate, and to construct the units. Construction had to be completed in 12 months. Licensee had the option of fixed payments or payments as development occurs. A full-time executive had to be hired within 30 days of the application acceptance.

Initial Franchisee Fee

The average initial franchisee fee was $20,000 for the development of each center. Initial deposit was $10,000 (to be cashed when the applicant was accepted) and the balance of the fee was due 10 business days after the receipt of building permits.

Royalty Fee

The royalty fee for the initial year was 5% of gross sales; thereafter, the royalty fee was 6%. No minimum royalty fee existed.

Support Services

National Advertising Fund: The required contribution was 1% of gross sales. A required total advertising commitment per unit was established at least 6% of gross sales.

Quality Control: Jiffy Lube International monitored and inspected the centers at least once a year to ensure that company-approved programs and practices were in use and being followed. An accountant, an advertising agency, and other support services inspected the centers annually.

Default Procedures: Default occurred when timely payments had not been made in any 12 month period, after JLI had given 30 days notice that such failure has already occurred. JLI provided reimbursements to franchisees who have defaulted and who had their units taken by JLI for tools, equipment, etc. at fair market value.

[4]Joseph E McCann and William G Cornelius, "How Acquisitions Fit Strategies of Young Firms," *Mergers & Acquisitions,* July–August 1987, pp. 39–44.

[5]Jiffy Lube International, Inc., Annual Report, March, 1987, p. 11.

initiated a centralized cash management system to monitor the franchisees. Hindman created a quality award, "The Best There Is," for the franchisees. Stephen Spinelli, president of the Association of Franchisees, explained that

> there are always points of contention in a franchise relationship and we had our fair share. However, Hindman had an ability to intercede personally at strategic moments and to force communication between top management and franchisees. His open door policy included making sure our door was open too.

The results were dramatic: 1987 sales revenues exceeded the original business plan. (See *Exhibit G*). By March 1987, JLI became the first quicklube company to advertise nationally. Touting the slogan, "We'll take care of you like family," a $5 million television campaign featured Dick Van Patten's family. Additionally, regional and local franchisees planned to spend $15 million on localized advertising effort. Just as Hindman had expected, the IPO raised public awareness. By February 1987, the stock had risen to $38 per share, which prompted management to declare a two-for-one stock split. Profits after tax more than doubled earlier projections, reaching $3.4 million of sales on $44 million. (see *Exhibit H.*)

As JLI's appetite for cash grew in July 1987, the company made a second public offering of 2,900,000 shares at $14.75 per share. The second offering raised $35 million. Most of the proceeds from the July offering went toward debt payments rather than fueling growth. (See *Exhibit I.*)

Financing was aided by a license from the Small Business Administration (SBA) to form the Jiffy Lube Capital Corporation (JLCC), a small business investment company. JLCC became a financing vehicle to purchase real estate and to develop more centers. JLI was entitled to borrow $4 of capital from the government, at a nominal interest rate, for each $1 of capital contributed to JLCC.

Exhibit G
Jiffy Lube International, Inc., Projected Operations

	1986	*1987*	*1988*	*1989*	*1990*	*1991*
Revenue:						
Sales by company-operated centers	$7,683	$10,169	$14,218	$18,840	$22,210	$23,954
Initial franchisee fees	3,630	4,527	4,735	5,048	5,215	2,706
Area development fees	2,000	500	0	0	0	0
Franchisee royalties	5,280	9,946	16,062	23,405	32,162	41,014
Sales of automotive products	8,880	15,789	24,489	34,623	46,169	56,561
Rental income from franchisees	2,328	3,010	3,701	4,440	5,137	5,442
Total revenues	$29,801	$43,941	$63,205	$86,356	$110,893	$129,677
Costs and expenses:						
Company-operated centers	6,377	8,440	11,801	15,637	18,434	19,882
Sales of automotive products	7,548	13,420	20,816	29,429	39,243	48,077
Rental expenses (interest)	1,711	1,546	1,502	1,433	1,341	1,332
General and administrative	8,880	14,399	20,341	26,163	31,694	35,221
Total costs and expenses	$24,516	$37,805	$54,460	$72,662	$90,712	$104,512
Income from operations	$5,285	$6,136	$8,745	$13,694	$20,181	$25,165
Other income (expense):						
Interest expense	(2,798)	(3,423)	(2,650)	(2,827)	(2,883)	(2,259)
Other	315	324	97	68	439	1,286
Income before income taxes	$2,802	$3,037	$6,192	$10,935	$17,737	$24,192
Income tax expense	951	1,518	3,096	5,465	8,868	12,096
Net income	$1,851	$1,519	$3,096	$5,470	$8,869	$12,096
Service centers in operation:						
Franchised	361	578	805	1,047	1,297	1,427
Company-operated	23	31	39	47	47	47

Exhibit H
Jiffy Lube International, Inc., Consolidated Statement of Operations (000)

	1987	*1986*
Revenue:		
Franchising:		
United States	$14,634	$8,546
International	1,457	0
Automotive products	13,505	8,792
Financing activity	6,495	4,288
Sales by cooperated centers	8,079	7,825
Total revenues	$44,170	$29,451
Costs and expenses:		
Franchising		
United States	10,168	9,281
International	411	0
Automotive products	12,415	7,492
Financing activities	5,670	4,065
Company-operated centers	8,172	6,548
Provision for credit losses	681	271
Total costs and expenses	$37,517	$27,657
Income from operations	$6,653	$1,794
Other income (expense):		
Other income	1,727	865
Corporate interest expense	(1,362)	(1,197)
Income before income taxes	$7,018	$1,462
Income tax (expense)	(3,333)	(720)
Income (loss) before extraordinary item	$3,685	$742
Extraordinary item	(219)	470
Net income (loss)	$3,466	$1,212
Earnings per share	$0.28	$0.16
Service centers	561	348
Company-operated	29	14

PLOTTING A FUTURE COURSE

In the summer of 1987, the prospects for Jiffy Lube International never seemed brighter. If Booz, Allen & Hamilton's estimates were correct, management and the board had significantly underestimated the quicklube market potential. The distinction between Booz, Allen & Hamilton's and Hindman's projections held enormous implications for the company and investors alike. Hindman and his team wondered whether their growth strategy was aggressive enough. Could it be too ambitious? Were the 1987 financial statements indicators of the future growth in the quicklube industry and JLI? Hindman paced the room one more time; the meeting was about to begin.

Exhibit I
Jiffy Lube International, Inc., Consolidated Balance Sheet (000)

	1987	*1986*
Assets		
Current assets:		
Cash and cash equivalents	$1,277	$2,474
Accounts and fees receivable	7,584	6,771
Notes receivable	4,682	1,811
	12,266	8,582
Less allowance for doubtful accounts	935	299
	11,331	8,283
Inventory	1,217	752
Other current assets	1,130	2,977
Total current assets	14,955	14,486
Notes and fees receivable	10,549	3,792
Assets of centers held for resale	2,663	0
Investments in/advances to affiliates	2,217	237
Assets leased to franchisees	57,383	7,694
Property and equipment	1,885	16,297
Intangible assets	9,104	6,228
Other assets	3,687	1,958
	87,488	36,206
Total assets	$102,443	$50,692
Liabilities and Stockholders' Equity		
Current liabilities:		
Accounts Payable/Accrued expenses	$9,167	$3,905
Notes Payable	1,981	2,403
Construction advances	0	2,331
Current portion of long-term debt	1,047	1,355
Total current liabilities	12,195	9,994
Long-term debt	26,684	19,707
Capital lease obligations	18,969	9,586
Other liabilities	5,099	4,646
	50,752	33,939
Stockholders' equity:		
Preferred stock, par value $50; 46,140 authorized shares, no shares issues or outstanding		
Common stock, par value $.025; Authorized—100,000,000 shares; Issued—11,760,828 shares (1987);	294	
—3,602,912 shares (1986)		180
Capital in excess of value	39,479	10,221
Retained earnings (deficit)	(277)	(3,467)
	39,496	6,934
Less cost of common stock held in treasury	0	175
Total stockholders' equity	39,496	6,759
Total liabilities and stockholders' equity	$102,443	$50,692

The Entrepreneur and the Troubled Company

17

Yes, I did run out of time on a few occasions, but I never lost a ball game!

Bobby Lane, great quarterback
in the 1950s and 1960s
of the Detroit Lions and the
Pittsburgh Steelers

RESULTS EXPECTED

Upon completion of this chapter,[1] you will have:

1. Examined the principal causes and danger signals of impending trouble.
2. Discussed both quantitative and qualitative symptoms of trouble.
3. Examined the principal diagnostic methods used to devise intervention and turnaround plans.
4. Identified remedial actions used for dealing with lenders, creditors, and employees.
5. Analyzed and chosen the investment bank to take EASEL Corporation public, as described in the case.

WHEN THE BLOOM IS OFF THE ROSE

This chapter is about the entrepreneur and the troubled company. It traces the firm's route into and out of crisis and provides some insight into how a troubled company can be rescued by a turnaround specialist.

As was seen in Chapter 1, sooner or later the competitive dynamics of the free enterprise system catch up with many smaller companies. This is a natural process of birth, growth, and death of firms. Even firms in the Fortune 500 are not immune to such forces. Today, over one-third of the Fortune 500 companies of 1970 no longer exist. Some have failed and gone bankrupt, others have been absorbed by larger firms, and still others have been acquired and dismantled.

Although there are similarities in the experiences of new and emerging companies and large companies that experience trouble, there are important differences. New and emerging firms need to approach crises more quickly and have less in the way of financial resources to help them. New and emerging firms deal with simpler strategic and organizational issues. Yet, these firms are more likely to commit errors in the area of financial planning and policy, to manage working capital poorly, to underutilize assets, and to have weak information systems. Finally, these firms are often too insignificant in the eyes of government to qualify for the kind of help Chrysler received.

[1] Special credit is due to Robert Bateman, Scott Douglas, and Ann Morgan for the material in this chapter. The material is the result of research and interviews with turnaround specialists and was submitted in a paper as a requirement for the author's Financing Entrepreneurial Ventures course in the MBA program at Babson College.

The author is especially grateful to two specialists, Leslie B Charm, chairman of Doktor Pet Centers, and Leland Goldberg, of Coopers & Lybrand, Boston, who contributed enormously to the efforts of Bateman, Douglas, and Morgan and to the material.

There is a saying among horseback riders that the rider who has never been thrown from a horse probably has never ridden one! This insight captures the essence of the ups and downs that can occur during the growth and development of a new venture.

Getting Into and Out of Trouble

Troubled companies face a situation similar to that described by Winston Churchill in *While England Slept*, "descending inconstantly, fecklessly, the stairway which leads to dark gulf. It is a fine broad stairway at the beginning, but after a bit the carpet ends, a little farther on there are only flagstones, and a little farther on still these break beneath your feet."

If a firm has in sight a good opportunity, crisis for such a firm is usually the result of management error, although external uncontrollable factors (such as the oil embargo of 1973) can precipitate crisis. In these management errors are found part of the solution to problems of the troubled company. It is pleasing to see that many companies—even companies that are insolvent or have negative net worth or both—can be rescued and restored to profitability.

The causes and signals of trouble described below, as well as the process of developing an action plan for turnaround, are usually more readily recognized by outsiders than those insiders who are immersed as part of the problem. However, the best single insurance policy to avoid such trouble, or at least to minimize the painful consequences, is to keep the company entrepreneurial in mind-set, culture, and management action.

Causes of Trouble

Trouble can be caused by external forces not under the control of management. Among the most frequently mentioned are recession, interest rate changes, changes in government policy, inflation, the entry of new competition, and industry/product obsolescence.

However, those who manage turnarounds find that while such circumstances define the environment to which a troubled company needs to adjust, they rarely account by themselves for an individual company failure. External shocks impact all companies in an industry, and only some of them fail. Others can survive and prosper.

Most causes of failure can be found within company management. Although there are many causes of trouble, the most frequently cited fall into three broad areas: inattention to strategic issues, general management problems, and poor financial/accounting systems and practices. There is striking similarity between these causes of trouble and the causes of start-up failure given in Chapter 1.

- ***Strategic issues***
  - *Misunderstood market niche.* The first of these issues is a failure to understand the company's market niche and to focus on growth without considering profitability. Instead of developing a strategy, these firms take on low-margin business and add capacity in an effort to grow. They then can find they run out of cash.
  - *Mismanaged relationships with suppliers and customers.* Related to the issue of not understanding market niche is the failure to understand the economics of relationships with suppliers and customers. Some firms allow practices in the industry to dictate payment terms, and so forth, when in fact they may be in a position to dictate their own terms.
  - *Diversification into an unrelated business area.* A common failing of cash-rich firms that suffer from the growth syndrome is diversification into unrelated business areas. These firms use the cash flow generated in one business to start another without good reason. As one turnaround consultant said, "I couldn't believe it. There was no

synergy at all. They added to their overhead but not to their contribution. No common sense!"

- *Mousetrap myopia.* Related to the problem of starting a firm around an idea, rather than an opportunity, is the problem of firms that have "great products" looking for other markets where they can be sold. This is done without analyzing opportunities.
- *The big project.* The company gears up for a "big project" without looking at the cash flow implications. Cash is expended by adding capacity and hiring personnel. When sales do not materialize or take longer than expected to materialize, there is trouble. Sometimes the "big project" is required by the nature of the business opportunity. An example of this would be the high-technology start-up that needs to capitalize on a "first-mover" advantage. The company needs to prove the product's "right to life" and grow quickly, to the point where it can achieve a public market or become an attractive acquisition candidate for a larger company, so that a larger company cannot use its advantages in scale and existing distribution channels, after copying the technology, to achieve dominance over the start-up.
- *Lack of contingency planning.* As has been stated over and over, the path to growth is not a smooth curve heading up. Firms need to be geared to think about what happens if things go sour – if sales fall or if collections slow. There need to be plans in place for layoffs and capacity reduction.

■ ***Management issues:***

- *Lack of management skills, experience, and know-how.* As was mentioned in Chapter 6, while companies grow, managers need to change their management mode from doing to managing to managing managers.
- *Weak finance function.* Often, in a new and emerging company the finance function is nothing more than a bookkeeper. One company was five years old, with $20 million in sales, before the founders hired a financial professional.
- *Turnover in key management personnel.* Although turnover of key management personnel can be difficult in any firm, it is a critical concern in businesses that deal in specialized or proprietary knowledge. For example, one firm lost a bookkeeper who was the only one who really understood what was happening in the business.
- *Big-company influence in accounting.* A mistake that some companies often make is to focus on accruals, rather than cash.

■ ***Poor planning, financial/accounting systems, practices, and controls:***

- *Poor pricing, overextension of credit, and excessive leverage:* These causes of trouble are not surprising and need not be elaborated. Some of the reasons for excess use of leverage are interesting. Use of excess leverage can result when growth outstrips the company's internal financing capability. The company then relies increasingly on short-term notes until a cash flow problem develops. Another reason is the use of guaranteed loans in place of equity for either start-up or expansion financing. One entrepreneur remarked that the guaranteed loan "looked just like equity when we started, but when trouble came it looked more and more like debt."
- *Lack of cash budgets/projections.* This is a most frequently cited cause of trouble. In small companies cash budgets/projections are often not done.
- *Poor management reporting.* While some firms have good financial reporting, they suffer from poor management reporting. As one turnaround consultant stated, the general ledger system "just tells where the company has been. It doesn't help *manage* the business. If you look at the important management reports – inventory analysis, receivables agings, sales analysis – they're usually late or not produced at all. The same goes for billing procedures. Lots of emerging companies don't get their bills out on time."

- *Lack of standard costing.* Poor management reporting extends to issues of costing, too. Many emerging businesses have no standard costs against which they can compare the actual costs of manufacturing products. The result is they have no variance reporting. The company cannot identify problems in process and take corrective action. The company will know only after the fact how profitable a product is.

  Even when standard costs are used, it is not uncommon to find that engineering, manufacturing, and accounting each has its own version of the bill of material. The product is designed one way, manufactured a second way, and costed a third.
- *Poorly understood cost behavior.* Companies often do not understand the relationship between fixed and variable costs. For example, one manufacturing company thought it was saving money by closing on Saturday. In this way, management felt it would save paying overtime. It had to be pointed out to the lead entrepreneur by a turnaround consultant that "he had a lot of high-margin product in his manufacturing backlog that more than justified the overtime."

  It is also important for entrepreneurs to understand the difference between theory and practice in this area. The turnaround consultant mentioned above said, "Accounting theory says that all costs are variable in the long run. In practice, almost all costs are fixed. The only truly variable cost is a sales commission."

THE GESTATION PERIOD OF CRISIS

Crisis rarely develops overnight. The time between the initial cause of trouble and the point of intervention can run from 18 months to five years. Rarely does intervention occur in less than a year.

What happens to a company during the gestation period has implications for the later turnaround of the company. Thus, how management reacts to crisis and what happens to morale determine what will need to happen in the intervention. A situation that usually develops is a demoralized and unproductive organization whose members think only of survival, not turnaround, and an entrepreneur who has lost credibility. Further, the company has lost valuable time.

The Paradox of Optimism

A typical scenario for a troubled company is as follows: The first signs of trouble (such as declining margins, customer returns, or falling liquidity) go unnoticed or are written off as teething problems of the new project or as the ordinary vicissitudes of business. For example, one entrepreneur saw increases in inventory and receivables as a good sign, since sales were up and the current ratio had improved. However, although sales were up, margins were down, and he did not realize he had a liquidity problem until cash shortages developed.

Although management may miss the first signs, outsiders usually do not. Banks, board members, suppliers, and customers see trouble brewing. They wonder why management does not respond. Credibility begins to erode.

Soon management has to admit that trouble exists, but valuable time has been lost. Furthermore, requisite actions to meet the situation are anathema. The lead entrepreneur is emotionally committed to people, to projects, or to business areas. Further, to cut back in any of these areas goes against instinct, because the company will need these resources when the good times return.

The company continues its downward fall, and the situation becomes stressful. Turnaround specialists mention that stress can cause avoidance on the part of an entrepreneur. Others have likened the entrepreneur in a troubled company to a rabbit caught in a car's headlights: The entrepreneur is frozen and can take no action. Avoidance has a basis in human psychology. One organizational behavior consultant who has worked on turnarounds said that, when a person under stress does not understand the problem and does not have the skills to deal with it, the person will tend to replace the unpleasant reality with fantasy. The consultant went on to say that the outward manifestation of this fantasy is avoidance. This consultant noted it is common for an entrepreneur to deal with pleasant and well-understood tasks, such as selling to customers, rather than dealing with the trouble. The result is that credibility is lost with bankers, creditors, and so forth. (Of course, these are the very people whose cooperation needs to be secured if the company is to be turned around.)

Often, the decisions the entrepreneur does make during this time are poor and accelerate the company on its downward course. To illustrate, the accountant or the controller may be fired with the result that the company is then "flying blind." One entrepreneur, for example, running a company that manufactured a high-margin product, announced across-the-board cuts in expenditures, including advertising, without stopping to think that cutting advertising on such a product only added to the cash flow problem.

Finally, the entrepreneur may make statements that are untrue or may make promises that cannot be kept. This is the death knell of his or her credibility.

Decline in Organizational Morale

Among those who notice trouble developing are the employees. They deal with customer returns, calls from creditors, and the like, and they wonder why management does not respond. They begin to lose confidence in management.

Despite troubled times, the lead entrepreneur talks and behaves optimistically. Employees hear of trouble from each other and from other outsiders. They lose confidence in the formal communications of the company. The grapevine, which is always exaggerated, takes on increased credibility. Company turnover starts to increase. Morale is eroding.

It is obvious there is a problem and that it is not being dealt with. Employees wonder what will happen, whether they will be laid off, and whether the firm will go into bankruptcy. With their security threatened, employees lapse into "survival mode." As an organizational behavior consultant explains:

> The human organism can tolerate anything except uncertainty. It causes so much stress that people are no longer capable of thinking in a cognitive, creative manner. They focus on survival. That's why in turnarounds you see so much uncooperative, finger-pointing behavior. The only issue people understand is directing the blame elsewhere.

At last, crisis can force intervention. The occasion is usually forced by the board of directors or a lender. For example, the bank may call a loan, or the firm may be put on cash terms by its suppliers. Perhaps creditors try to put the firm into involuntary bankruptcy.

PREDICTING TROUBLE

Since crises develop over time and typically result from an accumulation of fundamental errors, the question can be asked whether crisis can be predicted. The obvious benefit of being able to predict crisis is that the entrepreneur, employees, and significant outsiders, such as investors, lenders, trade creditors—and even customers—could see trouble brewing in time to take corrective actions.

There have been several attempts to develop predictive models. Two are presented below and have been selected because each is easy to calculate and uses information available in common financial reports. Since management reporting in emerging companies

Exhibit 17.1
Net-Liquid-Balance-to-Total-Assets Ratio

Net-Liquid-Balance-to-Total-Assets Ratio = NLB/Total assets
Where
NLB = (Cash + Marketable securities) − (Notes payable + Contractual obligations)

is often inadequate, the predictive model needs to use information available in common financial reports.

Each of the two approaches below uses easily obtained financial data to predict the onset of crisis as much as two years in advance. For the smaller public company, these models can be used by all interested observers. With private companies, they are useful only to those privy to the information and are probably only of benefit to such nonmanagement outsiders as lenders and boards of directors.

In considering the two models, it is important to note that the most frequently used denominator in all these ratios is the figure for total assets. This figure often is distorted by "creative accounting," with expenses occasionally improperly capitalized and carried on the balance sheet or by substantial differences between tangible book value and book value (i.e., overvalued or undervalued assets).

Net-Liquid-Balance-to-Total-Assets Ratio

This model, shown in *Exhibit 17.1,* was developed by Joel Shulman, a Babson College professor, to predict loan defaults.[2] Shulman found that his ratio can predict loan defaults with significant reliability as much as two years in advance.

Shulman's approach is noteworthy because it explicitly recognizes the importance of cash. Among current accounts, Shulman distinguishes between operating assets (such as inventory and accounts receivable) and financial assets (such as cash and marketable securities). The same distinction is made among liabilities, where notes payable and contractual obligations are financial liabilities and accounts payable are operating liabilities.

Shulman then subtracts financial liabilities from financial assets to obtain a figure known as the new liquid balance (NLB). NLB can be thought of as "uncommitted cash," cash the firm has available to meet contingencies. Because it is the short-term margin for error should sales change, collections slow, or interest rates change, it is a true measure of liquidity. The NLB is then divided by total assets to form the predictive ratio.

Nonquantitative Signals

Discussed in Chapter 16 were patterns and actions that could lead to trouble, indications of common trouble by growth stage, and critical variables that can be monitored.

There are also some nonquantitative signals that turnaround specialists use as indicators of the possibility of trouble. As with the signals discussed in Chapter 16, the presence of a single one of these does not necessarily imply an immediate crisis. However, once any of these does surface and if the others follow over the ensuing days and weeks, then trouble is likely to mount.

- Change in management or advisors, such as directors, accountants, or other professional advisors.

[2] A working paper by Joel Shulman, Wayne State University, Detroit, Michigan.

- Inability to produce financial statements on time.
- Accountant's opinion that is qualified and not certified.
- Changes in behavior of the lead entrepreneur (such as avoiding phone calls or coming in later than usual).
- New competition.
- Launching of a "big project."
- Lower research and development expenditures.
- Writing off of assets.
- Lowering of credit line.

THE THREAT OF BANKRUPTCY

It is unfortunate that the heads of most troubled companies usually do not understand the benefits of bankruptcy law. To them, bankruptcy carries the stigma of failure; however, the law merely defines the priority of creditors' claims when the firm is liquidated.

Although bankruptcy can provide for the liquidation of the business, it also can provide for its reorganization. Bankruptcy is not an attractive prospect for creditors because they stand to lose at least some of their money, so they often are willing to negotiate. The prospect of bankruptcy also can be a foundation for bargaining in a turnaround.

Voluntary Bankruptcy

When bankruptcy is granted under bankruptcy law (called *Chapter 11*), a firm is given immediate protection from creditors. Interest payments are suspended, and creditors must wait for their money. A trustee is appointed (sometimes the entrepreneur), and creditor committees are formed.

The great benefit of Chapter 11 is that it buys time for the firm. The firm has 120 days to come up with a reorganization plan and 60 days to obtain acceptance of the plan by creditors.

Under the reorganization plan, debt can be extended. Debt also can be restructured (composed). Interest rates can be increased, and convertible provisions can be introduced to compensate debt holders for any increase in their risk as a result of the restructuring. Occasionally, debt holders need to take part of their claim in the form of equity. Trade creditors can be asked to take equity as payment, and they occasionally need to accept partial payment. If liquidation is the result of the reorganization plan, partial payment is the rule, with the typical payment ranging from zero to 30 cents on the dollar, depending on the priority of the claim.

Involuntary Bankruptcy

In involuntary bankruptcy, creditors force a troubled company into bankruptcy. Although this is regarded as a rare occurrence, it is important for an entrepreneur to know the conditions under which creditors can force a firm into bankruptcy.

A firm can be forced into bankruptcy by any three creditors whose total claim exceeds the value of assets held as security by $5,000, and by any single creditor who meets the above standard when the total number of creditors is less than 12.

Bargaining Power

For creditors, having a firm go into bankruptcy is not particularly attractive. *Bankruptcy, therefore, is a tremendous source of bargaining power for the troubled company.* The reasons bankruptcy is not attractive to creditors are the following: Once protection is granted to a firm, creditors must wait for their money. Further, they are no longer dealing with the troubled company but with a trustee, as well as with other creditors. Even if creditors are willing to wait for their money, they may not get full payment and may have to accept payment in some unattractive form. Last, the legal and administrative costs of bankruptcy, which can be substantial, are paid before any payments are made to creditors.

Faced with these prospects, many creditors conclude that their interests are better served by negotiating with the firm. Since the law defines the priority of creditors' claims, an entrepreneur can use it to determine who might be willing to negotiate.

Since the trade debt has the lowest claim (except for owners), these creditors are often the most willing to negotiate. In fact, the worse the situation, the more willing they may be. If the firm has negative net worth but is generating some cash flow, the trade debt creditors should be willing to negotiate extended terms or partial payment, or both.

However, the secured creditors, with their higher priority claims, may be less willing to negotiate. Many factors affect the willingness of secured creditors to negotiate. Two are the strength of their collateral and their confidence in management. Yet, bankruptcy is still something they wish to avoid for the reasons cited above.

Bankruptcy can free a firm from obligations under executory contracts. This has caused some firms to file for bankruptcy as a way out of union contracts. Since bankruptcy law in this case conflicts with the National Labor Relations Act, the law has been updated and a good-faith test has been added. The firm must be able to demonstrate that a contract prevents it from carrying on its business. While most lawyers say that using bankruptcy law in this way is a questionable practice, some entrepreneurs have used it in this manner.

INTERVENTION

A company in trouble usually will want to use the services of an outside advisor who specializes in turnarounds.

The situation the outside advisor usually finds at intervention is not encouraging. The company is often technically insolvent or has negative net worth. It already may have been put on a cash basis by its suppliers. It may be in default on loans, or if not, it is probably in violation of loan covenants. Call provisions may be exercised. Creditors may be trying to force the company into bankruptcy, and the organization is demoralized.

The critical task is to quickly diagnose the situation, develop an understanding of the company's bargaining position with its many creditors, and produce a detailed cash flow business plan for the turnaround of the organization.

To this end, a turnaround advisor usually quickly signals that change is coming. He or she will elevate the finance function, putting the "cash person" (often the consultant himself) in charge of the business. All payments are put on hold until problems can be diagnosed and remedial actions decided upon. Creditors are called and informed that the company is experiencing difficulties.

Diagnosis

The task of diagnosis can be complicated by the mixture of strategic and financial errors. For example, for a company with large receivables, questions need to be answered about whether receivables are bloated because of poor credit policy or because the company is in a business where liberal credit terms are required to compete.

Diagnosis takes place in three areas: the appropriate strategic posture of the business, analysis of management, and "the numbers."

Strategic Analysis

The purpose of this analysis in a turnaround is to identify the markets in which the company is capable of competing and deciding on a competitive strategy. With small companies, turnaround experts state that most strategic errors relate to the involvement of firms in unprofitable product lines, customers, and geographic areas.

It is outside the scope of this book to cover strategic analysis in detail. (See the many texts in the area.)

Analysis of Management

Analysis of management consists of interviewing members of the management team and coming to a subjective judgment of who belongs and who does not. Turnaround consultants can give no formula for how this is done except that it is the result of judgment that only comes from experience.

The Numbers

Involved in "the numbers" is a detailed cash flow analysis, which will reveal areas for remedial action. The task is to identify and quantify the profitable core of the business.

- *Determine available cash.* The first task is to determine how much cash the firm has available in the near term. This is accomplished by looking at bank balances, receivables (those not being used as security), and the confirmed order backlog.
- *Determine where money is going.* This is a more complex task than it appears to be on the surface. A common technique is called *subaccount analysis,* where every account that posts to cash is found and accounts are arranged in descending order of cash outlays. Accounts then are scrutinized for patterns. These patterns can indicate the functional areas where problems exist. For example, it was noticed that one company had its corporate address on its bills, rather than the lock box address at which checks were processed. The result was that the practice was adding two days to its dollar days outstanding.
- Another technique is to calculate percent-of-sales ratios for different areas of a business and then analyze trends in costs. Typically, several of the trends will show "flex points," where relative costs have changed. For example, for one company that had undertaken a big project, an increase in cost of sales, which coincided with an increase in capacity and in the advertising budget, was noticed. Further analysis revealed this project was not producing enough in dollar contribution to justify its existence. Once the project was eliminated, excess capacity could be reduced to lower the firm's break-even point.
- *Reconstruct the business.* After determining where the cash is coming from and where it is going, the next step is to compare the business as it should be to the business as it is. This involves reconstructing the business from the ground up. For example, a cash budgeting exercise can be undertaken and collections, payments, and so forth determined for a given sales volume. Or the problem can be approached by determining labor, materials, and other direct costs and the overhead required to drive a given sales volume. What is essentially a cash flow business plan is created.
- *Determine differences.* Finally, the cash flow business plan is tied into pro forma balance sheets and income statements. The ideal cash flow plan and financial statements are compared to the business's current financial statements. For example, the pro forma income statements can be compared to existing statements to see where expenses can be reduced. The differences between the projected and actual financial statements form the basis of the turnaround plan and remedial actions.

The most commonly found areas for potential cuts/improvements are these: (1) working capital management, from order processing and billing to receivables, inventory control, and, of course, cash management; (2) payroll; and (3) overcapacity and underutilized assets. It is interesting to note that over 80 percent of potential reduction in expenses can usually be found in workforce reduction.

The Turnaround Plan

The turnaround plan not only defines remedial actions, but because it is a detailed set of projections, provides a means to monitor and control turnaround activity. Further, if the assumptions about unit sales volume, prices, collections, and negotiating success are varied, it can provide a means by which worst-case scenarios—complete with contingency plans—can be constructed.

Since short-term measures may not solve the cash crunch, a turnaround plan gives a firm enough credibility to buy time to put other remedial actions in place. For example, one firm's consultant approached its bank to buy time with the following:

> By reducing payroll and discounting receivables, we can improve cash flow to the point where the firm can be current in five months. If we are successful in negotiating extended terms with trade creditors, then the firm can be current in three months. If the firm can sell some underutilized assets at 50 percent off, it can become current immediately.

The turnaround plan helps address organizational issues. The plan replaces uncertainty with a clearly defined set of actions and responsibilities. Since it signals to the organization that action is being taken, it is of great help in getting employees out of their survival mode. An effective plan breaks tasks into the smallest achievable unit, so successful completion of these simple tasks soon follows and the organization begins to experience success. Soon the downward spiral of organizational morale is broken.

Finally, the turnaround plan is an important source of bargaining power. By identifying problems and providing for remedial actions, the turnaround plan enables the firm's advisors to approach creditors and tell them in very detailed fashion how and when they will be paid. If the turnaround plan proves that creditors are better off working with the company as a going concern, rather than liquidating it, they will most likely be willing to negotiate their claims and terms of payment. Payment schedules can then be worked out that can keep the company afloat until the crisis is over.

Quick Cash

Ideally, the turnaround plan has established enough creditor confidence to buy the turnaround consultant time to raise additional capital and turn underutilized assets into cash. It is imperative, however, to raise cash quickly. The result of the actions described below should be an improvement in cash flow. The solution is far from complete, however, because suppliers need to be satisfied.

For the purpose of quick cash, the working capital accounts hold the most promise.

Accounts receivable is the most liquid noncash asset. Receivables can be factored, but negotiating such arrangements takes time. The best route to cash is discounting receivables. How much receivables can be discounted depends on whether they are securing a loan. For example, a typical bank will loan up to 80 percent of the value of receivables that are under 90 days. As receivables age past the 90 days, the bank needs to be paid. New funds are advanced as new receivables are established as long as the 80 percent and under-90-day criteria are met. Receivables under 90 days can be discounted no more than 20 percent, if the bank obligation is to be met. Receivables over 90 days can be discounted as much as is needed to collect them, since they are not securing bank financing. One needs to use judgment in deciding exactly how large a discount to offer. A common method is to offer a generous discount with a time limit on it, after which the discount is no longer valid. This provides an incentive for the customer to pay immediately. Consultants agree it is better to offer too large a discount than too small a one. If the discount is too small and needs to be followed by further discounts, customers may hold off paying in the hope that another round of discounts will follow.

Inventory is not as liquid as receivables but still can be liquidated to generate quick cash. An inventory "fire sale" gets mixed reviews from turnaround experts. The most common objection is that excess inventory is often obsolete. The second objection is that since, for the small manufacturer, much inventory is work in process, it is therefore not in salable form and requires money to put in salable form. The third is that discounting finished-goods inventory may generate cash but is liable to create customer resistance to restored margins after the company is turned around. The sale of raw materials inventory to *competitors* is generally considered the best route.

One interesting option to the company with a lot of work-in-process inventory is to ease credit terms. It often is possible to borrow more against receivables than against inventory. By easing credit terms, the company can increase its borrowing capacity to perhaps enough to get cash to finish work in process. This option may be difficult to work out because, by the time of intervention, the firm's lenders are likely following the company very closely and may veto the arrangements.

Also relevant to generating quick cash is the policy regarding current sales activity. Increasing the total dollar value of margin, generating cash quickly, and keeping working capital in its most liquid form need to be guiding criteria. Prices and cash discounts need to be increased and credit terms eased. Easing credit terms, however, can conflict with the receivables policy described above. Obviously, care needs to be taken to maintain consistency of policy. Easing credit is really an "excess inventory" policy. The overall idea is to leverage policy in favor of cash first, receivables second, and inventory third.

Putting all accounts payable on hold is the next option. Clearly, this eases the cash flow burden in the near term. Although some arrangement to pay suppliers needs to be made, the most important uses of cash at this stage are meeting payroll and paying lenders. Suppliers may not like this solution, but a company with negative cash flow simply needs to "prioritize" its use of cash. Suppliers are the least likely to force the company into bankruptcy because, under the law, they have a low priority claim.

Dealing with Lenders

The next step in the turnaround is to negotiate with lenders. Lenders need to be satisfied that there is a workable long-term solution, if they are to continue to do business with the company.

However, at the point of intervention, the company is most likely in default on its payments. Or, if payments are current, the financial situation has probably deteriorated to the point where the company is in violation of loan covenants. It also is likely that many of the firm's assets have been pledged as collateral. To make matters worse, it is likely that the troubled entrepreneur has been avoiding his or her lenders during the gestation period and has demonstrated that he or she is not in control of the situation. Credibility has been lost.

It is important for a firm to know that it is not the first ever to default on a loan, that the lender is usually willing to work things out, and that it is still in a position to bargain.

Strategically, there are two sources of bargaining power. The first is that, to a lender, despite its senior claims, bankruptcy is an unattractive result. A low-margin business cannot absorb large losses easily. (Recall that banks typically earn 0.5 percent to 1.0 percent total return on assets.)

The second is credibility. The firm that, through its turnaround specialist, has diagnosed the problem and produced a detailed turnaround plan with best case/worst case scenarios, the aim of which is to prove to the lender that the company is capable of paying, is in a better bargaining position. The plan details specific actions (e.g., layoffs, assets plays, changes in credit policy, etc.) which will be taken.

There are also two tactical sources of bargaining power. First, there is the strength of the lender's collateral. The second is the bank's inferior knowledge of aftermarkets—and the entrepreneur's superior ability to sell.

The following example illustrates that, when the lender's collateral is poor, it has little choice but to look to the entrepreneur for a way out without incurring a loss. It also shows that the entrepreneur's superior knowledge of his business and ability to sell got himself and the lender out of trouble. One turnaround company in the leather business overbought inventory one year, and, at the same time, a competitor announced a new product that made his inventory almost obsolete. Since the entrepreneur went to the lender with the problem, it was willing to work with him. The entrepreneur had plans to sell the inventory at reduced prices and also to enter a new market that looked attractive. The only trouble was he needed more money to do it, and he was already over his credit limit. The lender was faced with the certainty of losing 80 percent of its money and putting its customer out of business or the possibility of losing money by throwing good money after bad. The lender decided to work with the entrepreneur. It got a higher interest rate and put the entrepreneur on a "full following mechanism," which meant that all payments were sent to a lock box. The lender processed the checks and reduced its exposure before it put money in his account.

Another example illustrates the existence of bargaining power with a lender who is undercollateralized and stands to take a large loss. A company was importing look-alike Cabbage Patch dolls from Europe. This was financed with a letter of credit. However, when the dolls arrived in this country, the company could not sell the dolls because the Cabbage Patch doll craze was over. The dolls, and the bank's collateral, were worthless. The company found that the doll heads could be replaced, and with the new heads, the dolls did not look like Cabbage Patch dolls. It found also that one buyer of dolls would buy all the inventory. The company needed $30,000 to buy the new heads and have them put on, so it went back to the bank. The bank said that, if the company wanted the money, key management had to give liens on their houses. When this was refused, the banker was astounded. But what was he going to do? The company had found a way for him to get his money out, so it got the $30,000.

In addition, lenders are often willing to advance money for a company to meet its payroll. This is largely a public relations consideration. The other reason is that, if a company does not meet its payroll, a crisis may be precipitated before the lender can consider its options.

However, it is important to be aware that, when the situation starts to improve, a lender then may call the loan. Such a move will solve the lender's problem but may put the company under. While many bankers will deny this ever happens, some will concede that such an occurrence "depends on the loan officer."

Dealing with Trade Creditors

In dealing with trade creditors, the first step is to understand the strength of the company's bargaining position. Trade creditors have the lowest priority claims should a company file for bankruptcy and, therefore, are often the most willing to deal. In bankruptcy, trade creditors often are left with just a few cents on the dollar.

Another aspect of the bargaining power a firm has with trade creditors is the existence of a turnaround plan. As long as a company demonstrates that it can offer a trade creditor a better result as a going concern than it can in bankruptcy proceedings, the trade creditor should be willing to negotiate.

Also, trade creditors have to deal with the customer relations issue. Trade creditors will work with a troubled company if they see it as a way to preserve a market.

The relative weakness in the position of trade creditors has allowed some turnaround consultants to negotiate impressive deals. For example, one company got trade creditors to agree to a 24-month payment schedule for all outstanding accounts. In return, the firm pledged to keep all new payables current. The entrepreneur was able to keep the company from dealing on a cash basis with many of its creditors and to convert short-term payables into what amounted to long-term debt. The effect on current cash flow was very favorable.

The second step is to prioritize trade creditors according to their importance to the turnaround. The company then needs to take care of those creditors that are most important. For example, one entrepreneur told his controller never to make a commitment he could not keep. The controller was told that, if the company was going to miss a commitment, he was to get on the phone and call. The most important suppliers were told that if something happened and they really needed payment sooner than had been agreed, they were to let the company know and it would do its best to come up with the cash.

The third step in dealing with trade creditors is to switch vendors if necessary. Inevitably, the lower priority suppliers will put the company on cash terms or refuse to do business at all. The troubled company needs to be able to switch suppliers, and its relationship with its priority suppliers will help it to do this, because they can give credit references. One firm said, "We asked our best suppliers to be as liberal with credit references as possible. I don't know if we could have established new relationships without them."

The fourth step in dealing with trade creditors is to communicate effectively. "Dealing with the trade is as simple as telling the truth," said one consultant. If a company is honest, there is not much a creditor can do, and at least it can plan.

Work-Force Reductions

With work-force reduction representing 80 percent of the potential expense reduction, layoffs are inevitable in a turnaround situation.

A number of turnaround consultants use the following guidelines: Turnaround specialists recommend that layoffs be announced to an organization as a one-time reduction in the work force and be done all at one time. They recommend further that layoffs be accomplished as soon as possible, since employees will never regain their productivity until they feel some measure of security. Finally, they recommend that a firm cut deeper than seems necessary. The reason for this is that if other remedial actions turn out to be difficult to implement, the difference may have to be made up in further reductions in the work force. For example, it is one thing to set out to reduce capacity by half and quite another thing to sell or sublet half a plant.

Longer-Term Remedial Actions

If the turnaround plan has created enough credibility and has bought the firm time, longer-term remedial actions can be implemented.

These actions will usually fall into three categories:

- *Systems and procedures.* Systems and procedures that contributed to the problem in the first place can be improved, or they can be implemented.
- *Asset plays.* Assets that could not be liquidated in a shorter time frame can be liquidated. For example, real estate could be sold. Many smaller companies, particularly older ones, carry real estate on their balance sheet at far below market value. This could be sold and leased back or could be borrowed against to generate cash.
- *Creative solutions.* Creative solutions that depend, of course, on the situation need to be found. For example, one firm had a large amount of inventory that was useless in its

current business. However, it found that if the inventory could be assembled into parts, there would be a market for it. The company shipped the inventory to Jamaica, where labor rates were low, for assembly, and it was able to sell very profitably the entire inventory.

As was stated at the beginning of the chapter, many companies—even companies that are insolvent or have negative net worth or both—can be rescued and restored to profitability. It is perhaps helpful to recall another quote from Winston Churchill: "I have nothing to offer but blood, toil, tears, and sweat."

*CASE—EASEL CORPORATION

Preparation Questions

1. Who should be a public company?
2. How much capital does EASEL need? When?
3. When is the right time for EASEL to pursue a public offering, and how should the process be managed? Concentrate on *Exhibits 6* and *9*.
4. Evaluate the request for quotation (RFQ) sent to investment bankers by EASEL and the responses. If EASEL were to pursue an IPO, which underwriter should they select?
5. At what price should EASEL go public? How many shares should be offered by the company and existing shareholders? What is your minimum price and number of shares you would offer?

EASEL CORPORATION

Doug Kahn, CEO of EASEL Corporation, had just concluded an hour-and-a-half phone conversation with a long-time friend who was also a professor at a well-known eastern business school. The call was precipitated by mixed messages coming from members of his board of directors. A group representing the five first-round (1981) venture capital investors was urging him to begin building relationships with investment bankers with the expectation that it would take a year or two to get ready if the initial public offering (IPO) window should open. Another group representing four later-round venture investors (summer 1987) felt much less pressure for liquidity and were not in favor of beginning the IPO process at this time, especially given the dormant IPO market of 1989. He wondered how best to handle this delicate process and the board differences. He was also more uncertain about the core issues: Should we be a public company at all? Are we ready enough for an IPO? Is the timing appropriate? How should the IPO process be managed?

It was December 21, 1989, over eight years since the company had raised its first round of venture financing. The early-round investors were particularly eager to realize liquidity in their investment. Some urged Doug, and CFO John McDonough, to attend the American Electronics Association financing conference, talk with some investment banks, and start "the courting process." After all, they reasoned, it would take a year or two for the underwriters to get to know EASEL, to gain confidence in the company's performance versus forecasts, and to build a solid relationship.

The past six years had seen a dramatic turnaround in the fortunes of EASEL Corporation, a small software company located on America's Technology Highway, the famed Massachusetts Route 128. Led by its new president, R. Douglas ("Doug") Kahn, a

*Associate in Research, Thomas A Soja prepared this case under the supervision of Professor Jeffry A Timmons as the basis for class discussion, rather than to illustrate either effective or ineffective handling of an administrative situation.

graduate of a well-known western business school, and patiently supported through several additional rounds of venture capital financing, EASEL had become a leader in computer-aided software engineering (CASE) tools used for the development of user-friendly graphical interfaces for IBM and IBM-compatible personal computers and workstations. Both the board of directors and management were committed to eventually realizing a gain on their investment, and under the right circumstances, a public offering was certainly one viable option. Unfortunately, since the stock market crash of October 1987, the IPO market for smaller companies had not been hospitable (see *Exhibit 13*).

Doug could foresee some of the immediate consequences of beginning to explore an IPO in terms of time, money, and effort he and his top managers would need to expend in the months ahead. Although the company was growing steadily and had just cemented a lucrative marketing relationship with IBM, there were still many operational challenges ahead. An eventual public offering was a possibility, but the thought of meeting the current challenges of growth while running the company under public scrutiny, with quarterly performance expectations, and the additional time devoted to managing relations with brokers, analysts, and investors was a daunting prospect.

COMPANY BACKGROUND

EASEL Corporation develops, markets, and supports software products that enable corporate data programmers to develop business applications featuring graphical user interfaces (GUIs). The EASEL product line is a graphical application development environment that enables programmers to design, prototype, and develop the personal workstation–based GUI and communications components of these applications. Applications developed with EASEL provide the end user with easy-to-use graphical displays and permit the user's IBM personal computer, P/S 2 or compatible (a personal workstation) to work in cooperation with other computing resources, including mainframes, minicomputers, servers, and local and wide area networks. Software products and the applications developed by using these products were run on either the DOS or OS/2 Presentation Manager operating systems.

EASEL markets its products to large business and governmental organizations for internal use and to independent software vendors that use the company's products to develop or enhance their own software products. A partial listing of EASEL customers is shown in *Exhibit 1*.

INDUSTRY BACKGROUND

The role of the personal computer is evolving from a personal productivity tool to an integral part of larger corporate information systems, communicating with other processors, remote applications, networks and databases. This evolution has resulted in the emergence of two important industry trends: demand for GUIs to larger corporate systems and movement toward a new information system architecture known as cooperative processing. Corporate management information systems (MIS) organizations and independent software vendors face major challenges in successfully exploiting these trends. Although GUIs and client/server architecture (CSA) can deliver dramatic productivity improvements and long-term savings, the implementation process can be costly and complex. In addition to cash outlays for new software, hardware, and networks, the organization must train both technical staff and end users, install new applications, and ensure compatibility with current applications, while at the same time not disrupting the conduct of daily business. Accordingly, the market is rapidly emerging for tools and services that can help smooth this transition.

Exhibit 1
Customer List

AMP, Inc.
The Babcock & Wilcox Company
Boeing Computer Services Division of the Boeing Company
Canada Wire & Cable Limited
Central and Southwest Services, Inc.
The Chase Manhattan Bank N.A.
Colonial Life & Accident Insurance Company
Continental Bank Corporation
Coors Ceramics Company
CPC International, Inc.
Domino's Pizza Inc.
DST Systems Inc.
Eastman Kodak Company
E. I. DuPont de Nemours & Co.
Federal Express Corporation
FMC Corporation
Ford Motor Company
General Electric Motor Business Group
Hill's Pet Products
International Business Machines Corporation
Inland Steel Company
Lechmere, Inc.
Lincoln National Corporation
Marine Midland Bank
Medicus Systems Corporation
Merck & Co., Inc.
Mobil Administrative Services Co., Inc.
Naval Avionics Centers
Navistar International Transportation Corporation
NCR Corporation
New York Life Insurance Company
Northern Telecom Canada Ltd.
Owens-Corning Fiberglass Corp.
Pennzoil Company
The Pillsbury Company
Pitt County Memorial Hospital, Inc.
Project Software & Development, Inc.
Roger's Communications, Inc.
Sterling Drug, Inc.
SunAmerica Financial, Inc.
Synetics Corporation
Tambrands, Inc.
Texaco
Toronto Dominion Bank
The Travelers Corp.
United States Department of Transportation
U.S. Shoe Company
Yellow Freight Systems, Inc.
Zimmer, Inc.

Graphical User Interfaces

GUIs replace the character-based interface of the PC as well as the block mode interface of the dumb terminal because they significantly enhance the ease-of-use of computers. The character-based interface of the DOS operating system, currently prevalent on the vast majority of the 50 million PCs installed worldwide, requires users to manipulate applications by typing characters at the keyboard. Since DOS only provides the infamous "C:>" prompt, software vendors, such as Lotus, Ashton Tate, and Software Publishing, have had to design their own unique screen design, menu structure, and command language. Consequently, the set of keystrokes required to save a file in 1-2-3 is completely different from the set of keystrokes required to perform the same task in dBase or Harvard Graphics. PC users must not only master typing skills, but also pore through thick manuals in order to learn different applications.

The block mode interface of most dumb terminals, such as IBM's ubiquitous 3270, is even worse. These terminals are most often utilized to access in-house–developed, back-office systems, such as accounting, personnel, or inventory management. Users here must not only type commands, but must also typically fill in an entire screen before sending it to the mainframe for a response. GUIs, such as Microsoft's Windows and Presentation Manager or Apple's Macintosh, enforce a consistent and colorful screen design, encompassing a rich set of pull-down menus, scroll bars, dialog boxes, icons, buttons, and windows for every application. Users can manipulate applications simply by pointing to menu items on the screen with a mouse, rather than by memorizing technical manuals and entering arcane keyboard commands.

GUIs can help improve the front-end of most applications; however, the CSA focuses on the back-end. It separates the database itself, stored on a central "server" (or servers), from the query and reporting tools which can reside on local "client" machines. An ideal

CSA configuration might involve a handful of servers with sophisticated database management software sending data across a network to several hundred PCs running Windows. The server might be a powerful PC running Microsoft's SQLServer database under the OS/2 operating system, a Sun workstation running Oracle under Unix, a DEC VAX running RDG under VMS, or an IBM mainframe running DB2 under MVS. Many large corporations have already invested trillions of dollars over the years to build mainframe applications and databases and now have the potential to leverage this investment by connecting their PCs to mainframes or by implementing hierarchies of servers connected in a complex network web. Cooperative processing uses the local processing power of the personal workstation with other computers that operate in independent environments to perform a single task combining the advanced user interfaces and local processing capabilities of personal workstations with the centralized power, control, and data storage capabilities of host computers and network servers. CSA maximizes the efficient end user functions of relatively inexpensive PCs, thus freeing its most expensive computers for its heaviest data processing tasks.

The Market for GUIs

While the benefits of GUIs and CSA are fast becoming known, the implementation process is still difficult. The connection of PCs, workstations, minicomputers, and mainframes involves much more than simply passing data back and forth. A corporation must often redesign the entire application to divide tasks among the different processors. Off-the-shelf GUI packages, such as spreadsheets and word processors, address end users' stand-alone computing needs but do not by themselves integrate with a corporation's back-office systems. Data processing staffs must develop customized codes for both the client and servers. Since these professionals have been designing and building databases for some time, server software is readily available. Database products have already evolved to automate this process. However, the creation of client software, especially for a GUI environment, is a completely new challenge for most data processing professionals. Graphical software requires the manipulation of every pixel on a computer screen and demands an intricate working knowledge of the computer and the operating system. The C and C++ programming languages are ideal for these tasks; however, it is estimated that only 5 percent of the 600,000 programmers in the United States and 1.1 million programmers worldwide have experience with these languages. Most business programmers have been schooled in COBOL, which is oriented to the creation of back-office systems, not graphical front-ends. Microsoft has tried to help the new Windows and PC programmers by delivering Software Developers' Kits (SDK) to ease the transition; however, these SDKs have more than 800 commands of their own. Most corporate industrial programmers do not have the skills, time, or inclination to master the SDKs.

Development tools and technologies such as the EASEL product line capture the benefits of graphical software applications and cooperative processing and improve programmer productivity. Most conventional programming tools, including fourth-generation languages (4GLs) and computer-aided software engineering (CASE) tools, traditionally have been used to develop mainframe- and minicomputer-oriented applications. EASEL's products are focused on the development of graphical and cooperative applications and, in particular, on the workstation components of these applications.

The market for CASE tools that can simplify or completely automate the process is projected to grow quickly, from approximately $40 million in 1990 to $200 million by 1995. EASEL's objective is to position the firm as the industry standard in the years to come.

THE PRODUCT LINE

EASEL has developed an entire product line dedicated to the creation of workstation, or client, components of GUI applications, as outlined in *Exhibit 2*. The tools run under the DOS and OS/2 Presentation Manager environments with a Windows version scheduled for delivery by the end of 1990. Applications developed with EASEL will be portable across all three environments. The EASEL tools enable data processing staffs to develop new graphical applications or freshen the face of existing back-office applications with a graphical look, thus preserving the corporation's investment in mainframe databases. EASEL's price points were relatively low for sophisticated CASE tools. The average initial price was typically $25,000 for a starter kit, which includes the development system, an application, training, several run-time modules, and a touch screen monitor.

The EASEL development system is a proprietary, high-level language that automatically generates a graphical program, freeing the programmer from the complexities of C or C++. In essence, a few short lines of EASEL code could substitute for a lengthy C program. EASEL offered full color, free-form drawing and a library of icons and artwork. Much like the applications which were developed on the system, it is also object-oriented and multitasking. EASEL's screen layout tools can ensure compliance with IBM Common User Access (CUA) guidelines. These detailed guidelines were an integral part of IBM's Systems Applications Architecture (SAA) and thus essential to most corporate computing scenarios. EASEL programs could accept input from a mouse, touchscreen, or keyboard without modification.

EASEL's communications offerings enable PC applications to link to host computers manufactured by IBM, DEC, Hewlett-Packard, Prime, and Data General. This feature is critical to EASEL's acceptance in the corporate world, and it differentiates it from other stand-alone personal workstation GUI tools.

EASEL has developed a set of packaged applications templates which enable new users to get started and familiarized with GUI's. EASEL/Office is a front end to IBM's PROFS, an electronic mail and calendar product. EASEL/View graphically displays data from personnel databases and EASEL/Spreadsheet Access creates interfaces from EASEL applications to Lotus 1-2-3, StockWatch provides a graphical interface to the Dow Jones News Retrieval service.

An EASEL run-time module is required for each PC that will run an EASEL application. While an EASEL customer may require only a handful of development systems to build applications, it may demand thousands of run-time versions for resale to all of the end users who will run those applications on their workstations. For example, a large automobile manufacturer has more than one thousand EASEL run-times scattered throughout its manufacturing plants.

Exhibit 2
EASEL Corp.'s Product Portfolio

Product	*Price*
EASEL Development System	$7,500
EASEL Communications Modules	$2,500
EASEL Runtime Systems	$350
Application Templates:	
EASELview	$12,000
EASEL OrgChart	$12,000
EASEL SpreadSheet Access	$6,000
StockWatch	$12,000

EASEL remarkets touch screen monitors in conjunction with its software offerings. It also provides consulting and training services. Training for new customers consists of a week-long course at an EASEL location. Consulting services include customized applications specification and coding of GUI designs by highly skilled EASEL technicians. While hardware sales accounted for 15 percent of EASEL's 1989 revenues, generating a gross margin of 50 percent, hardware will fall as a percentage of sales as software sales increase in the future. Consulting, training, and run-time product revenues represent 40 percent of EASEL's revenues and will grow in proportion of overall revenues.

EASEL applications perform a wide variety of tasks. The auto manufacturer has designed a quality control system to monitor and correct vehicle defects in real time. Other applications enable shop floor personnel to retrieve images of scanned mechanical drawings, and maintain control of their production process by monitoring visual images of materials movement. An insurance company has developed a personnel system that enables employees to review benefits programs and enter their selections interactively without complex manuals or training. In the executive suite, senior managers, who often lack typing skills or are simply not computer facile, can query data, review reports, and build graphs through a customized GUI. As the popularity of GUIs spreads, the applications for EASEL technology become more diverse.

Future product development revolves around the development of run-times for Windows 3.0, additional programmer tools such as debugging, testing and editing features, and possibly the development of linkages to other mainstream CASE products such as Knowledgeware's IEW.

ORGANIZATION

EASEL employed 116 regular full-time people, including 44 in sales, marketing, and related staff activities; 27 in product development; 18 in customer support; and 27 in management, administration, and finance. The backgrounds of executive officers and directors and the ownership structure of the company are summarized in *Exhibit 3*.

All of EASEL's software products had been developed substantially by its internal staff. The product development group produces a set of master diskettes and documentation for each product, which is then duplicated, assembled, and shipped by a manufacturing organization that consists of eight people. Hardware activities, including the mounting of touchscreens to monitors and building touchscreen controller boards, were performed primarily by subcontractors under the supervision of EASEL's manufacturing group. All quality control tests are performed in-house by EASEL personnel. EASEL usually purchased parts from single-source vendors but had potential alternative sources of supply for the manufacture and assembly of all hardware products. There had never been difficulties or delays in production of its hardware, software, or their related documentation, and EASEL normally shipped products within one week after receipt of an order.

MARKETING AND SALES STRATEGY

EASEL marketed its products through a direct sales force, value-added remarketers (VARs), and distributors. EASEL's direct sales force in four United States locations (Woburn, Massachusetts; Irvine, California; Parsippany, New Jersey; and Lombard, Illinois) consisted of 23 sales and sales support representatives and managers. EASEL was also building a telemarketing group whose primary function was to identify and qualify new leads and a tele-sales group to generate repeat business from the installed customer base.

EASEL also had a sales effort focused on independent software vendors. The vendors use the EASEL Development System to build or enhance their own applications

Exhibit 3
Current Ownership Structure and Management

Directors, Officers, and 5% Stockholders	*Shares Owned* Number (3)	Percent (2)
Oak Investment Partnerships (4)	1,298,776	34.9%
International Business Machine Corporation	463,184	12.4
Chancellor Capital Management, Inc. (5)	367,221	9.9
J. H. Whitney & Co. (6)	357,312	9.6
Massachusetts Capital Resource Corporation	219,999	5.9
J. F. Shea & Co.	199,999	5.4
Venturtech II, L. P. (7)	199,999	5.4
R. Douglas Kahn (8)	165,708	4.3
Jerome Jacobson (9)	16,000	*
Russell E. Planitzer (10)	2,911	*
Richard A. Carpenter	2,500	*
Robert E. Cook (11)	2,500	*
F. Duffield Meyercord (12)	2,500	*
Benjamin Robelen (13)	—	—
All officers and directors as a group (12 persons)(14)	972,252	23.8
Continental Illinois Venture Corporation	183,614	4.9
PaineWebber Group (15)	180,000	4.8
Leonard I. Hafetz	132,000	3.5

* = Less than 1%.

(1)Except as otherwise noted, each person or entity named in the table has sole voting and investment power with respect to all shares of Common Stock listed as owned by such person or entity.

(2)The number of shares of Common Stock deemed outstanding includes (i) 1,384,815 shares of Common Stock outstanding March 31, 1990 and (ii) 2,338,401 shares of Common Stock issuable upon the conversion of 5,421,524 shares of preferred stock outstanding as of March 31, 1990.

(3)(not applicable)

(4)Includes 545,713 shares held by Oak Investment Partners, L.P., and 753,063 shares held by Oak investment Partners II, L.P.

(5)Chancellor Capital Management, Inc., acts as investment manager for various entities and individuals and disclaims beneficial ownership of these shares.

(6)Includes 175,081 shares held by J. H.Whitney & Co. and 182,231 shares held by J. H. Whitney Associates, L.P., for which J. H. Whitney & Co. is the sole general partner. Excludes an aggregate of 9,486 shares previously distributed to partners and retired partners of J. H. Whitney & Co.

(7)Excludes 2,500 shares issuable upon exercise of outstanding stock options held by Mr. Meyercord, a general partner of Venturtech II, L.P., and a Director of EASEL.

(8)Includes 135,708 shares issuable upon the exercise of outstanding stock options on or before October 15, 1990.

(9)Includes 16,000 shares issuable upon the exercise of outstanding stock options on or before October 15, 1990. Mr. Jacobson, 68, has been a director of the company since May 1984. He is a private investor and business consultant and serves as an advisor to several venture capital funds. Mr. Jacobson is a director of Itel Corp. and Hercules Corp. In addition, he is also a director of several privately held companies.

(10)Includes 411 shares held by Mr. Planitzer and 2,500 shares issuable upon the exercise of outstanding stock options held by Mr. Planitzer exercisable on or before October 15, 1990. Excludes 357,312 shares held by J. H.Whitney & Co. (see footnote 6). Mr. Planitzer is a general partner of J. H. Whitney & Co. and has shared voting power with respect to the 357,312 shares. Mr. Planitzer, 46, has been a director of the company since January 1983. He is a general partner of J. H. Whitney & Co., a venture capital management firm. He serves as the chairman of the board of directors of Prime Computer, Inc., and Sage Software, Inc., In addition, he is also director of several privately held companies.

(11)Represents 2,500 shares issuable upon exercise of outstanding stock options exercisable on or before October 15, 1990. Mr. Cook, 48, has been a director of the company since May 1989. He has been the chair of the board of directors and chief executive officer of Systems Center, Inc. (formerly VM Software, Inc.), a software company.

(12)Includes 2,500 shares issuable upon exercise of outstanding stock options held by Mr. Meyercord, exercisable on or before October 15, 1990. Mr. Meyercord, 44, has been a director of the company since July 1986. He is the chair of Venturtech Management, Inc., a venture capital management firm, and is general partner of Venturtech II, L.P., a venture capital investment fund.

(13)Mr. Robelen, 61, has been a director of the company since May 1990 and is a private investor and business consultant. He was vice president, finance and administration, of Prime Computer, Inc., from 1973 to 1980. He is also a director of several privately held companies.

(14)Includes 348,530 shares issuable upon the exercise of outstanding stock options exercisable on or before October 15, 1990. See details of EASEL senior management below.

(15)Includes 120,000 shares held by PaineWebber Capital Inc. and 60,00 shares held by PW Partners L.P.

for resale and remarket EASEL Runtime Systems. They might also remarket EASEL Development System, generally in conjunction with these applications. This effort, known as the VAR business, had resulted in relationships with companies such as American Software, Inc., Computer Corporation of America, Consilium, Inc., Global Software, Inc., InfoData Systems, Inc., and Teseract Corporation. This VAR channel served to introduce EASEL to large accounts and set the stage for EASEL to sell its full product line.

Exhibit 3 (concluded)

EASEL Senior Management

Name	*Age*	*Position*
R. Douglas Kahn	37	President, chief executive officer, treasurer, and director
John P. McDonough	30	Vice president, finance and administration, and chief financial officer and clerk
Thomas J. Bilotta	38	Vice president, product development and support
Robert J. Gleason	38	Vice president, sales
John M. Canestraro	39	Vice president, product strategy
Stephen B. Sayre	38	Vice president, marketing

Mr. Kahn has been the president and chief executive officer and a director of EASEL Corp. since he joined the company in September 1984. Prior to joining EASEL, he held various positions at McCormack and Dodge Corp., a financial software company, serving as international vice president from 1981 to 1984. During his tenure at McCormack and Dodge, he built international sales from 0 in 1978 to $17 million in 1983.

Mr. McDonough joined EASEL in April 1985 as director of finance and administration and has served as vice president, finance and administration, and chief financial officers since July 1986. Prior to joining the company, he served as controller of Ovation Technologies, Inc., a software company, from 1983 to 1985, and as an accountant at Deloitte & Touche from 1981 to 1983. Mr. McDonough is a certified public accountant.

Mr. Bilotta has been vice president, product development and support, since joining the company in June 1985. From 1978 to 1985, he was a product line manager with Eikonix Corp., a manufacturer of digital imaging equipment and graphic arts systems.

Mr. Gleason has been vice president, sales, since joining the company in May 1987. Prior to that time, he was employed by Distribution Management Systems (DMS), a software company, as a product manager and as regional manager for Northeast sales from 1985 to 1986. In 1986, DMS was acquired by Cullinet Software, Inc., a software company, and Mr. Gleason continued to serve as regional manager for Northeast sales of the DMS subsidiary until 1987.

Mr. Canestraro has been vice president, product strategy, since July 1989. Prior to that time, he served as director of product management from January 1988 to July 1989 and as the director of customer service from January 1985 to January 1988. He joined the company in January 1984 as training manager.

Mr. Sayre has been vice president, marketing, since joining the company in September 1989. Prior to that, he served as vice president of Latin American operations of Cullinet Software, Inc., from 1987 to 1989, and as director of end user product marketing from 1986 to 1987. From 1984 to 1986, Mr. Sayre served as director of sales of Softbridge Microsystems Corporation, a software company.

In September 1986, EASEL had entered into an agreement with Comshare, Incorporated, under which EASEL granted Comshare a worldwide license to remarket EASEL and StockWatch but only in conjunction with Comshare products, in exchange for royalty payments form Comshare. That license was exclusive with respect to the remarketing of the DOS version of EASEL and StockWatch for use in Comshare's third-party decision support system (DSS) and executive information system (EIS) products, through April 1, 1992. Comshare was EASEL's largest VAR by far, contributing as much as 18 percent of revenues in 1988.

International sales represented a relatively untapped and potentially large opportunity for EASEL. Since English was the language of choice for computer programmers worldwide, the EASEL Development System did not have to be translated into foreign languages. In 1989, EASEL initiated an effort to develop distribution relationships with qualified independent software distributors outside the United States and Canada. In November 1989, it entered into an exclusive agreement with a distributor in the United Kingdom, and had also established relationships in Scandinavia and Venezuela. International sales accounted for less than 6 percent of sales.

THE IBM RELATIONSHIP

On April 7, 1989, EASEL entered into a multifaceted relationship with IBM. Under the terms of a marketing agreement, IBM was granted a perpetual license, which is exclusive through 1998, to market the OS/2 Extended Edition version of the EASEL Development

System and EASEL Runtime System. EASEL thereby became an official IBM program product, carried by all of its salespeople on a commission basis, under the IBM logo. The agreement gave IBM full pricing control over this version of the EASEL product line; however, IBM was to meet minimum revenue requirements each year after 1992 in order to maintain its exclusive distribution status, as outlined in *Exhibit 4*. IBM was also granted a nonexclusive license to market the DOS version of the EASEL Runtime System when the Runtime System was embedded in an IBM product. IBM was required to pay a royalty on the sales of any such products. IBM also purchased an unlimited worldwide site license to use the DOS, OS/2 Standard Edition and OS/2 Extended Edition of EASEL internally. To ensure that EASEL continued to develop its offering in line with IBM's strategic directions, IBM also agreed to pay EASEL for ongoing development work and enhancements.

IBM appointed EASEL as a marketing agent for the OS/2 Extended Edition version of EASEL. EASEL was to receive a 25 percent commission in connection with products licensed under this program. EASEL, in turn, appointed IBM as a marketing agent of the company for the DOS version of EASEL with a similar commission arrangement.

EASEL was also obligated under the agreement to provide maintenance services to IBM to assist in supporting its customers. Finally, IBM purchased a 10 percent equity stake in EASEL, valued at $2.5 million.

Exhibit 4
Financial Implications of the IBM Relationship

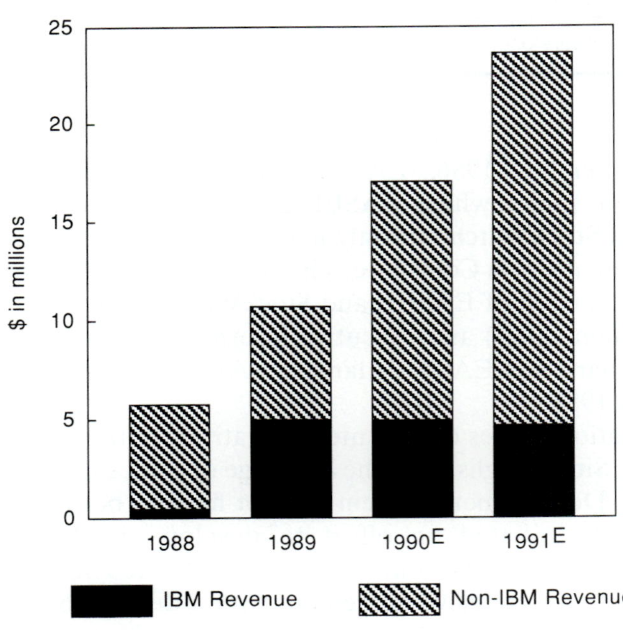

IBM/EASEL Revenue Streams

	1989A	*1990E*	*1991E*	*1992–1998E*
Licensing royalties	$1,500,000	$2,000,000	$3,000,000	$4,000,000
Internal use license	1,800,000	2,000,000	1,000,000	-0-
Maintenance services	225,000	750,000	500,000	500,000
Minimum IBM revenues	$3,525,000	$4,750,000	$4,500,000	$4,500,000

While the financial rewards of the IBM relationship were significant, the long-term strategic benefits were perhaps even more important. As a result of this relationship, EASEL had become an important element in IBM's Systems Application Architecture (SAA) strategy. In a June 5, 1990, external announcement, IBM described EASEL for OS/2 Extended Edition as a key Common User Access (CUA) enabler and had positioned EASEL as the 'recommended tool for the programmer implementing event-driven, graphical CUA either in creating a new front end for host applications or in creating OS/2 applications." This endorsement provided the credibility for EASEL to market its products to the corporate world and potentially establish EASEL as the defacto standard CASE platform. A potential drawback, however, was the loss of pricing control. EASEL had been priced at a significant premium over Knowledgeware's IEW workstation CASE tools, which were also similarly marketed by IBM. Only one month after entering the relationship, IBM had already cut the price of EASEL Development Systems by 50 percent, to $7,500, forcing EASEL to cut its own prices as well. Fortunately, sales volume had subsequently increased to more than compensate. However, it was a dramatic example of the control premium, or rather the lack thereof, which EASEL had to pay in order to gain the positive advantages from the IBM relationship.

Competition

Since GUIs were a relatively new development in the IBM world, there was still little competition from other CASE tool developers. The competition consisted mostly of an array of smaller companies, some of which had high-quality products, but lacked the distribution strength and product endorsement of IBM. These included GUIdance Technologies, Mozart Systems, MultiSoft, and Intelligent Environments. Asymetrix, founded by Microsoft's cofounder Paul Allen, had climbed into the limelight recently by delivering a Windows product, called Toolbook, which Microsoft was helping to promote. The Toolbook product, however, appeared to be more focused on the development of stand-alone PC applications, rather than on delivering links to host systems. IBM had recently signed an agreement with Metaphor Computing to establish Patriot Partners, which was charged with creating a complete applications development environment that would be portable across OS/2 and AIX (IBM's version of UNIX). Although that environment might eventually include some tools that would compete with the EASEL line, EASEL's products would likely be positioned under the Patriot umbrella. Patriot did not plan, however, to have any software available for at least two to three years, giving EASEL ample time to solidify its position in the marketplace.

In addition, traditional CASE vendors such as Knowledgeware, Texas Instruments, Sage Systems, or Index Technology might also look to enter the graphical software niche. Although it was believed at the time that none of those players currently had products under development, they did possess the financial resources to acquire any of EASEL's smaller rivals.

FINANCIAL PERFORMANCE

EASEL's relationship with IBM had already helped the company form a strong strategic and financial foundation for its future growth. IBM accounted for 46 percent of EASEL's 1989 revenues, up from just 7 percent in 1988, as illustrated in *Exhibit 4*. Because of IBM's May 21, 1989, price cut of 50 percent, EASEL was forced to drop the prices of its own offerings by a similar amount. Although non-IBM revenues were flat in 1989, unit volume had actually doubled in the last half of the year, immediately following the price cut. Unit growth continued to soar as its non-IBM revenue was projected to be up by more than

Exhibit 5 Financial Statements

Balance Sheet

	Year Ended December 31,		March 31,
	1988	1989	1990 (unaudited)
Assets			
Current assets:			
Cash and equivalents (1)	$845,410	$4,356,367	$4,120,769
Short-term investments (1)	722,699	976,700	—
Accounts receivable (less allowance for accounts of $24,000 in 1988, $45,000 in 1989 and $73,000 in 1990) (7)	1,276,477	1,980,367	2,820,640
Inventory (1)	135,401	187,660	140,156
Prepaid expenses and other	88,555	73,977	100,353
Total current assets	3,068,542	7,575,071	7,181,918
Property and equipment (1):			
Computer equipment	692,349	1,275,302	1,563,937
Office furniture and fixtures	72,143	610,771	677,021
Leasehold improvements	32,172	88,695	99,427
Total	796,664	1,974,768	2,340,385
Less accum. depreciation and amortization	478,222	821,352	966,821
Property and equipment net	318,442	1,153,416	1,373,564
Other assets:			
Capitalized software costs—net (1)	87,815	282,324	334,899
Deposits	47,417	44,196	44,196
Total other assets	135,232	326,520	379,095
Total assets	$3,522,216	$9,055,007	$8,934,577
Liabilities and Stockholders' Deficiency			
Current liabilities:			
Current portion of long-term debt (2)	$38,976	$38,976	$38,976
Accounts payable	401,115	501,643	461,991
Accrued compensation	355,035	505,690	217,845
Accrued expenses	34,256	296,523	410,177
Income taxes payable (3)	69,000	157,000	26,000
Deferred revenue (1) (7)	176,341	331,793	374,940
Total current liabilities	1,074,723	1,831,625	1,529,929
Deferred revenue—noncurrent (7)	—	464,750	429,000
Long-term debt (2)	55,218	12,519	3,249
Commitments (4) (6)			
Redeemable convertible preferred stock, at liquidation preference (4)	9,385,403	11,885,443	8,508,519
Stockholders' deficiency (5) (9):			
Common stock, $.01 par value; authorized 13,000,000 shares; issued and outstanding 378,011, 378,511, and 1,384,815 in 1988, 1989, and 1990, respectively	3,780	3,785	13,848
Additional paid-in capital	20,710	955	3,000,604
Deficit	(7,017,618)	(5,144,070)	(4,550,572)
Stockholders' deficiency	(6,993,128)	(5,139,330)	(1,536,120)
Total	$3,522,216	$9,055,077	$8,934,577

50 percent in the first half of 1990, compared to 1989 sales at the higher price point. Non-IBM service revenues were also booming, growing almost fourfold in 1990 to date. Due to non-IBM sales growth, IBM's contribution was expected to decline to 15–20 percent of EASEL's total revenues over the next two years. Total revenues for EASEL in 1989 were $10.7 million, and first-quarter results for 1990 were running at nearly double that of the first quarter of 1989, with an annualized $1.6 million profit after taxes. As of March 31, 1990, cash on hand was $4.1 million. Detailed financial statements are included in *Exhibit 5*.

Statements of Operations

	Year Ended December 31			Three Months Ended March 31	
	1987	*1988*	*1989*	*1989*	*1990*
Revenue:					
Product sales and license fees	$2,804,048	$5,055,483	$8,632,153	$1,590,015	$2,843,013
Customer support services	471,094	730,469	2,053,997	365,089	788,567
Total revenue	3,275,142	5,785,952	10,686,150	1,955,104	3,631,580
Costs and expenses:					
Cost of revenue	1,050,376	1,447,737	2,525,536	779,051	861,884
Sales and marketing	1,366,149	2,148,550	3,888,834	665,757	1,350,301
Research and development	609,826	616,447	1,110,881	246,702	337,303
General and administrative	689,064	998,872	1,474,813	203,310	505,385
Total costs and expenses	3,715,415	5,210,606	9,000,064	1,894,820	3,054,873
Income (loss) from operations	(440,273)	575,346	1,686,086	60,284	576,707
Interest income—net	69,912	58,876	366,462	26,082	93,791
Income (loss) before provision for income taxes and extraordinary items	(370,361)	634,222	2,052,548	83,366	670,498
Provision for income taxes	—	275,000	807,000	34,000	261,000
Income (loss) before extraordinary item	(370,361)	359,222	1,245,548	52,366	409,498
Extraordinary item—reduction of income taxes due to carryforward of prior years' operating losses	—	206,000	628,000	26,000	184,000
Net income (loss)	($370,361)	$565,222	$1,873,548	$78,366	$593,498
Income (loss) per common share:					
Income (loss) before extraordinary item	($0.71)	$0.11	$0.29	$0.01	$0.10
Extraordinary item	—	0.06	0.15	0.01	0.04
Net income (loss)	($0.71)	$0.17	$0.44	$0.02	$0.14
Weighted average number of common and common equivalent shares outstanding	520,078	3,425,211	4,333,586	3,991,143	4,319,900

Statements of Stockholders' Deficiency

	Common Stock		Additional Paid-in Capital	Deficit	Total
	Shares	*Amount*			
Balance, January 1, 1987	377,016	$3,770	$20,072	($7,212,479)	($7,188,637)
Exercise of stock options	200	2	248		$250
Net (loss)				(370,361)	($370,361)
Balance, December 31, 1987	377,216	3,772	20,320	(7,582,840)	(7,558,748)
Exercise of stock options	795	8	390		$398
Net income				565,222	$565,222
Balance, December 31, 1988	378,011	3,780	20,710	(7,017,618)	(6,993,128)
Issuance costs of redeemable preferred stock			(20,000)		($20,000)
Exercise of stock options	500	5	245		$250
Net income				1,873,548	$1,873,548
Balance, December 31, 1989	378,511	3,785	955	(5,144,070)	(5,139,330)
Unaudited:					
Conversion of redeemable preferred stock to common stock	937,589	9,376	2,965,978		$2,975,354
Exercise of stock options	68,715	687	33,671		$34,358
Net income				593,498	$593,498
Balance, March 31, 1990	1,384,815	13,848	3,000,604	(4,500,572)	(1,536,120)

(Continued)

Exhibit 5 ***(continued)***

Selected Financial Data

	Year Ended December 31					Three Months Ended March 31	
	1985	*1986*	*1987*	*1988*	*1989*	*1989*	*1990*
(In thousands, except per share data)							
Statements of operations data							
Revenue:							
Product sales and license fee	$816	$1,918	$2,804	$5,056	$8,632	$1,590	$2,843
Customer support services	137	245	471	730	2,054	365	789
Total revenue	953	2,163	3,275	5,786	10,686	1,955	3,632
Costs and expenses:							
Cost of revenue	528	788	1,050	1,448	2,526	779	862
Sales and marketing	1,004	824	1,366	2,149	3,889	666	1,351
Research and development	636	551	610	616	1,110	247	337
General and administrative	660	633	689	998	1,475	203	505
Total costs and expenses	2,828	2,796	3,715	5,211	9,000	1,895	3,055
Income (loss) from operations	(1,875)	(633)	(440)	575	1,686	60	577
Interest income (expense) – net	(12)	43	70	59	367	26	93
Income (loss) before provision for income taxes and extraordinary item	(1,887)	(590)	(370)	634	2,053	86	670
Provision for income taxes	–	–	–	275	807	34	261
Income (loss) before extraordinary item	(1,887)	(590)	(370)	359	1,246	52	409
Extraordinary item – reduction of income taxes due to carry-forward of prior years' operating losses	–	–	–	206	628	26	184
Net income (loss)	($1,887)	($590)	($370)	$565	$1,874	$78	$593
Income (loss) per common share (1):							
Income (loss) before extraordinary item	($3.71)	$1.15	($0.71)	$0.11	$0.29	$0.01	$0.10
Extraordinary item	–	–	–	0.06	0.15	0.01	0.04
Net income (loss)	($3.71)	$1.15	($0.71)	$0.17	$0.44	$0.02	$0.14
Weighted average number of common and common equivalent shares outstanding	509	516	520	3,425	4,334	3,991	4,320

	December 31					March 31	
	1985	*1986*	*1987*	*1988*	*1989*	*1989*	*1990*
Balance sheet data:							
Working capital	$600	$2,030	$1,588	$1,994	$5,743	$1,797	$5,652
Total Assets	1,204	2,474	2,289	3,522	9,055	3,645	8,935
Stockholders' deficiency	(6,585)	(7,189)	(7,559)	(6,993)	(5,139)	(6,915)	(1,536)

(1) See Note 1 of Notes to Financial Statements.

Exhibit 5 ***(continued)***

	Year Ended December 31			3 Months Ended March 31	
	1987	*1988*	*1989*	*1989*	*1990*
Statements of Cash Flows					
Cash Flows from operating activities:					
Net income (loss)	($370,361)	$565,222	$1,873,548	$78,366	$593,498
Adjustments to reconcile net income (loss) to net cash provided by (used for) operating activities:					
Amortization of capitalized software costs	—	9,857	49,187	2,018	28,448
Depreciation and other amortization	116,587	137,281	343,130	54,185	145,469
Increase (decrease) in cash from					
Accounts receivable	(686,514)	(224,869)	(703,890)	204,402	(840,273)
Inventory	(64,609)	(7,977)	(52,259)	21,692	47,504
Prepaid expenses and other	21,776	(26,878)	14,578	119,974	(26,376)
Deposits	(1,821)	(16,425)	3,221	(648)	—
Accounts payable and accrued expenses	186,356	395,050	513,450	66,461	(213,843)
Income taxes payable	—	69,000	88,000	(57,380)	(131,000)
Deferred revenue	45,128	121,843	620,202	49,467	7,397
Total adjustment	(383,097)	456,882	875,619	460,171	(982,674)
Net cash provided by (used for) operating activities	(753,458)	1,022,104	2,749,167	538,537	(389,176)
Cash flows from investing activities:					
Decrease (increase) in short-term investments	—	(722,699)	(254,001)	(242,799)	976,700
Purchase of property and equipment	(179,631)	(243,622)	(1,178,104)	(289,450)	(365,617)
Capitalized software costs	—	(97,672)	(243,696)	(27,463)	(81,023)
Net cash provided by (used for) investing activities	(179,631)	(1,063,993)	(1,675,801)	(559,712)	530,060
Cash flows from financing activities:					
Proceeds from issuance of preferred stock	—	—	2,480,040	—	—
Proceeds from issuance of stock options	250	398	250	—	34,358
Proceeds from issuance of notes payable	—	97,442	—	—	—
Repurchase of preferred stock	—	—	—	—	(401,570)
Repayments of debt	(47,078)	(15,334)	(42,699)	(14,343)	(9,270)
Net cash provided by (used for) financing activities	(46,828)	82,506	2,437,591	(14,343)	(376,482)
Net increase (decrease) in cash and equivalents	(979,917)	40,617	3,510,957	(35,518)	(235,598)
Cash and equivalents, beginning of period	1,784,710	804,793	845,410	845,410	4,356,367
Cash and equivalents, end of period	$804,793	$845,410	$4,356,367	$809,892	$4,120,769

(Continued)

Exhibit 5 ***(continued)***

Quarterly Results of Operations

	Three Months Ended								
	Mar 31, 1988	*Jun 30,* 1988	*Sep 30,* 1988	*Dec 31,* 1988	*Mar 31,* 1989	*Jun 30,* 1989	*Sep 30,* 1989	*Dec 31,* 1989	*Mar 31,* 1990
Revenue:									
Product sales and license fees	$ 912	$1,136	$1,280	$1,728	$1,590	$2,032	$2,401	$2,609	$2,843
Customer support services	139	179	168	244	365	327	680	682	789
Total Revenue	1,051	1,315	1,448	1,972	1,955	2,359	3,081	3,291	3,632
Costs and expenses:									
Cost of revenue	338	285	414	411	779	520	583	644	862
Sales and marketing	423	482	477	767	666	1,026	1,002	1,195	1,351
Research and development	130	146	150	190	247	175	284	404	337
General and administrative	169	194	220	415	203	316	466	490	505
Total costs and expenses	1,060	1,107	1,261	1,783	1,895	2,037	2,335	2,733	3,055
Income (loss) from operations	(9)	208	187	189	60	322	746	558	577
Interest income (expense)—net	11	14	14	20	26	87	135	119	93
Income (loss) before provision for income taxes and extraordinary item	2	222	201	209	86	409	881	677	670
Provision for income taxes	—	93	75	107	34	164	359	250	261
Income (loss) before extraordinary item	2	129	126	102	52	245	522	427	409
Extraordinary item—reduction of income taxes due to carry forward of prior years' operating losses	—	72	65	69	26	125	270	207	184
Net income (loss)	$ 2	$ 201	$ 191	$ 171	$ 78	$ 370	$ 792	$ 634	$ 593

Exhibit 5 ***(continued)***

Notes to Financial Statements

(1) Nature of Business and Summary of Significant Accounting Policies

Nature of Business

EASEL Corp. develops, markets, and supports software products that enable programmers to develop business applications featuring graphical user interfaces.

Revenue Recognition

Product sales and license fees—Revenue from product sales and license fees is generally recognized upon shipment of product. Minimum annual amounts due from IBM (Note 7) are recognized ratably during each year. Customer support services—Revenue from training and consultation services is recognized as the related services are performed. Maintenance revenue is recognized ratably over the term of the agreement.

Inventory

Inventory is stated at the lower of cost (first-in, first-out) or market. Inventory comprised the following:

	12/31/88	*12/31/89*	*3/31/90*
Raw materials	$ 63,556	$ 70,209	$ 35,747
Finished goods	71,845	117,451	104,409
Total	$135,401	$187,660	$140,156

Property and Equipment

Property and equipment are recorded at cost. Depreciation and amortization are provided on the straight-line method over the useful lives of the related assets (three to five years).

Capitalization of Software Costs

The company capitalizes certain software costs after technological feasibility of the product has been established. Such costs are amortized over the estimated life of the product (generally three years).

Cash and Short-Term Investments

Cash equivalents include short-term, highly liquid investments purchased with remaining maturities of three months or less. Short-term investments, which consist primarily of commercial paper and other money market instruments, are stated at cost, which approximates market value.

Income (Loss) Per Common Share

Income (loss) per common share is computed using the weighted average number of common and common equivalent shares outstanding during each period represented. Fully diluted and primary earnings per share are the same amounts for each of the periods presented.

Dilutive common stock equivalents consist of stock options (using the treasury stock method) and redeemable convertible preferred stock. Common stock issued and stock options granted subsequent to June 21, 1989 have been included in the calculation of common and common equivalent shares as if they were outstanding for all periods presented.

Interim Results (Unaudited)

The accompanying balance sheet at March 31, 1990, the statement of stockholders' deficiency for the three months ended March 31, 1990, and the statements of operations and cash flows for the three months ended March 31, 1989 and 1990, are unaudited.

(2) Long-Term Debt

Long-term debt comprised the following:

	12/31/88	*12/31/89*	*3/31/90*
Note payable to a bank—interest at prime rate plus 1.5% (12% at March 31, 1990); payments of principal and interest due through April 1991	$ 94,194	$ 51,495	$ 42,225
Less current portion	(38,976)	(38,976)	(38,976)
Long-term debt	$ 55,218	$ 12,519	$ 3,429

(Continued)

Exhibit 5 *(continued)*

Notes to Financial Statements (continued)

(3) Income Taxes

At December 31, 1989, the company had net operating loss carryforwards for financial reporting and federal income tax purposes of approximately $5,000,000, expiring through 2002. In addition, the company has tax credits of approximately $333,000 which may be used to offset future federal income taxes, if any, expiring through 2004.

(4) Redeemable Convertible Preferred Stock

At March 31, 1990, redeemable convertible preferred stock comprised the following:

Class A—$1.50 par value; 266,667 shares authorized, issued, and outstanding; liquidation preference, $400,000.
Class B—$5.36 par value; 82,932 shares authorized, issued, and outstanding; liquidation preference, $444,516.
Class C—$4.00 par value; 416,666 shares authorized, issued, and outstanding; liquidation preference, $1,666,666.
Class D—$1.00 par value; 3,497,297 shares authorized, issued, and outstanding; liquidation preference, $3,497,297.
Class E—$2.159 par value; 1,157,962 shares authorized, issued, and outstanding; liquidation preference, $2,500,040.

Rights Dividends and Preferences

Each share of Class A, Class B, Class C, Class D, and Class E preferred stock is convertible into .492, .727, .684, .400, and .400 shares of common stock, respectively. Conversion rates are subject to adjustment in certain circumstances. All classes of preferred stock are convertible at the holder's option and must be converted in the event of a public offering, provided that the net aggregate proceeds and per share price exceed $5,000,000 and $7.50, respectively.

In the event of a liquidation, Class D and Class E preferred stock are ranked prior to all other classes of stock. Class A, Class B, and Class C preferred stock are ranked behind Class D and Class E but prior to common stock. The preferred shares have per share liquidation preferences equal to their par values, plus any declared and unpaid dividends.

Preferred stock has voting rights equal to the number of shares of common stock into which it is convertible. Dividends, if any, are paid first to Class D and Class E stockholders, then on an equal basis to other classes of preferred stock, and finally to common stockholders. Dividends paid to Class D and Class E stockholders cannot be less than those paid to any other stockholders on a per share basis, and dividends paid to other preferred stockholders cannot be less than those paid to common stockholders.

Unless earlier converted, the company is required to redeem all Class A through D preferred shares and Class E preferred shares, in annual increments of one-third, beginning January 31, 1990, and January 31, 1995, respectively. The number of shares subject to redemption is cumulative and the redemption price is equal to the liquidation preference. The Class D and Class E stockholders rank prior to Class A, Class B and Class C stockholders in redemption. Redemptions of approximately $3,004,000 are required on January 31, 1991 and 1992, and $833,000 on January 31, 1995, 1996, and 1997.

The following table presents the redeemable convertible preferred stock activity from January 1, 1987, through March 31, 1990:

	Shares	*Amount*
Balance at January 1, 1987, 1988, and 1989	6,580,528	$ 9,385,403
Issuance of Class E	1,157,962	2,500,040
Balance at December 31, 1989	7,738,490	11,885,443
Conversions to common stock	(2,131,783)	(3,004,241)
Repurchases	(185,183)	(372,683)
Balance at March 31, 1990	5,421,524	$ 8,508,519

(5) Common Stock Options

The company has two stock option plans (1981 and 1986) under which options to purchase up to a maximum of 920,000 shares of common stock may be granted to certain employees, directors and consultants. The exercise price of incentive stock options may not be less than fair market value at the date of grant; the exercise of nonqualified options may not be less than the par value per share of common stock. Options become exercisable as specified at the date of grant and are generally subject to vesting over a four-year period.

Exhibit 5 ***(continued)***

Notes to Financial Statements (continued)

A summary of stock option activity is as follows:

	Number of Shares	*Exercise Price per Share*
Outstanding at January 1, 1987	241,082	$1.25–3.75
Granted	474,728	.50
Exercised	(200)	1.25
Canceled	(250,498)	1.25–3.75
Outstanding at December 31, 1987	495,112	$.50
Granted	170,440	.50
Exercised	(795)	.50
Canceled	(1,655)	.50
Outstanding at December 31, 1988	633,102	$.50
Granted	169,840	.75–1.25
Exercised	(500)	.50
Canceled	(1,100)	$.50–.75
Outstanding at December 31, 1989	801,342	$.50–1.25
Granted	51,800	2.50
Exercised	(68,715)	.50
Canceled	(4,076)	$.50–1.25
Outstanding at March 31, 1989	780,351	$.50–2.50
Exercisable at March 31, 1989	344,963	$.50–.75

One director of the company also holds an option to purchase 8,000 shares of common stock at $.50 per share. This option is fully exercisable at March 31, 1990, and expires in May 1994.

(6) Lease Agreements

The company leases office space under noncancellable lease agreements expiring on various dates through 1993. At March 31, 1990 future minimum lease payments under noncancelable operating leases are as follows: years ending December 31, 1990 (nine months), $424,886; 1991, $185,120; 1992, $116,950; and 1993, $31,016. Total rent expense under all operating leases was approximately $241,000, $270,000, and $442,000 for 1987, 1988, and 1989, respectively.

(7) Agreements with IBM

During 1989, the company entered into a series of license agreements with IBM, including a perpetual site license and a 10-year exclusive license to market certain of the company's products. As long as the exclusive license remains in effect, IBM is required to make minimum annual payments of $4,000,000 to the company. IBM may terminate its exclusive rights on four months' written notice. The company is entitled to additional royalties if sales of the product exceed certain cumulative minimums. A portion of the site license fee has been allocated to the five-year maintenance requirements of the agreement. Concurrently, IBM purchased 1,157,962 shares of EASEL Class E preferred stock.

Revenue from IBM comprised the following:

	Year Ended December 31,		*3 Months Ended March 31,*	
	1988	*1989*	*1989*	*1990*
Product sales and license fees	$373,140	$4,119,924	$368,995	$1,030,000
Customer support services	61,460	760,076	206,000	280,000
Total revenue	$434,600	$4,880,000	$574,995	$1,310,000

There was no revenue from IBM for the year ended December 31, 1987.

Amounts related to IBM included in the balance sheets were as follows:

	December 31,		*March 31,*
	1988	*1989*	*1990*
Accounts receivable	$38,642	$706,769	$1,285,044
Deferred revenue	–	$143,000	$ 143,000
Deferred revenue– noncurrent	–	$464,750	$ 429,000

(Continued)

Exhibit 5 ***(concluded)***

Notes to Financial Statements (concluded)

(8) Segment Information and Major Customers

The company is engaged in only one industry segment and export sales did not exceed 10% of the company's revenue during any period to date. One customer accounted for 10% and 14% and a second customer accounted for 13% and 18% of revenue for the years ended December 31, 1987 and 1988, respectively. A third customer (Note 7) accounted for 46% of revenue for the year ended December 31, 1989, and 29% and 36% of revenue for the three months ended March 31, 1989 and 1990, respectively.

(9) Event Subsequent to March 31, 1991

The company has obtained a $2,500,000 unsecured line of credit agreement with a bank replacing a previous line of credit which expired on May 31, 1990. Borrowing availability under the line is based on a percentage of domestic accounts receivable. The agreement requires, among other things, minimum levels of working capital, profitability, and tangible net worth. Interest on the line of credit is at the prime rate plus 0.5%. The credit is subject to renewal on May 31, 1991.

CONTEMPLATING A PUBLIC OFFERING

Since EASEL was a venture capital–backed company, the prospect of taking the company public someday had been present from the beginning of Doug's involvement. As a venture capital–backed company, management had two strong objectives: (1) to manage the continued growth of the company and (2) to manage the company with the intention of providing an opportunity to achieve investment liquidity on as favorable terms as possible, and not necessarily in that order. They began to think about a process which would enable them to choose an underwriting team with the eventual intention of going public (see *Figure 1*).

This prospect raised a number of questions in Doug's mind that he mulled over with his CFO, John McDonough. Among the issues on his mind were whether the company was ready to go public in terms of business maturity and in terms of management's ability. The market issues revolved around whether the company could achieve a favorable valuation because 1989 had not been strong for IPOs but seemed to be improving in 1990. To address some of these doubts, EASEL followed two courses of action. Doug and John's goal was to establish a relationship with several investment banks, to bring EASEL "into their field of vision," and to build a track record over the ensuing six to eight quarters. As part of the process they also began talking to the CEOs and the CFOs of some recent IPO companies to gain a perspective on what to expect in the IPO process such as, picking an underwriter, arranging the deal, and managing as a public company. Both activities were done at relatively informal levels involving lunch meetings or informal gatherings with investment bankers and company CEOs and CFOs.

EASEL was a corporate member of ADAPSO, a software industry trade association, therefore John and Doug had easy access to others who had gone through the process. They spoke to both computer hardware companies and to CASE and software tool companies. As a result of these meetings they got comfortable with the idea of becoming a public company and realized that it was not "rocket science" and felt they could do it as well.

By February 1990, there were some encouraging signs in the IPO market. At the board meeting that month, management recommended the formation of an IPO committee to work with them to explore the IPO process, including establishing contacts with investment banks in order to determine the suitability and appropriateness of the timing of an IPO (see *Figure 2*). Among the investment bankers they had spoken to during 1989 were Hambrecht & Quist, Alex Brown & Sons, Robertson, Stephens & Co., and Smith Barney, four sizable and reputable firms. They also spoke to some smaller firms such as Needham & Company and Wessels, Arnold & Henderson. One board member, who was not on the IPO committee, recommended talking to Donaldson, Lufkin & Jenrette based on his favorable impression of their software analyst, Scott Smith; as a result, EASEL began talks with them that month.

Figure 1
IPO Process Time Line—Early 1989

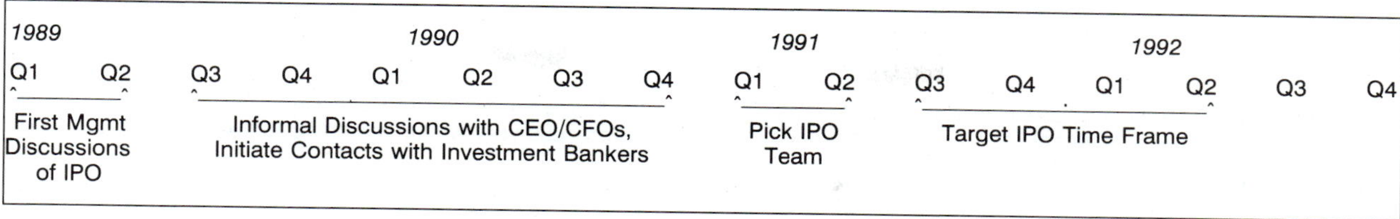

Figure 2 Time Line Update

By the end of March 1990, they had been the targets of some very persuasive sales pitches from the various investment banking teams which came out to EASEL's offices to discuss the possibility of an IPO. All the investment bankers were saying yes to a minimum $40 million valuation and some were considerably higher. They were all saying that they were willing to take the company public. EASEL Corp. was viewed by all as a quality company with a leading product in a growth market and all bankers felt confident in the management team. EASEL narrowed its choices to four finalists based on who the major players were in the software industry and positive opinions regarding the people from the respective banking teams.

They were faced with the decision of which and how many underwriters to pick. They wanted to make sure that if they chose more than one, whatever weaknesses one might have would be covered by another. Doug and John were very much aware that the investment bankers did this every day for a living and also appreciated the financial incentives behind their fee structures.

THE IPO PROCESS

Based on the CEO and CFO conversations that Doug and John had had over the past year, they were well armed with questions, some of which were not so easily answered by the wine-and-dine sales pitches they had been getting from various investment bankers. They put the questions into a "monster of an RFQ," or request for quotation. The RFQ detailed five pages of issues and questions regarding the deal to be struck, responsibilities and post-IPO support. (*Exhibit 6* presents a spatially condensed version of the RFQ.) They presented it to the IPO committee and the board. The reaction was, "We've never seen anything like it before, but it's just like you two to come up with an idea like that."

The RFQ turned out to be a litmus test of sorts. Three of the four firms "really went to town on it," said John. The firm of Hambrecht & Quist responded with a seven-and-a-half page proposal attached to an eight-tab, 54 page compendium of supporting documentation. (*Exhibit 7* outlines its contents.) None of the firms took a liking to the idea, however, because it required much work on their part and it somewhat bound them to follow through on whatever commitments they made if their proposal was accepted by EASEL. Coming down the stretch, John felt that one of the four firms would most likely be the lead on the offering, and as expected, that firm eagerly responded with a detailed proposal. It was now the end of April 1990 (see *Figure 3*), and all four proposals had now been received.

Exhibit 6
Request for Quotation (RFQ) Summary (condensed)

April 18,1990

Dear _______________ :

We appreciate the interest you have expressed in providing investment banking services to EASEL. In order to provide us with information to help us in the investment banker selection process, we would appreciate your written response to the following questions.

I. IPO Timing
- When and why would be the best time, given current market conditions?
- What financial performance would need to be achieved in order to feel comfortable with an IPO in the September time frame? Would you require an audit of interim financials in order to go public in 1990?
- How does your commitment committee operate and at what point in the process is the commitment obtained?

II. Pricing
- What offering price range would you select if the IPO were today? Please explain how you determined this price.
- How would you position EASEL among comparable software companies? Please indicate which companies you would add or delete from the list of companies which we believe to be comparable to EASEL (see p. 2).

III. IPO Process
- Please provide the names of the proposed investment banking team members and describe specific involvement of each person (drafting sessions, due diligence sessions, etc.)
- Which law firm would you select and who would be the lead attorney from the firm?
- Would you market the offering outside of the United States? Why or why not?
- What is your recommended mix of institutional versus retail buyers and why?
- Describe your recommended road show process. Please note anything unique or unusual relative to other investment banks.

IV. Research
- Who within your firm will be responsible for research? How long have they been with your firm? Is there any information that we should be aware of that would provide us comfort that this person will remain with your firm in the future? Please attach some reports developed by this individual in the past year.
- How would the analyst describe EASEL Corp. (positioning statement)? What is the analyst's opinion of the company's strategy? Will EASEL be included in the universe of software companies your firm tracks?
- When would you release the first research report?
- How often would research reports be released?

V. Fees
- Please provide a schedule of fees expected to be incurred.

VI. The Offering
- What percentage of shares would you feel comfortable allocating to existing investors? To management? What are your policies on selling stockholder indemnification? What are your policies on company reimbursement of selling stockholder expenses?
- What lockup provisions would you want in place for investors, management and employees?
- Management has received proposals from counsel as to the implementation of antitakeover provisions prior to an IPO including poison pill defense and a staggered board. What is your position on these provisions?

VII. Support
- Describe the scope of your trading operation and how you would support our stock in the market. Will you act as market maker? Who else would you recommend as additional market makers?
- What type and level of support would we receive after an IPO?

VIII. Other Information
- Please provide examples of the last five technology company IPOs you have managed or comanaged. Please provide IPO price and 30-day post-IPO price. Please also provide prospectus copies and CEO and CFO names and telephone numbers.
- Please provide any other information you would like us to consider.

We would appreciate six copies of your response to this request by April 30, which we will share with our IPO committee and board of directors. We may ask you to make a formal presentation to this committee at a later date.

Thank you for your continued interest and feel free to contact me if you should have any questions.

Sincerely,

John McDonough
Vice President and
Chief Financial Officer

Comparable Software Companies

Adobe Systems
Knowledgeware
Microsoft
Lotus
Oracle Systems
Informix

Consilium
Parametric Technology
Caere Corporation
BMC Software
Symantec

Exhibit 7
Outline of the Hambrecht & Quist Proposal Compendium

1.
   a. Personal computer industry spot report
   b. Ten Best Performing Technology IPOs of 1988 and 1989
   c. H&Q Executive Officers and Managing Directors
2.
   a. EASEL Valuation Projection
   b. Valuation Analysis of Selected Comparable Companies
3.
   a. IPO Team—H&Q (10 people listed, with profiles)
   b. IPO Team—Client References for each of the 10
   c. Sales and Trading—Distribution of Recent H&Q IPOs
   d. Example of an IPO Offering Summary
   e. Detailed Listing of Institutional Purchasers for the Example Offering
   f. Detailed Internal Memoranda for Two Comparable Company IPOs
4.
   a. Research Coverage of the Software Industry—Breakout by Five Analysts
   b. Research Support Plan
   c. Examples of Two Recent Company Research Reports
   d. Detailed Personal Computer Industry Review
5. Average Expenses of 10 1989 and 1990 IPOs Managed or Comanaged by H&Q
6. Listing of Emerging Growth IPOs, $10 million or Greater
7.
   a. Trading Support Plan—Coverage of the Software Universe
   b. Trading Support Plan—Aftermarket Commitment
8.
   a. Performance of IPOs Recently Handled by H&Q
   b. IPOs January 1, 1988, to April 25, 1990—H&Q
   c. IPOs January 1, 1988, to April 25, 1990—Alex. Brown
   d. IPOs January 1, 1988, to April 25, 1990—Donaldson, Lufkin & Jenrette
   e. IPOs January 1, 1988, to April 25, 1990—Robertson, Stephens & Co.

Figure 3
Time Line Update

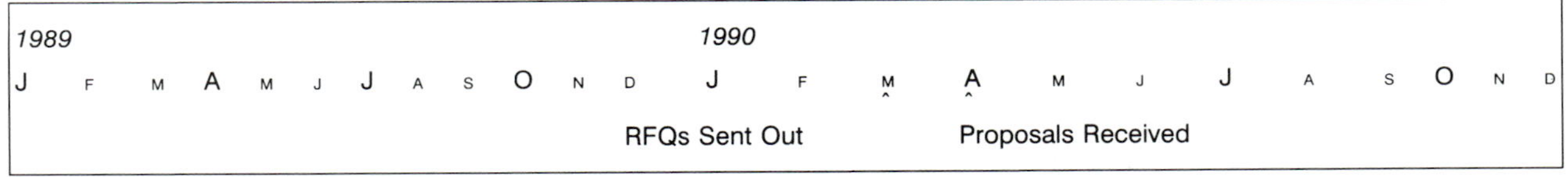

Results of the RFQ

A summary of some of the detailed material and information included in each proposal is shown in *Exhibit 8*. *Exhibit 9* provides a summary of key points from each of the four proposals. In addition to the issue of valuation and pricing of the shares, "value-added" in terms of research, sales, and aftermarket support was also of concern. *Exhibit 10* contains an analysis of the stock price performance of companies each firm had taken public from January 1, 1988, through April 25, 1990. By this analysis, H&Q IPOs had outperformed the other firms by far, averaging a 64 percent increase in stock price since IPO for their companies. If only software stocks were considered, the average increase was more than 100 percent.

Another analysis ranked investment bank research analysts, assigning first-team, second-team, third-team, and runner-up status to the top analysts at each of the nation's leading firms (*Exhibit 11*). By this ranking, Donaldson, Lufkin & Jenrette scored highest of the four, based on overall number (ranked No. 7 in 1989) of top analysts at their firm, and in terms of the number of All-America Team members as a percentage of their total number of analysts (ranked No. 3). Donaldson, Lufkin & Jenrette also had the third-highest-ranked

Exhibit 8
Details of Typical Proposal Items

EASEL Valuation Matrix

Calendar Year 1991 P/E Multiple	*Implied Post Offering Valuation ($MM)*	*Assumptions*	
16.0x	$64.4	1991 Profit before tax	$4,900
16.5	66.4	Incremental interest income	850
17.0	68.4		
17.5	70.4		
18.0	72.5	Pro forma pre-tax income	5,750
18.5	74.5	Income taxes at 30%	1,725
19.0	76.5	Pro forma net income	$4,025

Typical Research Support Plan

Written Reports
- Memo/Internal Report (2–6 pages)
  - After quiet period expires
  - After each quarter's results are announced (8 per 24 months)
- Spot Report (2–6 pages)
  - As appropriate (4 per 12 months)
- Full Company Report
  - Approximately every 12 months after IPO

Investor Contact (beyond reports)
- Sales Force
  - Regular updates from analyst at daily capital market reports
  - Direct access by management
  - Software focus, experience, and credibility
- Analysts' Contacts
  - Interactive relationship with investment community
  - Media and trade press exposure
- Investor Meetings
  - Informal road shows arranged by underwriter
  - Sponsorship at New York Society of Securities Analysts
- High-Tech Company Conferences
  - Institutional investor attendance
  - Breakout sessions for detailed question and answer
  - Company-sponsored dinners
  - Exposure to other corporate clients

analyst in the Information Technology/Software and Data Services sector, Scott Smith. None of the other three firms had an All-America Team analyst in this sector. D, L & J, however, had posted the lowest average post-IPO stock price performance of the final four (*Exhibit 11*).

Finally, as a measure of underwriting equity sales volume performance (*Exhibit 12*), Alex Brown & Sons scored highest among the four firms in terms of Book Manager Ranking (No. 2 overall, No. 5 without funds), and in terms of IPO Underwriter Rankings (No. 10 overall, No. 7 without funds). None of the other three firms made the cut of the top 15 firms in these categories for 1989.

THE IPO ENVIRONMENT

Following the October 1987 stock market crash, IPO activity had all but dried up and investors had continued to show indifference to IPO issues through 1988 and 1989. A *Wall Street Journal* article documented the relatively lower performance of small-cap stocks (i.e., those with total market valuation of less than $400 million) compared to the broader market (see *Exhibit 13*):

While the Dow Jones Industrial Average soared 160% and the Standard & Poor's 500-Stock Index soared 150% [from December 31, 1982, through December 31, 1989], the NASDAQ Compo-

Exhibit 8 ***(continued)***

Fees Matrix

Event	*Alex. Brown*	*DLJ*	*H & Q**	*RS & Co.*
SEC Registration Fee	$ 5,500		$ 4,636	$ 4,000
NASD Filing Fee	2,500		2,428	2,000
Accounting	50,000		95,449	80,000
Printing Expenses	60,000		85,347	150,000
Transfer Agent, Custodian, and Register Fees			6,056	10,000
Blue Sky Expenses	40,000		34,435	40,000
Legal Fees and Expenses	160,000		186,641	110,000
Road Show	10,000			
Miscellaneous			14,666	4,000
TOTAL	$328,000	$350,000	$429,658	$400,000

*An average composed of deals for Network General, Consilium, Vencor, Lattice, Solectron, Immunogen, Parametric, Hologic, Integrated Systems, and Syntellect.

Coverage of Software Universe by Hambrecht & Quist, Alex. Brown, Donaldson, Lufkin & Jenrette, and Robertson, Stephens & Co.

Company	*H&Q*	*ABS*	*DLJ*	*RS*
Adobe	T	T	T	T
Aldus	—	T	—	—
Autodesk	T	T	—	T
Caere	—	T	—	—
Consilium	T	—	—	—
Index Technology	T	T	—	T
Informix	T	—	T	—
Integrated Systems	T	T	—	—
Knowledgeware	—	—	T	—
Lotus Development	T	T	T	T
Microsoft	T	T	T	T
Oracle Systems	T	T	T	T
Parametric Technology	T	T	—	—
Sage Software	T	T	—	—
Structural Dynamics Research	T	T	—	T
Symantec	—	—	T	T
Number traded:	12	12	7	8

T = traded; — = not traded.

Continued.

site Index of over-the-counter issues rose just 96% and the Russell Index of 2,000 small stocks rose 89%.[1]

The article went on to point out that small-stock P/E ratios had fallen since 1988 and the stocks were "about as cheap as they had ever been." Analysts predicted that if interest rates remained low and small-company profits continued to improve, investors would come back. In April 1990, a few signs began to appear that small companies were once again becoming attractive investment opportunities and there was some renewed interest in IPO stocks by investors.

Later, *The Wall Street Journal* noted that "new technology issues [were] the darlings of the season."[2] According to Securities Data Corporation sources, 71 companies had gone public, raising $2.5 billion since January 1990, compared with only 46 over the same period

[1]"Stalled Secondaries – If the Smaller Stocks Historically Do Best, What's Going on Now?" *The Wall Street Journal*, March 13, 1990, p. A1. The Russell 2000 is an index composed of NASDAQ stocks tracked by Datastream/Worldview.

[2]"Initial Public Offerings Are Surging but Still Trail Levels Before '87 Crash," *The Wall Street Journal*, May 14, 1990, p. C6.

Exhibit 8 ***(continued)***

Valuation Analysis of Selected Comparable Companies

Company	*Ticker*	*FY End*	*LTM*	*Shares Out (Mil)*	*Price on 24 Apr*	*Earnings Per Share* LTM	*Earnings Per Share* CY90B	*Earnings Per Share* CY91P	*P/E Multiples* LTM	*P/E Multiples* CY90B	*P/E Multiples* CY91P
COMPUTER-AIDED SOFTWARE ENGINEERING											
Index Technology	INDX	Dec	Dec	4.8	$ 7.50	$0.50	$0.55	$0.75	15.0 x	13.6 x	10.0 x
Integrated Systems	INTS	Feb	Nov	7.9	11.63	0.28	0.40	0.57	41.5	29.1	20.4
Knowledgeware(a)	KNOW	Jun	Dec	11.8	19.25	0.77	0.94	1.20	25.0	20.5	16.0
Sage Software	SGS1	Apr	Jan	6.4	11.88	0.37	0.71	0.92	32.1	16.7	12.9
							Mean		28.4 x	20.0 x	14.8 x
PC SOFTWARE UTILITIES											
Caere	CAER	Dec	Mar	5.2	$24.25	$0.96	$1.15	$1.00	25.3 x	21.1 x	15.2
Symantec	SYMC	Mar	Dec	6.7	19.00	0.56	1.22	1.45	33.9	15.6	13.1
							Mean		29.6 x	18.3 x	14.1 x
DISTRIBUTED SYSTEMS: SOFTWARE											
Adobe Systems	ADBE	Nov	Feb	21.3	$38.75	$1.72	$2.10	$2.25	22.5 x	18.5 x	17.2 x
Aldus	ALDC	Dec	Dec	12.8	20.00	1.21	1.45	1.80	16.5	13.8	11.1
Informix	IFMX	Dec	Dec	12.6	12.00	0.48	0.95	1.55	25.0	12.6	7.7
Lotus Development	LOTS	Dec	Dec	42.8	30.75	1.61	2.35	2.75	19.1	13.1	11.2
Microsoft (b)	MSFT	Jun	Mar	121.1	57.25	2.09	2.55	2.95	27.4	22.5	19.4
Oracle Systems	ORCL	May	Nov	137.1	15.88	0.73	1.05	1.40	21.7	15.1	11.3
							Mean		22.0 x	15.9 x	13.0 x

[a] LTM earnings per share excludes one-time IBM license agreement payment of $2.4 million, or $0.15 per share.
[b] Reflects a two-for-one split effective April 13, 1990

in 1989, when $1.4 billion had been raised. In contrast, more than 200 companies had gone public in the same time period in 1983 and more than 175 in the first half of 1986.

According to the June 4, 1990, edition of *Going Public: The IPO Reporter*, IPO activity and stock performance had picked up in the first five months of 1990. *Exhibit 14* lists the IPO 100, which tracks the average price change in shares of the most recent 100 initial public offerings, including both companies and closed-end investment funds. By the end of May 1990, IPO stocks had increased in performance from approximately 5 percent to the 15 percent range as illustrated in *Exhibit 15*.

Among venture-backed company public IPOs, 19 companies had been brought to market through May 31, 1990, which raised $587 million, which was also up sharply from only $52.2 million raised by three companies in the first five months of 1989. The Venture Capital 100 (Venture Economics, Inc., Needham, Massachusetts) index also rose 14 percent in May, continuing the upward trend since the end of 1989. The Venture Capital 100 (VC 100) measures the stock price performance of a cross section of venture-backed companies which have gone public. These companies are chosen arbitrarily with respect to size, success, or growth prospects, and they represent 13 broad industrial sectors. Companies are removed when no longer publicly traded, or when traded for over 10 years. *Exhibit 15* shows the VC 100 index in comparison to the S&P 500 and Value Line Composite indices. Also included are recent performance data on the nine companies which represent the Computer Software and Service sector of the VC 100 index and a Software and Services Estimate Summary for several other publicly traded companies.

Following the recent IPO activity this year, 36 companies were in registration, showing the hope of continued confidence in IPO stocks by investors (*Exhibit 16*). Among those currently in registration were many technology companies, such as AICorp, a knowledge base/(CASE) tool software developer, and Micrografx, a software developer for IBM personal computers and compatibles (*Exhibit 17*). Another company which Doug and John had been closely watching had already gone public on December 7, 1989. A summary description of Parametric Technology and its offering is shown in *Exhibit 18*.

Exhibit 8 ***(concluded)***

EPS Growth Rate	EPS Growth Rate to CY91 P/E	Market Value ($MM)	LTM Revenues ($MM)	Mkt/ LTM Revenues	LTM Net Income ($MM)	Net Income Margin %	Latest Book Value	Mkt Value/ Book
36.4%	3.6 x	$ 36.0	$ 38.0	0.9 x	$ 2.3	6.1%	$ 31.5	1.1 x
42.5	2.1	91.8	11.1	8.3	1.8	16.2	16.9	5.4
27.7	1.7	227.2	50.1	4.5	8.6	17.2	43.1	5.3
29.6	2.3	76.0	23.9	3.2	2.3	9.6	28.2	2.7
	2.4 x			4.2 x		12.3%		3.6 x
39.1%	2.6 x	$ 126.1	$ 21.8	5.8 x	$ 42	19.3%	528.9	4.4 x
18.9	1.4	127.3	47.0	2.7	6.1	13.0	18.6	6.8
	2.0 x			4.2 x		16.1%		5.6 x
22.1%	1.3 x	$ 825.4	$ 133.0	6.2 x	$ 36.9	27.7%	$ 70.9	11.6 x
19.8	1.8	256.0	87.9	2.9	15.5	17.6	80.0	3.2
97.9	12.6	151.2	145.0	1.0	6.4	4.4	69.8	2.2
46.0	4.1	1,316.1	556.0	2.4	68.0	12.2	604.3	2.2
22.0	1.1	6,933.0	1066.7	6.5	244.6	22.9	826.2	8.4
43.8	3.9	2,176.5	852.4	2.6	98.0	11.5	318.2	6.8
	4.1 x			3.6 x		16.1%		5.2 x

These technology companies and the other IPO candidates followed closely on the heels of the broader rise in computer-related stocks on the Dow. Between December 29, 1989, and May 21, 1990, the Dow Jones (DJ) Computer Industry Index had risen 18.8 percent compared to only .98 percent for the Dow Jones Equity Market Index overall (*Exhibit 13*).[3]

As a subset of the computer industry, the DJ Software Group had earlier been shown to have been outperforming the DJ Equity Market Index as well. An analysis of these stocks indicated again that since the end of 1989, software stocks had similarly risen approximately 18 percent by mid-March at a time when the broader equity index had actually declined by approximately 4 percent (*Exhibit 13*).[4]

> The run in technology growth stocks had been fueled by so-called "value investors." These money managers roam through thousands of stocks in search of companies whose shares, by various value benchmarks, [had become relatively] cheaper than the overall market. . . . Lately, technology stocks have been popping up on value investors' computers that search the markets for cheap stocks. Earnings expectations, rather than underlying asset values had played a role as well.[5]

A caveat pointed out by one equities analyst was that "technology stocks go down as fast as they go up. One reason technology stocks had been trading at a cheaper value than the overall market was that they are known to be risky."[6] Another analyst termed technology stocks "a hair-trigger sector, . . . every technology company hits some sort of snag, and in a fair percentage of the cases it is a four-quarter snag. Investors don't want to hang around while the problem works out."[7]

[3]"Surging Technology Stocks Dazzle Analysts, Investors," *The Wall Street Journal*, May 22, 1990, p. C1.

[4]"Investment Insight—Industry Groups: Software," *The Wall Street Journal*, March 22, 1990, p. C1.

[5]Ibid.

[6]Ibid.

[7]Ibid.

Exhibit 9 ***Summary of the Four Underwriting Proposals***

	Robertson Stephens	*Alex. Brown*	*DLJ*	*H & Q*
Timing of research	Initial comprehensive report 25 days after IPO Quarterly reports—updates Interim reports—for significant events	Initial Report 60 days after IPO One major report/year Eight 1–2 pg. reports each year	Initial Report 25 days after IPO Quarterly and monthly coverage Major report annually	Initial Report 25 days after IPO Full stand-alone report within 15 months
Selling Stockholders				
Secondary shares	Up to 50%, prefer 25%–40%	Up to 50%	Up to 50%	Up to 35%
Management	No more than 18 to 20%	No more than 10 to 20%	No more than 10%	No more than 10%
Lockup	150 days for all offcrs, directors, >1% holders	180 days for management and >1% holders	180 days for management, selling and material holders	150–180 days
Antitakeover provisions	No issues, prefer "blank check" versus poison pill	No issues	OK, not in favor of poison pill	No issues, should consider blank check
Timing Recommendation	Sep 15, 1990	Sept./Oct. 1990	Sept./Oct. 1990	Q1 1991
Pricing comparables	Adobe, Mentor Autodesk, Microsoft BMC, Novell Cadence, Oracle Lotus, SDRC Knowledgeware	Caere Consilium Parametric Integrated Systems Knowledgeware	*GUI:* Microsoft *Quality:* Adobe *Applications development:* BMC Index, Caere Int. Systems, Consilium Knowlwre, Goal Systems Parametric, Oracle SAGE, Symantec (Integrated Systems Knowledgeware, Microsoft)	Index, Adobe Integrated Systems, Aldus Knowledgeware, Informix SAGE, Lotus Caere, Microsoft Symantec, Oracle
Recommended price	18–20X 1990 earnings	22.5X 1990 earnings	16–18X 1991 earnings	16–17X 1991 earnings
Total size	Not specified	Primary shrs up to 25%–30%, second. shrs could match	Primary shrs < 25%, second shrs could match	Not specified
Average change in price	+16% within 2 weeks of IPO	+29% within 30 days of IPO	+7% within 30 days of IPO	+16% within 28 days of IPO
Audited statements?	No	No	Yes	Yes
Road show	United States only	United States only	United States and Europe	Not specified
Law firm	Hale & Dorr	Goodwin Proctor & Hoar	Not specified	Hale & Dorr
Distribution	75%–80% institutional	60–70% institutional	Not specified	65 to 75% institutional
Research analyst	Rich Edwards	Chris Mortenson	Scott Smith	Bruce Lupatkin

Nevertheless, analysts and investment bankers expected "the IPO business to remain steady, [and] end the year slightly stronger than 1989."[8]

SUMMARY

Doug knew that even if the so-called IPO window was opening wider, it could also slam shut at any moment. While there were encouraging signs, he wondered whether to push ahead, and if so, which underwriter to choose.

[8]*The Wall Street Journal*, May 14, 1990, p. C6.

Exhibit 10
Comparison of Recent IPO Performance

Hambrecht & Quist
Initial Public Offerings
January 1, 1988, to April 25, 1990

Offer Date	*Issuer*	*Ticker Symbol*	*Dollar Amount (Mils)*	*Offer Price per Share*	*Stock Price on 4/25/90*	*Stock Price % Change Offer Date to 04/25/90*	*File Low*	*File High*	*% Chng Mid-File Price to Offer*	*Managing Underwriters*	*Description of Business*
2/26/88	Octel Communications	OCTL	$14.7	$ 7.00	$22.63	223.2	$ 6.00	$ 7.00	7.1	ABS:HG	Develop voice processing systems
6/23/88	Index Technology	INDX	19.2	12.00	7.50	−37.5	10.00	12.00	8.3	HQ;ABS;ROBERTSON	Computer software development
7/15/88	Homeowners Group	HOMG	13.5	9.00	10.00	11.1	9.00	11.00	−11.1	HQ	Real estate contract services
8/11/88	Novellus Systems	NVLS	15.2	8.00	16.00	100.0	7.00	9.00	0.0	BSC;HQ;NEEDHAM	Vapor deposition equipment
8/19/88	Synoptics Communications	SNPX	20.3	13.50	39.75	194.4	11.00	13.00	11.1	MS;HQ	Manufacturer computer network systems
2/2/89	Network General	NETG	15.2	8.00	25.00	212.5	7.00	7.00	12.5	ABS;HQ	Manufacture/market software network tools
5/9/89	Consilium	CSIM	14.0	9.00	19.00	111.1	7.50	8.50	11.1	HQ;SBHU	Develop computer software
7/11/89	Tocor	TOCRZ	30.0	12.00	18.00	50.0	12.00	12.00	0.0	PW;HQ(BOOK)	Health care products
9/19/89	Vencor	VCOR	14.5	8.50	7.50	−11.8	6.50	8.50	11.8	J.C.BRADFORD;HQ	Long-term hospital care
11/8/89	Lattice Semiconductor	LSCC	17.4	6.00	10.75	79.2	6.00	8.00	−16.7	DR:HQ	Develop/market program logic devices
11/15/89	Solectron	SLTN	11.1	6.00	9.75	62.5	8.00	10.00	−50.0	MLCM;HQ	Manufacture electronic system parts
11/16/89	Immunogen	IMGN	15.0	10.00	7.75	−22.5	10.00	12.00	−10.0	PW;HQ	Develop cancer treatment drugs
11/17/89	Receptech	RECP	27.0	12.00	5.50	−54.2	12.00	12.00	0.0	PBS;HQ	Develop immunology research prod
12/7/89	Parametric Technology	PMTC	20.4	12.00	23.00	91.7	8.00	10.00	25.0	ABS;HQ;WESSELS	Mechanical design software
3/1/90	Hologic	HOLX	16.8	14.00	18.50	32.1	11.00	13.00	14.3	HQ;NEEDHAM;ADAMS-HARKNESS	Manufacture X-ray systems
3/6/90	Integrated Systems	INTS	16.2	9.00	11.75	30.6	6.00	7.50	25.0	ABS;HQ	Develop/manufacture software
3/29/90	Syntellect	SYNL	28.0	15.00	17.00	13.3	11.50	13.00	18.3	ABS;HQ	Manufacture voice telephone systems
				Averages:		63.9%			3.3%		

(Continued)

Exhibit 10 ***(continued)***

Alex, Brown
Initial Public Offerings
January 1, 1988, to April 25, 1990

Offer Date	*Issuer*	*Ticker Symbol*	*Dollar Amount (Mils)*	*Offer Price per Share*	*Stock Price on 4/25/90*	*Stock Price % Change Offer Date to 04/25/90*	*File Low*	*File High*	*% Chng Mid-File Price to Offer*	*Managing Underwriters*	*Description of Business*
2/25/88	Geraghty & Miller	GMGW	$16.5	$ 7.50	$ 16.00	113.3	$ 7.00	$ 8.00	0.0	ABS;ROBERTSON	Groundwater resource services
2/26/88	Octel Communications	OCTL	14.7	7.00	22.63	223.2	6.00	7.00	7.1	ABS:HQ	Develop voice processing systems
6/7/88	Kinetic Concepts	KNCI	44.6	10.50	5.38	−48.8	10.00	12.00	−4.8	MS:ABS:OS	Manufacture specialized beds
6/23/88	Index Technology	INDX	19.2	12.00	7.50	−37.5	10.00	12.00	8.3	HQ;ABS:ROBERTSON	Computer software development
7/14/88	Babbages	BBGS	19.5	13.00	4.75	−63.5	10.00	12.00	15.4	ABS;ROBERTSON	Operate computer software stores
8/2/88	Environmental Control Group	ECGI	16.3	11.25	4.50	−60.0	10.00	12.00	2.2	ABS;JANNEY	Asbestos abatement service
8/11/88	Kinder-Care Learning Centers	KIND	42.0	7.00	3.13	−55.4	8.50	10.00	−32.1	ABS;DBL	Operate day care centers
8/12/88	BMC Software	BMCS	27.0	9.00	22.75	279.2	9.00	11.00	−11.1	ABS;ROBERTSON	Develop/market computer software
9/20/88	Casual Male	CMLE	12.5	10.00	0.50	−95.0	11.00	12.00	−15.0	ABS	Operate men's clothing stores
9/20/88	Weltek	WWTK	16.0	10.00	19.38	93.8	10.00	12.00	−10.0	MS;ABS	Manufacture semiconductors/circuit boards
10/20/88	Softsel Computer Products	SOFS	12.0	6.00	5.00	−16.7	7.00	9.00	−33.3	ABS;SBHU	Distribute computer hard/software
11/10/88	Genus	GGNS	10.0	5.00	4.25	93.8	5.50	6.00	−15.0	ABS;COWEN	Manufacture electrical machinery
2/2/89	Network General	NETG	15.2	8.00	25.00	−16.7	7.00	7.00	12.5	ABS;HQ	Manufacture/market software network tools
4/13/89	Bytex	BYTX	10.8	8.00	9.88	−15.0	8.00	10.00	−12.5	ABS;VOLPE	Manufacture switching system/ communication products
5/9/89	Goal Systems International	GOAL	23.4	9.75	13.13	212.5	9.00	10.50	0.0	MS:ABS	Design/develop computer software
5/11/89	Chempower	CHEM	27.3	13.00	16.13	23.4	11.00	13.00	7.7	ABS	Asbestos abatement services
6/8/89	Cirrus Logic	CRUS	33.4	10.00	11.13	34.6	8.00	9.50	12.5	GS;ABS;ROBERTSON	Manufacture VLSI products
6/29/89	Handex Environmental Recovery	HAND	16.8	14.00	19.00	24.0	12.00	14.00	7.1	ABS	Groundwater/soil contamination
7/7/89	Westcott Communications	WCTV	15.0	10.00	9.75	11.3	9.00	11.00	0.0	ROBERTSON;ABS	Informational programming
7/13/89	BEI Electronics	BEII	24.3	9.00	6.75	35.7	9.00	11.00	−11.1	ABS	Design/manufacture defense weapons
7/20/89	Cognex	CGNX	12.8	11.00	19.00	−2.5	8.50	10.00	15.9	ABS;NEEDHAM	Machine vision systems
7/27/89	GZA GeoEnvironmental	GZEA	13.2	12.00	11.75	−25.0	10.00	12.00	8.3	BSC;ABS	Environmental consulting service
8/3/89	Serv-Tech	STEC	16.9	13.00	NA	72.7	10.50	12.50	11.5	ABS	Maintenance to petrochem industry
8/10/89	Air & Water Technologies	AWT	68.0	17.00	21.50	−2.1	13.50	14.50	17.6	KP;ABS	Environmental services
8/18/89	BizMart	BZMT	34.0	10.00	13.13	NA	12.00	14.00	−30.0	ABS;ROBERTSON	Operates office products store
9/20/89	Electronic Arts	ERTS	16.6	8.00	12.75	26.5	8.00	10.00	−12.5	ABS:PW	Entertainment software
10/12/89	Rally's	RLLY	26.2	15.00	16.00	31.3	12.50	14.50	10.0	ABS;MONTGOMERY	Fast food restaurant
10/19/89	Caere	CAER	22.5	12.00	24.25	59.4	10.00	12.00	8.3	ABS;WER-SCHRODER	Manufacture recognition software
11/15/89	Urcarco	CARS	38.0	11.00	23.25	111.4	9.00	11.00	9.1	ABS;CAZENOVE	Used car retail lots

Exhibit 10 ***(continued)***

Alex, Brown
Initial Public Offerings
January 1, 1988, to April 25, 1990

Offer Date	*Issuer*	*Ticker Symbol*	*Dollar Amount (Mils)*	*Offer Price per Share*	*Stock Price on 4/25/90*	*Stock Price % Change Offer Date to 04/25/90*	*File Low*	*File High*	*% Chng Mid-File Price to Offer*	*Managing Underwriters*	*Description of Business*
11/30/89	Laserscope	LSCP	16.3	9.00	15.63	73.6	6.50	8.00	19.4	ABS;VOLPE	Manufacture surgical lasers
12/7/89	Parametric Technology	PMTC	20.4	12.00	23.00	91.7	8.00	10.00	25.0	ABS;HQ;WESSELS	Mechanical design software
12/14/89	American Capital & Research	ACRCA	30.7	8.50	9.38	10.3	10.00	12.00	−29.4	SLH;ABS;DBL	Environmental & engineer services
12/19/89	Borland International	BORL	22.5	10.00	15.38	53.8	9.44	9.44	5.6	GS;ABS	Develops/markets software
12/21/89	Exide Electronics Group	XUPS	15.0	12.50	8.50	−32.0	14.00	16.00	−20.0	ABS;DLJ	Manufacture electronic products
3/6/90	Integrated Systems	INTS	16.2	9.00	11.75	30.6	6.00	7.50	25.0	ABS:HQ	Develop/manufacture software
3/29/90	Syntellect	SYNL	28.0	15.00	17.00	13.3	11.50	13.00	18.3	ABS;HQ	Develop/market voice response system
4/3/93	Tetra Technologies	TTRA	23.5	10.00	12.25	22.5	9.00	11.00	0.0	PW;ABS;FIRST ANALYSIS	Recycling/water treatment
4/5/90	Pharmacy Management Services	PMSV	30.0	12.00	15.63	30.2	9.00	9.00	25.0	ROBERTSON;ABS	Medical cost containment
4/12/90	Sanifill	FIL	19.0	9.50	13.88	46.1	8.00	9.00	10.5	ABS;PENN-MERCHANT	Operate solid waste landfills
4/24/90	Orbital Sciences	ORBI	33.6	14.00	14.13	0.9	12.00	15.00	3.6	ABS;MLCM	Manufacture spaces products
			Averages:			35.4%			1.2%		

(Continued)

Exhibit 10 ***(continued)***

Donaldson, Lufkin, Jenrette
Initial Public Offerings
January 1, 1988 to April 25, 1990

Offer Date	*Issuer*	*Ticker Symbol*	*Dollar Amount (Mils)*	*Offer Price per Share*	*Stock Price on 4/25/90*	*Stock Price % Change Offer Date to 04/25/90*	*File Low*	*File High*	*% Chng Mid-File Price to Offer*	*Managing Underwriters*	*Description of Business*
6/6/88	Egghead	EGGS	$61.2	$17.00	$13.00	−23.5	$14.00	$17.00	8.8	DLJ;FBC	Retail computer software
10/19/88	American Steel & Wire	RODS	25.3	9.00	7.50	−16.7	9.00	10.00	−5.6	DLJ;PW	Manufacture steel products
6/23/89	Symantec	SYMC	16.5	10.50	19.25	13.3	9.50	11.50	0.0	ROBERTSON;DLJ	Software products
10/20/89	Knowledgeware	KNOW	37.5	12.50	20.00	60.0	10.50	12.00	10.0	MONTGOMERY;DLJ	Manufacture computer software
12/21/89	Exide Electronics Group	XUPS	15.0	12.50	8.50	−32.0	14.00	16.00	−20.0	ABS:DLJ	Manufacture electronic products
3/6/90	Sequoia Systems	SEQS	18.1	9.50	7.38	−22.4	9.00	11.00	−5.3	MLCM;DLJ;NEEDHAM	Manufacture computer systems
3/26/90	Tokos Medical	TKOS	24.0	12.00	11.25	−6.3	14.00	14.00	−16.7	ROBERTSON;DLJ	Outpatient/home health care
				Averages:		6.1%			−4.1%		

Exhibit 10 ***(concluded)***

Robertson, Stephens & Company
Initial Public Offerings
January 1, 1988, to April 25, 1990

Offer Date	*Issuer*	*Ticker Symbol*	*Dollar Amount (Mils)*	*Offer Price per Share*	*Stock Price on 4/25/90*	*Stock Price % Change Offer Date to 04/25/90*	*File Low*	*File High*	*% Chng Mid-File Price to Offer*	*Managing Underwriters*	*Description of Business*
2/25/88	Geraghty & Miller	GMGW	$16.5	$ 7.50	$16.00	113.3	$7.00	$8.00	0.0	ABS:ROBERTSON	Groundwater resource services
3/4/88	Vitalink Communications	VTTA	16.5	8.25	12.13	47.0	7.00	8.50	6.1	KP;ROBERTSON	Data communications products
5/6/88	Silk Greenhouse	SGHI	12.1	11.00	2.88	−60.8	10.00	11.00	4.5	ROBERTSON;RAYMOND	Market synthetic flowers/plants
5/17/88	Relational Technology	RELY	28.0	14.00	NA	NA	12.00	14.00	7.1	GS;ROBERTSON	Database management software
6/22/88	Dell Computer	DELL	29.8	8.50	8.63	1.5	8.00	9.50	−2.9	GS;ROBERTSON	Manufacture/design personal computers
6/23/88	Index Technology	INDX	19.2	12.00	7.50	−37.5	10.00	12.00	8.3	HQ;ABS;ROBERTSON	Computer software development
7/14/88	Babbages	BBGS	19.5	13.00	4.75	−63.5	10.00	12.00	15.4	ABS;ROBERTSON	Operate computer software stores
8/11/88	NeoRX	NERX	17.5	7.00	2.75	−60.7	7.00	9.00	−14.3	KP;ROBERTSON	Develop monoclonal antibodies
8/12/88	BMC Software	BMCS	27.0	9.00	22.75	279.2	9.00	11.00	−11.1	ABS;ROBERTSON	Develop/market computer software
5/11/89	Duty Free International	DFII	25.6	20.50	26.00	26.8	18.00	20.00	7.3	ROBERTSON;THOMSON	Duty-free merchandise retailer
6/8/89	Cirrus Logic	CRUS	33.4	10.00	11.13	11.3	8.00	9.50	12.5	GS;ABS;ROBERTSON	Manufacture VLSI products
6/23/89	Symantec	SYMC	16.5	10.50	19.25	83.3	9.50	11.50	0.0	ROBERTSON;DLJ	Software products
7/7/89	Westcott Communications	WCTV	15.0	10.00	9.75	−2.5	9.00	11.00	0.0	ROBERTSON;ABS	Informational programming
8/18/89	BizMart	BZMT	34.0	10.00	13.13	31.3	12.00	14.00	−30.0	ABS;ROBERTSON	Operates office products store
12/20/89	Ramsey-HMO	RHMO	21.8	10.00	8.88	−11.3	11.00	13.00	−20.0	ROBERTSON	Operates health maintanence organization
3/13/90	VeriFone	VFIC	52.8	16.00	20.25	26.6	12.00	14.00	18.8	MS;ROBERTSON;DWR	Manufacture transaction automation systems
3/26/90	Tokos Medical	TKOS	24.0	12.00	11.25	−6.3	14.00	14.00	−16.7	ROBERTSON;DLJ	Outpatient/home health care
4/5/90	Pharmacy Management Services	PMSV	30.0	12.00	15.63	30.2	9.00	9.00	25.0	ROBERTSON;ABS	Medical cost containment
				Averages:		24.0%			0.6%		

Exhibit 11
Institutional Investor* Magazine 1989 Analyst Rankings

Rank†			
1988	*1989*	*Firm*	*1989 Rank¶*
4	1	Merrill Lynch	8
	2	Goldman Sachs	1
3	3	First Boston	2
2	4	Drexel Burnham Lambert	4
7	4	Shearson Lehman Hutton	9
6	6	PaineWebber	5
8	7	Donaldson, Lufkin & Jenrette	3
5	8	Prudential-Bache Securities	6
10	9	Salomon Brothers	15
13	10	Morgan Stanley	12
8	11	Smith Barney, Harris Upham	12
11	12	Kidder Peabody	18
12	13	Dean Witter Reynolds	10
14	14	Wertheim Schroder	14
16	15	Sanford C. Bernstein	11
15	15	Cowen	7
16	17	C. J. Lawrence, Morgan Grenfell	16
20	17	Oppenheimer	19
18	19	Montgomery Securities	17
18	20	Bear Stearns	20
20	21	Alex. Brown & Sons	—
—	22	Mabon Nugent	—
—	22	Petrie Parkman	—
22	22	UBS Securities	—

Information Technology/Software and Data Services Analyst Rankings

First-Team	Richard Sherlund, Goldman Sachs
Second-Team	Stephen McClellan, Merrill Lynch
Third-Team	Scott Smith, Donaldson, Lufkin & Jenrette

Runners Up: Bahar Gidwani, *Kidder Peabody*; James Mendelson, *Morgan Stanley*; Terence Quinn, *Drexel Burnham Lambert*; David Readerman, *Shearson Lehman Hutton*; Charles Taylor, Jr., *Prudential Bache Securities*

*"The 1989 All-America Research Team," October 1989, p. 89.
†By overall number of total team positions (1st, 2nd, 3rd, runner-up).
¶By number of analysts on the team as a percentage of firms' total number of analysts (excluding fixed-income specialists).

Exhibit 12
The IPO Reporter **Underwriter Firm Rankings—1989**

IPO Book Manager Rankings

Full credit to book manager	**January 1, 1989–December 31, 1989**				**January 1, 1988–December 31, 1988**			
Manager	*Amount ($Millions)*	*Rank*	*%*	*Issues*	*Amount ($Millions)*	*Rank*	*%*	*Issues*
Goldman, Sachs	2,087.6	(1)	15.1	14	1,725.5	(6)	7.3	15
Alex. Brown & Sons	1,858.5	(2)	13.4	20	1,061.7	(7)	4.5	15
Prudential-Bache Capital Funding	1,834.7	(3)	13.3	11	3,193.8	(3)	13.4	12
Shearson Lehman Hutton	1,042.1	(4)	7.5	8	4,043.5	(2)	17.0	16
Merrill Lynch Capital Markets	1,031.6	(5)	7.5	13	4,348.2	(1)	18.3	28
PaineWebber	946.0	(6)	6.8	11	2,789.1	(4)	11.7	16
Wheat First Butcher & Singer	903.5	(7)	6.5	2	2,150.0	(5)	9.1	2
First Boston	646.0	(8)	4.7	6	548.8	(9)	2.5	9
Smith Barney, Harris Upham	615.6	(9)	4.5	10	513.2	(11)	2.2	3
Dean Witter Capital Markets	540.0	(10)	3.9	6	500.0	(12)	2.1	4
Salomon Brothers	348.9	(11)	2.5	7	517.3	(10)	2.2	7
Piper, Jaffray & Hopwood	303.0	(12)	2.2	5	345.1	(13)	1.5	4
Kidder, Peabody	188.0	(13)	1.4	3	126.2	(15)	0.5	5
Lazard Freres	178.0	(14)	1.3	2	—	(n/a)	—	—
Morgan Stanley	174.6	(15)	1.3	3	92.0	(17)	0.4	4
Industry Totals	13,821.5			245	23,750.1			280

IPO Underwriter Rankings

Full credit to book manager	**January 1, 1989–December 31, 1989**				**January 1, 1988–December 31, 1988**			
Manager	*Amount ($Millions)*	*Rank*	*%*	*Issues*	*Amount ($Millions)*	*Rank*	*%*	*Issues*
Goldman, Sachs	2,840.6	(1)	20.6	19	2,087.8	(15)	8.8	19
Prudential-Bache Capital Funding	2,839.3	(2)	20.5	17	3,316.4	(7)	14.0	14
Merrill Lynch Capital Markets	2,793.1	(3)	20.2	23	5,542.3	(1)	23.8	38
Legg Mason Wood Walker	2,742.9	(4)	19.8	10	2,427.8	(13)	10.2	11
Blunt Ellis & Loewi	2,505.0	(5)	18.1	10	2,754.4	(10)	11.6	18
Smith Barney, Harris Upham	2,360.6	(6)	17.1	18	4,033.0	(5)	17.0	13
A. G. Edwards & Sons	2,274.4	(7)	16.5	10	1,867.2	(17)	7.9	8
Dain Bosworth	2,208.4	(8)	16.0	10	2,634.5	(11)	11.1	11
Wheat First Butcher & Singer	2,106.5	(9)	15.2	8	4,927.8	(3)	20.7	9
Alex. Brown & Sons	2,091.8	(10)	15.1	28	1,199.8	(24)	5.1	20
Thomson McKinnon Securities	2,054.5	(11)	14.9	10	2,836.8	(9)	11.9	17
Kidder, Peabody	1,877.0	(12)	13.6	7	4,467.7	(4)	18.8	12
Shearson Lehman Hutton	1,653.1	(13)	12.0	11	4,968.9	(2)	20.9	24
John Nuveen	1,522.5	(14)	11.0	4	—	(n/a)	—	—
Piper, Jaffray & Hopwood	1,492.2	(15)	10.8	15	—	(n/a)	—	—
Industry Totals	13,821.5			245	23,750.1			280

*January 8, 1990 issue.

(Continued)

Exhibit 12 ***(concluded)***

IPO Book Manager Rankings Without Funds

Full credit to book manager	**January 1, 1989–December 31, 1989**				**January 1, 1988–December 31, 1988**			
Manager	*Amount ($Millions)*	*Rank*	*%*	*Issues*	*Amount ($Millions)*	*Rank*	*%*	*Issues*
Goldman, Sachs	1,977.6	(1)	31.7	13	1,725.5	(1)	28.8	15
Shearson Lehman Hutton	609.6	(2)	9.8	6	533.3	(3)	8.9	6
First Boston	586.2	(3)	9.4	5	308.8	(5)	5.2	6
Merrill Lynch Capital Markets	419.6	(4)	6.7	10	663.6	(2)	11.1	20
Alex. Brown & Sons	336.0	(5)	5.4	16	179.1	(10)	3.0	10
Prudential-Bache Capital Funding	303.9	(6)	4.9	4	305.8	(6)	5.1	4
Smith Barney, Harris Upham	291.6	(7)	4.7	8	—	(n/a)	—	—
Lazard Freres	178.0	(8)	2.8	2	—	(n/a)	—	—
Morgan Stanley	174.6	(9)	2.8	3	92.0	(13)	1.5	4
Bear, Stearns	126.4	(10)	2.0	4	33.2	(19)	0.6	2
PaineWebber	112.0	(11)	1.8	5	81.6	(14)	1.4	3
Kidder, Peabody	98.0	(12)	1.6	2	126.2	(11)	2.1	5
Oppenheimer	91.1	(13)	1.5	4	—	(n/a)	—	—
Salomon Brothers	85.4	(14)	1.4	3	327.4	(4)	5.5	5
D. H. Blair	83.2	(15)	1.3	16	40.0	(18)	0.7	9
Industry Totals	6,248.1			203	5,988.6			218

IPO Underwriter Rankings Without Funds

Full credit to each manager	**January 1, 1989–December 31, 1989**				**January 1, 1988–December 31, 1988**			
Manager	*Amount ($Millions)*	*Rank*	*%*	*Issues*	*Amount ($Millions)*	*Rank*	*%*	*Issues*
Goldman, Sachs	2,730.7	(1)	43.7	18	2,087.8	(1)	34.9	19
Merrill Lynch Capital Markets	1,486.1	(2)	23.8	16	1,677.7	(2)	28.0	28
Salomon Brothers	1,213.7	(3)	19.4	7	1,209.8	(4)	20.2	10
First Boston	755.1	(4)	12.1	7	790.9	(6)	13.2	8
Shearson Lehman Hutton	695.6	(5)	11.1	8	1,458.7	(3)	24.4	14
Morgan Stanley	616.2	(6)	9.9	6	1,147.6	(5)	19.2	9
Alex. Brown & Sons	569.3	(7)	9.1	24	293.2	(13)	4.9	14
Prudential-Bache capital Funding	536.0	(8)	8.6	7	428.4	(8)	7.2	6
Smith Barney, Harris Upham	345.6	(9)	5.5	11	124.0	(21)	2.1	5
Drexel Burnham Lambert	289.9	(10)	4.6	5	508.8	(7)	8.5	11
PaineWebber	235.6	(11)	3.8	9	358.7	(9)	6.0	10
Prescott, Ball & Turben	222.3	(12)	3.6	2	—	(n/a)	—	—
Bear, Stearns	184.4	(13)	3.0	5	201.0	(16)	3.4	6
Montgomery Securities	184.0	(14)	2.9	5	110.5	(23)	1.8	4
Lazard Freres	178.0	(15)	2.8	2	312.0	(11)	5.2	2
Industry Totals	6,248.1			203	5,988.6			218

Exhibit 13
Dow Jones versus Small Cap Computer and Software Stock Market Indices

Russell 2000 Index of Small Cap Stocks versus Dow Jones Industrial Average[a]

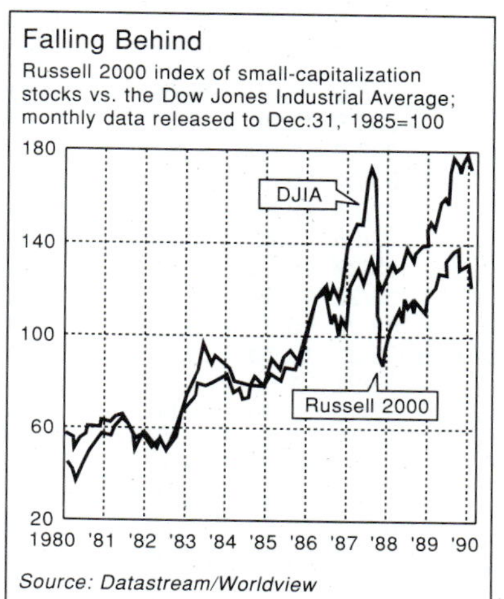

Dow Jones Computer Industry versus DJ Equity Market Index[c]

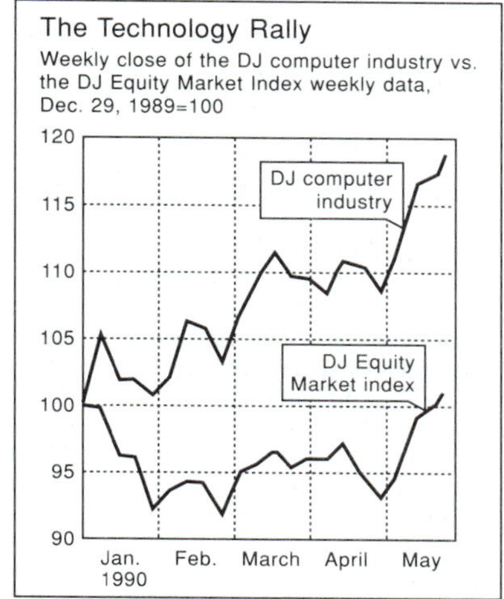

Dow Jones Software Industry Group versus DJ Equity Index[b]

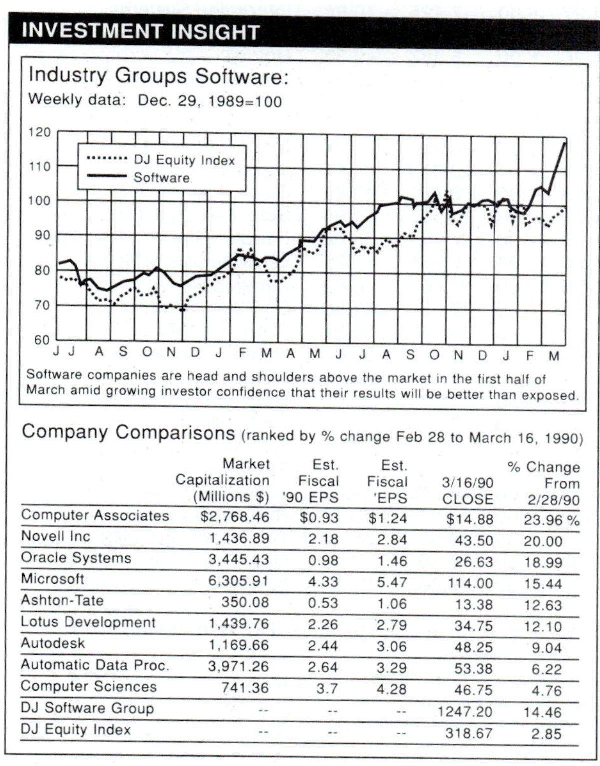

Software companies are head and shoulders above the market in the first half of March amid growing investor confidence that their results will be better than exposed.

Company Comparisons (ranked by % change Feb 28 to March 16, 1990)

	Market Capitalization (Millions $)	Est. Fiscal '90 EPS	Est. Fiscal 'EPS	3/16/90 CLOSE	% Change From 2/28/90
Computer Associates	$2,768.46	$0.93	$1.24	$14.88	23.96 %
Novell Inc	1,436.89	2.18	2.84	43.50	20.00
Oracle Systems	3,445.43	0.98	1.46	26.63	18.99
Microsoft	6,305.91	4.33	5.47	114.00	15.44
Ashton-Tate	350.08	0.53	1.06	13.38	12.63
Lotus Development	1,439.76	2.26	2.79	34.75	12.10
Autodesk	1,169.66	2.44	3.06	48.25	9.04
Automatic Data Proc.	3,971.26	2.64	3.29	53.38	6.22
Computer Sciences	741.36	3.7	4.28	46.75	4.76
DJ Software Group	--	--	--	1247.20	14.46
DJ Equity Index	--	--	--	318.67	2.85

[a]Stalled Secondaries—"If Smaller Stocks Historically Do Best, What's Going On Now?" *The Wall Street Journal*, 3-13-90, p. A1.
[b]Investment Insight—Industry Groups: Software, *The Wall Street Journal*, 3-22-90, p. C1.
[c]"Surging Technology Stocks Dazzle Analysts, Investors," *The Wall Street Journal*, 5-22-90, p. C1.

Exhibit 14
Recent IPO Activity

The IPO 100 A Review of the Initial Public Offering Aftermarket

Company Name	Date Public	IPO Price	Close on 5/30/90	Pcntg. Chge
Curragh Resources	05/24	10.00	8.125	−18.75
Chiles Offshore	05/24	14.50	14.75	+1.72
Templeton Global Utilities	05/23	12.00	12.125	+1.04
HealthInfusion	05/23	8.00	10.875	+35.94
Alliance Global Environment	05/23	15.00	16.75	+11.67
Thai Capital Fund	05/22	12.00	12.625	+5.21
Pinnacle Environmental	05/18	5.00	4.75	−5.00
Nuveen NY Muni Mkt Oppty Fund	05/18	15.00	15.00	same
Nuveen Calif Muni Mkt Oppty Fd	05/18	15.00	15.00	same
Mid-American Waste Systems	05/18	24.00	32.50	+35.42
Fountain Pharmaceuticals	05/15	1.00	1.047	+4.70
Club-Theatre Network	05/15	5.00	8.50	+70.00
Integrated Waste Service	05/14	5.00	8.50	+70.00
France Growth Fund	05/10	12.00	12.125	+1.04
RasterOps	05/09	12.00	17.00	+41.67
Lidak Pharmaceuticals	05/08	5.00u	5.625	+12.50
CMS-Data	05/08	5.00	6.375	+27.50
ACTV	05/04	5.50	8.00	+45.45
Dynasty Classics	05/03	11.25	15.25	+35.56
Immune Response	05/02	7.00	6.75	−3.57
IG Laboratories	05/02	7.50	6.75	−10.0
Aspect Telecommunications	05/01	14.50	18.125	+25.00
American Biogenetic Sciences	05/01	6.00u	7.375	same
Telebit	04/27	10.00	13.375	+33.75
STOR Furnishings International	04/27	8.00	7.125	−10.94
Europe Fund	04/26	15.00	15.125	+.83
California Jamar	04/26	6.00	5.437	−9.38
Wahlco Environmental Systems	04/25	13.00	16.00	+23.08
Safeway	04/25	11.25	12.375	+10.00
Home Federal Savings Bk–MO	04/25	7.25	7.937	+9.48
Fingerhut Companies	04/25	16.50	20.75	+25.76
Orbital Sciences	04/24	14.00	13.375	−4.46
BE Avionics	04/23	7.00	8.25	+17.86
Pacific-European Growth Fund	04/20	12.00	12.125	+1.04
Granite Construction	04/20	17.00	22.75	+33.82
Blackstone Advantage Term Tr	04/20	10.00	9.875	−1.25
Allstate Muni Income Opp III	04/20	10.00	10.062	+.62
Sullivan Dental Products	04/18	10.00	17.25	+72.50
Pool Energy Services	04/17	10.25	13.25	+29.27
Craftmade International	04/16	3.50	5.719	+63.40
Sanifill	04/12	9.50	17.875	+88.16
RMI Titanium	04/12	12.50	12.00	−4.00
Advanced Logic Research	04/11	13.00	17.50	+34.62
Jakarta Fund	04/10	12.00	13.75	+14.58
Medgroup	04/06	1.00	1.141	+14.10
Pharmacy Management Services	04/05	12.00	18.375	+53.13
Pinkerton's	04/04	14.00	19.625	+40.18
Tetra Technologies	04/03	10.00	13.50	+35.00
Peerless Productions	03/30	6.00u	5.50	−8.33
Irish Investment Fund	03/30	12.00	9.00	−25.00
Syntellect	03/29	15.00	19.625	+30.83
Emerging Germany Fund	03/29	12.00	9.375	−21.88
Medicis Pharmaceutical	03/28	1.00u	.937	same
Geneva Steel	03/27	10.00	11.875	+18.75
Tokos Medical	03/26	12.00	12.25	+2.08
Alliance New Europe Fund	03/26	12.00	10.25	−14.58
Pride L.P.	03/23	19.50	19.25	−1.28
Nuveen Municipal Market	03/22	15.00	14.25	−5.00
G.T. Greater Europe Fund	03/22	15.00	14.25	−5.00
American Adjustable Rate Term	03/22	10.00	10.125	+1.25
NDC Automation	03/21	1.00	1.219	+21.90
Devlieg-Bullard	03/16	7.00	6.50	−7.14
Bankers	03/16	9.00	12.75	+41.67
Viking Office Products	03/14	10.50	13.00	+23.81
Medical Nutrition	03/14	3.25	4.687	+44.22
Japan OTC Equity Fund	03/14	12.00	16.00	+33.33
VeriFone	03/13	16.00	20.50	+28.13
Tuboscope	03/13	8.50	8.00	−5.88
Delphi Financial Group	03/13	14.00	15.625	+11.61
Electronic Technology Group	03/12	4.50u	20.00	same
Santa Fe Energy Resources	03/08	18.25	18.625	+2.05
Interneuron Pharmaceuticals	03/08	2.00	2.641	+32.05
CII Financial	03/07	11.50	14.75	+28.26
Sequoia Systems	03/06	9.5	9.25	−2.63
Integrated Systems	03/06	9.00	13.50	+50.00
Indonesia Fund	03/01	15.00	15.50	+3.33
Hologic	03/01	14.00	24.50	+75.00
Teppco Partners	02/28	20.00	18.25	−8.75
Capucino's	02/28	5.00u	11.00	same
Future Germany Fund	02/27	18.00	14.625	−18.75
Digital Sound	02/27	8.50	9.375	+10.29
Intera Information	02/16	9.75	20.50	+110.26
Cisco Systems	02/16	18.00	23.50	+30.56
Seligman Select Muni Fund	02/15	12.00	11.50	−4.17
Reader's Digest Association	02/14	20.0	26.375	+31.88
Growth Fund of Spain	02/14	12.00	10.25	−14.58
Xenejenex	02/09	5.00	5.25	+5.00
Scudder New Europe Fund	02/09	12.50	10.375	−17.00
Cabot Oil & Gas	02/07	16.75	16.00	−4.48
Henley International	02/02	8.00	6.75	−15.63
I-flow	02/01	6.00u	3.187	−88.23
Hadson Energy Resources	01/31	13.00	9.75	−25.00
LifeSouth	01/29	10.00	—	—
TriCare	01/26	6.50	8.875	+36.54
Taurus MuniCalifornia Holdings	01/25	12.00	10.50	−12.50
Taurus MuniNewYork Holdings	01/25	12.00	11.25	−6.25
Summit Financial	01/25	10.00	10.25	+2.50
Twin Star Productions	01/24	3.00	10.562	+252.07
New Germany Fund	01/24	15.00	13.25	−11.67
Roberts Pharmaceuticals	01/23	6.00	5.75	−4.17

The IPO 100 Index measures the average price change in shares of the most recent 100 initial public offerings.

Not even an extended holiday weekend could keep the rampaging IPO index from peaking this week, up +15.77. Mid-American Waste Systems led the rather short list of 39 winners, climbing $3.00; while at −$.87, Aspect Telecommunications had the worst showing of all 29 losers.

IPO Market Performance

	Week Ending		
	5/30	5/23	5/17
IPO 100 Index	+15.7	+14.7	+11.1
% Trading Above IPO Price	52%	55%	52%
% Outperforming S&P 500	43%	46%	46%
Number of Issues Added	2	9	3

The IPO 100 (*Going Public: The IPO Reporter*, publ. by Investment Dealers' Digest, Inc., NYC), June 1990.

Exhibit 14 *(concluded)*

Annual IPO Data

	All Company IPOs			Venture Capital–backed IPOs			
	Number of Companies	*Total Raised*	*Market Value*	*Number of Companies*	*Total Raised*	*Market Value*	*Number of Venture Capital–backed Companies Acquired*
1980	95	$1,089	$ 5,717	27	$ 420	$ 2,626	28
1981	227	2,723	10,922	68	770	3,610	32
1982	100	1,213	5,466	27	549	2,374	40
1983	504	9,580	40,473	121	3,031	14,035	49
1984	213	2,545	10,792	53	743	3,495	86
1985	195	3,166	11,618	46	838	3,258	101
1986	417	8,190	31,616	97	2,118	8,434	120
1987	259	5,220	23,813	81	1,840	6,893	140
1988	96	2,392	11,759	35	756	3,122	135
1989	n.a.	n.a.	n.a.	39	996	3,900	136
5/90	n.a.	n.a.	n.a.	19	n.a.	n.a.	n.a.

Venture-Backed IPOs—May 1990*

Date	*Company*	*Size ($ Mil)*	*Post Value ($ Mil)*	*EPS*	*Period*	*Underwriters*	*Business*
1/29	Tricare Inc.	10.4	22.0	$ 0.44	5/31/89	Volpe & Covington	Medical related services
2/16	Cisco Systems, Inc.	50.4	226.0	0.34	7/31/89	Morg. Stanley/Smith Barney	Data communications
2/27	Digital Sound Corp.	40.0	143.0	0.26	12/31/89	Goldman, Sachs/Montgomery	Telephone equipment
3/1	Hologic, Inc.	16.8	53.0	0.46	9/30/89	H&Q/Needham/Adams, Hark.	Medical imaging
3/6	Integrated Systems, Inc.	16.2	71.0	0.21	2/28/89	Alex. Brown/H&Q	CAD/CAM/CAE systems
3/6	Sequoia Systems, Inc.	18.1	79.0	0.26	6/30/89	DLJ/Merrill Lynch/Needham	Fail-safe computers
3/13	Tuboscope Corporation	63.5	102.0	(1.08)	12/31/89	PaineWebber/Solomon	Energy related
3/13	VeriFone, Inc.	62.4	337.0	0.50	12/31/89	Mg St/Robtan, Steph/Dn Wit	Turnkey systems
3/26	Tokos Medical Corp.	24.0	139.0	0.06	12/31/89	Robertson, Stephens/DLJ	Healthcare services
3/29	Syntellect, Inc.	28.0	118.0	0.24	12/31/89	Alex. Brown/H&Q	Telephone equipment
4/3	TETRA Technologies, Inc.	23.5	106.0	0.20	12/31/89	Pn Web/Alex Br/First Analy	Environmental services
4/23	BE Avionics, Inc.	22.4	47.0	(0.13)	7/31/89	PaineWebber	Airline electronics
4/24	Orbital Sciences Corp.	33.6	130.0	(0.96)	12/31/89	Alex. Brown/Merrill Lynch	Space & launch vehicles
4/27	STOR Frnshngs Int'l, Inc.	18.0	51.0	(2.69)	3/31/89	Robtan, Steph/Bateman Eich	Warehouse-style retail
4/27	Telebit Corporation	20.4	57.6	0.49	12/31/89	Cowen & Co./Needham & Co.	Data transmission prdcts
5/1	Aspect Telecom Corp.	29.0	141.0	0.27	12/31/89	Morgan Stanley/H&Q	Telephone equipment
5/2	Immune Response Corp.	15.4	78.0	(0.63)	12/31/89	Dillon, Reed/Smith Barney	AIDS treatment drugs
5/9	RasterOps Corp.	22.4	58.0	0.06	6/30/89	Robertson, Stephens/DLJ	Color graphics systems
5/18	Mid-America Waste Syst Inc	72.0	240.0	0.27	12/31/89	Alex. Brown/Pru-Bache	Solid waste coll. and disp.

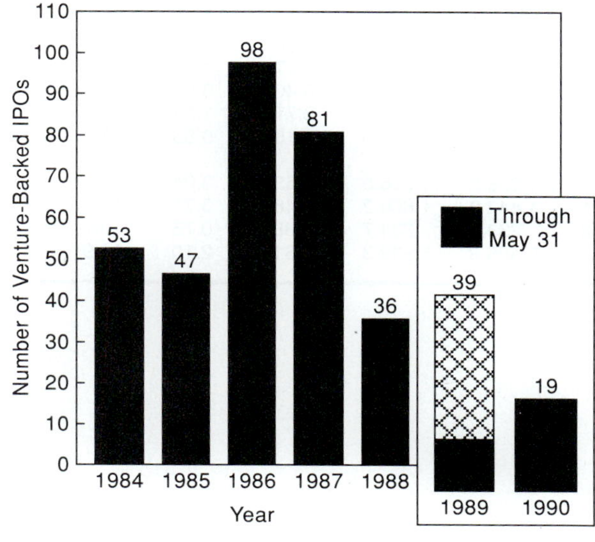

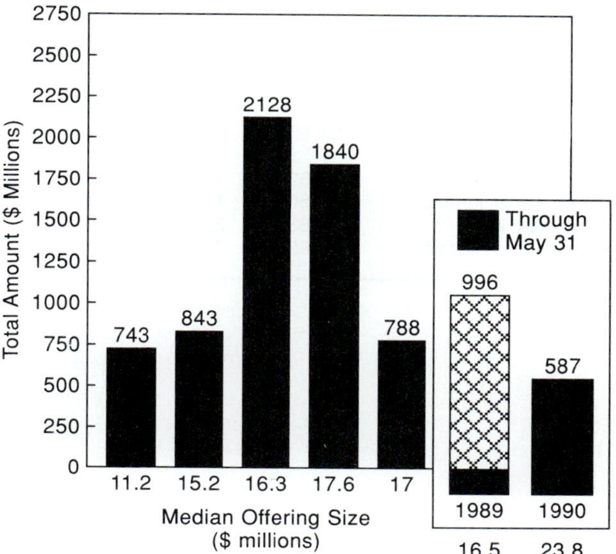

**Venture Capital Journal*, Venture Economics, Inc., Needham, MA.

Exhibit 15
IPO Aftermarket

Statistics of Venture Capital 100 Companies: Computer Software and Services

	P/E	*High*	*60-Month Low*	*5/31 Close or Bid Price*	*Change From 4/30/90*
BMC Software, Inc.	29	26	5 1/4	24	5 1/2
Information Resources, Inc.	—	32 3/8	8	14 5/8	1 3/8
Information Science, Inc.	28	3 3/4	0 3/16	0 5/16	0
Interleaf, Inc.	—	24 1/8	5 1/4	6 5/8	0 7/8
Lotus Development Corporation	19	39 3/4	5 1/16	37 3/4	3/4
Mediagenic	—	30	2	5 3/8	1 1/8
Pansophic Systems, Inc.	12	27 3/4	8 3/4	13 1/4	2 1/8
Relational Technology, Inc.	23	21 1/8	4 1/2	7 1/4	−0 7/8
SAGE Software, Inc.	38	20 3/4	4 1/2	14 1/8	2 1/4

Data of Selected Software and Service Companies

	Price 6/1/90	*% Since 12/29/89*	*Shrs Out (mil)*	*Mkt Cap ($ Mil)*	**Revenues**		**EPS**		**P/E**	
					C89(A)	*C90(E)*	*C89(A)*	*C90(E)*	*C89*	*C90*
Applic-Personal:										
Ashton Tate	12.25	−3.9%	26.6	325.8	265.3	232.5	(1.09)	(0.46)	NM	NM
Borland	17.25	74.6%	14.5	250.1	104.3	182.5	0.76	1.44	22.7	12.0
Corporate Software	13.51	38.5%	5.2	70.3	135.6	197.3	0.64	0.90	21.1	15.0
Egghead	16.49	46.5%	16.4	270.4	434.2	534.0	(1.35)	0.67	NM	24.6
Lotus	37.22	20.1%	43.0	1,600.5	556.1	683.7	1.61	1.80	23.1	20.7
Microsoft	75.15	72.7%	123.3	9,265.5	952.8	1,423.3	1.83	2.79	41.1	26.9
Software Publishing	26.26	61.6%	12.5	328.2	110.4	151.5	1.54	1.95	17.1	13.5
Symantec	23.26	50.0%	10.1	234.9	62.0	99.5	0.98	1.10	23.7	21.1
Applic-Corporate:										
Informix	14.61	−5.1%	13.6	198.7	145.0	189.0	0.48	0.80	30.4	18.3
Knowledgeware	24.24	53.9%	12.4	300.6	50.2	87.6	0.77	0.90	31.5	26.9
Oracle	19.90	−15.0%	131.4	2,615.4	753.8	1,040.2	0.65	0.40	30.6	49.8
System Software Assoc.	28.02	41.3%	12.0	336.2	98.6	124.1	1.03	1.41	27.2	19.9
Systems:										
BMC Software	25.00	24.0%	24.8	620.0	82.0	121.5	0.75	1.09	33.3	22.9
Computer Associates	14.87	18.9%	186.7	2,776.6	1,290.1	1,289.0	0.72	0.87	20.7	17.1
Goals Systems	17.24	11.2%	18.4	317.2	86.4	119.0	0.56	0.85	30.8	20.3
Legent	26.99	2.8%	21.4	577.6	142.8	176.7	1.17	1.60	23.1	16.9
On-Line Software	7.88	−19.1%	6.0	47.3	85.0	93.2	0.40	0.58	19.7	13.6
Pansophic	13.01	−29.8%	18.5	240.7	168.0	201.6	0.77	1.23	16.9	10.6
Systems Center	21.63	3.5%	10.1	218.5	76.9	111.0	1.15	0.85	18.8	25.4
Services										
Automatic Data	57.62	17.6%	74.4	4,287.1	1,698.5	1,736.0	2.62	3.04	22.0	19.0
Computer Sciences	49.50	−14.3%	15.9	787.1	1,442.9	1,660.2	3.46	3.71	14.3	13.3
Computer Task	11.63	27.5%	9.7	112.8	233.0	234.7	(0.88)	0.75	NM	15.5
Gen Motors-Class E	35.99	31.8%	240.0	8,638.5	5,466.8	5,929.3	1.81	2.10	19.9	17.1

Exhibit 16
Companies in Registration (from *Going Public: The IPO Reporter*, various dates)

	File Date	*$ Amt (mil)*	*Price Range Low-High*	*Shares (mils)*	*Expected Date*	*Underwriter*
Gensia Pharmaceuticals	4/27	25.0	9.00–11.00	2.5	6/4/90	Alex. Brown
Phibro Energy Oil Trust	3/12	100.0	25.00	4.0	6/4/90	Salomon Bros.
Share America	10/23/89	5.0	5.00	1.0	6/4/90	Grady-Hatch
Builders Express	3/1	6.0	2.00	3.0	6/7/90	D.H. Blair
AlCorp	5/14	18.0	7.00–9.00	2.25	6/11/90	Alex. Brown
Gamma International	4/6	10.2	3.00–3.30	3.2	6/11/90	Alex. Brown
Swift Transportation	5/21	19.8	11.00–13.00	1.65	6/25/90	Alex. Brown
Digital Systems Int'l	4/26	32.0	15.00–17.00	2.0	Ear Jun	D.L.J.
Fleer	4/19	20.4	11.00–13.00	1.7	Ear Jun	Smith Barney
Image Data	4/12	7.7	5.00–6.00	1.4	Ear Jun	Ladenburg
Auto Depot	4/30	6.8	1.50	4.5	Mid Jun	Global America
NSC	5/3	16.4	12.00–13.50	1.3	Mid Jun	Oppenheimer
Orthopedic Services	5/17	31.5	13.00–15.00	2.25	Mid Jun	Shearson Lehman
Micrografx	5/17	15.6	11.00–13.00	1.3	Lat Jun	Alex. Brown
Los Angeles Cookie	8/11/89	2.0	1.00	2.0	Jun 1990	Castleton
GB Foods	5/10	3.9	3.25	1.2	n/a	Stuart-James
Compana de Telef de Chile	5/23	n/a	n/a	n/a	n/a	Salomon
Alias Research	5/24	20.0	9.00–11.00	2.0	n/a	Robertson
Environmental Elements	5/25	34.5	14.00–16.00	2.3	Mid Jul	Kidder
Vidmark	5/24	17.6	11.00–12.50	1.5	Lat Jun	Sutro & Co.
CoHo Resources	5/24	n/a	n/a	3.5	n/a	Salomon
GolfAmerica	5/15	4.8	8.00	0.6	July	L.C. Wegard
Command Security	5/30	3.8	5.00	0.75	Lat Jun	Stuart-James
European Warrant Fund	5/24	80.0	12.00	6.67	Mid Jul	Oppenheimer
Mexico Advantage Fund	5/25	60.0	12.00	5.0	Lat Jul	Oppenheimer
Benchmark Electronics	5/15	10.2	8.25–10.25	1.1	n/a	Lovett
Wet Seal	5/15	n/a	n/a	2.5	n/a	First Boston
Fiesta Marcado	5/17	6.6	6.00	1.1u	Mid Jul	Global America
Foundation Health	5/17	39.6	11.00–13.00	3.3	Lat Jun	Merrill Lynch
J E Marniye & Sons	5/17	4.0	4.00	1.0u	n/a	L.C. Wegard
Sundowner Offshore Srvcs	5/18	21.5	7.50–9.00	1.3	n/a	Alex. Brown
ArctCo	5/21	35.2	10.00–12.00	3.2	Lat Jun	PaineWebber
Patriot Select Div Trust	5/11	105.0	15.00	7.0	n/a	Dean Witter
Banner Aerospace	5/14	161.5	16.00–18.00	9.5	n/a	Salomon
Pit Stop Auto Centers	5/3	2.63	7.50–10.00	0.3	n/a	Paulson
Horsehead Resource Dvmnt	5/9	35.75	10.00–12.00	3.25	Jun	Kidder

Exhibit 17
Summary of the AlCorp and Micrografx Offerings—In Registration

The AlCorp, Inc., Offering Filed 5-11-90

Common stock offered by the company	1,500,000 shares
Common stock offered by the selling Stockholders	750,000 shares
Total shares offered	2,250,000
Common stock outstanding after the offering	7,638,432 shares
Price	$7.00 to $9.00 per share
Use of proceeds	For working capital, other general corporate purposes, and possible acquisitions.
Underwriters	Alex. Brown & Sons Inc./Donaldson, Lufkin & Jenrette

Company Description

AlCorp develops, markets, and supports knowledge base/computer-aided software engineering (CASE) products which are used to develop and maintain knowledge base software applications which automate business processes that require judgment or are too complex or expensive for traditional programming methods. The products offer an integrated programming environment which enables users to reduce software development and maintenance costs and are integrated with standard hardware platforms, operating systems, and database management systems.

Their customers include Bethlehem Steel, British Telecom, Conrail, CSX, Dean Witter, DuPont, Frito-Lay, London Life, Mass Mutual, MCI, Mercedes Benz, The Travelers, The US Army and the US Department of State.

The company was founded in 1975, introduced its first product in 1981, and has received a number of rounds of financing since 1980 totaling over $18 million. Venture investors include Aeneas Venture Corp.(*), Atlas Associates, BancBoston Capital, Boston University, Chancellor Capital Management, Hancock Venture Capital (*), Harvard Associates, Inco Venture Capital Management, Newmarket Co. Ltd., Oak Investment Partners, Schroder Ventures, TA Associates(*), Utech Venture Capital Corp., Vista Ventures and Warburg, Pincus Ventures.

(*) = represented on board of directors.

($000, except per share amts)	Year Ended March 31			Three Months Ended			
	1988	*1989*	*1990*	*6-30-89*	*9-30-89*	*12-31-89*	*3-31-90*
Revenues	$9,505	$11,512	$15,109	$2,757	$3,005	$4,012	$5,335
Net income (loss)	1,025	54	1,012	(614)	(165)	418	1,373
Pro forma net income (loss) per common share	0.14	0.01	0.14	(0.08)	(0.02)	0.06	0.19

The Micrografx Inc., Offering Filed 5-17-90

Common stock offered by the company	703,434 shares
Common stock offered by the selling stockholders	596,566 shares
Total shares offered	1,300,000
Common stock outstanding after the offering	4,402,114 shares
Price	$11.00 to $13.00 per share
Use of proceeds	For working capital, other general corporate purposes and to retire bank debt.
Underwriters	Alex. Brown & Sons Inc./Donaldson, Lufkin & Jenrette

Company Description

The company develops, markets, and supports a line of personal computer graphics applications and systems software products for IBM personal computers and compatibles running under the Microsoft Windows, O/S 2 Presentation Manager, and Hewlett-Packard New Wave operating environments. The applications are designed for use for illustrations, data-driven graphics, basic drawing tools, reusable clip art libraries, and graphics translators. The system software products include graphics libraries, device drivers, and other development tools.

The company markets its products worldwide through distributors and dealers and directly to corporations, government agencies, and educational institutions. Systems software products are sold to hardware manufacturers, software developers, and customers who have purchased the company's applications software products. In fiscal 1990, international sales accounted for 45% of the company's net sales.

The company was founded in 1982 and has received two rounds of financing from TA Associates, which is also represented on the board of directors.

($000, except per share amts)	Year Ended March 31				
	1986	*1987*	*1988*	*1989*	*1990*
Net sales	$1,853	$2,220	$5,203	$11,581	$17,800
Net income (loss)	1	238	916	1,276	1,280
Pro forma net income (loss) per common share	–	0.07	0.26	0.35	0.32

Exhibit 18
Summary of the Parametric Offering—Actual

Parametric Technology Corporation Offering 12-7-89

Common stock offered by the company	1,365,226 shares
Common stock offered by the selling stockholders	334,774 shares
Total shares offered	1,700,000
Common stock outstanding after the offering	7,506,650 shares
Price	$12.00 per share
Use of proceeds	For working capital, other general corporate purposes, and possible acquisitions.
Underwriters	Alex. Brown & Sons Inc./Hambrecht & Quist/Wessels, Arnold & Henderson

Company Description

Parametric develops, markets, and supports a family of fully integrated software products for the automation of mechanical design, a complex, repetitive process encompassing a broad spectrum of engineering disciplines. These are essential to the development of virtually all manufactured products ranging from consumer products to jet aircraft. Parametric's mechanical design automation (MDA) products enable users to reduce the manufacturing time and costs for their products. The company believes that its Pro/Engineer product line offers better price/performance, greater ease of use and more complete integration of multiple engineering disciplines than any other available MDA products.

The company markets its products worldwide directly to strategic customers, through value-added resellers primarily to small and medium-size customers, and through original equipment manufacturers. Customers include Digital Equipment, Motorola, Sun Microsystems, General Motors, Mitsubishi, Chrysler, British Aerospace, Lockheed, Martin Marietta, Fisher-Price, Whirlpool, AT&T, and Northern Telecom.

The company was incorporated in 1985 and shipped its first product, Pro/Engineer, in January 1988. There are, in addition, approximately 11 other Pro/products such as Pro/Design, a conceptual design tool; Pro/Pro/Mesh, a finite element analysis preprocessor; and Pro/Interface, which allows designs to be transferred to other systems. Parametric has received financing from Adage Inc., Bessemer Venture Partners (*), Charles River Ventures (*), Draper Associates, and Oak Investment Partners.

(*) = represented on board of directors.

($ 000, except per share amts)

	Years Ended Dec. 31			*Nine Months Ended*		
	1985	*1986*	*1987*	*9-30-87*	*9-30-88*	*9-30-89*
Revenues	—	$7,882	$15,109	$39,383	$23,720	$70,120
Net income (loss)	(5,978)	(9,025)	(10,500)	(3,718)	(4,291)	592
Pro forma net income (loss) per common share	(1.06)	(1.06)	(0.92)	(0.24)	(0.29)	0.03

The Harvest and Beyond

18

And don't forget: Shrouds have no pockets.

The late Sidney Rabb
Chairman Emeritus,
Stop & Shop, Boston

RESULTS EXPECTED

After completing the chapter, you will have:

1. Examined the importance of first building a great company and thereby creating harvest options.
2. Examined why harvesting is an essential element of the entrepreneurial process and does not necessarily mean abandoning the company.
3. Identified the principal harvest options, including going public.
4. Analyzed the case, R. Douglas Kahn, known as Kevin Mooney in the earlier case (Chapter 5), and tracked his entrepreneurial career after his experience at PMI, Inc. (detailed Chapter 6 case).

A JOURNEY, NOT A DESTINATION

A common sentiment among successful entrepreneurs is that it is the challenge and exhilaration of the journey that gives them the greatest kick. Perhaps Walt Disney said it best: "I don't make movies to make money. I make money to make movies." It is the thrill of the chase that counts.

These entrepreneurs also talk of the venture's incredibly insatiable appetite for not only cash but also time, attention, and energy. Some say it is an addiction. Most say it is far more demanding and difficult than they ever imagined. Most, however, plan not to retire and would do it again, usually sooner. What is more, they also say it is more fun and satisfying than any other career they have had.

For the vast majority of entrepreneurs it takes 10, 15, even 20 years or more to build a significant net worth. According to the popular press and government statistics, there are more millionaires than ever in America. In 1994, as many as 2 million persons in the United States (or nearly 1 percent of the population) will be millionaires—their net worth exceeding $1 million. While these numbers may be true, a million dollars, sadly, is not really all that much money today, as a result of high inflation, and while lottery and sweepstakes winners become instant millionaires, entrepreneurs do not. The number of years it usually takes to accumulate such a net worth is a far cry from the instant millionaire, the get-rich-quick impression associated with lottery winners or in fantasy TV shows.

The Journey Can Be Addictive

In addition, the total immersion required, the huge workload, the many sacrifices for a family, and the burnout often experienced by an entrepreneur are real. Maintaining the energy, enthusiasm, and drive to get across the finish line, to achieve a harvest, may be, when the time comes, exceptionally difficult. For instance, one entrepreneur in the computer software business, after working alone for several years, developed highly sophisticated software. Yet, he was the first one to insist that he could not stand the computer business for another day. Imagine trying to position a company for sale effectively and to negotiate a deal for a premium price after such a long battle.

Some entrepreneurs, even with what most of us would agree has been raging success, wonder if the price of victory is too high. One very successful entrepreneur put it this way: "What difference does it make if you win, have $20 million in the bank—I know several who do—and you are a basket case, your family has been washed out, and your kids are a wreck?"

The opening quote of the chapter is a sobering reminder and its message is clear: Unless an entrepreneur enjoys the journey and thinks it is worthy, he or she may end up on the wrong train to the wrong destination.

FIRST BUILD A GREAT COMPANY

One of the simplest but most difficult principles for nonentrepreneurs to grasp is that wealth and liquidity are *results*—not a cause—of building a great company. They fail to recognize the difference between making money and spending money. Most successful entrepreneurs possess a clear understanding of this distinction; they get their kicks from growing the company. They know the payoff will take care of itself if they concentrate on the money-making part of the process.

Create Harvest Options

Here is yet another great paradox in the entrepreneurial process: Build a great company but do not forget to harvest. This apparent contradiction is difficult to reconcile, especially among entrepreneurs with several generations in a family-owned enterprise. Perhaps a better way to frame this apparent contradiction is to keep harvest options open and to think of harvesting as a vehicle for reducing risk and for creating future entrepreneurial choices and options, not simply selling the business and heading for the golf course or the beach, although these options may appeal to a few entrepreneurs. To appreciate the importance of this perspective, consider the following actual situations.

In the first instance, an entrepreneur in his 50s, Nigel, reached an agreement with a young entrepreneur in his 30s, Brian, to join the company as marketing vice president. Their agreement also included an option for Brian to acquire the company in the next five years for $1.5 million. At the time, the firm, a small biscuit maker, had revenues of $500,000 per year. By the end of the third year, Brian had built the company to $5 million in sales and substantially improved profitability. He notified Nigel of his intention to exercise his option to buy the company. Nigel immediately fired Brian, who had no other source of income, had a family, and a $400,000 mortgage on a house whose fair market value had catapulted to $275,000. Brian learned that Nigel had also received an offer from a company for $6 million. Thus, Nigel wanted to renege on his original agreement with Brian. Unable to muster the legal resources, Brian settled out of court for less than $100,000. When the other potential buyer learned how Nigel had treated Brian, they withdrew their $6 million offer. Then, there were no buyers. Within two years, Nigel drove the company into bankruptcy. At that point, he called Brian and asked if he would now be interested in buying the company. Brian suggested that Nigel go perform certain unnatural anatomical acts on himself!

In a quite different case, a 100-year-old, family business was approached by a buyer, who was willing to pay $100 million for the business, a premium valuation by any standard. Yet, the family insisted, it would never sell the business under any circumstances. Two years later, market condition changes and the credit crunch transformed slow-paying customers into nonpaying customers. The business was forced into bankruptcy, which wiped out 100 years of family equity.

It is not difficult to think of a number of alternative outcomes for these two firms and many others like them, who have erroneously assumed that the business will go on forever. By stubbornly and steadfastly refusing to explore harvest options and exiting as a natural part of the entrepreneurial process, owners may actually increase their overall risk and deprive themselves of future options. Innumerable examples exist whereby entrepreneurs sold or merged their companies and then went on to acquire or to start another company and pursued new dreams:

- Robin Wolaner founded *Parenting Magazine* in the mid 1980s and sold it to Time-Life.[1] Wolaner then joined Time and built a highly successful career there, and in July of 1992, she became the head of Time's Sunset Publishing Corporation.[2]
- After college, Douglas Ranalli[3] founded and built a student magazine, which he sold to a major publisher. After returning to school to get his MBA, he launched a second company, FAX International.[4] Ranalli was able to conserve his equity by having capital from his first venture.
- Jeff Parker built and sold two companies, including Technical Data Corporation,[5] by the time he was 40. His substantial gain from these ventures has led to an entire new career as a private investor who works closely with young entrepreneurs to help them build their companies.
- In mid-1987, George Knight, founder and president of Knight Publications,[6] was actively pursuing acquisitions in order to grow his company into a major force. Stunned by what he believed to be exceptionally high valuations for small companies in the industry, he concluded that this was the time to be a seller rather than a buyer. Therefore, in 1988, he sold Knight Publications to a larger firm, within which he could realize his ambition of contributing as a chief executive officer to the growth of a major company. Having turned around the troubled divisions of this major company, he is currently seeking a small company to acquire and to grow into a large company.

One could fill a book with numerous other examples. The entrepreneurial process is endless.

[1] This example is drawn from "Parenting Magazine," Harvard Business School Case 291-015.

[2] Lawrence M Fisher, "The Entrepreneur Employee," *The New York Times*, August 2, 1992, p. 10.

[3] For a more detailed description of Douglas Ranalli's first venture, as well as some of his thoughts on opportunity analysis, see "Doug Ranalli," Harvard Business School Case 391-027.

[4] See Chapter 12 case on his second venture.

[5] For TDC's business plan, see "Technical Data Corporation Business Plan," Harvard Business School Case 283-973, Revised November 1987. For more on TDC's progress and harvest strategy, see "Technical Data Corporation," Harvard Business School Case 283-072, Revised December 1987.

[6] For a detailed description of this process, see Harvard Business School Case 289-027, revised February 1989.

A Harvest Goal

Having a harvest goal and crafting a strategy to achieve it are indeed what separate successful entrepreneurs from the rest of the pack. Many entrepreneurs seek only to create a job and a living for themselves. But it is quite another thing to grow a business that creates a living for many others, including employees and investors, by creating value—value that can result in a capital gain.

Setting a harvest goal achieves many purposes, not the least of which is helping an entrepreneur get after-tax cash out of an enterprise and enhancing substantially his or her net worth. Such a goal also can create high standards and a serious commitment to excellence over the course of developing the business. It can provide, in addition, a motivating force and a strategic focus that does not sacrifice customers, employees, and value-added products and services just to maximize quarterly earnings.

There are other good reasons as well. The workload demanded by a harvest-oriented venture versus one in a venture that cannot achieve a harvest may actually be less and is probably no greater. Such a business, in fact, may be less stressful than managing a business that is not oriented to harvest. Imagine the plight of the 46-year-old entrepreneur, with three children in college, whose business is overleveraged and on the brink of collapse. Contrast that frightful pressure with the position of the founder and major stockholder of another venture who, at the same age, sold his venture for $15 million. Further, the options open to the harvest-oriented entrepreneur seem to rise geometrically in that investors, other entrepreneurs, bankers, and the marketplace respond. There is great truth in the old cliche that "success breeds success."

There is a very significant societal reason as well for seeking and building a venture worthy of a harvest. These are the ventures that provide enormous impact and value added in a variety of ways. These are the companies that contribute most disproportionately to technological and other innovations, to new jobs, to returns for investors, and to economic vibrancy.

Also, within the process of harvest, the seeds of renewal and reinvestment are sown. Such a recycling of entrepreneurial talent and capital is at the very heart of our system of private responsibility for economic renewal and individual initiative. Entrepreneurial companies organize and manage for the long haul in ways to perpetuate the opportunity creation and recognition process and thereby to ensure the process of economic regeneration, innovation, and renewal.

Thus, a harvest goal is not just a goal of selling and leaving the company. Rather, it is a long-term goal to create real value added in a business. (It is true, however, that if real value added is not created, the business simply will not be worth very much in the marketplace.)

Crafting a Harvest Strategy: Timing Is Vital

Consistently, entrepreneurs avoid thinking about harvest issues. In a survey of the computer software industry between 1983 and 1986, Steven Holmberg found that 80 percent of the 100 companies surveyed had only an informal plan for harvesting. The rest of the sample confirmed the avoidance of harvest plans by entrepreneurs—only 15 percent of the companies had a formal written strategy for harvest in their business plans and the remaining 5 percent had a formal harvest plan written after the business plan.[7] When a company is first launched, then struggles for survival, and finally begins its ascent, the farthest thing from its founder's mind usually is selling out. Selling out is often viewed by the entrepreneur as the equivalent to complete abandonment of his or her very own "baby."

[7] Steven R Holmberg, "Value Creation and Capture: Entrepreneurship Harvest and IPO Strategies," in *Frontiers of Entrepreneurship Research:1991,* ed. Neil C Churchill et al. (Babson Park, MA: Babson College, 1991), pp. 191–205.

Thus, time and again, a founder does not consider selling out until terror, in the form of the possibility of losing the whole company, is experienced. Usually, this possibility comes unexpectedly: new technology threatens to leapfrog over the current product line, a large competitor suddenly appears in a small market, or a major account is lost. A sense of panic then grips the founders and shareholders of the closely held firm, and the company is suddenly for sale—for sale at the wrong time, for the wrong reasons, and thus for the wrong price. Selling at the right time, willingly, involves hitting a strategic window, one of the many strategic windows that entrepreneurs face.

Entrepreneurs find that harvesting is clearly a nonissue until something begins to sprout, and again there is a vast distance between creating an existing revenue stream of an ongoing business and ground zero. Most entrepreneurs agree that securing customers and generating continuing sales revenue are much harder and take much longer than even they could have imagined. Further, the ease with which those revenue estimates can be cast and manipulated on a spreadsheet belie the time and effort necessary to turn those projections into cash.

At some point, with a higher potential venture, it becomes possible to realize the harvest. In terms of the strategic window, it is wiser to be selling as it is opening than as it is closing. Bernard Baruch's wisdom is as good as it gets on this matter. He has said, "I made all my money by selling too early." For example, in 1986, a private candy company with $150 million in sales was not considering selling. After contemplating advice to sell early, the founders recognized a unique opportunity to harvest and sold the firm for 19 times earnings, an extremely high valuation. Another example is that of a cellular phone company that was launched and built from scratch and began operations in late 1987. Only 18 months after purchasing the original rights to build and operate the system, the founders decided to sell the company, even though the future looked extremely bright. They sold because the sellers' market they faced at the time had resulted in a premium valuation—30 percent higher on a per capita basis (the industry valuation norm) than that for any previous cellular transaction to date. The harvest returned over 25 times the original capital in a year and a half. (Interestingly, the founders had not invested a dime of their own money.)

If the window is missed, disaster can strike. For example, at the same time as the harvests described above were unfolding, another entrepreneur saw his real estate holdings rapidly appreciate to nearly $20 million, resulting in a personal net worth, *on paper,* of nearly $7 million. The entrepreneur used this equity to refinance and leverage existing properties (to more than 100 percent in some cases) to seize what he perceived as further prime opportunities. Unfortunately, after changes in the federal tax law in 1986 and the 1987 stock market crash, there was a major softening of the real estate market in 1988. As a result, in early 1989, half of the entrepreneur's holdings were in bankruptcy, and the rest were in a highly precarious and vulnerable position because prior equity in the properties had evaporated, leaving no collateral as increasing vacancies and lower rents per square foot turned a positive cash flow into a negative one.

Shaping a harvest strategy is an enormously complicated and difficult area. Thus, crafting such a strategy cannot begin too early. For example, HTC, Inc., a company that became a leading innovator in developing vapor-phase technology for soldering printed circuit boards, began crafting its harvest strategy in 1977, when it was basically a one-person garage-shop venture with no marketable product, and when it had been able to raise venture capital of just $10,000 for 10 percent of the venture from a firm that was very reluctant to invest a dime. An advisor worked closely with the lead entrepreneur from the beginning, and he thus knew the intricacies of the market, the industry, the competitors, the customers, and the internal management capabilities of the firm intimately. In 1984, the company had grown to nearly $7 million in sales and was subsequently sold for $15 million cash to a larger firm.

In shaping a harvest strategy, some guidelines and cautions can help:

- *Patience.* As has been shown, several years are required to launch and build most successful companies; therefore, patience can be invaluable. A harvest strategy is more sensible if it allows for a time frame of at least 3 to 5 years and as long as 7 to 10.
- *Vision.* The other side of the patience coin is not to panic as a result of precipitate events. Selling under duress is usually the worst of all worlds.
- *Realistic valuation.* If impatience is the enemy of an attractive harvest, then greed is its executioner. For example, an excellent, small firm in New England, which was nearly 80 years old and run by the third generation of a line of successful family leaders, had attracted a number of prospective buyers and had obtained a bona fide offer for over $25 million. The owners, however, had become convinced that this "great little company" was worth considerably more, and they held out. Before long, there were no buyers, and market circumstances changed unfavorably. In addition, interest rates skyrocketed. Soon thereafter, the company collapsed financially, ending up in bankruptcy. Greed was the executioner.
- *Outside advice.* It is difficult but worthwhile to find an advisor who can help craft a harvest strategy while the business is growing and, at the same time, maintain objectivity about its value and have the patience and skill to maximize it. A major problem seems to be that people who sell businesses, such as investment bankers or business brokers, are performing the same economic role and function as real estate brokers; in essence, their incentive is their commissions during a quite short time frame, usually a matter of months. However, an advisor who works with a lead entrepreneur for as much as five years or more can help shape and implement a strategy for the whole business so that it is positioned to spot and respond to harvest opportunities when they appear.

HARVEST OPTIONS

There are seven principal avenues by which a company can realize a harvest from the value it has created. Described below, these most commonly seem to occur in the order in which they are listed. No attempt is made here to do more than briefly describe each avenue, since there are entire books written on each of these, including their legal, tax, and accounting intricacies.

Capital Cow

A "capital cow" is to the entrepreneur what a "cash cow" is to a large corporation. In essence, the high-margin profitable venture (the cow) throws off more cash for personal use (the milk) than most entrepreneurs have the time and uses or inclinations for spending it.

The result is a capital-rich and cash-rich company with enormous capacity for debt and reinvestment. Take, for instance, a health care–related venture that was started in the early 1970s that realized early success and that went public. Several years later, the founders decided to buy the company back from the public shareholders and to return it to its closely held status. Today the company has sales in excess of $100 million and generates extra capital of several million each year. This capital cow has enabled its entrepreneurs to form investing entities to invest in several other higher potential ventures, which included participation in the leveraged buy out of a $150 million sales division of a larger firm and in some venture capital deals.

Employee Stock Ownership Plan

Employee stock ownership plans (ESOPs) have become very popular among closely held companies as a valuation mechanism for stock for which there is no formal market. They are also vehicles through which founders can realize some liquidity from their stock by sales to the plan and other employees. And since an ESOP usually creates widespread ownership of stock among employees, it is viewed as a positive motivational device as well.

Management Buy Out

Another avenue, called a management buy out (MBO), is one by which a founder can realize a gain from a business by selling it to existing partners or to other key managers in the business. If the business has both assets and a healthy cash flow, the financing can be arranged via banks, insurance companies, and financial institutions that do leveraged buy outs (LBOs) and MBOs. Even if assets are thin, a healthy cash flow that can service the debt to fund the purchase price can convince lenders to do the MBO.

Usually, the problem is that the managers who want to buy out the owners and remain to run the company do not have the capital. Unless the buyer has the cash up front—and this is rarely the case—such a sale can be very fragile, and full realization of a gain is questionable. MBOs typically require the seller to take a limited amount of cash up front and a note for the balance of the purchase price over several years. If the purchase price is linked to the future profitability of the business, the seller is totally dependent on the ability and integrity of the buyer. Further, the management, under such an arrangement, can lower the price by growing the business as fast as possible, spending on new products and people, and showing very little profit along the way. In these cases, it is often seen that after the marginally profitable business is sold at a bargain price, it is well positioned with excellent earnings in the next two or three years. As can be seen, the seller will end up on the short end of this type of deal.

Merger, Acquisition, and Strategic Alliance

Merging with another firm is still another way for a founder to realize a gain. For example, two founders who had developed high-quality training programs for the rapidly emerging personal computer industry consummated a merger with another company. These entrepreneurs had backgrounds in computers, rather than in marketing or general management, and the results of the company's first five years reflected this gap. Sales were under $500,000, based on custom programs and no marketing, and they had been unable to attract venture capital, even during the market of 1982 to 1983. The firm with which they merged was a $15 million company that had an excellent reputation for its management training programs, had a Fortune-1000 customer base, had repeat sales of 70 percent, and had requests from the field sales force for programs to train managers in the use of personal computers. The buyer obtained 80 percent of the shares of the smaller firm, to consolidate the revenues and earnings from the merged company into its own financial statements, and the two founders of the smaller firm retained a 20 percent ownership in their firm. The two founders also obtained employment contracts, and the buyer provided nearly $1.5 million of capital advances during the first year of the new business. Under a put arrangement, the founders will be able to realize a gain on their 20 percent of the company, depending upon performance of the venture over the next few years.[8] The two founders now are reporting to the president of the parent firm, and one founder of the parent firm has taken a key

[8] This is an arrangement whereby the two founders can force (the put) the acquirer to purchase their 20 percent at a predetermined and negotiated price.

executive position with the smaller company, an approach common for mergers between closely held firms.

In a strategic alliance, founders can attract badly needed capital, in substantial amounts, from a large company interested in their technologies. Such arrangements often can lead to complete buyouts of the founders downstream.

Outright Sale

Outright sale is viewed by most advisors as the ideal route to go because up-front cash is preferred over most stock, even though the latter can result in a tax-free exchange.[9] In a stock-for-stock exchange, the problem is the volatility and unpredictability of the stock price of the purchasing company. Many entrepreneurs have been left with a fraction of the original purchase price when the stock price of the buyer's company declined steadily. Often the acquiring company wants to lock key management into employment contracts for up to several years. Whether this makes sense depends on the goals and circumstances of the individual entrepreneur.

Public Offering

Probably the most sacred business school cow of them all—other than the capital cow—is the notion of taking a company public.[10] The vision or fantasy of having one's venture listed on one of the stock exchanges, even over-the-counter, arouses passions of greed, glory, and greatness. For many would-be entrepreneurs, this aspiration is unquestioned and enormously appealing. Yet, for all but a chosen few, taking a company public, and then living with it, may be far more time and trouble—and expense—than it is worth.

After the stock market crash of October 1987, the market for new issues of stock shrank to a fraction of the robust IPO market of 1986 and a fraction of those of 1983 and 1985, as well. The number of new issues and the volume of IPOs did not rebound—instead they declined between 1988 to 1991. Then in 1992 and into the beginning of 1993 the IPO window opened again after a long dormant period (see *Exhibit 18.1*). During this IPO frenzy, "small companies with total assets under $500,000 issued more than 68% of all IPOs."[11] Previously, small companies had not been as active in the IPO market. (Companies such as Lotus, Compaq, and Apple Computer do get unprecedented attention and fanfare, but these firms were truly exceptions.) Recently, however, the SEC has been trying "to reduce issuing costs and registration and reporting burdens on small companies. The SEC began by simplifying the registration process by adopting Form S-18, which applies to offerings of less than $7,500,000, and reduced disclosure requirements."[12] Similarly, Regulation D created "exemptions from registration up to $500,000 over a twelve-month period."[13]

There are several advantages to going public, many of which relate to the ability of the company to fund its rapid growth. Public equity markets provide access to long-term capital, while also meeting subsequent capital needs. Companies may use the proceeds of an IPO to expand the business in the existing market or to move into a related market. The founders

[9] See several relevant articles on selling a company in *Growing Concerns*, ed. David E Gumpert (New York: John Wiley & Sons, 1984), pp. 332–98.

[10] The Big Six accounting firms, such as Ernst & Young, publish information on deciding to take a firm public. See also Richard Salomon, "Second Thoughts on Going Public," in *Trials and Rewards of the Entrepreneur,* ed. David E Gumpert (Boston: Harvard Business Review, 1983); and Safi U Quereshey, "How I Learned to Live with Wall Street," *Harvard Business Review*, reprint No. 91309.

[11] Seymore Jones, M Bruce Cohen, and Victor V Coppola, "Going Public," in William A Sahlman and Howard H Stevenson, eds., *The Entrepreneurial Venture* (Boston: Harvard Business School Publications, 1992), p. 394.

[12] Ibid., p. 395.

[13] Ibid.

Exhibit 18.1
Initial Public Offerings

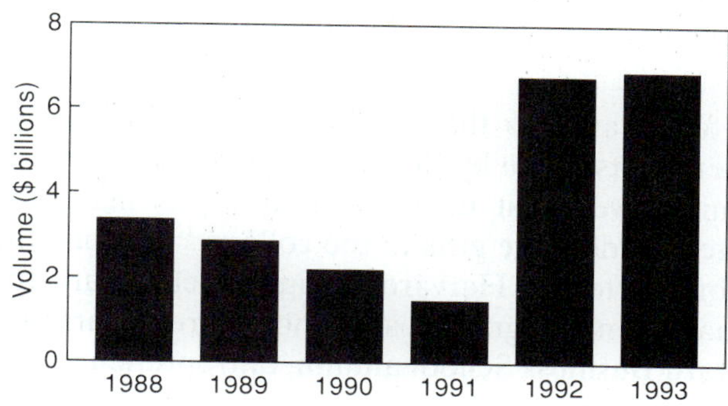

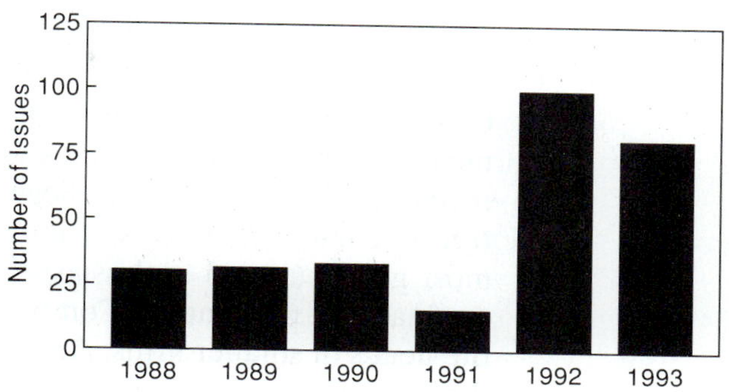

Source: Adapted from *Going Public: The IPO Reporter*, February 1993, p. 1.

and initial investors might be seeking liquidity, but it is important to note that SEC restrictions limiting the timing and the amount of stock that the officers, directors, and insiders can dispose of in the public market are increasingly severe. As a result, it can take several years after an IPO before a liquid gain is possible. Additionally, as Jim Hindman believed, a public offering not only increases public awareness of the company but also contributes to the marketability of the products, including franchises.

However, there are also some disadvantages to being a public company. For example, 50 percent of the computer software companies surveyed by Holmberg agreed that the focus on short-term profits and performance results was a negative attribute of being a public company.[14] Also, because of the disclosure requirements, public companies lose some of their operating confidentiality, not to mention having to support the ongoing costs of public disclosure, audits, and tax filings. With public shareholders, the management of the company has to be careful about the flow of information because of the risk of insider trading. Thus, it is easy to see why companies need to think about the positive and negative attributes of being a public company. When considering this decision, you may find it useful to review EASEL's Request for Quotation to identify the key components of the IPO process and to assess which investment bankers, accountants, lawyers, and advisors might be useful in making this decision.

Wealth-building Vehicles

The 1986 Tax Reform Act severely limited the generous options previously available to build wealth within a private company through large deductible contributions to a retirement plan. To make matters worse, the administrative costs and paperwork necessary to comply with federal laws have become a nightmare. Nonetheless, there are still mechanisms that can enable an owner to contribute up to 25 percent of his or her salary to a retirement plan each year, an amount which is deductible to the company and grows tax free. Entrepreneurs who can contribute such amounts for just a short time will, having Uncle Sam as a financial partner, build significant wealth.

[14] Steven R Holmberg, "Value Creation and Capture: Entrepreneurship Harvest and IPO Strategies," in *Frontiers of Entrepreneurship Research:1991*, ed. Neil Churchill et al., (Babson Park, MA: Babson College, 1991), p. 203.

BEYOND THE HARVEST

A majority of highly successful entrepreneurs seem to accept a responsibility to renew and perpetuate the system that has treated them so well. Somehow they are keenly aware that our unique American system of opportunity and mobility depends in large part upon a self-renewal process.

There are many ways in which this happens. Some of the following data often surprise people:

- *College endowments.* It was shown a few years ago that over half of MIT's endowment comes from gifts of stock and other assets made by the founders of companies. A recent study of Babson College alumni showed that up to eight times as many entrepreneurs, compared to other graduates, made large gifts to the college.[15] Among the most generous and enthusiastic contributors to the Harvard Business School are the graduates of the Smaller Company Management Program, a short nondegree course for the heads of smaller firms. Among Harvard Business School alumni, entrepreneurs lead the way.
- *Community activities.* Entrepreneurs who have harvested their ventures very often reinvest their leadership skills and money in such community activities as symphony orchestras, museums, and local colleges and universities. These entrepreneurs lead fund-raising campaigns, serve on boards of directors, and devote many hours to other voluntary work. One Swedish couple, after spending six months working with venture capital firms in Silicon Valley and New York, was "astounded at the extent to which these entrepreneurs and venture capitalists engage in such voluntary, civic activities." This couple found this pattern in sharp contrast to the Swedish pattern, where paid government employees perform many of the same services as part of their jobs.
- *Investing in new companies.* Postharvest entrepreneurs also reinvest their efforts and resources in the next generation of entrepreneurs and their opportunities. Successful entrepreneurs behave this way since they seem to know that perpetuating the system is far too important, and too fragile, to be left to anyone else. They have learned the hard lessons.

The innovation, the job creation, and the economic renewal and vibrancy are all results of the entrepreneurial process. The complicated and little understood process is *not caused* by government, though it is facilitated and/or impeded by it. Nor is it caused by the stroke of a legislative pen, though it can be ended by such a stroke. Rather, it is created by entrepreneurs, investors, and hard-working people in pursuit of opportunities.

Fortunately, entrepreneurs seem to accept a disproportionate share of the responsibility to make sure the process is renewed. And, judging by the new wave of entrepreneurship in the United States, both the marketplace and society once again are prepared to allocate the rewards to entrepreneurs that are commensurate with their acceptance of responsibility and delivery of results.

SEVEN SECRETS OF SUCCESS

The following seven secrets of success are included for your contemplation and amusement:

- There are no secrets. Understanding and practicing the fundamentals discussed here, along with hard work, will get results.

[15] John A Hornaday, "Patterns of Annual Giving," in *Frontiers of Entrepreneurship Research: 1984*, ed J Hornaday et al. (Babson Park, MA: Babson College, 1984).

- As soon as there is a secret, everyone else knows about it, too. Searching for secrets is a mindless exercise.
- Happiness is a positive cash flow.
- If you teach a person to work for others, you feed him or her for a year, but if you teach a person to be an entrepreneur, you feed him or her, and others, for a lifetime.
- Do not run out of cash.
- Entrepreneurship is fundamentally a human process, rather than a financial or technological process. *You* can make an enormous difference.
- Happiness is a positive cash flow.

CASE—R. DOUGLAS KAHN*

Preparation Questions

1. Evaluate the summary responses from the four underwriters.
2. How would you rank the four? Which would you select? Does this additional information alter your previous ranking?
3. What should be EASEL's walkaway share price and offering size?
4. What should be Kahn's priorities and actions in managing the IPO process?

TAKING EASEL PUBLIC

The responses to EASEL's request for quotation (RFQ) provided much food for thought. This case includes a sampling of the detailed responses to some of the key questions centering on the issues of timing, valuation, research support, EASEL's positioning in the public markets, the IPO marketing process and aftermarket support by the firms following completion of the IPO. Several of these issues were interdependent; a later offering date would result in a valuation based on higher earnings; however, there was no guarantee that the financial markets would continue to be friendly to IPOs. (See *Figure 1*).

Despite the original intent to go public in the Fall of 1990, Doug and John proposed to the IPO committee in early May that they proceed with the IPO "as soon as possible." They knew that once the decision was made to go forward, the process would consume 110 percent of top management's time and attention. The market clearly was gaining momentum; however, if that momentum should fade, it might take another year and a half or more to complete a deal. As a practical matter they wanted to limit the time drain to as short a time span as possible. Also, the IPO window was open unlike any time since the stock market crash of October 1987. P/E multiples were stronger than six months earlier. The sense was that valuations in the $40 million to $50 million range were reasonable. No one knew when it would, once again, slam shut.

Figure 1
Timeline Update

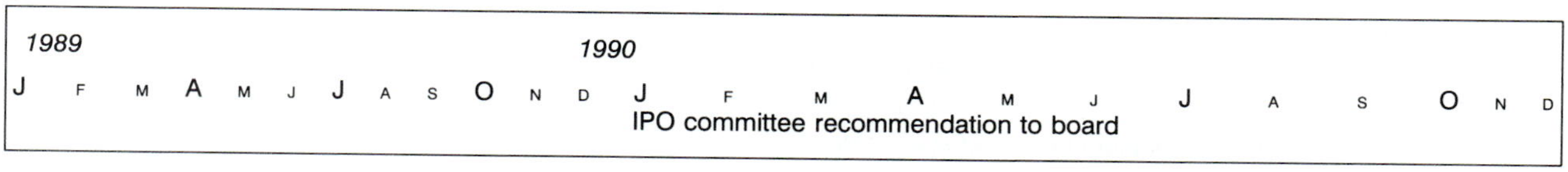

1989												*1990*											
J	F	M	A	M	J	J	A	S	O	N	D	J	F	M	A	M	J	J	A	S	O	N	D
															IPO committee recommendation to board								

*Associate in Research, Thomas A Soja prepared this case under the supervision of Professor Jeffry A Timmons as the basis for class discussion, rather than to illustrate either effective or ineffective handling of an administrative situation.

Preparation for an Offering

Ever since Doug's and John's arrival at EASEL, the company had been managed as if it already were a public company. Quarterly and annual projections were carefully planned and tracked. Consequently, there was a five-year history of detailed financial statements with more than 12 months of quarterly figures leading up to this time. That advanced preparation could potentially save time with the IPO audit team and avoid lengthy revisions to the company's financial statements.

The personalities of the individual team contributors were also expected to have an impact on how fast an offering memorandum could be written and finalized. Responses to the questions on the RFQ regarding each investment banker's choices for attorneys and accountants to work on the deal allowed Doug and John to get feedback on these choices from their board, EASEL's own attorneys and accountants, and other CEOs and CFOs. Enthusiasm or skepticism about their respective choices by the various advisors added another increment of comfort and knowledge to the decision process. The general opinions of several of the underwriter-designated accountants and attorneys was, "Those are the guys you want to have."

Conclusion

They asked the board for counsel on their choice of two underwriters. The reply was unexpected, but welcome: "Which ones do you want to work with? . . . Decide, then do it." They then proposed an aggressive schedule which represented a best-case scenario for taking the company public by the end of the summer. A final investment banking team would need to be chosen within the following week so that the preparation could formally begin. (See *Figure 2*.)

The following contains excerpts from the responses to EASEL Corporation's RFQ to take the company public. The actual "quotes" from each disguised investment bank contained considerably more detail, ranging from a 9-page response to a 54-page, eight-tab compendium.

The issues covered here, in depth, include *timing* of the IPO, *valuation* of the company, *research* support provided, each firm's *positioning statement* for EASEL, the *IPO marketing and road show*, and *aftermarket support*.

TIMING

Investment Bank I

The current market environment is extremely receptive to new technology offerings. We are advising clients which have the appropriate management infrastructure and financial performance to move forward on rapid time schedules toward a public offering. EASEL should proceed to the public markets as soon as possible.

Figure 2
IPO Schedule Presented at Early May IPO Committee Meeting

- "All Hands" meeting by end of May 1990
- File registration statement with SEC by end of June 1990
- "Road Show" last two weeks in July
- Public offering by August 15, 1990

In targeting the September/October time frame, we would be comfortable proceeding if the company continued to have a high degree of confidence in achieving or beating its Q3 plan. From an SEC perspective, a registration statement filed with Q2 financials would lose its effectiveness as of November 15. To provide ourselves with the appropriate flexibility to address unknown market conditions, we would want to proceed with a schedule which anticipated closing no later than October 30.

Investment Bank II

General Timing: A successful IPO depends on two things: a successful company in control of its business and a receptive market. We believe that no market-related factors can substitute for the fundamentals of a growing business which is well managed.

Control of Business: Public ownership with leading valuations requires a steady progression of earnings per share. The market is not forgiving of surprises. Revenue and profitability goals must be set and then met or exceeded. Operating results of the business should be "dead solid perfect" for the quarter to be reported immediately after the offering. There is nothing worse than to go through the offering marketing process generating enthusiasm for, and confidence in, the company, and then immediately to disappoint investors with a bad quarter. Investors react badly to such an event, and it takes an extremely long time to regain their confidence.

The current operating climate for the company is quite strong. If the business is expected to remain strong, do the deal into the operating strength, not after it. It is not worth the aftermarket risk of failed quarterly performance.

Market Receptivity: Since the beginning of 1988 (post-crash-of-1987 environment) equities have increased in value of 35 percent. They have been relatively flat for the past nine months with over-the-counter securities trending downward in that more recent timeframe. It is a reasonable environment for equities but uncertainty remains concerning the general market direction. The software equities subgroup is doing relatively well despite a number of bad earnings reports from several companies in the last 30 days. Software stocks have outperformed the market for the past 26 months and have been even stronger in the last 10 months.

We currently believe that the market is stronger for initial public offerings than one would believe merely by watching the financial markets in the newspaper. Institutions are flush with cash and are looking for new, quality ideas. They are prepared to commit cash to these stories if they can be convinced that management is strong and the company's strategy and ability to execute the business plan are first rate. The calendar for IPOs is moderately active currently and is expected to build as the year progresses.

Conclusion: It isn't often that business operating strength, equity market valuations, and the IPO markets are coincidentally strong. Focusing on the strength of the business issue, we advise EASEL to proceed with its initial public offering while also taking advantage of a receptive market.

Investment Bank III

The timing of an IPO is affected by equity market conditions, the general health of the software industry, and the business conditions faced by EASEL. The group of comparable, public software companies has exhibited sustained price strength through 1990, and we expect this trend to continue for the foreseeable future.

Equity Market Conditions: Enthusiasm for new equity issues is currently high. However, the equity capital markets are volatile at this time. The broad stock market averages have been negatively affected by the bond market, specifically the Treasury's benchmark issues recent break through the 9 percent yield level. The impact of these general trends is indirect but could be significant to the sustainability of an otherwise healthy new issues market.

EASEL should focus on current performance specifically within the technology sector. Currently, investor demand for new technology issues is strong. Many of the recent technology IPOs have been oversubscribed with strong aftermarket interest. Technology companies will continue to be able to access capital markets as long as the quality of new issues remains high.

Industry Conditions: Investor interest often comes in waves and is typically driven by the success, measured in both financial and stock market performance, of comparable companies. Software is one of the sectors which has generated the most IPO activity during the past two years. The number of offerings by software companies accounted for approximately 30 percent of the volume of all technology IPOs since January 1988. In addition, 6 of the 10 best performing IPOs completed in 1988 and 1989 were for software companies. The characteristics of software companies that appeal to the financial investor are (a) inherently high profit margins, (b) predictability of revenue and earnings growth, particularly in comparison to other high technology businesses, and (c) the tendency to develop protectable niche markets, often of considerable magnitude.

Business Conditions: Recently, investors have been excited about technology companies which exhibit sustainable long-term growth rates in excess of 40 percent with margins reflecting superior competitive positioning. In the software industry, this criterion generally translates to net margins in excess of 15 percent. EASEL is experiencing significant margin expansion through the four quarters of 1990, and in our opinion, the difference in margin (specifically 12 percent net income as a percentage of revenue for the projected September 30, 1990, quarter, assuming a 30 percent tax rate, versus 18 percent in the quarter ending December 31, 1990) argues for an offering based on year end results. Showing the December quarter results and proving the increased level of profitability will add to the credibility of the company's sustainable profit level and increase IPO valuation.

Conclusion: EASEL could certainly file an IPO based on its September 1990 results if current market conditions are sustained. However, the valuation vis-à-vis the comparable publicly traded stocks would reflect a discount due to the lower level of profitability on a historic and near-term projected basis. In addition, financial investors would perceive a greater amount of risk in the company's ability to achieve 15 percent or higher net margins given that the last reported quarter would show 12.3 percent net margin, fully taxed. Financial results for the quarter ending September 30, 1990, would need to show fully taxed net margins in the range of 15 percent to 17 percent in order to cross the minimum profitability hurdle for software companies and to lay the groundwork for a credible argument for margin expansion.

An IPO in the September/October time frame would necessarily be based on June 30 results; we do not believe that the optimal valuation for EASEL can be attained at that time.

Investment Bank IV

Market Conditions: The market is currently quite receptive to new issues of high quality technology companies, and especially of software companies.

Financial Position: EASEL is able to present rapid growth (over 50 percent projected in 1990) and expanding margins in a highly credible set of projections.

Valuation Comparisons: The valuations of the other segment-leading software companies, to which EASEL may be compared for valuation purposes, are all acting strongly (except Oracle).

Valuation Methodology: EASEL will begin in July to be valued at least partially, on the basis of 1991 projections. The weighting of 1991 versus 1990 will grow across Q3.

Time Constraints: While there is never an ideal time to undertake an offering in the context of competing demands for senior management resources, the summer is presumably a better time to undertake the bulk of the work.

Conclusion: We believe that EASEL should target its IPO schedule to draft the S-1 from mid-June to mid-July, file with the SEC about July 20–25 with 2nd quarter results, give the road show from September 6 to September 13, and offer the shares about September 15.

Performance Relative to Plan: We would expect EASEL to meet its targeted objectives, generally, without regard to timing of the offering. However plan performance is not binary: If you fall short, this factor alone does not require you to defer an offering. Understanding the reasons for the shortfall is more important in making the decision on timing.

VALUATION

Investment Bank I

Assuming a registration statement were filed today, we would propose a premoney valuation of approximately $40 million. This range is based on our feeling that EASEL should trade at a multiple of 25 × calendar 1990 earnings and that for pricing purposes, a 10 percent discount should be applied to this multiple. We have also assumed that the company will earn $1.8 million (reflecting a 35 percent tax rate) before deal interest in calendar 1990. Obviously, if the offering is delayed to later in the year and similar market conditions prevail, multiples for comparable companies will most likely be higher, resulting in a higher valuation for EASEL.

Investment Bank II

Methodology: Technology growth stocks are valued primarily in terms of multiples of future performance of earnings and revenues, generally for the 12 months following the offering. Due to the tone of the market, the time frame is often shortened to the completion of the current calendar year, or extended to include the following calendar year. Multiples of future revenues are a sanity check by investors.

The market also values technology growth stocks in a macro sense against the broader averages of industrial equities. The premium above or discount to these broader averages moves with the cycles of the technology equity market. Three groupings of software stocks have been chosen for comparison purposes:

Graphical User Interface	*Inner Circle of Quality*
Microsoft	Adobe
	BMC Software
Application Development	Caere
Index Technology	Consilium
Integrated Systems	Goal Systems
KnowledgeWare	Integrated Systems
Parametric Technology	KnowledgeWare
Sage Software	Microsoft
	Oracle
	Symantec

All the software groups are growing more rapidly than the broader market average. Graphical user interface commands a 50 percent premium to the S&P 400. Application development commands a 46 percent premium in its P/E of 1990 forecasted earnings. Historically, this relationship has moved in a range of a 50 percent premium to a 25 percent discount for software companies as a group compared to the broader market average.

	Market Multiples			
	CY90PE	*CY91PE*	*CY90Rev*	*CY91Rev*
Graphical user interface	23.2	16.8	5.0	3.7
Application development	22.6	15.4	1.8	1.3
Inner circle of quality	21.0	15.4	3.1	2.3
S&P 400 industrials	15.5	14.1	No Est.	No Est.
GUI premium to market	50%	19%	—	—
Applications development premium to market	46%	9%	—	—
Inner circle premium to market	35%	9%	—	—

CY90PE stands for calendar year 1990 price/earnings multiple, CY90Rev stands for calendar year 1990 revenue multiple, and so on.

Most of these companies are substantially larger than EASEL. Many of them have strong positions in their own competitive arenas, similar to the position that EASEL has in its own market. EASEL should be positioned as a company whose prospects for growth are strong, driven by secular trends in the software industry.

EASEL should carry a trading multiple of between 17× and 19× calendar 1991 earnings. The 1991 earnings multiple is the appropriate metric since we will be marketing the deal in the September/October time frame. Given successful close positioning against Microsoft and the best of the application development companies (Integrated Systems, KnowledgeWare, and Parametric Technology), the proposed trading multiple of 17× to 19× calendar 1991 earnings is a slight (12 percent) discount from the group. This accounts for EASEL's smaller size and lack of public trading history, as well as the need to be conservative. This trading multiple range translates to a $54 million to $60 million preoffering valuation trading range, assuming a 35 percent tax rate applied to forecasted operating income of $4.9 million for calendar 1991.

A reasonable market environment and strong institutional aftermarket buying interest should keep the underwriters' discount to between 5 percent and 8 percent. For your purposes, I would discount the above valuation ranges by 5 percent. A 10 percent discount in today's market would be conservative.

Conclusion: Investment Bank II proposes a preoffering filing valuation of $51 million to $57 million, reflecting a 5 percent discount to the above preoffering valuation trading range. Given the market positioning, strength of the investment story, and condition of the current IPO market, we believe this pricing is conservative and provides a strong aftermarket performance opportunity for the stock.

Investment Bank III

Emerging growth IPOs are valued primarily on projected 12-months earnings. For an offering based on either September 30 or December 31, 1990, results, the valuation benchmark would be projected 1991 earnings. The basis for our valuation model for EASEL is 1991 projected pre-tax income of $4.9 million. We assume that the company would earn approximately $850,000 in incremental, pre-tax interest income (for simplicity, we have assumed a full year of interest income at 8.5 percent on net proceeds to the company of $10 million). The average P/E multiple that the market is paying today for calendar 1990 earnings of CASE and PC software utilities stocks is 19.2×. We also assume that the market conditions will remain the same between now and year-end and that investors in early 1991 are paying approximately 19× calendar 1991 earnings.

CASE Software Stocks	*PC Software Utility Stocks*
Index Technology	Caere
Integrated Systems	Symantec
KnowledgeWare	
Sage	

IPO investors discount this P/E ratio between 10 percent and 15 percent for the risk inherent in buying a new, unseasoned stock. The resulting IPO filing multiple would thus be 16.3× to 17.2× projected 1991 earnings. This P/E results in an aggregate, postoffering valuation of approximately $65 million to $70 million.

With an effective marketing effort during the initial public offering, it has been our experience that the IPO discount can be closed; in fact, our most recent software IPOs have been priced above the filing range. We would expect EASEL stock to ultimately trade in line with the group of comparables and in fact could exceed them if the opportunities that the company has are well articulated. We expect the trading range would therefore be approximately $75 million or more.

Investment Bank IV

Valuation Methodology: Investment Bank IV's methodology in valuing EASEL focuses on:

1. Past and projected financial performance of EASEL—rate and sustainability of growth, predictability of earnings, and level of profitability.
2. Skill, experience, and functional breadth of the EASEL management team.
3. Comparison with other segment-leading software companies on the basis of
   a. multiple of estimated calendar 1990 earnings.
   b. multiple of estimated calendar 1990 revenues.
   c. multiple of estimated calendar 1991 earnings (when available).
4. IPO discount (10–15 percent) to the multiples of the relevant comparables to reflect the incremental risk associated with investors' lack of familiarity with EASEL and to stimulate aftermarket demand.

IPOs managed by Investment Bank IV have risen on average (weighted mean) 11.42 percent, 13.46 percent, and 22.18 percent two weeks after offering for initial offerings brought to market in 1988, 1989, and thus far in 1990, respectively. We want our offerings to be priced in, or above, the filing range. The stock price should recapture the 10–15 percent IPO discount in the first two weeks of trading.

Comparable Software Companies: EASEL has no directly comparable companies. We believe that EASEL should be positioned as the leading company in the market for GUI tools. For the purposes of pricing, we propose comparing EASEL to other segment-leading, publicly traded software companies (each of which may not necessarily be wholly comparable to EASEL in terms of size, distribution strategy, sales cost, average selling price, market growth, etc.) These are:

Adobe—desktop publishing software
Autodesk—desktop design software
BMC—mainframe utility software
Cadence—IC CAE software
KnowledgeWare—CASE software
Lotus—spreadsheet software
Mentor—ECAE software
Novell—network operating system software
Oracle—RDBMS software
SDRC—MCAE software

The P/E and price/revenue multiples for these stocks are:

Range of 1990 price/earnings multiples	12.0×–21.8×
Mean of 1990 price/earnings multiples	17.6×
Range of 1990 price/revenues multiples	1.4×–34.1×
Mean of 1990 price/revenues multiples	13.6×

The other companies on the list included in your letter are not, in our opinion, market leaders.

Offering Price Range: We would recommend a price range of 18× to 20× EASEL's 1990 earnings if the IPO were today. Assuming 1990 revenues of $16.6 million and fully taxed after-tax profit of $1.9 million, the resulting premoney valuation is $34 to $38.

RESEARCH

Investment Bank I

Kyle Maken will follow EASEL. Kyle heads Investment Bank I's software research group, has been with the firm for over four years, and plans to be employed with Investment Bank I for the foreseeable future. Kyle is very positive on EASEL's strategy and feels that it fits superbly with the Online Enterprise concept that our research staff has been studying and articulating over the last year. As a client, EASEL will be tracked among all software companies that we follow and will be invited to speak at our technology conference in the fall. A major report on the company will be issued concurrently with any statements made by analysts. Our analysts speak to the sales force each morning on relevant information about their companies. In general, you should expect one major report and eight shorter reports (one to two pages) per year.

Investment Bank II

Research coverage by a highly regarded analyst is of critical importance in stimulating and maintaining investor interest in an IPO. Investment Bank II's senior software analyst, Seth Thomas, has been with the firm for four years. He has been covering software companies for nine years, including time previously with the Gartner Group. Though you can never assure that an analyst will stay with a firm, you must understand that Investment Bank II is a research-oriented firm. Investment Bank II started as a research-only firm in 1959 and has used its superior research to grow and achieve its goals. We believe no other firm on the Street stresses and respects research as does Investment Bank II, which has ex-Investment Bank II research analysts as CEO, president, head of institutional sales, and head of research.

Number One Analyst: Seth is the most influential software research analyst on Wall Street. His rankings by *Institutional Investor* magazine and, more importantly, by Greenwich Survey poll of portfolio managers confirm this opinion. Seth's comments move stocks. When he initiates coverage of a stock, strong upward movement of the price occurs and trading volume increases. On several occasions he has published on a company in advance of when the company's investment banker has published. His motivation is to sponsor an investment idea to the institutional investment community. His opinions are independent of investment banking relationships. He is viewed by institutions as the authoritative view on the companies he sponsors. He is not viewed as an investment banking mouthpiece, like so many other analysts.

Research Sponsorship: Seth publishes as soon as he is legally allowed following the 25-day quiet period after the offering. He becomes the most knowledgeable about the company of any Wall Street analyst. On an on-going basis he publishes quarterly and covers the company in his industry monthly. He writes a major report on the company annually. He also speaks about the company to investors and on the morning sales calls when there are important things to report—interesting trade or financial press articles and new developments. He believes it is his job to be the most informed outside person on the company. He views that it is his job to keep the company's name of interest to the sales force and to investors.

In addition, you must realize that every IPO is a test of the credibility of the analyst. The buyers of the stock base much of their decision on that analyst, and even in the unlikely event that an analyst changes firms, the buyers are the same ones the analyst must go to in order to sell the next offering. His or her reputation is permanently related to your company.

For the past year, Seth has been sponsoring the theme of GUIs and their emergence of importance in the software marketplace. He has also sponsored the theme of adoption of application development tools.

Investment Bank III

Jack Victor will be responsible for the research coverage of EASEL. He joined the firm in 1984 and focuses on the distributed systems sector, both software and hardware. He is one of the five analysts that we have dedicated to coverage of the software industry. Jack has been with the firm for six years and is a key member of our research department from both an internal as well as a client perspective. Philip Holliday, managing director of research has been in the investment business for 16 years, including institutional sales positions at PaineWebber and Wertheim & Co. prior to joining Investment Bank III as an institutional salesman.

A list of the stocks which Jack Victor currently follows is shown below:

Adobe Systems	Compaq Computer	Microsoft
Aldus	Conner Peripherals	Oracle
Apple Computer	Informix	Quantum
Applied Magnetics	Lotus Development	Seagate Technology
AST Research	Maxtor	Software Publishing

Investment Bank III commits to cover all its corporate finance clients from a research standpoint as soon as the SEC quiet period ends. The first research report on EASEL will be immediately upon expiration of the quiet period (25 days following the offering.) This report will be Jack's first opportunity to present his views and his forecasts for the company in writing. It will be followed by spot reports as company developments warrant. A full stand-alone report dedicated to EASEL will be published within the first 15 months following the offering. Stand-alone company reports are published with sufficient elapsed time after an offering to avoid redundancy with the IPO prospectus.

Investment Bank IV

Analyst: Ed Richards—seven years experience. Ed, who was named a partner in December 1989, is responsible for software research. Prior to joining the firm in December 1983, he was at Hewlett-Packard where he was a marketing manager in the computer business development group. His responsibilities at HP over an eight-year period included marketing and strategic planning management for business computers, which included product marketing responsibilities for the HP 3000.

Research Reports: Investment Bank IV's research coverage of EASEL will include the following:

- Initial comprehensive report—to describe EASEL's strategy, markets, services, competitive position, and outlook, released at the conclusion of the quiet period, 25 days after the offering.
- Quarterly reports—to provide updates on the company's business.
- Interim reports—to explain significant events related to the Company such as competitive changes, important new business opportunities, and acquisitions, whenever they occur.
- First Fax—an Investment Bank IV innovation and the most timely written research product in the brokerage industry, it discusses current news or investment strategies for two–five companies and is delivered by facsimile to Investment Bank IV's top 150 institutional accounts once or twice daily.

In addition, as the head of the firm's research department, Tom Quist publishes a one- to three-page weekly overview in which he discusses specific themes driving the firm's investment strategy. EASEL will be highlighted in these pieces on an opportunistic basis.

The following summary illustrates Ed Richards' research output (number of reports) for selected software stocks in 1989.

Research Type	*BMC Software*	*Index Technology*	*Ingres*	*Legent**	*Novell*	*System Software Associates*
Stand-alone reports	2	—	—	1	1	1
First FAX	4	2	1	2	5	4
Weekly research	6	2	3	2	4	3
Internal research	21	10	24	9	41	15

*Coverage initiated August 1989.

POSITIONING STATEMENT

Investment Bank I

In positioning EASEL to potential investors, we prefer not to position the company against any particular company because there is no "pure play" similar to EASEL in the public markets. Our preference is to focus on a broader group of companies that are providing tools to end-users which dramatically alter the manner in which they use technology and information. Additionally, we would focus investors on technology companies with attractive financial models exhibiting high growth rates and strong operating margins. EASEL is offering next-generation technology that will substantially redefine how end users work with technology. EASEL can be positioned as a company that will reap significant benefits from its pioneering position in its marketplace. The key factors in the positioning will be the following:

1. Corporations have a huge investment in hardware technology which is growing less productive in relation to end users' desire to integrate all key internal systems and information.
2. End users have exhibited a growing demand to bring mainframe applications to their desktop in a user-friendly format.
3. EASEL products provide a single corporationwide standard for all current and future software.
4. EASEL products allow the elimination of multiple interfaces and presentation standards. It is the integration solution.
5. IBM's investment is a strong ratification of the company's strategy and underlying technology.
6. The company's high-quality customer base shows strong corporate demand and acceptance of the technology.
7. Multitiered distribution provides excellent market coverage in a cost-effective manner.
8. Financials ratify the business fundamentals: strong sales growth (over 50 percent) and high operating margins (trending to 20 percent).

We believe that Caere, Consilium, KnowledgeWare, Parametric, and Integrated Systems are the most relevant comparables. The other companies on the list which you provided are more mature, slower growing companies or younger companies that have not developed a strong following among investors.

Investment Bank II

Positioning EASEL: The future success of EASEL will be positioned against two themes: (*a*) the emergence of GUIs as the next major environment to enhance user productivity, and (*b*) the final arrival of programming development tools to address the application development backlog. Microsoft, the developer of Presentation Manager and Windows, is viewed as a world-class software stock. With the expected May 22, 1990, introduction of Windows 3.0, investors' awareness of graphical user interface should be heightened. By the September/October time frame, Windows 3.0 success should be acknowledged and EASEL's relationship with the implementation of GUIs for applications should be readily understood, accepted, and rewarded.

Application development automation has accelerated with the endorsement of a methodology by IBM with its AD/Cycle announcement. Highly attractive financial performance reported by Sage and KnowledgeWare reinforce the enormity of the business opportunity. Additionally, positioning EASEL as part of the industry move toward the use of program development tools, especially in the difficult area of GUI development, should further benefit the appreciation of the merits of the company's story and its valuation.

A select group of software stocks carry premium multiples due to investor perception of high growth rate opportunities, strong proprietary aspects of their products and technology, niche market positioning, quality management teams, and dependability of quarterly earnings performance. EASEL also possesses these attributes. Marketing the company's story and highlighting these factors will gain the company acceptance into this elite "inner circle of quality" by the institutional investment community. Additionally, investors will focus on four sets of issues when considering the offering. (1) Earnings visibility—the predictability of the company's business is most important to investors. (2) Sales and marketing are viewed as perhaps more important than product functionality in winning the battle in the commercial marketplace. (3) Competitive factors are perhaps more easily addressed in EASEL's case due to its market leadership position and opportunity to solidify its "industry standard" position. (4) Financial conservatism, especially in the area of revenue recognition, is increasingly a "hot button" for institutional investors. Interestingly, more attention is being focused on the strength of the balance sheet in enabling a company to have financial muscle to match its technology, product, and sales and marketing clout.

Investment Bank III

EASEL has the opportunity to define the market for graphical user interface software and tools and to position itself as the pioneer and leader in this exciting new software sector. We would position EASEL as a unique investment opportunity with closest comparability to the CASE and personal computer software companies against the general backdrop of other distributed systems software companies. The non-MIS user base of the computer-aided design and manufacturing stock (i.e., Parametric Technology and Consilium) make this group less comparable to EASEL, as the mainframe orientation of BMC Software also makes it a less relevant comparable.

Jack Victor's Positioning of EASEL: EASEL is positioned to be a principal beneficiary of two fundamental trends influencing information processing purchase decisions. The first of these trends is increasing customer emphasis on graphical forms of business communication. The deployment of intuitive GUI technology enables more-intuitive data manipulation and analysis as well as more-meaningful output creation. EASEL provides the necessary products and tools which enable the speedy creation of next-generation applications, thus ensuring the company an important role in this emerging environment.

An even more fundamental need exists within the information processing industry. Corporate decision makers should be able to make more-informed business decisions based on intuitive analysis of strategic corporate information in a timely manner. The implementation of this trend has taken several forms, most notably distributed processing schemes, along with the emergence of distributed data installations. EASEL products allow for the development of graphically oriented applications running under intuitive user interfaces that satisfy the need to make analysis of corporate data easier. These products also enable users to access data resident on a wide array of host computer platforms without requiring that the user understand host-based syntax.

EASEL is poised to benefit from two of the more powerful trends influencing the information processing industry. The company's products fall in the domain of both CASE and application development software products. Its overall positioning should allow management to exploit emerging opportunities while its OEM relationship with IBM should mitigate product risk.

Investment Bank IV

EASEL Positioning: EASEL is a leader in the computing world revolution that is enabling nontechnical end users to interact easily with sophisticated computer applications with minimal training. EASEL is a pioneer and leader in the development and marketing/sales of PC-based programming products for software developers to create intuitive, easy-to-use graphical user interfaces on end user applications. Applications developed with an EASEL GUI enable end users to easily access information from a variety of computers (including IBM mainframes) via a Macintoshlike interface on their standard IBM PC or compatible.

Two bottlenecks have been blocking the widespread adoption of GUIs by programmers: (1) learning to program a typical GUI is extremely difficult, in terms of both the learning curve and the radically different nature of the programming paradigm, compared with the traditional character-based program development environment, and (2) because there are a number of different GUIs emerging in the industry (e.g., Microsoft Windows for MS-DOS, Presentation Manager for OS/2, the Macintosh GUI, Open Look for AT&T/Sun, Motif from the Open Software Foundation, NeXTStep from NeXT), application developers (programmers) have to choose one computer system environment to work in, or duplicate their learning as they work with multiple GUIs.

The EASEL Development System enables programmers to easily and quickly build highly visual applications in a graphical user interface development environment (GUIDE). It features an object-oriented, device-independent, event-driven, nonprocedural programming language which is much richer than the typical GUI development tool.

Significantly, EASEL represents a breakthrough in solving the problem of how to develop an end user application that can run under more than one GUI such as Windows or Presentation Manager. EASEL allows an application to be developed one way and implemented under any industry-standard windowing system supported by EASEL, thereby allowing a development team to learn one GUI development environment—EASEL—and not every underlying GUI (Windows, Presentation Manager, etc.)

Furthermore, EASEL is oriented to application development for the IBM PC and PS/2, and it supports Presentation Manager, which is a foundation of the CUA specification of IBM's Systems Application Architecture (SAA) strategy.[1]

Understanding the significant opportunity for simplifying application development—if programmers worked with EASEL—IBM purchased a 10 percent stake in EASEL in 1989 and signed a long-term product development and licensing agreement with the company. EASEL has been joined by Bachman Information Systems, Index Technology, and KnowledgeWare to create a group of four computer-aided software engineering companies that are strategic partners of IBM, in each of which IBM has a minority investment. EASEL has become IBM's stated product of choice for the development of CUA-compliant applications that include graphics—which the majority of all new applications include.

EASEL is well-positioned to create an industrywide standard GUIDE that spans not only the IBM systems under SAA but also UNIX-based systems and systems for other

[1]The SAA is a concept for developing a unified programming environment for IBM's strategic computer systems (370 mainframes, midrange AS/400, and PS/2 personal computers); CUA describes how applications programs should look to the user—in terms of windows on the display screen, dialogue, graphics, and the like.

vendors, such as proprietary Digital VAX VMS systems. As a multisystem GUIDE, EASEL is unique in simplifying the development of visual applications that can span multiple operating systems and GUIs.

IPO MARKETING AND ROAD SHOW

Institutional Marketing Focus: Each of the investment banking proposals suggested a strong bias toward institutional investors, however varied by degree.

Investment Bank I

The percentage of institutional buyers will be in the range of 60–70 percent. While the overall markets are more heavily weighted to institutional ownership, we believe that the company will benefit by having a balanced mix of buyers. This will allow us to ration shares to institutional buyers thereby encouraging them to fill out their positions in the aftermarket. Such a mix will also provide the beginnings of broad-based retail knowledge and ownership in the company.

Investment Bank II

Institutions provide leadership in confirming valuation levels. Their participation is crucial to a successful offering. Retail investors do not spend the time to gain a fundamental understanding of the company and its business. They tend to buy into hot deals and tend to be quick sellers. Investment Bank II's approach is to concentrate on maximizing institutional demand for the offering. Retail demand will follow this strength.

Investment Bank III

We recommend that between 65 and 75 percent of the stock sold in the EASEL IPO be targeted to institutional accounts with the balance to retail investors. While retail investors are an important source of liquidity and investor diversification, successful IPOs are virtually always built on a strong foundation of institutional interest. In well-received transactions, institutional investors often subscribe as much as 10 percent of an offering each, with a commitment to continue to build a position in the aftermarket. This crucial aftermarket demand cannot be created with retail accounts.

Professional, institutional investors are a knowledgeable investing group. They are willing to pay higher multiples than nonsophisticated investors due to their ability to differentiate among seemingly comparable stocks and their expertise in managing risk. The institutional ownership of several of the software companies, such as Adobe, Informix, Microsoft, and Symantec, is in excess of 60 percent of the freely tradeable stock (or "float").

Investment Bank IV

We recommend that 75–80 percent of the offering be placed in institutional accounts. Institutions dominate emerging growth equity markets today and have the resources to understand the nuances of EASEL's strategy and positioning. They form their own investment opinions based on multiple sources of information. Retail accounts tend to be driven by a single broker who is motivated to move EASEL through accounts to generate multiple commissions. Institutions provide price and momentum leadership in an IPO.

(Institutional Marketing: Opinions also varied slightly on the advisability of a European road show.)

Investment Bank I

We typically sell approximately 20 percent of our initial public offerings outside the United States regardless of whether we organize road show visits in Europe. Our preference is to go to Europe only on offerings in which we expect to raise gross proceeds of at least $20 million. Smaller issues do not warrant the substantial expense for a relatively small amount of the offering. We generally prefer to organize luncheons and one-on-ones in Europe several months after the offering when the company has a business reason to be in Europe. The timing of this has the effect of building renewed support for the company's equity as the initial offering euphoria wanes.

Investment Bank II

Investment Bank II would recommend a two- to four-city European road show as part of the marketing program for the offering. European investors, especially those based in Edinburgh and London, are typically of longer-term perspective than their US counterparts. Given geographic remoteness from the United States, they realize that they will not get the first call on news about a particular company. They therefore tend to be investors rather than traders. They also tend to make investments based on management, belief in the business segment, and their philosophy that a multiyear commitment is necessary. These investors are, however, slow to invest, often choosing not to invest based on the first exposure to the story. The process must begin at some point, however, and the IPO is the place to start. The European road show may not yield large demand, but it will provide the important first step in gaining investor attention from a class of long-term, truly professional investors.

Investment Bank III

A significant portion of all the firm's offerings are placed with international buyers, and we anticipate selling between 10 and 20 percent of the EASEL offering to these accounts. International investors historically have had longer investment horizons, have been less liquidity conscious, and have had less concern for short-term performance than their domestic counterparts.

Investment Bank IV

We would like to market the offering outside the United States. European, and to a lesser extent Japanese, investors continue to be active buyers of high-quality emerging growth technology stocks. However, we generally recommend a European road show only when the offering is greater than $20 million. A smaller offering is not large enough to meet both domestic and European demand, and it would hurt EASEL with European investors to tempt such investors on a road show and then not be able to fill orders.

Road Show: All proposals agreed on the domestic road show agenda with minor exceptions. They would arrange for road show presentations in Boston, New York, Chicago, Minneapolis, Los Angeles, and San Francisco. Investment Bank III also included Baltimore, their home town, while Investment Bank IV omitted Los Angeles.

AFTERMARKET SUPPORT

Investment Bank I

Investment Bank I is committed to serving EASEL after an IPO. The firm's trading department has 9 principal traders and 14 coverage traders and makes a market in 294 OTC stocks. The firm's strong capital position ($27 million without prior authorization) allows it to maintain continuous markets in the securities of its clients and to take significant trading positions as needed to maintain orderly trading markets in its clients' shares. Investment Bank I is committed to maintaining the leading position as market maker in the common stock of its clients. With the exception of required regulatory withdrawals, the firm has never stopped making a market in a client's stock.

Upon completion of the offering, you should have at least 8 to 10 market makers. They will consist of members of the syndicate who take an active interest in the offering, the lead and comanager, and a number of firms which are exclusively traders. We will encourage key firms to make a market in the stock.

Investment Bank II

Market Making: Investment Bank II makes a market in approximately 125 OTC stocks. We only make markets in stocks that we cover in research. There is a close working relationship between the trading desk and research. The firm would be the most active market maker in EASEL stock. Investment Bank II is the most active market maker in software stocks covered by Seth Thomas. We recommend to other firms that they make a market in EASEL stock based on the strength of their research analyst covering the software industry.

Conclusion: Investment Bank II will be the Number 1 market maker in the company's stock. We will be the leader based in part on our capital and the expertise of the trading desk.

Investment Bank III

Investment Bank III focuses on the trading of approximately 200 emerging growth equities, including over 30 software stocks.

Retail Strategy: We recommend a small syndicate (9–12 members) made up only of firms that express a willingness to provide research support for EASEL. The syndicate would include high-quality, regional, retail-oriented firms.

In addition to research and trading support, the firm offers a broad spectrum of services. Investment banking services include general advisory assignments concerning capital structure, stock splits, dividend policy, follow-on offerings, convertible debt offerings, and corporate partnering transactions. In addition, we have a very active M&A effort dedicated to emerging growth situations. Being an Investment Bank III client also includes an annual presentation at the firm's technology conference in San Francisco.

Investment Bank IV

Investment Bank IV has 12 traders who make a market in 117 emerging growth stocks, 50 of which are corporate finance clients of the firm. We will commit to make a market in the stock of EASEL. We also will attempt to attract other market makers for the stock initially through the IPO syndication process and then among other firms whose research analysts you respect and would like to have cover EASEL stock.

Other Support: In addition to research and trading support, the firm's aftermarket support includes sponsored luncheons and one-on-one meetings in major financial centers (i.e., Boston, New York, Chicago, Los Angeles, San Francisco, London, and Paris), the firm's annual emerging growth conference, focused one-day conferences, arranged visits to the company by institutional analysts, research analyst road shows (at least twice a year), M&A assistance, 144 sales, and other financings such as private placements of equity or debt, secondary offerings, and debt refinancing.

CRAFTING A PERSONAL ENTREPRENEURIAL STRATEGY

PART VI

Acknowledging the extreme complexity in predicting or aligning people to careers, especially when both are constantly changing, and the difficulty in accurately measuring enough of the relevant variables to do so, principal tasks for an entrepreneur are to determine what kind of an entrepreneur he or she wants to become, based on his or her attitudes, behaviors, management competencies, experience, and so forth, and whether these fit with the requirements and demands of a specific opportunity.

At a practical and personal level, then, an aim of this book is to help you evaluate thoroughly (1) your *attraction* to entrepreneurship and (2) the *fit* between you and the demands of a particular opportunity. Seen frequently in business is the old adage, "What is one person's jam is another person's poison." Different people will investigate the same venture and come to opposite conclusions.

If there is a fit, then you can shape a strategy, including an action plan. It is fair to say that an entrepreneur's first 10 years out of school can make or break him or her in terms of how well prepared he or she is for serious entrepreneuring. While it may never be too late, evidence suggests that the most durable entrepreneurial careers, those found to last 25 years or more, were begun across a broad age spectrum but after the person selected prior work or a career to prepare for an entrepreneurial career.

Why leave it to chance when you don't have to? Isn't taking charge of your own life and career a part of the thrill and exhilaration of entrepreneuring in the first place? To help you in this, Chapter 19 provides an integrated self-assessment exercise.

As an entrepreneur who founded a rapidly growing database and information firm in the medical field put it, "Self-assessment is the hardest thing for entrepreneurs to do, but if you don't do it, you will really get into trouble." The reason is that if you do not do it, who will?

Crafting a Personal Entrepreneurial Strategy

19

If you don't know where you're going, any path will take you there.

The Koran

RESULTS EXPECTED

Upon completion of this chapter, you will have:

1. Looked at the self-assessment process.
2. Examined a framework for self-assessment and developed a personal entrepreneurial strategy.
3. Identified data to be collected in the self-assessment process.
4. Learned about receiving feedback and setting goals.

PLANNING REVISITED

A Personal Business Plan

Crafting a personal entrepreneurial strategy can be viewed as the personal equivalent of developing a business plan. As with planning in other situations, the process itself is more important than the plan.

The key is the process and discipline that put an individual in charge of evaluating and shaping choices and initiating action that makes sense, rather than letting things just happen. Having a longer-term sense of direction can be highly motivating. It also can be extremely helpful in determining when to say no (which is much harder than saying yes) and can temper impulsive hunches with a more thoughtful strategic purpose. This is important because today's choices, whether or not they are thought out, become tomorrow's track record. They may end up shaping an entrepreneur in ways that he or she may not find so attractive 10 years hence and, worse, may also result in failure to obtain just those experiences needed in order to have high-quality opportunities later on.

Therefore, a personal strategy can be invaluable, but it need not be a prison sentence. It is a point of departure, rather than a contract of indenture, and it can and will change over time.

This process of developing a personal strategy for an entrepreneurial career is a very individual one and, in a sense, one of self-selection. One experienced venture capital investor in small ventures, Louis L. Allen, shares this view of the importance of the role of self-selection:

Unlike the giant firm which has recruiting and selection *experts* to screen the wheat from the chaff, the small business firm, which comprises the most common economic unit in our business systems, cannot afford to employ a personnel manager. . . . More than that, there's something very special about the selection of the owners: they have selected themselves. . . . As I face self-selected top managers across my desk or visit them in their plants or offices I have become more and more impressed with the fact that this self-selection process is far more important to the *success or failure* of the company . . . than the monetary aspects of our negotiations.

Reasons for planning are similar to those for developing a business plan (see Chapter 11). Reasons for planning are that they help an entrepreneur to manage the risks and uncertainties of the future; that they help him or her to work smarter, rather than simply harder; that they keep him or her in a *future-oriented* frame of mind; that they help him or her to develop and update a keener strategy by testing the sensibility of his or her ideas and approaches with others; that they help motivate; that they give him or her a "results orientation"; that they can be effective in managing and coping with what is by nature a stressful role; and so forth.

Rationalizations and reasons given for not planning, like those mentioned in Chapter 11, are that plans are out of date as soon as they are finished and that no one knows what tomorrow will bring and, therefore, it is dangerous to commit to uncertainty. Further, the cautious, anxious person may find that setting personal goals creates a further source of tension and pressure and a heightened fear of failure. There is also the possibility that future or yet unknown options, which actually might be more attractive than the one chosen, may become lost or be excluded.

Commitment to a career-oriented goal, particularly for an entrepreneur who is younger and lacks much real-world experience, can be premature. For the person who is inclined to be a compulsive and obsessive competitor and achiever, goal setting may have the effect of adding gasoline to the fire. And, invariably, some events and environmental factors entirely beyond one's control may boost or sink the best-laid plans.

Personal plans fail for the same reasons as business plans, including frustration when the plan appears not to work immediately and problems of changing behavior from an activity-oriented routine to one that is goal-oriented. Other problems are developing plans that are based on admirable missions, such as improving performance, rather than goals, and developing plans that fail to anticipate obstacles, and those that lack progress milestones, reviews, and so forth.

A Conceptual Scheme for Self-assessment

Exhibit 19.1 shows one conceptual scheme for thinking about the self-assessment process, called the *Johari Window*. According to this scheme, there are two sources of information about the self: the individual and others. According to the Johari Window, there are three areas in which individuals can learn about themselves.

There are two potential obstacles to self-assessment efforts. First, it is hard to obtain feedback; second, it is hard to receive and benefit from it. Everyone possesses a personal frame of reference, values, and so forth, which influence first impressions of each other. It is, therefore, almost impossible for an individual to obtain an unbiased view of himself or herself from someone else. Further, in most social situations, people usually present self-images that they want to preserve, protect, and defend, and behavioral norms usually exist that prohibit people from telling a person that he or she is presenting a face or impression that differs from what the person thinks is being presented. For example, most people will not point out to a stranger during a conversation that a piece of spinach is prominently dangling from between his or her front teeth.

The first step for an individual in self-assessment is to generate data through observation of his or her thoughts and actions and by getting feedback from others for the

Exhibit 19.1
Peeling the Onion

	Known to Entrepreneur and Team	*Not Known to Entrepreneur and Team*
Known to prospective investors and stakeholders	Area 1 *Known* area (what you see is what you get)	Area 2 *Blind* area (we do not know what we do not know, but you do)
Not known to prospective investors and stakeholders	Area 3 *Hidden* area (unshared—you do not know what we do, but the deal does not get done until we find out)	Area 4 *Unknown* area (no venture is certain or risk free)

Source: Derived from an original concept called the "Johari Window" in D A Kolb, I M Rubin, and J M McIntyre, *Organizational Psychology: An Experiential Approach,* 2nd ed. (Englewood Cliffs, NJ: Prentice-Hall, 1974).

purposes of (1) becoming aware of blind spots and (2) reinforcing or changing existing perceptions of both strengths and weaknesses.

Once an individual has generated the necessary data, the next steps in the self-assessment process are to study the data generated, develop insights, and then to establish apprenticeship goals to gain any learning, experience, and so forth. Finally, choices can be made in terms of goals and opportunities to be created or seized.

CRAFTING AN ENTREPRENEURIAL STRATEGY

Profiling the Past

One useful way to begin the process of self-assessment and planning is for an individual to think about his or her entrepreneurial roots (what he or she has done, his or her preferences in terms of lifestyle and work style, etc.) and couple this with a look into the future and what he or she would like most to be doing and how he or she would like to live.

In this regard, everyone has a personal history that has played and will continue to play a significant role in influencing his or her values, motivations, attitudes, and behaviors. Some of this history may provide some useful insight into prior entrepreneurial inclinations, as well as into his or her future potential fit with an entrepreneurial role. It is safe to say that unless an entrepreneur is enjoying what he or she is doing for work most of the time, when in his or her 30s, 40s, or 50s, having a great deal of money without enjoying the journey will be a very hollow success.

Profiling the Present

It is useful to profile the present. Possession of certain personal entrepreneurial attitudes and behaviors (i.e., an "entrepreneurial mind") have been linked to successful careers in entrepreneurship. These attitudes and behaviors deal with such factors as commitment, determination, and perseverance; the drive to achieve and grow; an orientation toward goals; the taking of initiative and personal responsibility; and so forth.

In addition, various role demands result from the pursuit of opportunities. These role demands are external in the sense that they are imposed upon every entrepreneur by the nature of entrepreneurship. Discussed in Chapter 6, the external business environment is given, the demands of a higher potential business in terms of stress and commitment are given, and the ethical values and integrity of key actors are given. Required as a result of the demands, pressures, and realities of starting, owning, and operating a substantial business are such factors as accommodation to the venture, toleration of stress, and so forth. A realistic appraisal of entrepreneurial attitudes and behaviors in light of the requirements of the entrepreneurial role is useful as part of the self-assessment process.

Also, part of any self-assessment is an assessment of management competencies and what "chunks" of experience, know-how, and contacts need to be developed.

Getting Constructive Feedback

A Scottish proverb says, "The greatest gift that God hath given us is to see ourselves as others see us." One common denominator among successful entrepreneurs is a desire to know how they are doing and where they stand. They have an uncanny knack for asking the right questions about their performance at the right time. This thirst to know is driven by a keen awareness that such feedback is vital to improving their performance and their odds for success.

Receiving feedback from others can be a most demanding experience. The following guidelines in receiving feedback can help:

- Feedback needs to be solicited, ideally, from those who know the individual well (e.g., someone he or she has worked with or for) and who can be trusted.
- The context in which the person is known needs to be considered. For example, a business colleague may be better able to comment upon an individual's managerial skills than a friend. Or a personal friend may be able to comment on motivation or on the possible effects on the family situation.
- It is helpful to chat with the person *before* asking him or her to provide any specific written impressions and to indicate the specific areas he or she can best comment upon. One way to do this is to formulate questions first. For example, the person could be told, "I've been asking myself the following question . . . and I would really like your impressions in that regard."
- Specific comments in areas that are particularly important either personally or to the success of the venture need to be solicited and more detail probed if what the person giving feedback intended to say is not clear. A good way to check if a statement is being understood correctly is to paraphrase the statement.
- The person needs to be encouraged to describe and give examples of specific situations or behaviors that have influenced the impressions he or she has developed.
- Feedback is most helpful if it is neither all positive nor all negative.
- Feedback needs to be obtained in writing so that the person can take some time to think about the issues, and so feedback from various sources can be pulled together.
- The person asking for feedback needs to be honest and straightforward with himself or herself and with others. Time is too precious and the road to new venture success too treacherous to clutter this activity with game playing or hidden agendas.
- The person receiving feedback needs to avoid becoming defensive and taking negative comments personally.
- It is important to listen carefully to what is being said and think about it. Answering, debating, or rationalizing should be avoided.
- An assessment of whether the person soliciting feedback has considered all important information and has been realistic in his or her inferences and conclusions needs to be made.

- Help needs to be requested in identifying common threads or patterns, possible implications of self-assessment data and certain weaknesses (including alternative inferences or conclusions), and other relevant information that is missing.
- Additional feedback from others needs to be sought to verify feedback and to supplement the data.
- Reaching final conclusions or decisions needs to be left until a later time.

Putting It All Together

Exhibit 19.2 shows the relative fit of an entrepreneur with a venture opportunity, given his or her relevant attitudes and behaviors and relevant general management skills, experience, know-how, and contacts, and given the role demands of the venture opportunity. Again, although a considerable amount of research about the entrepreneurial mind and the role demands of entrepreneurship has been conducted in recent years, the precise identification of these variables remains elusive. Further, the need for specific "chunks" (i.e., managerial competencies, experience, know-how, and contacts) varies with each situation.

A clean appraisal is almost impossible. Self-assessment just is not that simple. The process is cumulative, and what an entrepreneur does about weaknesses, for example, is far more important than what the particular weaknesses might be. After all, everyone has weaknesses.

Thinking Ahead

As it is in developing business plans, goal setting is important in personal planning. Yet, few people are effective goal setters. Perhaps fewer than 5 percent have ever committed their goals to writing, and perhaps fewer than 25 percent of adults even engage in setting goals mentally.

Again, goal setting is a process, a way of dealing with the world. Effective goal setting demands time, self-discipline, commitment and dedication, and practice. Goals, once set, do not become static targets.

Exhibit 19.2
Fit of Entrepreneur and Venture Opportunity

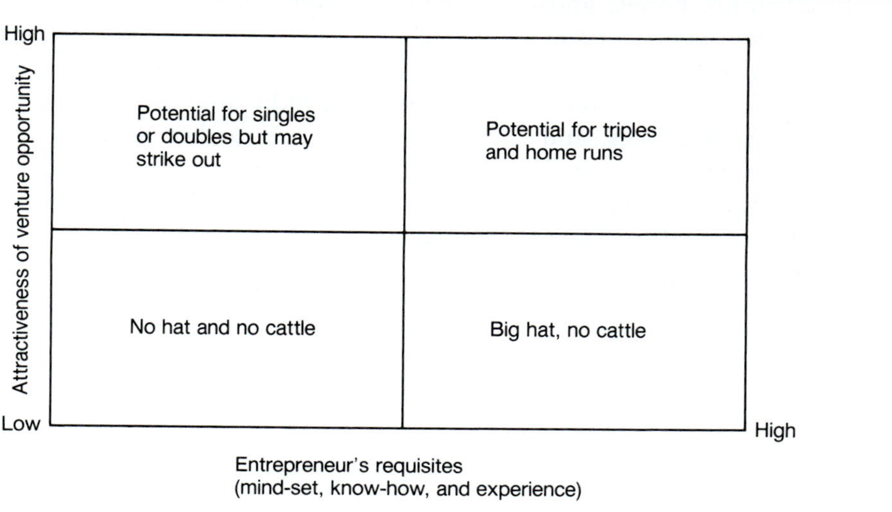

A number of distinct steps are involved in the goal setting process, steps that are repeated over and over as conditions change:

- Establishment of goals which are:
  - Specific and concrete (rather than abstract and out of focus).
  - Measurable.
  - Related to time (i.e., specific about what will be accomplished over a certain time period).
  - Realistic and attainable.
- Establishment of priorities, including the identification of conflicts and trade-offs and how these can be resolved.
- Identification of potential problems and obstacles that could prevent goals from being attained.
- Specification of action steps that are to be performed to accomplish the goal.
- Indication of how results will be measured.
- Establishment of milestones for reviewing progress and tying these to specific dates on a calendar.
- Identification of risks involved in meeting the goals.
- Identification of help and other resources that may be needed to obtain goals.
- Periodic review of progress and revision of goals.

EXERCISE—PERSONAL ENTREPRENEURIAL STRATEGY

The exercise that follows will help you in gathering data, both from yourself and from others, in evaluating the data you have collected, and in crafting a personal entrepreneurial strategy.

The exercise requires *active* participation on your part. The estimated time to complete the entire exercise is 1.5 to 3.0 hours. Those who have completed the exercise—students, practicing entrepreneurs, and others—report that the self-assessment process was most worthwhile. They hasten to add that completing the exercise was also a most demanding task. Issues addressed will require a great deal of thought, and there are, of course, no right answers.

Although this is a self-assessment exercise, it is useful to receive feedback. Whether you choose to solicit feedback and how much, if any, of the data you have collected you choose to share with others is your decision. Of course, the exercise will be of value only to the extent that you are honest and realistic in your approach.

And, again, a complex set of factors clearly goes into making someone a successful entrepreneur. No individual has all of the personal qualities, managerial skills, and the like, indicated in the exercise. And, even if an individual did possess most of these, his or her values, preferences, and such, may make him or her a very poor risk to succeed as an entrepreneur. It is worth repeating that the presence or absence of any single factor does not guarantee success or failure as an entrepreneur. Before proceeding, remember, "It is no embarrassment to reach for the stars and fail to reach them. It is a failure not to reach for the stars."

EXERCISE
PERSONAL ENTREPRENEURIAL STRATEGY

Name:

Date:

PART I—PROFILE OF THE PAST

STEP 1: EXAMINE YOUR PERSONAL PREFERENCES:

– What gives you energy, and why? These are things from either work or leisure, or both, that give you the greatest amount of personal satisfaction, sense of enjoyment, and energy.

Source of Energy	Reason

– What takes away your energy, and why? These create for you the greatest amount of personal dissatisfaction, anxiety, or discontent and take away your energy and motivation.

Source of Depletion	Reason

– Rank (from the most to the least) the items you have listed above:

Gives Energy	Takes Energy

– In 20 to 30 years, how would you like to spend an ideal month? Include in your description your desired lifestyle, work style, income, friends, and so forth, and a comment about what attracts you to, and what repels you about, this ideal existence.

– Review the Idea Generation Guide you completed in Chapter 2 and list the common attributes of the 10 businesses you wanted to enter and the 10 businesses you did not:

Attributes	
Would Energize	Would Turn Off

– Which of these attributes would give you energy and which would take it away, and why?

Attribute	Give or Take Energy	Reason

– Complete this sentence: "I would/would not like to start/acquire my own business someday because . . ."

– Discuss any patterns, issues, insights, and conclusions which have emerged:

– Rank the following in terms of importance to you:

	Important ⟵				⟶ Irrelevant
	5	4	3	2	1
Location					
Geography (particular area)					
Community size and nature					
Community involvement					
Commuting distance (one way): 20 minutes or less					
30 minutes or less					
60 minutes or less					
More than 60 minutes					

Lifestyle and Work Style *Size of business:* Less than $1 million sales or under 20 employees					
More than $1 million sales or 20 employees					
More than $10 million sales and 200 employees					
Rate of real growth: Fast (over 25%/year)					
Moderate (10% to 15%/year)					
Slow (less than 10%/year)					
Workload (weekly): Over 70 hours					
55 to 60 hours					
40 hours or less					
Marriage					
Family					
Travel away from home: More than 60%					

30% to 60%					
Less than 30%					
None					
Standard of Living Tight belt/later capital gains					
Average/limited capital gains					
High/no capital gains					
Become very rich					
Personal Development Utilization of skill and education					
Opportunity for personal growth					
Contribution to society					
Positioning for opportunities					
Generation of significant contacts, experience, and know-how					

Status and Prestige					
Impact on Ecology and Environment					
Capital Required From you					
From others					
Other Considerations					

– Imagine you had $1,000 with which to buy the items you ranked above. Indicate below how you would allocate the money. For example, the item that is most important should receive the greatest amount. You may spend nothing on some items, you may spend equal amounts on some, and so forth. Once you have allocated the $1,000, rank the items in order of importance, the most important being number 1.

Item	Share of $1,000	Rank
Location		
Lifestyle and work style		
Standard of living		
Personal development		
Status and prestige		
Ecology and environment		
Capital required		
Other considerations		

STEP 2: EXAMINE YOUR PERSONAL HISTORY:

- List activities (1) that have provided you financial support in the past (e.g., a part-time or full-time business, a paper route), (2) that have contributed to your well-being (e.g., financing your education or a hobby), and (3) that you have done on your own (e.g., building something).

- Discuss why you became involved in each of the activities above and what specifically influenced each of your decisions.

- Discuss what you learned about yourself, about self-employment, about managing people, and about making money.

– List and discuss your full-time work experience, including descriptions of specific tasks for which you had responsibility, specific skills you used, the number of people you supervised, whether you were successful, and so forth.

– Discuss why you became involved in each of the employment situations above and what specifically influenced each of your decisions.

– Discuss what you learned about yourself, about employment, about managing people, and about making money.

– List and discuss other activities, such as sports, in which you have participated and indicate whether each activity was individual (e.g., chess or tennis) or team (e.g., football).

– What lessons and insights emerged, and how will these apply to life as an entrepreneur?

– If you have ever been fired from or quit either a full-time or part-time job, indicate the job, why you were fired or quit, the circumstances, and what you have learned and what difference this has made.

– If you have ever changed jobs or relocated, indicate the job, why the change occurred, the circumstances, and what you have learned from those experiences.

– Among those individuals who have influenced you most, do any own and operate their own businesses or engage independently in a profession (e.g., certified public accountant)?

– How have the people above influenced you? How do you view them and their roles? What have you learned from them about self-employment? Include a discussion of the things that attract or repel you, the trade-offs they have had to consider, the risks they have faced and rewards they have enjoyed, and entry strategies that have worked for them.

– If you have ever started a business of any kind or worked in a small company, list the things you liked most and those you liked least, and why.

Liked Most	Reason

Liked Least	Reason

– If you have ever worked for a larger company (over 500 employees or about $50 million to $60 million in sales), list the things you liked most and those you liked least about your work, and why.

Liked Most	Reason

Liked Least	Reason

– Summarize those factors in your history that you believe are entrepreneurial strengths or weaknesses.

Strengths	Weaknesses

PART II—PROFILE OF THE PRESENT: WHERE YOU ARE

STEP 1: EXAMINE YOUR "ENTREPRENEURIAL MIND." That is, examine your attitudes, behaviors, and know-how:

– Rank yourself below. (See Chapter 5 for a discussion of these attitudes and behaviors.)

	Strongest ⟵ 5	4	3	2	⟶ Weakest 1
Commitment and Determination Decisiveness					
Tenacity					
Discipline					
Persistence in solving problems					
Willingness to sacrifice					
Total immersion					
Opportunity Obsession Having knowledge of customers' needs					
Being market driven					
Obsession with value creation and enhancement					

Tolerance of Risk, Ambiguity, and Uncertainty Calculated risk-taker					
Risk minimizer					
Risk sharer					
Tolerance of uncertainty and lack of structure					
Tolerance of stress and conflict					
Ability to resolve problems and integrate solutions					
Creativity, Self-reliance, and Ability to Adapt Nonconventional, open-minded, lateral thinker					
Restlessness with status quo					
Ability to adapt					
Lack of fear of failure					
Ability to conceptualize and to "sweat details" (helicopter mind)					

Motivation to Excel					
Goal and results orientation					
Drive to achieve and grow (self-imposed standards)					
Low need for status and power					
Ability to be interpersonally supporting (versus competitive)					
Awareness of weaknesses (and strengths)					
Having perspective and sense of humor					
Leadership					
Being self-starter					
Having internal locus of control					
Having integrity and reliability					
Having patience					
Being team builder and hero maker					

– Summarize your entrepreneurial strengths.

– Summarize your entrepreneurial weaknesses.

STEP 2: EXAMINE ENTREPRENEURIAL ROLE REQUIREMENTS:
– Rank where you fit in the following roles. (See Chapter 5.)

Strongest ←→ Weakest

	5	4	3	2	1
Accommodation to Venture Extent to which career and venture are No. 1 priority					
Stress The cost of accommodation					
Values Extent to which conventional values are held					
Ethics and Integrity					

– Summarize your strengths and weaknesses.

STEP 3: EXAMINE YOUR MANAGEMENT COMPETENCIES:

– Rank your skills and competencies below. (See Management Competency Inventory in Chapter 6.)

	Strongest ⟷				Weakest
	5	4	3	2	1
Marketing					
Market research and evaluation					
Marketing planning					
Product pricing					
Sales management					
Direct mail/catalog selling					
Telemarketing					
Customer service					
Distribution management					

Product management					
New product planning					
Operations/Production Manufacturing management					
Inventory control					
Cost analysis and control					
Quality control					
Production scheduling and flow					
Purchasing					
Job evaluation					
Finance Accounting					
Capital budgeting					
Cash flow management					

Credit and collection management					
Managing relations with financial sources					
Short-term financing					
Public and private offerings					
Administration Problem solving					
Communications					
Planning					
Decision making					
Project management					
Negotiating					
Personnel administration					

Management information systems					
Computer					
Interpersonal/Team Leadership/vision/influence					
Helping and coaching					
Feedback					
Conflict management					
Teamwork and people management					
Law Corporations					
Contracts					
Taxes					
Securities					
Patents and proprietary rights					

Real estate law					
Bankruptcy					
Unique Skills					

STEP 4: BASED ON AN ANALYSIS OF THE INFORMATION GIVEN IN STEPS 1–3, INDICATE THE ITEMS YOU WOULD ADD TO A "DO" LIST.

PART III—GETTING CONSTRUCTIVE FEEDBACK

Part III is an organized way for you to gather some constructive feedback. (If you choose not to get constructive feedback at this time, proceed to Part IV.)

STEP 1: (OPTIONAL) GIVE A COPY OF YOUR ANSWERS TO PARTS I AND II TO THE PERSON DESIGNATED TO EVALUATE YOUR RESPONSES. ASK HIM OR HER TO ANSWER THE FOLLOWING:

– Have you been honest, objective, hard-nosed, and complete in evaluating your skills?

– Are there any strengths and weaknesses you have inventoried incorrectly?

– Are there other events or past actions that might affect this analysis and that have not been addressed?

STEP 2: SOLICIT FEEDBACK. Give one copy of the Feedback Form to each person who has been asked to evaluate your responses.

Feedback Form

Feedback for:

Prepared by:

STEP 1: PLEASE CHECK THE APPROPRIATE COLUMN NEXT TO THE STATEMENTS ABOUT MY ENTREPRENEURIAL ATTRIBUTES, AND ADD ANY ADDITIONAL COMMENTS YOU MAY HAVE:

	Strong	Adequate	Weak	No Comment
Commitment and Determination				
Decisiveness				
Tenacity				
Discipline				
Persistence in solving problems				
Willingness to sacrifice				
Total immersion				
Opportunity Obsession				
Having knowledge of customers' needs				
Being market-driven				
Obsession with value creation and enhancement				

Tolerance of Risk, Ambiguity, and Uncertainty				
Calculated risk taker				
Risk minimizer				
Risk sharer				
Tolerance of uncertainty and lack of structure				
Tolerance of stress and conflict				
Ability to resolve problems and integrate solutions				
Creativity, Self-reliance, and Ability to Adapt				
Nonconventional, open-minded, lateral thinker				
Restlessness with status quo				
Ability to adapt				
Lack of fear of failure				
Ability to conceptualize and to "sweat details" (helicopter mind)				

Motivation to Excel				
Goal and results orientation				
Drive to achieve and grow (self-imposed standards)				
Low need for status and power				
Ability to be interpersonally supporting (versus competitive)				
Awareness of weaknesses (and strengths)				
Having perspective and sense of humor				
Leadership				
Being self-starter				
Having internal locus of control				
Having integrity and reliability				
Having patience				
Being team builder and hero maker				

Additional Comments

(Please make any comments you can on such matters as my energy, health, and emotional stability; my creativity and innovativeness; my intelligence; my capacity to inspire; my values; and so forth.)

STEP 2: PLEASE CHECK THE APPROPRIATE COLUMN NEXT TO THE STATEMENTS ABOUT ENTREPRENEURIAL ROLE REQUIREMENTS TO INDICATE MY FIT AND ADD ANY ADDITIONAL COMMENTS YOU MAY HAVE:

	Strong	Adequate	Weak	No Comment
Accommodation to Venture				
Stress (cost of accommodation)				
Values (conventional economic and professional values of free enterprise system)				
Ethics and Integrity				
Additional Comments				

STEP 3: PLEASE CHECK THE APPROPRIATE COLUMN NEXT TO THE STATEMENTS ABOUT MANAGEMENT COMPETENCIES, AND ADD ANY ADDITIONAL COMMENTS YOU MAY HAVE:

	Strong	Adequate	Weak	No Comment
Marketing				
Market research and evaluation				
Marketing planning				
Product pricing				
Sales management				
Direct mail/catalog selling				
Telemarketing				

Customer service				
Distribution management				
Product management				
New product planning				
Operations/Production Manufacturing management				
Inventory control				
Cost analysis and control				

Quality control				
Production scheduling and flow				
Purchasing				
Job evaluation				
Finance Accounting				
Capital budgeting				
Cash flow management				

Credit and collection management				
Managing lender relations				
Short-term financing				
Public and private offerings				
Administration Problem solving				
Communications				
Planning				

Decision making				
Project management				
Negotiating				
Personnel administration				
Management information systems				
Computer				
Interpersonal/Team Leadership/vision/influence				

Helping and coaching				
Feedback				
Conflict management				
Teamwork and people management				
Law Corporations				
Contracts				
Taxes				

Securities				
Patents and proprietary rights				
Real estate law				
Bankruptcy				
Unique Skills				
Additional Comments				

STEP 4: PLEASE EVALUATE MY STRENGTHS AND WEAKNESSES:

– In what area or areas do you see my greatest potential or existing strengths in terms of the venture opportunity we have discussed, and why?

Area of Strength	Reason

– In what area or areas do you see my greatest potential or existing weaknesses in terms of the venture opportunity we have discussed, and why?

Area of Weakness	Reason

– If you know my partners and given the venture opportunity, what is your evaluation of their fit with me and the fit among them?

– Given the venture opportunity, what you know of my partners, and your evaluation of my weaknesses, should I consider any additional members for my management team? If so, what should be their strengths and relevant experience?

– Please make any other suggestions that would be helpful for me to consider (e.g., comments about what you see that I like to do, my lifestyle, work style, patterns evident in my skills inventory, the implications of my particular constellation of management strengths and weaknesses and background, the time implications of an apprenticeship).

STEP 3: DECIDE IF ANY FEEDBACK IS PERTINENT AND HOW IT CHANGES YOUR ASSESSMENT.

PART IV—PUTTING IT ALL TOGETHER

STEP 1: REFLECT ON YOUR PREVIOUS RESPONSES AND THE FEEDBACK YOU HAVE SOLICITED OR HAVE RECEIVED INFORMALLY (FROM CLASS DISCUSSION OR FROM DISCUSSIONS WITH FRIENDS, PARENTS, ETC.)

STEP 2: ASSESS YOUR ENTREPRENEURIAL STRATEGY:

– What have you concluded at this point about entrepreneurship and you?

– How do the requirements of entrepreneurship—especially the sacrifices, total immersion, heavy work load, and long-term commitment—fit with your own aims, values, and motivations?

– What specific conflicts do you anticipate between your aims and values and the demands of entrepreneurship?

– How would you compare your entrepreneurial mind, your fit with entrepreneurial role demands, your management competencies, and so forth, with those of other people you know who have pursued or are pursuing an entrepreneurial career?

- Think ahead 5 to 10 years or more, and assume that you would want to launch or acquire a higher potential venture—what "chunks" of experience and know-how do you need to accumulate?

- What are the implications of this assessment of your entrepreneurial strategy in terms of whether you should proceed with your current venture opportunity?

- What is it about the specific opportunity you want to pursue that will provide you with sustained energy and motivation? How do you know this?

– At this time, given your major entrepreneurial strengths and weaknesses and your specific venture opportunity, are there other "chunks" of experience and know-how you need to acquire or attract to your team? (Be specific!)

– What other issues or questions have been raised for you at this point that you would like answered?

PART V—THINKING AHEAD

Part V considers the crafting of your personal entrepreneurial strategy. REMEMBER, GOALS SHOULD BE SPECIFIC AND CONCRETE, MEASURABLE, AND, EXCEPT WHERE INDICATED BELOW, REALISTIC AND ATTAINABLE.

STEP 1: LIST, IN *THREE* MINUTES, YOUR GOALS TO BE ACCOMPLISHED BY THE TIME YOU ARE 70.

STEP 2: LIST, IN *THREE* MINUTES, YOUR GOALS TO BE ACCOMPLISHED OVER THE NEXT SEVEN YEARS. (If you are an undergraduate, use the next four years.)

STEP 3: LIST, IN *THREE* MINUTES, THE GOALS YOU WOULD LIKE TO ACCOMPLISH IF YOU HAVE EXACTLY ONE YEAR FROM TODAY TO LIVE. Assume you would enjoy good health in the interim but would not be able to acquire any more life insurance or borrow an additional large sum of money for a "final fling." Assume further that you could spend that last year of your life doing whatever you want to do.

STEP 4: LIST, IN *SIX* MINUTES, YOUR REAL GOALS AND THE GOALS YOU WOULD LIKE TO ACCOMPLISH OVER YOUR LIFETIME.

STEP 5: DISCUSS THE LIST FROM STEP 4 WITH ANOTHER PERSON AND THEN REFINE AND CLARIFY YOUR GOAL STATEMENTS.

STEP 6: RANK YOUR GOALS ACCORDING TO PRIORITY.

STEP 7: CONCENTRATE ON THE TOP THREE GOALS AND MAKE A LIST OF PROBLEMS, OBSTACLES, INCONSISTENCIES, AND SO FORTH, THAT YOU WILL ENCOUNTER IN TRYING TO REACH EACH OF THESE GOALS.

STEP 8: DECIDE AND STATE HOW YOU WILL ELIMINATE ANY IMPORTANT PROBLEMS, OBSTACLES, INCONSISTENCIES, AND SO FORTH.

STEP 9: FOR YOUR TOP THREE GOALS, WRITE DOWN ALL THE TASKS OR ACTION STEPS YOU NEED TO TAKE TO HELP YOU ATTAIN EACH GOAL AND INDICATE HOW RESULTS WILL BE MEASURED. It is helpful to organize the goals in order of priority.

Goal	Task/Action Step	Measurement	Rank

STEP 10: RANK TASKS/ACTION STEPS IN TERMS OF PRIORITY. To identify high-priority items, it is helpful to make a copy of your list and cross off any activities or task that cannot be completed, or at least begun, in the next seven days, and then identify the single most important goal, the next most important, and so forth.

STEP 11: ESTABLISH DATES AND DURATIONS (AND, IF POSSIBLE, A PLACE) FOR TASKS/ACTION STEPS TO BEGIN. Organize tasks/action steps according to priority. If possible, the date should be during the next seven days.

Task/Action	Date Begin	Duration	Place

STEP 12: MAKE A LIST OF PROBLEMS, OBSTACLES, INCONSISTENCIES, AND SO FORTH.

STEP 13: DECIDE HOW YOU WILL ELIMINATE ANY IMPORTANT PROBLEMS, OBSTACLES, INCONSISTENCIES, AND SO FORTH, AND ADJUST THE LIST IN STEP 11.

STEP 14: IDENTIFY RISKS INVOLVED AND RESOURCES AND OTHER HELP NEEDED.

CASE—WHEN THE CIRCUS COMES TO TOWN[1]

Preparation Questions

1. What should Vic do now?
2. What should Fred do now?
3. Why is it so hard to complete the succession transition?
4. As a friend and adviser to each, what advice would you give them?

MORRIS ALPER, INC.
D. WHEN THE CIRCUS COMES TO TOWN

It was like a mid-life crisis in a marriage, we were asking ourselves, "Do we want each other anymore?"

—Victor R. Del Regno

On September 1, 1992, as he drove into work, Frederic M. Alper wrestled with a personal and professional dilemma. He had to decide whether or not to attend the wedding of Victor R. Del Regno's son. On the one hand, Fred had known both Vic and his son for over 15 years. But on the other hand, Fred and Vic no longer collaborated as they had in the past. In their almost 12 years of working together, they had never been more distant from one another. In fact, Fred thought about leaving the company altogether. Today, at the board meeting, he thought of announcing his early retirement.

Fred continued to deliberate, as he passed the company's new training and conference center. This building signified Morris Alper's commitment to the food industry. Although Fred liked the building and thought the idea of a training and conference center was incredible, he knew that he might not have spent as much money on it—and he would not have put the flag pole out in front. Morris Alper maintained a high reputation, but he had a more conservative posture under Fred's leadership. Now, with Vic in charge, things were different. Take for instance, the reserved parking spaces and the name of the company. Vic wanted reserved spaces for senior management. Additionally, Fred and Vic had decided that they would drop '& Sons' from the company name because of their no-nepotism policy. As Fred walked into the new Morris Alper, Inc. (MAI), building, he reflected that things were definitely changing and he sincerely felt that most of the changes were improvements.

Maybe it was best if he left the company, not because of the changes, but because he felt that he could not participate in the way he had hoped to, which was "on a kind of partnership basis, with a sense of respect and recognition that made him comfortable."

The 1991 Food Brokers Convention

In December 1991, Fred and Vic represented MAI at the industry convention. They had carefully planned which meetings each of them would attend. The planning had made the event a success for MAI. Both Fred and Vic felt that they had put their problems behind them. 1992 seemed full of promise for Fred as chairman and Vic as president. Principals and employees had adapted to the passing of the baton. The first six months of 1992 were smooth sailing for the most part.

[1] Research Associate Christine C Remey wrote this case under the supervision of Professor Jeffry A Timmons. Harvard Business School case 294-022 (revised 7/23/93).

Where Are You, When the Circus Comes to Town?

Fred observed that

> we have a saying, "Where are you when the circus comes to town?" Everybody in the broker business wanted to be involved when the circus came to town. As the president of a company, you have to delegate a lot of things, but when the circus comes to town, you want to be in the center. A new account was the circus and I wanted a little part in what the elephants were going to be doing. I certainly didn't need to be the main act.

In August 1992, MAI had an opportunity to represent Colombo Yogurt, a brand which held almost 25 percent of the New England market share. Colombo Yogurt had its own sales force and a product that generated consumer demand. If MAI could convince Colombo to use MAI, it would be very significant and a strategic new business for the company. Vic, with a team of managers, planned and executed the presentation. The first interview had gone well, but as usual they were asking, What can we do better?

As the managers prepared for the second interview, Vic spoke on the telephone with the Colombo national sales manager responsible for coordinating the interview, who also had developed a strong relationship with Fred over the years. After they discussed the strengths of the MAI presentation and the expectations for the second meeting, Vic asked, "Who would you like to see at the second interview?"

"Gee," the Colombo national sales manager responded, "It would be nice to have Fred there."

Vic responded, "Well, it is difficult to come in to the second interview, when you have not been there all along. Fred would have to catch up quite a bit, which could be disruptive this far into the process, plus Fred does not want to be viewed as a figurehead. We went through a similar situation in late 1991 with Nestle, where Fred had a very limited part in the interview and he was uncomfortable."

"Ok, Vic," said the Colombo national sales manager. "If you think that it would be awkward, I understand."

Vic hung up the phone, shared the highlights of his conversation with the managers, and continued to work on the presentation until late that night. The circus truly came to town when it came to new business. Vic finally called it a night, the final touches would have to wait until tomorrow. That night, Vic could not sleep—which is rarely the case. But that night something was eating at him. He had to tell Fred about his telephone conversation.

The next morning, Vic shared the whole story with Fred. Fred did not seem bothered at that moment. But as the days passed, Fred felt more and more bothered that the decision had been made for him, which caused him to question his place in the company. Fred said:

> Attending the meeting per se was not the important thing. I felt that the decision about my attendance was at least worthy of discussion. Since I had a special relationship with the national sales manager, my presence was suggested, and a corporate executive from Colombo's parent company would be at the second interview, which cast a more strategic tinge to the interview.

Over the next few weeks, more and more people at MAI were slowly pulled into conversations with Vic or Fred. Indirect messages were being passed between Vic and Fred. Vic felt undermined, wounded, and devastated that Fred felt Vic was threatening his value and purpose in the company.

Four days after the second meeting, according to Fred, Fred and Vic had each expressed that "the boil was broken. Each of us expressed to Jay Hughes and Alan Doyan, senior vice presidents and board members, that he was leaving. That was the best thing for the company.

It was not about who was right and who was wrong—just each felt that it was best for the company that he leave."

Jay Hughes arranged a board meeting as soon as possible to resolve this situation. Entering the MAI building, Fred had to decide what he would do not only at the board meeting today but about the wedding in two weeks.

APPENDIXES

I INFORMATION ABOUT RMA "PROJECTION OF FINANCIAL STATEMENTS" AND RMA STATEMENT STUDIES

II INFORMATION ABOUT *INDUSTRY NORMS AND KEY BUSINESS RATIOS,* PUBLISHED BY DUN & BRADSTREET

III "THE LEGAL PROCESS OF VENTURE CAPITAL INVESTMENT," BY RICHARD J. TESTA

IV SAMPLE TERMS SHEET

V OUTLINE OF AN INVESTMENT AGREEMENT

VI SAMPLE VESTING AND STOCK RESTRICTION AGREEMENT

VII SAMPLE LOAN AGREEMENT

VIII VASES AND FACES EXERCISE, BY BETTY EDWARDS

APPENDIX I—INFORMATION ABOUT RMA "PROJECTION OF FINANCIAL STATEMENTS" AND RMA STATEMENT STUDIES

The following is part of an article* about preparing and using "worksheet schedules" in completing an RMA form, "Projection of Financial Statements," and information from RMA Statement Studies.

Projection of Financial Statements—and the Preparatory Use of Worksheet Schedules for Budgets†

I don't know about other credit men, but without exception, all the budgets that I have seen were submitted without supporting schedules showing the source of the figures being used. Without this source, the budgets left me with an uneasy feeling of nebulous value and questionable accuracy, because it was impossible to check back any figures used.

I will be the first one to admit that I am not an expert in the preparation of "Projection of Financial Statements" (RMA Form C–117), but I'd say that it is impossible to complete these forms with any consistent degree of accuracy without the prior preparation of supporting schedules. In fact, the easiest, quickest—and possibly the only—way to complete the budget form is to sit down beforehand and gather up all the necessary information in a logical, concise, and intelligent manner in the form of "worksheet schedules." This article is directed primarily to the preparation and use of such schedules.

For purposes of illustration, I am going to deal with a hypothetical company, Sample Company, Inc. Starting out with (1) a 12/31/59 balance sheet and income statement (which the reader can find in the first column of the accompanying completed C–117) and (2) with certain additional pertinent financial facts (given below for the reader), my goal was to project Sample Company's financial statements monthly for 1960—i.e., to complete C–117. Each of the five schedules I had to prepare before tackling C–117 are reproduced in the article, and following the schedules, there is presented a line-by-line explanation of the entries made on C–117.

* Reprinted with permission. The Robert Morris Associates, 1616 Philadelphia National Bank Building, Philadelphia, Pennsylvania 19107.

† By Chester G Zimmerman, Director of Loan Review, American National Bank and Trust Company of Chicago, Chicago, IL. Reprinted from the April 1961 issue of the *Bulletin* (now *The Journal of Commercial Bank Lending*) published by Robert Morris Associates, The National Association of Bank Loan and Credit Officers, 1432 Philadelphia National Bank Bldg., Philadelphia, Pa. 19107. (Copyright © 1961 by Robert Morris Associates.)

Here are the necessary pertinent facts about Sample Company, established by competent management opinions:

Sales proposed (see Schedule A for detail by month)	$12,000,000
Cost figures—1959 percentages to be used	
Inventory supply on hand—45 days' supply, based upon next month's material costs with December inventory the same as at the beginning.	
Accounts receivable collections:	
January through April	15 days
May and June	30 days
July and August 50% in 30 days, 25% in 60 days, 25% in 90 days	
September 75% in 30 days, 25% in 60 days	
October through November	30 days
December	20 days
Trade payments every 15 days	
Additions to fixed assets (equally over the year)	$120,000 per annum
Depreciation (equally over the year)	$ 72,000 per annum
Direct labor, indirect labor, and manufacturing expenses paid every 15 days	
Sales expense—5% of sales—paid by end of month	
General and administrative expense—2.5% of sales—paid by end of month	
Minimum cash balances to be carried	$250,000
Monthly payments on long-term obligations	$ 5,000
Borrowing will be in multiples of	$ 50,000

The first logical schedule to be prepared ("A") would be the proposed sales, cost of sales, and other expenses making up the profit and loss figures for the coming year. These data complete the upper third of the form, and, because of the segregation of expenses, some details are brought forward to additional schedules to support cash projections and balance sheet data.

Schedule "A" projects by month:

- Cost of sales (85% based upon 1959 percentages)
- Material costs (80% of cost of sales based upon 1959 percentages)
- Direct labor costs (10% of cost of sales—1959 percentages)
- Indirect labor costs (5% of cost of sales—1959 percentages)
- Manufacturing overhead (5% of cost of sales—exclusive of depreciation—1959 percentages)
- Sales expense (5% of sales)
- General and administrative expense (2.5% of sales)

WORK SHEET SCHEDULES TO SUPPORT PROJECTION OF FINANCIAL STATEMENTS — SAMPLE COMPANY, INC.

SCHEDULE "A" — SALES AND COST OF SALES PROJECTED FOR 1960 (000) Omitted

Details	January	February	March	April	May	June	July	August	September	October	November	December	Totals
Net Sales	$ 800	$ 800	$1,500	$1,200	$ 800	$ 600	$ 400	$ 700	$ 1,000	$ 1,500	$ 1,500	$ 1,200	$12,000
Material Costs—80% of Cost of Sales	$ 544	$ 544	$1,020	$ 816	$ 544	$ 408	$ 272	$ 476	$ 680	$ 1,020	$ 1,020	$ 816	$ 8,160
Direct Labor—10% of Cost of Sales	68	68	128	102	68	50	34	60	84	128	126	102	1,018
Mfg. Overhead (Excl. Deprec.)													
5% of Cost of Sales	34	34	64	51	34	25	17	30	42	64	63	51	509
Indirect Labor—5% of Cost of Sales	34	34	64	51	34	25	17	30	42	64	63	51	509
Cost of Sales—85% of Sales	$ 680	$ 680	$1,276	$1,020	$ 680	$ 508	$ 340	$ 596	$ 848	$ 1,276	$ 1,272	$ 1,020	$10,196
Gross Profit	$ 120	$ 120	$ 224	$ 180	$ 120	$ 92	$ 60	$ 104	$ 152	$ 224	$ 228	$ 180	$ 1,804
Sales Expense—5% of Sales	$ 40	$ 40	$ 75	$ 60	$ 40	$ 30	$ 20	$ 35	$ 50	$ 75	$ 75	$ 60	$ 600
General & Admin. Expense—2½% of Sales	20	20	37	30	20	15	10	17	25	38	37	30	299
Operating Profit before Deprec. & Taxes	$ 60	$ 60	$ 112	$ 90	$ 60	$ 47	$ 30	$ 52	$ 77	$ 111	$ 116	$ 90	$ 905

Material Costs are brought into Schedule "C"

Direct Labor and Manufacturing Overhead are brought into Schedule "E"

Sales Expenses and General & Administrative Expenses are combined for Line 25

Depreciation is set forth on Line 12. Income Tax is provided at 50% (for ease in computation) and added to total of Line 48 less payments made on Line 27

Line 15 is net profit which is added to previous month balance of Line 56 for current month total for Line 56

SCHEDULE "B" — ACCOUNTS RECEIVABLE OUTSTANDINGS AND COLLECTIONS (000) Omitted

Details	January	February	March	April	May	June	July	August	September	October	November	December	Totals
Balance — Beginning of Month	$ 366	$ 400	$ 400	$ 750	$ 600	$ 800	$ 600	$ 400	$ 900	$ 1,450	$ 1,925	$ 1,500	
Add: Sales	800	800	1,500	1,200	800	600	400	700	1,000	1,500	1,500	1,200	$12,000
Total	$1,166	$1,200	$1,900	$1,950	$1,100	$ 1,400	$ 1,000	$ 1,100	$ 1,900	$ 2,950	$ 3,425	$ 2,700	
Balance — End of Month — Based on													
Collection Terms	400	400	750	600	800	600	400	900	1,450	1,925	1,500	800	
Cash Collections	$ 766	$ 800	$1,150	$1,350	$ 600	$ 800	$ 600	$ 200	$ 450	$ 1,025	$ 1,925	$ 1,900	$11,566
Collection Terms — in Days	15	15	15	15	30	30	50%—30 25%—60 & 90	50%—30 25%—60 & 90	75%—30 25%—60	30	30	20	

Monthly Cash Collections listed on Line 17

Balance — End of Month — listed on Line 36

SCHEDULE "C" — MATERIAL FLOW AND PURCHASES (000) Omitted

Details	January	February	March	April	May	June	July	August	September	October	November	December	Totals
Beginning Inventory	$ 788	$ 816	$1,530	$1,224	$ 816	$ 612	$ 408	$ 714	$ 1,020	$ 1,530	$ 1,530	$ 1,224	
Less: Materials Used from Schedule "A"	544	544	1,020	816	544	408	272	476	680	1,020	1,020	816	$ 8,160
Net Remaining before Required Purchases	$ 244	$ 272	$ 510	$ 408	$ 272	$ 204	$ 136	$ 238	$ 340	$ 510	$ 510	$ 408	
Add: Purchases Required	572	1,258	714	408	340	204	578	782	1,190	1,020	714	380	$ 8,160
Ending Inventory — 45 Days' Supply	$ 816	$1,530	$1,224	$ 816	$ 612	$ 408	$ 714	$ 1,020	$ 1,530	$ 1,530	$ 1,224	$ 788	

"Purchase Required" is always an amount which when added to the "net inventory" results in the pre-computed ending inventory

Ending inventories are set forth on Line 37

"Purchases Required" are brought forward to Schedule "D" to obtain cash disbursements and accounts payable at end of month

SCHEDULE "D" — ACCOUNTS PAYABLE — CASH FLOW — 15 DAY TERMS (000) Omitted

Details	January	February	March	April	May	June	July	August	September	October	November	December	Totals
Accounts Payable — Beginning of Month	$ 341	$ 286	$ 629	$ 357	$ 204	$ 170	$ 102	$ 289	$ 391	$ 595	$ 510	$ 357	
Add: Monthly Purchases Required — Schedule "B"	572	1,258	714	408	340	204	578	782	1,190	1,020	714	380	$ 8,160
Total	$ 913	$1,544	$1,343	$ 765	$ 544	$ 374	$ 680	$ 1,071	$ 1,581	$ 1,615	$ 1,224	$ 737	
Less Accounts Payable — End of Month	286	629	357	204	170	102	289	391	595	510	357	190	
Cash Disbursed on Trade Payables	$ 627	$ 915	$ 986	$ 561	$ 374	$ 272	$ 391	$ 680	$ 986	$ 1,105	$ 867	$ 547	$ 8,311

Accounts Payable — End of month are listed on Line 47

Cash Disbursed is listed on Line 22

SCHEDULE "E" — DIRECT LABOR, MANUFACTURING EXPENSES AND INDIRECT LABOR — ACCRUALS AND CASH DISBURSED (000) Omitted

Details	January	February	March	April	May	June	July	August	September	October	November	December	Totals
Accruals — Beginning of Month	$ 95	$ 68	$ 68	$ 128	$ 102	$ 68	$ 50	$ 34	$ 60	$ 84	$ 128	$ 126	
Add: Monthly Expense from Schedule "A" of 3 totals	136	136	256	204	136	100	68	120	168	256	252	204	$ 2,036
Total	$ 231	$ 204	$ 324	$ 332	$ 238	$ 168	$ 118	$ 154	$ 228	$ 340	$ 380	$ 330	
Less: Accruals — End of Month — Paid 15 days	68	68	128	102	68	50	34	60	84	128	126	102	
Cash Disbursed	$ 163	$ 136	$ 196	$ 230	$ 170	$ 118	$ 84	$ 94	$ 144	$ 212	$ 254	$ 228	$ 2,029

Cash Disbursed listed on Lines 23 and 24

Accruals — End of Month listed on Line 51

Sample Company, Inc.: Source of Figures for Budget Form

Line No.	*Source*
1	Sales from Schedule A
2	Material costs from Schedule A
3	Direct labor from Schedule A
4	Manufacturing overhead from Schedule A
5	Indirect labor from Schedule A
6	Cost of goods sold from Schedule A
7	Gross profit—Line 1 less Line 6
8	Sales expense—Schedule A
9	General and administrative expenses—Schedule A
11	Line 7 less totals of Lines 8, 9, and 10
12	Depreciation—from preliminary facts
13	50% for purposes of illustration (or current tax rate) or difference between Line 11 less Line 12
14	
15	Line 11 less total of Lines 12, 13, and 14
16	Balance of Line 33 (from previous month)
17	Monthly cash collections from Schedule B
20	Bank Loan Proceeds—an amount to be added (Line 20) to the difference of Line 21 less Line 32 to equal cash balances (Line 33) of not less than $250,000. Borrowings to be made in multiples of $50,000.
21	Totals of Lines 16 through 20
22	Cash disbursed on trade payables from Schedule D
23, 24	Cash disbursed from Schedule E
25	Total of Lines 8 and 9 above
26	Monthly amounts of fixed-asset additions from preliminary facts
27	Balance on Line 48 (from actual balance sheet) distributed in March and June, with 25% of the amount in excess of $100,000 of estimated income taxes payable in September and December
30	Balance on Line 49 (actual) distributed in accordance with terms of payment
31	When bank loans are outstanding, if Line 21 exceeds Line 32 (without Line 31 added in), any amount which reduces cash balances (Line 33) to not less than $250,000 should be placed in Line 31
32	Totals of Lines 22 to 31
33	The difference between Line 21 less Line 32—at no time to be less than $250,000
34	From Line 33
36	Balance—end of month—from Schedule B
37	Ending inventory—from Schedule C
39	Totals of Lines 34 through 38
40	Line 26 less Line 12 added to outstanding of previous month
41	No change—brought across from actual
44	No change—brought across from actual
45	Total of Lines 39 through 44
46	Total of Line 20 less total of Line 31 added to previous month balance
47	Accounts payable end of month from Schedule D
48	Previous month's balance plus Line 13 less Line 27
49	(Current maturities—term debt) year-end actual total less payments on Line 30, plus maturities of Line 53 becoming current obligations
51	Accruals end of month from Schedule E
52	Total of Lines 46 through 51
53	(Term debt) outstanding balance (from actual) less maturities becoming current obligations
54	(Total liabilities) total of Lines 52 and 53
56, 57	Previous month's outstanding balance plus Line 15
58	Total of Lines 54 and 56
59	Line 39 less Line 52

rma

'77 annual statement studies

fiscal year-ends 6/30/76 through 3/31/77

with other sources of composite financial data

Published by Robert Morris Associates, Philadelphia, Pa.

CHEMICALS & ALLIED PRODUCTS SIC# 5161					WHOLESALERS	DRUGS, DRUG PROPRIETARIES & DRUGGISTS' SUNDRIES SIC# 5122				
60(6/30-9/30/76)		105(10/1/76-3/31/77)				48(6/30-9/30/76)		67(10/1/76-3/31/77)		
0-250M	250M-1MM	1-10MM	10-50MM	ALL	ASSET SIZE	0-250M	250M-1MM	1-10MM	10-50MM	ALL
23	65	72	5	165	NUMBER OF STATEMENTS	16	26	58	15	115
%	%	%	%	%	**ASSETS**	%	%	%	%	%
7.9	7.7	6.9		10.9	Cash & Equivalents	9.6	5.5	3.6	8.9	6.6
34.3	35.0	33.6		30.4	Accts. & Notes Rec. - Trade(net)	30.3	28.4	32.3	26.8	29.1
32.2	28.8	24.6		28.5	Inventory	39.9	44.6	44.6	41.2	42.7
1.0	2.3	2.5		1.8	All Other Current	.7	1.2	2.0	1.9	1.9
75.4	73.9	67.7		71.6	Total Current	80.6	79.6	82.4	78.7	80.3
14.8	19.4	25.5		21.9	Fixed Assets (net)	8.3	12.2	11.8	16.4	14.3
.3	.7	.8		.6	Intangibles (net)	.0	1.0	.6	1.1	.9
9.5	5.9	6.0		6.0	All Other Non-Current	11.1	7.2	5.1	3.8	4.5
100.0	100.0	100.0		100.0	Total	100.0	100.0	100.0	100.0	100.0
					LIABILITIES					
12.6	10.2	9.5		7.6	Notes Payable-Short Term	10.9	10.6	13.3	3.6	7.9
4.0	2.8	3.5		2.5	Cur. Mat.-L/T/D	2.2	2.7	1.2	.9	1.1
22.2	26.0	28.4		29.5	Accts. & Notes Payable - Trade	30.4	31.2	29.2	26.9	28.0
10.2	5.4	5.4		4.6	Accrued Expenses	3.8	6.1	4.3	5.1	4.8
2.8	3.9	5.1		7.4	All Other Current	1.0	2.8	1.8	1.5	1.7
51.7	48.3	51.9		51.6	Total Current	48.3	53.4	49.8	38.0	43.4
15.8	12.1	10.2		9.3	Long Term Debt	16.1	7.4	9.5	8.2	8.7
2.2	2.0	2.4		2.5	All Other Non-Current	.0	7.2	1.3	3.2	2.5
30.4	37.7	35.5		36.6	Net Worth	35.6	32.0	39.4	50.6	45.3
100.0	100.0	100.0		100.0	Total Liabilities & Net Worth	100.0	100.0	100.0	100.0	100.0
					INCOME DATA					
100.0	100.0	100.0		100.0	Net Sales	100.0	100.0	100.0	100.0	100.0
64.9	75.6	80.5		79.5	Cost Of Sales	73.5	71.7	82.1	79.7	80.5
35.1	24.4	19.5		20.5	Gross Profit	26.5	28.3	17.9	20.3	19.5
29.1	21.3	16.2		16.3	Operating Expenses	23.3	25.3	15.0	16.2	16.0
6.0	3.0	3.2		4.2	Operating Profit	3.2	3.0	2.9	4.1	3.5
1.1	.6	.2		.3	All Other Expenses (net)	-.3	.4	.7	.3	.5
4.9	2.4	3.1		3.9	Profit Before Taxes	3.5	2.6	2.2	3.8	3.1
					RATIOS					
2.1	2.0	1.7		1.9		1.9	2.3	2.0	2.9	2.1
1.6	1.5	1.4		1.4	Current	1.7	1.6	1.7	2.1	1.7
1.1	1.2	1.1		1.1		1.5	1.2	1.3	1.8	1.4
1.2	1.1	1.1		1.1		1.5	1.1	.9	1.4	1.1
.9	.9	.8		.8	Quick	1.0	.7	.7	.9	.8
.6	.6	.6		.6		.4	.3	.6	.8	.5
26 14.3	28 13.1	33 10.9		31 11.7		23 16.1	22 16.9	28 13.1	29 12.6	27 13.5
41 8.8	36 10.1	46 7.9		42 8.6	Sales/Receivables	30 12.2	42 8.7	39 9.4	38 9.7	38 9.6
72 5.1	54 6.8	60 6.1		57 6.4		47 7.8	52 7.0	54 6.7	44 8.3	49 7.4
42 8.6	26 13.8	24 15.0		28 13.2		50 7.3	56 6.5	49 7.4	60 6.1	54 6.8
60 6.1	44 8.3	42 8.6		46 7.9	Cost of Sales/Inventory	74 4.9	79 4.6	62 5.9	63 5.8	68 5.4
87 4.2	73 5.0	64 5.7		70 5.2		104 3.5	118 3.1	87 4.2	69 5.3	87 4.2
7.9	7.6	10.4		8.3		7.7	6.1	6.9	5.0	6.6
8.9	13.9	14.9		13.9	Sales/Working Capital	9.2	8.6	10.7	7.5	9.3
44.4	34.3	38.9		36.9		20.0	21.0	16.4	9.4	15.1
13.0	11.8	12.1		12.1		7.4	13.8	10.1	29.4	11.3
(19) 6.0	(50) 3.2	(51) 4.7		(123) 4.7	EBIT/Interest	(12) 4.6	(23) 4.6	(43) 5.2	(12) 12.3	(90) 5.1
3.3	1.7	2.0		1.9		2.1	1.3	1.8	4.3	2.0
	4.1	5.6		4.9			4.7	11.2	27.4	8.9
	(32) 2.1	(41) 3.7		(83) 2.9	Cash Flow/Cur. Mat. L/T/D		(12) 2.9	(28) 2.8	(10) 8.4	(55) 2.9
	1.0	1.6		1.1			1.2	1.3	2.5	1.3
.1	.2	.3		.2		.1	.1	.1	.1	.1
.3	.5	.6		.5	Fixed/Worth	.2	.3	.2	.2	.2
1.6	1.2	1.0		1.1		.5	.9	.4	.5	.5
.8	.9	1.1		1.0		1.3	1.0	1.1	.6	1.0
1.9	2.2	1.9		2.0	Debt/Worth	1.7	1.7	1.7	1.0	1.6
7.3	3.5	3.6		3.6		2.4	5.0	2.9	1.4	2.9
88.5	35.1	36.0		37.5	% Profit Before Taxes/Tangible	52.2	37.8	28.9	29.0	34.2
(20) 45.0	17.1	(71) 23.3		(161) 22.4	Net Worth	(15) 31.1	(22) 16.2	17.5	19.7	(110) 18.1
15.3	10.8	10.3		10.8		8.2	9.2	10.1	7.5	9.8
21.1	10.8	13.9		14.1	% Profit Before Taxes/Total	19.0	13.7	11.0	14.0	13.8
10.7	5.4	8.3		7.4	Assets	10.9	6.7	7.3	10.0	7.8
4.4	3.0	3.2		3.2		3.7	3.0	2.7	2.0	3.3
65.2	60.8	41.9		53.3		113.6	85.9	81.8	51.6	81.2
29.2	20.5	14.9		17.8	Sales/Net Fixed Assets	48.0	26.8	42.6	33.4	36.3
11.7	9.6	9.3		9.7		14.5	16.0	22.3	23.1	17.7
3.9	4.0	3.8		3.8		3.8	3.8	4.0	3.5	3.9
2.7	3.2	2.8		2.9	Sales/Total Assets	3.1	2.7	3.2	3.0	3.1
1.9	2.3	2.3		2.2		2.6	1.9	2.4	2.8	2.4
.7	.4	.6		.5		.3	.4	.2	.3	.3
(19) 1.1	(61) .9	(70) 1.0		(155) 1.0	% Depr., Dep., Amort./Sales	(13) .5	(23) .7	(51) .4	(14) .5	(101) .5
1.9	1.7	2.1		1.8		1.0	1.3	.7	.9	.9
.9	.2	.2		.3		.7	.6	.4		.5
(18) 1.6	(36) 1.0	(43) .7		(100) .9	% Lease & Rental Exp/Sales	(13) 1.4	(18) 1.0	(36) .6		(74) .9
2.9	1.2	1.4		1.5		4.7	2.2	1.3		1.5
3.7	2.2	1.2		1.6		3.9	2.4	.9		1.3
(15) 6.5	(35) 3.4	(33) 1.7		(84) 3.1	% Officers' Comp/Sales	(13) 5.9	(14) 3.6	(25) 1.5		(54) 2.4
8.8	6.4	3.1		5.2		8.7	5.0	2.2		4.9
9612M	117496M	603504M	196173M	926785M	Net Sales ($)	8699M	43413M	662937M	800390M	1515439M
3346M	37519M	216024M	106577M	363466M	Total Assets ($)	2504M	14802M	206362M	267752M	491420M

M = $thousand MM = $million

DEFINITION OF RATIOS

INTRODUCTION

Below the common size balance sheet and income statement presented on each data page are series of ratios which have been computed from the financial statement data. Each ratio has three values: the upper quartile, median, and lower quartile. For any given ratio, these figures are calculated by first computing the value of the ratio for *each* financial statement in the sample. These values are then arrayed—"listed"—in an order from the strongest to the weakest. (We acknowledge that, for certain ratios, there may be differences of opinion concerning what is a strong or a weak value. RMA has resolved this problem by following general banking guidelines consistent with sound credit practice in its presentation of data.)

In such an array of ratio values, the figure which falls in the middle between the strongest and the weakest ratios is the *median*. The figure that falls halfway between the median and the strongest ratio is the *upper quartile*. The figure that falls halfway between the median and the weakest ratio is the *lower quartile*. The median and quartile values will always be shown on the data pages in the order indicated below:

Upper Quartile
Median
Lower Quartile

There are several reasons for using medians and quartiles instead of an average. One is to eliminate the influence which values in an "unusual" statement would have on an average. The method used more accurately reflects the ranges of ratio values than would a straight averaging method.

It is important to understand that the spread (range) between the upper and lower quartiles represents the middle 50% of all the companies in a sample. Ratio values greater than the upper or less than the lower quartiles, therefore, begin to approach "unusual" values.

For some ratio values, you will occasionally see an entry that is other than a conventional number. These unusual entries are defined as follows:

(1) *INF*—This stands for infinity, a value so large as to be beyond any practical value. It is the result of the denominator having the value of zero in a ratio calculation. With respect to the ratios sales/working capital, debt/worth, and fixed/worth, the value ± *INF* may occasionally appear as a quartile or median. This is the result of interpolation between positive and negative values in the nonlinear arrays typical of these ratios.

(2) *999.8*—When a ratio value equals 1,000 or more, it also becomes an "unusual" value and is given the "999.8" designation. This is considered to be a close enough approximation to the actual atypically large value.

(3) *−.0*—In a few places in this book, we encounter a negative value so minute that, when rounded, it becomes zero. We have used the symbol "−.0" to reflect this, but it is important to recognize that it is the result of rounding a *negative* number.

Throughout the *Statement Studies*, the ratio values have been omitted whenever there were less than ten statements in a sample. Occasionally, the number of statements used in a ratio array will differ from the number of statements in a sample because certain elements of data may not be present in all financial statements. In these cases, the number of statements used is shown in parentheses to the left of the array.

In interpreting ratios, the "strongest" or "best" value is not always the largest numerical value, nor is the "weakest" always the lowest numerical value. The following description of each of the ratios appearing in the *Statement Studies* will provide details regarding the arraying of the values.

The ratios in the *Statement Studies* are grouped into five principal categories: liquidity, coverage, leverage, operating, and specific expense items.

LIQUIDITY RATIOS

Liquidity is a measure of the quality and adequacy of current assets to meet current obligations as they come due.

CURRENT RATIO

Computation: Total current assets divided by total current liabilities.

$$\frac{\text{total current assets}}{\text{total current liabilities}}$$

Interpretation: This ratio is a rough indication of a firm's ability to service its current obligations. Generally, the higher the current ratio, the greater the "cushion" between current obligations and a firm's ability to pay them. The stronger ratio reflects a numerical superiority of current assets over current liabilities. However, the composition and quality of current assets is a critical factor in the analysis of an individual firm's liquidity.

The ratio values are arrayed from the highest positive to the lowest positive.

QUICK RATIO

Computation: Cash and equivalents plus accounts and notes receivable (trade) divided by total current liabilities.

$$\frac{\text{cash \& equivalents} + \text{accounts \& notes receivable (trade)}}{\text{total current liabilities}}$$

Interpretation: Also known as the "ACID TEST" ratio, it is a refinement of the current ratio and is a more conservative measure of liquidity. The ratio expresses the degree to which a company's current liabilities are covered by the most liquid current assets. Generally, any value of less than 1 to 1 implies a reciprocal "dependency" on inventory or other current assets to liquidate short-term debt.

The ratio values are arrayed from the highest positive to the lowest positive.

If the number of statements used in the calculation of this ratio differs from the sample size used in the asset category column, the sample size for each ratio will be printed in parentheses to the left of the array.

SALES/RECEIVABLES

Computation: Net sales divided by accounts and notes receivable (trade) .

$$\frac{\text{net sales}}{\text{accounts \& notes receivable (trade)}}$$

Interpretation: This ratio measures the number of times accounts and notes receivable (trade) turn over during the year. The higher the turnover of receivables, the shorter the time between sale and cash collection. For example, a company with sales of $720,000 and receivables of $120,000 would have a sales/receivables ratio of 6.0, which means receivables turn over six times a year. If a company's receivables appear to be turning slower than the rest of the industry, further research is needed and the quality of the receivables should be examined closely.

A problem with this ratio is that it compares one day's receivables, shown at statement date, to total annual sales and does not take into consideration seasonal fluctuations. An additional problem in interpretation may arise when there is a large proportion of cash sales to total sales.

When the receivables figure is zero, the quotient will be infinity (INF) and represents the best possible ratio. The ratio values are therefore arrayed starting with infinity (INF) and then from the numerically highest to the numerically lowest value. The only time a zero will appear in the array is when the sales figure is low and the quotient rounds off to zero. By definition, this ratio cannot be negative.

Days' Receivables: The sales/receivables ratio will have a figure printed in bold type directly to the left of the array. This figure is the days' receivables.

Computation: The sales/receivables ratio divided into 365 (the number of days in one year).

$$\frac{365}{\text{sales/receivable ratio}}$$

Interpretation: This figure expresses the average time in days that receivables are outstanding. Generally, the greater number of days outstanding, the greater the probability of delinquencies in accounts receivable. A comparison of a company's daily receivables may indicate the extent of a company's control over credit and collections. The terms offered by a company to its customers, however, may differ from terms within the industry and should be taken into consideration.

In the example above, 365 ÷ 6 = 61—i.e., the average receivable is collected in 61 days.

COST OF SALES/INVENTORY

Computation: Cost of sales divided by inventory.

$$\frac{\text{Cost of Sales}}{\text{Inventory}}$$

Interpretation: This ratio measures the number of times inventory is turned over during the year. High inventory turnover can indicate better liquidity or superior merchandising. Conversely it can indicate a shortage of needed inventory for sales. Low inventory turnover can indicate poor liquidity, possible overstocking, obsolescence, or in contrast to these negative interpretations a planned inventory buildup in the case of material shortages. A problem with this ratio is that it compares one day's inventory to cost of goods sold and does not take seasonal fluctuations into account. When the inventory figure is zero, the quotient will be infinity (INF) and represents the best possible ratio. The ratio values are arrayed starting with infinity (INF) and then from the numerically highest to the numerically lowest value. The only time a zero will appear in the array is when the cost of sales figure is very low and the quotient rounds off to zero.

Days' Inventory
The cost of sales inventory ratio will have a figure printed in bold type directly to the left of the array. This figure is the days' inventory.

Computation: The cost of sales/inventory ratio divided into 365 (the number of days in one year).

$$\frac{365}{\text{cost of sales/inventory ratio}}$$

Interpretation: Division of the inventory turnover ratio into 365 days yields the average length of time units are in inventory.

SALES/WORKING CAPITAL

Computation: Net sales divided by net working capital (current assets less current liabilities equals net working capital).

$$\frac{\text{Net Sales}}{\text{Net Working Capital}}$$

Interpretation: Working capital is a measure of the margin of protection for current creditors. It reflects the ability to finance current operations. Relating the level of sales arising from operations to the underlying working capital measures how efficiently working capital is employed. A low ratio may indicate an inefficient use of working capital while a very high ratio often signifies overtrading —a vulnerable position for creditors.

If working capital is zero, the quotient is infinity (INF). If working capital is negative, the quotient is negative. The ratio values are arrayed from the lowest positive to the highest positive, to infinity, and then from the highest negative to the lowest negative.

The value ± INF may occasionally appear as a quartile or median. This is the result of interpolation between positive and negative values in the nonlinear array typical of this ratio.

COVERAGE RATIOS

Coverage ratios measure a firm's ability to service debt.

EARNINGS BEFORE INTEREST AND TAXES (EBIT)/INTEREST

Computation: Earnings (profit) before annual interest expense and taxes divided by annual interest expense.

$$\frac{\text{Earnings Before Interest \& Taxes}}{\text{Annual Interest Expense}}$$

Interpretation: This ratio is a measure of a firm's ability to meet interest payments. A high ratio may indicate that a borrower would have little difficulty in meeting the interest obligations of a loan. This ratio also serves as an indicator of a firm's capacity to take on additional debt.

Only those statements which reported annual interest expense were used in the calculation of this ratio. If the number of statements used in the calculation of these ratios differed from the sample size used in the asset category column, the sample size for each ratio will be printed in parentheses to the left of the array. If there were less than 10 ratios in an array, no entry will be shown. The ratio values are arrayed from the highest positive to the lowest positive and then from the lowest negative to the highest negative.

CASH FLOW/CURRENT MATURITIES LONG-TERM DEBT

Computation: Net profit plus depreciation, depletion, and amortization expenses, divided by the current portion of long-term debt.

$$\frac{\text{Net Profit + Depreciation, Depletion, Amortization Expenses}}{\text{Current Portion of Long-Term Debt}}$$

Interpretation: This ratio expresses the coverage of current maturities by cash flow from operations. Since cash flow is the primary source of debt retirement, this ratio measures the ability of a firm to service principal repayment and is an indicator of additional debt capacity. Although it is misleading to think that all cash flow is available for debt service, the ratio is a valid measure of the ability to service long-term debt.

Only data for *corporations* which have the following items were used;

(1) Profit or loss after taxes (positive, negative, or zero)
(2) A positive figure for Depreciation/Depletion/Amortization expenses
(3) A positive figure for current maturities of long-term debt

If the number of ratios used differed with the total number of firms reported in a column, the sample size is printed to the left of the array. If less than 10 ratios were available, the array was not printed. Ratio values are arrayed from the highest to lowest positive and then from the lowest to the highest negative.

LEVERAGE RATIOS

Highly leveraged firms (those with heavy debt in relation to net worth) are more vulnerable to business downturns than those with lower debt to worth positions. While leverage ratios help to measure this vulnerability, it must be remembered that they vary greatly depending on the requirements of particular industry groups.

FIXED/WORTH

Computation: Fixed assets (net of accumulated depreciation) divided by tangible net worth.

$$\frac{\text{Net Fixed Assets}}{\text{Tangible Net Worth}}$$

Interpretation: This ratio measures the extent to which owner's equity (capital) has been invested in plant and equipment (fixed assets). A lower ratio indicates a proportionately smaller investment in fixed assets in relation to net worth, and a better "cushion" for creditors in case of liquidation. Similarly, a higher ratio would indicate the opposite situation. The presence of substantial leased fixed assets (not shown on the balance sheet) may deceptively lower this ratio.

Fixed assets may be zero, in which case the quotient is zero. If tangible net worth is zero, the quotient is infinity (INF). If tangible net worth is negative, the quotient is negative. The ratio values are arrayed from the lowest positive to the highest positive, infinity, and then from the highest negative to the lowest negative.

The value ± INF may occasionally appear as a quartile or median. This is the result of interpolation between positive and negative values in the nonlinear array typical of this ratio.

DEBT/WORTH

Computation: Total liabilities divided by tangible net worth.

$$\frac{\text{Total Liabilities}}{\text{Tangible Net Worth}}$$

Interpretation: This ratio expresses the relationship between capital contributed by creditors and that contributed by owners. It expresses the degree of protection provided by the owners for the creditors. The higher the ratio, the greater the risk being assumed by creditors. A lower ratio generally indicates greater long-term financial safety. A firm with a low debt/worth ratio usually has greater flexibility to borrow in the future. A more highly leveraged company has a more limited debt capacity.

Tangible net worth may be zero, in which case the ratio is infinity (INF). Tangible net worth may also be negative which results in the quotient being negative. The ratio values are arrayed from the lowest to highest positive, infinity, and then from the highest to lowest negative.

The value ± INF may occasionally appear as a quartile or median. This is the result of interpolation between positive and negative values in the nonlinear array typical of this ratio.

OPERATING RATIOS

Operating ratios are designed to assist in the evaluation of management performance.

% PROFITS BEFORE TAXES/TANGIBLE NET WORTH

Computation: Profit before taxes divided by tangible net worth and multiplied by 100.

$$\frac{\text{Profit Before Taxes}}{\text{Tangible Net Worth}} \times 100$$

Interpretation: This ratio expresses the rate of return on tangible capital employed. While it can serve as an indicator of management performance, the analyst is cautioned to use it in conjunction with other ratios. A high return, normally associated with effective management, could indicate an under-capitalized firm. Whereas, a low return, usually an indicator of inefficient management performance, could reflect a highly capitalized, conservatively operated business.

This ratio has been multiplied by 100 since it is shown as a percentage.

Profit before taxes may be zero, in which case the ratio is zero. Profits before taxes may be negative resulting in negative quotients. Firms with negative tangible net worth have been omitted from the ratio arrays. Negative ratios will therefore only result in the case of negative profit before taxes. If the tangible net worth is zero, the quotient is infinity (INF). If there are less than 10 ratios for a particular size class, the result is not shown. The ratio values are arrayed starting with infinity (INF), and then from the highest to the lowest positive values, and from the lowest to the highest negative values.

% PROFIT BEFORE TAXES/TOTAL ASSETS

Computation: Profit before taxes divided by total assets and multiplied by 100.

$$\frac{\text{Profit Before Taxes}}{\text{Total Assets}} \times 100$$

Interpretation: This ratio expresses the pre-tax return on total assets and measures the effectiveness of management in employing the resources available to it. If a specific ratio varies considerably from the ranges found in this book, the analyst will need to examine the makeup of the assets and take a closer look at the earnings figure. A heavily depreciated plant and a large amount of intangible assets or unusual income or expense items will cause distortions of this ratio.

This ratio has been multiplied by 100 since it is shown as a percentage. If profit before taxes is zero, the quotient is zero. If profit before taxes is negative, the quotient is negative. These ratio values are arrayed from the highest to the lowest positive and then from the lowest to the highest negative.

SALES/NET FIXED ASSETS

Computation: Net sales divided by net fixed assets (net of accumulated depreciation).

$$\frac{\text{Net Sales}}{\text{Net Fixed Assets}}$$

Interpretation: This ratio is a measure of the productive use of a firm's fixed assets. Largely depreciated fixed assets or a labor intensive operation may cause a distortion of this ratio.

If the net fixed asset figure is zero, the quotient is infinity (INF). The only time a zero will appear in the array will be when the net sales figure is low and the quotient rounds off to zero. These ratio values cannot be negative.

They are arrayed from infinity (INF) and then from the highest to the lowest positive values.

SALES/TOTAL ASSETS

Computation: Net sales divided by total assets.

$$\frac{\text{Net Sales}}{\text{Total Assets}}$$

Interpretation: This ratio is a general measure of a firm's ability to generate sales in relation to total assets. It should be used only to compare firms within specific industry groups and in conjunction with other operating ratios to determine the effective employment of assets.

The only time a zero will appear in the array will be when the net sales figure is low and the quotient rounds off to zero. The ratio values cannot be negative. They are arrayed from the highest to the lowest positive values.

EXPENSE TO SALES RATIOS

The following three ratios relate specific expense items to net sales and express this relationship as a percentage. Comparisons are convenient because the item, net sales, is used as a constant. Variations in these ratios are most pronounced between capital and labor intensive industries.

% DEPRECIATION, DEPLETION, AMORTIZATION/SALES

Computation: Annual depreciation, amortization, and depletion expenses divided by net sales and multiplied by 100.

$$\frac{\text{Depreciation, Amortization, Depletion Expenses}}{\text{Net Sales}} \times 100$$

% LEASE AND RENTAL EXPENSES/SALES

Computation: Annual lease and rental expenses divided by net sales and multiplied by 100.

$$\frac{\text{Lease \& Rental Expenses}}{\text{Net Sales}} \times 100$$

% OFFICERS' COMPENSATION/SALES

Computation: Annual officers' compensation divided by net sales and multiplied by 100.

$$\frac{\text{Officers' Compensation}}{\text{Net Sales}} \times 100$$

Only statements showing a positive figure for each of the expense categories shown above were used. If the number of statements used in an array differs from the sample population for an asset size category, the number of statements used is shown in parentheses to the left of the array. When there are less than 10 ratios, the array is not printed. The ratios are arrayed from the lowest to highest positive values.

SIC NUMBERS APPEARING IN THE STATEMENT STUDIES

SIC No.	Page	SIC No.	Page	SIC No.	Page
0161	186	2065	51	2512	59
0181	185	2074	56	2514	57
0211	182	2075	56	2515	56
0212	181	2076	56	2522	57
0251	183	2082	45	2541	58
0781	185	2084	46	2542	58
0782	185	2085	46	2621	85
0783	185	2086	183	2631	85
1211	182	2087	45	2642	84
1311	184	2091	51	2643	84
1381	193 & 200	2211	94	2648	84
1442	184	2221	94	2651	85
1521	191 & 199	2231	94	2652	85
1522	191 & 199	2241	97	2653	85
1541	191 & 199	2252	95 & 96	2654	85
1542	191 & 199	2253	96	2655	85
1611	192 & 199	2254	96	2711	89
1622	192 & 199	2257	96	2721	89
1623	197 & 202	2258	96	2731	87
1711	195 & 201	2261	95	2732	86
1721	194 & 200	2262	95	2751	87
1731	189 & 198	2272	97	2752	88
1741	193 & 200	2282	98	2761	88
1742	195 & 201	2311	42	2789	86
1743	197 & 202	2321	42	2791	90
1752	190 & 198	2327	41	2821	49
1761	196 & 201	2328	41	2831	47
1771	189 & 198	2335	43	2833	47
1791	196 & 201	2337	44	2834	47
1794	190 & 198	2341	44	2841	50
2011	54	2342	43	2844	49
2013	55	2351	39	2851	48
2016	54	2352	39	2861	48
2021	52	2371	39	2865	48
2022	52	2391	38	2873	47
2023	52	2392	40	2874	47
2024	52	2394	37	3021	91
2026	52	2421	63	3111	61
2033	52	2431	62	3143	60
2034	52	2435	61	3144	60
2037	53	2441	63	3161	60
2041	53	2451	100	3171	60
2048	55	2452	62	3172	60
2051	50	2511	58	3251	91

APPENDIX II—INFORMATION ABOUT *INDUSTRY NORMS AND KEY BUSINESS RATIOS,* PUBLISHED BY DUN & BRADSTREET

The following is summary information and a table of contents from the Library Edition, *Industry Norms and Key Business Ratios,* produced for libraries by Dun & Bradstreet as a reference tool.

Contents

	Page
Preface	
Background	i
Industry Norms for Financial Analysis	iii
Applications by Functional Area	iv
Calculations of the 14 Key Business Ratios	v
Special Bank Data	vii
Industry Overview	x
Industry Norms and Key Business Ratios	
Special Bank Data (SIC #s 6020, 6030, and 6710)	1
Agriculture, Forestry, and Fishing (SIC #s 0111–0913)	3
Mining (SIC #s 1041–1499)	14
Construction (SIC #s 1521–1799)	18
Transportation, Communication, Electric, Gas, and Sanitary Services (SIC #s 4011–4071)	24
Manufacturing (SIC #s 2011–3999)	37
Wholesale Trade (SIC #s 5012–5199)	126
Retail Trade (SIC #s 5211–5999)	141
Finance other than Banks, Insurance, and Real Estate (SIC #s 6121–6799)	157
Services (SIC #s 7011–8999)	167
Appendix—U.S. Standard Industrial Classifications	

Source: Dun & Bradstreet, 1983 Edition. Reprinted with permission.

Background

The Library Edition, *Industry Norms and Key Business Ratios,* hereafter referred to as *Industry Norms,* is specifically produced for libraries only as a reference tool. This book is made possible through the over 1 million financial statements in the Dun's Financial Profiles computerized database. This file consists of US corporations, partnerships, and proprietorships, both public and privately owned, in all size ranges, and includes over 800 different lines of business as defined by the US Standard Industrial Classification (SIC) code numbers. Our data are collected weekly, maintained daily, and constantly edited and updated by the Dun's Financial Profiles Department. All of these factors combine to make this financial information unequaled anywhere for scope and timeliness.[1]

It should be noted that only general data are supplied in the Library Edition; however, for more detailed asset/geographical breakdowns of these data, a set of industry norm books

[1] To provide the most current information available, fiscal years July 1–June 30 were utilized to calculate the Norms.

are also published by Dun & Bradstreet for the corporate marketplace in the following five industry volumes:

1. *Agriculture/Mining/Construction/Transportation/Communication/Utilities.*
2. *Manufacturing.*
3. *Wholesaling.*
4. *Retailing.*
5. *Banking/Finance/Insurance/Real Estate/Services.*

All five segments are available in three different formats (for a total of 15 books). The three formats are as follows:

1. *Industry Norms* for last three years ("Full File").
2. *Industry Norms* for the most recent year ("Partial File").
3. *Key Business Ratios* (only) for the most recent year.

Note that the *Industry Norms* books contain typical balance sheets and income statements, and common-size financial figures, as well as key business ratios. The *Key Business Ratios* books contain 14 indicators of performance.

Industry Norm Format

At the top of each industry norm will be identifying information: SIC code number and short title. Beside the year date, in parentheses, is the number of companies in the sample. The typical balance sheet figures are in the first column and the common-size balance sheet figures are in the second. The respective income statements begin with the item "net sales," and the respective key business ratios begin with the item "ratios." The latter are further broken down, or refined, into the median and the upper quartile and lower quartile.

The Common-Size Financial Statement

The common-size balance sheet and income statement present each item of the financial statement as a percentage of its respective aggregate total. Common-size percentages are computed for all statement items of all the individual companies used in the industry sample. An average for each statement item is then determined and presented as the industry norm.

This enables the analyst to examine the current composition of assets, liabilities, and sales of a particular industry.

The Typical Financial Statement

The typical balance sheet figures are the result of translating the common-size percentages into dollar figures. They permit, for example, a quick check of the relative size of assets and liabilities between one's own company and that company's own line of business.

After the common-size percentages have been computed for the particular sample, the actual financial statements are then sequenced by both total *assets* and total *sales,* with the median, or midpoint, figure in both these groups serving as the typical amount. We then compute the typical balance sheet and income statement dollar figures by multiplying the common-size percentages for each statement item by their respective total amounts.

(For example, if the median total assets for an SIC category are $669,599, and the common-size figure for cash is 9.2 percent, then by multiplying the two we derive a cash figure of $61,603 for the typical balance sheet.)

Key Business Ratios

The 14 key business ratios are broken down into median figures, with upper and lower quartiles, giving the analyst an even more refined set of figures to work with. These ratios cover all those critical areas of business performance, with indicators of solvency, efficiency, and profitability. They provide a profound and well-documented insight into all aspects for everyone interested in the financial workings of business—business executives and managers, credit executives, bankers, lenders, investors, academicians, students.

In the ratio tables appearing in this book, the figures are broken down into the median—which is the midpoint of all companies in the sample—and the upper quartile and lower quartile—which are midpoints of the upper and lower halves.

Upper-quartile figures are not always the highest numerical value, nor are lower-quartile figures always the lowest numerical value. The quartile listings reflect judgmental ranking; thus, the upper quartile represents the best condition in any given ratio and is not necessarily the highest numerical value. (For example, see the items total liabilities-to-net worth or collection period, where a lower numerical value represents a better condition.)

Each of the 14 ratios is calculated individually for every concern in the sample. These individual figures are then sequenced for each ratio according to condition (best to worst), and the figure that falls in the middle of this series becomes the median (or midpoint) for that ratio in that line of business. The figure halfway between the median and the best condition of the series becomes the upper quartile; and the number halfway between the median and the least favorable condition of the series is the lower quartile.

In a statistical sense, each median is considered the *typical* ratio figure for a concern in a given category.

APPENDIX III—THE LEGAL PROCESS OF VENTURE CAPITAL INVESTMENT*

Section I. General Considerations Relating to Legal Documentation

A key element in the attainment of a successful relationship between a young business enterprise and its venture capital investors is the careful crafting of the legal structure of the investment transaction. Venture capital investing is a long-term commitment of support to a company. As such, the parties involved in structuring and implementing the investment transaction must bring to the process a sensitivity to the changing and different objectives and requirements (financial, legal, personal, etc.) of the business and its principal participants.

The legal documents must foresee the evolution of the enterprise from a development stage start-up to a publicly held company or viable acquisition candidate. Not only do the investment documents represent a charter of the legal rights of the parties spanning the growth cycle of the business, but they also set the tone of the relationships between the management/entrepreneurs and the financial backers of the enterprise, serving as a model for resolution of their often differing interests.

Despite increasing standardization of the venture capital process, it remains, fundamentally, highly idiosyncratic, with each transaction reflecting the particular chemistry between entrepreneur and investor. Accordingly, there exists no such thing as the "perfect model" of legal documentation for the investment transaction. Each deal should be tailored to reflect the unique combination of styles and interests involved. Generally, however, each transaction will encompass the following common set of documents:

1. *The term sheet,* summarizing in broad strokes the principal financial and other terms of the investment.
2. *The investment agreement,* detailing the terms of purchase and provisions of the securities (equity or debt) being acquired.
3. *The stockholders agreement,* containing restrictions upon the transfer and voting of securities by management and (occasionally) investors.

*Section prepared by Richard J Testa, a partner in the Boston law firm of Testa, Hurwitz & Thibeault. He and his firm have served as counsel for many national and international venture capital firms as well as for a large number of high technology and other businesses that have been financed by venture capitalists.

4. *Employee stock purchase or stock option agreements,* governing the current and future allocation of equity in the business to key employees.
5. *Employee confidentiality and proprietary rights agreements,* assuring the retention by the business of its valuable trade secrets and business rights.
6. *Legal opinion* of company counsel.

Section II. The Term Sheet

The handshake "agreement" between investor and entrepreneur is often set forth in a written term sheet or letter of intent. Although the term sheet may take a variety of forms, from a cursory and informal letter to a more detailed and formal memorandum, it is intended to accomplish the following purposes:

1. To reflect the agreed-upon valuation of the business and to quantify the proposed allocation of that value between the entrepreneurs and investors.
2. To summarize key financial and legal terms of the transaction which will serve as the basis for preparing definitive legal documents.
3. On occasion, to impose enforceable legal obligations upon the parties, such as requiring payment of expenses in the event the investment does not close or prohibiting negotiations with other parties pending the completion of the transaction.

Above all, the term sheet should be used by the venture capitalist to elicit those concerns of the entrepreneurs which, if unaddressed and unresolved, might later develop into "deal killers." For example, if the venture capitalist intends to require that the entrepreneurs submit their stock ownership in the enterprise to buyback or forfeiture restrictions in the event they sever employment, such a condition should be covered in the term sheet since it encroaches in an area in which the entrepreneur will be especially sensitive. Similarly sensitive topics are the composition of the board of directors and matters relating to the terms of employment of the entrepreneurs.

A term sheet is particularly valuable for the entrepreneur who has never seen venture terms before. The new chief executive officer is being introduced to a large number of new concepts. By contrast, the venture capitalist is usually experienced and familiar with numerous levels of permutations on possible terms. The term sheet is particularly useful in bridging these differences in background knowledge and experience.

Although the term sheet is generally not a binding agreement to complete the investment, venture capitalists and entrepreneurs often consider a fully negotiated and agreed-upon term sheet, as a practical matter, to be sufficient evidence of their mutual commitment to warrant the advance of "bridge financing" by the investors.

Bridge financing is often employed to defray the essential expenses of a startup or development stage enterprise, while the lead venture capital investor completes the assembly of the investing syndicate or during the time necessary for the preparation of definitive legal agreements for the investment. On occasion, bridge financing will be advanced to fund a company while conditions to the permanent investment—such as the preparation of a complete business plan or the hiring of a new chief executive or other key employee—are being met.

Bridge financings ordinarily take the form of debt due on demand, convertible into whatever security is to be issued in the permanent financing at the time that financing takes place. Depending on the length of time that the bridge financing is anticipated to be in place, it may be secured by a security interest on company assets or guaranteed by company founders.

Section III. The Investment Agreement

A. Principal Purposes and Legal Consequences

The long-form investment agreement has four principal business objectives:

1. Most importantly, it sets forth the detailed substantive terms of the investment.
2. It serves as the basic disclosure document in which the relevant historical, business, financial, and legal data relating to the enterprise are set forth or referenced.
3. It presents, through the use of conditions precedent to closing, a "stop-action" photograph or image of the issuer that must exist at the time of closing. The level of detail of this photograph will vary depending upon the round of financing involved in the transaction and the simplicity or complexity of the company's operations.
4. It defines the several business parameters within which the enterprise must operate in the future. The several commandments to management range from relatively simple "thou shall nots" to complex "thou shalts."

The legal effect of the investment agreement is similar to that of many commercial contracts. The most common consequence of a breach of agreement in the capital investment context is the ability of the investor to refuse to close the transaction because of the company's failure to satisfy a condition precedent or the existence of a significant misrepresentation by the company. Once the closing has occurred, remedies in the nature of recision are rare. Moreover, while claims for damages do arise, they are uncommon in the high-risk venture area. Common remedies available for breach of covenant are specific performance and injunctive relief. As a practical matter, however, remedies that are self-executing, such as ratchet-down provisions in an antidilution formula or extraordinary voting rights granted to a class of preferred stock, are more formidable than those remedies that frequently amount to waving a stick in the air, such as provisions triggering accelerated repayment of debt securities, which investors may refrain from enforcing because to do so could impair the company's value as a going concern.

B. Description of the Transaction

The investment agreement memorializes the terms of the transaction. Consequently, the agreement should include a description of the securities being purchased, the purchase price, and a requirement that the securities be properly authorized.

If the investor acquires a note (whether or not convertible) or a stock purchase warrant, the form of the security should be attached as an exhibit to the investment agreement. If the investor acquires a class of stock other than conventional common stock, the terms of the class of stock as set forth in the corporate charter should be attached to the investment agreement as an exhibit.

If more than one investor participates in the financing, they may be listed or referenced in an exhibit to the agreement. In some cases, the company will execute separate but identical investment agreements with the other investors. Each investor's obligation to purchase may be conditioned on identical investment agreements having been executed simultaneously with every other investor, such agreements remaining unamended and in full force on the closing date, and the company having raised a specified minimum number of dollars in the offering.

In some transactions, the entire investment proceeds will not be made available to the company at a single closing. Investors may purchase securities in two or more installments over fixed periods of time, in which event the major condition precedent to closing each successive installment is the absence of any material adverse changes affecting the company since the initial closing. In a "staged" investment, the investors' obligation to purchase additional securities at subsequent closings is conditioned upon the company's attainment of certain financial or operational goals, such as reaching specified revenue levels or completing development work on a new product, as well as the absence of adverse changes. A staged investment serves as an incentive to management to proceed diligently with the development of its product as outlined in its business plan and enables the venture capitalist to target his investment with a maximum impact on the development of the business.

C. Representations and Warranties of the Company

It is a rare issuer company that is totally "clean," that is, a company which has no stated exceptions to the several business, financial, and legal topics addressed by the representation and warranty section of the investment agreement. Only a new start-up company with neither employees nor sales is likely to fall into this category. Since the venture capitalist has already conducted a thorough factual review of the company's business prior to issuing his term sheet or letter of intent, the representations and warranties are not intended to "screen" the company for suitability as an investment (although the disclosure of significant adverse information not previously known to the investor may scuttle the investment) but rather to provide full disclosure of the fine details of the company's operations which may be relevant in advising management with regard to the future conduct of the business.

The following list of specific representations and warranties are common in most venture capital investment agreements. Each category is prefaced by an affirmative declaration or affirmation of compliance, subject to stated exceptions which are normally appended as an exhibit.

1. *Organization and authority:* The company is properly organized, in good standing, and has legal authority to conduct its business.
2. *Corporate action:* All necessary actions under state corporate law, and under the company's corporate charter and bylaws, have been taken to authorize the transaction and issue the securities.
3. *Capitalization:* There is a description of the company's authorized capitalization and status of outstanding securities, including warrants, options and convertible securities. Any transfer restrictions, repurchase rights, or preemptive rights are also described.
4. *Governmental approvals:* All consents and approvals of governmental agencies necessary to complete the transaction and operate the business have been obtained. In particular, this covers compliance with state securities laws and labor and environmental regulations.
5. *Absence of litigation:* No litigation or other proceedings exist, or are threatened, which would adversely affect the company's business or the financing transaction.
6. *Employment of key personnel:* No restrictions exist relating to employment of key personnel or use of business information, particularly as a result of prior employment of such personnel by another enterprise.
7. *Compliance with other agreements:* No violations of the company's corporate charter, bylaws, or other valid agreements exist, or will exist as a result of the financing.
8. *Ownership of properties and assets:* The company possesses sufficient ownership rights in its business assets, particularly its patent, copyright, trademark, and other intellectual property rights, to conduct its business.
9. *Insurance:* The company holds valid insurance policies on the lives of certain of its key personnel and against risks normally insured against by businesses similar to the company.
10. *Taxes:* The company has paid all federal, state, and local taxes due and has filed all required tax returns.
11. *Environmental protection:* The company and its property are in compliance with all federal, state, and local environmental and health laws, including compliance with all

permit, license, and approval requirements and compliance with any laws, orders, or directives concerning cleanup of hazardous substances. Disclosure is made of potential environmental liability under various statutes.

12. *Financial information:* Audited and internal unaudited financial statements have been prepared in accordance with generally accepted accounting principles and fairly present the financial position and operating results of the company (statements as to specific categories of items, such as inventory valuation and status of accounts receivables, may be included). No adverse changes have occurred since the date of the most recent financial statements furnished. Provisions enacted in the tax reform act of 1986 limit a company's use of its net operating losses in certain circumstances when new investments are made in the company. A company that has net operating losses therefore may represent that such losses as set forth in current financial statements are available to offset future taxable income, and that the closing of the proposed transaction will not limit the company's use of such losses.
13. *Transactions with insiders:* Disclosure is made of any direct or indirect transactions between the company and its directors, officers, and stockholders.
14. *Third-party guaranties or investments:* Continuing financial involvements with third parties are absent.
15. *Compliance with federal securities laws:* That the transaction complies with federal and state securities laws, including the possibility that the transaction may be integrated with other securities sales, is certified.
16. *Registration rights:* Rights to cause the company to file any registration statement under the federal securities laws or any right to participate in any such registration statement are absent.
17. *Disclosure:* The business plan used to seek financing is generally accurate and complete as to historical information. There are appropriate disclosures of the assumption behind any forecasts. All material disclosures have been made to investors either in the business plan or in legal documents relating to the transaction.
18. *Brokerage:* Any finder's or broker's fees or commissions payable in connection with the transaction are disclosed.
19. *FIRPTA:* Investors who are not US taxpayers or who have partners who are not US taxpayers will want to assure themselves that their investment in the company will not be subject to US taxation under the Foreign Investment in Real Property Tax Act of 1980 (FIRPTA). They will require the company to represent that it is not a "United States real-property holding corporation," which is defined in FIRPTA (Internal Revenue Code, Section 987) to mean a company that holds US real estate worth at least 50 percent of the total value of its assets.
20. *ERISA:* All pension obligations of the company are disclosed, and the company represents that it is in compliance with the Employee Retirement Income Security Act of 1974 (ERISA).

D. Covenants and Undertakings of the Company

The covenants section of the investment agreement contains several affirmative and negative undertakings of the company relating to the future conduct of its affairs. Affirmative covenants are actions, positions, or results that the company promises to achieve or undertake. Negative covenants are actions, positions, or results that the company promises to avoid.

If, under the terms of the investment agreement, the board of directors is to be controlled by inside management, the covenants are frequently extensive. In an equity-oriented venture capital investment, however, where the investors will frequently control the board of directors, the covenants are often kept to a minimum. In such a situation, the affirmative covenants might merely provide that the investor will receive periodic financial information and will be represented on the board. The negative covenants might limit only the company's ability to amend its corporate charter or merge or sell its assets without the investor's consent. A venture capital firm with board control will generally rely upon this control to influence the development of a company and will not, as a rule, find it necessary to impose extensive contractual restrictions on the conduct of the business by insisting on strict affirmative and negative covenants.

Both affirmative and negative covenants may remain in effect as long as the investors hold any or a stated amount on percentage of the investment securities. If the investment agreement is properly negotiated from the company's side, however, most covenants will terminate upon the occurrence of certain events, such as completion of an initial public offering, conversion of convertible securities into equity, or mere passage of time.

Among the customary *affirmative* covenants that are found in venture capital investment agreements are the following:

1. *Payment of taxes and claims:* The company will pay all lawful taxes, assessments, and levies upon it or its income or property before they become in default. This covenant sometimes provides that all trade debt and principal and interest on debt securities acquired by the investor will be paid when due.
2. *Property and liability insurance:* The company will maintain insurance against hazards and risks and liability to persons and property to the extent customary for companies engaged in the same or similar businesses.
3. *Maintenance of corporate existence:* The company will maintain its corporate existence and all rights, licenses, patents, copyrights, trademarks, and the like, useful in its business, and will engage only in the type of business described in the business plan.
4. *Legal compliance:* The company will comply with all applicable laws and regulations in the conduct of its business.
5. *Access to premises:* The investor or the investor's representative will generally be permitted to inspect the company's facilities, books, and records. To the extent that confidentiality of corporate business information may be compromised by such rights of access, investors generally agree to confidentiality restrictions or to limiting access to lead or other major investors.
6. *Accounts and reports:* The company may be asked by the investor to agree to maintain a standard system of accounting in accordance with generally accepted accounting principles consistently applied, and to keep full and complete financial records.
7. *Repair and maintenance:* The company will keep all necessary equipment and property in good repair and condition, as required to permit the business to be properly conducted.
8. *Approval of budgets:* The investor will frequently require management to produce comprehensive annual budgets for approval by the investor or by the board of directors. Revisions of the budget during the year may also require advance approval.
9. *Protection of proprietary rights:* The company will agree to take all necessary steps to protect proprietary developments made in the future, including causing all key employees to sign confidentiality and proprietary rights and agreements.
10. *Compliance with key agreements:* The company will enforce its rights under key agreements, such as the stockholders agreement, and will cause future stockholders to become bound by the agreement.
11. *Life insurance:* The investor will often require the company to maintain insurance on the lives of key officers and employees. The face amount in some cases may be as much as the purchase price of the securities, and the insurance proceeds are often payable directly to the investor, particularly if the investor holds debt securities. Providing for

payment of insurance proceeds directly to the investor may cause the premium payments to be treated for tax purposes as payments of constructive dividends or additional interest to the investor.

12. *Stockholder meetings:* The investors may require that the by-laws of the company provide that the investors can call stockholders' and directors' meetings.
13. *Rule 144A information:* The company will agree, as long as it is privately held, to provide to potential third-party purchasers of the shares held by the investors upon request the information required to permit the investors to sell their shares to such a third party pursuant to the exemption from registration under the Securities Act provided by Rule 144A.
14. *Environmental matters:* The company will covenant to materially comply with any and all environmental laws which apply to it, its properties, and all activities thereon, including governmental directives to clean up hazardous contamination. The company will also agree to keep the investors informed regarding its discharge and handling of hazardous materials and any communications from any governmental entity relating thereto.
15. *Board of directors:* Venture capital firms will generally seek assurances that they will be represented on the company's board of directors. At times, the venture capitalist will also seek representation on or control of the audit, compensation, or other committees of the board of directors. The right to be represented on the board will ordinarily be backed up by voting agreements with the principal stockholders. If the investor is not to be represented on the board, the company may be required to notify the investor of the time and place of board meetings, to permit the investor or the investor's representative to attend such meetings and to deliver to the investor any written materials disseminated to directors. In March 1987, the Department of Labor's final regulations defining "plan assets" for purposes of the Employee Retirement Income Security Act of 1974 (ERISA) became effective. These regulations have resulted in an increased concern on behalf of certain venture capital funds whose investors are subject to ERISA (such as private pension funds) to exercise direct control (versus control through the lead investor of the venture capital syndicate) over portfolio investments. Consequently, affirmative covenants with regard to representation on a portfolio company's board of directors, the right to attend and receive information in connection with board meetings, the right to consult with management regarding the affairs of the company (even if no board representation is sought), and informational rights with respect to financial and operating data generally have been emphasized to a greater degree in venture capital agreements. Frequency of board meetings and financial arrangements for directors may also be covered.
16. *Financial and operating statements:* The company will invariably agree to provide the investor with detailed financial and operating information. The information to be provided may include annual, quarterly, and sometimes monthly reports of sales, production, shipments, profits, cash balances, receivables, payables, and backlog; all statements filed with the Securities and Exchange Commission or other agencies; notification of significant lawsuits or other legal proceedings; and any other information that the investor may need for the investor's own voluntary or involuntary filing requirements. Particularly where an investor is acquiring debt securities or preferred stock containing extensive financial and other covenants, financial statements are required to be accompanied by a certificate from the company's chief executive or financial officer and, in the case of audited financial statements, its auditors, to the effect that the company is in compliance with all provisions of the investment agreement. The right to receive financial information is often terminated when the company goes public in order to avoid dissemination of "inside" information. Although

companies generally concede the legitimate interests of investors to receive business information, negotiation over the scope and form of this information may be considerable in view of the operational burden and potential liabilities it can impose upon management.

17. *Current ratio, working capital, or net worth:* These covenants normally are included only in debt financings and are agreements to maintain the current ratio, working capital, or net worth, either at a minimum amount or as specified for various time periods. They may be keyed to projections made by the company; accordingly, care should be taken by the company in preparing the business plan to project financial results and conditions which management is comfortable in undertaking to attain on a contractual basis.
18. *Use of proceeds:* Often the company will agree to apply the proceeds received from the financing to a specified use. The investor will sometimes require that the proceeds be applied within a narrow area of the business in connection with a specific financing plan or may simply require that the funds be used for working capital.

In contrast to affirmative covenants, which generally exhort the company to undertake actions which it would ordinarily choose to take in the normal course, the negative covenants contained in the investment agreement serve to limit the company from actions it otherwise might be inclined to take, unless the investors have consented in advance. Typically these negative covenants relate to matters which would affect the fundamental nature of the business in which the investment has been made (e.g., mergers and acquisitions) or would alter the balance of control between the investors and entrepreneurs reached in the investment agreement (e.g., controls on dilution).

Since the negative covenants limit the scope of managerial flexibility, they are often the subject of sharp negotiation. This is all the more so because the investor's remedy upon material breach of a negative covenant often is quite dramatic—such a breach by the company may result in the immediate acceleration of indebtedness in the case of debt securities and may sometimes trigger recision rights in the case of equity securities. As suggested above, there is a trade-off between the degree of investor control of the voting power and board of directors and the strictness of the negative covenants imposed on the company. Many typical *negative* covenants are described below:

1. *Mergers, consolidations, and sale or purchase of assets:* Mergers, consolidations, acquisitions, and the like are generally prohibited without the investor's advance approval. Liquidation and dissolution of the company and the sale, lease, pledge, or other disposition of substantial assets without consent may also be barred. Restrictions may also be placed on the company's purchase of capital assets.
2. *Dealings with related parties:* The company will covenant that no transactions between the company and any officers, directors, or stockholders of the company shall be effected unless on an arm's-length basis and on terms no less favorable to the company than could be obtained from nonrelated persons. Approval of all transactions with affiliates by either the board or the investors may be required.
3. *Change in business:* The company will not change the nature of its business as described in its business plan.
4. *Charter amendments:* The investor may prohibit the company from amending its corporate charter or bylaws without the consent of the investor. More narrowly drawn covenants might prohibit only certain specified actions (such as a change in the capital structure) without the investor's consent.
5. *Distributions and redemptions:* The company typically agrees not to make any dividend distributions to stockholders. Dividends may be prohibited until a given date or may be limited to a fixed percentage of profits above a set amount. In addition, the company

may covenant not to repurchase or redeem any of its securities except in accordance with the terms of the securities purchased by the investor (e.g., redeemable preferred stock), employee plans (e.g., forfeiture of stock upon termination of employment), or agreements with stockholders (e.g., right of first refusal).

6. *Issuance of stock or convertible securities:* The investor may prohibit the company from issuing any securities that would result in dilution of the investor's position. This may include restrictions on the issuance of securities of the type purchased by the investor, and any securities convertible into such securities, at a price less than that paid by the investor. Alternatively, an "anti-dilution" formula may be employed so that such an issuance will automatically trigger an improved conversion rate for the securities purchased by the investor. Frequently these covenants are included in the terms of the securities themselves.
7. *Liens and encumbrances:* The investment agreement (generally for debt-oriented securities, including redeemable preferred stock) may provide for restrictions on liens, pledges, and other encumbrances of corporate assets, with exceptions for such liabilities as real estate mortgages. Separate restrictions can be placed on leases of real property or equipment.
8. *Indebtedness:* The company may agree to restrictions on future indebtedness, with exceptions for institutional senior borrowings, indebtedness on personal-property-purchase money obligations, and trade indebtedness, up to certain limits in the ordinary course of business. Again, this provision is most typical of investments in debt-oriented securities.
9. *Investments:* Restrictions against investing in other companies may be imposed by the investor. Exceptions are made for investments in wholly owned subsidiaries.
10. *Employee compensation:* The company may agree to limit employment and other personal service contracts of management or key personnel to a maximum term and a maximum amount of annual compensation. In addition, the investment agreement may prohibit the acceleration or termination of vesting schedules applicable to transfers of stock or stock options held by officers, directors, and employees.
11. *Financial covenants:* Negative financial covenants are frequently imposed upon a company in a debt-oriented investment, such as prohibiting key ratios or financial conditions from exceeding certain limits or limiting the company from incurring losses in excess of a certain amount. Semantics often determine whether a financial covenant is affirmative or negative in nature. Clear definition of financial and accounting terms is critical. Short of resulting in a default on securities, failure to comply with financial covenants may trigger adjustments in conversion ratios of securities or give rise to preferential voting or other rights for the investor. If such an adjustment in conversion ratio gives the investor an increased interest in the company's earnings or assets, however, the transaction may be treated under Section 305 of the Internal Revenue Code as payment of a taxable stock dividend to the investor. Hence, the investor must balance potential future tax liability against the additional security provided by such arrangements.
12. *FIRPTA:* Foreign investors may require the company to refrain from taking action which would cause the company to become a "United States real property holding company" and thus subject the investment to US taxation under FIRPTA. Alternatively, they may require notice prior to the company taking such action.

In addition to the numerous affirmative and negative covenants described above, the venture capital investment agreement will customarily contain a number of more complex undertakings by the company, which are generally set apart in the agreement. Two of the more typical of these covenants pertain to registration rights and rights to participate in future financings. Another such provision, indemnification of the investors for breach of the investment agreement, is also discussed briefly below:

1. *Registration rights:* Registration of the venture capital investor's securities for public sale under the Securities Act of 1933 and state securities laws represents the most advantageous vehicle for a venture capital investor to achieve liquidity and realize a return on his investment. The potential of an enterprise to achieve a size conducive to a public offering is an imperative of most venture capital investments. Accordingly, the right of the investor to participate in the public market for the company's securities is an area in which the venture capitalist will concede few limitations on the investor's flexibility of action. Registration rights are intricately bound up in the complexities of federal and state securities regulation and must be thoroughly understood by the investor and his or her counsel. The key elements of a registration rights provision in a venture capital investment agreement generally include the following:
   a. *Securities available for registration:* Registrable securities will invariably be limited to common stock, including shares issuable on conversion of other securities. After-acquired common stock may also be included. If the investor is participating in a second- or third-round financing, he or she must consider the extent to which his or her registration rights will be coordinated or "pooled" with registration rights granted to investors in previous financings. Investors in early rounds will wish to prevent the grant of registration right to future investors without their consent.
   b. *"Piggyback" registration rights:* Investors will have the right to include shares in any registration which the company undertakes either for its own benefit or for the account of other holders of securities. Exceptions are generally made for registrations involving employee stock plans or acquisitions. Piggyback registrations will frequently be unlimited in number on the theory that no significant burden is imposed on the company by requiring it to include additional shares in a registration which it is otherwise undertaking. Except for the company's initial public offering, investors may be guaranteed a minimum participation in piggyback registrations.
   c. *Demand registration rights:* Investors frequently obtain the right to require an issuer to register their shares upon demand and without regard to the registration of shares for the account of any other person. Demand rights assure the investor access to the public market. Theoretically, unrestricted demand registration rights enable an investor to force a company to go public. As a practical matter, however, demand rights are rarely, if ever, used to this end, although their presence may influence the decision of a company to go public. Demand rights often do not apply until after the company's initial public offering and usually do not become effective until some stated period after the investment. Because of the expense involved, demand rights may be limited in number unless registration is available on a short-form registration statement such as Form S–3. In addition, investors may agree that no demand for registration will be effective unless holders of a minimum specified percentage of registrable securities elect to participate, in order to avoid unduly small registrations.
   d. *Marketing rights:* Piggyback registration rights generally contain provisions enabling the underwriters managing the public offering to cut back the number of shares to be registered by selling security holders on a pro rata basis if, in the underwriters' opinion, such a cutback is necessary or desirable to market the public issue effectively. If security holders other than the venture capital investors also hold registration rights, the relative marketing priorities of the various groups, including management, in the event of a cutback must be addressed.
   e. *Indemnification:* Each party will agree to indemnify the other against liabilities for which it is responsible arising out of a registration. Although the extensive

indemnification provisions of an underwriting agreement will frequently supersede the terms of the investment agreement, the investment agreement is nevertheless important because underwriters will typically look to the company and any major selling shareholders for indemnification on a joint and several basis and will leave those parties to their own devices to allocate any liabilities among themselves.

f. *Procedural covenants:* Many registration rights provisions contain the company's pledge to undertake expeditiously certain procedural acts involved in a registration, such as participating in the preparation of a registration statement, qualifying the securities under state "blue sky" laws, and providing the investors with legal opinions and accountants' comfort letters.

g. *Availability of Rule 144:* The company will agree that once it has gone public, it will file all reports and take all other action necessary to enable the investors to sell shares in the public market under the exemption from registration contained in Rule 144 under the Securities Act of 1933, those shares not previously included in a registration statement pursuant to the investors' exercise of registration rights.

h. *Expenses of registration:* Because of the cost involved in a registration of securities, investors will typically require the company to agree at the time of the initial investment to bear the expenses of registration, exclusive of underwriters' discounts or commissions applicable to the investors' included shares.

2. *Rights to future financings:* Venture capitalists often insist upon a right to participate in future financings by the company. On the upside, this offers the investor an opportunity to maintain or increase his interest in the success of the enterprise; on the downside, the investor receives some protection against dilution or loss of the initial investment if financing must be sought under distress situations. The right to participate may include the following:

   a. *Rights of first refusal* to assume the entire financing (each investor on a pro rata basis with other members of the investor group).

   b. *Preemptive rights* to participate in the financing to the extent necessary to ensure that the investor's percentage ownership of the company's securities or value will be the same after the financing as before.

   c. *Rights of prior negotiation* to discuss and negotiate financing opportunities with the company prior to the company's offers of such opportunities to others.

First refusal and preemptive rights typically contain oversubscription rights to permit an investor to absorb any portion of the securities not subscribed for by another investor or security holder.

3. *Indemnification for breach of agreement:* Particularly in the case of start-ups, venture capital investors may require founders and/or top management to share personal responsibility for the representations and warranties made by the company in the investment agreement and to indemnify the investors for any breaches thereof. From the investors' point of view, imposing the specter of personal liability on the insiders can be an effective means of assuring complete and accurate disclosure of all material business information. Indemnification by insiders also circumvents the anomaly of investors seeking indemnification from the company funded by the capital which they have invested in the business. On the other hand, personal liability for disclosure matters which may be outside the reasonable knowledge of the entrepreneur may be an unfair burden to place on him or her. For this reason, in cases where personal responsibility for representations and warranties is desired, care should be taken to focus that responsibility in areas of special knowledge of the entrepreneur (ownership of proprietary rights, compliance with prior employment arrangements, etc.) and to distinguish between the risks assumed by the company and those assumed by the

individual (e.g., unqualified representations versus "best knowledge" representations). Termination of indemnification obligations often occurs after a stated period of time (usually not exceeding two years), or after the issuance of audited financial statements covering a one- or two-year period.

E. Conditions to Closing

The use in the investment agreement of "conditions precedent to closing" or, more appropriately, provisions requiring the company to satisfy specific conditions at or prior to the closing is a device with two principal functions. The most obvious is to guarantee that certain fundamentals relating to the securities and the particular transaction are in place, with receipt of favorable legal opinions being a classic example. In addition, conditions are used as negotiating tools to change or affect the financial or business operations of the company. For example, a common closing condition may involve the contemporaneous execution of a bank loan agreement satisfactory to the investor or the consummation of a significant commercial transaction with a customer.

Many venture financings contemplate a simultaneous signing of the investment agreement and closing. Consequently, there is no technical need for a set of conditions designed to cover the time period between execution of the agreement and a subsequent closing. Notwithstanding a simultaneous signing and closing, the use of express conditions serves to expedite the negotiations and to assist in completion of the closing process by serving as a checklist of actions to be taken in connection with the implementation of the transaction.

Closing conditions commonly seen in the capital formation process include opinion of counsel for the company; opinion of counsel for the investor; execution of the several ancillary agreements, including employment, noncompetition, and stock restriction agreements; elections and resignations of directors; and execution of compliance certificates by senior management. Descriptions of certain of these ancillary agreements and documents are included in Section V below.

Section IV. Terms of Investment Securities

A. General Considerations and Descriptions

Selection of the appropriate investment security for a specific transaction will depend upon the relative importance to the venture capitalist and the issuer of a number of factors, including the level of risk of the venture, investment objectives of the investors, capital requirements of the company, the relative interests and contributions of other security holders, the degree to which management control by the investors is desirable, liquidity of the securities, and so on. Among the securities which are commonly used in a venture capital financing are:

- Common stock.
- Convertible preferred stock.
- Convertible debt.
- Nonconvertible preferred stock or debt coupled with common stock or common stock purchase warrants.

Generally, the venture capitalists will prefer to invest in a senior security which is convertible into, or carries rights to purchase, common equity. A convertible senior security affords the investor downside protection, in terms of the opportunity to recover the investment on a priority basis through redemption, repayment, or liquidation preferences, with the upside potential of a liquid equity security traded at significantly appreciated values in the public market. Discussion of the relative merits and disadvantages of the various types of investment securities is beyond the scope of this article. Described in the following sections, however, are certain of the principal provisions of typical preferred stock and debt securities.

B. Principal Terms of Preferred Stock

Preferred stock is the investment security most frequently involved in venture capital financings because of the flexibility it offers the company and the investor in tailoring the critical issues of the investment—principally management control and recovery/return on investment. Typically the preferred stock utilized in a venture transaction is convertible into common stock and contains redemption provisions designed to enable the investor to recoup the investment if the enterprise fails to achieve its anticipated success. Convertible preferred stock provisions should address the following major issues:

1. *Dividends:* "Plain vanilla" convertible preferred stock does not generally carry mandatory dividend rights. Preferred will, however, participate with common to the extent dividends are declared. If dividends are desired, they may be on a cumulative or noncumulative basis. Cash flow considerations will affect the ability of a start-up to pay dividends.
2. *Liquidation:* Holders of preferred stock will have a priority claim to assets of the corporation over the common stockholders in a liquidation. The liquidation preference will typically equal the original purchase price of the security plus accrued dividends. Participating preferred may also share pari passu with common stock after the liquidation preference has been distributed. Convertible preferred stock provisions usually permit the investors to elect liquidation treatment in the event of a merger or acquisition.
3. *Voting rights:* Convertible preferred stock votes with the common stock on all matters and is entitled to one vote for each share of common into which the preferred may be converted. In addition, the holders of convertible preferred stock, voting separately as a class, may have the right to veto certain corporate transactions affecting the convertible preferred stock (such as the issuance of senior securities, mergers, acquisitions, and amendment of stock terms). Other preferential voting rights may include:
   a. Class vote for election of directors.
   b. Extraordinary voting rights to elect a majority of the board of directors upon a breach of the terms of the convertible preferred stock, such as a failure to pay dividends or make mandatory redemptions or default in the performance of financial or other covenants which may be contained in the convertible preferred stock provisions or underlying investment agreement.
4. *Conversion:* Holders of convertible preferred stock may convert their shares into common stock at their discretion (except as limited by automatic conversion obligations). Conversion provisions should address the following matters:
   a. Automatic conversion upon the occurrence of certain events, principally the completion of a public offering or the attainment of specified financial goals.
   b. Mechanics of conversion.
   c. Conversion ratio, usually expressed by a formula based upon original purchase price, which initially yields a one-for-one conversion factor.
   d. Adjustment of conversion ratio to take into account (1) stock splits, stock dividends, consolidations, and the like, and (2) "dilutive" common stock issuances, that is, sales of common stock at prices lower than those paid by the investors.
   e. Certification of adjusted conversion ratios by independent accountants.

The nature of the antidilution adjustments can have a dramatic effect on the number of common shares issuable upon conversion. "Rachet-down" antidilution provisions apply the lowest sale price for any shares of common stock (or equivalents) as the adjusted conversion value.

"Formula" or "weighted-average" antidilution provisions adjust the conversion value by application of a weighted-average formula based upon both sale price and number of common shares sold. Antidilution provisions generally carve out a predetermined pool of shares which may be issued to employees without triggering an adjustment of the conversion ratio.

5. *Redemption:* Redemption offers investors a means of recovering their initial investment and the issuer an opportunity to eliminate the preferential rights held by the holders of the senior security. Topics to be addressed include:
   a. Optional or mandatory redemption.
   b. Stepped-up redemption price or redemption premium designed to provide investors a certain appreciated return on the investment (NB: "unreasonable redemption premium" issue under IRC Section 305).
   c. Desirability of a sinking fund.
   d. Redemption call by the company.

It should be noted that the prospect of mandatory redemption or redemption upon call by the issuer may force the holders of convertible preferred stock to exercise their conversion privilege lest they lose the upside potential of the investment.

C. Principal Terms of Debt Securities

The purchase of debt securities will enable the venture capitalist to receive a current return on his or her investment through receipt of interest payments. In the case of a convertible debt instrument, the interest rate will be below market rates because of the equity feature coupled with it. Although the terms of convertible debt may be structured to resemble preferred stock in many aspects, significant differences between the two securities do exist. First, debt securities do not carry the right to vote for the election of directors or on other stockholder matters. Accordingly, the investor's ability to influence management of the company directly is diminished and the investor must resort to voting agreements and proxies in order to participate in the election of directors or, alternatively, rely on indirect means of influence such as the affirmative and negative convenants contained in the investment agreement. It should further be noted that the investor's status as a creditor of the company in any bankruptcy proceedings may be affected by principles of "equitable subordination" to the extent that such equitylike control is exercised. Second, the investor's right to receive interest under a debt instrument is more secure than the right to receive dividends on a preferred stock, inasmuch as payment of dividends may be restricted by state corporate laws relating to legally available funds and by the requirement that dividends must be declared by the board of directors. Finally, although a debt security may rank prior to preferred stock in terms of a claim on corporate assets in liquidation, this advantage is at the cost of creating a weaker balance sheet, which may have adverse effects in terms of trade and commercial bank credit, even where subordination provisions are present.

The following principal issues are generally addressed in the structuring of a venture capital investment in debt securities:

1. *Interest rate:* Interest will be at a fixed rate, below market if debt is convertible or coupled with common stock purchase warrants. Because of cash flow considerations of the issuer, interest payments may be deferred for a period of time.
2. *Repayment:* Repayment of principal is often scheduled in quarterly, semiannual, or annual installments commencing four to six years into the term, or in a single payment at maturity.

3. *Optional prepayment:* The company may elect to prepay the debt, often at a premium. Since prepayment will have the effect of extinguishing any conversion rights, the right to prepay will be deferred generally to such time as initial principal installments fall due. Issuance of stock purchase warrants in lieu of conversion will avoid this problem.
4. *Conversion:* The debt instrument may be converted into common stock at a fixed price at any time. Conversion terms, including antidilution provision, will be similar to those of convertible preferred stock.
5. *Subordination:* Debt is generally subordinated to bank and other institutional borrowings and may thus be viewed as equity by lenders. Complex subordination provisions are often required to regulate the relationships between senior lenders and subordinated noteholders in the event of defaults, insolvency, and the like.
6. *Affirmative and negative covenants:* Debt instruments are tied into extensive affirmative and negative undertakings by the company, which are usually contained in the purchase agreement. In addition to standard covenants used in a venture capital financing, these may include lengthy financial covenants of the variety typical in a commercial lending transaction.
7. *Defaults:* Defaults include material breaches of representations and warranties, breaches of covenants which are not remedied within a cure period, nonpayment of principal and interest on debt instrument, acceleration (cross-default) of senior debt, insolvency, and events of bankruptcy.
8. *Security:* Generally a debt instrument will be issued to a venture capitalist on an unsecured basis, although collateral is sometimes given in asset-based transactions such as leveraged buyouts. Another common exception to the general rule is an SBIC financing, in which adequate collateral and personal guarantees are often required.

Section V. Ancillary Agreements and Documents

A. Stockholders Agreement

The stockholders agreement is designed to control the transfer and voting of the equity securities of the company so that stable ownership and management of the enterprise may be maintained for the term of the investment. This is accomplished through restrictions on the sale of stock by insiders, which have the effect of limiting the stockholder group to persons who are known quantities to the investors, and through voting agreements, which assure that the balanced composition of the board of directors will be perpetuated. The principal provisions contained in a typical stockholders agreement to achieve these results are:

1. *Right of first refusal:* Key management stockholders will grant the company and/or the investors the right to purchase their shares on the same terms as those contained in a bona fide offer from a third party. Investors participate in the right of first refusal on a pro rata basis and have oversubscription rights to acquire any offered shares which are not picked up by another investor. Rights of first refusal are generally *not* extended to the company or insiders by the investors since the existence of such terms would tend to chill any sale of an entire block of shares by the investors to a third party. Transfers of shares by way of gifts to members of an insider's family or as collateral in a bona fide loan transaction are permitted, provided the transferee or pledgee also agrees to be bound by the agreement.
2. *Buyout provisions:* Some stockholder agreements provide that the company and/or the investors will have an option to purchase the shares of any insider at fair market value upon the occurrence of certain contingencies, such as death, personal bankruptcy, or attachment of shares by legal process. Detailed procedures, usually involving one or

more appraisals by disinterested persons, are provided to assure a fair valuation of the stock.

3. *Right to participate in insider sales:* Although philosophically at odds with a right of first refusal, a stockholder agreement may provide that the investors have a right to participate alongside management insiders in any sale to third parties. Although rarely exercised, this right limits the ability of management to bail out of the company leaving the investors at risk to recover their investment. Often this right of cosale is triggered only by a sale which would have the effect of transferring actual or effective voting control to a third party.
4. *Voting requirements:* All parties will generally agree to vote all shares for the election of directors in favor of specified nominees of the respective groups.

Restrictions under applicable state law need to be examined to determine the legality of stockholder agreements in any given jurisdiction, as well as to verify compliance with state procedural and substantive requirements. Unless otherwise limited by state law (10 years in Massachusetts), stockholder agreements will generally terminate upon the earlier of a public offering by the company or the expiration of a stated period of time.

B. Employer Stock Purchase Agreement

Venture capital investors typically insist that the appropriate equity incentives be implemented to attract, retain, and motivate key employees. Both the entrepreneurs and investors are willing to suffer dilution of their respective equity interests (anywhere in a range from 5 percent to 15 percent of fully diluted equity) to achieve this end. The investment agreement will specify a pool of shares to be set aside for employee purchases and exempt the issuance of those shares from the various negative covenants, antidilution provisions, and preemptive rights contained in the investment agreement and the terms of the investment securities. Establishment of appropriate employee stock plans is frequently a condition of closing of the investment. Incentive objections and tax considerations play a significant role in determining the shape of an employee equity program. Among the typical employee equity incentives are the following:

1. *Stock purchase plans*, providing for an outright sale to key employees, often at a bargain price, with the company's retaining an option to repurchase the shares on a lapsing basis (generally over four or five years) if the employee terminates employment for any reason.
2. *Incentive stock options*, enabling the employee to purchase shares with advantageous tax consequences at the fair market value on the date the option was granted.
3. *Nonqualified stock options*, which may be granted in amounts which exceed the aggregate dollar limitations for incentive stock options under the Internal Revenue Code and which may have exercise prices less than fair market value and other terms not available under incentive stock options.
4. *"Junior" common stock*, which is an equity security bearing only a percentage of the voting, dividend, liquidation, and other rights of a straight common stock and which is automatically converted into common stock upon the attainment of certain specified objectives, such as revenue and profit goals. Although "junior" common stock was a popular incentive vehicle through the end of 1983, its continued use and attractiveness as a method of compensating management have been called into question by recent actions taken by the Securities and Exchange Commission and proposed to be taken by the Financial Accounting Standards Board (FASB).

In all circumstances (other than incentive stock options) consideration must be given to the application of Section 83 of the Internal Revenue Code to issuances of stock to employees. Section 83 provides that an employee is required to recognize income in respect of property (including corporate securities) transferred in connection with the performance of services in an amount equal to the difference between the fair value of the property and the amount paid therefor. In the case of property subject to restrictions which lapse over time (such as forfeiture restrictions or repurchase options), the income is recognized at the time the restrictions lapse. Thus, an employee who acquires stock at a low purchase price in the early years of an enterprise and whose rights to those shares "vest" as forfeiture restrictions lapse over a period of years will recognize income based on the appreciated value of those shares as each installment lapses. Section 83(b) of the Code ameliorates the harsh effect of this provision by permitting a taxpayer to elect to include the value of the transferred property in income in the year of receipt by filing a special election.

In a recent decision (*Alves et al.* v. *Commissioner*, 79 TC 864, CCH Tax Court Reports Dec. 39, 501, 1982), the Tax Court applied Section 83 to a founding stockholder of a new company who acquired shares subject to a repurchase option granted to the company and exercisable upon his termination of employment prior to the end of a specified period. As a result of this decision, founding stockholders should consider taking the precaution of filing Section 83(b) elections when shares are initially acquired in order to prevent assessment of significant tax liabilities when those shares vest at appreciated values in later years.

C. Employee Confidentiality and Proprietary Rights Agreement

Protection and preservation of the "intellectual capital" of an enterprise are of paramount importance to the venture capital investor, especially where the portfolio company is engaged in product development activities on the leading edge of technologies. To secure the company's claim to its valuable proprietary and business rights, investors are increasingly requiring that founders and other key employees enter into confidential nondisclosure and invention agreements with the company. These agreements typically provide that the employee (1) will not disclose company trade secrets or rights to third parties or use such rights for any purpose, in each case other than in connection with the company's business; and (2) will disclose and convey to the company all inventions developed by the employee during the course of employment. Such agreements often contain acknowledgement that the individual is not bound by any obligations to a former employer which would prevent or restrict his or her employment with the company and his or her performance of services for the company does not involve the violation of the proprietary rights of any former employer. Founding stockholders may also agree to noncompetition covenants.

D. Legal Opinion

The favorable legal opinion of company counsel generally covers the legality of the securities, compliance with state and federal securities laws, and related matters. If the company is involved in litigation, company counsel may be requested to express a position. Likewise, if patents are critical to the company's business, a favorable opinion of patent counsel may also be required. A common error is to confuse the opinion of legal counsel with due diligence. Counsel is not a surety for business or legal uncertainties; the opinion is not a substitute for factual investigation.

APPENDIX IV—SAMPLE TERMS SHEET

BLACK BOX TECHNOLOGY, INC.

Summary of Principal Terms

Amount: $ ____________________

Security: ____ shares of convertible preferred stock ("preferred") at a price of $ ____ per share ("original purchase price")

Rights, Preferences, Privileges, and Restrictions of Preferred Stock

1. *Dividend provisions:* The preferred stock shall be entitled to dividends at the same rate as the common stock ("common") (based on the number of shares of common into which the preferred is convertible on the date the dividend is declared).
2. *Liquidation preference:* In the event of any liquidation of the company, the preferred will be entitled to receive in preference to the common an amount equal to the original purchase price.
3. *Redemption:* The company will redeem the preferred in three equal annual installments commencing six (6) years from the date of purchase by paying in cash a total amount equal to the original purchase price.
4. *Conversion:* The preferred will be convertible at any time, at the option of the holder, into shares of common stock of the company at an initial conversion price equal to the original purchase price. Initially, each share of preferred is convertible into one share of common stock. The conversion price will be subject to adjustment as provided in paragraph 6 below.
5. *Automatic conversion:* The preferred will be automatically converted into common, at the then applicable conversion price, in the event of an underwritten public offering of shares of common at a price per share that is not less than five times the original purchase price in an offering resulting in gross proceeds to the company of not less than $10 million.
6. *Antidilution provisions:* The conversion price of the preferred stock will be subject to adjustment to prevent dilution in the event that the company issues additional shares (other than the reserved employee shares described under "Reserved Employee Shares," below) at a purchase price less than the applicable conversion price. The conversion price will be subject to adjustment on a weighted basis which takes into account issuances of additional shares at prices below the applicable conversion price.
7. *Voting rights:* Except with respect to election of directors, the holder of a share of preferred will have the right to that number of votes equal to the number of shares of common issuable upon conversion of the preferred at the time the record for the vote is taken. Election of directors will be as described under "Board Representation," below.
8. *Protective provisions:* Consent of the holders of at least two-thirds of the preferred will be required for any sale by the company of a substantial portion of its assets, any merger of the company with another entity, each amendment of the company's articles of incorporation, and for any action which (*a*) alters or changes the rights, preferences, or privileges of the preferred materially and adversely; (*b*) increases the authorized number of shares of preferred stock; or (*c*) creates any new class of shares having preference over or being on a parity with the preferred.

Information Rights

The company will timely furnish the investors with annual, quarterly and monthly financial statements. Representatives of the investors will have the right to inspect the books and records of the company.

Registration Rights

1. *Demand rights:* If investors holding at least 50 percent of the preferred (or common issued upon conversion of the preferred) request that the company file a registration statement covering at least 20 percent of the common issuable upon conversion of the preferred, the company will use its best efforts to cause such shares to be registered. The company will not be obligated to effect more than two registrations (other than on Form S–3) under these demand right provisions.
2. *Registrations on Form S–3:* Holders of 10 percent or more of the preferred (or common issued upon conversion of the preferred) will have the right to require the company to

file an unlimited number of registration statements on Form S–3 (but no more than two per year).

3. *"Piggyback" registration:* The investors will be entitled to piggyback registration rights on all registrations of the company.
4. *Registration expenses:* All registration expenses (exclusive of underwriting discounts and commissions or special counsel fees of a selling shareholder) shall be borne by the company.

Board Representation

The board will consist of ____ members. The holders of the preferred will have the right to designate ____ directors, the holders of the common (exclusive of the investors) will have the right to designate ____ directors, and the remaining ____ directors will be unaffiliated persons elected by the common and the preferred voting as a single class.

Key Individual Insurance

As determined by the board of directors.

Preemptive Right to Purchase New Securities

If the company proposes to offer additional shares (other than reserved employee shares or shares issued in the acquisition of another company), the company will first offer all such shares to the investors on a pro rata basis. This preemptive right will terminate upon an underwritten public offering of shares of the company.

Stock Restriction and Stockholders Agreements

All present holders of common stock of the company who are employees of, or consultants to, the company will execute a stock restriction agreement with the company pursuant to which the company will have an option to buy back at cost a portion of the shares of common stock held by such person in the event that such shareholder's employment with the company is terminated prior to the expiration of 48 months from the date of employment; 25 percent of the shares will be released each year from the repurchase option based upon continued employment by the company. In addition, the company and the investors will have a right of first refusal with respect to any employee's shares proposed to be resold or, alternatively, the right to participate in the sale of any such shares to a third party, which rights will terminate upon a public offering.

Reserved Employee Shares

The company may reserve up to ____ shares of common stock for issuance to employees of the company (the "reserved employee shares"). The reserved employee shares will be issued from time to time under such arrangements, contracts, or plans as are recommended by management and approved by the Board.

Noncompetition, Proprietary Information, and Inventions Agreement

Each officer and key employee of the company designated by the investors will enter into a noncompetition, proprietary information, and inventions agreement in a form reasonably acceptable to the investors.

The Purchase Agreement

The purchase of the preferred will be made pursuant to a stock purchase agreement drafted by counsel to the investors and reasonably acceptable to the company and the investors, which agreement shall contain, among other things, appropriate representations and warranties of the company, covenants of the company reflecting the provisions set forth herein, and appropriate conditions of closing.

Expenses

The company will bear the legal fees and other out-of-pocket expenses of the investors with respect to the transaction.

APPENDIX V—OUTLINE OF AN INVESTMENT AGREEMENT

What follows is a detailed outline of the contents of a venture investment agreement. The main sections of a typical agreement are briefly described, and many of the terms that might appear in each section are noted. However, not all of the terms listed will appear in an investment agreement. Venture capital investors select terms from among those listed (and some not listed) to best serve their needs in a particular venture investment situation. For more detail on investment agreements we recommend the papers by Gardner and Stewart.*

1. Description of the Investment

This section of the agreement defines the basic terms of the investment. It includes descriptions of the:

a. Amount and type of investment.
b. Securities to be issued.
c. Guarantees, collateral subordination, and payment schedules associated with any notes.
d. Conditions of closing: time, place, and method of payment.

When investment instruments are involved that carry warrants or debt conversion privileges, the agreement will completely describe them. This description will include:

a. The time limits on the exercise of the warrant or conversion of the debt.
b. The price and any price changes that vary with the time of exercise.
c. Transferability of the instruments.
d. Registration rights on stock acquired by the investor.
e. Dilution resulting from exercise of warrants or debt conversion.
f. Rights and protections surviving after conversion, exercise, or redemption.

2. Preconditions to Closing

This section covers what the venture must do or what ancillary agreements and documents must be submitted to the investor before the investment can be closed. These agreements and documents may include:

a. Corporate documents (e.g., bylaws, articles of incorporation, resolutions authorizing sale of securities, tax status certificates, list of stockholders, and directors).
b. Audited financial statements.
c. Any agreements for simultaneous additional financing from another source or for lines of credit.
d. Ancillary agreements (e.g., employment contracts, stock option agreements, key individual insurance policies, stock repurchase agreements).
e. Copies of any leases or supply contracts.

3. Representations and Warranties by the Venture

This section contains legally binding statements made by the venture's officers that describe its condition on or before the closing date of the investment agreement. The venture's management will warrant:

*See W F Gardner, Jr., "Venture Capital Financing: A Lawyer's Checklist," *Business Lawyer,* January 1971, p. 997; and M D Stewart, "Venture Capital: Semi-Industry," *Venture Capital,* Publication 44–1092 (New York: Practicing Law Institute, 1973), p. 29.

a. That it is a duly organized corporation in good standing.
b. That its action in entering into an agreement is authorized by its directors, allowed by its bylaws and charter, legally binding upon the corporation, and not in breach of any other agreements.
c. If a private placement, that the securities being issued are exempt from registration under the Securities Act of 1933 as amended and under state securities law and that registration is not required under the Securities Exchange Act of 1934.
d. That the capitalization, shares, options, directors, and shareholders of the company are as described (either in the agreement or an exhibit).
e. That no trade secrets or patents will be used in the business that are not owned free and clear or if rights to use them have not been acquired.
f. That no conflicts of interest exist in their entering the agreement.
g. That all material facts and representations in the agreement and exhibits are true as of the date of closing (includes accuracy of business plan and financials).
h. That the venture will fulfill its part of the agreement so long as all conditions are met.
i. That any patents, trademarks, or copyrights owned and/or used by the company are as described.
j. That the principal assets and liabilities of the company are as described in attached exhibits.
k. That there are no undisclosed obligations, litigations, or agreements of the venture of a material nature not already known to all parties.
l. That any prior-year income statements and balance sheets are accurate as presented and have been audited and that there have been no adverse changes since the last audited statements.
m. That the venture is current on all tax payments and returns.

4. Representations and Warranties by the Investor

This section contains any legally binding representations made by the investor. They are much smaller in number than those made by the company. The investor may warrant:

a. If a corporation, that it is duly organized and in good standing.
b. If a corporation, that its action in entering into an agreement with the venture is authorized by its directors, allowed by its bylaws and charter, legally binding upon the corporation, and not in breach of any existing agreements.
c. If a private placement, that the stock being acquired is for investment and not with a view to, or for sale in connection with, any distribution.
d. The performance of his or her part of the contract if all conditions are met.

5. Affirmative Covenants

In addition to the above representations and warranties, the company in which the investor invests usually has a list of affirmative covenants with which it must comply. These could include agreeing to the following:

a. Paying taxes, fees, duties, and other assessments promptly.
b. Filing all appropriate government or agency reports.
c. Paying debt principal and interest.
d. Maintaining corporate existence.
e. Maintaining appropriate books of accounts and keeping a specified auditing firm on retainer.
f. Allowing access to these records to all directors and representatives of the investor.

g. Providing the investor with periodic income statements and balance sheets.
h. Preserving and providing for the investors' stock registration rights as described in the agreement.
i. Maintaining appropriate insurance, including key individual insurance with the company named as beneficiary.
j. Maintaining minimum net worth, working capital, or net assets levels.
k. Maintaining the number of investor board seats prescribed in the agreement.
l. Holding the prescribed number of directors' meetings.
m. Complying with all applicable laws.
n. Maintaining corporate properties in good condition.
o. Notifying the investor of any events of default of the investment agreement within a prescribed period of time.
p. Using the investment proceeds substantially in accordance with a business plan that is an exhibit to the agreement.

6. Negative Covenants

These covenants define what a venture must not do, or must not do without prior investor approval; such approval is not to be unreasonably withheld. A venture usually agrees not to do such things as:

a. Merge, consolidate with, acquire, or invest in any form of organization.
b. Amend or violate the venture's charter or bylaws.
c. Distribute, sell, redeem, or divide stock except as provided for in the agreement.
d. Sell, lease, or dispose of assets whose value exceeds a specified amount.
e. Purchase assets whose value exceeds a specified amount.
f. Pay dividends.
g. Violate any working capital or net worth restrictions described in the investment agreement.
h. Advance to, loan to, or invest in individuals, organizations, or firms except as described in the investment agreement.
i. Create subsidiaries.
j. Liquidate the corporation.
k. Institute bankruptcy proceedings.
l. Pay compensation to its management other than as provided for in the agreement.
m. Change the basic nature of the business for which the firm was organized.
n. Borrow money except as provided for in the agreement.
o. Dilute the investors' holdings without giving them the right of first refusal on new issues of stock.

7. Conditions of Default

This section describes those events that constitute a breach of the investment agreement if not corrected within a specified time and under which an investor can exercise specific remedies. Events that constitute default may include:

a. Failure to comply with the affirmative or negative covenants of the investment agreement.
b. Falsification of representations and warranties made in the investment agreement.
c. Insolvency or reorganization of the venture.
d. Failure to pay interest or principal due on debentures.

8. Remedies

This section describes the actions available to an investor in the event that a condition of default occurs. Remedies depend on the form an investment takes. For a common stock investment, the remedies could be:

a. Forfeiture to the investor of any stock of the venture's principals that was held in escrow.
b. The investor receives voting control through a right to vote some or all of the stock of the venture's principals.
c. The right of the investor to put his or her stock to the company at a predetermined price.

For a debenture, the remedies might be:

a. The full amount of the note becoming due and payable on demand.
b. Forfeiture of any collateral used to secure the debt.

In the case of a preferred stock investment, the remedy can be special voting rights (e.g., the right to vote the entrepreneurs' stock) to obtain control of the board of directors.

9. Other Conditions

A number of other clauses that cover a diverse group of issues often appear in investment agreements. Some of the more common issues covered are:

a. Who will bear the costs of closing the agreement; this is often borne by the company.
b. Who will bear the costs of registration of the investors' stocks; again, the investors like this to be borne by the company for the first such registration.
c. Right of first refusal for the investor on subsequent company financings.

APPENDIX VI—SAMPLE VESTING AND STOCK RESTRICTION AGREEMENT

Agreement, dated as of September 30, 1983, between Venture *x,* a Massachusetts corporation (the "company"), and Investor *y* (the "stockholder").

Whereas, the company has previously sold shares of its common stock ("common stock") to the stockholder; and

Whereas, the company is amending its Articles of Organization to remove certain provisions set forth therein which restrict the transfer of its common stock; and

Whereas, the parties desire to retain and impose certain restrictions on the shares of common stock presently owned by the stockholders and on any new, additional, or different shares of the capital stock of the company which may at any time be issued to the stockholder as a result of a recapitalization, stock dividend, split-up, combination, or exchange of or on the common stock of the company (collectively, all such common stock and any other such shares being referred to as "shares");

Now, therefore, in consideration of the covenants and agreements set forth herein, and the mutual benefits which the parties anticipate from the performance thereof, the parties agree as follows:

1. Repurchase of shares on termination of employment relationship. Subject to the lapse provisions hereinafter set forth, if at any time the stockholder's employment or consulting relationship with the company is terminated for any reason whatsoever, including death or disability, the company shall have the right (but not the obligation) to require the stockholder to sell to the company all or any part of the shares at the cash price paid by the stockholder therefor.

The company's right of repurchase set forth in this Section 3 to purchase part or all of the shares shall lapse as follows:

a. As to 100 percent of the shares on November 30, 1983, if at least $180,000 in funding has not been received by the company on or before such date.

b. If such funding has been received on or before such date, at the rate of 25 percent of such shares each year for four years effective annually on the anniversary of this agreement.

The company may exercise its right of repurchase of such shares by giving written notice to the stockholder or to his or her estate, personal representative, or beneficiary ("estate") at any time within 90 days of the termination of the stockholder's employment with the company, specifying the number of shares to be sold to the company. Such notice shall be effective only as to shares as to which the company's repurchase rights have not lapsed as of the date of such notice. Once such notice has been given, no further lapsing of such right of repurchase shall occur.

2. *Procedure for sale of shares.* In any notice given by the company pursuant to Section 1 hereof, the company shall specify a closing date for the repurchase transaction described therein. At the closing, the repurchase price shall be payable by the company's check against receipt of certificates representing all shares so repurchased. Upon the date of any such notice from the company to the stockholder or his or her estate, the interest of the stockholder in the shares specified in the notice for repurchase shall automatically terminate, except for the stockholder's right to receive payment from the company for such shares.

3. *Right of first refusal.* If the stockholder desires to sell all or any part of any shares as to which the repurchase rights of the company under Section 1 hereof have lapsed and an offeror ("the offeror") has made an offer therefor, which offer the stockholder desires to accept, the stockholder shall: (*a*) obtain in writing an irrevocable and unconditional bona fide offer (the "bona fide offer") for the purchase thereof from the offeror; and (*b*) give written notice (the "option notice") to the company setting forth his or her desire to sell such shares, which option notice shall be accompanied by a photocopy of the original executed bona fide offer and shall set forth at least the name and address of the offeror and the price and terms of the bona fide offer. Upon receipt of the option notice, the company shall have an option to purchase any or all of such shares specified in the option notice, such option to be exercisable by giving, within 30 days after receipt of the option notice, a written counternotice to the stockholder. If the company elects to purchase any or all of such shares, it shall be obligated to purchase, and the stockholder shall be obligated to sell to the company, such shares at the price and terms indicated in the bona fide offer within 60 days from the date of receipt by the company of the option notice.

The stockholder may sell, pursuant to the terms of the bona fide offer, any or all of such shares not purchased by the company for 30 days after expiration of the option notice, or for 30 days following a failure by the company to purchase such shares within 60 days of giving its counternotice of an intent to purchase such shares; provided, however, that the stockholder shall not sell such shares to the offeror if the offeror is a competitor of the company and the company gives written notice to the stockholder within 30 days of its receipt of the option notice stating that the stockholder shall not sell his or her shares to the offeror; and provided, further, that prior to the sale of such shares to the offeror, the offeror shall execute an agreement with the company pursuant to which the offeror agrees not to become a competitor of the company and further agrees to be subject to the restrictions set forth in this agreement. If any or all of such shares are not sold pursuant to a bona fide offer within the times permitted above, the unsold shares shall remain subject to the terms of this agreement.

The refusal rights of the company set forth in Section 3 of this agreement shall remain in effect until a distribution, if ever, to the public of shares of common stock for an aggregate public offering price of at least $3 million or more pursuant to a registration statement filed under the Securities Act of 1933, or a successor statute, at which time this agreement will automatically expire.

Because the shares cannot be readily purchased or sold in the open market, and for other reasons, the stockholder and the company acknowledge that the parties will be irreparably damaged in the event that this agreement is not specifically enforced. Upon a breach or threatened breach of the terms, covenants, and/or conditions of this agreement by any of the parties hereto, the other party shall, in addition to all other remedies, be entitled to a temporary or permanent injunction, without showing any actual damage, and/or a decree for specific performance, in accordance with the provisions hereof.

4. Adjustments. If there shall be any change in the common stock of the company through merger, consolidation, reorganization, recapitalization, stock dividend, split-up, combination, or exchange of shares, or the like, all of the terms and provisions of this agreement shall apply to any new, additional, or different shares or securities issued with respect to the shares as a result of such event, and the repurchase price and the number of shares or other securities that may be repurchased under this agreement shall be appropriately adjusted by the board of directors of the company, whose determination shall be conclusive.

5. Restrictions on transfer. The stockholder agrees during the term of this agreement that the stockholder will not sell, assign, transfer, pledge, hypothecate, mortgage, or otherwise encumber or dispose of, by gift or otherwise (except to the company), all or any of the shares now or hereafter owned by the stockholder except as permitted by this agreement.

The company may place a legend on any stock certificate representing any of the shares reflecting the restrictions on transfer and the company's right of repurchase set forth herein and may make an appropriate notation on its stock records with respect to the same.

6. Waiver of restrictions. The company may at any time waive any restriction imposed by any Section of this agreement with respect to all or any portion of any of the shares.

7. No Obligation as to employment. The company is not by reason of this agreement obligated to start or continue the stockholder in any employment or consulting capacity.

8. Successors and assigns. This agreement shall be binding on and inure to the benefit of the company's successors and assigns and the stockholder's transferees of the shares, heirs, executors, administrators, legal representatives, and assigns. Without limiting the foregoing, the company is specifically permitted to assign its repurchase rights under Sections 1, 2, and 3 hereof.

9. Notices. All notices and other communications provided for or contemplated by this agreement shall be delivered by hand or sent by certified mail, return receipt requested, addressed as follows:

If to the company:
If to the stockholder: At the stockholder's address, set forth below

or to such other address as the addressee may specify by written notice pursuant to this Section 10. Notices or communications sent by mail shall be deemed to have been given on the date of mailing. In the event of the stockholder's death or incapacity, any notice or communication from the company may, at the company's option, be addressed either to the stockholder at the stockholder's last address specified pursuant to this Section 10 or to the stockholder's estate.

10. Governing law. This agreement shall be governed by and construed in accordance with the laws of the Commonwealth of Massachusetts.

11. Amendments; waivers. Changes, amendments, or modifications in or additions to or waivers of any provision under or of this agreement may be made only by a written instrument executed by the parties hereto. Any waiver of any provision of this agreement shall not excuse compliance with any other provision of this agreement. Notwithstanding the foregoing, no course of dealing or delay on the part of either party in exercising any right shall operate as a waiver thereof or otherwise prejudice the rights of such holder.

The stockholder acknowledges that the issuance of the shares to the stockholder hereunder satisfies and discharges in full any previous understanding between the company and the stockholder regarding the issuance of the company's stock or option rights with respect thereto, and the stockholder waives any preemptive rights the stockholder has to purchase any capital stock of the company.

12. Captions. Captions are for convenience only and shall not be deemed to be a part of this agreement.

In witness whereof, the undersigned have caused this agreement to be executed as an instrument under seal as of the day and year first above written.

APPENDIX VII—SAMPLE LOAN AGREEMENT

BANK OF NEW ENGLAND, N.A.
TERM LOAN AGREEMENT

For value received and in further consideration of the granting by Bank of New England, N.A. ("Bank") to the undersigned ("Borrower") of a line of credit or of a loan or loans thereunder (all such loans, together with any existing loans from Bank to Borrower, being hereinafter collectively and separately referred to as the "Loan"), Borrower represents and warrants to and agrees with Bank as follows ("Agreement"):

SECTION 1. THE LOAN.

1.1 **Amount.** Bank will lend to Borrower, and Borrower will borrow from Bank $__________, with interest at ________% per annum.

1.2 **Evidence of Loan.** At the option of Bank, the Loan and the terms of repayment thereof, including the rate of interest, may be evidenced by a note or notes, or by Bank's books and records.

1.3 **Security and/or Guaranty.** The payment of the Loan may at any time or from time to time be secured and/or guaranteed wholly or partly separate and apart from this Agreement, but whether or not secured and/or guaranteed, all monies and other property at any time in the possession of Bank which Borrower either owns or has the permission of the owner thereof to pledge with or otherwise hypothecate to Bank, including, but not limited to, any deposits, balances of deposits or other sums at any time credited by or due from Bank, shall at all times be collateral security for all of the liabilities, obligations and undertakings of Borrower to Bank, direct or indirect, absolute or contingent, now existing or hereafter arising or acquired including, but not limited to, the payment of the Loan.

SECTION 2. WARRANTIES AND REPRESENTATIONS. Borrower hereby represents and warrants to Bank (which representations and warranties will survive the making of the Loan) that:

2.1 **Corporate Existence.** Borrower, if a corporation, is and will continue to be, a corporation duly incorporated and validly existing under the laws of the State of __________ and duly licensed or qualified as a foreign corporation in all states wherein the nature of its property owned or business transacted by it makes such licensing or qualification necessary. Borrower has obtained all required permits, authorizations and licenses, without unusual restrictions or limitations, to conduct the business in which Borrower is presently engaged, all of which are in full force and effect.

2.2 **Corporate Authority and Power.** If Borrower is a corporation, the execution, delivery and performance of this Agreement, any note or security agreement or any other instrument or document at any time required in connection with the Loan are within the corporate powers of Borrower, and not in contravention of law, the Articles of Organization or By-Laws of Borrower or any amendment thereof, or of any indenture, agreement or undertaking to which Borrower is a party or may otherwise be bound, and each such instrument and document represents a valid and binding obligation of Borrower and is fully enforceable according to its terms. Borrower will, at the request of Bank at any time and from time to time, furnish Bank with the opinion of counsel for Borrower with respect to any or all of the foregoing or other matters, such opinion to be in substance and form satisfactory to Bank.

2.3 **Financial Status.** All financial statements and other statements heretofore or hereafter given by Borrower to Bank in respect hereof are or will be true and correct, subject to any limitation stated therein, consistent with any prior statements furnished to Bank, and prepared in accordance with generally accepted accounting principles to represent fairly the condition of Borrower at the date thereof.

2.4 **Litigation.** There is not now pending or threatened against Borrower any action or other proceedings or any claim in which Borrower has any monetary or other proprietary interest nor do any of the executive or managing personnel of Borrower know of any facts which may give rise to any such litigation, proceeding or claim, except: __________

____

2.5 **Subsidiaries Affiliates.** If Borrower is a corporation it (a) owns 100% or ________% of the issued and outstanding stock of the following subsidiaries and/or affiliates: __________

____

____

(b) such stock shall be free and clear of any pledges, liens, or other encumbrances.

2.6 **Events of Default.** No event of default specified in Section 5.0 hereof, and no event which, with the lapse of time or notice, would become such an event of default, has occurred and is continuing.

2.7 **Title to Property.** Borrower has good and marketable title to all property in which Borrower has given or has agreed to give a security interest to Bank and such property is or will be free of all encumbrances except: __________

____

2.8 **Taxes.** Borrower has filed all tax returns required to be filed, has paid all taxes due thereon and has provided adequate reserves for payment of any tax which is being contested.

25-141-1 (5/82)

SECTION 3. AFFIRMATIVE COVENANTS. Borrower agrees that until payment in full of the Loan and performance of all of its other obligations under this Agreement, Borrower will, unless Bank otherwise consents in writing, comply with the following:

3.1 **Compensating Balances.** Bank shall be Borrower's main bank of deposit and Borrower shall maintain average aggregate collected balances in its deposit account or accounts with Bank of not less than ____________ per centum (____________%) of the outstanding unpaid balance of the Loan or Loans; such collected balances to be calculated net of any balances required to support demand deposit account activity costs. Balances shall be averaged ____.

3.2 **Commitment Fee.** Subject to the terms of this agreement Bank commits itself until ____________, 19_____, to lend to Borrower at any time or from time to time a sum or sums in the aggregate amount of $____________; and Borrower agrees to pay to Bank monthly in arrears a fee for Bank's said commitment in the amount of ____________ per centum (____________%) of the unused portion thereof so long as the same be outstanding. Borrower shall also, in addition to requirements of Paragraph 3.1 above, maintain collected balances in its deposit account or accounts with Banks of not less than ____________ per centum (____________%) of the unused portion of said commitment. Repayments on account of the Loan shall not operate to increase the unused portion of said commitment, except in the case of Revolving Loans.

3.3 **Financial Statements.** (a) Borrower will furnish to Bank quarterly statements prepared by Borrower within forty-five days of the close of each quarter, and within ninety days after the close of each fiscal year, an annual audit prepared by the equity method and certified by public accountants selected by Borrower and approved by Bank, together with a certificate by such accountants that at such audit date Borrower was acting in compliance with the terms of this Agreement. If Borrower is a corporation, consolidated and consolidating statements shall be furnished for Borrower and all subsidiary corporations, (b) Borrower shall indicate on said statements all guarantees made by it and (c) Borrower will upon request permit a representative of Bank to inspect and make copies of Borrower's books and records at all reasonable times.

3.4 **Insurance.** Borrower will maintain adequate fire insurance with extended coverage, public liability and other insurance as Bank may reasonably require as consistent with sound business practice and with companies satisfactory to Bank, which policies will show the Bank as a loss payee.

3.5 **Taxes and Other Liens.** Borrower will comply with all statutes and government regulations and pay all taxes, assessments, governmental charges or levies, or claims for labor, supplies, rent and other obligations made against it which, if unpaid, might become a lien or charge against Borrower or on its property, except liabilities being contested in good faith and against which if requested by Bank, Borrower will set up reserves satisfactory to Bank.

3.6 **Maintenance of Existence.** If Borrower is a corporation, it will maintain its existence and comply with all applicable statutes, rules and regulations, and maintain its properties in good operating condition, and continue to conduct its business as presently conducted.

3.7 **Notice of Default.** Within three (3) business days of becoming aware of (a) the existence of any condition or event which constitutes a default under Section 5.0 hereof, or (b) the existence of any condition or event which with notice or the passage of time, will constitute a default under Section 5.0 hereof, Borrower will provide Bank with written notice specifying the nature and period of existence thereof and what action Borrower is taking or proposes to take with respect thereto.

3.8 **Use of Proceeds.** Borrower shall use the proceeds of the Loan hereunder for general commercial purposes, provided that no part of such proceeds will be used, for the purpose of purchasing or carrying any "margin security" as such term is defined in Regulation U of the Board of Governors of the Federal Reserve System.

3.9 **Further Assurances.** Borrower will execute and deliver to Bank any writings and do all things necessary, effectual or reasonably requested by Bank to carry into effect the provisions and intent of this Agreement.

SECTION 4. NEGATIVE COVENANTS. Without the prior written approval of Bank, Borrower will not:

4.1 **Consolidation, Merger or Acquisition.** Participate in any merger or consolidation or alter or amend the capital structure of Borrower including, but not limited to, the issuance of additional stock, or make any acquisition of the business of another.

4.2 **Dividends.** Pay any dividends, **including stock dividends,** or make any distributions, in cash or otherwise, including splits of any kind, to any officer, stockholder or beneficial owner of Borrower other than salaries.

4.3 **Encumbrances.** Mortgage, pledge or otherwise encumber any property of Borrower or permit any lien to exist thereon except liens (i) for taxes not delinquent or being contested in good faith; (ii) of mechanics or materialmen in respect of obligations not overdue or being contested in good faith; (iii) resulting from security deposits made in the ordinary course of business; and (iv) in favor of Bank.

4.4 **Investments.** Invest any assets of Borrower in securities other than obligations of the United States of America.

4.5 **Disposition of Assets, Guarantees, Loans, Advances.** Sell, transfer or assign any assets of Borrower other than in the ordinary course of business or, except as hereinafter specifically permitted, (i) sell or transfer or assign any of Borrower's accounts receivable with or without recourse, (ii) guarantee or become surety for the obligations of any person, firm or corporation, or (iii) make any loans or advances except:

____

4.6 **Working Capital.** Permit its inventory to exceed ____________% of its Current Assets; permit its net Working Capital (excess of Current Assets over Current Liabilities) to be less than $____________ for the current fiscal year and for each subsequent fiscal year to be less than the amount for the prior fiscal year plus ____________% of Borrower's net income earned for the prior year, after provision for taxes, provided that there shall be no reduction in the required working capital for losses; or permit its Current Assets to be less than ____________% of its Current Liabilities, Current Assets and Current Liabilities to be computed in accordance with customary accounting practice except that Current Liabilities shall in any event include all rentals and other payments due within one year under any lease or rental of personal property.

4.7 **Liabilities.** Permit its total short and long term liabilities including borrowings to exceed ____________% of Borrower's **tangible** net worth, **said percentage to decrease** ____________% per year for the term of the Loan.

4.8 **Fixed Assets.** Make, or incur any obligation to make, any expenditures in any fiscal year for fixed assets by purchase or lease agreement the aggregate fair market value of which assets is in excess of $____________

4.9 **Compensation.** If Borrower is a corporation, pay to its officers and directors aggregate compensation in any fiscal year which exceeds $____________

4.10 **Employee Retirement Investment Secuirty Act of 1974 as amended ("ERISA"). Permit any pension plan to:** (a) engage in any "prohibited transaction"; (b) fail to report to Bank a "reportable event"; (c) incur any "accumulated funding deficiency"; or (d) terminate its existence at any time in a manner which could result in the imposition of a lien on the property of the Borrower. (The quoted terms are defined in Sections 2003(c), 302, and 4003, respectively, of ERISA.)

SECTION 5. DEFAULTS. If any one or more of the following "Events of Default" shall occur at any time, **Bank shall have the right to declare any or all liabilities or obligations of Borrower to Bank immediately due and payable without notice or demand:**

5.1 Any warranty, representation or statement made or furnished to Bank by or on behalf of Borrower or any guarantor or surety for Borrower was in any material respect false when made or furnished;

5.2 A failure to pay or perform when due any obligation, liability or covenant of Borrower or of any guarantor or surety for Borrower, under this loan agreement or any other indebtedness or obligation for borrowed money, or if such indebtedness or obligation shall be accelerated, or if there exists any event of default under any such instrument, document or agreement evidencing or securing such indebtedness or obligation, including, but not limited to, failure to perform the terms of this Agreement or of the note or notes evidencing the Loan;

5.3 The commencement of any proceeding under any bankruptcy or insolvency laws by or against Borrower, the appointment of a trustee, receiver, or custodian and, if any such proceeding is involuntary such proceeding has not been dismissed and all trustees, receivers, or custodians discharged within 30 days of its commencement or their appointment.

5.4 The service upon Bank of a writ in which Bank is named as trustee or Borrower or any guarantor or surety for Borrower;

5.5 If Borrower or any guarantor or surety for Borrower is a corporation, trust or partnership, the liquidation, termination or dissolution of any such organization or its ceasing to carry on actively its present business;

5.6 The death of Borrower or any guarantors or surety for Borrower, and if Borrower or any guarantor or surety for Borrower is a partnership, the death of any partner; or

5.7 A judgment or judgments for the payment of money aggregating in excess of $____________ is outstanding against Borrower or any guarantor or surety for Borrower and any one of such judgments has been outstanding for more than thirty (30) days from the date of its entry and has not been discharged in full or stayed.

SECTION 6. MISCELLANEOUS.

6.1 **Other Agreements.** This Agreement is supplementary to each and every other agreement between Borrower and Bank and shall not be so construed as to limit or otherwise derogate from any of the rights or remedies of Bank or any of the liabilities, obligations or undertakings of Borrower under any such agreement, nor shall any contemporaneous or subsequent agreement between Borrower and Bank be construed to limit or otherwise derogate from any of the rights or remedies of Bank or any of the liabilities, obligations or undertakings of Borrower hereunder unless such other agreement specifically refers to this Agreement and expressly so provides. This Agreement and the covenants and agreements herein contained shall continue in full force and effect and shall be applicable not only with respect to the Loan, but also to all other obligations, liabilities and undertakings of Borrower to Bank whether direct or indirect, absolute or contingent, due or to become due, now existing or hereafter arising or acquired, until all such obligations, liabilities and undertakings have been paid or otherwise satisfied in full.

6.2 **Waivers.** No delay or omission on the part of Bank in exercising any right hereunder shall operate as a waiver of such right or any other right and waiver on any one or more occasions shall not be construed as a bar to or waiver of any right or remedy of Bank on any future occasion.

6.3 **Expenses.** Borrower will pay or reimburse Bank for all reasonable expenses, including attorneys' fees, which Bank may in any way incur in connection with this agreement or any other agreement between Borrower and Bank or with any Loan or which result from any claim or action by any third person against Bank which would not have been asserted were it not for Bank's relationship with Borrower hereunder or otherwise.

6.4 **Notices.** All notices and other communications hereunder shall be in writing, except as otherwise provided in this Agreement, and shall be hand delivered or mailed by first-class mail, postage prepaid (in which event notice shall be deemed to have been given when so delivered or deposited in the mail), addressed (a) if to Borrower, to ____

____

and (b) if to Bank, to 28 State Street, Boston, Massachusetts 02106. Attention ____________________ The address of any party hereto for such demands, notices and other communications may be changed by giving notice in writing at any time to the other party hereto.

6.5 **Massachusetts Law.** This Agreement is intended to take effect as a sealed instrument and shall be governed by and construed according to the laws of the Commonwealth of Massachusetts.

6.6 **Successors and Assigns.** This Agreement shall be binding upon Borrower's legal representatives, successors and assigns and shall inure to the benefit of Bank's successors and assigns.

6.7 **Additional Provisions.** Borrower furthermore agrees to the following additional provisions: ______________________

____

____

____

____

____

____

____

____

____

____

IN WITNESS WHEREOF the parties hereto have caused this Agreement to be duly executed under seal this __________ day of ____________________, 19_____, at Boston, Massachusetts.

____
(Name of Borrower)

By _______________________________
Hereunto duly authorized
Title:

ATTEST:

By _______________________________
Hereunto duly authorized
Title:

____

BANK OF NEW ENGLAND, N.A.

By _______________________________
Hereunto duly authorized
Title:

DEMAND NOTE

$.. Boston, Massachusetts, ... , 19........

ON DEMAND, for value received, the undersigned, which term wherever used herein shall mean all and each of the signers of this note jointly and severally, promises to pay to BANK OF NEW ENGLAND, N.A., or order, at said bank, ...

.... Dollars,

with interest from the date hereof on the unpaid balance from time to time outstanding

CHECK APPROPRIATE BOX AND COMPLETE ITEM

☐ at the rate of .... per centum per annum,

☐ at the Large Business Prime Rate for commercial loans from time to time in effect at said bank plus .... per centum per annum,

☐ at the Small Business Base Rate for commercial loans from time to time in effect at said bank plus .... per centum per annum,

such interest to be payable .... in arrears.

The undersigned agrees to pay upon default costs of collection including reasonable fees of attorneys.

No delay or omission on the part of the holder in exercising any right hereunder shall operate as a waiver of such right or of any other right of such holder, nor shall any delay, omission or waiver on any one occasion be deemed a bar to or waiver of the same or any other right on any future occasion. Every one of the undersigned and every indorser or guarantor of this note regardless of the time, order or place of signing waives presentment, demand, protest and notices of every kind and assents to any one or more extensions or postponements of the time of payment or any other indulgences, to any substitutions, exchanges or releases of collateral if at any time there be available to the holder collateral for this note, and to the additions or releases of any other parties or persons primarily or secondarily liable.

The proceeds of the loan represented by this note may be paid to any one or more of the undersigned.

All rights and obligations hereunder shall be governed by the law of the Commonwealth of Massachusetts and this note shall be deemed to be under seal.

....
Borrower(s) - Print name or names

(by) ....
Signature

(by) ....
Signature

25-102-3 (5/82)

APPENDIX VIII—VASES AND FACES EXERCISE[1]

The exercise that follows is specifically designed to help you shift from your dominant left-hemisphere mode to your subdominant R-mode. The process could be described over and over in words, but only *you* can experience for yourself this cognitive shift, this slight change in subjective state. As Fats Waller once said, "If you gotta ask what jazz is, you ain't never gonna know." So it is with R-mode state: you need to experience the L- to R-mode shift, observe the R-mode state, and in this way come to know it.[2]

[1] Reprinted by permission of The Putnam Publishing Group from *Drawing on the Right Side of the Brain* by Betty Edwards. Copyright © 1989 by Betty Edwards.

[2] For those of you who can take the time, especially if you feel that you "can't draw a straight line," the author suggests that you find the book and try a further exercise.

Vases-Faces Drawing 1

You have probably seen the perceptual-illusion drawing of the vase and faces. Looked at one way, the drawing appears to be two faces seen in profile. Then, as you are looking at it, the drawing seems to change and become a vase. One version of the drawing is shown in *Exhibit A*

Before you begin. First, read all the directions for the exercise.

1. Draw a profile of a person's head on the *left* side of the paper, facing toward the center. (If you are left-handed, draw the profile on the right side, facing toward the center.) Examples are shown of both the right-handed and left-handed drawings (*Exhibit B*). Make up your own version of the profile if you wish. It seems to help if this profile comes from your own memorized, stored *symbols* for a human profile.
2. Next, draw horizontal lines at the top and bottom of your profile, forming the top and bottom of the vase (*Exhibit B*).

Exhibit A

Exhibit B

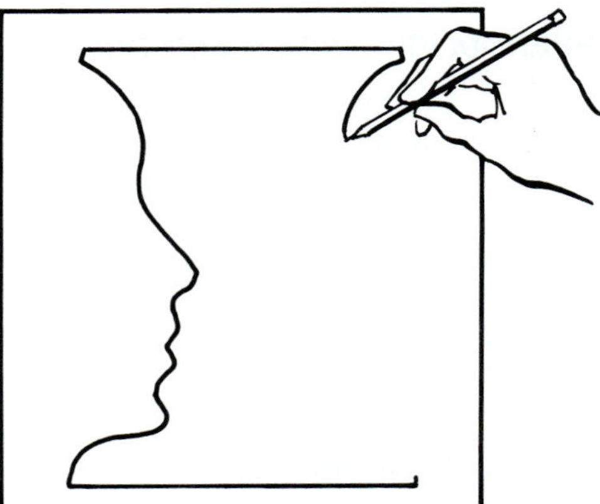

3. Now go back over your drawing of the first profile with your pencil. As the pencil moves over the features, *name them to yourself:* forehead, nose, upper lip, chin, neck. Repeat this step at least once. This is an L-mode task: naming symbolic shapes.
4. Next, starting at the top, draw the profile in *reverse.* By doing this, you will *complete the vase.* The second profile should be a reversal of the first in order for the vase to be symmetrical. (Look once more at the example in *Exhibit A*). Watch for the faint signals from your brain that you are shifting modes of information processing. You may experience a sense of mental conflict at some point in the drawing of the *second* profile. Observe this. And observe *how you solve the problem.* You will find that you are doing the second profile *differently. This is right-hemisphere-mode drawing.*

Before you read further, do the drawing.

After you finish. Now that you have completed the Vase-Faces drawing, think back on how you did it. The first profile was probably rather rapidly drawn and then, as you were instructed, redrawn while verbalizing the names of the parts as you went back over the features.

This is a left-hemisphere mode of processing: *drawing symbolic shapes from memory and naming them.*

In drawing the second profile (i.e., the profile that completes the vase), you may have experienced some confusion or conflict, as I mentioned. To continue the drawing, you had to find a different way, some different process. You probably lost the sense of drawing a profile and found yourself *scanning* back and forth in the space between the profiles, estimating angles, curves, inward-curving and outward-curving shapes, and lengths of line *in relation to* the opposite shapes, which now become *unnamed and unnamable.* Putting it another way, you made constant adjustments in the line you were drawing by checking *where you were* and *where you were going,* by scanning the space between the first profile and your copy in reverse.

In short, you began by drawing a symbol for a *face;* you concluded by drawing a *line* – the same result, but achieved by an entirely different process.

Index

Accountants, 341–42
Accounting, 221
Accounts receivable financing, 548
factoring form, 551–52
Achievement need, 187
Adaptability, 195–96
Adler, Fred, 41, 443
Administrative skills, 219
Advanced Energy Technology, Inc., 109
Advertising, 432
Affiliation need, 187
Affirmative covenants, 760–62
Agreements, 338
Air Florida, 101, 102
Alcorn, P., 291 n
Aldrich, Howard E., 333, 334
Alger, Horatio, 314
Allen, Fred T., 320
Allen, Louis L., 683–84
Allen, Paul, 619
Alper, David, 272
Alper, Frederic M., 265–67, 294–303, 323–27, 735–36
Alper, Morris, 265
Alves et al. v. Commissioner, 771
Ambiguity, 194–95
American Bank Directory, 547
American Bulletin of International Technology, 46
American dream, 3–6
American Management Association, 294
American Research and Development Corporation, 485
American Women's Economic Development Corporation, 49
Amortization, 99
Amos, Wally, 6 n, 25, 190
Angels, 481–83
Annual statement studies, 745–52
Anthanas, Anthony, 288
Antidilution protection, 523
Antidilution provisions
formula, 763
ratchet-down, 767–68
weighted-average, 768
Apple Computer, 97
Apprenticeship, 25–26
concept, 199–202
in family firms, 288
personal strategy, 201–2
windows of, 200–201
Arshad, Gulee, 476
Articles, source lists, 107
Assets, operating versus financial, 602
Association meetings, 48
Association of Collegiate Entrepreneurs, 49
Atkinson, John W., 187, 196
Attitudes, desired of entrepreneurs, 190–91
Attorneys, 337–40
Authoritarian personality, 198
Avoidance, 601

Babson, Roger, 575
Babson College's Academy of Distinguished Entrepreneurs, 5–6
inductees, 190–91
Babson Entrepreneurial Exchange, 48–49
Bankers, 340–41
Bankruptcy, threat of, 603–4
Bankruptcy law, 220, 339
Banks
debt capital relationship, 553–60
factors in selection, 554–55
financing by, 547
Banks—*Cont.*
information desired by, 556–57
lending criteria, 558
lending decision, 557
loan restrictions, 558
rejection of loan applications, 560
term loans, 549
Barnes, L. B., 287 n
Barnett, Frank, 286 n
Barnett, Sharon, 286 n
Barriers to entry, 101
Baruch, Bernard, 657
Bateman, Robert, 597 n
Baty, Gordon M., 341 n, 481 n, 554, 559 n
Bayer, Karl, 343–44
Bechtel, Steve, Jr., 288
Bechtel, Steve, Sr., 288
Bechtel, Warren, 288
Bechtel Corporation, 288
Beckhard, R., 283 n
Behaviors, desired of entrepreneurs, 190–91
Ben & Jerry's Homemade Ice Cream, Inc., 188
Beta measure of stock volatility, 447–48
Bhide, Amar, 15 n, 90 n, 314, 332
Big-project error, 599
Bilotta, Thomas J., 617
Biographical information sources, 108
Birch, David L., 13
Blakey, J., 521 n
Bloch, H. R., 6 n
Board of directors
alternatives to, 337
as a resource, 334–37
venture capitalist representation, 761
Body Shop, 88
Boesky, Ivan, 319
Bok, Derek, 313, 316
Bond, Alan, 6
Bookkeeping, 221
Bootstrapping, 480
Booz, Allen and Hamilton, 586–87
Borden, Neal D., 592
Bose, Amar G., 6, 190
Boston Computer Society, 49
Boston Globe, 480
Boulton, William B., 189
Boyd, David P., 195 n, 201 n, 254 n, 317 n
Bracker, Jeffrey S., 188 n
Bradford, David L., 194 n, 212, 213 n, 216 n, 583
Brain hemispheres, 785
Brainstorming, rules, 44
Breach of agreement indemnification, 765–66
Break-even chart, 164, 438–39
Breakeven point, 98, 100
Brechner, Bert, 198 n
Breen, J. Richard, 590
Bricklin, Dan, 42, 345 n
Bridge Capital Investors, Inc., case, 528–41
Bridge financing, 756
Brockhaus, Robert H., 22 n
Brown, Paul B., 522 n
Bruno, Albert V., 254 n, 335 n
Buffet, Warren, 543
Burn rate, 451
Burr, Don, 6 n
Burr, Egan and Deleage, 19, 376
Bush, George, 315
Bushnell, Nolan, 6 n, 9, 377
Business education, 216–17
Business environment, 88
Businesses; *see* Companies
Business plan
action steps, 385–86

Business plan—*Cont.*
case, 386–418
characteristics, 375–76
decisions, 378–79
goals and actions, 382–84
misunderstanding function of, 380
and outside professionals, 384–85
personal, 683–84
pitfalls, 379–82
preparation of, 418–19
segmenting and integrating information, 385
skills for writing, 383
uses of, 376–77
Business plan guide, 419–40
company-industry concept, 426–27
critical risks, problems, and assumptions, 436–37
design and development plans, 432–33
economics of, 430
executive summary, 425–26
financial plan, 437–39
management team description, 434–36
manufacturing and operations plan, 433–34
marketing plan, 430–32
market research and analysis, 428–30
overall schedule, 436
proposed company offering, 439–40
Business reconstruction, 605
Business strains, 289
Business Week, 283
Butcher, Charlie, 95
Buyback agreement, 264
Buyout provisions, 769–70
Bygrave, William D., 7 n, 18 n, 19 n, 20 n, 25 n, 94 n, 99 n, 335 n, 368, 483 n, 484 , 485 n, 487 n, 489, 498
Byrne, John A., 217 n, 316 n

Cabbage Patch dolls, 608
Caggianio, Christopher, 341 n, 342
Calian, Sara, 496 n
California Institute of Technology, 47
Campbell, Benjamin, 456 n
Canestraro, John M., 617
Capacity to inspire, 198
Capital, 332; *see also* Venture capital
abundance of, 579–80
process for raising, 380
staged commitment of, 517
strategies for raising, 449
users versus suppliers, 516–17
Capital asset pricing model, 447–48
Capital cow, 658
Capitalization, 439
Capital market context, 100
Capital markets, 449, 498
Capital requirements, 98–99
Carland, James, 189
Carland, Jo Ann C., 189
Carnegie, Andrew, 315
Carney, Karen E., 553
Carr, Albert Z., 313 n
Case, John, 45
Cash
quick cash, 606–7
uncommitted, 602
Cash burn, 580
Cash conversion cycle, 163–66
Cash flow, 448
assessment, 163–66
in financing strategy, 451–53
free, 99
methods for easing, 606–7
positive, 98
problems with, 599
and profit and loss, 100
Cash flow analysis
pro forma, 428
for turnaround, 605
Cash flow management, 221
Cash flow needs, 437
Cash flow projections, 345
Cavanagh, Richard E., 190 n
Cellular car phones, 91
Cellular One, 88, 95
Center for Entrepreneurial Leadership, 5
Chandler, Gaylen N., 189
Chapter 11 bankruptcy, 603
Charles Krug Winery, 290
Charm, Leslie B., 257, 334 n, 597 n
Chattel mortgages, 549
Choi, Audrey, 7 n
Churchill, Neil C., 6 n, 94 n, 176 n, 188 n, 194 n, 208 n, 213 n, 341 n, 376 n
Cisneros, Gustavo A., 251
Civil Service code, 320
Clifford, Donald K., Jr., 15 n, 190 n
Clinton, Bill, 4
Closely held corporations, 284
Closing conditions of investment agreements, 766
Coaching, 218
Cochran, Thomas P., 496 n
Cohen, Allan R., 194 n, 212, 213 n, 216 n, 583
Cohen, Herb, 521
Cohen, M. Bruce, 660 n
Cohesion, 255
Collection rates, 580
College endowments, 662
College and university courses in entrepreneurship, 5
Commercial bank financing, 547
Commercial finance companies, 550–51
Commitment, 191–92, 255–56
lack of, 380–81
of teams, 260
Common-size financial statement, 754
Communication skills, 219, 582–83
Community activities, 662
Companies
building, 654–58
characteristics, 215
Companies—*Cont.*
covenants and undertakings, 759–66
in crisis, 597–98
gestation period of crisis, 600–601
launched in 1991, 5
predicting trouble, 601–3
representations and warranties, 758–59
stages of growth, 10–16
threat of bankruptcy, 603–4
turnaround intervention, 604–10
venture modes and driving forces, 208–10
Company information, 105–6
Compaq Computer, 8
Competition, 48
assessment of, 429
case, 400–401
profile of, 167–68, 170–74
Competitive advantage, 101
profile, 144
Competitor intelligence, 105
CompuServe, 46
Conditional sales contracts, 549–50
Conditions precedent to closing, 766
Conflict management, 218
Conner, John T., 315
Consensus building, 582
Consultants, 108, 343–44
Consulting, 48
Consumer expenditures, 107
Contingency planning, 599
Contract law, 220
Contracts, 338
Control
degree of, 101
in family firms, 289
Convertible securities, 763
debt securities, 768–69
preferred stock, 767–68
Conway, Robert P., 493 n, 494 n, 497 n, 498
Coolidge, Calvin, 192
Cooper, Arnold C., 11 n, 26 n, 254 n
Coppola, Victor V., 550 n
Copyrights, 339
Cornelius, William G., 592 n
Corporate finance, compared to entrepreneurial finance, 509–12
Corporate law, 220
Corporations; *see also* Companies *and* Family ventures
research and development, 47
types of, 284–85
Cosale provision, 522
Cost analysis, 221
Coster, Betty, 185
Costing, poor management of, 600
Costs, 332
assessment, 160
fixed and variable, 101
flex points, 605
Cost structure, 98
Counterdependency, 199
Covenants, in loan agreements, 558–59
Covenants and undertakings, 759–66
Crane, Loretto, 203 n, 222 n
Crane, M., 293 n
Creative accounting, 602
Creative thinking, 43–44
Creativity, 195–96
innate, 197
unleashing, 44
Credibility, in family firms, 289
Credit
overextension, 599
sources of debt capital, 544–52
Credit and collection management, 221
Credit crunch of 1990–92, 100, 543
Credit environment, 543–44
Creditors
and threat of bankruptcy, 603–4
during turnaround, 607–10
Crisis
causes of, 598–600
diagnosis of, 604–6
factors leading to, 598–600
gestation period, 600–601
intervention, 604–10
predicting, 601–3
Crow, Trammel, 6 n
Cullinane, John, 6 n, 41, 304
Cullinet, Inc., 41
Current ratios, 762
Customer contacts, 48
Customers, mismanagement of relationships with, 598
Customer survey, 152–54

Danco, L., 291 n
Data General, 41
Data sources, 107
Deal-makers guide, 518
Deals
definition, 517–19
generic elements, 519
guidelines, 520–21
interpreting, 519–20
negotiations, 521–23
risk/reward management, 519
structuring, 517–21
successful, 518
Debt capital
accounts receivable financing, 548
bank financing, 547
banking relationship, 553–60
case, 562–72
chattel mortgages, 549
conditional sales contracts, 549–50
equipment loans, 549
factoring, 551–52
finance companies, 550–51
hazards, 561–62
interest calculation, 558
from leasing companies, 552
line of credit loans, 547–48
loan defaults, 602

Debt capital—*Cont.*
mezzanine financing, 493–94
plant improvement loans, 550
sources, 544–52
steps in obtaining loans, 554
tax problems, 562
time-sales finance, 548–49
trade credit, 546
unsecured term loans, 549
Debt problems, 599
Debt securities, principal terms, 768–69
Decision making
counterintuitive and unconventional, 213–14
during rapid growth, 580
skills, 219
Dees, J. Gregory, 4 n, 5 n, 316, 319
Degree of control, 101
Del Regno, Victor R., 265–67, 294–303, 323–27, 735–36
Department of Commerce, 4, 46
Design and development plans, 432–33
Desirability, 103
Determination, 191–92
Development
of human capital, 583
tasks, 148–50
Dialog database, 46
Differentiation, of rewards, 263
Digital Equipment Corporation, 92
Dingee, A. L. M., Jr., 190 n
Direct selling, 220
Discounted cash flow, 515
Disney, Roy, 90
Disney, Walt, 90, 516
Distribution channels, 104, 432
changes in, 89
Distribution management, 220
Distributors, 48
Diversification error, 598–99
Dividend distribution, 762–63
Dixon, Edward L., 46
Doriot, Georges, 19
Douglas, Scott, 597 n
Downey, Edward J., 265–67, 296, 300–301
Downside risk, 102
Driving forces, 208–10
Drucker, Peter F., 379 n
Dubini, Paola, 333, 334
Dumb Director Law, 336
Dun & Bradstreet, 753
Dunkelberg, W., 26 n
Dunkelberg, William C., 11 n
Dyer, W. G., Jr., 283 n

Early growth stage, in family firms, 286
Earnings before interest and taxes, 558
Earnings before interest but after taxes, 99
Easel Corporation, case, 610–51, 663–79
EBIAT; *see* Earnings before interest but after taxes
Economics
of business plan, 430
of high-potential ventures, 98–100
profile, 142–43
Edison, Thomas A., 92
Edwards, Betty, 45, 785 n
Egan, William, 19, 97, 376
Egnew, J. C., 27–28
Einstein, Albert, 92
Emerson, Ralph Waldo, 40
Emotional stability, 197
Employee benefit plans, 339
Employee compensation, 763
Employee confidentiality and proprietary rights agreement, 771
Employee Retirement Income Security Act, 759, 761
Employees
decline in morale, 601
as information sources, 108
work-force reductions, 609
Employee stock ownership plans, 498, 659
Employers, former, 48
Employer stock purchase agreements, 770–71
Employment, in large and small firms, 4
Encouragement, 583
Encyclopedia of Small Business Resources, 351
Ends-and-means issue, 321
Energy, 197
Enterprises; *see* Companies
Entrepreneur's Roundtable, 49
Entrepreneurial apprenticeship; *see* Apprenticeship
Entrepreneurial culture, 214–16
skills in building, 217–19
Entrepreneurial finance, compared to corporate finance, 509–12
Entrepreneurial Leadership Paradigm, 18–19
Entrepreneurial management, 207–10
assessment, 250–51
compared to leadership, 187
competence, 217–22
competency inventory, 235–49
examples, 583–86
knowledge needed by, 216–17
and organizational culture, 582–83, 582–83
for rapid growth, 211–16
and rate of growth, 576–79
Entrepreneurial mind, 24–26, 183–84
Entrepreneurial strategy
case, 735–37
exercise, 688–734
feedback, 686–87
goal-setting, 687–88
Entrepreneurial strategy—*Cont.*
profiles of past and present, 685–86
Entrepreneurial team, 101–2
Entrepreneurs
approach to resources, 331–34
and bank loan rejection, 560
bibliography on, 189
building net worth, 653–54
challenge of rapid growth, 573
company-building, 654–58
conflicts facing, 516–17
contribution to economy, 4–6
in crisis situation, 600–601
debt capital hazards, 560–61
desired behaviors and attitudes, 190–91
ethical dilemmas, 319–22
and ethics, 313–22
factors in bank selection, 554–55
harvest strategy, 656–58
high-potential ventures, 95–104
innate characteristics, 197–98
leadership and behavior, 186–87
loan agreement covenants, 558–59
main characteristics, 191–96
myths and realities, 22–24
negotiations, 521–23
personal business plan, 683–84
principles for greatness, 186–87
research on, 187–90
self-assessment, 684–85
successful, 24–25
Entrepreneur's creed, 202–3
Entrepreneurship
analytical framework, 15–22
courses in, 5
definition, 7–8
failure rule, 9–15
global trends, 7
intellectual and policy agenda, 9
practical agenda, 8
promise of growth, 13
threshold concept, 12–13
urgency of, 8
Equal inequality, 256
Equipment loans, 549
Equitec, 552
Equity, in family firms, 289
Equity capital
financing alternatives, 454–56
fund-raising traps, 523–27
initial public offering, 495–97
private placements, 494–95
Equity kicker, 493
Ernst and Young Guide to Raising Capital (Garner, Owen, and Conway), 498
ESOPs; *see* Employee stock ownership plans
Esprit, 290
Estee Lauder, 90
Ethical stereotypes, 314–15
Ethics, 184
ends-and-means issue, 321
entrepreneurial perspective, 318
exercise, 305–12
Kohlberg construct, 317–18
overview, 313–14
teaching of, 316–18
European Foundation for Entrepreneurship Research, 7
European Seed Capital Fund Network, 7
Executive summary of business plan, 425–26
Executory contracts, 604
Existing businesses, idea sources, 46
Exit mechanism, 100
Experience factor, 42–43
External environment assessment, 146

Facilities, 434
Factoring, 551–52
Failure, causes of, 598–600
Failure rule, 9–15
exceptions to, 11–15
and venture capital backing, 14–15
Fair Employment Practices Act, 320
Fairness, 256
in family firms, 289
Fama, Eugene, 447
Family dynamics, 289–90
Family-owned firms, 285
Family strains, 289
Family ventures
goals, 284–85
popularity of, 283
stages of growth, 286–87
succession issue, 290–91
success strategies, 291–93
teams, 288–91
types of firms, 284–85
types of involvement, 287–88
Fast, Norman D., 18 n, 19 n, 99 n
Fatal-flaw issues, 102
Fax International, case, 386–418
Feather, N. T., 187 n
Feedback, 686–87
Feeser, Henry R., 203 n
Fenchel Lampshade Company, case, 351–68
Fibercom Applications, case, 109–37
Fiber optics systems, 115–18
Fierman, J., 288 n
Finance
entrepreneurial versus corporate, 509–12
knowledge of, 221
Finance companies, 550–51
Finance function, weak, 599

Finance theory, 447–50
Financial Accounting Standards Board, 770
Financial assets, 602
Financial covenants, 763
Financial information, sources, 106
Financial life cycles, 454–56
Financial management myopia, 444–46
Financial plan, in business plan guide, 437–39
Financial ratios, 450
Financial resources, 21–22
  analysis or requirements, 345–51
Financial statements, 761–62
  exercise, 368–72
  projection of, 741–44
  typical, 754
Financing
  availability factors, 453, 487
  case, 528–41
  critical issues, 446–47
  debt capital, 543–72
  determining capital requirements, 450–53
  and fund-raising, 453–56
  future rights, 765
  main types, 453–54
  negotiations, 521–23
  owner's perspective, 447–50
  principles and predicaments, 443–50
  risk capital, 479–508
  strategies, 441
  strategy framework, 450–51
  structuring a deal, 517–21
  valuation, 509–17
Fireman, Paul, 6, 190
First Chicago method of valuation, 513–14
Fisher, Ken, 183–384
Fisher, Lawrence M., 655 n
Fisher, Roger, 521–22
Fit, 102, 191
  degree of, 103
  entrepreneurial, 681
  importance of, 18
  of partnerships, 183
Fixed costs, 101
Flanders, Ralph E., 485
Fleming, Dick, 6 n
Flexibility, 104, 332
  and rewards, 263
Fluid structures/procedures, 214
Forced buyout, 523
Ford, Edsel, 288
Ford, Henry, 288
Ford Motor Company, 288
Foreign Investment Real Property Tax Act, 759, 763
Fortune 500 firms, 4
Forum Corporation, 103
Foster, Bill, 256
Founders, 258–59
Founders of enterprises, 18–20
Fox, Harold W., 337 n
Fox International, case, 456–78
Franchise Opportunity Handbook (Department of Commerce), 46
Franchises, as idea source, 46
Franchising (Seltz), 46
Franchising, 338
Franchising Annual Handbook and Directory (Dixon), 46
Franchising Today, 46
Franchising World, 46
Frankenhuis, Jean Pierre, 343 n
Free cash flow, 99, 451–53
Freedom of Information Act, 108
Free enterprise system, 88
Fuld, Leonard M., 105, 109 n
Fundamental method of valuation, 513, 514
Fund-raising strategies, 450–51
  crafting, 453–56
  legal circumference, 523–24
  opportunity cost trap, 525–26
  status and size of venture firms, 524
  strategic circumference, 523
  traps for entrepreneurs, 523–27
  understanding costs, 526
  in unknown territory, 524–25
Furman, John R., 6, 190

Galbraith, John Kenneth, 207
Gallo, Ernest, 288
Gardner, W. F., Jr., 774
Garner, Daniel R., 493 n, 494 n, 497 n, 498
Garrett, Thomas, 313 n
Geographical location, 434
George, William W., 211 n
Giglierano, Joseph, 11 n
Gleason, Robert J., 617
Goals, 102
  establishing, 384
  failure to revise, 382
  of family firms, 284–86
  long-term, 450
  of teams, 260
  undefined, 381–82
Goal-setting strategy, 687–88
Godfrey, Joline, 6 n, 40
Going Public: The IPO Reporter, 634
Goldberg, Leland, 597 n
Gordon, Michael, 44
Gordon, William J. J., 44 n
Government regulations and reports, 339
Graham, Nicholas, 90
Grant, Alan, 18–19, 192–93
Graphical user interfaces, 612–13
Graphnet, Inc., 474
Great Game of Business (Stack), 584
Greco, Susan, 341 n, 342
Greed, 526
Grenier, L. A., 210 n
Gross margins, 99–100
Grousbeck, H. Irving, 332 n
Growth, 13; *see also* Rapid growth *and* Stages of growth
Growth rate, 97
  crises and symptoms, 577–78
  problem of, 579–80
Growth strategy, 427
Gumpert, David E., 18 n, 25 n, 46 n, 105 n, 107 n, 195 n, 201 n, 337 n, 341 n, 343 n, 344 n, 351, 354 n, 454 n, 455, 660 n
Gupta, Anil K., 208 n
Gustafson, Jerry W., 24 n

Hammer, Armand, 315
Handler, Wendy C., 283 n, 287 m, 290 n
Handy, Charles, 4
Harassment, by stockholders, 336
Harley, Judith W., 376 n
Harnett, Terry, 15–16
Harriman, Edward, 314
Harvard Business Review, 313, 343, 375, 447–48
Harvard Business School, 4–5, 257
  Owner/President Management Program, 313
  Small Company Management Program, 196
  teaching ethics, 316–17
Harvard Negotiation Project, 521
Harvest goal, 656
Harvest issues, 100, 653–63
  in business plan, 378
  case, 663–79
  profile, 143–44
Harvest mind-set, 256
Harvest options, 654–55, 658–61
Harvest-sharing, 256–57
Haslett, Brian, 262
Hayes, John L., 262
Head, Howard, 21–22, 39, 43, 90, 332
Head Ski, 22
Healey, Michael, 49–78
Health, 197
Helpers, in family firms, 287–88
Helping, 218
Hero-making ability, 213–14
Hershon, S. A., 287
Hewlett-Packard, 101
Hiatt, Arnold, 315
Higgins, Robert F., 479 n
High-growth stage, 210–11
  in family firms, 286
  problems of, 575
Highly-leveraged transactions, 543
High-potential ventures, 12
  characteristics, 95–104
  competitive advantage, 101
  economic criteria, 98–100
  fatal-flaw issues, 102
  harvest issues, 100
  industry and market issues, 96–98
High-potential ventures—*Cont.*
  management team issues, 101–2
  personal criteria, 102–3
  strategic differentiation, 103–4
Hill, James J., 314
Hindman, Jim, 499–503, 505, 509, 528–32, 537, 540, 586–94
Hindman and Company, case, 498–508
Hise, Phaedra, 553
Hofer, Charles W., 98
Hoffman, H. M., 521 n
Holmberg, Steven R., 656, 661
Home Depot, 103
Honda, Sochiro, 6 n, 190
Hopkins, Michael S., 522 n
Hornaday, John A., 25 n, 99 n, 188 n, 190 n, 194 n, 195 n, 202 n
Hoy, Frank, 189
HTC, Inc., 657
Hughes, Jay W., 265–67, 296, 323
Hugo, Victor, 139
Human behavior analysis, 186–87
Humphreys, Deborah S., 376 n
Hurlock, Burton C., 444 n
Huseby, Thomas, 491 n, 492

IBM, 40, 41
  and Easel Corporation, 617–19
Ideas
  compared to opportunities, 20, 87
  pattern recognition, 42–45
  sources of, 46–49
  as tools, 39–42
Impatience, 527
Implementation, 22
Impulsivity, 198
Inamori, Kazuo, 6
Inc. magazine, 46, 208, 313, 335, 337–38, 351, 373, 480, 498
Inc. 500 firms, 13, 14
Incentives, 262–65
  stock options, 770
Income statement, pro forma, 38
Incorporation, 338
Indebtedness, 763
Indemnification, 765–66
Industrial equipment leases, 552
Industry contacts, 48
Industry experience, 102
Industry guides, 105–6
Industry issues, 96–98
  in business plan, 426–27
  profile, 142
Industry Norms and Key Business Ratios (Dun & Bradstreet), 753–55
Industry turbulence, 580
Inexperience, 213
Influence, 217–18

Infomercials, 89
Informal investors, 481–83
Information
  on capital markets, 498
  gathering process, 105–9
  nonpublished sources, 108–9
  published sources, 105–8
  on resources, 351
  sources of, 46–49
  on venture capital investors, 490
Initial public offering, 439, 495–97
  case, 610–51, 663–79
  as harvest option, 660–61
Innovation, 4, 197
  by small firms, 88
In Search of Excellence (Peters and Waterman), 216
Insider sales, 770
Installment accounts receivable, 548–49
Insurance, 339
Integrity, 102
  and ethics, 321–22
  of teams, 255
Intellectual and policy agenda, 9
Intellectual capital, 771
Intellectual honesty, 102
Intellectual property protection, 339
Intelligence, 197
Interest calculation, 558
Internal rate of return, 99
Internal Revenue Code
  Section 83, 770–71
  Section 305, 763, 768
  Section 987, 759
Internal Revenue Service, 563
Intertec, 552
Inventions, 4
  personal identification with, 41
  by small firms, 104
Inventory
  control, 221
  liquidation of, 607
Inventory financing, 550–51
Investment
  legal process, 755–61
  in new companies, 662
Investment agreement
  closing conditions, 766
  covenants and undertakings, 759–66
  employee confidentiality and proprietary rights agreement, 771
  employer stock purchase agreements, 770–71
  legal opinion, 771
  principal purposes and legal consequences, 757
  representations and warranties, 758–59
  sample outline, 774–77
  stockholders agreement, 769–70
  transaction description, 757–58
Investment securities
  general considerations, 766–67
  principal terms on preferred stocks, 767–68
Investors
  conflicts with users of capital, 516–17
  dealing with, 491–92
  informal, 481–83
  required share of ownership, 511–12
  of venture capital, 490–92
Investor's rate of return, 511
Involuntary bankruptcy, 603
Invulnerability, 198
IPO Reporter, 498

Jansen, Erik, 189
Jiffy Lube, Inc., case, 499–508, 528–41, 586–95
Job evaluation, 221
Jobs, Steven, 18, 199
  created by entrepreneurs, 4
  created since 1973, 5
Joe Boxer Corporation, 90
Johari Window, 684–85
Johnson, John H., 25, 90
Johnson Publishing, 90
Johnsonville Sausage Company, 98, 585–86
Jones, Seymour, 660 n
Junior common stock, 770

Kahn, R. Douglas, 99 n, 610, 617
  case, 663–79
Kahn, Phillippe, 313–14
Kanter, Rosabeth Moss, 214–15
Kao, John J., 20 n
Kapor, Mitch, 18
Kasarda, John D., 319
Kaspar, 283
Kauffman, Ewing Marion, 5, 6, 185–86, 190–91, 583–84
Keillor, Garrison, 562
Kelley, Ed, 499
Kelley, Harold H., 260 n
Kent, C., 22 n
Ketchum, Bradford W., Jr., 337 n, 339 n
Key business ratios, 754–55
Key officer insurance, 523, 760–61
Kidder, Tracy, 41 n
Kirchhoff, Bruce A., 11 n, 13 n, 14
Kluge, John, 199
K-NET, 474
Knight, George, 655
Know-it-alls, 199
Kohlberg construct, 317–18
Kolb, D. A., 685
Kotter, John P., 187
Krentzman, Harvey C., 26, 200 n, 344 n, 576 n
Kroc, Ray, 6 n, 190
Kroeger, Carroll V., 210 n
Krueger, David E., 208 n
Kunkel, Scott W., 98
Kurtzig, Sandra L., 6, 190
Lammers, Teri, 90 n
Land, Edwin, 40
Langeler, Gerald H., 581
Lansberg, I., 293 n
Lead entrepreneurs, 18–19
Leadership
  entrepreneurial, 192–94
  and human behavior, 186–87
  and organizational culture, 582
Leadership paradigm, 192–93
Leadership skills, 217–18
Leasing companies, 552
Legal issues, 434
  and ethics, 320–21
  venture capital process, 755–71
Legal opinion, 771
Legal skills, 220
Lenders, 340–41, 544; *see also* Banks *and* Financing
  angels, 481–83
  during turnaround, 607–8
Lending criteria, 558
Lending decision, 557
Leverage, excessive, 599
Leveraged buyout, 659
Levinson, Daniel J., 201
Levinson, Harold, 291 n
Lexus, 103
Liability
  of board of directors, 336
  protection, 339
Licensing, 338
Liens and encumbrances, 763
Liles, Patrick R., 21 n
Line of credit, 547–48
Liquidation, 762
  costs, 166
  criteria, 550
  and preferred stock, 767
Liquidity measure, 602
Litigation, 339
Little, Royal, 6 n, 196 n
Loan agreement
  covenants, 558
  and personal guarantees, 559
  sample, 781–85
Loan defaults, 602
Loan restrictions, 558
Loans; *see* Debt capital *and* Financing
Lofblad, Robert, 49–78
Longsworth, Annie, 90 n
Lotus 1-2-3, 345
Lotus Development Corporation, 41–2
Low, Murray B., 12 n
Lowe, Edward, 6
Low-potential ventures, 96

Macho attitude, 198
MacMillan, Ian C., 333
Maeder, Paul A., 479 n
Mamis, Robert A., 90 n, 480
Management; *see also* Entrepreneurial management
  in high-potential ventures, 12
Management—*Cont.*
  as issue in company failure, 599
  turnaround analysis, 605
  turnover in personnel, 599
Management buyout, 659
Management by walking around, 210
Management information systems, 88–89
Management reporting, 599
Management skills, lack of, 599
Management team, 18–19
  assessment, 175–76
  business plan by, 385
  business plan description, 434–36
  importance of, 251–52
  issues, 101–2
  profile, 144
Manufacturing and operations plans, 433–34
Manufacturing management, 221
Marcus, Herbert, 291
Marcus, Stanley, 291
Marion Labs, 185–86, 583–84
Mariotti, Steve, 5
Market, in high-potential ventures, 12
Market capacity, 97
Market data, 107
Market development strategy, case, 388–91
Market forces, 88
Marketing, knowledge of, 220–21
Marketing plan, 430–42
Market issues, profile, 142
Market niche, 96
  misunderstood, 598
Market research, 220
  in business plan, 428–30
Market research firms, 108
Market share
  assessment, 158, 429
  attainable, 97–98
  as barrier to entry, 101
Market size, 90–92, 97
  assessment, 151–52
  case, 391
Market structure, 96–97
Market studies, 107
Marriott, J. Willard, Jr., 6 n, 102 n, 286
Marthinson, John, 6 n
Massachusetts Institute of Technology, 47
  Enterprise Forum, 49
Massachusetts Lawyers Weekly, 340
Maturity stage, 211, 575
  family firms, 286
Maugham, W. Somerset, 479
McCann, Joseph E., 592 n
McClelland, David C., 187, 190 n, 196
McCormack, Thomas J., 109, 133–35
McDonough, John, 610, 617, 663–64
McGovern, Patrick J., 6

McGowan, William G., 6, 190
McIntyre, J. M., 685
McKenna, Barrie, 89 n
Mentor Graphics, 581
Mentzer, Josephine Esther, 90
Mergers and acquisitions, 339, 659–60, 762
Merritt, John C., 6, 191
Mezzanine finance, 493–94
MGA Technology, Inc., 46
Michigan Lighting, Inc., case, 562–72
Microcomputers, 222
Miller, John B., 188 n
Miner, John B., 188 n, 194
Minimum resources, 21
Minority Enterprise Small Business Investment Companies, 492
Minority-owned businesses, 6
Mitton, Daryl, 194 n
Mondavi, Cesare, 290
Mondavi, Peter, 290
Mondavi, Robert, 290
Mooney, Kevin, case, 203–6, 222–33
Moore, John F., 28–29
Morale, decline in, 601
Morgan, Ann, 597 n
Morgan, J. P., 315
Morris, Jane, 488
Morris Alper and Sons, 95, 323–28
  case, 265–75, 293–303, 735–37
Motivation
  to excel, 196–97
  theory of, 187
Motivational-organizational fit, 194–95
Mousetrap fallacy/myopia, 40–41, 599
Murdoch, Rupert, 6 n
Muzyka, Daniel F., 20 n, 25 n, 94 n
Myers, Andrew D., 480 n

National Family Business Council, 293
National Foundation for Teaching Entrepreneurship to Handicapped and Disadvantaged Youth, Inc., 5
National Labor Relations Act, 604
National Patent Development Corporation, 46
National Science Foundation, 4, 88
Nayak, Chitra, 316 n
Needs, and motivation, 187
Negative covenants, 762–63
Negotiations, 219, 521–23
Nelton, Sharon, 286 n
NetExpress, Inc., 475
Net-liquid-balance-to-total-assets ratio model, 602
Network economics, 393–96
Networking, 48–49
Networks, 109
  in family firms, 292–93
Net worth, 762
New liquid balance, 602
New Product Development Services, Inc., 46
New-product planning, 221
Newsweek, 290
New ventures
  failure rate, 11
  rewards and incentives, 262–65
New York Times, 313
Nichols, Nancy A., 448
Nieman-Marcus, 291
Nonentrepreneurial mind, 198–99
Nonlinear events, 213
Nonparametric events, 213
Nonqualified stock options, 770
Nonquantitative signals of crisis, 602–3
Norris, Bill, 190
Norris, Floyd, 188 n
Not-for-profit research institutes, 47
NYNEX, 88

Oberfield, Alice, 5 n
Obstacles, anticipation of, 382
Oliver, 573
Olsen, Ken, 6 n, 92, 190
128 Group, 49
Operating assets, 602
Operating ratios, 106
Operating statements, 761–62
Operations, knowledge of, 221
Opportunities
  and analytical framework, 92–94
  and capital, 90
  compared to ideas, 87
  real time, 90–92
  recognition of, 87–90
  screening process, 139–81
  screening criteria, 93–104
  situational, 88
  strategic window, 657
  and team building, 259
Opportunity cost, 102–3
  trap, 525–26
Opportunity focus, 94–95
Opportunity obsession, 194
Opportunity orientation, 104
Opportunity overload, 579
Opportunity profile, 142–45
Opportunity recognition, 20–21
Opti-Com, 525
Organizational culture and climate, 580–83
Osborne, Adam, 8, 42
Osborne Computer, 8, 96
Other people's resources, 333–34
Outdoor Scene, Inc., 97
  case, 26–34
Outer control, 198
Out-of-cash time, 451–52
Outright sale, 660
Outside resources, 259
Owen, Robert R., 493 n, 494 n, 497 n, 498
Owens, Clint M., 136–37
Ownership, investor's required share, 511–12
Ownership dilution, 515

Paradox of optimism, 600–601
Parenting Magazine, 655
Parker, Jeff, 199, 476–77, 655
Patent brokers, 46
Patent law, 220
Patent Licensing Gazette, 47
Patents, 339
  idea sources, 46
Pattern recognition, 42–45
PC-Build, Inc., case, 49–78
Peer groups, 260
Pegasus Corporation, 46
People management, 218–19
Percent-of-sales ratios, 605
Perfectionism, 198–99
Performance, rewards for, 263
Perkins, Kleiner, 490
Perotti, Gian, 3 n
Personal business plan, 683–84
Personal criteria, 102–3
  profile, 144–45
Personal guarantees, in loan agreements, 559
Personnel administration, 219
Peters, Thomas J., 216
Peterson, Daniel, 564
Peterson, Jack, 562–72
Phillips, Bruce D., 13 n, 14
Piggyback registration rights, 764
Pilkington Brothers, 100
Pintendre Auto, Inc., 89
Piper, Thomas R., 316
Plain vanilla convertible preferred stock, 767
Planning
  ailments, symptoms, and cures, 381
  and business plan, 375–79
  personal business plan, 683–84
  pitfalls of, 379–82
  problems with, 379
Planning reviews, 382
Planning skills, 219
Plant improvement loans, 550
Posner, Bruce G., 554
Power need, 187
Practical agenda, 8
Pratt's Guide to Venture Capital Sources (ed., Schutt), 490, 498
Pratt, S. E., 19 n
Predictive crisis models, 601–3
Preemptive rights, 765
Preferred stock, mandatory redemption, 523
  principal terms, 767–68
Prentiss-McGraw, Inc., case, 222–33
Price, Country, 6 n
Pricing strategy, 431
  assessment, 155–56
  case, 399
  error of underpricing, 104
  knowledge of, 220
  poor policies, 599
Prime Computer, 183–84, 213
Prince tennis racket, 43
Private placement, 494–95
  after going public, 497–98
Problem solving, 219
Procedures, fluid, 214
Product description, 427
Production
  knowledge of, 221
  rescheduling, 221
Product licensing, 46–48
Product management, 220
Product pricing, 220
Professional contacts, 48
Profitability assessment, 160
Profit and loss, 100
Profits, after-tax, 98
Pro forma financial statements, 438, 605–6
Progress milestones, 382
Projection of Financial Statements (RMA), 741–44
Projections and forecasts, information sources, 106–7
Project management, 219
Promotion, 432
Proposed company offering, 439–40
Proprietary rights, 220
Psychological motivation, 187
Public filings, 108
Publicly owned corporations, 284
Public offering; *see* Initial public offering
Purchasing, 221
Purdue, Frank P., 6 n, 192

Quality control, 221
Quarterly earnings, 510–11
Quereshey, Safi U., 660 n
Quick cash, 606–7

Ranalli, Douglas J., 386, 655,
  case, 458–78
Rapid growth, 211–16
  challenge of, 573
  core management mode, 576–79
  and industry turbulence, 580
Ratchet-down antidilution provisions, 767–68
Rate of return, investor's, 511
Real estate law, 220
Real estate transactions, 339
Real time opportunities, 90–92
Redemption topics, 768
Reese, Pat Ray, 333 n
Registration rights, 523, 764–65
Regulation D, 660
  offerings, 482
  rules and applications, 497–98
Remey, Christine C., 4 n, 49 n, 265 n, 293 n, 323 n, 735 n
Remey, Donald P., 493 n, 590
Reorganization plan, 603
Representations and warranties, 758–59
Research and development, 4

Research and development stage, 575
Research Corporation, 46
Resource requirements, 21–22
Resources
accountants, 341–42
attorneys, 337–40
bankers and lenders, 340–41
board of directors, 334–37
characteristics, 329
consultants, 343–44
entrepreneurial approach, 331–34
financial, 345–51
information on, 351
marshalling and minimizing, 332
need assessment, 161–63
of other people, 333–34
Responsibility, acceptance of, 292
Return on equity mirage, 561
Return on investment, 98
Reverse engineering, 108–9
Reward system, 262–65
Rich, Stanley, 9
Right of first refusal, 765, 769
Rights of prior negotiation, 765
Rights to future financing, 765
Right Stuff (Wolfe), 8
Riklis, Ira, 288
Riklis, Meshulam, 288
Risk
reduced, 332
stated in business plan, 436–37
tolerance of, 194–95
Risk assessment, 178–79
Risk capital, 6
angels and informal investors, 481–83
central issues, 479–80
employee stock ownership plans, 498
initial public offering, 495–97
mezzanine finance, 493–94
private placement after going public, 497–98
private placements, 494–95
SBA program, 492–93
from small business investment companies, 493
timing, 480–81
Risk/reward management, 519
Risk/reward relationships, 449
Risk/reward tolerance, 103
RJR Nabisco, 583
R-mode state, 785
Roamer Plus, 95
Robber Barons, 314–15
Robert Morris Associates, 345
annual statement studies, 169, 745–52
Projection of Financial Statements, 741–44
Roberts, Edward B., 90 n
Roberts, Michael J., 332 n
Rock, Arthur, 19, 22
Rockefeller, John D., 315
Roddick, Anita, 6, 191
Rogers, Michele, 351–68
Rogers, Steve, 351–68
Role definition, 260
Role models, 26
Ronstadt, Robert C., 25 n, 202 n
Roper Survey, 5
Rosenstein, Joseph, 335 n
Rubenson, George C., 208 n
Rubin, I. M., 685

Sahlman, William A., 99 n, 259 n, 333, 340, 444 n, 512 n, 513 n, 517 n, 518, 561, 660 n
Sales contracts, conditional, 549–50
Sales management, 220
Sales strategy, case, 398–99
Sales tactics, 431–32
Salomon, Richard, 660 n
Samaras, John N., 344 n
Sander, Dale, 528 n
Sanders, Harlan, 9, 197
Sapienza, Harry J., 12 n, 335 n, 491
Sasser, John, 591, 592
Sayre, Stephen B., 617
Schein, Edgar A., 261 n
Schumpeter, Joseph A., 11
Schutt, David, 493 n, 498
Scott, David, 562–72
Scott, Richard, 564
Screening guide, 140–81
Screening opportunities, 139–81
Sculley, John, 216–17
Securities Act
registration rights, 764–65
Rule 144, 761, 765
Securities and Exchange Commission, 320, 526, 761, 770; *see also* Regulation D
filings with, 108
Securities law, 220
Selected Business Ventures, 46–47
Self-assessment, 684–85
Self-employed, number of, 3
Self-made millionaires, 481
Self-reliance, 195–96
Service management, 103, 220
Service policies, 432
Sexton, Donald L., 22 n, 319
Shad, John, 316–17
Shapero, Albert N., 11 n
Shapiro, Benson P., 267 n
Shaw, George Bernard, 22, 196
Shearson Lehman Brothers, 528, 531
Shellenbarger, Sue, 6 n
Sherman, Jeffrey J., 267 n
Short-term financing, 221
Shulman, Joel, 602
Silent revolution
American dream, 3–6
new era, 7
Simon, Herbert A., 42
Skinner, Susan, 254 n
Small Business Administration, 4, 292–93, 320
Small Business Administration—*Cont.*
on business survival rate, 13–14
7(a) Guaranteed Business Loan Program, 492–93
on women's ownership of companies, 6
Small business investment companies, 493
Smaller Business Association of New England, 49
Small firms
innovation by, 88, 88
inventions by, 104
Smith, Fred, 6 n, 18
Smith, Gary A., 109, 135–36
Smith, Norman R., 188 n
Smollen, L. E., 190 n
Smurfit, Michael W. J., 6
Socialized successors, 288
Soja, Thomas A., 610 n, 653 n
Solo entrepreneurs, 20
Sontheimer, Carl, 192
Sosnowski, Thomas P., 386, 465–70, 475
Sources of Industry Data, 105 n
Spinelli, Stephen, 499, 590, 593
Spinner, Art, 335, 336
Sprague, Peter J., 6 n, 207
Spreadsheet mirage, 445–46
Spreadsheet programs, 345–51
Springfield Remanufacturing Corporation, 584
Stability stage, 211, 575
Stack, Jack, 584
Staged capital commitments, 449, 517
Stages of growth, 210–16, 575–76
in family firms, 286–87
Stancill, James M., 345, 554
Standard costing, 600
Standard Industrial Classification codes, 106
Stark, Andrew, 316, 317 n
Starr, Jennifer A., 319, 333
Start-up stage, 210, 575
in family firms, 286
State of Small Business (SBA), 11
Statistics, sources of, 106
Stayer, Ralph, 585–86
Steiner, George A., 379 n
Stevenson, Dorothy, 102
Stevenson, Howard H., 3 n, 5 n, 7 n, 20 n, 24 n, 25 n, 94 n, 188, 196 n, 200, 201, 209, 219 n, 259 n, 313, 314, 331–32, 333, 334, 340, 660 n
Stewart, M. D., 774
Stock
initial public offering, 495–97
issuance, 763
Stock buyback agreement, 264
Stockholders agreement, 769–70
Stock market crash of 1987, 100, 511
Stock option plans, 770–71
Stock ownership, 263–64
Stock purchase plans, 770
Stock-vesting agreement, 264
Stoft-Nielsen, Jacob, Jr., 6
Strange, F. Leland, 39–40
Strategic alliance, 659–60
Strategic analysis, for turnaround, 605
Strategic differentiation, 103–4
profile, 145
Strategic issues, in causes of failure, 598–99
Strategic window, 657
Strategy; *see* Entrepreneurial strategy
Street smarts, 197
Stress
during crisis, 600–601
tolerance of, 103
Structures, fluid, 214
Subaccount analysis, 605
Subordinated debt capital, 493
Success, secrets of, 662–63
Succession, in family firms, 290–91
Sunk cost, 332
Suppliers, mismanaged relationships with, 598
Survival odds, 183
Survival problem, 9–11
Survival rate, 13–14
Swain, Frank, 5 n
Swanson, Robert A., 6
Symbus Technology, 480
Synetics, 43–44
Syrus, Publius, 376 n

Tabor, Richard, 480
Take-the-money-and-run myopia, 527
Task schedule, 180
Taxes, and stock options, 770–71
Tax law, 220
Tax planning, 339
Tax problems, 562
Tax Reform Act of 1986, 661
Team building
in family firms, 288–91
pitfalls, 260–62
process of evolution, 257–60
and success, 253–54
vision and attitudes, 254–57
Team creativity, 44–45
Team philosophy, 254–57
Team quality, 103
Teams
rewards and incentives, 262–65
value considerations, 264–65
Teamwork, 218–19, 255
Technical experience, 102
Technical skills, 222
Technology, 104
Technology Mart, 47
Teitz, Michael B., 13
Temes, Judy, 480 n
Templeton, John, 6 n
Term loans, unsecured, 549
Terms sheet, 756
example, 771–73
Testa, Richard J., 261, 755 n

Thibault, John W., 260 n
Threshold concept, 12–13
Thurston, Phillip, 197 n, 375 n, 378, 379 n
Tieken, Nancy B., 25 n, 190 n
Time and change, 213
Time-Life Corporation, 655
Time magazine, 315
Time-sales finance, 548–49
Time to close financing, 451–52
Timing, 18, 104, 449
 of family ventures, 286–87
 of harvest strategy, 656–58
 of operational activities, 163–66
 in reward systems, 263–64
 of risk capital, 480–81
Timmons, Jeffrey A., 3 n, 7 n, 9 n, 14 n, 18 n, 19 n, 20 n, 24 n, 25 n, 26 n, 46 n, 49 n, 87 n, 94 n, 99 n, 105 n, 107 n, 185 n, 188 n, 190 n, 196 n, 203 n, 209, 219 n, 222 n, 254 n, 258 n, 261 n, 265 n, 293 n, 313 n, 323 n, 335 n, 343 n, 376 n, 443 n, 454 n, 455, 456 n, 483 n, 484, 485 n, 487 n, 489, 491 n, 493 n, 498, 515 n, 516 n, 519 n, 523 n, 544 n, 545–46, 554, 556 n, 557, 580 n, 610 n, 653 n, 735 n
Tobin, Paul J., 95, 199, 383
Tompkins, Doug, 290
Tompkins, Susie, 290
Topolnicki, E., 290 n
Tracy, John, 351
Trade associations, 108
Trade contacts, 48
Trade credit, 546
Trade creditors, during turnaround, 608–19
Trademarks, 339
Trade shows, 48
Trouble; *see* Crisis
Truman, Harry, 103
Trust, 102, 219, 583
Turnaround
 and bankruptcy threat, 603
 case, 610–51
 intervention for, 604–10
Turnaround—*Cont.*
 long-term remedial actions, 609–10
Turnaround plan, 606–7
Twaalfhoven, Bert, 447 n
Twain, Mark, 7, 87
Tyler, Natalie T., 35 n

Uncertainty, 194–95
Underpricing, 104
Uniform Commerical Code, 549
Union contracts, 604
UNIVAC, 41
Universities, research by, 47–48
University Patents, 46
Upside issues, 102
Ury, William, 521, 522 n

Vachon, Michael, 487 n
Valuation
 discounted cash flow, 515
 First Chicago method, 513–14
 fundamental method, 513, 514
 methods, 449–50
 ownership dilution, 515
 rule-of-thumb methods, 515–16
 theoretical perspective, 511
 venture capital method, 512–13
Valuation multiples and comparables, 100
Value
 determinants of, 509–10
 psychological determinants, 511
Value-added banker, 554–55
Value-added potential, 100
Value chain, 157
Value creation, 22, 256
 long- versus short-term, 510–11
Values, 198
 entrepreneurial culture, 214–16
 of teams, 260
Vancil, Richard E., 294 n
Van Slyke, John, 337
Variable costs, 101
Vases and faces exercise, 785–87
Venkataraman, S., 12 n
Venture capital, 483–84; *see also* Capital *and* Risk capital backing, 14–15
 identifying investors, 490–92
 legal investment procedures, 755–71
 preferred stock issues, 767–68
 sources, 7
 staged capital commitments, 449, 517
Venture Capital at the Crossroads (Bygrave and Timmons), 498
Venture capital industry, 485–87
Venture capitalists; *see* Investors
Venture Capital Journal, 498
Venture capital method of valuation, 512–13
Venture Capital 100 Index, 100
Venture capital process, 487–90
Venture Economics, 14
Venture Finance, 498
Venture magazine, 46, 351, 482
Venture modes, 208–10
Venture opportunities; *see* Opportunities
Venture opportunity screening guide, 140–81
Ventures
 classes of, 139
 stages of growth, 210–16
 types of, 12
Venture team, 19
Veridical awareness, 196–97
Vesper, Karl H., 11 n, 22 n, 25 n, 45
Vesting and stock restriction agreement, 777–80
VisiCalc, 42, 345
Vision, 198, 217–18
 in team building, 254–57
Voltaire, 375
Voluntary bankruptcy, 603
Voting rights, 767
Waite, Charles P., 382 n
Waller, Fats, 785
Wall Street Journal, 46, 633, 636 n
Walt Disney Corporation, 90
Walters, Julian, 564
Wang, An, 6 n, 190, 315
Warranty policies, 432
Washout financing, 523
Waterman, Robert M., Jr., 216
Watson, Thomas, Jr., 286
Wealth-building options, 661
Weighted-average antidilution provision, 768
Werbaneth, Louis A., Jr., 341 n
Wetzel, William H., Jr., 454 n, 455, 483
Wexner, Leslie H., 6, 191
Wharton School, 317
Wholesalers, 48
Willard, Gary E., 208 n
Winston, Rudolph, Jr., 6 n
Winter, David G., 187 n, 190 n
Winters, O. B., 40
Wolaner, Robin, 654
Wolfe, Tom, 8 n
Women, company ownership by, 6
Woo, Carolyn Y., 11 n
Woodward, H. N., 210 n
Woodward, W. E., 315 n
Work-force reductions, 609
Working capital, 762
Wozniak, Steve, 199
Wright, Wilbur, 92

Xerox Corporation, 100

Yankelovich Partners, 6
Yeager, Chuck, 8
Yockel, Michael, 591 n
You Can Negotiate Anything (Cohen), 521
Youngman, Karl, 257, 334 n
Young Presidents Association, 293

Zimmerman, Chester G., 741 n